MW00845346

Handbook of Crisis and Emergency Management

PUBLIC ADMINISTRATION AND PUBLIC POLICY

A Comprehensive Publication Program

Executive Editor

JACK RABIN
Professor of Public Administration and Public Policy
School of Public Affairs
The Capital College
The Pennsylvania State University—Harrisburg
Middletown, Pennsylvania

1. *Public Administration as a Developing Discipline (in two parts),* Robert T. Golembiewski
2. *Comparative National Policies on Health Care,* Milton I. Roemer, M.D.
3. *Exclusionary Injustice: The Problem of Illegally Obtained Evidence,* Steven R. Schlesinger
4. *Personnel Management in Government: Politics and Process,* Jay M. Shafritz, Walter L. Balk, Albert C. Hyde, and David H. Rosenbloom
5. *Organization Development in Public Administration (in two parts),* edited by Robert T. Golembiewski and William B. Eddy
6. *Public Administration: A Comparative Perspective, Second Edition, Revised and Expanded,* Ferrel Heady
7. *Approaches to Planned Change (in two parts),* Robert T. Golembiewski
8. *Program Evaluation at HEW (in three parts),* edited by James G. Abert
9. *The States and the Metropolis,* Patricia S. Florestano and Vincent L. Marando
10. *Personnel Management in Government: Politics and Process, Second Edition, Revised and Expanded,* Jay M. Shafritz, Albert C. Hyde, and David H. Rosenbloom
11. *Changing Bureaucracies: Understanding the Organization Before Selecting the Approach,* William A. Medina
12. *Handbook on Public Budgeting and Financial Management,* edited by Jack Rabin and Thomas D. Lynch
13. *Encyclopedia of Policy Studies,* edited by Stuart S. Nagel
14. *Public Administration and Law: Bench v. Bureau in the United States,* David H. Rosenbloom
15. *Handbook on Public Personnel Administration and Labor Relations,* edited by Jack Rabin, Thomas Vocino, W. Bartley Hildreth, and Gerald J. Miller
16. *Public Budgeting and Finance: Behavioral, Theoretical, and Technical Perspectives, Third Edition,* edited by Robert T. Golembiewski and Jack Rabin
17. *Organizational Behavior and Public Management,* Debra W. Stewart and G. David Garson
18. *The Politics of Terrorism: Second Edition, Revised and Expanded,* edited by Michael Stohl
19. *Handbook of Organization Management,* edited by William B. Eddy
20. *Organization Theory and Management,* edited by Thomas D. Lynch
21. *Labor Relations in the Public Sector,* Richard C. Kearney
22. *Politics and Administration: Woodrow Wilson and American Public Administration,* edited by Jack Rabin and James S. Bowman
23. *Making and Managing Policy: Formulation, Analysis, Evaluation,* edited by G. Ronald Gilbert

24. *Public Administration: A Comparative Perspective, Third Edition, Revised,* Ferrel Heady
25. *Decision Making in the Public Sector,* edited by Lloyd G. Nigro
26. *Managing Administration,* edited by Jack Rabin, Samuel Humes, and Brian S. Morgan
27. *Public Personnel Update,* edited by Michael Cohen and Robert T. Golembiewski
28. *State and Local Government Administration,* edited by Jack Rabin and Don Dodd
29. *Public Administration: A Bibliographic Guide to the Literature,* Howard E. McCurdy
30. *Personnel Management in Government: Politics and Process, Third Edition, Revised and Expanded,* Jay M. Shafritz, Albert C. Hyde, and David H. Rosenbloom
31. *Handbook of Information Resource Management,* edited by Jack Rabin and Edward M. Jackowski
32. *Public Administration in Developed Democracies: A Comparative Study,* edited by Donald C. Rowat
33. *The Politics of Terrorism: Third Edition, Revised and Expanded,* edited by Michael Stohl
34. *Handbook on Human Services Administration,* edited by Jack Rabin and Marcia B. Steinhauer
35. *Handbook of Public Administration,* edited by Jack Rabin, W. Bartley Hildreth, and Gerald J. Miller
36. *Ethics for Bureaucrats: An Essay on Law and Values, Second Edition, Revised and Expanded,* John A. Rohr
37. *The Guide to the Foundations of Public Administration,* Daniel W. Martin
38. *Handbook of Strategic Management,* edited by Jack Rabin, Gerald J. Miller, and W. Bartley Hildreth
39. *Terrorism and Emergency Management: Policy and Administration,* William L. Waugh, Jr.
40. *Organizational Behavior and Public Management: Second Edition, Revised and Expanded,* Michael L. Vasu, Debra W. Stewart, and G. David Garson
41. *Handbook of Comparative and Development Public Administration,* edited by Ali Farazmand
42. *Public Administration: A Comparative Perspective, Fourth Edition,* Ferrel Heady
43. *Government Financial Management Theory,* Gerald J. Miller
44. *Personnel Management in Government: Politics and Process, Fourth Edition, Revised and Expanded,* Jay M. Shafritz, Norma M. Riccucci, David H. Rosenbloom, and Albert C. Hyde
45. *Public Productivity Handbook*, edited by Marc Holzer
46. *Handbook of Public Budgeting*, edited by Jack Rabin
47. *Labor Relations in the Public Sector: Second Edition, Revised and Expanded*, Richard C. Kearney
48. *Handbook of Organizational Consultation*, edited by Robert T. Golembiewski
49. *Handbook of Court Administration and Management*, edited by Steven W. Hays and Cole Blease Graham, Jr.
50. *Handbook of Comparative Public Budgeting and Financial Management*, edited by Thomas D. Lynch and Lawrence L. Martin
51. *Handbook of Organizational Behavior*, edited by Robert T. Golembiewski
52. *Handbook of Administrative Ethics,* edited by Terry L. Cooper
53. *Encyclopedia of Policy Studies: Second Edition, Revised and Expanded,* edited by Stuart S. Nagel
54. *Handbook of Regulation and Administrative Law,* edited by David H. Rosenbloom and Richard D. Schwartz
55. *Handbook of Bureaucracy,* edited by Ali Farazmand
56. *Handbook of Public Sector Labor Relations*, edited by Jack Rabin, Thomas Vocino, W. Bartley Hildreth, and Gerald J. Miller
57. *Practical Public Management*, Robert T. Golembiewski
58. *Handbook of Public Personnel Administration*, edited by Jack Rabin, Thomas Vocino, W. Bartley Hildreth, and Gerald J. Miller
59. *Public Administration: A Comparative Perspective, Fifth Edition*, Ferrel Heady
60. *Handbook of Debt Management*, edited by Gerald J. Miller

61. *Public Administration and Law: Second Edition*, David H. Rosenbloom and Rosemary O'Leary
62. *Handbook of Local Government Administration*, edited by John J. Gargan
63. *Handbook of Administrative Communication*, edited by James L. Garnett and Alexander Kouzmin
64. *Public Budgeting and Finance: Fourth Edition, Revised and Expanded*, edited by Robert T. Golembiewski and Jack Rabin
65. *Handbook of Public Administration: Second Edition*, edited by Jack Rabin, W. Bartley Hildreth, and Gerald J. Miller
66. *Handbook of Organization Theory and Management: The Philosophical Approach*, edited by Thomas D. Lynch and Todd J. Dicker
67. *Handbook of Public Finance*, edited by Fred Thompson and Mark T. Green
68. *Organizational Behavior and Public Management: Third Edition, Revised and Expanded*, Michael L. Vasu, Debra W. Stewart, and G. David Garson
69. *Handbook of Economic Development*, edited by Kuotsai Tom Liou
70. *Handbook of Health Administration and Policy*, edited by Anne Osborne Kilpatrick and James A. Johnson
71. *Handbook of Research Methods in Public Administration*, edited by Gerald J. Miller and Marcia L. Whicker
72. *Handbook on Taxation*, edited by W. Bartley Hildreth and James A. Richardson
73. *Handbook of Comparative Public Administration in the Asia-Pacific Basin*, edited by Hoi-kwok Wong and Hon S. Chan
74. *Handbook of Global Environmental Policy and Administration,* edited by Dennis L. Soden and Brent S. Steel
75. *Handbook of State Government Administration,* edited by John J. Gargan
76. *Handbook of Global Legal Policy,* edited by Stuart S. Nagel
77. *Handbook of Public Information Systems,* edited by G. David Garson
78. *Handbook of Global Economic Policy,* edited by Stuart S. Nagel
79. *Handbook of Strategic Management: Second Edition, Revised and Expanded,* edited by Jack Rabin, Gerald J. Miller, and W. Bartley Hildreth
80. *Handbook of Global International Policy,* edited by Stuart S. Nagel
81. *Handbook of Organizational Consultation: Second Edition, Revised and Expanded,* edited by Robert T. Golembiewski
82. *Handbook of Global Political Policy,* edited by Stuart S. Nagel
83. *Handbook of Global Technology Policy,* edited by Stuart S. Nagel
84. *Handbook of Criminal Justice Administration*, edited by M. A. DuPont-Morales, Michael K. Hooper, and Judy H. Schmidt
85. *Labor Relations in the Public Sector: Third Edition*, edited by Richard C. Kearney
86. *Handbook of Administrative Ethics: Second Edition, Revised and Expanded*, edited by Terry L. Cooper
87. Handbook of Organizational Behavior: Second Edition, Revised and Expanded, edited by Robert T. Golembiewski
88. *Handbook of Global Social Policy,* edited by Stuart S. Nagel and Amy Robb
89. *Public Administration: A Comparative Perspective, Sixth Edition,* Ferrel Heady
90. *Handbook of Public Quality Management*, edited by Ronald J. Stupak and Peter M. Leitner
91. *Handbook of Public Management Practice and Reform*, edited by Kuotsai Tom Liou
92. *Personnel Management in Government: Politics and Process, Fifth Edition,* Jay M. Shafritz, Norma M. Riccucci, David H. Rosenbloom, Katherine C. Naff, and Albert C. Hyde
93. *Handbook of Crisis and Emergency Management*, edited by Ali Farazmand
94. *Handbook of Comparative and Development Public Administration: Second Edition, Revised and Expanded*, edited by Ali Farazmand

Additional Volumes in Preparation

Handbook of Monetary and Fiscal Policy, edited by Jack Rabin and Glenn L. Stevens

Financial Planning and Management in Public Organizations, Alan Walter Steiss and 'Emeka O. Cyprian Nwagwu

Handbook of Developmental Policy Studies, edited by Stuart S. Nagel

Handbook of International Health Care Systems, edited by Khi V. Thai, Edward T. Wimberley, and Sharon M. McManus

ANNALS OF PUBLIC ADMINISTRATION

1. *Public Administration: History and Theory in Contemporary Perspective*, edited by Joseph A. Uveges, Jr.
2. *Public Administration Education in Transition*, edited by Thomas Vocino and Richard Heimovics
3. *Centenary Issues of the Pendleton Act of 1883*, edited by David H. Rosenbloom with the assistance of Mark A. Emmert
4. *Intergovernmental Relations in the 1980s*, edited by Richard H. Leach
5. *Criminal Justice Administration: Linking Practice and Research*, edited by William A. Jones, Jr.

Handbook of Crisis and Emergency Management

edited by

Ali Farazmand
Florida Atlantic University
Fort Lauderdale, Florida

Marcel Dekker, Inc. New York • Basel

ISBN: 0-8247-0422-3

This book is printed on acid-free paper.

Headquarters
Marcel Dekker, Inc.
270 Madison Avenue, New York, NY 10016
tel: 212-696-9000; fax: 212-685-4540

Eastern Hemisphere Distribution
Marcel Dekker AG
Hutgasse 4, Postfach 812, CH-4001 Basel, Switzerland
tel: 41-61-261-8482; fax: 41-61-261-8896

World Wide Web
http://www.dekker.com

The publisher offers discounts on this book when ordered in bulk quantities. For more information, write to Special Sales/Professional Marketing at the headquarters address above.

Current printing (last digit):
10 9 8 7 6 5 4 3 2 1

PRINTED IN THE UNITED STATES OF AMERICA

To my son, Cyrus

Preface

This encyclopedic handbook was conceived a few years ago, when I searched for a good book on the subject of crisis and emergencies. The fruitless search prompted me to think about a handbook that would present a collective body of literature on these two important features of public management. Several concerns serve as the rationale for this handbook. First was the growing multitude of crises facing our world at the turn of the new millennium—political, economic, environmental, personal, organizational, and institutional. Crises, especially revolutionary and lingering or creeping ones, disrupt order and destroy patterns of stability, yet they may be important manifestations of evolutionary processes.

Second was the need for a handbook that would address crises in a systematic way and offer solutions or approaches to study them. There was no single comprehensive book that would respond to such a pressing need. Lack of such a resource book as a reference or text has led to haphazard application of trial-and-error ideas, many of which have caused harm, and even disasters, instead of reducing crises. One of the fundamental benefits of such a book is the lesson one can draw from crisis cases and situations in order to avoid future errors.

The third concern was the lack of a reference text that would address the complex issues related to emergency management. Because of the paucity of knowledge about emergency management throughout the world, there is a great need for a book to guide practitioners, scholars, researchers, and students in this critically demanding field of public affairs and administration.

My urge to produce a comprehensive handbook on this subject became even stronger when I visited Iran in 1994, long after the revolution of 1978–1979 that had caused innumerable disruptions and produced new opportunities and challenges. As I presented to publishers in Iran my edited encyclopedic *Handbook of Bureaucracy*, fresh from the press, as well as my *Handbook of Comparative and Development Public Administration* (both published by Marcel Dekker, Inc.), the first question almost every one of them asked me was whether I had published a book on crises or emergency management. The pressing need for such a resource in postrevolutionary Iran was obvious, but I quickly found out that it was a need common among all nations and in public administration worldwide.

The purpose of this handbook is to present original materials on diverse issues and aspects of the twin fields of crisis and emergency management that would serve as a primary textbook for upper undergraduate and graduate courses in crisis management, emergency management, public policy on mitigation and disaster management or prevention, various kinds of emergency situations, public management, and more. A wide range of issues, cases, theories, and applications can be found in this book. Presentations include theoretical, analytical, practical, empirical, normative, and historical treatments. Levels of analysis include macro, micro, and macro/micro, covering a wide spectrum of discussions that address crises and emergencies in both a broad theoretical context and in terms of their practical applications around the globe.

The handbook is designed to inform a wide spectrum of audiences, including academic scholars, students, researchers, practitioners, public managers, and policy makers at all levels, from local to national to global, in the fields of crisis and emergency management around the world. Crises have always inflicted heavy costs on human lives, organizations, and governments. While some crises are natural and usually unpredictable, others are human-engineered and can be avoided or prevented through elimination of their sources. Some crises are by-products of sharp and rupturing incidents and they can be devastating, while others result from long-term processes that when exacerbated by a rupturing crises go out of control and produce massive chaos with unpredictable consequences. Crisis management is an essential and inevitable feature of human and organizational lives, but crisis management is an imperative function modern public management cannot afford to overlook or ignore. Crisis management leads to emergency management because it demands immediate and focused attention with concrete action strategies and urgent plans of action.

Similarly, emergency management has been a common practice of human and organizational life throughout history. As a major function of public management, emergency management dates back to the ancient times—for example, during the first world-state Persian Achaemenid Empire founded by Cyrus the Great (559–300 B.C.) and under the subsequent Parthian and Sasanian empires (240 B.C.–A.D. 651). During the long history of the ancient Persian Empire, public management and bureaucracy were well organized, well developed, and well practiced with high efficiency and effectiveness.

Strategic management and emergency management were among the key features of the Persian system, characteristics the empires that followed, especially the Romans, and the European nation-states, borrowed from heavily and passed on to modern public administration. Manifestations of this highly efficient public management in dealing with crises and emergencies were the high degree of alertness and preparation for flood control, disaster arrangement, resettlement programs after earthquakes and other disasters, building dams and water-way management systems, undergound irrigation canal systems stretching hundreds and thousands of miles away from the sources, and strong shelters for extreme weather conditions. Key features of this tradition were teamwork and team-based human activities to control natural and human-made disasters, crises, and emergencies.

Therefore, public emergency management has a long historical tradition, which has passed on lessons, skills, mechanisms, and organizational arrangements that will benefit forthcoming generations. Today, not only nation-states demand highly skilled teams and systems of emergency management, there is a global demand for concerted efforts to tackle crises and emergency situations of massive magnitude.

In the new millennium most major crises and emergencies are no longer national and local concerns; they are global concerns and require global attention. For example, problems causing atmospheric and environmental crises demand multinational and global cooperation, partnership building, and collective actions. Problems of labor, refugees, hunger, health, and wars require collective action of governments, nongovernmental organizations, and private citizens from all over the world before they turn into massive crises, chaos, or genocide. Unfortunately, globalization of capitalism has aggravated many of these global crises and increased the scale and number of problems that call for emergency management.

Crisis and emergency management has generally been neglected as a field of study in public administration. Only recently has it been recognized and pursued as an important area of public management (notice the ASPAs section on emergency and crisis management). Despite this recent recognition, however, the dual fields of crisis and emergency management are least recognized as areas of scholarly activity among the public administration and public policy communities. In the chaotic, rapidly changing, uncertain conditions that characterize the current world, crisis and emergency management becomes central to all activities of public and private organizations. Massive corporate and government downsizing may be considered a short-term solution to the long-term problems of economy and society, creating a creeping crisis that might be triggered by even small events in the future. Crisis and emergency management requires strategic, long-term vision and creative thinking in service of the broad common good, for all peoples of the global community—living in a "global village" requires the concern of all members of that community.

Scholars, researchers, experts, and practitioners from all over the world who follow these lines of thinking were invited to share their expertise and experience in this knowledge-based volume. They responded with enthusiasm and proposed chapter contributions. The result is the *Handbook of Crisis and Emergency Management*, a highly comprehensive volume of original materials designed to cover all levels of analysis and forms of crisis and emergency anywhere in the world, from personal to organizational, local to global, corporate to governmental, and natural to human-made. This is the first handbook to cover comprehensively crisis and emergency management.

The contributors and I certainly hope that this volume will serve as a major textbook for students and instructors in upper undergraduate and graduate courses in various curricula of public administration, public management, political science, management, public policy, and program management, and most importantly in the management of crisis and emergency management, in both public and private sectors, around the world. We hope that policy makers, government officials, corporate and business executives and managers, supervisors, employees, citizens, experts, professionals, academic researchers, scholars, and professional administrators and managers will find this a very informative, guiding, and valuable reference book.

Finally, I would like to acknowledge the contribution of several other individuals who have made possible the completion of this major project. First, I thank Jack Rabin, who provided support for this handbook from the beginning. His comments were both encouraging and assuring. Second, I wish to express my deep appreciation to all the contributors for their cooperation and timely submission of their manuscripts. Congratulations to all of them.

I also thank Marcel and Russell Dekker for accepting this project for publication. Moreover, the production editor, Elizabeth Curione, has been patient and cooperative through the completion of the handbook. She and I communicated frequently and cleared many confusions, resolved discrepancies, and coordinated the joint effort. My special appreciation to her. Further, I must express appreciation to all the staff members at Marcel Dekker, Inc., whose assistance has been valuable in the production process.

Finally, I thank my former graduate assistant Jack Pinkwoski and doctoral students in our school of public administration, who also provided assistance by preparing the data base on the contributors and performing related tasks.

I hope this handbook will serve as a valuable text and reference book for students, instructors, researchers, policy makers, and practicing public managers throughout the world.

Ali Farazmand

Contents

Part V Terrorism and Crisis/Emergency Management

Part VI Long-Term Strategic Plans for Prevention of and Preparedness for Crisis and Emergencies

Contributors

Yaser Adwan, Ph.D. Department of Political Science, University of Tennessee, Knoxville, Tennessee

Efraim Ben-Zadok, Ph.D. School of Public Administration, Florida Atlantic University, Fort Lauderdale, Florida

Dave Lee Brannon, J.D. Federal Defender's Office, Southern District of Florida, West Palm Beach, Florida

Pamela Tarquinio Brannon, Ph.D. Department of Adjunct and Continuing Education, Warner Southern College, Fort Pierce, Florida

Terry F. Buss, Ph.D. Department of Public Management, Suffolk University, Boston, Massachusetts

John Carroll, A.B.D., M.P.A. School of Public Administration, College of Architecture, Urban and Public Affairs, Florida Atlantic University, Fort Lauderdale, Florida

Jean J. Chu, M.S. Lithosphere's Tectonic Evolution Laboratory, Institute of Geology and Geophysics, Chinese Academy of Sciences, Beijing, People's Republic of China

Jeanne-Marie Col, Ph.D. Department of Economic and Social Affairs, The United Nations, New York, New York

Robert Cunningham, Ph.D. Department of Political Science, University of Tennessee, Knoxville, Tennessee

Robert E. Dewhirst, Ph.D. Department of Political Science, Northwest Missouri State University, Maryville, Missouri

David L. Dillman, Ph.D. Department of Political Science, Abilene Christian University, Abilene, Texas

Ali Farazmand, Ph.D. School of Public Administration, Florida Atlantic University, Fort Lauderdale, Florida

George O. Grant Office of Emergency Management, The City of Houston, Houston, Texas

Ashley Grosse Department of Political Science, Washington State University, Pullman, Washington

Gil Gunderson, Ph.D. Graduate School of International Policy Analysis, Monterey Institute of International Studies, Monterey, California

Mel Hailey, Ph.D. Department of Political Science, Abilene Christian University, Abilene, Texas

John R. Harrald, Ph.D. Department of Engineering, Institute for Crisis, Disaster, and Risk Management, George Washington University, Washington, D.C.

Ahmed Shafiqul Huque, Ph.D. Department of Public and Social Administration, City University of Hong Kong, Hong Kong, China

Karl Jamieson Irving, M.P.A., M.I.P.S. Department of Public Administration, School of Public Affairs, American University, Washington, D.C.

Rita Kabra, Ph.D. Open University, Kanpur, India

Behrooz Kalantari, Ph.D. Department of Public Administration, Savannah State University, Savannah, Georgia

Renu Khator, Ph.D. Environmental Science and Policy Program, University of South Florida, Tampa, Florida

Mohammad Mohabbat Khan, Ph.D. Department of Public Administration, University of Dhaka, Dhaka, Bangladesh

Pan Suk Kim, Ph.D. Department of Public Administration, Yonsei University, Wonju, Kangwon-do, South Korea

Gustav A. Koehler, Ph.D. California Research Bureau and Time Structures, Sacramento, California

Peter Koehn, Ph.D. Department of Political Science, University of Montana, Missoula, Montana

Guenther G. Kress, Ph.D. Department of Public Administration, California State University, San Bernardino, California

Jae Eun Lee, Ph.D. Department of Public Administration, Chungbuk National University, Cheongju, Chungbuk, South Korea

Leslie A. Leip, Ph.D. School of Public Administration, Florida Atlantic University, Fort Lauderdale, Florida

Randi L. Miller, Ph.D. Department of Sociology, California State University, San Bernardino, California

M. Celeste Murphy, Ph.D. School of Public Administration and Urban Studies, San Diego State University, San Diego, California

Emad Mruwat, M.S., M.A. Department of Political Science, University of Tennessee, Knoxville, Tennessee

Margaret S. Murray, Ph.D. Department of Urban and Regional Planning, Florida Atlantic University, Fort Lauderdale, Florida

David C. Nice, Ph.D. Department of Political Science, Washington State University, Pullman, Washington

Phyllis Bo-Yuen Ngai, M.A. Department of Curriculum and Instruction, University of Montana, Missoula, Montana

Fran H. Norris, Ph.D. Department of Psychology, Georgia State University, Atlanta, Georgia

Jack Pinkowski, Ph.D. Master of Public Administration Program, Wayne Huizenga Graduate School of Business and Entrepreneurship, Nova Southeastern University, Fort Lauderdale, Florida

Mohammad Habibur Rahman, Ph.D. Department of Public Administration, University of Dhaka, Dhaka, Bangladesh

Jasmin K. Riad Disaster Research Center, University of Delaware, Newark, Delaware

Masaru Sakamoto Faculty of Law, Ryukoku University, Kyoto, Japan

Alka Sapat, M.A., Ph.D. School of Public Administration, College of Administration, Urban and Public Affairs, Florida Atlantic University, Fort Lauderdale, Florida

Patricia M. Schapley Joint Center for Environmental and Urban Problems, Florida Atlantic University, Fort Lauderdale, Florida

Aaron Schroeder, M.P.A., Ph.D. Virginia Tech Transportation Institute, Virginia Polytechnic Institute and State University, Blacksburg, Virginia

Lorena Schwartz, B.A., M.P.A. Joint Center for Environmental and Urban Problems, Florida Atlantic University, Fort Lauderdale, Florida

Ellis M. Stanley, Sr., B.A. Emergency Preparedness Department, City of Los Angeles, Los Angeles, California

Steven D. Stehr, Ph.D. Department of Political Science, Washington State University, Pullman, Washington

Hugh W. Stephens, Ph.D. College of Social Sciences, University of Houston, Houston, Texas

Francis R. Terry, B.A., M.A., F.C.I.T., Mi.Mgt. Interdisciplinary Institute of Management, London School of Economics and Politics, London, England

Richard M. Vogel, B.A., M.A., Ph.D. Departments of History, Economics, and Politics, State University of New York at Farmingdale, Farmingdale, New York

Captain John Walmsley, R.E.H.S. U.S. Department of Health and Human Services, Region IX, San Francisco, California

Gary Wamsley, Ph.D. Center for Public Administration and Policy, Virginia Polytechnic Institute and State University, Blacksburg, Virginia

Robert Ward, Ph.D. Department of History and Political Science, Charleston Southern University, Charleston, South Carolina

William Lee Waugh, Jr., Ph.D. Department of Public Administration and Urban Studies, Georgia State University, Atlanta, Georgia

Frances E. Winslow, M.U.P., C.E.M., Ph.D. Office of Emergency Services, City of San José, San José, California

Habib Zafarullah, Ph.D. School of Social Science, University of New England, Armidale, New South Wales, Australia

Tim Ziaukas, M.A., M.F.A. Department of Communication Arts, University of Pittsburgh at Bradford, Bradford, Pennsylvania

1
Introduction
Crisis and Emergency Management

Ali Farazmand School of Public Administration, Florida Atlantic University, Fort Lauderdale, Florida

I. INTRODUCTION

The world has entered a new millennium facing tremendous uncertainties, chaotic changes, and significant crises of all kinds and various degrees of intensity that impose urgency and call for emergency management around the globe. It seems that the world has begun an age of unreason, in which all order is turned upside down. Governmental reports declare nation-states to be at major risk of losing territorial sovereignty and control of their independence in the age of globalization of capital and markets and political-military power that transcends national boundaries, defying conventional demarcation of statehood as well as popular democratic ideals (Ohmae 1995; Korten 1995; Farazmand 1999).

The rise of globalization of capital and its negative consequences for both developing and more developed nations of the industrialized West has produced many concerns that embrace economics, environmental ecology, labor, culture, traditions, governance, administration, and politics. Energized by technological innovations, globalization has produced some positive effects, such as bringing more markets and products to consumers with money and facilitating communication and travel among peoples and professionals around the globe. But it has also caused many devastating adverse consequences worldwide—increasing child labor, slave labor, wage slavery, environmental degradation, violation of human rights, loss of control over national and local resources, loss of the democratic rights of citizens to make independent decisions, and imposing powerlessness in the face of globalizing finance capital backed by the most powerful (and potentially deadly militarily) states—the United States and its European allies.

With the fall of the USSR—the only socialist superpower capable of checking the excesses of global capitalism and its hegemonic state, the United States—has come an exacerbation of the multidimensional crises facing peoples, nation-states, governments, and cultures under globalization. Under the one-world ideological system of capitalism and market-oriented and corporate elite–based governance, conflicts and crises are suppressed—at least on the surface, voices of opposition and protest are silenced, and alternative forms of governance and socioeconomic order are crushed by military and other coercive forces, all in the name of a self-proclaimed market supremacy and capitalist democracy in which the wealthy and corporate elites rule (Korten 1995; Farazmand 1999).

Crises are now being transformed into opportunities for further accumulation of capital throughout the world, which is now considered a ''global village'' ruled by the feudal barons of the new world order. *Profit*, *social control*, and *capitalism* are the key words of the new era. The global public is easily manipulated by omnipotent media, financial means, and other tools to present the new global reality, an artificial reality carefully and neatly crafted and promoted.

In this environment of globalization, critics have ample grounds to express concern. For example, Rifkin (1996) has announced ''the end of work,'' Wilson (1996) has argued about the loss of urban jobs, Mele (1996) and Knox (1997) have argued about the loss of the sense of community and urban infrastructure, Picciotto (1989) and Cox (1993) have discussed the loss of territorial sovereignty of nation-states, Korbin (1996) warns about the ''return back to medievalism,'' Fukuyama (1992) speaks of ''the end of history and of man,'' Huntington (1996) speaks of the ''clash of civilizations,'' Brecher and Costello (1994) warn of a ''global pillage,'' Parenti (1995) speaks of global ''corpocracy and plutocracy,'' Farazmand (1998, 1999) argues about ''the rise of wage slavery and mercenary systems of socioeconomic order,'' while Stever (1988) argues about the end of public administration—and the arguments go on. Crises of institutions are now reaching a higher level of criticality, especially the community and family institutions that form the backbones of society.

Popular books signal waves and shifting global paradigms away from stable patterns. The collapse of global systems and great powers, revolutionary changes, breakdown of family institutions and traditions, and environmental decay are but few such crises that should alarm us all. Information technology has also broken down barriers among nations, peoples, and organizations around the globe. No longer can organizations and governments rely on patterns of continuity and stability. No longer can individuals predict and feel secure about their futures. No longer can anyone escape the devastating impacts of crises—crises that have reached a new level and have been eroding the fundamental underpinnings and assumptions of humanity. But these crises are largely covered up by the military, communication, and financial arms of the globally dominant state. Feeling a sense of powerlessness and insecurity, therefore, peoples and groups seek alternative shelters for self-protection and expression in their attempts to escape from degradation, dehumanization, and exploitation. They are forced into practices of self-censorship, role playing, and pretension as the new culture of globalism and global order invades societies. Crises are therefore transformed into different forms and linger through different levels of criticality until they explode, perhaps globally all at the same time.

II. NATURE OF CRISES

Crises occur at all levels and appear in all guises. Some are long-term processes of deterioration and others are rapid ruptures; some have their origins and roots in the past while others are created by chance and the risks posed by a particular environment; some are caused internally while others are created externally. Some crises are creeping and lingering, based on illegitimacy and system entropies (the Shah's regime in Iran) while others may occur suddenly (the Stock Market Crash of 1929, causing the Great Depression). Crises come in a variety of kinds: economic crisis (note the chronic crises of debt among Latin American nations, the New York City fiscal crisis of 1974, or the Great Depression of 1930s); political crisis (revolutions in Iran, Russia, France, Nicaragua, and China as well as other wars); environmental crisis (ozone layer depletion, Bhopal and Chernobyl disasters in India and Russia, or the Three-Mile Island nuclear crisis in the United States); and organizational and leadership crises causing severe decline and death (Farazmand 1996), or moral bankruptcy and unethical conduct in public office (Clinton's presidency).

Crises involve events and processes that carry severe threat, uncertainty, an unknown outcome, and urgency. Crises scramble plans, interrupt continuities, and brutally paralyze normal governmental operations and human lives. Most crises have trigger points so critical as to leave historical marks on nations, groups, and individual lives. Crises are historical points of reference, distinguishing between the past and present. They leave memories for those involved in such events as disasters, hijackings, riots, revolts, and revolutions. Years, months, and days become historic points of demarcation, such as 1914, 1917, 1929, 1940, and 1978–79; and crisis events are memorable, such as the assassination of Rabin, the Cuban Missile Crisis, the Vietnam War, Nixon's presidency, the Middle East crisis, the Persian Gulf crisis, the hostage crisis, the "black Friday" and the February revolution (Iran), the October revolution (Russia), and so on (Rosenthal and Kouzmin 1993; Farazmand 1996).

Crises come in a variety of forms, such as terrorism (New York World Trade Center and Oklahoma bombings), natural disasters (Hurricanes Hugo and Andrew in Florida, the Holland and Bangladesh flood disasters), nuclear plant accidents (Three-Mile Island and Chernobyl), riots (Los Angeles riot and the Paris riot of 1968, or periodic prison riots), business crises, and organizational crises facing life-or-death situations in a time of rapid environmental change. Some crises can be managed successfully while others lead to failures and further disasters. Some lead to new and positive changes in society, while others lead to further calamities.

Some crises are caused by governmental and corporate actions (Exxon's oil leakage in Alaska or the Branch Davidian catastrophe in Texas, environmental pollution and decay, etc.) or inaction, leaving simple problems or conflicts that become transformed into major crises (the Balkan crises, prison riots, many African ethnic or tribal conflicts, massive epidemic health crises, or mass starvation and food crises, again as in Africa). Some events are creeping, with a particular small starting point, developing over time into full-scale crises. This is common among public and private organizations, whose elites "may convert their embarrassment over prolonged negligence into over-hasty and ill-conceived efforts to undo years of non-action and non-decision making" (Rosenthal and Kouzmin 1993:5).

Crises consist of "a short chain of events that destroy or drastically weaken" a condition of equilibrium and the effectiveness of a system or regime within a period of days, weeks, or hours rather than years. In this sense, a crisis is not the same as tensions, as referred to by many scholars, or the process-oriented crisis mentioned above. Therefore there are two types of crisis: a process-oriented one developing over a period of time, and the other a sudden rupture developing within weeks, days, hours, or even minutes (Farazmand 1996). The latter crisis is "fraught with far reaching implications. It threatens to involve large segments of society in violent actions" (Dogan and Higley 1996:5).

III. CHARACTERISTICS OF CRISES

A central feature of all crises is a sense of urgency, and in many cases urgency becomes the most compelling crisis characteristic. Situations change so dramatically and so rapidly that no one seems to be able to predict the chain of events or the possible outcomes. An important aspect of such crisis situations is the dynamics that evolve during days, hours, and even minutes. In a revolutionary crisis, such unpredictability, uncertainty, and change characterize the dynamics of the unfolding events. Leaders and decision-makers are often caught by surprises after surprises produced by many forces such as the masses, strength or weaknesses of the regime and the ruling elite, external or internal actors, climatic conditions, and national characters. Surprises characterize the dynamics of crisis situations (Farazmand 1996).

Some crises are processes of events leading to a level of criticality or degree of intensity generally out of control. Crises often have past origins, and diagnosing their original sources can help to understand and manage a particular crisis or lead it to alternative state of condition. Crises take many forms and display many patterns, such as defeat in international warfare, revolution, sudden breakdown of unstable democratic regimes, economic disaster, ''implosion,'' loss of foreign support resulting in the falling of a dependent regime—''temperature changes'' (Dogan and Higley 1996:9).

But, as mentioned above, some crises are sudden and are abrupt events that paralyze a regime, a community, or economic system. Understanding the dynamics of crises helps develop a better understanding of crisis evolution and its management. It requires serious crisis analysis, which in turn needs to go beyond a focus on human error as the origin of the crisis. Organizational, leadership, and systemic deficiencies must be diagnosed as effective approaches to crisis management. Many organizations develop over time a culture devoid of ability to detect environmental threats challenging their survival. And many crises develop as a result of managerial and leadership incompetence (Turner 1989 cited in Rosenthal and Kouzmin 1993:6; Perrow 1984). Public organizations are not immune from this maladaptation or bureaucratic culture inflicted by many bureau pathological deficiencies and vulnerabilities. Crises therefore are destructive, but they may also develop opportunities for a new order, changes that may produce positive results. Therefore, crises create their own antistheses, which may dialectically reinforce and complement forces of positive nature.

Key to crisis management is an accurate and timely diagnosis of the criticality of the problems and the dynamics of events that ensue. This requires knowledge, skills, courageous leadership full of risk-taking ability, and vigilance. Successful crisis management also requires motivation, a sense of urgency, commitment, and creative thinking with a long-term strategic vision. In managing crises, established organizational norms, culture, rules, and procedures become major obstacles: administrators and bureaucrats tend to protect themselves by playing a bureaucratic game and hiding behind organizational and legal shelters. A sense of urgency gives way to inertia and organizational sheltering and self-protection by managers and staff alike. This is the most devastating institutional obstacle in the management of any crisis. Successful crisis management requires: (1) sensing the urgency of the matter; (2) thinking creatively and strategically to solving the crisis; (3) taking bold actions and acting courageously and sincerely; (4) breaking away from the self-protective organizational culture by taking risks and actions that may produce optimum solutions in which there would be no significant losers; and (5) maintaining a continuous presence in the rapidly changing situation with unfolding dramatic events. Reason, creative thinking, and perseverance must lead those involved in crisis management and crisis resolution. Any error or misjudgment can lead to further disasters, causing irreparable damages to human lives.

Crisis management or resolution requires strategic thinking of contingencies. Crises also develop opportunities, which must be explored through mobilization of assets and forces available. The sense of urgency calls for immediate attention, action, and reaction. The primary function of any government is to protect the lives and property of citizens. Crises and emergencies generally test the competence of governments. Throughout the history of human civilizations, policymakers have sought to anticipate the unexpected ''in order to reduce the risk to human life and safety posed by intermittently occurring natural and man-made hazardous events'' (Petak 1985:3). This notion needs to be capitalized on as a noble policy and strategic choice of collective action. Unfortunately, not everyone thinks this way in a crisis situation; history is full of cases in which opportunists take advantages of chaos and disorders to enrich themselves, to take control of power bases, and to steal what does not belong to them.

Under normal bureaucratic situations, management literature points to decentralized and hands-off decision making as a good organizational strategy. But under crisis situations, this model of stable organizational behavior is ill-suited and becomes seriously problematic. It is interesting to note, ironically, that the crisis management literature points to a more centralized decision structure. ''In intense crises decisions should be made at the top of the organization because those at lower levels tend to 'suboptimize' based on their own interests, do not have all the information necessary, and are unaware of larger political or social issues or constraints'' (Averch and Dluhy 1997:85).

Literature refers to the desirability of the emergence of ''synthetic groups'' in a number of urban disasters (Wolensky and Wolensky 1990) operating as working coalition of key actors and agents at different levels to provide command and control systems and to facilitate damage assessment and resource deployment (Dluhy 1990). Absence of such command and control systems can cause severe problems and can add to crisis situations, as it did in Miami, Florida, during the Hurricane Andrew crisis in 1992. ''Dade County emergency managers had no way to enforce cooperation. . . . Organization chaos and weak command and control were the characteristic mode of the EOC [Emergency Operations Center] during the crisis period'' (Averch and Dluhy 1997:84). Despite the federal, state, and local government assistance in disaster management, empirical research shows that minorities, especially blacks and Hispanics, and immigrant workers, suffered most from the South Miami disasters caused by Hurricane Andrew. Crisis and emergency management was least effective for these groups, who had to rely on their family and relatives for help and assistance. Long after the crisis, their suffering continued in the forms of joblessness, loss of housing, hunger, diseases, socially and economically driven problems of crime, and a host of other associated crises (see studies in Peacock et al. 1997).

Contrasting evidence shows interesting observations of a swift and effective organizational response to the severe crisis and disaster situation caused by the 1989 earthquake in northern Iran, which caused a loss of over 50,000 lives, total destruction of two medium-sized cities and a number of towns, villages, and communities, plus devastating property losses. The Central Government Emergency forces were matched more than equally by massive popular forces of assistance by all means possible, and it was the initial ''command and control system'' of the national government—in a postrevolutionary situation still characterized by revolutionary spirit. Iran had gone through many crises since the revolutionary crisis of the 1978–79, including especially the 8-year-old defensive war against Iraq, and a degree of preparedness, coordination, and decision structure had already been developed in Iran both organizationally and politically. Research on organizational and managerial response to chaotic situations of crises reflect importance of central coordinating and command centers. This is an essential aspect of research on crisis and emergency management for the future.

The efforts of past decision makers, administrators, citizens, researchers, and all those involved in crisis and emergency management have provided the foundation for the current focus on this twin subfields of public administration in the United States and abroad. Not all emergency situations are caused by crises and, in fact, many have nothing to do with any crisis at all. But all crises cause emergency situations, which must be dealt with very carefully. As a central activity of public administration, emergency management is generally a process of developing and implementing policies and actions that involve: (1) mitigation—a course of action to detect the risk to society or the health of people and to reduce the risk; (2) preparedness—a response plan of action to reduce loss of life and to increase the chance of successful response to the disaster or catastrophe, etc.; (3) response—provision of emergency aid and assistance; and (4) recovery—provision of immediate support to return life back to normalcy (Petak 1985).

A more recent development in the fields of crisis and emergency management is the emergence of chaos theory in the social sciences, outlining—in social equivalence with the physical sciences—a state of chaos, disequilibrium, and disorder. Key to this multifaceted theory of social science, or chaos theory, is the prevalence of constant and rupturing changes that occur out of order, disturb system equilibria, and cause chaos, eventually leading to a renewed order. The cycle of chaos/disorder/order is an evolutionary process that contributes to the transformation of social systems, including organizations with political and managerial implications. Stability and equilibria carry with themselves potential forces of change and disruption, which trigger forces of system instability and disorder—political, organizational, economic, and institutional—and place them at the verge of chaos and disorder. Patterns of change and instability characterize this chaos. The key to understanding and managing these changes is application of nonlinear and multicausal or noncausal thinking within organizations and social systems. Long-term transformation results from short-term chaotic changes that cause system disequilibrium, a phenomenon that has major implications for crisis and emergency management around the world (for details on chaos theory, see for example, Loye and Eisler 1987; Lazlo 1987; Jantsch 1980; Prigogine and Stengers 1984; Kiel 1989. See also Koehler et al., Chapter 20, and Farazmand, Chapter 39, in this volume).

IV. PLAN OF THE BOOK

This encyclopedic handbook is designed to inform academic scholars, students, researchers, practitioners, public managers, and policy makers on the twin areas of crisis and emergency management around the world. It is divided into 3 major units, 11 parts, and 45 chapters. Except for one chapter, which is an updated and expanded version of an earlier article published in a first-rate refereed article, all chapters are original materials and contribute to our knowledge on the twin fields of crisis and emergency management with significant implications for all parties concerned.

Unit One focuses on crisis management and analyzes various theoretical and empirical issues at macro and micro levels. This is done in 3 parts and 14 chapters. Part I contains four chapters that deal with micro-macro issues of group and intergroup crisis management. Following the introduction, these chapters discuss comparatively the crisis of character in government and administration, intercultural communication training in refugee assistance crisis management, and motivation crisis in the context of nationalism, liberalism, and religion. This part sets the introduction for a deeper analysis of crisis and its management in all spheres.

Part II deals with macro issues and focuses on organizational and institutional crisis management broadly defined. By organization is meant broad, macroanalysis of the organization of economy, policy choices, management, organizational behavior, politics, state, and public service. Here, five chapters analyze crisis policy making, and human resource management, linkage disruption as a result of disaster impact upon economic structures, crisis in the U.S. administrative state, and global crisis in public service and public administration. Analysis of organizational and institutional crisis management sets the tone for understanding the various causes and consequences of crises as well as the nonlinear unpredictable changes that occur beyond human control and precipitate crises and make their management a more difficult and challenging task.

Part III discusses macro issues of political, economic, and social crises and their management worldwide. Five chapters discuss a number of issues such as immigration, refugees, and housing crisis management or resolution of civil wars through United Nations intervention, and a range of crises from the management of financial bankruptcy at the level of local government in California, to system crisis in Israel, to homeless policy crisis back in affluent America.

Unit Two focuses on emergency management at macro and micro levels of analysis. Five chapters discuss environmental and health related emergency management. Topics include fighting fires at sea, learning about disaster management from the cases of the Texas City to Exxon Valdez, public relations of crisis management through the cases of Bhopal in India to Exxon in Alaska, managing urban violence in hospital emergency departments, and metropolitan medical strikes team systems for emergency management in cases of responding to the medical demands of weapons of mass destruction/nuclear, biological, and chemical agents events. This part contains chapters with eye-opening discussions that illuminate everyone concerned in society and government at local, national, and global levels.

Part II analyzes macro and micro issues of emergency management with a focus on conceptual, practical, empirical, and policy aspects. Six chapters deal with a whole range of topics that include continuity of governments as a framework for emergency management, application of chaos theory to emergency management, the psychology of evacuation and policy design, the role of technology and human factors in emergency management, politics and management of environmental emergencies, and evolution of emergency management in America.

Unit Three addresses international case studies on crisis and emergency management from around the globe. This is done in six parts. Part I focuses on crisis and emergency management in the American continent, covering North, Central, and Latin America. Part I contains five chapters which deal with community recovery and reconstruction following disasters, the potential for disaster with case studies, American presidential crisis management under Kennedy (the Cuban Missile Crisis), bureaucratic analysis of emergency management, and lessons learned from the Three Mile Island and Chernybal reactor accidents. Part II deals with the 1989 rail disaster at Calpham in South London.

Part III focuses on crisis and emergency management in Asia and Africa. Here, seven chapters analyze such a wide range of topics and issues as emergency management in Korea, the 1994 plague outbreak in Surat, India with implications for disaster management, disaster management in Hong Kong, coping with calamities and managing disaster in Bangladesh, emergency management in Japan with lessons from the 1995 earthquake in the Hanshin-Awaji, early warning success for the 1976 Tangshan earthquake in China, and a case study of earthquake in Iran.

Part IV addresses crisis and emergency management in the Near/Middle East, with two chapters discussing the culture and crisis in Lebanon and transforming danger into opportunity: the case of Jordan and the Persian Gulf crisis of 1990; opportunity for whom? But disaster for the people and environment in the region. Part V discusses terrorism with ensuing crises and emergencies. Two chapters discuss managing terrorism as an environmental hazard, planning for weapons of mass destruction, as nuclear, biological, and chemical agents events.

Part VI contains four chapters that discuss long-term strategic plans for prevention and preparedness of crisis and emergencies. These include topics such as emergency managers for the new millennium, mitigating coastal hazards in Florida, planning for prevention and emergency preparedness, and managing refugee assistance crises in the twenty-first century, with an emphasis on intercultural communication factors.

Finally, subject and name indexes are provided, as well as a list of contributors to this volume.

REFERENCES

Averch, Harvey, Dluhy, Milan (1997). Crisis decision making and management. In Walter Gillis Peacock, Betty H. Morrow, Hugh Gladwin (eds.), *Hurricane Andrew: Ethnicity, Gender, and the Sociology of Disasters*. London and New York: Routledge.

Cox, R.W. (1993). Structural issues of global governance. In S. Gill (ed.), *Gramci, Historical Materialism, and International Relations*, 259–289. Cambridge, UK: Cambridge University Press.

Dluhy, M.J. (1990). *Building Coalitions in the Human Services*. Newbury Park, CA: Sage.

Dogan, Mattei, Higley, John (1996). Crises, elite change, and regime change, presented at the International Conference on Regime Change and Elite Change in El Paular, Spain, May 30–June 1.

Farazmand, Ali (1996). Regime change and elite change: The Iranian revolution of 1978–79, presented at the International Conference on Regime Change and Elite Change in El Paular, Spain, May 30–June 1.

Farazmand, Ali (1999). Globalization and public administration. *Public Administration Review* 59(*6*), 509–522.

Fukuyama, Francis (1992). *The End of History and the Last Man*. New York: Free Press.

Huntington, Samuel (1996). *The Clash of Civilizations and the Remaking of the World Order*. New York: Simon & Schuster.

Jantsch, E. (1980). *The Self-Organizing Universe*. New York: Pergamon.

Kiel, Douglas L. (1989). Nonequilibrium theory and its implications for public administration. *Public Administration Review*. November/December, 544–551.

Knox, Paul (1997). Globalization and urban economic change. *The Annals of the American Academy of Political and Social Science* 551 (*May*), 17–27.

Korbin, Stephen (1996). Back to the future: Neomedievalism and the postmodern digital world economy. *Journal of International Affairs* 51(2), 367–409.

Korten, David (1995). *When Corporations Rule the World*. Kumarian Press.

Lazlo, E. (1987). *Evolution: The Grand Synthesis*. Boston: Shambhala New Science Library.

Loye, David, Eisler, Riane (1987). Chaos and transformation: Implications of nonequilibrium theory for social science and society. *Behavioral Science* 32, 53–65.

Mele, Christopher (1996). Globalization, culture, and neighborhood change: Reinventing the Lower East Side of New York. *Urban Affairs Review* 17(*9*), 1663–1677.

Ohmae, Kenichi (1995). *The End of Nation States: The Rise of Regional Economics.* London: Harper Collins.
Peacock, G. Walter, Morrow, Betty H., Gladwin, Hugh (eds.) (1997). *Hurricane Andrew: Ethnicity, Gender and the Sociology of Disasters.* London and New York: Routledge.
Perrow, Charles (1984). *Normal Accidents: Living with High-Risk Technologies.* New York: Basic Books.
Petak, William J. (1985). Emergency management: A challenge for public administration. *Public Administration Review* 45(1), 3–6.
Prigogine, I., Stengers, I. (1984). *Order Out of Chaos.* New York: Bantam.
Reich, R.B. (1991). *The Work of Nations: Preparing for the 21st Century Capitalism.* New York: Simon & Schuster.
Rifkin, Jeremey (1996). *The End of Work.* G.P. Putnam's Sons.
Rosenthal, Uriel, Kouzmin, Alexander (1993). Globalizing an agenda for contingencies and crisis management: An editorial statement. *Journal of Contingencies and Crisis Management* 1(*1*), 1–12.
Stever, James (1988). *The End of Public Administration.* New York: International Publications.
Wolensky, R.P., Wolensky, K.C. (1990). Local government's problem with disaster management: A literature review and structural analysis. *Policy Studies Review* 9, 703–725.

2
The Crisis of Character in Comparative Perspective

David L. Dillman and Mel Hailey Department of Political Science, Abilene Christian University, Abilene, Texas

I. INTRODUCTION

We live in a time of crisis. Perhaps it has always been so and forevermore will be, but certainly the latter part of the twentieth century has been characterized by crises. For example, democratic governments in western Europe and the United States are experiencing a crisis of the welfare state in a wide variety of policy areas—health, education, pensions. Furthermore, most western democracies are challenged by a crisis of confidence in the institutions and capacity of government and perhaps in democracy itself. This chapter argues, with particular reference to the United States, that western governments are also afflicted by a crisis of character: the loss of confidence and trust in public officials and in the process of government generally, due to widespread perceptions of citizens that officials are either [1] unwilling or unable to maintain high standards of public morality or [2] unable or unwilling to maintain generally acceptable standards of private morality or [3] both.

We agree with the conclusion expressed by Dalton that "the crisis of government is, first of all, a problem of raising the performance of government institutions to match their potential" and "that if government could (or would) take decisive action to meet economic problems, protect the environment, and address other issues of long-standing public concern, popular satisfaction with government would increase" (Dalton, 1988, p. 242). However, we also argue that this perspective on the crisis of government in western democracies fails to account both for citizens' well-documented concerns about the character of government officials and the impact of character on citizens' evaluations of government. This chapter explores the nexus between how citizens perceive officials' character and their trust and confidence in government. Does the public's low regard for politicians and career officials have any consequences for governance? Do questions about an official's character influence public perceptions of his or her performance or, indeed, of the performance of government in general? In short, do citizens' perceptions that public officials are deficient in character contribute to a crisis of government?

By *character* we are referring to an individual's core traits or lifestyle. According to Renshon, "character represents a person's integrated pattern of responding to three basic life spheres or domains: what they will do with their lives, how they will do it, and their relations to others along the way" (Renshon, 1996, p. 39). Three core elements of character are ambition, integrity, and relatedness. Ambition, Renshon notes, is the domain of initiative and action. ''The basic concerns in this domain are the capacity, desire, and ability to invest oneself in accomplishing one's purposes'' (Renshon, 1996, p. 39). Ambition is necessary for achievement and productivity, but too much ambition—or too much inadequately controlled—may result in manipulative, self-serving behavior at the expense of others. If *ambition* refers to what people do with their lives, *integrity* refers to how they will do it. Stephen Carter suggests that integrity requires three steps: ''[1] *discerning* what is right and what is wrong; [2] *acting* on what you have discerned, even at personal cost; and [3] *saying openly* that you are acting on your understanding of right from wrong'' (Carter, 1996, p. 7). A person—a public official—of integrity is someone citizens feel they can ''trust to do right, to play by the rules, to keep commitments'' (Carter, 1996, p. 7). Integrity is central to the notion of character, ''not only because of its own fundamental importance, but because of its crucial role in shaping the other two character domains'' (Renshon, 1996, p. 40). The third element of character ''concerns one's stance toward relationships with others,'' which may range from antagonistic to friendly to intimate (Renshon, 1996, p. 45). The character of public officials is revealed not so much by what those interpersonal relationships are as by determining *why* they are what they are. For example, citizens do not want to be manipulated to serve the political or personal ends of public officials; rather, they desire respect and ''sympathy and compassion.''

Character issues are found in every political system. In the United States in recent years ambition has toppled at least one president and more than one presidential candidate; lack of integrity has led to government regulators ignoring ''the renaissance of sweated labour'' (Block, 1996, pp. 19, 26–28) and members of Congress using their ''public office for private purposes in a manner that subverts the democratic process'' (Thompson, 1993, p. 369); and underdeveloped citizen-official relations have denied ''the public their rightful role in self-governance'' (Denhardt, 1994, p. 2165). In contemporary Britain, inquiry after inquiry has sought to explain and contain declining standards in public life. The 1994 Nolan Committee, for example, was ''a creature of public concern, a response to the public's general dissatisfaction with politics and politicians, compounded by a perception of a collective flouting of expected or acceptable standards by public figures, or those in the public view, as they indulge in bed-hopping, self-enrichment, influence-peddling, and rule-bending'' (Doig, 1996, p. 51). ''In Japan, nine of the fifteen Prime Ministers who held office in the period 1955–1993 were involved in corruption scandals. At least half its members of Parliament, it is estimated, could have obtained their seats through the aid of illegal financing'' (Nelkin and Levi, 1996, p. 2). In Italy, corruption has become so rampant in recent years that the health of the economy is threatened. ''The latest studies estimate that the political parties may have siphoned off as much as $100 billion over the last decade—about a tenth of Italy's national debt'' (U.S. News and World Report, 1993, p. 44). The conclusion of the European Union's Court of Auditors in its 1994 annual report was: ''fraud, mismanagement, corruption: they are omnipresent in the European Union'' (Economist, 1994, p. 58), may also apply to every other region of the world. Character issues are ubiquitous.

Character, of course, is not just manifest by the presence or absence of sex or financial scandals, corrupt deals, fraudulent activity, or some other behavior that breaks a public trust for private gain. Any behavior that breaks the moral rules of the community, including generally accepted standards of private behavior, may give clues to one's character. The public official who does not keep commitments, who is not forthright, who, in the face of criticism, is not steadfast yet open to constructive compromise, or who is not consistent may lack character (see Carter, Chapter 3). In other words, citizens know that character is revealed in an official's quality of relationships and patterns of living, not just in his conformance or nonconformance to the law.

Nevertheless, it is also true that what becomes an issue and how it is resolved are particular to a given system. For example,

> Westerners are often critical of the apparent corruption of nepotism in developing countries such as Nigeria. Yet the strong links of Nigerians to the extended family and village throughout history produce behavioral norms that explain the prevalence of favoring family and friends in handing out government jobs and contracts. What outsiders decry as corruption among contemporary Nigerian politicians is simply the reflection of strong extended family and communal values present throughout history (Wilson, 1996, p. 19).

Disparate cultural norms and standards are not limited to differences between developed and developing countries; they also influence reactions to questions of character among countries in the affluent West. Thus, the circumstance that found the mistress of French President Mitterand standing next to his wife at Mitterand's funeral raised few eyebrows in France, while in the United States allegations of sexual impropriety have beleaguered President Clinton for years. Finally, standards may change over time in one country. For example, in the United States during the first half of the nineteenth century, ''It was not unusual, or considered improper, for members of Congress and for government employees to assist private parties in gaining favorable government action on claims before Congress or governments. Even Senator Daniel Webster demanded and got a substantial retainer from the National Bank for representing its interests in Congress with reference to the renewal of its charter'' (Roberts, 1985, p. 180). Today these actions of members of Congress would be considered ethical lapses and Webster's improprieties certainly illegal. They would raise questions about the politician's character. In short, there are core elements of character—integrity, trustworthiness, loyalty—that transcend culture and history, but the way that character is manifest and evaluated may differ over time and place. Because discussions of character must be embedded in its particular context, we turn to an exploration of character in the American polity.

II. CHARACTER IN THE AMERICAN REGIME

At the founding of the new American government, there was a concern that leaders of character were in short supply. Hence, James Madison wrote in the *Federalist Papers* (No. 51) in 1788:

> ''If men were angels, no government would be necessary. If angels were to govern men, neither external nor internal controls on government would be necessary. In framing a government which is to be administered by men over men, the great difficulty lies in this: you must enable the government to control the governed; and in the next place oblige it to control itself.''

Since angels do not govern, the founders knew that public trust had to be maintained in other ways. Thus, they provided for numerous institutional and procedural checks and balances—''ambition must be made to counteract ambition''—to constrain public behaviors.

At the same time, the founders were not unaware of the role of character in securing public confidence in government. To maintain public trust in the new government, George Washington "insisted that no consideration other than 'fitness of character' should enter into his nominations for public office, and the evidence indicates that in the main this prescription was upheld" (Mosher, 1968, p. 61). According to Frederick Mosher, " 'fitness of character' could best be measured by family background, educational attainment, honor and esteem, and, of course, loyalty to the new government—all tempered by a sagacious regard for geographic representation" (Mosher, 1968, p. 60). Though party identification and loyalty quickly became a prerequisite for nomination or appointment, reflecting the conventions of their English contemporaries, most high-level officials continued to be drawn from the elite strata of society. "But in sharp contrast with the British practice at the time, our early public service appears to have been remarkably free of corruption. The business of governing was prestigious, and it was anointed with high moral imperatives of integrity and honor" (Mosher, 1968, p. 61). Indeed, Leonard White concludes that "the moral standards of the Federalist public service were extraordinarily high—higher by far than those prevailing in the British public service. . . . Probably never in the history of the United States has the standard of integrity of the federal civil service been at a higher level, even though the Federalists were sometimes unable to maintain their ideals" (White, 1948, p. 514).

For subsequent years evaluations of officials' character has not been so sanguine. It is easy to forget that the current scandal is "part of a recurrent cycle of American corruption and reform" (Eisenstadt, 1989, p. 537). In the morality crusades of American politics, the character of our public officials is perpetually being condemned, remedies are advanced and promulgated, and character again condemned. Abraham Eisenstadt argues that "in every American age, there has been a group that has sounded the cry of corruption: the cry that political values are being debased, the political system subverted, public officials bought out" (Eisenstadt, p. 539). Much of the time these cries have found sympathetic ears.

Americans have always believed that character is a component of public leadership. If by the Jacksonian period partisanship was a dominating factor in appointments and elections, Francis Grund, an Austrian who settled in the United States during that period, observed that even so "the high premium at which morality is held in the United States consists in its influence on the elections of officers" (quoted in Eisenstadt, 1989, p. 541). "In Europe, said Grund, the statesman's 'wanderings are forgotten' in the face of the good he has done for his nation." In comparison, Grund noted,

> No such compensation takes place in the United States. Private virtue overtops the highest qualifications of the mind, and is indispensable to the progress of the most acknowledged talents. . . . The moment a candidate is presented for office, not only his mental qualifications for the functions he is about to assume, but also his private character are made the subject of criticism. Whatever he may have done, said, or listened to . . . is sure to be brought before the public (quoted in Eisenstadt, 1989, p. 541).

Grund in his time and Eisenstadt in ours have tapped into the importance of character in evaluating officials' performance. That is, the core of a public official's performance does not pertain to specific policy debates but rather to its quality: "the quality of a president's thinking about policy and the quality of the character elements he brings to bear on the political process" (Renshon, 1996, p. 248). Renshon's analysis of presidential performance can be generalized to other public officials as well.

All senior-level public officials, whether elected or appointed, must make decisions and mobilize support for their actions. Decision making requires judgment; mobilizing support requires political leadership. Most Americans would probably agree with Renshon that "judgment is not primarily a result of intelligence, but of character. Character, in favorable circumstances, reflects a president's [or some other public official's] realistic sense of himself as an able, honest, and related person" (Renshon, 1996, p. 250). Certainly, political leadership requires intelligence, energy, and communication skill. But if "leadership is essentially a relationship, then at its heart lie trust and trustworthiness" (Renshon, 1996, p. 256), qualities which are engendered by character. Could it be that Americans are distrustful of government because they have little sense that public officials possess the relational qualities that character demands? Is character an important criterion to citizens as they evaluate official behavior?

III. TWO CASE STUDIES: CHARACTER AND PUBLIC OPINION

American history is replete with examples of election campaigns, policy decisions, and administrative activity in which character issues significantly influenced the public's perceptions of a candidate's, official's, or government's performance. Two interesting examples are the presidential elections of 1884 and, more recently, 1996. One of the more distasteful campaigns for the presidency of the United States took place in 1884, an election where, ironically, the platforms of the two major parties were almost identical so the campaign was waged on "personal issues" (Garraty and McCaughey, 1983, p. 607). It was an election year where the Republican party refused to nominate an incumbent but accidental president, Chester A. Arthur, for reelection, choosing instead a man "blessed with almost every political asset except a reputation for honesty" (Bailey and Kennedy, 1979, p. 474). James G. Blaine, the "Plumed Knight" from Maine was a politician who had "become wealthy without visible means of support" (Garraty and McCaughey, 1983, p. 611). His dealings with the railroads were at least suspicious and possibly corrupt. That he was aware of his culpability is evident in a batch of letters written by Blaine and made public by James Mulligan that seemed to implicate Blaine in some very questionable dealings with the railroads. One letter, written to Warren Fisher (a Boston Railroad attorney), asked Fisher to sign an accompanying letter clearing Blaine of any wrongdoing. The cover letter to Fisher concluded with the phrase, "Burn this letter," a phrase that was to be repeated again and again by Democratic partisans in the campaign. Although the public integrity of Blaine was questionable, his private behavior as a good family man was impeccable. When the Democrats tried to find some dirt in the private life of Blaine, they came up with nothing definitive. A malicious rumor was spread that Blaine was the groom in a "shotgun" wedding, but the story lacked credibility.

Grover Cleveland, on the other hand, was seen as a person of remarkable public integrity. The *New York World* endorsed Cleveland for four reasons, "He is honest, He is honest, He is honest, He is honest" (Boller, 1984, p. 147). Although his public reputation as a reformer and trustworthy public servant was well deserved, shortly after the nomination of "Grover the Good" came the shocking revelation made public by the Republicans that Cleveland was the father of an illegitimate child. It appears that while Cleveland, a bachelor, was living in Buffalo, New York, he met and had sex with Maria Halpin, a widow. When Cleveland was approached by his supporters for some reassurance that this could not be so, Cleveland could not deny the charges and admonished his campaign workers, "Above all, tell the truth" (Boller, 1984, p. 148).

The problem for the voters, succinctly stated, was whether to elect a man with sterling public character but a questionable personal morality, or to elect a good family man and devoted husband and father but with a history of dubious and shady public dealings. It is reported that one Mugwump said, "We should therefore elect Mr. Cleveland to the public office which he is so well qualified to fill and remand Mr. Blaine to the private station he is admirably fitted to adorn" (Boller, 1984, p. 149). The public agreed with these sentiments but only by the thinnest margin. Cleveland won the popular vote by less than 25,000 out of nearly ten million cast. His margin of victory was less than one-half of one percent, winning 48.5 percent to Blaine's 48.2 percent. Furthermore, the election actually hinged on the outcome of balloting in New York, which Cleveland carried by a mere 1149 votes out of more than a million ballots cast. The decisive factor in New York was an unfortunate statement made by the Rev. Samuel D. Burchard, a Presbyterian minister, who, in the course of introducing candidate Blaine referred to the Democratic party as the one of "Rum, Romanism, and Rebellion." This hapless choice of words offended many Catholics who were potential Blaine voters but who consequently voted for Cleveland. Every schoolchild knows that the most quotable campaign slogan of 1884 was, "Ma, Ma, where's my Pa?" After the election the Democrats would retort, "Gone to the White House, ha, ha, ha!" The Democrats could claim victory, but it was a hollow one. Cleveland won, but without the support of the majority of the voters and with the unanticipated help of a Republican preacher. Cleveland ran for the presidency two more times but he never received a majority of the popular votes cast.*

The Cleveland/Blaine election has a very contemporary ring to it. In recent years the politics of character have become more and more pronounced. Areas that once were not vigorously or viciously reported in the press are no longer out of bounds with the media. When Gary Hart in 1987 invited the media to follow him around, the invitation was accepted. Hart's subsequent cry of "unfair" fell on deaf ears and the *Monkey Business* became a double entendre of his extra-marital activities. No longer were the marital indiscretions of presidents or presidential candidates kept private. As a matter of fact, retrospectives of Franklin Roosevelt's and John Kennedy's marital infidelities while in the White House became commonplace. Even Dwight Eisenhower was not immune from a late-in-life memoir by Kay Summersby, recounting her romantic involvement with the general. Is the public's interest in this kind of behavior strictly prurient or does having this information help the public make better judgments about public leaders? Then, of course, there is the case of Bill Clinton.

The election of 1996 was a long-drawn-out, tiresome affair, and in one sense every bit as distasteful as the election of 1884. Although there were some differences in the party platforms, the distinctions were increasingly blurred by candidates in search of the solid center. Also, always lurking in the shadow of the public pronouncements of the candidates was the question of the president's character. After the disastrous elections for the Democrats in 1994, President Clinton sought to maintain his own relevance (even defending the fact that he was still relevant). Health care reform was buried; welfare reform became the hot ticket. The economy was good, trust in the president precarious.

---

* In the election of 1892 when Cleveland recaptured the White House from Benjamin Harrison, he won with 46 percent of the popular vote.

The Republicans' ''Contract with America'' held center stage for a while, and the president shared a stage with the speaker of the House at a town hall meeting. A politically wounded, morally delinquent president seemed easy pickings for the Republicans; however, the ''comeback kid'' was simply down and not out. The Republican-controlled Congress tried to force the president's hand on the budget and the government shut down. Two centerpiece initiatives of the ''Contract with America'' (balanced budget amendment and term limits) failed. Slowly the president gained momentum as he moved to the center (or some say even to the right of center). Finally, his leadership was seen in a positive light after the tragic terrorist bombing in Oklahoma City.

The 1996 campaign season was rather disheartening for the Republicans. Probably the two most politically attractive candidates (Colin Powell and Jack Kemp) chose not to run. Yet there was a crowded field of second-tier candidates to challenge the front runner, Senator Robert Dole, the majority leader of the Senate.* The nine declared challengers created an environment for Dole that no candidate envies. His campaign was forced into heavy spending early in the process to fend off the challenges from within his own party. Furthermore, his own party seemed at war with itself. While Dole wanted the party to position itself in the center, the conservative element was camped out firmly on the right. Thus, Dole had the nomination but not the hearts of the Republican faithful. The San Diego convention exposed this weakness in the drafting of the abortion plank of the party platform. Later in September, candidate Dole would receive a polite but unenthusiastic reception at the annual convention of the Christian Coalition. Dole was being forced to the right, but he was not right enough for the religious right. His campaign started slowly and maintained the pace. The centerpiece of the campaign was his call for a 15% across-the-board tax cut. The American public was not buying it. Perhaps, reminiscent of V. O. Key's delightful thesis, ''the voters aren't fools,'' the electorate remembered and equated the 15% tax cut with the infamous ''Read my lips'' cry of candidate George Bush in 1988. In any event, Senator Dole eventually shifted tactics to something that he found personally distasteful but necessary. He raised the issue of the president's character. Should Bill Clinton be trusted in office with a second term?

President Clinton had a free ride through the primary season and into Chicago, where he received his party's nomination for the second time. The delegates at the Democratic Convention seemed concerned more with the new dance craze, the Macarena, than with the Republicans. It was a routine, upbeat affair. Perhaps the only concern came from the more progressive (liberal) elements in the party that President Clinton had moved too far to the right. After all, now the president was stating that he was personally in favor of school uniforms, the death penalty in certain cases, a balanced budget, voluntary school prayer, and greater control over the availability of pornography on television and the Internet; he was opposed to homosexual marriage. In addition, he signed a welfare reform bill that left many of his strongest supporters shocked and dismayed. To some political allies of the president and to some in the public, Clinton was showing a serious lack of integrity by taking policy positions they felt were inconsistent with his earlier claims.

The dark side of President Clinton's first term included ongoing investigations into Whitewater, ''Travelgate,'' charges of misuse of FBI files, the death of Vince Foster, and

---

* A list of declared Republican candidates challenging Senator Dole for the Presidential nomination included Lamar Alexander, Pat Buchanan, Robert Dornan, Steve Forbes, Phil Gramm, Alan Keyes, Richard Lugar, Arlen Specter, and Pete Wilson.

Paula Jones's sexual harassment claims. Each would prove to be an ever-present source of embarrassment to the President, but obviously not fatal to his reelection prospects.* The decent-but-dour Bob Dole was not able to overcome the charismatic-but-perceived-as-flawed character of Bill Clinton.

Yet Bill Clinton was, like Grover Cleveland, unable to convince a majority of the voters to cast their ballots for him. In the electoral college, the 1996 election was not close.† However, President Clinton would end up with only 49.2% of the popular vote. Additionally, voter turnout dropped to 49% in an era where traditional indicators (higher numbers registered, higher income, higher education) would suggest a higher turnout. (Burns, Peltason, Cronin, and Magleby, 1997, p. 228). It is clear that President Clinton's reelection was greatly aided by a relatively weak opponent and a strong economy. Thus, his re-election does not diminish the impact of lingering doubts about Clinton's character on voter turnout and on his ability to lead. Indeed, given his favorable circumstances, Clinton was reasonably expected to receive a majority of the votes.††

IV. THE SURVEY DATA REVIEWED

Like the case studies, public opinion polls suggest that character is an important factor as citizens evaluate officials and government. Certainly in the last 30 years the confidence of the American public in their government to act ethically and honestly has declined substantially. Writing in the late 1970s, Daniel Yankelovich noted,

> . . . Trust in government declined dramatically from almost 80% in the late 1950s to about 33% in 1976. . . . More than 61% of the electorate believe that there is something morally wrong in the country. More than 80% of the voters say they do not trust those in positions of leadership as much as they used to. In the mid-60s a one-third minority reported feeling isolated and distant from the political process; by the mid-70s a two-thirds majority felt that what they think "really doesn't count." Approximately three out of five people feel the government suffers from a concentration of too much power in too few hands, and fewer than one out of five feel that congressional leaders can be believed (quoted in Lipset and Schneider, 1987, p. 15).

More recently, a 1996 survey of American political culture by The Post-Modernity Project at the University of Virginia found that 70% of Americans believed that the overall level of moral and ethical standards had fallen, while only 6% said standards had risen (Hunter and Bowman, 1996, vol. 2, Table 4.E). At the same time, 81% of the public feel that "government is pretty much run by a few big interests looking out for themselves." This sentiment is up from 75% in 1992 and 60% in 1976 (Hunter and Bowman, 1996, vol. 1, p. 29). Similarly, a *Newsweek* poll in 1994 reported that 76% of the public thinks the United States is in a moral and spiritual decline (Fineman, 1994, p. 31).

---

* The issue of campaign finance irregularities (renting the Lincoln bedroom to 'fat cat' contributors, illegal contributions from foreign interests, soliciting funds in the White House, accepting campaign funds in the White House) is left for the second Clinton term.

† Clinton received 379 electoral votes compared to Dole's 159 electoral votes.

†† Under similar circumstances in the elections of 1964 and 1972, Presidents Johnson and Nixon, respectively, each received 61 percent of the popular vote. Watergate was not an issue until after the 1972 campaign.

The Post-Modernity Project survey found that citizens still retain high support for ''our system of government'' and the ''American creed.'' For example, ''there is widespread agreement (95 percent of all surveyed) with Tocqueville's dictum that 'democracy is only as strong as the virtue of its citizens' '' (Hunter and Bowman, 1996, vol. 1, pp. 6–7). At the same time large proportions of citizens do not believe that their leaders are particularly virtuous. The same survey found that 78% of Americans agree that ''our leaders are more concerned with managing their images than with solving our nation's problems'' and that ''most politicians are more interested in winning elections than in doing what is right'' (p. 26). A majority regard our governing elite as ''not people of character'' (Hunter and Bowman, 1996, vol. 1, p. 28).

Related findings show that the public's sense of political efficacy—their self-evaluation of their capacity to influence political events—''fell after 1960 for reasons apparently independent of education'' (Lipset and Schneider, 1987, p. 21). The Post-Modernity Project survey found that 70% of its respondents believe that ''most elected officials don't care what people like me think'' (Hunter and Bowman, 1996, vol. 1, p. 26) while 50% agree that ''people like me don't have any say about what the government does'' (vol. 1, p. 18).

> Interestingly, survey data from other parts of the globe report similar findings: In 1992, for example, an opinion poll in Japan revealed that 74 percent of Japanese accepted the notion that ''many dishonest people are running the country'' . . . A SOFRES poll in February 1995, equally revealed that, for 62 percent of the French citizens interviewed, ''the majority of politicians were corrupt.'' The same story can also be told of opinion about politicians and their parties in other countries, such as Belgium, Italy and Spain (Mény, 1996, p. 118).

Levels of citizens' confidence in government in most European nations and Japan falls below confidence levels in the United States (Lipset and Schneider, 1987, p. 410).

The numbers and trends are disturbing and should not be casually dismissed. They raise the questions: is there a link between the public's perception of falling moral standards among politicians and citizens' declining trust and confidence in government? Is government's authority and legitimacy at stake? A 1995 Washington Post/Kaiser Family Foundation/Harvard University survey found that 71% of their respondents trusted the government in Washington to do the right thing only some of the time. In a open-ended question as to why respondents often or sometimes did not trust the national government, 35% volunteered comments indicating their belief that politicians lacked honesty or integrity (Washington Post/Kaiser Family Foundation/Harvard University Survey Project, 1996, p. 11). The *Newsweek* poll asked ''Do questions about Bill Clinton's character hurt his ability to be an effective moral leader?'' In response, 72% of the respondents answered either ''seriously'' or ''somewhat'' (Fineman, 1994, p. 31). In reporting on the general patterns of public confidence in institutions, Lipset and Schneider argue that ''evidence of a direct relationship between confidence in institutions and evaluations of their ethical and moral practices may be found'' in the survey data (Lipset and Schneider, 1987, p. 77). First, they note that 10 of the 11 political institutions—state government, the White House, Senate, House, bureaucracy, etc.—are rated low on both honesty and integrity and their ability to get things done or efficiency (Lipset and Schneider, 1987, pp. 74–75). Second, politicians and bureaucrats are ranked near the bottom in an evaluation of the ethical and moral practices of various professions and are grouped with those institutions or professions garnering the least confidence.

As they analyze the survey results, Lipset and Schneider surmise that ''the principal difference between the positively regarded professions and the negatively evaluated ones would appear to be the varying importance of self-interest.'' Though politicians and public administrators ''claim to be serving the public good . . . many people apparently believe that those who go into public life do so in order to serve their private self interest, either by benefiting economically or by obtaining power'' (Lipset and Schneider, 1987, p. 80). Clearly this disjunction between what public officials claim and what citizens perceive may be in the minds of citizens a problem of integrity. Furthermore, the low feelings of efficacy reported by the surveys may suggest that citizens sense that the relational element of character is deficient.

V. CONSEQUENCES OF THE CRISIS OF CHARACTER

We do not claim that lower voter turnout or the inability of the winning candidate to capture at least a majority of the popular vote is primarily a result of voters' perceptions of politicians' character. However, we do claim that character plays an important role in voters' decisions. Clearly, the way that issues, character, and personality mix and, finally, impact the voting decisions is complex. Nonetheless, the conclusion of Campbell, Converse, Miller, and Stokes regarding the importance of character in the 1956 election of President Eisenhower remains instructive: ''It was the response to personal qualities—to his sincerity, his integrity, and sense of duty, his virtue as a family man, his religious devotion, and his sheer likableness—that rose substantially in the second campaign. These frequencies leave the strong impression that in 1956 Eisenhower was honored not so much for his performance as president as for the quality of his person'' (Campbell, Converse, Miller, and Stokes, 1980, p. 56). As citizens' evaluations of the character of candidates has fallen, it is apparent that at some point increasing numbers of the electorate are opting for none of the above.

Neither do we claim that citizens' perceptions of declining political character is the primary cause of falling confidence and trust in government. Nonetheless, we do argue that widespread concern about the character of public officials reinforces a rather permanent skepticism of government's ability to perform and is undermining the legitimacy of political and administrative actors. Finally, we do not claim that character issues are *now* undermining the legitimacy of government institutions (the regime), but it seems plausible that repeated revelations of violations of widely accepted standards in the personal and public lives of officials may threaten legitimate government. Yves Mény has concluded:

> The recognition that political systems, especially democracies, are based on values, which, when violated, weaken their legitimacy, implies that corruption [we would insert the broader notion, lack of character] ought not to be considered as a secondary phenomenon, or a benign evil. . . . Corruption [widespread lack of character on the part of public officials] brings destruction to any form of society, whether dictatorial or authoritarian and is particularly damaging to democratic governments (Mény, 1996, p. 112).

Furthermore, in Europe and the United States both, the widespread lack of confidence in government and the weakening of government's legitimacy may be an impetus for the rise of populist movements. Thus, discontent over character, though only one ingredient in a complicated recipe, may nonetheless be a significant factor ''in the resurgence of populism in many European countries [and the United States] and in the challenge this poses to elites and democratic institutions'' (Mény, 1996, p. 119).

Aristotle in his *Politics* reminds us, ''To live by the rule of the constitution ought not to be regarded as slavery, but rather salvation'' (Barker, 1946, p. 234). Thus, Aristotle gives advice as to how constitutions in both oligarchies and democracies are to be protected. One admonition is that ''rulers must not be permitted to use their position for their own profit''; the people are ''less offended at being excluded from public office than they are by the knowledge that their representatives are embezzling public funds'' (Harmon, 1964, p. 66). Petty lawlessness in government is destructive of good governance; thus, Aristotle tells us, leaders must be persons of high character (virtuous). Perhaps Aristotle is simply stating the obvious. But the difficulty lies in the fact that while only the virtuous should lead, it has certainly never been a given that only the virtuous do lead. Of course they do not. Statesmen and scoundrels will rule, and it is not always clear which is which. However, when the body politic believes that all (or most) politicians do not live by widely accepted personal standards and are not to be trusted, when citizens believe that too many public officials are looking after their own interests (and not the common good), when voters think that honesty and wisdom have given way to deceit and intrigue, then the system itself may be in jeopardy.

There may be no systematic linkage between character and these consequences. Perhaps the best that can be stated is that while character has not dominated the American political environment in the past and does not in the present, character does count. But even if this is all that can be claimed, it is enough to warrant countermeasures in political and organizational environments and practices in an effort to foster character development and more accurate citizen perceptions.

REFERENCES

Bailey, T. and Kennedy, D. (1979). *The American Pageant*, 6th ed. Lexington, MA: D.C. Heath and Company.

Barker, E. (trans. and ed.) (1946). *The Politics of Aristotle*. London: Oxford University Press.

Block, A.A. (1996). American corruption and the decline of the progressive ethos. In M. Levi and D. Nelkin (eds.), *The Corruption of Politics and the Politics of Corruption*, 18–35. Oxford: Blackwell Publishers.

Boller, Paul (1984). *Presidential Campaigns*. New York: Oxford University Press.

Burns, J.M., Peltason, J.W., Cronin, T.E., and Magleby, D.B. (1997). *Government by the People*, brief ed., 2nd ed. Upper Saddle River, NJ: Prentice Hall.

Campbell, A., Converse, P.E., Miller, W.E., and Stokes, D.E. (1980). *The American Voter*, Midway reprint. Chicago, University of Chicago Press.

Carter, S.L. (1996). *Integrity*. New York: Basic Books.

Dalton, R.J. (1988). *Citizen Politics in Western Democracies*. Chatham, NJ: Chatham House Publishers.

Denhardt, K. (1994). ''Character ethics and the transformation of governance.'' *International Journal of Public Administration* 17(*12*), 2165–2193.

Doig, A. (1996). ''From Lynskey to Nolan: The Corruption of British Politics and Public Service?'' In M. Levi and D. Nelkin (eds.), *The Corruption of Politics and the Politics of Corruption*, 36–56. Oxford: Blackwell Publishers.

Economist (1994). ''Europe: big buckets always leak most.'' *Economist* 333(*7890*), 58.

Eisenstadt, A.S. (1989). ''Political corruption in American history.'' In A.J. Heidenheimer, M. Johnston, and V.T. LeVine (eds.), *Political Corruption*, 537–556. New Brunswick, NJ: Transaction Publishers.

Fineman, H. (1994). ''The virtuecrats.'' *Newsweek*, June, 13.

Garraty, J.A. and McCaughey, R.A. (1983). *The American Nation*, 6th ed. New York: Harper & Row.

Harmon, M.J. (1964). *Political Thought from Plato to the Present*. New York: McGraw Hill Book Company.

Hunter, J.D. and Bowman, C. (1996). *The State of Disunion: The Post-Modernity Project*, Vols 1 and 2. Ivy, VA: Medias Res Educational Foundation.

Lipset, S.M. and Schneider, W. (1987). *The Confidence Gap*, rev. ed. Baltimore: Johns Hopkins University Press.

Mény, Y. (1996). ''Politics, corruption and democracy: The 1995 Stein Rokkan Lecture.'' *European Journal of Political Research* 30(*3*), 111–123.

Mosher, F.C. (1968). *Democracy and the Public Service*. New York: Oxford University Press.

Madison, J. (1788). *Federalist No. 51*.

Nelkin, D. and Levi, M. (1996). ''The corruption of politics and the politics of corruption: an overview.'' In M. Levi and D. Nelkin (eds.), *The Corruption of Politics and the Politics of Corruption*, 1–17. Oxford: Blackwell Publishers.

Renshon, S.A. (1996). *High Hopes: The Clinton Presidency and the Politics of Ambition*. New York: New York University Press.

Roberts, R. (1985).''Lord, protect me from the appearance of wrongdoing.'' In D. Rosenbloom (ed.), *Public Personnel Policy*, 177–192. Port Washington, NY: Associated Faculty.

Stille, A. (1993). ''World report: a scandal too big to ignore.'' *U.S. News and World Report* 114(*15*), 43–44.

Thompson, D.F. (1993). ''Mediated corruption: the case of the Keating five.'' *Public Administration Review* 87(2), 369–381.

Washington Post/Kaiser Family Foundation/Harvard University Survey Project (1996). ''Why don't Americans trust the government?'' (Washington: Kaiser Family Foundation).

White, L.D. (1948). *The Federalists*. New York: Macmillan Company.

Wilson, F.L. (1996). *Concepts and Issues in Comparative Politics*. Upper Saddle River, NJ: Prentice-Hall.

3
Preparing for Diversity in the Midst of Adversity

An Intercultural Communication Training Program for Refugee-Assistance Crisis Management

Phyllis Bo-Yuen Ngai Department of Curriculum and Instruction, University of Montana, Missoula, Montana

Peter Koehn Department of Political Science, University of Montana, Missoula, Montana

I. INTRODUCTION

In today's diverse world, emergencies increasingly occur in a context of cultural as well as institutional pluralism. Consequently, persons already involved in refugee-assistance crisis management, as well as new recruits, must be in a position to engage effectively in intercultural communication.

The development of intercultural communication competency requires specialized preparation—preferably in advance of assignment in the case of agency staff and integrated with local-level assistance activities for community members. In this chapter, the authors present their design for a model training program that is specifically intended to build intercultural sensitivity and communication skills among persons responsible for refugee assistance crisis management. We assume that participants in the program will include a mix of nongovernmental organization (NGO) workers and governing-board members, government employees, refugees selected by their community, leaders chosen for training by local host communities, and volunteers.

The overall goals of our model intercultural communication training program are (1) to enhance communicative and behavioral competency in dealing with refugee assistance crises and (2) to facilitate the management of such crises by harnessing the power of diverse cultural perspectives. In the multicultural working environment that characterizes refugee assistance, competency in intercultural communication involves attaining specific diagnostic and transaction skills. Mastery of these skills enables program graduates to select and apply appropriate intercultural communication guidelines in essential strategic information exchanges (see Chapter 45 in this volume). The second major objective of the training program concerns promoting appreciation for and utilization of the synergistic potential of intercultural communication among staff and community members who engage one another from diverse perspectives.

A. Training Criteria

In the management of refugee assistance crises, the performance of essential functions—including needs and vulnerabilities assessment, resource identification and mobilization, service provision, conflict management, and accountability—requires effective intercultural communication training for expatriate staff, locally recruited assistance workers, and community members. In designing the overall program, coordinators should bear in mind that (1) emergencies ''provide opportunities to train local people in skills that increase their capacities to deal with subsequent crises and/or development efforts'' (Anderson and Woodrow 1989:79, 83) and that (2) trainees constantly learn from the explicit and implicit communication of insights and lessons they receive in the field.

In the current multicultural refugee assistance environment, therefore, an intercultural communication training strategy should (1) promote understanding among staff members possessing different nationality, ethnic, and religious backgrounds; (2) involve selected participants from the affected local community(ies); (3) enhance organizational goal attainment; (4) integrate the field experiences of expatriate and local NGO personnel; (5) be useful both for specific multicultural-workplace situations and when interacting with a dispossessed clientele; and (6) enable trainees to impart the principal lessons of their training experience to fellow refugee assistance workers from the same and different cultural backgrounds. These six criteria should be applied in designing each training intervention and in assessing outcomes.

B. Preprogram Assessment

Although this chapter presents components and considerations for a model training program that are based primarily upon lessons from the study and practice of intercultural communication, actual programming must be tailored to the specific clientele. Thus, the first stage of the training process always must involve needs and capabilities assessment. All participants should be invited to take part in a needs and capabilities identification exercise in advance of the course.[1] In the case of refugee assistance crisis management

[1] The importance of refugee participation and consultation in all stages of decision making regarding their training constituted a recurring emphasis among participants at a 1994 International Symposium dedicated to refugee training. The experienced practitioners and other experts in attendance agreed that refugee needs, identified through careful assessments that involve refugees themselves (specifically including women and the elderly), should drive the implementation of training programs (Koehn 1994:6, 64). Specific recommendations included the following: (1) ''training should be a community-based process of learning, empowerment, and enhancing self-esteem which takes place within a planning/learning/change spiral where all are teachers and learners'' (ibid. 70); (2) ''in order to be sustainable, training in administration and management should be future-oriented and participatory, accommodating people-oriented planning with involvement of all players at all stages . . .'' (ibid. 69–70); (3) training needs should ''reflect the socio-economic, cultural, as well as human-resource needs of the country of origin and the refugees themselves'' (ibid. 72); and (4) appropriate training should include the incorporation and modification of traditional practices (ibid. 68).

training, trainees are expected to arrive with a multiplicity of cultural backgrounds and to share elements of a working environment that principally is defined by demands for emergency relief and sustainable development. The trainees' common working environment is likely to involve a dispossessed and traumatized clientele in need of assistance, considerable local autonomy, demands for continuous vertical and horizontal communication, goal attainment that is contingent upon effective communication, frequent pressure for on-the-spot decisions and innovative responses, the primacy of informal interaction, logistical complexity, shortages of vital equipment and supplies, a high degree of uncertainty (including basic uncertainty over the duration of one's mission), and lack of physical security.

As part of the needs and capabilities assessment process, each group of prospective trainees should be surveyed separately. The survey should emphasize encounters with previous intercultural communication problems and approaches to cross-cultural adaptability as well as participant awareness, knowledge, concerns, expertise, experience, abilities, and desired skills (also see Pedersen 1994:28–30). The survey should result in an inventory that guides trainers in tailoring the program to the specific backgrounds and needs of each group of trainees. In preparation for program sessions, trainers should integrate trainee doubts and questions into anonymous and hypothetical incidents and situations for analysis and small-group discussion. For instance, if potential trainees mention in the survey that certain types of intercultural conflicts have presented difficult problems to deal with, trainers can design directly relevant conflict management training sessions. Trainers should aim at addressing trainees' concerns and interests by offering practical advice throughout the training program. Moreover, program coordinators should use the survey results to identify trainees whose practical experiences, knowledge, and adaptability skills will enable them to serve as valuable resource persons (also see Anderson and Woodrow 1989:318–319).

II. MODEL PROGRAM ACTIVITIES AND COMPONENTS

The intercultural communication training program set forth here primarily is designed for refugee assistance workers who possess some formal education. It consists of five principal training activities: (1) multicultural knowledge and awareness building, (2) developing intercultural communication skills, (3) emotion sharing, (4) training of trainers, and (5) postcourse assessment and follow-on activities.

The first aspect of the model program—enhancing knowledge and awareness—sharpens trainees' cross-cultural sensitivity and adaptability. This enables participants to identify, understand, and cope with the dynamics of cultural differences and adjustments. The second training activity—developing communication skills—provides trainees with concrete and ready-to-use techniques needed for the exchange of vital information and for effective interaction in culturally diverse crisis management situations. Building intercultural communication skills requires an extensive training effort. In the discussion of this activity, therefore, we present an eightfold training design linked to specific teaching approaches that promise to be especially conducive for learning. The third dimension of the model program—emotion sharing—aims to equip participants with skills that facilitate management of the negative emotions (e.g., trauma, stress, frustration, fear, and depression) that frequently are encountered in refugee assistance crisis situations. The next sections of this chapter provide a step-by-step discussion of the proposed training model, including the training-of-trainers and postcourse assessment and follow-on activities.

III. MULTICULTURAL KNOWLEDGE AND AWARENESS BUILDING

The primary objectives of the first training activity are to raise general awareness among trainees about culturally influenced behavior, including differing cultural perceptions, and to promote individual capacity to engage in culturally specific adjustments. Joseph Bastien (1995:85–86) shows, for instance, that "it is only after doctors and nurses understand people's cultural perceptions of . . . vaccinations that they can communicate cross-culturally in terms that the people understand."

A helpful first step in knowledge and awareness building is to expose the trainees' "own stereotypes, prejudices, misconceptions, or a combination of these, about members of cultural groups that are different from their own" (D'Andrea et al. 1991:144). For instance, participants can be engaged in an ice-breaking exercise that generates "a degree of embarrassment and a desire to learn more about culture and cultural differences" (Brislin and Yoshida 1994:27; also see Pedersen 1994:34, 66, 74–75). It also is useful for trainees to discuss personal experiences, participate in role plays and role reversals, and explain videotaped or enacted intercultural interactions from the perspective of learning to value, respect, and become comfortable with cultural differences (Sue 1991:102; also see Pedersen 1994:27, 39).

In the training model developed by the authors, knowledge and awareness building includes mastery of cultural continuum identification and placement, sociocultural map construction, opening and revising culturally specific communication data files in one's mind, and cultural adjustment action planning. We suggest that knowledge building begin by introducing cultural dimensions in the form of continuums that present different behavioral patterns. The six cultural dimensions selected by the authors for this purpose are set forth in Table 1. The trainer next describes the characteristics of the two defining points on each dimension (see Chapter 45) and points out that countless variations exist between the extremes of each continuum.

Once trainees achieve a firm grasp of the six cultural dimensions, they should be invited to locate the prevailing pattern of their own culture at a point along each continuum

Table 1 Selected Cultural Dimensions

Dimension	Continuum
Context	High -- Low
	H.K. U.S.
Contact	High -- Low
	U.S. H.K.
Power distance	High -- Low
	H.K. U.S.
Uncertainty avoidant	High -- Low
	H.K. U.S.
Masculine/feminine	Masculine -------------------------------------- Feminine
	H.K. U.S.
Collectivistic/individualistic	Collectivist ------------------------------------ Individualist
	H.K. U.S.

based on personal understanding and the exchange of information and insights. In Table 1, the authors placed the United States (U.S.) on each continuum as an example.

The next step, illustrated in Table 1 by reference to Hong Kong (H.K.), is to fit the other culture(s) that trainees must interact with on each continuum. Acquiring accurate and culturally sensitive understanding of unfamiliar behavioral styles requires prior study and ''in-depth understanding of social groups, their history, their political dynamics, and their cultural characteristics'' (Eade and Williams 1995:253, 813). Gains in understanding can be achieved through reading, the presentation of empirical data regarding the specific culture(s) one is working with, panel discussions, interviews with experts, exposure to audiovisual resources, field trips accompanied by expert debriefings, attribution training, bicultural observation, and cultural immersion (Pedersen 1994:37, 39–40). The ongoing participatory process of constructing a sociocultural ''map'' of the geographic area one operates within (Eade and Williams, 1995:253–255) can be particularly useful in building knowledge about an unfamiliar local culture. Trainees should be guided through this process in order that the compilation of reliable sociocultural maps becomes a culture-specific tool they are capable of utilizing and comfortable with in the field.

The entire *continuum-placement* exercise is designed to assist trainees both in developing heightened sensitivity regarding behavioral variations across cultures and in ''seeing'' the extent to which specific cultures are different from and similar to each other. It also provides an opportunity for trainers to discuss the effects of ethnocentrism and prejudice and to comment on the presence of alternative cultural patterns and the importance of overcoming stereotypes.

After trainees are guided through peer-group discussion and individualized coaching to place the cultures they are dealing with on each continuum, the trainer should provide them with a handout that summarizes *communicative* differences at each end of the six cultural dimensions set forth in Table 1.[2] Trainees should learn how to use this handout to identify predominant communication styles within the particular culture(s) at issue.

This type of knowledge training resembles opening *culture-specific data files in the minds* of trainees. Trainers should emphasize that such ''mind'' files are neither complete nor final, and that each only refers to the dominant pattern of communication. When working in an unfamiliar culture, retrieving the appropriate cultural data file will provide program graduates with valuable hints for understanding local communication styles. Practitioners also should be prepared to modify the knowledge files in their minds during the continuous process of learning about a culture in situ.

Next, trainees should be guided on how to construct a personal *cultural adjustment action plan*. This training component focuses on the blending of cognitive and behavioral dimensions. The actual preparation and periodic modification of each participant's dynamic cultural adjustment action plan will be based upon the outcome of his or her culture-specific assessment and on the expectations and communication styles one encounters in the crisis management field site (also see Ngai and Koehn 1998:49–50; Pedersen 1994: 135–137).

Table 1 and the communication styles handout serve as useful tools that trainees can take back with them to their workplace. Although the two devices provide only generalized information about six different communication styles across cultures, they also constitute magnifying glasses that allow trained assistance personnel to observe and understand their

---

[2] This handout should be adapted from Table 1 found in Chapter 45.

multicultural work situations more clearly and to monitor and adjust their own intercultural behavior. In sum, the knowledge- and awareness-building dimensions of the training program are intended to equip trainees with capabilities in intercultural perception, learning, information gathering, decision making, and adjustment that will be of lifelong value in crisis management. With this background in place, the training program next turns to developing skills in intercultural communication.

IV. DEVELOPING INTERCULTURAL COMMUNICATION SKILLS

The principal overall objectives of the second part of the training program are to provide emergency management practitioners with the sending and receiving skills needed to ''improve and increase intentional communication across cultures'' (Pedersen, 1994:69) and with the ability to realize the benefits of cross-cultural synergy when managing refugee assistance crises. If successful, this part of the training program will equip crisis-assistance personnel to engage in interculturally sensitive planning and to reach participatory decisions that are shaped by the unique cultures and customs of the involved refugee and host community populations.

In light of its principal objectives, the second part of the intercultural communication training program focuses on developing skills in eight key areas: intercultural nonverbal communication, written and verbal expression, information gathering and sharing, multicultural organization communication, interaction with clients of diverse cultures, reaching agreement in intercultural contexts, intercultural conflict management, and harnessing cross-cultural synergy. The instructional approach would include a structured learning mix of informative presentations about each skill; skill clarification through case-study preparation and analysis; the joint development of new forms of practice decision-making; rehearsal, with feedback, via role-playing, simulations, and action training; and the transfer of skills to crisis management situations through on-the-job training (see Pedersen 1994: 41). Decisions on which skills and approaches to emphasize should be based on the outcome of the needs/capabilities assessment and on the particular set of cultures represented in the program. In the following discussion, the authors elaborate on the eight components of their model skill-based curriculum and link promising instructional approaches to each training objective.

A. Component 1: Intercultural Nonverbal Communication

Nonverbal communication scholars suggest that people communicate mainly through nonverbal cues. Intercultural interactions present one context in which nonverbal misunderstandings frequently emerge due to lack of awareness and training. As Pedersen (1994: 91) points out, ''persons from another culture may grossly misinterpret a simple gesture, expression, or implied attitude owing to a different cultural viewpoint. Hints, clues, understatements, and appropriate omissions are some of the more subtle tools of communication that present barriers to multicultural communication.''

To enable participants to avoid costly misunderstandings and to facilitate effective intercultural communication (see Ngai and Koehn 1998:49–50; Sue 1991:103), this training component first raises participant awareness of cultural differences in communicating through facial expressions, gazes, gestures, posture, body movement, space, dress, touch, vocalics, and the use of time. The importance of subtle nonverbal cues and barriers in communicating across cultures is demonstrated. Then, trainers assist crisis managers develop personal skills in observing, accurately understanding, facilitating feedback (Pedersen 1994:91), and utilizing appropriate nonverbal behavior to prevent misunderstanding and to enhance the intercultural communication of intended messages.

Approach: Implicit-cultural-messages exercises (see Pedersen, 1994:82–83). Explaining and sharing one's culture through drawing (see Pedersen, 1994:84–85). Presentations and videos on reading and transmitting cultural nonverbal cues and on confused interpretations. Joint examination and reflection on the results of a nonverbal communication survey conducted among trainees. Sign and gesture exercise. Trainee role plays guided by articulate cultural resource persons (Pedersen, 1994:37–38) of unfamiliar nonverbal behavior in multicultural work situations. Peer reactions and coaching. Modeling and demonstrations with videotaped feedback.

B. Component 2: Written and Verbal Expression

Although spoken English currently is the prevailing language of international and intercultural communication, its verbal expression differs widely across cultures and even within countries. Understanding important variations enables crisis managers to avoid costly misunderstandings and misinterpretations. This component should develop enhanced behavioral sensitivity to cultural differences in verbal communication logic and behavior—including equivocation, requesting, compliance gaining, taboo topics—and prepare participants for necessary linguistic adjustments. Training in public and media relations should emphasize effective public speaking in specific cultural and political contexts.

This component also emphasizes mastery of effective business writing skills in English—the predominant language of formal communication within and among NGOs, and between NGOs and host-government agencies. Guidance should be provided in the concise and unambiguous drafting of documents such as situation reports (see Eade and Williams 1995:959–960), grant applications, budget requests, news releases, contracts and other legal documents, and interinstitutional agreements (see Siegel 1985:116). Furthermore, this component should introduce methods of designing educational materials that present topics in a language and style that are easily understood in the client culture (see Taylor 1979:441).

Approach: Presentations on cultural differences in oral expression—including informality versus formality, high involvement versus high consideration, fast and slow messages, cross-gender communication. Training in culturally appropriate linguistic initiation and response for the work environment and in the effective use of questions. Role plays using intercultural verbal exchanges.

Presentations on effective English-language professional writing skills. Adopting an audience-oriented strategy is particularly important in multicultural settings. Explore cultural differences in organizing and presenting information and ideas. Video on "power writing." Writing exercises with feedback from trainers and learning from others' mistakes. Practice editing. Writing-improvement goals should be set so that they "stretch" trainees but are attainable (see Anderson and Woodrow 1989:84–85).

C. Component 3: Information Gathering and Sharing

This component involves at least five training objectives:

1. Identifying which information is needed for problem solving and decision making in the particular humanitarian-assistance context

2. Learning how to locate essential information in a foreign environment
3. Developing competency in gaining access to reliable sources of information in different cultural contexts
4. Ensuring the physical security of staff and valuable organizational resources through networking
5. Building individual and institutional capacity to alert persons from diverse cultures and different organizations, sectors, and levels about impending crises

Approach: Handouts on crucial information needs given the specific crisis management context. Training in locating and consulting available sources of useful data and in PALM, or participative learning methods (Eade and Williams 1995:254–255). Presentations on information access in relevant emergency situations and on message-networking techniques. Case-study analysis and small-group discussion among trainees regarding appropriate cross-cultural teaching/learning styles and ways to overcome obstacles to information gathering and sharing.

D. Component 4: Multicultural-Organization Communication

This session deals with methods of effective interorganizational and cross-sectoral communication and networking in decentralized multinational and multicultural settings. Trainees learn how to assess organizational culture and develop skills in communicating across levels and within multicultural intraorganizational groups and teams. In addition, trainers introduce the importance of cross-cultural competency when one is engaged in processes of transparent decision making, interest articulation, and the identification of major stakeholder groups and their interests, power bases, and limitations (see Siegel 1985: 116). Training also is provided in communication strategies for effective leadership in multicultural settings—including team building and teamwork, problem resolution, making meetings work, networking, and functioning as an effective voice in mobilizing resources from community, government, and donor sources.

Approach: Presentations on effective organizational-communication strategies in the multicultural workplace. Case-study analysis and small-group discussion of organizational communication problems. Group work with critical incidents involving refugee assistance personnel from diverse cultural backgrounds that requires that a decision be reached and an intervention plan be developed, admits no easy or clear-cut answers, and projects serious consequences (Pedersen 1994:81). Action training using actual or simulated policy dilemmas and intercultural communication barriers. Groups or work teams analyze problems and the likely impacts of alternative actions, propose a detailed set of recommended actions in priority order, decide upon and implement a problem-solving strategy, and assess outcomes and side effects. For example, an interorganizational committee of refugee assistance managers devises an agreed-upon procedure for improving communication linkages among NGOs, central and local government agencies, refugee and host community institutions. More complex challenges of a multi-sector and/or multilevel nature can be introduced as participants develop their analytical and problem-solving abilities.

E. Component 5: Interaction with Clients of Diverse Cultures—Local Capacity Building

This component presents sensitizing background on relevant refugee populations, including the antecedents of their dislocation and their experiences with trauma, depression, uprootedness.[3] Training also is provided in effective means of (1) dealing with culture shock, distrust toward strangers, and insecurity in cross-cultural relationships; (2) creating valued participatory linkages that span cultures (see, for instance, Phillips 1993:107–108); (3) conveying information-gathering, organizing, and analyzing skills (Anderson and Woodrow 1989:47–48); (4) building intercultural rapport, acculturation skills (Bemak et al. 1996:249–251), self-esteem, and empowerment (see Eade and Williams 1995:879; Koehn 1994:70; Bemak et al. 1996:259); and (5) inculcating concepts of self-reliance. Important related elements for refugee assistance staff and volunteers are (1) sensitivity training regarding gender/age roles (and role reversals) and the importance of communicating with the ''appropriate group for the most effective impact'' (Anderson and Woodrow 1989:67; Bemak et al. 1996:251); (2) learning ''the skill of respectful and careful listening'' in culturally unfamiliar contexts; that is, being ''ignorant but teachable'' (Anderson and Woodrow 1989:86); (3) developing interculturally sensitive planning—reaching participatory decisions that reflect understanding of the specific cultures and customs of involved refugee and host community populations; and (4) training in how to establish early-warning systems that centrally involve diverse communities (Lusty 1979:353).

Approach: Presentations on developing interculturally sensitive information models (see Bastien 1995:85). Knowledge sharing with informed resource persons that accurately and comprehensively explicates the particular refugee experience and promotes political and cultural awareness (Bemak et al. 1996:255, 258). Role plays that simulate critical interaction, acculturation, and role confusion situations with and among refugee and host communities (see, for instance, Bemak et al., 1996:253; Pedersen, (1994: 68–69). Critical incidents that feature crisis management personnel and refugees from culturally diverse backgrounds. Small groups of trainees and experienced trainers discuss and analyze alternative approaches to difficult cases and incidents. Action training that builds skills in developing self-reliant community involvement in needs assessment, project selection (Hyden et al. 1996:44–45), and project appraisal (van Bergen 1995:26). Enhancing the capacity of local participants ''to learn from their own environment and experience'' by encouraging ''methods of experimentation . . . that are appropriate to the cultural context and that can become permanent systems for the discovery and communication of knowledge'' (Anderson and Woodrow 1989:81).[4]

F. Component 6: Reaching Agreement in Intercultural Contexts

Trainees are informed regarding culture-general and culture-specific factors that inhibit and facilitate cross-cultural agreement reaching. Then, this component offers training in negotiation strategies for reaching agreement in dynamic multicultural settings, with special attention devoted to the nonverbal elements of intercultural negotiation (see Ngai and Koehn 1998). The program should emphasize adaptive and inventive skills. Successful

---

[3] The trauma experiences of politically dislocated migrants include deprivation of basic needs, physical injury and torture, incarceration, and witnessing killing and acts of human cruelty. Among refugees, such stresses occur prior to dislocation, during flight, and throughout the resettlement (and, if it occurs, repatriation) process (Bemak et al. 1996:248–251).

[4] Bemak et al. (1996:260) maintain, for instance, that mental health professionals need to be knowledgeable and respectful of traditional practices, and to assess them critically, with a view toward ''establishing 'treatment partnerships' that provide the refugee with the rich combination of healing sources from the culture of origin and culture of resettlement.''

trainees will develop competency in negotiation and persuasion across cultures. Skills in working with interpreters and cultural informants also are likely to prove useful (Pedersen 1994:34).

> **Approach**: Using reference criteria that are directly related to intercultural agreement-reaching situations, culturally different partners attempt to predict the other person's reactions and responses (see, for instance, Pedersen 1994:87–88). Presentations and videos on effective intercultural-negotiation strategies. Role plays and behavioral rehearsals. Modeling and demonstrating intercultural negotiation and agreement-reaching skills with feedback aided by audiovisual resources (Pedersen 1994:32). Individual practice with interpreters and cultural informants (Pedersen 1994:35). Facilitated action training.

G. Component 7: Intercultural Conflict Management

Training in ways of preventing and containing intercultural conflicts. This component should enable participants to identify potential sources of conflicts (e.g., language choice in working and social relations) and effective communication responses in the multicultural work environment. It also involves training in network-management, relationship-building, conflict-management, and balance-restoration (see Pedersen 1994:200) strategies in multicultural settings. Participants should develop competency in mediation across cultures. Where appropriate, this component should include training in dispute resolution and restoring reciprocity among culturally mixed communities receiving non-indigenous or returning refugees (see Koehn 1994:82, 78).

> **Approach**: Provide background on the refugee-settlement process and on the principal players involved (see Pedersen 1994:34). Presentations and videos on effective intercultural conflict management and mediation strategies. Discussion of conflict-management and balance-restoration styles in different cultures. Case-study analysis. Critical incidents and decisional situations involving conflicts among persons from culturally different backgrounds, using teamwork and comparative problem solving. Microskill training that "builds on basic foundation skills toward more advanced [integrative] skills" (Pedersen 1994:41). Videotaped role playing in simulated conflict and mediation situations with feedback from trainers and trainees. Action training in the use of inclusive communication strategies within work groups and among agency staff and community members.

H. Component 8: Harnessing Cross-Cultural Synergy

Emergency-assistance practitioners report that people are more receptive to change, to learning about capabilities and vulnerabilities, and "to considering new ways of doing things" in the aftermath of disaster (Anderson and Woodrow 1989:14, 62, 83). Participants should emerge from the intercultural-communication training program aware that emergency situations provide an opportunity to improve local conditions and that many promising culture-bridging options arise in crisis settings even when resources are limited (van Bergen 1995:27).

Facilitating creative and constructive input from a variety of perspectives requires the creation and maintenance of a climate that supports the articulation of challenges to agency thinking and customary practices (Eade and Williams 1995:821). Moreover, the establishment of dynamic networks among autonomous organizations that share common concerns reveals that information diversity serves as a source of strength and as a vital aid to cooperation in crisis management (Eade and Williams 1995:379). In this component, therefore, trainees should develop (1) learning skills that emphasize receptivity to new and different ideas and approaches; (2) competency in multicultural group decision making through problem and constraint identification, testing hypotheses about contributing factors and opportunities, generating creative alternative approaches and analyzing the consequences of each, and in selecting a viable alternative and evaluating the impact of its implementation (see Levin 1997:5); and (3) the ability to tap the power of diverse perspectives and change possibilities through networking, community empowerment, and the judicious selection of multicultural-communication styles and strategies from a wide repertoire of practical alternatives (see Pedersen 1994:36).

> **Approach**: Training in identifying the advantages and power of diversity, in developing listening and adaptation skills, and in avoiding cultural chauvinism and stereotyping. Critical incidents/opportunities with team initiatives; reports back to the entire group of trainees. Involvement in realistic group-problem-solving exercises. Completion of challenging projects by multicultural groups engaged in goal-directed interaction. Facilitated action training.

V. EMOTION SHARING AND INTERCULTURAL COMMUNICATION

Emergency and crisis situations ensure that humanitarian-assistance personnel operate in a stressful and rest-deprived work environment. The pressures, workload volume, and burden of responsibilities they assume are likely to be exceptionally heavy. The *Oxfam Handbook of Development and Relief* adds that ''they may witness atrocities and immense suffering; and may themselves be close to individuals who are killed, detained, tortured or bereaved'' (Eade and Williams 1995:849, 973). Consequently, refugee assistance workers often experience feelings of ''helplessness, guilt or anger . . .'' (Eade and Williams 1995:849, 973). In exceptional situations, NGO staff encounter death threats and are vulnerable targets for kidnapping and assassination (Burge 1995:157). Insecurity and fear for one's own life exert a debilitating toll on vulnerable crisis managers. In one extreme case, ''the perilous nature'' of providing assistance for Rwandan refugees in Zaire in 1994 ''was a regular agenda item in coordination meetings in Goma and in conversations among international and national staff'' (Minear and Guillot 1996:65).

Service in a different culture with minimal local support adds to the extreme and prolonged level of emotional distress that many crisis managers encounter in the field. Thus, expatriates who are living and working in isolation from their primary support system(s) are likely to experience refugee assistance as particularly emotionally taxing. The *Oxfam Handbook of Development and Relief* cautions that in such crisis-management situations ''People may not themselves recognise the ways in which their responses and behaviour are stress-related. A common reaction is to take refuge in work—by working long hours without proper breaks, and failing to relax or take leave. The individual's health and ability to function may seriously suffer'' (Eade and Williams 1995:973).

One important purpose of the intercultural communication training program, therefore, should be to prepare crisis managers to recognize and respect the early stages of stress among themselves as well as among other humanitarian assistance workers. Learning how to establish an organizational culture that ensures that staff are assigned manageable workloads, guarantees sufficient and undisturbed leaves, and enables assistance personnel "to articulate their concerns and know that they will be listened to sympathetically" (Eade and Williams 1995:973) constitutes another valuable dimension of the model program. The training effort also must provide managers with the communication skills required to reassure staff that protection of their own health and assessment/decision-making capacities are genuinely valued as an agency priority. Such training assumes even greater urgency in situations where refugee-assistance personnel and their families are exposed to armed conflict, personal physical dangers, and/or organized harassment (see Eade and Williams 1995:973). Then, crisis managers need to possess the ability to prepare precise and cautious guidelines for travel in dangerous circumstances (see, for instance, the checklist of considerations set forth in Eade and Williams 1995:974–975), to arrange police escorts, armed protection, and reliable advance-warning communication systems (Juma 1995:111), and to ascertain what constitutes an unreasonable risk of continued involvement in a refugee-assistance capacity (Eade and Williams 1995:974).

In addition, intercultural communication training needs to equip humanitarian assistance workers with skills that will enable them to cope emotionally with a stressful multicultural workplace. Among those working overseas, in particular, the ability to deal with one's feelings and emotions largely conditions the outcome of group interaction (Brislin and Yoshida 1994:83). For many people, talking and writing about disturbing experiences constitutes an effective emotion management technique. We recommend, therefore, that this dimension of the training program help trainees discover the comforting effect of writing therapy and, concomitantly, develop a willingness to share their feelings with trusted others. The integration of writing therapy with sharing across cultures promises to be especially beneficial in the refugee-assistance context.

One effective way to operationalize this approach is to encourage every trainee to keep a diary or journal from the onset of the comprehensive training program that records how she or he *feels* about incoming information regarding the multicultural crisis management work situation. For instance, a trainee may write in his or her journal that the isolated refugee camp is (is likely to be) a depressing and fear-provoking place, or that he or she is (is likely to be) frustrated by the slow response rate exhibited in emergency situations by people from culture *x*. Each participant will be paired throughout the program with a partner from a different culture with whom he or she shares journal entries. At the beginning of each training day, trainers should allocate half an hour for trainees to read their partner's journal and to talk with, listen to, advise, and console each other about how they felt about the new information acquired on the previous day. Such intercultural sharing allows trainees to learn to express their feelings about what happens in crisis management situations, to prepare psychologically for emotional distress, and to develop the practice of seeking out and reflecting upon insights from a different cultural perspective. Also, this part of the training effort helps trainees develop the habit of expressing their feelings, especially disturbing feelings, in writing. Journal exchange enables trainees both to learn from another perspective and to be able to receive and provide emotional support. In short, the journal-entry exchange process amounts to a simulation exercise through which trainees acquire emotion management skills that are transferable to their work environment.

To supplement the emotion sharing process, trainers are encouraged to invite experienced field personnel to share some of their traumatic experiences and successful coping strategies. These accounts should be directed at reinforcing the trainee's emotional preparation and coping ability. In addition, the specific suggestions offered by experienced field personnel could prove invaluable to trainees in future crisis management situations.

We further recommend that, near the conclusion of the training program, trainers work with trainees to identify a suitable postcourse communication partner from a different culture for each participant serving in a crisis management position. Communication partners, who will function as trusted listeners and emotional supporters, generally should be available to one another in the field. However, trainees should be aware that communication with their trusted confidant can be disrupted by emergency conditions, technology failures, or other complications. Thus, trainers also need to remind trainees of the therapeutic power of writing, especially in times of isolation. A diary would be a meaningful end-of-training gift for each trainee to take with them to their assigned site.

VI. TRAINING OF TRAINERS

In order that the intercultural communication training program reach as many as possible of those involved in refugee assistance crisis management, it should include a major training-of-trainers activity. Participants should be aware of their on-going responsibility in this regard from the outset of the program. In light of this responsibility, each program participant should devote particular attention to training needs and capabilities assessment, curriculum application, training methods, materials development, and the management and evaluation of training programs (Collins 1993:342). They also should experience guided role plays involving peer training in the eight key curriculum components and be provided with essential training materials. Finally, the training program should encourage participants to appreciate the value of learning by teaching at the grass-roots level (van Bergen 1995:26).

In the field, trainees as trainers should promote cascading knowledge and empowerment as well as the transfer of portable skills—such as "organizing, problem-solving and tangible production skills" (Anderson and Woodrow 1989:327; also see Koehn 1994: 70). This goal is maximized by adopting a community- or team-focused approach whereby program graduates serve as formal and/or informal training team leaders. Emphasis should be placed on conveying information about useful techniques in a culturally sensitive manner that inspires skill transfer among community members (see Anderson and Woodrow 1989:238).

VII. POSTCOURSE ASSESSMENT AND FOLLOW-ON ACTIVITIES

The postcourse outcomes assessment should apply the training criteria set forth at the beginning of this chapter and be related to the principal objectives of the program and the participants. It should incorporate the trainees' end-of-course written and oral evaluations and suggestions. A thorough assessment would utilize trainee articulation and application of evaluative criteria (Levin 1997:5), focus interviews, portfolio analysis, participant and co-worker questionnaires, and on-site observations (also see Eade and Williams 1995:371).

Assessment should be linked to mastery of specific intercultural communication skills during and immediately following the training course. This process should include formative evaluations that are tightly linked to desired training outcomes (see, for instance,

Pedersen 1994:35–36). Among refugee assistance workers, competence in crisis management further requires the ability to interact flexibly and strategically with culturally diverse partners in implementing pragmatic and timely interventions. Thus, postcourse assessments also should expect to encounter demonstrated effectiveness in crisis decision making through the application of multicultural information sharing and group problem-solving techniques. When assessing intercultural communication and interaction in crisis management settings, however, both training program coordinators and participants must always bear in mind that "the ability to recover from mistakes is more important than perfection . . ." (Pedersen 1994:204).

The ongoing dimensions of the training program should include guided individual apprenticeships and the informal daily communication of tips and insights following conclusion of the formal training course (see Perille and Trutat 1995:8; Anderson and Woodrow 1989:85). In these learning-by-doing situations, local field staff and/or seconded technical/professional personnel teach trainees and vice versa (Yamamoto 1995:140–141). In addition, experienced trainers should visit trainees at their work site(s) to offer advice and constructive criticism on approaches to handling various crisis-management challenges and on promising adaptations in light of local workplace conditions (see Xiao 1996:57–60, 69–70). All follow-up efforts should emphasize the inculcation of skills in lifelong-learning.

At approximately annual intervals after delivery of the training course, additional assessments should be conducted with participants and with trainee-trained field workers. This long-term assessment process can be based on questionnaires, interviews, participant portfolios, and field observations. In addition to serving as a guide for additional follow-up training where needed, the results should be used to identify gaps and strengths in the overall training exercise that it would be valuable for program coordinators to address or enhance.

VIII. CONCLUSION

Effective intercultural communication in refugee-assistance crisis management requires an appropriate and continuous training program. The vision of a model program presented here devotes attention to both content and learning-process considerations. The content recommendations, which are linked to specific training approaches, are intended to address the practical communication needs that increasingly arise among field workers engaged in refugee and other humanitarian assistance capacities given the multicultural nature of today's relief and development crises.

Readers are encouraged to draw liberally from the model presented in this chapter when designing an intercultural-communication training program that is tailored to a specific clientele. The authors would especially welcome reports from practitioners on training outcomes when elements of the program design and methodology presented here are employed and adapted in culturally diverse circumstances.

REFERENCES

Anderson, Mary B., and Woodrow, Peter J. (1989). *Rising from the Ashes: Development Strategies in Times of Disaster*. Boulder Co: Westview Press.

Bastien, Joseph W. (1995). ''Cross cultural communication of tetanus vaccinations in Bolivia.'' *Social Science and Medicine* 41(*1*), 77–86.

Bemak, Fred, Chung, Rita Chi-Ying, and Bornemann, Thomas H. (1996). ''Counseling and psychotherapy with refugees.'' In Paul B. Pedersen, Juris G. Draguns, Walter J. Lonner, and Joseph E. Trimble (eds.), *Counseling Across Cultures*, 4th ed., 243–265. Thousand Oaks, CA: Sage Publications.

Brislin, Richard, and Yoshida, Tomoko (1994). *Intercultural Communication Training: An Introduction.* Thousand Oaks, CA: Sage Publications.

Burge, Alun (1995). ''Central America: NGO coordination in El Salvador and Guatemala 1980–94.'' In Jon Bennett (ed.) *Meeting Needs: NGO Coordination in Practice*, 145–165. London: Earthscan Publications.

Collins, Paul (1993). ''Civil service reform and retraining in transitional economies: strategic issues and options.'' *Public Administration and Development* 13(*3*), 323–344.

D'Andrea, Michael, Daniels, Judy, and Heck, Ronald (1991). ''Evaluating the impact of multicultural counseling training.'' *Journal of Counseling and Development* 70(*1*), 143–150.

Eade, Deborah, and Williams, Suzanne (1995). *The Oxfam Handbook of Development and Relief.* Vols. I and II. Oxford: Oxfam.

Hyden, Goran, Koehn, Peter, and Saleh, Turhan (1996). ''The challenge of decentralization in Eritera.'' *Journal of African Policy Studies* 2(*1*), 31–51.

Juma, Monika K. (1995). ''Kenya: NGO coordination during the Somali refugee crisis, 1990–93.'' In Jon Bennett (ed.), *Meeting Needs: NGO Coordination in Practice*, 89–115. London: Earthscan Publications.

Koehn, Peter (compiler and editor). (1994). *Final Report of the International Symposium ''Refugees and Development Assistance: Training for Voluntary Repatriation.''* Missoula, MT: Office of International Programs, University of Montana.

Levin, Henry M. (1997). ''Accelerated education for an accelerating economy.'' Wei Lun Visiting Professor lecture presented at The Chinese University of Hong Kong, September 26.

Lusty, Tim (1979). ''Notes on health care in refugee camps.'' *Disasters* 3(*4*), 352–354.

Minear, Larry, and Guillot, Philippe (1996). *Soldiers to the Rescue: Humanitarian Lessons from Rwanda*. Paris: Organisation for Economic Co-operation and Development.

Ngai, Phyllis Bo-yuen, and Koehn, Peter (1998). ''Cross-cultural management: the pitfalls of unspoken signals'' *World Executive's Digest* (January) 49–50.

Pedersen, Paul (1994). *A Handbook for Developing Multicultural Awareness*, 2nd ed. Alexandria, VA: American Counseling Association.

Perille, J.M., and Trutat, J.M. (1995). ''Does aid have a future?'' *The Courier* 152 (*July/August*), 6–8.

Phillips, Brenda D. (1993). ''Cultural diversity in disasters: sheltering, housing, and long term recovery.'' *International Journal of Mass Emergencies and Disasters* 11(*1*), 99–110.

Siegel, Gilbert B. (1985). ''Human resource development for emergency management.'' *Public Administration Review* 45(2), 107–117.

Sue, Derald Wing (1991). ''A Model for Cultural Diversity Training.'' *Journal of Counseling and Development* 70(*1*), 99–105.

Taylor, Alan J. (1979). ''Emergency sanitation for refugees.'' *Disasters* 3(*4*), 435–442.

van Bergen, J.E.A.M. (1995). ''District health care between quality assurance and crisis management: possibilities within the limits, Mporokoso and Kaputa District, Zambia.'' *Tropical and Geographical Medicine* 47(*1*), 23–29.

Xiao, Jin (1996). ''The relationship between organizational factors and the transfer of training in the electronics industry in Shenzhen, China.'' *Human Resource Development Quarterly* 7(*1*), 55–73.

Yamamoto, Hideki (1995). ''An NGO perspective on empowerment of humanitarian assistance.'' *International Education Forum* 15(2), 138–141.

4
Formation of Motivation Crisis

Liberalism, Nationalism, and Religion in Israel

Efraim Ben-Zadok School of Public Administration, Florida Atlantic University, Fort Lauderdale, Florida

I. INTRODUCTION

For Habermas, a *social system* comprises the economics, politics, or socioculture of a society—or the society itself. A social system ultimately operates through voluntarily accepted values and communication and not only through hierarchy and command of institutions. Central to its operation is *social integration*: that is, social relationships among individuals through verbal and nonverbal communication. From this perspective, the system is a *life world* that is symbolically organized around normative structures (institutions and values) (Habermas 1975:3–6).

The social integration of a society depends mainly on the outputs of the sociocultural system because of the motivation that it supplies to the *political system* in the form of legitimation. The outputs that determine motivation and supply legitimation originate in the leading normative structures of the sociocultural system. These structures are culture, history, art, literature, language, science, morality, religion, and ideology (Habermas 1975: 48, 75–92).

When the existing supply of legitimation does not meet the demand of the political system, the result is a *legitimation crisis*. This can be broken only through a *motivation crisis*, resulting from disturbances in the sociocultural system itself. Such disturbances make the output of the system dysfunctional to the political system and produce a legitimation deficit. Both the legitimation and motivation crises are *identity crises*. That is, individuals in the system are not sure of their direction and the purpose they serve (Habermas 1975: 45–50).

The disturbances in the sociocultural system originate in the problematic output of the political system, produced when the social integration of the political system is endangered by a threat to its integration. Such a threat appears when the political system suffers from a reduced capacity to master its environment through its functional mechanisms (Habermas 1975:24–25, 48).

The main characteristic of the motivation crisis is a lack of action-motivating meaning and a loss of purpose for individuals in the political, educational, and occupational systems. This also involves erosion of the old traditions that produced motivation, a lack of alternative new traditions, and an overemphasis on universalistic values that lead to new needs that are not satisfied (Habermas 1975:48–50).

Perhaps because the structures of the sociocultural system are normative and its characteristics are intangible, it is difficult to determine whether a motivation crisis actually exists. Commentaries on Habermas confirm that this is indeed the case for a legitimation crisis in the political system, where structures are even more obvious and defined. Kateb (1984:181) explains that even the legitimation crisis itself is not necessarily a clearly manifest condition and could be implicit. People might not be aware of it and they are surprised when drastic political changes take place. Connolly (1984:11–12) explains that Habermas's "crisis tendencies in advanced capitalism" is an account of a potential crisis that is neither inevitable nor easy to detect. It is an account of a variety of subtle institutional developments that press toward the formation of legitimation crisis in capitalism. Following this logic, the formation of a motivation crisis is also subtle and hard to detect.

The formation of motivation crisis in the Israeli sociocultural system has been under way since the late 1980s and continued after the 1996 general elections. This is the central argument of this chapter. The motivation of individuals in the system was reduced; less of it was generated to the political system, thereby creating a legitimation deficit there. This increasing deficit threatened the system with a legitimation crisis. Behind this development were suppressed tensions and contradictions among the three normative structures in the sociocultural system: the Jewish religion and the ideologies of liberalism and nationalism.

The tensions and contradictions originate in the political system. Trying to maintain social integration, the system managed two opposing processes simultaneously. The first process, the growing political power of the religious parties, strengthened religious norms and weakened secular-national and liberal norms. The second process, the shrinking significance of territorial religious nationalism in the West Bank, weakened religious norms and strengthened secular-national and liberal norms. Each process, in addition, had its own internal political ambivalence and vagueness.

The formation of motivation crisis since the late 1980s and the two processes are elaborated in Sections IV to VIII of this chapter. A brief history of the Israeli sociocultural and political systems in the prestate period, before 1948, is provided in Section II. The big compromise of the political system that tied nationalism and religion (thus weakening liberalism) to secure its legitimacy in the 1950s is described in Section III.

II. HISTORY OF THE SOCIOCULTURAL AND POLITICAL SYSTEMS

Three normative structures of the Israeli sociocultural system have played central roles in the system since its inception. These are the Jewish religion and the ideologies of liberalism and nationalism. These three structures were always the most vital sources for the production of individual motivation and the supply of legitimation to the Israeli political system.

The deepest roots of the two-century-old Israeli sociocultural system are in the Jewish religion, which dominated the Jewish sociocultural system until the end of the eighteenth century. The Jewish sociocultural system was the only one available to Jews at the time unless they assimilated or converted. Communication within the system was based on Judaism, a monotheistic religion founded in 2000 B.C. That is, culture, history, art, literature, language, and morals were all interpreted through religion.

Until the end of the eighteenth century, the religious affiliation of individuals defined their legal access to the economic, occupational, educational, and political systems. Jews were excluded from these systems because their religion was considered to be inferior. That is, they were viewed as a minority religion with beliefs that contradicted those of the Christian and Moslem majority. Jews in Europe, the Middle East, and North Africa lived in secluded small towns and urban ghettos, having only limited contacts with the larger society (Avineri 1991:13–17). They maintained the social cohesiveness of their dispersed communities through the sociocultural system that they all shared, with the Jewish religion at its center. This religion was not distinct from Jewish nationality.

Paradoxically perhaps, Jews did not experience much tension between their religion and the lack of opportunities in the systems from which they were excluded. Their religion defined their legal and social status and they had no chance to break out of their own society (Avineri 1991:18–19). Their religious affiliation could hardly be denied even when assimilation into the general society was possible and was exercised by them.

In the wake of the American and French revolutions, the Christian society began to change. Both revolutions held religion to be an individual matter, irrelevant in defining personal or group access to business, employment, education, or politics. The status of the Jews began to change. The United States was the first to grant them full civil and political rights. Most European countries abolished the restrictions on Jews and granted their rights, though not to full extent.

The new liberalism opened the door for Jews to the general society—an entry that was widened during the early nineteenth century, with the Enlightenment. European Jews began to make successful strides in business, journalism, academia, and the arts. For many, however, the long-awaited breakthrough to the outside world raised new problems. First, they found that the old anti-Semitism, rooted in centuries of Christian theological preaching, was there to stay. Second, they found that the new anti-Semitism, aimed against their new social status, had risen owing to their daily contact with the outside world. The Jews realized that integration and even assimilation into the general society would not solve their problem. European liberalism, in short, was not a solution to anti-Semitism (Safran 1981:16–18).

That feeling was confirmed after Captain Dreyfus, a Jewish officer in the French army, was publicly stripped of his rank and given a dishonorable discharge. Dark anti-Semitic clouds covered the 1895 trial in the country that was supposed to be the model of European liberalism. Some eastern European countries, where Jews never gained as much freedom as was possible in the west, applied new repressive measures against them at the time. A wave of violent anti-Semitic pogroms covered Russia. Jews had their homes and properties confiscated and many emigrated to more promising lands, such as the United States and South America.

These events demonstrated that European liberalism was linked to nationalism within the European sociocultural systems. The free and "enlightened" French, Germans, or Poles were also conscious of their own culture, history, art, literature, language, and morality. They interpreted these normative structures more and more through their own national (rather than religious) symbolism. National and liberal symbols became the main sources of legitimation for European political systems.

European nationalism also represented self-determination in the context of a defined geographical unit—the land. In its more dogmatic forms, it was compounded by values taken from emerging philosophies of evolutionism, historicism, and racism. These philosophies maintained that society was a natural living organism formed by centuries of blood relations, common culture, history, and language (Goodwin 1982:8–9).

The Jews, who were distinct and secluded for centuries, had little share in European nationalism and none in its dogmatic forms. To be considered as equal in any European society, however, they also had to identify with the nationalism of the specific sociocultural system. To do so wholeheartedly, to assimilate, Jews had to disassociate themselves from their old and established sociocultural system. For most of them, such a drastic change was difficult, emotionally and intellectually complex, and with no guarantee for genuine acceptance into the general society (Avineri 1991:19–22). European nationalism, in short, was certainly not a solution to anti-Semitism.

By the end of the nineteenth century, disappointed in liberalism and nationalism, European Jews began to develop their own solution to anti-Semitism: Zionism, a political movement based on the very same ideologies. With respect to liberalism, the Zionist political system, the forerunner of its Israeli counterpart, claimed that Jews were entitled to freedom and equality and to the achievement of full civil and political rights. With respect to nationalism, the Zionist political system further claimed that Jews were entitled to social and cultural self-determination in their own national home. That is, Jews were entitled to develop their culture, history, art, literature, language, and morality in their country (Safran 1981:19–23). They were supposed to interpret all these through national and liberal symbols, following the European experience. That was the original intent of the largely secular Zionist leadership.

From the very beginning, however, the mainstream of the political system also interpreted nationalism through symbols of Jewish religion. The religious interpretation had a long history, was tied to nationality, was readily available, and came naturally. It immediately proved effective in motivating individuals and in supplying legitimation to the system (Shapiro 1996:52–54). Liberal, national, and religious symbols thus dominated the political system from its inception and were replicated into the emerging Israeli sociocultural system.

That mix of symbols was not accepted without a powerful emotional debate. Crucial to the future of the movement was the debate between the national and religious norms, a debate that threatened to tear the political system apart when the location of the national home came on the agenda. The pragmatic founder of the movement and the head of the system, Theodor Herzl, toned down the religious connection to the Land of Israel and considered territories other than Palestine as a national home. He was even inclined to accept a territory in East Africa, an alternative that faced the bitter opposition of many, especially religious Jews. Only after his death, when the Seventh Zionist Congress of the movement convened in 1905, did the spiritual connection and the deep popular religious attachment to Israel prevail (Safran 1981:20). The political system, concerned with its legitimation, confirmed overwhelmingly that the national home must be built in Palestine.

The implementation of this policy began soon thereafter and Jews immigrated to Palestine in increasing numbers. Since the 1920s, after many countries imposed restrictions against Jewish immigration, Palestine became one of the few places of refuge and the only one where a sovereign national home could be achieved. Under British rule (1918–1948) and Zionist leadership, the Jewish community in Palestine gained civil and political rights and enjoyed full cultural and religious autonomy. For all practical purposes, the Zionist political system continued to develop liberal norms, and also national norms tied with religious ones. That mix was replicated into the sociocultural system. Even in the formal educational system—culture, history, art, literature, and language were all taught in a blurred style with no intellectual boundaries drawn between nationalism and religion.

III. THE COMPROMISE OF THE POLITICAL SYSTEM IN THE 1950s

A natural opportunity to draw the boundaries between national and religious norms arose in 1948, when the Zionist movement accomplished its goal and the state of Israel was established. The Zionist political system was now formalized into the state political system. The latter was expected to promote liberalism and nationalism, as in other western democracies; to make the distinction between nationalism and religion; and to allow religion a communicative role only and not within formal state affairs. These principles were to be absorbed into the sociocultural system and replicated there to generate motivation in the form of legitimation back into the state political system. This scenario appeared to be the alternative that could be accomplished in 1948, when most Israelis were of European origin and secular.

This alternative of a separation between nationalism and religion in a secular democracy was entertained in the political system throughout the 1950s. In sharp contrast was the other alternative, of a strong bond between the two in a genuine theocracy. But the mainstream alternative, which quickly prevailed and filled up the normative vacuum in the political system, was a pragmatic compromise between the two. It maintained the centuries-old tie between the national and religious norms of Judaism, yet the tie was loosened to meet the needs of a secular liberal democracy.

From time to time, the debate concerning which alternative should be pursued by the political system took the course of minimizing the role of religion by drawing its boundaries with nationalism, promoting secular nationalism, and thus strengthening the liberal norms of state building. Under these circumstances, tension was heightened due to an incompatibility between the political system and its sociocultural counterpart, in which religion combined with nationalism played a central role. The political system then reacted nervously to the possibility of a legitimation deficit due to a crisis of motivation in the sociocultural system, which might fail to generate the requisite degree of motivation in the form of legitimation.

Throughout the 1948 War of Independence and the mass in-migration of the 1950s, the mainstream pragmatic compromise between religion and nationalism was pursued. Religion was promoted at the expense of weakening the norms of secular nationalism and liberalism (Shapiro 1996:54). Behind this formula stood the Labor party (Mapai at the time), and Prime Minister David Ben-Gurion, who led the political system. Lacking its independent sources of legitimation, the young system exploited the religious source to unify the people and prevent a dangerous inter-Jewish struggle in the midst of a turbulent period of state building. Religion was to continue its historical role in preserving Jewish identity and stressing the commonality among immigrants coming from Jewish communities all over the world. Religion thus filled up the legitimacy vacuum, played a central role in formal state affairs, and became an integral element of emerging Israeli nationalism.

To ensure the link between Judaism and nationalism and, not less important, to limit the power of the Arab minority, the leadership of the new state ruled out the writing of a formal constitution. Instead, a constitution was to be built gradually through a series of

Basic Laws, 11 of which were enacted between 1958 and 1992. To date, Israel is still one of the few members of the United Nations with no formal constitution, and two generations have been socialized without the educational impact of a constitution. Religion, in fact, was granted more importance than a constitution as an integrative mechanism for state building.

Israel followed the *millet* system of the Ottoman Empire, which was largely continued by the British Mandate in Palestine. Freedom was granted to all religions, with each having its own courts and exclusive jurisdiction over marriage, divorce, alimony, and other personal matters. British Mandate local-level laws and regulations of public religious observance were also continued in Israeli communities. The only observance laws enacted on a national level, however, were those affecting the Jewish community. Chief among them were laws regarding the observance of the Jewish Sabbath, holidays, and dietary rules (Edelman 1994:48–72).

The dominant mode of the 1950s was that of formal religious liberty, with Judaism functioning as the official religion in practice. In the absence of a constitution, any significant attempt to separate state and religion was aborted by Labor. The leadership of the party did not realize the implications of its legitimacy-seeking behavior for the coming years. It adopted religion as an integral part of Jewish nationalism, the only type of nationalism to be represented by the state. It enacted the 1950 Law of Return, granting every Jew the right to immigrate to Israel, and the 1952 Citizenship Law, granting every Jewish immigrant Israeli citizenship. Step by step, an ''ethnic democracy'' emerged, with Jews at the center and Arabs as a minority with equal citizenship rights but no opportunities to exercise their nationalism (Peled 1992).

To ensure the supply of legitimacy, the Labor leadership consistently blurred and converted religious symbols into national symbols in its political rhetoric. That was also the standard in the formal education system. Religion became essential for communication in both the political and the sociocultural systems. This development has benefited the religious parties, which increased their pressures to infuse religion into state affairs (Shapiro, 1996:52–61). Labor demonstrated little resistance to the pressures. A secular-religious division in the midst of state building was too risky for the party.

The Labor-led government also needed the votes of the religious parties in the parliament (Knesset). The partnership that developed between the ruling party and the religious parties throughout the 1950s became the cornerstone of the Israeli political system. The religious parties, with an average of something below one-sixth of the total electoral power, were always the vital block required to form the parliamentary majority upon which the secularly controlled left or right coalition governments could be built. With the exception of a few interim periods, the religious parties always served as key power brokers in the ruling coalition government. The religious parties used their bargaining leverage to acquire a privileged status for the Jewish religion in state affairs and to take over disproportionately large slices of the government budget.

Within a short time, Orthodox women and yeshiva (theological college) students were exempted from compulsory military service. A state-funded religious school system was developed independently from the general education system. A state-funded rabbinical court system, in charge of personal matters like marriage and divorce, was developed independently within the judicial system. Its judges were trained and certified by the Rabbinical Council, the chief interpreter of religious law, which in practice became a quasi-legislative body. The council also licensed marriage, divorce, and kosher dining establishments (conforming to the Jewish dietary laws). It maintained synagogues, cemeteries, and public baths.

The national and local offices of the Rabbinical Council, the rabbinical court system, and the religious school system (in part) were all budgeted by the Ministry of Religions, which was always controlled by the religious parties. That was usually the case also for the Ministry of Interior, in charge of the implementation of the Population Registry Law. The ministry was involved in a series of ''Who is a Jew'' Supreme Court cases because of the *Halakha* (Jewish religious law) interpretations of its bureaucrats in registering the citizenship, nationality, and religion of individuals.

The mixing of state and religious affairs by the leadership was accepted favorably by most Israelis, and the sociocultural system thus continued to generate motivation to the political system. Much support for that mix was given by the mass of Jewish immigrants from the Islamic countries of the Middle East and North Africa. They came from *millet* systems and maintained traditional values. Not less important, Israelis generally supported that pattern because they had favorable attitudes toward Judaism. In 1962 and again in 1969, some 74% of respondents to a survey reported that they observed religion at least to some extent and 43% indicated that the government should maintain public life in accordance with Jewish religion (Arian 1985:335).

The mixing of state and religious affairs in the political system continued well into the 1980s. The sociocultural system supplied the required legitimation, much of it through the production of ''civil religion.'' That is, the transformation of religious values and symbols into national ones drew nonobsevant Israelis into their historical heritage (Liebman and Don-Yehiya 1983). In 1981, one-half of Israeli respondents said that the government should maintain public life in accordance with Jewish religion (Arian 1985:335). In 1989, the same proportion identified themselves as keepers of Jewish religion and tradition, and 70% reported that they observed religion to some extent (Dowty 1991:10–11).

IV. THE FORMATION OF THE MOTIVATION CRISIS, 1988–1996

The balance between the Israeli political and sociocultural systems began to shake in the late 1980s. Both systems were overloaded with centuries-old repressed tensions among liberalism, nationalism, and religion. The last four decades of statehood accelerated the production and accumulation of subtle contradictions. The peace process under way with Jordan and the Palestinians increased government and public attention to domestic social issues.

These historical tensions and contradictions surfaced time and again on the agenda of the political system. They were promoted by the clash between two opposing processes simultaneously under way in the system and by the ambivalence inherent within each process. These processes touched the heart of Israeli liberal, national, and religious norms and threatened to retard the overall functioning of the system.

The first process was the growing political power of the religious parties between the 1988 and 1996 elections to the Knesset, and especially the new legislative and executive power of the ultra-Orthodox parties. That process strengthened religious norms and weakened secular-national and liberal norms. The second process was the shrinking significance of territorial religious nationalism, which led to the gradual decline of Gush Emunim, the head group of religious Jewish settlement in the West Bank. That process, in contrast to the first one, weakened religious norms and strengthened secular-national and liberal norms. This cumulative process reached a most violent peak by the end of 1995 with the assassination of Prime Minister Rabin.

The political system handled the two processes through a series of incremental short-range responses. The system never had a comprehensive conception of how to deal with its contradictory state–religion imperatives. Its short-range political compromises in this area consistently resulted in the suppression of normative questions. The government, the leading mechanism in the system, lost steering capacity whenever a policy area related to one of the two processes was on the agenda. The confusion spilled over to other policy areas and endangered system integration.

The contradiction between the two processes left an open gray area (vacuum) in the symbolic life-world of the political system. Politicians in the system were unsure about their direction. They were transmitting ambiguous messages about the two processes and, as a result of the distorted communication, their social integration was weakened. The confused and fuzzy communication was absorbed into the sociocultural system and created much disturbances there. Citizens in the system were not sure what political goals their liberal, national, and religious norms served and whether what they were doing was contributing to state or religion. That loss of purpose raised many questions for them. They were in need of clarity and closure, especially regarding their identification with state and religion.

The two processes ultimately led to a reduced motivation among individuals—a reduction sufficiently harmful to begin the formation of motivation crisis in the sociocultural system. The system generated a decreasing amount of legitimation to the political system. This supply cut produced some legitimation deficit in the political system. If the motivation crisis under way was to continue and if the deficit was to grow, a legitimation crisis would erupt.

The two processes are analyzed below: first, the growth of the political power of the religious parties and, second, the decline of religious nationalism. Finally, the most violent expression of this decline, the Rabin assassination, is elaborated.

V. GROWTH-RELATED CRISIS FORMATION: RELIGIOUS POLITICAL POWER AND THE ULTRA-ORTHODOX

The growing political power of the religious parties between the 1988 and 1996 elections to the Knesset was one important process contributing to the formation of the motivation crisis. At the heart of this process was the new legislative and executive power of the ultra-Orthodox parties, acquired as a result of their electoral success.

The religious parties increased their power in the Knesset from 11.4% of the total vote in 1984 to 15.4% in 1988. After a small decrease to 13.8% in 1992, their vote increased dramatically to 20.0% in 1996. In 1988, a total of 13 of the 18 religious seats in the Knesset (120 seats) were occupied by the ultra-Orthodox parties. In 1996, these numbers reached a climax of 14 out of 23. Moreover, since 1988 the ultra-Orthodox parties shared power in Israeli coalition governments. In the past, these parties were small, and they excluded themselves from such a partnership because they opposed the idea of a Zionist state (Herzog 1995:82–84; *Ma'ariv* 1996b).

The electoral advances of the more extreme ultra-Orthodox parties and their control of powerful ministries such as Interior and Religion, increased their influence over government policy and endowed them with increasing budget allocations (Willis 1995). It also increased the demands of the religious sector as a whole to enforce its rules over state affairs. Even the two new Basic Laws of 1992 did not escape the religious pressures. The first, Human Dignity and Freedom, did not include judicial protection of religious freedom or the right of conscience. The second, Freedom of Occupation, was amended in 1994 to preclude a successful court challenge by companies seeking to import nonkosher meat (Edelman 1996:28–29).

The rising new religious power was not exploited by the religious community without problems. As in the past, the political system did not meet all the religious demands, and many state–religion policies remained undecided and unclear. Not less important, the system clearly downsized policies supporting territorial religious nationalism, yet it continued its ambiguous behavior in that area (more on that later).

Many in the religious community were left confused. They were not sure about the direction of the government and felt that their new political power was not reflected in its policies. Their questions were not answered by a government they had ceased to trust. Their uncertainty and alienation ultimately burst out in the form of public protest, disobedience, violence, and crime. Much of the social unrest erupted in local communities where the ultra-Orthodox were attempting to enforce strict religious observance on their secular neighbors. The secular community, just as confused about government policies, tried to protect its way of life. Fierce struggles took place around the observance of the Sabbath and kosher laws. Not less emotional were confrontations around modest clothing in public, posters of models in bathing suits, and the sale of pornographic magazines (Lehman-Wilzig 1992:115–128; Shilhav 1993).

VI. DECLINE-RELATED CRISIS FORMATION: TERRITORIAL RELIGIOUS NATIONALISM AND GUSH EMUNIM

The shrinking significance of territorial religious nationalism by the late 1980s, a cumulative process since the early part of the decade, was another important factor contributing to the development of a motivation crisis. At the heart of this process was the decreasing power of Gush Emunim.

The political system began to promote religious nationalism after the 1967 Arab–Israeli war and lent it strong support until the early 1980s. This type of nationalism provided the system with a greater degree of legitimacy because it supported the continuous occupation, on the basis of a security and defense rationale, of the territories that had been captured during the war. Religious nationalism, advocating expansion to the limits of the biblical boundaries of the Land of Israel, was especially instrumental in building the Jewish settlement in the West Bank, a region taken from Jordan in the war. But this nationalism was less useful to the political system in the early 1980s and became disruptive to government peace initiatives with Jordan and the Palestinians by the end of the decade.

Throughout the 1970s, religious nationalist groups sponsored by Labor and Likud governments were building settlements in the West Bank in order to strengthen the Israeli presence there, with a view to the inevitable negotiations to come on the future of the area. The spearhead of the settlement enterprise was a small group called Gush Emunim (‘‘Bloc of the Faithful’’). The Gush was a fundamentalist social movement of young people with much support in the more moderate religious community. Its ideology was the transformation of the materialistic western values of consumption, prevalent in Israeli society, into individual fundamentalist messianic and spiritual beliefs. This platform was to be fulfilled through self-actualization, primarily by settling the Land of Israel. The target area for the Gush settlement was the biblical core—Judea and Samaria, also known as the West Bank.

Since the early 1980s, this broad social platform of the Gush was deemphasized and the movement began its transformation into a regional interest group, mainly concerned with the economic well-being of West Bank settlements. The transformation was caused primarily by the government's dwindling political support for the settlements and its significantly reduced budgets, largely earmarked for the expansion of the physical infrastructure rather than for the construction of new settlements. Behind the new political economy was the 1984–1990 National Unity Government, led jointly by Likud and Labor. Because Labor was the powerful junior partner in this coalition, the religious parties as a whole lost much of their crucial bargaining leverage (Goldberg 1993).

The growing power of the ultra-Orthodox parties since 1988 did not help the Gush. These parties concentrated their efforts on domestic legislation and, unlike the rest of the religious community, had little interest in settlement. Most important, the whole political system slowly shifted course toward peace negotiations over the West Bank. The Gush's presence in the region presented a big problem to the government.

The Gush's settlers and public opinion were both confused. The political system did not meet the Gush's demands. Public opinion since the late 1980s viewed the expansion to the limits of the biblical boundaries of the Land of Israel as less and less important (Shamir and Shamir 1996). At the same time, the Gush still represented the national (if not the religious) ambition of a significant proportion in the public. The centrality of the Likud in the political system, its responsiveness to the domestic legislation pressures of the ultra-Orthodox, and the mixed signals regarding the peace process only added to the confusion.

Joined by many frustrated Israelis, the settlers reacted through a series of violent demonstrations. They felt exploited by a government that lacked interest in their faith and left them exposed to Arab terror in the West Bank with no choice but self-defense. They organized a number of vigilante groups approved by the Gush's rabbis and launched anti-Arab terror attacks in the West Bank. One group was the Jewish Underground, known for its bomb attacks on Arab mayors, the assault on the Islamic College, and actions against Arab civilians. Another group was the Nation of Judah, which conspired against the government and prepared to stay in the West Bank in case of Israeli withdrawal. The government's hesitant prosecution of the illegal acts included interrogations, arrests, and trials (Lehman-Wilzig 1992:62–65; Lustick 1988; Reiser 1991).

The anger and confusion of the settlers grew when the Likud-led government joined the 1991 Madrid summit conference on the peace process. The struggle with the government reached a new peak when Madrid's resolutions were reinforced in 1992 by the first Labor-led government since 1977. Prime Minister Yitzhak Rabin marked a departure from the Likud's hard line, yet he was also considered a hard-line politician within Labor. Actually, in his first term as premier, between 1974 and 1977, the Gush started its major penetration into the West Bank. The new Rabin government rejected the idea of a Palestinian state but signed an agreement in September 1993 for Palestinian self-rule in the West Bank and Gaza Strip. The agreement left unclear the political future of the West Bank Jewish settlement.

On February 25, 1994, Baruch Goldstein, a settler, opened fire in a Moslem mosque in Hebron, killing 29 Arabs at morning prayers. Goldstein was then killed by security forces. His grave immediately became a shrine to Gush settlers. His request for closure on the future of the holy land was granted temporarily. For the next few months the peace process was paralyzed, with many in the religious community keeping quiet about the massacre. But the Rabin government proceeded to sign a peace treaty with Jordan in October 1994.

VII. DECLINE-RELATED CRISIS FORMATION: TERRITORIAL RELIGIOUS NATIONALISM AND THE RABIN ASSASSINATION

The significance of territorial religious nationalism continued to shrink in 1995. This cumulative process accelerated the development of a motivation crisis which reached a violent peak with the assassination of Prime Minister Rabin at the end of the year.

Earlier that year, the protest against the government's peace policy was widened. The settlers were joined by many in the religious community and the right wing. The less organized secular left wing, led by groups such as Peace Now, responded with progovernment rallies. Public opinion on the future of the West Bank was frequently interpreted as a dead-end split (Shamir and Shamir 1996). The hesitant government continued to steer the peace process, but it lost direction periodically owing to the political divisions and hurdles.

Antigovernment rallies were called in the name of the holiness of the Land of Israel and religious nationalism, but they benefited the right wing as a whole. Likud leaders who opposed the withdrawal from the West Bank attended the rallies. They were silent when the violent crowd demonized Rabin as a ''traitor'' and ''murderer'' and when the prime minister was caricatured with a hooked nose dripping blood (as a Jew in the Nazi paper *Der Sturmer*) and was pictured in the uniforms of both an SS officer and of Palestinian leader Yasser Arafat (*New York Times* 1995). The escalation in verbal and visual violence expressed the anxiety of people feeling ignored by leaders who were blocking the channels of communication.

The communication breakdown culminated in a powerful explosion of physical violence—the assassination of Rabin on November 4, 1995. The assassin, Yigal Amir, a funded student in a state-funded religious university, was a fundamentalist Jew who took the law into his own hands, hoping to stop the withdrawal from the West Bank. He represented the Gush's absolute and nonnegotiable position on the holiness of the Land of Israel, a position denied by the Rabin government.

For Amir, the Gush, and many others in the religious community, the Land of Israel and its boundaries were sanctified by God to the Jewish people. Any attempt by the state to surrender parts of the land, let alone to an enemy, was viewed as an act against God's will and a betrayal of the Jewish people. Accordingly, Rabin did exactly that when he began the Israeli withdrawal from Judea and Samaria, the West Bank. He also had to be killed because handing the holy land to the Palestinians represented a mortal danger to the Jewish settlers there.

''I acted alone on God's orders, and I have no regrets,'' said the 25-year-old Amir after the assassination (*New York Times* 1995). ''I know Jewish law and '*din rodef*' means that if you have tried everything else and nothing works, then you have to kill him!'' That was his explanation to the court referring to the ritual command—''the judgment of the pursuer''—to kill anyone, even the prime minister, who intends to act against the Jewish people and to cause the death of Jews (*Jewish Journal* 1996).

Amir's viewpoint that the holy land must remain under Israeli control was shared by the Likud-led opposition, yet with one important difference. The Likud came to it from the uncompromising national-historical and security viewpoints that dominated the Israeli right wing. After the assassination, eager to control the potential electoral damage, Likud leaders quickly dropped their ''national'' terminology, which could easily be confused with religion. In their effort to promote the ''security'' terminology in the public discourse, they were joined by Labor leaders, the media, and the Israeli public.

In no time, the debate on the political future of the West Bank was transformed from its secular-religious and security contents into a left-right security-only content. In other words, stricken by the fear of a potential legitimation deficit due to a sincere state-religion subjective debate, the political system as a whole switched the debate to an objective-technical one, around the strategic importance of the West Bank. Religion, again, was made a nonissue, to be swept under the rug.

The leader of the Likud, Benjamin Netanyahu, claimed that Rabin had been ''slain by a madman,'' a diagnosis later denied by the court (*New York Times* 1995; *Ma'ariv* 1996a). Amir was instantly an outcast, outside of the ''rational'' left-right debate on the West Bank. His deep fundamentalist motive, Jewish ownership of the holy land, was left undiscussed. The political system skillfully suppressed his question and prevented the potential eruption of a legitimacy crisis.

That suppression was one more important inducement to the subtle formation of a motivation crisis. For Amir and many frustrated religious Israelis, God's given norm, the eternal holiness of the land, was superior to the secular state's norm of security and defense, which was subject to the politics of the day. For them, secular norms and politics were not only informed by God's will but also subject to it. They were left with no response from the political system to their claim that the state was subject to religion. Secular Israelis were also left puzzled by a system that chose not to come to grips with such an antiliberal challenge.

VIII. THE FORMATION OF MOTIVATION CRISIS CONTINUED: POST–1996 ELECTIONS

Neither religious nor secular Israelis received any answers from the Labor-led caretaker government headed by Shimon Peres, which served between the Rabin assassination and the early elections on May 29, 1996. Both the assassination and its religious magnitude were rarely mentioned during the elections campaign. The two leading parties were afraid of alienating voters and of losing the support of the religious parties. At the same time, security disasters occupied the attention of the media and the public. These were the Hamas massacres in the heart of Israel and the Hezbollah Katyusha attacks at the northern border. Ironically, the Israeli public was well aware of the Islamic fundamentalist motivation behind the Arab terror.

After the 1996 elections, Israelis did not receive much clarification on the direction of the left-right tied debate regarding the West Bank. The vote for the Knesset and the prime minister were razor-edge close: 34 and 32 seats to Labor and Likud, respectively; and 50.5 and 49.5% to Netanyahu and Peres, respectively (*Ma'ariv* 1996b). Netanyahu, the election's campaign underdog who became the new prime minister, was considered to be a pragmatic politician. He was greatly constrained, however, by his government's coalition with the religious parties. The Likud-led government quickly lost control of the fragile peace process and periodically became deadlocked with Palestinian negotiators. By the end of 1996, the government was still delaying its withdrawal from the West Bank town of Hebron (where 450 settlers lived amid 120,000 Arabs) owing to pressure from religious nationalists (*New York Times* 1996).

Israelis received at least one clarification after the elections. The three religious parties raised their power dramatically to 23 Knesset seats or close to 20.0% of the total vote. Their interests in the West Bank were generally compatible with those of the Likud. Their extreme demands for state–religion domestic legislation and religious enforcement in local communities, however, surprised the Likud politicians, who were concerned with the secular democratic foundations of the state (*Ma'ariv* 1996c). Right- and left-wing politicians constantly voiced their opinion in favor of a Likud-Labor National Unity Government in order to meet the religious demands. Nonetheless, by the end of 1996, the religious parties were still in government. The balance of the political system clearly tended to favor the religious right.

These political clouds and fluctuations produced much tension for both secular and religious Israelis. They were uncertain about their political goals and felt growing concern about the purpose they served in the society and in the economy. They were confronting each other more and more in demonstrations around the peace process and around the lifestyle of their local communities. The state–religion status quo since the 1950s was under an unprecedent threat. Israeli academia and media were constantly assessing the possibility of a violent *kulturkampf*, which now seemed more realistic than ever before (*Ma'ariv* 1996d; Yedioth Aharonot 1996).

This formation of motivation crisis in the sociocultural system drastically undermined the supply of legitimacy to the political system. The increasing deficit of legitimacy threatened to bring a legitimation crisis.

IX. CONCLUSION

The Jewish religion, and the idealogies of liberalism and nationalism, have all played central roles in the Israeli sociocultural system over the last two centuries. They were always the most vital sources for the motivation of individuals and the provision of legitimacy to the Israeli political system and its Zionist predecessor. Religion and nationalism were firmly linked by the political system of the 1950s in order to secure its legitimacy after the establishment of the state of Israel. Religion was thus given a special status and became involved in formal state affairs. Secular nationalism and liberalism were weakened in turn.

This process continued well into the late 1980s. However, an opposite, simultaneous process has also been under way in the political system. It included the weakening of religion and the strengthening of secular nationalism and liberalism. The clash of the two processes, and the internal ambivalence inherent in each process, produced many tensions and contradictions in the political system. The system experienced a legitimacy deficit (which might lead to a legitimacy crisis) because its own problematic actions reduced the supply of motivation in the form of legitimation from the sociocultural system.

The extent of that reduction was enough to initiate the formation of motivation crisis in the sociocultural system. This process has been under way since the late 1980s and continued after the 1996 elections. That has been the main thrust of this chapter.

Behind this development lie decades of tense relationships between state and religion and between secular and religious Israelis. These relationships were repressed by decades of military and economic struggle, a series of politically convenient institutional and legal arrangements, and an overall supporting public opinion. The repression was instrumental in promoting Jewish unity.

The tensions and repressions surfaced and social cohesiveness decreased as progress was made toward peace, the economy continued to flourish and Israel began to focus more and more on its social problems. At present, the tie between religion and nationalism excludes many secular Jews, not to mention non-Jews, who constitute close to one-fifth of Israel's population. Many view this tie as unnecessary in modern Israel, where Jewish culture, history, art, literature, and language are preserved through secular institutions, primarily the public schools. Many feel that religion should not define formal public life and that its state-funded institutions must cease their control over private life.

The present developments mark a struggle on the meaning of the Israeli state—a struggle that will become more visible and vocal. Clearly, a stronger sense of belonging and solidarity must be provided to all Israelis. That can be accomplished only by realigning state–religion relationships and drawing the boundaries among liberalism, nationalism, and religion.

REFERENCES

Arian, Asher (1985). *Politics and Government in Israel*. Tel Aviv: Zmora-Bitan (Hebrew).

Avineri, Shlomo (1991). *Varieties of Zionist Thought*. Tel-Aviv: Am Oved Publishers (Hebrew).

Connolly, William (1984). ''Legitimacy and modernity.'' In W. Connolly (ed.), *Legitimacy and the State*, 1–19. New York: New York University Press.

Dowty, Alan (1991). ''Religious-secular accommodation in Israeli politics.'' Paper presented at the annual meeting of the American Political Science Association, Washington, D.C.

Edelman, Martin (1994). *Courts, Politics, and Culture in Israel*. Charlottesville, VA: University Press of Virginia.

Edelman, Martin (1996). '''Protecting' the majority: religious freedom for non-Orthodox Jews in Israel.'' In F. Lazin and G. Mahler (eds.), *Israel in the Nineties: Development and Conflict*, 13–33. Gainesville, FL: University Press of Florida.

Goldberg, Giora (1993). ''Gush Emunim new settlements in the West Bank: from social movement to regional interest group.'' In E. Ben-Zadok (ed.), *Local Communities and the Israeli Polity: Conflict of Values and Interests*, 189–208. Albany: State University of New York Press.

Goodwin, Barbara (1982). *Using Political Ideas*. New York: Wiley.

Habermas, Jurgen (1975). *Legitimation Crisis*. Boston: Beacon Press.

Herzog, Hanna (1995). ''Penetrating the system: the politics of collective identities.'' In A. Arian and M. Shamir (eds.), *The Elections in Israel 1992*, 81–102. Albany: State University of New York Press.

Jewish Journal (1996). March 13.

Kateb, George (1984). ''On the 'legitimation crisis.' '' In W. Connolly (ed.), *Legitimacy and the State*, 180–200. New York: New York University Press.

Lehman-Wilzig, Sam N. (1992). *Wildfire: Grassroots Revolts in Israel in the Post-Socialist Era*. Albany: State University of New York Press.

Liebman, Charles S., and Don-Yehiya, Eliezer (1983). *Civil Religion in Israel*. Berkeley, CA: University of California Press.

Lustick, Ian S. (1988). *For the Land and the Lord: Jewish Fundamentalism in Israel*. New York: Council on Foreign Relations.

Ma'ariv (1996a). March 3.
Ma'ariv (1996b). June 2.
Ma'ariv (1996c). June 7.
Ma'ariv (1996d). September 13.
New York Times (1995). November 6.
New York Times (1996). December 31.
Peled, Yoav (1992). "Ethnic democracy and the legal construction of citizenship: Arab citizens of the Jewish state." *American Political Science Review* 86, 432–443.
Reiser, Stewart (1991). "Sovereignty, legitimacy, and political action." In I. Lustick and B. Rubin (eds.), *Critical Essays on Israeli Society, Politics, and Culture*, 63–73. Albany: State University of New York Press.
Safran, Nadav (1981). *Israel: The Embattled Ally*. Cambridge, MA: Harvard University Press.
Shamir, Michal, and Shamir, Jacob (1996). "Value preferences in public opinion in Israel." *Megamot* 37(*4*), 371–393 (Hebrew).
Shapiro, Yonathan (1996). *Politicians as a Hegemonic Class: The Case of Israel*. Tel Aviv: Sifriat Poalim (Hebrew).
Shilhav, Yosseph (1993). "The Emergence of Ultra-Orthodox Neighborhoods in Israeli Urban Centers." In E. Ben-Zadok (ed.), *Local Communities and the Israeli Polity: Conflict of Values and Interests*, 157–187. Albany, NY: State University of New York Press.
Willis, Aaron P. (1995). "Shas—The Sephardic torah guardians: religious 'movement' and political power." In A. Arian and M. Shamir (eds.), *The Elections in Israel 1992*, 121–139. Albany: State University of New York Press.
Yedioth Aharonoth (1996). September 22.

5

Crisis Policy Making

Some Implications for Program Management

David C. Nice and Ashley Grosse Department of Political Science, Washington State University, Pullman, Washington

I. INTRODUCTION

Students of public policy making have long recognized that crises are a powerful influence on many public policy decisions (Edwards and Sharkansky 1978:280–282; Lineberry 1978:62–63; Nice 1994:21; Sharkansky 1970:175–178). As Plato (1975:164) wrote in his last major book, "Accidents and calamities . . . are the universal legislators of the world." Crises act as *focusing events*, demanding public attention to a policy failure or problem (Kingdon 1995:94–100). A great war, a major depression, or an epidemic may set into motion a number of important changes in public policies. Crisis management is, in turn, made more complex by the tendency for crises to foster policy changes, which leave managers struggling with changing policy guidance in addition to the difficulty of coping with the crisis itself. Crisis decisions also involve dynamics that often produce additional complications for program managers. In this chapter, we review the ways in which crises foster policy change, discuss the special aspects of crisis decision making that may complicate program management, and explore some examples of crisis policies that have encountered implementation problems.

II. CRISES AS FORCES FOR POLICY CHANGE

Crises tend to encourage policy change in a number of ways, although the specific dynamics may vary from one crisis situation to another. At the outset, a crisis increases the likelihood that an issue will reach the policy agenda and receive serious attention from public officials (Anderson 1994:93; Edwards and Sharkansky 1978:101–102; Kelman 1987:39; Kingdon 1995:16–17; Nice 1994:21). In the sometimes fierce competition for attention, a visible, dramatic problem is often difficult to ignore. Indeed, those who are interested in drawing attention to an issue may try to present it as a crisis and frighten people in order to attract media coverage, increase the issue's visibility, and push aside issues already receiving attention (Davis 1993:11–12; Kingdon 1995:96). Often groups that have not had financial resources or political backing in policy debates take advantage of the drama by defining a situation as a disaster or crisis and attaching powerful and emotive symbols to the situation and the defenders of the current policy. The public relations spin on a crisis is critical for stimulating a cry of public outrage and the demands for policy change that follow. The battle for advocates of policy change is to convince others that the event is directly related to a policy failure and that viable policy solutions exist. However, crises open a policy window for only a limited time (Kingdon 1995:168–170). The media may turn their attention away and/or the public may become bored long before real change makes its way to the agenda, making policy change unlikely.

Crises do not automatically receive attention from officials. Disasters in less visible policy domains are likely to receive less than prompt attention. Some conditions are difficult to measure or may have multiple facets that are difficult to understand or compare. Environmental disasters can sometimes be more ambiguous in their effects on people, thus prompting a wait-and-see attitude. A dramatic event may be dismissed as an isolated occurrence that is unlikely ever to occur again. A crisis is more likely to be noticed if people regard it as a public responsibility, work actively to draw attention to it, and regard it as part of a broader pattern indicating a problem or an early warning of future difficulties. Conversely, a crisis is less likely to receive attention from public officials if the problem is perceived as a private-sector matter or powerful groups try to keep it off of the policy agenda (Edwards and Sharkansky 1978:107–109, 282; Kelman 1987:40–41; Kingdon 1995:97–99). If a problem alarms a large number of people, however, officials may fear that ignoring it may adversely affect their careers.

Crises also foster policy change by stimulating the search for new ideas and new approaches (Cyert and March 1963:278–279; March and Simon 1958:173–174; Nice 1994:21–22; Rose 1993:50–60). When things seem to be going reasonably well, the burden of meeting day-to-day responsibilities may leave little time, energy, or inclination for exploring alternative strategies. Searching for alternative approaches may create the impression that existing approaches are somehow deficient—an impression that may anger some people. Searching for alternatives may also create the expectation of a dramatic change. If the search ultimately fails to yield that change, officials may have a serious public relations problem on their hands, as the Clinton Administration found when health care reform was rejected by Congress. Under normal circumstances, then, searching for new approaches may often be a low priority. An obvious crisis or disaster, by contrast, is likely to make expending the time and effort needed for discovering new approaches seem much more worthwhile.

Crisis further encourage policy change by creating pressure for prompt action. Forces for policy change are sometimes deflected by delaying tactics, which can take many forms, from appointing a commission to study an issue to changing the subject to another issue to Senate filibusters and protracted litigation. The presence of a crisis, however, may cause officials to fear that failure to act relatively quickly may endanger their political careers (Edwards and Sharkansky 1978:101–102, 108–109; Eyestone 1978:153–155; Polsby 1984:168). In that situation, the risks and uncertainty that often discourage policy change may be offset by concerns that appearing unresponsive will enrage the public.

In a related vein, a widely perceived crisis may facilitate adoption of policy changes by increasing the public's willingness to be led, at least for a while. Under normal circumstances, proposals for change are vulnerable to being picked apart by critics who oppose any change or who favor change in the abstract but dislike one or more provisions in a specific proposal. Given the many veto points in the American political system, opponents have many opportunities to obstruct proposals for change. The presence of a crisis may encourage people to be less critical about specific provisions in a proposal and more willing to give political leaders who are grappling with a problem a bit more room to maneuver (Davis 1993:11–12; Polsby 1984:169).

Crises also foster policy change by spurring the mobilization of new political groups, which help to draw attention to problems, encourage officials to search for new policy options, and goad officials into acting on the problem promptly. In addition, as officials search for political support in order to help them survive the crisis, they may feel more inclined to pay attention to groups that had previously been ignored (Gamson 1975:112–119; Truman 1951:31, 44, 57). The result is likely to be more policy changes.

Bear in mind that not all crises produce major policy shifts. If a crisis produces too much stress and anxiety, the result may be apathy and paralysis rather than policy change. A problem may be regarded as a private matter, or citizens may lack confidence in the ability or willingness of public officials to handle the problem appropriately. Officials may not know how to handle the problem, or they may not be able to agree on a suitable response. Opponents of policy change may continue to block action even in a crisis situation. At most, then, a crisis creates an opportunity for adopting new policies, but that opportunity must be successfully managed in order to yield actual policy change (March and Simon 1958:184; Nice 1994:23–24; Polsby 1984:170–171).

III. PROBLEMATIC RESIDUES OF CRISIS POLICY MAKING

Although crises can substantially influence policy decisions, the dynamics of crisis policy making can produce a number of problems for program managers. One fundamental difficulty results from the fact that the sense of crisis will eventually fade. A policy adopted during a crisis situation may lack a firm, underlying base of support. People may have been willing to be led during the crisis, but the end of the crisis may lead to greater skepticism and more criticism. Complaints regarding the cost of the new initiative or the difficulty of dealing with the problem grow louder and more numerous. The excitement and enthusiasm felt by people who are battling a grave emergency are eventually replaced by a sense of doing a more routine job on a routine basis. Elected officials and administrators with the most interest in the issue may eventually leave, and their replacements may have other interests. Officials and the public gradually lose interest in the issue as other matters claim their attention (Anderson 1994:96–97, 265; Bullock 1984:198–202; Eyestone 1978:155–156; Kingdon 1995:103–105, 168–169; Lineberry 1978:62; March and Simon 1958:199; Toqueville 1945:267–268). The result may be a policy initiative that eventually withers as the crisis is replaced by more normal, less supportive conditions.

Crisis policies may also encounter difficulty because the pressure to act quickly and people's greater willingness to be led in a crisis may lead to the adoption of policies that paper over serious political conflicts. As the sense of crisis fades, those submerged conflicts may resurface. Consequently, program managers may find themselves caught in a crossfire of conflicting and incompatible expectations, and the formal policy adopted during the crisis may provide little guidance regarding how to handle those conflicts (Edwards 1980:151–152; Eyestone 1978:153–156; Mazmanian and Sabatier 1983:41).

A further source of difficulty for crisis policies results from the combination of pressure to act quickly and the high levels of emotional stress that accompany crisis situations. Officials may feel pressed to act before there is adequate time for collecting information, analyzing it, or assessing policy options in depth. The need to act quickly may leave too little time for convincing some skeptics or accommodating their concerns. The stress of dealing with the crisis, the uncertainty that it brings, and the fear of adverse effects on political careers may lead officials to ignore possible flaws in a proposal and avoid rigorous discussion of the proposal for fear of antagonizing their colleagues and heightening their own sense of vulnerability. In addition, the pressure to act quickly may lead to a strong bias in favor of options that can be found quickly and put into action rapidly rather than other options that might perform more effectively but take more time to find or implement. The pressure to act quickly to deal with the most visible parts of a crisis may lead to the failure to consider other, less visible aspects of the problem or how the new policy will mesh with other, existing programs (Buchanan 1978:36; Eyestone 1978:155; Janis 1972: 197–210; Lineberry 1978:62–63; Pressman and Wildavsky 1979:126–127, 138–139). The result may be the adoption of a policy that is seriously flawed in one or more respects. Program managers may, consequently, face great difficulty in trying to make the policy function effectively.

Crisis policies may also encounter difficulty due to a fundamental dilemma: the pressure to act quickly to deal with a problem that may not be fully understood and without sufficient time to do thorough exploration or development of proposals may lead to policies that are not very clear or specific. Policy makers may not have time to develop clear program goals or priorities, and the need for flexibility to cope with a problem that is not clearly understood and that may be changing further discourages clarity and precision. However, vague policies with unclear goals are often prone to implementation problems, as administrators struggle with unclear and conflicting expectations and a policy that gives them little clear guidance. The availability of new resources accompanied by unclear policy guidelines may give too much play to political groups trying to advance their individual agendas rather than deal with the crisis at hand (Bullock 1984:194–196; Edwards 1980: 150–152; Lineberry 1978:62–63).

The group dynamics that encourage policy change in a crisis may also carry the seeds of subsequent difficulties. The mobilization of new groups and the policy gains of previously excluded groups may eventually lead to a countermobilization of other groups who disagree with the new direction that government is pursuing (Truman 195:59,107). Some of those groups might have been caught off guard initially or might have been reluctant to raise objections during the crisis period, but their opposition is likely to surface eventually. The new initiatives adopted to deal with the crisis may, therefore, be undercut by established groups seeking to regain the upper hand and eliminate policy provisions that they find objectionable.

A final source of difficulty that crisis policy making may pose for crisis managers arises from the tendency for new policies to need an initial shakedown phase. Administrators need time to develop and learn new procedures. Initial timetables for action may be unrealistic; the new policy must be fitted in among other programs, and relationships with other relevant public and private sector actors must be established. The basic policy may need to be modified in various ways as administrators gain experience with its operation. Personnel may need to be trained or retrained if carrying out the new program requires new skills. Surviving this shakedown phase under crisis conditions and competing for resources with older, more established programs can be very difficult (Edwards 1980: 150–152; Edwards and Sharkansky 1978:304–305; Peterson et al. 1986). A review of some policies adopted under crisis conditions illustrates the difficulties that crisis policies can pose for program managers.

IV. ENERGY POLICY

One example of the difficulties that crisis policy decisions can encounter is energy policy in the United States. For many years, U.S. energy policy was based on the assumption of cheap, abundant energy from domestic sources and the premise that private-sector decision making was generally preferable (Cochran et al. 1993:90; Dye 1984:182), although many public policies, such as transportation policies, had important implications for energy use. Energy policy was rarely a visible issue for many years.

Beginning in 1970, U.S. crude oil production began a long-term decline. More dramatically, two oil embargoes in the 1970s highlighted the risks of American dependence on imported oil and contributed to both inflation and unemployment. Although the oil embargoes angered the public, much of the anger was directed at the oil companies or the U.S. government. Pressures to do something about the energy crisis began to build, but the energy issue had many different facets, and policy makers were far from certain regarding what policy remedies, if any, would be most appropriate (Cochran et al. 1993: 94–95; Davis 1993:6–20; Palumbo 1994:346–349).

From 1973 through 1980, the federal government adopted a series of measures designed to deal with various aspects of the energy crisis. The measures included lower highway speed limits, automobile mileage standards, creation of the Department of Energy and the Strategic Petroleum Reserve, tax incentives to encourage energy conservation, decontrol of oil prices, and funding to encourage development of alternative energy sources (Cochran et al. 1993:98–100; Davis 1993:109–116; Dye 1984:184–185).

A recurrent problem that these measures (as well as other proposed measures) faced was the high degree of conflict among different groups with different interests regarding energy issues. People in oil-producing states and people in states that produced no oil had different views regarding higher oil prices. Residents of sparsely populated states were less pleased with lower speed limits than were people in densely populated states. Environmentalists criticized expansion of energy production on public lands. Established energy companies did not welcome government's more prominent role. Underlying these group conflicts were a host of conflicts over the objectives and priorities that energy policy should serve. Should we emphasize production or conservation, energy independence or environmental protection, reliance on proven technology or reliance on future technological breakthroughs? (Cash and Rycroft 1985:435; Dye 1984:184, 191–192; Davis 1993: 110; G.A.O. 1988:69.)

Policy makers trying to deal with the energy crisis were also plagued with considerable uncertainty and stress. Would Americans be willing to change their modes of living to reduce energy consumption? How long would they remain interested in the energy issue? How cohesive would the Organization of Petroleum Exporting Countries (OPEC) be in the future? What technological breakthroughs would the future bring, and when would they occur? How accurate were future projections of energy supplies and needs? Given that energy affects many people's lives in many ways, officials knew that energy problems might endanger their careers, as the unfortunate experiences of Presidents Ford and Carter indicated. How could the many connections from energy to other public policies, from defense and foreign policy to transportation and the environment, be untangled? (Davis 1993: 4, 10–19.)

Although the energy policies of the 1973–1980 period apparently helped to encourage energy conservation and efficiency to some degree (along with a number of other factors), those policies encountered a number of difficulties. Leaders of the U.S. automobile industry grumbled about higher gas mileage standards. Many American drivers began exceeding the speed limit. Leaders of the oil industry resented government intrusion, although they did not resent government tax subsidies. The economic problems of the 1970s and early 1980s led to a growing preoccupation with the economy, and many other issues, including abortion, affirmative action, and crime, clamored for attention. Interest in energy issues began to subside.

The energy policies of the 1970s fared poorly in the 1980s and 1990s. The Reagan Administration pressed for more market-oriented energy policies in a variety of ways. Funding and staffing for energy programs were cut substantially, and regulations affecting energy industries were weakened. National speed limit guidelines were loosened and later eliminated entirely, which led to higher speed limits in most states. The public became increasingly fond of vehicles with relatively poor gas mileage ratings (Cash and Rycroft 1985:437–441; Cochran et al. 1993:98–111; Davis 1993:116; Dye 1984:191; Palumbo 1994:376–377).

In a number of respects, the developments since 1980 present a troubling picture. Crude oil imports to the U.S. rose by nearly 40% from 1980 to 1994, and proven U.S. petroleum reserves fell by more than 24% in the same time period; U.S. crude oil production fell by 24% from 1980 to 1995 (derived from *American Almanac 1996*: 702–704). Oil imports account for a large proportion of the U.S. trade deficit in recent years. Most known petroleum reserves are in the Middle East, which has been plagued with numerous conflicts over the years. The U.S. transportation system continues to have a huge appetite for oil, and much of the transportation system cannot readily be converted to other energy sources in the short term. The combination of heavy reliance on imports and the concentration of much U.S. energy processing in a small number of locations creates a high degree of vulnerability to sabotage or other disruptions due to natural causes (Clark and Page 1981:41, 84, 108, 226; Cochran et al.: 109–110; G.A.O. 1988:3, 10, 18–21, 24, 39–48). In spite of numerous signs of difficulty in the U.S. energy situation, the energy issue has apparently returned to the nonissue status that it had prior to 1973.

A. Environmental Policy

A fundamental public policy conflict that lawmakers face is our desire to protect America's pristine environment and to ensure a high level of energy production so as to maintain economic stability. With the onset of the energy crisis and the emphasis on economic growth significant pressure existed to postpone compliance deadlines and to relax environmental standards and rules (Cochran 1996:138–139). A disastrous case of such pressures involved the building of the Alaska pipeline and the subsequent oil spills in and around Prince William Sound. In 1968 Atlantic-Richfield Company (ARCO) announced the discovery of the largest oil field in North America found in Prudhoe Bay, Alaska (Lord 1992: 3). They estimated that as much as 25 billion barrels of oil and another 30 trillion cubic feet of natural gas lie in Prudhoe Bay. The oil industry quickly began planning a transportation system to move the oil through an 800-mile overland pipeline to an ice-free port on the Gulf of Alaska at Valdez. Valdez is infamous for storms, drifting ice, narrow passages, and submerged reefs; arguably treacherous waters for supertankers. Not everyone was enamored with the idea and pipeline approval was not quick to come. In particular fishermen and native Alaskans raised strong concerns about the pipeline. In addition, the National Environmental Protection Act (NEPA), passed in 1969—which required an assessment of social, economic, and environmental impact of activities on federal lands—was holding the process up with expensive ecological studies of the North Slope and pipeline corridor. With Spiro Agnew casting the tie-breaking vote, Congress in 1973 exempted the pipeline project from many of NEPA's environmental restrictions. Alyeska, a consortium of seven oil companies, the state of Alaska, and the federal government, were all promising the American public the safest pipeline and tanker system in the world. Interior Secretary Rogers Morton assured Congress that their goal was to protect the environment. Morton claimed to those who were concerned about possible damage to Prince William Sound that tankers would have double bottoms and sophisticated electronic equipment to ensure safe operations. In response Alaska created its Department of Environmental Conservation to make certain industry held to its pledges. When the first oil was loaded on the tankers at Valdez double bottoms were not required, nor had the Coast Guard installed full-coverage radar or any other electronic surveillance in Prince William Sound.

In 1976 the State of Alaska attempted to flex its muscles by passing a law that would give the state broad authority to regulate tanker traffic in state waters. The oil industry challenged the law and a district court ruled against the state on grounds that it preempted federal authority.

By the 1980s the Coast Guard and the State of Alaska started raising concerns about Alyeska's steadily declining ability to deal with a medium or large size oil spill. Shortly after, Alyeska dismantled its team dedicated solely to oil spill response in an effort to cut costs due to losses in the oil shipping industry. Alaska responded by requiring the consortium to submit a contingency plan that would include their response to a scenario of a 200,000-barrel spill (8.4 million gallons). They begrudgingly complied, protesting that such a spill could only be expected once every 241 years. Between 1977 and 1989 tanker traffic in Prince William Sound failed to send off any serious alarms. In the Port of Valdez and the Prince William Sound area, 440 mostly minor spills were reported (Lord 1992: 7).

However, the citizens of Valdez were becoming concerned the industry had become sloppy. Two months before the *Exxon Valdez* spill, the mayor of Valdez, John Devens, was alerting others to the fact that the ships making the Valdez run constituted 13% of the nation's total tanker traffic but accounted for 52% of its accidents (Davidson 1990: 7). The town of Valdez tried to build up its own oil spill protection, procuring booms and skimmers. However, under state and federal law, the principal responsibility for spill prevention and response rested on the industry. As it turned out, the people of Valdez had good reason to be concerned about oil spill response.

Shortly after midnight on March 24, 1989, the tanker *Exxon Valdez* (Exxon's newest and most advanced single-hull tanker), carrying more than 50 million gallons of crude oil, ran aground and ruptured its tanks on Bligh Reef, making Prince William Sound the site of the largest oil spill ever. Observers said that once the supertanker was damaged, the crude oil escaped so rapidly that it appeared to boil as it rushed to the surface. Approximately 11 million gallons of crude oil escaped, mucking the shores and bringing a swift death to the wildlife of that area.

By all accounts Alyeska failed to carry out its contingency plan. They were completely unprepared, as had been warned. Despite repeated assurances that response equipment was *en route*, Alyeska did not place its oil-containment barge on site for 14 hours (Kelso and Brown 1991:13). Alyeska finally transferred the responsibility of spill response to Exxon, which had never reviewed the contingency plan. Exxon was attempting to respond ad hoc to a crisis of enormous proportions. When Exxon's difficulties became obvious, fishermen and officials of the Alaska Department of Environmental Conservation organized their own response effort. The ability of the organizations to manage the crisis in a coordinated fashion was hampered by the national attention to the crisis. The media and environmentalists wanted to blame Exxon, and Exxon, in turn, blamed the state of Alaska and the Coast Guard for refusing to approve the use of chemical dispersants. Because this was literally untrue, this strategic act of diversion eroded Exxon's relationship with the state.

The nation was horrified by pictures of oil-covered sea otters and dying birds. The fact that this had happened in a place most Americans regard as the last wild, beautiful, pristine part of the country did not help the oil industry's case. The *Exxon Valdez* had focused the nation's attention on the failure of environmental policy—in particular water pollution policy.

Federal oil spill policy was disjointed, with no less than three separate funds established to defray the costs of oil spill response and cleanup. Liability limits were relatively low, and no clear lines of responsibility were drawn to ensure appropriate response to a large oil spill (Birkland 1997:16). In direct response to the *Exxon Valdez* oil spill, Congress passed the Oil Pollution Act (OPA) of 1990. This law combined the separate funds into one large federal fund—the national Oil Spill Liability Trust fund, increased liability limits, and specified clearer lines of authority. The OPA also provided new requirements for contingency planning by both government and industry. The government plan included a three-tier approach among federal, state, and local officials. In addition, Congress passed legislation requiring double hulls for the U.S. tanker fleet to be phased in during the next 20 to 25 years. Congress and the state of Alaska have also taken measures to address vehicular traffic systems. The Alaska legislature strengthened the state's response preparedness standards and the penalties for failing to carry out approved contingency plans. "Per barrel" penalties for those who spill oil were also increased.

The policies enacted in the wake of the *Exxon Valdez* disaster were numerous and left the industry virtually silenced during the proceedings. Strong opposition by Exxon and others representing the oil industry would not have been strategic for the public relations war they had already lost. However, the coming years will be telling for the strength of those polices. When the disaster occurred, many environmental groups received a surge in new membership and donations. But crises mobilize groups for only a limited time. The enacted policies have and will undoubtedly continue to be challenged by an industry seeking less regulation. As of November 1997, the Oil Pollution Act of 1990 was challenged and upheld by the U.S. Court of Appeals.

V. FREEING THE SLAVES

The issue of slavery was a source of tension in American politics for many years. The principle of equality that the Declaration of Independence proclaimed was difficult to reconcile with slavery, and the authors of the U.S. Constitution struggled with a number of slavery-related issues in drafting the Constitution. Further conflicts erupted over organizing territorial governments, admitting new states, runaway slaves, and the political power gained by slave states as a result of counting each slave as three-fifths of a person for determining the allocation of seats in the House of Representatives and votes in the electoral college (see Nice and Fredericksen 1995:107–110, and the studies they cite).

As opponents to the expansion and even existence of slavery became more vocal and better organized and as defenders of slavery became increasingly alarmed by the activities of antislavery forces, tensions increased. Following Lincoln's election, southern states began seceding from the Union. When the Civil War erupted, the Lincoln Administration and Congress initially expressed the view that their objective in the war was the reunification of the country and upholding of the Constitution. The abolition of slavery was not an official objective, and sentiment in the North and in the Union Army was apparently mixed on the issue of slavery (Catton 1960:100–107, 174; Jordan et al. 1987: 375).

As the war dragged on, abolition of slavery became a more attractive policy option, in part because it would weaken the Confederate war effort (Catton 1960:174). Abolition rested on a rather diverse coalition, including people who believed that slavery was morally wrong, people who believed abolition would militarily weaken the South by depriving the southern economy of much of its labor force, and people who wanted to punish the South and southern slave owners especially. In addition, the abolitionist coalition included many people with significant racial prejudices. Abolition emerged in a series of stages, from laws encouraging Union troops to recognize the freedom of runaway or abandoned slaves to the Emancipation Proclamation and, finally, the Thirteenth Amendment (Blake 1972:315).

Abolishing slavery raised a host of other, related issues. Most of the former slaves had little or no formal education, a situation that reflected southern state laws forbidding the education of slaves. Many had agricultural skills but owned no land. Ending slavery meant that southern blacks would count as entire persons rather than as three-fifths of a person each. That change would enhance the political power of the South in the U.S. House and electoral college; should that enhanced power be enjoyed only by southern whites, many of whom had supported secession, or should blacks vote? Should blacks enjoy legal and social equality or be relegated to second-class status? Could generations of racial prejudice be overcome? (Brogan 1990:361–362; Henretta et al. 1987:498–499; ''Report on the Joint Committee on Reconstruction'' 1982:17–20).

Immediately after the Civil War, southern state governments controlled by whites adopted ''black codes'' designed to limit the rights and freedoms of blacks; legislative weapons were reinforced by violence and intimidation. Congress responded with Reconstruction, which attempted to protect black rights to some degree. The Freedmen's Bureau worked to increase black access to education, health care, and land, along with providing other kinds of aid, and laws and Constitutional amendments were adopted to combat discrimination (Blake 1972:316; Martin et al. 1989:485–488).

The efforts to protect black rights and help blacks in the transition from slavery to freedom encountered many difficulties. Southern whites pressured the Freedmen's Bureau into limiting its activities in some areas; the bureau was finally abolished in 1872. White racists attacked and undercut efforts to educate blacks, and initiatives designed to provide blacks with farmland were eroded by concerns over the sanctity of private property. Northerners gradually lost interest in Reconstruction and became more concerned with economic growth and development, particularly with the recession that began in 1873. The U.S. Supreme Court narrowed the applicability of the Fourteenth Amendment and civil rights laws designed to combat discrimination. Critics denounced corruption in the Reconstruction governments of the South and called for a return to a more limited role for the national government regarding the conduct of state government. Although Reconstruction involved a very complex and difficult bundle of tasks, which could not realistically be carried out quickly or easily, many people in the North became discouraged by its seemingly slow progress. The great pain and trauma produced by the Civil War and its aftermath were not entirely conducive to calm negotiation or reasonable problem solving (Blake 1972: 316–320; Brogan 1990:373–380; Catton 1960:274–275; Henretta et al. 1987:496–500; Jordan et al. 1987:374–388; Washington 1995:40).

With the Compromise of 1877, Reconstruction came to an end. Southern whites regained control of state and local governments in the South, and they manipulated the electoral machinery to push blacks out of the electorate. Violence and intimidation, along with laws requiring segregation in many aspects of life, eroded the status of blacks. Many found themselves in debt and trapped in sharecropping arrangements that left them with little better living standards and little more mobility than in the slave era (Blake 1972: 320; Brogan 1990:380–382; Henretta et al. 1987:501–502; Jordan et al. 1987:392–396; Martin et al. 1989:493, 506–507). The failure to develop and sustain an overall plan to protect black rights after the Civil War helped to lay the groundwork for many of the social problems facing the United States in the twentieth century.

VI. SAVING PASSENGER RAIL SERVICE

After the 1920s, passenger rail service in the United States began a long-term decline that was interrupted by World War II. The decline resumed after the war, with passenger volume, the number of passenger trains, and the number of routes being served all declining. The nation's railroads tried a variety of approaches to attract passengers, from investing in new equipment to discount fares. Financial losses from passenger service averaged approximately $500 million annually by the end of the 1960s (Bradley 1985:23–40; Hilton 1980:2–5; Nice 1996:95).

A number of factors contributed to the decline of passenger trains, including increasing competition from automobiles and airplanes; improvements in both modes were due in part to massive government subsidies for road and air transportation. The railroads were hampered by inefficient labor policies, and as financial losses mounted, railroad management gradually lost interest in providing passenger service unless some sort of governmental help became available. Modernization of equipment and facilities grew less common after the mid-1950s (Hilton 1980:8–11; Morgan 1959:14–51; Nice 1996:96–98; Stover 1970:196–218).

By 1969, the nation's major railroads began to press for some form of financial aid from the federal government to support passenger rail service or for approval to terminate almost all remaining passenger trains. Some discussions regarding a possible response took place in Congress and the U.S. Department of Transportation. Those discussions developed a greater sense of urgency when the huge Penn Central Railroad, which provided much of the passenger rail service in the Northeast, filed for bankruptcy in June 1970. In October of the same year, Congress passed legislation creating Amtrak (originally called Railpax), a quasi-public corporation. It began operations in May 1971 (Bradley 1985:41–43; Phillips 1972:10–11; Nice 1996:99; Weaver 1985:90–93).

The manner in which Amtrak was created contributed to a number of significant problems that the system faced. The failure to act on the problems of passenger trains until they were on the verge of extinction meant that much of the nation's passenger rail equipment was obsolete and in poor condition. The speed with which Amtrak was created left little time for an accurate inventory of equipment or advance planning to ease the transition from private to quasi-public service. Partly to ease that transition, most of the employees providing passenger services remained in the employment of private railroads. The routes to be served had not been decided by the time the legislation passed, nor was there time to develop even a general consensus regarding the goals of the system. Some supporters emphasized the need to modernize the system and improve services,but others were concerned about containing costs. A number of conflicts centered on the distribution of service (Nice 1996:99; Zimmerman 1981:3–6).

Dealing with those various problems was a major preoccupation of Amtrak's managers in its early years. They had to oversee development of more modern passenger equipment, a process that took a number of years. Amtrak's management gradually shifted to directly employing personnel, rather than relying on employees of the railroads, in order to gain more effective control over operations and improve labor productivity. Amtrak also shifted from reliance on private railroads for maintenance and servicing to having its own service facilities, and it acquired the Northeast Corridor (from Boston to Washington, D.C.), which has developed into the fastest passenger rail route in the United States. Amtrak created the first nationwide, computerized reservation system for passenger rail travelers in order to improve customer convenience (Bradley 1985:64–120; Nice 1996: 100–101; Weaver 1985:251–254; Zimmerman 1981:39, 68).

Amtrak has succeeded in reversing the long-term decline in passenger-train ridership in the United States and has gradually improved its financial performance (Nice 1996: 102–103). However, continued controversies over federal subsidies (in contrast to the steady flow of federal highway aid) have produced enormous variations in Amtrak's capital funding from year to year (National Railroad Passenger Association 1994:12–13). As a result, Amtrak has sometimes been forced to keep old equipment in operation longer than is desirable. In addition, funding problems led to termination of service on two routes in 1997; disputes over the distribution of service have continued to surface periodically. Moreover, Amtrak has continued to face occasional calls for its termination; it has not achieved the political security enjoyed by federal highway programs or governmental support of the sort given to aviation. Here, again is a crisis policy that lacks the political base needed for a reasonably secure existence.

VII. CONCLUSIONS

Making crisis policy is a fact of life for policy makers. The widely accepted view among lawmakers is that government policy has been and will always be a function of crisis (see Kingdon 1995). The fact that we live in an increasingly interdependent technological world has made crises and disasters a normal part of our everyday existence (Perrow 1984:3). The implications for policy making and implementation are numerous. Crises act as catalysts for policy change in that their very existence alerts others to problems. They can be *focusing events*, capturing the attention of the public, often telling a causal story that informs the public through emotive symbols and information. Cries of public concern and outrage may follow and have the potential to foster policy change. If a crisis remains a salient topic that is viewed as a public problem, it is more likely to reach the political agenda and lead to the adoption of policy changes. However, the very nature of making policy during a crisis may lead to problems for lawmakers and the program managers who must implement the policy changes. Because of the ephemeral nature of how long situations will be defined by the public as crises, people may abandon their willingness to accept certain solutions that may be perceived as too costly or too complicated to adopt.

The end of the crisis may lead to greater skepticism and more criticism. Policy makers and program managers may have to suffer the wrath of groups that were excluded from the search for policy solutions during the crisis. Often, when normal conditions are restored, the political base for policy changes becomes so eroded that a policy initiative falls apart. Another troublesome area for policy makers and program managers is how to implement vague policies with unclear and or conflicting goals. In their haste, lawmakers—being cognizant of the policy window that surrounds a crisis—frequently write vague policies so as to garner the support of their colleagues in approving a particular policy solution. Then program managers are left to implement the policy changes, which may take significant resources from other programs and be learning-intensive under crisis conditions.

REFERENCES

Anderson, James (1994). Public Policymaking. 2nd ed. Boston: Houghton Mifflin.

Birkland, Thomas (1997). ''The Exxon Valdez oil spill as focusing event: politics, policy, and symbols.'' Paper presented at the 1997 Meeting of the American Studies Association, Washington, D.C., October.

Birkland, Thomas (1997). ''The political uses of events: a theory of event politics.'' Paper presented at the 1997 meeting of the American Political Science Association, Washington, D.C., September.

Blake, Nelson (1972). *A History of American Life and Thought*, 2nd ed. New York: McGraw-Hill.

Bradley, Rodger (1985). *Amtrak*. Poole, United Kingdom: Blandford.

Brogan, Hugh (1990). *The Penguin History of the United States of America*. London: Penguin.

Buchanan, Bruce (1978). *The Presidential Experience*. Englewood Cliffs, NJ: Prentice-Hall.

Bullock, Charles III (1984). ''Conditions associated with policy implementation.'' In Charles Bullock III and Charles Lamb (eds), *Implementation of Civil Rights Policy*. Monterey, CA: Brooks/Cole.

Catton, Bruce (1960). *The Civil War*. Boston: Houghton Mifflin.

Clark, Wilson, and Page, Jake (1981). *Energy, Vulnerability and War*. New York: Norton.

Cochran, Clarke, Mayer, Lawrence, Carr, T.R., and Cayer, N. Joseph (1993). *American Public Policy* 4th ed. New York: St. Martin's.

Creger, Ralph, and Combs, Barry (1981). *Train Power*. Independence, MO: Independence Press.

Cyert, Richard, and March, James (1963). *A Behavioral Theory of the Firm*. Englewood Cliffs, NJ: Prentice-Hall.

Davidson, Art (1990). *In the Wake of the Exxon Valdez*. San Francisco: Sierra Club Books.

Davis, David (1993). *Energy Politics*, 4th ed. New York: St. Martin's.

Dye, Thomas (1984). Understanding Public Policy. 5th ed. Englewood Cliffs, NJ: Prentice Hall.

Edwards, George (1980). *Implementing Public Policy*. Washington, D.C.: Congressional Quarterly.

Edwards, George, and Sharkansky, Ira (1978). *The Policy Predicament*. San Francisco: W.H. Freeman.

Eyestone, Robert (1978). *From Social Issues to Public Policy*. New York: Wiley.

Gamson, William (1975). *The Strategy of Social Protest*. Homewood, IL: Dorsey.

G.A.O. (1988). *Energy Security: An Overview of Changes in the World Oil Market*. Washington D.C.: General Accounting Office.

G.A.O. (1989). *International Energy Agency*. Washington D.C.: General Accounting Office.

Henretta, James, Banlee, W. Elliot, Brody, David, and Ware, Susan (1987). *America's History to 1877*. Chicago: Dorsey.

Hilton, George (1980). *Amtrak*. Washington, D.C.: American Enterprise Institute.

Janis, Irving (1972). *Victims of Groupthink*. Boston: Houghton Mifflin.

Jordan, Winthrop, Litwack, Leon, Hofstadter, Richard, Miller, William, and Aaron, Daniel (1987). *The United States*, 6th ed. Englewood Cliffs, NJ: Prentice Hall.
Lord, Nancy (1992). *Darkened Waters: A Review of the History, Science, and Technology Associated with the Exxon Valdez Oil Spill and Cleanup*. Homer, AK: Homer Society of Natural History.
Kash, Don, and Rycroft, Robert (1985). "Energy policy: how failure was snatched from the jaws of success." *Policy Studies Review* 4, 433–444.
Kelman, Steven (1987). *Making Public Policy*. New York: Basic Books.
Kelso, Dennis, and Brown, Michele (1991). "Policy lessons from Exxon Valdez spill." *Forum for Applied Research and Public Policy* 6 (winter), 13–19.
Kingdon, John W. (1995). *Agendas, Alternatives, and Public Policies*, 2nd ed. New York: Harper Collins.
Lineberry, Robert (1977). *American Public Policy*, 2nd ed. New York: Harper & Row.
March, James, and Simon, Herbert (1958). *Organizations*. New York: Wiley.
Martin, James, Roberts, Randy, Mint, Steven, McMurry, Linda, and Jones, James (1989). *America and Its People*. New York: Harper Collins.
Mazmanian, Daniel, and Sabatier, Paul (1983). *Implementation and Public Policy*. Glenview, IL: Scott, Foresman.
Mohr, Lawrence (1969). "Determinants of innovations in organizations." *American Political Science Review* 63, 111–126.
National Railroad Passenger Corporation (1994). *Annual Report*. Washington, D.C.: National Railroad Passenger Corporation.
Nice, David (1994). *Policy Innovation in State Government*. Ames: Iowa State University Press.
Nice, David (1996). "Passenger rail service: decline and resurgence." *Transportation Quarterly* 50(*4*), 95–106.
Nice, David, and Frederickson, Patricia (1995). *The Politics of Intergovernmental Relations*, 2nd ed. Chicago: Nelson-Hall.
Palumbo, Dennis (1994). *Public Policy in America*, 2nd ed. Fort Worth: Harcourt Brace.
Perrow, Charles (1984). *Normal Accidents: Living with High-Risk Technologies*. New York: Basic Books.
Peterson, Paul, Rabe, Barry, and Wong, Kenneth (1986). *When Federalism Works*. Washington, D.C.: Brookings.
Phillips, Don (1972). "Railpax Rescue." In Harold Edmonson (ed.), *Journey to Amtrak*, Milwaukee, WI: Kalmbach.
Plato (1975). *The Laws*. London: Penguin.
Polsby, Nelson (1984). *Political Innovation in America*. New Haven, CT: Yale University Press.
Pressman, Jeffrey, and Wildavsky, Aaron (1979). *Implementation*, 2nd ed. Berkeley, CA: University of California Press.
Rose, Richard (1993). *Lesson-Drawing in Public Policy*. Chatham, NJ: Chatham House.
"Report on the Joint Committee on Reconstruction,".
Sharkansky, Ira (1970). *Routines of Politics*. New York: Van Nostrand Reinhold.
Stover, John (1970). *The Life and Decline of the American Railroad*. New York: Oxford.
Tocqueville, Alexis de (1945). *Democracy in America*. Vol. 1. New York: Vintage.
Truman, David (1951). *The Governmental Process*. New York: Knopf.
U.S. Congress (1982). "Report of the Joint Committee on Reconstruction, June 20, 1866." In Richard Hofstadter and Beatrice Hofstadter (eds.), *Great Issues in American History*, Vol. 3.
Phillips, Don (1972). "Railpax rescue." Harold Edmonson (ed.), *In Journey to Amtrak*. Milwaukee, WI: Kalmbach.
Washington, Booker T. (1995). *Up From Slavery*. New York: Dover.
Weaver, Kent R. (1985). *The Politics of Industrial Change*. Washington, D.C.: Brookings.
Zaltman, Gerald, Duncan, Robert, and Holbek, Jonny (1973). *Innovations and Organizations*. New York: Wiley.
Zimmerman, Karl (1981). *Amtrak at Milepost 10*. Park Forest, IL: PTJ Publishing.

6

Disaster Impact upon Urban Economic Structure

Linkage Disruption and Economic Recovery

Richard M. Vogel Departments of History, Economics, and Politics, State University of New York at Farmingdale, Farmingdale, New York

I. NATURAL DISASTER AND THE URBAN ECONOMY

Natural hazards such as earthquakes, floods, and hurricanes present the modern city, the setting of the urban economy, with the continual threat of serious and sometimes cataclysmic disaster. Alongside possible physical impact and destruction, employment and income may be affected—the result of damage to economic infrastructure, individual firms, and population displacement. In the aftermath of the disaster, recovery consists of three primary concerns—replacement of damaged infrastructure and housing, recovery of employment and income, and the recovery of economic structure. Local officials, planners, and government authorities are generally able to address the first two issues more easily than the last.

In a sense, location is the principal cause of urban vulnerability to a particular natural hazard. That does not, however, imply that the problem could be solved by simply moving or relocating the city. This solution fails to take into account the viewpoint or wishes of the city's inhabitants, especially if a sense of place or home is an important component of individual utility. It also ignores the fact that geographic location may also be one of the principle underlying factors responsible for urban growth.

Traditional urban analysis ascribes city location to factors such as natural resource availability, ocean and river transportation, transhipping points, transportation costs, and as a commercial center. Modern economic geographers and economists link urban growth and development to external economies, economies of agglomeration, subcontracting activities, the urban center's role in information exchange, and intellectual spillovers (Glaeser 1994; Storper 1995; Porter 1993; Scott 1993; Scott 1988). Briefly stated, growth and development occurs as a result of these linkages and externalities. In turn, continued growth depends upon the deepening and expansion of these linkages and externalities. Additionally, one urban area may grow more rapidly than another region as a result of these endogenous factors of growth.

The modern city can continue to grow and expand even after the original reason for the city's location has become unimportant. New enterprise, though, is built within and expands the bounds of the urban area. Many of the factors that make a particular city or urban area an attractive location for the firm and the individual, however, are geographically rooted.

Goods and services produced within the urban economy may be for local consumption and produced primarily with local inputs (intraregional trade). The urban economy though, sits within a broad framework of regional, national, and international trade. Thus, the goods and services produced will also make use of extraregional inputs and are traded outside of the region (interregional trade). Production and trade is located and carried out in the geographic space of the city. Thus, the structure of the urban economy has an important spatial component to it.

As a result of the spatial structure of regional production and transactions, the urban economy is vulnerable to tremendous upheaval and displacement arising from a major disaster event. Vulnerability arises from three primary sources. The first source is direct impact damage and losses. In this case, regional economic activity (or some portion of it) may be temporally idled as a result of loss of infrastructure, capital loss, and displaced population and labor. Second, temporary disruptions of economic activity may also result in changes in the pattern of intraregional and interregional trade. And last, a large scale disaster event may also cause breaks in the regional structure of production, and regional economic linkages—in turn causing further changes in intraregional and interregional trading patterns.

The focus of this paper is on the effects of natural disaster upon urban economic structure. While a number of man-made and technological situations may have a significant impact upon the community, the underlying basis of the disaster lies directly within the control of the social, political, and institutional setting (Bogard 1989). With natural disaster, the vulnerability of the urban area arises from two sources. One is the social, political, and institutional setting. The other source of vulnerability, though, is the natural disaster agent itself—i.e., hurricane, flood, drought, earthquake, etc.—outside of human control (Vogel 1996; Bates and Peacock 1993).

There is no uniform or codifiable set of effects of natural disaster upon the urban economy owing to the uniqueness of each disaster event as well as the generally unique nature of the impacted regional economy. A natural disaster such as a hurricane may cause severe physical damage or only slight wind damage. Additionally, this damage may be widespread across the community or isolated to specific geographic locations, e.g., affecting primarily residential areas or agricultural sites. Direct damage and impact, as well, may be sectorally isolated, primarily affecting one sector of the urban economy but not others owing to the geographic range of disaster impacts, the location of economic activity, and spatial structure. The urban economy may feel a wider impact from the disaster due to loss and disruption in sectoral linkages and intraregional and interregional trade relationships.

From the above discussion, it becomes apparent that measuring economic recovery following a disaster is not a simple and straightforward matter of evaluating regional aggregates like unemployment, regional gross domestic product (GDP), or regional income. The problem is that while regional aggregates may eventually reattain and push above their previous levels, the underlying structure of the economy may be completely different. These differences arise as a result of sectoral impacts and changes in sectoral and trade linkage relationships. In the next section of this paper I discuss a generalized set of short- and long-run economic effects of a disaster on the urban economy. Section III further develops the concept of growth in the urban economy and how natural disaster may affect both the nature and rate of growth. In Sect. IV, several methods of evaluating and measuring economic disaster's effect on the urban economy and its structure are discussed and outlined. Section V is an application of this methodology as applied to the particular case of Miami, Florida, following the impact of Hurricane Andrew in August, 1992. The basic conclusions and proposals from this study are presented in Sect. VI.

II. ECONOMIC IMPACT OF NATURAL DISASTER

A. Natural Disaster Impact

A natural disaster can be thought of as an exogenous force that impacts the regional and urban economy. In many cases inhabitants, including investors and businesses of the area, may be aware of the potential risk they face from the particular hazards in the region (tropical storm, hurricane or typhoon along many coastal areas, earthquake hazard, or flood hazard in a flood plain) and may have some combination of structural and nonstructural mitigation programs in place. As such, these plans or programs influence economic activity to some degree by defining and restricting available business locations through, for example, zoning. Structural flood control reduces the hazardous conditions to more tolerable levels and thus brings more area into human use and habitation. Urban vulnerability, however, may increase as a result of the now partially protected flood plains being put to more intensive use (White 1974).

Through structural and nonstructural mitigation, hazards are partially endogenized into the economic growth process, but not the actual disaster event. While the attempt to insulate the region from disaster does affect regional growth and structure, the occurrence of an actual disaster event is, with very few exceptions, unexpected, unanticipated, and unplanned for. Despite a number of good disaster simulations, such as Borkan and Kunreuther (1978), Ellson et al. (1984), or Gordon and Richardson (1992), actual loss and damage from impact is almost impossible to predict a priori.

The disaster event gives rise to two general levels of economic impact—direct and indirect. Direct impacts, as the name suggests, are simply damages directly attributable to the disaster agent, such as loss of life, injury, capital losses, crop damage, and damage to public and residential structures. Indirect impact takes the form of changes in flow activity, business interruption, changes in employment due to structural and capital loss, and changes in regional and interregional demand and supply relationships, to name but a few (Vogel 1996; Albala-Bertrand 1993). Predisaster mitigation strategies are primarily directed toward minimizing direct disaster losses, while the primary goal of postdisaster recovery efforts are mainly restoration and replacement of lost infrastructure, residences, and capital. In addition, the economic impact of disaster must be evaluated in terms of its short- and long-run consequences.

B. Short-Run Impact

Short-run impacts have the most noticeable effects and are often of the greatest concern to local officials. The principal economic effects of natural disaster are (1) changes in employment levels (positive and negative), (2) changes in income (positive and negative), and (3) inflationary pressures.

1. Changes in Employment

In the short run, unemployment may increase or decrease. There are two forces at work here. The disaster event may have heavily damaged or destroyed industrial sites or the central business district. This would result in a loss of employment (temporary or permanent, dependent on businesses rebuilding and remaining in the area). The increase in unemployment may be counteracted by what has been termed disaster's "silver lining," a reconstruction boom (Denslow 1992; West and Lenze 1994; Guimares et al. 1993). Reconstruction in the community can fuel additional economic activity through increased spending on construction supplies, furnishings, services, and a multiplier effect as employment and consequently income in construction and ancillary sectors increase.

Disaster's effects upon employment though are tenuous and are highly dependent on the areal extent of damage and sectoral impact. Additionally, they depend on the immediate predisaster conditions of the economy, economic trends within the region, and resource mobility within the economy. A postdisaster change in employment may be due to factors other than the natural disaster, such as recession or expansion in the rest of the country. Resource mobility and the availability of resources in the community are key elements to a reconstruction boom. In some instances, and such is the case with Hurricane Andrew and Miami, there was a high degree of resource availability and mobility. Reconstruction surged, fueling further economic activity. There was a cost, though, to surrounding communities as firms and additional construction labor resources flooded into Dade County, delaying projects in other parts of the state and the Southeast for up to 1½ years. The reconstruction effect was also felt more at the state level than the urban economic region level because of the high mobility of the construction industry. In the lesser developed nations, though, factor mobility and (un)availability is very often the root cause of a further weakening of employment levels, choking off an already depressed economy.

2. Changes in Income

The disaster may also impact income in the short run. Income is affected through several channels. Income in the first instance will directly reflect changes in employment and unemployment. Firms, though, may not increase or decrease the number of individuals employed, but instead simply adjust employee hours (cutbacks or increases in the number of hours worked). Transfer payments into the community may increase, and disaster aid may additionally affect income. Income from rents, capital, and proprietors income may all be affected as well, owing in part to direct impact damages, and also to things such as temporary population displacement and changed traffic patterns. As with employment effects, income may move in either a positive or a negative direction and is highly dependent upon sectoral and geographic damages.

While there is still considerable debate about employment and income effects, even in the short run (Albala-Bertrand 1993; Guimaraes et al. 1993), disasters tend to cause a short-run decrease in wealth. Insurance coverage, because of deductibles and exclusions, is typically incomplete. Even with additional government disaster relief and assistance, households may have to dip into savings and other holdings in order to completely rebuild damaged homes or replace lost property. From a business perspective, disaster damage represents an immediate amortization of the affected capital stock. For the firm and the household, the disaster can cause unreimbursed losses to wealth and capital in the short run.

3. Inflationary Pressures

Disaster impact may also cause inflationary pressures in the affected urban economy. Again, the degree of pressure is highly dependent on the areal extent and level of damage and the predisaster state of the urban economy. If, for example, vacancy rates are low and a large proportion of the housing stock is either destroyed outright or rendered temporarily unusable, this would create greater upward pressure on rental rates and home prices than a situation with higher vacancy rates. Upward price pressures can occur in other markets as well. Goods such as chainsaws or portable generators may have a tendency to rise in price following hurricanes. This tendency, especially in the developed world, is tempered by the ease of mobility of the particular good or goods and whether or not the good is in ready supply in the rest of the country. Additionally, sellers may not wish to antagonize existing customers by raising the price (even with an increase in demand) of a particular good and may thus face charges of price gouging, and losses in customer goodwill (Douty 1977). Thus, supermarkets and large chain stores may keep the price of bottled water or batteries at predisaster prices, partially due to the issue of customer goodwill. Additionally, though, they may not increase prices because of a ready supply at other locations within the distribution network, mobility, and the ease of consumers to find alternate sources for the goods. Other sectors, such as housing, with lesser degrees of the mobility, will exhibit greater upward pressure in prices.

C. Long-Run Impact

A disaster may have further long-run impact on the urban economy. While certainly not limited to these effects, the principal long-run consequences of natural disaster are (1) permanent changes in employment and income, (2) acceleration of preexisting economic trends, and (3) changes in growth and development.

1. Permanent Changes in Employment and Income

As was the case with short-run consequences, the effect on the urban economy depends in large part on the immediate pre-disaster state of the regional, national, and world economy, and the areal and sector specific level of disaster impact. These effects, as well, are highly interrelated to one another, the major cause of these changes being rooted in changes in the underlying sectoral and spatial structure of the urban economy. Sectoral and spatial linkage disruptions can result in the alternation of structural relationships within the urban economy. These changes will, in turn, affect employment, income, and the underlying determinants of growth within the urban economy.

Long-run changes in sectoral and total level of employment outside of any preexisting trends within the urban economy is attributable to a number of factors. One cause may be from incomplete sectoral or economic recovery. While it is rare for a community not to be rebuilt, some individuals and firms may choose to leave the area or not rebuild. Additionally, some intraregional sectoral and intersectoral linkages may have been disrupted by the disaster. Surviving firms will find alternate sources of supply for these inputs. This, in turn, places new competitive pressures on local firms in the supply chain at a time when they are least able to respond. Sectoral linkages and intraregional trade may be weakened in this case. If these new trade patterns remain in place, this can cause further sectoral decline in employment and income (Gordon and Richardson 1993; Albala-Bertrand 1993; Cochrane 1975).

2. Acceleration of Trends

The disaster may accelerate preexisting trends in the urban economy as well. In this circumstance, the disaster's impact serves as the catalyst for accelerated sectoral expansion or sectoral decline. Acceleration of trends can result as firms may take the opportunity to expand their more profitable operations as they reconstruct and rebuild. Trend acceleration also may arise through price and valuation changes. In many urban areas, land-intensive activities such as farming or mining continue to exist. While these activities may still be profitable to operate, there may exist strong development pressures within the urban economy. Following the disaster, changes in price and land valuation may force the owners and operators of these land-intensive activities to reevaluate their operations. What had been a steady decline of these sectors now may be accelerated.

3. *Effect on Long-Run Growth and Development*

Disaster's effect on long-run growth and development of the urban economy works primarily through changes in the region's underlying structure. These changes in growth and development may not be readily apparent in the aggregate measures of economic activity. Sectoral shifts in economic activity may affect the distribution of income but not total income. Disaster-induced changes within the patterns of regional trade will affect the nature of growth. The community may change from one with a high level of linkages between sectors and firms within the area, to one with a reduced level of linkages. These changes will affect not only the urban economy but the institutional, social, and political relationships within the community.

III. EVALUATION OF DISASTER'S IMPACT ON URBAN ECONOMIC STRUCTURE

A. The Urban Economy

The urban economy reflects a spatially complex set of production and trade activities. Households and firms within this urban landscape locate themselves through both a market process allocating land on the basis of willingness to pay as well as through an institutional, legal, and political framework, as exemplified by zoning and licensing requirements. Out of this process evolves the resulting patchwork of residential, industrial, and mixed-use neighborhoods; business, commercial, and shopping districts; government complexes; and the like that we call a city.

Economic activity within the urban economy takes place through many different channels. Firms within the region employ local labor, which generates wage income. Additionally, firms will employ capital, material inputs, and services (general and specialized, i.e., accounting, engineering, machining, etc.) of both regional and nonregional (from outside the community) origin. Thus, additional income in the form of profits will be created in the community through intraregional trade. Likewise, final goods and services will be traded intraregionally and interregionally. Strong backward and forward linkages between firms and sectors within the region imply that the success of one sector or firm (operating in the region) will have additional positive multiplier effects on income and employment within the region.

Linkages within and between sectors and firms arise from a number of sources. Among them are labor and human capital resources in the region and transportation costs of inputs. These are the classic explanations for firm location. Additionally, agglomeration and external economies of scale may arise by firms being in close proximity to each other. These effects may occur as a result of the fact that a number of similar types of firms within one region allow for specialized inputs and facilities to become feasible or profitable. Scott (1993) views these scale effects to be an important reason for the dominance of Los

Angeles in the commercial film industry of the United States. He additionally found, though, that if one link within the region weakens enough, it may have far-reaching effects on the rest of the sector, or associated sectors. Illustrating this problem is the fact that film animation, owing to cost pressures, moved out largely of Los Angeles, which had been the center for film animation through the mid-sixties, the seventies, and the eighties.

While sectoral and firm linkages are one important aspect of the regional economy, sector and firm location are another important aspect. Many firms will move to locations in relation to client and customer base—retail establishments, restaurants, personal services (i.e., beauty salons, barbershops, etc.). If, due to a disaster, a large part of the population temporarily moves from the neighborhood or area, these firms could suffer a dramatic loss of business. And if the neighborhood never recovers, then the area business may either move or go out of business as well.

Firms location decisions will also take into consideration the proximity of related businesses or infrastructure location (transportation, port facilities). Retail firms located in shopping centers and malls exhibit this types of behavior. In manufacturing and service industries, locating near related businesses can facilitate face-to-face communications and subcontracting activity. Communications, subcontracting, and the ability of subcontractors to respond quickly are key elements in a system of flexible production (Storper 1995; Scott 1993; Porter 1993).

Disaster may negatively affect these interfirm relationships. If some of the firms within the production process fail to recover, the competitive advantage of the region can be lost. This is an especially important concern in a world of global competition. The factors responsible for global firms locating in a particular city or region will be based upon concerns such as transportation costs, labor costs, infrastructure, human capital, externalities of informational linkages, as well as these region specific synergies that arise from proximity, subcontracting, and the vertical and horizontal integration of production processes within the region.

B. Growth in the Regional Economy

The classic conception of growth and development centers around the concepts of savings, investment, capital, and technology (Chenery 1986). Obviously, a natural disaster event may affect all of these variables. In the region, though, while savings may be affected as individuals tap savings due to extraordinary expenditures, savings rates themselves are not likely to change. The disaster's effect on capital can be viewed as an acceleration of the amortization schedule, capital which firms would have had to replace anyway. Individuals and firms investment decisions are fundamentally related to the concepts of risk and profit.

The occurrence of a major natural disaster event does not change the underlying probability of an event occurring. Nor does it directly change the underlying profitability of a particular activity. It can, however, indirectly affect profitability through its effect on the synergistic structure of industry within the region. Additionally, while event probability is unchanged, the disaster may have a temporary effect on expectations. Natural disasters are normally not at the forefront of political and economic decision making (Rossi et al. 1982). In essence, long-run investment will likely be unchanged, but the composition (type of activities invested in) of investment may be different.

Technology, the last element of classic growth models, is also possibly affected by a natural disaster. Technological change, or the adaptation of new technology in the affected region may occur. There were reports of new technologies and techniques being adopted in Alaska, after the 1964 earthquake, and after Hurricane Hugo in Puerto Rico (Kunreuther and Fiore 1966; Aguirre and Bush 1992). While technology transfer may take place as a result of the recovery process, it is not the ''norm.'' Capital replacement that embodies new technologies, though, is the primary channel for technological change and adaptation to take place. Thus, the disaster may speed up the adoption of new technology and techniques. The overall effect then, depends largely on the level of capital loss, and the amount of technological change embodied in new replacement.

Regional growth and development, though, is more than just a process of savings and investment. The urban metropolis forms a set of functional and spatial complexes through which expanding divisions of labor and increasing spatial and temporal linkages can create spatial economic agglomerations and deepening external economies. This implies that the regional economy and its industrial complexes are self-reinforcing (Scott 1988; Storper and Walker 1989; Porter 1993; Glaeser 1994). The synergy between local economic actors and the arising economic complex may give rise to comparative advantage even in the face of poor natural resource endowments.

Growth in the urban economy is additionally tied to national and international economic growth, while, from the previous discussion, it is apparent that one city or urban economy may vary from another city's economy because of self-reinforcing regional internal factors. Consequently, urban economic activity will be driven by a combination of international, national, and regional economic factors. National and international economic conditions will affect the regional economy through interregional trade linkages, which will, in turn, affect local employment, income, and consumption. The degree to which the regional economy is driven by external economic activity depends largely upon the strength of these interregional trade linkages. Thus, the urban economy is subject to the same recessionary and expansionary forces as the national and international economy. Recession or expansion, however, will be felt differently in different urban areas across a country.

In the aftermath of a natural disaster, the community is forced to address a number of important issues. Once critical emergency services and immediate life safety issues have been addressed, the community can turn its attention to the problems of cleanup and community and economic restoration. Any decisions made, though, may have unforeseen consequences on future regional growth and development.

IV. EVALUATING DISASTER'S IMPACT

A. Simulating and Modeling Natural Disaster's Impact

The regional economy can be simulated and modeled using a number of different techniques. Which particular method the analyst chooses to use though depends largely upon two main criteria: (1) what specific issues are being addressed and (2) what type of data are available or obtainable. The second issue takes on additional meaning or power when applied to the natural disaster situation.

The primary method of quantitative analysis used in the past to measure the economic impact and effects of a natural disaster involved single-equation regression-models techniques (e.g., Friesima et al. 1979). Single-equation regression models offer the analyst a great deal of flexibility in situations where data are fairly limited or extremely difficult to obtain. One of the serious drawbacks that arises with single-equation models, though, is specification biases due to their inability to capture the full level of simultaneity of both the general level of economic activity as well as the situation created by a natural hazard event (Ellson et al. 1984; Guimaraes et al. 1993).

To overcome these obstacles, a number of analysts turned to input-output (I/O) models and their related extension, computer general equilibrium (CGE) modeling, to analyze the disaster scenario (Albala-Bertand 1992; Gordon and Richardson 1992). I/O analysis and CGE modeling give the analyst the ability to model the regional economy with a very high degree of simultaneity and detail. They are also quite useful in a general preevent simulation where specifically impacted areas can be readily identified. In application, however, I/O and CGE models can be difficult to apply due to extensive data requirements and their rigid structure. The actual hazard event may result in the destruction of entire sectors of an economy or the introduction of entirely new technologies. In such a case, the use of I/O and CGE approaches could require the construction of not one but two input-output tables as well as extensive survey data and additional data requirements.

The other primary method of simulating the regional economy is with a regional econometric forecasting model (REFM). A REFM extends regression analysis techniques into a system of simultaneous equations. This method takes advantage of regression analysis' flexibility in the presence of limited data availability. It additionally allows the urban economy to be examined in a fully simultaneous manner. The REFM can be sectorally and spatially disaggregated, though not to as fine a level of detail as I/O and CGE models. In an applied setting, though, forecasting models are much more readily adaptable than are I/O and CGE. Chang (1983, 1984), Guimares et al. (1993), and West and Lenze (1994) all illustrate the use and capabilities of an REFM in assessing the impact of natural disaster.

Disaster simulations of all types—i.e., REFM models (Roberts et al. 1982; Ellson, Millman, and Roberts 1984), input-output modeling (Cochrane 1975; Haas, Cochrane, and Kates 1974; Albala-Bertrand 1993)—and CGE modeling (Brookshire and McKee 1992), while important in their own right, also highlight some of the fundamental difficulties associated with applied hazards research. Within the framework of a simulation model, analysis is based upon well-specified damage and impact scenarios as well as upon a preestablished economic database. The analysis of an actual disaster event though is generally not as clear-cut, due to the lack of predisaster baseline, the difficulties associated with impact and damage assessment, and uneven, unbalanced, or asymmetrical disaster impacts as opposed to well-defined damage and impact (West and Lenze 1993).

Simulation has also brought to the fore the idea that economic analysis of the disaster event should be undertaken in the vein of "with and without," not "before and after." Beginning with Ellson et al. (1982), the basis of economic analysis is a "with and without" form of analysis. In essence, and as demonstrated by Guimaraes et al. (1993), and West and Lenze (1994), the economic analysis of the disaster situation and its attendant recovery period must include not only "pre and post" (before and after) event economic conditions at the level of impacted region but also take into consideration general economic conditions and trends outside of the affected area. Thus, the question of the impact or effect of the disaster upon the local economy must be analyzed in light of general cyclical activity in the economy as a whole.

B. Toward a Functional Econometric Model

An econometric forecasting model, while it lacks the complete level of detail I/O and CGE models contain, is better able to cope with the dynamic aspect of natural hazards.

Depending upon data limitations, the framework of an econometric model allows for some flexibility with regard to the level of spatial and sectoral disaggregation. This, though, is the major difficulty with empirical analysis of an actual event.

Disaggregation is, conceptually, fairly easy to accomplish. The regional model is divided into smaller submodels for spatial disaggregation, i.e., county and cities within the county, which can then be estimated simultaneously. Sectoral disaggregation is accomplished by splitting sectoral employment and income within the model (or submodels) from one-digit standard industrial classification (SIC) to two- or three-digit SIC, i.e., split trade into wholesale and retail trade. The model (or submodels) can also be placed into a block structure such as income, employment, labor force, housing market, and government, allowing for greater level of analysis of interaction in the urban economy.

Within the framework of the regional econometric forecasting model, the urban region is essentially treated as if it were a small, open, independent economy. Because of this openness, economic activity in the model is driven by both regional and national factors using an output-income approach. The precise block structure and level of aggregation (spatial and sectoral), from an empirical viewpoint, depends on the amount of data available—the higher the degree of disaggregation, the greater the amount of statistical data required.

The forecasting model outlined below, follows the suggestion of Taylor (1982; West and Lenze 1994) and uses a relatively simple but simultaneous structure of the regional economy. Following a natural disaster, estimation of a fully disaggregated model is impractical due to data availability and limitations and the possible lack of preexisting economic baseline analysis.

The model is composed of five simultaneous blocks: employment, income, demographic and labor force, retail sales, and housing. Block interaction is shown in Figure 1. Economic activity in the model is driven by national variables as well as regional variables.

The primary blocks of the system are employment, income, and labor force. In the model, employment and income are disaggregated to the one-digit SIC level. Disaggregation at the one-digit SIC level captures the major trends within the regional economy, while reducing data requirements (especially availability, and length of series) that a fully disaggregated structure would pose.

Equations within the employment block are specified as functions of both national and regional income variables, sectoral employment lagged one period, wage rate, sectoral specific variables (e.g., mortgage rate, interest rates, number of visitors, etc.), and seasonal quarterly dummy variables. Functionally, sectoral employment takes the form:

$$EMP_{i,t} = f(EMP_{i,t-1}, GDP_t, RY_t, Z_t)$$

where $EMP_{i,t}$ is employment in sector i at time t, GDP_t is real U.S. gross domestic product at time t, RY_t is regional income at time t, and Z_t represents sector-specific variables. Sectoral employment is forecast for construction, FIRE (finance, insurance, and real estate), manufacturing, services, trade, TCP (transportation, communications, and utilities), farm, mining, and government.

The labor force block uses a simple structure to estimate the regional unemployment rate. Total labor force is estimated as a function of the labor force participation rate, GDP, national unemployment rate, and average earnings lagged one period. Total employment is estimated as a function of total sectoral employment, population, GDP, and quarterly seasonal dummy variables. The total number of unemployed is then calculated by subtracting total employment from total labor force.

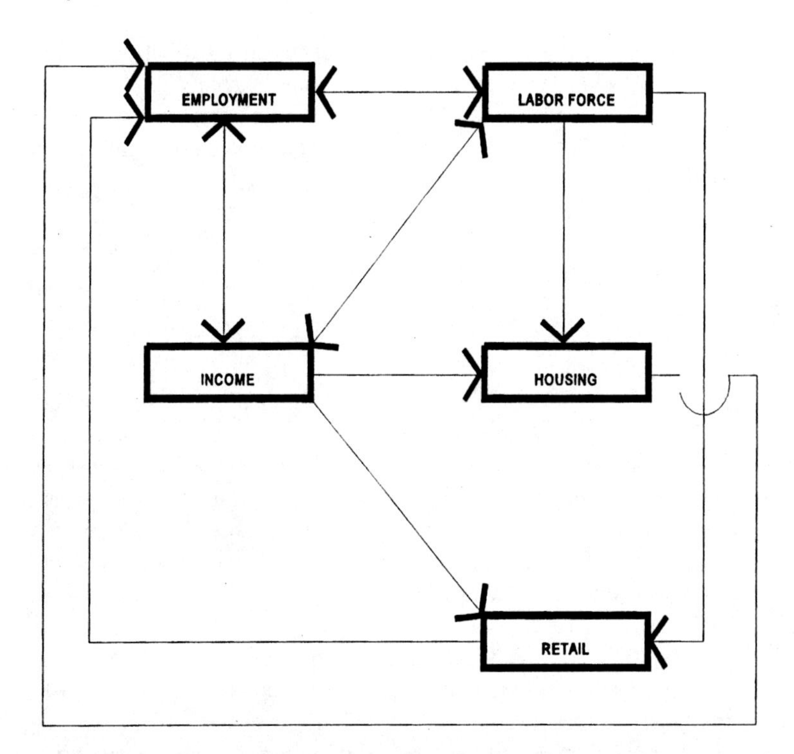

Figure 1 Linkage schematic of the Dade County forecasting model.

In the income block, sectoral income from wages and salaries is calculated as a function of sectoral employment and the wage rate. The national average sectoral wage rate is used here as a proxy for the regional wage rate. Total regional income is estimated as a function of total regional income from wages and salary, GDP, interest rates, and the exchange rate.

The remaining two blocks of the model consist of one equation to estimate retail sales, and a housing and construction sector block. Retail sales is taken to be a function of regional income, GDP, tourism, CPI, the exchange rate index, and quarterly seasonal dummy variables. The housing block consists of four equations estimating the change in the housing stock, single- and multifamily housing starts, and the average price of single-family housing. Housing starts are forecast as functions of population, mortgage rate, GDP, and regional income. The price of housing is forecast as functions of housing prices lagged one period, CPI, tourism, and the change in the housing stock.

The model outlined above uses a fairly straightforward and simple structure. It is similar in form to ones used by Roberts et al. (1982), and Guimaraes et al. (1993). Regional activity is the result of endogenous factors such as regional income and regional prices. It additionally is the result of exogenous factors such as GDP, interest rates, and exchange rates.

This particular model, called the Dade County Econometric Forecasting Model (DCEFM), consists of 57 equations, in five blocks (see Vogel 1996). The model could be further aggregated or disaggregated and additional blocks added, depending on the complexity of the urban area under study and available data. The model can be estimated using regression procedures. As applied to the case of Hurricane Andrew in the next section, the model was estimated using the 3SLS procedure over a 10-year period. Quarterly data for the 10-year period 1982–1992, prior to the hurricane, were used to estimate the parameters of the model. A 2-year forecast, 1992, second quarter, through 1994, third quarter, is presented with the "without" Andrew estimates and compared against the actual "with" Andrew data.

V. APPLICATION TO DADE COUNTY, FLORIDA—HURRICANE ANDREW

A. Preliminaries

Natural disaster's effects on the urban economy arise from direct physical impact and the consequent disruption of normal economic activity. Before its effects in a particular community can be understood, prevent economic structure, growth, and activity must be established. Economic analysis of the situation then is a three-step process—establish predisaster baseline, survey and measure disaster damage, and evaluate "pre and post" disaster positions. Using the "with and without" framework as well, the disaster's effect on the urban economy is evaluated in light of exogenous changes in economic activity outside of the region, such as recession or recovery.

The DCEFM is estimated to its preevent baseline and then used to generate economic postdisaster baseline "without" the disaster, but it takes into account economic events outside of the region. Structural linkages reveal themselves through the influence of endogenous variables such as regional income on sectoral employment. Economic activity, though, is generated through the combination of endogenous and exogenous variables.

Changes in activity and structure within the urban/regional economy can be established in several ways. Economic activity changes can be inferred by comparing actual and forecast levels of sectoral and aggregate employment and income against one another. Structural changes can be established by comparing the composition of actual and forecast employment and income against one another. Additionally, postdisaster trend sectoral growth or decline can be compared against baseline forecast trend.

B. The Miami-Dade Metropolitan Statistical Area

The following analysis of Hurricane Andrew's economic impact is based on a functional concept of a city/urban economy and not the political boundaries of the city proper. This is the case with Miami-Dade County, Florida, a region composed of 27 different cities and municipalities. The urban economy, though, cannot be separated or completely isolated to any one geographic location or municipality with Miami as its focal point.

Miami-Dade County is a region with a population of 1.93 million people. It is a triethnic, trilingual community, with 49.2% of its population Hispanic and 20.6% African American. Total personal income before the hurricane was $34.7 billion, and per capita income was $17,823. The county had a total labor force of 976,000 persons.

The Miami-Dade County economy is fairly diverse, with a gross regional output in excess of $70 billion. While tourism is still the largest component of the local economy, there are significant levels of activity in wholesale and retail trade, finance, insurance, and real estate, manufacturing, and transportation, communications, and utilities (Carvajal and Bueso 1989; Metro-Dade County 1992). In 1992, with a labor force of 976,000 people, the unemployment rate stood at 10%, with 878,000 persons unemployed. By sector, employment was composed of 30.4% in services, 26.6% in trade, 14.6% in government, 9.8% in transportation and utilities, 7.3% in FIRE (finance, insurance, and real estate), and 3.6% in construction (Beacon Council 1993:55).

Southern and southwest Dade County has been dominated by three main components. One is agriculture, primarily centered around the Homestead and Florida City. It represents approximately $504 million in gross regional output, and 15,000 persons employed. The second component was Homestead Air Force Base (HAFB), accounting for employment of 11,000 and links to the county accounting for an estimated $405 million in local impact (Metro-Dade County 1992:16). Last, this part of the county has been facing increasing residential development pressures from encroaching urban sprawl.

At the time that Andrew struck the county, unemployment was at 10%. Job growth in the county had slowed, while population and labor force had continued to rise. A weak construction sector, combined with local banking's retrenchment from the real estate sector, further exacerbated the downward trend in local manufacturing. The failures of three major employers in the area—Southeast Bank, Eastern Airlines, and Pan American Airlines—through their multiplier impact caused additional decline in retail and wholesale trade (Denslow et al. 1992).

C. Hurricane Andrew's Impact

Damage and impact to Dade County as a result of Hurricane Andrew was extensive. While the death toll resulting from the storm was extremely low, with 15 deaths directly attributable to it, it resulted in temporarily displacing approximately 353 thousand persons (Smith and McCarthy 1994). The southern part of the county was the most deeply impacted area, which includes a land area of approximately 1100 square miles. In this area, the most deeply affected municipalities were Coral Gables, Homestead, and Florida City, including the heart of Dade County's agricultural complex.

In terms of loss and damage to structures, the most dramatic impact of the hurricane was to housing. Metro-Dade County (1993:7–8) reports that 107,876 homes were damaged, 90% of the mobile homes in South Dade were destroyed, and 47,000 housing units were destroyed. In the months following the hurricane, the vacancy rate in the South Dade area fell from 4.9% in August of 1992, when the storm struck, to 1.4% in May 1993. Concurrent with the decreasing vacancy rate, apartment rental rates in the area rose an average of 10% over this same period (Metro-Dade 1993:8).

West and Lenze (1993) estimate the total physical and structural damages to the county as $22.571 billion. Almost two-thirds of the damages stem from loss to residential structures and contents. Of the $10.4 billion in damage to residences and $5.3 billion in residential contents loss, $8.253 billion and $3.308 billion respectively was rereimbursed through insurance. Federal assistance into the area, exclusive of loans, amounted to $2.624 billion.

In the South Dade area, in terms of economic activity, of the approximately 8800 businesses in operation before the Hurricane, a year later, only 6324, had reopened in the area (Beacon Council 1993b). Another 550 had moved their operations outside of the hurricane impacted area. In terms of employment, this translates into a loss of 19%, from pre-Andrew levels, with employment in the area from these reopened businesses at 75,000 persons.

D. Andrew's Impact on Employment

Direct employment impacts attributable to Hurricane Andrew should manifest themselves as sharp deviations, either positive or negative, within the third and fourth quarters of 1992 when compared against forecasted employment figures. Medium- and long-term effects will manifest themselves in a similar fashion. According to some analysts, full recovery from a major natural disaster could take anywhere between 2 and 10 years (Kates and Pijawka 1977). In the case of Hurricane Andrew, state forecasters and analysts suggested that Dade County economic activity should return to its pre-Andrew forecast track by late 1995 or early 1996 (Lenze and West 1993).

Dade County nonfarm employment during the quarter Andrew struck experienced an overall and immediate decrease. Over the next three quarters, employment continued to increase (Figure 2). After four quarters, the local economy, in terms of total nonfarm employment, begins to converge with the ''without'' Hurricane Andrew forecast. This would suggest that the economic stimulus, resulting from the hurricane, was isolated to only a few sectors of the economy, or that some geographic factors played an important part in the question of economic stimuli.

Not surprisingly, the greatest impact and lingering effects of the Hurricane occurred in the construction sector (Figure 3). Sectoral employment showed a sharp increase, with strong expansion running through the fourth quarter of 1993, before beginning to taper off. The forecasts for the region indicate a slow but steady rise in construction employment, while actual employment levels rose well beyond the baseline forecasts.

Transportation, communications, and public utilities (TCP) was also greatly affected by Andrew. While, TCP employment in the first quarter of 1992 had bottomed out in Dade County, by the second quarter it was beginning to rebound. Sectoral employment in the quarters following Hurricane Andrew, through second-quarter 1994, rose well beyond the forecast level of employment for this sector.

The farm sector, with its heart in southern Dade County, the area most affected by the hurricane, also suffered some of the greatest immediate and short-term employment losses. However, employment levels rebounded to forecast levels by the first quarter of 1994.

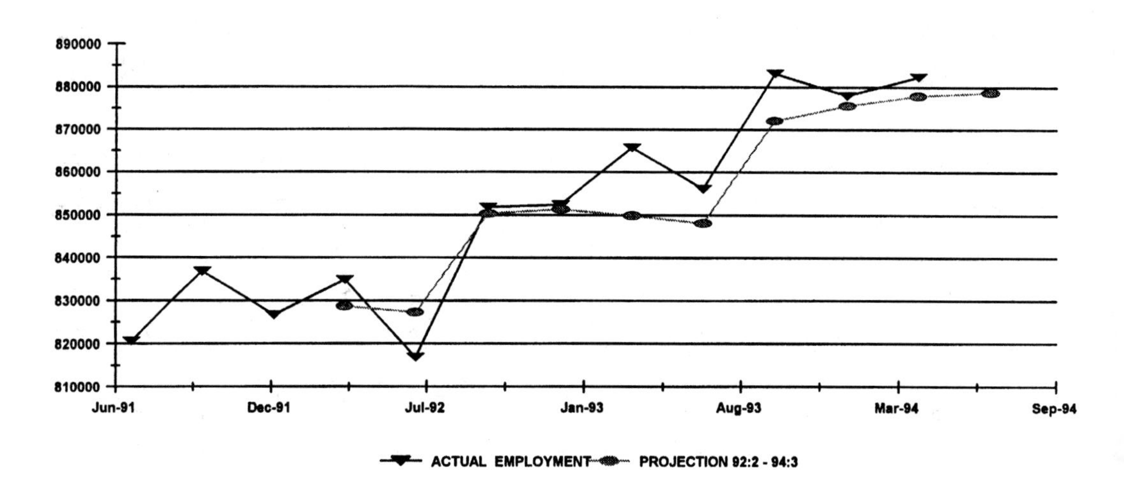

Figure 2 Total non-farm employment.

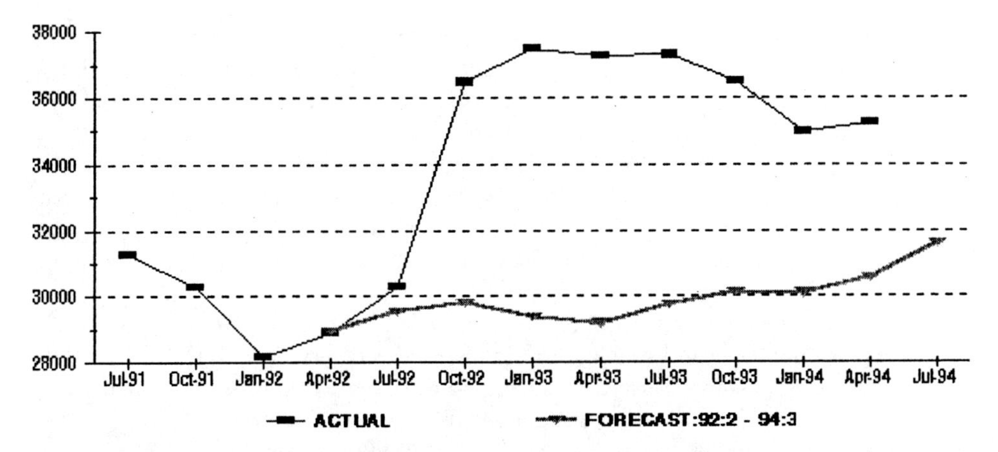

Figure 3 Sectoral employment: Construction.

Finance, insurance, and real estate (FIRE) was the only other major sector of the economy to suffer noticeable while not severe effects resulting from the hurricane. In the quarters immediately following Hurricane Andrew, while forecast employment rose, actual employment continued on a downward trend, reaching its trough during the first quarter of 1993. At that point, it begins to follow and eventually converge with the forecast track of the economy. This course is consistent with the reconstruction period following the disaster event. As cleanup and repair activities to affected structures and areas progressed and economic and social activity began to return to normal, this sector of the economy rebounded as well.

Employment in manufacturing, service, and government sectors showed no significant deviation from their baseline economic forecast. Outside of a small drop in service employment from the second to the third quarters of 1992, Hurricane Andrew caused no other measurable impact.

Overall, the baseline employment forecasts for Dade County for 1992, second quarter, through 1994, third quarter indicate that there was a one-quarter negative impact upon employment. This impact had the effect of reducing total county employment by approximately 15,000 individuals. However, with national economic recovery already in full swing, it is difficult to attribute too much of the increase in employment levels over the 2 years following Andrew (with the exception of the construction sector) to the stimulus resulting from reconstruction.

E. Miami-Dade and Structural Adjustment

Comparative analysis from baseline forecasts to actual event statistics points to four general conclusions. Employment and income suffered a one-quarter negative impact as a direct result of the hurricane. Sectoral employment in construction, TCP, and agriculture were the most deeply affected sectors over the period of analysis. The overall path of total employment though, through the forecast period, did not vary significantly from baseline projections. General trend and the underlying patterns to the paths for total regional income and sectoral wage income appears to show little change. However, wage and regional income data did, in general, follow these existing paths, albeit at elevated levels through the forecast period.

Even though damage and impact losses were severe, Hurricane Andrew's economic impact on aggregate economic activity, based upon a DCEFM-generated baseline, was surprisingly limited. In the 2-year period following the disaster, employment and income in the construction sector was elevated by approximately 17% above baseline and agricultural employment was 8% below baseline. While construction, agriculture, mining, and TCP sectors showed the most dramatic changes following Andrew, they make up only 13.5% of total employment and 16% of total county wage income. Total employment registered only a 0.38% increase over baseline, with total wage income registering an increase of 2.36%.

The variations in employment reported in Table 1 illustrate the limited nature of the impact and stimulus towards employment in the local economy from Hurricane Andrew. Reported figures for mining are misleading, as they represent a sectoral decline due to environmental and developmental pressures within the county. The hurricane's impact though, may have accelerated the conversion of land to other uses.

Income variation over the period illustrates similar results as those for employment, although the results for income tend to show a slightly greater amount of variation (see Table 2). Sectoral wage income shows an overall increase of 2.36% and sectoral gains of 17% in construction, 8.15% in TCP, 3.42% in FIRE, and 3.15% in service. Total regional income registered a 6.24% gain over baseline as well; however, overall existing trend in the growth of income followed national activity, baseline trends, and preexisting seasonal variation.

Impact upon and adjustment to economic activity as a result of the hurricane, especially major structural changes and shifts in the direction of growth, would also manifest themselves in large alterations in the structure of production as measured through sectoral employment and income as a percentage of total employment and income.

Minor variation in the percentage distribution of employment and income by sector following Andrew are revealed by these figures (Table 3). In general though, these figures are fairly representative of continuing trends in the composition of economic activity. The construction sector, as expected, is elevated above baseline in both employment and in-

Table 1 Average Variation in Employment from Baseline Forecasts, 1992–1994

Sector	Average employment (actual)	Percent variation from baseline
Agriculture	11,813	−8.89
Construction	35,676	+17.54
FIRE	63,316	−1.46
Government	125,153	−2.15
Manufacturing	80,919	−0.78
Mining	487	−28.13
Service	255,173	+1.01
Trade	229,243	−0.82
TCP	70,888	+4.62
Total	872,668	+0.38

Key: FIRE, finance, insurance, and real estate; TCP, transportation, communications, and utilities.

Table 2 Percentage Variation in Sectoral Wage Income, 1992–1994

Sector	Percent (size) of total wage income	Percent variation in income
Agriculture	0.78	−7.98
Construction	4.22	+17.09
FIRE	9.64	+3.42
Government	18.38	−1.25
Manufacturing	9.22	+0.01
Mining	0.08	−15.55
Service	31.22	+3.15
Trade	15.46	−1.94
TCP	11.00	+8.15
Total wage income		+2.36
Total regional income		+6.24

Key: FIRE, finance, insurance, and real estate; TCP, transportation, communications, and utilities.

come by approximately 0.6 percent. Initial impact quarters did show a slightly greater variation from baseline measure. However, major sectoral shifts never materialized, suggesting that county production structure did not undergo severe sectoral change or upheaval.

Structural change and alteration in the pattern and sectoral distribution of employment and income are all suggested as the possible consequences of a natural hazard (Guimaraes et al. 1993; Albala-Bertrand, 1993; West et al. 1994). Simulation and theoretical analysis of the disaster scenario, especially with the use of stylized impact damages, indicate that from an economic perspective, while physical loss is of great concern, disruption

Table 3 Percentage of Employment by Sector: 1992–1994 (Average)

Sector	Actual	Forecast baseline
Agriculture	1.35	1.51
Construction	4.09	3.43
FIRE	7.26	7.39
Government	14.34	14.73
Manufacturing	9.27	9.38
Mining	0.06	0.08
Service	29.24	29.06
Trade	26.27	26.65
TCP	8.12	7.75

Key: FIRE, finance, insurance, and real estate; TCP, transportation, communications, and utilities.

to the economic sphere should have a larger and more deleterious effect (Cochrane 1975; Ellson et al. 1982; Richardson 1992). With Hurricane Andrew and Dade County, the level and direction of economic activity does not appear to have changed course.

VI. CONCLUSION

Many urban areas across the world face some degree of vulnerability due to the threat of natural hazard. Economic development and population growth within an urban area raises its vulnerability to physical loss and social dislocation. Actual levels of destruction and damage are functions of an event's speed, severity, and the specific zone of impact. Economic impact depends not only on these same factors but also on the magnitude of disruption, dislocation, resource availability, and the level of built-in response mechanisms.

Linkage disruption represents the principal source of economic vulnerability from natural disaster. The case of Hurricane Andrew discussed in Sect. V illustrates this situation well. Hurricane Andrew caused more than $20 billion in damages—one of the most costly disasters in the United States in the twentieth century. Physical damages though, were primarily restricted to residential and agricultural sectors. Additionally, the bulk of direct hurricane impact was geographically limited to the southern portion of the county. Generalized linkage disruption did not occur with Hurricane Andrew, as Dade County's economic infrastructure was virtually untouched.

Not all of the channels for disruption can be captured using a tool such as a regional econometric forecasting model. The level of sectoral and spatial aggregation incorporated into the model preclude direct measurement below the threshold of the simulation. While it is possible to disaggregate an urban economy from its larger to underlying constituent parts—i.e., county, to city, to specific census tract levels—the difficulty in obtaining the requisite statistics often preclude complete disaggregation. Linkages within smaller communities or neighborhoods are difficult to simulate.

Disaster impact can cause damages to firms, households, individuals, and infrastructure. Neighborhoods within the urban economy reflect the interrelationships between individuals, households, firms, and infrastructure. Although the movement of firms and individuals within the urban complex may constitute changes in spatial relationships, they do not necessarily imply structural change or changes in growth. Over time, neighborhoods within the urban area may undergo periods with varying degrees of growth and development. The urban economy, though, is the result of an evolutionary process.

Natural disasters such as earthquakes and hurricanes have the propensity to cause abrupt and sudden change. As a result of this abrupt change, disaster presents the greatest challenge to neighborhoods. Neighborhood recovery, though, is related to more than just impact damage. Individual access to resources, insurance coverage, and the nature of preexisting trends within neighborhoods and communities will also contribute to neighborhood recovery. Abrupt change from a disaster then places peripheral neighborhoods and communities in decline at risk of only partial recovery or accelerated decline.

Structural change within the urban economy attributable to natural disaster may arise from a number of causes, among them direct physical impact and linkage disruption. As both the level of sectoral impact and area of physical impact increases, the greater is the possibility of structural change. In the short run, with major natural disaster, there is certainly some temporary alteration of economic activity within the urban area. At the neighborhood level, natural disaster does affect the interrelationship of individuals, households, and firms. Disasters' effects on spatial structure and long-run growth is an area that requires further study.

REFERENCES

Aguirre, B. E., and Bush, D. (1992). Disaster programs as technology transfers: the case of Puerto Rico in the aftermath of Hurricane Hugo. *International Journal of Mass Emergencies and Disasters* 10(*1*), 161–178.

Albala-Bertrand, J. M. (1993). *Political Economy of Large Natural Disasters.* Oxford, UK: Clarendon Press.

Barnard, Jerald R. (1985). *Measuring Business Losses from Flooding.* Iowa City, IA: University of Iowa, Institute of Economic Research.

Bates, Frederick L. and Peacock, W. G. (1989). Long term recovery. *International Journal of Mass Emergencies and Disasters* 7 (*November*), 349–365.

Bates, Frederick L. and Peacock, W. G. (1993). *Living Conditions, Disasters, and Development.* Athens, GA: The University of Georgia Press.

Beacon Council (1994). *Miami's Multinational Business Community.* Miami, FL: The Beacon Council.

Beacon Council (1993). *Miami Business Profile, 1993–1994.* Miami, FL: Florida Media Affiliates, Inc.

Berke, Phillip R., Beatley, T., and Clarence Feagin, C. (1993). Hurricane Gilbert strikes Jamaica: linking disaster recovery to development. *Coastal Management* 21, 1–23.

Bernknopf, R. L. et al. (1988). An economic and geographic appraisal of spatial natural hazard risk: a study of landslide mitigation rules. *Environment and Planning A* 20(*5*), 621–631.

Bernknopf, R. L., Brookshire, D. S., and Thayer, M. A. (1990). Earthquake and volcano hazard notices: an economic evaluation of changes in risk perceptions. *Journal of Environmental Economics and Management* 18(*1*), 35–49.

Bogard, W. (1989). *The Bhopal Tragedy: Language, Logic, and Politics in the Production of a Hazard.* Boulder, CO: Westview Press.

Borkan, B. and Kunreuther, H. (1978). Towards a community disaster model for policy analysis. *Mass Emergencies* 3, 1–22.

Brookshire, D. S. et al. (1985). Test of the expected utility model: evidence from earthquake risks. *Journal of Political Economy* 93(*2*), 369–389.

Brookshire, D. S. and McKee, D. L. (1992). Other indirect costs and losses from earthquakes: issues and estimation. In J. Milliman and S. G. Etty (eds.), *Indirect Economic Consequences of a Catastrophic Earthquake.* Washington, D.C.: Development Technologies, Inc.

California Department of Insurance, California Residential Earthquake Recovery Fund Program (1992). *Exploratory Study on Insurance for Small Business Earthquake Losses.* Sacramento, CA: California Department of Insurance (prepared pursuant to Chapter 1165, Statutes of 1990).

Carvajal, M. J. and Bueso, R. E. (1989). *Urban Growth and Provision of Services in South Florida: Estimated Consequences of a Moratorium on New Construction.* Discussion Paper No. 85, Discussion Papers in Economics. Miami, FL: Department of Economics, Florida International University.

Chang, S. (1979). An econometric forecasting model based on regional economic information system data: the case of Mobile, Alabama. *Journal of Regional Science* 19(*4*), 437–447.

Chang, S. (1983). Disasters and fiscal policy: hurricane impact on municipal revenue. *Urban Affairs Quarterly* 18(4 June), 511–523.

Chang, S. (1984). Do disaster areas benefit from disasters? *Growth and Change* 15(*4*), 25–31.

Chenery, H. (1986). Growth and transformation. In H. Chenery, S. Robinson, and M. Syrquin (eds.), *Industrialization and Growth: A Comparative Study.* New York: Oxford University Press.

Cochrane, H. C. (1975). *Natural Hazards and Their Distributive Effects*. Monograph #NSF-RA-E-75-003. Boulder, CO: University of Colorado, Institute of Behavioral Science.

Cochrane, H. C. (1980). Post-disaster reconstruction in Darwin, Australia. *International Review* 3(*1*), 64–73.

Cochrane, H. C., Haas, J. E., Bowden, M. J., Kates R. W. (1974). *Social Science Perspectives on the Coming San Francisco Earthquake: Economic Impact, Prediction and Reconstruction*. Working Paper No. 25. Boulder, CO: Institute of Behavioral Science, Natural Hazard Research.

Cochrane, H. C., Revier, C. F., and Takioshi Nakagawa, T. (1979). *Inflationary Changes in Construction Cost*. Report under Grant No. ENV 76-24169. Boulder, CO: Department of Economics, Colorado State University.

Dacy, D. C. and Kunreuther, H. (1969). *The Economics of Natural Disasters*. New York: The Free Press.

Denslow, D., West, C. T., and Lenze, D. (1992). Before the storm: Dade's economy was in the doldrums. *Economic Leaflets* 51(*9*), 1–5.

Denslow, D., West, C. T., Lenze D. (1993). Forecasting economic recovery from natural disaster: the case of Hurricane Andrew. *Economic Leaflets* 52(*8*), 1–3.

Doherty, N., Kleffner, A. E., and Kunreuther, H. (1991). *The Impact of a Catastrophic Earthquake on Insurance Markets*. Boston: Earthquake Project, National Committee on Property Insurance.

Douty, C. M. (1977). *The Economics of Localized Catastrophe: The 1906 San Francisco Catastrophe*. New York: Arno.

Ellson, R., Milliman, J., and Roberts, R. B. (1984). Measuring the regional economic effects of earthquakes and earthquake predictions. *Journal of Regional Science* 24(*4*), 559–579.

Fair, R. C. (1984). *Specification, Estimation, and Analysis of Macroeconometric Models*. Cambridge, MA, and London: Harvard University Press.

Friesema, P. H., Caporaso, J., Gerald Goldstein, G. et al. (1979). *Aftermath: Communities After Natural Disasters*. Beverly Hills, CA: Sage Publications.

Fronstin, P. and Holtmann, A. G. (1994). The determinants of residential property damage caused by Hurricane Andrew. *Southern Economic Journal* 61(2), 387–397.

Geipel, R. (1991). *Long-Term Consequences of Disasters: The Reconstruction of Friuli, Italy, in Its International Context 1976–1988*. New York: Springer-Verlag.

Girard, C., and Peacock, W. G. (1997). Ethnicity and segregation: post-hurricane relocation. In W. G. Peacock, B. H. Morrow, and Gladwin H. (eds.). Hurricane Andrew: Ethnicity, Gender, and the Sociology of Disasters. New York: Routledge.

Glaeser, E. L. (1994). Cities, information, and economic growth. *Cityscape* 1(*1*), 9–47.

Gordon, P., and Richardson, H. W. (1992). *Business Interruption Effects of a Major Earthquake in the Newport/Inglewood Fault Zone (NIFZ)*. Boston: The National Committee On Property Insurance.

Guimaraes, P., Heffner, F. I., and Woodward, D. P. (1993). Wealth and income effects of natural disasters: an econometric analysis. *Review of Regional Studies* 23(2), 97–114.

Haas, J. E., Cochrane, H. C., and Eddy, D. G. (1976). *The Consequences of Large-Scale Evacuation Following Disaster: The Darwin, Australia Cyclone Disaster of December 25, 1974*. Working Paper No. 27. Boulder, CO: Natural Hazard Research, University of Colorado.

Haas, J. E., Kates, R. W., and Bowden, M. J. (eds.) (1977). *Reconstruction Following Disaster*. Cambridge, UK, and London: The MIT Press.

Howe, C. W. and Cochrane H. C. (1993). *Guidelines for the Uniform Definition, Identification, and Measurement of Economic Damages from Natural Hazard Events*. Program on Environment and Behavior Special Publication No. 28. Boulder, CO: Institute of Behavioral Science, University of Colorado.

Kates, R. W. and Pijawka, D. (1977). From rubble to monument: the pace of reconstruction. In

J. E. Haas, R. W. Kates, and M. J. Bowden (eds.), *Reconstruction Following Disaster*, 1–24. Cambridge, UK, and London: The MIT Press.

Kunreuther, H. (1996). *The role of insurance in dealing with catastrophic risks from natural disasters.* Paper Presented at the Competitive Enterprise Conference on Insurance, Washington D.C., January 12, 1996. Philadelphia: The Wharton Risk Management and Decision Processes Center, Working Paper Number 95-12-15.

Kunreuther, H., and Fiore E. S. (1966). *The Alaskan Earthquake: A Case Study in the Economics of Disaster.* Arlington, VA: Institute for Defense Analyses.

Kunreuther, H., Lepore, J., Louis Miller, L., et al. (1978). *Interactive Modeling System for Disaster Policy Analysis.* Boulder, CO: Institute of Behavioral Science, University of Colorado.

Lande, P. S. (1994). Regional industrial structure and economic growth and instability. *Journal of Regional Science* 34(*3*), 343–360.

Lord, D. J. (1991). Propety damage and retail sales impacts of Hurricane Hugo. *Area* 23(*3*), 229–237.

Metro-Dade County (1992). *Economic Recovery Strategies, Phase II: Short Term Strategies.* Miami, FL: Metro-Dade County.

Metro-Dade County (1992). *Economic Recovery Strategies, Phase One: Long Term Strategies.* Report of the Economic Development Administration, Economic Development Administration Adjustment Strategy Grant no 04-59-03929. Miami, FL: Metro-Dade County.

Milliman, J. W., and Roberts R. B. (1985). Economic issues in formulating policy for earthquake analysis. *Policy Studies Review* 4(*4*), 645–654.

Nigg, J. M., and Tierney K. J. (1990). *Explaining Differential Outcomes in the Small Business Disaster Loan Application Process.* Preliminary Paper No 156. Newark, DE: University of Delaware, Disaster Research Center.

Peacock, W. G. and Girard, C. (1997). Ethnic and racial inequalities in disaster damage and insurance settlements. In W. G. Peacock, B. H. Morrow, and Gladwin, H. (eds)., Hurricane Andrew: Ethnicity, Gender, and the Sociology of Disasters. New York: Routledge.

Peacock, W. G., Killian, C. D., and Bates, F. L. (1987). The effects of disaster damage and housing aid on household recovery following the 1976 Guatamalan earthquake. *International Journal of Mass Emergencies and Disasters* 5(*March*), 63–88.

Roenigk, D. J. (1993). Federal disaster relief and local government financial condition. *International Journal of Mass Emergencies and Disasters* 11(2), 207–225.

Roberts, B. R., Milliman, J. W., and Ellson, R. W. (1982). *Earthquakes and Earthquake Predictions: Simulating Their Economic Effects.* Technical report prepared for National Science Foundation, PFR 80-19826. Columbia, SC: College of Business Administration, University of South Carolina.

Rossi, P. H., Wright, J. D., and Weber-Burdin, E. (1982). *Natural Hazards and Public Choice.* New York and London: Academic Press.

Scott, A. J. (1988). *Metropolis: From the Division of Labor to Urban Form.* Berkeley, CA: University of California Press.

Scott, A. J. (1993). *Technopolis: High-Technology Industry and Regional Development in Southern California.* Berkeley, CA: University of California Press.

Smith, S. K. and McCarty, C. (1994). The demographic impact of Hurricane Andrew in Dade County. *Economic Leaflets* 53(*8*), 1–6.

Storper, M. (1995). Territorial development in the global learning economy: the challenge to developing countries. *Review of International Political Economy* 2(*3*), 394–424.

Storper, M. and Walker, R. (1989). *The Capitalist Imperative: Territory, Technology, and Industrial Growth.* Oxford, UK, and New York: Blackwell.

Taylor, C. A. (1982). Econometric modeling of urban and other substate areas: an analysis of alternative methodologies. *Regional Science and Urban Economics* 12, 425–448.

Vogel, R. M. (1996). *Regional Growth, Structural Change, and Natural Disaster*. Unpublished Ph.D. dissertation. Florida International University, Miami.

West, C. T., and Lenze, D. G. (1993). Modeling Natural Disaster and Recovery: An Assessment of Regional Data and Impact Methodology in the Context of Hurricane Andrew. Unpublished manuscript. University of Florida, Bureau of Economic and Business Research,

West, C. T. and Lenze, D. G. (1994). Modeling the regional impact of natural disaster and recovery: a general framework and a specific application to the case of Hurricane Andrew. *International Regional Science Review* 17(2), 121–50.

West, C. T., Lenze, D. G., and Glenn R. S. (1993). *The Florida Long-Term Economic Forecast, 1992. Vol. 2: Metropolitan Statistical Areas*. Gainesville, FL: Bureau of Business and Economic Research.

White, G. F. (1974). Natural hazards research: concepts, methods, and policy implications. In G. F. White (ed.), *Natural Hazards—Local, National, Global*, 3–16. New York, London, Toronto: Oxford University Press.

7
Crisis in the U.S. Administrative State

Ali Farazmand School of Public Administration, Florida Atlantic University, Fort Lauderdale, Florida

I. PROLOGUE

These days, hardly anyone discusses the administrative state, much less the crisis that it has gone through. This chapter is a reprint of an article published in *Administration & Society* in 1989. The decades of 1980s was a period of globally designed structural changes that affected public sectors around the world. Under two ultra-right-wing conservative political leaders, Ronald Reagan in the United States and Margaret Thatcher in Britain, a worldwide anti–public sector crusade was launched under the banner of antibureaucracy and antigovernment. It shrank the realm of public spheres, public sector, and public administration not only in the United States and Britain but also around the world. Under the directions and pressures of these two countries, the World Bank (WB) and International Monetary Fund (IMF) instructed almost all developing and underdeveloped nations to adopt ''structural adjustments,'' ''deregulations,'' ''privatization,'' and commercialization of their public sectors, public enterprises, and public administration. Therefore, the administrative state came under relentless attacks, causing severe diminution and crises in its institutional and legitimacy foundations.

Interestingly, it was the same world organizations and same global governments that pressured developing countries to nationalize industries and take leading role by the state in running their economies and carry out national development projects. Key to this earlier development was massive growth and expansion of the bureaucracy, administrative, and welfare state. Public enterprise also grew dramatically, and public corporations expanded. This was still in the so-called Cold War era, in which the two world-system powers, America and the USSR, competed against and checked each other in international arena. The late 1970s brought economic decline in world capitalism and, along with other crises in political and social systems, institutional crises paralyzed corporate America as well. With the acceleration of the globalization of capital at the turn of the 1980s, when the two ultraconservative leaders of the western capitalism began their global crusade against state capitalism and against the public sector, the crisis of the administrative state intensified.

As will be seen later in this chapter, the administrative state had already come under attack from a variety of sources, including some academics and corporate elites. The latter wanted to structurally alter the power structure and the organization of society and economy with a monopolistic way in favor of corporate power structure. Therefore, privatization was launched as a global strategy of globalization, and its aim has been to shrink the public sector, set it for failure so more public sector functions could be taken by corporate elites, and to expand the chaotic corporate market sector, full of instability and disorder. Bureaucracy was an antithesis of disorder for decades, and that is how the corporate capitalism grew and prospered in the twentieth century.

The administrative state became a major target of the corporate power structure led by the elites whose interests dictated such massive structural adjustments in and outside of the United States. With the fall of the USSR, there was no reasons for the continuity of the welfare administrative state; it was time to totally dismantle it. This indeed happened, but there was a point that most scholars and researchers have either ignored or are unaware of: the public bureaucracy and the administrative state was reshaped dramatically by the conservative crusaders, their mission and purposes of serving broad public service/ public interests or common good were replaced by particularistic interests of the big business corporate elites, whose dominance and control of most powerful organizations and economy of the nation and of the world have frightened many observers. The service-oriented side of the administrative state was slashed by massive programmatic and budget cuts, while the functions of military, policing, social control, criminal justice, and court systems were expanded. Today, there are more police forces, more budget allocations for the policing functions, and a lot more that designed to control the citizen public and to provide stability and order that are essential to the smooth function of the market sector.

Therefore, the bureaucracy and administrative state did not vanish; they were reformulated and reemerged as entrepreneurial leadership structure. With the fall of the USSR, the name administrative state has become virtually extinct, and its place has been supplanted by the coercive corporate welfare state. But what was the nature of crisis in the administrative state? The rest of this chapter addresses this question.

This article argues that the U.S. administrative state is in a legitimacy and institutional crisis, that this crisis can be understood in relation to the concurrent crises facing the socioeconomic and political systems in America, that the current crisis is a result of the inherently contradictory role of the administrative state in American society, and that the politics-administration interface and the new political administration theory of the 1980s have had major consequences for the administrative state and for the society. Finally, the article briefly suggests an alternative solution to the problems of administrative state in America.[1]

The administrative state in this study refers to the complex of institutions (departments, agencies, organizations) of the executive branch of the federal government, with the exclusion of the Department of Defense. Strong evidence shows that the administrative

---

[1] This article is an updated and expanded version of the original paper "Politics of the Federal Bureaucracy and Administrative Theory under Reagan," presented at the 47th National Conference of ASPA in Anaheim, California, March 13–16, 1986. Information has been collected from several sources. Interviews were conducted with 35 federal officials (former and present) at the MSPB, Office of Special Counsel, senior staff members of the Congress, scholars in the field, and federal employees' union officials. Also government documents on the subject were carefully examined at the OPM Library and the Library of Congress, scholarly works in the field were reviewed, and other official and unofficial reports and secondary information were examined. Because of space limitations, a detailed analysis of the historical context of the administrative state has been neglected. I have done this elsewhere. See Farazmand, *Crisis in the U.S. Administrative State: A Political Economy Analysis* (Praeger, forthcoming).

state is facing another crisis of legitimacy. For example, Rosenbloom (1983: 225) argues that ''accumulation of legislative, executive, and judicial functions in administrative agencies runs counter to the deeply ingrained desire within the political culture for a system of checks and balances.'' Caiden (1983: 1) contends that public administration is defenseless against accusations of being ''parasitic, unproductive, inefficient, wasteful, incompetent, corrupt, and above all unnecessary.'' B. Rosen (1986), Goodsell (1985), Rohr (1986), H. Rosen (1985), and Schroeder (in ASPA, 1987a) discuss aspects of the current crisis and defend a strong role of the administrative state in society because they recognize the threat.

The first step toward understanding the crisis is to explain the rise of the administrative state and its legitimacy problem in an historical context.

II. SYSTEM LEGITIMACY AND THE RISE OF THE ADMINISTRATIVE STATE

A central characteristic of the American political system is its consistent inconsistency: Policies and programs of one period dominated by one political party are often either removed or drastically changed in another period dominated by another party. This inconsistency in the system and its policy process has affected the role of the state in general and the administrative state in particular in American society since the creation of the Republic. Therefore, the role of the administrative state has for two hundred years been unclear, a problem that ''again confronts the nation as it moves into a new international economic and technological order'' (Carroll 1987:106). The consistent inconsistency of the system has contributed to the second central characteristic: the ''reactive'' nature of the policy process and policy politics (Greenberg 1986).

Public administration has existed in the United States since the colonial period because no government can govern without administrative organizations. But the real rise of the administrative state is generally dated from the 1880s and particularly to the 1930s (Nelson 1982; Rohr 1986; Skowronek 1982; Stillman 1987). What has caused this phenomenon? Briefly stated, the socioeconomic conditions of American society in the post-Civil War period were characterized by increasing inequality and a lack of real freedom, compounded by the problems of corruption, the spoils system, recurring business cycles, and the growing power of the national government through force and administrative governance (Rohr 1986; Stillman 1987). However, three major forces seem to have contributed significantly to the rise of the administrative state since the late nineteenth century: the farmers' movement, the labor movement, and the Civil Service and Reform Movement. As Stillman (1987:5) notes, ''The administrative state began much less auspiciously . . . with the aggressive agitation by aggrieved midwest farmers over what they viewed as imposition of unfair, gouging rates by monopolistic railroads. It was a nasty fight, almost a classic Marxian economic contest between classes.'' Also the Grange movement and other lower-class demands made possible the passage of the Interstate Commerce Commission (ICC) in 1887 to remedy these intense socioeconomic problems.

Similarly, the labor movement had a major contribution to the rise of the administrative state. The rise of the industrial union, the Knights of Labor, in the late nineteenth century, and its continuous demand for major socioeconomic changes in the society is a good example. The economic panic of 1873 worsened the ''insecurities'' of the now almost ten million nonagricultural workers, who also were threatened by technological advancement in the system of mass production. Therefore, the activism of the labor movement, especially under the leadership of the Knights of Labor, challenged the status quo since ''it proposed workers cooperatives to replace capitalism and wanted to do away with the wage system'' (Rosenbloom and Shafritz, 1985:76). While the Knights of Labor organization was dissolved in Chicago's Haymarket Square, some of its ''goals eventually came to fruition; among them were the 8 hour day, the abolition of child labor, the creation of a national bureau of labor statistics, and weekly payday'' (Rosenbloom and Shafritz 1985:76).

But the Civil Service and Reform Movement seems to have made the greatest contribution to the rise of the administrative state. Space limitations here preclude adequate analysis of the spoils system and the consequent reform movement that resulted in the 1883 Civil Service Reform (Pendleton Act). It is sufficient to say that this movement had a tremendous impact on public administration.

Thus the reactive system and its government responded to the societal forces' potential of challenging the system. This response was delivered through the growing intermediating administrative state. As Stillman (1987:6) notes, it ''provided a much needed *constitutional corrective* [emphasis added], offering enhanced individual freedom through the positive enlargement of the public sphere to check and balance unrestrained private power on individuals, groups, and society as a whole. It effectively supplemented, not supplanted, the Constitution. . . ,'' which, as an economic document, addressed ''the interests of those who wrote it'' (Beard 1986:vi).

A central contradiction of the capitalist economy is that ''wages, a cost of production, must be kept down; wages, a source of consumer spending, must be kept up'' (*Dollars and Sense* [1976], quoted in Parenti 1983). This contradiction is a ''source of great instability, leading to chronic overproduction and underconsumption'' (Parenti 1983:17). Without the intervention of the federal government in the management of the business cycle, many convincingly argue, the country ''would continuously face collapse,'' undermining system legitimacy. From the end of the Civil War to the Great Depression of 1929, ''the American economy suffered sixteen major recessions or depressions'' (Greenberg 1986:296).

The Great Depression of the 1930s was so severe that ''none of the supposed 'self-correcting' feature of the free market was sufficient to bring the nation out of the doldrums'' (Greenberg 1986:296). The economic crisis of the 1930s was a potential threat to the legitimacy of the economic system and the political authority, and the enlargement of the administrative state was an inevitable and necessary consequence. The labor movement again questioned the legitimacy of the laissez-faire economic system, and its sociopolitical activism caused major threats to the political authority. The New Deal policies of the 1930s were aimed not only at rescuing the collapsing business sector, but also at preventing a massive social upheaval and buying legitimacy. For example, Rosenbloom and Shafritz (1985:24) note that ''the crash of 1929 and its aftermath seemed to many to require a radical reorganization of the society. It appeared as though the capitalist system had failed.'' Parenti (1983:85) reports that ''actually the New Deal's central dedication was to business recovery rather than social reform. . . . Faced with massive unrest, the federal government created a relief program that eased some of the hunger and starvation and—more importantly from the perspective of business—limited the instances of violent protest and radicalization.''

Similarly, Piven and Cloward (1971:46, 1985) argue that the policies of the New Deal were a response to the political unrest of millions of Americans in misery. Once the threat subsided as a result of government aid, they argue, ''large numbers of people were put off the rolls and burst into a labor market still glutted with unemployed. But with stability restored, the continued suffering of these millions had little political force.'' For example, while the Wagner Law was a positive response to labor pressure in the 1930s, the Taft-Hartley Act limited the rights of labor in the 1940s (Rosenbloom and Shafritz 1985). Greenberg (1986:315) argues that the Social Security Act was ''Franklin Roosevelt's response to the threats represented by widespread factory takeovers, the 'share the wealth' plan of Huey Long, and the popular Townsend movement.'' Witte (1962:v) reports the very large movement led by Frances Townsend of California who advocated a broad-based social reform and welfare plan. His petition was signed by 25 million people. Others also argue that the relief measures of the 1930s and 1960s were instruments of social control of the poor and disenchanted people whose potential threat to the system legitimacy was recognized.

The growth of the administrative state, then, became a reality in response to problems of legitimacy and system crisis. The Keynesian revolutionary macroeconomic policies advanced ideas for solving the problems of unemployment, economic growth, and distribution of income in society; and the government, through its now large administrative state, became the coordinator of the system.

The administrative state further grew when the military and international role of the United States grew at an unprecedented rate, putting the country on a ''*permanent war footing* since 1941. Well over one-half of all budget expenditures since that date have been devoted to military activities'' (Greenberg 1986:297 [emphasis in the original]). The Vietnam War and the domestic social upheavals made the enlargement of the administrative state possible even further. The massive federal grants-in-aid flew from the federal government and Lyndon Johnson's War On Poverty and Great Society programs required major administrative actions to provide relief services and meet the challenges of civil rights and other movements of the urban poor.

The growth of the administrative state began to be seriously questioned in the 1970s. The end of the Vietnam War in the 1970s that produced many losses, the Watergate scandal and the political crisis of the Presidency, the energy crisis of 1973 through 1974, the two victorious revolutions in Nicaragua and Iran, the hostage crisis, the budget and trade deficits crisis, double-digit inflation, double-digit unemployment, and other problems associated with the general performance of the government as the solver of all problems and as the driving force of society had a tremendous negative impact on the public perception and attitude toward government, causing a major ''confidence gap'' and a ''crisis'' in the system. This crisis was aggravated by the economic recessions and many international political and economic challenges (Downs and Larkey 1986; Fainstein and Fainstein 1984; Feinberg 1983; LaFaber 1984; Lipset 1987; Parenti 1983; Schott 1984). Thus the crisis and confidence gap about government performance widened. But the main target of criticism and attack became the administrative state and the government.

III. REACTION TO AND THE CRISIS IN THE ADMINISTRATIVE STATE

The rise and expansion of the administrative state has aroused significant reaction from many directions, which, along with other factors, have contributed to the diminution of its infant legitimacy. The following is a brief account of these reactions and sources of the crisis.

A. Reactions

Judicial reaction. The federal judicial response to the rise of the administrative state has been characterized by an initial hostility and eventual "partnership" in which the courts have become more intrusive. The Roosevelt Court was the first to face the major administrative expansion created by the New Deal. Citing several cases like *Wyman v. James, Spady v. Mount Vernon, U.S. v. Richardson, Branti v. Finkel,* and *Schecter Poultry v. U.S.*, Rosenbloom (1987, 1986:130) clearly shows the initial hostility of the judiciary toward the administrative state. Rosenbloom (1983:225) notes that this strain on the separation of powers has contributed to a "crisis of legitimacy in public administration."

Politicians' reactions. Being primarily interested in getting elected and reelected and enjoying the privileges of political power, the politicians—both conservative Republicans and liberal Democrats—have attacked the administrative state and its bureaucracy in general without making a distinction between the military-security bureaucracy and the general, public service bureaucracy. This lack of distinction has often confused the problems of the large size and "pathological" behaviors of the bureaucracy. The politicians (members of Congress, presidents, and their political appointees) have much to gain politically from attacking the administrative state and its bureaucracy by blaming it for their policy failures (Greenberg 1986; Jones 1983).

The conservatives' attack on bureaucracy has usually been based on the classical economic theory of limited government and market supremacy. They argue that big government is a strain on the free market system, that government limits the freedom of choice, that the bureaucracy is a major source of economic problems, and that it endangers democracy. The general expression is "getting the government off our back" (Boas and Crane 1985; Butler et al. 1984; Salaman and Lund 1981; Stockman 1987). The conservative attacks, however, have been consistently paradoxical. Rather than questioning the "outcome" of the administrative state activities "(who benefits?), conservatives examine the inputs (who directs the process? how much does government regulation cost?) and outputs (what is the total benefit?)" (Fainstein and Fainstein 1984:311); and their solution to the problem of bureaucracy is privatization and deregulation. The Reagan presidency seems to be the best representative of this ideological argument. As a group of contemporary observers of American government state, in a document known as the "Blacksburg Manifesto," in the 1980s: "we have also allowed public administration to be diminished by the headlong rush to adopt a policy or program perspective excessively focused on output without a balanced concern for the public interest. Output and the public interest are often erroneously assumed to be synonymous" (Wamsley et al. 1987:302). Public agencies can generate high outputs in the short run, but they may do so at the expense of their own "infrastructure and capabilities" (Wamsley et al. 1987:302), as well as long-term public interests. Public agencies should not be compared with private corporations that achieve output often at the expense of social equity, environment, and labor well-being without being accountable to anyone for their harmful actions.

While the conservative politicians' attacks on the "welfare state" have had tremendous negative impacts on the administrative state (as will be shown later), they have, ironically, both contributed to and significantly benefited from bureaucratic growth. In times of socioeconomic and political crises, they joined the liberal politicians to expand the welfare state because the state was vital to the continuous accumulation of capital and maintaining social control and political stability. As one of the top conservative politicians, former OMB Director David Stockman, put it: ''The conservative opposition helped build the American welfare state brick by brick during the three decades prior to 1980.'' Regarding the expansion of Medicare and Social Security, Stockman adds, ''Over two decades an average of 80 percent of House Republicans and 90 percent of Senate Republicans voted for these expansions'' (Stockman 1987:442, 447). According to an observer of American politics, the ''mainstream'' Americans have always had a ''consensus'' on matters of politics and policy: ''Republican opposition to the New Deal was simply a matter of time-lag, . . . By the time the Republicans regained office—in order to regain office—it was necessary for them to catch up with the consensus. Eisenhower came to administer the welfare state, not dismantle it'' (Wills 1971:509). It was the ''mainstream'' consensus that made the conservative Richard Nixon an ultimate liberal, who had to continue the American tradition of ''liberalism'' (Wills 1971:Chap. 6).

Thus the last three decades of state intervention in the economy both domestically and internationally benefited the conservative as well as liberal politicians and their ''big'' interest groups. The recent crisis in the stock market crash of 1987, and the urgent call for government intervention into the marketplace, is another good example.

The liberal reaction to the administrative state has been mainly based on a concern for representative democracy. Liberals, unlike conservatives, recognize the need for the administrative state, or welfare state, for political and socioeconomic reasons. Their acceptance of the interventionist state in society and economy reflects their concern for the possible undesired consequences of the crisis-ridden, unchecked, inequality-generating system of the marketplace. They object, however, to the exercise of power by the bureaucracy because of its unelected position. The liberal politicians reserve the right of government policymaking for the elected members of the system. They too have contributed to both the rise and diminution of the administrative state, as the bureaucracy has always served them as an easy target for attacks during election campaigns. Almost every presidential candidate has promised voters that he or she would ''fix'' the problem of uncontrolled bureaucracy, again making no distinction between the military-security bureaucracy and the general, public bureaucracy (Goodsell 1985; Greenberg 1986; H. Rosen 1985; Rourke 1986b).

Media reaction. The media and press have also contributed significantly to the crisis of the administrative state. State agencies have often become the targets of attack for government inefficiency, waste, corruption, red tape, and other stereotypes. Owned and controlled by major corporate and influential business concerns, television and the press usually induce a negative public image of the administrative state, and its performance. On the other hand, little criticism is offered of corporate waste, fraud, crime, inefficiency, and market failures. They distinguish between the public and private bureaucracies, and promote a negative public perceptions of the welfare state (Downs and Larkey 1986; Goodsell 1985; Parenti 1983).

Public reaction. The public response has been based on the general image of the administrative state shaped primarily by politicians, business leaders, and the media, and secondarily by contacts with the bureaucracy at different levels. The political values of liberal democracy, limited government, liberty, and free enterprise have, as parts of American political culture, influenced the views of the public that government is bad, and this is reinforced through the political socialization process (Greenberg 1986; Hartz 1986; Rosenbloom 1986). As a result, the public has a distasteful, hostile reaction to the administrative state and the bureaucracy (without making any distinction between the two public bureaucracies). They do not seem to realize that the very survival and expansion of the private, corporate sector requires a strong national administrative state (Macpherson, 1987).

Business reaction. While business, especially the corporate sector, has often reacted negatively to the rise and expansion of the administrative state, its self-interest has sometimes pointed in the other direction. For example, business supported the policies of the New Deal to rescue it from the collapse of the 1930s, "but as the New Deal moved toward measures that threatened to compete with private enterprises and undermine low wage structures, businessmen withdrew their support and became openly hostile" (Parenti 1983: 85). Despite the continued protection of the state in domestic areas (subsidies, contracts, protective regulations, tax credits, stability, and order) and the international sphere (military interventions in countries threatening the interests of the transnational corporations, concessionary gains secured through government negotiations, and so on), business has remained hostile toward those parts of the administrative state that form the welfare state. This same state rescued major corporations such as Chrysler, Exxon, Union Oil, and others by "giving several billion dollars" to them since the 1970s (Stockman 1987:415). Another example of state protection is Ronald Reagan signing a "bill paying dairy farmers $1,300 per head *not to milk their cows*" (Stockman 1987:418 [emphasis in the original]).

Academic reaction. Fascinated by the notion of representative democracy through election, the academicians have also made their contribution to the legitimacy crisis of the administrative state, some intentionally and others unintentionally. The main argument of the academic critics has been that the center of power in the twentieth century has shifted from the elected legislative branch to the administrative state. This, they argue, has endangered democracy, representation, and accountability. They claim that the separation of power has "collapsed," and that the characteristics of the bureaucracy (as defined by Max Weber) run counter to democratic values (Nackmias and Rosenbloom 1980; Rosenbloom 1983; Wilson 1986). Therefore, the "fourth branch" (Meier 1987) of government has become a giant force of political as well as organizational power that makes policy, implements it, and adjudicates differences. As a result, a "bureaucratization" (Nackmias and Rosenbloom 1980) of the three branches of government along with the other parts of society has taken place, and America has become the captive of a "professional state" whose members are neither elected by nor accountable to the public. Perhaps among the best representatives of this position are Frederick Mosher (1968), James Wilson (1986a, b), Francis Rourke (1986), and the conservative scholars in economics and public administration associated with public choice theory, namely, William Niskanen (1971), Vincent Ostrom (1973), and those of the Heritage Foundation think tank (Butler et al., 1984; Salaman and Lund 1981). Others such as Ralph Hummel (1982) and Fred Thayer (1981) have criticized the nature of corporate as well as public bureaucracy from psychological, political, and philosophical points of view. While the former groups have directly contributed to the crisis in the administrative state, the latter group's consistent criticism has also had an indirect effect on the administrative state. Similar "corrosive influence" upon the administrative state came from humanistic psychology and a variety of cultural dynamism during the 1960s (Wamsley et al. 1987:303).

Leftist intellectual reaction. The Marxist reaction rests on the argument that in advanced capitalist America, the administrative state is a strong instrument serving the ruling class, and that the role of bureaucracy and state in society is determined by the economic requirements of capital accumulation. They attack the bureaucracy for its lower-class oppression and parasitic nature (Miliband 1969; O'Connor 1973; Offe 1985a, 1985b; Poulantzas 1978). From this perspective, the capitalist welfare state "(1) is largely devoted to enhancing the process of capital accumulation rather than directly increasing the welfare of the masses; (2) it provides social benefits only as they are necessary for capitalist legitimation; (3) it is the servant rather than the master of the capitalist class" (Fainstein and Fainstein 1984:310–311).

B. Other Sources of the Crisis

One source of the administrative crisis is the very ambiguous meaning of the administrative state itself. For example, "welfare state" has variably been defined as a "particular state in the development of society," as a "way of life," as a "set of social and economic policies," as "the mode and pattern of government, . . . and expansion of bureaucratic system," and as "not only a product of government action but also a type of society where families fulfill an important role" (Shiratori 1986:193–197). Various types of welfare states are identified by emphasizing freedom, autonomy, values, affluence, and fraternity. The concept is thus confusing. Is the military-security state part of the administrative-welfare state? How is bureaucracy differentiated from the welfare state?

Another source of the crisis is the distinction between the public and private sectors. Convincing arguments have been made for differentiating public from private sectors in terms of organization, accountability, responsibility, constitutionality, legality, and so on (Allison 1987; Perry and Kraemer 1983). Yet the boundary has been blurred and most of what the public sector does is through the private corporate sector, and much of what the private sector does is subsidized, assisted, and protected by the public sector (Goodsell 1985; Greenberg 1986). This has led some theorists to claim that "all organizations are public" (Bozeman 1987). The public does not know that many of the problems of the administrative state are actually caused by the private sector. The bureaucracy and the administrative state are expected to do impossible things and to perform functions with multiple and unclearly defined goals. It also takes social costs of the market mechanism. Nevertheless, the public bureaucracy has been charged with inefficiency, corruption, red tape, and lack of accountability and political responsiveness. These charges have come from every direction.

Another source of the crisis is the Constitution itself. It does not even mention either administration or bureaucracy; rather it emphasizes the separation of powers. Thus the lack of constitutional legitimacy has always made the administrative state an easy target for political criticism (Rohr 1986). Consequently, "the history of the modern administrative process can be seen, then, as having been marked by an extended sense of crisis" (Freedman 1978:9). Further, as Wamsley et al. (1987:302) state, public administrators themselves have also contributed to the diminution of the administrative state. "For their part, public administrators have been entirely too timid in pressing their rightful claim to legitimacy." They have also been "hesitant about extending the agency perspective in pursuit of a broader definition of the public interest" and in defending the legitimacy of the administrative state through their administrative behavior that would lead to building "trust among citizens" (Wamsley et al. 1987:302).

Still another source of administrative crisis is the nature of its role in modern capitalist society. To maintain its relative legitimacy, the modern state has to play two simultaneous but often contradictory roles: The economic role of providing the optimal conditions for capital accumulation (even through coercive intervention at home and abroad) and the sociopolitical role of maintaining order, stability, and social control. A balanced performance of these two roles would be ideal, but it is rarely achieved and seems almost impossible because any such balanced administrative action will require an equal division and exercise of power by the administrative state in society. It also requires an autonomy from private business, especially the corporate sector, a constitutional legitimacy, and an ability to take from capital and distribute it to those whose consent is necessary for system maintenance.

None of these requirements can be satisfactorily met, because the modern state is not and never has been neutral. The administrative state is dependent on and is mainly controlled by capital; it does not have a recognized status of constitutional legitimacy; and it is always subject to charges of limiting capital accumulation and liberty. This is because taking from capital and giving to others for system maintenance decreases capital accumulation and would enlarge the public sector that may seek autonomy and,in an alliance with a massive clientele, attempt to challenge the corporate sector (Connolly 1984; Habermas 1984; Held et al. 1983). This would be destructive to the reign of the corporate sector. The business sector would not tolerate it, as it never has. However, reality shows that the state usually takes over unprofitable but ''necessary operations and/or is absorbing the cost of looking after that part of the labor force which technological change has made redundant'' (Macpherson 1987:67).

The ''incoherent'' nature of the modern administrative welfare state has also been explained by economist Kenneth Arrow (1963), who shows the problem of internal contradictions in defining a democratic ''social welfare function.'' The welfare state is also called impossible, according to Heidenheimer et al. (1983:330), because ''it fails to satisfy socialist criteria for production organized around social needs rather than profit motives . . . [and] the welfare state also fails to satisfy conservative criteria for maximizing individual liberty. It does not leave people, as Milton Freedman put it, 'free to choose,' and it neither fully accepts nor rejects market mechanisms.'' The result is a legitimacy crisis of the state in general and the administrative state in particular.

The last source of crisis in the administrative state is the problems facing the economic and sociopolitical systems. As discussed earlier, the international politico-economic challenges facing the United States and the internal crises emanating from major economic recessions and depressions and political crisis, and so on, of the 1970s and 1980s, have resulted in a ''confidence gap'' on the part of the masses and, therefore, a general crisis in the system. Evidence is abundant, Skolnick and Currie (1985) suggest, that the ''crisis in American Institutions'' covers the family, environment, workplace, health, education, welfare, and national security. Schott (1984) shows the ''persistence of economic problems in capitalist states.'' Greenberg (1986), Parenti (1983), Habermas (1984), Connolly (1984), Thayer (1984), Macpherson (1987), and others also show how significant the legitimacy crisis in America is. Generally, this blame has been shifted to the government and its administrative state.

IV. CONFIDENCE GAP AND POLITICS-ADMINISTRATION INTERFACE IN THE 1980s

The confidence gap resulted in the ''triumph'' of politics to restore system legitimacy in the 1980s. The rise of the conservative-right to power under the leadership of Republican ''crusaders'' (Stoessinger 1985) was made possible by two broad phenomena: the diversion of public attention from internal crises to the external threat of the Soviet Union and the spread of communism and a constant attack on the administrative welfare state. Both have been advanced in the names of democracy, liberty, and American supremacy as the leader of the free world. The principles of limited government, market supremacy, deregulation, supply-side economics, ideology, and global military might have been accompanied by a resumption of cultural and religious fundamentalism. This has been instrumental in rallying millions of uninstructed voters behind Ronald Reagan, who promised to restore American military and economic dominance in the global sphere (Carroll et al. 1985; Levine 1986; Newland 1983, 1987).

The triumph of politics has been of four types: (1) interest group politics, which has emphasized the maximization of the interests of the strongest supporters of the Republican regime both financially and politically at home and abroad; (2) partisan politics, which has emphasized traditional, conservative Republican values of politics, economics, and culture; (3) policy politics, which has advanced to enhance both the special, big interest group politics and partisan politics; and (4) bureaucratic politics, which has served as a power instrument to enhance the above three types of politics (Cigler and Loomis 1986; Dye and Zeigler 1987; Joe and Rogers 1985). The triumph of conservative politics over administration has further aggravated the legitimacy crisis of the administrative state, which over decades had gained a professional legitimacy for public administration as a self-conscious enterprise.

A. Reagan's Political Administration

The Reagan administration's unprecedented attacks on the federal bureaucracy and administrative state have resulted in a theory and style that Chester Newland (1983) properly calls "political administration." The major tenets of this political administration, most of which have been made bipartisan, include: ideological orientation of Reaganism; limited government; personalized presidency; supply-side management; privatization of public service; internationalized, warfare-security-oriented state; politics-administration dichotomy; overcentralization of policymaking led from the White House; high level of politicization of the bureaucracy and civil service; excessive practice of patronage and spoils system in the civil service; excessive and illegal use of partisan activities in the civil service; emphasis on conservative regime-enhancement; "Government of Enemies"; deregulation; corporate protectionism; antilabor and antiunionism; and attempts to reverse many policies and Supreme Court rulings of the past that were aimed at reducing economic injustice and serving the general public interest (ASPA 1986b; Goodsell 1985; Heclo, 1984; Levine 1986; Newland 1983, 1987; Parenti 1983; Perlmutter 1984; B. Rosen 1986; Rubin 1985).

B. Tools of Regime Enhancement

The following have been used as major tools for politicizing the federal bureaucracy and civil service, serving the "particular," big economic interests of the corporate sector, and achieving regime-enhancement: (a) extensive use of budget and program cuts, impoundments, deferrals, and recisions to "shrink" the size of the federal nonmilitary agencies while enlarging the military-security bureaucracy (Stockman 1987: epilogue), making it, as Keller reports, "the world's largest bureaucracy run out of control" (Keller 1985); (b) extensive use, and abuse, of the provisions of the Civil Service Reform Act of 1978, especially the Performance Appraisal and the Senior Executive Service systems, to reward the ideological, political, and personal loyalists, to co-opt potential supporters, and to get rid of unwanted personnel (Levine, 1986; Newland, 1983; H. Rosen, 1985); (c) extensive use, and abuse, of RIFs (reduction-in-force) to cut the size of the federal work force, which has resulted in the subsequent congressional and public employees' union protests (ASPA 1986c, 1985; Rich, 1986a, 1986b; U.S. Government, MSPB-OPM, 1984). "The current administration has brought an ideological dimension to the process" of RIFs. Consequently, "the process has been upgraded to a policy level" (Rich 1986b:3).

Other tools include (d) extensive use, and abuse, of reassignments of non-Republican, career personnel to undesirable positions and geographical locations ("described as Siberia") as a mechanism for inducing resignation and co-optation (H. Rosen 1985:chaps. 4–8). A good example of this policy-level practice is the case of the reassignment for resignation of Dr. Maxine Savitz, a Senior Executive Service (SES) career appointee in the Department of Energy in 1982 (U.S. Congress 1983a, b). A congressional hearing concludes that through "RIFs, reorganizations, and unprecedented attrition, those offices and programs in disfavor with the Department of Energy management have been crippled by inadequate staff, shifting managers, and poor productivity due to the removal of qualified personnel and a severely demoralized work force" (U.S. Congress 1983b:1).

Other tools of control include: (e) extensive ideological socializations and indoctrination for political appointees and their key administrators; (f) attempts to dismantle certain agencies with weak clienteles, while increasing the budget of agencies with powerful clienteles (e.g., Veterans Administration); (g) reorganization; (h) overcentralization of the federal bureaucracy by eliminating the middle-level managerial positions and concentration of policy functions in the White House; and (i) separation of policy from administration (Carroll 1987; Newland 1983; B. Rosen 1986; H. Rosen 1985).

While the administration has systematically rejected pro-poor protection, it has provided protection to the big business and corporate giants—through deregulation, billions of dollars in subsidies, guaranteed loans, tax credits, relaxation of labor laws, and attempts to reverse past legislation and Supreme Court decisions intended to limit the abusive power of the private sector in personnel actions (ASPA 1985; Stockman 1987:chap. 12, epilogue). The recent EEOC decision to abandon hiring goals and timetables and the administration's attempt to nullify some of the provisions of the Civil Rights Act of 1964 are but two examples (ASPA 1986b:1, 4). According to a member of the U.S. Civil Rights Commission, the agency has lost its credibility "and become a little Beirut in the Potomac . . . [and] is no longer an important voice on behalf of national goals and ideals" (quoted in ASPA 1986b:1, 4). Partisan politics have been highly promoted and the Hatch Acts of 1939 and 1940 have been extensively used to punish those public employees and their union officials who participated in voting registration activities and/or endorsed Democratic candidates during the 1984 presidential election.

Whistle-blowing has become a most dangerous action in the federal bureaucracy, leading to quick dismissal without protection. Even congressional members advise whistle-blowers to make their disclosures anonymously, and the Reagan appointee in charge of protecting whistle-blowers advised them in 1984: "Unless you're in a position to retire or are independently wealthy, don't do it. Don't put your head up, because it will get blown off" (H. Rosen 1985:93). This problem has recently caused Congress to pass another law to "ensure that civilian employees of government contractors are afforded job protection, and in some cases monetary rewards, for turning in unscrupulous contractors" (ASPA 1986a:1, 4). In short, the triumph of conservative particular interest politics under Reagan has had dramatic impact on the administrative state.

C. The Impacts and the Crisis

Some of the major impacts of Reagan's policies on the administrative state are the following.

Loss of expertise and institutional memory. Strong evidence indicates that a large number of well-trained, highly competent professional career personnel, whose commitment to public service has served several presidents, are no longer in the civil service. Many have been separated by reorganization and RIFs (especially at GS 5–13), 49% of whom are minorities and women (U.S. Congress 1984:2–3). Many others have been reassigned either to undesired locations and positions or demoted (e.g., people with Ph.D.s to clerical jobs). More important, many others have left public service and have taken higher-paying executive positions in large corporations. This is especially true in the case of SES: by March 1983 40% of these invaluable public servants had left civil service, 22% were planning to leave, and 72% indicated that they would not recommend federal government careers to their children. By mid-1984, 45% of the SES executives "had left the government" (Goodsell 1985:174–175; Heclo 1984:12–14; Levine and Hansen 1985). This is an historical phenomenon in the American political system.

While the institutional memory, the "leadership core," and the expertise of the administrative state (nonmilitary-security) have been drastically reduced, the Reagan administration has not been able to fill many key positions of the bureaucracy because ideologically committed Reaganites have been reducing in number. The result has been a crippling of organizational competence (Goodsell 1985; *New York Times* May 3, 1985: A19; H. Rosen 1985). Thus the administration has achieved two objectives: (1) transferring the institutional competence of the administrative state to the private, corporate sector, and (2) advancing market efficiency as the slogan against the crippled bureaucracy (Farazmand 1985; Pfiffner 1987).

Efficiency. With severe budget cuts, loss of expertise, job insecurity (many civil servants have been replaced by temporary and unqualified persons), and dominance of unqualified and inexperienced political appointees, the crippled bureaucracy has naturally suffered efficiency problems, and thus become subject to further public and political criticisms (Fainstein and Fainstein 1984; Farazmand 1985; H. Rosen 1985).

Morale and motivation. Devastating adverse impacts have been inflicted on the morale of career personnel and their motivation for initiative, creativity, and innovation in public management. A highly hostile and suspicious environment created by the political appointees has caused alienation, extremely low morale, and a feeling of degradation among the career people (Denhardt 1987; Downs and Larkey 1986; Farazmand 1985). As one postal employee put it, "Working for the U.S. government today is like being a Jew in Germany when Hitler came to power. You are defenseless, blamed for all the problems of the country, and used politically as best suits the objectives of the Administration rather than the American people" (quoted in Goodsell 1985: 171). But professionally unqualified persons have been promoted in the bureaucracy in violation of civil service laws. The bureaucracy and civil service have become more than ever an instrument of Republican regime-enhancement headed by the "government of enemies" (Heclo 1984; Stockman 1987: epilogue). As Charles Levine (personal interview, August 1985) put it, "the time of neutral competence is over."

Minorities and women. Minorities, younger, nonveteran, and female personnel have been affected most by the changes in the administrative state. According to a congressional document, about one-half (49%) of all the RIFs have hit the minorities, 54.6% of these minority women. Other groups follow the minorities (U.S. Congress 1984: executive summary and pp. 1–10). Charges of pervasive discrimination and prohibited personnel actions have increasingly been documented in past years (ASPA 1987b; U.S. Congress 1983a, 1983b).

Corruption. Bureaucratic corruption by political appointees and their partisan administrators in office has been pronounced. The almost daily disclosure of these corruptions have ranged from favoritism to partisan preference, to patronage and "selling" the privilege of seeing the president to business leaders for contributions to the *contras*, to waste and billions of dollars of kickbacks, return of favors to corporate contractors, "conflict of interest," and bribery (Rep. Barry Anthony on ABC's *Nightline*, April 29, 1987; Farazmand 1985, 1986; Newland, 1987; Parenti 1983:96–97).

Quality of service. Overwhelming evidence suggests that the phenomena outlined above have had, and will increasingly have, significant negative impacts on the quality of public service. This is especially true with the privatization or contracting out ("selling out") of public service (Downs and Larkey 1986; Farazmand 1985, 1986; Goodsell 1985; U.S. Congress 1983b:1–111). Evidence supports Howard Rosen's (1985) argument that private companies bid on public service contracts with lower cost first, then once granted contracts and subsidy, they start raising prices, perform poorly, provide lower-quality service, violate safety regulations, and fail to meet schedules, practice substandard compensation, are not accountable to the public, and the government loses control over companies' output. The result is poor service and no accountability (Farazmand 1985, 1986; Kettl 1988; Perlmutter 1984; Stern 1984).

The famous report of the Peter Grace Commission, whose findings have been seriously questioned by congressional investigations and by independent researchers, proposed a comprehensive privatization of American government. As Goodsell (1985:174–175) put it, its ideas "extend to items deeply imbedded in the citizens' personal relationship with government, such as readiness to save our lives, . . . its provision of the coin of the realm, . . . its trust in our word, . . . and its own fiduciary promises. Should the values inherent in such relationships be subject to cost comparisons and motivated by profit-seeking?" Another expert, Chester Newland (1987:54), reports that "cost overruns, excessive prices, performance failures, and corruption in space, defense, and other national government contracts have become routine, increasing as deinstitutionalization and politicization have advanced" under Reagan.

Deinstitutionalization of public service as a result of privatization and replacement of the welfare state with the warfare state (with a budget increase of 40%) by the Reagan administration have returned to the corporate sector some of the favors that the "BIG money" and "particularistic interests" paid during the presidential and congressional elections in the 1980s (Newland 1987:45, 53). Congressional criticism of the officials in the Department of Commerce shows "the automatic approval of decisions already made outside the Government in business and industry" (quoted in Parenti 1983:299). While the "Nixon administration" was a "business administration" and its "mission" was to "protect American business," (according to Nixon's Secretary of State William Rogers; quoted in Greenberg 1986:302), the Reagan administration has undoubtedly been BIG business administration (Newland 1987:45–53; Stockman, 1987: Epilogue). Privatization has reduced the American citizens down to "consumers" of the marketplace (Frederickson and Hart 1985). While Peter Grace's plan for privatization has been implemented by Reagan, children of the Boston area have been dying of leukemia caused by Grace's chemical company's contamination of water wells (CBS, February 3, 1986; *Washington*

Post, June 1, 1988:A3). Other aspects of the loss of public service can be shown by statistics: collapsing public bridges (57,000 in 1987 compared to 15,000 in 1983) (CBS, June 4, 1987); massive unemployment (about 7%–14%, including hidden unemployment) (Greenberg 1986:319); and massive growing poverty (according to James Carroll, in 1983, "22.2 percent of all children in the United States were living in poverty. . . . These children constitute 40 percent of all poor people, . . . and 22 percent of its [nation's] youth" (Carroll 1987:112). Crisis in education, health, environment, and so on should also be noted (Skolnick and Currie 1985; Thayer 1984).

V. CONCLUSION

The triumph of politics over administration in the 1980s under the Reagan presidency, a response to the sociopolitical and economic crises, has resulted in a significant diminution of an administrative state already facing a legitimacy crisis. This crisis has had and will continue to have major political and socioeconomic consequences in the United States. The important question today is: Will the administrative state survive the current crisis? It is a conclusion of this article that despite the current crisis, the administrative state and its bureaucracy will ultimately survive and rise again. The survival and revival of the administrative state is inevitable and necessary because it is functional to system maintenance and system legitimacy; and the pervasiveness of state is a global phenomenon (Kazancigil 1986).

The corporatization and commercialization of American government in the 1980s have had and will continue to have extensive social costs (market failures of externalities, unemployment, and so on) in the inherent crisis-ridden nature (business cycles) of the market system, requiring protective intervention from the state. In short, the highly centralized corporatization of America, including the agricultural sector, will enlarge the working class and the poor by millions. This army of unemployed and unskilled will join the millions of others already displaced by rapid technological advancement. Such a massive pool of unemployed and underemployed will likely represent a "potentially disruptive and explosive mixture, . . . and the principal instrument for treatment of this explosive mixture under modern capitalism is the system of welfare" (Greenberg 1986:320). Thus the corporate sector will need the administrative system to absorb the social costs of the marketplace, to cool the explosive mixture, and to provide system legitimacy through relief programs. In the words of David Stockman (1987:413), the White House has also recognized "the political necessities of the welfare state." The administrative state will be needed, as it always has been, to provide stability, system enhancement, and system legitimacy.

Contrary to the charges of the opponents of the administrative state, evidence suggests that in fact the administrative state has been more productive, more efficient, more equitable, more accountable to the public, and more responsible to political and policy goals than has the private sector (Abrahamson 1987:360–363; Downs and Larkey, 1986; Goodsell 1985; Perlmutter 1984; Rose and Shiratori, 1986; H. Rosen, 1985; Thayer, 1984). According to the ASPA's President Robert B. Denhardt, "Over the past 20 years governmental productivity has increased 1.5% a year, almost double the national average" (Denhardt, 1987:2). As John Logue (1979:85) points out, "The welfare state is the victim of its success, not of its failures."

Calls for revival of public service have been made recently by a growing number of academicians, practitioners, and legislators, and alternative approaches to administration have been suggested by some public administration scholars (Carroll 1987; Denhardt 1987; Goodsell 1985; Rep. Schroeder—ASPA, 1987a). This article suggests an Integrated Model of Public Administration, which embraces politics as well as administration. For two centuries, the relationship between politics and administration has been one of the most controversial issues of American government. No government in modern society can govern without an administrative system, and no administrative system is politically neutral (Waldo 1984). A reassessment of the Constitution (prepared for its *time*) is needed to grant the administrative state a legal legitimacy, and to make it an equal partner in the institutional structure of the governance in America. Such an administrative state will have to be representative of different social classes and of ethnic and racial segments of the population. A politico-economically representative administrative state will be actively involved in making as well as implementing policy. An integrated administrative system will be professionally competent, politically more accountable, more responsive to public need, and more sensitive to public interests. It will also be a powerful instrument of system maintenance and system legitimacy. Elsewhere (Farazmand 1989) I have discussed in detail the major aspects of a proposed Integrated Theory of Public Administration that outlines the principal foundations for legitimizing the administrative state. For the purpose of this article, the proposed Integrated Theory of Public Administration emphasizes the "guardianship," "trusteeship," and "agency" roles of the administrative state and public administrators in serving the general public interests, not the particular partisan interests, and in promoting constitutional principles of democracy and social justice. Some of these aspects of the administrative state have already been suggested by others (Rohr 1986; Waldo 1986a; Wamsley et al. 1987).

It seems appropriate to use Dwight Waldo's (1986b:468) words that "public administration, seeking to solve problems in a very real world, is importantly involved in creating the political theory of our time. I am confident that this will be the verdict of the history." Long-term damage to public service and administration has already been done. A joint effort by public administrationists, a politically conscious public, and politicians is badly needed now to change the current trend. Fortunately, there are signs of such effort. As Scymour Lipset (1987:23) concludes, Americans remain "dissatisfied with the performance of their leaders in powerful nongovernmental institutions, . . . [and] the continuing confidence gap could easily give rise to an era of progressive policies aimed at reforming the structure of private power in the United States."

ACKNOWLEDGMENT

I wish to thank the following for their encouraging feedback and helpful comments on the earlier draft of this manuscript: Dwight Waldo and Jesse Burkhead of Syracuse University, Fred Thayer of the University of Pittsburgh, and Charles Goodsell of VPI. I am also grateful to the anonymous referees for their review of and comments on the manuscript.

REFERENCES

Abrahamson, M. A. (1987). "Executive personnel systems in government: how are they doing?" *Public Administration Rev.* (July/August): 360–363.

Allison, G. T. (1987). ''Public and private management: Are they fundamentally alike in all unimportant respects?'' pp. 510–529 in J. M. Shafritz and A. C. Hyde (eds.) *Classics of Public Administration*. Chicago: Dorsey Press.

American Broadcasting Corporation (1987). *Nightline* program on ''Iran-Contras.'' (April 29).

American Society for Public Administration (1985). ''Congress may block new OPM personnel policies.'' *Public Administration Times* (July 15): 2.

American Society for Public Administration (1986a) ''New law will reward civilian whistleblowers.'' *Public Administration Times* (November 1): 1, 4.

American Society for Public Administration (1986b). ''EEOC abandons hiring goals, time-tables.'' *Public Administration Times* (March 1): 1, 4.

American Society for Public Administration (1986c). ''National council adopts policy on RIFs.'' *Public Administration Times* (January 15).

American Society for Public Administration (1987a). ''Schroeder Bill would target public service.'' *Public Administration Times* (August 1): 1, 8.

American Society for Public Administration (1987b). ''NAPA panel criticizes federal hiring practice.'' *Public Administration Times* (May 1): 1, 3.

Arrow, K. (1963). *Social Choice and Individual Values*. New Haven, CT: Yale Univ. Press.

Beard, C. A. (1986). ''The Constitution as an economic document,'' pp. 57–62 in R. Nivola and D. H. Rosenbloom (eds.) *Classic Readings in American Politics*. New York: St. Martin's.

Boas, D. and E. H. Crane [eds.] (1985). *Beyond the Status Quo: Policy Proposals for America*. Washington, DC: CATO Institute.

Bozeman, B. (1987). All *Organizations Are Public: Bridging Public and Private Organization Theories*. San Francisco: Jossey-Bass.

Butler, S. M., M. Sanera, and W. B. Weinrod [eds.] (1984). *Mandate for Leadership 11: Continuing the Conservative Revolution*. Washington, DC: Heritage Foundation.

Caiden, G. G. (1983). *The need for a theory of public administration*. Presented at the annual meeting of the American Society for Public Administration Conference, New York.

Carroll, J. (1987). ''Public administration in the third century of the Constitution: supply-side management, privatization, or public investment.'' Public Administration Rev. (January/February), 106–114.

Carroll, J., L. P. Fritscheller, and B. Smith (1985). ''Supply-side management in the Reagan administration.'' *Public Administration Rev.* (November/December), 805–815.

Cigler, A. J. and B. A. Loomis (1986). *Interest Group Politics*, 2nd ed. Washington, DC: Congressional Quarterly Press.

Columbia Broadcasting Company (1986). ''What killed Jimmy Anderson.'' *60 Minutes XVIII* (25) Final—March 2.

Columbia Broadcasting Company (1987). ''Special report: labor unions and management lockouts of the companies.'' CBS Evening News (June 4).

Connolly, W. [ed.] (1984). *Legitimacy and the State*. New York: New York Univ. Press.

Denhardt, R. B. (1987). Assert value of public service. *Public Administration Times* (July 15), 2.

Downs, G. W. and P. D. Larkey (1986). *The Search for Government Efficiency: From Hubris to Helplessness*. New York: Random House.

Dye, T. R. and H. Zeigler (1987). *The Irony of Democracy: An Introduction to American Politics*, 7th ed. Monterey, CA: Brooks/Cole.

Fainstein, N. and S. B. Fainstein (1984). ''The political economy of American bureaucracy,'' pp. 309–315 in F. Fischer and C. Sirianni (eds.) *Critical Studies in Organization and Bureaucracy*. Philadelphia: Temple Univ. Press.

Farazmand, A. (1985). Personal interviews with about 35 federal employees, congressional staff members, members of the Federal Merit System Protection Board, union representatives, and several scholars in the federal government. (August and December).

Farazmand, A. (1986). *Politics of the federal bureaucracy and administrative theory under Reagan: a summary*. Paper presented at the 47th National Conference of ASPA in Anaheim, CA, March 13–16.

Farazmand, A. (1989). *Crisis and legitimacy in the federal administrative state: toward an integrated theory of public administration.* Presented at the 1989 annual meeting of the American Political Science Association. Atlanta, GA, August 29–September 3.

Farazmand, A. (forthcoming) *Crisis in the U.S. Administrative State: A Political Economy Analysis.* New York: Praeger.

Feinberg, R. E. (1983). *The Intemperate Zone: The Third World Challenge to U.S. Foreign Policy.* New York: Norton.

Frederickson, G. and D. Hart (1985). "The public service and the patriotism of benevolence." *Public Administration Rev.* (september/october): 547–553.

Freedman, J. O. (1978). *Crisis and Legitimacy: The Administrative Process and American Government.* New York: Cambridge Univ. Press.

Goodsell, C. (1985). *The Case for Bureaucracy*, 2nd ed. New York: Chatham House.

Greenberg, E. S. (1986). *The American Political System* 4th ed. Boston: Little, Brown.

Habermas, J. (1984). "What does a legitimation crisis mean today? Legitimation problems in late capitalism," pp. 134–155 in W. Connolly (ed.) *Legitimacy and the State.* New York: New York Univ. Press.

Hartz, L. (1986). "The concept of liberal society," pp. 15–21 in R. Nivola and D. H. Rosenbloom (eds.) *Classic Readings in American Politics.* New York: St. Martin's.

Heclo, H. (1984). "A government of enemies?" *Bureaucrat* 13 (fall): 12–14.

Heidenheimer, A. J., H. Heclo, and C. T. Adams (1983). Comparative Public Policy: *The Politics of Social Choice in Europe and America*, 2nd ed. New York: St. Martin's.

Held, D. and associates [eds.] (1983). *States and Societies.* New York: New York Univ. Press.

Hummel, R. P. (1982). *The Bureaucratic Experience*, 2nd ed. New York: St. Martin's.

Joe, T. and C. Rogers (1985) *By the Few, For the Few: The Reagan Welfare Legacy.* Lexington, MA: Lexington Books.

Jones, C. (1983). *An Introduction to the Study of Public Policy*, 3rd ed. Monterey, CA: Brooks/Cole.

Kazancigil, A. [ed.] (1986). *The State in Global Perspective.* Paris: UNESCO; Brook-field, VT: Gower.

Keller, B. (1985). "Weinberger on the political siege, but few expect change of course," *The New York Times* (July 23): 1, A15. Copyright © 1985 by The New York Times Company. Reprinted by permission.

Kettl, D. F. (1988). *Government by Proxy: (Mis?) Managing Federal Programs.* Washington, DC: Congressional Quarterly Press.

LaFaber, W. (1984). *Inevitable Revolutions: The United States in Central America.* New York: Norton.

Levine, C. (1986). "The federal government in the year 2000: administrative legacies of the Reagan years." *Public Administration Rev.* 46(*3*), 195–215.

Levine, C. and M. G. Hansen (1985). "The centralization tug-of-war in the new executive branch." Presented at the World Congress of the International Political Science Association, Paris, July 15–20.

Lipset, S. M. (1987). "The confidence gap during the Reagan years, 1981–1987." *Pol Sci Q* (spring), 1–23.

Logue, J. (1979) "The welfare state: the victim of its success," p. 85 in S. R. Graubard (ed.) *The State.* New York: Norton.

MacPherson, C. B. (1987). *The Rise and Fall of Economic Justice.* New York: Oxford Univ. Press.

Meier, K. J. (1987). *Politics and the Bureaucracy: Policy Making in the Fourth Branch of Government*, 2nd ed. Monterey, CA: Brooks/Cole.

Miliband, R. (1969). *The State in Capitalist Society.* London: Weidenfeld & Nicolson.

Mosher, F. C. (1968). *Democracy and the Public Service*, 2nd ed. New York: Oxford Univ. Press.

Nackmias, D. and D. Rosenbloom (1980). *Bureaucratic Government: U.S.A.* New York: St. Martin's.

Nelson, W. E. (1982). *The Roots of American Bureaucracy, 1830–1900.* Cambridge, MA: Harvard Univ. Press.

Newland, C. (1983). "A mid-term appraisal—the Reagan presidency: limited government and political administration." *Public Administration Rev.* 43(*1*), 1–21.

Newland, C. (1987). "Public executives: imperium, sacerdotium, collegium? Bicentennial leadership challenges." *Public Administration Rev.* 47(*1*), 45–56.

Niskanen, W. A. (1971). *Bureaucracy and Representative Government.* Chicago: Aldine Atherton.

O'Connor, J. (1973). *The Fiscal Crisis of the State.* New York: St. Martin's.

Offe, C. (1985a). *Disorganized Capitalism: Contemporary Transformation of Work and Politics.* Cambridge, MA: MIT Press.

Offe, C. (1985b) *Contradictions of the Welfare State.* Cambridge, MA: MIT Press.

Ostrom, V., Jr. (1973). *The Intellectual Crisis of Public Administration in America.* University, AL: Univ. of Alabama Press.

Parenti, M. (1988) *Democracy for the Few* (5th ed.). New York: St. Martin's.

Perlmutter, F. D. (1984). *Human Services at Risk: Administrative Strategies for Survival.* Lexington, MA: Lexington Books.

Perry, J. L. and K. L. Kraemer (1983). *Public Management: Public and Private Perspectives.* Palo Alto, CA: Mayfield.

Pfiffner, J. (1987). "Political appointees and career executives: the democracy-bureaucracy nexus in the third century." *Public Administration Rev.* 47(*1*), 57–65.

Piven, F. F. and R. Cloward (1971). *Regulating the Poor.* New York: Pantheon.

Piven, F. F. and R. Cloward (1985). "The relief of welfare," pp. 428–445 in J. H. Skolnick and E. Currie (eds.) *Crisis in American Institutions*, 6th ed. Boston: Little, Brown.

Poulantzas, N. (1978) *State, Power, Socialism.* London: New Left Books.

Rich, W. C. (1986a). "Political context of a reduction-in-force policy: on the misunderstanding of an important phenomenon." *Public Administration Q (spring)*: 7–21.

Rich, W. C. (1986b). "Reduction-in-force: issues and perspectives—a symposium: introduction." *Public Administration Q.* (spring): 3–6.

Rohr, J. (1986) *To Run a Constitution: The Legitimacy of the Administrative State.* Lawrence, KS: Univ. Press of Kansas.

Rose, R. and R. Shiratori [eds.] (1986) *The Welfare State East and West.* New York: Oxford Univ. Press.

Rosen, B. (1986) "Crises in the U.S. civil service." *Public Administration Rev.* 46(*3*), 195–215.

Rosen, H. (1985) *Servants of the People: The Uncertain Future of the Federal Civil Service.* Salt Lake City: Olympus.

Rosenbloom, D. H. (1983). "Public administration theory and the separation of powers." *Public Administration Rev* 43(*3*), 219–221.

Rosenbloom, D. H. (1986). "The judicial response to the rise of the administrative state," pp. 129–150 in F. Lane (ed.) *Current Issues in Public Administration*, 3rd ed. New York: St. Martin's.

Rosenbloom, D. H. (1987). "Public administrators and the judiciary: the new partnership." *Public Administration Rev* 47(*1*), 75–83.

Rosenbloom, D. H. and J. M. Shafritz (1985). *Essentials of Labor Relations.* Reston, VA: Reston.

Rourke, F. E. (1986a). "The presidency and the bureaucracy," pp. 71–89 in F. Lane (ed.) *Current Issues in Public Administration*, 3rd ed. New York: St. Martin's.

Rourke, F. E. [ed.] (1986b). *Bureaucratic Power in National Policy Making*, 4th ed. Boston: Little, Brown.

Rubin, I. S. (1985). *Shrinking the Federal Government: The Effects of Cutbacks on Five Federal Agencies.* New York: Longman.

Salaman, L. M. and M. S. Lund (eds.) (1981). *The Reagan Presidency and the Governing of America.* Washington, DC: Urban Institute.

Schott, K. (1984) Policy, *Power and Order: The Persistence of Economic Problems in Capitalist States.* New Haven, CT: Yale Univ. Press.

Shiratori, R. (1986). "The future of the welfare state," pp. 193–206 in R. Rose and R. Shiratori (eds.) *The Welfare State East and West.* New York: Oxford University Press.

Skolnick, J. H. and E. Currie (1985) Crisis in American Institutions (6th ed.). Boston: Little, Brown.

Skowronek, S. (1982). *Building a New American State: The Expansion of National Administrative Capacities, 1877–1920.* Cambridge: Cambridge Univ. Press.

Stern, M. J. (1984). "The politics of American social welfare," pp. 3–21 in F. D. Perlmutter (ed.) *Human Services at Risk: Administrative Strategies for Survival.* Lexington, MA: Lexington Books.

Stillman, R., II (1987). "The Constitutional bicentennial and the centennial of the American administrative state." *Public Administration Rev.* 47(*1*), 4–8.

Stockman, D. A. (1987). *Triumph of Politics: The Inside Story of the Reagan Revolution.* New York: Avon.

Stoessinger, J. G. (1985). *Crusaders and Pragmatists: Movers of Modern American Foreign Policy,* 2nd ed. New York: Norton.

Thayer, F. C. (1981). An End to *Hierarchy and Competition: Administration in the Post-Affluent World,* 2nd ed. New York: Franklin Watts.

Thayer, F. C. (1984). *Rebuilding America: The Case for Economic Regulation.* New York: Praeger.

U.S. Congress (1983a). Civil Service Oversight: Hearings Before the Subcommittee on Civil Service of the Post Office and Civil Service, House of Representatives, 98th Congress, First Session, March 9 and 10. Washington, DC: Author.

U.S. Congress (1983b). "DOE prohibited personnel practices." Joint Hearing before the Subcommittee on Energy Conservation and Power of the Committee on Energy and Commerce and the Subcommittee on Civil Service of the Committee on Post Office and Civil Service, House of Representatives, 98th Congress, First Session, April 19. Washington, DC: Author.

U.S. Congress (1984). *Federal Government Service Task Force, Report of Fiscal 1984 Reduction-in-Force Activity in Non-Defense Agencies: Executive Summary.* Washington, DC: Author.

U.S. Government [OPM-MSPB] (1984). "Roundtable monograph: significant actions of the OPM: a labor-management dialogue." Report of the U.S. MSPB—Office of Management Systems Review and Studies, August.

Waldo, D. (1984) The Administrative State: *A Study of the Political Theory of American Public Administration,* 2nd ed. New York: Holms & Meier.

Waldo, D. (1986a). "Afterward: thoughts in retrospect—and prospect," pp. 165–185 in B. Brown and R. J. Stillman II, eds. *A Search for Public Administration: The Ideas and Career of Dwight Waldo.* College Station: Texas A&M Univ. Press.

Waldo, D. (1986b). "Bureaucracy and democracy: reconciling the irreconcilable," pp. 455–469 in F. Lane (ed.) *Current Issues in Public Administration,* 3rd ed. New York: St. Martin's.

Wamsley, G. L. and associates (1987). "The public administration and the governance process: refocusing the American dialogue," pp. 291–317 in R. C. Chandler (ed.) *A Centennial History of the American Administrative State.* New York: Free Press.

Washington Post (1984), July 7.

Washington Post (1988), June 1.

Wills, G. (1971). *Nixon Agonistes.* New York: New American Library, Inc.

Wilson, J. Q. (1986). "The bureaucratic state," pp. 427–447 in P. S. Nivola and D. H. Rosenbloom (eds.) *Classic Readings in American Politics.* New York: St. Martin's.

Witte, E. E. (1962). *Development of Social Security Act.* Milwaukee: University of Wisconsin Press.

8

Global Crisis in Public Service and Administration

Ali Farazmand School of Public Administration, Florida Atlantic University, Fort Lauderdale, Florida

I. INTRODUCTION

Public service has been one of the oldest and most cherished institutions of human history. In fact, civilization, administration, and public service have always developed together, one reinforcing the other. Throughout history progress has been made toward improving the human lot, for which public service and administration have played a key role. Real progress in such a direction was made during the last two centuries when social, economic, political struggles and innovations led to overall progress in human conditions for citizens worldwide. The rise of the modern nation-states and the growth of professionalism—along with development in education and economic progress—also contributed to some degree to this human progress around the world.

The rise and expansion of modern capitalism, especially corporate capitalism, raised serious concern about the adverse consequences of this historical development. Subsequent struggles by working-class peoples and middle-class professionals worldwide, as well as the rise of world socialism, resulted in a minimal social safety net. The modern welfare state has absorbed many of the grievances raised by deteriorating human conditions for the mass of citizens, in the midst of a prosperity enjoyed by the few elites.

With the rise and expansion of the welfare state and the accompanying interventionist state worldwide, public service and administration grew and expanded all over the capitalist world. This situation resembles to a very small degree the features of socialist countries in place throughout the twentieth century up to the big wave of structural changes that began to appear in the 1980s. Until then, public service and administration were cherished, as they contributed to civilization, corrected constitutional and political as well economic wrongs, and helped balance the excesses of market capitalism. However, with the accelerated rate of technological and economic globalization of capital and the rise of the strategic globalization policy of privatization, public service and administration became the targets of relentless attacks from corporate capitalists, conservative business and political elites promoting the ideology of market supremacy, and scholars and policy advisors.

With the fall of the USSR, the diminution and crisis of public service progressed at a new, accelerated pace. Thus, the global system of corporate capitalism pronounced a death sentence on all that had been achieved through public service and administration over decades—in fact, over centuries. As a result of sweeping privatization, what had been considered ''public'' and the public sphere was attacked under the banner of efficiency and anti–public sector sentiment. This has been enforced through supranational organizations such as the World Bank, the International Monetary Fund, and the World Trade Organization, all of which are heavily influenced by the leading and most powerful governments—the United States and its key western allies. Public service has therefore been sacrificed for the rapid accumulation of capital, while the character of the state and administration has been changed in favor of strong police security and military systems to promote and protect corporate interests worldwide. The result has been a global crisis of public service and administration, with three distinct manifest dimensions: crises institutions, image, and legitimacy.

This chapter outlines this global crisis of public service and administration by addressing the nature of the crisis, its core dimensions, and the factors causing the current crisis in public service worldwide. Consequences and suggestions for policy decisions and administrative action are beyond the limits of this discussion. A major thesis of the chapter is that while there is a need for reform and improvement in public service delivery and administration worldwide, the root causes of the crisis of public service and administration are both political and economic. Much of the historical progress toward the betterment of human conditions is now expected to be lost, and people everywhere have become disposable commodities or tools of the new globalization of capital in search of rapid growth in profits.

Consequently, public service and administration have been transformed from institutions with long historical traditions into a corporate, coercive state institutions enforcing the new rules of the corporate welfare state at local, national, and global levels. The global crisis of public service is now connected with other crises impairing the human condition: environmental degradation and destruction, child labor, mercenary labor, violations of basic human rights, furtherance of mass poverty, malnutrition, and wage slavery all over the world.

II. THE NATURE OF THE PUBLIC SERVICE CRISIS

Public service is experiencing a crisis globally, nationally, and locally. This global crisis of public service has many dimensions, some of which are discussed in this chapter. Fundamentally speaking, understanding this crisis of public service requires a deeper understanding of the underpinnings that shape the contemporary global trends and changes in socioeconomic and political systems as well as in the global power structures that have been causing much of the public service crisis experienced all over the globe. It must also be understood in connection with other crises facing the entire planet earth and all global humanity: financial crisis, moral and ethical crisis, environmental crisis, institutional crisis, political and cultural crises, and a host of other crises that affect public service and administration worldwide.

This global crisis of public service has not yet reached its critical point. In fact, it has a fairly long way to go before it reaches the criticality that is needed for fundamental social action and qualitative change. The multitude of contemporary quantitative changes—innovations in technologies, increasing numbers of nation-states, breakdowns in traditional structures—that have produced some degrees of qualitative changes in human history have had profound effects on the lives of billions of global citizens. However, many of these changes have produced fruits that have only benefited a small number of individuals and governments, who have declared the entire globe their own realm. At the center of this small group are some of the most powerful globalizing barons backed and promoted by the military and political-coercive muscles of the globally hegemonic states: the United States and its European allies. Here, both ethnocentrism and superpower arrogance appear to have dominated the psychological as well as the political and economic environment of the globe.

The core of this globalization enterprise has focused its onslaught on the realm of public service, public interest, and the public sphere all over the world. Behind this global onslaught is the dogmatic, self-proclaimed ideology of global capitalism, which is equated with market-based governance, administration, and democracy. The traditional historical progress, of the last four centuries or so, against worker exploitation, human serfdom, child labor, human rights abuse, and other violations of human dignity have all of a sudden become matters of nonsense, or irrelevant, as new concepts of corpocracy and market idolatry are invented and propagated. The traditional domains of public service have been claimed and occupied by this new globalizing ideology, and a neo-colonization has penetrated deeply into the heart of public service and those areas in which the unprotected have traditionally sought a level of sheltering.

Today, the public service image is totally tarnished by this globalizing ideological corporatism, and both its institutional capacity and philosophical identity have come under serious question. With the governmental elites—elected and nonelected alike—joining as accomplices and, in fact, major partners of this global corporate strategy, public service and administration have become critically impaired and driven deep into a major crisis that has reached a global scale. In fact, expressions such as "The Quiet Crisis of the Civil Service" (Levine and Kleeman 1988), "Crisis in the U.S. Civil Service" (Rosen 1986), "Crisis in the U.S. Administrative State" (Farazmand 1989), "The Legitimacy Crisis" (Brown 2000), "Crisis of Morale. . . ." (Ban 2000), and others are important explanations for and evidence of this global crisis, but they only scratch the surface of the crisis that face public service and administration worldwide.

To understand and explain deeply the core of this global phenomenon, we need to bring the big picture into our discussion and analyze the nature of the current crisis in public service and the other pervasive crises mentioned earlier within a broad theoretical framework at the macro level. Here, a global political economy analysis is needed in order to explain the cause and effect of the crisis and to outline implications for corrective social action.

III. DIMENSIONS OF THE CRISIS

Three dimensions make up the current global crisis of public service and administration: those of image, institution, and legitimacy or philosophy.

A. The Image Crisis

Public service has always been valued as a major part of human civilization. This has been due to many factors, including the nature of humankind as a social creature with concern for both the common good and self interest. The state and public sector have always played a leading role in providing this common good and public service.

The rise and expansion of the modern state has also contributed significantly to the growth and expansion of public service. This has been accompanied by the increasing bureaucratization and professionalization of the modern state, as Weber (1946; 1984) predicted. Professionalization has added many values to the administrative and organizational values. Ironically, some of these administrative values have, during the last few decades, come into conflict with the long cherished human values of citizenship and democratic principles. Professionalization of public service and administrative systems has indeed changed the nature of modern organizations by implanting deeply the instrumental rationality that has dominated societies as well as organizational life around the globe (Farazmand 1994a).

This dominance has been more prevalent in the western societies of the United States and Europe than in developing nations. Rationalism and positivism have become part of the western culture, whereas the normative values are still dominant in most developing countries' cultures. However, there seem to be two trends: globalization and cultural convergence of this instrumental rationality, especially through the current government reinvention and reengineering, on the one hand, and on the other, the concurrent counterpressures from below against this rampant instrumental rationality in developed nations such as the United States and Europe. The result has been a clash of major values underlying the administrative systems and public service around the world, with the invading values of corporate capitalism and self-interest individualism.

Public service received high values during and after World War II in both developed and developing nations. In the former countries, professionalization of public service reached the highest stage as bureaucratization of society increased and the role of government and state became more pronounced. This was even more important in underdeveloped and developing countries as these nations freed themselves from the yoke of colonialism and nation-building became a top priority for national development and independence. Nation-building was followed by institution-building, which meant development of infrastructure in society and bureaucratization and administrative capacity building for implementation of national goals. Building of administrative capacity also meant expansion of public service and the growth of the administrative state. In both developed and developing nations under capitalism, the administrative welfare state grew significantly in response to the increasing needs and demands of citizens.

The rise of the USSR and expansion of socialism also forced the capitalist nations to adopt mixed economies with a growing welfare state. The Cold War rivalry and competition between capitalism and socialism weakened both systems from within and made them more vulnerable to external pressures. Eventually, the fall of the USSR and other socialist states resulted in a reconsideration of societal, organizational, and economic arrangements. As the dominant type of economic system, capitalism appears to have risen to the top as the social and economic system in the world, with the United States and some European nations as the leaders of this global environment. Capitalist ideologies have claimed a supremacy of the marketplace, private enterprise system, and administrative rationality. However, this new global trend has at the same time been accompanied by the pressures from below by the mass of citizens who seek empowerment, smaller government and less governmental intrusion in their private lives, democratization of policy, citizenship, and public service. Everywhere, ordinary people resist the empty claims and pressures against public service institutions and demand corrective action through community and global solidarity movements.

The result has been a clash of political citizenship values on the one hand and the professional administrative values, on the other. Thus, public service has been badly damaged in terms of institutional capacity, quality, and public image. Corruption has also plagued public service, which has provoked massive resentment and protest against such practices. Resolving this conflict requires a reconciliation of, and exercise of, administrative ethics with citizenship ethics. It is through this integration that the image of public service can be revived and enhanced.

B. The Institutional Crisis

Institutional crisis appears when an institution loses credibility, organizational capacity, and ability to function as a viable institution in connection with its environment. An institution may lack organizational capacity, or an organization may exist but have been politically deinstitutionalized, or its time and viability may simply have passed. In any of these cases, an institutional crisis may be manifest. A market or a government may face institutional crisis when they either lack or lose organizational and legitimacy bases. Without organization and credibility, an institution is shaky and fragile, while an organization without institutionalization is much more fragile and subject to easy breakdown.

The public service values and images have been tarnished severely ever since the rise of the new global corporatism and its corollary strategic design of privatization, antigovernment and anti-bureaucracy, anti–civil service, and antieverything that is ''public'' around the world. This is a phenomenon that is totally unprecedented in modern history. Even the ancient civilizations of powerful empires and underdeveloped societies did not experience the current level of hostility toward what is ''public'' and public service and administration. Why? This is a big question that requires broad, theoretical, and philosophical answers.

To return to the central point of our discussion, the institutional crisis of public service began with the massive onslaught on public service, bureaucracy, and public administration since the 1980s. Led by two major representative speakers of the neocorporate elites of global capitalism, American, Ronald Reagan, and British, Margaret Thatcher, a global crusade was started with a global political economy agenda that aimed to fundamentally turn around the structural changes and transformations that had taken place for many decades in the twentieth century. They were the key speakers of the new global capitalist elites and of globalization that now demanded (1) sweeping privatization; (2) questioning the viability and values of public service through governmental organizations and institutional arrangements; (3) reconfiguration of organizational structures of society (public and private sectors); and (4) reduction of the modern state and public administration into a police state for social control, maintenance of order, and promotion of the surplus accumulation of capital, the ultimate objective of capitalism, dominated by globalizing financial capital.

As part of this globalization process, the modern states began experiencing numerous strategic deinstitutionalizations of the administrative state. This was done by both policy and administrative actions aimed at breaking the institutional capacity of the modern administrative state. It includes the social and economic areas long established and characterized as the welfare administrative state, and a massive ideological, psychological, and propagating onslaught on the legitimacy of the modern public service, administrative state, and public administration.

Through massive downsizing, reductions in force, destabilization of the civil service structure, businesslike reforms, and all out propaganda campaign against public service administration, with drastic cutbacks in public personnel and service expenditures, the institutional capacity of administration has been destroyed or seriously diminished. It is to the point of driving it to failure in order to support the false claims of market supremacy over the public sector. The net effect has been an effective strategic implementation of the deinstitutionalization of public service and administration and, consequently, a crisis of public service worldwide.

C. The Legitimacy Crisis

The legitimacy crisis has been featured by many aspects of the worldwide assault on public service and administration as inefficient, ineffective, unaccountable, undemocratic, unelected, bureaucratic, and wasteful. Much of these slandering assaults have come from the business sector, especially the business corporate elites, including the corporate media and press, but they also have come from critical organizational and management theorists who aspire to improve organizational life and to improve public service productivity, responsiveness, and accountability to citizens. However, the intellectual suppliers of this worldwide anti–public service and administration have been the neoclassical conservative economic advocates of the rational choice or ''public choice theory'' (see for example, Buchanan and Tullock 1962; Niskanen 1971; Savas 1987; and others).

The legitimacy crisis also has roots in the philosophical and conceptual grounds of the conservative Lockean view of antigovernment, private property and private business, and limited government intervention in the economy and society. Further, the legitimacy crisis is rooted in the political culture of the western Anglo-Saxon, Anglo-American, mostly American political culture in which private property and self-interested individualism as well as a culture of possessive consumerism prevail. This is a phenomenon propagated intensely by corporate, business, and power elites in pursuit of global dominance of market capitalism. The notion of public service, as it has existed and was cherished for several millennia, is generally alien to American culture. Therefore, public service and administration never became rooted in American political culture. Sadly, it is this corporate-dominated culture of anti–public service and administration that is now being imposed upon developing countries and less developed nations by various means of coercion—military, security, economic, social, and cultural—and through the globalization of economics and politics. Therefore, globalization of corporate capital and of the hegemonic state power of the United States and its European allies are transcending a global crisis of public service in favor of marketization, corporatization, privatization, and a self-interested, possessive capitalist culture.

IV. CAUSES AND CONSEQUENCES OF THE PUBLIC SERVICE CRISIS

Elsewhere (Farazmand 1989, 1997), I have discussed in some detail a number of factors that have contributed to the rise, growth, and expansion of the modern administrative state, with which also came an unprecedented degree of professionalization of public bureaucracy and public service. The role of governments in society, economy, and administration grew dramatically. Governments became the engines of national development, of private sector development, of providing public goods, and of solving problems as well as protecting individual rights.

Professionalization of the administrative state and public service has been a common phenomenon of both capitalism and socialism. In the capitalist countries, mixed economies grew and the domain of public-private sectors became gradually expanded, with a blurring of boundaries between the two sectors. The competing values of the public-private sectors also merged to an extent. Yet, the public service values and the commitment and aspirations of those pursuing to public service career remained strong. This was also the case in the United States and some other nations, where the rampant political corruption of the nineteenth and early twentieth centuries resulted in a major reform movement known as the Progressive movement. It sought to eliminate political and governmental corruption by the application of a modern bureaucratic and administrative rationality based on neutral competence, efficiency, and effectiveness.

These professional administrative values replaced much of the values of the earlier political machine systems prevalent around the nation. Then, professionalization of bureaucracy and civil service followed and resulted in the separation of politics and administration (Thayer 1997). The politics-administration dichotomy was a dominant mode and philosophy in the administrative state and public service (Van Riper 1997; Frederickson 1993). However, despite major improvements in public service delivery and in professionalization of public administration, another major dilemma was produced by the mythical dichotomy of politics and administration (Riggs 1994).

The dichotomy put professional administrators in a major position of vulnerability in that they should not be involved in policy decision making or be engaged in activities considered in the domain of politics, however defined. The democratic values of responsiveness, responsibility, and accountability became major political values claimed to be in conflict and clashed with the administrative values of professionalism, efficiency, and effectiveness. Consequently, despite the major earlier strands, the administrative state and the public service and administration came under attacks from an array of crusaders of political values of democracy.

These anti–public service, antibureaucracy, and antigovernment trends have had major ideological, political, social, and economic underpinnings beyond the space limitations of this chapter (see Farazmand 1989 for a detailed discussion). Consequently, a severe decline of the public service followed both in terms of institutional capacity and of its image in the United States and around the world. The result is a major crisis of public service and of professionalism in public administration around the world. The contributing critics of public service and administration came from many backgrounds, from left to right, and many factors contributed to this crisis.

A. Causes of the Public Service Crisis

The causes of the current worldwide crisis in the public service are many. Most of the factors or causes listed here are identified with terms beginning with the letter C. Some of these factors are macro, national, and even international and they influence shaping of the environment in which public service and administration are provided. Others are microspecific and relate to the profession of public service and public administration, organizationally, individually, and professionally. The ordering of these factors is arbitrary and does not reflect any significance.

1. Crisis of Legitimacy

This is a political and ideological crisis afflicting regimes and political systems in which the consent of people is not sought and the forms or styles of governance are accompanied by dictatorial rule with consequences including repression, corruption, and other manifestations of abuse of power. Regimes not enjoying legitimacy—the popular consent or perception and attitudes of citizens toward a government—often have little credibility among citizens, and the public service bureaucracy tends also to be perceived negatively by citizens. Lack of accountability, transparency, and responsiveness, compounded by moral and ethical scandals at highest levels of governmental leadership are few reasons why citizens form negative perceptions toward their governments. Simply put, citizens lose confidence and credibility in their governmental and corporate leadership. This has been manifest in the United States for the last 30 years (see Lipset 1987; Brown 2000).

Crisis of legitimacy also refers to the crisis or lingering problem of the administrative state in the United States, where its largeess and policy-making roles have been criticized by many. Legitimacy crisis has roots in the political culture of the American-dominated corporate power structure, which favors corporate, market capitalism and small government (see Henry 1995; Rosenbloom 1995). It also takes root in the philosophical grounds of the role of government in society, especially of the Lockean view of government. Governments and corporate elites around the world in both industrialized and developing countries suffer a crisis of legitimacy (Brown 2000; Lipset 1987), and this has contributed heavily to the current global crisis of public service and administration.

2. Corruption

Corruption is a multifaceted and pervasive phenomenon of many forms and degrees. A major impact of corruption is its immediate delegitimation effect on the government, regime, and state bureaucracy. The image of public service suffers seriously under a corrupt system of governance. Simply put, there is no trust in a government perceived to be corrupt. It also suffers when sectors of the public service are contaminated by corruption. Examples are the Department of Housing and Urban Development (HUD) scandals in the United States in the 1980s, bribery and other forms of corruption, the Pahlavi regime under the late shah of Iran, deposed by the popular revolution of 1978–79, or the Somoza regime in Nicaragua, and the Marcos regime in the Philippines. Other examples abound.

Corruption may also have a destabilization effect on governments and political regimes. Corruption in public service and administration may benefit a few people, but its negative effect on society's productivity is significant. Corruption also tends to widen the gap between rich and poor, therefore having an inequity and injustice effect. All forms of corruption take a big toll on the image of the public service and administration (Gould 1991). As a universal problem, corruption has been a major contributor to the current crisis of public service around the globe.

3. Capitalism

Capitalism has also contributed to both corruption and the public service crisis in at least two ways. It has promoted businesslike forms of corruption as a way to increase the bottom line. It has also induced forms of corruption in making contracts with public organizational elites. Bribery and kickbacks are but two examples. Conflict of interest is another common example. Few Americans know that, for example, the members of the legislature in Florida, as in most other states, can be and are on the payroll of private corporations. Since most of these legislators come from the well-to-do class of business/legal elites, their success in election has also been produced by strong support of the corporate power elites, who in turn expect or demand passage of laws favoring those class interests. Conflicts of interest are massively reported as private dealings and corporate representation disproportionately affects ordinary and poor citizens. The nature of capitalism promotes business induced corruption in various forms such as bribery, conflicts of interest, special favors, kickbacks, etc.

The second way in which capitalism has caused crisis in public service is the private, corporate sector's antigovernment, antibureaucracy, and probusiness slogans that have eroded the public service institutions' image and legitimacy. This has often been under the banner of business efficiency and free market choice (e.g., the public choice theorists' arguments; see Farazmand 1994a,b). The idea that "money talks" seems to have had an influence on peoples' perception of business and government bureaucrats dealing with private corporations, especially the "iron triangles."

Iron triangles (IT) have special places in capitalist societies. A typical IT is found, for example, in the department of defense, including the bureaucratic elites, related legislative members, and corporate business elites producing weapon systems. They are present in every policy area and dictate policy choices in favor of powerful business interests whose protection and promotion are directly linked to the main functions of governmental officials, from the top chief of state, the president or other form of leadership, to the lowest possible level of organizational hierarchy. Capitalism inherently promotes corruption and causes erosion of public service and administration. By nature, it is anti–public service because under capitalism the rich and business elites can afford to buy almost anything. Whereas the middle class and working lower classes as well as the poor who are unable to work are in serious need of public goods and services such as education, health, transportation, and enabling socioeconomic opportunities. The latter group cannot afford to buy these things in marketplace where money is the only purchasing power.

4. Cutbacks

Massive cutbacks in public sector expenditures have been a major, responsible factor contributing to the current crisis of public service and administration worldwide. Cutbacks in the public sector have occurred in at least five major forms: (1) cutbacks in public investments of infrastructure development, or public works; (2) massive cutbacks on social service programs necessary for sustenance of a large number of citizens in need of assistance; (3) cutbacks of organizational capacity such as personnel and operational expenditures; (4) cutbacks in institutional and operational capacities of governmental regulatory functions; and (5) cutbacks in the enabling role of government to provide economic and social opportunities for the vast majority of citizens. Cutbacks have hurt deeply public service and administration systems worldwide.

5. Communism

Communism provides equitable and massive public services, but equalization and leveling off sometimes are not valued by citizens who take them for granted and are enticed by anticommunism propaganda of the capitalist regimes. The inability of communism to effectively repel the capitalist regime propaganda, its lack of dynamism in producing luxury and appealing goods and services, and its preoccupation with self-defense and protection against the various forms of onslaught of capitalism, have made the system vulnerable.

Therefore, it has contributed to some degree to the current crisis of public service in two ways. Its lack of incentives for individual creativity and opportunity for personal development under some existing socialist systems has been compounded by the poverty-level standard of living. Often, public service is viewed by people as being poor in quality as opposed to the privately provided goods and services in mixed economies—regardless of the fact that most public services were provided free of charge. The fall of the leading socialist states, including especially the USSR, has also fueled the anti–public service and anti-bureaucracy fervor among peoples and private sector–corporate elites in capitalist nations.

6. Cost

Costs, especially cost overruns, have been a major cause of public service decline and crisis. Most governments of the world have been operating with significant budget deficits for the last decade or so. A national budget deficit has a major negative impact on the image of the public service. Cost overruns in government procurement and other activities—e.g., $700 for toiled seats in the Pentagon in the 1980s—badly tarnished the image of the bureaucracy and public service in the eyes of citizens.

Cost also means that monopolistic government bureaucracies are not efficient in delivering services, and that many public services are too costly, especially social services. These latter perceptions have often been fueled mainly by corporate business elite circles in order to discredit the public sector organizations, but the shortcomings and excesses or wastefulness of some government bureaucracies cannot be ignored; they must be exposed for transparency and accountability purposes.

7. Conflict of Interest

Conflict of interest arises when members of the public service engage in contractual or other governmental transactions with certain private contractors with whom the officials—both political and career—have private interests. Conflict of interest occurs in many forms, and they may contribute to major cost overruns.

8. Corporatism

This has been another cause of crisis in public service. It has promoted the corporate ideology of private enterprise against government regulation and administrative processes. Corporatism has roots in political economy in that its ideological underpinnings dictate corporations as the best and ideal form of organizational arrangement of society.

Corporatism also means corporations as the alternative to formal traditional governance and administration of economy, social services, and legal and professional establishments. Here government intervention may be desirable, under this notion, to help serve the interests of the dominant, corporate power structure which claims to run the economy and provide goods and services in the marketplace. Corporatism feeds on the rhetoric slogans of freedom, liberty, market, and financial gains. Yet, the fundamental question of corporatism begs the explanation of who benefits from these rosy concepts, average citizens or the privileged corporate elites and business class of rich and affluent? The latter benefits from the anti–public service and anti–public sector organizational arrangements because it is alien to the social and economic problems that the underprivileged or average citizens face on daily basis. The corporate ideology attempts to terminate the alternative concepts to the social and economic orders that may be attractive or utilitarian to a broad based populace. Simply put, it is a door shut to the world outside while classification inside is both constantly tightening or rigidified and opportunities tend to strangle the mass citizenry with ''a race to the bottom.''

In such a microcosmic world of corporate isomorphism, the broad ''public sphere'' in which social breathing allows common citizens to think and search for alternative identity is constantly shrinking in favor of ''idolism,'' a notion that subscribes to worshiping of repressive corporate idols in control of the destiny of masses of citizens. It is this isomorphous ''idolic corporatism'' that is both stifling and deepening the crises that have already reached a level of criticality worldwide with numerous manifestations in the environment, ecosystems, population, governance, and administration, and destructive migrations (Parenti, 1994; Weiner 1995). Only a massive punctuation of glacial magnitude is needed, and will be inevitable, to breakdown this idolic isomorphism. A heavy price will be paid by humanity before such a social breakdown occurs in this idolic corporatism, a phenomenon that social chaos theory attempts to explain. In the meantime, public service crisis will continue to deepen with casualties everywhere around the world (Brecher and Costello 1994).

9. Colonialism and Neocolonialism

Most developing countries were subjected to colonialism in the last centuries. Colonialism has left major legacies of economic, political, and bureaucratic corruption in newly independent nations, most of which lack a developed free market system, an indigenous administrative and civil service system, and an independent political elite. The result has been a de facto colonialism and continuation of the colonial bureaucratic presence in many nations of Africa and Asia. The public sector is often perceived as instruments of former colonial powers.

This phenomenon has also been observed in twentieth century countries experiencing neo-colonialism and imperialism. Many political, administrative, military, and business elites of these developing countries are under the heavy influence of the powerful Western powers such as the United States, Britain, and France. Many regimes in these nations are perceived by their people and intelligentsia as puppets of the foreign powers. Consequently, their state and bureaucratic systems lack popular legitimacy and credibility due to mass corruption and repressive behavior, as well as due to their subservience to foreign neocolonial powers. Consequently, their public service and administration are heavily affected by the global domination of corporate elites, and the globally dominating governing elites whose primary interests are promotion of financial accumulation of surplus capital and political-military control of the world, creating and promoting the isomorphous ideology of idolic corporatism worldwide.

10. Cold War

The Cold War also drained the institutional and fiscal capacities of the both capitalist and socialist systems. Indeed, the expansion of the public service and welfare state in capitalist nations with a mixed economy has been perceived and attacked as part of the ideological cold war strategy. The Cold War took a toll on the public service image—by being viewed as socialistic—in capitalist nations. The ideology of idolic corporatism had found the welfare state useful while at the same time it was opposed to its behavioral and structural consequences of public service and administration. This duality and conflicting feature of idolic corporatism has been embodied in American political culture that is shaped by corporate elites.

11. Culture

Some cultures have an inherent tendency to promote the anti–public service image. This is particularly true in countries like the United States, in which corporatism and private enterprise system appear to dominate the American individualistic and political culture. Unlike the case in other nations, public service has never been valued widely in the United States, where it is the weakest in the world. Idolic corporatism has planted very deeply a sense of antipublic and proindividualism in American culture, which is now also invading the world far beyond its territory (see, for example, Triandis 1995; Macpherson 1987; Bellah et al., 1985).

12. Commercialization and Commodification

These have similar effect on the public service image and legitimacy in the United States and many other nations. This trend appears to dominate the cultures and societies at a global level, but its origins are the United States and Britain. Commercialization and commodification have intellectual roots in the contemporary neo-conservative public choice (misleadingly called "public choice," while it should be called "elite choice" or "affluent choice") theory and practical roots in Anglo-American idolic corporatism with isomorphic manifestations. Money as an ultimate means of exchange and transaction process has become a gospel of all interactions and social relations, including of human body and soul, of culture and identity, of pride and existence, and everything else (see Parenti 1994 for the "land of idols in America").

Commercialization has degraded and devalued humanity and human dignity as well as all other phenomena and objects in the universe; objectification of all that exists and their valuation by commercial means of exchange, that is the price. Both intellectual and practical roots of commercialization and commodification have contributed to the current crisis of public service and administration, and they are being spread throughout the world by means of both global capital and global coercion of the hegemonic state power.

13. Consumerism

This is another ideological phenomenon dominating the current reforms and reinvention programs of governments and public service around the globe. It is a major by-product of the idolic corporatism, as well as being its major basis of expansion and promotion. Originated in the United States, this conservative, neoclassical, public-choice theory ideology places individual consumers at the center of the debate and claims a legitimacy for consumer sovereignty. Its market-oriented consumer ideology is being extended to the public sector forcing governments and public administrators to view people as consumers, not citizens or owners (Schachter 1997).

This public-choice ideological perspective has in fact degraded citizenship and reduced citizens to consumers in the marketplace. The result has been the loss of trust in and appreciation for public service, especially those services and goods that are not quantifiable, measurable, and have no price tags, such as police protection, defense, social services, professor-student and doctor-patient relationships and the like. As an ideological extension of idolic corporate capitalism, consumerism is advanced to a level of false identity with individual fantasies for perceived ultimate power and control. In such an artificial environment, idolic corporatism thrives and feeds on mass citizenry with short term, partial and "only now" means of subsistence turning them into consuming animals (like pigs; the more they are fed, they more meet they produce for sale and profit). This would allow the inventories of the idolic corporatism to produce more for further consumption and further surplus accumulation of capital. Consequently, the rich get richer and the poor get poorer.

Once unable to consume, unable to work as wage slave, the modern ordinary citizen is reduced to disposable objects that can be auctioned in the real world of commodity consumerism, where others can offer pennies in exchange for bodies and souls through prostitution, drug dealings, and wage slavery. The utility of mass human beings stops when they are no longer useful to surplus accumulation of capital under idolic corporatism. The public service and administration crisis deepens as consumerism is expanded ideologically and practically worldwide.

14. The Confidence Gap

The erosion and loss of public confidence in governments, democratic as well as authoritarian, and in their governing elites has also contributed to the erosion of the public service image, the institutional and legitimacy crisis worldwide. Although this confidence gap has been experienced in private sector leadership (Lipset 1987), it is the public service that has suffered the most (Farazmand 1989).

Much of this confidence gap is rooted in the legitimacy crisis in corporate and government leadership in the capitalist world, but it has been masked by events and changes in other global socioeconomic and political systems; thus, the spillover of the masked crises to public service and administration has been both expansive and profound. Hard at work, the globalizing idolic corporatism has obstructed continuing historical progress through various systems and has at least temporarily claimed a global hegemony. This confidence gap cannot be filled by injection of more idolic symbolism, as people around the world demand substantive improvement in their lives, communities, and the quality of the environment that must sustain them. The result is a continuing crisis of public service, and there is no break in sight.

15. Careerism

This has also caused public service crisis in that many self-serving and self-conserving bureaucrats are engaged in activities or inactivities aimed at preserving and promoting personal careers at any cost. This has at times been at the expense of public service, public interests, therefore contributing to the loss of public trust in the civil servants who may be viewed as guardians of public interests. Many senior civil servants refused to speak up or resist the political pressures and intimidation tactics of the Regan presidency simply to protect their "careers." By refusing to act professionally against immoral, illegal, or unethical political decisions of their bosses, these career civil servants simply violated their basic professional principles and compromised their professional integrity and trusteeship of general public interests.

Similarly, many Danish bureaucrats who cooperated with the Nazi forces during the occupation may be viewed as violating their ethical and moral principles as professional administrators. In the eyes of many citizens, many civil servants are viewed as careerists who are after their personal interests only. Certainly, the public-choice theorists as well as corporate elites, including of the media, have strongly perpetuated this idea. Careerism is a major delegitimating problem in public service. Similarly, carelessness on the part of some public servants has contributed to the crisis of public service.

16. Coercion and Control

By nature, most public organizations are coercive in their relationship with the public. The argument that the public/citizens have become the captives of the administrative state has received considerable attention of experts on modern public administration (Rosenbloom 1995). As a result, citizens have been learning to become a bureaucratic-self in order to deal effectively with the governmental bureaucrats (Rosenbloom 1995). The coercive behavior of public organizations emanates from the monopolistic and authoritative nature of government. Citizens have little choice but to pay the required taxes and dues.

The bureaucratic nature of most public organizations makes them highly control oriented. Organizational control performs essential functions of system maintenance and system enhancement in modern governance and administration. However, overcontrolled-oriented organizations tend to become dysfunctional and long-run delegitimizers. Examples are the Shah's regime in Iran and Marcos's regime in the Philippines. Simply stated, public bureaucracies become instruments of regime enhancement at the expense of public interests and citizen welfare (Farazmand 1989, 1997).

17. Clientelism

A major feature of the "iron triangle" operation, this has also fed to the problem of corruption, conflict of interest, and preferential treatment leading to organizational injustice and abuse of public trust. Clientelism seems to have dominated the political process and the power elite configurations in the United States and most other capitalist nations. Clientelism serves particularistic, private, and strong interest groups at the expense of the broad general public interests. It is discriminatory and unfair, and erodes the public trust in government and its administrators.

18. Character and Conduct

Problems of morality have also been major contributing factors in the public service image crisis. Official conduct and the personal character of public officials—both political and career—are significant symbols of public trust: good character and conduct present a positive image in public service while bad character and unethical conduct portray negative images of public service and administration; they have negative impacts on governance and administration, with implications for system legitimacy. It is absolutely inconceivable for citizens to expect high public officials to be engaged in immoral and unethical behavior such as sexual scandals in public office, as President Bill Clinton did, or others may have done.

These are prime examples of violations of public trust, public confidence, and conduct as well as character. But unethical sexual behaviors are not the only examples of poor character or conduct; diverting public resources to and simply engaging in organization and support of criminal organizations and training criminals to destroy villages, kill innocent people, and destabilize economies and political systems of other nations personally deemed unfriendly is another violation of ethical conduct at the international level. No system can claim to be democratic while at the same time thwarting legitimate democratic governments and violating the democratic human rights of citizens outside of its boundaries, no matter what the rationale would be.

Western capitalist democracies have engaged in numerous bloody interventions in developing countries against legitimate and democratically elected public figures whose policies and preferences had favored indigenous national public interests rather than foreign multinational corporate interests. Under various pretexts, the United States and many western Europeans powers have supported some of the most repressive and fascist regimes in the world. By implication, therefore, the concepts of good character and ethical conduct can and should also apply to national governmental behavior as well as to the individual public official's personal behavior.

19. Civil Service Crisis

This has also occurred as a result of many forces attacking public bureaucracy and the administrative or welfare state. The largesse of the administrative state in the twentieth century aroused significant oppositions from left to right who criticized it on different grounds. Politicians, academics, media reporters, press, and the general public all have contributed to the decline and crisis of civil service in many countries around the world, including the United States. Their main argument has focused on the fact that career civil servants are nonelected officials who enjoy job security and are not accountable for their actions, and that they are involved in policy making as well as implementation, and this is undemocratic.

Such an argument has come from a variety of academic and political circles from the mainstream to the right circles (see, for example, Wilson 1986; Mosher 1968; and the public choice theorists such as Buchanan and Tulluck 1963; Downs 1962; Niskanen 1971; and Ostrom 1973; for details of this theoretical literature, see Farazmand 1997, 1989). The crisis in civil service has automatically contributed to the crisis in public service around the world. The more recent challenge to civil service systems has come from the conservative corporate ideological basis of idolic capitalism and market-based values. These values include efficiency at any cost to public interests, temporary and contractual employment, disregard for civil service protection, wage-earning jobs, abolition of job security, abolition of employee unions, and disregard for politic responsiveness and political responsibility in serving the public interests.

The whole notion of the civil service system has come under question or abolition. The U.S. 1978 Civil Service Reform Act was a prime example of turning right toward conservative, businesslike, public personnel system in which the civil service system is pushed to the back burner in favor of maximizing market values of efficiency and privatization of public services for profit accumulation of capital, again, enhancing the idolic corporate capitalism. This ideological trend is now being pushed worldwide as globalization and global privatization are being implemented.

20. Privatization

Privatization has been a global strategy of globalization process which has been transforming the entire world of nations, their governments, and their cultures into a corporate capitalism of grand scale. Armed with antigovernment, antibureaucracy, anti–public service forces and in favor of businesslike organizations, market corporatism, and private sector values, privatization of public services and of public enterprises began to take a global crusade in the early 1980s. Pursued by two conservative right-wing political representatives of the big, globalizing corporate elites, American President Ronald Reagan and British Prime Minister Margaret Thatcher started the crusade of transforming the public sector into an expanded realm of the corporate sector claiming a global domain with no restriction.

A number of supranational organizations, such as the International Monetary Fund (IMF), the World Bank (WB), and the World Trade Organization (WTO) have been used by the U.S. government as powerful instruments to force developing countries and European nations into this global strategy of capitalist transformation. This global trend of privatization has had devastating consequences for public service and administration worldwide, shrinking the public sector, undermining the institutional capacity of governments to perform their key functions, and causing a severe crisis in legitimacy, performance, and image of the public service and administration (see Farazmand, 1999b for details on privatization). If privatization has been bad for public service, then globalization, as it has already done, will continue to cut deep into many aspects of governance, administration, and what has traditionally been considered public service and administration.

21. Globalization

Globalization has become a worldwide phenomenon with transcending forces of integration aimed at global restructuring around the ideological corporate capitalism with accompanying global governance and cultural convergence. Different perspectives and meanings of globalization explain the concept, but the most important and common of all is the concept of globalization of capital accumulation by globalizing firms and transnational corporations that do not recognize territorial boundaries and market products through multiple sources of technological means.

Through global factories, global production, global marketing, and global financing, transnational corporations are now able, with the aid of the technological innovations, to make transactions anywhere in the world instantaneously. They are backed and promoted by the globalizing powerful state of the United States and other powerful allies with their military and security might, intimidating developing nations and crushing any government or group in their way for surplus accumulation of capital at rapid rates. Although nothing is new about globalization, for it has been around for many decades, it is the rapid rate of profit maximization by transnational corporations that has made globalization a political and economic phenomenon that never existed before.

A key requirement of globalization is facilitation or way-paving through the global strategies of privatization, deregulation, de-governmentalization and shrinkage of the public sector to the bone, limiting the government role to policing and social control, corporatization, marketization, cheap labor forces, cheap natural resources, and structural reforms in favor of corporate business operations without constraints. The forces of global finance, backed and promoted by the United States and other big and powerful capitalist governments, enter anywhere on the globe they deem profitable and leave whenever they decide, leaving behind destruction in labor structure, environment, economy, and community. Consequently, globalization has caused one of the most severe sources of global crisis in public service and administration. This is a trend that will likely continue for many years to come. Degradation of the human condition, destruction of the ecological system, deterioration of living conditions of the working people, and reduction of human beings into disposable market commodities have forced millions of global citizens into a "race to the bottom" (see Farazmand 1999a, Korten 1995, and Brecher and Costello 1994 for details on globalization).

22. Other Trends Deepening the Public Service Crisis

The current global trends that have further deepened the public service crisis may be identified by the following D's and R's: The D's include deregulation, decentralization and devolution, debureaucratization, degovernmentalization, and democratization. The R's of public service and governments have included reinvention, reinstitutionalization, realignment, and reconfiguration of public-private sector boundaries, reengineering, reparticipation of the public in decision making, reorganization of the bureaucracy, redefinition of the term *public* in society and administration, reform of governmental and administrative systems including the civil service system making it more businesslike, reinstitutionalization, redevelopment, readjustment, and more. These have been the phenomena of government reform since the late 1970s, but especially since 1980s. Central to all these problems and causes of the current public service crisis has been a problem of corruption, calling for an ethical movement in public service and administration around the globe.

B. Consequences of the Crisis

Consequences of the current global crisis in public service and administration are many, some of which have already been touched upon throughout this chapter. Briefly stated, public sector infrastructures are in the process of destruction, a trend that will continue as long as the major causes of the crisis are not abated. These public infrastructures have evolved over thousands of years and they have been made possible by sacrifices in human lives as well as in massive investments by various societies; their development has been imperative for sustaining and growth of human civilizations. Without such public infrastructures, no stability and no prosperity could have been achieved. They have up to recently sustained and promoted the viability of private businesses as well as public sector institutions.

But these public infrastructures are now under severe threat of destruction for profit accumulation purposes. Moreover, humanity and citizenship are in danger as everyone and everything is now put up for grabs in the marketplace. Health, education, and economic and social opportunities are squeezed and will be lost to the vast majority of citizens and their children who comprise the brains and labor forces of the future civilizations. Obviously, not everyone or every nation is affected equally by the destructive crisis under way; citizens of the less developed nations will suffer most.

The gap between the north and the south will be widened very deeply, and the gap between rich and poor among all nations will also enlarge, making it very difficult if not impossible for the average, hard-working citizens to sustain a decent life. Consequently, more institutions of family and community will break down in the wake of market chaos, causing further crises in societies. The future generations will suffer, but the few powerful business elites and their children will be enhanced by all opportunities in politics, education, administration, governance, and control of resources. They are the few who rule the many (Parenti 1995). Humanity is heading for a return back to medieval feudalism (Korbin 1986), a socioeconomic system characterized by few ruling feudal barons, a mass of serfs unable to change their destiny, and a village surrounded by other feudal villages, and so on. Today, the global village is ruled by few corporate elites and the global governing elites/barons are ruling the world; there is little or no opportunity to escape. Until 1990, the two world systems—capitalism led by the United States and socialist systems led by the USSR—checked each other's excesses and their rivalry served global citizens with a degree of calculated, and fragile, security and a minimum extent of public service in the capitalist world. With the fall of that superpower, there is no matching power to stand the abuses of the globalizing corporate barons and the exploitative, anti–public service wall of the colonizing hegemonic power of the western capitalism under the U.S. corporate leadership. Despite some positive consequences of this new global world order and corporate hegemony, critics argue, the road to serfdom is widening and shortening, unless something is done locally, nationally, and globally (Korten 1995; Farazmand 1999a). Unless a global movement of human networks for resistance and reversal of the process takes place, which I believe is inevitable and is already in progress, the road to serfdom for billions of people will be shortened even faster.

V. CONCLUSION

There is a global crisis in public service and administration. To some, especially to the neoconservatives and establishment oriented theorists and practitioners, there is no such a thing as a crisis. To them, the new conservative view of public service and administration is summarized in the ''new public management,'' and ideological rhetoric of business managerialism applied to public sector, shrinking it to the bone, stripping it from institutional and financial capacity, and setting it up for failure. This is a global strategy of corporatization, privatization, marketization, and commercialization that is pursued by powerful corporate elites who have captured all realms of life, society, economy, and public service. It is a global strategy to capture all public realms and to turn human citizens into consumers of corporate products, for more profits, more surplus accumulation of capital, and in doing so has reduced citizens of the world into ''consumer pigs,'' feeding them with as much as possible to make fatter for more profit return.

The global crisis in public service is felt institutionally, financially, politically, organizationally, and psychologically. The global crisis of public service and administration is accompanied and accentuated by other crises facing societies both in the West and East. Crisis in education, family, health, community structure, and other areas are only manifestations of the global crisis caused and perpetuated by the small corporate elites, whose global design of corporate hegemony is set to conquer the entire world and its population, turning them into disposable objects for profit accumulation.

The global crisis of public service and administration can be cured if there is a global brake on the greedy and destructive forces of corporate capitalism. This globalizing destructive force of late capitalism has swept away whatever was achieved over decades and even centuries for the general welfare of societies, their average people, and their social systems so that a general harmony could be achieved by the majority of citizens. The welfare administrative state was in part responsible for providing a safety net for the poor and underprivileged, so that the upper class elites could enjoy the benefits of tranquility, peace, and prosperity. With the fall of the USSR as the leader of the socialist world, which had at least served as a deterring force against the excesses of globalizing corporate elites, there are no global checks deterring the new giant power structure of globalizing transworld corporate elites who have made claim on all corners of the world as their realm of profit seeking crusade.

Public service has been sacrificed for private elite interests, and public means are being used for private corporate ends. In this process, governments are forced by both home supporting governments of the globalizing states—such as the U.S. government—and the local subsidiaries (read the business and military elites) to facilitate this globalizing exploitation of public means for private ends, using governmental forces—police, military might, and media propaganda—to promote this global crusade against average, hardworking citizens of the globe. The consequences will catch up the entire globe—including the powerful and shameless elites—and everywhere through epidemics, crises in education and health care, family destruction, increased violence, crimes, and imprisonment of society and people, including especially in the United States and western Europe.

The current trend of global crisis in public service and administration can be turned around by exerting grass-roots pressures from below, by people around the world. Governments need also to revisit their policy options and must play the role of an enabling environment for self-organizing organizations and institutions, for citizens to challenge both corporate and government institutions, and to exercise their democratic rights of self-determination. There are many ways to start, and this chapter has mentioned a few.

REFERENCES

Ban C. (2000). The crisis of morale and federal senior executives. In M. Holzer (ed.), *Public Service: Callings, Commitments, and Contributions*. Boulder, CO: Westview Press.

Bellah R., Madson R., Sullivan W., Swiddler A., Tipton S. (1985). *Habits of the Heart: Individualism and Commitment in American Life*. Berkeley, CA: University of California Press.

Brecher J., Costello T. (1994). *Global Village or Global Pillage*? Boston: South End Press.

Brown P. (2000). The legitimacy crisis and the new progressivism. In M. Holzer (ed.), *Public Service: Callings, Commitments, and Contributions*. Boulder, CO: Westview Press/ASPA, pp. 105–111.

Buchanan J., Tullock G. (1962). *The Calculus of Consent*. Ann Arbor, MI: University of Michigan Press.

Caiden G. (1991). Administrative reform. In A. Farazmand (ed.), *Handbook of Comparative and Development Public Administration*. New York: Marcel Dekker, pp. 367–380.

Caiden G. (1994). Getting at the essence of the administrative state. In A. Farazmand (ed.), *Handbook of Bureaucracy*. New York: Marcel Dekker, pp. 65–78.

Downs A. (1967). *Inside Bureaucracy*. Boston: Little & Brown.

Gould D. (1991). Administrative corruption: Incidence, causes, and remedial strategies. In A. Farazmand (ed.), *Handbook of Comparative and Development Public Administration*. New York: Marcel Dekker, pp. 467–483.

Farazmand A. (1989). "Crisis in the U.S. administrative state." *Administration & Society* 21(2), 173–199.

Farazmand A. (1991). State Tradition and public administration in Iran in ancient and modern perspectives. In A. Farazmand (ed.), *Handbook of Comparative and Development Public Administration*. New York: Marcel Dekker, pp. 255–272.

Farazmand A. (1994a). Organization theory: An overview and appraisal. In A. Farazmand (ed.), *Modern Organizations: Administrative Theory in Contemporary Society*. Westport, CT: Praeger, pp. 1–54.

Farazmand A. (1994b). The new world order and global public administration: A critical analysis. In J.-C. Garcia-Zamor R. Khator (eds.), *Public Administration in A Global Village*. Westport, CT: Praeger, pp. 62–81.

Farazmand A. (1997). Institutionalization of the new administrative state/role: A political economy analysis. Paper presented at the Annual National Conference of the American Political Science Association (APSA), Washington, DC, September 1–4.

Farazmand A. (1999a). Globalization and public administration. *Public Administration Review* 57(*6*), 209–222.

Farazmand A. (1999b). "Privatization or reform? Public enterprise management in transition. *International Review of Administrative Sciences* 65, 551–567.

Finer H. (1990). Administrative responsibility in democratic government. In W. Richter et al. (eds.), *Combating Corruption, Encouraging Ethics*. Washington, DC: ASPA, p. 44.

Frederickson G. (1994). Research and knowledge in administrative ethics. In T. Cooper (ed.), *Handbook of Administrative Ethics*. New York: Marcel Dekker, pp. 31–46.

Friedrick C. J. (1990). Public policy and the nature of administrative responsibility. In W. Richter et al. (eds.). *Combating Corruption, Encouraging Ethics: A Sourcebook for Public Service Ethics*. Washington, DC: American Society for Public Administration (ASPA), pp. 43–44.

Gould D. (1991). Administrative corruption: Incidence, causes, and remedial strategies. In Farazmand A. (ed.), *Handbook of Comparative and Development Public Administration*. New York: Marcel Dekker, pp. 467–483.

Hummel R. (1987). *Bureaucratic Experience* 3rd ed. New York: St. Martin's Press.

Korbin S. (1986). Back to the future: Medievalism and the postmodern digital economy. *Journal of International Affairs* 52(2), 367–409.

Korten, D. (1995). *When Corporations Rule the World*. West Hartford, CT: Kumarian Press.

Levine C. and Kleeman R. (1988). The quiet crisis of the civil service: The federal personnel system at the crossroads. Occasional paper. Washington, DC: National Academy of Public Administration.

Lipset, S. (1987). The confidence gap during the Reagan years: 1981–1987. *Political Science Quarterly (spring)*, 1–23.

Macpherson C. B. (1987). *The Rise and Fall of Economic Justice*. New York: Oxford University Press.

Mosher, F. (1986). *Democracy and the Public Service*, 2nd ed. New York: Oxford University Press.

Niskanen W. (1971). *Bureaucracy and Representative Government*. Chicago: Aldein Atherton.

Peters G. (1994). Government reorganization: A theoretical analysis. In A. Farazmand (ed.), *Handbook of Bureaucracy*. New York: Marcel Dekker, pp. 165–182.

Ostrom V. (1974). *Intellectual Crisis in American Public Administration*. University, AL: University of Alabama Press.

Parenti M. (1994). *Land of Idols*. New York: St. Martin's Press.

Parenti M. (1995). *Democracy for the Few*, 6th ed. New York: St. Martin's Press.

Riggs F. (1994). Global forces and the discipline of public administration. In J.-C. Garcia-Zamor and R. Khator (eds.), *Public Administration in A Global Village*. Westport, CT: Praeger, pp. 17–44.

Rosenbloom D. (1995). *Public Administration: Understanding Management, Law, and Politics*.

Savas P. (1987). *Privatization: The Key to Better Government*. Chatham, NJ: Chatham House.

Thayer F. (1997). The U.S. Civil Service: 1883–1978 (I.R.P.). In A. Farazmand (ed.), *Modern Systems of Government: Exploring the Role of Bureaucrats and Politicians*. Thousand Oaks, CA: Sage Publications, pp. 95–124.

Triandis H. (1995). *Individualism and Collectivism*. Boulder, CO: Westview Press.

Van Riper P. (1997). The Pendleton Act of 1883 and the professionalization in the U.S. public service, in A. Farazmand (ed.), *Modern Systems of Government: Exploring the Role of Bureaucrats and Politicians*. Thousand Oaks, CA: Sage Publications, pp. 196–211.

Waldo D. (1980/1990). *The Enterprise of Public Administration*. Navota, CA: Chandler & Sharp Publisher.

Weber M. (1946). *From Max Weber: Essays in Sociology*. H. H. Gert and C. Wright Mills (trans. and eds.). New York: Oxford University Press.

Weber M. (1984). Bureaucracy. In F. Fischer and C. Cirianni (eds.), *Critical Studies in Organization and Bureaucracy*. Philadelphia: Temple University Press.

Weiner, M. (1995). *The Global Migration Crisis: Challenge to States and to Human Rights*. New York: Harper Collins.

Wilson, J. Q. (1986). "The Bureaucratic State," in P. S. Nivolas and D. H. Rosenbloom (eds.), *Classic Readings in American Politics*. New York: St. Martin's Press.

9
Immigrants, Refugees, and the Affordable Housing Crisis in South Florida

Margaret S. Murray Department of Urban and Regional Planning, Florida Atlantic University, Fort Lauderdale, Florida

I. INTRODUCTION

A significant demographic change occurring in the United States today is related to the influx of refugees and immigrants during the past several years. Because of changes in immigration legislation that formerly favored European immigrants, more immigrants today come from developing countries in Latin America and Asia. In the 1950s, less than one-third of the legal immigrants came from these areas,by the 1980s this number exceeded 80%. A large percentage of these immigrants are attracted to traditional port-of-entry states and cities. The number and nature of these immigrant households affects the demand for housing, particularly in the states that have received a large proportion of newcomers—California, Texas, and Florida (Frey 1996). Moreover, many of these recent immigrants lack the education or the job-related skills needed to obtain employment that will provide the resources needed to live in these areas and to secure adequate housing without some type of financial assistance. Continual pressure on low-income housing markets has created a housing crisis related to the affordability, quality, and crowding of housing units in these states.

The purpose of this chapter is to consider the potential effect of recent U.S. federal legislation on the ability of immigrants to secure adequate, affordable housing. The legislation has raised the possibility of making the housing crisis much more difficult to manage. If immigrants lose some or all of their existing welfare support, we must consider how they will deal with the problem of obtaining affordable housing. This chapter focuses on one of the areas in the United States receiving a significant flow of immigrant newcomers, southeastern Florida. After considering the affordable housing crisis and its effect on the immigrant population, a summary of immigration trends both nationally and in the state of Florida is presented. The next section focuses on federally sponsored welfare programs in the United States and on new federal legislation directed at incoming as well as resident immigrants. This is followed by a brief review of literature relevant to the housing issues of affordability, quality, and crowding, with particular emphasis on the housing of minority populations. The final section examines the potential impact of the new federal legislation on the housing situation of immigrant households in southeastern Florida and offers some suggestions for managing the housing crisis.

II. IMMIGRANTS AND THE AFFORDABLE HOUSING CRISIS

When we consider the word *crisis*, we usually think about a problem that demands immediate resolution. However, unlike many crisis situations, housing solutions take a long time to work out. For example, while the demand for housing may increase at a fairly rapid rate, the supply of housing increases much more slowly. Developers must perceive that the demand exists, land must be made suitable for development, and financing must be arranged. Even then, housing takes a relatively long time to construct. Meanwhile, prices increase and families tend to seek short-term solutions to the problem. Selecting a smaller housing unit or one of lower quality are two of these solutions. In spite of the length of time that it takes to solve housing problems, the word *crisis* is commonly used in reference to housing.

A more immediate aspect of the housing crisis involves households that either do not have the income to support available housing or lose jobs and are faced with eviction from their housing units. Zarembka (1990), in her book *The Urban Housing Crisis*, sees the housing situation as an affordability crisis exacerbated by problems of displacement and discrimination. Displacement occurs when housing formerly available to low-income households is demolished or revitalized. Demolition usually reduces the overall number of units, while revitalization makes them unavailable to low-income persons.

The housing crisis impacts recent immigrants in a number of ways. In addition to the difficulties associated with finding employment that produces sufficient earnings to pay for housing, immigrants may not understand U.S. housing markets and may be further limited by language barriers. Racial and ethnic discrimination is prevalent. Immigrants may not perceive housing options available to them and may seek the ease associated with living in ethnic enclaves in spite relatively high cost and poor quality.

III. IMMIGRATION TRENDS

The present level of immigration has led to apprehension over the United States' ability to assimilate large numbers of aliens. The demographic impact of this flow raises concerns about employment, health, education, and housing. Although the impact of immigration is not equally distributed across the country, the concern seems widespread. This section is included to acquaint the reader with the trend in immigration both nationally and in the state of Florida.

A. National Trends

The number of immigrants entering this country yearly during the past 30 years has grown substantially, reaching a high of 1.8 million in 1991. This number includes 1.1 million aliens currently residing in the country who became permanent residents under the provisions of the Immigration Reform and Control Act of 1986 (INS 1996). According to the Immigration and Naturalization Services (INS), the number of legal immigrants coming into the country in 1995 was 720,496. This number increased by 27% in 1996, to 915,900, including 128,565 refugees. In addition to legal immigrants and refugees, illegal or undocumented aliens constitute a sizable portion of nonnatives residing in this country. While not directly considered in the context of this chapter, it is important to note that estimates place them at around 25% of the total alien population.

The rapid increase in the immigrant population came about for two primary reasons. Amendments to the 1952 Immigration and Nationality Act that were passed in 1965 identified family reunification as the main preference category for entry, and the overall number of visas was substantially increased. Another factor contributing to the rapid growth of the foreign-born population in the United States was the number of refugees entering the country. Refugees now constitute 7% of the alien population, in contrast to a much smaller percent of earlier groups. The early refugee flows were largely Cuban and Indo-Chinese (Jensen 1989). More recently, refugee groups include Amerasians and their families from Vietnam, members of the former Soviet Union, and people from Laos, Romania, Ethiopia, Cuba, and Iran (Sullivan 1992). Until 1965, the dominant justification for granting entry into the United States was tied to employment-based skills. During that period, established quotas favored European immigrants.

B. Trends in Florida

The alien population tends to concentrate geographically in a limited number of urban areas in the port-of-entry states. Florida, one of the high-immigration states, attracted 62,023 aliens in 1995 and 79,461 in 1996. This represents more than 10% of all aliens coming into the country in those years.[1] Of the 1996 immigrants, 41,527 (52.3%) indicated the intention to reside in Miami and 10,290 (13%) indicated locating in Fort Lauderdale (INS 1997). This classifies the Miami–Fort Lauderdale area as a high-immigration area. This is an area containing large numbers of immigrants participating in low-paid service and unskilled blue-collar occupations (Frey 1996). The largest percentage of 1995 immigrants coming into south Florida are from Cuba: 28%. Haitians make up the second largest group at 9.8%.

The total immigrant population in Florida is extremely diverse but heavily weighted toward newcomers from Latin American countries. Figure 1 illustrates this diversity. This

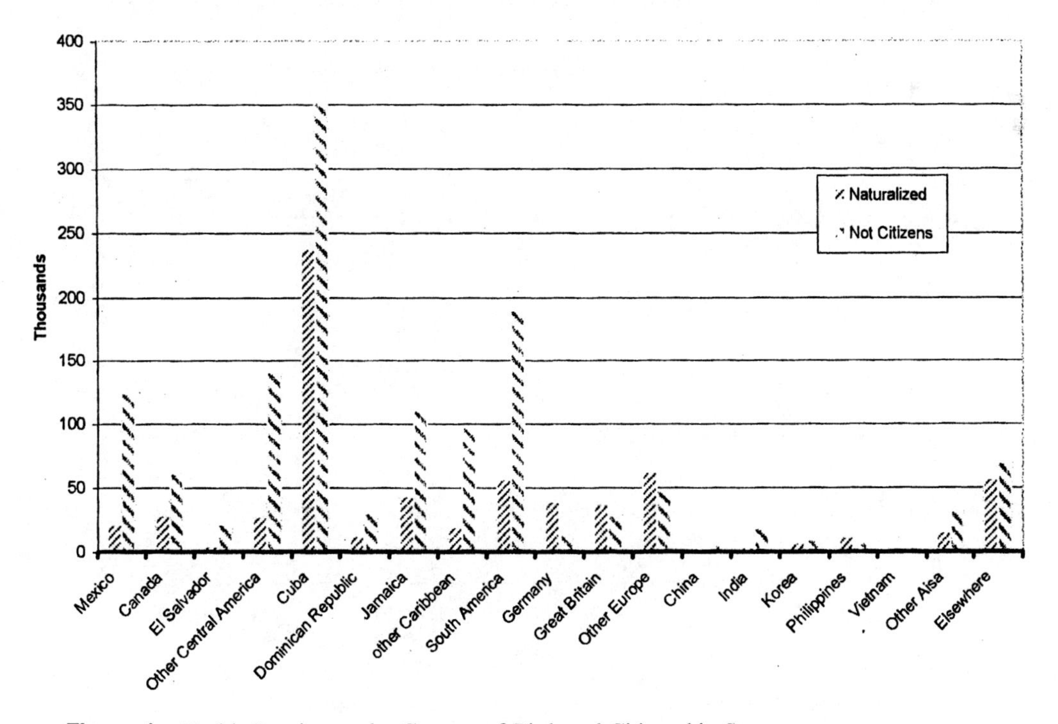

Figure 1 Florida Immigrants by Country of Birth and Citizenship Status.

figure identifies the country of origin for non-native-born residents of Florida in 1995. Also indicated in the figure is the relationship between the number of immigrants who are naturalized citizens and those who remain noncitizens. Various theories speculate on reasons for the large number of noncitizen immigrants. One theory suggests that many immigrants of Cuban origin see themselves as exiles who plan to return to Cuba once Castro is no longer in power. Another theory gives more consideration to the characteristics of many of these immigrants and suggests that age, infirmity, and lack of language skills prevents them from acquiring the knowledge necessary to meet the requirements for citizenship.

Figure 2 further explains citizenship status by illustrating the number of immigrants living in Florida by year of entry who have become naturalized citizens. Newcomers must reside in the United States for a minimum of 5 years prior to applying for citizenship. In addition to the residency requirement, they must pass an examination based on U.S. history and American government. Following recent federal legislation affecting legal immigrants' ability to qualify for various welfare benefits, a large number of eligible immigrants applied for citizenship and were naturalized.

C. Immigrant Poverty Levels

Numerical data do appear to support a greater incidence of poverty among immigrants arriving in this country after 1965 (Jensen 1989) than among pre-1965 immigrants or in the native population. This apparent increased level of poverty fuels concern that immi-

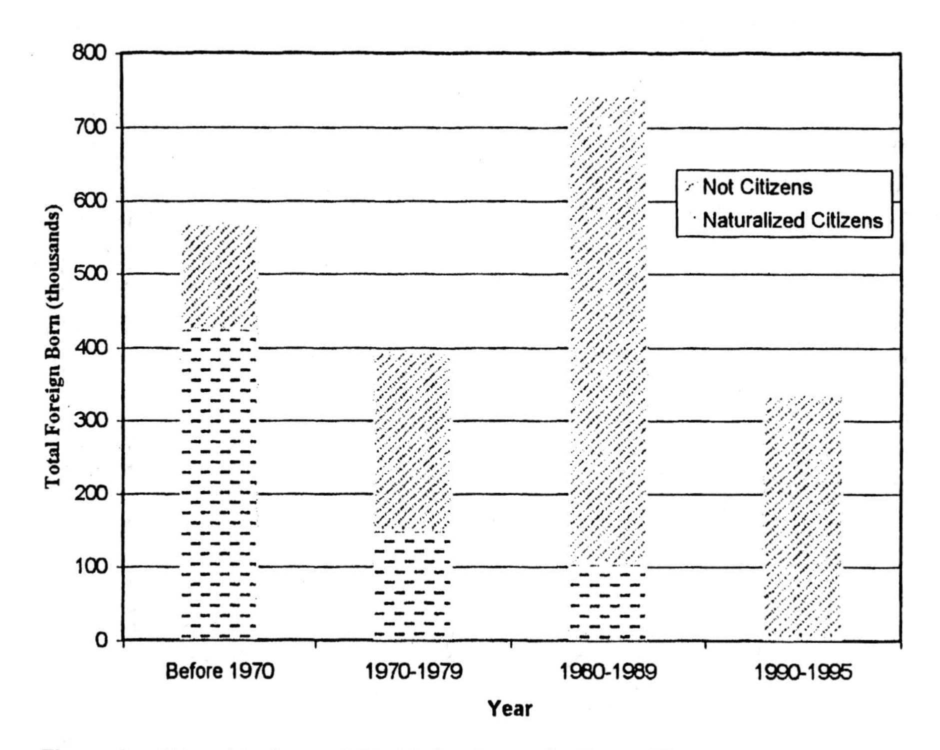

Figure 2 Citizenship Status of Florida Immigrants by Year of Entry.

grants may place a higher burden on public assistance programs than they return in taxes, thus causing a net drain on public resources.

Figure 3 indicates the percent of immigrants classed as poor in relation to their year of entry. From this chart, we see that poverty status is highest for the most recent immigrants; however, the percentage of immigrants below poverty is lower for naturalized citizens for all years. In comparison, slightly more than 14% of the native-born population are below the poverty level. When we consider all years of entry prior to 1990, the naturalized citizens are as well off or slightly better off than the native population. These numbers are analyzed further in an in-depth analysis conducted by Francine Blau (1984). She examined the immigrant poverty issue and found that, over time, immigrants are less likely to receive public assistance than are a comparable group of natives.

Assimilation theory suggests that immigrants are transitionally poor. That is, their poverty status is brief, not chronic. Once culture and language adjustments are accomplished, immigrants become able to provide for themselves and their families on a par with natives (Segalman and Basu 1981). This theory reflects the traditional view of the United States as the land of opportunity. While this is a fairly romanticized view of opportunities available to the immigrant population, it does seem to be true for many of Florida's immigrants. Although the rate of poverty for immigrants residing in this country for 5 years or less is almost 40%, the average poverty rate for those living here more that 5 years is considerably lower. However as noted in Table 1, there is a substantial difference in poverty rates for naturalized and nonnaturalized immigrants. The latter group exhibits a substantially higher poverty level for all entry periods except the 5-year period from 1990 to 1995. In this period, the number of naturalized citizens is very low owing to their general ineligibility for citizenship. The higher poverty rate coupled with the noncitizen status may indicate a lack of assimilation in the noncitizen group.

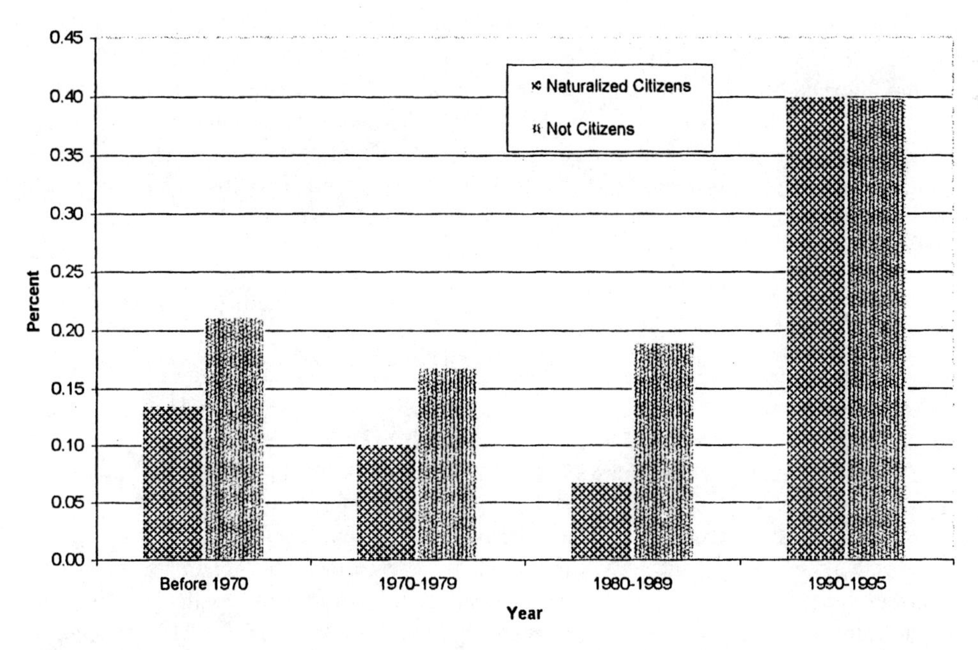

Figure 3 Poverty Status of Florida Immigrants in 1994 by Year of Entry.

Table 1 Percent of Florida Immigrants Below the Poverty Level by Year of Entry

	Before 1970	1970–1979	1980–1989	1990–1995
Naturalized	13.41	10.07	6.73	40.00
Noncitizens	21.13	16.80	18.96	39.88
Average	15.34	14.25	17.25	39.89

Source: U.S. Bureau of the Census, 1997.

IV. FEDERALLY FUNDED WELFARE PROGRAMS

The U.S. federal government supports a number of major and minor programs to help the needy. Welfare programs began in the period following the Depression of the 1930s and were greatly expanded during the Johnson[2] Administration under the auspices of the "Great Society." These programs are need based[3] and divided into cash and noncash, or "in kind," types of support. The direction in which government moves at any one time in the provision of assistance to the poor is largely driven by ideological views of purposes appropriate for government action. The hodgepodge of welfare programs that exists today represents the views of the competing ideologies that have dominated U.S. government over time (Hays 1995). Conservatives generally endorse programs that support the direction the market is taking on its own, while liberals tend to favor more active intervention and redistribution programs.

A. Cash-Based Assistance Programs

The two major programs that have provided direct cash benefits to low-income families and individuals were Aid to Families with Dependent Children (AFDC) and Supplemental Security Income (SSI). AFDC and SSI also commanded the largest proportion of budget dollars allocated to means-based transfer payments. These programs provided the most financial support to low-income families and are the ones whose withdrawal will most affect immigrant families. As discussed below, AFDC was recently replaced by a new program designed to provide benefits for a limited time and to encourage recipients to move into the labor market. Prior to the passage of the 1996 welfare legislation, these programs did not specifically exclude immigrants.

B. In-Kind Assistance Programs

The federally funded food stamp program is one of the most widely utilized noncash assistance programs in the United States. This program is administered by the U.S. Department of Agriculture and provides the equivalent of about $76 worth of food stamps per individual per month. The food stamps are exchanged at grocery stores for food items only; nonfood items must be purchased with actual currency.

Facilitating the acquisition of housing by the American population has been a priority of the U.S. government since the passage of the Homestead Act in the nineteenth century. Subsequent legislation, at both the state and federal levels, confirmed this country's desire to foster policies that contribute to obtaining decent, affordable housing. A major piece of legislation, the National Housing Act of 1934, created the Federal Housing

Administration, which greatly revised the manner in which we finance housing. This was followed by the 1937 Housing Act, which created a mechanism to provide public housing for low-income households. A number of additional pieces of legislation enacted during the years from the postwar period to the 1980s continued to support this nation's concern with housing. Although some advocates of low-income housing discredit much of this legislation as too little or poorly focused, it did aid in bringing decent, affordable housing within the reach of many low-income households.

During the 1980s and into the 1990s, the federal government withdrew support for much housing activity and placed more of the responsibility with the state governments. Current federal housing policy focuses on giving the states more responsibility for making decisions about how to best serve the housing needs of their low-income population through Community Development Block Grant (CDBG) funds. A number of states have responded to lower levels of funding by developing initiatives to meet their own low-income housing needs. For example, in 1992, the state of Florida initiated a program that is funded by an additional tax on deeds to real property. This program, the State Housing Initiatives Partnership (SHIP), funnels money directly to local communities that design housing programs to meet specific local needs.

SHIP has had a dramatic impact on specific aspects of the housing crisis by providing aid for programs such as home purchase assistance, home rehabilitation, and new home construction. Because of its focus on problems at the local level, individual communities have established partnerships with local not-for-profit organizations, lending institutions, and private sector builders and developers to provide services under the program. These partnerships have enhanced the development of low- and moderate-income housing by building on the strengths of the participants.

C. Welfare Use by Immigrants

In contrast to a previous section documenting the relatively higher poverty rates among recent immigrants, this section considers the receipt of public assistance by immigrant groups both nationally and in the state of Florida. The breakdown of immigrant groups into naturalized citizens and noncitizens permits comparison between these populations and with the native-born population. Table 2 reports the receipt of various types of assistance on a national level, while Table 3 is specific to Florida. In both tables, we find somewhat higher use of welfare by non-citizen immigrants than by either the naturalized

Table 2 Percent of U.S. Population Receiving Assistance by Citizenship Status

Type of Assistance	Total population	Native born	Naturalized	Noncitizens
Public assistance income	0.04	0.03	0.03	0.07
AFDC income	0.02	0.02	0.01	0.03
SSI	0.02	0.02	0.02	0.03
General welfare	0.00	0.00	0.00	0.01
Received Medicaid	0.12	0.12	0.06	0.16
Received food stamps	0.11	0.11	0.06	0.16

Key: AFDC, Aid to Families with Dependent Children; SSI, Supplemental Security Income.
Source: U.S. Bureau of the Census, 1997.

Table 3 Percent of Florida Population Receiving Assistance by Citizenship Status

Type of Assistance	Total population	Native born	Naturalized	Noncitizens
Public assistance income	0.03	0.03	0.04	0.07
AFDC income	0.01	0.01	0.00	0.01
SSI income	0.02	0.02	0.03	0.06
General welfare	0.00	0.00	0.00	0.01
Received Medicaid	0.12	0.12	0.09	0.13
Received food stamps	0.12	0.12	0.10	0.16

Key: AFDC, Aid to Families with Dependent Children; SSI, Supplemental Security Income.
Source: U.S. Bureau of the Census, 1997.

or native-born population. In spite of popular opinion to the contrary, these tables illustrate the relatively low use of welfare benefits in the total population. Only two programs, Medicaid and Food Stamps, provide assistance to more than 4% of the total U.S. population. Noncitizens consistently receive welfare benefits at a higher rate than do either native-born or naturalized citizens. This higher rate reinforces evidence that recent immigrants have lower levels of education and fewer job-related skills than did earlier immigrant groups. As a result, these new immigrants have little chance of escaping poverty.

Welfare use in the state of Florida closely mirrors receipt of assistance at the national level. The only significant exceptions are in SSI and Medicaid among noncitizens. SSI provides money for many elderly noncitizens who are not able to work. Since many elderly immigrants reside in Florida, it is not surprising that this number is higher. One would expect Medicaid usage to reflect the larger number of elderly immigrants; however, it is somewhat lower than the national percentage.

A degree of ambivalence exists in this country with respect to the poor and social programs to alleviate poverty. Although support for welfare programs is drawn closely along the ideological lines that divide liberals and conservatives, broadly shared views about the impact of program outcomes encourages the formation of coalitions that lead to the enactment of social programs (Hays 1995). However, programs for the poor are also frequently perceived to foster a spirit of dependency among recipients, and the effort to limit these programs is a consistent theme in the U.S. Congress. In 1996, both the issue of welfare dependency and that of welfare use by immigrants became objects of emerging legislation. The next section provides a description of these new laws and considers the potential effect on housing associated with the legislation.

V. 1996 FEDERAL LEGISLATION AFFECTING IMMIGRANTS

The immigration policy debate grew out of questions like: What are the numbers? What is the impact of immigration on U.S. labor markets? What should be done about illegal immigrants entering the country? Do immigrants consume more in resources than they contribute to the tax base? To link immigration legislation with welfare legislation is to struggle with issues of native-immigrant differentials in poverty and transfer program participation. These questions and issues provided the impetus for the enactment of two significant pieces of legislation by the 104th Congress of the United States. The specific, impact of this legislation is difficult to predict, however, given the shortage of housing affordable to immigrants and welfare recipients, the impact will undoubtedly be significant.

A. Immigration Legislation

On September 30, 1996, President Clinton signed into law the *Illegal Immigration Reform and Immigrant Responsibility Act* (IIRIRA).[4] This sweeping piece of legislation is considered to be the strongest revision to the existing immigration laws that has occurred in decades. It was widely supported by the conservative members of the U.S. Congress yet received substantial support from liberal members as well. The lengthy document affects both legal and illegal immigrants. Although the focus of this chapter is the effect of the legislation on legal immigrants and refugees, prior to that discussion, it may be a good idea to present a few of the issues that affect illegal immigrants under the new law. For example, illegal immigrants will not be eligible for any public support programs such as social service block grants, Medicaid or food stamps, housing, unemployment, or financial support to attend college. In addition, if an alien overstays a tourist visa by more than 180 days but less than 1 year, that alien is ineligible to apply for a new visa for a period of 3 years. If the overstay exceeds 1 year, the overstayer will be denied a new visa for at least 10 years and may be permanently barred from reentering the United States.

The new law similarly affects legal immigrants in that they are denied food stamps and many kinds of government support, including SSI, as of August 1997. If the legal immigrant attempts to obtain other forms of public assistance within 5 years of becoming a resident, he or she may be classed as a public charge and subsequently deported. Furthermore, immigrants currently receiving SSI risk losing that income if they do not meet certain requirements (National Conference of State Legislatures 1997). Asylees and refugees are not subject to this ruling for the first 5 years that they are in the United States. At the end of 5 years, they are placed in the same category as legal immigrants and subject to the same regulations.

Residents of the United States who agree to sponsor immigrants must be able to show an annual income equal to or exceeding 125% of the poverty level adjusted for family size (Tasoff, 1996). The 1995 poverty level for a family of four was $15,455. Prior to the passage of this welfare bill, sponsors were not obligated to provide support for the immigrants they sponsored. Under the new legislation, a sponsor's income is deemed or considered available to the immigrant for the necessities of life, thus reducing access to government assistance.

B. Welfare Legislation

A few months before President Clinton signed the immigrant reform bill, he signed a welfare reform bill that significantly changes the U.S. welfare system. The Personal Responsibility and Work Opportunity Reconciliation Act[5] (PRWORA) of 1996 is both an attempt to reform the welfare system and a mechanism to help reduce the federal deficit. Estimates suggest that the bill will save the federal government $55 billion over a 6-year period, and much of that savings will come from cutting help to poor legal immigrants. (Super et al. 1996). These cuts include a reduction in food stamps, benefits to poor immigrant children, the elderly, and those who have become disabled after coming to this country. The bill also sharply curtails aid to citizens. The existing Aid to Families with Dependent Children (AFDC) is being replaced with a block grant program, Temporary Assistance to Needy Families (TANF). This program gives the states more discretion in spending the fixed amount of money that the federal government allocates to them.

Under the new law, SSI aid to the elderly and disabled immigrants is cut off until they become U.S. citizens. As pointed out by a number of analysts, a large proportion of these people are physically unable to work or mentally unable to acquire sufficient knowledge to obtain citizenship (Super et al. 1996; Fix and Zimmermann 1995). Once SSI is cut off, Medicaid, the federal health insurance program for low-income individuals, is also cut off. The law does make exceptions for immigrants who have 40 quarters of employment in the United States.

Together, these two bills have the potential to severely curtail the low-income immigrant's ability to afford decent housing. Distinctions are being drawn between natives and immigrants in ways never before seen in this country (Fix and Zimmermann 1995). Historically noncitizen immigrants have been eligible for assistance programs on a par with natives and naturalized citizens. This has been true in spite of a 1978 law that required deportation of any immigrant receiving welfare during the first 5 years of U.S. residency. A Supreme Court ruling essentially invalidated the 1978 law by stating that recipients must have an opportunity to repay the government for benefits, and no mechanism is in place that meets this provision. However, the new legislation will undoubtedly make housing matters worse unless states deal with the problems on an individual basis.

C. The Florida Response

Concern for the plight of the low-income immigrant population in Florida following the 1996 legislation focused on the potential loss of SSI and Food Stamps by elderly noncitizen residents. The Florida legislature passed a program—called the Legal Immigrant's Temporary Income Bridge Program—designed to provide temporary income assistance to legal immigrants of age 65 and older. Only those residents who are in the process of becoming citizens or are seeking an exemption from the obligation to become citizens are eligible for the program. It is estimated that about 38,880 legal immigrants in Florida are over age 65 and depend on SSI for their basic income. The average monthly payment is $342 (Hirth 1997). However, the bill provided that this benefit would be revoked if the federal government renewed the SSI benefits. The compromise budget act of 1997 did reinstate SSI benefits to elderly and disabled legal immigrants, thus relieving Florida of the obligation. As the cutoff date for receipt of food stamps neared, Florida's governor, Lawton Chiles, pushed for and received an allocation of state money to support a food stamp program for the same group. Another "clarification" that came out of the final federal budget reconciliation bill that was signed into law on August 5, 1997 gave Cuban and Haitian entrants and Amerasian noncitizens status as refugees for purposes of eligibility for benefits.

A number of immigrant advocacy groups in Florida have worked to facilitate the process of immigrants becoming citizens since the passage of the federal legislation. Citizenship alone, however, does not guarantee an endless stream of welfare benefits to immigrants. Once naturalized, they become subject to the same requirements as native-born welfare recipients. That is, most federally generated benefits to nondisabled, working-age individuals are restricted to a 2-year time limit without working and a 5-

year lifetime limit. Additionally, immigrants arriving in this country after August 1996 are permanently banned from SSI and food stamps. Other means-tested benefit programs (TANF or Medicaid, for example) are denied to immigrants for the first 5 years of U.S. residency.

VI. HOUSING PROBLEMS

The affordability of housing for low- and even moderate-income groups is a prevalent topic in much of the housing literature. In the past several years, research focusing on the affordability crisis overshadowed research directed at many other typical housing problems, such as the physical condition of housing and discrimination in housing markets (Linnemnan and Megbolugbe 1993). While the cost of housing remains central to housing policy discussions, today there is a renewed interest in the relationship between affordability and quality. Apgar (1996) points out that between 1974 and 1993 there was a substantial increase of households described as worst-case needs—rental households paying more than 50% of their income for housing but living in structurally inadequate housing. Many of these worst-case households are immigrant households. The relationship between immigration and the housing crisis is only beginning to receive the attention of scholars and policy makers.

A. Housing and Immigrants

There is little empirical research specifically targeted at evaluating the housing situation of immigrants in the United States. The studies that do exist are directed more toward ethnic/racial differences in housing attainment and not in the housing choices of immigrants per se (see, for example, Rosenbaum 1996, Galster 1990, Fix and Struyk 1989). In an attempt to remedy that situation, Alba and Logan (1992) studied home-ownership patterns among Hispanics and other ethnic groups in the United States. They found that the ability to speak English substantially increased the probability of home ownership in median and upper-income households. Another important finding of their study was the influence of the local market situation for Puerto Ricans and Cubans. That is, in communities with a high proportion of these immigrant groups, submarkets tend to form which facilitate the formation of ethnic enclaves.

Work by Kirvo (1995) compares Anglo and Hispanic households in order to examine housing inequality. His analysis includes immigrant characteristics, such as Spanish-language use, duration of residence in the United States, household economic characteristics, location in an area with a heavily immigrant context, and local market conditions. The results point out the importance of these characteristics on two main issues, home ownership and crowding. Importantly, Kirvo's study indicates the need to consider the differences between Hispanic populations with respect to immigrant characteristics such as family structure in making comparisons about housing attainment.

In trying to adapt to life in a new country, many immigrants locate in ethnic enclaves where networks of kin and countrymen support newcomers. The traditional American dream of owning one's own home is not lost on immigrants (Johnson et al. 1997). Initially, the barriers of poverty, limited education, and limited information about the home-buying process restrict the immigrants ability to achieve that dream. However, as duration of residency in the United States increases, so does the home-ownership rate.

The percentage of immigrants living in owner-occupied dwellings is presented in Figure 4. Slightly over 70% of Florida's native-born residents live in owner-occupied residences. This compares with a home-ownership rate of over 80% for naturalized citizens who have been in this country for 25 years or more. Noncitizen immigrants' level of home ownership is significantly lower than that of naturalized citizens. Again, this figure excepts immigrants who have lived in Florida for 5 years or less and are generally not eligible for citizenship.

B. The Housing Crisis in South Florida

The geographic focus of much of the subsequent discussion in this chapter is south Florida. Over 65% of the immigrants coming into Florida choose to reside in this part of the state. The cities of Miami and Fort Lauderdale form the nuclei of a densely populated urban area bounded on the south and east by the Atlantic Ocean and on the west by the environmentally fragile Everglades. South Florida is quite literally running out of suitable land on which to build housing. Estimates derived from current building-permit activity suggest that by the year 2010 all of the buildable vacant land will be used.

Continued population growth coupled with the scarcity of land place intense pressure on housing markets. Demand for housing exceeds supply, and prices have continued to rise. The shortage of affordable rental housing units is most severe. According to the 1990 U.S. Census of Population and Housing, over 43% of renters and 27% of owners in this region faced housing costs of 30% or more of household income. Based on average 1995 rental figures, it would take an income of almost $20,000 per year to support a housing

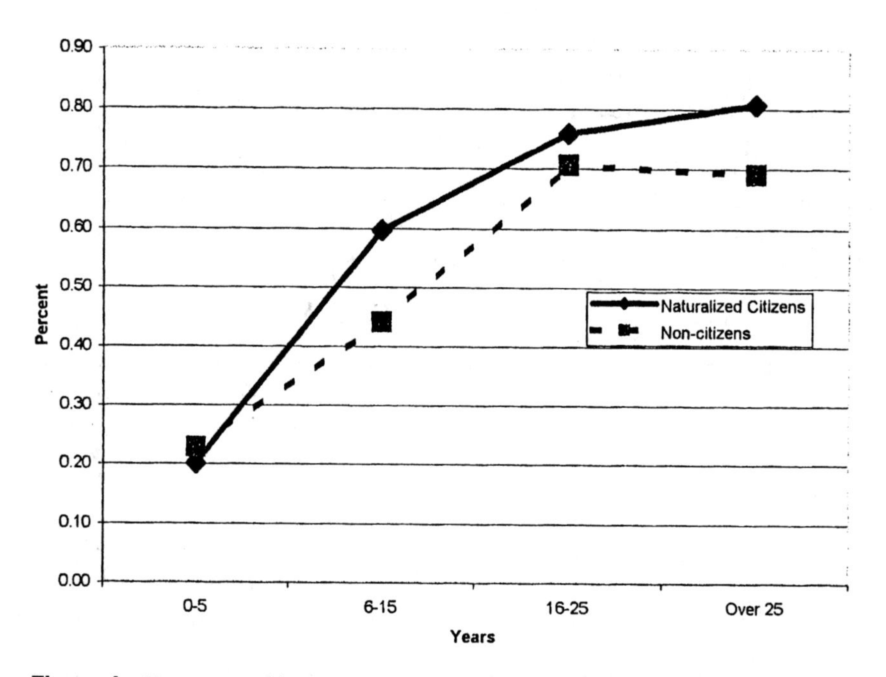

Figure 4 Homeownership Rates of Florida Immigrants by Years of Residency.

unit at the 30% of income rate. Additionally, overcrowding occurs in almost 20% of the renter-occupied dwellings.

VII. EFFECT OF WELFARE LOSS ON IMMIGRANTS' ABILITY TO AFFORD HOUSING

To understand the effects of the loss of welfare on the ability of immigrants to afford housing, one must first realize how including noncash benefits in the ratio of housing costs to income shifts the emphasis of housing problems from one of supply to one of demand. Koebel and Krishnaswamy (1993) found that noncash transfers significantly reduced the problems associated with housing affordability for low-income renters. They estimated the value of food stamps, other fungible noncash transfers such as health care, and housing assistance on the income of poverty level households. They discovered that noncash transfers reduced the affordability ratio of poverty households by 13% (p. 510). That is, poverty level renters who appeared to be paying 54.6% of income for housing were actually paying 42.2% when transfer payment were counted as income.

The importance of cash transfer payments such as AFDC (now TANF), general assistance, and SSI as income available to support housing needs is more readily accounted for in the affordability ratio. Additionally, these programs contain implicit and even explicit shelter allowances (Burchell and Listokin 1995). For example, AFDC benefits are frequently adjusted upward in high-housing-cost markets.

The significance of the relationship between transfer payments and the affordability of housing is particularly important for immigrant families. Most of the immigrants now residing in the United States will no longer receive federal transfer payments,[6] and immigrants arriving after August 1996 will not be eligible for any welfare support for their first 5 years of U.S. residency. For the first group, the potential cutoff of both noncash and cash transfer payments will force immigrant families to either spend more of their limited resources for those items formerly covered by transfer payments or to turn to charitable organizations for help. In either event, one must conclude that the amount of income available to support housing will decline. The second group, more recent immigrants, will be forced from the outset to allocate income differently than did earlier immigrant groups. Without any chance of obtaining benefits, new immigrants will be forced to occupy lower quality housing and live in a more overcrowded situation than did earlier immigrants. The issue of equity is also relevant to this discussion particularly in south Florida. Since Cuban and Haitian immigrants are largely exempt from the abrupt cutoff of welfare benefits, they will be able to maintain a higher standard of living than will immigrants from other countries with similar incomes.

VIII. ADDRESSING THE EFFECTS OF WELFARE REFORM

While federal policy is made at the national level, it is implemented at the local level. States have the authority to determine if noncitizen legal immigrants qualify for Medicaid, TANF, and other state assistance programs. The Florida legislature is making choices that will determine who gets aid and how this will impact local administrative and fiscal status. Because of the concentration of immigrants in south Florida, these decisions are particularly important to local communities in the area. These communities may experience significant losses to small businesses and a loss of rent to low-income housing providers.

New demands will be placed on community-based heath care, social service, and nonprofit organizations. Local public housing authorities (PHAs) administer public housing units and housing voucher programs. These programs require that tenants pay 30% of their income to support their housing. The amount of revenue generated by these payments will decline as tenant income declines, causing actual housing costs for PHAs to increase. To accommodate this increase, PHAs will then have to reduce the number of public housing units or vouchers offered. Some qualified immigrants currently receiving housing assistance may continue to receive it; however, the PHAs may no longer have a unit or a voucher for them. The welfare reform legislation will also create an additional burden for providers who now must verify an immigrants eligibility for some housing subsidies with the Immigration and Naturalization Service.

IX. SUMMARY AND CONCLUSIONS

The combined effects of the immigration and welfare legislation will worsen the existing housing crisis for Florida's immigrant households. Income reduction associated with the reduction or loss of welfare assistance will ultimately force immigrant households to reduce their housing consumption. The state legislature can ameliorate some of the negative effects by through careful crafting of new legislation. The *Personal Responsibility and Work Opportunity Reconciliation Act* permits the use of state funds to replace some of the benefits lost, but only after legislation is passed to address this use.

Service provision at the local level will be determined by laws enacted at the state level. South Florida has a significant network of direct service providers and community organizations that can work to diminish the negative impact of the federal legislation. Kramer (1997) points out that the costs to local communities in humanitarian, public health, economic, and fiscal terms will be great, particularly in areas like south Florida, with its large concentration of immigrant populations (p. 4). She stresses the need for continual monitoring and reevaluation of the effects of these new ways of helping low-income immigrants. Local providers may encounter additional costs and look to the state to offset the additional expense.

To adequately combat the housing problems that arise as a result of the immigration and welfare reform legislation, service providers should:

Provide public information on the availability of housing
Find ways to preserve and rehabilitate existing low-income housing
Locate sources of low-interest loans to help immigrant families move to homeownership
Form coalitions with providers of auxiliary services for job training, language development, and naturalization services

Immigrant families without access to welfare benefits will not be cast adrift in south Florida. However, benefits will undoubtedly be reduced, and it will take aggressive outreach on the part of local service providers to reach many of the needy immigrant households, particularly the elderly and infirm. Coalition building between service providers and intergovernmental cooperation will be crucial to the success of housing programs. The impact of the loss of income on housing will be significant for immigrant households.

Helping immigrant households afford housing will be a continued challenge to service providers and an indicator of the success of the welfare reform program.

ENDNOTES

1. The other high immigration states are California, New York, Texas, and Illinois.
2. Lyndon Baines Johnson served as U.S. president following the assignation of J. F. Kennedy and was subsequently elected for an additional term.
3. Transfers from the federal government to individuals are classed as either means tested or non-means tested. Means tested or need-based transfers are tied to an official definition of poverty and standards of minimally adequate levels of food, housing, and health care. Non-means-tested programs such as Social Security and unemployment are largely supported by direct payments to the program. The income level of the recepient is not a consideration in distributions.
4. This law is officially known as Public Law 104–208.
5. Known officially as Public Law 104–193.
6. States can elect to provide some supplemental assistance to immigrants and many have. However, the amount of such assistance is generally below that of the federal government.

REFERENCES

Alba, R. D. and Logan, J. R. (1992). Assimilation and stratification in the homeownership patterns of racial and ethnic groups. *International Migration Review* 26, 1314–1341.

Apgar, W. (1996). *The State of the Nation's Housing 1996.* Cambridge, MA: Joint Center for Housing Studies at Harvard University.

Blau, F. (1984). The use of transfer payment by immigrants. *Industrial and Labor Relations Review* 37, 222–239.

Fix, M. and Zimmermann, W. (1995–1996). *Immigrant Families and Public Policy: A Deepening Divide. Policy and Research Report.* Washington, D.C.: The Urban Institute, Winter.

Fix, M. and Struyk, R. J. (1989). *Clear and Convincing Evidence: Measurement of Discrimination in America.* Washington, D.C.: The Urban Institute Press.

Frey, W. H. (1996). Immigration, domestic migration, and demographic balkanization in America: new evidence for the 1990s. *Population and Development Review* 22, 741–763.

Galster, G. (1990). Racial discrimination in housing markets during the 1980s: a review of the audit evidence. *Journal of Planning Education and Research* 9, 165–175.

Hays, R. Allen, (1995). *The Federal Government and Urban Housing: Ideology and Change in Public Policy*, 1–35. Albany, NY: State University of New York Press.

Hirth, D. (1997). "Florida to sue U.S. on welfare cutoffs." *Sun-Sentinel*, April 23.

Immigration and Naturalization Services (1997). *Immigration to the United States in Fiscal Year 1996*, last modified May 13, 1997. (http://www.ins.usdoj.gov/public/stats/977.html)

Jensen, L. (1989). *The New Immigration.* Westport, CT: Greenwood Press.

Johnson, Stephen J., Katimin, M., and Milczarski, W. J. (1997). Homeownership aspirations and experiences: immigrant Koreans and Dominicans in northern Queens, New York City. *Cityscape* 3, 63–90.

Kirvo, L. J. (1995). Immigrant characteristics and Hispanic–Anglo housing inequality. *Demography* 32, 599–615.

Koebel, C. T. and Krishnaswamy, A. (1993). The impact of noncash transfers on rental affordability. *Journal of Urban Affairs* 15, 505–513.

Kramer, F. D. (1997). Welfare reform and immigrants: recent developments and a review of key state decisions. *The Welfare Information Network.* (http://www.welfare info.org/kramer.htm).

Linnemnan, P. D. and Megbolugbe, I. F. (1992). Housing affordability: myth or reality? *Journal of Urban Studies* 29, 369–392.

National Conference of State Legislatures (1997). March 13. (http://www.ncsl.org/ststefed/welfare/imigrant.htm).

Rosenbaum, E. (1996). Racial/ethnic differences in home ownership and housing quality. *Social Problems* 41, 403–427.

Segalman, R. and Basu, A. (1981). *Poverty in America: The Welfare Dilemma.* Westport CT: Greenwood Press.

Super, D. A., Parrott, S., Steimnetz, S. and Mann, C. (1996). *The New Welfare Law*, Washington, D.C.: Center on Budget and Policy Priorities. August 13.

Sullivan, L. W. (1992). *Report to the Congress for Fiscal year 1992.* Washington, D.C. Office of Refugee Resettlement, Administration for Children and Families.

Tasoff, R. J. (1997). *Short Summary of the New Immigration Law.* (http://www.DGKSney.com/tasoff/010-p03.htm)

Tienda, M. and Jensen, L. (1986). Immigration and public assistance participation: dispelling the myth of dependency. *Social Science Research* 15, 372–400.

U.S. Bureau of the Census. (1990). *Census of Population and Housing, 1990.* Washington, D.C.

U.S. Bureau of the Census. (1997). *Current Population Reports, Citizenship Status.* Washington, D.C.

Zarembka, A. (1990). *The Urban Housing Crisis.* Westport, CT: Greenwood Press.

10
Managing "Complex Emergencies"
U.N. Administration and the Resolution of Civil Wars

Karl Jamieson Irving Department of Public Administration, School of Public Affairs, American University, Washington, D.C.

I. THE MANAGEMENT OF CONFLICT AND PEACE

As president, Woodrow Wilson was instrumental in the establishment of the first collective institution to manage global conflict, the League of Nations, carefully designed to counter manifestations of crisis with precise applications of particular forms of conflict resolution, with little regard to politics and power (Murphy 1994:878–880). Wilson's work as a scholar in the field of public administration remains a controversial legacy to this day—a bold assertion that the "field of administration is a field of business . . . removed from the hurry and strife of politics" (Wilson 1887). Now we find the concept coming full circle as scholars and practitioners seek to produce a more efficient United Nations to govern the realm of international peace and security. Recent commentary on the future of global governance cautions against a fully Wilsonian image—Rosenau (1995), for instance, speaks of the importance of "bottom-up" as opposed to hierarchical "top-down" processes. Nevertheless, while there have been studies and reports concerning individual elements of U.N. financing, the international civil service, and bureaucratic operations (Heady 1998), there has been a dearth of research in recent decades of the administrative processes of executive management in global governance. According to one of the American godfathers of the field of public administration, Chester Barnard (1938:235 and 290), it is essential for the successful administration of policy for the chief executive to analyze the organization and its environment as a whole on a continuous basis in order to maintain the cooperative organizational endeavor at hand. Similarly, Petak (1985:6) stresses that "the public administrator, as emergency manager, must have the conceptual skill to understand . . . the total system." This chapter provides such a holistic view of international administration dealing with "complex emergencies"—large-scale suffering among civilian populations resulting from violent civil conflict (see Annan 1997: para. 180)—through comprehensive missions assisting with their political resolution.

The turn of the past decade witnessed an ambitious flurry of U.N. peace operations, most with a bold new emphasis on civilian activity in support of the implementation or even ongoing negotiation of peace accords. Notable failure in Somalia and elsewhere, however, led to an equally precipitous decrease in exuberance regarding the international management of conflict and peace, most evident with regard to the collective response—or lack thereof—to the Rwandan crisis of 1994. There could not have been a clearer example of Anthony Downs' (1972) model of public policy cycles, where support for new programs tends to decline either as a more mature understanding develops of the costs (fiscal and otherwise) of addressing the problem or after an almost inevitable administrative fiasco occurs within the public spotlight. Following a 1997 coup d'état in Cambodia, 3 years after completion of a 3-year U.N. operation, the large headline on the front page of the *Washington Post* read, "$3 Billion Effort Fails to Pacify Cambodia." At a time when President Bill Clinton was actively trying to get the Republican majority in the Congress to arrange for payment of U.S. arrears to the organization, this particular headline was potentially as detrimental to the long-term outlook of multidimensional U.N. peace operations as the 1993 images of U.S. soldiers being dragged through the streets of Mogadishu and into the living rooms of the American public via the Cable News Network (CNN). Cambodia had been the most ambitious U.N. peace operation ever—previously dubbed by scholars and practitioners alike as one of the more successful of the "second generation" of peacekeeping-related activity. That it would fail in the longer term raised serious questions regarding the improvisation, implementation, and impact of such complex operations.

"Lessons learned" in the peacekeeping and international relations literature mainly blamed shortcomings on piecemeal aspects of the convoluted and fluid management task involved in supporting states through transition from violent to peaceful means of political conflict. An overemphasis by scholars and practitioners on isolated problem areas can lead analysis to neglect (1) the larger context of political constraints to proposed reform, as the problems themselves may be inherent to the public nature of the organization; (2) a crucial perspective comprising the three areas of organizational goals, capacity, and environmental fit simultaneously and over time; and (3) the important stages of crisis management prior to and especially following that of response. As Indar Jit Rikhye (1992) argues, peace operations "should be planned and managed as integral parts of one forward-looking process that encompasses peacemaking, peacebuilding, and peacekeeping." This essay describes the difficulties facing operations encompassing these tasks through the stages of crisis management—mitigation and preparedness, response, and recovery. It explores the prescriptions of pundits to date, as well as the significance of the public administration/public management literature for the international management of conflict and peace, given Van Wagenen's (1971) assertion that "the similarities overwhelm the differences between national and international administration." It is my contention that many pathologies afflicting U.N. operations are due to the inherent infusion of politics with administration; that the inability of the executive to balance mission, capacity, and environment is the main cause of failure; and that stages of crisis other than that of response are critical to lasting effectiveness of U.N. crisis management outputs. The implication is that executive administration of the international governance process with regard to the emergence of states from a system of violent civil conflict is one more of ongoing negotiation than hierarchical bureaucracy, confirming the observation of Cox and Jacobson (1973) that the implementation of international programs is largely an extension of both organizational and international politics.

II. THE EVOLUTION OF U.N. PEACEKEEPING

The Allied powers established the United Nations at the end of the Second World War as a means to manage conflict on a collective basis, aiming to correct the deficiencies of its predecessor, the League of Nations. The intent was to give the new system the "teeth" necessary to deal with a belligerent state, through a Security Council given primary responsibility over matters concerning the maintenance of international peace and security (U.N. Charter, Art. 24), and the authority to impose economic sanctions and even organize multilateral armed force against aggression (U.N. Charter, Arts. 41, 42). Another body, the General Assembly, was to help maintain peace through advancements in human development over the longer term. The system was designed in part by the same group of individuals who constructed the New Deal system of the U.S. federal bureaucracy, so it is not surprising that it would include a set of semi-autonomous bodies of functional groupings loosely attached to the General Assembly (Burley, in Ruggie 1993). While the secretary-general would be "chief administrative officer" (U.N. Charter, Art. 97), the General Assembly would set the budget and regulate personnel (U.N. Charter, Arts. 17, 101). The secretary-general's role in conflict management was formally limited to reporting threats to the peace to the Security Council (U.N. Charter, Art. 99), but in practice the secretary-general came to rely on the *implicit* powers of this role, together with his position as chief executive, to establish enquiries, facilitate dialogue, and even, on rare occasions, arbitrate disputes (Irving 1993; Rivlin and Gordenker 1993). The secretary-general naturally came to wield executive authority over U.N. peace operations under Art. 98 of the Charter, which the organization's designers included with the assumption that there would be a proliferation of tasks the Security Council and General Assembly would need to delegate.

The League of Nations had engaged in the mediation of disputes, the deployment of protective forces, and even in temporary territorial administration between the two world wars (see Chopra in Weiss, 1995; Ratner 1995). The United Nations became involved in such activities almost from the start, setting up a special commission to monitor borders in the Balkans in 1947 to prevent the Greek civil war from spreading to its intervening neighbors. The first officially recognized U.N. peacekeeping operation was an unarmed force established to observe the truce and then armistice at the close of the first Arab-Israeli war in 1948. Peacekeeping became an accepted facet of regular U.N. activity beginning with the operation established in 1956 following the failure of collective security with regard to the Suez Canal crisis, owing to the threat of veto in the Security Council. The General Assembly, in accordance with the "Uniting for Peace" resolution (U.N. Doc. A/RES/377(V), 1950) circumvented the gridlocked Security Council by establishing an operation to observe a cease-fire between Egypt and Israel (U.N. Doc. A/RES/998, 1956). From this operation has come the model of "classic" peacekeeping, with the following core characteristics: consent of the host state government, strict impartiality with regard to the disputing parties, and use of force restricted to self-defense in the last resort. The number and scope of operations grew in the 1960s under the entrepreneurial leadership of Secretary-General Dag Hammarskjold, even entailing full transitional authority of West Irian from Netherlands colony to Indonesian territory, but serious superpower controversy over the expansive operation in the Belgian Congo and failure of the Cyprus or Middle East operations to break the intractability of those conflicts kept expectations low for this particular conflict management tool in the ensuing decades.

With the demise of the Cold War in the late 1980s, however, the number of ongoing U.N. peace operations and the breadth of their tasks rapidly proliferated to levels surpassing that of all previous operations combined. In addition to the auspicious and unprecedented period of time without a veto in the Security Council, there were an increasing number of local conflicts suddenly unbridled by superpower politics; an increasing number of states where parties to civil conflict reached accords with a view to carrying out democratic elections; a public audience in western states able to watch once distant crises of starvation and slaughter live on television; public fanfare over a 1988 Nobel Peace Prize award to U.N. peacekeepers; and a growing sense among international decision makers that international law had developed to the point where intervention in internal conflict was justified in cases of widespread humanitarian crisis. Moreover, the gravity of these crises was overwhelming, with the half-decade of 1989–1994 producing one-fifth of all wartime casualties since World War II, the vast majority of these among civilian populations (Smith 1997:9–10). These factors helped lead to the establishment of numerous concurrent "second-generation" or "multidimensional" U.N. peace operations—i.e., those "responsible for overseeing or executing the political solution of an internal conflict, with the consent of the parties" (Ratner 1995:17) with a civilian chief of mission embodied in a special representative of the secretary-general, beginning with observation of multiparty elections in Namibia in 1989. Incoming secretary-general Boutros Boutros-Ghali labeled these "comprehensive peace operations" (Pick 1992). The Security Council in 1992 requested a report from the secretary-general on the new prospects of peacekeeping, and Boutros-Ghali unexpectedly laid out an ambitious typology of U.N. conflict management and resolution, ranging from *preventive diplomacy* (negotiation prior to extensive violent conflict) and the more traditional *peacekeeping* (commonly referred to as "classic" peacekeeping or "first generation") to *peacemaking* (both mediation and *peace enforcement*) and postconflict *peacebuilding* (including governance reforms) (Boutros-Ghali 1992).

The intricate nature of the conflict environment and this new range of responsibilities increased the complexity of the overall management effort. U.N. management of conflict and peace has much in common with U.S. public management, given similarities in separation of powers and aspects of federalism. A crude parallel can be drawn to a U.S. federal government body, such as the Environmental Protection Agency (EPA), where the department secretary (the secretary-general) simultaneously must deal not only with the conflicting interest groups concerned (the disputing parties) and his or her own staff (the Secretariat), but with the authorizing legislation of Congress and any White House policy directives (Security Council resolutions); congressional appropriations committees [committees of the General Assembly, such as the Committee on Administrative and Budgetary Questions (ACABQ, or Fifth Committee)]; other agencies with overlapping concerns such as the National Park Service (other bodies of the U.N. system such as the U.N. High Commission for Refugees or the World Bank); other intergovernmental organizations such as the National Governors' Association (other intergovernmental organizations such as the International Committee of the Red Cross); field offices (offices of the special representatives or military field commanders); private interest groups (nonprofit organizations); and, finally, the national news media and public opinion (the international news media and public opinion). This analogy also holds with regard to policy implementation, as both rely on a compliance game with two or more conflicting parties—although in the domestic U.S. government sphere, parties that fail to abide by agreements made take up conflict via civil litigation rather than military combat. Hill and Malik (1996:17), in fact, describe U.N. peacekeeping as "clearly a regulatory system." Moreover, the legal and historical environment of peace operations is in transition, with great uncertainty over authority and procedure, similar to, say, the new public policy and public management dilemmas in dealing with the issue of "acid rain" in the 1970s.

III. RESPONDING TO CRISES OF CIVIL CONFLICT

The U.N. Charter clearly forbids general involvement in the domestic political activity of states [Art. 2(7)], and the charters of other organizations relevant to transitions from conflict to peace, such as the International Bank of Reconstruction and Development (World Bank) and the U.N. Development Program (UNDP), officially prohibit such engagement as well. The Universal Declaration of Human Rights of 1948 and the International Covenant on Civil and Political Rights of 1966 were largely treated as domestic obligations not open to outside enforcement except in 1968, when the Security Council imposed economic sanctions upon the white minority government of Rhodesia, setting the precedent for a politically tenable connection between civil and political rights and the maintenance of international peace and security. Swift changes with regard to the willingness of the United Nations to intervene in civil conflict demonstrated the adage that the Security Council tends to make decisions "not according to objective criteria but, rather, according to what the international political traffic will bear" (Weiss 1995:201). The Security Council can authorize multilateral intervention in state sovereignty to protect the peace under Article 42 in Chapter VII of the U.N. Charter but needs to meet its prerequisites. This requires a finding of a "threat to the peace" under Article 39; a call for provisional measures such as negotiation and mediation under Article 40; and an assessment that nonforcible measures such as economic sanctions under Article 41 are inadequate to achieve an end to the threat. Under Chapter VII, there are avenues other than all-out force as used in the Persian Gulf war, such as the operations in Somalia and Bosnia-Herzegovina, established in part to ensure unfettered access of humanitarian aid. Short of a formal finding of a threat to the peace, under provisions for the pacific settlement of disputes in Chapter VI of the charter, the secretary-general as a semiautonomous international actor is free to mediate with disputing parties and gain their consent to the establishment of a force to undertake the monitoring of a cease-fire, or other aspects of guaranteeing or implementing a political agreement among them. Owing to the inherent character of a possible need to use force to defend the integrity of the operation and not just the lives of those engaged in such endeavors, however, scholars have dubbed these "chapter six-and-a-half" operations, with some arguing that their legal authority is dubious.

For management assistance with peace operations, Secretary-General Dag Hammarskjold originally established two undersecretaries without portfolio, later designated undersecretaries general for special political affairs in 1961. While one acted as personal mediator for the secretary-general, the other oversaw field operations and mediations. In 1988, all mediation activity was separated completely from peacekeeping operations, so there was little to no input from those responsible for implementation into the form and scheduling of operations used to guarantee peace accords, and the Senior Planning and Management Group has not been sufficient to overcome such problems (Durch 1993: 62). Nor was there much communication between Security Council members authorizing operations and Secretariat members who had to design them (Berdal 1995:234). In implementation, the Field Operations Division in the Department of Administration and Management was in charge of transport, logistics, communications, and budgets, often leading the chief administrative officer and the military force commander to be at odds, serving as a serious constraint for commanders facing changing environments (Allan 1996:27; Durch 1993:65; Jonah 1991). Multiple operation components in the field, as in the Cambodia operation, with no transparent intercomponent coordination process among them, has led to numerous turf battles detrimental to wider operation success (Ratner 1995:196). In 1993, all logistical responsibility related to peace operations was consolidated into a new Department of Peacekeeping Operations (DPKO). The Department of Political Affairs took on all responsibility for the political affairs relating to a given operation, "leaving the DPKO with the nuts and bolts" of planning responsibility and authority (Durch 1995: 158).

The Secretariat has been seriously overtaxed by the sheer number and size of the second-generation operations. At the height of its involvement in the resolution of civil wars at the end of 1994, the United Nations had active operations in more than a dozen areas of the globe, utilizing over 70,000 military, 2000 civilian police, and 2000 civilian personnel from nearly 80 countries, at an annual cost well over $3 billion—one-third the total cost of all prior U.N. operations (see Boutros-Ghali 1995). Meanwhile, there were a couple dozen other crises of international conflict with which U.N. personnel were dealing in some manner or another, and more than 50 other countries in which crises were either imminent or festering. At this time, however, there were barely 100 officials in the Office of the Secretary-General, well under half serving in the Department of Peacekeeping Operations (see Durch 1995:158). "There is no defense ministry on earth that has a soldier to support ratio like that" (Shashi Tharoor quoted in Stewart 1995). After vociferous complaints from field officers in the former Yugoslavia that they were unable to reach anyone at U.N. Headquarters in New York after hours, the Secretariat set up a new 24-hour situation room and a planning and coordination group. There have also been serious problems of coordination between different national groupings of U.N. peacekeeping troops. Planning and coordination has been even more difficult with the rise in the level of "co-contracting" of operation tasks and leadership with regional organizations or individual member states (see Genus:115). The Somalia operation in particular exacerbated these problems, as there were in essence two separate multilateral operations working simultaneously, one led by the United Nations, the other by the United States. This use of chapter VII has led to difficulties in authority, with the secretary-general complaining about Security Council propensity to "micromanage" peace operations in Somalia and the former Yugoslavia through constantly changing, counterproductive mandates (Boutros-Ghali 1995). In the latter case, for instance, there were no fewer than 60 Security Council resolutions, leading the Belgian Commander Lt.-Gen. Francis Briquemont to quip, "I don't read the Security Council resolutions any more . . . because they don't help me" (quoted in Ramsbotham and Woodhouse 1996:183).

With the panoply of actors involved in crises of international conflict, of course, there are other coordination difficulties with which the U.N. Secretariat must contend. There are other organizations within the larger "family" of the U.N. system involved, including the U.N. Children's Fund, the UNDP, the U.N. Disaster Relief Office, the U.N. High Commission for Refugees (UNHCR), the World Food Programme, the Food and Agriculture Organization, the International Monetary Fund (IMF), and the World Bank. According to a 1995 report of the Joint Inspection Unit (1995)—the only independent U.N. systemwide inspection, evaluation, and investigation body—the network of committees and subsidiary bodies has been a "cumbersome structure where agencies pushed their agendas while others defended their turf." Recent secretary-general Kofi Annan backed away from a plan to bring the United Nation's multiple humanitarian relief agencies together under the Geneva-based UNHCR, due to resistance from the various agency heads, and instead named the head of the new—and thus weak—Department of Humanitarian Affairs (DHA, established in 1992) in New York as "emergency relief coordinator" to help with negotiations over operations with state governments, ostensibly leaving agencies on the ground to go about their business without the hassle of political complications (see Annan 1997; Mortimer and Lambert 1997). The Administrative Committee on Coordination and the Committee on Program and Coordination, which generally meet only a few times a year, have largely been forums for general discussion among these agencies rather than an effective means for coordination and consultation (De Soto and Del Castillo 1994). DPKO heads a peace operation task force that includes the DHA, the economic departments, and the Department of Administration and Management (Annan 1997). The new post of deputy secretary-general is also intended to help ensure "intersectoral and interinstitutional coherence of activities" (U.N. Press Release, GA/9388, 1997). Problems encountered in several of the early 1990s peace operations, with non-governmental organizations (NGOs) setting up their own parallel infrastructure and contributing to the war economy by hiring armed guards (Sapir and Deconnick 1995), have led to the formation of such bodies as the regional "Partnership in Action" consultations between the UNHCR and the International Council of Voluntary Agencies, which included global conferences involving nearly 200 NGOs from over 80 countries (Ramsbotham and Woodhouse 1996: 152–153).

Some of these agencies, such as the UNDP and the World Bank, have found it difficult to diverge from standard operating procedure of developing and implementing programs through consultation solely with government actors, leading other signatories of peace accords to cry foul (Holiday and Stanley 1993). Media attention and poor public relations by the organization have exacerbated the natural tendency to "soldier on" even in the face of open defiance (see Durch 1993), specifically with respect to carrying on with planned elections despite a deteriorating security situation (Kiernan 1993). This type of phenomenon may have led, in Somalia and elsewhere, to counterproductive "mission creep" in response to rapidly changing environments without much reevaluation of the new circumstances (Doyle 1996:60; Hill and Malik 1996; Bertram 1995:416). In most situations, there have been little to no means provided for dispute settlement between the conflicting parties in situations where disputes are bound to arise in the implementation of peace accords and operational means to uphold them (Diehl 1993:160; Cliffe 1994: 84–89). U.N. inability to deal with recalcitrance on the part of one actor often has led to foot-dragging on the part of another (e.g., Doyle 1995). Troops and other officials have become a main target for the frustrations of all sides, with abductions and killings in Cambodia and elsewhere (Kiernan 1993). There have been episodes of peacekeeping troops involved in torture, prostitution of minors, drug and gun smuggling, and organization of black markets, even by troops touted as being well disciplined (Hill and Malik 1996:132–133; Kirshenbaum 1994; Heininger 1994; Ramsbotham and Woodhouse 1996; et al.). Furthermore, the income disparity that results from a large influx of international activity on a local level has tended to promote a political economy of corruption, counter to the operational goals of promoting civil society to reestablish peace and security (Doyle 1995).

IV. MITIGATING AND PREPARING FOR CRISES OF CIVIL CONFLICT

Obviously, it would be better if serious crises could be resolved *before* a U.N. operation needs to be put into place. The *mitigation* stage of crisis management is tightly constricted with regard to multilateral intervention in civil conflict, however, as the U.N. Charter states in Article 2(7) that ''[n]othing contained in the present Charter shall authorize the United Nations to intervene in matters which are essentially within the domestic jurisdiction of any state or shall require the Members to submit such matters to settlement under the present Charter.'' The activity of the organization is therefore limited entirely to ''preventive diplomacy'' at the whim of the parties in conflict. There was a proposal in 1985 to establish U.N. ''embassies'' or a permanent commission of good offices to facilitate negotiations among disputing parties, but this has yet to be realized (Broms 1987:89). An Office of Research and Collection of Information started operating in 1988, but it has been understaffed and underequipped, and has had little access to information of organizations outside the U.N. Secretariat in New York (Durch and Blechman 1992). More recently, the secretary-general has sought to institute a ''global watch'' through sector-specific early-warning systems for humanitarian emergencies developed by individual agencies (Annan 1997). While the explicit identification of preventive diplomacy as a U.N. tool at this stage of conflict management in *An Agenda for Peace* gave it some needed attention and provided an impetus to strengthen the organization's capacity to deal with it, it has taken a long time for real reforms to be made in this direction. A new section was set up in 1997, but its effectiveness remains to be seen. Other states and organizations seeking to help with diplomatic efforts may get in the way of U.N. attempts to expand such activity too far, however, even though their own interests can complicate already sophisticated problems of early political settlement (Smith 1985; Weller 1992). Furthermore, the ruling parties understandably tend to feel that entering into negotiations with an opposition group implicitly ''legitimizes'' the latter's appeals, and the conflict may not be ''ripe'' for negotiation, or one of the parties may have a problem accepting the impartiality of the United Nations from the start (see Zartman 1995). On the military side of mitigating activity, the emplacement of U.N. troops in Macedonia to prevent the spread of the conflict in the former Yugoslavia set a precedent for ''preventive deployment,'' but this remains the only such U.N. operation to date.

The crisis management stage of *preparedness* holds a greater potential for improvement in U.N. operations, in terms of both financial and personnel resources, and logistical planning. In addition to an already small and decreasing budget for general U.N. activities, with some of the largest contributors in serious arrears, there is a relatively small annual cap on discretionary spending by the secretary-general. Furthermore, proposed operation budgets have to pass through the ACABQ, and even if everything goes through smoothly, approval takes a minimum of several weeks following authorization of the operation design by the Security Council. Furthermore, the ACABQ has demonstrated a preoccupation with member states' concern for the bottom line rather than political or operational consequences of their actions (Durch 1995:152). Any serious disagreement between the Security Council and the secretary-general as to funding outlays can lead to months of delay in deployment (e.g., Angola—see U.N. Doc. S/23191, 1991). The General Assembly in 1993 established a voluntary Peacekeeping Reserve Fund of $150 million as a cash-flow mechanism to ensure rapid start-up of new operations (U.N. General Assembly Res. A/48/622), but payment shortfalls by contributing states regularly occur here as well (Beigbeder 1997: 101). Moreover, due to the organization's overall funding problem, the secretary-general has needed to regularly borrow from peace operation budgets to keep the organization—which operates entirely on a pay-as-you-go basis—afloat (UNDPI 1997). The secretary-general has proposed a voluntary revolving credit fund of up to $1 billion for the organization to address this problem (Annan 1997) which could be of some assistance, but the touted switch to results-based budgeting techniques will not likely do much for the funding of temporary activities as second-generation peace operations.

Even with adequate funding, it has been difficult for the United Nations to obtain the necessary personnel for operations. On the military side, a renewal of calls for the establishment of a standing U.N. force from scholars and former U.N. officials in the early 1990s (e.g., Urquhart 1993) was strongly opposed by outside political forces. After compliant by the secretary-general over the continuing problem of finding enough governments willing to provide troops in a timely fashion, a model standby forces arrangement was devised in 1993, and agreements have now been signed with over 50 countries (Knight 1998). None of the states with such arrangements, however, offered any of their designated forces for an operation in Rwanda when the secretary-general made a formal request for them to do so in 1994 (Tharoor 1996:24). Military personnel that *are* obtained for operations may not be adequately trained or prepared for peace operations. The International Peace Academy, a private organization in close association with the United Nations, has conducted some limited training for a number of years, and other organizations, including the DPKO and nongovernmental organizations, have begun such training as well (Annan 1997; Durch 1993), but much training of peacekeepers is still performed in an uncoordinated manner by the separate contributing member states (Findlay 1996). Lack of training is exacerbated by a dearth of informational briefings in the field at start-up (Hill and Malik 1996:102). As U.N. remuneration for troop contributors is made on an equitable per capita basis regardless of the normal pay rate of the contributing states themselves, some developing countries are eager to send *any* troops so as to profit through pocketing excess per diem, no matter how qualified or suitable—let alone accompanied by sufficient supplies and equipment. As for civilian personnel, it has proven difficult to find individuals qualified to assist in political and administrative transitions, particularly those also familiar with the workings of the U.N. system, and both military and civilian personnel have had inadequate language skills or cultural knowledge for the state where they were deployed (Ratner 1995:167 and 194–195; Fetherston 1994). A new roster of qualified civilian staff for second-generation peace operations has been developed, however, comprising over 5000 names (Hill and Malik 1996:172).

Beyond the problems of obtaining an adequate level of funding and staffing, there is still the problem of procurement and logistics planning. Developing countries ravaged by decades of war do not generally offer much by way of supplies, and operations require as a basic minimum vehicles, communication equipment, prefabricated housing units, electrical generators, water and food, and general office supplies (Heininger 1994:42). The recent development of "start-up kits" of commonly used equipment left over from previous operations being stockpiled in a single location in Italy should help alleviate some prior difficulties in the future (see U.N. Docs. A/50/907 and A/50/985, 1996). Procurement rules requiring equal access by member states and the requirement of choosing the lowest bid has led, among other examples, to late arrivals of fire trucks without hoses and spotlights without bulbs (Harrell and Howe 1995:200). A completely new bidding process has been conducted for each operation, taking as long as 6 months to advertise for bids, review bids received, and to await delivery of material and services (Durch, 1995:159). As many as 50 steps were required for a battalion commander in the field to receive a requested item (Berdal 1993). In 1994, an independent review was conducted of U.N. procurement processes for peacekeeping operations (Beigbeder 1997), and some streamlining has been instituted as a result (Annan 1997). Lack of preparedness for contingencies has created problems for the critical responsibility of troop demobilization, as they are often ill equipped themselves to move to designated demobilization areas in remote parts of the country, and lack food, shelter, and proper clothing when they arrive (e.g., Angola—see U.N. Docs. S/23191, 1991; S/23671, 1992; and S/24145, 1992). Some observers have criticized U.N. operations for not utilizing existing operational networks of nongovernmental organizations, although in some cases agencies such as UNHCR had a preexisting presence that helped them in dealing with the conflicting parties (Heininger 1994:49). Incremental decision making during the response stage of crisis management can lead to difficulties in poor logistical preparedness as well. In Cambodia, for example, following international pressure on the mission in Cambodia to arrest civil rights violators, the special prosecutor began issuing warrants, but there was no jail, no means of capturing suspected criminals by force, or an impartial court system in place to try them (Doyle 1995:47).

V. RECOVERING FROM CRISES OF CIVIL CONFLICT

In the *recovery* stage of crisis management, the U.N. organization suffers somewhat from the same problems narrowing its options in the mitigation stage. Once a new national political system is firmly in place, the United Nations cannot get involved without the government's consent. Nevertheless, Boutros-Ghali has emphasized a rationale for international involvement in the end game of transitions from civil violence to peace, stating that "the United Nations, having invested much effort in helping to end the conflict, can legitimately express views and offer advice about actions the Government could take to reduce the danger of losing what has been achieved" (Boutros-Ghali 1995). The secretary-general set precedence for a follow-up mission to seek continued settlement in the governance uncertainties following violent conflict with the Office of the Secretary-General in Afghanistan and Pakistan, after U.N. observation of the Russian pullout in 1990. Durch and Blechman have supported the idea of follow-up missions, as has Sullivan (1994:83–84). In the cases of peace operations in the early 1990s, however, concerted U.N. activity in the spotlight of major state politics ended as soon as large-scale fighting had halted and elections had taken place. Governance reforms became the province only of separate initiatives by agencies such as the UNDP, which only recently established a division on governance—largely taking the place of rather than complementing similar activities of the World Bank, whose governance subdivision has involved itself less in such activity across the globe in recent years.

The concentration of those designing and implementing U.N. peace operation activity during the recovery stage of crisis management largely has been on troop demobilization, the formation and training of a new national police force, the retraining of judicial officials, human rights education, electoral and land reform legislation, and some infrastructure revitalization. What U.N.-system activity remains upon pullout of a peace operation can show a general lack of organizational coordination, as different bodies operate separately from peace accord implementation, sometimes resulting in conflicting efforts. There was no dialogue between the Bretton Woods institutions and negotiators of the comprehensive peace accords in El Salvador, for instance—the World Bank and IMF set conditionality for their postwar loans on governmental reforms entailing budget cutbacks and downsizing of the civil service, despite the need to implement legal reform and rehabilitation programs under the accords (De Soto and Del Castillo 1994:72–73). It is hoped that the Department of Political Affairs, now acting as convenor of the new executive committee on peace and security and focal point of postconflict peacebuilding strategy in collaboration with the other executive committees, will be able to alleviate some of these problems (Annan 1997: Action 5).

In terms of crisis management, the organization itself needs to undergo recovery in learning from its recent experience. While it should be commended for the establishment of "lessons learned" units in its peacekeeping department and elsewhere, much that is found in U.N. reports closely mirror much of the findings in the contemporary peacekeeping literature (see DPKO 1997). A few authors in that literature have attempted to approach the issue of collective security using heavily quantitative methods, coming to the broad conclusion that the United Nations is not very effective at minimizing or ending conflict, except in certain cases that have become very volatile and garnered the captivated interest of the superpowers (Haas 1987 and 1991; Wilkenfeld and Brecher 1984 and 1997). The more qualitative research in the literature stresses the need for (1) a relatively clear mandate with feasible goals and adequate superpower support for operation success (Berdal 1995; Fetherston 1994; Durch 1993; Evans 1993; Rikhye 1992; Mackinlay 1989; Urquhart 1987); (2) decentralized decision making and more rapid procurement and improved intraorganizational relations (Durch 1996; Berdal 1995; Doyle 1995; Ratner 1995; Heininger 1994; Durch 1993); and (3) enhanced cooperation with independent actors, including effective coordination of macro-level responsibilities and the development of good relations with the disputing parties themselves (Allan 1996; Durch 1996; Doyle 1995; Ratner 1995; Schear 1995; Fetherston 1994; Diehl 1993; Durch 1993; Evans 1993; Ruggie 1993b; Heiberg 1991; Urquhart 1987). Such prescriptions echo the current global trend in public administration for agencies to be more enterprising and results-oriented, decentralized and anticipatory, and competitive and customer-driven (e.g., Caiden 1991; and Osborne and Gaebler 1992; Gore 1993; Peters and Waterman 1982). Chayes, Chayes, and Raach (1997) even explicitly posit the potential applicability of such new business management tenets for U.N. peace operations. Parallel to the above, they advocate incorporation of a shared clarity of vision and allocation of adequate resources, decentralization of operational responsibility, and direct involvement of the principal parties affected by peace operations to generate a rolling consensus in implementation. They acknowledge, however, that certain political forces operate against the adoption of their suggestions in practice.

Some pundits argue that involvement of the parties in conflict precludes military means of peace enforcement as a static, dichotomous variable outright, due to the almost certain consequent loss of perceived impartiality (Allan 1996; Hill and Malik 1996; Tharoor 1996; Fetherston 1994; Lyons 1994; Ruggie 1993b; Rikhye 1992)—"impartiality works best where intervention is needed least" (Betts 1994:28). There is thus a strong emphasis on the classical aspects of U.N. peacekeeping—neutral, lightly armed troops positioned with the consent of the disputing parties—as *de minimus* characteristics for a successful peace operation. Allan (1996:142) argues that an operation "cannot survive" without them, and Boutros-Ghali (1995), in his humbling follow-up to *An Agenda for Peace* (1992), acknowledged that these are "essential" principles for successful operations. On the other hand, the anticipation of a loss of perceived neutrality from the affected party has led to indecisiveness and unwillingness to use force in situations when it might have proven an effective tool of conflict management, as demonstrated by the contrast of the U.N. inability to counter the genocide in Rwanda and the successful, although limited, use of force by France to help alleviate it (Murphy 1996:217, 242, and 259). With or without enforcement, however, a few scholars note that the use of dispute settlement mechanisms to determine rules of permissible behavior and detect violations would improve the likelihood of sustained implementation of peace accords (Crocker and Hampson 1996; Doyle 1996; Irving 1996; Ratner 1995; Zartman 1995; Diehl 1993). This concern over disputing parties' ability to work through ongoing transition misunderstandings and transgressions on their own leads Mackinlay (in Weiss 1995:5) and Crocker and Hampson (1996:63) to admonish the thought that one could develop a working democracy without disarming the military leaders of opposing factions—''[p]eace builders should not be sent where there is no peace to build'' (Bertram 1995:415). Indeed, Ratner (1995:2) cautions that harmonization of the three separate U.N. roles of ''administrator, mediator, and guarantor'' can be difficult as ''they have inherent incompatibilities that are exacerbated if the parties begin to withhold their cooperation.''

VI. IMPLICATIONS OF THE PUBLIC MANAGEMENT LITERATURE

In the early days of the field of public administration in the United States, Wilson (1887), Goodnow (1900), and Gulick (1937) argued that there was or should be a separation between politics and administration. White (1926) insisted that the study of administration should start from a base of management rather than law. Such views persist to this day, and have even come to appear in the peacekeeping literature. Doyle and Suzuki (in Weiss 1995:143) admonish that there may have been ''a professional tendency to negotiate rather than direct'' in the Cambodian peace operation, and Chopra (1995:80) argues that the special representative of the secretary-general ''could no longer afford to be a diplomat . . . [as] . . . executive powers had to be exercised, not negotiated.'' Some in the field of public administration point out, however, that organizational relations in a public context are based more on bargaining rather than hierarchy (see Milward 1994). Wilson (1885), Willoughby (1927), and Koenig (1964) all lamented the lack of unified direction over the administration because of the existence of a second ''manager'' in the form of Congress. Neustadt (1960) noted that because the U.S. government is one of ''separated institutions sharing powers,'' presidential control is exercised mainly through the art of persuasion. As policy formulation and evaluation are a shared activity, public governance holds inherent constraints for those seeking management efficiency (see Bozeman 1993; Nutt and Backoff 1992; Allison 1980; Rainey et al. 1976). First, ambiguous mandates made to please multiple constituencies with vague, shifting, and conflicting interests limit the chief executive's options and access to resources to implement them. Resulting goals tend to be not only confusing but conflicting. Second, the chief executive has little by way of autonomous control to develop system coherence, integration, and coordination among functional separations and different levels of authority during implementation, exacerbated by the difficulty of designing clear, acceptable, and effective performance measures. Public administration takes place within a ''jurisdictional jungle,'' and private sector management techniques simply ''cannot cope with this pluralism'' (Nutt and Backoff, 1992:47). Third, decision making comes to rely on disjointed incrementalism that hinders effective, long-term responsiveness to those affected by policy, who in turn may hold varying degrees of veto power at multiple points of implementation. As ''politics goes all the way through administration'' (Dimock 1937), and policy is ''made and remade endlessly'' (Lindblom

1959; see also Friedrich 1937), strategies are ''more likely to be emergent than intended'' (Rainey 1997:169). Simply put, ''[I]mplementation is evolution''(Majone and Wildavsky 1978:114). In a system of decentralized government authority such as the United States—or the United Nations—attempts to solve administrative problems in isolation from political ones thus are likely to prove relatively ineffectual (see Long 1949).

Perry and Rainey (1988) posit that inherent problems in public management limit the portability of efficiency-raising concepts from the private sector particularly with regard to strategic direction. Touval (1994) does note with regard to U.N. responses to crises of conflict that a dependence upon consensus results in little opportunity for flexibility in strategy, which tends to lack coherence from the start. As Gawthrop (1969:253) argues, a public organization must weigh political desirability in addition to operational feasibility, generally biased in favor of the former. These dynamics significantly affect a chief executive's ability to maintain what contemporary management scholars have dubbed the ''strategic triangle''—fluid connection between the organizational development of a vision, the capacity to achieve that vision, and adaptability to the changing environment upon which such achievement depends. Allison (1984) describes the import for executive management of the strategic level, where objectives and operational plans to meet them are made; the internal management level, including organization and staffing; and the external management level, concerning autonomous units of the organization, independent organizations, and parties whose action or approval or acquiescence is required. Rein and Rabinovitz (1977:39) describe the three basic forces affecting implementation as legal authority, bureaucratic capacity, and external consent; while Moore (1995:71–72) argues that strategy must be politically sustainable, operationally feasible, and substantively valuable—simultaneously focusing managerial attention upward, downward, and outward, respectively. This three-pointed concept stems in part from Simon (1945), who describes three participants in governance—entrepreneurs, employees, and customers—with the first negotiating ''contracts'' with the last two. As they are all central to the organization's success over time, the interactions among the three elements of the strategic triangle should be seen as *linked* negotiations in which the executive head must engage simultaneously and keep in ''strategic alignment'' (Lax and Sebenius 1986). Genus (1995:7) notes the prevalent suggestion in the management literature for a ''fit'' between an organization's mission, resource capabilities, and wider environment. As Simon (1945:17) himself put it, the executive must keep the contracts in ''equilibrium'' and ensure that they are ''sufficiently advantageous . . . to maintain inducements to keep others in organized activity with him.''

Authors in the sparse literature on management in the face of crisis argue that straight hierarchical command and control is even more inappropriate in emergency management, as intergovernmental jurisdictions tend to be more numerous and public expectations for government intervention more unrealistic (Sylves and Waugh 1996). There is a temptation for crisis managers both to limit action to remedy surface problems and consider management a purely technical affair (Lagadec 1993:39). Examination of crisis management is split into the four stages into which the earlier sections of this essay have been divided: mitigation and preparedness, where steps are taken to minimize the risk of crisis occurrence and train, identify and assemble available resources, and develop interorganizational arrangements of contingency response for a crisis that may nonetheless occur; response, where the organization takes action to end a crisis that has occurred and minimize its damage to organizational interests, with an eye to minimizing recovery problems; and recovery, where the organization provides community support, adjusts to the crisis experience and new environment and, more importantly, takes steps to ensure that the situation does not relapse into crisis (National Governors' Association 1978)— ''[y]our net task as a crisis manager is to return to normalcy . . . [and] . . . find ways to avoid repetition of the incident''(Nudell and Antokol 1988:23).

This recovery stage is crucial to postconflict administrative transitions as politics tends to run rampant through public administration in developing countries even more than in developed ones (Peters 1996). Scott (1989:136–137) notes that most political demands in new states are not amenable to the legislative process, and that in developing countries in general it is during the administrative policy phase that public demands are typically made (see also Grindle 1980:15, fn. 19). Civil service systems tend to dominate the policy process of states that have experienced a sustained period of political instability (Riggs 1963). The conduct of elections without adequate mechanisms to maintain the confidence of factions in ongoing reform can easily result in shallow democratic systems, or ''delegative democracies,'' in which whoever wins leadership governs as he or she sees fit, constrained only by a limited term of office (O'Donnell 1994). Heidenheimer and colleagues (1989) maintain that informal channels of influence naturally increase in new systems of governance, while Migdal (1988) and Agh (in Pridham and Lewis 1996) hold that power elites move in to fill up the vacuum in the bureaucracy created by recent civil conflict. Valenzuela (1992) refers to ''reserved domains'' of power in the bureaucracy in governance transitions, akin to Weber's (1952) observation of a continuation of bureaucratic machinery after violent change. In some instances, as in Mozambique and Cambodia, for example, local administration can be constituted in the form of two parallel and conflicting systems of local government, or new government ministers may be impeded from their work by remaining bureaucrats of the former ruling party (see Olojede 1995; Jeldres 1993). Successful stabilization of democratic means of settling political conflict thus requires greater assurance of depoliticization and accountability, as transitions can exacerbate already existing problems of government administration in developing countries (Linz and Stepan 1996). A small group of elites tend to dominate in all societies of the globe; the key here is to develop suitable means of accountability particularly to maintain the confidence of competing factions in the substantive aspects of reform (Bachrach 1971; Hoston 1992). In the words of Di Palma (1991:10), ''removal of the breakdown potentials from the competitive issue'' is crucial in the heightened tension of transitional society. When one's management problem includes acting not only as administrator and mediator but as guarantor of a transition from violent to peaceful means of political conflict, ignoring lingering control of administration is not only dangerous but also unethical.

VII. MANAGING THE COMPLIANCE PROCESS

Ernst Haas (1964:103) has argued that international administration, ''instead of appearing as a heroic ordering of chaos, assumes the form of continuous negotiation.'' Chayes and Chayes (1991:313) find bargaining to be a continuous aspect of living under any international regulatory agreement. Yet this is not a phenomenon unique to global governance. Writing about management in general, Chester Barnard (1938:215, emphasis added) states that the function of the executive is that of ''*maintaining* the organization in operation'' via continual development and manipulation of an ''economy of interests.'' It has been argued that public administration should be seen as ''bargaining *within* negotiated order'' (Barrett and Fudge 1981:24), and that it is the function of the civil administrator ''to enable disputes to be carried on within reasonable bounds'' (Heclo and Wildavsky 1974:

375). Nutt and Backoff (1992:37) suggest that strategic managers in public organizations need to "build in negotiation and bargaining opportunities." Comfort (1996) states that "any perceived failure in emergency management most often reflects a breakdown in [the] process of intergovernmental communication and interdependent action." With regard to EPA and other regulatory policy in the United States, both implementation and enforcement are based on cooperative negotiation, with threat of sanctions as a tool of bargaining leverage used only in the last resort, often followed by more cooperative negotiation (e.g., Downing 1983). "[L]aw is not administered in a vacuum, but in an environment composed of all those who have an interest in the application or the nonenforcement of the statute." Even in the private sector, the perceived importance of top-down efficiency is changing: "Now we see that a successful strategy is simply a sustainable deal among a variety of stakeholders" (Harvard Business School Professor Malcolm Salter, quoted in Moore 1995:69).

What strategic management by the United Nations needs most—particularly in dealing with parties that have been killing one another—is a greater appreciation for Barnard's economy of interests over the longer term. If the goal of the United Nations is to bring about a lasting *resolution* and not just a superficial *settlement* of civil war, it needs to remain aware of, and address, the parties' alternatives to *continued* agreement (see Lax and Sebenius 1991:109–110). There is a need to continually assess whether the main interests of the parties are being addressed by the policy as implemented (Rupesinghe 1996:166–167), including the possibility one of the parties may be relying on intervention from the political oversight body to change the policy in a manner beneficial to them if they decline to comply with the original policy (Hill and Weissert 1995). Mediators arguably have a professional ethical obligation to ensure the stability of an agreement they help produce (Susskind and Cruikshank 1987), which generally requires procedures to resolve misunderstandings and other ongoing disputes that often arise even without any change in circumstances (Ury et al. 1991). Effective implementation of a public program requires not only sustained support from those providing resources but from those affected by the program (Mazmanian and Sabatier 1989:41–42). Policies with both a high level of ambiguity and a high level of conflict in particular require attention to both top-down and bottom-up implementation processes, the former through focus and incentives, the latter through coalition bargaining (Matland 1995:168–170). If successful implementation of public policy is the "cost-effective use of appropriate mechanisms and procedures in such a way as to fulfill the expectations roused by the policy and retain general public assent" (Lewis, in Lewis and Wallace 1984:215), continued consent of the main conflicting parties is necessary for success by definition. Mediators are accepted "not because of their impartiality but because of their ability to influence, protect, or extend the interest of each party"(Bercovitch 1996:26; see also Princen 1987). This is not an easy thing to accomplish, as the complexity of multiple interests in public administration tends to evolve as an ecology of interaction, which yields results that are not always intended or anticipated (Long 1962). Success in such processes tend to be determined not by the observed value of particular static, independent variables, but *how these variables affect the bargaining relationships* in the overall organizational endeavor to achieve a stable political resolution to violent civil conflict. The participating actors' resources, "rules of the game," and perceptions and beliefs all affect this interactive order, with values of these variables themselves somewhat dependent upon choices made by others as the process moves along (see Lane 1997). Given the right balance of expanding the zone of possible agreement through positive incentives and the alteration of perceptions of the zone through negative incentives, a mediator can even maneuver around problems such as ripeness (Lax and Sebenius 1986:59). The goal of strategic management is to carefully maintain this complex progression of social exchanges along the ''edge of chaos'' (see Waldrop 1994). As Lagadec (1991:40) notes, ''Managing a crisis is not a frantic rescue operation to be undertaken when there is virtually nothing else to be done. Rather, it is a way of acting on a threatening process as that process unfolds. The goal is to avoid slipping into a vicious circle and losing all control.''

A peace operation intended to help parties move their political conflict from the battlefield to legislative, executive, and judicial offices does not fail simply because it is has an unclear mandate, because it has logistical problems, or because a tendency toward incrementalism leads to confrontation limiting its responsiveness to those ostensibly benefiting from its services. These are all problems common to much of domestic public management in the United States. Difficulties in continued compliance these factors cause are overcome not from calls for greater business management efficiency through some artificial and superficial separation of administration from politics. Rather, ongoing politics is the key to successful administration. Implementation relies upon strong political support from those providing direction and resources, those coordinating and carrying out operations at headquarters and in the field, and from those affected by and assisting with the operation. This requires, however, ongoing consensus of these groups over causal theory and values behind objectives (Mazmanian and Sabatier 1989). Haas and Haas (1995) argue that since such consensus has yet to exist regarding the nexus of conflict management, humanitarian assistance, and democratization, integrated programs such as second-generation peace operations are bound to fail. Simon (1945:177) cautions, however, that if an attempt is not made to assign management values ''consciously and deliberately, then it is achieved by implication in the decisions which are already reached.'' May (1985:47) warns that without organizational learning, there will develop a mismatch between strategy, resources, and responsibility. The proper values seem clear—Boutros-Ghali (1995: para. 22) states that the goal of U.N. peace operations is ''to ensure that the original causes of war are eradicated.'' This can be done only through careful regard to the interests of those responsible for decision making at all three corners of the strategic triangle over time. Overall, the management of a modern U.N. peace operation should be regarded by policy makers as a continuous and tenuous balancing exercise of multiparty, multilevel negotiation and mediation supported by credible pressures as well as incentives. Martin (1993) crafted a useful typology of different types of negotiation games, consisting of collaboration, focusing on maintenance; coordination, requiring facilitation; suasion, which need linkage and protection of interests; and assurance, in which uncertainty and suspicion must be allayed. With regard to executive management, the strategic level requires collaboration, the internal level coordination, and the external level suasion and assurance. The chief executive—in the case of U.N. crisis management, the secretary-general together with his staff and special representatives—bears a central role as mediator, not just for the formally conceived operation but for the entire *cooperative effort* over time, bargaining upward, inward, and outward.

REFERENCES

Agh, A. (1996). From nomenclatura to clientura: the emergence of new political elites in East-Central Europe. In G. Pridham and P. Lewis (eds.), *Stabilizing Fragile Democracies: Comparing New Party Systems in Southern and Eastern Europe*. London: Routledge.

Allan, J. (1996). *Peacekeeping: Outspoken Observations by a Field Officer*. Westport, CT: Praeger.
Allison, G. (1980). Public and private management: are they fundamentally alike in all unimportant respects? Proceedings for the Public Management Research Conference, November 19–20, 1979. OPM Document 127-53-1. Washington, D.C.: Office of Personnel Management.
Annan, K. (1997). *Renewing the United Nations: A Program for Reform: Report of the Secretary-General*. U.N. Doc. A/51/950.
Bachrach, P. (1971). *Political Elites in a Democracy*. New York: Atherton Press.
Barnard, C. (1938). *Functions of the Executive*. Cambridge, MA: Harvard University Press.
Barrett, S. and Fudge, C. (1981). *Policy and Action: Essays on the Implementation of Public Policy*. New York: Methuen.
Beigbeder, Y. (1997). *The Internal Management of United Nations Organizations*. New York: St. Martin's Press.
Berdal, M. (1995). United Nations peacekeeping in the former Yugoslavia. In D. Daniel and B. Hayes (eds.), *Beyond Traditional Peacekeeping*. New York: St. Martin's Press.
Berdal, M. (1993). Whither peacekeeping. *Adelphi Paper* no. 281, October.
Bertram, E. (1995). Reinventing governments: the promise and perils of United Nations peace building. *Journal of Conflict Resolution* 39(*3*), 387–418.
Betts, R. (1994). The delusion of impartial intervention. *Foreign Affairs* 73(*6*), 20–33.
Boutros-Ghali, B. (1995). *Supplement to An Agenda for Peace: Position Paper of the Secretary-General on the Occasion of the Fiftieth Anniversary of the United Nations*. U.N. Document S/1995/1.
Boutros-Ghali, B. (1992). *An Agenda for Peace: Preventive Diplomacy, Peacemaking and Peace-Keeping*. Report of the Secretary-General. U.N. Document A/47/277.
Bozeman, B. (ed.) (1993). *Public Management: The State of the Art*. San Francisco: Jossey-Bass.
Broms, B. (1987). The role of the United Nations in the peaceful settlement of disputes. In United Nations Institute for Training and Research (UNITAR), *The United Nations and the Maintenance of International Peace and Security*. Boston: Martinus Nijhoff.
Burley, A.-M. (1993). Regulating the world: multilateralism, international law, and the projection of the New Deal regulatory state, in J. Ruggie (ed.), *Multilateralism Matters: The Theory and Praxis of An Institutional Form*. New York: Columbia University Press.
Caiden, G. (1991). *Administrative Reform Comes of Age*. New York: W. DeGruyer.
Chayes, A. and Chayes, A. H. (1991). Compliance without enforcement: state behavior under regulatory treaties. *Negotiation Journal* 7, 311–336.
Chayes, A. H., Chayes, A., and Raach, G. (1997). Beyond reform: restructuring for more effective conflict intervention. *Global Governance* 3(2), 117–145.
Chopra, J. (1998). Introducing peace-maintenance. *Global Governance* 4(*1*), 1–18.
Chopra, J. (1995). U.N. civil governance in trust. In T. Weiss (ed.), *The United Nations and Civil Wars*. Boulder, CO: Lynne Rienner.
Cliffe, L. (1994). *The Transition to Independence in Namibia*. Boulder, CO: Lynne Rienner.
Comfort, C. (1996). Book review. *American Political Science Review* 90(*3*), 659–660.
Cox, R. and Jacobson, H. (1973). *The Anatomy of Influence: Decision Making in International Organization*. New Haven, CT: Yale University Press.
Crocker, C. and Hampson, F.O. (1996). Making peace settlements work. *Foreign Policy* 104, 54–71.
Damrosch, L. F. (ed.) (1993). *Enforcing Restraint: Collective Intervention in Internal Conflicts*. New York: Council on Foreign Relations Press.
Daniel, D. and Hayes, B. (eds.) (1995). *Beyond Traditional Peacekeeping*. New York: St. Martin's Press.
de Soto, A. and Del Castillo, G. (1994). Obstacles to peace building. *Foreign Policy* 94, 69–83.
Diehl, D. (1993). *International Peacekeeping*. Baltimore: Johns Hopkins University Press.
Dimock, M. (1937). The study of administration. *American Political Science Review* 31(*2*), 28–40.
DiPalma, G. (1991). Parliaments, consolidation, institutionalization: a minimalist view. In U. Liebert

and M. Cotta (eds.), *Parliament and Democratic Consolidation in Southern Europe: Greece, Italy, Portugal, Spain, and Turkey* London: Pinter.

Downing, P. (1983). Bargaining in pollution control. *Policy Studies Journal* 11(*4*), 577–586.

Downs, A. (1972). Up and down with ecology—the issue-attention cycle. *Public Interest* 28(*2*), 38–50.

Doyle, D. (1996). Managing global security: the United Nations not a war maker, a peace maker. In C. W. Maynes and R. Williamson (eds.), *Foreign Policy and the United Nations System*. New York: W. W. Norton & Company.

Doyle, D. (1995). *UN Peacekeeping in Cambodia: UNTAC's Civil Mandate*. Boulder, CO: Lynne Rienner.

Doyle, D. and Suzuki, A. (1995). Transitional Authority in Cambodia. In T. Weiss (ed.), *The United Nations and Civil Wars*. Boulder, CO: Lynne Rienner.

DPKO (U.N. Department of Peacekeeping Operations) (1997). *Multidisciplinary Peacekeeping: Lessons from Recent Experience*. Available from the Lessons Learned Unit.

Durch, W. (1996). *UN Peacekeeping, American Policy, and the Uncivil Wars of the 1990s*. New York: St. Martin's Press.

Durch, W. (1995). Structural issues and the future of UN peace operations. In D. Daniel and B. Hayes (eds.), *Beyond Traditional Peacekeeping*. New York: St. Martin's Press.

Durch, W. (ed.) (1993). *The Evolution of UN Peacekeeping: Case Studies and Comparative Analysis*. New York: St. Martin's Press.

Evans, G. (1993). *Cooperating for Peace: The Global Agenda for the 1990s and Beyond*. St. Leonards: Allen & Unwin.

Fetherston, A. B. (1994). *Towards a Theory of United Nations Peacekeeping*. New York: St. Martin's Press.

Findlay, T. (ed.) (1996). *Challenges for the New Peacekeepers*. SIPRI Research Report No. 12. New York: Oxford University Press.

Friedrich, C. (1937). *Constitutional Government and Politics*. New York: Harper and Brothers.

Gawthrop, L. (1969). *Bureaucratic Behavior in the Executive Branch: An Analysis of Organizational Change*. New York: The Free Press.

Genus, A. (1995). *Flexible Strategic Management*. New York: Chapman & Hall.

Goodnow, H. (1900). *Politics and Administration: A Study in Government*. New York: Macmillan.

Gore, A. (1993). *Common Sense Government: Works Better and Costs Less, Third Report of the National Performance Review*. Washington, D.C.: U.S. Government Printing Office.

Graham, L. (1993). The Dilemmas of managing transitions in weak states: the case of Mozambique. *Public Administration and Development* 13(*4*), 409–422.

Grindle, M. (1980). *Politics and Policy Implementation in the Third World*. Princeton, NJ: Princeton University Press.

Gulick, L. (1937). Notes on the theory of organization. In L. Gulick and L. Urwick (eds.), *Papers on the Science of Administration*. New York: Institute of Public Administration.

Haas, E. (1964). *Beyond the Nation State: Functionalism and International Organization*. Stanford, CA: Stanford University Press.

Haas, P. and Haas, E. (1995). Learning to learn: improving international governance. *Global Governance* 1(*3*), 255–284.

Hampson, F. O. (1996). *Nurturing Peace: Why Peace Settlements Succeed or Fail*. Washington, D.C.: United States Institute of Peace Press.

Harrell, M. and Howe, R. (1995). Military issues in multinational operations. In D. Daniel and B. Hayes (eds.), *Beyond Traditional Peacekeeping*. New York: St. Martin's Press.

Heady, F. (1998). Comparative and international public administration: building intellectual bridges. *Public Administration Review* 58(*1*), 32–39.

Heady, F. (1996). *Public Administration: A Comparative Perspective*, 5th ed. New York: Marcel Dekker.

Heclo, H. and Wildavsky, A. (1974). *The Private Government of Public Money*. London: Macmillan.

Heiberg, M. (1991). Peacekeeping and local populations. In I. J. Rikhye and K. Skjelsbaek (eds.), *The United Nations and Peacekeeping: Results, Limitations and Prospects—Lessons of 40 Years of Experience*. New York: St. Martin's Press.

Heidenheimer, A., Johnston, M., and LeVine, V. (1989). *Political Corruption: A Handbook*. New Brunswick, NJ: Transaction Books.

Heininger, J. (1994). *Peacekeeping in Transition: The United Nations in Cambodia*. New York: The Twentieth Century Fund Press.

Herring, E. P. (1936). *Public Administration and the Public Interest*. New York: McGraw-Hill.

Hill, J. and Weissert, C. (1995). Implementation and the irony of delegation: the politics of low-level radioactive waste disposal. *The Journal of Politics* 57, 344–369.

Hill, S. and Malik, S. (eds.) (1996). *Peacekeeping and the United Nations*. Brookfield, VT: Dartmouth.

Holiday, D. and Stanley, W. (1993). Building the peace: preliminary lessons from El Salvador. *Journal of International Affairs* 46, 415–438.

Hoston, G. (1992). The activist state and the challenge of democratization: a comparative historical perspective. In P. Volten (ed.), *Bound to Change: Consolidating Democracy in East Central Europe*. New York: Institute for EastWest Studies.

Irving, K. (1996). The United Nations and democratic intervention: is "swords into ballot boxes" enough? *Denver Journal of International Law and Policy* 25(*fall*), 41–70.

Irving, K. (1993). *Stars on the Ceiling: The U.N. Secretary-General and the Mediation of International Disputes: A Portfolio of Individual Papers*. Cambridge, MA: n.p.

Jeldres, J. (1993). The UN and the Cambodian transition. *Journal of Democracy* 4(*4*), 104–116.

Joint Inspection Unit of the United Nations (1995). U.N. Docs. A/50/126, A/50/572, and E/1995/20.

Jonah, J. (1991). The management of UN peacekeeping. In I. J. Rikhye and K. Skjelsbaek (eds.), *The United Nations and Peacekeeping: Results, Limitations and Prospects—Lessons of 40 Years of Experience*. New York: St. Martin's Press.

Key, V. O. (1940). The lack of a budgeting theory. *American Political Science Review* 34(*December*), 1137–1144.

Kiernan, B. (1993). *Genocide and Democracy in Cambodia: The Khmer Rouge, the United Nations and the International Community*. New Haven, CT: Yale University Press.

Kirshenbaum, G. (1994). "Who's watching the peacekeepers? Charges of abuse and exploitation tarnish the image of U.N. troops," *Ms.* (*May/June*), 10–15.

Knight, W. A. (1998). Establishing political authority in peace-maintenance. *Global Governance* 4(*Jan–Mar.*), 19–40.

Lagadec, P. (1993). *Preventing Chaos in a Crisis: Strategies for Prevention, Control and Damage Limitation*. translated by J. Phelps from *La gestion des crises*, 1991. New York: McGraw-Hill.

Lax, D. and Sebenius, J. (1986). *The Manager as Negotiator: Bargaining for Cooperation and Competitive Gain*. New York: Basic Books.

Lewis, D. and Wallace, H. (eds.) (1984). *Policies into Practice: National and International Case Studies in Implementation*. London: Heinemann Educational Books.

Lindblom, C. (1959). The science of "muddling through," *Public Administration Review* 19(*spring*), 79–88.

Linz, J. and Stepan, A. (1996). Toward consolidated democracies. *Journal of Democracy* 7(*April*), 14–33.

Long, N. (1962). *The Polity*. Chicago: Rand McNally & Company.

Lyons, G. (1994). A new collective security: the United Nations and international peace. *The Washington Quarterly* 17(2), 173–199.

Lyons, G. and Mastanduno, M. (eds.) (1995). *Beyond Westphalia? State Sovereignty and International Intervention*. Baltimore: Johns Hopkins University Press.

Mackinlay, J. (1993). Problems for U.S. forces in operations beyond peacekeeping. In W. Lewis, (ed.), *Peacekeeping: The Way Ahead?* Report of a Special Conference, McNair Paper 25. Washington, D.C.: Institute for National Strategic Studies.

Mackinlay, J. (1989). *The Peacemakers: An Assessment of Peacekeeping Operations at the Arab-Israel Interface*. London: Unwin Hyman.

Mainwaring, S., O'Donnell, G., and Valenzuela, J. S. (1992). *Issues in Democratic Consolidation: The New South American Democracies in Comparative Perspective*. Notre Dame, IN: University of Notre Dame Press.

Martin, L. (1993). The rational state choice of multilateralism. In J. Ruggie, (ed.), *Multilateralism Matters: The Theory and Praxis of An Institutional Form*. New York: Columbia University Press.

Majone, G. and Wildavsky, A. (1978). Implementation as evolution. In H. Freeman (ed.), *Policy Studies Review Annual*. Beverly Hills, CA: Sage Publications.

Matland, R. (1995). Synthesizing the implementation literature: the ambiguity-conflict model of policy implementation. *Journal of Public Administration Research and Theory* 5, 145–174.

May, P. (1985). FEMA's role in emergency management: examining recent experience. *Public Administration Review* 45(6), 40–48.

Mazmanian, D. and Sabatier, P. (1989). *Implementation and Public Policy*. New York: University Press of America.

Migdal, J. (1988). *Strong Societies and Weak States: State-Society Relations and State Capabilities in the Third World*. Princeton, NJ: Princeton University Press.

Milward, H. B. (1994). Implications of contracting out. In P. Ingraham and B. Romzek (eds.), *New Paradigms for Government: Issues for the Changing Public Service*. San Francisco: Jossey-Bass.

Moore, M. (1995). *Creating Public Value: Strategic Management in Government*. Cambridge, MA: Harvard University Press.

Mortimer, E. and Lambert, R. (1997). "Unraveling the UN," *Financial Times*, October 17, p. 19+.

Murphy, C. (1994). *International Organization and Industrial Change: Global Governance Since 1850*. New York: Oxford University Press.

Murphy, S. (1996). *Humanitarian Intervention: The United Nations in an Evolving World Order*. Philadelphia: University of Pennsylvania Press.

National Governors' Association (1978). *Emergency Preparedness Project Final Report*. Washington, D.C.: U.S. Government Printing Office.

Nudell, M. and Antokol, N. (1988). *The Handbook for Effective Emergency and Crisis Management*. Lexington, MA: Lexington Books.

Nutt, P. and Backoff, R. (1992). *Strategic Management of Public and Third-Sector Organizations: A Handbook for Leaders*. San Francisco: Jossey-Bass.

O'Donnell, G. (1994). Delegative democracy. *Journal of Democracy* 5(*January*), 55–69.

Olojede, D. (1995). "Putting Mozambique back together." *Newsday*, September 10.

Osborne, D. and Gaebler, T. (1992). *Reinventing Government*. Reading, PA: Addison-Wesley.

Perry, J. and Rainey, H. (1988). The public private distinction in organization theory: a critique and research strategy. *Academy of Management Review* 13(2), 182–201.

Petak, W. (1985). Emergency management: a challenge for public administration. *Public Administration Review* 45(6), 3–7.

Peters, G. (1995). *The Politics of Bureaucracy*, 4th ed. White Plains, NY: Longman.

Peters, T. and Waterman, R. Jr. (1982). *In Search of Excellence: Lessons from America's Best-Run Companies*. New York: HarperCollins.

Picco, G. (1994). The U.N. and the use of force: leave the secretary general out of it. *Foreign Affairs* 73(5), 14–18.

Pick, H. (1992). "World leader demands Europe work harder for peace." *The Guardian*, May 23, 16.

Pressman, J. and Wildavsky, A. (1973). *Implementation*. Berkeley, CA: University of California Press.

Princen, T. (1987). International mediation—the view from the Vatican. *Negotiation Journal* 3(*4*) 347–366.

Rainey, H. (1997). *Understanding and Managing Public Organizations*, 2nd ed. San Francisco: Jossey-Bass Publishers.

Rainey, H., Backoff, R., and Levine, C. (1976). Comparing public and private organizations. *Public Administration Review* 36, 233–246.

Raman, K. V. (1977). *Dispute Settlement Through the United Nations*. Dobbs Ferry, NY: Oceana Publications.

Ramsbotham, O. and Woodhouse, T. (1996). *Humanitarian Intervention in Contemporary Conflict: A Reconceptualization* Cambridge, MA: Polity Press.

Ratner, S. (1995). *The New UN Peacekeeping: Building Peace in Lands of Conflict after the Cold War*. New York: St. Martin's Press.

Rein, M. and Rabinovitz, F. (1977). *Implementation: A Theoretical Perspective*, Working Paper No. 43. Cambrdge, MA: Joint Center for Urban Studies.

Riggs, F. (1963). Bureaucrats and political development: a paradoxical view. In Joseph LaPalombara (ed.), *Bureaucracy and Political Development*. Princeton, NJ: Princeton University Press.

Rikhye, I. J. (1992). *Strengthening UN Peacekeeping: New Challenges and Proposals*. Washington, D.C.: U.S. Institute of Peace.

Rikhye, I. J. and Skjelsbaek, K. (eds.) (1991). *The United Nations and Peacekeeping: Results, Limitations and Prospects—Lessons of 40 Years of Experience*. New York: St. Martin's Press.

Rivlin B. and Gordenker, L. (eds.) (1993). *The Challenging Role of the UN Secretary-General: Making "The Most Impossible Job in the World" Possible*. Westport, CT: Praeger.

Rosenau, J. (1995). Governance in the twenty-first century. *Global Governance* 1, 13–43.

Rosenbloom, D. (1993). Editorial: have an administrative Rx? Don't forget the politics. *Public Administration Review* 53(*6*), 503–506.

Ruggie, J. (ed.) (1993). *Multilateralism Matters: The Theory and Praxis of An Institutional Form*. New York: Columbia University Press.

Ruggie, J. (1993). The United Nations: stuck in a fog between peacekeeping and enforcement. In W. Lewis (ed.), *Peacekeeping: The Way Ahead*? McNair Paper no. 25. Washington, D.C.: Institute for National Strategic Studies.

Rupesinghe, K. (1996). Mediation in internal conflicts: lessons from Sri Lanka. In J. Bercovitch (ed.), *Resolving International Conflicts: The Theory and Practice of Mediation*. Boulder, CO: Lynne Rienner.

Sapir, D. and Deconnick, H. (1995). The paradox of humanitarian assistance and military intervention in Somalia. In T. Weiss (ed.), *The United Nations and Civil Wars*. Boulder, CO: Lynne Rienner.

Schear, J. (1995). Beyond traditional peacekeeping. In D. Daniel and B. Hayes (eds.), *Beyond Traditional Peacekeeping*. New York: St. Martin's Press.

Schneider, S. (1995). *Flirting with Disaster: Public Management in Crisis Situations*. Armonk, NY: M. E. Sharpe.

Scott, J. (1989). Handling historical comparisons cross–nationally. In A. Heidenhelmer, M. Johnston, and V. LeVine, *Political Corruption: A Handbook*. New Brunswick, NJ: Transaction Books.

Simon, H. (1947). *Administrative Behavior*. New York: Macmillan Co.

Smith, D. (1997). Towards understanding the causes of war. In K. Volden and D. Smith (eds.), *Causes of Conflict in the Third World*. Oslo: North/South Coalition and International Peace Research Institute.

Smith, W. (1985). Effectiveness of the biased mediator. *Negotiation Journal* 1(*4*), 363–372.

Stewart, J. (1995). "U.N. learns hard lessons on peacekeeping: new direction after Somalia," *San Francisco Chronicle*, March 28, 1995, p. A1+.

Sullivan, J. (1994). "How peace came to El Salvador." *Orbis* (Winter) 83–98.

Susskind L. and Cruikshank, J. (1987). *Breaking the Impasse: Consensual Approaches to Resolving Public Disputes*. New York: Basic Books.

Sylves, R. and Waugh, W. Jr. (eds.) (1996). *Disaster Management in the U.S. and Canada: The Politics, Policymaking, Administration and Analysis of Emergency Management*, 2nd ed. Springfield, IL: Charles C Thomas.

Task Force on Ethical and Legal Issues in Humanitarian Assistance. (1994). *The Mohoak Criteria for Humanitarian Assistance in Complex Emergencies.* New York: World Conference on Religion and Peace.

Thakur, R. and Thayer, C. (1995). *A Crisis of Expectations: UN Peacekeeping in the 1990s*. Boulder, CO: Westview Press.

Tharoor, S. (1996). The future of peacekeeping. In J. Whitman and D. Pocock (eds.), *After Rwanda: The Coordination of United Nations Humanitarian Assistance*. New York: St. Martin's Press.

Touval, S. (1994). Why the U.N. fails. *Foreign Affairs* 5(2), 44–57.

UNDPI (U.N. Department of Public Information). (1997). *The UN financial crisis: at a glance*, U.N. Doc. DPI/1815/Rev. 11.

Urquhart, B. (1993). "Needed—A UN volunteer military force." *New York Review of Books* 40(*June 10*), 3–4.

Urquhart, B. (1987). United Nations peacekeeping operations and how their role might be enhanced. In UNITAR (U.N. Institute for Training and Research), *The United Nations and the Maintenance of International Peace and Security.* Dordrecht, The Netherlands: Martinus Nijhoff.

Ury, W., Brett, J., and Goldberg, S. (1991). Designing an effective dispute resolution system. In J. W. Breslin and J. Rubin, (eds.), *Negotiation Theory and Practice*. Cambridge, MA: Program on Negotiation Books.

Van Wagenen, R. (1971). In R. Jordan (ed.), *International Administration: Its Evolution and Contemporary Applications*. New York: Oxford University Press.

Weiss, T. (ed.) (1995). *The United Nations and Civil Wars*. Boulder, CO: Lynne Rienner.

Weller, M. (1992). The International response to the dissolution of the Socialist Federal Republic of Yugoslavia. *The American Journal of International Law* 86, 569–607.

White, L. (1926). *Introduction to the Study of Public Administration*. New York: Macmillan.

Whitman, J. and Pocock, D. (eds.) (1996). *After Rwanda: The Coordination of United Nations Humanitarian Assistance*. New York: St. Martin's Press.

Wildavsky, A. (1964). *The Politics of the Budgetary Process*. Boston: Little, Brown and Co.

Wilson, W. (1887). The study of administration. *Political Science Quarterly* 2(2), 197–222.

Zartman, W. I. (ed.) (1995). *Elusive Peace: Negotiating an End to Civil Wars*. Washington, D.C.: The Brookings Institution.

11

Managing Through a Crisis

A Case Study of the Orange County, California, Bankruptcy

M. Celeste Murphy School of Public Administration and Urban Studies, San Diego State University, San Diego, California

I. INTRODUCTION

On December 6, 1994, Orange County, California declared bankruptcy, creating the single largest county bankruptcy in U.S. history. In a land where million-dollar homes on sprawling cliffs overlook the bright blue waters of the Pacific Ocean, the sudden declaration of bankruptcy came to many public officials and private citizens as quite a surprise. This financial crisis call sent shock waves through Wall Street and the entire nation. Many people asked, then and now: How could such an economically prosperous area go bankrupt? This case study will explore the main factors leading up to Orange County's declaration of bankruptcy, as well as the consequences, impacts, and preventive measures that could have helped avoid such a financial crisis. Additionally, this case study will review the currently proposed county bankruptcy recovery plan.

II. METHODOLOGY

The data collected for this paper was compiled through personal and telephone interviews, newspaper reports, government documents, and journal articles. The paper is based on nine focused, face-to-face personal interviews and seven telephone interviews conducted during the months of July 1995 and March 1996 in Orange Country, California. The personal interviews were conducted on site at the offices of city and county officials. The telephone interviews were conducted from an apartment in Newport Beach, California. The questionnaire used to focus the interviews consisted of 15 questions (see Appendix A) designed to determine the factors leading up to the bankruptcy, the role of specific individuals leading up to the bankruptcy, the impacts of the bankruptcy upon the cities within the county, preventive actions that could have been taken to avoid the bankruptcy, and possible postbankruptcy solutions. Each interview lasted approximately 45 minutes and was not tape-recorded. All documentation of the interviews consisted of handwritten notes and quotations. All city and county officials interviewed were sent a personal letter,

1 month prior to the interview, requesting the opportunity to interview them for the purpose of determining the causes of the Orange County bankruptcy. Upon the author's arrival in Orange County, individuals were contacted and formal arrangements for the interviews were made.

In order to obtain a well-rounded sense of the impacts of the bankruptcy on different sectors of the citizenry within the county, interviewees represent the interests of both the public and private sectors. Selection criteria for interviewees included one or more of the following: (1) a top-level Orange County official, (2) an Orange County official whose position directly involved budgeting and/or financial management, (3) a top-level administration policy city official, (4) a city official whose position directly involved budgeting and/or financial management policies, (5) a representative of business interests of the county, (6) a representative of the voting population of the county, (7) a representative of general citizens' interests, (8) a representative of schools and or colleges within the county, and (9) a representative of the private financial advisor to the county.

III. OVERVIEW OF ORANGE COUNTY

The land that currently makes up the political jurisdiction of Orange County was discovered and settled by Don Hernando Cortez in 1519 (Ramsey 1973:1, 58). In 1870 Dr. W.N. Hardin of Anaheim, California, brought the first orange to the county, later leading to a thriving agriculture-based economy. Orange County prospered from its agricultural industry, beginning with grapes in 1875 and followed by oranges and raisins. When the county was created, owing to the economy's dependence upon agricultural production, a five-member Board of Supervisors was appointed to oversee the five agricultural regions which today make up Orange County (Popejoy 1995). Originally part of Los Angeles County, Orange County did not split from Los Angeles County until 1889, after the strong leaders of the county felt they were not receiving proper representation in county government and that their specific problems were frequently neglected and overlooked (Ramsey 1973).

In 1995 the Orange County economy had a value of $82 billion (Moore 1995). As the economic structure of the county has changed, it has come to rely less on agricultural production and more on the expansion of high-tech firms such as Rockwell, TRW, and Unical (Moore 1995). According to the president of Orange County's Economic Development Consortium, Ken Moore, "It still remains an entrepreneurial county" (Moore 1995). Today Orange County is an ethnically diverse county. Hispanics rank second to whites in population, and Asians rank third (California County Projection 1994). Over one-third of the population in the county is made up of foreign immigrants. Financially, the county's per capita income ranks slightly above the state's per capita income. In 1993 Orange County's per capita income was $24,737, while California's was $21,517 (California County Projections 1994;iii). Other economic indicators, such as taxes from general and retail sales, showed growth in the economy from 1980 to 1990 (California County Projections 1994:iii).

As the county's economic structure has changed, several high-ranking county officials have come to believe that the government's present organizational structure is antiquated and should be restructured (Bergenson 1995; Popejoy 1995). Specifically, individuals within county and city government as well as civic organizations favor the appointment of a county chief executive officer (CEO) to provide executive leadership in county affairs (Bergenson 1995; Coloma 1995; Haddad 1995; Huston 1995; Popejoy 1995; Ream 1995).

Further discussion of county government reform will follow a review of the main factors contributing to Orange County's bankruptcy.

IV. FACTORS CONTRIBUTING TO ORANGE COUNTY'S BANKRUPTCY

In 1978 California passed Proposition 13, which limited revenue generated from local property taxes throughout the state (Lucier et al. 1980:193; Mittermeier 1995). At the same time this measure put greater demands upon local governments throughout the state to search for new ways to generate revenue to fund the many services local governments offer. Additionally, according to the Federal Mandate Accountability and Reform Act of 1994, during the 1980s and 1990s, the federal government promulgated and legislated numerous intergovernmental mandates. The combination of these two factors—Proposition 13 and increased federal intergovernmental mandates—forced counties across the country to search for new, creative sources of revenue to maintain a sufficient level of public services; in the case of Orange County, it led to a gamble with public funds.

In an era when innovative government financing and ''reinventing government'' (Gaebler and Osborne 1992) is encouraged, Orange County, like other counties across the nation, tried to raise revenue without raising taxes. This strategy provoked then Orange County Treasurer Robert L. Citron to turn to high-risk investments such as derivatives. A derivative is ''a financial instrument that is valued according to the expected price movements of an underlying asset, which may be a commodity, a currency, or a security'' (Oxford University Press 1993:82). Investing in derivatives when interest rates were low allowed the investment portfolio of the county treasurer to earn an average interest rate of 8.52% and at times as much as 5 percentage points higher than the interest earned by the state of California on its investments. These high interest rates provided the county with a healthy source of revenue. In fiscal year 1994–1995, a total of 35% of the ongoing general fund revenue for the county was from interest earnings (Huntington Beach 1995). Thus, as earnings continued to increase, county officials, such as the board of supervisors, were not inclined to question Citron's investment practices. However, as interest rates continued to rise, as determined by the Federal Reserve, the county's portfolio value significantly decreased. The fact that the county's portfolio value was highly dependent upon a stabilization or decrease in interest rates was clearly stated by Citron in the Treasurer's Annual Financial Statements of 1993 and 1994 to the Board of Supervisors (Citron 1992: 2,3,5; 1993:2,3). Thus, unlike the fiscal crisis of New York City in 1975 (Bahl and Duncombe 1992; Glassberg 1981; Gordon 1977), in Philadelphia in 1976, and in Cleveland in 1978 (Inman 1983), the Orange County bankruptcy was caused primarily by the high-risk investment practices of the county treasurer.

Numerous other factors contributed to Orange County's bankruptcy. According to a current Board of Supervisors member, ''There were two factors which contributed to the bankruptcy: 1) lack of oversight [there was] not an accountable system and 2) failure of disclosure to investors . . . i.e. more questions should have been asked'' (Bergenson 1995). Additionally, there was an investment oversight committee, which Citron refused to meet with (Mittermeier 1996). Supervisor Bergenson, who took office shortly after the bankruptcy also added, ''The Treasurer and Assistant Treasurer had total control and trust by the county'' (Bergenson 1995).

Another factor contributing to the Orange County bankruptcy was the use of a financial maneuver by the treasurer called ''leveraging.'' A leveraged fund is ''a mutual or investment fund whose charter allows it to borrow money in order to increase its securities portfolio'' (Aveneyon 1988:278). This investment strategy is speculative in nature: since interest and expenses on loans are fixed, the stockholders will receive a very high rate of return if investments bring a high rate of return. However, if the return is low, the stockholders will receive an even lower return on investments (Aveneyon 1988:278). Through leveraging, the treasurer was able to take $7.57 billion and leverage it 2.7 times into $20.5 billion (Merrill Lynch 1995:3). Citron also used reverse repurchase agreements, which are enforceable agreements between a seller and a buyer. These agreements require the seller to buy back what is being sold within a certain period of time or at a specific price and under specific conditions (Aveneyon 1988:397). Leveraging and the use of reverse repurchase agreements without matching maturities helped contribute to the country's current fiscal problems.

Dan Villella, finance director of Huntington Beach, California, believes the causes of the Orange County bankruptcy were ''Citron's investment practices, the leveraging of his investments, borrowing to get a higher return rate, and the fact that the Treasurer took a loan on his borrowing'' (Villella 1995). The fact that the treasurer's investment practices turned sour raised questions among county residents about his qualifications to be treasurer in the first place. ''Mr. Citron was an *elected* official with no qualifications other than to get elected'' (Huston 1995). Janet Huston, executive director of the League of California Cities, Orange County Division, states, ''The Board of Supervisors had responsibility for county funds. . . . The Board was not involved in the county's investment policy'' (Huston 1995). Orange County's director of management and budget saw the problem as ''a lack of sophisticated understanding of Orange County's fiscal program county-wide. For example, it was believed that the county had a sophisticated Treasurer, who understood what he was doing. If he were sophisticated, then he was driving his portfolio on ego'' (Branca 1995). Branca's and Huston's views raise the important issue of which standards, if any, elected officials must meet in order to serve in public office.

The president of the Orange County League of Women Voters questioned the role of the state government in financing solutions to local problems. ''The state used to fund local governments, but recently the state has been pulling back. The state was extracting $6.5 million more from the county than it was putting in'' (Haddad 1995). Thus, the net effect was that Orange County sent money annually to the state and the county received only a portion of what it collected and sent to the state.

The one significant event preceding the county's declaration of bankruptcy, on December 6, 1994, involved First Boston, which was selling the collateral the bank had invested in the county after finding insufficient cash within the county treasury's account (Huntington Beach 1995). This action by First Boston caused the treasurer to become concerned about other investors withdrawing their money or demanding the liquidification of collateral, which would, in turn, lead to a run on the investment pool (Popejoy 1995). ''Declaring bankruptcy allowed the county to freeze the funds and stop the investment banking firms from liquidating the collateralized agreement for the Reverse Repurchase Agreements. However, many banks liquidated them anyway'' (Popejoy, 1995). In total there were 187 investors (individuals, banks, investment firms, and cities) who invested $7.57 billion in the investment pool (Citron 1993:2,3). All but two cities within the county, several cities outside the county, school districts, and others made up the investment pool.

The bankruptcy cost $1.69 billion or 22.3% of the total investment (Huntington Beach, 1995).

Some believe the main financial advisor to the county, Merrill Lynch, shares a considerable part of the blame for the bankruptcy. Former county Chief Executive Officer William Popejoy stated:

> A number of investment firms contributed to the loss and failed to protect the interests of the county. When you sell to a municipality you have a responsibility to it. After a written warning by Merrill Lynch (ML) to Citron, warning him of the volatility of the county's investment in derivatives, ML continued to buy Citron the same funds they warned him about and underwrote a huge bond issue for $600 million. Warning letters about the high volatility of the county's investment portfolio were never sent to the county Board of Supervisors. ML's actions run contrary to the advice they provided to the county. (Popejoy 1995)

Current county CEO Janice Mittermeier reinforces Popejoy's belief by stating ''Merrill Lynch is extremely culpable. However, this is not to say that the county people aren't responsible'' (Mittermeier 1996). Presently, the county is suing Merrill Lynch for $ 2 billion (*Orange County Register* May 3, 1995). These actions by Merrill Lunch raise the important issue of corporate responsibility. Should Merrill Lynch have continued to sell the county derivatives, knowing the risk involved in such an investment? Merrill Lynch paints quite a different picture of the financial relationship between the Orange County and the investment firm. Peter Case, Merrill Lynch's vice president of the Southern California District, offered his thoughts on the issue:

> ML had a 20-year relationship with Orange County. . . . In 1992 ML began to discuss at least a dozen times the high percentage of derivatives in the county's investment portfolio. . . . In 1993 ML suggested to Citron to include in his report to the Board of Supervisors the amount of leverage in the portfolio. . . . Also, in 1993 ML offered to buy back the derivatives from the county, and Citron came back to ML and turned down the offer. . . . The problem was with leverage. Derivatives had the volatility of a five-year treasury bond. . . . ML was not aware that Citron was skimming interest and had secrets accounts. ML feels that it does not have to act as the supervisor of the Treasurer. That's the role of the Board of Supervisors. (Case 1995)

Citron reported in his 1993 and 1994 Annual Financial Statements to the Board of Supervisors his use of reverse repurchase agreements and leveraging. The 1994 report included a mention of the 20% possibility that the treasurer's forecast of interest rate fluctuation was wrong (Citron 1994). It is also clearly stated in both the 1993 and 1994 reports that the future success of the county's investments was dependent upon interest rates stabilizing or declining. These statements about the dependency of the county's continued financial success upon interest rates were warning signs to the board of supervisors about the high volatility of the county's investment portfolio. These statements were not questioned by the board of supervisors.

City and county officials, as well as county leaders of civic organizations, feel the Securities Exchange Commission, the rating agencies, and auditors (both internal and external) share the blame with Merrill Lynch (Royalty 1995; Watson 1995). According to the executive vice president of Orange County's Taxpayers' Association:

> The county needed better auditors. Peat Marwick, one of the big six accounting firms audited Orange County and concluded everything was fine. They, too, are culpable.

> . . . The Board of Supervisors should have insisted upon a more thorough audit. But since Citron lied, they [the Supervisors] can be personally forgiven. They would be fired if this were in private business. . . . Also, equally liable are city managers, mayors and city council members who put money in the investment pool unquestioningly. (Royalty 1995)

Others blame the county's reporting policies for the bankruptcy (Uberaga 1995). The city manager for Huntington Beach, California, assessed the situation this way: "There should have been more explicit reporting mechanisms, both internal and external . . . more detailed reports of where the money was invested. . . . The county could have had an ongoing outside investment council" (Uberaga, 1995).

V. PREVENTIVE MEASURES THAT MIGHT HAVE HELPED AVOID THE BANKRUPTCY

There are several preventive measures that could have helped avoid such a large-scale municipal bankruptcy. According to Santa Ana City Manger Dave Ream, whose city had $150 million invested in the Orange County portfolio and is still waiting for the 20% the county owes the cities ($28 million for Santa Ana), "There needed to be an investment oversight committee. The state balanced its budget on the backs of the counties. When the state was in trouble in 1990, Orange County raised the risk level of its investments. In 1991 the pool was opened up for outside investors. There needs to be a central core to handle the day-to-day business of the county" (Ream 1995). Like Ream, many citizens and public officials feel strongly that there is a need for more disclosure of financial information. There are varied municipal accounting principles throughout the 50 states, yet the only provisions of the federal securities laws that are applicable to the municipal securities issuer are the "antifraud provisions" (Hansen 1977). Thus, in the case with Orange County, if the investment procedures of the county treasurer were made public, the disclosure of this information could have called public attention to the matter much earlier.

Others raise questions about the auditing procedures of the county. These procedures permit a single person to serve as both auditor and controller. As noted by former County CEO William Popejoy, "The Auditor is elected and should be appointed. The Auditor served as the Controller too. Thus, there were no internal checks on the investments. The Controller writes checks and the Auditor checks the checks written. In this case he is serving in two positions" (Popejoy 1995). The question again is raised about the appropriateness of the current structure of the Orange County government. Should the auditor and controller be two separate positions instead of one? If so, could this new structure have prevented the bankruptcy? Current county CEO Janice Mittermeier believes that, instead of changing to a system of appointing county officials, the county could impose minimum qualifications to run for office (Mittermeier 1996). However, this still does not guarantee that "risk takers" will not be elected to office.

As the bankruptcy has unfolded, former Treasurer-Tax Collector Robert Citron has been replaced by his opponent in the previous election, James Moorlach. Both Citron and former Assistant Treasurer Matthew Raabe, who has also been replaced, have pleaded guilty to six counts of fraud in connection with investment practices that led to the bankruptcy. Citron's felony charges include misappropriation of public funds, falsifying public documents, and misleading investors. He faces up to 14 years in prison and up to $10 million in fines (*Orange County Register*, May 8, 1995). Raabe reportedly directed county treasury staff to divert extra interest earnings from the shared investment pool into the County General Fund, where Citron then leveraged them to produce additional earnings. Additionally, Raabe participated in a series of investment deals in 1993 and 1994 that allowed certain schools and other favored agencies to receive extra earnings at the expense of pool participants (*Orange County Register*, May 17, 1995).

VI. CONSEQUENCES OF THE ORANGE COUNTY BANKRUPTCY

There are many direct and indirect consequences of the Orange County bankruptcy. One direct consequence is the county's debt of $1.7 billion it must repay to pool investors. However, on May 19, 1995, investors in nearly $1 billion of the county's bonds agreed to postpone demand for repayment on their debt for 1 year, making full repayment due in June 1996 (Sterngold 1995:19). An indirect consequence resulting from this direct consequence is that bondholders have agreed to accept a significantly lower interest rate during the next year, because the county simply does not have the money to pay the full market rate. A second direct consequence, as mentioned previously, is the county's lawsuit against Merrill Lynch for bad financial advice, which costs the county extensive legal fees as a result of the ongoing litigation. The third direct consequence is that the county's bonds have received a "D" (default) bond rating, mainly because of the county's postponement of its debt obligation to investors (Martinez 1995). Standard & Poor lowered the county's once perfect rating because the county's deal to rollover its debt to bond investors does not stipulate how the county will produce the money to pay the interest due. This default rating for Orange County makes it the third largest municipal bond default in U.S. history, behind the Washington Public Power Supply System in 1983 and the New York City bond default in 1975. The fourth consequence of the bankruptcy is the conflict of interests it created among county officials. As a result of these conflicts, William Popejoy resigned as CEO of the county in July 1995, citing a lack of financial and management autonomy from the Board of Supervisors, as they increasingly reinvolved themselves in the micromanagement of the county (Lait 1995; p. A1). Finally, one of the more politically sensitive consequences is that several members of the board are facing a recall by the voters.

VII. IMPACTS OF THE BANKRUPTCY

The bankruptcy has impacted the county's cities, other cities, and school districts in a number of ways. On May 2, 1995, Orange County won Bankruptcy Court approval to disperse $5.7 billion to more than 200 cities, schools, and government agencies, holding off a possibly disastrous string of municipal defaults and bankruptcies (Johnson and Owen 1995). The investment pool settlement provides investors an average of 77 cents on the dollar in cash, with school districts receiving an additional 13 cents in recovery notes or a total of 90 percent of their total principal investment. Cities received 80 cents per dollar or 80 percent of their total principal investment (Ream 1995).

However, this settlement does not eliminate the bankruptcy. Actually, there are two bankruptcies. One is for the failed investment pool; the other is for the county itself. The May 1995 settlement helps to remedy the investment pool bankruptcy. The county bankruptcy must still be addressed, with its bondholders awaiting $1.275 billion and vendors holding $100 million in unpaid bills; there are also other creditors who need repayment. On July 7, 1995, Wall Street investors voted to extend repayment dates on $800 million, which triggered Standard & Poor to lower the county's bond rating to "D." This default rating will hurt the county's ability to attract investors to invest in any local projects. Thus, in order to help the county's short as well as long-term financial future, the county is hoping that its newly developed recovery plan, to be voted on on May 8, 1996, will boost the county's current bond rating. Hopefully, as with the New York City fiscal crisis, the Orange County fiscal crisis will not lead to a fundamental or long-standing change in risk perceptions of investors that will result in higher interest rates in the municipal bond market (Kidwell and Trzcinka 1982). However, only time will tell. Thus far school districts within the county have been repaid the largest percentage of any investors, with a 90% repayment. However, according to Newport-Mesa School District Director of Fiscal Services Mike Fine, schools have definitely been forced to make sacrifices due to the bankruptcy. According to Fine:

> Not counting the loss in principal the immediate impact of the bankruptcy was $5 million in interest lost. The School Board adopted a plan to help in the bankruptcy which called to: 1) sell surplus school sites, providing $4.5 million, 2) cut the budget by $3 million, 3) increase lease revenue by vacating school owned sites. . . . In addition, we set up a budget committee of 23 people. The committee went through 66 items and ranked them in order of things that could be cut first to last. We decided to cut rates per child which run from $46 for K–6 to $76 for 9–19. Now schools have $10 less per child. . . . Also, we eliminated elementary school counselors and 12 classified positions and laid off four management people. . . . We cut back on travel and conferences eliminated the Administrative Intern Program, reduced the heat in the swimming pools, eliminated two of five car phones in addition to grades 9–12 school bus transportation. Our main goal was no change in class size. We laid off no teachers. Our cuts were as far away from the classroom as possible. . . . However, these cuts only address the principal revenue, not the $5 million in interest revenue still not paid. (Fine 1995)

The Newport-Mesa School District originally invested in the county due to the high-interest yield. The school district, along with three other investors, invested with the firm Rauscher, Pierce and Refsnes. The other investors were Irvine, North Orange County Community College, and the Orange County Department of Education for a total investment of $200 million. Fine contends that the firm did not warn the districts about the county's intent to utilize derivatives and leveraging, nor were they aware of the extent of their volatility. Newport-Mesa School District and the other three investors are asking the investment firm to repay them the several-million-dollar profit the firm earned from the investment deal. Thus, like the financial relationship between Orange County and Merrill Lynch, the public entity is holding the private investment firm responsible for its loss of funds. Jim McIlwain, vice president of administrative services for Orange Coast College, which enrolls about 23,000 students as part of the Coast Community College District, stated that the district, consisting of three community colleges, had $22 million invested in the county fund (McIlwain 1995):

> The State sent the money to the County. We had no choice with the investment. The Coast District has received 90 percent of our money back. The three colleges in the Coast District lost $2.2 million. This 10 percent still not repaid has not affected the colleges. However, we don't know about the future. We see increased state funding as an alternative. Some colleges in the County invested additional money in the pool, for example Fullerton and Cypress College. (McIlwain 1995)

Cities do not appear to be feeling the severity of the bankruptcy at this time. According to the city manager of Huntington Beach, Michael Uberaga, when asked how the bankruptcy had impacted Huntington Beach, he responded, "Through the deferral or elimination of capital projects. Also, there's been a one percent reduction in the Operating Budget. . . . Psychologically the bankruptcy has affected our community by validating the right wing mentality of such organizations as the Committee of Correspondence, which views government as ineffective and incompetent" (Uberaga, 1995). According to the Finance Director of the city of Santa Ana, Rod Coloma, "The Orange County bankruptcy hasn't impacted the city. We are downsizing [which the city was in the process of doing before the bankruptcy]. . . . The population has increased 50 percent in the last 12 years. Currently, we have $30 million in capital improvements for jail and water bonds, that will not get done" (Coloma 1995). It is evident from the responses given by the city officials of both Huntington Beach and Santa Ana that the bankruptcy up until now has had little impact upon these two cites. The main impacts have been on the postponement of capital projects.

Other indirect impacts of the bankruptcy have been the decrease in the number of housing sales within the county and layoffs of county and noncounty employees. According to a report by Dataquick Information System, monthly home sales dropped in volume from 3000 in April 1994 to 2143 in April 1995. The decrease in home sales is from 39% the previous year to 35% (*Orange County Register*, May 4, 1995) However, in February, 1996 home sales increased 31%, the biggest monthly sales increase in nearly 2 years (Vrana 1996). This sudden increase in sales is partially attributed to the recently proposed bankruptcy recovery plan. In reaction to the impact on the real estate market, the bankruptcy prompted former Orange County Chief Executive Officer William Popejoy to announce the layoffs of 1040 county employees in March 1995 (Lait 1995:A1). Popejoy's budget proposal also called for eliminating 563 vacant positions, for a total savings of $188 million (Lait 1995:A1). These cuts reduce the county's original operating budget by 40.6% (Lait 1995:A1). The general manager for the Orange County Employee's Association (OCEA) noted, "The County had 18,000 employees [before the bankruptcy]. They've eliminated 4,000 positions and laid off 1,500 employees, 800 of them were OCEA people. Most of the cuts were unfilled positions, therefore, most were done by attrition. The county Sheriff's Department took a 40 percent cut in general fund contributions and the District Attorney took a 50 percent cut in general fund contributions" (Mittermeier 1996).

To ease the pain of the layoffs, the county set up a counseling office to find jobs and counsel the laid off employees. Popejoy is interested in helping laid off employees get jobs (Sawyer 1995). Orange County took the approach of both downsizing and rightsizing its government through a combination of layoffs and voluntary attrition. Voluntary attrition is more cost-effective and healthy for organizational morale than layoffs (Greenhalgh and McKersie 1980: p. 315; Zaffane and Mayo 1994). The counseling and outplacement services offered to laid off employees will not only ease the pain for the people directly affected but it will also help relieve the stress for the retained employees (Zaffane and Mayo 1994). However, owing to the large number of employees who were involuntarily laid off, some of the resulting personnel turmoil could detract from whatever gains the county achieved (Seglem 1992).

Ken Moore, president of Orange County's Economic Development Consortium, reports some of the positive and negative impacts of the bankruptcy on the Orange County economy. "Business people who provide services to the county may be directly impacted, but some of the positive signs are plans of Rockwell, TRW and Unical to expand. Also,

Chapman University reported there will be positive job growth for the first time in four to five years'' (Moore 1995). Thus, it is evident that the Orange County bankruptcy has had a wide impact upon both the public and private sectors of the county's economy. While the public sector is downsizing, the private sector is expanding its operations. Therefore, possibly the growth in the private sector will help off set some of the negative side effects the bankruptcy has had on the public sector.

VIII. VIABLE SOLUTIONS TO THE ORANGE COUNTY BANKRUPTCY

After a year of turmoil, on December 12, 1995, the county proposed a viable bankruptcy recovery plan made up of five main elements: (1) the reallocation of the Bradley-Burns sales tax, (2) the transfer of motor vehicle fuel taxes, (3) the reallocation of property taxes (beaches, harbors and parks), (4) the reallocation of property taxes (flood control), and (5) the reallocation of taxes (development authority) (Orange County 1996). Now to review each of the five points.

The first point of the recovery plan allows the county to reallocate and or retain a portion of the Bradley-Burns Sales Tax currently allocated to the Orange County Transportation Authority (OCTA) or to the Orange County Transit District (OCTD) in the sum of $38 million per year for 15 years. The second point is the allocation to the OCTA $23 million of the county's yearly apportionment of Motor Vehicle Fuel Taxes for 16 years. This allocation of funding to OCTA will help to offset some of the impacts of the reallocation of the funds from the Bradley-Burns sales tax. The third point of the recovery plan involves the reallocation to the county of property taxes currently allocated and paid to the Orange County fund known as Harbors, Beaches and Parks, equaling an amount of $4 million per year for 20 years. The fourth point of the plan involves the reallocation to the county of property taxes currently allocated and paid to the Orange County Flood Control District for an amount of $4 million per year for a 20 years. The fifth point of the plan involves the transfer from the Orange County Development Agency (OCDA) to the county's general fund $4 million per year for 20 years. Each of the five list points began on July 1, 1996. In addition to the implementation of the above stated recovery plan, voted on on May 8, 1996, the county introduced zero-based budgeting as a form of internal budget reform. Ms. Mittermeier says that this form of budgeting requires each county department to justify every dollar it spends (Mittermeier 1996).

The current recovery plan has come as an alternative to several other strongly opposed plans. On June 27, 1995 the county overwhelmingly voted down Measure R, a 0.5-cent sales tax which that translated into $50 per $10,000 spent by each person within the county. The tax would have generated approximately $130 million per year to help the county solve its financial problem (Orange County 1995). Thus, the citizens of Orange County expressed their antitax sentiment, as did the citizens of California in 1978 with Proposition 13 (Lucier et al. 1980:193). One of the reasons for the overwhelming defeat of Measure R is the feeling that the citizens' money is not being well spent, as well as a distrust of public officials. Robert Behn of Duke University points out that taxpayers demand lots of services but are reluctant to allow their governments to spend their money to provide them (Lemove 1992). David Osborne notes that during time of severe fiscal crisis, raising taxes may not only be impossible but also counterproductive (Walters 1992). The problem Osborne notes is mainly caused by the disillusionment constituents feel toward government. Change may be accepted more easily as a fiscal crisis recedes and recovery begins. However, recovery sometimes is impossible without increasing taxes or raising fees. Another reason for the opposition to Measure R is the issue of equity. A sales tax is a regressive form of taxation and may tend to drive business elsewhere if it becomes too burdensome, thus reducing the tax base (Inman 1992; Pechman 1971). Therefore, the amount of revenue generated from the tax stabilizes as tax rates continue to rise, which reduce the municipality's tax base (Inman 1995). Those interest groups interviewed for this chapter who expressed support for Measure R were the Orange County Taxpayers Association, the Orange County Women's League of Voters, and the Orange County Employees Association (Haddad 1995; Royalty 1995; Sawyer 1995). However, conservative groups like the Committee of Correspondence and the Citizens Bureau of Investigation opposed the tax (Uberaga 1995).

While Orange County residents are opposed to new taxes, as are large portions of residents in California and throughout the United States, many people do not realize that of all major industrialized countries, the United States has the lowest total tax burden, at 32.6% of the national wealth produced each year (Wood and Benson 1991:147). In comparison, the Japanese pay 35% of their wealth; Britain, 39%; and Germans, 42% (Wood and Benson 1991:147). Despite the low tax rate in contrast to other industrialized countries, most Americans continue to feel overtaxed.

IX. PREVENTATIVE MEASURES: IMPLICATIONS FOR OTHER LOCAL GOVERNMENTS

In order for Orange County to avoid another bankruptcy, county and national officials are discussing how the county could have prevented the bankruptcy. There are many measures other local governments should consider to avoid the same problems faced by Orange County. Much like New York City in its fiscal crisis of 1975, Orange County needed better managerial accountability (Viteritti 1978). In the Orange County government, the treasurer took much of the blame for the fiscal crisis. Yet if a better system of managerial and financial accountability had been in place, as was implemented in New York City, with its Financial Management System that integrates its budgetary and accounting systems (Viteritti 1978), maybe the county could have avoided such a disastrous fiscal crisis. Because of the unregulated entrepreneurial environment in which Citron was investing, greater discretionary accountability should have been used by Citron. When there is a lack of meaningful threats or sanctions from the external environment, public officials must take personal and professional responsibility for anticipating emerging standards of acceptable professional behavior and organizational performance, considering long-term risks as well as short-term benefits (Kearns 1995). In the case of the Orange County situation, Citron did not exercise proper discretionary accountability.

In interviews the majority of local officials and citizen groups throughout the county supported of more oversight—for example, establishing an investment policy and improved reporting procedures for local governments (Branca 1995; Haddad 1995; Huston 1995; Moore 1995; Ream 1995; Sawyer 1995; Uberaga 1995). Others suggested the need for better auditing procedures (Bergenson 1995; Royalty 1995). When asked about the possibility of imposing new regulations upon the municipal securities market to prevent municipal governments from investing in high risk securities, such as derivatives, the current Orange County CEO expressed her opposition to imposing national regulations upon local officials (Mittermeier 1996). Instead, Ms. Mittermeier favors having the Securities and Exchange Commission (SEC) examine the private sector and the way it deals with municipalities (Mittermeier 1996). However, as noted by Kearns (1995) in the wake of the Orange County bankruptcy, government agencies should anticipate the formulation of these new standards and thus position themselves for the potential development of these new regulations by playing an active role in the creation of new laws.

Several other preventative measures that have been suggested by several county and city officials relate to restructuring the county government to allow for a more accountable and effective system. Marian Bergenson is one of five members of the County's Board of Supervisors who has proposed the plan of replacing the current county structure of a part-time, elected Board of Supervisors and a full-time CEO with a full-time appointed county executive officer (Bergenson 1995: July 3). In her outlined proposal, titled "Orange County 2001," Supervisor Bergenson expresses the county's need for greater centralized authority in one person for running the day-to-day operations of the county, separating the responsibility of setting policy for ensuring delivery of regional services to the part-time governing board (See Appendixes B and C for comparison of old and newly proposed county structure). Bergenson believes this new structure should enhance accountability within the system through more defined roles and responsibilities of county officials. There is wide support for restructuring county government through a full-time county executive officer among county and city officials as well as citizen's organizations (Bergenson 1995; Branca 1995; Huston 1995; Moore 1995; Popejoy 1995; Ream 1995; Royalty 1995).

An alternative government restructuring proposal involves regionalization of city services (Villously 1995; Watson 1995). This proposal would involve a number of cities within the county joining together to collaborate in service provision, giving less responsibility for service delivery to the county. Bergenson also suggested the possibility of revolving private auditors instead of using the same private auditing firm year after year, which might enhance objectivity.

Three other methods of government reform suggested as preventative measures are (1) reducing the number of elected officials in county government by replacing them with appointed officials, (2) developing minimum qualifications for elected officials to run for office, and (3) separating the position of Auditor/Controller into two separate positions (Haddad 1995; Mittermeier 1996; Popejoy 1995; Ream 1995; Uberaga 1995; Watson, 1995). The main reason given for replacing elected officials, such as the treasurer, with an appointed official is to set certain standard qualifications for people who will fill these positions as well as provide for greater fiscal and managerial accountability. The city and county officials interviewed for this study felt that Citron held the position of treasurer–tax collector knowing he was elected by the people and thus felt only accountable to those who elected him.

Additionally, several individuals interviewed felt elected officials have trouble downsizing (Ream 1995). Thus, more efficiency may be gained through more appointed positions. However, the current county CEO believes elected officials can also be required to met certain minimum requirements before running for public office (Mittermeier 1996). The preventative measure of separating the offices of Auditor/Controller into two offices is seen as another way to lead to greater accountability. Separating the tasks of writing the checks and verifying the checks which have been written for the county makes good financial management sense (Popejoy 1995).

In order to help other municipalities around the county from facing a similar financial situation as Orange County, further research is needed in a number of areas. These areas include (1) a survey of numerous local governments' financial auditing procedures, (2) a survey of the types of investment policies in place in local governments, (3) a survey of numerous local governments to determine the level of accountability of elected and appointed officials and whether or not local government officials feel the government would run more effectively with fewer elected officials and more appointed officials, and (4) a survey of the number of local governments that have minimum requirements for elected officials to run for office and the effectiveness of the governments that have these minimum standards.

X. SUMMARY

Some may view the Orange County bankruptcy as one of the most financially disastrous situations for local government in U.S. history. However, it may also be regarded as a laboratory for experimentation in public policy, administration, and management. Beginning in 1978 with the passage of Proposition 13, California has taken the lead in reforming the way government conducts its business and provides services to its citizens. The Orange County bankruptcy is the result of many contributing factors such as (1) a lack of proper oversight by the Board of Supervisors, (2) fraudulent reporting by the treasurer–tax collector, (3) the lack of proper financial background of county officials, (4) a lack of disclosure of financial transactions between the county treasure–tax collector and outside investment firms, (5) a lack of accountability by those responsible for ensuring the safe investment of county funds, (6) a lack of disclosure of key financial information to the investors, both within and outside of the county, and (7) perhaps inappropriate governmental structure.

While the causes of the bankruptcy are numerous, so are the components of the county's current recovery plan. The current plan, voted on on May 8, 1996, clearly outlines the path for the county's economic survival. The plan calls for an internal reallocation of county resources together with the newly introduced zero-based budgeting strategy. These new approaches to financial management demonstrate the county's true commitment to economic survival. The county voters clearly displayed, on June 27, 1995, the less than likely chance of certain tax measures being passed to help solve the bankruptcy problem. At a time of financial crisis, voters become disillusioned with public officials and express their anger by opposing any additional taxes. The voters in Orange County feel that those who created the county's current financial situation must come up with a miracle solution to resolve the problem, one which does not involve increasing taxes. Thus, the current recovery plan meets the criteria set forth by the voters. However, what many voters do not realize is the small tax increase Measure R would have called for ($50 per $10,000 spent). This is much less than the amount of money it will now cost the county in legal fees and loss of business for private sector developers and realtors. One of the other long-term negative effects of voting down Measure R is the poor public image painted by the media of the county. The image is one of a jurisdiction that is financially irresponsible. The other long-term effects of the bankruptcy have yet to be seen. Some city officials within the county even feel that the county will never regain the confidence of investors (Ream 1995).

Some people may question the treatment of Orange County by Standard & Poor or the SEC, both of which had a direct relationship with the county by respectively providing consistently high ratings for the county's bonds and approving the county's handling of municipal bonds up to the time of the bankruptcy. However, as a spokesperson for Standard & Poor pointed out, ". . . we rely on those providing reliable information . . ."

(Martinez 1995:A10). In this case, the treasurer–tax collector was providing false information, which was not detected to be such by the rating agency or the SEC. Some critics argue (including the city manager of Santa Ana, Ream) that the county declared bankruptcy too early.

XI. CONCLUSION

There are several lessons to be learned from the Orange County bankruptcy. One lesson is the need to restructure the county government by appointing a county executive officer to manage the day-to-day affairs of the county and either appoint or elect a part-time County Board of Supervisors. As suggested in Marian Bergenson's proposal ''Orange County 2001,'' this new system would help improve accountability and oversight within county government through the day-to-day micromanagement of a county manager, leaving the responsibility for setting public policy to the board of supervisors. Another possible lesson of the bankrupt is the need for the SEC to create stronger national laws regulating the municipal securities market to prevent municipal governments form investing in high-risk securities, such as derivatives. It will take time to heal the financial wounds the bankruptcy has inflicted upon Orange County. However, owing to the county's strong economic base and numerous assets which include prime California coastal real estate and ideal weather, it will be hard for the county not to rebound. The combination of a more efficiently structured county government and a more tightly regulated municipal securities market are two key points this author has chosen among the many lessons to be learned from studying the Orange County bankruptcy.

REFERENCES

Aveneyon, E. (1988). *Dictionary of Finance*. New York: Macmillian Publishing Co., 278, 397.
Bahl, R. and Duncomb, W. (1992). Economic change and fiscal planning: the origin of the fiscal crisis in New York State. *Public Administration Review*, 52(6), 547–558.
Bergenson, M. (1995, July 7). Personal interview. C. Murphy.
Bergenson, M. (1995, July 3). ''Orange County 2001.''
Branca, F. (1995, July 7). Personal interview. C. Murphy.
(1994). *California County Projections*. Palo Alto, CA: Center for Continuing Study of the California Economy.
Case, P. (1995, July 5). Personal interview. C. Murphy.
Citron, R. (1993). *Annual Financial Statement*. Orange County, CA, pp. 2, 3.
Citron, R. (1992). *Annual Financial Statement*. Orange County, CA, pp. 2, 3, 5.
Coloma, R. (1995, July, 17) Personal interview. C. Murphy.
Federal Mandate Accountability And Reform Act of 1994. August 10, 1994. 103rd Congress, 2nd Session.
Fine, M. (1995, July 12). Personal interview. C. Murphy.
Gaebler, T. and Osborne, D. (1992). *Reinventing Government: How the Entrepreneurial Spirit Is Transforming the Public Sector*. New York: Penguin Books.
Glassberg, A. (1981). The Urban Fiscal Crisis Becomes Routine. *Public Administration Review* (Special Issue) 41, 165–171.
Greenhalgh, L., McKersie, R., and Levine, C. (1980). *Managing Fiscal Stress: The Crisis in the Public Sector* Chatham, NJ: Chatham House Publishers, Inc.

Gordon, A. (1977). Lessons From a Municipal Fiscal Crisis. *CPA Journal*. 47(*11*), 25–28.
Haddad, C. (1995, July 11). Personal interview. C. Murphy.
Hansen, D. (1977). Municipal accounting and disclosure. *Management Accounting*. 58(*11*), 23–24.
(1995). "Transforming local government: Orange County bankruptcy."
Huston, J. (1995, July 18). Personal interview. C. Murphy.
Inman, R. (1995). How to have a fiscal crisis: lessons from Philadelphia. *American Economic Review* 85(*2*), 378–388.
Inman, R. (1992). "Can Philadelphia escape its fiscal crisis with another tax increase?" *Business Review: Federal Reserve Bank of Philadelphia*, Sept./Oct., pp. 5–18.
Inman, R. (1983). "Anatomy of a fiscal crisis." *Business Review: Federal Reserve Bank of Philadelphia*, Sept./Oct., pp. 15–22.
Johnson, G. and Owen, S. (1995, May 3). "Bankruptcy Court OKs $5.7 billion O.C. pool payout." *Los Angeles Times*, May 3, p. A1.
Kidwell, D. and Trzcinka, D. (1982). Municipal bond pricing and the New York City fiscal crisis. *Journal of Finance* 37(*5*), pp. 1239–1246.
Lait, M. (1995). "Popejoy calls for 1,040 layoffs." *Los Angeles Times*, March 8, pp. A1, A14.
Lait, M. (1995). "Fed-up Popejoy calling it quits." *Los Angeles Times*, July 13, pp. A1, A16.
Lemove, P. (1992). Tailoring local governments to the 1990s. *Governing*. July, 28–31.
Lucier, R. and Levine, C. (1980). *Managing Fiscal Stress. The Crisis in the Public Sector*. Chatham, NJ: Chatham House Publishers, Inc.
Martinez, G. (1995). "House panel to probe O.C. recovery effort." *Los Angeles Times*, July 26, pp. A10.
Martinez, G. and Rosenblatt, R. (1995). "O.C. bankruptcy move too early, critics testify." *Los Angeles Times*, July 27, p. A14.
Merrill Lynch (1995). *Setting the Record Straight: The Facts on the Orange County Bankruptcy*.
McIlwain, J. (1995, July 12). Personal interview. C. Murphy.
Mittermeier, J. (1996, March 6). Personal interview. C. Murphy.
Moore, K. (1995, July 12). Personal interview. C. Murphy.
Orange County (1995). *Draft Resolution of Measure R*.
Orange County (1996). *Joint Agreement of the County of Orange*. The Official Investment Pool Participants' Committee, The Official Subcommittee of Orange County Cities of the Official Investment Pool Participants' Committee and Each Option A Pool Participant for Resolution of Claims Against the County of Orange. p. 12.
Orange County Register (1989). "The story of Orange County." p. 76.
Orange County Register (1995, May 3). "Where county investors stand after settlement." p. 13.
Orange County Register (1995, May 1). "Key bills stemming from the O.C. bankruptcy." p. 2.
Orange County Register (1995, May 4). "Home sales: April is the cruelest month." p. B1.
Orange County Register (1995, May 8). "Profiles in crisis." p. 9.
Orange County Register (1995, May 17). "Raabe indicted." p. 6.
(1993). *A Dictionary of Finance*. New York: Oxford University Press.
Pechman, J. (1971). Fiscal federalism for the 1970's. *National Tax Journal* 24(*3*), 281–290.
Popejoy, W. (1995, July 13). Personal interview. C. Murphy.
Ramsey, Merle and Mable (1973). *The Reflections in Orange*. Laguna Beach, CA: Mission Printing Co.
Ream, D. (1995, July 17). Personal interview. C. Murphy.
Royalty, R. (1995, July 17). Personal interview. C. Murphy.
Sawyer, J. (1995, July 12). Personal interview. C. Murphy.
Seglem, L. (1992, July). Turning state street upside down. *State Legislatures* p. 23.
Sterngold, J. (1995). "Debt-Plagued County Likely To Get Relief." *The New York Times*, May 20, pp. 19–20.
Uberaga, M. (1995, July 11). Personal Interview. C. Murphy.
Villella, D. (1995, July 11). Personal Interview C. Murphy.

Viteritti, J. (1978). New York's management plan and reporting system: a descriptive analysis. *Public Administration Review* 38(4), 376–381.
Vrana, D. (1996). "O.C. home sales up 31% while prices level out." *Los Angeles Times*, March 6, pp. A1, A12.
Walters, J. (1992). Reinventing government: managing the politics of change. *Governing December*, 29.
Watson, D. (1995, July 11). Personal Interview. C. Murphy.
Wood and Benson. (1991, October 13). "Government's role as provider wanes: the fading American dream." *Orange County Register*, October 13, p. 147.
Zaffane, R. and Mayo, G. (1994). Rightsizing: the strategic human resource management challenge of the 1990s. *Management Decision* 32(9), 5,8.

Appendices

ORANGE COUNTY INTERVIEW SURVEY

1. What were the main significant factors leading up to the December 6 declaration of bankruptcy by Orange County?
2. What part did you play in the events leading up to the O.C. bankruptcy? Did you provide any financial advice? Did the city manager seek any financial advice from you or did you provide any financial advice or non-financial advice to anyone?
3. How has your city been impacted by the O.C. bankruptcy so far and what will be the future impacts?
4. What preventative measures could have been taken by Orange County to have avoided the bankruptcy?
5. Do you feel the Board of Supervisors could have prevented the bankruptcy?
6. Do you think the Board of Supervisors should be maintained?
7. How do you feel about the Charter County proposal?
8. What do you see as some of the viable solutions to help pull O.C. out of its current fiscal state? (a) importing garbage, (b) ½ cent sales tax, (c) state bailout?
9. In what ways in your opinion will municipalities be affected by the bankruptcy?
10. Have you laid off any employees?
11. Do you have a downsizing policy?
12. What is the financial future of Orange County? What are some of the strategies the County will use to avoid another bankruptcy? How will the County regain the confidence of investors?
13. Has the bankruptcy caused concern about raising taxes among the citizens within your municipalities or their economic well being?
14. Have you or any friends of yours been laid off or had their salary reduced?
15. Could you give me a name of another individual who could provide me with information regarding the bankruptcy?

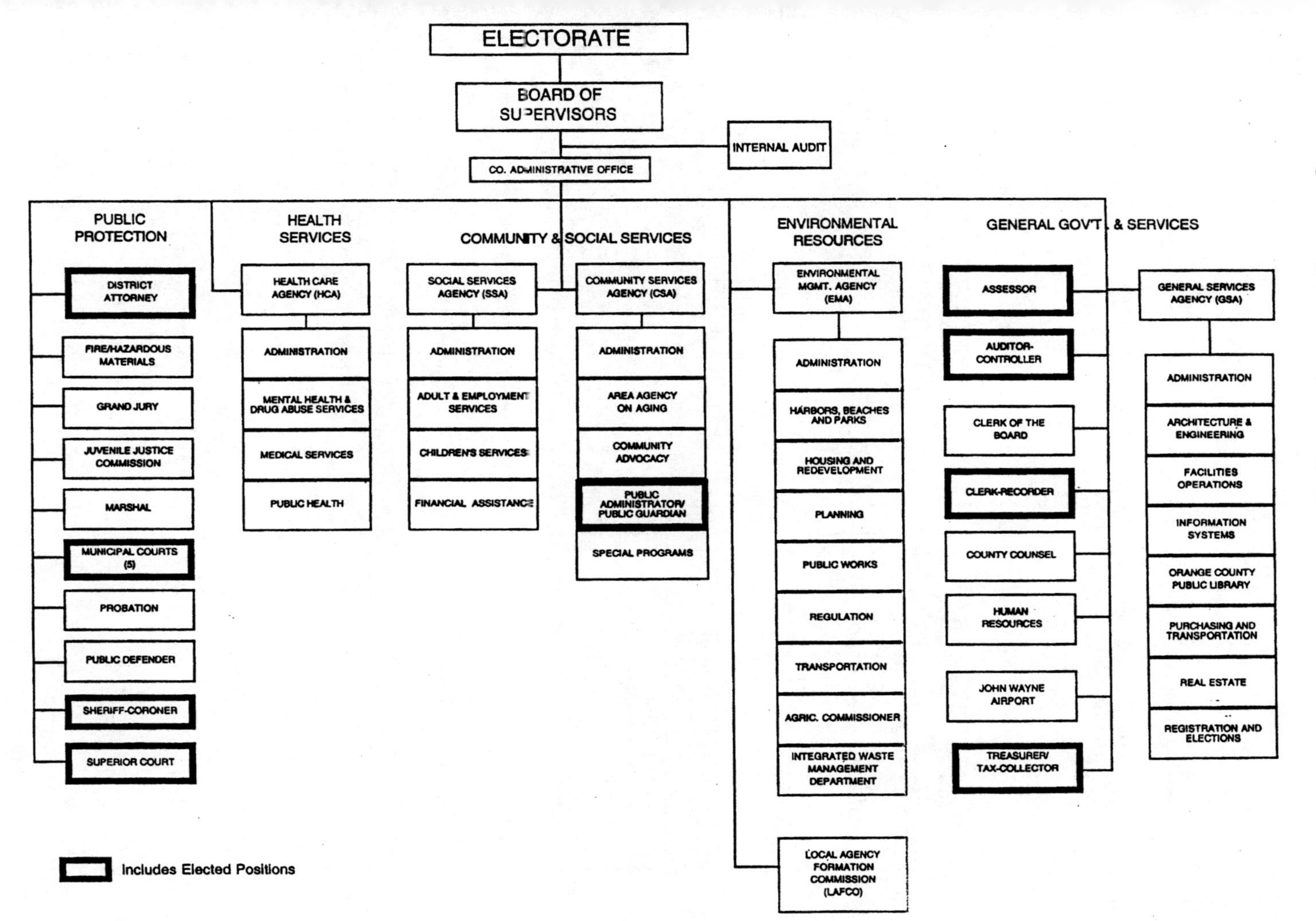

Source: Orange County, 1995.

Orange County 2001 Function Chart

Orange County Cities

Former County Operations
Police Services
Local Planning and Land Use
Housing
Libraries

State of California

Former County Operations
Elections and Registration
Treasury and Investment
Department of Education
Property Tax Administration
Courts & Marshal

Note:
Structure will require legislation relating to the cessation of county powers, the modification of OCTA, and the consolidation of all non-school special purpose districts.

County Mayor
4-year elective term of office
Chairs ORSA Board

Orange Regional Services Authority

Governing Board
Eight Commissioners + Mayor
Part-Time, Elected by District

ORSA Operations

Division of Health and Human Services
Health Care
Social Services

Division of Public Facilities
Regional Planning
Flood Control
Parks and Recreation
Sanitation and Waste Management
Water

Division of Public Protection
Coroner
District Attorney/Public Defender
Fire and Emergency Management
Jail Administration (Sheriff/Warden)
Probation

Division of Transportation
Airport
Roads and Freeways
Transit

Source: Bergenson, M. July 3, 1995.

12

System Crisis: The 1973 War Crisis in Israel

Efraim Ben-Zadok School of Public Administration, Florida Atlantic University, Fort Lauderdale, Florida

I. INTRODUCTION

Israel is a "security society." It is a society facing constant threats and risks to its survival; a society where security and defense greatly affect every aspect of life including most institutions, values, people, and lifestyles. The military and civil activities of the Israeli security system penetrate those of all other systems and can reach up to one-third of the government's total budget in a given year (Arian 1985: 59–65, 304–313). These activities are the main task of a government that dominates the economy through one of the most powerful bureaucracies in all democracies (Sharkansky 1989).

Since its inception in the late nineteenth century, Israeli society has had a turbulent military history. Before and after it achieved statehood in 1948, it fought hundreds of border skirmishes and other battles against its Arab neighbors. In the last five decades, these limited engagements culminated in five all-out Arab-Israeli wars: in 1948 (Independence), 1956 (Sinai), 1967 (Six Days), 1973 (Yom Kippur), and 1982 (Lebanon). The significance of these wars and the periods between them in shaping the society, its politics, and its economics is obvious in any analysis of Israeli history (e.g., Congressional Quarterly 1986: 7–17; Gilbert 1993; Safran 1981).

Israel had two crucial victories in 1948 and 1956 and a decisive brilliant victory in 1967. These three wars were perceived by Israelis as successful. Thereafter, the "security society" became confident of its military supremacy in the Middle East and its long-term survival. The 1973 war, however, was perceived by Israelis as a failure—or, at least, not a clear-cut success (Galnoor 1982:37–39). Their military confidence was shattered. The war threatened the very physical existence of their society and posed the most dangerous challenge to their security.

The 1973 war was extensively documented. It was the first war on television in a country that adopted that medium only in 1968. Its story was told in newspapers, novels, poems, and songs. The war was covered in historical, military, strategic, political, and social studies by both laypeople and academics.

Nonetheless, the most common concept used to describe the war and its implications for Israel, the concept of "crisis," still suffers from a lack of systematic analysis of its political and social dimensions (the military and strategic dimensions have been covered). As the 25th anniversary of the 1973 war has passed, perhaps the time is ripe for a more systematic analysis of the "crisis" concept and its political and social dimensions. This chapter constitutes such an effort.

Section II of the chapter is a theoretical discussion of Habermas's *social system crisis* concept and its application to three Israeli systems—society, politics, and security. Section III is a brief review of the history and development of the three systems before 1948 (the pre-state period). This review is the necessary background required to understand the operation of these systems in the 1973 war crisis. The following discussion analyzes the war crisis itself in the Israeli army and the at-large security system (Section IV), in the government and the at-large political system (Section V), and in the society (Section VI). Section VII concludes with the management of the crisis.

II. A THEORY OF SOCIAL SYSTEM CRISIS

Habermas opens with an explanation of the *social system* and its components. A society is a social system that includes other social systems (subsystems), such as economics, politics, and culture. A social system ultimately operates through voluntarily accepted values and communication and not only through hierarchy and command of institutions. Therefore it is difficult to determine the boundaries of the system (Habermas 1975: 3–6).

The application to Israel is clear. The Israeli society, its politics, and its security are all social systems with values and communication channels that stretch far beyond their institutions and cover Israelis, Jews, and non-Jews in Israel and abroad. The boundaries of the three systems' activities are hard to define. Their substantive content, however, is easier to define. It is the "security" content that is at the heart of their values, communication, and institutions.

Central to Habermas's social system operation is the interconnection between its two components: social integration and system integration. *Social integration* is related to the institutions in which individuals are socially related through verbal and non-verbal communication. From this perspective, the social system is a life world which is symbolically organized around normative structures (institutions and values). *System integration* is related to the specific steering performance of a self-regulated social system. From this perspective, the social system is considered in terms of its capacity to maintain its (hard-to-define) boundaries and existence by mastering its complex turbulent environment through nonnormative functional mechanisms (Habermas 1975:4–5).

Accordingly, Israel's three systems—the "security society," its politics, and its security are social systems organized around institutions in which individuals are related through social-horizontal rather than mechanical-hierarchical communication (social integration). The institutions and values of each system focus on the norms of security and, ultimately, on the preservation of physical life and survival (*life world*). The continued existence of each system depends on the steering performance of its functional mechanisms, primarily the Israeli government and the army (system integration).

After explaining the social system and its components, Habermas proceeds to elaborate on the sources of a *social system crisis*. It begins when a threat to *social integration* and a danger to *system integration* lead to disintegration (Habermas 1975:24–25). A threat to social integration appears when the communication of Israeli institutions and values, which deal with norms of preservation of life and survival, evolves around their difficulties in the delivery of normative promises for continued security. Such a threat appears as a result of a danger to system integration. Such a danger occurs when the security society, its political, or its security system suffers from a reduced capacity to master its environment through the government or the army.[1]

Habermas's social system crisis incorporates themes from Marx and the social sciences. From Marx it draws on the social-scientific approach. Accordingly, crisis arises through incompatible structurally inherent system imperatives that cannot be integrated hierarchically. From the social sciences it draws on the system theory approach. Accordingly, crisis arises when the structure of the system allows for fewer problem-solving options that are necessary to the existence of the system (Habermas 1975:2–3).

Habermas continues to elaborate on the nature of the crisis itself. Temporarily unresolved steering problems clearly disturb the operation of the functional mechanisms. This danger to *system integration* threatens *social integration*. Problems of social disintegration and instability develop and incompatible interests become antagonistic. The crisis is then endemic and cannot be resolved through existing learning mechanisms. To maintain itself, the social system must significantly alter its life world. A new moral-political content of communication, which goes beyond the limits of the precrisis content, then develops and gradually becomes dominant. In the cases where it drives out its predecessor, the normative structures (institutions and values) clearly change or are built anew (deHaven-Smith 1988: 85–88; Habermas 1975:24–31).

The application to Israel is that the reduced steering capacity of the government or the army decreases their effectiveness in operation. This danger to system integration threatens social integration. That is, social disintegration, instability, and antagonistic interests become prevalent in the "security society," its political, and its security system. Each system appears incapable of delivering security to Israelis. The crisis is then endemic. The old practices of the systems become obsolete. To maintain itself, each system must significantly alter its life world. That is, institutions and values in the system must clearly change or be replaced through the introduction of new symbols of life preservation and survival.

III. HISTORY OF ISRAELI SOCIAL SYSTEMS

The pre-state (pre-1948) period shaped the content of communication, institutions, and values of the three Israeli systems—the security society, its politics, and its security. A brief review of the development of the three systems during that period allows us to understand their operation in the 1973 war crisis.

Until the end of the eighteenth century, European Jews constituted a "closed society"—they were excluded from the general society and suffered discrimination. In the wake of the American and French revolutions, and especially with the Enlightenment of the eighteenth century, Jews began to enter the general society. They soon discovered that the new European liberalism was inseparable from nationalism. In order to enjoy the benefits of liberalism in France, for example—that is, to enjoy full equal status in this society—Jews had to identify with French national history and culture. That posed enormous difficulties to the Jews—a "closed society" for centuries with its own national history and culture. The failure of assimilation was illustrated in the dishonorable discharge of Captain Dreyfus from the French army in the famous 1895 trial, which shook Europe. The post-trial impression was that anti-Semitism was sentenced to stay in Europe (Avineri 1991:13–24).

Disappointed by European liberalism and nationalism, Jews began to formulate their own solution to anti-Semitism at the end of the nineteenth century. It was Zionist liberal nationalism, an ideology of freedom and equality in the context of Jewish national history and culture. Central to the ideology was its implementation in a national home in a defined territory (Palestine) in order to protect and preserve a society that had been persecuted for centuries. Moreover, the implementation of the ideology, according to European nationalism, could only be in a sovereign political system with a strong security and defense system to protect the society (Avineri 1991:182–215; Safran 1981:14–23).

Thus, the first task of Zionism, the political movement nourished by the ideology, was to develop its social systems with functional mechanisms for political independence, security, and defense. The movement organized its own political system with two major mechanisms: the World Zionist Organization and the Jewish Agency. The organization represented Jewish communities worldwide and the agency was its Palestine's branch. The agency led the Jewish community in Palestine until independence, when it transferred most of its functions to the government of the new state.

The movement also organized its security system with two functional mechanisms: a massive settlement and a strong army. Jewish settlements were founded throughout Palestine, especially in frontier areas along the border of the future state, where the presence of settlers strengthened security and defense (Ben-Zadok 1985). Three illegal underground military organizations were established during British rule over Palestine (1918–1948), and after independence these were united into one army—the Israel Defense Forces (IDF) (Safran 1981:44–45).

Both systems, politics and security, were capable of maintaining themselves in the complex pre-state environment through the successful steering of their functional mechanisms. That is, both systems achieved a reasonable degree of system integration. The environment, however, rapidly became extremely turbulent toward the establishment of the state in 1948. That was due to the extermination of the Jewish community in Europe in World War II and the conflict with the Arab neighbors in Palestine. These dangers to system integration, to the steering capacity, threatened social integration. That is, the communication of institutions and values focused on the possibility that both systems might not be able to deliver the promised security. The symbolic organization of each system, the life world, could become unstable and disintegrate.

When the first Arab-Israeli war began in 1948, however, the political and security systems demonstrated successful steering and were skillful in preventing system crisis. By that time, the security content began to dominate Israeli communication. The perception and concept of "security society" soon prevailed (Shapiro 1996:23–25, 70–73). A feeling of relative safety followed in communication patterns. The actual crisis broke out well into the state period—on its 25th anniversary.

IV. SECURITY SYSTEM CRISIS

On October 6, 1973, at 1:55 p.m., some 150 Egyptian planes penetrated into the Sinai Peninsula and began to bomb Israeli airfields and military installations there. A few minutes later, over 1000 Egyptian artillery guns opened fire and the first wave of 8000 infantrymen crossed the Suez Canal toward the Israeli positions along the entire East Bank. At the same time, some 700 Syrian artillery guns, with aircraft support, opened a heavy barrage directed at the Israeli fortifications in the Golan Heights. A few minutes later,

45,000 Syrian infantrymen and 600 tanks began to attack Israeli positions along the entire front. The 1973 Arab-Israeli had begun.

The war ended on October 24, 1973, with a cease-fire on both fronts. Egypt and Syria lost an estimated 11,200 soldiers, between two and three times that many were wounded, and 9000 were taken as prisoners of war. They also lost about 500 planes and 2000 tanks. Israel lost 2552 soldiers, between two and three times that many were wounded, and close to 350 were taken as prisoners of war. It also lost 114 planes and 800 tanks. Egypt captured some territory from Israel on the east bank of the Suez Canal. Israel gained some territory from Egypt on the west bank of the Canal and from Syria in the Golan.

At the minimum, the results above represent a partial success to both sides in the war. At the maximum, the results indicate that Israel ultimately had the upper hand. This is especially so in light of the initial heavy setbacks that the IDF had suffered from the concerted Arab's surprise attack in the midst of Yom Kippur—the Day of Atonement, day of prayer and fasting—the holiest day in the Jewish calendar. Close to defeat, the IDF managed to recover and turned the war close to a victory.

But these results do not tell the whole story. Despite early warnings, the Israeli military intelligence failed. The Arabs' advantage of surprise won them big initial gains. The IDF was caught off guard on Yom Kippur and shown to be vulnerable. The army, the central functional mechanism of the security system, suffered a great initial loss of steering capacity to control its environment. The crisis then began in the army and rapidly spilled over to the at-large security system, which lost much of its steering capacity. These steering problems are described below.

The initial shock of the Arab offensive threw the IDF off balance. The prewar conception of the research division of the military intelligence (in charge of analysis and evaluation) was that Egypt and Syria would not go to war with Israel because they were unsure about their capacity for a successful attack. This rigid conception was broken when the war erupted and left the army confused. New positions, not included in the contingency plans, were hastily created in the first days of the war. High-ranking reserve officers returned to service. They were placed immediately as the ''supervisors advisers'' of the younger high-ranking service officers, an act that questioned the confidence in the latter. Frequent breaks occurred in the high ranks of the command chain. The noted example was General Arik Sharon, who was called on by his superiors for refusal to carry out orders (Peri 1983:251–252).

Loss of steering and danger to system integration was also reflected in the relations between the major mechanisms of the security system: the military and the Ministry of Defense.[2] The generals questioned and sometimes ignored the instructions of Minister of Defense Moshe Dayan. They doubted his authority and were puzzled about his role, which had never been clearly defined. Dayan himself, with shattered preconceptions after the surprise attack, rapidly and extremely changed the hierarchy and command patterns several times during the war. He began to give ''ministerial advice'' to the generals. That was a clear change from his prewar pattern of giving specific operational orders that ignored the chain of command and bypassed the military chief of staff, David Elazar. Dayan suddenly gained confidence and returned to that old pattern in the second week of the war, when the army began to recover from the initial shock. Throughout the war, however, climatic tension disrupted the communication between him and Elazar. Some generals preferred to take orders directly from the minister of defense. Others refused to bypass the authority of the chief of staff (Peri 1983: 252–254).

These incompatible structural imperatives resulted in hierarchical disintegration, which quickly dominated the confused system. The entire code for system operation was altered and remained vague, rife with contradictions, until the end of the war. Strategies were constantly replaced by tactical trials and improvisation. The life world of the system—its confidence in its power to deter, and its ability to maintain Israel's survival—became shaky.

V. POLITICAL SYSTEM CRISIS

Social systems are interdependent. The security system crisis quickly expanded to the political system. The government, the central functional mechanism of the political system, was unprepared for the Arab offensive and had no contingency plan for an Arab initial success in a war against Israel. The government's outdated conception from the 1967 war, which is described below, explains much of its initial loss of steering in 1973.

First, a political system crisis of 3 weeks preceded the military confrontation in 1967. Second, the 6 days brief war erupted with an Israeli government decision ordering a series of intense preemptive air strikes on the airfields of Egypt, Syria, and Jordan. The air forces of all three countries were virtually destroyed during the first day of the war and their ground forces remained at the mercy of the Israeli air force. Third, Israel captured the Sinai Peninsula and Gaza Strip from Egypt, the Golan Heights from Syria, and the West Bank from Jordan. The small country gained much more early-warning space and a stronger strategic-political position. Fourth, these stunning achievements, which drastically changed Middle East geopolitics, cost Israel a minimum of 766 dead and 2811 wounded soldiers.

The contrast in 1973 was dramatic. The political and the security system crises began simultaneously with the latter absorbing most of the initial shock. Only hours before war erupted, the surprised government began to consider a preemptive attack yet finally made its biggest mistake by deciding against it. Much of this decision was based on the fear of a loss of international support, which was a dominant factor in the 1967 prewar diplomacy, and on the early-warning space gained in that war. The government also continued to rely in 1973 (at least at the beginning) on the 1967 concept of a brief war with minimum losses and decisive outcomes.

The decision against a preemptive attack determined the course and result of the war. The war extended to 19 days with great losses and indecisive outcomes. At the end, Israel faced more direct threats to its security and a weaker strategic-political position than before (Safran 1981: 278). The decision not to attack first was ultimately made by Prime Minister Golda Meir. She writes in her memoirs that after much agony and hesitation she made this decision relying primarily on the assessments of the military intelligence and the minister of defense, Dayan. Moreover, she claims that throughout the decision-making process, her healthy political instincts were very much at odds with the assessments of three chiefs of staff. Their military experience and input, however, were crucial in her decision (Meir 1975:353–360). This influential role of the 1973's chief, Elazar, and two retired ones who served as ministers in Meir's government, Dayan and Chaim Bar-Lev, points out the disproportionate influence of high-ranking officers (in service or retired) and military inputs in the political decisions of the Israeli government.

This intervention raises another structural problem in the political system: the vast gray area of responsibility between the army and the government. According to the Agranat Commission (the national inquiry commission of the 1973 war), there was a lack of clear definitions of the authorities and functions of the IDF, the Ministry of Defense, the Israeli government, and heads of all three agencies. The Commission concluded that the government authority to operate the IDF was vaguely defined. Specifically, whereas the government (cabinet) as a whole had such formal power, its minister of defense lacked such formal power over the IDF. The minister, therefore, was not more responsible over the IDF than any other minister in the government (Peri 1983:131–142).

In the lack of clear civil authority over the military, the political system remained diffuse and indecisive. Its boundaries were never clearly drawn. It had major communication barriers with the at-large security system and the military. Its authority was limited and its steering lost direction.

The political system also suffered a weakening strategic-political position in the international environment after the war. Egypt and Syria improved their positions and were successful in breaking the diplomatic stalemate. The Arab front against Israel became more united. Even moderate states like Saudi Arabia and Kuwait cut their oil supplies to the West in order to increase pressure on Israel. European and African governments severed or broke relations with Israel. The United States, Israel's chief supporter, concerned with its oil flow and its position in the Middle East, pressed hard for Israeli concessions. American political, economic, and military support became more and more conditioned upon such concessions through international negotiations.

The Israeli political system came to the negotiation table heavily concerned with its isolation in the international community and with the readjustment of its ends to the new environment. Its immediate military concern was the daily artillery exchanges on the Egyptian and Syrian fronts and the risk that the war might resume any day. First on its agenda was the drawing of disengagement and buffer zones between the fighting forces as well as early-warning arrangements to monitor their movements. With active American mediation headed by Secretary of State Henry Kissinger, an agreement for disengagement of military forces was signed with Egypt on January 18 and with Syria on May 31, 1974.

Meanwhile, the crisis at home continued. The cost of the war was close to $10 billion. The long mobilization of the reserve forces affected the economy, which slowed down, with soaring prices, runaway inflation, and increased national debt. The failed deterrence power and lack of preparation of the army were reported in the media. The communication breakdowns and rivalries in the top echelon of the security system leaked out. The performance during the war of the at-large security system, the army, the government, and particularly the performance of the minister of defense all became the target of angry public protest. The public demanded an official inquiry on the war activities of all agencies involved.

For the first time in Israel's history, the basic accountability and reliability of the political system in the security domain was questioned. The system's life world was shaken and the Israeli public actually labeled this transformation as "earthquake." And that was only the beginning.

In the national elections on December 31, 1974, the ruling Labor party lost only five seats. Under much turmoil in the public and in the party and a growing demand for Dayan's resignation and for new faces in government, Meir finally managed to present a government on March 10, 1974, with Dayan as minister of defense and minor personnel changes. The political system did not adjust to the new environment. The crisis continued.

The biggest system breakdown took place only after the Agranat Commission submitted its interim report on April 2, 1974. Meir's government with Dayan, and the top military echelon headed by Elazar and the chief of intelligence who absorbed most of the criticism of the controversial report, all resigned shortly thereafter. The crisis continued with a caretaker government. It somewhat subsided only after a new Labor government, with a minimal margin in the parliament, was presented by Yitzhak Rabin on June 3, 1974.

VI. "SECURITY SOCIETY" CRISIS

The security and political systems are parts of the larger system of society. Their crises naturally impinged on the society but were only the initial stimulants to the very different crisis there. It began with an angry and persistent movement of reserve soldiers who returned home in winter 1973. They were disturbed with the yet unpublicized performance problems of the army during the war, and they found it difficult to return to civil routine. The movement had stimulated large public protest and demand for the resignation of the leaders who were accountable for the results of the war.

Not less important was the public request to subject the security and political systems to the inquiry of an independent judicial body. In a society where security, foreign affairs, and a host of related domestic issues were conducted far from the public view, the work and the reports of the Agranat Commission on the most sensitive security issues set at least two important precedents. First, the military and the government went under an unparallel in-depth judicial investigation of a public body. Second, the inquiry process itself and the published parts of the commission's report exposed public servants and opened the flow of official information, also on issues other than the war, to a degree unknown before (Galnoor 1980:141–144).

The war, the public protest, and the work of the commission became major catalysts for a number of important sociopolitical changes in the 1970s. To begin, the political process and leaders came under a more sophisticated public scrutiny. The number of exposures of both leaks and corruption cases in government were thus heightened. Into the power vacuum entered extraparliamentary groups on the left (e.g., Peace Now) and the right (e.g., Gush Emunim), and they were organized as social movements rather than parties. Finally, new forms of active citizen participation in grassroots politics (e.g., local planning) mushroomed in Israel.

With these changes, the content of communication began to change. The revelations of the lack of responsibility in the public sector and the new forms of single-interest citizen participation all impinged on the old life world of collective identity around the institutions and values of security in the society. The limited delivery capacity of all social systems shattered the prewar feelings of relative security and self-confidence. Apprehension and uneasiness around the question of physical existence dominated the public discourse. The survivor underdog image of 1967 was replaced with that of a society under siege with continuous mobilization, heavy toll of dead, and huge economic strains (Eisenstadt 1985: 387–402).

Although new meaning to security symbols seemed essential, the very centrality of the symbols was not questioned because they still provided the base for survival. Yet, the reinterpretation of the symbols was complicated by the acceleration of several new western trends for which the war served as a powerful catalyst and which continued into the 1980s. Chief among them were trends of individualism and materialism that raised the need for revision in the old communication content of collective cohesiveness around the institutions and values of the "security society." Specialized sectors pressed for the redistribution of economic and status rewards and tried to benefit themselves from a "society pie" which was more "open to grab" due to the power vacuum created by the crisis. More defined distinctions were drawn among class, ethnic, culture, and lifestyle groups. A relative social heterogeneity replaced the old homogeneity of the "security society."

An important symbolic reinterpretation process which continued into the 1980s evolved around the land itself. On one hand, the value of the historic territory was reconfirmed after the 1967 war and Jewish settlements were established in the Sinai, Gaza Strip, West Bank, and Golan Heights. On the other hand, the value of the same physical territory as a secure base for survival was confirmed as fragile in 1973. Thus, the old consensus around the centrality of the land was broken.

The public discourse then turned to a debate over the land and its relation to the fundamentals of Zionism. On each side of the mainstream debate, an extreme reinterpretation of the connection to the land has been popularized into the 1980s. On one side, it was the fundamentalist right-wing (e.g., Gush Emunim) reinterpretation which called for aggressive Jewish settlement in the historic land despite the Arab inhabitants. On the other side, it was the reinterpretation of Israelis from all walks of life that Jews can be safe in territories other than Israel, where the conflict with the Arabs seemed endless. These Israelis constituted the bulk of the immigration wave to western countries, which accelerated dramatically after the war.

VII. CRISIS MANAGEMENT

The new communication contents described in the previous section shaped the public discourse into the 1980s. They were instrumental for crisis management in all social systems. The physical territory as the base for survival and the "security socicty" as the salient feature of private and public life have remained the dominant communication contents in Israel. The 1973 war crisis pointed out that these contents were practically irreplaceable for the public as a whole. At the same time, they had to be drastically revised and modified. The 1982 war in Lebanon required a further albeit smaller revision.

Crisis management in the system of society involved slow and long content revisions and social changes, which continued into the 1980s. Their seeds are indicated in the previous section and are self-explanatory. Crisis management in the security and political systems involved specific strategies, all implemented in the 1970.

After the Rabin government entered office in June 1974, it began a 3-year rehabilitation program of the IDF. It was funded by the United States, which practically became the sole supplier of military aid, for $1.5 billion a year. It included the import of massive machinery and high technology. The combat forces were also enlarged.

Following the recommendations of the Agranat Commission, the military-civil constitutional balance was restored. The mechanisms of civil control over the army were restructured. The communication channels between the Ministry of Defense and the IDF improved. Nonetheless, the bureaucracy in the Ministry still lacked control over the IDF's finance, procurement, intelligence, strategic planning, and research (Ben-Meir 1995).

The Rabin government also took steps to save the economy from collapse. The war had tremendous negative economic impacts. The immediate problems were the low productivity and the international oil crisis. Later, defense imports reached a climax, along with huge trade deficits. Economic growth was stifled and a decade-long inflation process began with a record of 56% in 1974 (25% before the war). The government reduced wages, increased taxes (mainly on import duties), devalued the local currency to 43% against the dollar in November 1974, and reformed the cost-of-living allowance policies in July 1975 (Plessner 1994:10–11, 206–231).

The most important role of the Rabin government was naturally in the management of the political system crisis. The background of the prime minister himself was crucial in restabilizing the system. First, Yitzhak Rabin symbolized the physical security and survival of Israelis. His glamorous military career culminated as the chief of staff of the IDF in the 1967 war. Some military analysts held him to be the architect of the victory. Public opinion viewed him as the number-one hero of the legendary war and held his 1967 victory as the ultimate contrast to the problematic course and outcome of the 1973 war (Slater 1996:132–174).

But there was more to Rabin than restoring the public confidence in the old life world of the security and political systems. Rabin was a new type of Labor leader. He was the first young (age 52) native-born premier. In a sharp contrast to his predecessors in office, he was a competent professional who emerged from the army ranks with no political power base in the Labor party. He was not ''contaminated'' by politics, including the politics of the 1973 war, when he served as the ambassador to Washington (Slater 1996:175–268).

Rabin had his own weaknesses and many conflicting interests within his government. But during his tenure, the political system stabilized to some extent. He was a second-generation Labor leader, a member of a pragmatic and efficient specialized elite. His native-born generation never centralized political power, lacked the cohesiveness of the first-generation pioneer elite from Europe, and enjoyed a more lucrative lifestyle (Eisenstadt 1985:404–411). Rabin came in the right time to manage the crisis. But in the long run, his term in office presented the tip of the sinking iceberg of all Labor elites, for which the war served as a powerful catalyst. The political system crisis, which became more moderate, still continued.

The corruption in Labor after decades in power, the splitting of its reform faction into a new party (the Democratic Movement for Change), the course and outcome of the war, and some unique events just before the May 1977 elections all haunted the Labor party in the polls. A month later, for the first time in the history of the political system, a new right-wing Likud-led government came to power. Its first task was to continue to manage the political crisis, which later on gradually subsided.

VIII. EPILOGUE

The management style of the new Likud government was very different than that of Labor. Not much changed, however, in the communication contents of the political system. Prime Minister Menachem Begin introduced high emotional tones regarding the historic connection to the land. But he only pursued more aggressively the settlement policy initiated by Labor in the territories captured in 1967. His nationalistic platform, much more than that of Labor, promoted military force as a political tool. But for the life world of the political system, the change was more one of degree than of kind. Indeed, during its second term in office, the Likud was already muddling in an unnecessary war in Lebanon.

Left or right wing in power, the ''security society'' system crisis seemed to be managed to a reasonable extent with an old-new mix of communication contents. Recovery was under way and the system's continued existence seemed secure again. At the same time, its decades-long isolation circle was gradually breaking. In 1979, Israel and Egypt signed a peace treaty. The treaty eventually led to the Israeli-Palestinian self-rule agreement of 1993 and the Israeli-Jordanian peace treaty of 1994. Israel and Syria also opened negotiations. New and different communication contents, perhaps those of ''peace society,'' began to emerge in a slow trial-and-error fashion. A new life world, perhaps, began to be written.

ENDNOTES

1. Habermas's concept of *social system crisis* focuses on the case of economic crisis in liberal capitalism, which, in the final analysis, turns into a *legitimation crisis*. The analysis here employs Habermas's epistemology only and focuses on the case of security (rather than economic) crisis. Furthermore, the 1973 war crisis is not viewed here as reaching the level of a legitimation crisis.
2. *Defense* is the common word used in English. *Security*, interestingly, is the word actually used in Hebrew.

REFERENCES

Arian, Asher (1985). *Politics and Government in Israel*. Tel Aviv: Zmora-Bitan. (Hebrew)

Avineri, Shlomo (1991). *Varieties of Zionist Thought*. Tel Aviv: Am Oved Publishers. (Hebrew)

Ben-Meir, Yehuda (1995). *Civil-Military Relations in Israel*. New York: Columbia University Press.

Ben-Zadok, Efraim (1985). National planning—the critical neglected link: one hundred years of Jewish settlement in israel. *International Journal of Middle East Studies*, 17(*3*), 329–345.

Congressional Quarterly (1986). The Middle East. Washington, D.C. *Congressional Quarterly*, 6th ed.

deHaven-Smith, Lance. (1988). *Philosophical Critiques of Policy Analysis: Lindblom, Habermas, and the Great Society*. Gainesville, FL: University of Florida Press.

Eisenstadt, Shmuel N. (1985). *The Transformation of Israeli Society*. Boulder, CO: Westview Press.

Galnoor, Itzhak (1980). Transformations in the Israeli political system since the Yom Kippur war. In A. Arian (ed.), *The Elections in Israel-1977*, 119–148. Jerusalem: Jerusalem Academic Press.

Galnoor, Itzhak (1982). *Steering the Polity: Communication and Politics in Israel*. Beverly Hills, CA: Sage.

Gilbert, Martin (1993). *Atlas of the Arab-Israeli Conflict*. New York: Oxford University Press.

Habermas, Jurgen (1975). *Legitimation Crisis*. Boston: Beacon Press.

Meir, Golda (1975). *My Life*. London: Weidenfeld and Nicolson.

Peri, Yoram (1983). *Between Battles and Ballots: Israeli Military in Politics*. Cambridge: Cambridge University Press.

Plessner, Yakir (1994). *The Political Economy of Israel: From Ideology to Stagnation*. Albany, NY: State University of New York Press.

Safran, Nadav (1981). *Israel: The Embattled Ally*. Cambridge, MA: Harvard University press.

Shapiro, Yonathan (1996). *Politicians as an Hegemonic Class: The Case of Israel*. Tel Aviv: Sifriat Poalim. (Hebrew).

Sharkansky, Ira (1989). The Overloaded State. *Public Administration Review* 49(*2*), 201–204.

Slater, Robert (1996). *Rabin of Israel: Warrior for Peace*. London: Robson Books.

13

Homeless Policy Initiatives

Managing or Muddling Through the Crisis?

Leslie A. Leip School of Public Administration, Florida Atlantic University, Fort Lauderdale, Florida

I. INTRODUCTION

Some forty years ago, Charles Lindblom (1959) wrote his landmark article entitled ''The 'Science' of Muddling Through.'' Lindblom purported that the rational-comprehensive method, or the root method, for policy making is impossible for complex problems because policy makers do not possess the intellectual capabilities, sources of information, time, and money necessary to use the root method. The second method, that of successive limited comparisons, or the branch method, was defined by Lindblom as ''continually building out from the current situation, step-by-step and by small degrees'' (p. 80). Many scholars[1] have further developed the study of public policy, and the branch method, now termed *incremental policy formulation*, still holds explanatory power for understanding how public policy is made in the United States. Lindblom claimed that the branch method is what is practiced, and this assertion still holds true for current homeless policy formulation.

The federal government has attempted to address the homeless problem by developing an array of public policies that have created a plethora of programs and services. The policies that were constructed during the early 1980s primarily focused on emergency food and shelter programs, which assisted people after they became homeless. It became clear that the provision of emergency care only did not adequately address the problem, because the numbers of homeless people increased to crisis levels. A more comprehensive policy, under the Stewart B. McKinney Act, was developed in 1987, but the focus remained on emergency and remedial programs. This policy created many unintended consequences, the most important being management problems. In order to deal with that situation, the federal government consolidated policies and many programs were eliminated or reorganized in the early 1990s. The homeless crisis continued to grow and policy makers began to realize that a new approach was needed. This approach, the ''Continuum of Care'' strategy, was developed by the Department of Housing and Urban Development (HUD) in 1994, and it resulted in a holistic approach for managing the homeless crisis. Since 1994, legislation has been created based on the Continuum of Care strategy, and many of the homeless programs and the corresponding funding have been reorganized. The major public laws that have been enacted over the past 15 years are listed on Table 1.

Table 1 Legislation for Homeless Initiatives and Programs

Year	Legislation Title	Purpose of Legislation	Managing Agencies
1983	Emergency Jobs Appropriations Act	To provide funds to states and local governments for emergency food and shelter programs	Federal Emergency Management Agency (FEMA)
1987	Stewart B. McKinney Act	To provide funds to states and local governments for housing, health, education, training and veteran programs	See Table 2 for comprehensive list of managing agencies.
1990	National Affordable Housing Act (Title VIII)	To incorporate housing programs into the Shelter Plus Care (SPC) umbrella	Department of Housing and Urban Development (HUD)
1990	McKinney Homeless Assistance Act	To develop programs for homeless children and reauthorize appropriations for homeless programs	Department of Health and Human Services (HHS)
1992	Housing and Community Development Act	To reauthorize funding for SPC, training, health care and youth programs included in the McKinney Act	Departments of HUD, Labor, HHS, Education
1992	Comprehensive Service Programs for Homeless Veterans Act	To establish a pilot veteran's program and reauthorize funding for the Homeless Veterans' Reintegration program	Department of Veterans Affairs (DVA)
1993	HUD Demonstration Act	To create the Innovative Homeless Initiatives Demonstration program and to have the HUD secretary provide assistance to the National Community Development Initiative	Department of Housing and Urban Development
1994	Human Services Amendment Act (Title II)	To extend the authorization of appropriations for the Emergency Community Services Homeless Grant program	Department of Health and Human Services
1996	DVA, HUD, and Independent Agencies Appropriations Act	To reauthorize appropriations for programs and eliminate the Adult Education program and Emergency Services Grants program	FEMA and Departments of HUD and HHS
1997	Homeless Housing Programs Consolidation and Flexibility Act (has not become public law)	To amend the McKinney Homeless Assistance Act in order to consolidate the federal programs for housing assistance for the homeless into a single block grant program. To require the secretaries from several departments to coordinate their efforts	Departments of HUD, HHS, Labor, Education, and Veterans Affairs
1997	Homeless Assistance and Management Reform Act (has not become public law)	To facilitate the management of the homeless assistance programs of HUD by merging programs into one fund	Department of Housing and Urban Development

Each of these laws was developed based on the situation at hand, step by step, and by small degrees.

The changes in homeless policy that have occurred lead to an intriguing research question: Are the policy initiatives that have been developed to address the homeless crisis allowing all levels of government to manage the crisis, or are governments muddling through the crisis? The purpose of this chapter is to examine federal policies that address homelessness in order to understand how all of the levels of government have managed the homeless crisis. This chapter explicates important management lessons, and government administrators and policy makers can use this information to more effectively manage and diminish other types of social crises.

II. HOMELESS POLICY DEVELOPMENT 1970–1989

During the 1970s, the homeless problem was not viewed as a crisis by the federal government (Robertson and Greenblatt 1992), and there was no attempt by the federal government to develop a comprehensive policy that could be used to manage the homeless problem at the national level. Local and state governments were primarily responsible for dealing with the homeless population in their respective areas. Many governments relied on churches and charities to provide emergency shelter and food to the homeless while the governments provided other types of assistance, such as Food Stamps Program. There was no systematic approach for developing programs that would meet all the needs of the homeless populations, and this resulted in a piecemeal approach for managing the homeless populations in cities around the nation. Therefore, the lack of federal government policy and the local government piecemeal approach resulted in governments muddling through the management of the homeless crisis during the 1970s.

The nation appeared to awaken to the problems of the homeless in the early 1980s. A variety of events and coalition building that drew attention to the homeless problem occurred. The Coalition for the Homeless was formed in 1980, the National Coalition for the Homeless was formed in 1982, and the Hands Across America program began in 1986. As a result, there was more media attention that helped to bring the homeless problem to policy agendas at the federal, state, and local levels.

There were also several studies of homeless populations completed during the early 1980s, which demonstrated the severity of the homeless problem in cities around the United States. Various homeless advocate groups used these studies to illustrate the expansion of the homeless crisis and draw national attention to the problem. Homeless populations in specific cities such as Los Angeles (Robertson et al. 1985), Chicago (Chicago Department of Human Services 1983), Baltimore (Fischer et al. 1986) and Phoenix (Brown et al. 1983) were examined.

In addition to the specific city studies, larger studies were completed. The members of the Community for Creative Non-Violence (CCNV) completed a survey in 1982 that indicated that 2.2 million people lacked shelter (Hombs and Snyder 1982). The findings from this study were challenged because the sampling methods did not follow scientific standards. As a result, the Department of Housing and Urban Development (HUD) began to gather official data on the homeless. HUD spent 6 months reviewing 100 local and national studies and conducting more than 500 interviews with homeless providers in 60 cities. The report determined that on an average night from December 1983 to January 1984, there were between 192,000 and 586,000 homeless people, with the most reliable estimate being 250,000 to 350,000 (U.S. Department of Housing and Urban Development 1984). The Urban Institute conducted the first national study of urban homeless populations. A random sample of 1704 homeless people was selected and interviewed. The findings suggested the total U.S. homeless population to be between 500,000 and 600,000 (Burt and Cohen 1989).

These studies illustrated the contradictions about counting the homeless. Counting the homeless is important because without accurate data it is difficult to gauge how big and costly assistance programs must be. According to S. Anna Kondratas, a former assistant secretary at HUD, "the numbers are of critical political significance at the federal level. If the U.S. is swamped with millions of homeless Americans (according to the CCNV study), then a better case can be made for treating the matter as a federal problem. If the numbers are closer to the HUD figures, then the main burden of responsibility for the homeless is with state and local governments and private organizations" (Kondratas 1985:6). There has never been a consensus on the number of homeless in the United States because of the difficulties that arise from defining who is homeless and the methodology necessary for actually counting the homeless (Pear 1988; Fannie Mae 1991).

The increase in coalition building, media attention, and research influenced the growth of the internal structure of the policy subsystems involved in this policy arena. Using Sabatier's (1988) language, the "advocacy coalitions"[2] in the homeless policy arena began taking shape in the early 1980s. The combination of the growing numbers of homeless people and the formation of advocacy coalitions resulted in the federal government adding this issue to their agenda.

The first congressional committee meeting on the homeless crisis was held in 1983, and Congress passed the Emergency Jobs Appropriations Act. The purpose of this policy was straightforward—to provide funds to state and local governments enabling them to create emergency food and shelter programs that would assist people who were living on the streets. The Federal Emergency Management Agency (FEMA) was authorized to manage these programs, and the emphasis was on remedial care, not preventive care. Many state and local governments did receive funds from FEMA for food and shelter programs, but the programs did not meet many of the needs of the homeless populations (DeKoven 1995).

In the late 1980s, the federal government extended its role in the homeless policy arena, and this had a profound impact on the management of homeless policy. Many unforeseen management problems resulted from the profusion of new programs and the administrative procedures of the programs.

Congress considered several bills that broadened the federal role in helping the homeless in 1987. The legislation that eventually became law was the Urgent Relief for the Homeless Act; it was renamed as the Stewart B. McKinney Homeless Assistance Act in honor of the congressman from Connecticut. There were nine titles under this act, and the initial authorization was $490.2 million. The McKinney Act was amended and reauthorized for 1989 and 1990, and these amendments authorized existing programs to use funds for activities aimed at preventing homelessness. For the first time, people at risk of becoming homeless could receive emergency funds to pay back rent, utilities, and other costs (Wasem 1991).

The McKinney Act was the first attempt at developing a comprehensive strategy for dealing with the variety of homeless population needs. The programs and provisions of the McKinney Act for 1987–1989 were as follows: (1) the emergency food and shelter program; (2) housing assistance program; (3) community-based mental health services;

(4) substance abuse programs; (5) health care programs; (6) education and training programs; (7) community services to provide follow-up and long-term services; (8) veteran's provisions; (9) grants for groups to renovate or convert unused federal property into shelters; and (10) provisions dealing with Aid to Families with Dependent Children and Unemployment Compensation.

Title II of the McKinney Act established the Interagency Council on the Homeless as an independent agency in the Executive branch. The council's primary responsibility was to coordinate and manage the variety of assistance programs provided by the federal departments. Table 2 is a listing of the federal programs that were developed as the result of the McKinney Act and the federal departments responsible for administering the programs. Appropriations were given to all of the federal departments to create programs for the homeless. A brief review of the funds allocated to three of the departments illustrates the increased role of the federal government. Although all of the fiscal years have not yet been discussed, this information provides an understanding of the amount of money that has been allocated for homeless programs over the past nine years.

The Department of Housing and Urban Development administers many programs that in some way assist the homeless. The main programs are the Emergency Shelter Grants program, the Supportive/Transitional Housing program, Supplemental Assistance (funded through 1992), Section 8 Single Room Occupancy program, and the Shelter Plus Care program. Funding increased from just under $200 million in 1989 to $1 billion in 1995. It decreased to just over $800 million in 1996 and has remained stable from 1996 to 1998 (Interagency Council on the Homeless 1991; National Coalition for the Homeless 1998). The president's request for 1999 funding for the HUD Homeless Assistance Programs was $1.15 billion, the House of Representatives' funding request was $975 million, and the Senate's funding request was $1 billion.

The Departments of Health and Human Services (HHS) and Labor administer several programs that in some way help the homeless. The main HHS programs are the Emergency Community Services program, Projects for Assistance in Transition from Homelessness (PATH), alcohol and drug demonstrations, mental health demonstrations, health care for the homeless program, and family support centers. The main Department of Labor program is the Job Training for the Homeless program. In 1989, just over $50 million was allocated to the Department of Health and Human Services and the Department of Labor (Interagency Council on the Homeless 1991; National Coalition for the Homeless 1998). The dramatic increase in 1991 funding, from $90 million in 1990 to $1.6 billion in 1991, is the result of developing PATH. Funding has remained between $140 million and $160 million since 1991. The funding requests for 1999 indicate minimal increases.

These are only the appropriations for three departments; the other eleven, federal departments have also received millions of dollars for homeless programs.[3] All of the federal departments had dissimilar requirements for the applications for funds that state and local governments could receive, and this put a burden on governments applying for funding because the application process was cumbersome and time-consuming. In addition, the individual programs were administered differently for each state and local government. Some states and localities submitted proposals for all types of assistance programs, and others submitted proposals for only one or two assistance programs. This turned into an immense amount of record keeping that the Interagency Council on the Homeless, federal departments, and state and local governments had to conduct. According to a General Accounting Office report, this management structure was one of the problems with

Table 2 Federal Homeless Assistance Programs

Type of Program	Managing Agency
Emergency services	
Emergency Food and Shelter Grants Program	Federal Emergency Management Agency
Emergency Shelter Grants Program	Department of Housing and Urban Development
Emergency Community Services Homeless Grant Program	Department of Health and Human Services
Nonemergency Housing	
Supportive Housing Program	Department of Housing and Urban Development
Section 8 Single Room Occupancy Dwellings	Department of Housing and Urban Development
Shelter Plus Care Program	Department of Housing and Urban Development
Supplemental Assistance for Facilities to Assist Homeless	Department of Housing and Urban Development
Surplus Federal Property	Department of Housing and Urban Development
Shelter for the Homeless	Department of Defense
Homes for the Homeless Program	Department of Agriculture
HOME Investment Partnership Program	Department of Housing and Urban Development
Housing Opportunities for Persons with AIDS	Department of Housing and Urban Development
Housing Improvement Program	Department of the Interior
Mental health services	
Project for Assistance in Transition from Homelessness	Department of Health and Human Services
Community Mental Health Projects	Department of Health and Human Services
Community Projects for Alcohol and Drug Abuse Treatment	Department of Health and Human Services
Community-Based Psychiatric Residential Treatment	Department of Veterans Affairs
Victim Assistance Program	Department of Justice
Education and training	
Adult Education for the Homeless	Department of Education
Education for Homeless Children and Youth	Department of Education
Job Training for the Homeless	Department of Labor
Homeless Veterans Reintegration Projects	Department of Labor
Children and youth	
Aid to Families with Dependent Children	Department of Health and Human Services
Runaway and Homeless Youth Program	Department of Health and Human Services
Drug Abuse Prevention Youth Program Youth	Department of Health and Human Services
Transitional Living Program for Homeless Youth	Department of Health and Human Services
Office of Juvenile and Delinquency Prevention	Department of Justice
Social services and prevention	
Family Support Centers	Department of Health and Human Services
Child Support Enforcement Program	Department of Health and Human Services
Supplemental Security Income	Department of Health and Human Services
Post Office Program	U.S. Postal Service
Weatherization Assistance Program	Department of Energy
Abuse Treatment of Homeless Individuals	Department of Health and Human Services
Volunteers in Service to America	Federal Domestic Volunteer Agency
Nutrition services	
Special Supplemental Food Program	Department of Agriculture
Commodity Assistance for Charitable Institutions Program	Department of Agriculture
Commodities for Soup Kitchens Program	Department of Agriculture
Temporary Emergency Food Assistance Program	Department of Agriculture
Food Bank Program	Departments of Defense and Transportation

the Stewart B. McKinney Act. "Local service providers were dissatisfied with some of the aspects of the McKinney Act program, such as the burdensome application and record-keeping requirements" (U.S. General Accounting Office 1994:1).

Although there was an effort by the federal government to increase their role and improve homeless policies during the 1980s, management and coordination of the assistance programs were still lacking. By the end of the 1980s, over 60 homeless programs were administered by 14 federal departments that had to coordinate with local governments, nonprofit organizations, and private organizations. As a result, there were problems with coordinating efforts between the different governments and organizations, duplicating of services, and keeping funding procedures straight. State and local governments had to muddle their way through the application procedures, the funding structure, and the administrative operations. These management problems were the impetus for the incremental reorganization of administrative responsibilities in the 1990s.

III. HOMELESS POLICY DEVELOPMENT 1990–1998

During this period, some of the homeless assistance programs were reorganized so that the burdens of the application and administrative procedures were reduced. From 1990 to 1992, the management of policies was still complicated and laborious; however, changes that were made in policies between 1993 and 1997 reduced management problems. Furthermore, proposed legislation from the most recent Congress will, if passed, have profound implications on the administration and management of homeless programs. The proposed legislation may allow state and local governments to effectively manage the homeless crisis as opposed to continuing to muddle through the crisis. Although proposed policies may improve the management and maintenance of services for the homeless, the legislation does not provide permanent solutions (affordable housing, livable wages, comprehensive health care) that can address the root causes of homelessness.

A. 1990–1994 Legislation

In the early 1990s, policies were developed that addressed specific needs of the homeless populations around the nation. A plethora of research on the homeless was completed in the early 1990s, which focused on single aspects of homelessness. These studies brought attention to the many different problems that homeless people faced. The relationship between housing policy and homelessness was examined (Sclar 1990; Leavitt 1992; Ringheim 1993). Morse and Calsyn (1992), Breakey (1992), Frazier (1992), and Koegel and Burnam (1992) investigated the problems the mentally-ill homeless population faced. The relationship between drug abuse and homeless people was explored (Schutt and Garrett 1992; Wilhite 1992; Schmidt 1990). McChesney (1992), Merves (1992), Robertson (1992), Petry and Avent (1992), and Bassuk (1992) examined problems surrounding homeless families, homeless women with children, and homeless youths. Some scholars completed research on the medical care for the homeless and the health of homeless people (Brickner et al. 1992; Jaheil 1992).

In addition to these scholarly works on homelessness, the U.S. Bureau of the Census, for the first time in the history of the nation, included an assessment of the homeless population in the 1990 census. On March 20, 1990, surveyors went to 39,000 sites and counted the homeless. The sites that were included in the survey ranged from emergency shelters to refuges for runaways. The count of homeless people from the census was 459,209. The census officials emphasized in their report that the count was only a numerical snapshot of the homeless on March 20, not an estimate of the total number of homeless (U.S. Census Bureau 1992). These studies demonstrated the necessity for addressing the increasing homeless population and the various needs of the population.

In 1990, Congress enacted two laws related to the reauthorization of the McKinney Act for 1991 and 1992. Title VIII was added to the National Affordable Housing Act of 1990, which contained housing provisions, a statutory authority over McKinney programs provision, and a provision requiring HUD to complete a study on converting programs into a block grant. Three new programs were placed under the Shelter Plus Care (SPC) umbrella. Provisions for Section 8 single occupancy, rental assistance, and Section 202 handicapped housing were folded into the act.

The second law was the McKinney Homeless Assistance Act of 1990. The statutory authority for all non-HUD McKinney Act programs was established in the law. Housing provisions, a health care program for homeless children, and a program to prevent the splitting of children and homeless parents were also included in the law.

The House and Community Development Act was enacted in 1992, and it reauthorized the McKinney Act. For 1993, $1.1 billion was appropriated for federal homeless assistance programs. An increase of $156 million for HUD's Shelter Plus Care Program was included in the act. The Department of Labor's Job Training for the Homeless Demonstration Program received an increase of $3.2 million for a total of $12.5 million. The Health Care for the Homeless Program administered by the Department of Health and Human Services received an increase of $2 million for a total of $58 million. A total of $21 million was appropriated for the Access to Community Care Effective Services and Support Program (ACCESS), which is a program for people who are homeless and have severe mental illness and substance abuse problems. Family support centers to help families with housing received a total of $6.9 million. Congress also approved $150 million for Support Housing and $100 million for Housing Opportunities for People with Aids Program administered by HUD, $24 million for the Community Support Program, and $62 million for three programs for Runaway and Homeless Youth administered by Department of Health and Human Services.

Congress also passed the Comprehensive Service Programs for Homeless Veterans Act in 1992. This public law established a pilot program to improve and expand the provision of services to homeless veterans and extended existing assistance programs for veterans. In addition, the law amended the McKinney Homeless Assistance Act to authorize appropriations for the Homeless Veterans' Reintegration Project.

Congress passed the HUD Demonstration Act in 1993 and the law authorized appropriations for homeless programs for 1994. The act directed the Secretary of HUD to carry out the Innovative Homeless Initiatives Demonstration program through 1994. Washington, D.C., Miami, Philadelphia, Denver, and Los Angeles were selected as the cities for the Homeless Initiative Demonstration program. In addition, it authorized the HUD secretary to provide assistance to the National Community Development Initiative for grants to local community development organizations for training and capacity building, technical assistance, community development, and housing assistance.

The Human Services Amendments Act was passed in 1994. Title II (Community Services Block Grant Amendments) Section 206 amended the Stewart B. McKinney Homeless Assistance Act to extend the authorization of appropriations for the Emergency Community Services Homeless Grants program.

The McKinney Act was also amended to terminate the Interagency Council on the Homeless. The appropriations for the council were not renewed for 1994, and the tasks of the council were assumed by a Working Group of the White House Domestic Policy Council. The new Council/Working Group consists of 17 agencies and is chaired by the secretary of HUD. The duties of the Council/Working group include (1) planning and coordinating all federal activities and programs to assist the homeless; (2) monitoring and evaluating assistance to homeless persons provided by other levels of government and the private sector; (3) ensuring that technical assistance is provided to help communities and organizations assist the homeless; and (4) disseminating information on federal resources available to assist the homeless (U.S. Department of Housing and Urban Development Web Site 1997).

All of the laws that were passed between 1990 and 1994 provided the authority to combine and reorganize the programs for the homeless that were originally established by the McKinney Act in 1987. Nine principal programs and projects have been categorized as the result of the different pieces of legislation: (1) FEMA Emergency Food and Shelter Program; (2) HUD Homeless Assistance Programs (Emergency Shelter Grants, Supportive Housing, Shelter Plus Care, Section 8 SRO Moderate Rehabilitation); (3) the Projects for Assistance in Transition from Homelessness (PATH) program; (4) Adult Education for the Homeless program; (5) Education for Homeless Children and Youth program; (6) Health Care for the Homeless; (7) Homeless Veterans Reintegration project; (8) Emergency Community Services Grants; and (9) the ACCESS demonstration program.

The management and administration of homeless assistance programs did change during this period as a result of consolidating programs and the creation of the Council/ Working Group. The main change was on the management of the funding structure, not on reducing the duplication of services and coordination of services. State and local governments were able to apply for funding for a variety of programs that were incorporated into block grants.

The demonstration programs that were developed during this period were used to test different approaches to addressing the homeless crisis. The results were used as a foundation for policy development from 1995 until the present.

B. 1995–1998 Legislation

Several pieces of legislation had an impact on the homeless crisis during this period. The majority of policies emphasized the consolidation of programs, which helped to coordinate the administration of homeless programs. The focus of policy development was based on a new approach, the Continuum of Care model, established by the Clinton Administration and the Department of Housing and Urban Development. This model was grounded on the understanding that homelessness is not caused merely by a lack of shelter but also by a variety of underlying, unmet physical, economic, and social needs (Schwartz 1997). In addition to this shift in focus, the management of homeless programs greatly improved during this time because of the effort made by federal departments to provide information for funding and planning via the Internet.

In 1996, a public law titled "The Department of Veterans Affairs, Housing and Urban Development and Independent Agencies Act," was passed. The programs included in the act were the FEMA Emergency Food and Shelter Program, HUD Homeless Assistance Programs, and low-income housing programs. The PATH Program received $20 million for 1996 and 1997. The National Heath Care for the Homeless Program was reauthorized as Section 330 (h) of the U.S. Public Health Service Act in 1996. In addition, the Housing Opportunities for Persons with AIDS (HOPWA) received appropriations. During this time, the Adult Education for the Homeless Program was eliminated, but the Education for Homeless Children and Youth Program was reauthorized. The Homeless Veterans Reintegration project did not receive any appropriations for 1996 and 1997. The Emergency Community Services Grants program was also eliminated.

As a result of the Innovative Homeless Initiatives Demonstration program established by the HUD Demonstration Act of 1993, the most recent homeless policy development has been based on the Continuum of Care approach. This new approach consisted of two key elements: (1) a coordinated community-based process of identifying needs and building a system to address those needs and (2) increased funding to provide communities with the resources needed to build the system of care (Cuomo 1997).

The Office of Community Planning and Development (CPD) at HUD contracted with Barnard-Columbia Center for Urban Policy to conduct a study of the implementation of the Continuum of Care. The study showed that the implementation of the new approach resulted in (1) substantial increases in funding from both government and non-government sources; (2) an increase in the number of homeless people assisted; and (3) an increased emphasis on transitional and permanent housing relative to emergency assistance (Fuchs and McAllister 1996). According to the study, the Clinton Administration's homeless strategy was an ''effective partnership between federal and local governments, non-profits, and the private sector'' (Cuomo 1997:1).

A major part of the Continuum of Care effort was the inclusion of community development plans. Andrew Cuomo, Secretary of HUD, stated in a letter that

> HUD recognizes that for a homeless assistance strategy to be effective, it must be linked to a community's overall development plan. We have been working with communities to forge comprehensive community development strategies—strategies that recognize the best solutions come from the bottom up, from within the community, by empowering residents to become real stakeholders in the future of their neighborhoods. Therefore, we ask that all projects seeking funding be a part of a single Continuum of Care strategy to help homeless persons move to self-sufficiency within their community or state. (Cuomo 1997, p. 1)

HUD has provided the structure for the community development plans as well as assistance for creating the plans to state and local governments.

These community development plans have been implemented in all 50 states and hundreds of cities across the nation. The plans have five major components: (1) the citizen's summary; (2) the community profile; (3) housing and community development needs (which includes housing market conditions, affordable housing needs, homeless needs, public and assisted housing needs, barriers to affordable housing, and community development needs); (4) a 5-year housing and development strategic plan; and (5) a 1-year action plan (Department of Housing and Development Web Site 1997). The community development plans have provided the states and cities an opportunity to assess the housing situations in their areas and courses of action to use to manage their strategies to deal with the homeless crisis.

The community development plans that include the Continuum of Care strategy are the basis for the majority of applications for HUD competitive grants; hence the amount of proposal development time has been reduced. Furthermore, HUD has issued a Notice of Funding Availability (NOFA) for a wide range of programs based on the Continuum of Care strategy and all of the applications and funding information are available via the Internet, HUD software, or on paper. According to the National Coalition for the Homeless, HUD's efforts have "greatly enhanced local collaboration of housing and services programs to reduce duplication of effort and insure that a community develops a holistic response" (National Coalition for the Homeless Web Site 1997:1).

The bills that have been recently put forth by Congress clearly reflect the Continuum of Care approach and the need to consolidate programs. One piece of proposed legislation is the Homeless Housing Programs Consolidation and Flexibility Act. The purpose of the bill is to "amend Title IV of the McKinney Homeless Assistance Act to consolidate the federal programs for housing assistance for the homeless into a single block grant program that ensures states and communities are provided sufficient flexibility to use assistance amounts effectively" (U.S. House of Representatives 1997:1).

At the beginning of the act, congressional findings about the homeless crisis and the management of the crisis are clearly stated as the impetus for the legislation. Under Section 2 of the bill the following findings are stated:

1. The United States faces a crisis of individuals and families who lack basic affordable housing and appropriate shelter.
2. Assistance from the federal government is an important factor in the success of efforts by state and local governments and the private sector to address the problem of homelessness in a comprehensive manner.
3. There are a multitude of federal government programs to assist the homeless; many of the federal programs for the homeless have overlapping objectives, resulting in multiple sources of federal funding for the same of similar purposes.
4. While the results of federal programs to assist the homeless generally have been positive, it is clear that here is a need for consolidation and simplification of such programs to better support local efforts. (U.S. House of Representatives 1997:1–2)

One of the ways the Homeless Housing Programs Consolidation and Flexibility Act addresses the problems stated above is by amending the Stewart McKinney Act so federal agencies can coordinate their efforts. The act calls for the Secretaries of HUD, Health and Human Services, Labor, Education, Veteran Affairs, and Agriculture to consult and coordinate in order to ensure that assistance for federally funded activities for the homeless can be provided (U.S. House of Representatives 1997:10). The consulting and coordinating is suppose to lead to less duplication of services and to the simplification of programs so that local governments have the flexibility to effectively and efficiently manage their efforts.

Another piece of proposed legislation, the Homelessness Assistance and Management Reform Act of 1997, was developed to "facilitate the effective and efficient management of the homeless assistance programs of the Department of Housing and Urban Development, including the merger of such programs into one performance fund" (U.S. Senate 1997:1). If this piece of legislation is passed, facilitating the effective and efficient management of homeless programs would be accomplished by taking seven steps which are outlined in the legislation. First, community-based, comprehensive systems would be created to maximize a community's ability to implement a coordinated system to assist homeless individuals and families. Second, authorizations under the McKinney Act would be reorganized into a Homeless Assistance Performance Fund. The third step would be to assist state and local governments, in partnership with private nonprofit service providers, to use homeless funding more efficiently and effectively. Fourth, provisions of federal homeless assistance would be simplified and made more flexible. Fifth, the manner in which the secretary distributes homeless assistance would be made more efficient and equitable. The reduction of the federal role in decision making for homeless assistance programs would be the sixth step. Finally, the seventh step would be to reduce the costs to governmental jurisdictions and private nonprofit organizations in applying and using assistance (U.S. Senate 1997).

This bill also formalized the Continuum of Care System, which would be created by local and state homeless assistance boards. Each Continuum of Care System would include a series of components. The first component is a system of outreach and assessment, including drop-in centers, 24-hour hotlines, and counselors designed to engage homeless individuals and families into the Continuum of Care System. The second component is a system of emergency shelters with essential services. Transitional housing with appropriate supportive services to help ensure that homeless individuals and families are prepared to make the transition to increased responsibility and permanent housing is the third component. The fourth component is creating permanent housing to help meet the long-term housing needs of homeless individuals and families. A system of coordination of assistance provided by federal, state, and local programs is the fifth component. The final component is a system of referrals for subpopulations of the homeless to the appropriate agencies, programs, or services necessary to meet their needs (U.S. Senate 1997).

All of the legislation that has been passed or recently proposed reflects the effort by the federal government to change the management of homeless assistance programs to a strategic and systematic approach. There has been a concentrated effort to provide assistance with strategic planning in order for state and local governments to systematically manage the homeless crisis in their communities. There has also been a push toward consulting about homeless assistance programs so that there will be less duplication of services, which leads to a more efficient use of funding. Finally, efforts have been made to consolidate and simplify the funding processes so that state and local governments have the flexibility to meet the specific needs of the homeless populations in their communities. The actual effects of the most recent policies on the management and administration of assistance programs for the homeless is yet to be assessed, but the foundation has been established for improvement.

IV. DISCUSSION

During the past two decades, the changes in focus of homeless policy initiatives have resulted in a shift from all levels of government muddling through the homeless crisis to governments managing the crisis. Although the management of the homeless problem has improved, there are few future federal policies that indicate that the root causes of homelessness will be addressed. The purpose of this section is to analyze the policy patterns in order to illustrate the inadequacies of past policies and explicate possible policy choices of the future.

In the 1970s, there were no federal policies that directly addressed the homeless problem. State and local governments held the responsibility of creating services to assist the homeless population in their states and localities. As a result, numerous charitable and nonprofit organizations and public sector services assumed the role of providing emergency shelter and food to the homeless in cities around the United States. There was no national systematic plan for the development of services, hence there was no federal foundation for proactive policy that could be used to address the growing problem of homelessness in the United States.

The lack of a federal foundation for services for the homeless ushered in the piecemeal policy approach in the early 1980s. Furthermore, the number of homeless people on the streets dramatically increased in the early 1980s and the problem was brought to the attention of the American public via advocacy coalition development and exposure. The Emergency Jobs Appropriation Act of 1983 only provided emergency shelter and food services for people after they became homeless; it by no means established any proactive policy to address the root causes of homelessness. Using Edelman's (1964) policy typology, this policy was symbolic because there was little material impact on the homeless population and no real tangible advantages. The piecemeal approach only allowed governments to muddle through the homeless crisis because there was no systematic policy that provided funding for all types of services.

The McKinney Act of 1987 was a means to develop a comprehensive policy and provide a variety of services, not just emergency shelter and food. However, many of the services followed the pattern of remedial care. During this period, defining, counting and studying the homeless population became important. There was very little consensus about the homeless population and their needs. Policy makers did not have a clear understanding of the root causes of homelessness, and this influenced them to focus on the management of services, not on the alternatives that would ameliorate the homeless crisis.

The unintended consequence of the McKinney Act was that management problems, such as confusing funding procedures and time-consuming record keeping, emerged because 14 federal departments had to administer numerous programs in the 50 states and hundreds of cities. Although the Interagency Council on the Homeless was created to coordinate the efforts of the federal departments, it had a minimal impact on the management problems that appeared from the McKinney Act. Millions of dollars were appropriated during this period; however, some of the monies had to be spent on management costs. These management problems were the reason for incrementally consolidating homeless assistance programs in the early 1990s, and funding procedures and record keeping became less confusing and time-consuming. The pattern of focusing on policy changes for management procedures, not the root causes of homelessness, was reinforced during this period.

During the mid 1990s, policy makers launched pilot programs to test new approaches for addressing the homeless problem. This was the first attempt to use the continuum-of-care approach, and it was the most important change in focus that resulted in state and local governments being able to manage the homeless crisis. This systematic approach has allowed governments to create strategic plans to address specific homeless population needs in their communities. The recent, proposed legislation would enhance the systematic approach because the policies permit state and local governments to more fully develop their community-base, comprehensive systems of assistance for homeless people. The legislation would lead to less duplication of services, which would ultimately lead to more efficient uses of funding.

The main problem that still exists, however, is that these federal policies primarily focus on the management of homeless programs, not on dealing with the root causes of homelessness. Housing policies still do not ensure that all low-income Americans can have access to housing that costs less than 30% of their income. In order for this to occur, the federal government needs to implement a set of policies utilizing direct subsidies and the tax code to ensure that affordable housing is offered to all Americans. Employment and income policies still do not provide for all Americans to have the income necessary for adequate housing. The federal minimum wage should continue to be increased until it can lift the average family out of poverty, and federal disability payments should be large enough to bring recipients' incomes up to the poverty line. Health care policies still do not guarantee comprehensive health care services to all poor Americans. The federal government needs to preserve and expand the entitlement to Medicaid in order for health care services to be available to poor Americans. The Medicaid managed care arrangements should include accommodations for the difficult circumstances of the homeless population, and the providers should be paid for providing health care to the populations with special needs. Even though there is hope for the future management of homeless programs, there is still much improvement that needs to be made the numerous policies that affect the homeless and poor populations of America.

This chapter illustrates that policy formulation for the homeless crisis began as a ''muddling through'' process. Looking toward the future, there is hope that the homeless crisis can be effectively managed, but housing, employment and income, and health care policies that address the root causes of homelessness still need to be improved.

There are some important lessons to be learned from understanding the evolution of homeless policy initiatives. First, coordination of policy initiatives should be emphasized, so that all of the people in governments and organizations involved in a social crisis can discuss the approaches necessary to address the problem. Second, policymakers should focus on preventive policies, not remedial policies, in dealing with a social crisis. Most social crises are complex webs that are a result of numerous problems that must be addressed, and remedial policies do not ameliorate these problems. Third, preventive policies should be formulated into a holistic approach that allows state and local governments to incorporate a strategic plan to manage the social crisis. Finally, support for the holistic approach must be available from the federal government in order for state and local governments to manage any social crisis in an effective and efficient way.

ENDNOTES

1. See Thomas Dye (1984), *Understanding Public Policy* (5th ed.), Englewood Cliffs, NJ: Prentice-Hall; Guy B. Peters (1993), *American Public Policy: Promise and Performance*, 3rd ed. Chatham, NJ: Chatham House; James E. Anderson (1990), *Public Policymaking: An Introduction*, Boston, MA: Houghton Mifflin.
2. Sabatier purported that the term *advocacy coalitions* is the most useful way to refer to the aggregation of actors involved in policy changes over a long period of time. These actors consist of elected and agency officials, interest group leaders, and researchers.
3. The total sum of funding for all homeless programs provided by the 14 federal departments was $1.475 billion in 1995, $1.090 billion in 1996, $1.096 billion in 1997, and $1.107 billion in 1998.

REFERENCES

Bassuk, E. L. (1992). Women and children without shelter: The characteristics of homeless families. In M. J. Robertson and M. Greenblatt (eds.), *Homelessness: A National Perspective*. New York: Plenum Press.

Breakey, W. R. (1992). Mental health services for homeless people. In M. J. Robertson and Greenblatt M. (eds.), *Homelessness: A National Perspective*. New York: Plenum Press.

Brickner, P. W., McAdam, H., Vivic, W. J., and Doherty, P. (1992). Strategies for the delivery of medical care: Focus on tuberculosis and hypertension. In M. J. Robertson and M. Greenblatt M (eds.), *Homelessness: A National Perspective*. New York: Plenum Press.

Brown, C., MacFarlane, S., Paredes, R., and Stark, L. (1983). *The Homeless of Phoenix: Who Are They? And What Do They Want*? Phoenix, AZ: Phoenix South Community Mental Health Center.

Burt, M. B. and Cohen, B. E. (1989). *America's Homeless: Numbers, Characteristics and the Programs That Serve Them*. Washington D.C.: The Urban Institute Press.

City of Chicago. (1983). *Homelessness in Chicago*. Chicago: Department of Human Services, Social Services Task Force.

Cochran, C. L. and Malone, E. F. (1995). *Public Policy Perspectives and Choices*. New York: McGraw-Hill.

Congressional Research Service. (1992). The Homeless. *CQ Researcher 2*. (29). pp. 665–688.

Cuomo, A. (1997). Letter from the Office of the Secretary of the Department of Housing and Urban Development [On line]. Available: (http://www.hud.gov) [1997, November 20].

DeKoven, W. L. (1995). A status report on hunger and homelessness in America's cities. Report submitted to the U.S. Conference of Mayors.

Edelman, M. (1964). *The Symbolic Use of Politics*. Urbana, IL: University of Illinois Press.

Fannie Mae (1991). Counting the Homeless: The methodologies, policies and social significance behind the numbers. *Housing Policy Debate 2*(3).

Fischer, P. H., Shapiro, S., Breakey, W. R., Anthony, J. C., and Kramer, M. (1986). Mental health and social characteristics of the homeless: A survey of mission users. *American Journal of Public Health 76*, 519–524.

Frazier, S. (1992). Homelessness and mental disorder: The federal response. In M. J. Robertson and M. Greenblatt (eds.), *Homelessness: A National Perspective*. New York: Plenum Press.

Fuchs, E. and McAllister, W. (1996). *The Continuum of Care: A Report on the New Federal Policy to Address Homelessness*. Report submitted to the Department of Housing and Urban Development.

Hombs, M. E. and Snyder, M. (1982). *Homelessness in America, A Forced March to Nowhere*. Washington D.C.: Community for Creative Non-Violence.

Jahiel, R. I. (1992). Health and health care of homeless people. In M. J. Robertson and M. Greenblatt (eds.), *Homelessness: A National Perspective*. New York: Plenum Press.

Interagency Council on the Homeless (1991). *Federal Programs to Help Homeless People*. Washington D.C.

Koegel, P. and Burnam, M. A. (1992). Problems in the assessment of mental illness among the homeless: An empirical approach. In M. J. Robertson and M. Greenblatt (eds.), *Homelessness: A National Perspective*. New York: Plenum Press.

Kondratas, S. A. (1985). A strategy for helping the homeless. *The Heritage Foundation Backgrounder 431*, 6.

Leavitt, J. (1992). Homelessness and the housing crisis. In M. J. Robertson and M. Greenblatt (eds.), *Homelessness: A National Perspective*. New York: Plenum Press.

Lindblom, C. E. (1959). The ''science'' of muddling through. *Public Administration Review 19* 79–88.

McChesney, K. Y. (1992). Homelessness families: Four patterns of poverty. In M. J. Robertson and M. Greenblatt (eds.), *Homelessness: A National Perspective*. New York: Plenum Press.

Merves, E. S. (1992). Homeless women: Beyond the bag lady myth. In M. J. Robertson and M. Greenblatt (eds.), *Homelessness: A National Perspective*. New York: Plenum Press.

Morse, G. A. and Calsyn, R. J. (1992). Mental health and other human services needs of homeless people. In M. J. Robertson and M. Greenblatt (eds.), *Homelessness: A National Perspective.* New York: Plenum Press.

National Coalition for the Homeless (1997). *Position Paper on HUD McKinney Reauthorization.* (http://nch.ari.net/hr217.html)

National Coalition for the Homeless (1998). *Funding for Homeless Assistance Programs.* (http://nch.ari.net/appchart.html)

Pear, R. (1988). Data are elusive on the homeless. *The New York Times*, March 1, p. B6.

Petry, S. D. and Avent, H. (1992). Stepping Stone: A haven for displaced youths. In M. J. Robertson and M. Greenblatt (eds.), *Homelessness: A National Perspective.* New York: Plenum Press.

Ringheim, K. (1993). Investigating the structural determinants of homelessness: The case of Houston. *Urban Affairs Quarterly 18*(4), 617–640.

Robertson, J. M. (1992). Homeless and runaway youths: A review of the literature. In M. J. Robertson and M. Greenblatt (eds.), *Homelessness: A National Perspective.* New York: Plenum Press.

Robertson, M. J., Ropers, R. H., and Boyer, R. (1985). The homeless in Los Angeles County: An empirical assessment. Los Angeles, UCLA School of Public Health. Reproduced in *The Federal Response to the Homeless Crisis.* Hearings before a Subcommittee of the Committee on Government Operations, House of Representatives, 98th Congress. Washington, D.C., GPO [GPO Item No.: 1016-A, 1016-B (microfiche)]. pp. 984–1108.

Robertson, M. J. and Greenblatt, M. (1992) *Homelessness: A National Perspective.* New York: Plenum Press.

Sabatier, P. (1988). An advocacy coalition framework of policy change and the role of policy-oriented learning therein. *Policy Sciences 21*, 129–168.

Schwartz, R. (1997). *HUD Continuum of Care for Homeless.* (http://www.hud.gov/comcare.html#-policy)

Schutt, R. K. and Garrett, G. (1992). The homeless alcoholic: Past and present. In M. J. Robertson and M. Greenblatt (eds.), *Homelessness: A National Perspective.* New York: Plenum Press.

Schmidt, L. A. (1990). Problem drinkers and the welfare bureaucracy. *Social Service Review.* September, 390–406.

Sclar, E. D. (1990). Homelessness and housing policy: A game of musical chairs. *American Journal of Public Health 80*, 1039–1040.

U.S. Census Bureau (1992). *Fact Sheet for 1990 Decennial Census Counts of Persons in Selected Locations Where Homeless People Are Found.* Washington D.C.

U.S. Department of Housing and Urban Development (1984). *A Report to the Secretary on the Homeless and Emergency Shelters.* Washington D.C.

U.S. Department of Housing and Urban Development (1997). *McKinney Homeless Housing Assistance.* (http://www.hud.gov/sec5.html)

U.S. Department of Housing and Urban Development (1996). *Listing of the Community Development Plans.* (http://www.hud.gov/cpes).

U.S. General Accounting Office (1994). *Homelessness: McKinney Act Programs Provide Assistance but Are Not Designed to Be the Solution.* Washington D.C.

U.S. House of Representatives (1997). *Homeless Housing Programs Consolidation and Flexibility Act.* (ftp://ftp.loc.gov/pub/thomas/c105/h217.ih.txt).

U.S. Senate (1997). *Homelessness Assistance and Management Reform Act.* (http://www.hud.gov/hamrabil.html)

Wasem, R. (1991). Homelessness and the federal response, 1987–1991. *CRS Report for Congress.* Washington D.C.: Library of Congress.

Wilhite, J. (1992). Public policy and the homeless alcoholic: Rethinking our priorities for treatment programs. In M. J. Robertson and M. Greenblatt (eds.), *Homelessness: A National Perspective.* New York: Plenum Press.

14

Smoke on the Water: Fighting Fires at Sea

Pamela Tarquinio Brannon Department of Adjunct and Continuing Education, Warner Southern College, Fort Pierce, Florida

Dave Lee Brannon Federal Defender's Office, Southern District of Florida, West Palm Beach, Florida

I. INTRODUCTION

Vessels, whether military or civilian, cannot execute their mission, be it war or peace, if they are not afloat. All of these ships are essentially metal boxes with compartments of fuel and oil and hot, constantly operating machinery. Ships operate in a rolling and pitching environment that is driven by weather. Modern vessels still must maintain their watertight integrity and still must keep their essentially combustible nature under control. Thus a degree of preparedness and alertness is necessary to keep every vessel operating in the face of the routine dangers of the sea. Both military and civilian vessels must be prepared to deal with ''the routine emergency''—an oxymoronic term.

Preparedness may be defined as ''developing a response plan and training first responders to save lives and reduce disaster damage, including the identification of critical resources'' (Petak 1985:3). This includes having sufficient material to effectively carry out assigned tasks. Alertness can be defined as the quality of being vigilant, and ''readiness for action, defense or protection'' (Joint Chiefs 1988:24). Preparedness and alertness became central facts of life for the U.S. military in the wake of the Japanese attack on Pearl Harbor on December 7, 1941. These additions to the national psyche were internalized for times of peace as well, as shown in an article in the *Honolulu Star-Bulletin* on December 7, 1945, which indicated the attack was ''a day of terrible warning, never to be forgotten, ever at hand, to keep us alert that it must not happen again'' (Prange et al. 1986:550).

Civilian maritime disaster can also result from a lack of preparedness and alertness. The White Star Passenger Liner *Titanic* ignored ice warnings from at least four other ships as it proceeded from Ireland en route New York (Ballard 1987). Despite these warnings, ''a complacency, an almost arrogant casualness, that permeated the bridge'' kept the great ship moving along at full speed (Lord 1987:53). Registering 22.5 knots at 11:40 p.m. on the night of April 14, 1912, *Titanic*'s lookouts observed ice dead ahead. The crew of the new state-of-the-art and supposedly unsinkable vessel were at last forced to take action. The ship attempted to turn to port but brushed an iceberg approximately 100 feet high. The ship began to take on water as its hull plating, the steel sheets making up the exterior of the hull, were damaged by the contact with the ice. Fifteen hundred people died as a result of that complacency (Lord 1976).

This chapter examines three components needed to deal with one of the most serious dilemmas that can befall a ship—fire at sea. These components are training, esprit among the crew, and equipment. Military (Coast Guard and Navy) and civilian (*Sultana* and *All Alaskan*) examples of fires at sea illustrate the three components. Additionally, the Coast Guard examples demonstrate four types of crises that can befall a ship when it has a fire.

II. TRAINING

A. Military Training

The devastating power of nuclear weapons made alertness even more imperative in the nuclear age. The speed of modern weapons has pushed this need for alertness even further. The Japanese striking force took 10 days to reach Pearl Harbor from the Kuriles; today it would take an intercontinental ballistic missile less than 1 hour (Prange 1981).

Modern warfare, with its exponentially increased destructiveness on the one hand and its dramatically increased tempo on the other, is much less forgiving of inexperience and mistake than the pre-World War II military. This was not immediately apparent after the Second World War or even after the Korean conflict, but it became obvious in Vietnam. The Air Force discovered during the Korean conflict it downed 13 Migs for every U.S. plane shot down, but in Vietnam it was was scoring only 2 enemy aircraft for 1 American (Bolger 1986). Both the Air Force and the Navy realized that their fighter pilots were not adequately trained for the reality of aerial combat in the missile age. The Air Force analysis of the situation yielded the conclusion that pilots had their best chance for survival after the completion of their first 10 missions (Bolger 1986). The solution was to provide those 10 missions relatively risk-free with realistic training. Both the Air Force, with its Red Flag training program, and the Navy, with Top Gun, adopted realistic training to fill their needs for aviators.

This infusion of concern for preparedness and alertness for major military activity can only be achieved if individual units are prepared to respond to the severe challenges of their assigned tasks in wartime. The Army adopted the same concept as the Air Force and Navy—that of providing realistic training on a half-million acres of desert training ground at the National Training Center at Fort Irwin, California (Bolger 1986).

The success of Desert Storm reflected an educational component that had been added to training. The educational component was initiated in 1973, when the Army created the Training and Doctrine Command. This Command was tasked with setting uniform training standards for individuals and units, operating the Army's school system, establishing material needs and organizations for the next war, and writing operational doctrine (Clancy 1997). The creation of the School for Advanced Military Studies (SAMS), which is accredited to award master's degrees in military arts and sciences, provided the "Jedi Knights" who planned Desert Storm. (Clancy 1997:111). SAMS provided the theory that guided the practical skills honed at Fort Irwin.

Surface ship training is also conducted realistically with intensive exercises that challenge all elements of the ship's organization. These exercises test the readiness of every part of the ship, from weaponry to navigation to the engineering plant to damage control. The exercises also include realistic battle problems testing the fighting skill of the crew. The Navy's Atlantic Fleet, and those Coast Guard units stationed on the East and Gulf Coasts, journey to Guantanamo Bay, Cuba. Pacific Fleet units and Coast Guard cutters located on the West Coast travel to Pearl Harbor. This intensive training, called

Refresher Training, or REFTRA, is simultaneously dreaded and sought after as a tough test of the ship's and crew's capability.

This level of sophistication is necessary for the military to perform the major task assigned to them—the use of armed force as an instrument of national policy. The armed forces function in a world where machines operated by young persons are often operating at very high performance levels, doing stressful things in normal operations: e.g., a nuclear submarine operating at great depths, an aircraft operating at high speed, or merely a ship moving across the face of the waters. (It is always useful to recall Samuel Johnson's comment that being aboard ship is like being in prison, with the added risk of drowning.)

The importance of military training to fighting fires at sea is illustrated by the examples discussed below: the Coast Guard's *Glacier*, the British Navy's *Sheffield*, and the U.S. Navy's *Stark*.

B. Civilian Training

The United States has a strong maritime tradition, although it is not often spoken of today, and a merchant fleet is integral to that tradition. This American tradition traces back to the whaling fleet, the clipper ships, and the American cargo vessels that date from colonial times. The Coast Guard has statutory authority over vessels under construction, pursuant to Title 46 of the United States Code (U.S.C.), Section 361. The following sections address other issues: the inspection of vessels after their construction, 46 U.S.C. 494; the training and certification of seamen, 46 U.S.C. 2; and the training and certification of officers, 46 U.S.C. 224. The Coast Guard has therefore promulgated regulations requiring realistic training, using simulators and other training aids, under Part 28 of Title 46 of the Code of Federal Regulations (C.F.R.). However, this training is affected by the tension existing in any government effort to mandate businesses to engage in expensive training for their employees. Prior to the *All Alaskan* fire discussed below, such training requirements effectively ended at the officer level. Since that fire, amendments have spread the level of training down to the seamen who are fighting the fire.

Of course, businesses may provide more for their personnel than the minimums required by the government. Mobil Shipping and Transportation Company, Mobil Oil's shipping subsidiary, views the training and motivation of their crews as the most important factor in ship safety and is willing to spend the money for competent people (Southerland 1996).

The importance of civilian training to fighting fires at sea is illustrated by the *All Alaskan* example discussed below. In 46 C.F.R. 28.270, the Coast Guard requires the provision of instruction and drills concerning firefighting at least once a month aboard commercial fishing vessels.

In 46 C.F.R. 28.265, the Coast Guard requires the posting, in conspicuous areas, of emergency instructions for fighting fires. Those instructions contain information such as shutting off the air supply to the fire and maneuvering the vessel to minimize the effects of the wind on the fire.

III. ESPRIT DE CORPS

Esprit de corps may be defined as the ''spirit of a body, a sense of pride, honor, etc., shared by those in the same group or undertaking'' (Guralnick 1984:478). It is a concept that can provide a look at the human dimensions of crisis situations.

Intensive training, particularly when difficult, builds tremendous esprit de corps and gives units not only the expertise but also the cohesion necessary to face the shock of combat or disaster. An illustration of this can be seen in the difficult and realistic training conducted by the Japanese Navy prior to the Second World War. This training was described in a document of the Imperial Japanese Navy translated by the U.S. Naval attaché in Tokyo in 1937:

> Leaving home ports the latter part of January and carrying out intensive training for the greater part of the year in the stormy Pacific or in out-of-the-way gulfs where human habitations are extremely scarce, with hardly a day of rest other than two or three days at anchor for recreation after . . . sometimes more than a month of operating. . . . There are no Saturdays or Sundays, especially when under way, where one drill follows another—literally a period of no rest and no sleep. This is because if we are not under way we cannot carry out actual battle training, and so with a tenacious and tireless spirit we are striving to reach a superhuman degree of skill and perfect fighting efficiency. (Morison 1948:24.)

Training hard to win a badge of proficiency is a constant staple of World War II movies that illustrate the building of a unit.

Katz and Kahn (as cited in Berkely and Rouse 1994) suggested that knowing why a particular task is required and the result of that task can help to raise the effort of the individuals who perform the task. This can lead to improved productivity and efficiency. The results of the Hawthorne experiments led researchers to conclude that individuals need to feel that they are important—to their unit, their army, their country, etc. They need to know that they are participating members of a cohesive work group and not just isolated individuals performing tasks by themselves (Starling 1986).

Esprit de corps develops not only as the result of "good" training but also because of good leadership and its influence on subordinates. Shafritz and Russell (1997) acknowledged that "it has been known since ancient times that unit cohesion is the glue that holds armies together" (p. 200). Troops need to know why they are doing what they are doing. They need to believe that their leaders will fight beside them, and die with them if necessary. Berkely and Rouse (1994) have termed this "interpersonal credibility: when the personnel within the organization believe that an individual understands and cares about what happens to them" (p. 222).

Kirkland and associates (1993) explored this dimension of esprit de corps in their study of commanders' priorities and the psychological readiness of their troops. Esprit de corps is one dimension of psychological readiness; psychological readiness is one characteristic affecting the performance of a military unit. The other characteristics are tactical proficiency, operability of equipment, and adequacy of logistical support.

The authors analyzed and compared the results of two surveys conducted by the U.S. Army: self-described priorities of company commanders and perceptions of the members of the commanders' units. Although cause and effect could not be determined, since the surveys were administered at the same time, an association was demonstrated between commanders' priorities, their emphasis on morale, and the psychological readiness of their units. "The data indicate that commanders who emphasize Morale issues have units with stronger Company Commitment, Vertical and Horizontal Bonding, Confidence in Leaders, General Well Being, Confidence in Self and Weapons, and Work Satisfaction" (p. 588). The authors also found a "strong association between psychological readiness and trust, respect, caring, and empowerment" (p. 590). Commanders who were able to influence their subordinates positively in these areas were more likely to have successful units under their command.

Examples of esprit de corps and leadership skills in crisis situations are illustrated below, in the military examples.

IV. EQUIPMENT

Equipment, of course, must be up to the standards of the disaster. A recurring theme discussed in the examples below is that the equipment operates differently under the stress of a real emergency than it does in drills, and that each new crisis seems to indicate that different or additional equipment is necessary.

For example, the self-contained breathing apparatus (SCBA) is required under 46 C.F.R. 28.205(e) to provide a minimum of 30 minutes of air as well as to be equipped with a face plate and a spare bottle. However, the air supply can be depleted in less time when an individual is under exertion. This is illustrated in the *All Alaskan* example below. In addition to the SCBA, a firefighter's outfit must also contain an attached lifeline, a flashlight, a helmet, boots, gloves, protective clothing, and a fire axe.

With technological development and changes in budgets, equipment concerns are constantly changing. Technical expertise, such as the training discussed above, is also required to properly operate and maintain firefighting and safety equipment.

Equipment carried on board ships varies from ship to ship and service to service. For example, 46 C.F.R. 28.315 requires fire hose on commercial fishing vessels less than 79 feet in length to be at least 5/8 inch in diameter, of good commercial quality, and equipped with a corrosion-resistant nozzle designed to produce either a solid stream or a spray. For those vessels 79 feet or greater, the regulations also require that the hose be lined.

The *Sheffield* incident, the *Sultana* tragedy, and the *All Alaskan* fire, described below, illustrate the necessity of having enough safety equipment in working condition to handle fires at sea.

V. MILITARY EXAMPLES

A. Coast Guard

These examples are drawn from one of the authors' experiences aboard a Coast Guard icebreaker in the mid 1970s, prior to the full post-Vietnam revolution in realistic training.

The U.S. Coast Guard Cutter *Glacier* was 21 years old when she proceeded to the Antarctic for Operation Deep Freeze in 1975. The ship was powered by 10 diesel generators located in three different engine rooms, which provided electricity to two electric motors located in a fourth compartment called Main Control. This system required extensive wiring and, due to the basic design, the age of the vessel, and a hard operating schedule of a 3-month Arctic and a 6-month Antarctic deployment every year, fires were a common event aboard ship. This was a substantial difference from the routine on most Coast Guard vessels where fire is, of course, viewed as the ultimate internal crisis at sea. A number of fires took place during the 6-month deployment, the first approximately 3 hours after sailing. Four other fires, however, offer lessons illustrating four different types of crises.

1. The Unrecognized Crisis

(a) Problem. The first crisis fire took place approximately 1 week after departure from California en route New Zealand. The exhaust gases from the diesel engines were vented through the stack immediately behind the bridge. The stack would become coated with residue, and this residue sometimes caught fire. A stack fire would burn hot and could burn for awhile; this was such a fire.

(b) Response. Every United States government vessel tests all ships alarms and whistles every day at noon, with the test proceeded by an announcement over the public address (p.a.) system that the following was a test. The alarms aboard *Glacier* consisted of the general alarm (''battle stations'' in old World War II movies), the chemical alarm for chemical attacks, and the collision alarm. The alarms aboard *Glacier* had an unfortunate habit of sticking when tested, and the p.a. system sometimes cut in and out. On this particular day, the officers and crew were at lunch as the noon hour approached. The general alarm sounded and all hands continued eating, assuming the regular test schedule. The general alarm continued and catcalls started, yelling at the p.a. speaker (as a stand-in for the bridge team) to turn the alarm off. Everyone assumed that the p.a. system had malfunctioned, causing the crew to miss the announcement that this was a test, and that the alarm had stuck. Everyone assumed the routine and did not consider the unusual, an actual problem. Finally, someone said, ''We just may really have a fire here, let's go!'' and everyone scrambled to their assigned positions.

(c) Lessons Learned. The leadership skill required in this situation was simple: somebody had to make a decision that there was a crisis in order to get everyone moving. The staff skills needed are simple to express but more difficult to internalize: ''Do not assume the situation, find out the reality. Do not fall into routine but realize that disaster can literally strike at any moment.'' This requires management to develop a training program ensuring that personnel are prepared mentally to respond to the unrecognized crisis.

This is called *the unrecognized crisis* because all the indicators of the crisis were present and the parties still did not understand that they were in a crisis. Plausible explanations were offered to maintain a noncrisis explanation of the situation.

2. The Gradually Worsening Crisis

(a) Problem. Approximately 2 months into the voyage, the ship was in Antarctic waters. After completing its first task of opening a resupply channel into the American McMurdo Station, *Glacier* was proceeding past the Ross Ice Shelf heading for oceanographic operations in the Weddell Sea. (The Ross Ice Shelf appears as a surreal object. It is a wall of ice, as high as 150 feet, extending from horizon to horizon for a distance of some 400 miles.) During the evening a report reached the bridge that smoke had been sighted in several compartments and the general alarm was promptly sounded. In their haste to get to their stations, many people reported in shirtsleeves, not taking the time to put on jackets and hats.

(b) Response. As the damage control parties searched for the fire, the crew impatiently waited for the fire to be discovered and extinguished. As the search continued without success, people began to be concerned. It was observed that the closest help was 3 days away. Other personnel commented on the fact that the seawater temperature was 31 degrees. (Due to the presence of salt, seawater freezes at temperatures below 32 degrees). The ice shelf was also observed to be too high to allow people to get atop the shelf from either the ship or the life rafts should the crew have to abandon ship. Life expectancy in the icy waters was not more than 10 minutes. A noticeable rise in tension on the bridge followed as everyone waited for the engineers to locate and solve the problem. Soon it was discovered, as a result of their methodical approach, that the fire was relatively minor but took place in a isolated space which was well ventilated, allowing quantities of smoke to spread to a number of other compartments before it was discovered.

(c) Lessons Learned. The leadership skills required here are those that go to preventing a panic when the situation seems to be getting worse rather than better. Leadership must maintain a calm, confident manner and must keep all personnel occupied with some task. The staff must keep the focus on working the problem and must not take counsel of their fears. From a procedural point of view, personnel must keep working in a methodical manner, avoiding skipping steps that could leave problem areas open.

This is called *the gradually worsening crisis* because the situation continues to worsen as time goes by. The normal conception of a crisis involves a ''bad event'' that is over and then the focus is on recovery. In the gradually worsening crisis, the bad event continues over time.

3. The Assumed Crisis

(a) Problem. Another 2 weeks passed. At 2:30 in the morning a sudden call came to the bridge with a simple statement, ''Main control is ablaze!''

(b) Response. The general alarm was sounded and the ship was galvanized into action. The fact that it was 2:30 a.m. convinced everyone that the alarm was both real and potentially catastrophic. Duty stations were rapidly manned and the reality of the situation was discovered. A minor fire had broken out directly behind the control board in main control; it had been extinguished immediately by the people on the scene. They had ordered their messenger to relay the word to the bridge that there was a fire and the fire was out. In the excitement of the moment, the messenger relayed the word of the fire but did not mention that it had been extinguished.

(c) Lessons Learned. Leadership must make sure that correct information is passed and then must take an active role in calming personnel. The staff must avoid an overreaction. Procedurally, this situation requires communication verification procedures.

This is called *the assumed crisis* because a crisis does not actually exist except in the minds of the personnel. Thus, it is the opposite of the unrecognized crisis.

4. The Blasé Crisis

(a) Problem. A particular problem arises when the organization is used to dealing with crises. By this point in the cruise, 5 months into the 6-month deployment, fires were not exactly unforeseen events. At approximately 9:00 p.m., the officers were assembled in the wardroom to watch the nightly movie, a social event of some importance in those days preceding the video cassette recorder. The messenger entered from the watch, the movie was stopped, and the lights turned on. The messenger told the captain that there was a small fire in the boiler room.

(b) Response. The officers turned their heads from the screen, listened to the messenger, assumed that the watch would deal with the problem, and turned back to the screen. The captain, naturally incensed at this response, yelled, ''Gentlemen, we have a fire! Get to your stations!''

(c) Lessons Learned. Leadership must not allow past success to breed overconfidence, particularly when the problems have been coming thick and fast. Staff has the responsibility to maintain awareness of the possible consequences of disasters and must therefore keep fresh in their approach. Procedurally this situation requires standard procedures to be observed in all cases.

This is called *the blasé crisis* because the officers had fallen into a habit of thinking of any fire as a problem that could be handled easily. Their success had given them an overconfidence that actually could cost precious minutes, making the difference between success and failure.

B. British Navy

In April 1982 the Argentine government decided they would settle their long-standing dispute with Great Britain over the Falkland Islands by seizing the islands by military force. A conflict then ensued that matched ships of the Royal Navy against the Argentine Air Force.

The Royal Navy, faced with budgetary problems, had made the decision to invest heavily in defensive electronics rather than in redundant systems, armor, and damage control. The strategy was to prevent a hit on the ship in the first place, as opposed to surviving the hit (Cordesman and Wagner 1990b). A casualty of the strategy was the *H.M.S. Sheffield*, a type 42 destroyer.

1. Problem

On May 4, 1982, two Super Etendard aircraft of the Argentine Navy flew from the Rio Grande Naval Air Base to attack a target detected by its electronic emissions as a type 42 destroyer of the Royal Navy. Unaffected by any electronic interference, the Super Etendards each launched one Exocet air-to-surface missile at radar targets at a distance of 27 nautical miles and returned to base. One missile struck its target (Scheina 1987).

2. Response

The missile's warhead did not explode, but its rocket fuel did catch fire. Eleven men were killed directly by the missile strike. The hit knocked out all electrical power and the main water supply, leaving *Sheffield* without lights, communications, weapons, or any ability to move other than to drift. The crew fought the fire with buckets on ropes at first. The buckets were dropped overboard and hoisted back filled with seawater, which was then thrown into the fire. Even after other vessels came to the assistance with portable pumps, it was clear that the battle against the fire was lost. Despite the best efforts of the crew, at least eight of whom lost their lives by staying at firefighting and damage control work until their escape routes were blocked, the ship was lost (Middlebrook 1987).

3. Lessons Learned

This case involved a *gradually worsening crisis* as the fire continued to spread in spite of the firefighting work of the crew. Good training, for which the Royal Navy has an international reputation, and tremendous esprit de corps, which literally kept men at their stations until they died, were frustrated by a lack of proper equipment. This situation was based upon a strategic decision to pay less attention to remedial efforts in favor of preventive measures. These preventive measures had no impact on the Argentine attack, and the lack of remedial measures made the loss of *Sheffield* inevitable. Had the warhead exploded, there is every reason to believe that the loss of life would have been greater and the ship would have sunk sooner.

C. U.S. Navy

After the fall of the Shah of Iran, Iraq and Iran engaged in conflict over the strategic Persian Gulf. Because of the oil assets of this region, world attention became focused on this struggle. Neither side was able to win a decisive victory. Each began to put pressure on the other by attacking third-country tankers trading in oil of the other country (Cordesman and Wagner 1990a).

In May 1987, the Iran-Iraq War was 7 years old; the U.S. Navy and other western countries were engaged in protecting the Persian Gulf tanker traffic from both Iranian and Iraqi forces. The prime focus, however, for the U.S. Navy involved attacks by Iranian small craft and mines against tankers carrying out Iraqi oil. U.S. Navy vessels patrolled in the Persian Gulf to provide a defense against Iranian attacks. The Iraqis, meanwhile, were using their aircraft, armed with Exocet missiles, to strike tankers carrying Iranian oil. Some of the tankers were heavily damaged, particularly if the missile strike forced the outbreak of a fire (Cordesman and Wagner 1990a).

1. Problem

The guided missile frigate *U.S.S. Stark* was attacked by an Iraqi aircraft with two French-made Exocet air-to-surface missiles. The *Stark* was outside the Iraqi Exclusion Zone and no challenge or identification was ever made by the Iraqi pilot. He apparently merely fired upon the first radar target he acquired. American forces had tracked the aircraft beginning at 7:55 p.m. throughout its mission. The *Stark* herself tracked the aircraft from at least 8:55 p.m. through the time the missiles struck the vessel at 9:09 p.m. Thirty seven sailors were killed; eleven more were seriously wounded (Cordesman and Wagner 1990a).

2. Response

The firefighting effort was heroic but almost insufficient. Despite *Stark*'s possession of nearly twice its complement of firefighting equipment, emergency breathing apparatus only functioned in a limited fashion. The crew had also only limited training in the use of this equipment. There was no proper clothing and a lack of power-cutting devices. Aluminum ladders melted from the severe heat and fire spread by heat radiation. Although power was not lost, the fire situation brought the ship to all stop (Cordesman and Wagner 1990a).

3. Lessons Learned

This is an example of *the blasé crisis*. Iraqi attacks had become routine and it was assumed that this was another routine attack on a merchant vessel. When the Iraqi pilot made a mistake and attacked the first target that came into view, no one was prepared to react in the very short time available.

Complacency on the part of senior officers aboard the *Stark* and a reduced readiness effort were blamed as the cause of the successful Iraqi attack. The Iraqi attacks on merchant vessels were routine, but this time the attack was misdirected at a U.S. naval vessel. Thus many of the systems designed to detect such attacks were either not on (for example, an audio alarm of incoming missiles was turned off, as the crew found it distracting) or, in the case of radars, not being monitored as the crew turned to other tasks (Cordesman and Wagner 1990a).

Study of the situation generated requirements for more breathing aids, more bulkhead cutting equipment, more night-vision and thermal sensors, more emergency radios, improved firefighting uniforms, and more pumps. The fact, however, that general damage control training was high and that lessons had been learned from the British experience in the Falklands is probably what allowed the ship to survive two Exocet missile strikes, while one had been sufficient for the sinking of the *Sheffield* (Cordesman and Wagner 1990a).

VI. CIVILIAN EXAMPLES

A. The Sultana

An incident that has been called America's greatest maritime disaster is little known today except as a footnote to the Civil War. The sidewheel steamer *Sultana* exploded on April 27, 1865, on the Mississippi River near Memphis, Tennessee. This resulted in a loss of life greater than that of the *Titanic* disaster, which occurred 47 years later (Potter 1992).

1. Problem

The *Sultana* was overcrowded with Union soldiers who had recently been released from Confederate prison camps and were headed home to Tennessee, Virginia, Indiana, Kentucky, Ohio, and Michigan. The number of passengers was over 2400, which was more than six times the legal capacity of 376. These passengers came aboard at Vicksburg and crowded every inch of deck space, including the roof of the cabin. Additional cargo included 70 to 100 mules and horses and 100 hogs, all of which were housed on the main deck.

During the journey, the chief engineer discovered a leak in one of the boilers and insisted that repairs be made when the ship docked at Vicksburg. A local boilermaker was called in, discovered a bulge on the middle boiler, and recommended replacement of some of the boiler plates. He was persuaded ''to limit his repairs to a patch measuring only twenty-six by eleven inches'' (Potter 1992:51). He is on record as observing that all the boilers appeared to have been burned by an insufficient supply of water.

At approximately 2:00 a.m. on the morning of April 27, 1865, three of the four boilers aboard the *Sultana* ''erupted with a volcanic fury that resounded across the countryside'' (Potter 1992: 81).

2. Response

Many passengers were thrown into the air and eventually into the cold waters of the Mississippi. The explosion tore through the decks directly above the boilers; fragments of the boilers, bricks, pipes, and machinery were driven through the upper decks like shrapnel; scalding steam, boiling water, hot ashes, and flaming coals covered the passengers; and the ship's superstructure collapsed from the blast. Estimates are that the entire ship was in flames in about 20 minutes (Potter 1992).

Approximately 1800 individuals perished from the explosion, although the exact number has never been known. In comparison, the number of passengers lost on the *Titanic* was 1522. With regard to lifesaving equipment aboard, the *Sultana* carried 76 cork-filled life preservers, one yawl, and a single metal lifeboat (Potter 1992).

3. Lessons Learned

The captain of the *Sultana* was one of the minority owners of the ship and apparently in some financial need. He was eager to transport the soldiers for the fees that could be received: $5 per enlisted man and $10 per officer. He felt that the *Sultana* should rightly receive its share of liberated prisoners since the ship belonged to a line that had contracted with the government to transport freight and troops. The *Sultana* was also in competition with ships from other lines for the transportation of troops at the end of the Civil War. Additionally, the soldiers were eager to return home by the fastest route possible and were willing to endure the crowded conditions.

The investigations afterward fixed the cause of the accident to the poor condition of the boilers, including an insufficient amount of water, and the failure of the repair work done earlier in the journey. Other factors that might have contributed to the disaster included the light wood used in the construction of the decks, which not only collapsed under the weight of the troops after the explosion, but also fueled the fire; the coating of paint, which consisted of combustible materials such a turpentine and benzine; and the use of an experimental boiler design, which increased the possibility of overheating (Potter 1992).

This is a *blasé* type of crisis. Although aware of the boiler problem and the inadequacy of the repair, the crew of the *Sultana* proceeded as if nothing could happen to them. This blithe assumption that everything would turn out fine because they always had in the past appears to be one of the most dangerous conditions in the *blasé* crisis.

B. The *All Alaskan*

Fish processing vessels begin to process the fish they have caught while the ship is still at sea. Thus, they are a mixture of factory and ship, with the increased perils that can come from a floating workshop.

The *All Alaskan*, a fish processing vessel owned by All Alaskan Seafoods, Inc., was under way off Unimak Island in the Bering Sea, north of the Aleutian Islands, on July 24, 1994, when a fire broke out aboard the ship. The master of the vessel, concerned about fire safety, had instituted a roving fire watch as the ship got under way. The watch consisted of a crew member, with the sole responsibility of looking for fires, who circulated the ship every half hour. The watch continued 24 hours per day while the vessel was under way and not actively processing. These safety precautions were more than the regulations required (NTSB 1995).

1. Problem

The fire watch discovered an unusual smell in hold number 3, which might have been caused by overheating, at about 12:30 a.m. For the next 8 1/2 hours the fire watch detected the smell every half hour. On 10 occasions during this same time frame, engineering crew members also detected the odor. Neither the master nor the chief mate were ever notified about the smell. The ship's electrician was not called to deal with the problem. No efforts were made to isolate the hold. No efforts were made to turn the electrical circuits off and on to determine the source of the odor (NTSB 1995).

The chief mate was having breakfast at 5:30 a.m. after having been relieved by the master, who was standing watch from 6:00 a.m. to 6:00 p.m., when he overheard the assistant engineer discussing a smell and an electric motor. The chief mate did not notify the master, felt the engineers were "always looking for a peculiar smell of some sort," and went to bed, obviously unconcerned about the situation (NTSB 1995:48).

Approximately 15 to 20 minutes after the fire watch on duty from 8:00 a.m. to 12:00 p.m. passed through hold number 3, a refrigeration technician noted smoke around the door to that hold (NTSB 1995).

2. Response

The chief mate was in charge of the fire team. However, an able-bodied seaman and a deckhand immediately went to the scene of the fire in an unplanned effort. When they came to hold number 3, they felt the door to determine if it was hot and did not detect any unusual amount of heat. Each wore a self-contained breathing apparatus and a firefighting coat. The able-bodied seaman carried a fire extinguisher. The two crew members did not discuss any plan either about fighting the fire or fleeing the scene if that became necessary. When they opened the door, smoke and flame came roaring out of the open door upon them and the open door became a chimney, feeding oxygen to the blaze. The fire extinguisher was useless to fight such an inferno (NTSB 1995).

The able-bodied seaman was able to make his way out of the flames and smoke, exhausting his air supply in less than the advertised 30-minute endurance. The deckhand, unfortunately, exhausted his air supply before he was able to get out of the compartment. When his body was discovered, the burn pattern disclosed that he was still wearing his breathing apparatus when he died (NTSB 1995).

The ship burned out of control and eventually was abandoned by the crew. The fire continued to burn for several days prior to burning itself out. The fire died of fuel exhaustion; it was not extinguished by the crew. Vessel and cargo damage ran from $25 to $31 million (NTSB 1995).

3. *Lessons Learned*

The NTSB concluded that the probable cause of the fire was "the failure to isolate heat tape from combustible rigid polyurethane insulation and the lack of heat tape standards for fish processing vessels" (NTSB 1995:v). Additionally, the lack of formal firefighting standards and training contributed to the severity of the fire and the loss of life. The quick assault on the fire prevented a more methodical approach that might have contained the fire.

With regard to heat tape, the NTSB made recommendations to the Coast Guard, to All Alaskan Seafoods, Inc., and to the Commercial Fishing Industry Vessel Safety Advisory Committee that vessels using heat tape should make sure that the tape is physically separated from the polyurethane foam and other combustible materials.

The lack of training of the able-bodied seamen and the deckhand were factors that had great impact on this fire. First, since the crew members were not formally trained, they did not realize that the insulation on the door defeated their efforts to determine the presence of the fire by touching the door. Second, their lack of training may very well have resulted in the death of the deckhand, since they made no use of any lifelines—a procedure included in formal training. The Coast Guard requires only licensed officers on private fishing vessels to receive formal firefighting training. However, after the investigation of this incident, the NTSB recommended that formal training in marine firefighting and emergency equipment use be required for all crew members assigned to fire teams of fishing vessels (NTSB 1995).

Another contributing factor was the lack of procedures with regard to detecting and reporting unidentified odors. After this incident, the NTSB recommended to All Alaskan Seafoods, Inc., that they institute written procedures for fire watch duty, that they provide their firm's team members with formal training, and that they make sure that crew members are familiar with safety procedures and emergency equipment (NTSB 1995).

Contributing to the severity of the fire was the casual treatment by the fire watch as well as the engineers and the chief mate of the preliminary symptom of the fire in the form of the consistent smell of something overheating. The master's institution of fire watch procedures over and above those required by regulations did not deal with this problem.

This is an example of *the unrecognized crisis*. Despite the master's efforts to encourage fire safety and despite the smell of something burning, both strong indicators of danger, the crew of the *All Alaskan* failed to seriously consider the possibility of a fire. All hands involved in the matter sought solutions to the problem of the smell of something overheating other than the possibility that something might be on fire. Their attitude of ''It can't happen here'' led to a fatal fire that almost sank the ship.

VII. CONCLUSIONS

Some common threads run through these situations. First, frequent, realistic training is required. Staff must be trained such that the correct action becomes routine in time of stress. This cannot be resolved by the provision of instructional sheets that personnel have to find at the moment of crisis. Training must be based in reality to enable personnel to diagnose a crisis and apply the appropriate procedures as an automatic response. The clerical staff cannot be expected to remember, for example, what folder contains the bomb-threat response.

Flin and colleagues (1996) have drawn the following conclusion regarding realistic training from their work with installation managers on offshore oil sites:

> All high-reliability industries should seek to provide a training regime whereby experience of decision making in challenging situations can be gained in a nonjeopardy environment and whereby on-site commanders and their support teams can hone skills, such as communication and situation assessment, that underpin efficient emergency management. (p. 275)

Such training can be tedious and time-consuming but, when the real crisis comes, the parties will respond appropriately and catastrophe, if not averted, will be handled the best way possible.

Second, ''crises provide opportunities for leaders to demonstrate fortitude, commitment to employees, and other values and basic assumptions'' (Rainey 1996:160). Leadership has to remain calm, confident of success, and consistently aware of the risks of the situations. Leadership has the most difficult task of never relaxing, never making assumptions, and never being anything less than clear-headed. Staff must be methodical in their approach, always conscious of possibilities of disaster and yet confident in their abilities to deal with the problem. Procedurally this requires one item that is simple in its requirement yet difficult in its execution.

Third, training and leadership for crisis situations must be accompanied by the right kind and the right amount of well-maintained and appropriate equipment. This equipment will always be in the process of being refined and developed. The equipment must be designed to be operated by personnel under stress, thus taking into account such things as increased consumption of air due to heavy breathing, the need for simplicity of operation, and the possible use of excessive force due to adrenalin surges. This mandates constant attention to both the quantity and quality of equipment. No complacency can be brought to this issue.

There are various types of crises that appear in the lives of people and organizations. These crises are different in their particulars and in their potential effect, but they have some elements in their timing and course which are similar. This chapter has presented situations regarding fires at sea, and has classified the crises into four types: unrecognized, gradually worsening, assumed, and blasé. This classification can also be applied to other nonmaritime organizational settings, and is useful for the conceptualization of emergency situations and the type of management and preparation that would be needed for them.

The fundamental lessons of the sea are unchanging. But, human nature being what it is, they must be relearned from time to time. In December 1944 the U.S. Third Fleet was the most powerful surface fleet in the world, having just decisively defeated the Imperial Japanese Navy in October in the Battle of Leyte Gulf. Yet, on December 17 and 18 that fleet encountered a typhoon that sank three destroyers, destroyed 146 aircraft, and significantly damaged at least six other major naval vessels. Eight hundred men were killed by the power of the sea (Morison 1959: 59–81). The subsequent Court of Inquiry in this natural disaster generated a letter from Fleet Admiral Chester Nimitz that summed up preparation for catastrophe masterfully:

> . . . both seniors and juniors must realize that in bad weather, as in most other situations, safety and fatal hazard are not separated by any sharp boundary line, but shade gradually from one into the other. There is no little red light which is going to flash on and inform commanding officers or higher commanders that from then on there is extreme danger from weather, and that measures for ship's safety must now take precedence. . . . The time for taking all measures for a ship's safety is while still able to do so. Nothing is more dangerous than for a seaman to be grudging in taking precautions lest they turn out to have been unnecessary. Safety at sea for a thousand years has depended on exactly the opposite philosophy (Calhoun 1981:222–223).

REFERENCES

Ballard, R. D. (1987). *The Discovery of the Titanic*. Toronto: Madison Press Books.

Berkley, G. and Rouse, J. (1994). *The Craft of Public Administration*. Madison, WI: Brown & Benchmark Publishers.

Bolger, D. P. (1986). *Dragons at War: 2–34 Infantry in the Mojave*. Novato, CA: Presidio Press.

Calhoun, C. R. (1981). *Typhoon: The Other Enemy: The Third Fleet and the Pacific Storm of December 1944*. Annapolis, MD: Naval Institute Press.

Clancy, T. and Franks, F. (1997). *Into the Storm*. New York: G. P. Putnam's Sons.

Code of Federal Regulations, Title 46.

Cordesman, A. H. and Wagner, A. R. (1990a). *The Lessons of Modern War: Vol. II. The Iran-Iraq War*. Boulder, CO: Westview Press.

Cordesman, A. H. and Wagner, A. R. (1990b). *The Lessons of Modern War: Vol. III. The Afghan and Falklands Conflicts*. Boulder, CO: Westview Press.

Flin, R., Stewart, K., and Slaven, G. (1996). Emergency decision making: The offshore oil and gas industry. *Human Factors* 38(2), 262–278.

Guralnick, D. B. (ed.). (1984). *Webster's New World Dictionary of the American Language*, 2nd. college ed. New York: Simon & Schuster.

The Joint Chiefs of Staff (1988). *U.S. Department of Defense Dictionary of Military Terms*. New York: Arco.

Kirkland, F. R., Bartone, P. T., and Marlowe, D. H. (1993). Commanders' priorities and psychological readiness. *Armed Forces & Society*, 19(*4*), 579–598.

Lord, W. (1976). *A Night to Remember*. Toronto: Bantam Books.

Lord, W. (1987). *The Night Lives On*. New York: Jove Books.

Middlebrook, M. (1987) *Task Force: The Falklands War, 1982*, rev. ed. New York: Viking Penguin Books.

Morison, S. E. (1948). *History of United States Naval Operations in World War II: Vol. III. The Rising Sun in the Pacific: 1931–April 1942*. Boston: Little, Brown and Company.

Morison, S. E. (1959). *History of United States Naval Operations in World War II: Vol. XIII. The*

Liberation of the Phillipines: Luzon, Mindanao, the Visayas. 1944–1945. Boston: Little, Brown and Company.

National Transportation Safety Board (1995). *Marine Accident report. Fire on Board. U.S. Fish Processing Vessel All Alaskan near Unimak island, Alaska. Bering Sea. July 24, 1994.*

Petak, W. J. (1985). Emergency management: A challenge for public administration. *Public Administration Review*, 45 (*special issue*), 3–7.

Potter, J. O. (1992). *The Sultana Tragedy*. Gretna, LA: Pelican Publishing Company.

Prange, G. W. (1981). *At Dawn We Slept: The Untold Story of Pearl Harbor*. New York: McGraw-Hill Book Company.

Prange, G. W., Goldstein, D. M., and Dillon, K. V. (1986). *Pearl Harbor: The Verdict of History*. New York: McGraw-Hill Book Company.

Rainey, H. G. (1996). Building an effective organizational culture. In James Perry (ed.), *Handbook of Public Administration*, 2nd ed., 151–166. San Francisco: Jossey-Bass Publishers.

Scheina, R. L. (1987). *Latin America: A Naval History 1810–1987*. Annapolis, MD: Naval Institute Press.

Shafritz, J. M. and Russell, E. W. (1997). *Introducing Public Administration*. New York: Longman.

Southerland, D. (1996). Mobilizing the fleet. *The Washington Post*, June 23, p. H1.

Starling, G. (1986). *Managing the Public Sector*, 3rd. ed. Pacific Grove, CA: Brooks/Cole Publishing Company.

United States Code, Title 46.

15

From *Texas City* to *Exxon Valdez*

What Have We Learned About Managing Marine Disasters?

John R. Harrald Department of Engineering, Institute for Crisis, Disaster, and Risk Management, George Washington University, Washington, D.C.

Hugh W. Stephens College of Social Sciences, University of Houston, Houston, Texas

I. INTRODUCTION

Harbors and navigable waterways are places of high risk for hazardous materials transportation disasters. For one thing, these are locations of large amounts of flammable, toxic, explosive materials. Risk is all the greater because differences in organization, procedures, techniques, equipment, and vocabulary between landside and waterside environments create a perceptual and organizational void at the water's edge. Without a determined effort to bridge these differences, integrated contingency planning necessary for effective response to sudden-onset disasters typical of hazardous materials emergencies is extremely difficult.

Both of these factors, plus complacency about the possibility of a catastrophe, were present in two of the greatest maritime transportation disasters in U.S. history. The first occurred in April 1947 when two ships loaded with ammonium nitrate fertilizer—the same substance used at the Oklahoma City and the World Trade Center bombings—blew up at the Texas City docks. The explosions and their aftereffects killed almost 600 persons, injured 3500 more, and inflicted property damage on the order of $100 million ($700 million in today's values). The second happened in March 1989, when the supertanker *Exxon Valdez* ran aground on Bligh Reef, rupturing several of the ship's tanks and disgorging 240,000 barrels of crude oil into the pristine waters of Prince William Sound, Alaska. In both cases, inept response efforts exacerbated the damage caused by the initial event. Such was the chaos after the explosion of the first ship at Texas City, the *S.S. Grandcamp*, that everyone overlooked the threat of the *S.S. High Flyer*, which also had fertilizer in its cargo. It caught fire and blew up 16 hours after the *Grandcamp*. Although casualties from the second explosion were modest, serious additional damage was inflicted upon industrial facilities and residences in the vicinity of the docks. While no lives were lost when the *Exxon Valdez* went aground, inadequate response allowed the oil slick to spread over much of the sound and caused widespread environmental degradation, $2 billion in cleanup costs, and billions more in damage settlements.

Measured by devastation and the shock and surprise of those at the scene as well as the general public, these were clearly disasters of the first magnitude. Different in many respects, the two nevertheless featured parallel failures in prevention and response. In neither instance did those on the scene appear to have been particularly concerned about operational risks and consequences of failure prior to their onset. Risk assessment and contingency planning for a serious emergency was absent at Texas City and only perfunctory at Valdez. Consequently, when an unusual concatenation of circumstances triggered catastrophe, the sudden crises were greeted with surprise, delay, and confusion, thereby exacerbating their harmful effects.

The question then arises: what was learned about disaster management in the forty-two intervening years between the *Texas City* and *Exxon Valdez* disasters and do recent legislative initiatives embody effective solutions? This assumes some urgency when one understands that in the interim, public- and private-sector organizations have made considerable efforts to develop information and institute safety measures about the production, storage, and transportation of hazardous materials. Four major policy or administrative failures present in most disasters are at issue in these two marine disasters:

Antecedent complacency in a situation of acute exposure to hazards, and consequent failure to monitor risk levels and institute basic mitigation measures
Inadequate contingency planning, particularly toleration of fragmented jurisdiction among major stakeholders
Ad hoc response and gaps and overlaps in agency efforts
Deficient information management among major stakeholders and poor media relations between the stakeholders and the general public

We begin with a brief description of the major features of the two disasters. Three criteria of preparedness and response are at issue. The first, awareness of risk, is designed to assess the relationship between the presence of hazards and recognition of vulnerability among those at the scene prior to the disaster. The second is contingency planning, including assumptions and the action plan in place to marshal organizational, financial, and physical resources for response. Incident response is the final criterion, examining the accuracy, timeliness, and integration of activities when the crises erupted.

A description of events at Texas City establishes the baseline of comparison. After surveying what happened in the *Exxon Valdez* incident, we discuss the common features of both disasters in terms of vulnerability and risk and then of response. Vulnerability and risk address the probability of a disaster actually occurring and its impact. Response encompasses three stages: resource mobilization, integration of agency efforts, and production, the last designating the point in the response when stable patterns of action are achieved. Then, we briefly describe legislative initiatives and regulatory measures about oil spills since *Exxon Valdez*, which bear upon management of major disasters and an evaluation of the results. These demonstrate that many vital shortcomings about risk awareness, contingency planning, and crisis response discerned at Texas City and Valdez are not yet institutionalized in disaster management.

II. TEXAS CITY

A. Background Conditions

Texas City is located on the west side of Galveston Bay, some 10 miles north of the City of Galveston and 40 miles south of Houston. It has a deep-water port in a landlocked harbor and, in 1947, had three quays, two of which handled break-bulk commodities and one petroleum. Land communications were good. The Texas City Terminal Railway Company (Terminal Railway), which owned the docks, had six miles of railway connected to the main trunk lines between Galveston and Houston.

Increasing hazard levels from expanded petrochemical production was the reciprocal of steady economic growth, which began in the 1930s. Helped by government efforts to expand petrochemical production prior to the onset of World War II, Texas City was very much an oil town by 1947, home to four major refineries, two aviation gasoline units, two chemical companies, a boxcar transfer terminal, and a tin smelter (Benham 1987:30). The population had mushroomed from 6000 persons in 1940 to an estimated 16,000 after the war and might have been greater had not a housing shortage obliged many workers to commute from neighboring towns. In addition to petroleum products and bulk cargoes of cotton, grain, and tin ore, in mid-1946 the port began to handle large quantities of ammonium nitrate fertilizer produced at government ordnance plants in the midwest, destined for western Europe.

Production, storage, and transport of petrochemicals always carries the risk of explosion, fire, or toxic contamination. At Texas City, the physical proximity of docks, chemical production, tank farms, and residences created the potential for disaster. Although separate zones existed for industrial, residential, and commercial activities, most of the new facilities were built immediately inland from the waterfront (Stephens 1997:10). The resulting congregation of facilities with large quantities of hazardous materials adjacent to the docks and part of the town's residential area dramatically increased the chance that a serious fire or explosion would initiate a devastating chain reaction. Moreover, some 25 blocks of residences and several tank farms were located within 4000 feet of dock 0, where the *Grandcamp* was moored, and the Monsanto chemical plant was within 1000 feet.

The prevailing social climate also enhanced risk and abetted the absence of preparations for a serious emergency. Direct evidence on this matter is elusive, but postwar Texas City appears to fit Paul Shrivastava's (1991:322) description of a period of "munificence" that often precedes a disaster, marked by a social and political environment emphasizing growth and opportunity at the expense of other concerns. At a time when much of the rest of the country was mired in a recession, it was variously described as "young and thriving" and a "boom town." At issue was the indifference of experts as well as public complacency about hazardous materials risks in general and ammonium nitrate fertilizer in particular. Moreover, no federal agency, including the U.S. Coast Guard, was enforcing safety standards for movement of hazardous substances through U.S. ports, including Texas. This was 40 years before Bhopal, an age of technological innocence, when hazardous materials production and transportation were not nearly as extensive as today and regulatory pressures were minimal (Wenk 1986:17). Moreover, although fires had occurred at refineries and on ships, nothing serious had ever happened before.

B. The Incident

Those who do not feel at risk are unlikely to prepare for potential trouble. Although some preparations existed for the annual hurricane threat, Texas City had no contingency plan for calamitous industrial accidents. Consequently, while shortfalls in response efforts are predictable under such circumstances, it is useless to search for weaknesses in assumptions of contingency planning or gaps and overlaps in organizational competence. Such response capability as did exist was highly fragmented; the municipal government and the Terminal

Railway had no specific understanding about firefighting responsibilities or enforcement of safety rules, such as prohibitions against smoking at the docks. Refinery firefighting teams and the town's volunteer fire department of 29 men and four trucks had effectively fought fires at refineries and even in ships moored at the docks. But nothing was in place that could have quickly and accurately brought extensive resources to bear in a manner required to cope with sudden and unpredictable events caused by large-scale explosions and fires.

While it is important to identify precursor factors—such as high risk, complacency about hazardous materials, and an absence of contingency planning—the manner in which the Texas City disaster was triggered is important as well. Ammonium nitrate will explode only when subjected to extreme heat and pressure. This is precisely what happened on the morning of April, 16, 1947, when a fire started among 880 tons of fertilizer contained in 100-pound sacks loaded in number 4 hold of the *S.S. Grandcamp*. When hand-held extinguishers failed to snuff out the smoldering fire, in an effort to put out the fire by depriving it of oxygen, the ship's master ordered the hold sealed and steam injected into it. Within the confines of the hold, the rising temperature and pressure initiated thermal decomposition of the fertilizer and produced large amounts of combustible gas. At 8:30 a.m., a half hour after the fire was discovered, the hatch covers blew off and reddish smoke billowed out of the ship.

Soon thereafter, the volunteer fire department arrived and began directing streams of water onto the deck. Attracted by the unusual color of the smoke, a crowd of about 300 onlookers gathered at the head of the slip. The ship's turbine was undergoing repair at the time and no tugs or fireboats were available to assist in moving the ship away from the docks or suppressing the fire. At 9:12 a.m., approximately an hour after the fire began, the *Grandcamp* disintegrated in a prodigious blast heard 150 miles away. A huge, black, mushroom-shaped cloud billowed 2000 feet into the sky. Fragments of the ship, some weighing several tons, scythed through stevedores and spectators while numerous pieces were hurled out to a distance of a mile. Pipes and tanks of flammable product were ripped open by falling shrapnel, starting secondary fires and explosions. Almost all structures within a half-mile of the docks were turned into rubble. At the Monsanto plant across the slip from the *Grandcamp*, 145 of 450 shift workers were killed outright. Flaming balls of sisal and cotton, also part of the ship's cargo, showered down upon refineries and homes. The *High Flyer*, a freighter at an adjoining slip with fertilizer in its cargo, was torn from its moorings by the force of the blast and drifted over to lodge against another ship, the *Wilson B. Keene*.

C. The Response

Hazardous materials transportation disasters originating from fire and explosion commonly feature low predictability, rapid onset, and severest damage during the initial stages. Successful coping action therefore demands rapid, focused response. This is a function of contingency planning. The confused, ad hoc nature of response for the first 24 hours starkly exhibits the awful costs of surprise and absence of preparedness at Texas City.

Everyone within 20 miles immediately realized something awful had happened when the *Grandcamp* exploded. In Galveston, shock waves shattered glass and knocked people to the ground, and buildings swayed in Baytown, 15 miles distant. The huge column of thick, black smoke and refinery and oil tank fires served as a beacon for those from neighboring communities who immediately converged on Texas City. Despite a spontaneous and generous outpouring of assistance, including excellent law enforcement activities and medical treatment, and despite heroic actions by individuals and groups, consistent response efforts were not initiated for 24 hours.

The lack of either a disaster plan or prearranged mutual aid was painfully evident. No concerted effort toward fire suppression was achieved for at least 48 hours following the initial blast. The wonderful examples of personal initiative and heroism that marked the early hours of rescue and salvage work lacked the necessary direction in many cases (Tryon 1947:2).

Particularly vexatious was the organizational void between land and marine activities. This void hampered integrated search and rescue amid the smoke and fires at the docks and, by hindering damage assessment and identification of secondary hazards, led to the explosion of the *High Flyer* 16 hours after the *Grandcamp*. Recall that the force of the latter's explosion tore the *High Flyer* from her moorings in an adjoining slip, and it had lodged against another ship. Its cargo included not only ammonium nitrate fertilizer but also a larger consignment of sulfur. Smoke from oil fires and fumes from the sulfur prompted the crew to leave the ship at about 10 a.m. For the next 9 hours, no one gave the ship much thought, perhaps because it was partially obscured by thick clouds of smoke. Whatever concern those on land had about the *High Flyer's* condition was not relayed to Coast Guard boats in the turning basin. No one noticed this threat until fires broke out in its holds at about 4 p.m., but 3 more hours passed before tugs from Galveston arrived and attempted to pull this ship from the slip. This failed, and at 1:10 a.m. on April 17, the *High Flyer* blew up at the docks in an explosion witnesses thought was even more powerful than that of the *Grandcamp*. Casualties were light because search-and-rescue workers were evacuated from the waterfront, but refineries and tank farms were showered with glowing shrapnel, collapsing more storage tanks and setting off synergistic reaction of fires.

Not until about noon on the April 18 did response begin to take on a semblance of order, when municipal officials were able to assume direction of recovery operations, supported by the Salvation Army, Red Cross, and detachments from the U.S. Fourth Army and nearby military bases. Progress was made in extinguishing fires at tank farms and, a day later, at the docks. Fittingly, a pall of black smoke hovered over Texas City for 5 days, until the last of the fires were extinguished and the immediate emergency was over.

III. THE EXXON VALDEZ

A. The Incident

The *Exxon Valdez* ran aground on Bligh Reef just after midnight on March 24, 1989. The ship departed from the outbound traffic lanes as it left the port of Valdez to avoid ice from the Columbia Glacier. The Coast Guard Vessel Traffic System watchstander granted the deviation; after all, the *Exxon Valdez* was the only major vessel under way in Prince William Sound at the time. The Vessel Traffic System radar, which was the major means of providing a warning about collision, did not track the ship as it began deviating from accepted track lines. Having excellent resolution but relatively short range, this radar provided good coverage of the Valdez Narrows, perceived as the highest-risk area, but not of Prince William Sound. The human component of safety was diminished as well. As the ship began its unusual maneuver, the watchstander at the Vessel Traffic System began the process of changing the watch. The watch consisted of only one person instead of the usual two, a result of cost cutting by the Coast Guard. Moreover, no pilot was on the bridge of the *Exxon Valdez* as the ship traversed the inbound lane—the Coast Guard and the state of Alaska allowed the state pilot to disembark prior to Bligh Reef instead of the entrance to the sound at Hinchinbrook provided that a ship's officer qualified as a Prince William Sound pilot was on board. Captain Hazelwood met this requirement but was in his cabin catching up on paperwork. In the event, the third mate on the bridge failed to alter course to the south in spite of repeated reports by the lookout of a red light (on Bligh Reef) off the starboard bow, and the *Exxon Valdez* was still accelerating to sea speed when it went aground on the reef.

Despite the fact that 25% of all crude oil supplied to the United States flowed through the Trans Alaska Pipeline and was transshipped through the Port of Valdez and Prince William Sound, the possibility of a catastrophic spill was not taken seriously. When notified of the grounding, the manager of the Alyeska Pipeline Service Terminal, who had overall responsibility for oil spill emergencies, alerted his response team and then returned to bed. Complacency extended beyond this one person. As a cost reduction measure and with the permission of the state of Alaska, full-time emergency response had been downgraded several years before to a collateral duty of the team. The worst-case scenario envisioned in Alyeska's contingency plan was a 200,000 barrel spill released from a tanker over a 10-hour period under ideal weather conditions. In contrast, the *Exxon Valdez* actually lost 240,000 barrels in 3 hours, well beyond the imagination of anyone who shared responsibility for designing or approving this plan. The state had approved the plan despite its obvious lack of resources to execute even a minimal response. The parent oil companies represented in the Alyeska consortium were equally guilty of complacency. For example, an *Exxon USA* (1977:17) article reads: ''while exercising every precaution to prevent an oil spill [in Prince William Sound] Alyeska had detailed plans to clean up a spill should one occur.'' Plans did not included resources; there was only one barge to store recovered oil in Valdez and it was not in service when the ship went aground. As protection against harsh weather, booms and skimmers were stored ashore.

B. The Response

Insufficient resources doomed response efforts from the outset. But, just as the absence of a planned organizational response condemned Texas City to 24 hours of chaos, an inability to form a functioning response was the other major contribution to failure at Valdez. The Coast Guard, the state of Alaska, Alyeska Pipeline, and Exxon all had contingency plans prescribing an organizational structure that was to be formed and procedures to be followed in event of a serious emergency. The plans of the state and Alyeska assumed that the latter's response force would coordinate response efforts to any spill in Prince William Sound. Coast Guard plans assumed that the Coast Guard's predesignated on scene coordinator (OSC), the commanding officer of the U.S. Coast Guard Valdez Marine Safety Office, would assume this role and would supervise Alyeska's spill response operations. This was congruent with the National Contingency Plan (NCP) for all oil spills within U.S. jurisdiction. The NCP creates a complex support system for the federal OSC: environmental, scientific, and technical support is to be provided by the National Oceanographic and Atmospheric Administration (NOAA); Coast Guard technical expertise is available from the National Strike Force. Additional federal and state support can be arranged through the interagency Regional Response Team (RRT) or the National Response Team.

None of the major organizational elements embodied in federal or Alyeska plans were executed. Unanticipated events quickly obviated any hope that the plan would prove viable in any important respect (NRT Report 1989; Alaska Oil Spill Commission 1990; Harrald et al. 1990). Exxon's crisis management team, headed by Frank Iarossi, the president of Exxon Shipping, was assembled and dispatched to the scene within hours of the spill. Despite the fact that none of the existing contingency plans anticipated that the affected oil company, not Alyeska, would assume the overall management function, the Exxon team assumed responsibility for oil spill response and salvage of the *Exxon Valdez* when it arrived the day after the disaster began. Relations were further occluded when the Coast Guard raised the level of its presence by dispatching Captain Glenn Haines, chief of the Seventeenth Coast Guard District's Marine Safety Division and the chairman of the Regional Response Team for the Alaska Region, to relieve Commander Steve McCall, the predesignated OSC. Further escalation of rank followed when Captain Haines was replaced as OSC by Rear Admiral Ed Nelson, the Seventeenth District commander. After several weeks of negative media evaluation, President Bush directed Admiral Paul Yost, commandant of the Coast Guard, to go to Valdez and take charge of the federal response effort. He eventually turned over responsibility to Vice Admiral Clyde Robbins, commander of the USCG, Pacific Area.

Other elements acted in similar fashion. Coast Guard plans for Valdez anticipated that in the event of a major spill, state and federal activities would be coordinated through the RRT, Alaska being represented by its Department of Environmental Conservation (DEC). Like the haphazard nature of group contributions at Texas City, Governor Cowper and DEC Commissioner Dennis Kelso came to the scene, while the state of Alaska created its own independent on-scene organization. The Alaska Division of Emergency Services set up a command post in Valdez on March 25, but this was never used by the state's DEC and was eventually abandoned. As other state agencies asserted jurisdiction, Governor Cowper created a "mini-cabinet" in Juneau to coordinate activities. The RRT actually met in Valdez within 24 hours of the spill but never functioned as an effective support mechanism for the federal OSC.

The Federal OSC organization underwent additional change when Vice Admiral Robbins assumed command upon Admiral Yost's departure. Exxon and state organizations were also evolving and determining their relationships with each other. It is important to note that none of the organizational structures and interrelationships that evolved following the spill resembled what had been contemplated in preexisting contingency plans. The net result of organizational turmoil was a delay of 3 weeks before a stable, functional decision-making organization evolved. But by then, the opportunity for effective response to the oil spill had passed. The complexity of the tripartite arrangement between federal, state, and Exxon officials obviated timely and accurate decision making. Frank Iarossi has since publicly criticized the concept of "crisis management by committee." The fact that an internal Coast Guard report (Sherikon 1989) identifies over 16 significant formal external relationships and 16 critical formal relationships just within the Coast Guard itself testifies to the confusing organizational web that emerged at Valdez.

IV. VULNERABILITY AND RISK

Emergency planners are often justifiably criticized for preparing for the last major disaster. Unfortunately, when low-probability, high-consequence events are at issue, history is not often a valid guide to hazards and the vulnerabilities they create. Low-probability events that have not occurred must be envisioned by means of creative vulnerability assessment. For instance, we now understand our vulnerability to significant oil spills from tankers. Nonetheless, we find it difficult to focus on other equally and perhaps more probable technological disasters, such as release of toxic materials from maritime incidents and tank ruptures at storage and transshipment facilities located in harbors.

Consider for a moment the nature of risk. Risk has two components: the probability of occurrence and the impact of the event. Managing risk for low-probability, high-consequence events is extremely complex. It includes both preventive measures focusing on reduction of the likelihood of occurrence and mitigation measures focusing on minimizing the impact of the event if it actually occurs. Inconsistencies in public perceptions of risks are an additional problem. That is, if an event has not occurred, people tend to focus on the low probability and dismiss the risk and its impact, thereby ignoring the expense of efforts to avoid or mitigate a disaster. After a low-probability event occurs, what Wenk (1986) terms ''the politics of risk'' sets in: the public switches its focus to the impact of the disaster and acts as if it were inevitable, professing to understand low-probability causal chains that were previously ignored or overlooked.

Both the Texas City disaster and the *Exxon Valdez* oil spill demonstrate that maritime risk should be managed in a broad systems context capable of including both landside and waterside activities. At Texas City, locating oil storage facilities and refineries near the waterfront added unnecessarily to the potential impact of an accident involving a powerful explosive like ammonium nitrate fertilizer, which originated in the maritime environment. At Valdez, storage tanks receiving oil from the pipeline were capable of holdings only a few days' throughput. This amounted to inadequate buffering, because the Coast Guard Captain of the Port (COTP) could not close the port to tanker traffic under adverse maritime conditions without effectively shutting down the pipeline and disrupting the production and flow of north slope oil. Since approximately 25% of the U.S. supply of crude was flowing through Valdez, a shutdown could have had a profound and severe impact upon the national economy as well. In other words, port closure was not something a midlevel Coast Guard officer could easily do; in fact, when the COTP did close the port because of adverse weather, he quickly received a call from the secretary of energy. Needless to say, that particular COTP never did so again. In sum, the close proximity of the docks to industrial operations and residences at Texas City and tightly coupled oil-transfer arrangements at Valdez created what Perrow (1984) terms ''the catastrophic potential of a high risk system.''

Unlike Texas City, where a sense of risk and preparations for a serious emergency were virtually absent, the initial system established in Valdez did embody a significant vulnerability assessment. It included a mandatory Vessel Traffic System, separate lanes for incoming and outgoing vessels, pilotage requirements, and extensive pollution response regulations. But, as time passed without disaster, the focus of concern shifted from the possibly serious consequences of a spill to the lower probability that one would actually occur and the high cost of maintaining preventive systems. Deterioration set in when the Coast Guard, the state of Alaska, and private sector entities began ignoring the possibility of a serious spill in Prince William Sound and focused their attention on the port of Valdez and the Valdez narrows.

Texas City was vulnerable because no one realized the explosive potential of ammonium nitrate fertilizer and basic preparedness and response functions were absent. In the *Exxon Valdez* case, system vulnerability was enhanced because major stockholders failed to perform as expected. Alyeska fell short in preparing to combat a major oil spill in Prince William Sound and the state of Alaska acquiesced to this critical breach of conditions for the operation of the pipeline/tanker link between the North Slope and west coast refineries. There was no plan to specify an operational response organization or set up unambiguous functional relationships between the Coast Guard, the state of Alaska, and the oil companies. For its part, the Coast Guard's oil spill response capabilities were severely diminished by budget cuts and redirection of assets to the war on drugs during the 1980s, while research on pollution response as well as funds for development and acquisition of material disappeared.

In sum, Valdez and Texas City are instances where hazardous products were moved through areas with a high potential for severe emergencies and where complacency, abetted by prosperity, increased risks. The fact that complacency at Texas City derived from ignorance about the explosive potential of ammonium nitrate fertilizer and at Valdez emanated from the potential impact of an accident to its low probability made little practical difference; in both situations, the prevailing sense of vulnerability was diminished and preparedness undermined in turn.

V. RESPONSE

Like the disaster at Texas City, the *Exxon Valdez* spill was an unanticipated, sudden-onset technological disaster. In such instances, successful coping actions require immediate, focused response efforts. In neither case was there any warning prior to the incident triggering the disaster. But requisite organizational structures and resources were not in place, causing widespread confusion initially and only a remedial, reactive response thereafter. At Texas City, hundreds of people were allowed to congregate at the end of the pier, only a few hundred feet from the burning *Grandcamp*. In the confusion that followed its explosion, the threat of fertilizer in the cargo of the *High Flyer* was overlooked until even remedial action was impossible. After the *Exxon Valdez* ran aground, confusion reigned; organizational response was slow and poorly focused as large numbers of responders deployed along the sensitive shoreline of Prince William Sound. Ad hoc remedial measures, such as the hot washing of beaches, ultimately may have done more harm than good.

These two instances of maritime crises—and others besides—demonstrate that major ports must have the ability to mount a rapid, integrated, multiorganization response supervised by a predesignated individual. For an oil spill, the local Coast Guard captain of the port (COTP) fulfills this role as on-scene coordinator under authority of the National Contingency Plan. During the initial period following the crisis, OSC is faced with three critical requirements: (1) mobilizing resources, (2) forming the response team, and (3) directing initial response actions. If successful, the response quickly passes through three other stages: mobilization and initial response, integration, and production. The success of the mobilization effort depends upon the adequacy of the plan and the ability of the unit to immediately execute its tasks. Effective notification and mobilization in a plan requires that response scenarios be based on realistic vulnerability assessments and allocation of appropriate resources for each scenario of the disaster. The organizational system uses feedback from the external environment (initial assessment) to formulate resource requirements. These resources must be acquired and mobilized within the time constraints of the external event—that is, the triggering incident. Feedback mechanisms must already exist if the response organization is to perform the initial evaluation effectively. The fact that activities must bridge differences in equipment, organization, and orientation between landside and waterside environments in all three phases necessarily complicates matters.

Integration, the second stage of response in a crisis, encompasses the period required for responding forces to arrive on the scene and integrate particular activities. Bruce Tuckman (1965) points out that all groups involved in response pass through several stages: orientation, internal problem solving, growth, and productivity and control—or, in his terms, "forming," "storming," "norming," and "performing." Given the sudden eruptions of crises at Texas City and Valdez, the elapsed time for the entire integration stage was too long to be effective, consuming 2 days in the former instance and a week in the latter. A similar delay in organizational integration was a major reason for the tardy federal response to Hurricane Andrew (Carley and Harrald 1993). Although the elements of preplanning, training, and exercising critical stakeholders were lacking at Texas City, even though nominally present at Valdez, these were not sufficiently viable to support a rapid, integrated response by the several stakeholder organizations.

Mere specification of desired organizational outcomes will not ensure integrated action during a crisis. Several conditions may prevent or limit integration, all of which were present in the two case studies: task complexity, organizational incompatibility, and political incompatibility. Let us briefly explain each of these.

Task complexity inhibits coordination during the available time when sufficient resources or capabilities are not yet available. Given the importance of *some* response, this may lead to the formation of ad hoc organizations which engage in experimental problem solving. (Dynes and Quarantelli 1968). Task complexity is rife when firefighting, search-and-rescue, salvage and pollution responses encompass both land and maritime environments. Differences in skills, organizational orientations, and legal jurisdictions are potential impediments. A fundamental drawback to integrated response in the United States is that expertise for these tasks resides in a variety of formal organizations. For instance, in the maritime environment, the Coast Guard has responsibility for rescue and pollution response, but salvage is left to the private sector. Maritime firefighting is a shared local, state, and federal responsibility. The Texas City disaster stands as a prime example of both impediments and criticality of integrated firefighting that spans the landside-waterside divide. Salvage was the major issue after the *Exxon Valdez* went aground; this was better understood by Exxon Shipping and the Coast Guard than by state and private environmental organizations. During the *Mega Borg* oil spill in the Gulf of Mexico off Galveston, the lack of adequate firefighting and salvage resources as well as the location and control of these resources became public issues.

The second major impediment to integrated response is organizational incompatibility. This may assume one or more of several dimensions based on differences in culture, geography, or functions and technology. All are likely to be present in emergencies at ports, navigable waterways, and estuaries. The ability of military units to communicate well with each other and with uniformed state and local police but not with other civil groups or private organizations during Hurricane Andrew illustrates the influence of organizational cultural norms. This is not a new problem. The fact that it is overcome only with difficulty is demonstrated by the inhibiting presence of organizational incompatibilities at Texas City in 1947 and again in Valdez in 1989.

A third issue affecting integrated response is political incompatibility. The point here is that responding organizations may not operate according to the same processes or decision-making criteria. In an extreme case, decision authority may be withheld from participants by the parent organization. A more typical example would be conflict that could arise between organizations oriented toward centralized, autocratic decision making that are suddenly obliged to cooperate with other stakeholders commonly operating in a decentralized mode. This extends to the difficulties that spill response groups, port safety, and security, are likely to encounter under the pressure of an emergency. At Texas City, this type of incompatibility obviated meaningful cooperation among a variety of organizations with a stake in port safety, including the Coast Guard, Army Engineers, dock operators, ship captains, shipping agents, and stevedores. Decision making for the organization created to respond to the spill created by the sinking of the *Tenyo Maru* at the entrance to the straits of Juan de Fuca explicitly included the Makah Indian tribe because its lands were affected; not surprisingly, the tribe's decision criteria and process were significantly different from those used by federal and state response teams (U.S. Coast Guard 1991).

The third and final stage of response is production. In the case of pollution, this is reached when response organizations stabilize and attain the capability to operate routinely in formulating and adjusting tactical plans on a short-term basis. The response phase is not actually terminated at this point, but the system, task environment, and information flows are stabilized. Successful outcomes are possible but not assured. In order to achieve success, the dimensions of success and measures of effectiveness must be defined and broadly accepted by participants and observers. This implies that the manner in which success is defined is critical to any assessment of preparedness and response. Its definition during *Exxon Valdez* was, in effect, abdicated to the media, meaning that success became a moving threat and responders were unable to counter the resulting perception of failure. For weeks following both crises, neither of these efforts achieved a routine, consequently missing opportunities for effective initial actions that might have limited damage.

VI. LEGISLATIVE INITIATIVES

The Texas City disaster, together with concerns about sabotage during the Korean War, led to the creation of the Coast Guard Port Safety program by President Truman in 1950. This assigned the Coast Guard captain of the port significant powers over the movement of vessels in the port under his jurisdiction. These responsibilities were extended by the Ports and Waterways Safety Act of 1972. None of this, however, enhanced federal maritime firefighting or salvage capability. It also failed to resolve a major shortcoming inherent in the Texas City disaster—response efforts impaired by jurisdictional problems between different levels of government when emergencies encompass both landside and waterside facilities.

Legislative action and organizational change stemming from the Exxon Valdez incident was of similar character. The Oil Pollution Act of 1990 (OPA 90), the formation of the Marine Spill Response Corporation (MSRC), and legislation by coastal states were designed to effect major changes in oil spill response in the United States. Response organizations are now able to mobilize more and better equipment and provide more trained personnel at the site. The MSRC, a private sector initiative funded by major oil transporters, will invest approximately $1 billion in oil spill response equipment stockpiled at various points and deployed under the direction of one of five regional centers. The Coast Guard has augmented its response capability by creating the National Response Unit and stockpiling its own equipment at various sites. The creation of an independent national oil spill response organization, the National Response Corporation, to compete with the MSRC was announced in November, 1991.

Under the aegis of OPA 90, local area and regional contingency plans set higher and more comprehensive planning requirements for transporters—those who store oil and for governmental entities as well. This act requires that local area or port teams be created to coordinate federal, state, and industry plans executed locally. The Coast Guard and the Environmental Protection Agency have revised the National Contingency Plan to reflect OPA 90 requirements. The former agency has drafted regulations specifying the required content of industry and local area contingency plans. One by one, coastal states are drafting their own oil spill legislation that will create their own unique spill response organizations.

These initiatives mean that responding organizations have access to an unprecedented stock of resources and support from a complex array of plans and organizations for ensuing spills. The question is, however, whether responsible agencies have given sufficient consideration to organizational matters, which are complex but critical in mobilizing and integrating resources at a spill scene with sufficient rapidity. In addition to neglecting jurisdictional and functional differences between land and marine environments, these do not deal forthrightly with inconsistencies between the National Contingency Plan and other federal crisis management plans and neglect lessons derived from theoretical research about organizational design for crisis decision making.

VII. CONCLUSION

Texas City and *Exxon Valdez* are two disasters separated by a considerable period of time and by differences in the nature of the event. The preparation and response of organizations involved have four common characteristics:

The first is *complacency* in the face of acute exposure to hazards. The combination of petrochemical operations in close proximity to docks handling ammonium nitrate fertilizer created a veritable powder keg in Texas City, yet plans and resources required for disaster response did not exist. With respect to the *Exxon Valdez* incident, over 25% of the total crude oil supplied to the United States made its transit through Prince William Sound. Millions of private and public dollars were spent on oil storage and transshipment facilities in Valdez, to build the oil tankers, and to establish the Coast Guard Vessel Traffic system. Plans were written and drills held, but these were based on the mistaken assumption that a massive oil spill would never happen. When the oil spill did occur, Alyeska's response was as inadequate as the efforts of Texas City's volunteer fire department.

The second characteristics was the adverse impact of *fragmented jurisdiction* on the response efforts. As discussed earlier, the fundamental dichotomy at Texas City was a failure to attain a modicum of integration between landside and waterside functions and responsibility necessary to coordinate response efforts. During the *Exxon Valdez* affair, it became painfully evident that the National Contingency Plan could not resolve roles and responsibilities among federal, state, and private sector groups. A unified response effort was never organized; the response that evolved was conducted by coordinating committees throughout.

The third characteristic of preparation and response was *poor information processing and management*. In neither disaster did the responders accurately assess the situation during the phase of maximum damage. Information transfer between organizations was slow, informal, and distorted. As a result, different portions of the respective response efforts were operating with different mental models of the problem. Information transmitted to the public by responders also came in a slow and fragmented manner. In both disasters, the media obtained their own information and formed their own view of the event, which was transmitted to outsiders converging on the scene; as a result, it had a significant impact upon response efforts.

The fourth and final characteristic of both events was the *ad hoc nature of the response*. This was probably inevitable, given the preexisting conditions of complacency and fragmented responsibility. These ensured that responders would not be prepared, would not have adequate plans for the situation they confronted, and would not be able to communicate with each other. Contingency plans for an oil spill did exist at Valdez, but they quickly proved unrealistic and were discarded. At least 24 hours passed after the explosion of the *Grandcamp* before an effort to coordinate response even began at Texas City. However ingenious, spontaneous organizations, strategies, and tactics failed to achieve the degree of coordinated activity required for effective action.

It would be nice to believe that OPA 90 and revisions in the National Contingency Plan have ushered in a new era in maritime disaster response. The results to date are mixed. Two major oil spills have occurred since the *Exxon Valdez*, suggesting that, under certain conditions, successful coordinated response in the maritime environment is attainable. The *American Trade* spill occurred prior to OPA 90, and the *Morris J. Berman* spill came 5 years after the act was passed.

The U.S. flag tanker *American Trader* grounded on one of her anchors, spilling approximately 9500 gallons of Alaska crude oil into the waters off Huntington Beach, California, on February 7, 1990. Unlike the *Exxon Valdez* response, federal (Coast Guard), state, and corporate (British Petroleum) response efforts involving over 1300 persons were closely coordinated and organizationally grounded within the Incident Command System (Rolan and Cameron 1991; Card and Meehan 1991). OPA 90, it was hoped, would encourage the evolution of coordinated response on this scale.

The grounding of the tank barge *Maurice J. Berman* 200 yards off Punta Escambron, Puerto Rico, several years later yielded different results. Although the spill response was successful and the Unified Command System prescribed by OPA 90 was established, organizational deficiencies severely hampered the effort. The federal on-scene coordinator observed that "the lack of coordinated planning and dialogue among various sectors of the response community before the incident continues to hamper the collective ability of responders to come together quickly and effectively in an emergency situation" (Ross 1995).

Perhaps the most significant conclusion is that there was little difference in the outcome of an event where there was no preparation (Texas City) and where preparation was based on false premises (Valdez). Particularly in technological disasters where warnings are brief, onset is rapid, and most damage occurs in the early stages, successful coping will turn upon realistic and careful risk and vulnerability analysis as well as upon the presence of organizational viability.

REFERENCES

Alaska Oil Spill Commission (1990). *SPILL: The Wreck of the* Exxon Valdez *and Implications for Safe Marine Transportation*.

Benham, Priscila M. (1987). Texas City: port of industrial opportunity. Ph.D. dissertation. University of Houston, Houston, TX.

Card, James C. and Meehan, John A. (1991). Response to the *American Trader* oil spill. *Proceedings, 1991 International Oil Spill Conference*, 305–311. Washington, D.C.: American Petroleum Institute.

Carley, Kathleen M. (1990). The organizational structures most responsive to Crises. Working paper, Oakland, CA: National Research Council Workshop on Organizational Issues in US Nuclear Policy.

Dynes, Russell and Quarantelli, E. L. (1976). *Organizing for Response: The Unresolved Problem.* Report number 17. Newark, DE: Disaster Research Center, University of Delaware.

Exxon (1997). Protecting Prince William Sound: Impressive protective measures safeguard an impressive body of water which tankers must traverse with cargoes of Alaskan oil. *Exxon USA* 16.

Harrald, John R., Marcus, Henry, and Wallace, William (1990). The *Exxon Valdez*: An assessment of crisis prevention and management systems. *Interfaces* 20, 14–30.

Perrow, Charles (1984). *Normal Accidents: Living with High-Risk Technologies*. New York: Harper Torchbooks.

Rolan, Robert G, and Cameron, Keith H. (1991). Adaptation of the Incident Command System to oil spill response during the *American Trader* spill, *Proceedings, 1991 International Oil Spill Conference*, 267–272. Washington, D.C.: American Petroleum Institute.

Ross, Robert G. (1995). Spill response management and the *Morris G. Berman* spill: The FOSC's perspective. 687–693. *1995 International Oil Spill Conference*. Washington, D.C.: American Petroleum Institute.

Sherikon, Inc. (1989). *Tank Ship Exxon Valdez: Oil Spill Management Analysis Debrief.* Washington, D.C.

Shrivastava, Paul, Danny Miller, and Miglani, Angil (1991). The evolution of crises: Crisis precursors. *International Journal of Mass Emergencies and Disasters*. 9, 321–337.

Stephens, Hugh W. (1997). *The Texas City Disaster, 1947.* Austin, TX: University of Texas Press.

Tryon, George (1947). "The Texas City disaster." *National Fire News* 359(2–3), 6.

Tuckman, Bruce (1965). Developmental sequence in small groups. *Psychological Bulletin* 63, 384–392.

U.S. Coast Guard (1991). *On-Scene Coordinator's Reports*: Tenyo Maru *Oil Spill*. Washington, D.C.

U.S. National Response Team (1989). *The Exxon Valdez Oil Spill: A Report to the President*. Washington, D.C.

Wenk, E. (1986). *Tradeoffs: Imperatives of Choice in a High-Tech World*. Baltimore, MD: Johns Hopkins University Press.

16

Environmental Public Relations and Crisis Management

Two Paradigmatic Cases—Bhopal and Exxon

Tim Ziaukas Department of Communication Arts, University of Pittsburgh at Bradford, Bradford, Pennsylvania

I. INTRODUCTION

The 1980s witnessed the early development of a subgenre of public relations—crisis management—spawned in large part by the 1979 nuclear accident at Three Mile Island and the communication challenges that occurred nearly simultaneously. Hyde points out (1993: 108) that "TMI was the seminal event for the development of a vast body of crisis communications literature and practice. It was also the single event that glaringly demonstrated the lack of crisis planning by industry." This emerging subgenre of public relations was, in turn, refined and reinforced by a series of crises that occurred during the 1980s and early 1990s, ranging from product tampering to environmental and natural disasters and set against a backdrop of burgeoning media outlets and exponentially expanding access by an increasingly sophisticated public. These crises include the tragedy of cyanide-laced Tylenol that struck Johnson & Johnson in 1982 and again in 1986; Pepsi-Cola's syringe-in-the-cans episode in 1993, the Ashland oil spill near Pittsburgh; United Way of America's fund-raising problems following the disclosure that its president used the organization's funds for personal expenses; the incidents of racial discrimination at Denny's restaurant chain; and many others. These events and the various reactions to them resulted in the refinement of the principles of crisis management, which has been one of the characteristics of the evolution of public relations throughout the 1980s and 1990s. Two important examples of environmental crisis communications, however, have emerged from this developmental period as near-allegorical illustrations of crisis management theory. The gas leak at Union Carbide's plant in Bhopal, India, in 1984 and the *Exxon Valdez* oil spill in March 1989 have become paradigmatic case studies. The Bhopal tragedy remains the worst industrial accident in human history (Cassels 1993); the *Exxon Valdez* oil spill has the distinction of being the most economically expensive environmental accident of all time (Small 1991). This chapter examines these cases, which occurred during a nascent phase in the development of crisis management.

II. WHAT IS A CRISIS AND WHAT IS CRISIS MANAGEMENT?

Hearle (1993:397) defines a crisis as "a situation that, left unaddressed, will jeopardize the organization's ability to do business," while Mitroff and colleagues (1996:7) call it "an event that can destroy . . . an entire organization." Caywood and Stocker (1993:411) define a crisis as "an immediately unexpected event or action that threatens the lives of stakeholders and the ability of the organization to survive." Crisis management, according to Kreps (1986: 233) is "the use of public relations to minimize harm to the organization in emergency situations that could cause the organization irreparable damage." Fearn-Banks (1996:2) adds that crisis management "is a process of strategic planning for a crisis or negative turning point, a process that removes some of the risk and uncertainty from the negative occurrence and thereby allows the organization to be in greater control of its own destiny."

A survey by the public relations firm of Porter/Novelli (Wilcox et al. 1998), however, underscores the overriding element in all public relations activities in general and in crisis management in particular: telling the truth. The overriding element is to establish and maintain credibility throughout the crisis and into the postcrisis phase. In other words, all who participate in crisis management must tell the truth as precisely, as quickly, and as completely as possible. Without the truth, there is no true communication, and the crisis will generally develop into a much graver situation. In the Porter/Novelli survey, 95% of the respondents said they were more offended by a company's lying about a crisis than by the situation that triggered the crisis initially.

The basic principles of crisis management as they have evolved over the past two decades may be summed up in the following key elements, some of which overlap and, in the chronology of any crisis, may happen simultaneously.

1. *Preparation and Anticipation*. It is essential to plan for crises before they happen. Practitioners should require a written crisis plan (frequently updated) that identifies the crisis management team. As Mitroff et al. point out, many crisis teams are made of up representatives from these areas: legal, finance, operations, security, public affairs or public relations, health and safety, and human relations. In all cases, an official spokesperson should be designated, from whom all official internal and external information should come. In addition, it is essential to anticipate the needs of important constituents. Ultimately, the crisis team must develop a plan that will enable it to act ethically while adapting to evolving situations involving many unknowns.
2. *Admission*. As Seitel (1998:459) declares: "Tell it all and tell it fast"—perhaps the number-one rule in crisis communications. Accepting responsibility in public at the earliest possible time is essential for maintaining or restoring credibility. Never shift the blame or engage in scapegoating. While legal consequence must be considered, fear of litigation is not an ethically valid excuse for avoiding responsibility and blame.
3. *Action*. Not deciding or not acting is, in fact, a decision and an action. At the beginning of any negative event, a "fire curtain" is generally drawn across the client in crisis. (The metaphor comes from the theater, where a heavy curtain comes down in the event of a fire to separate the audience from the stage.) If the curtain is not drawn back through effective communications, the team may "hunker down" and develop a siege mentality. This paralysis is often perceived as arrogance. A window of opportunity exists in the very early stages of the

crisis ''during which the company's response is absolutely crucial to the way [it will be] perceived'' (Yagoda 1990:49). Further, as Mitroff et al. contend: ''[t]he key to whether an organization will be perceived as a hero, victim or villain is its ability to respond quickly with genuine care and concern'' (1996: 16). Now, however, particularly in light of the burgeoning ubiquity of networked computers, the size of the window is being reducing to minutes. Swift action requires effective planning.

4. *Location*. Particularly at the time of crisis, the president or CEO embodies the corporation. Despite the fact that it might make practical sense to keep him or her at headquarters, the president at this time rises to a mythic level, and his or her actions must represent the company. The CEO generally should be on site to see, to feel, and to report to significant publics, especially the media. As Yagoda (1990:49) points out: ''The most important corollary states that each of these responses [to significant publics] should be embodied in the person of the company's chairman.''
5. *Cooperation*. ''Stonewalling,'' a generally naive form of information control, is characterized by a lack of cooperation. The implied hope of stonewalling seems to be that by ignoring the problem, the crisis will disappear. This is generally ill advised. ''Coverage will proceed, regardless of whether it is aided, hindered, or ignored by the people with public relations responsibilities'' (Seib and Fitzpatrick 1995:109–110). Seitel confirms (1998:459) that ''As a general rule, when information gets out quickly, rumors are stopped and nerves are calmed.'' As Wilcox et al. suggest, the monitoring of all media coverage to determine what messages are being delivered and the manner in which the crisis is being positioned is essential.
6. *Communication*. The ''public'' in *public relations* is plural. It is essential to communicate often and regularly with significant publics, especially the oft-forgotten internal public. Internal publics, especially employees who are trying to maintain normalcy while the crisis rages, have the most believable version of events to offer external publics.
7. *Prediction*. At least some members of the communications team should be thinking about and working on what is to happen when the crisis is over. Practitioners should be building and maintaining relationships with publics for the postcrisis period and beyond.

The communications tactics successfully and unsuccessfully employed during Union Carbide's handling of the tragedy of Bhopal and Exxon's handling of the disaster at Valdez have contributed significantly to the development of these principles. This contribution is evidenced not only by the considerable literature each event has produced but also by the fact that each event often dramatically illustrated how effective the employment of these elements or principles can be—or how ignoring them can be disastrous—in the unfolding of a major catastrophe.

III. THE TRAGEDY AT BHOPAL

The name *Bhopal* has entered the vernacular as a synecdoche for environmental disaster. The explosion and subsequent leak of toxic gas is, according to Cassels (1993:ix), ''the worst single-incident industrial catastrophe in history.''

At the time of the gas leak, Union Carbide, an American multinational chemical corporation with nearly $9 billion in annual sales, had about 700 operations in 38 countries and employed 100,000 people (Kurzman: 4–5). The company produced petrochemicals and carbon products; its line of consumer products included Glad trash bags, Eveready batteries, Prestone antifreeze, and others.

The tragedy at its Bhopal plant and its ensuing communications challenges underscored not only the ethical concerns of reacting to and attempting to rectify an event that resulted in a great loss of human life but also illustrated the considerable complications of handling communications between two different cultures. Overall, the Bhopal catastrophe is, as Shrivastava contents (1992:ix), ''an event of such vast social and technological scope and deep human significance [that it] defies explanation based on traditional concepts and theories.''

A. The Background and the Event

In retrospect, disaster—both industrial and communications—seemed inevitable. The Bhopal plant was owned and operated by Union Carbide of India Ltd. (UCIL), a subsidiary of the Union Carbide Corporation (UCC). UCIL was established in the 1920s with a flashlight battery plant in Calcutta (Cassels:13–14). Following the establishment of India as in independent state in 1947, the Indian government pursued a policy of as much Indian ownership and employment in multinational subsidiaries as possible. UCC, for example, reduced its share of UCIL to 50.9% during the four decades between separation from the British Crown and the Bhopal disaster (Baker 1993:47). So while India's Ministry of Industry had granted the licenses for the operation of industrial plants, the safety standards were to be reinforced by the state governments, which, in Bhopal's case, was Madnya Pradesh, ''the Middle Province.'' The Indian oversight of the Bhopal plant was clearly insufficient. *The New York Times* reported after the disaster that the office charged with overseeing the Union Carbide plant at Bhopal had ''only two inspectors, both mechanical engineers with little knowledge of chemical hazards'' (Reinhold 1985:A1).

The pesticide that the Bhopal plant produced was to have helped in India's ''green revolution''—that is, its attempt to produce enough food to feed its huge population. Bhopal, a city of 700,000 people in central India 360 miles south of New Delhi, was chosen for the plant since the city was located in one of India's poorest regions, one with an urgent need to modernize. Many of Bhopal's residents earned a per capita income of less than the equalivent of $100 a year (Kurzman 1987:21).

On the night of December 2 and in the morning of December 3, 1984, a series of human, mechanical, design, and technical errors, flaws, failures, and deficiencies caused a highly toxic substance, methyl isocyanate (MIC), used in the production of pesticide, to be released into the air of Bhopal. The scenario of how water, some of which should have been used to wash out pipes, was added to a tank containing the unstable MIC, causing it to explode, has yet to be resolved (see Shrivastava and Cassels for chronologies of the event). Whether the water was accidentally flushed into the MIC tank or deliberately added by a disgruntled employee is in question, although UCC's claim of sabotage seems questionable in light of its inability to muster much evidence (see especially Shrivastava, 1992 :124–126). What is not in dispute is that the explosion sent 45 tons of hot gas, foam, and liquid through the plant's stack and out into the city of Bhopal. The effects of the poisonous explosion were immediate and devastating.

''Remarkably,'' Shrivastava contends, ''no one knows how many people actually died in the Bhopal disaster'' (1992:54). Sen and Egelhoff (1991:77) point out: ''An analysis of circumstantial evidence, based on shrouds sold and cremation wood used, estimate the number of deaths at 10,000,'' yet estimates from India's government put the number of deaths at 1754, India's media at 2500, American media at 2500, and relief organizations at 3000 to 10,000; other accounts range from 6000 to 10,000. Unofficial estimates (Kurzman) suggest that about a half-million people were exposed to the gas and dust generated by the leak; 300,000 people were psychically affected by the gas, 60,000 of them seriously. Cassels points out that as victims have gradually succumbed to the injuries caused by the disaster in subsequent years, the toll stood at 3500 by 1987 and 4000 by 1992.

B. Crisis Communications and Union Carbide

1. Preparation

Fortune (Kirkland, 1985:52) reported that ''Carbide lacked a pre-existing corporate plan for coping with a catastrophe of this magnitude.'' Sen and Egelhoff maintain (1991:80) that ''no crisis management plans were in place, and that Carbide did not have information on the various consequences of a major MIC leak.'' However, the degree of control that the American company had over the Indian-operated plant is in question. For example, Baker claims that, in light of the Indian government's desire to have the plant employ as many people as possible, modernizations that could have saved lives were not made. Workers at Bhopal relied on ''reading'' the degrees to which their eyes watered to determine possible gas leaks! This violated UCC policy, to be sure. In any case, Warren M. Anderson, chairman of UCC, would eventually admit that the Bhopal plant operated at a level of safety standards that would not have been permitted in the United States (Cassels). Despite UCIL's obvious inability to enact a sufficient crisis plan to deal with the actual disaster, UCC's checkered handling of the communications crisis fared somewhat better. This is true despite the fact of the understandable difficulty in evaluating crises as horrific as Bhopal in terms of effective tactics in either the court of law or the court of public opinion.

2. Admission

Anderson held the first press conference on the Bhopal tragedy on the afternoon of December 3, hours after the story broke, at UCC's headquarters in Danbury, Connecticut. Anderson accepted moral responsibility for the tragedy (Baker), but it is unclear exactly what that meant; he was, however, less willing to embrace the legal (and fiduciary) responsibility. According to Sen and Egelhoff (1991:76), UCC ''tried to shift the blame to the Indian subsidiary, claiming mismanagement, thereby fueling the opinion that the U.S.-based multinational did not even care about its own subsidiary's reputation, since it was in a developing company.'' Given the complicated relationship between the parent company and its subsidiary, shifting the blame here seems to have been an effective strategy, if not an especially ethical one. UCC sowed the seeds for winning the media relations battle in the developed countries, especially the United States, while distancing itself from the potentially fatal fiduciary responsibilities to the Bhopal victims. Underlying all of Anderson's decisions, it may be presumed, was his statement immediately following the disaster and reported in *Chemical Week*: ''Shareholders will be protected'' (''Bhopal: the endless aftershocks,'' 1984:33).

3. Action and Location

Under Anderson, nevertheless, UCC appeared to move swiftly to contain the disaster, get assistance to those in medical need, and communicate its problems and plans to a world that was horrified by the tragedy and demanding information. Among the important actions taken by UCC was halting production of MIC at a plant in Institute, West Virginia (which would not be resumed until May 1985); converting the guest house at the Bhopal plant into an orphanage; announcing that the Bhopal plant would not reopen without the consent of the appropriate Indian officials; and offering an immediate $20 million in relief for the victims. This money was never used because UCC required health data in return, which would be used in court proceedings (see Sen and Egelhoff 1991:75).

UCC's public relations staff decided early that, ''Anderson should make the dramatic gesture of going to India, together with the technical team that would be sent'' (Kurzman 1987:95). Anderson's trip to India, whether a show of concern or a publicity stunt, was given added drama when he was arrested shortly after he arrived. He was released after 6 hours, following intercession by the Indian government. Anderson's showing in India was not lost on his U.S. audience, however, since UCC management must have been aware that it was playing to two different publics, one in the developed world and another in India. In the United States, the *Wall Street Journal* reported that

> Mr. Anderson's trip was the cornerstone of Union Carbide's early response to the disaster in Bhopal. . . . And though his visit didn't turn out as expected, it has already earned generally high marks as the kind of swift, decisive action that experience shows is necessary to manage such corporate crises successfully (Winslow 1984:29).

4. Cooperation

From the beginning of the tragedy, Union Carbide proved to be generally open, frank, and accessible to the media, a major key to their overall successful strategy. The major point of access was in Danbury, Connecticut, with other ''special events'' designed to illuminate UCC's operations to the media. By mid-December, for example, the company conducted a press tour of the temporarily shutdown MIC-producing plant in Institute, West Virginia, to explain the process and the product of the plant. The company received praise from the national media for its open forthrightness (Baker 1993).

5. Communications

Within 2 days of the disaster, UCC's chief operating officer appeared on closed-circuit television ''to assure employees that the company was doing everything possible to address the needs of the victims'' (Winslow 1984:29). A videotape of the speech was then sent to all 500 UCC locations around the world. In addition, Anderson himself communicated directly to his internal and base public: the employees. He produced another videotape that was sent to all UCC plants around the world (except Bhopal), updating employee on the efforts and actions of UCC's top management. He visited many plants as well, making pleas for understanding: ''We have a lot to prove and the world is watching,'' he'd say. ''What I have seen so far gives me enormous confidence that Carbiders will meet the test'' (Kurzman 1987:172).

Beginning on Wednesday, December 5, all flags at U.S. UCC locations were flown at half-mast, and this continued until December 12. At noon (EST) December 5, all employees were asked to observe a moment of silence for the victims of Bhopal. These internal communications strategies not only offered UCC's employees a way in which to show their emotion and concern but also identified them as an important public during the company's moment of tragedy.

6. Prediction

UCC appears to have made a decision to maintain its base in America and abandon its commitment and, some could say, responsibilities, in India. Sen and Egelhoff (1991:77) conclude that ''Carbide appears to have . . . focused . . . on maintaining its image with financial investors and the developed world.'' Kurzman (1987:181) bluntly states, ''In the final analysis, UCIL was expendable.''

In 1989, the Supreme Court of India ordered a final settlement of $470 million ($425 million from UCC and $45 million from UCIL)—''many times larger than any previous damage award in the history of India'' (Baker 1993:46).

IV. THE DISASTER OF THE *EXXON VALDEZ*

The disaster resulting from the *Exxon Valdez* running aground in Alaska's Prince William Sound generated more comprehensible emotions in the face of despoiled beauty, environmental disaster, and the enormous loss of plant and animal life. Even with a number of previous disasters, including Bhopal, to serve as models, Exxon officials proved to be historically inept at handling the communications aspect of this environmental disaster.

A. The Background and the Event

Shortly after vast amounts of oil were discovered in Alaska in the 1960s, the passage of the Trans Alaska Pipeline Authority Act of 1973 cleared the way for the oil companies to build a pipeline, remove the oil, and ship it to market (Smith 1992). The oil companies were represented by Alyeska, a consortium of seven companies including Exxon, which, at the time of the spill, was one of five largest American companies, with sales of $80 billion.

Alyeska made Valdez its home port, the site where oil from the pipeline would be loaded into tankers and shipped. Valdez was the gateway to the interior of Alaska, and the village was long known as the ''little Switzerland of Alaska,'' both for its beauty and for the string of mountains that circled it. By the time of the spill, 70 to 75 tankers were making their way to Valdez each month, transporting 13% of the national total tanker traffic (Davidson 1990) through Prince William Sound, one of the most fertile and delicate ecosystems in the world. Following the accident, the *New York Times* described the ecosystem of the sound as ''one of the richest marine environments in North America, with magnificent fjords, tree-lined coasts, rock pinnacles jutting out of the water and beaches teeming with sea lions, seals, whales and sea birds'' (Mauer 1989:22).

It was the consortium Alyeska, not the any individual oil company, however, that was charged with developing and implementing a contingency plan for responding to the oil spills that would inevitably occur. A pollution specialist testified during the 1971 Department of Interior hearings that Alyeska would develop and have the ability to implement a plan to effectively handle spills, making ''operations in [the] Port of Valdez and Prince William Sound the safest in the world'' (Davidson 1990:81).

By March 23, 1989, some 12 years after oil began to flowing through the pipeline, 8548 tankers had embarked from the terminal (Smith 1992:77). The *Exxon Valdez*, filled to capacity, was the 8549th. The captain of the tanker, 42-year-old Joseph Hazelwood, had worked for Exxon Shipping for 19 years and had successfully completed the 5-day Long Beach–Valdez run more than 100 times (Fearn-Banks). The ship was 3 years old.

Shortly before midnight on Thursday, March 23, 1989, Hazelwood radioed into the Coast Guard that he was moving the 987-foot tanker from the outbound shipping lane into the inbound one to avoid ice. He then put Third Mate Gregory Cousins in charge, with orders to return to the outbound lane when the ship approached Busby Island. Hazelwood left the bridge and returned to his cabin. Cousins did not make the turn in time and shortly after midnight the tanker ran aground on Bligh Reef and began to spill what would eventually be 11 million gallons of crude oil into Prince William Sound (see Davidson 1990; Small 1991; and Smith 1992 for chronologies of the event). Cousins was not licensed to pilot the tanker out of the sound; his action was a violation of federal law and Exxon policy.

The devastation was enormous: 1100 miles of shoreline contaminated; over 36,000 birds, nearly 1000 otters (Small); and damage to other marine life and plants as well. The National Wildlife Federation claimed that "the long-term environmental consequences of the Prince William Sound oil spill will far exceed those of Chernobyl or Bhopal" (Smith 1992:78).

B. Communications Crisis and Exxon

1. *Preparation*

Although Alyeska was charged with handling a crisis of this nature, from the beginning it was Exxon, whose people and equipment caused the accident, and, very significantly, whose name was on the tanker, that felt compelled to fill the leadership—and communications—void, a move that, however ineptly done, has gone largely unappreciated. (One wonders how differently the scenario might have played out if the ship had been called the *Alyeska Valdez*.) Lukaszewski reports (1992:202) that "the most common observations are that Exxon apparently was not ready to deal with a spill of this magnitude and that Exxon was reluctant to talk about what it was doing and how it was going to go about resolving the problem." Exxon CEO Lawrence G. Rawl actually declared himself to be "technologically obsolete" (Fearn-Banks 1996:146), so unprepared were he and his company to deal with the intense reaction of the media, the environmentalists, and the other interested publics.

2. *Admission*

Lukaszewski points out (1992:202) that perceptions developed that Exxon was slow to react to the disaster, both "to managing the spill itself as well as communicating about the spill publicly." To exacerbate the problem, after it was revealed that Hazelwood had not only undergone treatment for alcoholism but had been drinking the day of the accident, one of the more public and demonstrable actions that Exxon took was to summarily fire him on March 31. This was perceived by some as "scapegoating" by Exxon, because the company had not clearly accepted responsibility itself and was attempting to shift the blame to others. However, as *Time* magazine (Behar 1989:43), in a July 24, 1989, cover story on the event, pointed out: "Nearly four months after the spill, there is no proof that Hazelwood was drunk when his ship ran aground. In fact, his crewmates say that he was not . . . . A more plausible theory is that he was drinking in the hours after the accident occurred."

When Rawl finally spoke publicly, after a week's delay—an eternity on the crisis communications clock, he pointed a finger again and shifted blame to the others, telling *Fortune* magazine: ''It was the state and the Coast Guard that really wouldn't give us the go-ahead. . . . The basic problem we ran into was that we had environmentalists advising the Alaskan Department of Environmental Conservation that the dispersant could be toxic . . . '' (''In ten years'' 1989:33). Exxon had, as it turned out, accepted responsibility for the spill. On the front page of the Sunday *New York Times* of March 26, 1989, five paragraphs into the story, one reads: ''Frank Iarossi, president of the Exxon Shipping Company, said Exxon accepted full financial responsibility for the damage'' (Mauer). Exxon's acceptance was part of a story headlined ''Alaska Aide Assails Oil Industry for 'Inadequate' Response to Spill.'' The oil company's responses clearly required action from someone in a higher position than Iarossi to be heard above the fray.

3. Action

Paradoxically, Exxon, in fact, seems to have acted reasonably quickly in a number of areas yet seemed unable to communicate the nature or effectiveness of those actions. Exxon did act quickly, dispatching Frank Iarossi, president of Exxon Shipping, from Houston to Valdez. Iarossi's Herculean efforts are richly detailed in a number of the chronologies (especially Davidson). But Iarossi was paralyzed by Exxon's dense corporate structure; the disappearance of Alyeska, which seemed to abdicate its responsibility; and the complicated regulations and permission required for the various forms of cleanup efforts. Small concludes:

> Ironically, the Exxon cleanup effort by and large was probably the most that one could expect. Ironically, the expenditures by this giant corporation was probably *more* than one would expect. And yet, the black eye in public was as great and as lasting as probably any other in American corporate history. (1991:12)

4. Location and Cooperation

Among Exxon's more infamous mistakes were those made in location and cooperation: both in the on-site presence of senior management and in the location of the media relations center, both of which affected its cooperation with the media and both were disastrous for the oil giant.

Iarossi was in Valdez working through the tangle of requests and permissions to attempt to arrive at a possible method to deal with the spill—dispersants were environmentally dangerous and required special permissions, equipment for skimming was not forthcoming, burning posed other risks—and then, 3 days after the spill, the weather turned bad and Exxon's chances of containing the spill got worse. Iarossi had also been holding regular press conferences in an attempt to keep the media informed. While Iarossi served as the closest thing to official spokesperson for Exxon, CEO Rawl, meanwhile, remained out of sight, undoubtedly busily concerned with the disaster, but his low profile led many to believe that he, and by extension, the corporation he ran, were not concerned with the spill and its devastating effects. Rawl finally made his first public comments on March 30, a week after the spill; he went to Alaska April 14, some 3 weeks after the accident, but by then public opinion had hardened. The *Wall Street Journal* noted that ''Mr. Rawl's lack of visibility is just one striking note in a decidedly mixed crisis-management effort'' (Sullivan and Bennett 1989:B1).

Those who made the decision that Rawl not go to Alaska, however, may have been correct in some measure, despite violating a crisis communications principle. Rawl was known for not liking publicity and the media, and, when he finally did surface, he showed little skill in handling the situation, the finger-pointing mentioned in *Fortune* being only the first instance. Other examples of Rawl's media relations disasters abound. He snapped at Kathleen Sullivan, a reporter from *CBS Morning News*, who asked a question about an Exxon report: Rawl carped that he was too busy (and it seemed too important) to know the details of the cleanup plan; again in *Fortune* magazine, in what seemed another attempt to shift the blame, he said ''in World War II we lost 16 times more oil off the East Coast of the U.S. in the early months of 1942 when our tankers were torpedoed, and there was no permanent damage to the shoreline'' (''In ten years . . .'' 1989:52).

In addition, beyond Rawl's inept handling of media relations, Exxon seemed to defy the media to get their version of the story with another blunder. The other decision that sealed Exxon's media relations fate was designating Valdez as the media center for all official Exxon responses. While reporters would, of course, remain in the remote Alaskan town, one with limited electronic access, Exxon should have held its briefings in New York or its headquarters city, Houston, to make it as easy as possible for the media to get its side of the story. Even a writer for *Oil & Gas Journal*, an industrial publication generally not as critical as the mainstream media, complained: ''Exxon did not update its media relations people elsewhere in the world . . . it told reporters it was Valdez or nothing'' (Small 1991:20).

The *Wall Street Journal* captured the ludicrous state of the giant oil company's unpreparedness and lack of cooperation: ''Exxon's usual public-relations office for its U.S. operations—one man and an answering machine in Houston—was swamped with calls . . . '' (Sullivan and Bennett 1989:B1).

5. Communication

Two pieces of communication, one an ad in the form of an ''open letter'' designed to articulate Exxon's concern and response to the American public from its chairman, and the other a memo intended for an internal audience, proved particularly disastrous for Exxon's crisis communications effort.

The full-page advertisement/''open letter'' was purchased for publication on April 3, 1989, in more than 100 media outlets. The ad copy read in full:

> AN OPEN LETTER TO THE PUBLIC
>
> On March 24, in the early morning hours, a disastrous accident happened in the waters of Prince William Sound, Alaska. By now you all know that our tanker, the *Exxon Valdez*, hit a submerged reef and lost 240,000 barrels of oil into the waters of the Sound.
>
> We believe that Exxon has moved swiftly and competently to minimize the effects this oil will have on the environment, fish and other wildlife. Further, I hope that you know we have already committed several hundred people to work on the cleanup. We also will meet our obligations to all those who have suffered damage from the spill.
>
> Finally, and most importantly, I want to tell you how sorry I am that this accident took place. We at Exxon are especially sympathetic to the residents of Valdez and the people of the State of Alaska. We cannot, of course, undo what has been done. But I can assure you that since March 24, the accident has been receiving our full attention and will continue to do so.
>
> (signature)
> L. G. Rawl
> Chairman
>
> (Exxon logo)

The ad was undoubtedly written by a committee, and the syntax is designed to distance the audience and alleviate any guilt on the part of the oil company. Passive voice tends to remove all involvement (and responsibility), in the ''mistakes-were-made'' school of guilt diffusion: ''a disastrous accident happened'' in the first sentence and at the end that same accident ''has-been-receiving'' constructions do not place any Exxon people—much less Rawl, the person from whom the language was presumably coming—anywhere near the passively constructed event. The letter also suggests too ''internal-looking'': the ''We believe that Exxon has moved swiftly . . .'' and ''We at Exxon are especially sympathetic . . . '' elements suggest self-absorption. Do the people for whom the ad is intended really care what Exxon thought of itself or its actions? Should Rawl not have cared more about what the public thought rather than telling them what Exxon thinks? Overall, Rawl's attempt to ''minimize'' the spill is apparent (he should have avoided that word in any context for this occasion). Further, his diction is too tidy for the realities of the event. The letter says that the oil was ''lost,'' like a key, implying that it would be easily ''found,'' picked up, and fixed. Finally, the apology, as the *O'Dwyer's PR Services Report* (Lukaszewski 1992:205) suggests in its ''edited'' version of the letter: at 10 days after the accident, the letter itself came too late, and at the beginning of the last paragraph of the letter, the apology came too late as well.

Then, in another public relations disaster, an internal memo leaked to the press gave the appearance that Exxon was at best insincere about its commitment to the cleanup, that it had one public stand at odds with its internal, actual plan. Exxon's Valdez general manager, Otto Harrison, issued a memo dated July 19, 1989, to company managers, writing that Exxon's ''only commitment for the spring of 1990 is to survey the shorelines'' (Davidson 1990:210), that Exxon would determine the nature of its demobilization, and that it would also determine when it was done. He suggested that what other, non-Exxon people said or did was superfluous: ''These are not negotiable points,'' Harrison wrote to his (he imagined) internal audience, ''In discussion on these matters, you should stress the safety and operational factors. We are willing do discuss those factors. We are not willing to discuss the decision.'' Again, Exxon's commitment to cleaning up the spill was thrown in doubt. Later Harrison said, ''In PR terms, that's the dumbest thing ever did . . . . We're going to put it right, and we're not abandoning Alaska'' (Small 1991:14). Clearly, if anyone was working on the postcrisis aspect of the *Exxon Valdez* oil spill, it was not apparent to many.

In many ways Exxon paid dearly for both the spill and the company's inability to communicate its actions. It plummeted from 8th to 110th on *Fortune* magazine's list of America's most admired companies. As of April 1990, Exxon had spent $2 billion in cleanup costs and another $200 million in claims (Small 1991:10). In 1995 a federal judge refused to overturn a $5 billion verdict in punitive damages brought by 14,000 plaintiffs (''Exxon verdict . . . '' 1995). The title of William J. Small's classic essay on the handling of the spill, published in the *Public Relations Review*, puts the incident in a nutshell: ''Exxon Valdez: How to Spend Billions and Still Get a Black Eye.''

V. CONCLUSIONS

The disasters at Bhopal and Valdez each cost a great deal in both the court of law and the court of public opinion, yet, it should be pointed out, despite the immensity of each disaster, that both companies are still in working condition. Paradoxically, Exxon seems to have fared worse than Union Carbide in the crisis communications aspects of the disasters, particularly in the American media, despite the enormous loss of life at Bhopal. This paradox remains a point of inquiry. The horrors of Bhopal were, literally, half a world away from the United States and the staggering human toll was so numbing that some may have dismissed the incident out of hand. Additionally, the tragedy in India would enter history as "Bhopal" (not "Union Carbide's Bhopal"), unlike the *Exxon Valdez*, an incident and a ship, now along with Noah's Ark, the *Santa Maria* and the *Titanic*, among the most famous in history and a constant reminder of who did what where. UCC's Anderson undoubtedly responded more competently than the largely absent and often petulant chairman of Exxon, Rawl. Yet was this enough to have the incident at Valdez pull ahead of Bhopal as the most infamous environmental disaster of the century? According to Lukaszewski,

> The magnitude of *Valdez* managed to eclipse this century's other giant, nonwar, nonnaturally caused environmental disaster, Union Carbide's deadly explosion in Bhopal. . . . Public reaction to the *Valdez*'s massive environmental damage and destruction of wildlife clearly overshadowed the fact that no human deaths resulted from either the tanker's spill, the effects of the spill, or the cleanup operations that lasted nearly two years . . . [In short, n]o environmental disaster in the 20th century has captivated the world's attention to the extent of the *Exxon Valdez* oil spill in March 1989. (p. 187)

I contend that the answer to this confounding riddle of why—in the face of Bhopal—*Exxon Valdez* holds such a commanding position in the history of environmental disaster lies within the handling or mishandling of its crisis communication. The inquiry into this paradox will undoubtedly continue as crisis communication enters into a more mature stage—one brought about in some part by these two justly famous paradigmatic cases.

REFERENCES

Baker, L. W. (1993). *The Credibility Factor: Putting Ethics to Work in Public Relations*. Homewood, IL: Business One Irwin.

Behar, R. (1989). *Time*, July 24, 42–47.

Bhopal: The endless aftershocks. (1984). *Chemical Week*, December 19, 33–40.

Cassels, J. (1993). *The Uncertain Promise of Law: Lessons from Bhopal*. Toronto: University of Toronto Press.

Caywood, C. and Stocker K. P. (1993). The ultimate crisis plan. In J. A. Gottschalk (ed.), *Crisis Response: Inside Stories on Managing Image Under Siege*. Detroit: Visible Ink.

Davidson, A. (1990). *In the Wake of the* Exxon Valdez: *The Devastating Impact of the Alaska Oil Spill*. San Francisco: Sierra.

"Exxon verdict is upheld" (1995). *The New York Times*, January 29, A17.

Fearn-Banks, K. (1996). *Crisis Communications: A Casebook Approach*. Mahwah, NJ: Erlbaum.

Gottschalk, J. A. (1993). *Crisis Response: Inside Stories on Managing Image Under Siege*. Detroit: Visible Ink.

Hyde, C. R. (1993). Meltdown on Three Mile Island. In J. A. Gottschalk (ed.), *Crisis Response: Inside Stories on Managing Image Under Siege*, 107–121. Detroit: Visible Ink.

"In ten years you'll see 'nothing'" (1989). *Fortune*, May 8, 50–52.

Kirkland, R. J. Jr. (1985), "Union Carbide: Coping with catastrophe." *Fortune*, January 7, 50–53.

Kreps, G. L. (1990). *Organizational Communication: Theory and Practice*. New York: Longman.

Kurzman, D. (1987). *A Killing Wind: Inside Union Carbide and the Bhopal Catastrophe*. New York: McGraw-Hill.

Lukaszewski, J. E. (1992). The *Exxon Valdez* paradox. In J. A. Gottschalk (ed.), *Crisis Response: Inside Stories on Managing Image Under Siege*, 185–213. Detroit: Visible Ink.

Mauer, R. (1989). ''Alaska aide assails oil industry for 'inadequate' response.'' *The New York Times*, March 26, A1, A22.

Mitroff, I. I., Pearson, C. M., and Harrington, L. K. (1996). *The Essential Guide to Managing Corporate Crises: A Step-by-Step Handbook for Surviving Major Catastrophes*. New York: Oxford.

Reinhold, R. (1985). ''Disaster in Bhopal: Where does blame lie?'' *The New York Times*, January 31, A1, A8.

Rogers, R. (1993). Anatomy of a crisis. In J. A. Gottschalk (ed.), *Crisis Response: Inside Stories on Managing Image Under Siege*, 123–139. Detroit: Visible Press.

Seib, P. and Fitzpatrick, K. (1995). *Public Relations Ethics*. Fort Worth, TX: Harcourt Brace.

Seitel, F. P. (1998). *The Practice of Public Relations*, 7th ed. Upper Saddle River, NJ: Prentice-Hall.

Sen, F. and Egelhoff, W. G. (1991). ''Six years and counting: Learning from crisis management at Bhopal.'' *Public Relations Review*, 17(*1*), 69–83.

Shrivastava, P. (1992). *Bhopal: Anatomy of a Crisis*, 2nd ed. London: Chapman.

Small, W. J. (1991). ''Exxon Valdez: How to spend billions and still get a black eye.'' *Public Relations Review*. 17(*1*), 9–25.

Smith, C. (1992). *Media and Apocalypse: News Coverage of the Yellowstone Forest Fires, Exxon Valdez Oil Spill, and Loma Prieta Earthquake*. Westport, CT: Greenwood.

Sullivan, A. and Bennett A. (1989). ''Critics fault chief executive of Exxon on handling of recent Alaskan oil spill.'' *Wall Street Journal*, March 31, B1.

Wilcox, W. K, Ault, P. H., and Agee, W. K. (1997). *Public Relations: Strategies and Tactics*, 5th ed. New York: Longman.

Winslow, R. (1984). ''Union Carbide mobilizes resources to control damage from gas leak.'' *The Wall Street Journal*, December 10, 29.

Yagoda, B. (1990). ''Cleaning up a dirty image.'' *Business Monthly*, April, 48–51.

17
Metropolitan Medical Strike Team Systems

Responding to the Medical Demands of WMD/NBC Events[1]

Frances E. Winslow Office of Emergency Services, City of San José, San José, California

Captain John Walmsley U.S. Department of Health and Human Services, Region IX, San Francisco, California

I. BACKGROUND

The Defense Against Weapons of Mass Destruction Act of 1996, sponsored by Senators Nunn, Lugar, and Domenici, mandated that certain agencies of the federal government conduct activities to counteract terrorism, among these "to provide enhanced support to improve the capabilities of State and local emergency response agencies to prevent and respond to such incidents at both the national and the local level."

Under the Emergency Response Assistance Program section of the Nunn-Lugar-Domenici Domestic Preparedness (DP) program legislation, six federal agencies were directed to participate in a joint effort to enhance the capabilities of local governments to conduct initial medical response to weapons of mass destruction/nuclear, biological, chemical (WMD/NBC) mass casualty events. In early 1997, headquarters representatives of the Department of Defense (DoD), Department of Energy (DoE), Department of Health and Human Services (DHHS), U.S. Environmental Protection Agency (EPA), Federal Emergency Management Agency (FEMA), and the Federal Bureau of Investigations (FBI) formed a Senior Interagency Coordination Group (SICG), cochaired by FEMA and DoD, that was tasked with the implementation of the Nunn-Lugar-Domenici DP program. The SICG's objective was to facilitate interagency cooperation and to coordinate the various types of support or assistance that each federal agency was able to bring to the program. The SICG met regularly to steer the DP program at the federal headquarters level.

The six federal partner agencies brought an impressive array of assets and capabilities to the table and were mandated important responsibilities. DoD was made responsible for training, expert advice, WMD/NBC help-line assistance, loan of WMD response equipment, creation of a Domestic Terrorism Rapid Response Team, conduct of exercises, establishment of a chemical/biological agent database, support to the Department of Justice, and the interdiction of WMD agents. DOE offered specialized technical support in the event of nuclear terrorist events and nuclear awareness and technical response training programs. DHHS called for a systems approach to the local health and medical services response to WMD events and embarked on a strategic plan to develop partnerships to improve local health and medical system capability while improving the federal capability to rapidly augment state and local response. The EPA, in addition to its regular responsibilities to assist state and local governments in the response to hazardous materials incidents, offered training in a number of aspects of hazardous materials (hazmat) response under its Emergency Response Training Program. The Bureau of Justice Assistance received funding to contribute grant assistance to metropolitan fire and emergency services departments to enhance their response to terrorist attacks. The FBI offered training in federal/community law enforcement integration at WMD incident sites and courses in crime scene awareness and recognition. FEMA, along with its normal emergency response coordination responsibilities, offered counterterrorism training grants to states and pertinent training from the Emergency Management Institute and the National Fire Academy.

The SICG also was instrumental in developing the list of cities that were selected to participate in the DP program. In general, cities were selected on the basis of population size, but Honolulu, Hawaii, and Anchorage, Alaska, were included because of their status as important cities in remote geographical areas. Washington, D.C., was included in the list because of its importance to national security and the perception that increased risk for terrorist activity existed in the nation's capitol. The final list of cities was arrived at with input from the staffs of Senators Nunn and Lugar.

Each city included in the DP program was able to determine for itself the extent to which other adjacent local jurisdictions or counties would be invited to participate with the city in this enhancement effort. Direct state government representation was not included in the program.

II. DHHS DEVELOPMENT PROGRAM

DHHS made the decision to fund 27 cities, each with \$300,000 to \$350,000, for Metropolitan Medical Strike Team Systems (MMSTS)[2] development in the first year of the DP program. Although DHHS originally conceived of this response enhancement plan as focusing on the development of a Metropolitan Medical Strike Team (MMST) in each of the selected cities, the Department soon realized the importance of focusing on a larger systems approach to response. Thus, the MMSTS development program became one in which the interface between hazmat response, emergency medical services, medical facilities, mental health and crisis counseling, and the functions of the local medical examiner became integral to the concept of response enhancement.

DHHS initiated the MMSTS development program in the Washington, D.C., metropolitan area and offered the district's efforts as a prototype for the other MMSTS cities to use in the development of their own medical response systems. In order to provide an enhanced WMD preparedness posture for the 1996 Summer Olympics in Atlanta, Georgia, and for the Summit of Eight meeting in Denver, Colorado in 1997, MMSTS development work for these two cities was put on a fast track and initiated before that of the remaining cities.

At the regional level, loosely organized SICG counterparts, composed of regional representatives of the same six federal partner agencies, were established in the 10 federal geographic regions. These regional advisory groups were organized with the objective of translating the DP program, as it was developed at the headquarters level, to the local jurisdictions that were selected to receive response enhancement assistance from the federal government. Also at the regional level, federal project officers were assigned to oversee the MMSTS contracts that provided DHHS funding to the cities for the purposes of developing enhanced WMD medical response teams and systems and acquiring WMD response-enhancing equipment and pharmaceuticals.

The MMSTS development effort was intentionally designed to allow each participating city the flexibility to create a MMST and a supporting MMST system that would be compatible with the city's standing emergency response procedures. Two basic approaches to doing this evolved: augmentation and enhancement.

III. TEAM AND SYSTEM DESIGN

The Washington, D.C., metropolitan area (WMA), as the first locale to develop an MMSTS, chose the augmentation approach and created a specialized freestanding WMD medical response team. It could be rapidly called together and deployed to augment the local response capabilities of any of the various local jurisdictions that were included in the WMA's MMSTS development effort. A system was also developed that provided an interface between the team and the infrastructures that supported it. This approach worked well in a situation where a number of different political jurisdictions were involved in the development process.

In contrast, some other cities opted for the enhancement approach and developed MMSTs that consisted of on-duty personnel who received special WMD training to enhance their regular response skills. Under the enhancement approach, on-duty staff responded as part of their regular assignments and as they normally would except that their enhanced skills included specialized WMD response capabilities and awareness. Under this approach, a system was also developed that provided an interface between the team and the infrastructure that supported it.

Although the MMSTS development process was purposefully made flexible to allow each city to develop a team and system that could work within the framework of already extant emergency response systems, some common elements emerged in the cities' strategies. For a number of the cities' MMSTs, a structure was developed that included some or many of the following elements: field medical operations, emergency medical services operations, hazmat operations, decontamination operations, medical information/research, logistics, hospital coordination and support, and law enforcement. Within these elements, the critical team functions of WMD agent detection, sampling and identification, and victim extraction, triage, decontamination, treatment, and transport to definitive care were addressed. In addition to these functions, the larger "system" response effort addressed the following elements: hospital preparedness for multicasualty WMD events; mental health crisis counseling; storage, maintenance, and transport of WMD antidotes; use of appropriate medical protocols; maintenance of and access to specialized WMD response equipment; handling of deceased victims; emergency communications; and development of the command and control function.

In general, MMSTs tended to be staffed by 35 to 40 people, often including positions for team leader, safety officer, administrative officer, public information officer, medical operations physician, and several operations sector leaders.

Another key element of each city's MMSTS design was the interface with state and federal response systems. DHHS required each city to set forth how it would interface with these systems and how it would plan for forward movement of patients into the National Disaster Medical System, the federal system designed to transport and provide medical treatment for patient loads that exceed a city or state's ability to provide hospital care.

IV. MMSTS MISSION STATEMENT

A number of the MMSTS cities adopted all or part of the WMA mission statement which is included here:

> It is the mission of the MMST to respond to, provide support for, and provide assistance to local and regional jurisdictions to effectively address responder safety issues, incident management, and public health consequences of NBC incidents that result from accidental or deliberate acts. This support and assistance includes providing planning and training to response personnel prior to an NBC incident, identification of the offending substance via available technology, off-site management consultation service, and where needed, response to the scene or secondary site to assist with incident management and medical care during an NBC incident. These activities will be conducted in collaboration with and supported by Federal, State and local authorities.

V. DHHS CONTRACT AND ASSISTANCE

The technical aspects of WMD response were new to a number of the cities participating in the MMSTS development program. In order to help the cities deal with the current and evolving response issues and technologies in this field, DHHS hired a contractor to provide technical assistance on WMD/NBC response planning and equipment acquisition to the MMSTS cities. The contractor created a five-phase MMSTS development plan for use by the cities that included the following steps: (1) preliminary coordination of local agencies/departments; (2) development of a mission statement, concept of operations, and organizational structure; (3) delineation of strike team operations; (4) establishment of staffing and equipment requirements; and (5) conduct of training. The contractor provided considerable technical assistance concerning specialized WMD/NBC response equipment for personal protection, hazardous agent detection, mass decontamination and patient movement.

The DHHS contract with each city called for the submission of a set of deliverables that included four elements: a plan for training the MMST and the personnel in the larger MMSTS that interfaced with it; a plan for how the MMSTS would be developed over the contract period; a concept of operations document; and lists of proposed pharmaceuticals and WMD response equipment to be procured with DHHS funds. Each city was given approximately 15 months to plan for, staff, train, and procure equipment and pharmaceuticals for an operational MMSTS.

VI. FEDERAL GOVERNMENT RESOURCE CONTRIBUTIONS

Three of the federal partner agencies developed ongoing relationships with the selected cities: the FBI, DoD, and DHHS. Each brought resources into the selected cities to provide practical assistance in the development of the MMST and the MMSTS.

The FBI provided extensive briefings for the city staff, not only those in law enforcement, as in the past, but also for the fire, emergency planning, and medical personnel who would have to assist in the development of the MMSTS concept of operations. A local special agent was assigned as liaison with the city's MMSTS development team. A tabletop exercise to explore the interface between FBI resources and local government resources was created and provided by the FBI. Bringing together top police staff members with FBI leaders from the local area as well as regional and national offices built a spirit of cooperation. The controversial issues of control of the crime scene and the establishment of joint command were sensitively handled through an open exploration and resolution of concerns. Finally, the Bureau of Justice Assistance offered a competitive grant program for additional equipment to enhance the MMSTS response capabilities.

The DoD worked with contractors to translate military training on battlefield NBC events to a civilian teaching environment. Courses on first-responder awareness, first-responder operations, hazardous materials technician, emergency medical technician, incident command at an NBC event, and hospital response were taught in a train-the-trainer format for 4 consecutive days, with most offerings repeated three times. All the expenses for the instructors and training resources were borne by DoD, but the cost of facilities, refreshments, and, most significantly, personnel time to attend the classes was the responsibility of the receiving agency.

On the final day of the training, a tabletop exercise was held to permit resource leaders from federal, state and regional agencies to discuss their resources and capabilities that would be available to the city if a WMD/NBC event occurred. This facilitated discussion led to a better understanding of the range of assistance potentially available and the constraints of location and travel times for the arrival of these resources. This information reinforced the importance of locally available first response capabilities.

The DoD also provided to each of the selected cities a cache of training supplies and equipment valued at approximately $300,000. In addition to teaching materials, such as slides and a CD-ROM of Power Point presentations and student books, training equipment could be selected by the city. The range of training equipment included hazmat personal protective equipment and detection equipment; decontamination resources; and communications equipment. This cache enabled the city to deliver the training to all appropriate city personnel.

Most cities included neighboring jurisdictions in the DoD train-the-trainer opportunity. Departmental training officers from fire and law enforcement agencies throughout the county, ambulance company trainers, hazardous materials response teams, public health service personnel, public health nurses, emergency medical services, and medical examiner/coroner staff members were included in the training classes. The specialized hospital classes were generally offered at different hospital sites to make attendance as convenient as possible for hospital personnel.

The DHHS provided specific guidance on the development of a MMSTS within a city through the Washington, D.C., model. A project officer was assigned to each MMSTS to assist with local issues in the development of the plan. A contract between DHHS and each city provided for the procurement of a cache of equipment and supplies to support the MMST and also some elements of the wider system. Equipment acquisition plans were focused on personal protective equipment for first responders, decontamination equipment for victims and first responders, medical support equipment such as stretchers, chemical weapon detection equipment, and communications gear. Pharmaceutical acquisition focused on antidotes needed in large quantities within a short period after the WMD/

NBC event and medical equipment to support the team. The selected city is the custodian of all the equipment and pharmaceuticals and is responsible to DHHS for its maintenance and replacement for team "sustainment."

VII. LOCAL GOVERNMENT CONTRIBUTIONS

Cities selected for the MMSTS development staffed their teams from existing local resources. The variety of governmental structures in different states has often resulted in the necessity to partner with other governmental jurisdictions and private entities to create the full MMSTS. Teams have been developed using only the resources within one city, using a combination of city and county resources, sometimes including private resources and even using locally stationed federal resources to fill out the complement of team positions.

A complete MMSTS requires some resources that are under the direct jurisdiction of the selected city and others that may be either under the jurisdiction of another governmental entity or in private ownership. For example, in San Jose, California, the city was able to provide the required fire/rescue, hazmat, and law resources from among its own personnel. Under California law, emergency medical response is divided between the city and the county in which it is located. Within the San Jose Fire Department, all firefighters are emergency medical technicians who can provide the basic-life-support level of medical care. In addition, every engine and truck carries a paramedic who can provide advanced life support.

Transportation of the victims from the scene to definitive care is provided by a privately owned ambulance company under contract to the county for emergency response services. Patients are billed directly for this service. The same for-profit company also provides nonemergency medical transportation services privately. Control of the emergency medical transportation resources rests with the county's Emergency Medical Services Department, which also certifies the EMTs and paramedics within its jurisdiction and oversees ambulance licensure within the county. The county oversees the development and implementation of the Mass Casualty Incident Plan. Through this plan, the transport of patients to specific hospitals is controlled based on hospital capacity and availability of specialized resources.

In addition, the public health function rests with the county. Public health laboratories and communicable disease surveillance are conducted by the county. A disease-related disaster would require investigative work by the county public health entities. A health or disease-based disaster declaration would be issued by the county health officer, county executive, or the county board of supervisors even if it occurred only within the city's boundaries.

The medical examiner/coroner is also a county employee with a separate department. Care of the deceased victims, forensic pathology, and investigation of the deaths would be a county coroner function.

Hospitals would be an integral part of a WMD/NBC response. There is one county hospital in San Jose. The rest of the hospitals in the city and the county are nongovernmental, and most are part of for-profit or managed care systems.

Thus, in San Jose, California, development of a MMSTS requires the cooperation of two levels of government and a variety of private businesses (hospitals and the ambulance company). The county contract with the ambulance company for emergency medical transportation ensured their participation in some of the training opportunities provided through the DoD's Nunn-Lugar DP activities. However, as a profit-making enterprise, the cost of this training in personnel time was a significant issue for them.

Furthermore, few hospitals participated in the Nunn-Lugar DP program because of the high cost of personnel time and the perceived lack of direct benefit to the hospital. As more hospitals are operated as profit-making entities, resources are concentrated on activities that enhance the financial bottom line of the parent organization.

Successful MMSTS communities have to find incentives to bring together the groups required to field a complete MMST system. City-controlled resources, such as police, fire, and emergency management, realize the importance of training and equipping for all credible disaster events. The MMSTS program provided for training of personnel in the specialized response capabilities required by WMD/NBC events, and for federal funding for specified equipment and supplies. For most cities, this training and equipping builds on an existing foundation of investigative, response, and planning activities. Hazardous materials response teams, bomb squads, and paramedics all have related knowledge and training that the WMD/NBC program enhances.

Bringing in the county as a partner required an understanding of the roles and responsibilities that would be affected by a WMD/NBC event. The FBI's presentation on the threat of domestic terrorism provided a strong basis for county resource allocation to WMD/NBC training. While the DoD train-the-trainer program was available to county staff, there was no funding through Nunn-Lugar DP programs for enhancement of county equipment resources. The personnel costs for staff to receive the training were also a county expense. However, as a governmental entity the county realized the necessity of participation.

The private business community did not have the same imperative to participate. While the Joint Commission on Hospital Accreditation currently requires that hospitals have some hazardous materials response capabilities, they are minimal. Hazardous materials responses are seldom practiced. Key staff members may not be aware of the hazardous materials response plan, or even of how to evaluate a patient for exposure to a WMD/chemical agent. However, since the training on WMD/NBC is not mandated, few hospitals are investing in sending their personnel to either the DoD training, or to shorter, locally sponsored training. While offering training for hospital providers is included in the MMSTS's training plan, obtaining participation by the hospital staff members is at best problematic. Such training takes staff time, a bottom-line expense, and generates no revenue in any foreseeable period of time.

VIII. THE FUTURE OF MMSTS

Enhanced awareness of the threat of domestic terrorism will provide an incentive for the maintenance of established MMSTSs. Under the Domestic Preparedness Program, additional cities are having their response capabilities enhanced through training and federal partner guidance. At present there is no funding for supplies or equipment for the cities being added after the first 27. Given the expense of the specialized WMD response equipment, it seems unlikely that these cities will achieve parity in preparedness levels with the initial 27 cities through local funding sources alone. However, the DoD training in awareness and medical skills related to WMD/NBC should improve first-responder safety and patient evaluation.

The first 27 cities have a goal of long-term MMSTS sustainment. While the enhanced training will benefit the cities far into the future, the perishable equipment and pharmaceuticals may not be replaced when they expire, based on the availability of municipal funds and the competing demands for this scarce resource. Recent Presidential Decision Directives have begun the development of a national stockpile of some critical pharmaceuticals. Cities using the MMSTS to acquire multiple use equipment will find it easier to maintain and replace both the equipment and the staff's proficiency with it. For example, some cities used part of the DHHS contract funding to purchase more sets of the same type of personal protective equipment (PPE) that is currently used by their hazmat teams. This will allow the medical care givers and decontamination team to be protected from WMD/NBC agents, using the extra equipment supplied by the DHHS funds. The PPE, however, can be used through the normal hazmat team response cycle, and replaced through the normal departmental supply system, preventing the stockpiling of what, in future years, would have been old, or outdated, equipment. Similarly, acquisition of gas detectors with broad capabilities permits the hazmat team to use the equipment frequently, both maintaining their proficiency in its use, and justifying its maintenance and updating from city funds. Conversely, a single purpose detector would be warehoused and become outmoded, with staff losing familiarity with its operation except for annual ''refreshers.''

The first 27 cities have made remarkable progress in their MMSTS development efforts with a small amount of money, pressing time frames, and meager development staff. It is anticipated that all of the original 27 cities will have an operational MMSTS by the close of calendar year 1998. This represents a significant enhancement of domestic terrorism response capabilities.

ENDNOTES

1. The opinions expressed in this paper are those of the authors alone. They do not reflect the opinions of the governmental entities by which they are employed.
2. This name was created by the original group in Washington, D.C. Most fire departments now use the Incident Command System, which has consistent nomenclature. A strike team is a group of similar equipment. Since a MMST is defined as a team of members from a variety of professional backgrounds, the more correct nomenclature is *Metropolitan Medical Task Force*, terminology adopted by some cities. For simplicity, MMST and MMSTS are used in this paper.

18

Managing Urban Violence Cases in Hospital Emergency Departments

Terry F. Buss Department of Public Management, Suffolk University, Boston, Massachusetts

I. INTRODUCTION

Urban violence—intentional injury resulting from shootings, stabbings and beatings[1]—is out of control in America. Every year about 25,000 people die from interpersonal violence, making homicide the 11th leading cause of death (Anderson et al. 1996). For young people aged 15 to 24 years of age, homicide is the third leading cause of death. For African-American males, odds of being murdered are 1 in 20, compared to 205 for white males. For each homicide victim, 90 additional people are injured in nonfatal criminal assaults (U.S. Department of Justice 1987). Nearly 600,000 reported violent crimes occur annually, a figure fairly constant from 1973 to 1995, after which numbers began to fall (Bastian 1993). Perhaps twice that many violent crimes go unreported. Costs to society of urban violence are estimated by the National Research Council at $285 billion (Reiss and Ross 1994). Large urban areas, small cities, and even rural areas all suffer from unacceptably high levels of interpersonal violence (Bachman 1992).

Health care providers, especially in public health and emergency medicine, view urban violence as an epidemic similar to plague and AIDS (Novello et al. 1992; Smeltzer and Redeker 1995). According to the National Academy of Science, intentional injury is the nation's leading public health problem. In 1986, the surgeon general held a national conference of medical experts to address the issue (Cron 1986). So pressing is the problem that the editors of 11 leading medical journals devoted one entire issue each attacking violence from their discipline's perspective (American Medical Association 1992). Typical of articles in these journals was, "Violence in America: A Public Health Emergency—Time to Bite the Bullet Back" (Koop and Lundberg 1992).

Hospital emergency departments[2] (EDs), particularly trauma centers,[3] serving cities bear the brunt of interpersonal violence often jeopardizing their very existence (Morrissey et al. 1991; Organ 1993; Smith et al. 1992; Trunkey 1990; Legorreta et al. 1993). Many urban trauma centers closed, and others are at risk (Daily et al. 1992; Fleming et al. 1992; Mondargon 1992). Urban violence victims consume scarce resources denied to others—car accident or heart attack victims, for example (Ryan et al. 1993).

The nationwide cost of injury for 1988 was $180 billion, 10% attributable to urban violence (Rice and MacKersie 1989). Gunshots in 1995 alone cost $4 billion to treat. Unsponsored trauma care, much of it for urban violence, totaled $1 billion in 1988, or

10% of all unsponsored care (Champion and Mabe 1990). In Youngstown, Ohio, 279 inpatients who were victims of urban violence cost $3,330,000 to treat, or $14,300 per patient (Buss et al. 1995). In a Chapel Hill study, 200 urban violence victims incurred $2 million in hospital charges; two-thirds were uninsured and the insured patients had only 30% of their expenses covered (Clancy et al. 1994). Gunshot wounds treated in California average $58,271, according to one study (Kizer et al. 1995). More than half of these patients were uninsured, with two-thirds of the rest on Medicaid. In 1988, Arizona hospitals alone provided $221 million in uncompensated care (Mondragon 1992).

Better case management, early intervention, and prevention, combined with health and human service integration, might improve what are now dismal prospects for hospital emergency departments. But, in spite of the problem's gravity, relatively little is known about how to manage urban violence cases (Koop 1988; Kellermann 1994; Kellerman 1996; Reiss and Ross 1994) and what works in making things better is not often undertaken (see Koop 1988). For example, the literature barely addresses urban violence committed on females (Lake 1993). Physicians treat victims' injuries but offer little else, while others who would like to do more are stymied by constraints, not the least of which is cost.

Effective emergency management of urban violence in the ED depends on (Mercey and O'Carroll 1988:1):

Surveying the nature and extent of the problem
Identifying groups at risk
Exploring why groups are at risk
Designing programs targeted at risk reduction
Evaluating program effectiveness

This encyclopedic review of the urban violence field in an ED context departs substantially from most literature in the field. Most reviews are discipline-based and hence somewhat narrow in scope. Criminal justice looks at deterrents, sanctions, and rehabilitation, but it ignores health care. Sociologists examine causal relationships often in criminal justice and health care but ignore EDs. Medical researchers focus on treatment using medical models but ignore nonmedical issues. And public health tries to take a more comprehensive view but has not progressed much beyond the talking stage. No literature reviews, to my knowledge, try to bring these disparate disciplines together.

In the sections below, I employ the public health model of disease control as a way to organize this vast, unconnected literature. The chapter looks first at surveillance activity, then victim characteristics and how and why people became victims. This is followed by a review of efforts to target programs at victims. The paper concludes with an overview of why programs seem not to work and what remains to be done. I draw on a wide variety of literature from many sources to cover the field. I supplemented these materials throughout with published (Buss et al. 1995; Buss and Abdu 1995) and unpublished data from a study of urban violence victims receiving care in Youngstown, Ohio[4] designed to take an interdisciplinary look at this pressing emergency management problem.

II. SURVEYING URBAN VIOLENCE

The purpose of surveillance activity is to clearly identify what is happening in the environment—both externally and in the ED itself—so that resources can be allocated effectively and efficiently. Of considerable importance is identifying change in patterns of violence that might affect resource allocation over time.

In 1992, the National Hospital Ambulatory Medical Care Survey (NHAMCS), comprising the most complete data on EDs, found that EDs nationwide admitted 1,554,000 victims of homicide and assault (Burt 1995). Some 588,000 people were victims of fighting, brawling, or rape; another 173,000 were victims of penetrating wounds and 731,000 were assaulted but not classified.

Study results from Youngstown mirrored those in most other studies (Buss et al. 1995). About two-thirds of patients presented with penetrating wounds, about three-fourths resulting from gunshots and only 28% from knives (22%) or sharp instruments (6%). Blunt instruments accounted for a mere 10% of wounds. Some 23% of wounds resulted from punches, kicks, and burns. Attacks are typically serious: in Youngstown, 64% felt that their lives were in danger during the attack.

III. AT-RISK GROUPS

Not all segments of society are equally affected by urban violence. Effective emergency management requires concentration of scarce resources on those most at risk. Understanding groups at risk is especially important in this field, where a great deal of mythology, misperception, and misinformation abound (Kelley et al. 1997).

A. Victims or Losers?

An emerging consensus across the literature is that victims of urban violence presenting in hospital EDs are mostly not victims in the usual sense of the word. Rather, they are similar to their attackers except that they were on the losing end of a fight (Rivara et al. 1995; Lauritsen et al. 1991).

B. Criminal Records

As further evidence that victims are not generally innocent bystanders or helpless targets, research shows that victims have criminal records, often reflecting violent crimes. Most studies (e.g., Singer 1986; Morrissey et al. 1991) find anywhere from one-third to three-fifths of victims have criminal records. In the Youngstown study, for example, 41% of inpatient victims had criminal records. Of these, 37% had committed a crime of violence—assault or murder (27.2%), domestic violence (4.9%), or rape (6.2%). Also, of those with criminal records, 13.6% had a drug conviction and 23.5% were sentenced for driving under the influence.

C. Repeat Victims

Some observers accept the notion that urban violence is epidemic, but they equate it instead with a chronic disease rather than a single random, episodic event. Urban violence studies typically show that between 20 and 50% of those presenting at EDs are repeat victims (Morrissey et al. 1991; Goins et al. 1992; Sims et al. 1989; DeMuth 1989; Buss and Abdu 1995; Cesare et al. 1990; Litacker 1996; Smeltzer and Redeker 1995; Wintemute and Wright, 1992). In a study of firearm injuries in Stockholm, Sweden, researchers found that patients were likely to return with a subsequent firearm injury in the future. They coined the phrase *chronic trauma syndrome* to capture this phenomenon (Ponzer et al. 1996).

One of the factors prompting research in the Youngstown study was that trauma surgeons in the ED began to complain that they recognized their sutures on victims returning with new wounds.

D. When and Where Assault Occurs

When and where victimization occurs plays out in treatment in hospital EDs. Most urban violence cases present at EDs in late evening, especially on weekends and holidays (Greenberg and Schneider, 1992; Greenberg et al. 1991; Cesare et al. 1990). The reason is simple: people tend to blow off steam on evenings and weekends, consuming alcohol and drugs in the process. Because most do not work at those times, they can stay awake late at night joy-seeking. And the night conceals criminal activity.

Other researchers concerned about staffing EDs have looked at less obvious factors. In one study, Coates and colleagues (1989) analyzed possible effects of a full moon on violence caseloads. They found no statistically significant differences for full-moon and non-full-moon days with respect to caseloads, types of injuries, severity of injuries, and length of stay. Other researchers studied impacts of welfare check distribution (Brunette et al. 1991). ED caseloads were high following the issuance of welfare checks but then declined in the days following check distribution. Greenberg and Schneider (1992) found that African-American males were more likely to murder or be murdered on Thursdays, something they could not satisfactorily explain. Still others have explored weather, calendar events, and even biorhythms finding modest correlations (see Brunette et al. 1991).

Although drinking and drugs are associated with urban violence, victims are most likely injured not in bars or pool halls but near their homes, especially women, and in public places, especially roads, for men (Ellis, 1997). In Youngstown, for example, only 14% were attacked in a bar or like facility.

E. Demographics

1. National Studies

According to the National Ambulatory Medical Care Survey in 1992, more than one-half of the victims were at least 25 years of age. One-third were aged 15 to 24 years, with the lion's share beyond the teen years. Only one in ten was below age 15. About three-fifths were males and only one-third were African Americans. Statistics suggest that urban violence as played out in EDs is not exclusively a young, male, African American problem associated with gangs in the poor inner city, as is often perceived (Koop and Lundberg, 1992).[5]

2. Selected Local Studies

The demographic picture is much more complex at the local level as well: victim groups are segmented. Victims in Youngstown, for example, were more likely to be young males, African American, poor, single, unemployed, and high school dropouts (Buss et al 1995). But only 14% of urban violence victims possessed all eight of these attributes, while 70% possessed at least five. Figures can be misleading. The average age of Youngstown victims was 32 years. One-third were white; one-third earned incomes above the federal poverty level; and one-third were married. Most had finished high school, although they were poor students overall. Cesare and coworkers (1990), in a study of assault injuries in Hartford, found that 48% were African American, 72% were male, and average age was 30 years. In the Shreveport study of recurrent trauma victims with wounds, penetrating 88% were unemployed, 95% were male, and 94% were African American (Morrissey et al. 1991). In a study of assault injuries in Los Angeles, researchers found that 90% of patients were ethnic minorities aged 25 to 30 (Klein et al. 1991). In a study of victims of firearm injuries in Stockholm, Sweden, physicians found that the average victim was young and single, often an immigrant, and with a likely criminal record (Panzer et al. 1995).

F. Health Insurance

Patients without health insurance or on Medicaid or publicly subsidized health insurance are much more likely to be victims of urban violence than those who are insured, an obvious connection to poverty and unemployment (Mackersie et al. 1995; Payne et al. 1993; Luna et al. 1988).

IV. EXPLAINING HIGH-RISK BEHAVIOR

Once at-risk groups have been identified, reasons for their deviant behavior must be explained as a precursor to developing policy or programs to reduce and better manage urban violence in EDs. Numerous explanations, all with some credibility, can be gleaned from the literature, each having implications for emergency management.

A. Alcohol and Drugs

Victims of urban violence presenting in EDs likely have abused alcohol and/or drugs (Buss et al. 1995; Brookoff et al. 1993; Budd 1989; Haberman and Natarajan 1986; Herve et al. 1986; Holt et al. 1980; Meehan and O'Carroll 1992; Organ 1993; Pernanen and Heath 1991; Thal et al. 1985; Rivara et al. 1989; Lindenbaum et al. 1989). From the NHAMCS study, researchers found that when a patient's record included an alcohol or drug-related note, the injury was three times more likely to be an intentional injury or to have caused the victim's death (Burt 1995). ED visits related to alcohol or drugs were six times more likely to be caused by violence (Burt 1995). Thum and coworkers (1973) detected alcohol in 56% of ED patients injured in assaults. Rivara et al. (1989) found that 54% of assault victims were on drugs. Lindenbaum et al. (1989) found illicit drugs present in the toxicology screens of 80% of violent crime-related cases. Sims et al. (1989) found that 63% of patients with repeat trauma visits to the ER had abused alcohol or drugs.

The high incidence of substance abuse among victims of urban violence poses problems in managing patients in emergency, especially for trauma sugeons (Mackersie et al. 1988; Waller 1990). Drugs and alcohol may precipitate unusual clinical problems, often mistakenly diagnosed (Goins et al. 1992). Patients on alcohol or drugs may inaccurately report symptoms or may be unconscious and unable to report (Enderson et al. 1990). Patients with head injury trauma may be misdiagnosed as having a psychiatric disorder when they had actually been abusing substances (Sloan et al. 1989). Expensive tests and screens may be required to diagnose such patients accurately (Jurkovich et al. 1992). Surgery can affect patient physiology. Patients mixing cocaine, alcohol, and other substances may be adversely affected by common medications (Lipman 1980) or during general anesthesia (Lindenbaum et al. 1989). ED personnel may be at risk of HIV infection (Eposito et al. 1991). Drug and alcohol abuse may be associated with secondary illnesses: poor nutrition, heart and liver disease, sexually transmitted disease, cognitive impairment, hepatitis, psychiatric disorders, seizures, and numerous other medical problems (Blanken 1993; Brody et al. 1990; Cregler and Mark 1986; General Accounting Office 1991). Drugs and alcohol may place urban trauma victims at greater risk of infection generally (Gentilello et al. 1993).

A shortcoming of most medical studies is that they tend to underestimate substance abuse, because not everyone presenting in the ED as a victim of urban violence is screened for alcohol and drugs. In our study in Youngstown, we combined data from toxicology screens and patient self-reports to get a better measure of substance abuse prevalence (Buss et al. 1995). Combined medical records and self-reports showed that 70% of victims were under the influence of alcohol or drugs when attacked. Of those under the influence, 62% were drinking, 12% took drugs, and 26% consumed both.

Many victims have medical histories of alcohol and drug abuse. In our Youngstown study, medical records revealed that 57% had alcohol problems and 44% had drug abuse histories (Buss et al. 1995).

Attackers are just as likely to be abusing substances as victims of attack (Buss et al. 1995). In Youngstown, 60% of victims reported that their attackers were on drugs or alcohol.

B. Psychiatric Disorders

Victims with psychiatric problems are a small but nonetheless an important patient population. The nexus between psychiatric disorder and violence has rarely been studied (Rund et al. 1981; Silverman et al. 1985). In our Youngstown study, only 6% of victim medical records indicated any psychiatric episode associated with urban violence (Buss et al. 1995), but 12% of victims had been treated for some form of psychiatric disorder in the past.

Psychiatric problems also pose difficulties in ED management. Substance abuse may trigger mental health problems in victims with psychiatric disorders. Substance abuse may mask psychiatric disorders requiring treatment. Conversely, psychiatric disorders may mask injuries requiring treatment. For example, an internal head wound may go unnoticed because of behavioral or emotional problems displayed by patients.

C. Subculture of Violence

Studies have identified the apparent symmetry between victim and offender. Violent behavior tends to be a reciprocal exchange in which assault is followed by retaliation, usually in efforts to resolve interpersonal or intergroup conflict. In short, members of the subculture of violence expect to attack and be attacked (Singer 1986; DuRant et al. 1994). Singer (1986) found that among Philadelphia youths 26 years of age or younger who were victims of assault, two-thirds admitted to having seriously attacked someone else. In a study of adolescents in the Bureau of Justice's National Crime Survey of Victimization, Lauritsen and coworkers (1991) found that persons are more likely to be victims when they come into contact with members of demographic groups that share a disproportionate share of offenders. Kuhlhorn (1990) studied violent offenders incarcerated in Sweden and their victims, concluding that offenders are statistically significantly more deviant and demographically different than their victims. At the same time, victims are significantly different from normal populations. Offense activity can be considered as a characteristic of lifestyles or as a routine activity which increases the risk of victimization because of the motives, vulnerability, or culpability of the people involved in those activities (Lauritsen et al. 1991:268). Offenders make ideal targets for crime because they can be victimized with relative impunity: victims are less likely to call police and if they do call they have less credibility (see also, Sparks 1982). And recreational pursuit of drinking is associated with victimization (see Jensen and Brownfield 1986).

Some researchers suspect that child abuse and family violence predispose people to behave violently as they grow older: violence begets violence (Maxwell and Widom 1996; Widom 1989, 1992). Child abuse and family violence is not unique in poor neighborhoods, but that combined with poverty predisposes people to violence.

In the Youngstown study, the culture of violence was all too evident. Two-fifths of those studied were repeat victims of violence. One-third were victims of robbery or burglary when attacked. One-fifth owned a gun. One-third carried a knife or gun, and 15% had used weapons against another person in the past year. Two-fifths fought to defend themselves. Nine of ten believed that violence was getting worse in their neighborhood. Two-thirds could not have avoided assault in their view. Three-fifths knew their attacker, and one-half saw the attacker following the assault. Sixty percent of assaults were carried out by one attacker, but 14.3% involved two attackers, 12.2% three, and 9.5% involved a gang.

Perhaps two anecdotes from Youngstown will shed light on this subculture. During our study, a gang brought one of its pledge members into our ED for treatment of a knife wound. Gang members thought it might be a good show of machismo and commitment to have the injured member stitched up without anaesthetic. In another case, a gang shot a rival gang member, drove him to the emergency department, and threw him out the door of the moving vehicle.

D. Locational Factors

Proximity to crime has a direct effect on victimization risk that is not mediated by lifestyle factors (Garofalo 1987; Lauritsen et al. 1991). Men are more likely to be injured on the street and women at home (Kingma 1994). Assaultive firearm-related injuries peaked sharply after 8 p.m. and usually occurred on roads or in other public places (Baker et al. 1996).

V. TARGETING AT RISK GROUPS

Programs and policies aimed at reducing urban violence are common in many cities, especially in law enforcement, civic groups, religious groups, youth programs, and schools. But there are few attempts organized with EDs as a focus or major participant (reasons for which are discussed in the next section). Some proposals for targeting in emergency rooms include the following:

A. Focusing on Substance Abuse

Some experts in emergency medicine are beginning to view urban violence—and trauma generally—not as a disease but rather as a symptom of substance abuse (Lowenstein et al. 1990; Sims et al. 1989). The implication: treat substance abuse and reduce urban violence.

To better address the substance abuse problem, many observers recommend mandatory toxicology screens for all victims of urban violence to improve initial diagnosis, counseling, treatment, rehab and follow-up (McNagny and Parker 1992; Rich and Singer 1991; Sloan et al. 1989; Lindenbaum et al. 1989).

Once screened for substance abuse, this targeting model calls emergency medicine physicians to immediately counsel victims against substance abuse behaviors. Some studies have noted modest success from counseling. After initial counseling, patients are referred to in-house or extramural substance abuse programs (Gentilello et al., 1988). In-house programs may begin while patients are recovering in hospital, or they may be offered along with rehabilitation services that many patients require (Waller 1990).

Above all, under this model, emergency medicine physicians must avoid making substance abuse problems worse. When ignoring possible substance abuse behaviors in favor of more immediate concerns in emergency treatment, emergency physicians are likely to prescribe pain-killing medications to patients who are likely to misuse them. These medications promote drug abuse and may likely end up on the streets to be sold to others.

B. Focusing on Holistic Care

Some experts in the field recognize the pervasiveness of the substance abuse problem in treating urban violence but believe that much more needs to be done (Koop and Lundgren 1992). In addition to substance abuse treatment and referral, emergency medicine physicians ought to treat the whole patient, not just the injury. Along with alcohol and drug screening, psychiatric assessments, social work evaluations, and comprehensive physical workups should be conducted. The idea: restore the victim to health. This model replicates the family practice model where the general practitioner focuses not only on disease and injury but also on improving or maintaining health status.

At present, no ED of which I am aware pusues the holistic model. Some do focus on identifying and treating psychopathology and substance abuse. Buss and colleagues (1995) found that only 10% of urban violence victims were referred to substance abuse programs. Lowenstein and coworkers (1990), in their study of ED trauma patients in Denver, found only 13% were referred to a psychiatrist, mental health worker, or alcohol rehab facility. In the Youngstown study as elsewhere, referrals to mental health programs were not widely used (Buss et al. 1995; Lowenstein et al. 1990).

VI. EVALUATING EMERGENCY DEPARTMENTS

Why, given the severity of urban violence as a problem, do emergency medicine physicians generally do so little about it? Why are the models above—substance abuse and holistic care—not pursued? Answers to the question are not surprising:

1. *Data bases for management are inefficient and inaccurate*. EDs keep poor records, so much so that it is difficult to understand the nature and extent of urban violence in emergency medicine (Winn et al. 1995; Coben et al. 1996; Lloyd and Graitcer 1989; Moss and Wade 1996; Rutledge 1995; Shepherd et al. 1993).

Managing the system with accurate data is a low priority. The system cannot improve because it lacks the where with all to direct and evaluate itself with meaningful performance data.

2. *Screening for substance abuse and psychopathology is not a priority and is considered problematic and unnecessary.* ED physicians are neither trained, encouraged nor required to screen for substance abuse nor psychopathologies (Lowenstein et al. 1990; Lewis et al. 1987; Reyna et al. 1985). Some question (1) the legality of universal screening, (2) the exorbitant cost of universal screening, and (3) whether universal screening is cost-effective. Many do not believe it necessary (Simel and Feussner 1988).
3. *Focus is not on urban violence patients.* In most EDs all patients are treated the same. Because urban violence cases are atypical compared to other emergency visits, they are not well served by standard operating procedures (Bell et al. 1994).
4. *Focus is only on treatment of injuries.* Emergency medicine physicians are not trained to treat injured patients holistically, as is the case in many family medicine programs, for instance. Rather, emergency medicine physicians are trained to treat injuries then send patients home or to other hospital departments. Until medical schools add the necessary training to their curriculum, existing patient management strategies will not change. Only 26% of trauma surgeons in a nationwide study reported involvement in programs to reduce violence through the ED (Tellez and Mackersie 1996). A study of emergency medicine physicians revealed that because of their lack of training, they were very likely to not diagnose common psychopathologies (Silverman et al. 1985).
5. *Emergency medicine is not general practice.* Most emergency medicine physicians seem to self-select into their field. They are drawn by the excitement of saving lives in crisis situations. They do not relish practicing more pedestrian forms of medicine. Most do not like treating violent patients who are notorious for being violent against hospital staff, noncompliant, abusive, and uninsured (Lowenstein et al. 1990; Cembrowicz and Shepard 1992).
6. *Health care funding does not support emergency medicine intervention.* Even if emergency physicians were to take a more holistic approach to patient management—doing comprehensive assessments, making referrals and following up, becoming involved in interdisciplinary treatment teams—health care funding sources like Medicaid, Medicare, and private insurers would not fund these additional services (Lowenstein et al. 1990).
7. *Health and human service delivery systems are not integrated.* There is little or no sharing of information on or coordination of services for urban violence victims across health care, criminal justice, substance abuse programs, social services, and education providers (Cron 1986). Confidentiality, turf battles, differences in treatment philosophy, and resources thwart sharing. Nor can any of these agencies compel urban violence victims to participate in services of other agencies. So, once victims leave EDs or hospital inpatient services, they are lost.
8. *Most emergency medicine physicians are apathetic about prospects for systemic change.* Although many EDs have concern for urban violence, many are apathetic, seeing themselves as powerless cogs in an unfriendly system. Most are reactive by training (Shepherd et al. 1995).

9. *Heroic treatment models will not solve the urban violence problem.* Many emergency medicine physicians believe that comprehensive models—substance abuse or holitic care—will not solve the problem. After treatment, patients still must return to the culture of violence where they are likely to victimize or be victimized. The ED is perceived by many to be a revolving door. Solutions for urban violence lie in much larger societal issues outside the purview of either the ED or health care system generally.

VII. WHAT NEEDS TO BE DONE

Looking at the literature on urban violence and EDs, some common themes emerge that offer possible resolutions to the problem. Presumptions are that emergency medicine physicians have (1) initial contact with victims who no other health and human service providers may see; (2) a captive audience in victims, who because of their injuries, cannot flee after emergency treatment; (3) authority to refer victims to a wide variety of health and human services; and (4) access to victims as they participate in rehab programs. In other words, emergency medicine physicians have access to victims as they pass through or could pass through a continuum of care from emergency to rehabilitation. EDs are key (Roizen 1988). How can emergency medicine physicians participate more fully at all stages of the continuum to reduce urban violence?

1. Emergency medicine physicians must assume a proactive posture in addressing urban violence, not a reactive one (Shepherd et al. 1995).
2. The concept of victim must be dropped in favor of a term that better captures the reality of victimization. Perhaps simply *violent assault patients* would help.
3. A consensus on the problem must be widely adopted. Most knowledgeable observers now opt for treating injury from urban violence as a symptom of substance abuse (McCarthy and Robinson 1985). This will be difficult to accomplish, because the traditional role of emergency medicine physicians would have to be abandoned for a totally new approach to medicine.
4. Under the substance abuse model, a comprehensive strategy must be adopted by health care institutions (Koop 1986). To begin with, data on urban violence patients must be widely and accurately gathered, extensively shared and reported, and acted upon in decision making and planning (Uva 1990; Bell et al. 1994; Coben et al. 1996; Dutton et al. 1996; Lloyd and Graitcer, 1989; Rutledge 1995; Sinauer et al. 1996). Next, ED and hospitals must formulate policies for identifying, evaluating, treating, and referring urban violence patients. A holistic model of treatment is required. In the ED, at a minimum, emergency medicine physicians must gather detailed event history, develop risk profiles, and assess total health needs (Koop 1986). Alcohol, drug, and psychiatric screens/assessments must be done (Rund et al. 1981; Reyna et al. 1985; Elsea et al. 1984; Sloan et al. 1989; Conway 1996).
5. Emergency medicine physicians must counsel patients having alcohol, drug, or psychiatric problems while in their immediate care, and they must refer patients to appropriate in-house and extramural substance abuse and mental health services, always with aggressive follow-up. This will be difficult unless health

care finance practices change to allow emergency medicine physicians to be reimbursed for services rendered.

6. EDs must work more closely with law enforcement to share data and deliver services. Because of rights to privacy and agency turf concerns, this is unlikely to occur in the system. But there are models that might prove effective, like drug courts, for example. In exchange for not serving hard time for substance abuse offenses, offenders agree contractually to participate in substance abuse programs with clearly established performance goals, which, if violated land offenders back in jail. It might be possible to develop similar agreements between "victims" and the health care and criminal justice systems.

What are the prospects that the emergency care system can be reformed as above? Not good. Its been 14 years since Surgeon General Koop called for a concerted effort to tackle the problem of urban violence, and little has changed in that interval.

ENDNOTES

1. Medical researchers typically exclude suicide, self-inflicted injury, and rape from urban violence definitions, not because they are unimportant but because they have their own classifications. Similarly, domestic violence and child abuse are often treated separately. But these definitional conventions are not uniformly adhered to, especially by nonmedical researchers. Therefore a major problem in the literature is that we are often comparing apples and oranges.
2. For some years now, *emergency department* has replaced the outdated *emergency room*.
3. Trauma centers are the Cadillacs of emergency departments. There are three categories, levels I, II, and III: a regional resource center, a community center, and a rural trauma hospital. To obtain the designation of trauma center, an institution must devote substantial resources, being prepared to treat any injury with state-of-the-art equipment and high-level skill. Trauma centers must periodically pass rigorous accreditation inspections by teams of experts. See Eastman (1992).
4. About 300 victims of urban violence, treated in a level I trauma center and admitted from 1989 to 1991 as inpatients to St. Elizabeth Hospital Medical Center in Youngstown, Ohio, were studied. The study included personal and telephone interviews as well as analyses of medical and billing records. The study was funded by St. Elizabeth's.
5. These figures probably understate involvement by this group, since they also include rape, domestic violence, child abuse, and other injuries that are less gang-related.

REFERENCES

American Medical Association (1992). *Violence*. Washington, DC: author.

Anderson J. F., Grandison T., Dyson L. (1994). Victims of random violence and the public health implication. *J Crim Justice* 24, 379–391.

Bachman R. (1992). Crime victimization in city, suburbs and rural areas. NCJ-135943. *Bull Bureau Justice Stat*, June.

Bastian L. D. (1993). Criminal victimization. *Bull Bureau Justice Stat*, October.

Bell C. C., Jenkins E. J., Kpo W., Rhodes H. (1994). Response of emergency rooms to victims of interpersonal violence. *Hosp Commun Psychiatry* 45, 142–146.

Blanken A. J. (1993). Measuring use of alcohol and other drugs. *Public Health Rep* 108, 25–30.

Borduin C. M., et al. (1995). Multisystemic treatment of serious juvenile offenders. *J Clin Psychol* 63, 569–578.

Brookoff D., Campbell E. A., Shaw L. M. (1993). The under-reporting of cocaine-related trauma. *Am J Public Health* 83, 369–374.

Brunette D., Kominsky J., Ruiz E. (1991). Correlation of emergency health care use. *Ann Emerg Med* 20, 739–742.

Budd R. D. (1989). Cocaine abuse and violent death. *Am J Drug Alcohol Abuse* 15, 375–386.

Burt C. W. (1995). *Injury Related Visits to Hospital Emergency Departments*. Washington DC: National Center for Health Statistics, Advance Data, #261, February 1.

Buss T. F., Abdu R., Walker J. R. (1995). Alcohol, drugs, and urban violence in a small city trauma center. *J Subst Abuse Treat* 12:75–83.

Buss T. F., Abdu R. (1995). Repeat victims of violence in an urban trauma center. *Violence Victims* 10, 183–194.

Cembrowicz S. P., Shepard J. P. (1992). Violence in the accident and emergency department. *Med Sci Law* 32, 118–122.

Cesare J. et al. (1990). Characteristics of blunt and personal violent injuries. *J Trauma* 30, 176–182.

Champion H. R., Mabee M. S. (1990). *An American Crisis in Trauma Care*. Washington DC: Wash Hospital Surgical Critical Care Services, 1990.

Cherpitel C. J. S. (1988a). Drinking patterns and problems associated with injury status in emergency room admissions. *Alcoholism* 12, 105–110.

Cherpitel C. J. S. (1988b). A study of alcohol use and injuries. *Ann Emerg Med* 12, 288–299.

Clancy T. V., et al. (1994). The financial impact of intentional violence on community hospitals. *J Trauma* 37, 1–4.

Clark D., McCarthy E., Robinson E. (1985). Trauma as a symptom of alcoholism. *Ann Emerg Med* 14, 274–280.

Coates W. et al. (1989). Trauma and the full moon. *Ann Emerg Med* 18, 763–765.

Coben J. H. et al. (1996). Evaluation of the emergency department logbook. *Ann Emerg Med* 28, 188–193.

Conway T. (1996). The internist's role in addressing violence. *Arch Intern Med* 156, 951–956.

Cregler L. L., Mark H. (1986) Medical complications of cocaine. *N Engl J Med* 315, 1495–1499.

Cron T. (1986). The surgeon general's workshop on violence and public health. *Public Health Rep* 101, 8–14.

Daily D. T., Teter H., Cowley R. A. (1992). Trauma center closures. *J Trauma* 33, 539–547.

DeMuth W. E. (1989). Comment. *J Trauma* 29:946–951.

DuRant R. H. (1994). Factors associated with the use of violence among urban black adolescents. *Am J Public Health* 84, 612–617.

Eastman A. B. et al. (1994). The economic status of trauma centers on the eve of health care reform. *J Trauma* 36, 835–844.

Eastman A. B. (1992). Blood in our streets. *Arch Surg* 127, 677–681.

Ellis W. W. (1997). *Interpersonal violence*. Washington, DC: Congressional Research Service, 97-96-GOV.

Elsea W. R., et al. (1984). Violence and trauma. *Urban Health* June 26–51.

Enderson B. L., Reath D. B., Meadors J., Dallas W., et al. (1990). The tertiary trauma survey. *J Trauma* 30, 666–670.

Eposito P. J., Maier R. V., Rivara F. P., Carrico C. J. (1991). Why surgeons prefer not to care for trauma patients. *Arch Surg* 126, 292.

Fleming A. W., et al. (1992). Injury and violence in Los Angeles. *Arch Surg* 127, 671–676.

Garofalo J. (1987). Reassessing the lifestyle model. In M. R. Gottfredson (ed), *Positive Criminology*. Newbury Park, CA: Sage, 1987.

General Accounting Office (1991). *Urban Violence*. Washington, DC: GAO.

Gentilello L. M., Duggan P., Drummond D., et al. (1993). Acute ethanol intoxication increases the risk of infection following penetrating abdominal trauma. *J Trauma* 34, 669–675.

Gentilello L. M., et al. (1988). Major injury as a unique opportunity to initiate treatment in the alcoholic. *Am J Surg* 156, 558–561.

Goins W. A., Thompson J., Simpkins C. (1992). Recurrent intentional injury. *J Natl Med Assoc* 84, 431–435.

Greenberg, M., Schneider D. (1992). Blue Thursday? *Public Health Rep* 107, 264–268.

Greenberg M., Naus J., Schneider D., Wartenberg D. (1991). Temporal clustering of homicide. *Ethnicity Dis* 1, 342–350.

Guyer B. et al. (1990). Injury surveillance. *J Trauma* 30, 470–473.

Haberman P. W., Natarajan G. (1986). Trends in alcoholism & narcotics abuse from medical examiner data. *J Studies Alcohol* 47, 316–317.

Herve C., Gaillard M., Roujas F. (1986). Alcoholism in polytrauma. *J Trauma* 26, 113–1126.

Holt S. et al. (1980). Alcohol and the emergency service patient. *BMJ* 281, 638–640.

Jensen G. F., Brownfield D. (1986). Gender, lifestyle, and victimization. *Violence Victims* 1, 85–99.

Jurkovich G. J., Rivera F. P., Gurney J. G., Seguin D., et al. (1992). Effects of alcohol intoxication on the initial assessment of trauma patients. *Ann Emerg Med* 21, 704–708.

Kellermann A. L. et al. (1996). Injuries due to firearms in three cities. *N Engl J Med* 335, 1438–1444.

Kellermann A. L. (1984). Firearm-related violence. *Am J Public Health* 84, 541–542.

Kelley B. T., Huizinga D., Thornberry T. P., Loeber R. (1997). *Epidemiology of Serious Violence*. Juvenile Justice Bulletin, Office of Juvenile Justice and Delinquency Programs, June.

Kingma J. (1994). Site of accidents for victims of assault. *Psych Rep* 75, 1361–1362.

Kizer K. W. et al. (1995). Hospital charges, costs, and income. *JAMA* 273, 1768–1773.

Klein S. R. et al. (1991). Socioeconomic impact of assault injuries. *Am Surg* 57, 793–797.

Koop, C. E. (1986). The Leesburg Amendment. *Public Health Rep* 101, 1.

Koop C. E., Lundberg G. D. (1992). Violence in America: A public health emergency. *JAMA* 267, 124–125.

Kuhlhorn E. (1993). Victims and offenders of criminal violence. *J Q Criminol* 6, 51–59.

Lake E. S. (1993). An exploration of the violent victim experiences of female offenders. *Violence Victims* 8, 41–51.

Lauritsen J. L., Sampson R. J., Laub J. H. (1991). The link between offending and victimization among adolescents. *Criminology* 29, 265–291.

Legorreta A. P. et al. The high cost of trauma care. *J Assoc Acad Minn Phys* 4, 52–55.

Lewis D. C., Niven R. G., Czechowicz D. (1987). A review of medical education in alcohol and other drug abuse. *JAMA* 257, 2945–2948.

Lindenbaum G. A., Carroll S. F., Daskal I, Kapusnick R. (1989). Patterns of alcohol and drug abuse in an urban trauma center. *J Trauma* 29, 1654–1658.

Lipman A. G. (1980). Keeping up to date on drug-alcohol interactions. *Mod Med* 20, 129–130.

Litacker D. (1996). Preventing recurring injuries from violence. *Am J Public Health* 86, 1633–1636.

Lloyd L. E., Graitcer P. L. (1989). The potential for using a trauma registry for injury surveillance. *Am J Prev Med* 5, 34–37.

Lowenstein S. R., Weissberg M. P., Terry D. (1990). Alcohol intoxication, injuries, and dangerous behaviors. *J Trauma* 30, 1252–1258.

Luna G. K. et al. (1988). The medical and social impact of nonaccidental injury. *Arch Surg* 123, 825–827.

Mackersie R. C. et al. (1995). High-risk behavior. *Arch Surg* 130, 844–849.

McNagny S. E., Parker R. M. (1992). High prevalence of recent cocaine use. *JAMA* 267, 1106–1108.

Meehan P. J., O'Carroll P. W. (1992). Gangs, drugs and homicide in Los Angeles. *Am J Dis Child* 146, 683–693.

Mercy J. A., O'Carroll P. W. (1988). New directions in violence prediction. *Violence Victims* 3, 285–301.

Mondragon D. (1992). Hospital costs of societal violence. *Med Care* 30, 453–470.

Morrissey M. C., Byrd R. C., Deitch E. A. (1991). The incidence of recurrent penetrating trauma in an urban trauma center. *J Trauma* 31, 1536–1538.

Nelson C. R., Stussman B. J. (1994). *Alcohol and Drug Related Visits to Hospital Emergency Departments*. National Center for Health Statistics, Advance Data, #251, August 10.

Organ C. H. (1993). Trauma. *Arch Surg* 127, 651.

Payne J. E. et al. (1993). Outcome of treatment of 686 gunshot wounds. *J Trauma* 34, 276–281.

Pernanen K., Heath D. B. (1991). *Alcohol in Human Violence*. New York: Guilford.

Ponzer S., Bergman B., Brismar B. (1995). Sociodemographic characteristics and criminality in victims of firearm injuries. *J Trauma* 38, 845–850.

Ponzer S. B., Bergman B., Brismar B. (1996). Morbidity and injury recurrence in victims of firearm injuries. *Public Health* 110, 42–46.

Rapaport A., Feliciano D. V., Mattox K. L. (1980). An epidemiologic profile of urban trauma in America. *Texas Med* 8, 44–50.

Reiss A. J., Roth J. A. (eds) (1993). *Understanding and Preventing Violence*. Washington, DC: National Academy Press.

Reyna T. M., Hollis W. H., Hulsebus R. C. (1985). Alcohol-related trauma. *Ann Surg* 201, 194–197.

Rice D. P., Mackersie E. J. (1989). *Cost of Injury*. San Francisco: University of California.

Rich J. A., Singer D. E. (1991). Cocaine-related symptoms in an urban ED. *Ann Emerg Med* 20, 616–621.

Rivara F., Mueller B. A., Fligner C., et al. (1989). Drug use in trauma victims. *J Trauma* 29, 462–470.

Rivara F. P. et al. (1995). Victim as offender in youth violence. *Ann Emerg Med* 26, 609–614.

Roizen J. (1988). Alcohol and trauma. *Ann Emerg Med* 12, 21–66.

Rund D. A., Summers W. K., Levin M. (1981). Alcohol use and psychiatric illness in emergency patients. *JAMA* 260, 1240–1241.

Rutledge R. (1995). The goals, development, and use of trauma registries. *Surg Clin North Am* 75, 305–326.

Ryan M. et al. (1993). Medical consequences of gang-related shootings. *Am Surg* 59, 831–833.

Sampson R. J., Lauritsen J. (1990). Deviant lifestyle, proximity to crime and offender-victim link. *J Res Crime Delinq* 27, 110–139.

Shepherd J. et al. (1995). Should doctors be more proactive as advocates for victims of violence. *BMJ* J 311, 1617–1621.

Shepherd J. et al. (1993). Trends in urban violence. *J R Soc Med* 86, 87–88.

Silvermann J. J., Peed S. F., Goldberg S., Hammer R. M., Stockman S. J. (1985). Surgical staff recognition of psychopathology in trauma patients. *J Trauma* 25, 544–546.

Simel D., Feussner J. (1988). Blood alcohol measurements in the emergency department. *Am J Public Health* 78, 1478–1479.

Sinauer N., Annest J. L., Mercy J. A. (1996). Unintentional, nonfatal firearm-related injuries. *JAMA* 275, 1740–1743.

Singer S. (1986). Victims of serious violence and their criminal behavior: sub-culture theory and beyond. *Violence Victims* 1, 61–70.

Silverman J. J., Peed S. F., Goldberg S., et al. (1985). Surgical staff recognition of psychopathology in trauma patients. *J Trauma* 25, 544–546.

Simel D. L., Feussner, J. R. (1988). Blood alcohol measurements in the emergency department. *Am J Public Health* 78, 1478–1479.

Sims D. W., Bivins B. A., Obeid F. N., et al. (1989). Urban trauma: a chronic recurrent disease. *J Trauma* 29, 940–946.

Sloan E. P., Zalenski R. J., Smith R. F., et al. (1989). Toxicology screening and urban trauma patients. *J Trauma* 29, 1647–1653.

Smeltzer S. C., Redeker N. (1995). A framework of trauma and trauma recidivism. *J Trauma Nurs* 2, 93–99.

Smith R. S., Fry W. R., Morabito D. J., Organ C. H. (1992). Recidivism in an urban trauma center. *Arch Surg* 127, 668–670.

Soderstrom C. A. (1996). Substance abuse common among seriously injured trauma center patients. *JAMA* 275, 1744–1750.

Tellez M. L., Mackersie R. C. (1996). Violence prevention involvement among trauma surgeons. *J Trauma* 40, 602–606.

Thal E., Bost R. O., Anderson R. J. (1985). Effects of alcohol and other drugs on traumatized patients. *Arch Surg* 120:708–712.

Trunkey D. D. (1990). What's wrong with trauma care? *Bull Am Coll Surg* 75, 10.

Thum D., Wechsler H., Demone H. (1973). Alcohol levels of emergency service patients. *Criminology* 10, 487–497.

Uva, Jane L. (1990). Urban violence: a health care issue. *JAMA* 253:138–139.

Widom C. S. (1992). *The Cycle of Violence: Research in Brief.* Washington, DC: National Institute of Justice.

Winn D. G., Agran P. F., Anderson C. L. (1995). Sensitivity of hospital E-coded data. *Public Health Rep* 110, 277–281.

Wintemute G. J., Wright W. (1992). Initial and subsequent hospital costs of firearm injuries. *J Trauma* 33, 556–560.

19

A New Use for an Old Model

Continuity of Government as a Framework for Local Emergency Managers

Hugh W. Stephens College of Social Sciences, University of Houston, Houston, Texas

George O. Grant Office of Emergency Management, The City of Houston, Houston, Texas

I. INTRODUCTION

One of the major problems presently confronting local emergency managers (coordinators) is the difficulty of placing their duties in the context of local government and devising integrated programs to fulfill them. This is a product of a paucity of thought and action in emergency preparedness before the early 1980s and a proliferation of organizing concepts and programs since.

The scope of the field and our ability to manage serious emergencies has improved significantly over the past 25 years. Until the early 1980s, concern about disasters was confined to civil defense against nuclear attack. The preeminent legislation of the Cold War period, the Civil Defense Act of 1950, focused upon the threat of Soviet nuclear attack and ignored all-hazards planning. Federal funding was restricted to medical self-help, shelter management, radiological protection, and fallout shelter programs. Local governments interested in preparing for serious but less formidable natural and technological emergencies could not obtain federal or state program support. Indeed, substantial change in the way this country prepares for emergencies did not begin until 1979, when President Carter issued an executive order establishing the Federal Emergency Management Agency. Local emergency managers welcomed this shift, but ensuing concepts and programs spawned policy and program guidance issues that needed resolution. Until the early 1980s, the concept of Continuity of Government (COG) was virtually the only source of policy and program guidance, even though it was directed to maintaining the constitutional order in event of nuclear attack. In order to justify their positions, local coordinators of necessity became active participants as first responders rather than planners when emergencies occurred. COG provided some guidance, but it could not help set the role of emergency management as an element of local government or provide guidance in formulating programs.

Despite many valuable intellectual and programmatic advances in the field since 1979, the authors believe that emergency managers (coordinators) still confront this difficulty. Paradoxically, this now derives from a proliferation of concepts during the past 25 years together with an absence of a core organizing framework. We will demonstrate that, reinterpreted in an all-hazards context, COG can help coordinators cut through much of the existing confusion. It is a logical cornerstone of local emergency management because it assumes that government plays the key role in maintaining community viability during disaster. Consisting of seven major elements or activities, COG is comprehensible to coordinators and local officials, who must provide overall direction and support.

The essence of the problem is that new concepts and elaboration of old ones leave coordinators uncertain as to the precise nature of their responsibilities and how to fulfill them. While elaboration lends realism and sophistication to emergency management, the proliferation of detail tends to obscure essential relationships within and between organizations at all levels of government. Indeed, the authors have encountered growing evidence that, confronted by a welter of detail, some coordinators encounter difficulty in formulating comprehensive, integrated plans appropriate to the complexity of serious emergencies. This is also true of local government officials who must set policy goals for coordinators in their jurisdiction and whose support is critical for successful implementation. Although federal programs are outside the scope of this essay, by way of illustration it is worth noting that many of the difficulties the Federal Emergency Management Agency (FEMA) encountered in responding to Hurricane Andrew originated from ambiguous procedures within the National Response Plan. At issue were questions about direction and management of outside resources, particularly after the hurricane had obliterated local government infrastructure.

The COG model should alleviate these difficulties because it provides a core framework, improves conceptual clarity, and offers comprehensible guidelines for local disaster policy and programs. Shifted from the nuclear war to Comprehensive Emergency Management (CEM) and adapted to local government, the elements of the model suggest several significant questions political leaders and coordinators should consider in organizing or evaluating their jurisdiction's emergency plans. These are:

Who is authorized to take charge of the jurisdiction's response effort if the mayor or city manager is killed, seriously injured, or absent in during an emergency requiring a local disaster declaration?

What special powers can these officials exercise in an emergency?

Are all officials aware of the place from which emergency response and recovery efforts will be directed and the location of the alternate site?

Are vital community records secure and are those resources, personnel, and facilities immediately available which are required to initiate response and recovery?

COG should also alleviate two underlying problems that constantly beset coordinators. First, it provides a framework capable of demonstrating the unique and fundamental demands of emergency response to mayors, city managers, and other decision makers. Second, it should facilitate identification of inconsistent perceptions and relationships among departmental representatives at the Emergency Operations Center (EOC) and between the EOC and incident commanders in the field, which often arise during a disaster.

In order to demonstrate these possibilities, we first identify complications embodied in two prevalent models—the Integrated Emergency Management System (IEMS), appropriate to EOC operations, and the Incident Command System (ICS), designed for field operations. Next, we note difficulties these models pose in delineating relationships between local political and administrative policy makers and their emergency management coordinators. Finally, we suggest how a modified COG provides coordinators with a useful way of increasing mutual understanding among departmental representatives at the Emergency Operations Center (EOC) and between the EOC and incident commanders at the scene of emergencies. The word *suggest* is used advisedly, since this is not a complete blueprint but a preliminary effort designed to stimulate further thought and refinement.

II. THEORETICAL DEVELOPMENTS AND THEIR COMPLICATIONS

Emergency management is shedding elements derived from its long-held emphasis upon civil defense. Begun in 1950, the overriding concern of this program was ensuring the survival of legitimate government in the United States in event of Soviet nuclear attack and providing protection for its citizens. Natural disasters did receive some attention, but mainly in the form of congressional legislation for relief on a case-by-case basis. While state and local governments evolved generic contingency plans for hurricanes, earthquakes, tornadoes, and floods, these were usually confined to public safety and relief. The creation of FEMA in 1979 and formulation of Comprehensive Emergency Management (CEM) as a general objective in 1981 marked the beginning of a reorientation in government concerns about emergencies. This extended the scope of consideration to all types of natural and industrial disasters and all phases of the disaster cycle, not just relief. It is no less significant that these innovations have also pervaded state and local emergency policy because of FEMA's ability to exert its influence through financial assistance and training programs.

In 1983, FEMA formulated the Integrated Emergency Management System (IEMS) concept as an implementation strategy for CEM. With greater emphasis upon hazard analysis and capability assessment, IEMS shifted emergency management into a more active mode. The original model specified six major generic functions that local governments must perform to some degree in any emergency (McLouglhlin 1985: 168–171). These are mitigation, hazard analysis, capability assessment, planning, capability maintenance, response, and recovery.

Preparedness for nuclear attack was speculative and never put to the test, but this is not the case for natural and industrial disasters. These not only happen but do so relatively often, so the shift in orientation raises the challenge of how to translate theory into practice. To date, the results have not been at all promising, mainly because of the complexity of disaster preparedness and response. For instance, the emergency plans of jurisdictions using IEMS transmute its 6 functions into at least 15—and often more—specific functions, each of which is covered in a separate annex.

Warning, communications, evacuation, law enforcement, health and medical, damage assessment, hazardous materials response, transportation, and EOC direction are structured along departmental or agency lines for the most part. The "integrated" aspect of IEMS is more than a recognition that these functions and the activities they engender are interrelated; it also implies that success requires cooperation and coordinated activity among agencies within jurisdictions and between governmental entities. The other major innovation in the field is ICS. Originally formulated by the U.S. Forest Service, ICS has been adopted as the standard response model by the National Fire Academy and is extensively used among local fire services. It is also mandated by the Environmental Protection

Administration and the Occupational Safety and Health Administration (OSHA) for all organizations handling hazardous materials.

Whereas IEMS is appropriate for EOC operations and coordinators, as its name implies, ICS is a management system designed to integrate response activities of several agencies at the scene of a particular emergency, ICS divides the spectrum of on-scene activities into five functions: command, operations, logistics, planning, and finance, which are implemented as the situation requires. More narrow in scope than IEMS, the five ICS functions nevertheless can elaborate to as many as 36 "positions." Success requires advanced planning and testing to attain common terminology, modular organization, integrated communications, consolidated action plans, and unified command. When these are in place, component organizations, such as fire service, police, or public works, can coalesce at one command post and operate within the same organizational framework while retaining their integrity with respect to fiscal matters, agency roles, and organizational procedures. (Auf der Heide 1989:157) Given the intricacies of this model and its emphasis upon rapid, focused response—usually under fire or police direction—establishing close cooperation with those in the EOC who have different responsibilities has proved difficult.

III. PROBLEMS FOR COORDINATORS

The variable nature of emergencies as well as the complexity of the models has complicated the task of translating theory into reality and developing readily understandable programs. Coordinators encounter problems communicating their goals and needs to the major groups with whom they must work. From the coordinator's perspective, five major relationships are at issue (Waugh 1993:19–22):

1. With local government executives, be they county judges, mayors, or city managers and their councils. The fact of the matter is that priorities of local executives are often different and incompatible with the requirements of successful emergency management. They are unlikely to grasp its essentials easily. A major conclusion of the General Accounting Office study of Hurricane Hugo and the Loma Prieta earthquake was that state and local elected and appointed officials in the affected areas often lacked the knowledge and skills required for disaster response and recovery. (Weseman and Moore 1993:2) The coordinator must bridge these differences because leadership sets policy and authorizes programs that determine capabilities.
2. With heads of departments or agencies having major emergency response or recovery duties, such as Fire, Police, Public Works, and Health. Differing orientations can impede necessary cooperation and create severe strains under the stress of a prolonged emergency.
3. With departmental or agency representatives assigned to the EOC who do not grasp IEMS as an operational framework and do not understand the responsibilities either of the coordinator or representatives from other departments of the local government.
4. With administrative and operational relationships to the Incident Commander(s) and the team in the field because of misperceptions and hampered by conflicting priorities;

5. With communications and requirements originating from incident commanders or teams at the scene of emergencies who operate in the context of ICS to coordinators and others at the EOC whose concerns derive from IEMS. This is the obverse of (4).

Problem 1 derives from the difficulty of explaining the intricacies of disaster management to generalists despite the potentially vital nature of the subject to the entire jurisdiction. Problems 2 and 3 occur in all sorts of organizations, not just those concerned with managing disasters. Mutual ignorance and indifference are likely to rise whenever specialists are thrown together to accomplish a larger purpose. Their perceptions and the management styles of departments or agencies with emergency duties may not mesh well with each other or with those of a generalist like a coordinator, who has overall responsibility. The problems embodied in points 4 and 5 also derive from differences in magnitude since the focus of IEMS is more general than that of ICS. IEMS addresses mobilization of resources and support whereas ICS is focused upon response to a specific situation. For example, phrases such as ''basic plan of action'' and ''overall development of staff and equipment'' characterize EOC operations, while ''incident'' and ''span of control'' are in the vocabulary of ICS. IEMS is concerned with''disaster analysis,'' ICS with ''damage assessment.'' Be they overt or subtle, conflicts arise from the management mentality of ''handling'' emergencies at the EOC verses the operational mentality of the incident command team at the scene handling ''its'' emergency. Everyone seemingly agrees that responsibility should shift from ICS to EOC when an incident escalates into a major emergency and the EOC is activated, but determining the appropriate point amidst and the confusion of the moment is not easy.

IV. ADAPTING CONTINUITY OF GOVERNMENT

Let us now consider an adaptation of the COG designed to alleviate these sorts of difficulties. Recall that it is the complexity of emergencies that limits the utility of IEMS and ICS as readily comprehensible guides. IEMS comprises 6 basic functions and at least 15 particular activities performed by at least a dozen identifiable agencies. ICS is somewhat less complicated, consisting of 5 functions, but potentially expandable to a maximum of 36 positions. For both planning and response, elaboration increases the potential for confusion about relationships and tasks between the numerous stakeholders involved. Local political and administrative leaders find it difficult to formulate clear-cut emergency policy and programs and coordinators are hard put to provide guidance for departmental representatives at the EOC and with responders at the scene of a disaster. Perhaps this was why FEMA's committee on IEMS saw fit to form an ICS/EOC Interface Curriculum Advisory Committee in 1991 to investigate this relationship.

Given this contradiction between comprehensives and practicality, what is to be done? Here, we turn to a device called ''strategic simplification.'' It designates a process by which theories, models, or even operating systems are adapted to growing complexity through identification of critical linkages between ideas or essential components of systems. Once essential relationships are identified, appropriate elaborations can be added to fit particular situations without losing overall coherence. For instance, physics became more readily comprehensible when older, cumbersome models of the universe set forth by Ptolemy and Copernicus were discarded for the general formulations of Newton and

Einstein. Here, in a much more modest endeavor, we seek to ''cut through'' the complications of IEMS and ICS by proposing a framework designed to

Represent the essence of preparedness planning for major emergencies at all governmental levels as well as between levels
Be internally consistent and readily-understandable to coordinators and others who will participate in overall management of emergencies
Build on existing wisdom which is suitable for elaboration and adaptation to all types of emergencies and circumstances

For those who wish to make a detailed comparison, the original seven preparedness and planning actions of COG are set forth in Executive Orders 11490 (1969) and 12656 (1988). These are also elaborated in FEMA manual CPG 1–10, *Guide for the Development of a State and Local Continuity of Government Capability*. They are as follows:

1. Line of succession for key governmental personnel
2. Predelegation of authority
3. Emergency action plans
4. Emergency operations center (EOC)
5. Alternate operating center
6. Protecting government personnel, resources, and facilities
7. Safeguarding vital records

Some will find the choice of COG ironic, since it served as the rationale for civil defense against nuclear attack. Our modifications represents a shift not in subject matter but in the scale of concerns and emphasis—from concern about governmental institutions to ensure the survival of the legitimate political order to maintaining governmental leadership and services of local authority. COG is particularly appropriate for large-scale events like Hurricane Andrew or the Midwest floods of 1993, which severely strain the viability of communities and degrade the ability of local governments to maintain order and initiate recovery. Although the safety and welfare of the civil population is the ultimate concern, we wish to emphasize that COG is focused upon sustaining government capabilities. Even in nonnuclear disasters, only government has the inherent power to mobilize and direct the full range of community effort and assistance.

V. THE MODIFIED COG FRAMEWORK

A. Designate Line of Succession for Key Governmental Positions

While it is unlikely that civil order at the state level will be eliminated during the course of a catastrophic disaster, extensive casualties among local officials could jeopardize coordinated action during the critical early stage of a disaster. This requires designation of a line of succession in advance and provision for an interim authority in a ''worst case'' scenario where virtually all officials are killed or disabled. If not already covered by state law, a common standard and procedure should be established for such contingencies. Since county and municipal chief executives are often absent from their jurisdictions in the line of duty, standing operating procedures (SOPS) should require that key officials keep their coordinator informed of their location. The reciprocal is that coordinators should begin monitoring the location of key officials as soon as a credible threat develops. These considerations extend to department heads as well as personnel designated for service at the EOC. A corollary of this is that successor officials who may not have had a role in formulating emergency management programs should possess at least a rudimentary understanding of what is involved.

B. Ensure That Legal Provisions Exist for Full Exercise of Emergency Powers

In the absence of a nuclear attack threat, disruption of constitutional order will not be a concern. At issue are standing procedures and special ordinances which permit local officials to exercise powers necessary to maintain order and provide essential services amidst the confusion and stress of a catastrophic disaster. We refer particularly to the ''evaluation criteria'' set forth in CPG 1–10 apply, especially laws and ordinances that define authority of senior officials and chiefs of emergency services. More particular concerns are also pertinent, such as SOPs for emergency organizations, impact of state declarations of local emergency, food distribution rules, and identification of essential governmental functions which must continue without interruption. Local executives and their coordinators must understand that some of these functions—controls on population movements, use of private property, and curfew enforcement among them—could impinge upon response operations at the scene of an emergency. Special efforts are necessary to anticipate potential conflicts between coordinators and incident commanders arising from their respective responsibilities. One item not covered in CPG 1–10 should requires careful specification in local emergency plans—authority to make or release statements to the mass media about damage, casualties, and governmental actions.

C. Specify Essential Emergency Powers for Key Officials

This element addresses basic actions that officials should take or at least consider as a disaster evolves. These actions are usually embodied in checklists or SOPs designating their duties in an emergency, including assigned locations. We confine our observations to three points on this matter. First, procedural matters illustrate the difference between the nuclear scenario of the ''old'' COG and the all-hazards orientation of the modified COG. That is, nonnuclear emergencies can arise virtually anywhere and at any time, including those which have modest beginnings as fires or rainstorms. Hence, plans should embody the fact that transmitting alerts or calls for assistance ''up the line'' from police or firefighters at the scene of an emergency to other department or agency heads or the coordinator is no less important than getting directives from senior officials ''down the line'' to incident commanders. Second, the warning in CPG 1–10 about the importance of integrating emergency notification procedures into existing SOPs of departments is well taken. This applies especially to those who will send representatives to the EOC when it is activated. Mutual adjustments may ease the potential for conflict between department personnel and coordinators, but clearly this is often a source of conflict. The third point is that notification procedures will inevitably cause difficulties among the players at the EOC and between the EOC and incident commanders. When a judgment is made that an emergency is so serious that the EOC must be activated and perhaps a disaster declaration issued, alterations occur in the duties and behavior of officials that are no less profound than the differences in priorities of IEMS and ICS.

D. Set Emergency Operations Center Requirements

An absence of the nuclear threat diminishes self-sufficiency and security requirements for EOCs which were so important a part of CPG 1–10. But EOCs remain the "nerve centers," the primary source of direction and control for all government emergency activities in the revised COG. While this changes the criteria somewhat, selecting a location and incorporating construction standards that minimize vulnerability to physical damage and disruption remain important. What does not change at all is the necessity of having physical facilities, equipment, and organizational arrangements in the EOC which can fulfill the extensive demands of IEMS. The essence of viable EOC operations are reliable communications—with political leaders, with response agencies, with the general public, and with outside sources of assistance—and a continual ability to collect and assess information about damage and secondary hazards. Surely, physical interruption of communications and consequent misunderstandings about damage of secondary hazards provides the greatest opportunity for misunderstandings and conflicts between coordinators and incident commanders. Moreover, preparations, including staffing, must be sufficient to allow the EOC to activate on relatively short notice in case an incident suddenly escalates into a major emergency.

E. Set Plans for an Alternate Emergency Operations Center

Since the absence of the nuclear threat reduces security and self-sufficiency requirements for EOCS, the question of the possible shut-down of the primary center becomes less important. Nevertheless, EOCs will not be invulnerable: physical access may be cut off for a period of time, backup power sources may fail, or storms or floods may seriously damage facilities. The Alternate EOC (AEOC) should have enough space, equipment, and accessibility to carry on essential communications and control activities. The emergency plan should clearly identify this facility and those departments of local government involved should draft detailed relocation arrangements.

F. Protect Vital Records

Modern society and its governments cannot operate without comprehensive, detailed demographic, legal, property, and financial data. Of the seven basic functions of COG, records preservation is important to response and is fundamental to recovery. Again, even without the extensive devastation of a nuclear attack, hurricanes, floods, and earthquakes are capable of wiping out vital local government archives, whether in printed form, on microfilm, or in computer files. For instance, local administration and justice in Hillsboro, Texas, were disrupted for a considerable period of time when the County Court House burned down and vital records were destroyed. Coordinators will certainly want to make special arrangements to store and retrieve information directly pertinent to EOC operations as well as records needed by police, fire, health, public works, and other departments. And, although coordinators are unlikely to be assigned primary responsibility for records protection in their jurisdiction, it is in their interest to ensure that records which are "vital" have been explicitly identified, stored in secure facilities, and that a system exists which continually copies these and sends them to a remote site, such as the state archives.

G. Sustain Essential Governmental Resources, Facilities, and Personnel

CPG 1–10 emphasized stockpiling and physical dispersal of officials, facilities, equipment and supplies. While still useful, for catastrophic disasters, we believe the emphasis should be shifted toward identifying and monitoring stocks of equipment and expendable supplies for response and the early phases of recovery. Stockpiling is less important and might well be limited to those items which cannot be readily obtained from either public or private sources in the locality. These concerns are already present in emergency plans, but our intent is to get local authorities and their coordinators to look at the problem in its entirety and ensure they have critical resources. The resource inventory will vary according to the nature of existing hazards and other factors particular to any given jurisdiction. Equipment requirements will probably extend to all modes of transportation, debris removal and heavy rescue, as well as chemical analysis and radiological monitoring devices. Insofar as personnel matters are concerned, since duties of key officials are covered under Section V.C above, this reminds us to consider likely needs for additional personnel and their employment as emergency operations expand, particularly during recovery. These would include organized and unorganized volunteers, federal and state officials, National Guard contingents, and relief officials from other jurisdictions. Another concern are facilities, including fire and police communications centers, utility and transport nodes, and potential sites for shelters and disaster assistance centers.

Experienced coordinators will quickly recognize that of the seven factors, this one will have the most immediate and profound effect upon relations between coordinators and incident commanders. More than adequate amounts are at issue here: priorities of incident commanders are set by the particular crisis they confront, whereas the coordinator must consider the needs of the entire community over a longer period of time. If conflicts are to be kept to a minimum, ''real-time'' information is needed about how key personnel are being employed, availability of particular equipment items and supplies in high demand, and the condition and use of particular facilities.

VI. SUMMARY AND CONCLUSION

Recall that we began with the assertion that elaboration of emergency management models in the interests of greater realism and comprehensiveness have had a paradoxical effect. That is, their complexity has tended to confuse local political leaders and emergency management coordinators about their fundamental responsibilities. A major part of confusion and uncertain derives from differences in the scope of IEMS and ICS, even though the former is more general and the latter is focused upon response requirements of particular incidents. As a result, coordinators are confronted with several difficulties: local political and administrative leaders who do not understand the nature of their responsibilities during serious emergencies; heads of agencies or departments having major emergency responsibilities who adhere to their own priorities; departmental representatives assigned to the EOC who are neither cognizant of IEMS as the framework of operations nor of the coordinator's responsibilities; administrative and operational relationships with incident commanders in the field because of misperceptions and conflicting priorities; the obverse of Section V.D, wherein communications and requirements originating from incident commanders at the scene of emergencies operating in the context of ICS to often conflict with the perception of coordinators and others at the EOC whose concerns derive from the wider concerns of IEMS.

We believe that the COG model provides a way of ''strategically simplifying'' and sorting out the essence of these complex relationships. Substantively speaking, COG itself is significant because even as the scenario shifts from the nuclear war to all hazards, government remains the focal point of efforts to save lives and prosperity and retain social cohesion during disaster. We believe this perspective should alleviate those difficulties described above because it is both comprehensible to those unfamiliar with emergency management and useful as a conceptual base from which to elaborate the mutual responsibilities of major governmental stakeholders. We wish to emphasize that COG is not a blueprint for organization and action: emergency plans and standing operating procedures must still be formulated and tested. And, while COG has little bearing upon even more fundamental circumstances such as basic matters as minimalist government and insufficient public awareness, it should alleviate one of the major weaknesses in emergency management noted several years ago by Charles E. Fritz—better integration of its functions into the daily routine of government (1992).

REFERENCES

Auf der Heide, Erik (1989). *Disaster Response: Principles of Preparation and Coordination*. St. Louis: C. V. Mosby Company.

Fritz, Charles E. (1992). Review of T. Drabek and G. Hoetmer, (eds.), *Emergency Management: Principles and Practice for Local Government. International Journal of Mass Emergencies and Disasters* 10, 219–224.

McLoughlin, David (1985). A framework for emergency management. *Public Administration Review* 45, 165–172.

U.S., Federal Emergency Management Agency (1987). *Guide for the Development of a State and Local Continuity of Government Capability*. CPG 1–10 July 10.

Waugh, W. (1993). Coordination or control: organizational design and the emergency management function. *Disaster Prevention and Management* 2, 17–21.

Weseman, M., Moore, A. (1993). The role of elected/appointed officials in disaster response: managing your worst nightmare. Paper presented at the ASPA/CASU 54th National Training Conference, July 17–21, San Francisco, California.

20

What Disaster Response Management Can Learn from Chaos Theory

Gustav A. Koehler California Research Bureau and Time Structures, Sacramento, California

Guenther G. Kress Department of Public Administration, California State University, San Bernardino, California

Randi L. Miller Department of Sociology, California State University, San Bernardino, California

I. DISASTER CHARACTERISTICS THAT DISORDER ORGANIZATIONS

Major disasters have a low probability of occurring, but when they do, they can have devastating consequences. Designing response structures for such events is a difficult task, particularly when public resources are limited. Typically, the effort to organize a disaster response structure involving multiple public, private, and nonprofit agencies is hampered by a number of unpredictable factors. One or more of the following factors may apply in an emergency response situation.

The type of disaster that could occur at any time is unpredictable. Clearly, disasters such as earthquakes and hazardous materials releases are inherently unpredictable. And while hurricanes, tornadoes, civil disturbances, and floods are somewhat more predictable, the exact time when, for example, casualties will occur or when medical transport is needed remains unknown.

Where a disaster will occur is often unpredictable. The exact location of a disaster cannot be predicted and the way it will geographically progress is unknown in advance. For example, the path of a tornado or of a civil disturbance cannot be precisely predicted, causing considerable variation in the number and severity of injuries.

How a disaster will unfold in geographic space over time is often unknown. The rate at which disaster extends itself geographically over time can effect the generation of injuries and deaths.

The type and distribution of injuries in space and time are often unknown. Particular types of disasters have specific injury profiles. For example, an earthquake produces lacerations and crush injuries. A hazardous materials incident can produce inhalation injuries.

But the lack of knowledge of the space-time distribution of where the disaster occurred and the rate at which it is proceeding makes it difficult to predict the profile of injuries particularly if, for example, an earthquake and a hazardous materials release occur simultaneously.

Which elements of the emergency response system will be damaged, how they will be damaged, and the resulting delay in their response are unpredictable. For example, medical resources such as personnel, supplies, ambulances, hospital beds, and communication links can be overwhelmed, damaged, or distorted. Their location, distribution of response units, and availability is often not congruent with the type, volume, and distribution of injuries. Furthermore, the initial starting conditions of any one agency affect the way its own structure emerges and how it relates to other agencies.

Self-organizing efforts by citizens, responders in the field, and other emergency organizations at the state, federal, nonprofit and private sector levels may create unexpected communications paths and response structures. Following a disaster, people in the area organize themselves to rescue neighbors and perform other immediate disaster response activities. Responders, hospital staff, fire personnel, and others will be repairing their disrupted and damaged systems and creating new and often unplanned organizations for delivering disaster relief services. Volunteer organizations and other private response groups may suddenly appear and demand that their needs be immediately met.

Information about the entire emergent disaster response structure or even parts of the response (including how it extends across the community, city, and operational area, as well as the status and organization of the regional, state, and federal responses) is incomplete. A disaster response structure is ''emergent'' because it did not fully exist prior to the disaster. The response involves the birth of new units or the restructuring of old ones at the work group, organizational, interorganizational, community, or regional level that are more or less adaptive to a particular circumstance within the disaster (Comfort 1994; Drabek 1987; Koehler 1995). It is difficult to identify what and where the new structures are or how old ones have changed as well as to identify the form of intergroup and interagency connections.

Preexisting strains between organizations may be exacerbated. Preexisting strains between organizations due to competition, organizational placement, routine underfunding and understaffing of disaster preparedness, and other factors may make interorganizational coordination more difficult (Drabek 1989).

Because of initial starting conditions and varying resource demands, critical activity rates within and between organizations drive each other and the overall response in unpredictable and complex ways. A disaster response depends on tight and effective coordination between many different public and private organizations. For example, citizen self-organizing rescue efforts, ambulance companies, law enforcement, hospitals, pharmaceutical supply houses, surface and air transport, military forces, and federal, state, and local government agencies may be included in any disaster response. The rate of victim rescue affects how quickly transport vehicles must be identified and dispatched, which, in turn, affects how many injured people are waiting for care in hospital emergency departments, emergency department staffing, and so on (Koehler 1992). These factors are driven by the availability of communications, health care personnel and supplies, as well as by whether transport can move necessary resources to where they are needed.

The various ways in which a disaster disrupts both individual organizations and collective efforts to develop a disaster response system points to several critical issues in disaster and emergency management.

1. The best efforts of disaster managers to develop a disaster response system may achieve relatively poor results because:
   a. The problems they face at the onset of the disaster are often ambiguous, unclear, and shifting.
   b. Information is unavailable, unreliable, problematic, and subject to multiple, competing interpretations.
   c. Resources are limited, not immediately available, and are being used up at unknown rates.
   d. Lacking a clear problem definition as to where the most injured are located, a profile of the injuries, and measures of success relative to how the entire response is proceeding makes it difficult to systematically prioritize resources during the earliest part of the response.
   e. Attempts to organize may actually be counterproductive due to incomplete knowledge about the nature of the disaster and the availability of resources.
2. Simple relationships, even deterministic ones, appear to generate indeterminate behaviors because of varying response rates between individuals and organizations.
3. The application of simple rules (e.g., all messages requesting assistance must come to a specific message center and not go directly to response organizations) can generate complex results (e.g., message delivery is slowed, increasing problems with obtaining resources in a timely manner).
4. Small changes appear to have an amplifying effect across the entire response, resulting in large changes later.

Due to some or all of these factors, the planned emergency response system will probably not be the one that emerges. The one that does emerge will, most likely, have a tendency to be locally self-organizing, somewhat unpredictable in its interorganizational linkages, and likely to succeed or fail in unpredictable ways.

Managing disasters is indeed a daunting task. Can chaos theory provide insights as to why these organizational phenomena occur? If so, are there strategies that management can adopt that may improve the nature of the disaster response? This paper addresses these questions by first looking at how chaos theory helps us understand the process that causes disaster organizations to become disordered. Second, the paper discusses appropriate strategies for the management of nonlinear events such as disasters. Third, it arrives at key lessons disaster response managers can learn from chaos theory. After a review of the limitations of chaos theory for disaster management, the paper concludes with a presentation of options for future administrative and legislative action in California and elsewhere.

II. WORKPLACE RULES, FIELDS OF ACTION, AND ORGANIZATIONAL MORPHOGENESIS

Disaster workers are in constant motion at various locations as they simultaneously apply various management systems (e.g., the Incident Command System in California) and develop tactics to organize and implement their response. Generally, they are applying policies, work processes, work behaviors and attitudes, or "workplace rules" within a "field of action" (Kiel 1994). *Workplace rules* are rules for interorganizational coordination and communication, as with an emergency operations center (EOC). The *field of action* is defined as the physical workplace and the external environment. The field of action is multidimensional and highly complex. In the case of a disaster, the field of action is influenced by the initial conditions that an organization finds itself in following the often abrupt onset of disaster. Kiel (1994) tells us that ''It is the interaction of the [workplace] rules of motion with the field of action that determines the direction and result of motion in the workplace. The dynamic created by the interaction of the 'rules' and the 'field of action' lead to agency outputs and performance (p. 50).''

A change process links the emergent organizational and system-wide disaster response structure with the one that existed prior to the disaster. As the field of action changes, so changes the organization's functions and accompanying work rules, which, in turn, change its structure. Organizational survival and the emergence of the response system are related to these self-organized adaptive activities (Jantsch 1980). Often the emergent structure stabilizes long enough to provide some range and level of services before changing back to its preresponse form (Thom 1972).

Our earlier discussion of what happens to an organization following a disaster and its efforts to form a disaster response system, as well as the limits of rational management, could be interpreted to mean that there are no rules or characteristic stages that define the disaster management process. Furthermore, we do not fully understand how interagency structures emerge when faced with a disaster situation (Drabek 1987). While there is a large literature that carefully describes and characterizes organizations and interoganizational behavior at various points in this process, there is no general theoretical explanation for the process of disaster organization emergence, structure, stability, reintegration into the day-to-day system, and cross-system interaction. In what follows, we hope to show that chaos theory may shed some light on the processes associated with the emergence of disaster response organizations.

The development of a time-based, process-oriented map of how organizations change under extreme conditions, such as those prevailing in a disaster, might reveal deeper or more fundamental aspects of the organizational change process in disaster situations. Workplace rules and the field of action create unique variations that emerge from these deeper processes. In a way, the problem is analogous to how an individual organism grows. While each individual is different, they are also members of a particular species and exhibit a general body plan. Their individual growth process (morphogenesis) obeys very specific rules that guide growth from an egg to an adult and on through death (Abraham 1985; Lincoln et al. 1982). These deeper rules guide the formation of organs, bones, etc., so that functioning but different and adaptable individual organisms emerge. Is there a similar set of organizational morphogenic rules that map the process of how an organization is disorganized and then reorganized? Can we look below the surface features of a disaster and find more general principles that can be used to speed the response along? Are there similar rules that apply to the ''morphogenesis'' of large-scale response systems (Quarantelli 1987)? The term *morphogenesis* will be used to refer to this deeper set of organizational response system dissolution/reforming rules. We will assert, for the sake of discussion, that such morphogenic rules exist and present some preliminary empirical evidence of how they might work.

In summary, our hypothesis is that effective disaster response management involves the creative application of morphogenic and workplace rules within the disaster field of action. In so doing, an effective disaster response pattern emerges (self-organizes to a significant degree) in space and time to meet a qualitative objective such as saving lives.

III. CHAOS THEORY AND THE RULES OF ORGANIZATIONAL MORPHOGENESIS

Disaster response organizations and response systems are dynamic systems. A dynamic system consists of two parts: a rule or ''dynamic,'' which specifies how a system evolves, and an initial condition or ''state'' from which the system starts. Some dynamic systems, such as those being discussed here, evolve in exceedingly complex ways, appearing to be irregular and initially to defy any rule. The next state of the system cannot be predicted from the previous one.

In mathematical theory, the change from order and predictability into unpredictability or chaos for dynamic systems is governed by a single law. Furthermore, the ''route'' between the two conditions is a universal one. According to Pietgen and colleagues (1992): ''Route means that there are abrupt qualitative changes—called bifurcations—which mark the transition from order into chaos like a schedule, and universal means that these bifurcations can be found in many natural systems both qualitatively and quantitatively'' (p. 584). Put another way, chaos is a type of nonlinear behavior emerging along a universal route. At a certain point along this route (''close to the edge of chaos'') organizations become highly sensitive to initial conditions and may abruptly change.

The effect of a disaster on organizations and response systems and the form(s) they take appears to be influenced by the initial conditions they experience following the disaster. Having said this, we still do not know if such organizations or systems move from a relatively stable state into a chaotic one or if they are simply adjusting their behavior within a given and predictable set of possibilities consistent with each organization's work rules (Holden 1986). The two conditions are very different and require different management strategies; in the earlier case the existing management strategy is useful; in the latter, a new one is necessary to deal with an emergent process and accompanying structure. The application of chaos theory to other social phenomenon can be helpful in clarifying this issue (Brown 1994; DiLorenzo 1994; Gregersen and Sailer 1993; Kronenberg 1994). If it cannot be empirically shown that at least some disaster response organizations and response systems come close to or enter into chaos, then disaster management has little to learn from chaos theory. More to the point, does the ''single law'' and ''universal route'' apply to a disaster response?

By applying the logistic equation to appropriate disaster response data, it is possible to determine if a disaster organization or response system traces the universal route to chaos (Priesmeyer and Cole 1995). Priesmeyer and Cole (1995) provide a detailed discussion of how the logistic equation is applied to a large number of phenomena to produce what is called a logistic map. Using disaster exposure data provided by Bosworth and Kreps (1986), Priesmeyer and Cole (1995) show that disaster organizations follow the logistic map in their response. The logistic map shows that as the level of activity increases and the environment becomes more turbulent, the organization moves from a relatively steady state through a bifurcation point and on to the edge of chaos.

If the environment becomes even more disordered, requiring the commitment of even more resources or their exhaustion, the organization is forced to move through various structural states until chaos sets in. Prediction of the next organizational structure becomes progressively more difficult. In terms of individual or interorganizational interactions, a series of ever increasing self-reinforcing ''errors'' are made by participants, deviating from established workforce rules and their relationship to the disaster's field of action (Koehler 1995). These continuously repeated errors become amplified and redefine the functions of the organization, which in turn redefines its structure. The errors increase the organization's sensitivity to small changes in the environment (sensitivity to initial conditions), which in turn cause large changes in the organization's structure. Thus "... process and structure become complementary aspects of the same over-all order of process, or *evolution*. As interacting processes define temporary structures . . . so structures define new processes, which in turn give rise to new temporary structures" (Jantsch and Waddington 1976:39).

To summarize what happens to management efforts at and following a bifurcation point:

The relationships between work rules, the field of action, and the environment become more and more unpredictable.

Problems of varying magnitude and the efforts to address them ("errors") may generate large structural changes in the organization.

The organization's functions and structures may lock onto one of two or more states or may oscillate between them.

Eventually bifurcations and accompanying oscillations become so complex that they cannot be distinguished from chaotic conditions.

> When chaos occurs a . . . system does not retrace prior identifiable sequences of behavior and does not evidence obvious patterns in its behavior. Chaotic behavior thus appears extremely disorderly since patterns over time, a symbol of orderliness, do not appear to exist. Chaotic behavior simply skips from one identifiable point to the next, yet never extends outside clear and distinct boundaries. (Kiel 1995:189)

Priesmeyer and Cole (1995) suggest, however, that disaster systems do *not* enter chaos. Instead, they tend to exist at the edge of chaos.

At or near the boundary of chaos it appears that the ordered structure of a disaster response agency loosens, potentially making new behavior possible. It is at the edge of chaos that sufficient fluidity is achieved by continuous "error," allowing for new work rules and a redefined field of action to emerge and be absorbed into a new but not necessarily more adaptive organizational structure (Kaufman 1993). Organizational changes traced by the logistic map do not necessarily lead to a rational emergent process or structure; they simply undergo certain characteristic changes at certain points which workers and managers must respond to. Interestingly, such changes often can lead to structures with an increased level of organization, which are more complex and capable of accomplishing more work, than the previous ones. Kiel (1989) suggests that "this is due to its increased capacity to attract, utilize, and organize available energy for its creation and maintenance" (p. 545). Recent work in evolutionary theory and simulation studies supports the view that organisms at the edge of chaos tend to be highly adaptive (Kaufman and Goerner 1994).

It may be that this new or adaptive response structure emerges from a "phase transition" at the edge of chaos. There are two types of phase transitions: first order and second order (Waldrop 1992). A first order phase transition involves a sharp change from one physical state to another. An example is the rapid transformation of water to ice. The change is very abrupt and well defined. A second order phase transition takes more time to accomplish and is less precise. Once a second order phase transition starts, no clear cut structure remains or immediately emerges but there are lots of little structures coming into and going out of existence. Efforts to establish a "better" order or to select a particular organizational structure among many possible ones are management's task. This structure is reinforced by what is called a path-dependent process; that is, once the structure begins to aggregate, there is a tendency to direct resources towards that aggregation rather than to other alternative ones (Arthur 1990; Arthur et al. 1987). Both of these concepts—phase transition and path-dependent processes—are important to understand how large, geographically extended structures may emerge.

Drawing together what has been said about the edge of chaos:

At least during the first 24 hours after an event, disaster organizations appear to exist at the edge of chaos, a position that allows maximum adaptability.

Very small changes or ''errors'' can have large organizational consequences.

The accumulation of errors could lead to a second-order phase transition characterized by a period of disconnected organizational fragments that eventually come together to form the new organization or system.

More complex and adaptive structures may emerge from a phase transition but they are not necessarily more efficient.

Path-dependent processes may play an important role in reinforcing an emergent organizational structure.

Although the logistic equation is very simple and carries little information about the individuals, organizations, and systems we are interested in, it seems to map the essential information about how these systems become disorganized and why they take the form that they do. Priesmeyer and Cole (1995) show that disaster responses are clearly nonlinear and at the very edge of chaos, therefore nonlinear tools and chaos theory are useful for developing disaster management techniques.

IV. CHAOTIC SYSTEMS MANAGEMENT THEORY

Management techniques appropriate for organizations prior to a bifurcation point do not work well once an organization reaches this point or moves to the edge of chaos. Prior to the bifurcation point the variations occurring in the environment fall within the organization's change capabilities. The management task at the bifurcation point is to dampen the disrupting structural oscillations. The challenge at the edge of chaos is how to creatively interpret the options and choose among a multitude of possibilities that will, via a second-order phase transition, effectively recouple the organization to other organizations and its environment. Kiel (1995) tells us: ''Most importantly, during times of high instability such as disasters and occasions when emergency services reach peak levels of activity it is essential to recognize that stability can only be regained by developing strategies that are themselves unstable. In short, we must match the instability of these environments with management practices and organizational strategies that are dynamic and fluid'' (p. 2).

According to Kiel (1994), there are three ways to deal with chaos:

Alter organizational parameters so that the range of fluctuations is limited. In this case, management tries to reduce the amount of change going on within the system by reducing the effect of critical behavioral and other factors on the system. The goal is to reduce uncertainty and to increase predictability so that management goals can be achieved. However, this approach is unlikely to work for an organization at the edge of chaos since the number of factors that are affecting the organization may be very large, and their relative importance to the emergence of the new organizational structure cannot be predicted.

Apply small perturbations to the chaotic system to try and cause it to organize. This approach requires some understanding of how the various perimeters of the organization's system work and what the effect of a small perturbation might be. A highly unstable system may require a small effort—a nudge—to cause self-organization to begin. Appropriate lines of communication rather than the control of hierarchical structures characterize this approach (Comfort 1994). Adequate communications provide timely information about the progress of the disaster and about the current state of local efforts. The nudge can be as simple as a single person taking charge and making decisions (Weick 1985).

Change the relationship between the organization and the environment. This requires continuous tracking of the relationship between critical conditions in the environment and key organizational perimeters. As changes occur organizational perimeters are adjusted in a continuous feedback process. For example, the relationship between the number of injured and available transport is closely watched so that as one increases or decreases, so does the other. This approach could be a way of refining the second possibility above. In this case, self-organizing processes are consciously shaped to bring the emergent structure more in line with environmental conditions and management goals.

For organizations at the edge of chaos, a combination of the last two options may be useful. As we have noted, the aggregation of organizational fragments at the edge of chaos into a new response structure may be initiated by an unexpected or unpredictable event. Kiel (1994) suggests that "as with variation beyond the control limits in quality measurement systems, that variation should not be considered a problem in management systems but rather an opportunity to learn why the variation occurred" (p. 22).

In this case, the disaster response manager is looking for variations driving the self-organizing process—the fluctuations—in a direction that appears to meet his or her immediate goals. Such a fluctuation can be either positive—something is being built—or negative—there is a silent area that has not reported. This phase transition or evolution of a response organization or extended response structure to a more adaptive one is a learning process. Good information about variations in the environment and the capacity to learn and visualize based on that information are key manager attributes. These skills include the capacity to "see" beyond the immediate present and construct a longer-term future horizon that may serve to reduce resource waste through continuous short term adjustments. Such skills are necessary to build in variation and to construct and adjust work rules relative to the field of action for optimal performance under changing environmental conditions (Jantsch 1980).

Kiel (1994) suggests that "we practice variation by perhaps using diverse teams to try diverse methods on essentially the same disaster or emergency problem" (p. 23). Relatively autonomous "messy" or multidiscipline work teams in the field may be able to identify and use relatively large amounts of data to do problem solving and create individual or coordinated response structures that respond to the immediate needs of their clients, be they victims or other response organizations. Teams should be messy or unstable in the sense that their membership is drawn from across functional areas constituted to solve a service delivery problem. According to Kiel (1994) "This suggests less of a focus on traditional structuring by functional area and instead consideration of where functional units converge to create outputs and services'' (Hammer and Champy 1993:200). Teams drawn from a single functional area (medical but not transportation for example) may tend to too narrowly define the issue and may have an overly rigid view on how to address it.

Sensitivity to initial conditions and the inability to predict exactly what form an organization will take at the edge of chaos suggests that it is impossible to predict which pattern for organizing the response is best. Provocative research cited by Loye (1995) finds that groups do a better than average job of predicting future events. The research suggests that groups are able to create a chaos ''gestalt'' that is able to predict a likely outcome. Messy groups, particularly since they are composed of individuals drawn from each element of a problem, seem particularly well suited for developing and implementing options beyond the edge of chaos.

The creation of relatively autonomous, messy groups to solve problems in the field suggests a very flat, decentralized disaster management structure. A multilayered, hierarchical structure will tend to restrict information flow at each point as it climbs upward, concentrate and restrict decision making away from the field, and reduce innovation and flexibility. A flat structure allows for the fluid and rapid flow of information, particularly if multiple information linkages are possible. Experiments by Hershey and colleagues demonstrate that a flat organization tends to produce the least disorder in information flow resulting in higher efficiencies than hierarchical organizations (Hershey et al. 1990).

These suggestions appear consistent with the four factors that increase the resilience and adaptiveness of the complex system that extends across the disaster. They are (1) a capacity for creative innovation among organizational units that interact as a system to achieve a common goal; (2) flexibility in relationships between the parts of a system and the whole; (3) interactive exchange between the system and its environment; and (4) a crucial role for information in increasing either order or chaos, regularity or random behavior within the system (Comfort 1994:158).

V. KEY LESSONS FOR DISASTER MANAGERS

Several key management lessons for public disaster response managers emerge from the application of chaos theory to disaster management:

No general theory of disaster management as a set of prescriptive rules is likely. Generally, the implication of chaos theory is that ''no grand theory of management is likely to appear.'' By extension, no grand theory of disaster management will appear that applies to all disasters and all environments particularly in varying social time contexts (Kiel 1994).

All levels of the disaster response should be flexible and adaptive. The capacity to develop a self-organizing response involves the whole system from top to bottom.

Managers should look for the unusual, the variation, and the fluctuation that indicates that a new form is emerging. It is necessary to be open to learning and therefore adapting to what is needed in the new environment. This style of decision making relies on rapid, adequately networked communications and on an ''exploratory, experimental process based on intuition and reasoning by analogy'' (Stacey 1992:13–14). Overall, disaster strategy implementation may be more successful when it involves a series of "nudges" directed at reinforcing favorable fluctuations in the field and collaboration with other response efforts rather than implementing an overall, highly structured plan.

Support disaster infrastructure formation processes that enable the response to rapidly organize itself. Managers need to quickly identify the infrastructure processes that contribute to the emergent response. The logistic map and the associated rules of morphogenesis may point to the kinds of *disorder* that will occur. On the other hand, the literature suggests that there are rules that may contribute to the emergence of large-scale systems. Infrastructures that support the response process should support a pattern that is likely to help local "messy" groups. For example, the provision of a horizontal, deeply redundant communications system with sufficient capacity for the immediate mobilization of large numbers of personnel and supplies and transportation assets based on the disaster profile, might be such an "infrastructure-like" process that contributes to the emergence of a disaster-wide response. Consistent with a flat structure and local decision making, messy groups should be able to draw on this infrastructure and avoid hierarchical approval structures.

Self-correcting processes that track environmental changes relative to response infrastructure and messy group efforts are important. Continuing success involves creative interaction with what is emerging in the environment. Building on existing strengths to support the response is important. However, this effort should be flexible enough to avoid the negative possibilities of path-dependent processes which tend to reinforce existing operations rather than being flexible enough to respond to emergent needs.

Strategies should be incremental and process-oriented so that they speed the self-organization of the response. Due to the large number of interactions and feedback loops, it is very difficult to predict the detailed course of the response or to develop a comprehensive strategy. "But, on an incremental or local basis, the effects of feedback from one time period into the next are often perfectly clear. This is a powerful argument for planning strategies that are incremental rather than comprehensive in scope and that rely on a capacity for adaptation rather than on blueprints of results" (Cartwright 1991:54).

Managers should take the role of catalyst to cause self-organization to occur. By having access to information and communications and by making it available to key trained responders, it may be possible to speed the effective formation of local response networks.

Management values provide the deepest source of order in an organization. "A commitment to service, a desire to excel, a drive to improve, and a dedication to having open organizations that let democracy flourish are essential management values in a world of increasing complexity" (Kiel 1994:218). It may be that the level of employee commitment to change and their ability to cooperate and form messy teams may reduce the time an organization is disorganized (Kiel 1989).

Reward employees for creativity. Successful adaptation often involves making second-order phase shifts. Because the effect of sensitivity to initial conditions and the effects of choices made cannot be predicted, the creation of different visions about what should be done should be encouraged. No single organizational vision for the entire disaster is possible in such an environment. Attention could be given to which skills are needed to make a system emerge. Employees should be rewarded for risk taking and experimentation that creates different options and for making such shifts. Managers should focus on ". . . changing agendas of strategic issues, challenges, and aspirations" (Stacey 1992:13–14)

The politics of the disaster response need to be addressed. The politics of the disaster response should minimize the ongoing stresses and strains between organizations to prevent unnecessary fractures in the overall response. This approach involves top level managers dealing with the politics of coordination and consensus building across organizational and political jurisdictions (Stacey 1992).

VI. LIMITATIONS OF CHAOS THEORY FOR DISASTER MANAGEMENT

The application of chaos theory to disaster management has a number of significant limitations:

The question of how helpful chaos theory is for disaster management needs further empirical investigation. As shown, the application of chaos theory to disaster management has some preliminary empirical support. The concepts make metaphorical sense and seem to be consistent with disaster management experiences. However, several questions remain. For example: (1) How do we know when an organization is at the bifurcation point? (2) When does an organization actually enter chaos or pass through a bifurcation point? (3) Can these be rigorously defined and empirically observed?

Every response agency that is responding to a disaster does not come to the edge of chaos. Some programs adapt using existing management systems. Thus different management systems apply to varying organizational situations throughout the disaster area.

Management flexibility as a response to chaos has its own costs (Kaufman 1985).

Resources are needed to maintain the capacity to act in different ways on short notice. When a disaster occurs, reserved resources, if immediately committed, could make a significant difference.

Technical expertise and functional specialization may be particularly important for certain types of disasters such as hazardous materials events. Under these circumstances, generalists may simply not know what to do.

An overcommitment to flexibility can result in rigidity, particularly when decisive action in a single direction is required. Such organizations can also be indecisive and not be able to make critical decisions quickly.

The formation of messy groups may weaken important bonds between workers (i.e., friendship, self-interest, habitual behavior) that hold the organization together.

Leadership that constantly revises its direction may find itself challenged, resulting in increased disorder.

Management skills may not be the answer to why response organizations are successful. It may be that sensitivity to initial conditions and fortunate relationships with other organizations have more to do with a successful response than disaster management skills (Kaufman 1985).

Computer chaos modeling is not the same thing as creative risk-taking by disaster responders and cannot replace chaos management techniques. Efforts to simulate the course of a disaster and to use the information to manage it may restrict the creativity of individuals to develop the most appropriate local response. Complex predictive models have many problems with validity and prediction that temper their applicability even though they may be useful for investigating how sensitive critical elements might be to initial conditions (Oreskes et al. 1994).

Chaos theory does not address many other organizational and interagency problems that condition the emergence and effective operation of disaster response systems. A review of the disaster research cited in this paper shows exactly how complex a disaster response is.

VII. ADMINISTRATIVE AND LEGISLATIVE OPTIONS

Based on the preceding discussion, the following are potential options for administrative and legislative action in California and elsewhere.

A. Research and Evaluation

The science of complexity research, which includes chaos theory, may be a useful avenue to further disaster research and should be encouraged with research grants.

Design a PC-based disaster simulation program that could be used to investigate the sensitivity to initial conditions of key components of the response for various types of disasters.

Encourage researchers to validate Priesmeyer's finding that a disaster response is chaotic for various disasters and different types of public, private, and nonprofit organizations at the state, operational area, city, and field level. Such research should seek to link existing sociological, psychological and other organizational studies of disasters to chaos theory.

A high priority could be given to the collection of time series data during a disaster response. Time series data are important for understanding how a disaster response organizes.

B. Communications and Steering

Inventory and coordinate state, local, and private emergency communication systems. Various levels of government, private agencies, amateur radio operators, and others collectively represent a potential network that could provide the necessary communications links to cause the rapid formation of a disaster response. Often elements of these communications systems have failed, been overloaded, or cannot intercommunicate. These limitations and failures need to be identified and eliminated. Disaster exercises that bring up and stress elements of the entire system and run according to disaster response plans should be conducted. Providing communications to messy groups and coordinating them into a network could be included.

Consideration could be given to parallel communication systems that connect key decision makers and resource storage areas, allowing local responders to obtain the supplies they need with a minimum of higher level regulation. Highly centralized communications systems for ordering, coordinating and delivering resources may not support the rapid emergence of large-scale disaster networks.

C. Statutory and Regulatory Review

Statutes and regulations that limit cross-jurisdictional coordination and resource sharing should be identified and reviewed to determine if they hinder the formation of response networks.

D. Disaster Management

The California Legislature has attempted to deal with the disruptive effects of disasters on response organizations. EMS, and other state and local government response agencies are required by statute (Section 8607 of the Government Code) to use the Standardized Emergency Management System (SEMS), when responding to emergencies involving multiple jurisdictions or multiple agencies. Local governments must use SEMS to be eligible for state reimbursement of response-related personnel costs. This legislation was passed to address interagency coordination and other response management problems occurring during the 1991 East Bay Hills Fire in Oakland. Generally, law enforcement, fire, and other response organizations had problems organizing themselves in compatible ways, making it difficult to identify or coordinate similar functions and resources.

SEMS seeks to address interagency coordination problems by providing a five level hierarchical emergency response organization (field, local government, operational area, region, and state) that facilitates:

The flow of emergency information and resources within and between involved agencies at all five organizational levels
The process of coordination between responding agencies
The rapid mobilization, deployment, use and tracking of resources

This hierarchical structure uses the Incident Command System (ICS), the Multi-Agency Coordination System, the state's Master Mutual Aid agreement, the Operational Area Satellite Information System, and a specific designation of operational areas to integrate the disaster response. Each agency organizes itself around a set of common ICS defined functions (command/management, operations, planning/intelligence, logistics, and finance/administration), specifies objectives that it seeks to accomplish (management by objective is required), and uses preestablished systems to fill positions, conduct briefings, obtain resources, manage personnel, and communicate with field operations.

The preceding discussion of the applicability of chaos theory to disaster management suggests that a number of state-related management options should be evaluated to determine their response utility for ICS and SEMS:

Integrate SEMS and ICS training with chaos management training options. SEMS and ICS are analogous to the command and control structures of an army. Ideally, these management systems provide a common command and control structure (SEMS) and nomenclature for each unit (ICS). Commanders at headquarters or in the field are not told how *to tactically* coordinate with other units or how to arrange the units into an effective formation on the battlefield to win a particular engagement. Tactics and the deployment of forces are battle-specific. Similarly, SEMS and ICS help to organize the various components of a disaster response. They create an adaptive priority setting and resource management structure, but do not define which tactics might be most useful for organizing individual components into an overall response system for a *particular* disaster. The Office of Emergency Services has moved in this direction by decentralizing its operations away from the State Operations Center to Regional Emergency Operations Centers. As noted above, it is what is unique about a disaster that disrupts the response. Disaster managers should be trained in skills that increase their ability to adapt to changing situations.

Identify and evaluate various critical interorganizational interfaces and rates of interaction that regulate the response infrastructure's self-organizing process. Agencies' ability to self-organize and mobilize resources is all directly related to how quickly the response emerges. Relationships to be examined might include: state SOC interactions between public and private response and resource agencies and resource agencies with each other, state/region interactions; region/operational area interactions and setup of critical operations and their support; and operational area/emergent field structures and their identification and support.

Consider reducing the number of layers of government required to approve the allocation of resources and personnel, and allow existing and emergent organizations in the field to request and approve distribution of state and other resources locally.

Consider developing and training a new group of field responders who would be seen as information brokers. Their purpose would be to identify locally emergent groups, determine inadequate communication linkages, consider the need to coordinate resources, and other similar functions. They would be dispatched with the appropriate communications equipment immediately following a disaster.

E. Disaster Response Training

State disaster scenarios should be scripted to emphasize the progress of the disaster by showing emergent fluctuations, process problems, and disaster infrastructure issues relative to the demands being serviced by EOCs close to the disaster.

Field exercises should be linked to EOC operations and emphasize communications, self-organization processes to address unexpected problems, formation of messy groups to deal with process problems, and the like. The emphasis would shift to supporting self-organizing processes and disaster infrastructure issues.

State and operational area EOC strategy setting could involve tracking the emergence and efficiency of the response infrastructure relative to localized incremental goals and needs. By attending to the emergence of the response infrastructure and how locally set priorities and resource allocations are shaping these responses, it could be possible to quickly improve the operation of the emergent processes and structures.

State and operational area EOC status reports could emphasize the emergence of disaster infrastructure and overall fluctuations across the disaster area. There would be less of a focus on individual functional area accomplishments and more emphasis on process, emergent organizations, and the implications of localized strategies and resource use rates.

Disaster managers and responders could be trained to visualize the whole of the response; do process mapping; form messy groups; engage in-group problem solving; and be functionally cross-trained. The overall goal of the suggested modifications in disaster training would be to produce a creative generalist who is able to visualize large portions of the response, understand the role of process in developing infrastructure, and capable of forming and working in messy groups to solve problems.

Disaster response managers could be trained to resolve likely interorganizational disputes, differences in social timing, political turf, and other issues that could seriously disrupt a response.

AUTHOR'S NOTE

Gustav A. Koehler is the Senior Policy Analyst of General Law and Government for the California Research Bureau. Guenther G. Kress is a Professor of Public Administration at California State University San Bernardino. Randi L. Miller is a Professor of Sociology at California State University, San Bernardino.

Many of the concepts, ideas, and management lessons presented in this chapter were first introduced at an invitational conference on what disaster managers can learn from chaos theory. The conference was convened by the California Research Bureau on May 18–19, 1995.

REFERENCES

Abraham, R. Q. (1985). *On morphodynamics*. Santa Cruz, CA: Ariel Press.
Arthur, B. (1990). Positive feedback in the economy. *Scientific American* 263, 92–99.
Arthur, B., Ermoliev, Y., and Kaniovski, Y. (1987). Path-dependent processes and the emergence of macro-structure. *European Journal of Operational Research* 30, 294–303.
Bosworth, S., and Kreps, G. (1986). Structure as process: Organization and role. *American Sociological Review* 51, 699–716.
Brown, C. (1994). Politics and the environment: Nonlinear instabilities dominate. *American Political Science Review* 88, 292–303.
Cartwright, T. (1991). Planning and chaos theory. *Journal of the American Planning Association* 57, 44–56.
Comfort, L. (1994). Self-organization in complex systems. *Journal of Public Administration Research and Theory* 4, 393–410.
DiLorenzo, V. (1994, June). Chaos theory and legislative dynamics. Paper presented at the meeting of the Canadian Political Science Association, Calgary, Alberta, Canada.
Drabek, T. (1987). Emergent structures. In R. Dynes, B. De Marchi, and C. Pelanda (eds.), *Sociology of Disasters*, 261 Milan, Italy: Franco Angeli.
Drabek, T. (1989). Strategies used by emergency managers to maintain organizational integrity. *Environmental Auditor* 1, 139–152.
Gregersen, H., and Sailer, L. (1993). Chaos theory and its implications for social science research. *Human Relations* 46, 777–802.
Hammer, M., and Champy, J. (1993). *Reengineering the Corporation: A Manifesto for Business Revolution*. New York: Harper Collins.
Hershey, D., Patel, V., and Hahn, J. (1990). Speculation on the relationship between organizational structure, entropy, and organizational function. *Systems Research* 7, 207–208.
Holden, A. (1986). *Chaos*. Princeton, NJ: Princeton University Press.
Jantsch, E. (1980). *The self-Organizing Universe*. New York: Pergamon Press.
Jantsch, E., and Waddington, C. (eds.). (1976). *Evolution and Consciousness: Human Systems in Transition*. Reading, MA: Addison-Wesley.
Kaufman, H. (1985). *Time, Chance, and Organizations*. Chatham, NJ: Chatham House.
Kaufman, S. (1993). *The Origins of Order*. New York: Oxford University Press.
Kaufman, S., and Goerner, S. (1994). *Chaos and the Evolving Ecological Universe*. Longhorne, PA: Gordon and Breach.
Kiel, L. D. (1989). Nonequilibrium theory and its implications for public administration. *Public Administration Review* 49, 544–551.
Kiel, L. D. (1994). *Managing Chaos and Complexity in Government*. San Francisco: Jossey-Bass.
Kiel, L. D. (1995, May). Chaos theory and disaster response management: Lessons for managing periods of extreme instability. Paper presented at the meeting of the conference What Disaster Response Management Can Learn from Chaos Theory, California Research Bureau.
Koehler, G. (1992). A computer simulation of a California casualty collection point used to respond to a major earthquake. *Prehospital and Disaster Medicine* 7, 339–347.
Koehler, G. (1995). Fractals and path dependent processes: A theoretical approach for characterizing

emergency medical responses to major disasters. *Proceedings of the Society for Chaos Theory in Psychology* 199–216.

Kronenberg, P. (1994, June). Chaos and re-thinking the public policy process. Paper presented at the meeting of the Chaos and Society Conference, Universite du Quebec a Hull, Hull, Quebec, Canada.

Lincoln, R., Boxshell, G., and Clark, P. (1982). *A dictionary of Ecology, Evolution and Systematics*. Cambridge, UK: Cambridge University Press.

Loye, D. (1995). How predictable is the future? The conflict between traditional chaos theory and the psychology of prediction, and the challenge of chaos psychology. In R. Robertson and A. Combs (eds.), *Chaos Theory in Psychology and the Life Sciences*, 345–358. Hillsdale, NJ: Lawrence Erlbaum Associates.

Oreskes, N., Shrader-Frechette, K., and Belitz, K. (1994). Verification, validation, and confirmation of numerical models in the earth sciences. *Science* 263, 2840.

Peitgen, H., Jurgens, H., and Saupe, D. (1992). *Chaos and Fractals*. New York: Springer-Verlag.

Priesmeyer, H. and Cole, E. (1995, May). Nonlinear analysis of disaster response data. Paper presented at the meeting of the conference ''What Disaster Response Management Can Learn from Chaos Theory, California Research Bureau.

Quarantelli, E. (1987). What should we study? Questions and suggestions for researchers about the concept of disasters. *International Journal of Mass Emergencies and Disasters* 5, 285–310.

Stacey, R. (1992). *Managing the Unknowable: Strategic Boundaries Between Order and Chaos in Organizations*. San Francisco: Jossey-Bass.

Thom, R. (1972). *Structural Stability and Morphogensis*. Redwood City, CA: Addison-Wesley.

Waldrop, M. (1992). *Complexity: The Emerging Science at the Edge of Order and Chaos*. New York: Simon & Schuster.

Weick, K. (1985). Sources of order in underorganized systems: Themes in recent organizational theory. In Y. Lincoln (ed.), *Organizational Theory and Inquiry*, 128. Beverly Hills, CA: Sage Publications.

21
The Psychology of Evacuation and the Design of Policy

Jasmin K. Riad Disaster Research Center, University of Delaware, Newark, Delaware

William Lee Waugh, Jr. Department of Public Administration and Urban Studies, Georgia State University, Atlanta, Georgia

Fran H. Norris Department of Psychology, Georgia State University, Atlanta, Georgia

I. INTRODUCTION

Evacuation policy is a very salient issue among communities along the East and Gulf Coasts of the United States, and for good reason. There are 2700 miles of barrier islands from Maine to Texas (Leavenworth 1986), many barely above sea level and with limited egress, such as Galveston Island and the barrier islands of the Carolinas and Georgia. There are also thousands of more miles of low-lying coastline, much of it heavily developed. Many of the islands and much of the coast are vulnerable to tidal surges brought on by hurricanes and even lesser storms. Evacuation of the islands and coastal communities has historically been problematic for officials. Inhabitants have to be convinced of the danger posed by storms and persuaded to leave homes and possessions. Visitors have to be convinced of the danger and persuaded to forego vacations and the excitement of the disaster. Officials typically have little lead time to organize orderly evacuations, particularly when there are few bridges and/or ferries to the mainland or to larger islands and the adjoining land itself is low and prone to flooding. A recurring nightmare of emergency managers is having evacuees trapped on congested highways or housed in insecure facilities vulnerable to wind and water as a hurricane makes landfall.

Fortunately, quite a bit is known about evacuation behavior and how to plan and implement an evacuation. After each major disaster operation, the attention of emergency managers focuses on the "lessons learned." They debrief one another to identify the strengths and weaknesses in the disaster operations so that they can reduce errors and improve performance during the next emergency. In that manner, policies evolve and programs become more effective. That incremental process of trial and error represents the theory of policy design, and it is, in fact, what happens for the most part. However, policies are often based on the assumptions of individuals about cause-effect relationships and the ultimate outcomes of policy decisions as well as on the predisposition of organizations to make particular policy choices. As a result, policy is often based on faulty judgments about how people respond to crises and how they interpret the warnings and advice given by authorities.

That is no less true of emergency management decision making than it is of decision making in other political arenas. A frequent criticism of emergency management policies has been that the civil defense origin of many disaster agencies has encouraged a command-and-control orientation that is ill suited to civilian disaster operations. In effect, authorities assume that they need only issue warnings loudly and clearly and order evacuations when the level of risk or probability of disaster reaches a predetermined level. They expect that civilians will respond appropriately. As has been the experience in recent disasters, that is not always the case and may seldom be the case. Indeed, it may not be enough that authorities provide reasonable justification for their orders. Emotion, social connections, and a variety of other psychological variables affect crisis decision making and should be both anticipated and addressed in the design of evacuation policies. Authorities are often surprised by the lack of attention to their warnings and the tendency for at least some residents to put themselves at risk rather than to follow evacuation orders. To some extent, the problem is a familiar one in that some people will always respond in a manner contrary and often opposite to that which is desired. Experienced evacuation planners know that some people will head south when the evacuation route heads north. They also know that some people will stock their coolers with beer and wine and invite friends and neighbors to a ''hurricane party'' even when there is a mandatory evacuation order.

Coherence and consistency may also be lacking in the plans and how they are communicated to those to be evacuated. The organizational culture engendered by former military personnel and the hierarchical structures created to support the civil defense programs of the 1950s and 1960s may conflict with the orientations of other emergency management personnel and organizations and thereby reduce the effectiveness of disaster operations. Differences in organizational culture will affect communication, decision making, risk taking, and a variety of other administrative behaviors (Waugh 1993). To be fair, some agencies, too, have been criticized as being too ''scientific'' and failing to consider how to help the public and emergency managers understand the information that they provide. Emergency managers may receive conflicting information, too much information, or too little information. While the professionalization of the field is encouraging emergency managers to develop political and management skills as well as technical skills, the learning process takes time.

This chapter examines the problem of designing effective evacuation policies to minimize the risk of human casualties in hurricanes and the fit between current evacuation policies and the social psychology of evacuation. In other words, it addresses the question of how public officials might design an evacuation policy that is sensitive to both individual and collective decision processes concerning whether, when, and how to evacuate and the concerns that the policy makers themselves have. Policy recommendations are drawn from the comparison of expected individual and collective behaviors and the expectations of emergency managers in issuing evacuation orders. It is important to note that any policy suggestion in this chapter must first be pretested and evaluated on the specific region or population before implementation. The cases and literature upon which the analysis is based are largely American and significant differences would be expected in another culture and even from one region of the United States to another.

II. EVACUATION RESEARCH

Evacuation is very complex and involves many types and levels of interaction among individuals and collectives within the threatened area and among residents, emergency managers, and other government officials. This complexity is paralleled in the researchers who have attempted to explain the phenomena of how individuals decide whether to flee or fight a storm. Among the analysts who have addressed this complicated issue are researchers in geography, political science, economics, psychology, communications, and sociology. Disaster research is increasingly multidisciplinary and involves a variety of methodological approaches. From an empirical standpoint, some of the research leaves much to be desired (i.e., it is not peer-reviewed and has research design flaws; also variables are defined and measured differently). However, from an open-minded theoretical standpoint, this combination of fields and methodologies has an advantage. The advantage is apparent when the same finding (e.g., families will evacuate only when together) occurs across all of the studies. [For complete reviews of evacuation literature see Quarantelli (1980) and Aguire (1993).]

First we examine the research literature that has focused on individuals and evacuation. The individual section is divided into two parts, stable and unstable research findings. *Stable* means that the research result has been found in a significant number of studies. *Unstable* means that the research results differ in many studies. This categorization is not a value judgment. Unstable results are not negative and they usually deal with oscillating variables. These topics may be new to the evacuation field, need updated information, or need more research. The sections are summarized by policy suggestions. The stable results we discuss first are gender, family, risk perception and stress, the psychological effects of predictions, hurricane knowledge and terminology, social influences, and prior evacuation and experience.

A. Stable Results

1. Gender Differences

Gender differences appear consistently in the literature, with women being more likely to evacuate (Riad et al. 1998) and to have evacuation intentions (Riad 1997). Women are more likely to perceive a disaster event or threat as serious or risky (Cutter 1992; Howe 1990; Leik et al. 1982; Flynn et al. 1994; Fothergill 1996; Riad et al. in press). Women are more likely to receive communications about risk, due to their social networks, and to respond with protective actions, such as evacuation (Fothergill 1996). There is some indication that women more than men prepare their families and communities for disasters (Fothergill 1996). An effective evacuation policy would include ways of specifically targeting women with evacuation information (e.g., put materials in places frequented by women).

2. Family

Family variables have been important components of evacuation (Houts et al. 1984; Drabeck and Stephenson 1971), most likely because families tended to evacuate as a unit (Perry 1979). Consistent with past research, Riad and Norris (1998) found that individuals who had intentions to evacuate had family who wanted to leave.

3. Risk Perception and Stress

People who do not feel as though they are at risk will not evacuate. Many of the evacuation models of decision making have focused on risk perception as a key component (Perry and Lindell 1991; Houts et al. 1984). In an analysis using a combined sample of participants from studies of Hurricanes Hugo and Andrew, both category 4 hurricanes, Riad et al. (in press) examined the reasons people gave for not evacuating and found that 33%

of the sample believed that the hurricane was not a serious threat, and 25% were confident in their safety. Riad and Norris (1998) found that high perceived risk was the most important variable in predicting evacuation intention.

Sociologists have a long history of examining warning messages. Individual decision processes prior to evacuation are usually based upon the nature of the warning (e.g., source, credibility, ambiguity, etc.), confirmation (i.e., finding a second source of information or repeat of initial warning by a credible source), and then mobilization (Drabek 1994:127–146). [For detailed discussions on warnings, see Nigg (1995), Mileti and Sorenson (1988), and Sorenson and Mileti (1988).]

These warnings or fear communications get people to assess the severity of the threat, the probability that the threat will hit, and the efficacy of a coping response. If the communication is confusing, anxiety may increase (Maddox and Rogers 1983). In Riad (1997), two out of three individuals who were the most anxious intended to evacuate. Similarly, two out of three individuals who were the least anxious did not intend to evacuate. Individuals with medium levels of anxiety were split evenly on evacuation intention.

Actions that increase the level of anxiety or that increase the credibility of the warning should increase the likelihood of evacuation. The practice of police asking individuals for the name of their next of kin or asking them to fill out a toe tag form might achieve the desired effect. A worthwhile research topic could address whether asking this question ever changes people's minds. A challenge for policy makers and researchers is how to come up with a way to increase risk perception ethically and safely, thereby increasing evacuation compliance without unreasonably scaring the individuals.

4. *Psychological Effects of Predictions*

Keeping in mind the interdisciplinary nature of this chapter, it is pertinent to mention research conducted in social and cognitive psychology. This massive body of literature has shown that individuals depend on heuristics when making predictions under uncertain conditions (e.g., a hurricane warning), and this reliance sometimes lead to correct decisions but can lead to incorrect systematic errors (Kahneman and Tversky 1984). Often we try to adopt shortcuts that seem to simplify complex problems. Fiske and Taylor (1991) say that we are cognitive misers because we conserve cognitive energy by ignoring relevant information, fall back on learned behavioral patterns, or accept the ''good enough'' option (Aronson 1992). These shortcuts can produce prejudice, bias, and a feeling of superiority that may extend to controlling damage from nature. Heuristics are often used when we do not have time to think carefully about an issue, when we are so overloaded with information that we cannot process the information fully, and when we have little other information. Theoretically this can explain some of the responses we see to evacuation. However, it still needs to be tested empirically.

The following example from the floods in Grand Forks shows how individual heuristics and scientific predictions can give people too much of a sense of control. Some researchers have called this ''misplaced concreteness.'' In Grand Forks a prediction for the Red River to crest at 49 feet was interpreted as certain; however, the river crested at 54 feet. The dikes protecting the city had been built up with sandbags to contain a 52-foot crest. There was no prior experience because the river had never risen this high before. The citizens were surprised when they saw the water coming down the street. Whether the problem is climate change, earthquakes, droughts, or floods, the tendency to overlook uncertainties, margins of error, and ranges of probabilities can lead to damaging misjudgments (Stevens 1998).

5. Knowledge and Terminology

Individuals often do not know what the terms *watch* and *warning* mean. A problem arises when threat awareness is high but the understanding and interpretation of hurricane terminology is low. Most individuals use the media to keep informed. In one study, as many as 99% of 210 individuals surveyed used the radio or television to keep informed (Riad 1997). These numbers are not retrospective because these individuals were asked about their evacuation intentions while under a hurricane warning. From another part of the sample, the pre–post sample (n = 96), 97% updated themselves often and 50% of the individuals did not know what a watch was and 15% did not know what a warning was.

With the worldwide web, it is very easy to look up strike probabilities. A future research question could address how individuals interpret these strike probabilities and how much faith individuals put in them. Dow and Cutter (1998) state that researchers need to rethink the older evacuation decision-making models because they are not in keeping with technological advances. They further suggest that coastal residents may be becoming more sophisticated in their risk assessments because they use the weather channel and the Internet to help them make evacuation decisions.

From a policy standpoint, it is important to point out that many politicians like to set up educational preparedness programs. These programs often teach an individual the difference between a watch and a warning. A major problem is that many of these programs are not evaluated for their effectiveness.

6. Social Influences and Support

In emergency situations, people look to others to help them with their decision-making process. For example, victims of crime often talk to someone immediately after the crime, and this interaction seems to have a large effect on their decision to report or not to report the crime to the police (Greenberg and Ruback 1992). This stable research finding extends to evacuation decision making. The greater one's contacts in the community, the more one is likely to receive information regarding a threat (Perry 1979). Consistent with this notion, Drabek and Boggs (1968) found that having a small social network was a characteristic of individuals who did not evacuate. Riad et al. (in press) found that social support that includes access to a network was a predictor of evacuation. Decisions regarding evacuation and other disaster responses are influenced significantly by the kinship support network (Drabek 1969; Bolin and Bolton 1986; Perry et al. 1981).

Social psychology has examined affiliation under stressful conditions. Festinger's (1954) social comparison theory holds that we need to see other people's behavior to clarify our own. Schachter concludes, "misery doesn't love just any kind of company, it loves only miserable company" (1959:24). People want to affiliate in order for them to have access to emotional comparison, cognitive clarity, and support. Riad (1997) found that blacks were more likely to affiliate than whites and they affiliated for emotional support.

Individuals also use others to interpret warnings. Drabek (1997) described six social constraints that affect how messages are processed. These are prior disaster experience, proximity, source credibility, family structure, observation of the threat, and interaction with others.

If social influence is this powerful, it needs to be examined as a way to encourage individuals to evacuate. It is theoretically possible that something as simple as a phone call could encourage individuals to evacuate. This may also be an intervention point to calm highly anxious individuals and help them with their decision-making processes. From a policy perspective, phone calls could be an easy intervention point. The Community Alert Network (CAN) is an organization that provides community call-down systems that alert the public to hazards by automatically ringing their home phones. This computer-generated system can call thousands of individuals in an hour. The message usually contains the voice of a recognizable authority figure and specific instructions; if the individuals want to speak to a person, they can contact the operator. The CAN network has responded to many different types of situations (e.g., hurricane evacuations, plant explosions, Amtrak derailments, prison escapes, chemical plant leaks, flood warnings, etc.). This automated system could be manipulated to be more personable (i.e., customized for neighborhoods). In the past, CAN has found that some individuals do not want to be called and some individuals may not have a phone. This problem must be examined further. The system has been evaluated but not in response to an actual evacuation. These results suggested that a test call was very effective in communicating emergency preparedness information to those who received it (Conn and Rich 1993). For more information on the effectiveness of different types of warning systems including call-down systems, see Rogers and Sorenson (1988).

7. Prior Evacuation and Experience

Prior evacuation more than prior experience has been shown to be a predictor of future evacuation (Riad et al. in press). In another study, Riad (1997), found those who had prior evacuation experience (52.6%) perceived more risk, were more prepared, had higher levels of efficacy, were more likely to say that others would influence their decision to evacuate, and were more likely to have evacuation intentions. Individuals who have prior evacuation experience have an evacuation repertoire because they know what to do and how to act, feel as though they can accomplish the action, and perceive enough risk to intend to evacuate to begin with (Riad 1997).

In sum, the more stable evacuation findings involve gender, family, risk perception and stress, the psychological effects of prediction, hurricane knowledge and terminology, social influences and support, and prior evacuation and experience.

B. Unstable Results

Now we are going to examine some of the more unstable findings from the evacuation literature. These variables are ethnicity, resources, territoriality, children, age, and pets.

1. Ethnicity

Different ethnic findings are reported in the evacuation literature (Riad et al. 1997; Perry 1981). This may be because different population subgroups may have different rates of evacuation (Moore 1963). An important ethnic difference in one study was that the white population was less likely to evacuate than the black population (Riad 1997). Early studies suggested that blacks were more likely to evacuate because they possess larger kinship and community networks than whites (Perry 1979). There is some evidence that ethnic groups link and integrate their elderly, which helps in evacuation (Quarantelli 1985). Perry and Lindell (1991) interviewed 182 evacuated flood victims and 123 evacuees from a train derailment carrying hazardous material and found that ethnic group membership was not a significant factor in explaining evacuation compliance. However, Riad et al. (1997) found that both Latinos and whites were more likely to evacuate than blacks. Ethnic differences could be confounded with resources especially if lower income individuals tend to evacuate because they live in less sturdy housing. Policy needs to take into account different ethnic groups living within an area.

2. Resources

One would expect that a major factor in evacuation decisions would be the individual's resources. Not having access to a car, money, and other essential resources would logically be an obstacle to evacuation. However, while a lack of resources certainly presents problems, the research suggests that individual resources are not important predictors of evacuation intentions (Riad 1997). Socioeconomic status, physical stress, and efficacy were found to be unrelated to evacuation intentions as well. In fact, another study that examined the reasons for not evacuating for Hurricanes Hugo and Andrew found that not having a car and not having money only accounted for 0.9% of the population that did not evacuate (Riad et al. in press). Evidently, while lacking the resources to evacuate might affect the decision to do so, relatively few people lacked sufficient resources to participate in the evacuations for Hugo and Andrew. Resources seem to be more of a driving issue on the communal level (e.g., building enough shelters, buying computer equipment). Future research must target populations that truly do not have any resources (e.g., the homeless) to determine what kinds of assistance must be provided and to whom.

3. Territoriality

Sometimes individuals may experience conflicting motivations in that although they perceive risk, it may be for their territory rather than for themselves. Wachtendorf (1998) believes that individuals who are defending their property are in fact protecting their sense of identity. Riad et al. (in press) mentions that individuals who do not have other social ties may use their property as a means to reduce stress. Of course this hypothesis must still be tested. Owners were less likely to have evacuation intentions and tended to be more concerned about looting (Riad 1997). The same study showed that individuals who lived in Savannah, Georgia, were more attached to and proud of their homes. These individuals were less likely to have evacuation intentions. Individuals who had evacuation intentions appeared to be less embedded in the community (Riad 1997). As mentioned before, some individuals may be more attached to their home/community than others. It is possible that individuals who are more embedded in the community find it harder to leave.

Officials need to assure the safe and quick return of evacuees. A new fear after Hurricane Opal was that residents would not be allowed to reenter quickly enough. One emergency manager recommended that homeowners be allowed in as quickly as possible following disasters so that they could let officials know what was wrong with their property (e.g., gas leaks, water main breaks, etc.). His logic was that homeowners can determine what is wrong with their homes much more quickly than anyone else. In Riad (1997), community-level officials said that their citizens did have trouble returning home after Hugo. They also believed that not allowing individuals in quickly may cause people not to evacuate in the future and that "reentry" is a constant issue. When they deem it safe for individuals to return home depends on the damage to the areas hit. Quick reentry and a way to reduce looting or the fear of looting would also encourage those individuals who are territorial and reluctant to leave.

4. Children

Relocation or evacuation decisions are often related to concern for children as well, even if parents do not feel threatened enough themselves to evacuate (Kirschenbaum 1996).

Moreover, having children encourages preparedness (Turner 1986), so that people are better prepared to leave. Given the concern for child safety, it is suggested that warnings be communicated through children, via school, to make sure that the risk was heeded and to encourage parents to prepare for evacuation.

5. Pets

In recent years, considerable attention has been paid to the ''pet factor.'' Because shelters have seldom accepted house pets, residents often chose to stay home with their ''children'' rather than to leave them alone in a house or apartment. However, Riad et al. (in press) found that only 1.6% of their sample gave having to take care of a pet as a reason for not evacuating. But after a train derailment and spill of hazardous material evacuated the town of Weyauwega, Wisconsin, Heath (1998) found that 32% of households that did not evacuate all pets attempted to rescue their pets before the spill was contained and the area was considered safe.

The conflicting research may well be a result of differences in how pets are perceived. Rural residents are apparently much less likely to view their pets in the same way as more urban and suburban residents. For many pet owners, their dogs and cats are their ''children'' and they will endanger their own lives in order to protect them from harm. For others, particularly rural residents who may have farm animals or many pets, the relationship may be viewed very differently. Concerns were raised following hurricane evacuations of urban residents in Florida and the impact of pets on evacuation decisions may be much stronger in such communities. In any case, the lesson received enough attention that at least one organization specializes in pet rescue operations following disasters and more and more emergency shelters are arranging with local veterinarians to provide facilities for pets in or near the shelters for their owners. Protocols are also being developed to facilitate the reunion of owners and pets separated during disasters. Providing for pet care and pet rescue may or may not encourage residents to evacuate, but it will remove a possible obstacle for some residents. It may also be an important concern relative to reentry. Residents may be more willing to leave pets if they are assured that they can return quickly to their homes to take care of their animals.

C. Evacuation Research Summary

Consistent and stable findings should help in making policy recommendations. However, it is not that simple; there are hundreds of variables that can influence an individual's evacuation decision. These variables exist at both the individual level (i.e., prior evacuation experience inducing future evacuation) and the community level (i.e., significant number of new residents who do not have evacuation experience). The community influences can intervene and influence individual evacuation decision making. Let us not forget possible situational influences either. For example, individual reactions to a category 1/2 hurricane could be dramatically different than a category 3/4 or 5 hurricane.

Evacuation research is never concluded. For example, Dow and Cutter (1998) report that more individuals in their sample relied on the media than other people. This finding is very interesting and may tell us something about our changing culture and society. As cultures and communities grow and change, scientists must remain aware of how old research findings and new theories and findings could influence positive evacuation, and they must make policy suggestions on the basis of such data. On the other hand, policy makers should pay more attention to evacuation research and assign it a priority in high-risk areas. Outlined below are some community variables and issues we should keep in mind when designing evacuation policy and conducting evacuation research.

1. Population Growth

Along the mainland, there are many miles of populated lowlands with similar exposures. For decades, experts have expressed great concern about the potential devastation of a major hurricane in south Florida and, in some measure, their fears were realized when Hurricane Andrew came ashore in 1994. But, the storm could have been far more devastating had it hit Miami Beach or the densely populated areas to the north more directly. This issue must be examined with more of the population moving and vacationing along coastal communities. For example, the new casinos on the coast of Mississippi not only bring in new employees who may not have evacuation experience from hurricanes but also attract a great many tourists as well. Casinos, resorts, and even small towns with motels along interstate highways that may become large population centers at night or on the weekend need to have staffs trained to respond to disasters and to direct the evacuation of guests. Emergency managers will need to plan for inexperienced evacuees.

The most obvious way to minimize risk is to reduce the number of people living in the most hazardous areas and thereby reduce the need for mass evacuations. However, restricting development on barrier islands and along beaches is easier to recommend than it is to implement, as South Carolina officials learned when they tried to implement a beach management program following Hurricane Hugo (Waugh 1990; Mittler 1993).

2. Consistent Evacuation Policies

One problem with evacuation policies is that there is no consistency from one state to another. In some states, evacuation orders are issued by state authorities only. In other states, evacuation orders can be issued by local authorities, sometimes based on decision rules promulgated by state authorities and sometimes on their own. The power to order evacuations depends on whether the community has a centralized or decentralized emergency management system. A study comparing government evacuation decision making in Georgia and South Carolina illustrates this point.

South Carolina has a centralized emergency management system, meaning that power and authority come from the top down. The governor gets recommendations from both the local and state emergency managers when deciding whether to issue voluntary or mandatory evacuations. However, the governor has the final word on the evacuation decision. One respondent commented that the procedure changes depending on who is in office. Some governors more than others feel it is their responsibility to take care of the state and not leave the evacuation decision to local counties. Another respondent stated that she believed the centralized system of South Carolina cuts down on confusion with both local residents and tourists.

Georgia, on the other hand, operates with a decentralized system, meaning that the local emergency officials in conjunction with the county commissioners and other elected officials are in complete control. The state emergency agency is available as backup support. The local and state officials are accountable only within their agencies and the local emergency management does not report to the state. The person in charge of making the final evacuation decision is the chair of the county commission. However, the governor can override the decision of the county commissioner if necessary. The point of this illustration is that evacuation policy is by no means consistent. This discrepancy can confuse individuals who are visiting or live in those areas.

3. *Media Influences*

One problem with news coverage of hurricanes is that the focus tends to be on the eye of the storm rather than the surrounding winds. There can be severely damaging winds, including tornadoes, hundreds of miles from the storm's eye. Another problem is that many individuals rely on reporters' interpretations of the threat. The National Hurricane Center does an excellent job of informing individuals with updates on many different shows, from the news to the weather channel. However, many of these good influences are undone by reporters who may inadvertently encourage individuals to go surfing or to have hurricane parties. Social psychology has long shown how the media influence us (Aronson 1992). When reporters show a family who stayed during a hurricane, others think they may safely do so next time as well. This could especially occur with individuals who are not experienced with evacuation.

A case example of the media influence was seen when Hurricane Hugo hit South Carolina in 1989. The reports of damage in the Caribbean gave impetus to residents to evacuate the barrier islands relatively early. Still, many coastal residents held hurricane parties and remained in the storm's path. The coverage of approaching storms by local and national news media, including the impressive use of satellite photography and other meteorological technologies by television weather people, may not convey information to residents in a manner that they can understand. In fact, the media's focus on the "eye" of the storm, rather than on the leading edge of the storm system—with its high winds (including tornadoes) and precipitation—may delay evacuation decisions.

Not all media coverage is negative, of course. Auf der Heide (1989) says that the media can act as a friend by providing information to the public (e.g., warning information, disaster information, preparedness information) and that they can stimulate donations, encourage mitigation measures, and possibly reduce injuries. A good example of news coverage can be found on a videotape of the Channel 4 news team of WTVJ during Hurricane Andrew. This news team has been credited with saving lives, and other reporters should view their reportage. The "media as foe," however, can distort facts and provide bad examples. It may be a good idea for reporters to examine the disaster literature to understand what effect they could be having on the public. One suggestion is for disaster researchers to hold a conference with the media to discuss some of these issues and the media's critical role in disaster communication.

4. *Technology*

The common wisdom and operational imperatives for hurricane evacuation have evolved as predictive capabilities regarding landfalls, tidal surges, and wind speeds have improved. Computer models, historical experience, and simple logic can identify the major risk areas and provide probabilities of damage. Fortunately, the worst fears of the experts were not realized during the Hurricane Andrew disaster. But they might be realized in the next major storm. The National Weather Service (NWS) and Federal Emergency Management Agency (FEMA) have identified high-risk coastal communities and are assisting local governments in developing mitigation strategies, including evacuation plans. NWS SPLASH (Special Program to List the Amplitude of Surges from Hurricanes) and SLOSH (Sea, Lake, and Overland Surges from Hurricanes) models have been used to plan evacuation routes. Some local communities also use HURREVAC and the Inland Wind Computer Model.

Dr. William Gray's annual predictions based on rainfall in western Africa, El Niño current in the Pacific Ocean, westerly equatorial stratospheric winds, and barometric pressures in the Caribbean in the spring give decision makers some notion of the level of general threat each year. But the predictions give little guidance regarding specific landfall locations. While hurricanes have landfall cycles, tending to move from the East Coast to Mexico and Texas over a period of decades, the risk to particular communities is still hard to assess. Based on the history of landfalls, however, there is growing concern about the risk to south Florida and to communities along the East Coast. Probabilities of landfalls are based on aerial surveillance, barometric pressures west and north of the storm path, and other factors. The probabilities of landfalls were added to hurricane warnings in 1983 to encourage voluntary evacuations and to better communicate increasing risk.

5. Mitigation

Operational strategies have also evolved as building standards, land-use regulations, and public education have increased the survivability of coastal populations. One of the early "lessons learned" was from the devastating Galveston hurricane in 1900, which killed approximately 6000 residents. Thereafter, the town was literally raised higher and a seawall was built. Those actions were relatively progressive for the time and have served reasonably well, although storm surges have breached the wall and caused flooding in recent years and the limited points of access to the island still make evacuation difficult (Waugh 1990). In some cases, such as the catastrophic cyclone in Bangladesh that killed over 300,000 in 1970, mitigation strategies have been difficult to find. Low-lying lands with little or no cover for threatened populations afford little opportunity for government to intervene to reduce risk. Poor farmers have little choice but to cultivate in high-risk areas. Evacuation is complicated by the dispersed rural population, the inaccessibility of many farms and communities, and the lack of an effective warning system, but it may be the only solution.

Prior to Andrew, experts had expressed concern about the tremendous population growth and the nature and extent of development in south Florida and had pointed out the greatly increased exposure of lives and property. There were also concerns that residents were unfamiliar with severe storms and unappreciative of their danger. As the Andrew experience confirmed, in many cases coastal communities lacked effective land-use regulation and enforcement of building codes. Even when standards were adequate, they were not enforced effectively (Waugh and Hy 1996).

Another concern with building codes and land-use regulation is that often policies are established in response to a disaster event. These policies seem to last for a while and then revert. For example, after Hurricane Camille, a category 5 storm, hit in 1969, there were new building code regulations that prohibited a building to exceed three stories. Now that regulation has been changed and there are multistory hotels being built along the Mississippi coast. This is not the first time mitigation efforts to minimize damage have taken a step backward.

A new effort in mitigation is Project Impact. The FEMA project gives communities "seed money" to become more disaster-resistant. The Project Impact communities that are threatened by hurricanes should take into consideration evacuation planning and coordinate evacuation policies with other disaster preparedness efforts in their communities.

6. Emergency Management Responsibility, Resources, and Power

Hurricanes are not a seasonal issue (e.g., preparedness needs to be implemented ahead of time), nor are they only a coastal issue (e.g., inland flooding). Regarding information and education on preparedness, the emergency managers said that this is their job when there is no threat. One state official said she speaks to anyone anytime, but she feels as though individuals listen only right before a hurricane.

Many emergency managers are finding themselves responsible for mitigation as well as preparation, response, and recovery. Many coastal counties have evacuation behavioral and transportation analyses to aid in decision making. These behavioral analyses are supposed to occur every 5 years and, in the absence of clear priorities, some lower-risk areas may be in line to get the analyses before higher-risk areas. This could have detrimental effects with the increase of coastal populations. In 5 years, population growth and development can significantly alter the distribution of risk in a community. More frequent analyses may be needed in such cases. Another problem with the behavioral analyses is that in some areas the types of questions are mandated by policy makers who do not know the research. The restriction on what the researcher can ask severely limits the usefulness of the behavioral part of the analysis.

Emergency managers accomplish a great deal on often very low budgets. Better equipment and more personnel are driving resource issues. There seems to be a mind set that emergency managers can ''do it all.'' This is probably because emergency managers are a very competent, responsible group. However, the resources available to emergency managers change from county to county. Some emergency managers have state-of-the-art offices with a lot of useful equipment while others barely have what they need to do their jobs.

Here is a good example of emergency management resources and how they can be improved: while one hurricane was threatening, officials traveled to the migrant labor camps to warn migrant workers. Emergency management was not confident that the labor workers were receiving the information through the normal designated channels. However, when they drove up (in a sheriff's car), all of the workers ran into the woods and the officials went in after them trying to explain (in English) that they were not there to arrest illegal immigrants. Since then, the problem has been fixed because officials have access to someone who speaks Spanish and they do not arrive at migrant labor camps in a sheriff's car (Riad 1997).

Emergency managers have a lot of power during an event but do not have enough power or resources during nondisaster times to make policy decisions that could affect evacuation. During disasters, they are the authority and everyone listens to their instructions. ''During operations we make it happen, the authority and power is often more than enough.'' However, regarding preparedness ahead of time (e.g., requiring businesses to have plans) they have no authority or control (Riad 1997).

7. Legal Issues

A central issue is whether there is a legal basis for making evacuations mandatory, and if so whether it is better to force evacuations or to keep them voluntary. Local authorities might also consider their responsibilities to residents who decide to ride out the storms in their homes or businesses. The decision to stay may be an individual one; but if a rescue is necessary, it can be dangerous for public safety personnel themselves. In some cases, it may not be reasonable to try to protect people from themselves. Of importance to policy makers is the issue of legal liability for decisions (Miller 1991). When local officials are exercising their own discretion rather than simply carrying out state policies, they may be held legally liable. Federal and state officials enjoy ''sovereign immunity'' and thus are protected from personal lawsuits. For local officials, evacuation orders may well result in lawsuits brought by business and property owners who suffer economic losses and by individuals who suffer physical injury, particularly if the evacuation proves unnecessary or there is some question about its necessity or conduct.

8. *Vertical Evacuation*

Given the limited lead time in the best of circumstances, officials in low-lying communities are having to opt for vertical evacuation and ''hardened'' facilities, such as schools or hotels, that can accommodate large numbers of people. Moving entire populations out of harm's way is simply not feasible given limited time, the potential for flooding well inland (particularly along rivers and creeks and across lowlands), the danger of leaving evacuees exposed to high winds along the evacuation route, and the logistics of moving large numbers of people in a short period of time. In a study to determine people's attitudes about vertical evacuation, Ruch (1991) found that 80% of individuals in Galveston and 84% in Tampa said they would use vertical evacuation, although 20% of those in Galveston and 16% of those in Tampa said they would not use it. Most of these individuals felt their homes were safer or they would opt for horizontal evacuation in the case of a major hurricane.

9. *Special-Needs Populations*

Chatham County, Georgia has a Special-Needs Registry. This registry is for individuals who are home-bound either because of illness or severe handicap and who have absolutely no one else who can help them in an emergency situation. Individuals have a form they must fill out at the city hall to qualify for this service. There was no budget for this service in 1997. This type of a registry is an excellent idea and a simple policy suggestion; however, it must have resources to maintain it.

10. *Collective Evacuation Decisions*

As Thomas Drabek (1994) concludes, evacuation decisions by tourism executives are characterized by the same process of warning, confirmation, and mobilization. However, while business executives face a similar decision process, it is made more complex by the involvement of customers, staff, and the business owners and general managers to whom the executives are responsible. Inquiries and expressions of concern by customers may be met initially with passive reassurance, referrals to local emergency management officials, or proactive recommendations for evacuation. The executives tend to rely more heavily on confirmation by local emergency management officials rather than the media and are more likely to exhibit denial in the absence of a mandatory evacuation order. Managers of hotels and restaurants are understandably concerned about lost revenue and fear legal liability for their recommendations to customers. The managers are caught between the option of simply waiting for customers and staff members to make evacuation decisions on their own and the option of closing the facility and thereby forcing them to leave. For the firm, evacuation is generally the owner's or general manager's decision, but the decision may be made for him or her if customers leave and/or substantial numbers of the staff join their families and/or choose to evacuate.

Customers are concerned about the loss of deposits, changing their travel plans, and whether to seek shelter or return home. They often have little understanding of the hazard itself or have no knowledge of local emergency procedures, even though provisions may have been made to move them to secure facilities through vertical evacuation, designated public shelters, or accommodations in other, more secure hotels. Many businesses do not have clear plans for their employees.

11. Evacuation Policy

Ideally, emergency managers would have a systematic means of (1) assessing disaster risk, (2) communicating the danger to residents credibly, (3) assuring that residents pack appropriately and secure their homes and businesses, and (4) providing guidance and support for an orderly evacuation along safe routes to safe shelters. Evacuations should be implemented early enough to minimize risk but not so early as to increase the costs to businesses unnecessarily or to overtax the shelter and food programs. To the extent that the evacuations can be phased, with the residents in the most dangerous areas leaving first, risk can be reduced and the evacuation itself can be managed better. All of this presupposes effective planning, preparation, and implementation of the plan, with appropriate involvement by community leaders.

The reality of evacuation decision making is that warnings may not be heeded or will be heeded by some but not all; the level of risk may be difficult to judge and communicate credibly; communication with all residents may be difficult or impossible; some residents may evacuate without packing needed medicines and other supplies; and some residents simply may not have the means to evacuate. Also, evacuations can be expensive and dangerous. Quite apart from the costs of shutting down coastal businesses, evacuees incur costs for food and lodging and fear losses from looters.

Evacuation is physically demanding and may pose health risks to the elderly and infirm while also increasing the likelihood of accidental injury and death. Damage and distress from not evacuating can be avoided. Despite the common elements in all or nearly all hurricanes, evacuation policies have to be designed for the particular demographics of the community and the geography as well as offering flexibility to accommodate the peculiarities of each storm. We need to have updated information on both individual and community-level factors in order to encourage evacuation.

III. CONCLUSIONS: DESIGNING AN EFFECTIVE EVACUATION POLICY

Designing a policy that accommodates the psychology of evacuation as well as minimizing the exposure of people to hazards is a challenge. In order to meet those conditions, policy makers need to:

1. Address the reasons why people may choose not to evacuate, such as evaluating the strength of intended shelters and identifying most secure shelters (even if they do not offer adequate protection) and accommodating evacuees with pets.
2. Address the reasons why people may delay evacuation decisions, such as providing frequent situation reports and recommending decision points for evacuation preparation and actual evacuation.
3. Facilitate the social process of decision making by including families in discussions of risk and, as much as possible, organizing evacuations by neighborhood.
4. Focus attention on risk to children, the elderly, and other special populations from the disaster and from a lengthy recovery process (e.g., days or weeks without electricity).
5. Choose spokespersons who can communicate clearly and with appropriate emotional content communicate the risk to individuals, families, communities,

etc., rather than persons who simply convey factual information without giving cues concerning how it might be interpreted.

6. Remind hospitality and other business owners of the OSHA requirement (29 CFR 1910) that each firm have a written disaster evacuation plan, assist in the development of plans, and facilitate the integration of individual firm plans into the community evacuation plan.
7. Maintain and encourage social support networks. Evacuation is also part of the recovery process and, therefore, keeping families together and, to the extent possible, recommending that neighbors and others within particular communities be housed together in shelters would reduce stress and aid in the psychological recovery of individuals.
8. Update behavioral and transportation analyses more often.
9. Use scientific and technical information, including probabilities of landfalls and other events, judiciously to inform the public and the media concerning risk and the potential need for evacuations.
10. Provide a credible but reasonable assessment of the risk that individuals and families may be taking if they do not comply with evacuation orders.
11. Emphasize the uncertainty of events (e.g., flood level, wind speed, etc.) and the limits of individual and community precautions, so that individuals understand that the level of risk is unpredictable and their own resources and capabilities may be inadequate.
12. Educate the public and the media concerning disasters based upon the kinds of information that they are likely to use in making their preparedness and evacuation decisions, such as interpreting weather broadcasts.
13. Communicate the warning through a credible source, preferably a known person or agency, and do so directly and personally.
14. Build upon past disaster experience, particularly experience with evacuation itself.
15. Consider differences in ethnic groups, particularly the size and cohesiveness of families, when issuing evacuation information and orders.
16. Include information on protecting property from looters, providing for the reentry of residents to their communities as soon as possible following the disaster, and involving owners in damage assessment to the extent possible.
17. Use schools, day-care centers, and other facilities for children in communicating risk and evacuation procedures to parents to reinforce their concern about the safety of their children.
18. Involve the media in the emergency communication system so that they understand the information that they receive and communicate it effectively to the public.
19. Evaluate educational programs and provide more women with materials necessary to make informed evacuation decisions for their families.
20. Address the special needs of individuals.

Attention to those issues should increase the likelihood of compliance with evacuation orders and the effective implementation of evacuation plans. Of course, attention should also be paid to the need to (1) invest more resources in state and local emergency management efforts, including evacuation planning; (2) restrict development in hazard-prone areas, e.g., floodplains, to minimize exposure to risk; (3) spend the time and money to rebuild correctly (i.e., putting power lines underground) to mitigate future disasters;

and (4) base evacuation and other emergency plans on the largest number of residents and visitors or guests that might be expected and anticipate that they will have little understanding of the hazard and the risk that it poses. The psychology of evacuation includes both the application of knowledge about hazards and risk-reducing behaviors and normal human responses to uncertainty, fear, and excitement. Just as hurricanes and other hazards may be somewhat unpredictable, people may well behave in ways contrary to their own interests as well as the interests of policy makers. No matter what emergency managers may wish, some people will evacuate into the teeth of the storm rather than away from its danger, and some will stay at home. However, as scientists and policy makers, it is our duty to use what we know about evacuation to reduce the loss of life and cost to society as much as we can.

REFERENCES

Aronson, E. (1992). *The Social Animal.* New York: W.H. Freeman & Co.

Aguirre, B.E. (1991). Evacuation in Cancun during Hurricane Gilbert. *International Journal of Mass Emergencies and Disasters*, 9(*1*), 31–45.

Bolin, R. and Bolton P. (1986). *Race, Religion, and Ethnicity in Disaster Recovery.* Monograph #42. Boulder, Co: Institute of Behavioral Science, University of Colorado.

Cutter, S. (1994). *Environmental Risks and Hazards.* Englewood Cliffs, NJ: Prentice Hall.

Dow, K. and Cutter, S.L. (1998). Crying wolf: repeat responses to hurricane evacuation orders. *Coastal Management* 26, 237–252.

Drabek, T. (1969). Social processes in disaster: family evacuation. *Social Problems* 16(*winter*): 336–349.

Drabek, T.E. and Stephenson, J.S. (1971). When disaster strikes. *Journal of Applied Social Psychology* 1(*2*), 187–203.

Drabek, T. (1986). *Human System Responses to Disaster, An Inventory of Sociological Findings.* New York: Springer-Verlag.

Drabek, T. (1994). *Disaster Evacuation and the Tourist Industry.* Monograph #57. Boulder, CO: Institute of Behavioral Science, University of Colorado.

Festinger, L. (1954). A theory of social comparison processes. *Human Relations* 7, 117–140.

Fiske, S.T. and Taylor, S. (1991). *Social Cognition.* New York: McGraw-Hill.

Fothergill, A. (1996). Gender, risk, and disaster. *International Journal of Mass Emergencies and Disaster* 14(*March*): 33–56.

Greenberg, M.S. and Ruback, R.B. (1994). *After the Crime: Victim Decision Making.* New York: Plenum Press.

Heath, S.E. and Glickman L.T. (1998). Human evacuation and pet ownership in disasters. School of Veterinary Medicine, Purdue University. Presented at the Natural Hazards Workshop, Boulder, CO.

Kahneman, D. and Tversky, A. (1973). On the psychology of prediction. *Psychological Review* 80, 237–251.

Kirschenbaum, A. (1996). Residential ambiguity and relocation decisions: population and areas at risk. *International Journal of Mass Emergencies and Disasters* 14(*March*): 79–96.

Leavenworth, G. (1986). The Barrier Island gamble: is Galveston a catastrophe waiting to happen? *Insurance Review* (September), 40–43.

Maddox, J. and Rogers, R. (1983). Protection motivation and self-efficacy: a revised theory of fear appeals and attitude change. *Journal of Experimental Social Psychology* 19, 469–479.

Mittler, E. (1993). The public policy response to Hurricane Hugo in South Carolina. Boulder, CO: University of Colorado, Natural Hazards Research and Applications Information Center, Working Paper #84.

Moore, H., Bates, F., Layman, M., and Parenton, V. (1963). *Before the Wind: A Study of Response to Hurricane Carla*. National Academy of Sciences/National Research Council on Disasters, Study #19. Washington, D.C.: National Academy of Sciences.

Nigg, J.M. (1995). *Risk Communication and Warning Systems*. Article #285. Newark, DE: Disaster Research Center, University of Delaware.

Perry, R.W., Lindell, M.K., and Greene, M.R. (1981). *Evacuation Planning in Emergency Management*. Lexington, MA: D.C. Health.

Perry, R.W. (1979). Evacuation decision-making in natural disasters. *Mass Emergencies* 4, 25–38.

Perry, R.W. (1985). *Comprehensive Emergency Management: Evacuating Threatened Populations*. Greenwich, CT: JAI Press.

Quarentelli, E.L. (1980). *Evacuation Behavior and Problems: Findings and Implications from the Research Literature*. Monograph #16. Newark, DE: Disaster Research Center, University of Delaware.

Quarantelli, E.L. and Popov, K. (1993). *Proceedings of the United States-Former Soviet Union Seminar on Social Science Research on Mitigation for and Recovery from Disasters and Large Scale Hazards*. Monograph #25. Newark, DE: Disaster Research Center, University of Delaware.

Riad, J.K. (1997). Hurricane threat and evacuation intentions: an analysis of risk perception, preparedness, social influence, and resources. Unpublished dissertation, Department of Psychology. Atlanta, GA: Georgia State University.

Riad, J.K. and Norris, F.H. (1998). Hurricane threat and evacuation intentions: an analysis of risk perception, preparedness, social influence, and resources. Manuscript under review.

Riad, J.K., Norris, F.H., Ruback, B.R. (In press). Predicting evacuation in two major disasters: risk perception, social influence, and access to resources. *Journal of Applied Social Psychology*.

Ruch, C., Miller, H.C., Haflich, N.M., Farber, N.M., Berke, P.R., and Stubbs, N. (1991). *The Feasibility of Vertical Evacuation: Behavioral, Legal, Political, and Structural Considerations*. Monograph #52. Newark, DE: Institute of Behavioral Science, University of Colorado.

Schacter, S. (1959). *The Psychology of Affiliation*. Stanford, CA: Stanford University Press.

Sorensen, J.H. and Mileti D.S. (1988). Planning and implementing warning systems. In M. Lystad (ed.), *Mental Health Response to Mass Emergencies*. New York.

Sorensen, J.H. and Mileti, D.S. (1988). Warning and evacuation: answering some basic questions. *Industrial Crisis Quarterly* 2. Amsterdam.

Stevens, W.K. (1998). "When scientific predictions are so good they're bad." *New York Times*.

Rich, R. and Conn, W. (1993). Using a "call down" system to disseminate emergency preparedness information. Center for Environmental and Hazardous Materials Studies, Virginia Polytechnic Institute and State University. *Hazardous Materials Dialog*. 4(2).

Wachtendorf, T. (1999). Defending property. Defending identity from disaster: Arendt, Goffman, and the symbolic meaning of property. Paper to be presented at the Eastern Sociological Society, March 1999.

Waugh, W.L. Jr. (1998). Emergency management. In *Encyclopedia of Tourism*, London: Routledge Publishers.

Waugh, W.L. Jr. (1993). Co-ordination or control: organizational design and the emergency management function. *International Journal of Disaster Prevention and Management* 2(December), 17–31.

Waugh, W.L. Jr. (1990). Hurricanes. In W.L. Waugh, Jr., and R.J. Hy (eds.), *Handbook of Emergency Management: Policies and Programs Dealing with Major Hazards and Disasters*. Westport, CT: Greenwood Press.

Waugh, W.L. Jr. and Hy, R.J. (1996). The Hyatt skywalk disaster and other lessons in the regulation of building. In *Disaster Management in the U.S. and Canada*. Springfield, IL: Charles C Thomas Publishers.

22

The Role of Technology and Human Factors in Emergency Management

Francis R. Terry Interdisciplinary Institute of Management, London School of Economics and Politics, London, England

I. INTRODUCTION

Late-twentieth-century technology has unquestionably made the conditions of peacetime human existence more bearable, more prosperous, and more enjoyable. Developments in pharmaceuticals and medical care as well as in food production, communications, and transport are some of the most obvious areas in which technology has made vast impacts on the majority of people's lives over the past 50 years. Yet accidents, emergencies, and disasters continue to plague human existence. Indeed our perception of them may well have been heightened by the very technology of communications which also brings to us a wider range of information services than ever before.

On the other hand, the application of modern technology on an industrial scale carries with it the risk of catastrophic malfunction, leading to an emergency of some kind. An emergency is defined here simply as a *sudden critical juncture demanding immediate remedial action*. In seeking to prevent emergencies in an industrial context, which is the main focus of this chapter, we can distinguish between:

1. Failures of the technology itself; that is, a physical inadequacy for the intended purpose, which arises at some point as a consequence of weakness in design, poor manufacture, build up of stress or wear in the course of operation, or a variety of other possible causes
2. Failures of control; that is, a defective or inappropriate interaction between human beings and the technology

It is possible for emergencies arising from technical failure to be safeguarded against in a variety of ways—for example, by employing "fail-safe" principles in design or backup features such as triplication. Indeed, the standards of performance expected from modern industrial technology are typically very high, since people are understandably reluctant to trust machines to "think" and the potential for accidental injury and death may be considerable. Much greater reliability and confidence levels are demanded from technology than we normally require from our fellow human beings.

II. THE NEED FOR INSTITUTIONAL FRAMEWORKS

Failures of human control are much more problematic. ''Control,'' incidentally, is taken to include the conceptualization, design, and initial application of technology as well as the operation of it in practice. As Graumann (1974) has written, any technological device, whether a simple instrument or a complex computer system, is an ''agendum'' that, owing to its specific technical features, presents itself with a specific demand structure that has been incorporated into it by its designer. Man (woman)/machine interaction can therefore be viewed as a virtual social interaction between the operator and the machine's designer. Such interaction can be conceptualized as a communication process (Quintanilla 1987), subject to the same uncertainties of understanding and defects in comprehension as other, more direct forms of communication. Thus, however mechanized or automated a device may be, there is inevitably at some point a human interface with it, and this is a potentially dangerous source of weakness.

As in the case of physical failure, there are remedies that the technology itself can provide which may help to guard against such dangers. ''Intelligent'' systems can eliminate misuse, mindless error, or inconsistent decisions, thus helping to reduce the chance of an emergency, but the system may still be vulnerable to eventual failure through inadequate maintenance (Flin 1996). Despite significant advances in psychological research (see, for example, Rasmussen et al. 1987; Hockey 1996), the human/machine interface remains a critical problem area in the prevention of emergencies.

Society's response to this problem has been to evolve institutional frameworks and social mechanisms that seek to prevent or mitigate the effect of failures of the human/machine interface as well as the effect of failures in the operation of the machinery itself. Institutional frameworks may be imposed externally, in the form of independent inspectorates or audit bodies, or they may be located in-house (U.K. Health & Safety Executive 1991). Their functions constitute a form of regulation. The trend in Europe is for in-house organizational units to assume increasing importance in the prevention and control of emergencies—for example, through safety management systems. Instituting a safety management system would typically involve consideration of:

Organizational structure
Management and personnel standards
Training for operations and emergencies
Safety assessment
Design assessment
Procedures for operations, maintenance, modifications, and emergencies
Management of safety by contractors to the organization in respect of their work
Involvement of the work force in safety
Accident and incident reporting, investigation, and follow-up
Monitoring and auditing of the operation of the system
Systematic reappraisal of systems in the light of experience internally and across the industry more generally (Cullen 1988)

Despite the comprehensive appearance of such a system, a failure in any one or more of the functions listed could allow a problem at the human/machine interface to trigger an emergency. Even if institutional frameworks and social mechanisms worked with the precision and reliability that we expect of the technology itself, there would still be problems.

III. REGULATING BEHAVIOR AT THE HUMAN/TECHNOLOGY INTERFACE

We can demonstrate this by examining how the behavior of an operative is regulated at the interface with technology in a particular case. In the railroad industry, failure of the correct interaction between human actors on the one hand (locomotive engineers, dispatchers, and signalers) and control technology on the other has the potential for very serious accidents and emergencies to arise.

The response of railroad organizations is, first, to operate a recruitment and training policy designed to ensure that all staff are fully trained and tested for competency before commencing their duties. At the initial selection stage, the recruit is tested for his or her capacity to absorb and retain the necessary training; to carry out routine tasks consistently; and to respond appropriately in the event of an emergency. The selection process includes medical and possibly psychometric tests. Subsequent training is designed to ensure that the required competencies can be deployed in a wide range of working conditions and situations.

For the locomotive engineer, for example, it would comprise:

Knowledge of the traction equipment, including operating characteristics and fault diagnosis and treatment

Train handling knowledge, i.e., understanding the characteristics of operation with particular loads

Route knowledge, including locations of signals and stations, crests and bottoms of grades, turn-outs and sidings

Knowledge of all relevant rules, special instructions and procedures (Health & Safety Executive 1993)

Once the engineer is employed, a further set of institutional checks is maintained on his performance. Health status has to be monitored regularly and training has to be refreshed or updated. Performance on the job is monitored in various ways, to ensure compliance with current standards, and this may be through random inspection, self-reporting of incidents, or simulator driving, to name some examples. Safety officers, safety drills, welfare services, and support services all have their part to play.

One particular source of risk in the railroad context (though it is also present in many other industries) concerns fatigue. There is widespread acceptance in the industry, enshrined in all manner of directions and rules, that the number of hours spent at work is positively correlated with fatigue and that this, in turn, leads to an increasing risk of accident. On the British railroad system, no employee is allowed to work more than 12 hours in any day or 72 hours per week and shall not work more than 13 days out of 14. The pattern is similar across other European countries, with additional restrictions imposed on locomotive engineers' hours—a maximum of 9 applies in the U.K. case. Nevertheless, fatigue is still identified as a major cause of accidents and emergencies.

The problem is partly that there is no generally recognized definition of fatigue and there are few objective measures of it. Indeed, as Dyer-Smith (1997) observes, we could substitute *stress*, *boredom*, or *lack of motivation* for the word *fatigue*, and the same supposed relationship between hours of work and proneness to accidents would hold good. A review of recent literature on accidents, however, reveals that they do not necessarily increase in frequency the longer an operative works. The study of bus drivers by Pokorny et al. (1981) showed that there is a concentration of accidents in the third and fourth hours of work. A study by Hamelin (1987) of truck drivers suggests that risks are actually highest in the first 4 hours of duty unless the total work period exceeds 12 hours. Wharf (1993) found a distinct peak of ''signal passed at danger'' incidents among railroad engineers in the second hour of duty. Folkard (1996a and 1996b) found a similar peak in a more general review of industrial injury rates.

It is hypothesized by Dyer-Smith (1997) that the explanation of the 2- to 4-hour peak lies in the interaction of *engagement* and *habituation*, two effects that he describes as individually linear but acting in opposite directions. When an operative starts duty, he or she is usually mentally alert and concentrating on the task in hand; in other words, engagement is high. If the task, such as driving, is familiar and routine, habituation sets in over time. Given predictable stimuli, says Dyer-Smith, performance of the task demands diminishing mental resources as responses become virtually automated. We can all think of behavior patterns that become routine and mental processes that lose none of their effectiveness by becoming unconscious. The 2- to 4-hour peak could be attributable to the fact that while engagement is falling off, automatization is not yet at maximum efficiency. Within this ''window,'' the potential for failure in the human/machine interface is heightened.

It is difficult to know what implications this research has for the design of institutions and procedures concerned with preventing accidents and emergencies. At the least, we could say that an awareness of the 2- to 4-hour peak might caution operatives in safety-critical areas to be especially on their guard. Technological aids to vigilance might be improved. Further research might illuminate the risks at work from boredom and fatigue and approaches might be found to meet them.

The conclusion from the argument so far, and it is a somewhat depressing one, is that while technology itself—along with institutional frameworks of regulation, inspection, monitoring, etc.—is a considerable insurance against emergencies arising from failures at the human/machine interface, it cannot guarantee perfect safety. As a result, much interest in emergency management focuses on the containment of risk. In other words, having been forced to accept that somewhere along the line failure may sooner or later occur, we seek to quantify the risks and minimize them wherever possible.

IV. LIVING WITH RISK

It is important to note that risks may be *tolerated* as the price of securing certain benefits, and that this may be done in the belief that the risks are being controlled. The knowledge that nearly 4000 people die every year in road accidents across the United Kingdom, with injuries to many more, does not discourage people from incurring the risks associated with driving. To say that we tolerate a risk does not mean that we ignore it or regard it as negligible but that it is a factor that needs to be kept under review and further reduced if possible. If we say that a risk is *acceptable*, on the other hand, it means that, in relation to life or work, we are willing to take it more or less as it is. A woman who wants a child will not change her mind if she learns that the average chance of death due to pregnancy and childbirth is around one in 10,000.

We may define *risk* as the chance that some event that affects us adversely will occur. To take a risk means deliberately incurring that chance, while estimating a risk involves defining the adverse event precisely and establishing a means of calculating how often it is likely to happen in particular circumstances. When we use the word *chance*, we usually mean the probability of something happening. *Risk*, then, may be defined as *the chance of an adverse event happening and the consequences of that event taken together*. Before continuing, we need to consider three further points.

First, there is no such thing as a total absence of risk. Whether we exploit modern technology to the full or abhor it, we continually experience various kinds of risk, even by remaining at home. One may fall downstairs and break a leg. In performing other kinds of activities, we would experience other types and levels of risk. Second, we should remember that however remote a risk may seem, it could nevertheless occur. The chance of being struck by lightning in the United Kingdom is about one in 10 million, but it still might happen to any one of us. Remote risk is therefore not the same as no risk at all. Finally, as individuals, our chances inevitably vary according to a whole range of factors, such as where we live, how fit we are, how old, how observant, etc.

In normal conversation, the word *risk* is quite often used to emphasize the consequences rather more than to the probability. If we see a driver speeding through an intersection at the moment when the traffic lights change to yellow or red, we might say ''that's risky''—meaning not so much that there is a high *probability* of a collision but that it will have dangerous *consequences* if it does happen. We should therefore include a third component in estimating risk: the *severity* of the consequences. This third aspect becomes more and more important as the number of people potentially affected by any given risk increases.

It is possible to draw a distinction between risks that we *voluntarily* incur as a result of individual choice and risks that are imposed on us *externally* by governments, commercial firms, and other agencies. There are also significant risks from natural causes, and public bodies may take action to control these risks—as, for example, in London, where the local authority constructed a barrage across the river Thames estuary to reduce the risk of flooding when there is a freak high tide.

V. INSTITUTIONAL FRAMEWORKS AND RISK CONTROL

Regulatory institutions may seek to control risks that are voluntarily incurred if enough people are affected by them. Thus, local and national governments make road improvements in an effort to reduce the risk of accidents. But institutional frameworks have a major, and often a more problematic, role in seeking to manage the risks from applying modern technology in an industrial context. These risks may have implications that are quite as severe as those that are voluntarily incurred or stem from natural causes. They include risks from the siting of nuclear and chemical plants, refineries, dams, defense installations, and certain types of waste repository. Even though there may be compensating benefits from the existence of such facilities, which contribute in some way to a better life for all, society demands that they are regulated in the interests of controlling risk. Table 1 shows a comparison of the risk of death from all causes as against certain categories of accident arising from the application of industrial technology on a large scale.

We might note in passing that most people apply quite different criteria to involuntary risks as compared to voluntary ones. They expect the former to be reduced to much lower levels and they often believe in an implicit right to know how risks from potentially hazardous technology are being controlled. The presence of risk can vary considerably according to location, and the benefits may be unevenly distributed: a decision to construct a nuclear power station, for example, imposes risks on people nearby, but the availability

Table 1 Some Risks of Death Expressed as Annual Experiences (U.K. Figures)

	Risk as annual experiences
Dying from all causes	
Average over whole population	1 in 87
Men aged 55–64	1 in 65
Women aged 55–64	1 in 110
Men aged 35–44	1 in 578
Women aged 35–44	1 in 873
Boys aged 5–14	1 in 4,400
Girls aged 5–14	1 in 6,250
Dying from cancer	
Average over whole population (Great Britain)	1 in 374
Death by all violent causes	
(Accidents, homicides, suicides, others—average over population of Great Britain)	1 in 2,700
Death by accidents (all Great Britain)	1 in 4,200
Death by road accident	
(Average over population of Great Britain)	1 in 10,204
Death by gas incident	
(fire, explosion or poisoning—average over population of Great Britain)	1 in 1,100,000
Death by lightning	1 in 10,000,000
Death by industrial accident	
Deep sea fishermen on U.K. registered vessels	1 in 750
Extraction of oil and gas	1 in 990
Extraction of minerals and ores	1 in 3,900
Coal extraction	1 in 7,100
Construction	1 in 10,200
Agriculture	1 in 13,500
All manufacturing industry	1 in 53,000
Metal manufacturing	1 in 17,000
Instrument engineering industry	1 in 1,000,000
All service industries	1 in 150,000

Sources: Central Statistical Office. (1991). *Annual Abstracts of Statistics*. London: HMSO.
Health & Safety Commission. (1991). *Annual Report*. London: HMSO.
Department of Transport Marine Accident Investigation Branch. (1991). *Annual Report 1990*. London: HMSO.

of cheap power may be spread over a much wider area. Risks may be shifted in time: for example, tolerable risks at the present may be traded against higher levels of risk in the future. A balance has also to be struck between saddling industries and businesses with an excessively heavy framework of supervisory institutions and allowing those same industries and businesses to fall below what the public considers a tolerable level of risk (Royal Commission on Environmental Pollution 1976).

Against this background, it is all too easy to assume that regulatory institutions should be composed of highly qualified experts, taking decisions on behalf of citizens who are busy with their own lives and prefer to believe that the risks from industrial applications of technology are negligible, or who are not interested in finding out exactly what the risks are. On the other hand, however competent the experts may be and however small the statistical risks of an emergency, public perceptions are inclined to be different. Creating institutional frameworks necessarily implies placing a degree of trust in officialdom to act on the citizen's behalf; and that trust has to be maintained consistently with public perceptions (Starr 1985).

It may be argued that regulatory institutions, as well as the industries exploiting modern technology, have a responsibility to inform and educate the public even if they are not particularly interested or concerned about risk (Slovic 1986). But even then, public expectations about the level of risk that can be tolerated will differ according to the hazard involved, while individuals' knowledge and feelings about risk will quite legitimately vary. Opinions about the value of benefits obtained will also vary, and ethical views of certain activities may differ too. In a democratic society, such factors have to be given due weight in emergency management.

VI. THE CASE OF NUCLEAR POWER

In the United Kingdom, debate about such issues has surfaced periodically in response to actual emergencies or the fear of potential emergencies. One example in this second category is the question of whether or not to construct further nuclear power stations. In the early 1980s, the former nationalized electricity undertaking, the Central Electricity Generating Board (CEGB), put forward proposals for a new nuclear station on the coast of Suffolk in eastern England. The station was to be of the pressurized water reactor (PWR) type widely used in the United States but relatively untried in the British environment. Public consultation was extensive, leading to a wide-ranging public inquiry spread over 2½ years. The report of the inquiry, conducted by Sir Frank Layfield, an eminent judge, was submitted to the secretaries of state in 1986; approval to construct was subsequently given and the station is now working.

The public inquiry was the largest and most expensive of its kind, bringing together leading scientists, lawyers, environmentalists, and officials to give and to hear testimony. The report of the inquiry is one of the most compendious sources of information on all aspects of the development of nuclear stations. Among his recommendations, Layfield called for the Health & Safety Executive (HSE) to "formulate and publish guidelines on the tolerable levels of individual and social risk to workers and the public from nuclear power stations." He averred that "the opinion of the public should underlie the evaluation of risk; there is at present insufficient public information to allow understanding of the basis for the regulation of nuclear safety" (Layfield 1987).

This was a remarkable recommendation on two counts: it acknowledged for the first time that public opinion as much as expert opinion had a place in the assessment of risk from an industrial facility, but it also implicitly criticized the promoters of the scheme for failing to raise public understanding to a point where it could sensibly formulate such an opinion. Layfield perhaps was overoptimistic. He seems to have believed that, with more information, a fair and rational compromise between promoters and objectors would be found. In reality, many objectors felt defeated but found themselves powerless to resist further.

VII. THE REGULATION OF RISK

The HSE did nevertheless publish the guidelines that had been called for (Health & Safety Executive 1992a), and they deserve critical examination. They constitute an invaluable case example of how a regulatory institution seeks to control the risks arising from the application of a potentially dangerous technology. The HSE's guidelines lay down a series of tests to be applied in regulating risks from industrial plants: (1) Whether a given risk is so great or the outcome so unacceptable that it must be refused all together; (2) Whether the risk is, or has been made, so small that no further precaution is necessary; or (3) If a risk falls between these two states, that it has been reduced to the lowest level practicable, bearing in mind the benefits flowing from its acceptance and taking into account the costs of any further reduction. The injunction laid down in safety law is that any risk must be reduced so far as reasonably practicable, or to a level which is "as low as reasonably practicable" (the ALARP principle).

Procedures like these conform to commonsense expectations, but they do not go very far in specifying how risk should be controlled in specific situations. On the other hand, it has to be recognized that not everything can be measured with the greatest degree of accuracy. Where a risk can be quantified, a definite standard of performance should be fixed; and where measurement is not possible, expert assessment or judgment is called for. In its application of these procedures, the HSE puts the onus on employers to take responsibility: "At the core of any organisation's activities for safety is the need to manage its own undertaking in an appropriate way" (Health & Safety Executive 1991). Although management is expected to take responsibility and be vigilant in identifying opportunities for improvement, the HSE may insist that there is a basic standard of achievement or a particular requirement to be met—even if the costs involved threaten the viability of the business concerned.

In considering the risks of large-scale injury and death from industrial plant, it is characteristic of regulatory institutions, including the HSE in Britain, to insist that the owners of the plant should carry out and submit for examination the basic assessment (Health & Safety Executive 1992b). The executive may then require additional measures to be taken. The assessment procedure recommended by HSE starts with the technology itself, by examining the overall design and reliability of the process and the risk of plant failures, which should so far as possible be quantified. Since it is not always possible to show how an overall design or an individual component will perform under extreme circumstances or in every situation, expert judgment may have to be relied on in deciding what reinforcement is needed to cope with the unexpected. Physical components may need to be strengthened or additional, backup components may be incorporated to provide *redundancy*.

Redundancy will not necessarily guard against design faults, which might be repeated in every component of that type; consequently, it may be necessary to rely on components that perform a similar function but are designed independently. We call this *design diversity*. HSE maintains (Health & Safety Executive 1992a) that design diversity can be very effective in the case of simple devices, since different versions almost invariably fail independently of one another. But in more complex situations, it appears to deliver only a modest level of protection from risk. For example, experiments on diverse computer software have suggested that there is a tendency for different designers, working separately on the same problem, to make similar errors. We note that even in these early stages of the assessment, human factors impinge on the application of the technology at every turn.

Next, the technology has to be examined in the physical context of the plant. This implies close scrutiny of the quality standards applied to design, construction, operation, and maintenance of the plant. Quality management is a subject in itself and, while important in the overall control of risk, is not discussed further here. We pass on to the organizational context, which covers the psychological and physical dimensions of work in the plant, together with the operational and management procedures above them. As the British Health & Safety Executive has expressed it, ''While the 'hardware' of safety . . . must be of a high standard, technical excellence is not enough and, on its own, will not ensure a consistent safety performance. In most high-technology industries . . . the underlying causes of accidents are organisational'' (Health & Safety Executive 1993). Human beings are, of course, themselves a source of risk, as we have seen from the railroad industry example, but there are subtler aspects to be considered as well. Management may be able to motivate and lead the work force in identifying new risks or countering unnecessary risks (Barrett 1997). The importance of repeated analysis, communication, consultation, and reporting in dealing with risk-related issues (Misumi 1978) should be stressed.

VIII. RISK ASSESSMENTS

Although all these approaches have value in minimizing the risks within an industrial plant, the external implications of failure have also to be assessed. Such an assessment can be considered at two levels—*individual* and *societal*. In the first case, the key task is to calculate the risk to any random individual who lives within a defined distance of the plant or who follows a pattern of life that might expose him or her to the consequences of an accident. This entails, first, an estimation of the likelihood of a failure occurring in the plant at all. Data need to be collected and maintained on experience with similar plants and processes elsewhere and on the characteristics of those failure situations that have occurred in order to gain a picture of reliability.

The results of specific failures then have to be evaluated. How much toxic gas, radioactivity, inflammable substance, etc., would be released? How would these releases affect a hypothetical person at a particular location, either outdoors or indoors? What would be the effect of weather conditions? How would population density and transport patterns possibly multiply the effect on a single individual? Having examined the chances of harm from all significant causes of failure and preferably quantified them, an overall summation can be made of the risk from the plant. When such ''individual risk'' calculations have been made, they enable us to say, for example, that ''a person who lives within a half-mile radius of the plant has a chance of x per year of being injured from a significant accident at that plant.'' It is perhaps easy to forget that emergencies do not result only in death or survival: they may lead to a reduction in life expectancy relative to the norm as well as to immediate pain or suffering.

The consequences of a major emergency may go much wider than injury to individuals. For example, in the case of the Chernobyl nuclear accident, there were health effects internationally, and there were major disruptions to life in all its forms locally. Not least, there was a loss of plant and electricity production, which had considerable economic impact. Though less dramatic—certainly less newsworthy—than a mass killing at a single moment, large numbers of accidental deaths over a long period of time (and other deleterious effects from plant failures) are just as much a matter of public concern. These societal risks, as we call them, could in principle be evaluated just as individual risks are and assigned monetary values. It would then be possible to talk in terms of the costs of an emergency and perhaps to set this against a calculation of the benefits accruing in financial and other ways from the existence of the plant.

Such calculations would be fraught with problems and involve placing values on things that are not only difficult to estimate in themselves but also difficult to weigh with each other. Nonetheless, at the simplest level, we might say that no benefit, however large, would lead us willingly to accept the kind of costs produced by a calculation of the societal risks—unless the benefit took the form of avoiding some even greater misfortune. In making this comparison, we should, of course, have to estimate the probability of incurring the costs in question. The two factors can be combined by multiplying the costs likely to be incurred by the probability of their being incurred in order to produce a measure of *detriment.*

If such a measure were obtained, it would enable the relative detriment of pursuing different technological solutions to reach a particular goal to be compared. For example, it might enable us to evaluate the detriment from industrial activities that gave rise to the risk of accidents against the detriment from continuing with some more insidiously harmful processes. The comparison between nuclear and coal-burning power plants in ecologically sensitive areas is one obvious application that springs to mind. Unfortunately, we are a long way from common agreement on the methodology for performing such complex calculations. There are no recognized accounting or valuation standards that would apply. Estimation of the probability of remote events is an inexact science. The best we can probably do is to estimate what chance there is of a given number of people losing their lives from an emergency of a specified type and comparing this with other, similar risks that are ordinarily accepted or well known.

IX. CONCLUSION

Technology has a seductive appeal for us. It offers the promise of comfort, prosperity, and many other enhancements to human existence. We recognize the potential for emergencies to arise from its application on an industrial scale, and a range of strategies is pursued to lessen such occurrences. In an organized society, it is also a rational and effective response to create institutions that regulate the risky area at the interface between technology and human behavior. Research, analysis, and experience of past emergencies has helped these institutions—whether internal units or external agencies—to understand the dimensions of risk and to implement appropriate preventive measures, controls, and sanctions.

Nevertheless, all the risks from utilizing technology on a large scale cannot be reliably contained. The potential effects of an emergency may involve a much wider field than the workforce on the spot: the public at large, sometimes over a wide area, may be vulnerable. This raises questions about public understanding and participation in the regulatory process, and about the calculation of individual and societal risk from industrial plants and the like. There are clear limits to the extent of protection available to us in harnessing technology, and while those limits might be pushed further out by research and experience, the danger is that prevention of emergencies becomes an ever-growing bureaucratic exercise. Where the point of diminishing returns sets in—that is, where the costs of regulation exceed the resources of the operating organization—is not only a matter of economics but is, as we have seen, powerfully influenced by social factors.

REFERENCES

Barrett, D. (1997). *The 1997 Review of Crisis and Risk Management*. London: Infoplan International.

Cullen, The Hon. Lord. (1988). *The Public Inquiry into the Piper Alpha Disaster*. London: Department of Energy.

Dyer-Smith, M. (1997). Boredom and fatigue in transport industries. *Proceedings of the Chartered Institute of Transport* 6(*1*), 48–53.

Flin, R. (1996). *Sitting in the Hot Seat—Leaders and Teams in Critical Incident Management*. Chichester, U.K.: John Wiley & Sons.

Folkard, S. (1996a). Diurnal variation. In G.R.J. Hockey, ed., *Stress and Fatigue in Human Performance*. New York: John Wiley & Sons.

Folkard, S. (1996b). Black times: temporal determinants of transport safety. In L. Hartley, ed., *Fatigue and Transport Engineering: Enforcement and Education Solutions*. Freemantle, W.A.: Murdoch University.

Hamelin, P. (1987). Quoted in Folkard, S. (1996b).

Health & Safety Executive (1991). *Successful Health and Safety Management*. London: HMSO.

Health & Safety Executive (1992a). *Tolerability of Risks from Nuclear Power Stations*. London: HMSO.

Health & Safety Executive (1992b). *Safety Assessment Principles for Nuclear Plants*. London: HMSO.

Health & Safety Executive (1993). Ensuring safety on Britain's railways—A report submitted to the Secretary of State for Transport. London: Department of Transport.

Hockey, G.R.J. ed., (1996). *Stress and Fatigue in Human Performance*. New York: John Wiley & Sons.

Layfield, F. (1986). *Report of the Sizewell 'B' Public Inquiry*. London: Department of Energy.

Misumi, J. (1978). The effects of organizational climate variables, particularly leadership variable and group decision making on accident prevention. Munich: 19th International Congress for Applied Psychology.

Pokorny F. et al. (1981). Quoted in Folkard, S. (1996b).

Quintanilla, S.A.R. (1987). New technologies and human error: social and organizational factors. In J. Rasmussen et al., eds., *New Technology and Human Error*. New York: John Wiley & Sons.

Rasmussen, J., Duncan, K., and Leplat, J. (1987). *New Technology and Human Error*. New York: John Wiley & Sons.

Royal Commission on Environmental Pollution. (1976). *Sixth Report—Nuclear Power and the Environment*. London: HMSO.

Slovic, P. (1986). Informing and educating the public about risk. *Risk Analysis* 6(*4*), 403–415.

Starr, C. (1985). Risk management, assessment and acceptability. *Risk Analysis* 5(*2*), 57–102.

23

The Intergovernmental Dimensions of Natural Disaster and Crisis Management in the United States

Alka Sapat School of Public Administration, College of Administration, Urban and Public Affairs, Florida Atlantic University, Fort Lauderdale, Florida

I. INTRODUCTION

Every year thousands of communities and cities across the United States are affected by natural disasters. In the last decade alone, natural disasters such as floods, hurricanes, and earthquakes have claimed the lives of thousands and have led to billions of dollars being spent on response and recovery. For instance, the federal government spent almost $120 billion (in constant 1993 dollars) on disaster assistance between the fiscal years 1977 and 1993 (Joint Task Force 1995). Likewise, state expenditures on natural disasters increased by 56% between the fiscal years 1992 and 1994, and states spend approximately $1.6 billion in emergency management per year (NEMA 1994; Cabot 1996). In light of the rising cost of natural disasters and the devastation caused by them, there is a growing consensus that the current approach to natural disasters needs reworking. To further the goal of finding a new approach to disaster management, a number of reports and legislative initiatives have appeared that focus on reworking approaches to disaster management. In particular, two major trends stand out clearly in these efforts to improve disaster management. First, attention has increasingly focused upon hazard mitigation as opposed to recovery as a solution to the problems caused by natural disasters (FEMA 1994, 1995a, 1995b; NAPA 1994). Second, the focus on mitigation has been accompanied by an increasing emphasis on the devolution of responsibilities to the state and local levels (FEMA 1996a, 1996b).

While the first of these issues (i.e., mitigation strategies) has received a fair amount of attention, relatively less scholarly work has been done on the second issue of analyzing how states have coped and will cope with their new responsibilities, particularly in the area of mitigation. The gaps in the literature leave several questions unanswered, namely: How have states been handling their responsibilities in disaster management and in mitigation? Will the devolution of powers to state governments be successful? Will states be willing to shoulder more policy responsibilities? How will states cope with these new burdens on their political, economic, and social structures?

To answer these questions, neglected in prior studies of disaster management, this chapter focuses on the role of the 50 states in disaster management and mitigation and analyzes the determinants and constraints to devolution. Section II below is a brief discussion of the factors that have led to a renewed emphasis on devolution and mitigation in emergency management in the United States. Section III presents a description of the main aspects of federal legislation and administrative regulations dealing with mitigation at the national level. To answer the main research question posited in this essay, I examine existing efforts made by state governments to cope with natural disasters in Section IV. Next, I turn to the problems that states might encounter by analyzing the factors that could hinder or help state efforts to cope with emergencies. Using theories pertaining to the role of state political institutions, political elites, interest groups, and citizens, I analyze the potential influence of these factors on state commitment and capacity to manage mitigation effectively. The chapter ends with a brief conclusion.

II. DEVOLUTION AND MITIGATION

As discussed earlier, there has been a renewed emphasis in emergency management on two issues: devolution and mitigation. The reasons underlying this emphasis are as follows:

First, the costs of natural disasters have been important in spurring policy makers to recognize the importance of preventive measures to lessen the impact of disasters on life and property. Over the past decade alone, disasters such as Hurricane Andrew, Fran, and more recently Hurricane Georges have resulted in millions of dollars worth of damage (Beatley 1996; Beatley and Brower 1996). These events galvanized policy makers at the federal, state, and local levels to pay more attention to mitigation and prevention. For instance, these events added to the growing recognition among policy makers that unplanned communities and growing populations, particularly in hazard-prone zones, are likely to worsen the impact of disasters on human lives and property. Second, the rising costs associated with natural disasters have led policy makers at the federal level to search for means to cut these costs. One solution has been to reexamine cost sharing between federal, state, and local governments. As in other policy areas, devolution from the federal to the state levels has been seen as means of reducing the burden placed on federal actors. Third, related to this issue, is the growing perception on the part of federal legislators that federal disaster assistance policies may act as a disincentive to states to shoulder the responsibility for disaster preparation, response, and recovery. The report of the bipartisan task forces of the Senate and House released in 1994 (supported by similar reports from the House and Senate) concluded that current federal disaster assistance policies in some instances may discourage individuals, communities, and state governments from taking action to prepare for, respond to, and recover from disasters (U.S. Senate Bipartisan Task Force on Funding Disaster Relief 1994; U.S. House of Representatives 1994; U.S. Senate 1995). Finally, devolutionary trends in other policy areas ranging from welfare to the environment have influenced the policy-making process with respect to disaster management as well (Donahue 1997). Devolution has been increasingly emphasized as a panacea to all ills ailing federal government, particularly since 'Reaganomics' took hold in the 1980s. Ideologically then, it is seen as being desirable to both federal and to some state actors. This prevailing ideology has affected the terms and parameters of the debate in emergency management as well.

For these reasons, a "pound of prevention as opposed to an ounce of cure," along with devolution, have become the new *mantras* of the disaster management pundits and experts. These ideas have been put into practice through federal legislation and administrative regulations, which are examined next.

III. FEDERAL LEGISLATION AND ADMINISTRATIVE REGULATIONS DEALING WITH MITIGATION AND STATE RESPONSIBILITIES

The federal government has undertaken several measures to reflect the increased emphasis placed on mitigation and to increase state efforts in this area. The most important of these measures has been the passage of the Stafford Act of 1988, which mandated state adoption of hazard mitigation plans and allocated money for hazard mitigation. In addition, the Federal Emergency Management Agency has also developed implementation rules and policy responses to federal legislation. Of these, two of the most important are the implementation regulations promulgated by the Federal Emergency Management Agency (FEMA) for the Hazard Mitigation Grant Program (HMGP) (under the Stafford Act of 1988) and for the Flood Mitigation Assistance Program (FMAP) (created under the Flood Insurance Reform Act of 1994). In addition, the adoption of a National Mitigation Strategy by FEMA helps coordinate these different programs. In this section, I briefly review provisions of the Stafford Act relevant to mitigation activities at the state level, followed by a brief review of the relevant rules and policies adopted by FEMA.

A. The Stafford Act of 1988

The Stafford Disaster Relief and Emergency Assistance Act of 1988 emphasized three major means of undertaking mitigation: (1) Section 409 mitigation plans; (2) Section 404 mitigation grants; and (3) Hazard Mitigation Survey Teams and Interagency Hazard Mitigation Teams (the latter were established under a 1980 Office of Management and Budget Directive and incorporated into Section 206 of the Stafford Act) (Godschalk 1996).

Under Section 409 of the Stafford Act, states are required to prepare state disaster mitigation plans as a condition of eligibility for federal disaster assistance. The 409 plans require states and their localities to identify hazard risks and to adopt programs and policies to reduce such current and future risks. FEMA can, under the provisions of this section, condition disaster assistance funds on the implementation of state 409 plans. However, while this provision exists, FEMA has seldom used it to coerce states in implementing its 409 plans.

The Stafford Act requires that state 409 mitigation plans contain elements addressing the following issues (Godschalk 1996; Kaiser and Goebel 1996):

- Assessment of natural hazards
- Hazard mitigation goals and objectives
- Analysis of existing policies, and state and local capabilities to mitigate hazards
- Proposed strategies, programs, and actions
- Proposed approach to implementation
- Proposed approach to monitoring of implementation and hazard conditions
- Proposed approach to evaluation of plan and implementation
- Proposed approach to updating the plan

While Section 409 deals with planning, Section 404 of the Stafford Act deals primarily with fiscal issues and aimed to solve funding issues with respect to mitigation. Under this section, the HMGP was created. This program provides federal matching funds for state and local mitigation projects (Joint Task Force 1992). A more detailed discussion of the HMGP follows in Section III.B, below.

Incorporated into the Stafford Act is also a provision to facilitate mitigation planning and implementation in the wake of a flood-related disaster (developed by the U.S. Office of Management and Budget and subsequently incorporated into the Stafford Act). This provision established a procedure for activating postdisaster mitigation teams of federal, state, and local representatives. Thus, following every disaster, an Interagency Hazard Mitigation Team is called into action. The main mission of this team is to quickly formulate a postdisaster report that identifies hazard mitigation opportunities and recommends actions. The team does this by reporting immediately to the disaster scene and reviewing the damage. The team recommendations are then intended to act as a feedback mechanism and guide the state in the preparation of its 409 hazard mitigation plan and its 404 hazard mitigation grants application. The Stafford Act also provides for federal/state Hazard Mitigation Survey Teams for non-flood-related disasters. The functions of these teams are similar to those of Interagency Hazard Mitigation Teams (Godschalk 1996:6).

B. Mitigation Policies and Programs Adopted by the Federal Emergency Management Agency

To facilitate the implementation of federal legislation dealing with mitigation and the devolution of responsibilities to the state level, the Federal Emergency Management Agency has promulgated a number of regulations and policies. Some of the most important among these are regulations for the HMGP and the Flood Mitigation Assistance Program. In addition, the development of a National Mitigation Strategy in 1994 has been crucial to achieve mitigation goals and develop partnerships with state and local governments, along with citizens and the private sector. These are reviewed briefly in turn.

1. The Hazard Mitigation Grants Program: Implementation Rules

As discussed above, the HMGP was created in 1988, by Section 404 of the Stafford Disaster Relief and Emergency Assistance Act. While the Act provides for funding mechanisms, it is FEMA that implements this legislation. More specifically, it is FEMA that assists state and local communities in implementing long-term mitigation measures following a presidential disaster declaration. To meet this objective, FEMA can fund up to 75% of the eligible costs of each project. The state or local cost-share match does not need to be cash; in-kind services or materials may also be used. Federal funding under the HMGP is now based on 15% of federal funds spent on the public and individual assistance programs (minus administrative expenses) for each disaster with the passage of the Hazard Mitigation and Relocation Assistance Act of 1993 (FEMA 1995a, 1995b).

The HMGP can be used to fund projects to protect either private or public property as long as the projects in question comply with program guidelines and fit within the overall mitigation strategies of the state and local governments involved. Examples of projects that may be funded include the retrofitting of existing structures to protect them from future damage, the acquisition or relocation of structures from hazard-prone areas, and the development of state or local standards designed to protect buildings from future damage. Eligibility for funding under the HMGP is limited to state and local governments, certain private nonprofit organizations that serve a public function, authorized tribal organizations, and Alaska Native villages or organizations (FEMA 1995a, 1995b, 1996a).

Over $2 billion has been invested in mitigation projects under FEMA's HMGP since 1993. However, many of these projects are not completed yet because of requirements for multiple agency review by states and FEMA, misunderstanding of project eligibility, and inadequate local plans to develop the projects. To improve management of the HMGP, FEMA has recently promulgated a new set of implementation rules. Under these new rules, a "dual management system" is created to encourage states to develop their mitigation capabilities. More specifically, under this new system, a state, based on its mitigation capabilities, is classified as either a "managing" state or a "coordinating" state at the time of a declared disaster. If a state is classified as a "coordinating state," it will require a FEMA sign-off on projects. However, if it is designated to be a "managing state," the state will be given final authority for project fund dispersal. The classification categories are based on several factors or criteria such as the presence of a full-time permanent hazard mitigation officer, an approved state mitigation planning process and documentation, and the ability to provide technical assistance on mitigation techniques (FEMA 1996a:18–19).

Under the new rules promulgated by FEMA, there is also greater clarification about the eligibility of projects, communities, and hazards addressed by HMGP projects. In particular, these new rules provide for a shift away from structural to nonstructural projects, which is again part of a larger national trend in hazard mitigation. Hence, projects that would invest in major structural works or the building up of areas through artificial beach replenishment are considered more or less "taboo." The rationale behind this rule is the avoidance of additional development that could exacerbate existing problems in coastal areas. Moreover, structural approaches to mitigation have been discredited by existing research, which clearly shows that such measures are costly, have a negative impact on the environment, and render people more vulnerable to the damaging effects of natural disasters (Interagency Floodplain Management Review Committee 1994; Faber 1996; Federal Interagency Floodplain Management Task Force 1992a, 1992b).

2. The Flood Mitigation Assistance Program: Implementation Rules

The Flood Mitigation Assistance Program was created under the National Flood Insurance Reform Act enacted in 1994. Similar to the HMGP, implementation rules adopted by FEMA for the Flood Mitigation Assistance Program clarify eligible project funding, describe procedures and criteria for allocating funds, and generally seek to provide states with greater flexibility in program implementation.

Three types of grants are provided under this program: planning assistance grants, project implementation grants, and technical assistance grants. To be eligible for funding, a locality or state must have a Flood Mitigation Plan in place. The rule also stipulates what must be included in a Flood Mitigation Plan. The preparation of these plans themselves renders a state or locality eligible for the first type of grant—i.e. planning assistance grants. In some cases, a state's 409 plan or a local plan prepared under the Community Ratings System fulfills eligibility requirements for further funding (FEMA 1996b; Godschalk 1996).

Planning assistance funds are allocated through FEMA's regional offices by a competitive process. Other funds in this program are also allocated through FEMA's regional offices: the allocation is weighted according to the number of repetitive loss structures and the number of flood insurance policies in force. Examples of eligible projects are elevation, acquisition, demolition, or relocation, minor structural projects, and certain forms of beach nourishment. Similar to the HMGP program, structural measures and artificial beach replenishment are strongly discouraged.

3. *The National Mitigation Strategy*

The National Mitigation Strategy represents the first major attempt at the federal level to put forth a systematic agenda to develop a strategic plan for mitigation. FEMA began to develop the plan in 1994 based on a series of national mitigation forums involving a vast number of organizations, citizens, and public and private organizations. The resulting document presents a vision for the future, a set of principles underlying the main strategy, an overall national mitigation goal, and a series of more specific mitigation objectives. While somewhat difficult to isolate from the overall strategy, which is comprehensive in its scope, some of the major aspects of this strategy are critical to developing state capacities in mitigation. The relevant parts of the National Mitigation Strategy that apply to state capacities in mitigation are as follows:

The strategy is based on the principle that all mitigation is local and that the building of new federal-state-local and public-private partnerships is the most effective way of implementing measures to reduce the impact of natural hazards.

One of the objectives of the Mitigation Action Plan of the National Mitigation Strategy aims to encourage state and local governments to develop sustained administrative structures and resources for mitigation programs, to adopt and enforce building code and land use measures, and to conduct ongoing public information campaigns on natural hazard awareness and mitigation.

The strategy also calls for the federal government, in partnership with state and local governments, to provide leadership, coordination, research support, incentives, and resources to encourage communities, businesses, and individuals to undertake mitigation to minimize potential disasters and to employ mitigation strategies during the recovery process following disasters.

States and localities are also encouraged to prepare a risk assessment and to create disaster funds.

The strategy also laid down that within 5 years of its adoption, infrastructure funds and other federal assistance would be conditioned on the local adoption and enforcement of building codes and "life-cycle maintenance plans" for community buildings.

While these are some of the main elements of the National Mitigation Strategy relevant to the role of state and local governments, the strategy also contains a number of other measures that clearly renders it a watershed document in the history of U.S. mitigation policy. Moreover, the strategy is one of the main elements through which the goals of mitigation and the devolution of responsibilities to state governments are to be achieved. However, the strategy also has a number of flaws. A major drawback of the National Mitigation Strategy as formulated is that it relies more on rhetoric than reality. It is overly ambitious and some of the strategies laid down to achieve the stated goals may not be conducive to their effective implementation. As discussed further on, the unclear and ambiguous nature of some of the goals and strategies can hinder the achievement of mitigation and pose obstacles to the assumption of greater responsibility by state governments.

IV. STATE EFFORTS IN DISASTER MANAGEMENT

While federal actors play an important role in hazard mitigation and disaster management, emergency management in the United States is a shared responsibility of governments at the federal, state, and local levels. The review of federal legislation and of FEMA policies discussed above elucidates the role that states must play in emergency management: for instance, state and local governments are mandated to undertake or are given incentives to undertake certain mitigation measures. Mandated measures include the development of state 409 plans and the HMGP program. In addition, as the federal legislation discussed in the previous section indicates, states are given incentives to develop disaster funds for mitigation and undertake general measures to improve their mitigation capabilities. If we are to understand how states will cope with greater responsibilities in the future, it is important to first understand how states measure up so far in these areas. Below, state efforts in the development of 409 plans, measures undertaken under the HMGP program, and expenditures undertaken for mitigation purposes are examined.

A. State 409 Plans

Studies undertaken recently by a team of scholars at the University of North Carolina—Chapel Hill (Godschalk 1996; Healey and Berke 1996; Kaiser and Goebel 1996; Young et al. 1996; Berke and Bohl 1996; Beatley 1996) provide an excellent and comprehensive analysis of state 409 plans. In their assessment of the content and quality of state 409 plans, these scholars find that, in general, state 409 plans are at their strongest in describing and assessing present hazards, but they are much weaker in assessing risk in a systematic manner and assessing the vulnerability of people and property to hazards. Moreover, they find that mitigation action proposals tend to stress measures that are the easiest to implement, such as promoting awareness and providing technical assistance, rather than actions that are more effective but that require greater political commitment, cost more, and intervene more directly in the development process (such as acquisition of property at risk, land use regulations, and the protection of community infrastructure). Implementation proposals were mostly very general and broad rather than specific, while most plans do not emphasize monitoring, the evaluation of implementation, and the changing status of hazards and vulnerability. While most plans met the pro forma requirements of the Stafford Act, the overall quality of plans was mediocre in their assessment and most plans were descriptive rather than being goal- and objective-oriented (Kaiser and Goebel 1996). In short then, the adoption of these plans appear to be purely symbolic rather than real and seem to be mainly for the purposes of fulfilling federal mandates to qualify for fund assistance.

B. State 404 Funds: The HMGP Program

As mentioned above, the Hazard Mitigation Grants Program (HMGP) was created under Section 404. This program provides federal matching funds for state and local mitigation projects. These grant funds are contingent upon disaster declarations and are limited to a percentage of the federal public assistance monies made available. FEMA committed about $437 million in the years between 1998 and 1995 for this program and approved approximately 905 applications. Despite these impressive numbers, the 404 program has been riddled with problems. In an evaluation of the HMGP, a joint task force of the

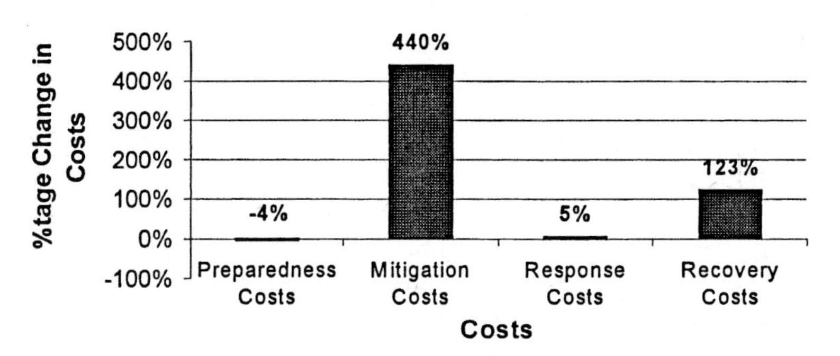

Figure 1 Changes in state costs for comprehensive emergency management, 1992–1996. (From National Emergency Management Association 1996.)

National Emergency Management Association and the Association of State Floodplain Managers found a number of problems with it: a lack of hazard mitigation principles and guidance, difficulties in state coordination, a slow pace of implementation, and failure of states and localities to identify mitigation opportunities before disasters occurred.

C. State Expenditures for Hazard Mitigation

Analysis of state expenditures on disaster management was recently undertaken by the Council of State Governments and the National Emergency Management Association (NEMA/CSG Report 1996). Figure 1 presents the results of the analysis of state expenditures. As can be seen from this figure, states significantly increased spending for comprehensive emergency management. In particular, state expenditures for mitigation increased by 440% between 1992 and 1996.

Figure 2 presents a graphical overview of state mitigation expenditures over the years 1992 to 1994. As seen in this graph, overall state spending totaled $130,217,433 in 1992. This figure rose to $206,135,652 in 1994. On average, states spent approximately $4,481,210 on mitigation activities in 1994. Analysis by the National Emergency Management Association also shows that, contrary to the perceptions of federal actors, the number of state disaster declarations outnumbered the number of federal declarations in the years 1992 to 1994.

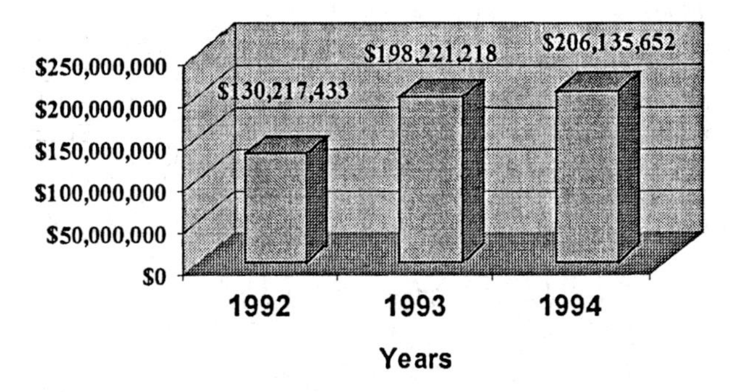

Figure 2 State mitigation expenditures, 1992–1994. (From National Emergency Management Association 1996.)

These reductions in federal declarations and the increase in state declarations have had a major impact on state pre- and postdisaster spending. When compared to federal payments by FEMA to state and local governments for predisaster expenses, state predisaster expenses were found to be higher. State costs for predisaster emergency management in the 3-year period from 1992 to 1994 totaled $1,934.1 million, while FEMA expenditures totaled $367 million. Similarly, state costs for response and recovery rose dramatically between 1992 and 1994 from $609.4 million to $953.5 million (NEMA/CSG Report 1996:15).

V. FACTORS AFFECTING STATE CAPABILITIES IN DISASTER MANAGEMENT

While the discussion above indicates that states have been making progress in improving their capabilities in disaster management, it also indicates that this progress has been slow. While states have improved their capabilities, they still face problems in developing their mitigation capabilities. To understand how states will cope with the devolution of even greater responsibilities in the area of emergency management, it is important to understand the issues and factors that affect state capabilities and willingness to assume greater responsibilities in the management of natural disasters. I focus on the issues affecting the policy readiness of state governments by analyzing them through various theoretical lenses. In particular, I analyze the influence of and theoretical issues related to the following factors: (1) problem severity and exposure to natural hazards (2) the ability and capacity of states; (3) the role of interest groups; and (4) the importance of administrative and political elites.

A. Problem Severity

One major influence on state emergency management is the magnitude of the problem itself or the susceptibility of the state to natural disasters. States such as California, Florida, Texas, and Louisiana, which have experienced earthquakes, floods, and hurricanes, are more likely to be sensitive to the need to adopt mitigation measures. Indeed, researchers have long regarded problem severity as a significant influence on state regulation and the adoption of innovations (Walker 1969; Gray 1973; Hilgartner and Bosk 1988; Hedge and Scicchitano 1993; John 1994; Nice 1994). In general, problem severity can spur state policy makers to address a problem. For instance, disasters can act as "focusing events" or crises that can galvanize policy makers into action (Kingdon 1984).

However, the assumption that objective indicators of need will prod policy makers is somewhat simplistic and neglects dynamics intrinsic to the policy process. Previous research has demonstrated that policy making is not based only on scientific findings of need but also on perceptions of that need (Berke and Beatley 1992; Ringquist 1997). The manner in which issues of need are framed, defined, and perceived by policy makers will very likely determine the actions taken by them. In addition, policy makers have to be cognizant of measures available to craft effective remedies to solve the problem.

With respect to natural hazards and disaster management in particular, the importance of subjective perceptions of need and problem severity factors become even more complicated and acquires special importance. A number of scholars have noted, time and again, the low saliency and priority attached to natural hazards by policy makers (Rossi et al. 1982; Burby 1985; Burby et al. 1991; Kunreuther and Kleffner 1992). This renders the adoption of mitigation measures difficult. For instance, scholars have found that in states such as Washington and Missouri, there has been considerable resistance to instituting seismic building codes for residential structures despite studies showing their importance in reducing future losses. Moreover, few residents adopted any mitigation measures voluntarily because they did not perceive an earthquake to pose a credible threat (Drabek et al. 1983; Kunreuther and Kleffner 1992). Others might not voluntarily adopt mitigation measures because budget constraints combined with relatively short time horizons may discourage individuals from adopting expensive cost-effective mitigation measures. Furthermore, even if scientists and experts judge risks as being important, elected officials may be less supportive of management or mitigation actions that are costly or politically unpopular (Mushkatel and Nigg 1987; Lambright 1982). If the capacity to implement mitigation actions does not exist, it may be difficult for states to undertake such policies (Mittler and Alesch 1996).

In view of the latter considerations, it is likely that the presence of other factors—such as institutional capacity and resources, interest group support, and institutional commitment—are also necessary for policy makers to take action in mitigation and disaster management (Mittler 1988). I discuss these factors next.

B. Capacity and Ability of State Officials

While elite attitudes and their commitment may be important in understanding whether states will be effective in undertaking new responsibilities in emergency management, their ability and capacity to do so will also be important. *Ability* refers to the actual capacity of state governments and agencies to effectively adopt and implement emergency management and mitigation policies. In other words, the funding and staffing levels available to plan and carry out mitigation efforts. With respect to capacity, changes that have taken place over the years at the state level have been positive to a large extent. In particular, over the past decade or so, state institutions have increased in size and capacity, strengthening their ability to deal with new problems and pioneer new public policies in a host of areas (Van Horn 1989, 1993; Bowman and Kearney 1986; Elazar 1984).

For instance, state legislatures have become increasingly professional and have increased their institutional capacity considerably in the last 25 to 30 years. Rosenthal (1993, 1996) has documented the "rise of the legislative institution" in the states from the rural-dominated political backwaters of the 1950s to the modern, more professionalized and representative institutions of today. The reform and revitalization in state legislatures resulted in the strengthening of institutional capacity and the increasing professionalism of its members (Rosenthal 1993:116–117). Since the 1970s there has also been a dramatic increase in professional staffing. Fiscal staffs, audit and evaluation staffs, caucus and partisan staffs, and legislative and district aides greatly enhanced the ability of legislators to delve more deeply into policy issues, increased oversight capabilities, and enabled legislators to assess the effectiveness of government programs (Rosenthal 1993, 1996). There has also been an improvement in legislative facilities with the construction of new office buildings to provide space for standing committees, staff, and members. Legislators also began spending more time on their jobs, both in and out of session. Moreover, professionals are replacing former groups of "citizen legislators." As per estimates by Rosenthal, approximately two-fifths of the nation's legislators are largely in professional legislatures or moving gradually toward the professional model (Rosenthal, 1996:110). Theoretically, more professional state legislatures will have greater resources, better-educated members, and higher compensation levels. Hence they will have more resources and information to examine emergency management issues in detail and adopt policies to deal with mitigating natural hazards (Grumm 1971; Lester et al. 1983; Ringquist 1993).

In addition to institutional capacity, fiscal capacity is also important. The greater the resources available to a state, the more likely it is that the state can afford to undertake more stringent regulation or adopt policy innovations (Williams and Matheny 1984; Lowry 1992; Ringquist 1993). However, it is important to keep in mind that while the fiscal health of a state may enable a state to plan and implement mitigation policies, it may lead us to develop facile conclusions regarding the use of such resources by states. It is necessary to also analyze the complexities of the relationship between fiscal health and state mitigation policies. For instance, it is conceivable that if achieving economic development is extremely important to state officials, they may be less willing to adopt mitigation policies that interfere with goals of economic growth. The conflict between goals of economic development and emergency management can be seen, for example, in coastal states. A number of states along the coast have allowed development to continue unimpeded and unrestricted, even though such development is susceptible to coastal hazards and is damaging to the environment (Beatley 1992; Platt et al. 1991; Platt 1994). Similarly, states have allowed development to occur in flood plains despite evidence that such development can be destroyed in the event of a natural disaster.

Thus, even if states have the ability, they may not be willing to use it. Moreover, state emergency management officials often have to counter powerful interests who may oppose emergency management or mitigation measures that are not in their interest. Interest groups may play a powerful role, and it is these actors that I turn to next.

C. Interest Groups

States may face natural disasters and have the capacity to deal with them. However, interest groups may oppose emergency management or mitigation measures if such measures impose costs on them. Theoretically, scholars have acknowledged the role of interest groups in policy making to be vitally important. Theories of interest group influence on policy makers range from those that see interest groups as predominant (Stigler 1971; Bernstein 1955; Bauer et al. 1964) to those that posit interest groups as not exercising any more influence over regulatory policy than any other actors or bureaucrats (Meier 1988; Derthick and Quirk 1985). The former perspective assumes that certain groups of people, who are organized and economically powerful, will have the capability to dominate policy at the subnational level. While this view is compatible with the Madisonian perspective of private parochial interests at the state level modifying policy outcomes, it has been modified considerably to account for characteristics of interest groups, such as size and density, that could affect their capabilities to exert influence over state regulation (Aggarwal et al. 1987; Lowery and Gray 1994). The motivations and actions of other political actors, bureaucrats, and other interest groups themselves have also been found to be important in influencing policy outcomes (Wilson 1989; Mushkatel and Weschler 1985; Petak and Atkinson 1982). Moreover, the evidence on state regulation indicates that interest groups of regulated interests often choose the level of government to lobby (Teske 1994).

The technical complexity of some of the issues involved in the adoption of mitigation measures tends to enhance the importance of interest groups in this area. Technical complexity can lead to what Wilson (1989) characterizes as "interest-group" politics or policy making that is characterized by the presence of interest-group conflict, with little involvement by other actors outside the system. For instance, mitigation measures such as the adoption of building codes are important. However, building codes are technically complex and there are a number of organized interest groups such as building contractors, design professionals, the insurance industry, structural engineers, architects, energy conservation groups, consumer advocacy groups, and environmental groups that stand to lose or gain from the adoption of wider coverage or more stringent hazard provisions (May 1997; May et al. 1995; Cohen and Noll 1981). For instance, previous studies of building code regulations at the state and local level have shown that interest groups have been important in influencing regulation. Noam (1982) found that the dominance of groups, both advocates and opponents of regulation, was a critical factor in choosing local over national codes. In his study of state oversight of local building regulations, similarly, May (1997) finds strong support for interest group activities in influencing state regulatory choices. Thus, it is important to consider the presence and activity of interest groups in analyzing state emergency management. If such interest groups are powerful, state emergency management officials as well as state elite policy makers need to be motivated and committed to achieving the goals of mitigation.

D. Commitment by Institutional Elites

An important factor determining the activism of states in emergency management is motivation of states to adopt policy innovations is the attitude of institutional elites. The importance of elites in the policy-making process is theoretically supported by the elite perspective of policy analysis. The elite theory of the policy process is closer to the neo-pluralist view: neo-pluralists, such as Lindblom (1977, 1990) challenged the pluralist notion that power was diffuse and argued instead about the privileged position of business. Put in a nutshell, elite theorists argue that power is concentrated in elites who use the resources of their respective organizations to manage and impose order on society. Political and economic stability in society, according to this perspective, does not come about because of a common political culture and some particular set of values. Instead, stability albeit superficial, is created by a forced consensus that is managed and reinforced by the elite. Key decisions regarding policy are thus made by primarily by elites. Popular and electoral politics are, for the most part, mainly symbolic and concerned with middle-level policy issues, according to the elite perspective (Mills 1956; Farazmand 1994, 1999). In short, this perspective stresses the role of the elite in the policy process.

The motivation of institutional actors and elites is also stressed in theories that emphasize the importance of institutions in policy and governance (Noll and Owen 1983; Moe 1989; North 1990; Van Horn 1996). Institutional theories posit that government actors can act independently of interest group pressures and other factors. According to this view, government actors are not merely advocates and representatives of the views and attitudes of various interest groups; rather the attitudes and views of these actors influence the manner in which they process information and affect independently the policies they put in place (North 1990; Van Horn 1996). Institutional theories also recognize that informational constraints and computational limitations of political actors prevent actors from making purely "rational decisions" that are independent of the actor's subjective representation of the decision problem (Alston et al. 1996; North 1990; Cohen and Olson 1972; Cyert and March 1963). Thus, the attitudes and ideological views of state legislators, governors, and bureaucrats can influence and shape the types of disaster management and mitigation policies that are adopted.

Given the theoretical importance of elite attitudes, one would expect that when state emergency management officials are committed to adopting mitigation policies, there would be a greater likelihood of such policies being adopted. This expectation is supported to some extent by the existing evidence. For instance, researchers have found that one explanation for the variation in the adoption and implementation of state 409 plans discussed above, has been the differing levels of political and organizational willingness on the part of the states to support and pursue hazard mitigation goals and policies (Berke and Bohl 1996).

Elite attitudes towards other groups involved in emergency management can also be important. This is particularly true in the case of emergency management, given that such management is a function of intergovernmental coordination and involves actors at the federal, state, and local levels (Sylves and Waugh 1996; Burby et al. 1997). The perceptions of state officials toward local governments as well as toward federal actors in terms of the roles that each play in mitigation and in emergency management in general may be crucial to achieving the necessary coordination. In achieving this coordination, miscommunication can often occur. For instance, federal actors, particularly in Congress, tend to believe that the federal government does more than its fair share in disaster management, while states do not do as much (U.S. House of Representatives 1994). On the other hand, state officials counter that such allegations are unfair and that states do indeed commit resources and energy to building and maintaining capabilities to protect the lives of citizens from natural and artificial hazards (NEMA 1996).

Such misunderstandings can be costly. For instance, over $2 billion has been invested in mitigation projects under FEMA's Hazard Mitigation Grant Program since 1993. Many of these projects are not completed yet because of misunderstanding of project eligibility, requirements for multiple agency review by states and FEMA (i.e., overlapping jurisdictional responsibilities) and inadequate local plans to develop the projects.

With respect to state-local relations, similar forms of miscommunication may occur. To avoid such miscommunications, some states clearly define the role of local governments. For instance, some states maintain the tradition of home-rule laws that give local governments great power in emergency management and other policy areas. However, in other cases, the division of responsibilities is less clear. Thus, even if administrative and political elites are committed and view a problem as being serious, confusion or misperceptions about the level of government that is responsible for taking action can lead to inactivity. For example, as Mittler (1988:106) points out, in states like Louisiana, even though key state figures rated hurricane issues as very serious, the state legislature has consistently viewed hurricane and flood control as local problems. Moreover, even though issue salience was high in Louisiana, it did not lead to legislation on nonstructural mitigation because structural approaches had been historically prominent.

In short, to understand whether states will respond effectively to new responsibilities and take charge in mitigation and emergency management, it is necessary to recognize that the 50 American states are extremely diverse in their political, economic, and social environments. States vary across a number of dimensions and some crucial differences exist in terms of the severity of the problem they face, their capacities and abilities to overcome these problems, their commitment to do so, and the attitudes of elite policy makers.

VI. CONCLUSION

With the rising costs and destruction associated with disasters, exacerbated by phenomena such as El Niño, efforts by the federal government to devolve responsibility to the states and to improve state capacities in emergency management have increased. Within this context, mitigation actions in particular are viewed as being extremely important in disaster management. While state spending for emergency management has increased considerably over the last few years, states, nonetheless, vary considerably in their adoption of mitigation measures and in terms of the resources they commit to mitigation funding. In order to understand the effectiveness of federal efforts to encourage states to shoulder greater responsibilities in disaster management, I argue that it is important to take into account various state-level factors, such the severity of the problem, the ability and capacity of states, and the role of interest groups and of administrative and political elites. These factors are explored in some detail in this paper, and the manner in which they relate to state mitigation policies are analyzed. Using theories of interest group and elite behavior, I find that it is crucial to take these actors into account in understanding the intergovernmental dimensions of emergency and crisis management in the United States.

ACKNOWLEDGMENT

This research was funded in part by the National Science Foundation, NSF Grant No. CMS9813611.

REFERENCES

Aggarwal, Vinod K., Robert O. Keohane, and David B. Yoffie. (1987). The dynamics of negotiated protection. *American Political Science Review* 81(*June*), 345(22).

Alesch, Daniel J. and William J. Petak. (1986). *The Politics and Economics of Earthquake Hazard Mitigation*. Institute of Behavioral Science Monograph No. 3. Boulder: University of Colorado.

Alston, Lee J., Thrainn Eggertsson, and Douglass C. North (1996). *Empirical Studies in Institutional Change*. Cambridge, U.K.: Cambridge University Press.

Bauer, Raymond A., Ithiel de Sola Pool, and Lewis Anthony Dexter. (1964). *American Business and Public Policy*. New York: Atherton.

Beatley, Timothy (1996). *National Trends in Mitigation Policy: An Evolving Framework*. Working Paper #6. Chapel Hill, NC: Center for Urban and Regional Studies, University of North Carolina at Chapel Hill.

Beatley, Timothy (1992). *Risk Allocation Policy In the Coastal Zone: The Current Framework and Future Directions*. Washington, D.C.: Office of Technology Assessment, U.S. Congress.

Beatley Timothy and David Brower (1996). *Hazard Mitigation in Florida Following Hurricane Andrew*. Working Paper #13, Chapel Hill, NC: Center for Urban and Regional Studies, University of North Carolina at Chapel Hill.

Berke, Philip R. and Timothy Beatley (1992). *Planning for Earthquakes: Risk, Politics, and Policy*. Baltimore: Johns Hopkins University Press.

Berke, Philip R. and Charles C. Bohl (1996). *Policy, Capacity, and Commitment in Hazard Mitigation: Intergovernmental Linkages*. Working Paper #7, Chapel Hill, NC: Center for Urban and Regional Studies, University of North Carolina at Chapel Hill.

Bernstein, Marver (1955). *Regulating Business by Independent Commission.* Princeton, NJ: Princeton University Press.

Bowman, Ann O'M., and Richard C, Kearney (1986). *The Resurgence of the States.* Englewood Cliffs, NJ: Prentice Hall.

Burby, Raymond J. (1985). *Flood Plain Land Use Management: A National Assessment.* Boulder, CO: Westview Press.

Burby, Raymond J. with Beverly A. Cigler, Steven R. French, Edward J. Kaiser, Jack Kartez, Dale Roenigk, Dana West, and Dale Whittington (1991). *Sharing Environmental Risks: How to Control Governments' Losses in Natural Disasters.* Boulder, CO: Westview Press.

Burby, Raymond J., Peter J. May, and Robert Paterson (1997). Improving compliance with regulations: choices and outcomes for local government. Journal of the *American Planning Association.* (Forthcoming)

Cabot, Sandra (1996). "The art of readiness: results of a national survey reveal that many disaster costs are absorbed at the state and local levels." *State Government News,* January, pp. 18–21.

Chubb, John (1985). The political economy of federalism. *American Political Science Review* 79, 994–1015.

Cohen, Linda and Roger Noll (1981). The economics of building codes to resist seismic shock. *Public Policy* 29(*1*), 1–29.

Cohen, Michael, James March, and Johan Olsen (1972). A garbage can model of organizational choice. *Administrative Science Quarterly* 17(*March*), 1–25.

Cyert, Richard M. and James G. March (1963). *A Behavioral Theory of the Firm.* Englewood Cliffs, NJ: Prentice-Hall.

Derthick, Martha and Paul Quirk (1985). *The Politics of Deregulation.* Washington, D.C.: Brookings Institution.

Donahue, John D. (1997). *Disunited States.* New York, NY: Basic Books.

Drabek, T.E., Alvin Mushkatel, and T. Kilijarrel (1983). *Earthquake Mitigation Policy: The Experience in Two States.* Boulder, CO: Institute of Behavioral Science, University of Colorado.

Elazar, Daniel J. (1984). *American Federalism: A View from the States,* 3rd ed. New York: Harper & Row.

Faber, Scott (1996). *On Borrowed Land: Public Policies for Floodplains.* Cambridge, MA: Lincoln Institute of Land Policy.

Farazmand, Ali (1994). Organization theory: an overview and appraisal. In Ali Farazmand, (ed.), *Modern Organizations: Administrative Theory in Contemporary Society.* 3–43. Westport, CT: Prager Press.

Federal Emergency Management Agency (1998). *Promoting the Adoption and Enforcement of Seismic Building Codes: A Guidebook for State Earthquake and Mitigation Managers.* Washington, DC: FEMA 313.

Federal Emergency Management Agency (1996a). Proposed Rule for Hazard Mitigation Grant Program, 44 CFR Part 206, RIN Disaster Assistance; Hazard Mitigation, April 1.

Federal Emergency Management Agency (1996b). *Proposed Rule for Flood Mitigation Assistance Program.* 44, CFR Part 78, RIN 3067-AC45, April 1.

Federal Emergency Management Agency (1995a). *National Mitigation Strategy.* Washington D.C. January.

Federal Emergency Management Agency. (1995b). *Mitigation: Cornerstone for Building Safer Communities.* The Report of the Mitigation Directorate for Fiscal Year 1995, Washington, D.C.

Federal Emergency Management Agency (1994). *A Multi-Objective Planning Process for Mitigating Natural Hazards.* Denver, CO: FEMA Region VIII.

Federal Interagency Floodplain Task Force (1992a). *Floodplain Management in the United States: An Assessment Report*: Vol. 1. *Summary Report.* Washington D.C.: FEMA.

Federal Interagency Floodplain Task Force (1992b). *Floodplain Management in the United States: An Assessment Report*: Vol. 2. Washington D.C.: FEMA.

Godschalk, David R. (1996). *Assessing Planning and Implementation of Hazard Mitigation Under the Stafford Act: Study Approach*. Working Paper #1, Chapel Hill, NC: Center for Urban and Regional Studies, University of North Carolina at Chapel Hill.

Gray, Virginia (1973). Innovation in the states: a diffusion study. *American Political Science Review* 67, 1174–1185.

Grumm, J. 1971. The effects of legislative structure on legislative performance. In R.I. Hofferbert and I. Starkansky (eds.), *State and Urban Politics*. Boston: Little, Brown.

Healey, Mark and Philip Berke (1996). *Opinions of State Hazard Mitigation Officers About Mitigation Planning and Implementation: Report of A Survey*. Working Paper #2. Chapel Hill, NC: Center for Urban and Regional Studies, University of North Carolina at Chapel Hill.

Hedge, David M. and Michael J. Scicchitano (1993). The states and environmental regulation in the 1980's: a test of the New Federalism. In Fred A. Meyer, Jr., and Ralph Baker (eds.), *State Policy Problems*. 129–145. Chicago: Nelson-Hall.

Hilgartner, Stephen and Charles L. Bosk (1988). The rise and fall of social problems: a public arenas model. *American Journal of Sociology* 94(*1*), 53–78.

Insurance Institute for Property Loss Reduction (1995). *Summary of State Mandated Codes*. Boston: Insurance Institute for Property Loss Reduction. [Now called the Institute of Business and Home Safety (IBHS).]

Interagency Floodplain Management Review Committee (1994). *Sharing the Challenge: Floodplain Management into the 21st Century*. Washington D.C.: GPO.

Joint Task Force on the Hazard Mitigation Grant Program (1992a). *Mitigation Grant Program: An Evaluation Report*. National Emergency Management Association, Association of State Floodplain Managers, and FEMA, September.

Joint Task Force on the Hazard Mitigation Grant Program, (1992b). *The Hazard Mitigation Grant Program: Summary Summaries*. National Emergency Management Association, Association of State Floodplain Managers, and FEMA, September.

John, DeWitt (1994). *Civic Environmentalism: Alternatives to Regulation in States and Communities*. Washington, DC: Congressional Quarterly Press.

Kaiser, Edward J. and Mathew Goebel (1996). *Analysis of Content and Quality of State Hazard Mitigation Plans Under Section 409 of the Stafford Act*. Working Paper #3, Chapel Hill, NC: Center for Urban and Regional Studies, University of North Carolina at Chapel Hill.

Kingdon, John W. (1984). *Agendas, Alternatives, and Public Policies*. Boston: Little, Brown and Company.

Kunreuther, Howard and Anne E. Kleffner (1992). Should earthquake mitigation measures be voluntary or required? *Journal of Regulatory Economics* 4, 321–335.

Lambright, Henry W. (1982). *The Role of States in Earthquake and Natural Hazard Innovation at the Local Level: A Decision-Making Study*. Syracuse, NY: Science and Technology Policy Center.

Lester, James P., James Fronke, Anne Bowman, and Kenneth Kramer (1983). Hazardous waste politics and public policy: a comparative state analysis. *Western Political Science Quarterly* 36, 258–285.

Lindblom, Charles (1977). *Politics and Markets: The World's Political Economic Systems*. New York: Basic Books.

Lowery, David, and Virgina Gray (1995). The Population Ecology of Gucci Gulch, or the Natural regulation of interest groups in the American states. *American Journal of Political Science* 39(*February*), 29.

Lowry, William (1992). *The Dimensions of Federalism*. Durham, NC: Duke University Press.

May, Peter J., Dan Hansen, and Mark Donovan (1995). *State Building Code and Energy Administration: Report to Respondents to a National Survey of State Agencies*. Seattle, WA: Department of Political Science, University of Washington.

May, Peter J. (1997). State regulatory roles: choices in the regulation of building safety. *State and Local Government Review* 29(2), 70–80.

Michaels, Sarah (1992). New perspectives on diffusion of earthquake knowledge. *Earthquake Spectra* 8(*1*), 159–175.

Mills, C. Wright (1956). *The Power Elite*. New York: Oxford University Press.

Mittler, Elliot (1988). Agenda-setting in non-structural hazard mitigation policy. In Louise Comfort (ed.). *Managing Disaster: Strategies and Policy Perspectives*. Durham, NC: Duke University Press.

Mittler, Elliot and Daniel J. Alesch (1996). A reassessment of state roles in disaster mitigation and management. National Science Foundation Grant Proposal: Division of Civil and Mechanical Systems.

Moe, Terry (1989). The Politics of Bureaucratic Structure. In John E. Chubb and Paul E. Petersen (eds.), *Can the Government Govern*? Washington, DC: Brookings Institution.

Mushkatel, Alvin H., and Joanne Nigg (1987). Effect of objective risk on key actors' support for seismic mitigation policy. *Environmental Management* 11, 77–87.

Mushkatel, Alvin H., and Louis F. Wescler (1985). Intergovernmental implementation of building codes with lateral force provisions. *Policy Studies Review* 4, 680–688.

National Academy of Public Administration (NAPA) (1994) *Review of Actions Taken to Strengthen the Nation's Emergency Management System*. Washington, D.C.: NAPA, March.

National Emergency Management Association and Council of State Governments. (1996). *NEMA/CSG Report on State Emergency Management Funding and Structures*. Lexington, KY: Council of State Governments, February.

Nice, David (1994). *Policy Innovation in the States*. Ames, IA: Iowa State University Press.

Noam, Eli (1982). The choice of governmental level in regulation. *Kyklos: The International Review of Social Sciences*, Fasc. 2, 278–291.

Noll, Roger and Bruce M. Owen (1983). *The Political Economy of Deregulation: Interest Groups in the Regulatory Process*. Washington, D.C.: American Enterprise Institute for Public Policy Research.

North, Douglass (1990). *Institutions, Institutional Change and Economic Performance*. Cambridge University Press.

Petak, William J. and Arthur A. Atkisson (1982). *Natural Hazards Risk Assessment and Public Policy: Anticipating the Unexpected*. New York: Springer-Verlag.

Platt, Rutherford H. (1994). Evolution of coastal hazards policies in the United States. *Coastal Management* 22, 265–284.

Platt, Rutherford H., Timothy Beatley, and Crane Miller (1991). The folly at Folly Beach and other failings of U.S. coastal erosion policy. *Environment* 33, 7–9, 26–32.

Rosenthal, Alan (1989). The legislative institution transformed and at risk. In Carl E. Van Horn (ed.), *The State of The States*. 69–101. Washington, D.C.: Congressional Quarterly Press.

Rosenthal. Alan (1993). The legislative institution: in transition and at risk. In Carl E. Van Horn (ed.), *The State of The States*. 115–148. Washington, D.C.: Congressional Quarterly Press.

Rosenthal, Alan (1996). The legislature: unraveling of institutional fabric, In Carl E. Van Horn (ed.), *The State of the States*. 108–142. Washington, DC: Congressional Quarterly Press.

Ringquist, Evan J. (1993). *Environmental Protection at the State Level: Politics and Progress in Controlling Pollution*. Armonk, New York: M.E. Sharpe.

Rossi, Peter H., James D. Wright and Eleanor Weber-Burdin (1982). *Natural Hazards and Public Choice: The State and Local Politics of Hazard Mitigation*. New York: Academic Press.

Stigler, George (1971). The theory of economic regulation. *Bell Journal of Economics and Management Science* 2, 3–21.

Sylves, Richard T. and William L. Waugh, Jr. (1996). *Disaster Management in the U.S. and Canada: The Politics, Policymaking, Administration, and Analysis of Emergency Management*, 2nd ed. Springfield, IL: Charles C Thomas.

Teske, Paul (1994). The state of state regulation. In David Rosenbloom and Richard Schwartz, eds. *Handbook of Regulation and Administrative Law*. 117–137. New York: Marcel Dekker.

U.S. House of Representatives (1994). *Report on the Bipartisan Task Force on Disasters*. Washington, D.C.: Congress of the U.S., December 14.

U.S. Senate. (1995). *Report on the Senate Task Force on Funding Disaster Relief*, Washington, D.C.: U.S. GPO, March 15.

U.S. Senate Bipartisan Task Force on Funding Disaster Relief (1994). *Federal Disaster Assistance*. Washington, D.C.: Congressional Research Service, General Accounting Office, November.

Van Horn, Carl E. (ed.) (1989). *The State of the States*. Washington, D.C.: Congressional Quarterly Press.

Van Horn, Carl E. (ed.) (1993). *The State of the States*, 2nd ed. Washington, D.C.: Congressional Quarterly Press.

Van Horn, Carl E. (1996). *The State of the States*, 3rd ed. Washington, D.C.: Congressional Quarterly Press.

Walker, 1969. The diffusion of innovation among the American States. *American Political Science Review* 63, 880–899.

Williams, Bruce and Albert Matheny (1984). Testing theories of social regulation: hazardous waste regulation in the American states. *Journal of Politics* 46, 428–458.

Wilson, James Q. (1989). *Bureaucracy*. New York: Basic Books.

Young, Kevin, Mark Healey, and David Godschalk (1996). *Opinions of Federal Hazard Mitigation Officers about Mitigation Planning and Implementation: Report of a Survey* Working Paper #5. Chapel Hill, NC: Center for Urban and Regional Studies, University of North Carolina at Chapel Hill.

24
The Evolution of Emergency Management in America: From a Painful Past to a Promising but Uncertain Future

Aaron Schroeder and Gary Wamsley Virginia Polytechnic Institute & State University, Blacksburg, Virginia

Robert Ward Department of History and Political Science, Charleston Southern University, Charleston, South Carolina

I. INTRODUCTION

This chapter traces the evolutionary maturation of emergency management in America. It has been a slow and torturous process of "coming of age," made all the more difficult by the unique peculiarities of America's democratized, constitutional, and federal republic and made more urgent by the implacable extension of our "built environment" into harm's way. The chapter also shows that what is evolving in emergency management, more often than not unconsciously, is a "network entity," similar in some respects to "network organizations" that have developed in the private sector but different in other respects. It has the Federal Emergency Management Agency (FEMA) at its center but is a complex network with a distinctive political economy and a "network management process," if we understand that "management" in this sense is something quite different from the command-and-control characteristics usually connoted by the word. The chapter concludes with some questions concerning the future of emergency management, FEMA, and the network of which FEMA is the center.

II. THE TORTURED EVOLUTION

Extensive loss of lives and suffering, destruction of property, and disruption of essential services resulting from forces of nature, actions of enemies, and civil disorders have been fundamental aspects of human existence throughout recorded history. Societies have always sought to mobilize collective action to react to them and to cope with them, but until relatively recently in human history the ability to cope and expectations as to what could be done were miniscule. Things changed, however, as the "developed" societies entered the modern era. An Austrian official responsible for emergency management notes that ". . . catastrophes . . . were always regarded as punishment inflicted by God, but hand in hand with scientific progress the principles of cause and effect were gradually understood, and it was also realized that measures had to be undertaken to prevent and remedy disasters of all kinds'' (Fustenhofer 1993).

Indeed, in the waning years of the twentieth century, which is perhaps the apogee of modernism or perhaps just past it, there has been a quantum leap in people's expectations as to what their governments can do about such things. Not only do they expect a response but they expect far more in the way of a response. Not only do they expect a response after the fact and help in coping, but they expect warnings and prevention. In fact, their expectations of response grow ever closer to that of ''being made whole again'' and to assurances that causes will be found and ''corrected.'' Nor have government officials done much to abate this trend in expectations. Indeed, it is fair to say they have contributed to it. An American scholar's observation of several years ago now seems a vast understatement: ''The fatalistic assumption that natural disasters will happen and all we can do is cope is slowly being altered, leading to increased reliance on government action.'' (Cigler 1991:313).

As the nation's population has steadily grown, so has our typically modernist assumption that humans can control nature and the uniquely American optimism concerning our ability to control social forces. There has also been a steady shift in attention and expectations to the national level of government, despite growing rhetoric and symbol manipulation asserting that the contrary is, or should be, taking place, and this paradox is reflected within emergency management and FEMA itself. There has also been a great deal of burden shifting from state to state behind a fog of rhetoric asserting that the national government should not intervene by leveraging states to take preventive measures; simultaneously, there has been a parallel stream of rhetoric calling for more effective disaster response from the national government. To these trends, constants, and contradictions bearing on emergency management and our built environment, one must add the American faith, which has only begun to show the faintest signs of wavering, that our space is limitless.

If one stirs these ingredients vigorously, the result is a pregnant mixture of heedlessness, risk, vulnerability, and contradictory expectations of government help whenever the forces of nature and our built environment collide. We seem oblivious to the fact that this government, of which we now have such extensive if paradoxical expectations, is the same government in which we profess little confidence and indeed which we increasingly scorn and revile. A 1996 political cartoon captured some of this ironic mixture. It showed a couple struggling to stay afloat above their flooded home (no doubt built in a flood plain and uninsured). A sign has floated up from where they had previously proudly displayed it in their yard. It demands ''Get government off our backs!'' As a boat manned by a FEMA official speeds to the rescue, the homeowner, oblivious to the contradiction, exults—''Thank God, a government bureaucrat!''

This ironic mixture has led us to extend our built environment—freeways, housing tracts, and skyscrapers—into places that can only result in disasters: on seismic fault lines, in flood plains, on seaside and lakeside cliffs; within the 25-, 50-, 75-, or 100-year tide or flood marks; into the potential path of rock, mud, or snow slides; at the feet of active volcanoes; in areas where the wet season's lush vegetation turns to explosive tinder in the dry season; into ''tornado alleys'' and the traditional paths of hurricanes. The list of the ways we have put our lives and property at risk is endless and growing exponentially.

And there is more. Although the once looming specter of a thermonuclear holocaust has receded, we must now contend with domestic and international terrorism, which can strike at any time and place and without warning turn skyscrapers, huge office complexes, shopping malls, sports stadiums, and subways into disaster sites in an instant. Additionally, there is the specter of emergencies arising from ''normal accidents,'' which inevitably result from the breakdown of the interconnected and tightly coupled systems of incredible complexity constituting the infrastructure of our ''built environments''—power outages, chemical spills, air traffic failures and delays, Y2K impacts (Perrow 1984). Finally, there are emergencies in the form of civil disorders—phenomena we prefer to think do not occur in a democratic society but which have always been a part of our existence and which we have no reason to believe will not be a part of our future (NAPA 1993:10).[1]

All of these can lead to only one conclusion: as we continue to extend our built environment into the path of powerful forces of nature, we will face an increasing number of events that we call emergencies, crises, disasters, or catastrophes. And as that number increases, so does our expectation that our government, at all levels but certainly at the national level, should and must ''do something'' about them—rhetoric to the contrary notwithstanding.

Despite the historic persistence and future inevitability of disasters and emergencies, and the perhaps overly optimistic belief that something can and should be done about them, Americans, as our contradictory rhetoric demonstrates, have never settled the question concerning the role of the federal government in dealing with such incidents. Instead, the question is being answered by inexorable though largely unconscious evolution in response to a number of forces and under the press of events. Although the federal government has long played a role in these matters, it is the specific form of the federal involvement that has been and to some degree remains at issue.

Nor have we completely settled how emergency management should be organized. Particularly at the national level but at other levels as well, there are seemingly intractable problems of organization, administration, and coordination. How can one agency be given the power and jurisdiction necessary for effective disaster planning and coordination of response and recovery operations without giving it more power in times of both nonemergencies and emergencies than other participants in the political process are willing to grant it? What should be the role of the National Guard, the U.S. Department of Defense, the Red Cross, the Salvation Army? And what about all the other microemergency systems that exist? Petrochemical industries, the U.S. Forest Service, utility companies, nuclear power plants, the oil-shipping industry, the Department of Defense and many others have emergency systems that they have developed. Can these somehow be effectively coordinated?

III. ENDURING PROBLEMS OF EMERGENCY MANAGEMENT

Underlying the issues of defining and organizing emergency management are some problems associated with the function that are unique in their intensity and in their enduring nature. They endure because they are rooted in human nature, American attitudes toward long-range planning, the dynamics of power in the executive branch of government, and the short-term perspective of the American political process.

Generally, emergencies and disasters are easily dismissed as things that are unlikely to happen, more likely to happen to someone else, or liable to happen on ''someone else's watch.'' As a consequence of these attitudes, there is a tendency on the part of elected officials to procrastinate or delay action that would prepare us for the next traumatic event. Senator Diane Feinstein of California offered an example of this. When she was mayor of San Francisco, she was approached by administrators responsible for Candlestick Park, who told her that inspections revealed the stadium to be dangerously vulnerable to an earthquake and that, if a quake occurred during a sports event, there would probably be a major loss of life. Repairs that could prevent this would be very expensive. Senator Feinstein candidly admitted that her first thought was, ''This isn't likely to happen while I am mayor. In fact, it may never happen. Besides, the cost will distort all the other budget priorities. Perhaps it can simply wait'' (U.S. Senate 1993). Nonetheless, she reluctantly agreed to have the repairs made. Months after the repairs had been made, an earthquake did indeed strike during a baseball game. There was considerable damage, but thanks to the recent repairs, nobody was killed or seriously injured. Nobody can say how often officials fail to take the action that then-Mayor Feinstein did, but probably more often than we like to admit.

Americans have also never seemed to value long-range planning and training, which are essential to emergency management. Although they have come to accept the necessity of these things in the military in order to protect citizens from threats from abroad, they have not yet developed an appreciation for their need in protecting citizens from hazards that can befall them ''at home.'' As a result of this underlying attitude, emergency management agencies are generally underfunded for planning, training, and exercises, even though these activities are every bit as essential for their effectiveness as they are for military organizations.

Emergency management also requires coordination of a wide range of organizations and activities, both public and private. Everyone acknowledges the critical need for such coordination in an emergency, but in fact no one wants to be ''coordinated,'' nor is it clear just what the term means in practice. Statutory authority is not easily transformed into legitimate political authority, and emergency management agencies are very seldom given anything but statutory authority to ''coordinate'' in the event of an emergency or disaster—which everyone prefers to believe is unlikely. Statutory power is a necessary but insufficient condition for real power to coordinate. Finally, emergency management has almost no natural constituency base (with the possible exception of insurance companies) until an emergency or disaster occurs. Except for those persons and agencies with responsibilities in emergency management, who are modest in number and influence, the function has no generally attentive, supportive set of constituents or clients, which is so important to the survival and effectiveness of public agencies. (NAPA 1993,17; Long 1949).

The never-ending problem facing anyone attempting to develop an emergency response is that every emergency is somewhat unique and will involve a certain degree of ad hoc organizing, mission learning, and, inevitably, mistakes. As one experienced emergency manager put it ''No matter how hard you try, sometimes you can't get a better grade than C+'' (Wamsley 1992–1993). Yet in spite of the imperfect nature of disaster planning, response will be performed in the full view of the media and ultimately the public. While emergency management seeks to develop a constituency to support their efforts, it is often caught between the imperfect nature of scientific planning, the unpredictable nature of emergencies, and the underlying expectation of citizens for unlimited security and protection.

IV. AN OVERVIEW OF EMERGENCY MANAGEMENT'S HISTORIC EVOLUTION

In spite of the systemic problems associated with emergency management within the United States, federal involvement in emergency management has a long history in this country. As early as 1786, the federal government, under the original Articles of Confederation, projected troops into a civil disorder brought about by Shays's Rebellion in western Massachusetts. This level of civil disorder response continued through the Whiskey Rebellion of 1792, the New York draft riots of 1863, the 1894 Pullman strike in Chicago, the "race riots" of the late 1960s, and even to current times with the 1992 Los Angeles riots.

Although dealing with civil disorder has always been an accepted role for the federal government, federal intervention in natural disasters has a history of nearly equal length. Starting as early as 1803 with congressional disaster relief to the city of Portsmouth, New Hampshire, federal involvement in natural disasters has slowly but steadily grown. While federal efforts in this area were modest during the nineteenth and early twentieth centuries, federal resources were used in response to or recovery from no less than 100 natural disasters between 1803 and 1950 (Drabek and Hoetmer 1991). During the twentieth century, the federal involvement initially took the form of little more than the congressional chartering of the Red Cross in 1905, federal troops to help maintain order in the wake of the San Francisco earthquake of 1906, and the granting of authority to the Army Corps of Engineers over flood control in the Mississippi Valley after the horrific 1927 flood.

Starting in 1916, civil defense began to emerge as part of emergency management, and a succession of new laws and organizations appeared during World War II. Finally, the specter of atomic warfare led America's political leaders to pass into law the Federal Civil Defense Act of 1950. It gave the federal government the authority to initiate planning and provide state and local governments with "guidance, coordination, assistance, training and matching grants for the procurement of supplies and equipment." This was undeniably a major impetus to the evolution of emergency management. During the Eisenhower Administration, no less than three major reports (Gaither, Rockefeller, and Rand) called for civilian shelter programs as part of the nation's overall defense strategy. Emergency management would eventually take on the role not only of helping civilians survive an attack but also of assuring that a functioning government and its officials would survive as well. The pattern of the federal government stimulating and funding state and local efforts was a major evolutionary step. The best way to organize federal efforts remained an open question, however, and a bewildering array of organizations followed one another during the 1950s, '60s, and '70s.

In spite of the expansion of federal involvement in emergency management and the subsequent professionalization of the field, federal emergency management response programs were constantly under political attack for being both inadequate and fragmented in their responses. Eventually, during the 1970s, this political dissatisfaction led to the creation of the Federal Emergency Management Administration (FEMA) under President Carter's Administration. While FEMA was originally viewed as "one agency/one official/one point of contact" for dealing with emergency management, the great expectations for the agency were quickly dashed as the systemic problems of coordination and a variety of dysfunctions associated with partisan and institutional politics plagued the agency's operations. During the 1980s, the agency's credibility steadily declined, and both congressional and executive support for emergency management reached a nadir by the early 1990s.

The agency's state of decline and lack of credibility eventually reached a crisis point during Hurricane Andrew in 1992. The decision by the Bush Administration to turn to the secretary of transportation as a special presidential representative to head up relief efforts and to massively involve the armed forces only emphasized the total lack of confidence in FEMA's capabilities.

In the wake of disaster, there were calls from Congress to either abolish the agency, to turn the emergency management over to the military, or to disperse elements of the program to other organizations within both the federal and state levels of government (Wamsley and Schroeder 1996:235–244). The congressional call for change marked a critical juncture for FEMA and saw the agency, under a new president and a new agency head, begin to move toward a more effective response position. Today FEMA, and emergency management in the United States, has begun to take on a new direction and development, one that seeks to achieve, finally, that level of comprehensive response that the United States has been searching for since its very beginning as a nation.

There have been many changes in FEMA and its operations, but probably the most significant development has been the recognition, by the administration of FEMA, that while it may have a statutory charge to "coordinate" disaster efforts, it lacks the necessary legitimacy and power to exercise that authority to "control" disaster response efforts. There seems to be a growing awareness that in order to accomplish the goal of coordination, FEMA must rely upon the voluntary cooperation and assistance of a wide range of other government agencies spanning both the horizontal and vertical dimensions of our complex federal system. In order to accomplish this goal of coordination, the "new" FEMA, sometimes consciously and sometimes unconsciously, has begun to reposition itself within a new organizational format and structure that, in many ways, resembles types of network organizations found in the private sector. The dawning realization within FEMA that a new approach was needed was convergent with, if not always the result of, several other contextual changes.

V. THE NATIONALIZATION OF DISASTERS

While natural disasters have occurred regularly over the course of American history, the use of a presidential declaration of a disaster had limited application until the 1980s. While disasters such as the San Francisco earthquake of 1906 and civil disorders occasionally called for federal involvement, many other natural disasters of equal impact were handled on the local or state level, with little or no federal assistance offered to help cope with the trauma following such events. For instance, in 1927, the flooding of the lower Mississippi River threatened the safety of everyone living in the Mississippi Delta area. Rather than calling for federal assistance, the banking community of New Orleans took matters into their own hands and dynamited the levies below New Orleans in order to divert water away from the city and into the lower Mississippi Delta region. The subsequent flooding of the delta, caused by the dynamiting of the levies, left over 100,000 persons homeless. The response by President Coolidge and his disaster manager, future President Herbert Hoover, was to merely offer the flood victims moral platitudes but leave the Red Cross and the State of Louisiana to help the survivors (Barry 1997).

Generally, the involvement of the federal government in disasters was limited, but starting in the 1980s, disasters began to be increasingly defined as matters of national concern. By 1993 over 70 requests for presidential disaster declarations were being received each year, and the number continues to increase annually. People engaged in emergency management widely believe that this trend is not necessarily due to an increase in nature's wrath, although El Niño and La Niña effects do seem to be increasing as global warming also increases. Rather, there is a growing consensus that this increase in defining natural disasters as ''national'' and calling for a national response is due to advent of ''live,'' ''action,'' and ''on the scene'' coverage by national media; a related need for presidents to appear to be ''strong'' leaders that take action in response to the needs of citizens; and heightened politicization (not necessarily partisan) of the disaster declaration and response process in general. One FEMA official emphasized the point to which things had gone by wryly remarking that ''. . . in Texas they want a declaration every time a cow pisses on a flat rock.'' While the decision by the federal government to increase its role in disasters probably has fueled the politicization of the process, neither one of these two factors, presidential needs, or climate changes, would, by themselves, have led to this level of escalation if it had not also been for the increase in immediacy directly attributable to the expansive nature of media coverage. Disasters are, in fact, ''newsworthy'' and as such help to sell newspapers, radio and television access, and even web pages.

A. The Camcorder Policy Process and the Nationalization of Disasters

Prior to the advent of television, news was conveyed to the general population through a mix of written media, still photographs, radio coverage, and short newsreel clips shown in movie theaters. While written coverage and radio broadcasts could inform citizens in a timely fashion, there still remained a time lag between the event's occurrence and the actual information reaching the public. This time lag factor began to change with the advent of television. At first television coverage was also limited due to the lack of technological ability to broadcast directly from the field. Starting in the late 1960s, though, this technological handicap began to dissolve as satellite linkages, coupled to portable broadcast units, began to be adopted by all the major television networks. Today the broadcast industry has the ability to cover events from the field in a real-time environment; it is not only able to report on the event as it is unfolding but also to place its coverage in the middle of the event as it is actually occurring.

The time lag factor that historically limited news coverage has now disappeared, and in its place we often find ourselves viewing events as they actually occur. Consider CNN's coverage of the Gulf War from Baghdad, as we watched the U.S. Tomahawk missiles bombard the Iraqis' military complexes, or nightly news broadcasts from the major networks as Belgrade's center was hit with multiple air raids. This immediate media coverage has become a factor in the policy arena as it affects natural disasters. Within a matter of hours from the time that a natural disaster strikes an area and in some cases even before the disaster touches ground, our national networks are on the ground, directly broadcasting details of the destruction that is either anticipated or has occurred. Often the media arrive even before the designated disaster response units are fully mobilized.

Further compounding the pressure on disaster response efforts is the fact that as they work to assess the damage and determine what resources should come into play, they do so under the watchful eye of the media. In many ways a stopwatch is ticking as the public, through the eye of the media, watches the developing response and assesses the speed with which the agencies deliver aid and support to the affected area. The media themselves also add to the problems of disaster response. The unrelenting competition for viewers and "market share" fuels efforts to find and on occasion even create "stories" that will captivate and titillate the average viewer and affect viewers' preferences for one network over another.

The insatiable demand for audiences drives the media toward exaggeration and fuels the pressure for live national coverage. Disasters that in the past would have been viewed as local in nature are suddenly projected as either regional or national disasters. Take, for example, the media coverage concerning tornadoes over the past several years. Although tornadoes are common local events occurring each spring in many portions of our country, during recent years the national media projected the development of tornado damage as great national events. Instead of scattered tornado strikes in South Dakota, Mississippi, Georgia, North Carolina, Oklahoma, and New York that were doubtless disasters but just as assuredly local events, they were suddenly portrayed by the national media as national disasters—an assault by nature threatening the entire country due to possible climatic changes.

As the cameras roll and the public watches the events unfold, a "milling process" occurs in which public perceptions are developed concerning the effectiveness of government's response to the problem (Schneider 1992). The normal process of funneling aid and resources into the area are often seen as too slow or "bureaucratic," especially as the media personalize the event by presenting interview after interview of individual victims and families bemoaning their lack of physical support within an atmosphere of personal and community shock. As the perception of the lack of effective response develops through the media, elected officials feel compelled to step forward and assume the "strong person" role, seeking to gain the political mantle of "leadership" that can "jump start" the presumably ineffective government bureaucracy. As the disaster reaches a "national" level through the media coverage, the level of political actors engaged in the "strong person" process escalates, until finally it reaches the highest elected offices of the land. All the while this escalating milling process occurs, the agencies designated to deal with the disaster are publicly undermined and yet are left to deal with the problem after the politicians and the media have left to pursue more lucrative ratings (NAPA 1993:18).

The end result of camcorder policy development is that the emergency management agencies, at all levels of government, are vulnerable to being stigmatized as ineffective and inept in the public eye. Still, the siren's call of media coverage is a tantalizing lure for any elected official, especially if one can project an image to a national audience. This national audience potential fuels efforts to have the disaster escalated to a national level, and the device chosen for such escalation is a presidential declaration, which is often followed by a presidential or vice presidential "inspection tour" of the stricken area. In our new media age, the national executive is often more than happy to oblige local and state officials.

B. The "Photo-op" Presidency and Nationalization of Disasters

Disasters are traumatic and leave people in need of psychological reassurance and support. These needs may be as great as or greater than their physical and material needs. It is thus to be expected that people will look to and expect a strong leader—someone who symbolizes strength and potential succor. Executive figures at all levels—mayors, governors, and especially presidents—are natural focal points for such postdisaster psychological needs. Probably incumbents of the office of president have most avidly sought to meet this need and thus assume the mantle of the strong leader. The nationalization of disasters is inextricably linked with the expansion of the president's role as a symbolic leader and the related phenomenon of the ''photo-op presidency.''

The reasons for this are historic and complex but lie within a number of factors unique to the office of the president (Lane and Wamsley 1998). The first is that the offices of the president and vice-president of the United States are the only two elected offices in the United States that are voted on by the national voting public. Thus the office of the president theoretically stands at the pinnacle of all elected offices in terms of citizens' choices for elected officials. No other elected office can thus make as powerful a legitimacy claim, despite the fact that anyone who thinks about it for a moment realizes that by no means ''all'' citizens or even all voting citizens preferred a given electee. Presidents can claim, even if they receive less than a majority of all the votes of potential voters, that they represent the ''voting'' majority's preferences and wishes. Thus they have a decided edge when they make the claim that all elected officials make implicitly and explicitly—to speak for ''the American people.'' Of course, the congressional leadership can claim that ''collectively'' they also represent the voting majority's preferences, but no individual congressperson or senator can claim to represent the majority of the voting public. Thus, historically, every president has claimed to be *the* national leader and that their agenda should be the national agenda.

The second factor involved in the strong leader complex is the fact that every president has tried to make Presidency the equivalent of a chief executive officer analogous to a corporate CEO. Unfortunately, both scholars and practitioners of public administration have enthusiastically endorsed this change (Lane and Wamsley 1998) The authors of the Constitution clearly did not have such a notion in mind, for they intentionally created a system of fragmented authority: horizontally powers were not simply divided but made shared and overlapping between branches; vertically they were made shared and overlapping between levels. In essence our system creates an ongoing struggle between all branches and levels of government over authority and rights of office.

A close reading of the Constitution makes it abundantly clear that the authors thought of the legislative branch, not the executive, as the ''first among equals.'' Unfortunately, both scholars and practicing public administrators have also endorsed this change enthusiastically. (Lane and Wamsley 1998). But of the three branches (at all levels), the executive has always had the greatest prospect for expanding its role and increasing its power. Alexander Hamilton, the indefatigable proponent of ''energy in the executive,'' recognized that the potential for this expansion was inherent in the potential unity of the position and in the nature of administration which involves the crucial capacity to act (Green 1987). Presidents, governors, and mayors (in the strong mayor form of government) have historically seized upon oversight of administrative structures to expand their role and powers. This has held true despite the fact that shared powers enables legislative bodies to exercise joint oversight of the agencies through confirmation of many appointments, oversight of administration inherent in legislating, and through budgetary oversight and power to appropriate (Lane and Wamsley 1998). This pattern of expanding executive power has held true at all levels of government, but we need only focus on the national level for purposes of this chapter.

While political pundits may decry the usurpation of Constitutional authority by ambitious presidents, the media will seize every opportunity to create the presidential sound bite so essential to television's theatrical staging and to sustaining or increasing viewer ratings. For their part, presidents also recognize the significance for their power of the theater and drama provided by television news and take every opportunity to create the "photo opportunities" needed to project the image of a strong, forceful, and dynamic leader. Few events offer such potential for dramatic staging as a natural disaster, where the "chief executive officer" can stand in the midst of rubble, offering assistance and compassion to the citizen victims on behalf of all the citizens of the nation. The heroic leader, clad in the symbolic khakis of military command, can be instantaneously dropped into the scene of disaster by helicopter, with a bevy of media representatives broadcasting every dramatic minute as he at least appears to "take charge." Lost, though, in the political theater starring the president as disaster hero, are all of the essential administrative and policy decisions that must both precede and follow that moment. Invisible as well are policies and programs that could be developed to deal with emergency management on a longer-term basis, especially such things as taking preventive action that avoids or mitigates disasters.

C. Presidential Disaster Declarations, Free Riders, and Nationalization

The problem with being a "hero," of course, is that you have to do something heroic. When President Coolidge's personal representative, future President Hoover, stood in the mud of the flooded Mississippi Delta in 1927, had his picture taken with the devastated Cajun locals, and then boarded his train back to Washington, neither Coolidge nor Hoover were seen as heroes. In fact, Huey Long was able to use the lack of presidential leadership during the flooding to mount a political assault on Louisiana's state government, eventually seizing the mantle of hero for himself and creating a political dynasty (Barry 1997). But presidential resources for heroism have grown considerably since the time of Coolidge, and today presidents have the tools needed to do heroic deeds in the form of presidential declarations of disasters and release of emergency funds. These can be dramatic and politically profitable if handled effectively.

Depending on the terms of the declarations made under the Stafford Act, presidents can make available between 75 and 100% funding for repairs to private homes, reimbursement for the deductible part of homeowners insurance, between 75 and 100% of the cost of repairing public buildings and infrastructure, and 75 to 100% of the cost of debris removal. It also makes available low-interest loans to small businesses. Raising the limit on federal funds made available beyond 75% (normally matched with a 25% levy from the state government) is possible if a state's average per person expenditure on mitigation has exceeded $64. The reason for the federal matching requirement, of course, was to encourage state and local governments to develop mitigation and disaster response plans prior to an actual disaster occurring. The basic idea behind the match was that with proper planning and zoning and building code requirements at the local and state levels, the impact of natural disasters could be lessened and the cost to both federal and state governments decreased. Unfortunately this logic is undercut by another clause within the Stafford Act, which allows not only a presidential waiver for the state match requirement and an increase in the percentage of federal aid but also a reduction of the average expenditure per person on mitigation required of a state in order to receive the federal funds.

Thus the president can, at his own discretion, nullify all the previous match and expenditure requirements that were established to encourage local and state mitigation and response plans (NAPA 1993). And state leaders, knowing this, have pressed as hard as possible for all they can get. With the cameras rolling, the disaster victims standing in shock, and all of the local and state officials surrounding the president in the role of strong leader, the temptation is often too great for the president to resist opening up the federal largesse. While this plays well on the evening news and CNN and potentially boosts a president's poll ratings, it also undercuts the incentive for mitigation measures by state and local communities before a disaster strikes by raising the possibility that an area will be able to receive aid regardless of its slighting of mitigation and response efforts. In effect, when a disaster does strike, it sets in motion is something like a game of Monopoly, in which everyone except the American taxpayer has the potential to acquire a ''forgiveness of sins'' card. While some states take the mitigation and planning process seriously, others bet on the likelihood that if something happens, the federal government will cover the costs. Thus states such as California will make a serious attempt to develop and maintain an effective emergency management system while other states will not only underfund emergency management, but will use their representatives in Congress to attack FEMA for not giving them 100% of the recovery costs when a disaster strikes. Since the funds are federal and raised from across the width and breadth of the country, the states that experience relatively fewer or less frequent disasters or put greater effort into mitigation and response end up covering a large portion of the costs of states that experience more frequent disasters or put less effort into mitigation and response. This means that they are effectively and unfairly shifting the fiscal burden away from the citizens of some states to those of another. In essence, some become ''free riders.''

The inevitable end result of the conjunction between the process of presidential aggrandizement, the evolutionary changes in news media, and the ''free rider'' mentality of some states is that state and local variances allow the building of high-rise hotels and casinos into sand dunes along hurricane coasts, river cities refuse to construct flood walls, nuclear power plants are built on earthquake faults, and farmers till flood plains—and, of course, the American taxpayer foots the bill. In the end, all the political actors—presidents, governors, and mayors—come out looking like heroes and strong leaders while the media help to perpetuate the fiscal shell game. But presidents benefit the most, and since the presidency is a national office and the national fiscal resources are the greatest, the overall result is the nationalization of disasters on both political and fiscal terms.

Eventually, though, the media do leave, and presidents, along with other elected officials, look for new opportunities to be seen as leaders. FEMA, along with the other government agencies at all levels charged with dealing with the disaster, are left to struggle with the disaster's aftermath, which often lingers for years. FEMA needs the support of the president for the ''longer haul,'' but often his or her agenda is full of other more pressing problems. This lack of sustained presidential attention has so far been dealt with through the placement of persons who it was assumed could be political ''sentinels''; persons whose major qualification has been that of political and personal loyalty rather than knowledge of either the politics of Washington or emergency management. While plausible enough in theory, the placement of presidential sentinels within FEMA has created historical problems that, ultimately, work to undermine not only the agency's effectiveness and legitimacy but also presidential authority.

VI. FEMA'S NEED FOR "MUSCLE," THE PRESIDENT'S NEED FOR "SENTINELS"

FEMA, in relation to the entire federal government, is not a large agency. Fewer than 3000 employees seek to cover the entire spectrum of disaster problems across the United States. In addition to disaster problems, FEMA is also charged with being the lead agency for civil defense response. Yet FEMA's primary mission is to coordinate the response of all federal agencies to emergencies and disasters. In essence, this very small federal agency is charged to direct and coordinate the response efforts of the largest and most powerful cabinet departments within the federal government. In terms of its size and presidential support for most of its history, one can only view FEMA's relationship to the other agencies of the federal government as the equivalent of a chicken trying to dance with elephants. Obviously, an agency this small desperately needs a powerful advocate or ''muscle'' to back up its efforts to coordinate much more powerful agencies, and it needs it on a sustained basis through the day-to-day skirmishes of bureaucratic trench warfare as well as the dramatic moments of coordinating disaster response. The natural source, indeed the only possible source, of such support is, of course, the president.

Yet historically presidents have paid little attention to FEMA's role of coordinating federal efforts in natural disasters. The reasons for presidential neglect can be summed up in three factors. First, natural disaster response was never seen as a primary federal responsibility until the communications media changed public perception. Indeed, FEMA was always careful to describe itself as the ''responder of last resort'' after local and state authorities were overwhelmed and requested federal assistance. Second, natural disasters are episodic, the chance for presidential heroism brief and fleeting, and once a disaster is over, other more pressing political issues rise in the priorities of presidential attention. Unfortunately, the short time horizon of the partisan political world gives presidents, and for that matter governors, mayors and city managers, little reason to be interested in FEMA until a disaster has occurred. Third, FEMA's responsibility for natural disaster response was, until relatively recently, seen as marginal next to its responsibilities for dealing with population protection and government continuity in the event of a nuclear Armageddon.

Thus, from its very creation in 1978, FEMA and natural disasters were placed on a low-priority level within the White House and the larger executive office of the president. Still, a president does not like to look less than a strong leader when a natural disaster occurs and is also not willing to give up supposed presidential control over any aspect of the federal administrative structure. Thus, presidential political appointments of sentinels were used to achieve at least the reassuring semblance of control over the agency and at least the illusion that an effective response would be forthcoming when needed. Unfortunately, the results has been more illusory than real, in part because presidents were not willing to fight for adequate budgets and to intervene to back up the agency in its daily struggle to coordinate disinterested agencies that did not want to be coordinated in either planning or response. Perhaps equally important was the failure of some presidents to appoint persons in whom they had great trust or more often their failure to recruit persons whom they trusted *and* who had significant knowledge concerning emergency management.

A. To Politicize is Not to Control, or Why Sentinels Haven't Worked

Both Democratic and Republican administrations have used presidential political appointees as a means of downward penetration and presumed ''control'' of the federal administrative structure and extending presidential control. Congress, for its own reasons, has allowed the process to continue, and even to be expanded (Light 1995). It is easy to forget—indeed, the White House Personnel Office and the president's staff often seem to forget—that the more important presidential appointments require Senate confirmation and that this has serious consequences for control. This makes the appointment of loyal and competent sentinels to the top position to look after the emergency management function problematic; even more important, it makes it nearly impossible for the person at the top of the agency to manage it in an integrated and effective manner. For "presidential appointees" are not actually the president's alone. They are in fact a product of a joint process and as such have long been used as weapons in partisan conflict and in the struggle between the executive and legislative branches of the federal government. The Senate has used the confirmation process to influence the type of person selected to oversee various programs and to strike its own political bargains with the soon-to-be incumbent program head. The House, for its part, has used partisan political linkages with appointees and its key role in the budgetary process to extend its leverage and oversight of agencies and their programs (Oleszek, 1989). This is discussed further below. For now we only want to point out that this, in the past, has left both the FEMA director and the president with something considerably less than control; indeed, it often leaves them struggling for mere cooperation (Wamsley and Schroeder, 1996).

B. FEMA's Congressional Problem

If FEMA's problems with the President can be characterized as too little attention or inconsistent attention, the agency's problems with Congress might be characterized consistently as too much attention. The problem of conflict between agency efficiency, presidential control, and congressional oversight is of course ongoing for all federal programs, but in the case of FEMA the problem is extraordinary and has had profound consequences. The roots of the problem can be traced directly back to the original creation of FEMA under the Carter Administration. Prior to 1978, the program areas of the present FEMA were handled by seven separate agencies of the federal government. The dispersion of the programs across these various departments added to the problem of developing a comprehensive, coordinating function. In order to offset the problem, the Carter Administration sought to amalgamate the various programs under one roof. The underlying belief within the administration was that such an amalgamation would result in a synergistic effect. As one person who had been present at the time of the reorganization put it: "It was assumed that all these programs were related, not at their cores, but at their margins; and that their relations at the margins could create an important synergism" (NAPA 1993:15).

The basic idea was that lessons learned from responding to disasters would lead to improvements in both preparation and mitigation planning for future disasters. The difficulty facing the Carter Administration, however, in developing this new "synergistic" organization was that creation of such an agency would require the rewriting of existing separate laws into a comprehensive statute. In order to develop such a new statute, numerous congressional committees, which had oversight on the separate seven agencies, would have to be consulted and formal approval obtained. Such a prospect appeared to be daunting, considering the political factors related to each committee and the interest groups involved in each area. The specter of committee and subcommittee turf battles stretching on for years was a chilling one. To avoid this obstacle, the Carter Administration's reorganization project staff attempted to achieve their goal by the use of an "end run" approach around the congressional committees. Rather than seeking formal legal integration within a new organization, the Carter Administration simply transferred the specific programs housed in each of the separate agencies into the newly created FEMA, where each would continue to operate on the basis of its existing statutory turf. As a further means of avoiding the ruffling of congressional feathers, the administration also transferred each of the program's political executive positions, along with the sitting incumbent into the new agency. The effect was a ''confederation'' or ''umbrella'' agency with all the pathologies inherent in the genre.

The final result was that FEMA came into existence fragmented, with hermetically sealed program compartments each overseen by a political appointee with his or her own links, not just to the president but also to both congressional committees and the interest groups concerned with the specific program. Even though FEMA was charged with coordinating and linking the various programs, internally each program stood alone, with only the slightest traces of commitment to any shared mission and little or no reason to engage in coordination. Thus FEMA was born with 30 political appointees, 9 of whom required Senate confirmation by six separate committees, each with its own particular program interests and influence groups. The consequence of political appointees linked to congressional committees created avenues within the agency for various interest groups to foster their own agendas. These vertical agenda avenues are referred to within the agency as ''stovepipes'' (NAPA 1993:41–43).

C. Congressional Particularism and FEMA's Fragmentation

Congress is an institution based on particularism as opposed to universalism (Heaphey and Kronenberg 1966:16). It fulfills its systemic role and does its work by breaking big, seemingly incomprehensible problems down into simple and understandable terms upon which bargaining and decision making can be based. Harold Lasswell's aphorism concerning politics in general expresses the particularistic calculus of Congress perfectly. For the members of Congress everything can ultimately be reduced to ''who gets what, when and how,'' or even more pointedly, ''what will it do for me, my district or state, or my party, when will it do it, who will it specifically benefit or hurt and how?'' (Lasswell 1936). These are particularistic questions that require particularistic answers: particular persons, particular geographic places, particular funds, particular laws and programs. After all, it was former Speaker Tip O'Neill who epitomized the outlook of particularism when he said that ''all politics are local.'' They are not, or ought not to be, of course, but Congress, particularly the House, tends to see politics that way. It is Congress's particularistic view of the world and way of doing business that more than anything else has sustained FEMA's fragmented state and troublesome stovepipes.

FEMA's programs are authorized and operated in accord with a myriad of enabling legislation, appropriation acts, executive orders, and National Security Directives (NAPA 1993:124–125). Consequently, a myriad of committees and subcommittees with very particular interests have jurisdiction over its activities. In 1992 the director stated that 16 committees and 22 subcommittees of Congress had oversight over its programs and appropriations (NAPA 1993:75). But even this figure is questionable. Committee jurisdictions shift, however slowly and slightly, and additionally, there are numerous other committees that have jurisdiction over other federal agency programs providing assistance to disaster victims (e.g., the Department of Agriculture and the Small Business Administration) (Gilmour and Halley 1994; Oleszek 1989). Although numerous authorizing committees have jurisdiction over some aspect of emergency management, there is no single committee that has comprehensive oversight responsibility for FEMA. In fact, one FEMA document states of emergency management in general, that about ''two-thirds of the House and Senate Committees get involved'' (NAPA 1993:75). The problem assumes nightmare proportions when one considers that within these committees there are many subcommittees each of which has its own micro-piece of jurisdiction over some aspect of FEMA that is even narrower than the concerns of the full committee. The fragmentation is so pervasive that no one has an overall perspective as to where individual programs fit within the broad framework of federal emergency management.

As a result, FEMA's mission is continually altered and shaped in a piecemeal fashion by diverse events: the influence of various constituencies, partisan changes in control of the houses of Congress, changes in committee members and staffers, and differing congressional interest. Adding to the problems of congressional fragmentation is the confirmation process for political appointees referred to above. Since each of the program areas has a precedent-setting existence prior to the creation of the agency, and since all of the political appointees bring with them contacts with the various interest groups and congressional committees overseeing the operation, a self-perpetuating stasis is created that is based on previous decisions and basic shared assumptions. Thus behavioral contracts, committee demands, and expectations have already been established between congressional subcommittees and committees and the appointees as to how each of the program responsibilities should be carried out (or how their stovepipes should be maintained). Under these conditions, if the FEMA director tries to change the course of the agency, the largest obstacle will be his supposedly subordinate political appointees and their congressional and interest group allies. The appointees will do whatever they have to do in order to ensure the structural integrity of their stovepipes and their alliances outside the agency, and if the director proposes anything that sounds like it may create a ''leak'' or a ''connection'' with another stovepipe, they will be quick to let the relevant members of Congress know. Congressional committees, in turn, have the ability to make the director's life miserable. The end result of this situation has, in the past, been an agency mired in turf wars and lacking the ability to develop a unified mission and the teamwork necessary to pursue it.

D. FEMA's Problem of Living Down Its Reputation

By 1992, the watershed year for FEMA, the agency was saddled with a reputation for inefficiency, ineptness, cronyism, ''pork barrel'' politics, scandal, and corruption. A good deal of this was deserved; much was not. The worst of its reputation was acquired under one director, Louis Guiffreda in the early 1989s. Two directors, Julius Becton and Wallace Stickney, followed Giuffreda and worked to turn things around, but with little or no effect. While there were accomplishments, ultimately there was little to show for their efforts. Reputation is a precious commodity within the beltway, and once a negative one is acquired, it is difficult to erase. As one observer commented, ''Once an agency is on the ropes in this town, it is really hard to recover'' (NAPA:49).

The agency's culture was tending more toward defensiveness in terms of its actions and programs. This was understandable, for it faced increasing external criticism of both its operations and justification for continued existence. It was becoming obvious that a major change in both operations and external relations were necessary if the agency was to survive. While key groups within the agency were prepared to attempt to change the organization, it faced the daunting task of overcoming 14 years of well-deserved skepticism concerning both its intentions and administrative competence. In order to understand and fully appreciate this reputational problem, one must take an even closer look at the emergence and early years of the operation of FEMA and the disastrously significant events of the 1980s.

During the 1960s and early 1970s, the nation faced a series of major natural disasters.[2] In all cases, the inadequacies of the federal government to respond to the crises became painfully evident. But the legislation passed to adjust disaster response actions, instead of improving the system, further fragmented the various programs.

During this same period of time, emergency management emerged as a professional field of both academic study and public service. This progression toward professionalization occurred at the same time that the various governors began to voice their concerns over the inability of the federal government to effectively assist state governments during these disasters. Eventually, in 1977, the National Governors' Association initiated an evaluation of emergency management and in 1978 issued a critical report calling for more professionalism and a comprehensive national emergency policy as well as the creation of a federal agency that would concentrate the functions then dispersed throughout several agencies (National Governors' Association 1978). The issuance of the governors' report also corresponded to the Carter Administration's reorganization project, which eventually led to the establishment of FEMA in early 1979 despite considerable objections from Congress (President of the United States 1978).

The Carter Administration's plan for the reorganization of emergency management envisaged direct oversight by the White House through the director of FEMA as an independent executive agency. Under the original plan, the FEMA director was to serve as the chair of a White House emergency management committee. The committee was to include the assistant to the president for national security and was to directly advise the president on ways to meet national emergencies. Unfortunately, the original plan was never established (NAPA 1993:14–17).

As indicated above, the president's reorganization project decided to avoid a fight with congressional committees by ''cobbling together'' existing programs. FEMA was formally authorized as a federal agency on April 3, 1979, with a full budgetary line allocation set for the upcoming 1979–1980 fiscal year but without the proposed ties to the presidency or any structural integration. By the time that FEMA's budget allocations were formalized, the Carter Administration found itself in a losing presidential campaign against Ronald Reagan.

The defeat of Carter by Reagan in November of 1979 placed the entire process of developing FEMA on hold as the presidential transition dominated the attention of the administrative branch. Uncertainty was ratcheted higher when the Reagan Administration delayed the selection of a new permanent director for FEMA while it considered what role FEMA should play in the newly emerging ''Reagan philosophy of government.''

President Carter had appointed John Macy, a highly respected public administrator, as his first director. Whatever progress Macy might have been able to make was nullified, however, by the looming transition and his untimely death. Nonetheless, he had initiated a professional and nonpartisan evaluation of the agency's programs by a newly organized program analysis unit. It had analyzed each of FEMA's programs and outlined the potential options for their future direction. The Reagan transition team, however, announced that the briefing books that resulted were to be ''trashed,'' and in a remarkable meeting the top career staff were told that they were to blame for the agency's problems and would all ''be gone'' in short order.

The transition team used the provisions of the Civil Service Reform Act of 1978—which allowed more flexibility in assigning, reassigning, and removing civil servants—to move career staffers to dead-end and unpalatable jobs that would lead them to resign and to open up positions for political appointees or noncareer senior executive service positions—i.e., political appointees.[3]

Finally, in April 1981, a director, Louis O. Giuffrida, was named for the agency. Giuffrida was a long-time associate of Ed Meese, an influential "insider" during Reagan's years as California's governor, and an insider in the new president's administration as well. There is little doubt among persons in FEMA at that time that Giuffrida owed his appointment to his connection to Meese. Giuffrida had been Reagan's chief advisor and organizer for California's civil defense and emergency management training programs. The California Emergency Management Agency was, and is to this day, a far larger organization in terms of operations than FEMA. But it is important to note that Giuffrida had not been director of the California agency. Had he been, things might have unfolded differently. His position involved little operational or managerial experience. It seemed that a far greater source of influence on the new director was his background in the army's military police, from which he retired with the rather prosaic rank of lieutenant colonel, and his subsequent rise to the rank of a general in the California National Guard.

Along with the naming of Giuffrida as the director of FEMA, the Reagan Administration also shifted the major emphasis of the agency. As envisioned by the Governors' Conference and the Carter Administration, FEMA had dealt primarily with floods, droughts, hurricanes, and other natural disasters. In addition, FEMA would have also had a secondary role within the broad civil defense structure, especially in terms of providing civilian support and protection in the event of a nuclear war. For the Reagan Administration, which saw "government as the problem," and with its focus on the Cold War struggle with the "evil empire" of the U.S.S.R., it was natural to switch the priorities that the Carter Administration and the National Governors' Association (NGA) had envisioned and to make civil defense the primary mission, while downplaying federal involvement in areas of domestic national life like responding to natural disasters. Coming from California, with its well-developed capacity to respond to natural disasters, the Reagan Administration may have lost sight of the importance of the federal government in performing and enhancing the states' capacities to perform such functions.

In any event, civil defense and the continuity of government were further emphasized due to the personality and background of Giuffrida, who quickly, and no doubt to his considerable pleasure, became known within the agency as "the general." Giuffrida saw emergency management's main priority being the sustaining of civilian life and the continuity of government after the outbreak of a nuclear war, and he advocated those priorities both within the White House and to Congress. Backing up the new emphasis for FEMA, the Reagan Administration proposed a 7-year $4.2-billion program, which involved FEMA in "provid(ing) for survival of a substantial portion of the population in the event of a nuclear attack" and a highly classified program to assure the continuity of government.

The Reagan landslide had not produced a Republican Congress, however—just a slim Republican majority in the Senate. Reagan's proposal for shifting FEMA's priorities occurred during a time when some members of Congress, most notably some Democrats, were beginning to call for a nuclear weapons freeze and greater efforts at "détente" with the Soviet Union. FEMA, which up to this point in time had been a "backwater" agency, suddenly found itself thrust into the national limelight of a debate over both foreign policy and national defense.

Giuffrida and the other Reagan political appointees within FEMA wasted no time in beginning to develop the new agency priority and a culture to match it. A broad-based national ''crisis evacuation'' plan was developed calling for the evacuation of 400 ''risk area'' cities with populations of more than 50,000. Under the plan, it was assumed that the outbreak of a nuclear war would become apparent over several weeks, and would allow the nation time to evacuate millions of people from ''risk areas'' into safer ''host areas'' in the countryside. The goal of the plan was to save 70 to 80% of the population in the event of a nuclear war. Critics in Congress and other quarters insisted that the plan was unrealistic and pointed out that panic, traffic jams, and chaos would envelop every major American city if a nuclear war loomed in the near future. In spite of the congressional criticism, Giuffrida and the agency's other political appointees insisted that they had a ''legal and moral'' responsibility to develop the plan, and proceeded to direct the majority of the agency's resources toward that end. (New York Times 1982).

Soon FEMA took on the aura and all the trappings of a national security agency. The hallways of the agency were cluttered with signs saying ''Security is Everybody's Business''; an entire floor of the agency and various other facilities were devoted to the continuity of government and maintained at the highest level of security. Some key officials took to wearing side arms on a daily basis. The security focus, which critics labeled a ''fixation,'' was so pervasive that, by 1985, the Information Security Oversight Office was reporting that over 30% of FEMA's documents were classified as ''top secret,'' as opposed to 1% receiving such classification within the Defense Department and 5% within the CIA (Washington Post, 1986:F19).

Some of the agency's security concerns may well have been justified. The full story behind the agency's ''national security emergency preparedness'' operations has never been declassified, but if there was any validity in the things said about those operations in public access media, it would justify to some degree the claim of those involved: that it represented a serious strategic concern to the Soviet Union and that it was easily vulnerable to compromise with its only protection being the secrecy it could maintain. Be that as it may, the rationale and justification were swamped by what was perceived by ''old line'' national security agencies to be play-acting and posturing by the ''new kid on the block.'' The National Guard connection of Giuffrida and his coterie did little to enhance his standing with the regular officers in the armed forces who predominate in the Department of Defense, or, for that matter, with any of the other career civilian counterparts in the many other national security agencies.

What further damaged FEMA's reputation in the national security realm, however, was its attempt to extend itself into policy realms for which it lacked clear authority, credentials, or enough power backing by the White House, thereby making itself vulnerable to being scorned, attacked, or simply ignored. Or, to put it differently, in some instances it could be said that FEMA had statutory standing to do something but simply lacked the authority, credibility, or power backing to make others take it seriously. As an example of the first instance, when the nuclear-freeze debate intensified, FEMA began to develop an anti–nuclear freeze educational program aimed at both adults and children. In one instance, the agency issued a brochure for grade-school children that asked them to color in the items they would need in a fallout shelter. On another occasion, anti–nuclear freeze films produced by the conservative American Security Council Foundation were purchased by the agency and distributed to civic clubs around the United States (Washington Post

1985:A7). These moves, of course, were like waving a red flag at a metaphorical bull: in this instance, the Democrats in Congress, other national security agencies, and the Washington media.

At the height of the Giuffrida administration, over three-quarters of the agency's resources were directed toward the civil defense/anti–nuclear freeze and continuity of government programs (NAPA 1993). Naturally and unfortunately, the emphasis on civil defense was done at the expense of developing the capacity to better deal with natural disasters. Rather than improving the federal response to natural disasters, FEMA's procedural setup, or lack of a credible one, led to a series of allocations and designations for local disasters, perceived to have political influence behind them.[4] Compounding the problem of disaster designation was the fact that no standardized method was established to evaluate disasters and determine if an area was eligible for disaster relief. The General Accounting Office in 1982 recommended that FEMA develop computer models to standardize the assessment process, but FEMA refused to allocate funds for the programming of a new system. In addition to a lack of damage standards, FEMA also refused to assess the damage for such a designation until after the entire disaster event was over, thus delaying aid until well after the gravest and most damaging period had passed. Needless to say, the lack of effective disaster response to the various states further fueled the conflict between FEMA and Congress, especially in terms of the congressional members whose home states received little or no federal aid (Washington Post 1982).

While the conflict over whether civil defense or natural disaster should be emphasized strained relations between FEMA and Congress, the agency suffered further damage through the process of arbitrary removal and appointment of agency personnel. The Reagan Administration had adopted the Nixonian philosophy concerning the federal bureaucracy or civil service with a vengeance. Under Nixon's view of government in his second term, two basic premises were determinant as to who should be employed by the government and what restraints should be placed on their actions. The first premise was that "protection of the national interests . . . requires undivided loyalty to the president and unquestioning obedience to his orders" (Seidman and Gilmour 1986:109). The second premise was "The bureaucracy or civil service represents the principal threat to presidential power. Members of the civil service cannot be trusted because they are either disloyal or have divided loyalties" (Seidman and Gilmour, 1986:109). The Nixonian view was effectively summed up by John Ehrlichman when he said: "There shouldn't be a lot of leeway in following the President's policies. It should be like a corporation, where the executive vice presidents (the Cabinet officers) are tied closely to the chief executive, or to put it in extreme terms, when he says jump, they only ask how high" (Seidman and Gilmour 1986:121).

In essence, the Reagan Administration adopted the Nixonian philosophy related to the civil service but added an additional qualifying factor: "The three criteria we followed were, was he a Reagan man? Two, a Republican? And three, a conservative? Probably our most crucial concern was to ensure that conservative ideology was properly represented" (Newland 1987:45). FEMA very quickly became a prime example of the Nixon/Reagan philosophy.

Two weeks after the Reagan Administration took office, the acting FEMA Director, Bernard Gallagher, fired four top FEMA officials. Gallagher, who had never worked with the officials, never interviewed them, or even reviewed their personnel files sent a memo to White House Counselor Edwin Meese III not only recommending the firing of the four officials but also recommending their replacements based on party affiliation. None of the replacements had any experience in managing disaster relief. In addition, Gallagher accused the former FEMA officials of fouling up the Three Mile Island nuclear emergency and based their termination on those grounds. It was only after the firing that it was discovered that the officials either had not been employed with FEMA at the time of Three Mile Island or had been assigned to other divisions not involved in the emergency (Washington Post 1983).

When Giuffrida took over as the director of FEMA, he proceeded to follow the White House example and rebuilt the upper levels of the agency around personal loyalty and cronyism. Over a dozen of the highest-ranked positions within the agency were filled by individuals with either direct ties to Giuffrida or the military police. The agency's executive administrator, deputy director, assistant deputy director, and all of Giuffrida's assistants were former army policemen who had served with Giuffrida and his associates over the years that he had been in the army and National Guard. FEMA officials were ordered to hire ''old military friends'' as either employees or consultants for the agency. Jobs were created for various ''friends'' and job descriptions were intentionally rewritten to qualify these individuals for existing agency openings. In addition, these people often received the highest salaries available for their job classifications. When questioned by the press on the propriety of such hirings, FEMA spokesman James L. Holton replied, ''It was natural that (Giuffrida) looked for people he could trust'' (Washington Post 1985: A4). Within the agency, objections to Giuffrida's hiring practices were met with swift retribution. FEMA's original personnel director decided to take early retirement rather than participate in the charade, and his successor, a 20-year personnel veteran, was quickly transferred to the nuclear war division when he objected to the hiring practices. Eventually, the personnel job was given to a former finance director who had no experience with personnel administration (Washington Post 1985:A4).

While the hiring practices of Giuffrida and his staff were troubling, even more serious was the general attitude that pervaded the upper administration in terms of dealing with the fiscal trust they were charged to maintain. Very quickly the agency's budget became a source for personal perquisites and questionable outside expenditures. The offices of the upper-level officials were soon sporting color television sets, hide-a-beds, loveseats, sofas, and leather chairs. A training center building was modified to include private apartments with fireplaces, wet bars, cherry-wood cabinets, expanded bathrooms, and, in one instance a special ''pasta kitchen'' for Giuffrida's gustatory pleasure. ''Friends,'' who were also paid as ''consultants,'' were provided with rent-free housing at the training center, and government cars with chauffeurs were used by the top political appointees to commute from home to office on a daily basis (Washington Post 1985:A4). In one instance a tawdry scandal surfaced in congressional hearings involving the director of FEMA's training center, who had allegedly put pressure on his female chauffeur for sex. In addition, overseas trips to Israel and Mexico also included first-class travel for wives, all at the agency's expense. FEMA funds were even used to award noncompetitive grants to unrelated institutes of which Giuffrida was an ''unpaid advisor'' (Washington Post 1985:A1).

While these examples of ''petty'' personal corruption were serious, of a far more serious nature was the use of the agency's budget for both political contributions and political payoffs. The attendance of FEMA officials at political fund-raising events sponsored by the National Republican Club were paid for by agency contractors, who then billed the expenses back to the agency, claiming that the expenses were incurred when such officials attended unspecified ''conferences.'' Attendance at various fund-raising social receptions sponsored by conservative groups were also billed back to the agency by contractors. FEMA's food service contractor also catered champagne lunches and receptions for various Reagan officials to court corporate donors for political campaigns (Washington Post 1985:A1) Even more troubling, though, was the use of agency funds to award contracts for outside consulting work to groups having direct and indirect political and personal connections to the agency's administration.

Multi-million-dollar consulting contracts were awarded to companies whose officials had direct personal contacts with Giuffrida. Not content with obtaining the contracts, these firms proceeded to double bill the agency for equipment rentals and to award personal bonuses (Washington Post 1984). In addition, noncompetitive grants were used to award contracts to longtime friends and associates of the agency's upper-level management (Washington Post 1985). Once again, objections were met with a quick transfer to lesser jobs, and refusals to sign-off on shoddy contract work often resulted in forced resignations (Washington Post 1986).

The abuses within the agency eventually led to the opening of investigations by the Justice Department, the House Government Operations Subcommittee, and the House Science and Technology Committee. Eventually, in September 1985, Giuffrida resigned as director of FEMA and Julius W. Becton was appointed its new director. While the resignation of Giuffrida was generally seen as a positive move for the agency, the legacy of Giuffrida's administration would continue to haunt FEMA for the next 8 years. By the late 1980s, FEMA's reputation was compromised almost past redemption. In general, FEMA was referred to as a ''turkey farm'' of the federal government—a place for incompetent political appointees. Congress, because of FEMA's past record, tightened its oversight of the agency and its programs and began to micromanage every aspect of the agency's operations. And while FEMA continued to emphasize its civil defense role, the fall of the Soviet Union and the end of the Cold War left it with little direction or purpose in that realm.

The election of George Bush to the presidency did little to alleviate FEMA's problems. Wallace Stickney, former head of the New Hampshire Department of Transportation and a close personal friend of John Sununu (the White House chief of staff), was appointed the new director of FEMA. In general, though, Stickney was considered to be weak and inexperienced and was personally ''uninterested in the substantive programs of FEMA.'' During his term in office, Stickney was virtually invisible except when he would reluctantly go to Capitol Hill to defend the agency against its increasing number of critics. Unfortunately, Stickney, in 1991, forced a FEMA employee who had publicly acknowledged he was gay to reveal the names of other FEMA employees who were gay, threatening him with failure to receive a security clearance. The outcry from both the gay community and Congress about the ''blackmail'' forced Stickney to shred the list but once again reinforced the perception of FEMA as a political turkey farm (Time 1993:22).

In 1989 and 1990 both the Loma Prieta earthquake in California and Hurricane Hugo in South Carolina once again called for the federal government (i.e., FEMA) to respond. FEMA's obvious incompetence in responding to both disasters led South Carolina Senator Ernest Hollings to declare that FEMA was made up of ''the sorriest bunch of bureaucratic jackasses I've ever known'' (Congressional Quarterly Weekly Report 1992). In spite of FEMA's lackluster performance, lawmakers decided to give the agency ''another chance'' and continued funding for the agency. But in 1992 the final chance for the agency appeared in the guise of Hurricane Andrew, and the agency's response had far-reaching consequences for its future.

E. The Turning Point

In June, 1992, The House Appropriations Committee issued a damning report concerning FEMA. The report found that the agency's morale not only was low but that there was outright bureaucratic war within the agency between the political appointees and the career officials. The committee's report not only accused the upper administration of mismanagement and incompetence but also publicly labeled the agency as a ''dumping ground'' for political appointees. While Stickney retorted that the report was full of ''innuendo . . . downright gossip and hallway speculation,'' he nonetheless faced powerful congressional forces opposed to the continuation of the agency's existence. Norman Y. Mineta (D-Calif.), upcoming chairman of the House Public Works Committee, had publicly declared his intention to ''write legislation that will have Congress rebuild this system.'' After the 1990 Loma Prieta earthquake, Mineta had declared that FEMA ''could screw up a two-car parade.'' An even more powerful threat came from Sen. Barbara A. Mikulski (D-Md.), chairman of the appropriations subcommittee, with powerful leverage over the agency. Mikulski was demanding that the General Accounting Office conduct a full study of the disaster relief system, with the intention of opening hearings for a complete overhaul of the system within 1 year. (Congressional Quarterly 1992).

In addition to the congressional discontent, 1992 was a presidential election year, and while the Bush Administration, still basking in the glow of the Gulf War victory, was confident of being reelected, it was not a time to offer the Democratic party the opportunity to criticize any aspect of federal administration. In many ways, 1992 was a year for FEMA to ''lay low'' and mend political fences. But while Stickney and the Bush administration may have wanted to avoid a Congressional confrontation over FEMA, Mother Nature had another less welcome agenda. In the early morning of August 24, 1992, Hurricane Andrew slammed into southern Florida and proceeded to cut a 50-mile swath of damage and havoc across the state. In less than 24 hours, Hurricane Andrew left over 200,000 residents homeless, 1.3 million people without electricity, and all the residents of southern Florida with a scarcity of food, clean water, shelter, and medical assistance.

President Bush and FEMA Director Stickney immediately helicoptered into the damaged area and declared it a disaster area eligible for federal relief; then they returned to Washington. While the declaration was initially seen as a hopeful development, the full extent of the damage was only beginning to emerge. Andrew had not only destroyed the fabric of social life in southern Florida but had also wreaked havoc with the public safety infrastructure and shown that the system at all levels was inadequate to deal with a disaster of Andrew's magnitude. The homeless victims of Andrew also included the emergency management and public safety personnel of the devastated areas, who now, along with the rest of the local population, were desperately seeking food, water, and shelter. Not only were the power grids and water pumping systems disabled, but streets were choked with debris and the emergency response equipment and public communications networks had also been seriously damaged. Panic, devastation, and shock pervaded both the citizenry and public officials of southern Florida, all under the ubiquitous and unblinking eye of the national television networks, which were broadcasting directly from the heart of the damaged areas.

Very quickly, the county and state emergency management systems were overwhelmed and without the capacity to assess their needs and prioritize them. Pleas from local officials to state officials to ''send everything'' were met by replies from state officials that ''we can't send *everything*—what do you *need*?'' For 3 days after the hurricane hit, southern Florida waited for relief from somewhere, but the state system seemed immobilized and FEMA, operating from its normal posture of ''responder of last resort,'' was waiting for state officials to ask for assistance and to say what they needed. FEMA did not even send in a damage assessment team to evaluate what resources should be brought into play; instead, it waited for formal requests from the state to come through normal channels.

While FEMA waited, the state government's damage assessment system was failing because the local public safety personnel, who would normally report the damage, were overwhelmed with trying to meet the life-support needs of citizens, reestablish some kind of organizational functioning and capacity, and meet the immediate needs of themselves and their families (NAPA 1993:28; Wamsley 1992–1993). Finally, after 3 days of mounting frustration over the lack of a meaningful disaster response, Kate Hale, Dade County's director of emergency preparedness, held a news conference and publicly pleaded to the nation over the national broadcasting networks: ''Where the hell is the cavalry on this one? We need food. We need water. We need people. For God's sake, where are they?'' (Newsweek 1992:23). The politically explosive sound bite was a perfect example of the camcorder policy process in action. It landed like a scud missile in the Oval Office, where by that time President Bush's reelection campaign was lagging behind Bill Clinton's in the polls. The ''heroic'' presidential visit to Florida only 3 days before now appeared to have been a hollow gesture by a weak and ineffective leader, reminiscent of Calvin Coolidge.

With 25 electoral votes at stake in the key state of Florida, the president needed to respond in a forceful manner, and he did (Wamsley 1992–1993). Within 24 hours of the Hale statement, President Bush dispatched 7000 federal troops to southern Florida. Within a week, the total number of army, navy, air force, and coast guard personnel dispatched would reach nearly 20,000, along with 19 generals and admirals (Newsweek 1992:23). In addition to ''sending in the troops,'' President Bush designated Andrew Card, the secretary of transportation, as his ''personal representative'' to assume leadership for all federal response and recovery activities in Florida and to coordinate with state and local authorities. At least symbolically, which is sometimes the most important dimension in politics and administration, FEMA Director Stickney, and FEMA generally, were pushed aside and made to look nonessential (Wamsley 1992–1993). FEMA was, of course, heavily involved in the response and recovery effort, but the public perceptions created by the ''bypass'' of FEMA were devastating for the agency. One event scarcely noted in the swirl of events was a visit to the disaster response headquarters by candidate Clinton, who avoided all publicity and simply sat and listened at several meetings (Wamsley 1992–1993).

That same September, Senator Mikulski included in the ''notes'' to an appropriation bill a requirement that FEMA fund a study by the National Academy of Public Administration of itself and the entire emergency management system. The notes further required that FEMA transmit the study to Congress without any changes by a date certain. By this time, the overwhelming majority of both the House and Senate were calling for a change in the wake of Hurricane Andrew, and the bill was quickly authorized. Not content in having just one study conducted, Senator Mikulski began to prod the General Accounting Office (GAO) into conducting another study of FEMA. While the GAO and the White House were reluctant to conduct such a study, Mikulski used her position as chairman of the appropriations subcommittee to force the GAO into action. Mikulski's subcommittee oversaw the GAO budget, and she threatened to slash the GAO's budget unless it conducted the study. Both the NAPA and GAO study groups worked on the evaluation of FEMA, sharing data back and forth. In the meantime the Inspector General's Office within FEMA was stirred to action and began an analysis, and NAPA shared much of its findings with that organization. In the early part of 1993, all three reports were issued.

Both the NAPA and GAO reports called for a major redesign of both FEMA and the system of federal emergency management response. Two key elements in the reports called for FEMA to abandon its traditional posture of "responder of last resort," take a proactive stance in terms of its natural disaster mission, and replace the large number of political appointees within the agency with career civil servants who were professionals trained in providing emergency responses to disasters. While the two studies were developing, the presidential election process reached its conclusion. In a stunning defeat, George Bush lost the election and Bill Clinton returned the White House to Democratic control after 12 years.

Congressional hearings centered on the three reports took place in early 1993. There was a solid consensus among the three reports as to a necessary reform agenda. Indeed, the chairman of one committee remarked that he had never heard such agreement among witnesses as to what should be done (Wamsley 1993). Things clearly were headed toward the comprehensive reform bill that Senator Mikulski intended to introduce. As often happens, this course of action was overtaken by events. The Clinton transition team asked for and received complete briefings from the NAPA study team, and from comments of the team it seemed clear that President-Elect Clinton was aware of many of the recommendations of the NAPA team, the GAO, and the inspector general of FEMA. Within weeks it became known that James Lee Witt was to be the new director of FEMA. Although the media found some amusement in the fact that he was from Wild Cat Holler in Yell County, Arkansas, there was also acknowledgment of the fact that Witt would be the first FEMA director with direct experience in dealing with emergency management, having served as director of the Arkansas State Office of Emergency Services under then-Governor Clinton. He may also have been the first director to have a personal relationship with *and* the confidence of a president as a result of his effective performance.

The NAPA study team briefed Witt and some of his close associates thoroughly before the announcement of his nomination. Whether the findings and forthcoming recommendations coincided with his own ideas or he was quickly absorbing them and planning to adopt them can never be known. It is, after all, one of the important skills of political executives and administrators generally that they be able to listen without making clear until the right moment what their own thoughts are. In any event, Witt immediately upon his appointment began to implement the overwhelming majority of those things recommended by the NAPA and GAO reports, with a few important exceptions.[5] Witt immediately proved in other ways that he was a highly skilled political executive of the type FEMA had long needed so desperately. First, as mentioned above, he insisted and obtained from the president and the White House Personnel Office what at the time he called "a veto," or refusal rights on political appointees. Second, the week after his nomination was announced, he remained on Capitol Hill, listening and talking to the chairpersons of each of the myriad committees and subcommittees important for FEMA, the committees' ranking minority members, and the key staffers of both the majority and minority members of the committees and subcommittees. Third, the Monday following his week on Capitol Hill, he stationed himself at the entrance to FEMA and introduced himself and shook hands with every employee who arrived for work. With that one simple act he wiped away much of the bitterness and dissension, and a nascent union that had been born of all the employees' bitterness shortly dissolved. Fourth, he met with all FEMA's members of the senior executive service and made it clear that he would value their assistance in turning the agency around. Fifth, he called for an "all hands" meeting with the FEMA Washington staff, the top officials in the regional offices, and randomly selected lower-level staff from the regional offices. In the meeting he made it clear that he considered it the beginning of a new FEMA and needed and expected their support to make it so. Witt, of course, has done much more, key aspects of which are discussed later in this chapter. These dramatic first gestures were incredibly important, however, and warrant mention as part of the historic watershed for FEMA and emergency management in America. Much of the future of both will depend upon appointing to the directorship of FEMA political executives with Witt's skills.

The debacle surrounding Hurricane Andrew, the issuance of the two reports, the extensive congressional hearings, and finally the appointment of Witt as director all signaled a watershed for FEMA. They also mark the beginning of an effort to develop a much different agency—indeed, a new structural arrangement in government that challenges traditional concepts of organization and management.

VII. THE OLD MODELS NO LONGER APPLY—AN OPPORTUNITY TO REINVENT AND REDESIGN A "NETWORK" OF SERVICE DELIVERY

The reality of public sector program implementation today is simply this: any implementation that is attempted in the name of "enhancing public service" will necessarily involve stakeholders external to the implementing organization (e.g., the local community, the private sector, other public sector agencies, or quasi-public entities). James Lee Witt, coming as he did from a state department of emergency management, knew this to be the case. That is, simply put, any concept of a program's implementation following a linear, top-down, centralized within-the-agency approach will most likely fail. In an environment comprising conflicting and semioverlapping functions and powers, differing motivations for involvement, and no single authority with a span encompassing all stakeholder parties, traditional ideas such as unity of purpose, line of authority, and span of control are quite difficult to apply. That is, the context of effective, large-scale action in federal emergency response has been steadily moved away from a concept of unified organization to a concept more appropriately described as an interorganizational "network."

This was the circumstance of FEMA, in spades, when it found itself faced with a major reorganization and repurposing following Hurricane Andrew. Simply put, an appropriate response to the needs of the organization could not be made by simply reshuffling the boxes of an organization chart that supposedly depicted internal administration. Instead, a complete reformulation of FEMA's reason for being and operation was called for, and this, in turn, depended on a restructuring of its relations with "relevant others." New relationships would have to be established (politically and operationally) with entities external to the organization. That is, the agency's environment required that it reach out beyond itself and establish what can now be referred to as a network organization. In order to respond appropriately in a timely fashion, with all necessary resources, FEMA, a comparatively small agency, *must* effectively coordinate all the available resources of the federal government *and* integrate these resources with state and local level resources already on the ground—this in a world where all actors applaud ''cooperation'' just as long as they do not have to be coordinated by someone else.

In their book *Managing Complex Networks*, Kickert et al. (1997) provide a detailed analysis of public administration's maturation beyond a traditional ''rational central rule'' to a multiactor model and then to a network concept of governance. There has also been much discourse in the American literature of the late 1970s and 1980s concerning the related concepts of ''top-down'' vs. ''bottom-up'' models of governance. The central thesis of all this work is that these different approaches to governance provide a lens through which the administrator views and acts upon the world. One may even refer to them as ''theories in use'' (Argyris and Schon 1978). By assessing the shortcomings of trying to apply a ''centralized top-down'' or ''multiactor bottom-up'' model of understanding to FEMA's circumstance, we can discern the necessity of using another, more complex model, the network, for understanding more clearly what has happened and where we are today.

A. From a Top-Down to a Bottom-Up to a Network Model

What has been referred to as the ''rational central rule'' or ''top-down'' model of governance is characterized by processes of public policy making and governance marked by a presumed division between politics and administration, one that portrays politics as the reaching of policy consensus by interested political entities and administration as the application of scientific knowledge to policy design and a program of implementation: a process of governance where decision making is unambiguous and authoritative and implementation is nonpolitical, technical, and potentially programmable (Landau 1979; Sabatier 1986; Wamsley and Schroeder 1996; Kickert et al. 1997:7).

This top-down model has also been referred to as the ''conventional'' model of governance, as it focuses explicitly on the relation between the agent and the objects to be ''steered'' or ''controlled.'' The policy process, thus, is characterized by a supposedly stark division between politics and administration—between those who make the rule and those who enforce the rule. The implementation phase is considered to be a nonpolitical, technical, and potentially programmable activity. Such a concept of governance is easily compatible with America's naïve conception of democracy and often the starting point for any new governmental agency. That is, a political body (in FEMA's case, the U.S. Congress) supposedly decides that there is a need that must be addressed by the establishment of a new agency (the political act). The agency is then supposed to venture forth to objectively ''implement'' the ''clear'' will of the establishing body (the administrative act). As can be discerned by the preceding history of this particular agency, because there was no clear policy that shaped the initial mission and political aspects of this agency, these features were thoroughly institutionalized in the higher percentage of political appointees than any other agency. That is, there was not established a discernible separation between the political enactors and the administrative implementers. This is not to say that this should have necessarily been the case but simply to say that the original conceptualization of FEMA operations was probably rather flawed.

Separating of the concepts of politics and administration is, of course, not new. In fact, Sun Tzu, author of the military and later management classic *The Art of Warfare*, written in approximately 400 B.C., states that ''enlightened rulers deliberate plans while capable generals execute them'' (Wee et al. 1996:149). In public administration literature, we often attribute such a conceptual divide to the writings of early-twentieth-century scholars in praise of the wonders of the industrial revolution. This is, of course, ridiculous. Such an attempted conceptual divide has probably existed since the first tribal/clan leader told somebody else to do something he did not want to do himself or wanted it done "exactly" as instructed. To be fair, however, it may certainly be argued that what such a conceptual divide *means* in terms of the *roles* played by those *doing the telling* and those *doing the doing* has changed significantly following the industrial revolution. What had changed, in Sun Tzu's terms, is the concept of what constituted a "capable" general. To Sun Tzu, the political leader gives an order something akin to "go and defeat my enemy." The general in this case is left with a very high level of discretion to determine the appropriate subgoals to be achieved and the strategies and behaviors necessary to achieve those goals. In this sense, the term *capable* has a very rich and wide-ranging meaning. In the writings of early-twentieth-century scholars of public administration, usually typified by those of Woodrow Wilson and Frederick Taylor, the capable general, or in this case administrator, is one who faithfully applies the rigorous scientific management techniques derived of industrial capitalism, *not* one who decides, at any stage, what should be produced and how. In this case, the capable administrator has a very limited and narrowly drawn role. The inherent assumption in this case is that that which is left over from the earlier meaning of Sun Tzu's capable general (i.e., what is left if we subtract the modern meaning from Sun Tzu's meaning) is somehow handled by the modern-day political entity giving the administrator a specific order. If we now consider that such orders are being handed down from within a constitutional democracy of divided power, where directives are seldom if ever any more specific than the order of Sun Tzu's political leader (e.g., go and defeat my enemy, or, better, go and fix the problem with the federal emergency management system), then the inadequacy of such a limited and narrowly drawn role should become evident. If we now go a step further and consider working within one of the most politically influenced agencies in the federal bureaucracy, then the inadequacy becomes pronounced in bold type.

In terms of implementation research, borrowing from the classic top-down implementation model of Mazmanian and Sabatier, causes of implementation failure can be discerned by starting with the policy decision (from the top) and asking four questions that highlight the flaws in the approach. These questions are:

Were the actions of officials and target groups consistent with the objectives and procedures of the decision?
To what extent were the objectives attained?
What were the principal factors affecting outputs and inputs?
How was policy reformulated over time on the basis of experience? (Sabatier 1986: 22)

To ensure a successful implementation, using this top-down model would require meeting six conditions:

Clear and consistent objectives
An adequate causal theory of the problem being addressed
A legally structured implementation process to enhance official and target group compliance
Committed and skillful implementing officials
Support of interest groups and sovereigns

Changes in socio-economic conditions that do not undermine political support or the causal theory (Sabatier 1986:23).

The many disadvantages of using such a model in approaching governance situations (especially the management of FEMA) have been well documented (Elmore 1979; Landau 1979; Barrett and Fudge 1981; Hanf 1982; Hjern and Hull 1982; Wamsley et al. 1996). For our purposes, however, the most obvious are that the model presupposes that there is one central top level agent(s), the policy maker(s), who has been able to reach a final and clear consensus among all stakeholders, and that such a person has access to all necessary information regarding a situation, as well as all information pertaining to potential solutions. That is, the key actor is the policy maker at the top. All other actors are considered either obedient instruments (best case) or potential impediments on which compliance needs to be enforced (worst case). There is no regard for the attitudes, values, and interests of the entities that will be responsible for implementation, nor the ambiguities of the policies that reveal themselves through the process of implementation.

The U.S. Congress, in establishing FEMA, was tacitly using the top-down, centralized model of governance. There was no provision that FEMA should be the overarching coordinator of a diverse range of resources spread throughout the federal and state governments. Quite the contrary, FEMA was originally conceived as a means of last resort to bail out the states when they needed it (and the thought was that they would not need it that much).

Another problem with this model is that it presumes a clear distinction between formulation and implementation of a policy. Unfortunately, when no preeminent authority is dictating clear objectives of a policy, as is inevitably the case in America, those objectives tend to be renegotiated many times during the implementation process itself. *That is, while the legislative stage in policy making creates what purports to be goals and objectives, what the end result is going to look like is simply not foreseeable.* For example, today FEMA considers itself to be "forward leaning," meaning that it does not wait to be called into action by the state. FEMA gets the resources in place on the assumption that they will be called upon. A 3-day gap between disaster startup is no longer acceptable. This new policy of action has not been congressionally dictated. It is a policy decision originating from *within* the agency to effectuate better response and reduce the potential for political assault.

In general, the top-down model neglects the inherently political nature of the most critical aspect of governance, known as administration or policy implementation. Additionally, others have argued that efforts to achieve central coordination and control leads generally to increased bureaucratization and diminished effectiveness and efficiency (Landau 1979; Van Gunsteren 1976; Hanf and Toonen 1985; Schroeder and Wamsley 1996). Martin Landau and Russel Stout probably summarize it best when they write,

> [w]e began with a vision: If a domain of tasks can be mapped to a formal logic, and if that logic orders the behavior of a large and complex organization, then that organization becomes a decision machine whose operations are entirely unambiguous and whose output occasions no surprise. To create such an organization is a monumental feat, requiring an intelligence of the order of Laplace's demon; or, as Madison might have put it, "So perfect a system is not for men" (p. 148).

Generally speaking, from a structural standpoint, the inadequacy of this model for FEMA operations is not terribly surprising. Starting off, we face the immutable wall of constitutional federalism dictating two broadly defined areas of authority, federal and state. We then have at both levels a further dissection of authority into executive, legislative, and judicial spheres of control. If that were not enough, we then have, again at both levels, a division of authority according to the functions or content of the action to be taken. That is, we have many different governmental agencies that address different functions (e.g., Emergency Management, Transportation, Social Welfare). Each of these agencies purportedly reports directly to the chief executive. In reality, and in fact constitutionally, these agencies also report to content-specific congressional committees and are often under the watchful eye of a monitoring judiciary (that is, the separation of powers at both the federal and state levels is often reflected within federal and state agencies). Additionally, in many states, we add the third ''local'' level of government which reflects much of the same complexity just discussed.

Supporting this system of split or shared power is the right of these various levels of government to maintain ''fiscal autonomy.'' In essence, each level of government has a base of taxing authority, which allows it to raise the necessary funds required to operate. Thus, at every level there is a source of both legal and fiscal authority supporting it. That is, at the get-go, there is need to conceptualize FEMA operations from the perspective of a more dynamic model.

B. The Multiactor Bottom-Up Model

The ''multiactor'' or ''bottom-up'' model, in direct reaction to the perceived problems of hegemony of the ''top-down'' model, represents a ''radical plea for decentralization, self-governance, and privatization'' while at the same time calling for a central government to ''give more attention to the problems of local actors to provide them with more resources. In this model, governance is seen as an essentially political process in which local entities barter according to their personal interests and purposes'' (Kickert 1997:8). This phase is clearly seen in the 1960s and 1970s in both the United States and Europe. In the United States, this model can be seen being employed in both the Great Society and New Federalism approaches of the Johnson and Nixon administrations. In Europe, a decentralizing theme can be clearly seen in many a country's reaction to the overburdening of public resources by the centrally administered socialist welfare state.

Such an approach is often referred to as a ''bottom-up'' approach because the perspective chosen is that of the implementing bodies and target groups, as opposed to a central overhead agent. Both models assume central and peripheral actors, but in the bottom-up model, power shifts away from the center to the periphery. The interests of these local, or bottom, actors are the point of departure for evaluations of public policy and its administration. Quite unlike the centralized top-down approach, this approach asserts that governance requires both policy making and administration that are seamless and, in their essence, *political* processes.

A general bottom-up model of analysis was developed by Benny Hjern and his colleagues Porter, Hanf, and Hull in their works of the late 1970s and early 1980s. This model was developed in direct reaction to the perceived shortcomings of the top-down approach. Generally, this model is driven by a need to operate in policy areas with multiple public and private actors. The model dictates four general steps to be taken by an analyst: (1) Identify the network of actors involved in service delivery in one or more locals; (2) ask about goals, strategies, activities, and contacts of each actor; (3) use these contacts to develop a network technique to identify local, regional, and national actors involved

Table 1 Three Perspectives on Public Policy Making and Governance

	Perspectives		
Dimensions	The Centralized Top-Down Perspective	The Multiactor Bottom-Up Perspective	The Network Perspective
Object of analysis	Relation between central ruler and target groups	Relation between central ruler and local actors	Network of actors
Perspective	Central ruler	Local actors	Interaction between actors
Characterization of relations	Authoritative	Centralized versus autonomous	Interdependent
Characterization of policy process	Neutral implementation of ex ante formulated policy	Political processes of interest representation and informal use of guidelines and resources	Interaction process in which information, goals and resources are exchanged
Criterion of success	Attainment of the goals of the formal policy	Local discretionary power and obtaining resources in favor of local actors	Realization of collective action
Causes of failure	Ambiguous goals; too many actors; lack of information and control	Rigid policies; lack of resources; nonparticipation of local actors	Lack of incentives for collective action or existing blockages
Recommendation for governance	Coordination and centralization	Retreat of central rule in favor of local actors	Management of policy networks; improving conditions under which actors interact

Source: Adapted from Kickert et al. (1997:10).

in planning, financing, and execution of relevant governmental and nongovernmental programs; and, (4) map, from the bottom up, the network of actors relevant to implementation, all the way to the top policy makers (Sabatier 1986:22).

This model, while attempting to address the shortcomings of its predecessor, unfortunately is disappointing in that it is, like its predecessor, rather inconsistent and one-sided. Like the top-down model, it tends to overemphasize the ability of one side to dictate the actions of the other; in this case, the periphery, as opposed to the center. This approach can also be charged with being both ahistorical and atheoretical. That is, it takes the existing members of an implementation structure as a given without analyzing why they are there or who else should be there given the history of the structure. It also does not start from an explicit theory of the factors affecting its subject of interest. It is solely the prisoner of the perceptions and activities of the participants. At best, one may say that this approach ''offers little more than a plea for the radical retreat of government (in which case the baby is thrown out with the bath water) or an argument for central rule for the benefit of local actors'' (Kickert 1997:9). Generally, we may state that it represents a direct reaction to the top-down model, as opposed to a complete model for understanding effective policy implementation. Or, as Sabatier puts it, ''Their networking methodology is a useful starting point for identifying many of the actors involved in a policy area, but it needs to be related via an explicit theory to social, economic, and legal factors which structure the perceptions, resources, and participation of those actors'' (Sabatier 1986:35).

In fact, working with an expanded ring of stakeholders to establish an operational network for response is exactly what James Lee Witt intuitively set out to do with the establishment of the Federal Response Plan to national emergencies—the coordinate policy for resource sharing between federal agencies. The bottom-up model, however, would neglect the actual control and influence that was exerted from the ''central actor''—that is, FEMA—in establishing this stakeholder network. In fact, given the political language often used in describing bottom-up theory, such direction from the center would be considered a bad thing.

Both the top-down and bottom-up approaches, because they have been motivated by different concerns, do not directly address the need to actually work in multiactor situations. The top-down approach is primarily interested in the effectiveness of specific government programs and the ability of elected officials to guide and constrain and shape the behavior of civil servants and target groups. The bottom-up approach is primarily concerned with accurately mapping the strategies of actors in certain problem/issue areas. The bottom-up approach has *not* been primarily concerned with efficient implementation of a policy (that is, getting it done). The top-down approach sees public administrators as impediments to the will of political actors. The bottom-up approach is not concerned with getting the policy implemented in any timely fashion (just so long as more peripheral actors are involved). That is, they both fail to provide an adequate model of what has happened at FEMA under Witt. *We are left, therefore, in need of a model that takes into consideration the concerns of both the top-down and bottom-up approaches.*

That is, what we have come to in the case of FEMA is a need for consideration of policy making taking place in *networks* consisting of various actors (federal agencies, state agencies, local agencies, individuals, special-interest groups, public organizations, private organizations, nonprofits, etc.), none of whom have the individual power to autonomously determine the strategies of all the other actors. The policy processes is not viewed as the implementation of ex ante formulated goals, but as an interaction process in which actors exchange information about problems, preferences and means, and trade-off goals and resources (and in doing so make conscious and unconscious adjustments to one another).

Such an approach, what we may call a ''network perspective,'' builds on the bottom-up criticisms but attempts to be more realistic in its understanding of the role of a ''central'' actor as catalyst. In this model, while the central agency is no longer envisioned as holding a superior, hegemonic position, it is nonetheless viewed as being on at least an equal footing with other interested entities and of having special responsibilities for catalyzing, convening, synthesizing, and in general exerting leadership in the public interest. Additionally, failure of effective operations in this model is considered to be the result of the existence of blockages to collective action and a lack of incentives to cooperate. Such an assessment of contributing factors for failure begins to form the role of a center network administrator—an entity that is not only an agent of an executive with responsibility for implementing a program, but also an agent responsible for creating incentives for and evoking cooperation between interested parties and for identification of potential blockages that these parties, working collectively, will have to overcome. This network approach to understanding the development of FEMA and emergency management to date works very well in comparison to the older models of understanding. This is especially so given the actual circumstances surrounding FEMA when Witt took over. At that point in time the public sector was beginning to be affected by the new forms of management processes and organizational formats that had been emerging in the private sector. Additionally, the ''reinventing government'' movement, along with process reengineering applications, moved to the forefront of administrative consideration at both the federal and state levels of government. Driving this development were several factors which have come to dominate both the public and private sector's view of the emerging information society.

First, both the public and private sectors were being influenced not only by advances in technology, but also by the accelerating rate at which these new developments are emerging within both our organizational and social structures. While these new technologies have allowed organizations to reach out beyond the physical constraints of time and distance, they have also challenged existing organizational and social relationships. Traditional forms of organizational interaction, which required direct person-to-person contact, are quickly disappearing as mediating technologies allow for immediate interaction across both distance and time.

Second, technological development has also had a profound impact on worker productivity, leading to major gains in worker outputs in both the public and private sectors. While the increase in productivity is welcomed, it has also led to the problem of creating an excess in the capacity of production for both the public and private sectors. The private sector's response to over capacity has been a movement toward major mergers between firms. But the public sector's inability to breach the federalist system of split constitutional powers has presented the public sector with the problem of both reducing and redistributing public sector capacity, yet at the same time being unable to do so due to the constitutional ''rights of place'' held by local, state, and federal governments. This factor, more than any other, speaks to FEMA's necessary use of a network model of governance to carry out its mission. Given the facts of a constitutional/federal democratized republic, there is simply no other way to manage large-scale emergency management effectively.

Third, customer and consumer expectations have risen due to the developments in technological innovation. The creation of new products and services, linked to the new technological platform, have allowed for an increase in the number and quality of choices available through the marketplace. Issues such as quality, value, and breadth of services are now major factors in customer choice. This level of rising customer expectations of choice is also reflected in the public markets for governmental services. While constrained by existing laws, regulations, and rules, public organizations face a citizenry now seeking and expecting a wider choice in the methods and types of government services that are offered. The days of ''one size fits all'' public equity is now being replaced by experimentation and innovation at all levels of government. That is, people want their emergency response now, and they want it in a form that is specific to them. This fact makes the necessity of well-coordinated networks of service delivery all the more important.

Last, an additional factor influencing both public and private sectors is the nature of the new technology. The marriage of computers and telecommunications has allowed for organizational control and oversight to be extended beyond the mere limits of geographic space. Where before supervision and control were directly linked to physical proximity, now supervision and control can be exercised through the technology, and this is not limited by distance. This capability is obviously a necessary ingredient in multiparty, multijurisdiction coordination.

All of the above factors began to impact thinking regarding the organization and structuring of government services during the early 1990s. What became evident, though, was that adapting existing organizational structures to these new forces would require a different type of focus than previously used in past governmental reform efforts. The focus of this new effort would have to be a total revamp of existing organizational processes and cross-cutting of organizational lines in order to utilize existing capacity located within another agency or group. The view of governmental processes would have to be extended at both the work and social levels and seen as a total systems concept involving all levels and operations of government. This new ''network'' view of governmental ''redesign'' would include a wide range of factors, including formal organizational structure, work practices, formal and informal groups, group operating styles and decision assumptions, personnel and group selection processes, individual and group socialization practices, and both individual and group career development.

The target of this new process would also be different than the target for past ''reform'' movements. Past reform had generally been associated with strengthening constitutional executive authority over the operations of government, often at the expense of the constitutional legislative authority. (Wamsley et al. 1996:265–271; Lane and Wamsley 1998). This new process, ''Reinventing government,'' on the other hand, would be focused on developing employee motivation and improving the level of services and quality within government services while maintaining the existing levels of resource allocations. To accomplish this end of creating scale without increasing the level of mass, the new process would have to rely on a complex network model that would cross-cut existing governmental structures.

C. Technological Capabilities

The basis for experimentation, in this case, is achieved through the application of three technological capabilities inherent within these new communications and automation platforms. These three new developments are communication, linkage, and knowledge enhancement.

In essence, the new platforms allow for communication to deliver all formats of information on a global level, thus freeing organizations from both time and distance constraints that have limited pervious organizational forms. Both human and technical resources can be ''remixed'' at will based on environmental feedback and without the constraints of distance.

The remix process if facilitated by the linkage factor, allows organizations to link their various technical platforms together across other organizational boundaries. What has started out as an internalized process within organizations, is now facilitated through linkage to outside organizations, thus increasing the possibilities of mixing and matching organizational subunits, production processes, individuals, work teams, and customers. In such an environment, external and internal organizational boundaries are either blurred or discarded, and fosters the development of even more alliances and networks.

Finally, by combining both an increase in communication with linkage to other organizations, the information for decision making and analysis is suddenly enhanced, and value is added to the overall base of data available to the network. To aid in this enhancement process, advanced applications such as expert systems, artificial intelligence, robotics, and object oriented data are brought into play against the knowledge base, forming a new level of analysis previously unknown to management and decision makers.

When all three ''technological capabilities'' are added together, one creates an entity in which the organizational assets, knowledge, and computing power are distributed across intra- and interorganizational boundaries. Rather than resources residing in a single location or controlled by a select group, resources are distributed across the organization and indeed across organizations and reside in multiple locations. Since the resource allocation is distributed across the network, the nature of roles and authority within the individual organizations are altered.

Organizational performance and output become highly interdependent owing to the need to tap resources from various levels of the network, which are often under the control or supervision of different groups. In such an environment, organizational roles often change, with personnel operating as leaders at one time and just as quickly shifting to a following role. By changing the location of resource allocations and role performance of organizational members, one creates an organizational interaction no longer based on command and control, but rather highly dependent of ''need.'' The network, in a sense, is ''self-organizing,'' and structures initiation, communication, and coordination based on the end process, not the organizational hierarchy. In such a dynamic environment, coordination can only be fostered through development of shared goals, common motives, and shared ''values,'' both management and personal, between organizational and network members.

Thus, at the base of these networks, resides a set of values that cross-cut organizational subunits and other organizations. The new value system seeks to replace the older ownership and control of information and resource mentality with one that fosters a sharing of resources and information—a form of collaboration. In addition, the authority of individual knowledge takes precedent over the authority of an individual's organizational position within the hierarchy. And finally, rather than viewing the environment as a factor that should be reacted to in a negative manner, the new value promotes the environmental stress as a learning and growth process full of potential for organizational and personal development. (Cohen and Mankin 1998:154–178). When the new network format is merged with the new systems model, plus the new technological capability, and overlaid with the new network values, one creates entity that, in essence, is the sum of the members attitudes, the management processes, the work processes, the network structure, and the technological platform.

Witt's assumption of office in 1993 corresponded with the emergence of these new network concepts and governmental redesign, issues. While it is not clear how self-consciously he drew upon these developments, they were nonetheless important in providing a favorable context for the decision process of the agency. To save FEMA from extinction was going to require a major reinventing FEMA process, and one that recognized the new organizational and technological design factors that had emerged into society.

D. Laying the Foundation for a Network Approach Within FEMA

In order for Witt to reorganize FEMA, he was faced with an immediate problem that could not be avoided. The basic problem was reestablishing credibility with Congress in order to at least delay the proposed demissioning of the agency. In order to accomplish the delay with Congress, though, Witt needed to first deal with personnel, and specifically with placing people with disaster expertise into positions of authority within the agency.

Witt was aided in the personnel process by the very positions which up to that point had been the bane of FEMA's existence: the gaggle of political appointment positions the agency had acquired. Resignations and firings of 35 political appointees within the agency in January 1993—3 months before he was appointed the new director of FEMA—cleared the way for him to quickly appoint persons with backgrounds in emergency management. In addition to the departure of incumbent political appointees, Witt, in accepting the director's position, also was able to gain a critical concession from President Clinton. In his discussions with Clinton and White House staffers, Witt insisted upon and received assurance that he could assess the credentials of all FEMA political appointees and a promise that his recommendations for appointment would be given top priority. Immediately after that meeting he described this as a ''veto'' over anyone the White House Personnel Office recommended—something he seemed to construe as ''refusal rights'' (Wamsley 1993). As a result of the negotiations with the White House, Witt was able to quickly assemble a group of persons experienced in emergency management to fill the political executive positions of FEMA (Ward 1998).

Once Witt had dealt with the competency of ''political'' employees of the agency, he then turned his attention to the ''career'' employees. In order to deal with the problem of low employee morale, Witt directly tackled the issue of FEMA's reputation as a political dumping ground and the conversion of federal merit jobs to scheduled political appointments. He immediately halted the practice of making political appointments to senior executive service (SES) positions and returned the agency to a commitment to merit or career professionalism within the SES similar to other agencies. This single action quickly dampened the resentment among higher-graded career employees who had previously watched as positions to which they aspired for years were handed to political outsiders with no emergency management experience.

Witt also began the process of cross-training his entire upper-level staff. Whether he was following the recommendations of the NAPA study, acting on intuition or taking a cue from traditional Japanese management practices is not known, but he pulled managers from their jobs and rotated them through other positions. He began to advocate the concept of managerial competency based on every manager spending some time in each aspect of the agency and sharing their different perspectives and ideas across the spectrum of the agency's subunits. In order to put clout in behind his managerial ideas, Witt also altered the performance management system, making evaluations quarterly instead of annual, and allowing supervised employees to participate in the supervisor's evaluation. In essence, career advancement for managers within FEMA now also depended in part on their employees' evaluations of their management and leadership skills and their mastery of an overall agency perspective—a ''total system'' view of FEMA's mission.

Witt's move with regard to political appointees and career personnel accomplished two significant effects. The first, in terms of the political appointees, was to assure the agency that the individuals filling the political positions had at least a modicum of expertise within the area of their supervision. While the appointees would no doubt continue to have alliances and coalitions with program and congressional constituencies, they would be operating with some professional knowledge of each program area.

More significant, though, was Witt's cross-training program with the agency's career employees. By cross-training the employees and shifting them from program to program, Witt effectively undermined the ''stovepipes'' within the agency. Rather than advancing within a specialized program area, employees now had to advance on the basis of demonstrating an agencywide ability. Career and personal loyalties no longer were linked solely to the various separate programs, but now were linked to the agency's overall performance. In addition, by having supervised employees involved in the evaluation process, Witt developed another level of personnel performance based on creating greater employee involvement in the agency, and placing responsibility for that increased involvement directly on the head of each supervisor. Teamwork, as well as program knowledge, now became a critical criterion for advancement within the agency. While the political stovepipes still exist, their efficacy was greatly reduced. Witt finally was able to begin the process of program integration which had been effectively avoided since the agency's inception under the Carter Administration. (Ward 1998)

Witt's restructuring of the personnel system was met with some resistance, especially among the long-term managers who saw it as an attack on their power. Still, even among the reluctant managers, it was widely accepted that a major change was long overdue. In order to deal with the resistance, Witt proceeded to also undermine the traditional funding streams for the various programs. Over the 15 years of FEMA's existence, 18 separate funding streams had been developed for states to receive federal disaster funds. The ways of receiving federal funds evolved over the years to meet specific needs and had become entangled in a web of red tape, program self-perpetuation, and inefficiency.

Witt consolidated the 18 funding streams into two streams. Next he announced that the funding from the two streams was to be awarded states based on their development of a comprehensive agreement with FEMA, which outlined each states specific objectives and tasks in support of the broader disaster objectives of FEMA. By consolidating the funding streams and connecting their allocation to state and federal plans for disaster relief and response, Witt effectively undercut the traditional resource base for the stovepipes, further weakening the reluctant managers who resisted the agency wide changes (Ward 1998).

While Witt's moves with regard to political appointees, career personnel, and funding streams allowed for the early development of a team approach within the agency and an undermining of the stovepipes' resources, he still faced the problem of deflecting the congressional movement toward agency demissioning. Once again, he was fortunate in assuming the post of director at a time when the agency was already beginning to take steps to improve its emergency performance.

E. The Reputational Context

Many of the higher-level FEMA officials, especially the career professionals, had taken the Hurricane Andrew presidential rebuff personally. While they were unable to gain the support of the previous director, Stickney, to institute an agencywide reorganization, they had begun to modify specific operational methods under their personal control and discretion.

Plans were drafted to begin the process of placing both disaster resources and staff into potential disaster areas before an actual emergency was declared. Rather than waiting for a state request for assistance, state officials were advised ahead of time on what resources were in their vicinity and what processes needed to be followed in order to request that such resources be mobilized. Additionally, FEMA officials began to consult regularly with both state and local officials, seeking their advice on what types of responses would be required in the event of a disaster. To foster communication, each regional office of FEMA assigned a specific employee to serve as a liaison to the state and local emergency management offices within the regional coverage (Congressional Quarterly 1993).

The staff planning soon paid off for the agency. Shortly after Witt took over as Director, FEMA was offered an opportunity to redeem itself and to prove to Congress that it still was a viable and effective force. The spring of 1993 saw the midwestern states of Wisconsin, Minnesota, Iowa, Illinois, and Missouri hit with a series of floods which quickly turned into a national disaster declaration.

Even before the flooding rivers had reached their crests, FEMA began to preposition both resources and staff into the flooding states. FEMA regional emergency operations managers helped the various states prepare the papers needed to secure ongoing assistance. FEMA also sent out preliminary assessment teams to Wisconsin, Minnesota, Iowa, Missouri, and Illinois. FEMA officials also began offering supplies, such as tents, purified water, inoculation devices and mobile homes, to local and state officials without waiting for state requests for assistance. Once the emergency declaration was issued, FEMA officials held daily conference calls with state and regional emergency managers, and in the hardest-hit areas FEMA agents talked to state officials almost every hour. FEMA also granted states more independent authority to determine how resources were allocated and instituted a preliminary disaster assistance center with a direct telephone application system (Ward 1998).

The new FEMA approach did not go unnoticed. Indeed Witt had been shrewd enough to appoint a first-rate public relations expert to his congressional relations staff whose job was to be sure anything positive about the agency and Witt *was* noticed. For the first time in a long time, congressional voices spoke out with praise for the agency. "FEMA's doing a great job," said House Majority Leader Richard A. Gephardt of Missouri. Rep. Neal Smith, Democrat of Iowa said "They got on the ball right away." Even professional emergency management officials at the state level offered praise. "This is the first time we have had this kind of coordination in my experience," said Jim Franklin, director of emergency management in Minnesota, and a 25-year state government veteran. "They think like we do, not like the bureaucrats." Still, doubts about FEMA's long-term commitment remained in existence, and were evident in the additional comment that Iowa Representative Smith made in his praise of the agency: "I don't know if it will last" (Congressional Quarterly 1993).

In spite of the improved performance with the midwestern floods, FEMA still faced the prospect of a major congressional overhaul. Senate bill S995 had been introduced by Senator Barbara A. Mikulski (D-Md.) and the chairman of the senate appropriations subcommittee, which called for a complete revamp of the nation's emergency management system. Specifically, Mikulski sought to reduce the number of political appointees, clarify the channels of liaison between FEMA and the Department of Defense by separating civil defense and continuity of government activities from those dealing with natural disasters, and create block grants that high-risk states could use to train local officials to combat disasters without authorization from FEMA. Mikulski's view of the agency saw FEMA still operating under the older Reagan Civil Defense model rather than a newer natural disaster model. "The old FEMA is still functioning under a Cold War framework, under which more money goes into preparing for nuclear war than for the disasters ordinary Americans in our communities are going to face" (Congressional Quarterly 1993).

Mikulski's bill was largely based on the two study reports of FEMA conducted by the Government Accounting Office (GAO) and the National Academy of Public Administration (NAPA). Both studies found that FEMA, and emergency management in general, faced three critical problem areas. The first was that FEMA lacked a method of comprehensive assessment of damage, coupled to an effective provision of disaster assistance. The second was claimed to be a lack of explicit authority for FEMA to mobilize the broad multiorganizational array of federal emergency response once a disaster warning was issued. (Others maintained that this was more a matter of ambiguity than a lack.)[6] And the third was a lack of adequate training and funding for state and local governments to develop effective responses to catastrophic disasters.

Both GAO and NAPA further clarified the three main areas of weakness when they testified at Senate committee hearings in May, 1993. In the hearings, both organizations recommended seven additional changes that would be required in developing an effective federal response. The first recommendation called for a greater involvement by the president and White House in disaster response, and the assurance of a swift, effective response to disasters. The second recommendation was the immediate deployment of FEMA disaster assessment teams in an emergency. The third was clearer legislative authorization for FEMA to mobilize resources for catastrophes. The fourth recommendation followed from the third, and called upon the Department of Defense to integrate their resources relevant to disaster response (particularly the National Guard) into a broad federal response system. The fifth recommendation called on FEMA to move toward a comprehensive emergency management charter, and away from a national civil defense program. The sixth area of improvement called for increased flexibility of funding to state and local governments to improve their own disaster response programs. And the seventh and final area of recommendation called on FEMA to assure Congress, and the nation that the top management positions of the agency were filled by individuals with sufficient professional backgrounds and experience to handle disaster response.

The Mikulski hearings were extensive and whatever might be said of them, they resulted in a thorough review of the implications of aspects of the legislation—implications that called for more work on the bill. As a consequence, Mikulski's original bill, S995, was withdrawn, and the committee spent the next year redrafting a new version of the bill. The one year reprieve gave Witt time to work on various aspects of FEMA's problems, and to also move the agency toward a better public and political image.

During the first 100 days of Witt's tenure, he continued to improve his relations with Congress. He met again with the chairs and staffers of all the key congressional committees overseeing the various FEMA programs. During this time he publicly testified before six congressional committees and subcommittees. In addition to mending fences with Capitol Hill, Witt forcefully continued his reorganization of FEMA's structure. His efforts in this area were so effective, that after only six months in the position he felt confident enough to ask NAPA to review the agency's operations in light of their previously critical report. The report was guardedly positive and encouraging.[7] Also aiding FEMA during the 1-year reprieve was the continuing effective response of the agency to a series of natural disasters. Within 15 months, FEMA effectively responded to 17 separate declarations of disasters.[8]

In spite of FEMA's impressive improvements, and the public/political relations efforts of Witt, the Mikulski committee continued their development of a new legislative agenda for FEMA. Finally, on August 18, 1994, the Senate governmental affairs committee approved a bill aimed at recasting the central mission of FEMA. The new bill, S1697, attempted to shift the focus of FEMA away from nuclear attack-related disasters, and instead focus the agency on providing relief after natural disasters. It would have required both the president and FEMA to submit plans to Congress for providing federal disaster assistance, and establish chains of command for disaster response. The submitted plans would have specified both federal duties in an emergency, and the response relationships that would be established between the federal government, various state and local governments, and any related private agencies. The bill would have also specified ways in which

FEMA itself would be reorganized, including the relocation of regional offices to high-risk areas. In addition to the above provisions, the bill also established a targeted grant program which allowed state and local governments to better prepare for emergencies. The measure authorized $200 million each year through fiscal 1998 for this grant program. While originally scheduled to be voted on by the Senate after the Labor Day recess, the bill was delayed due to the upcoming Fall congressional election. (Congressional Quarterly 1994).

However, the fall 1994 congressional elections proved a disaster for the Democratic majority in Congress. In a stunning defeat, they lost control of both the House and the Senate to the Republicans. One of the senatorial casualties of the election was Senator Mikulski's position as chair of a key subcommittee of Senate Appropriations—a position from which she had been waging guerrilla warfare against FEMA or, to be fair, against what she saw as its problems.

The new Republican majority had another plan for government, far different than the previous Democratic majority, a plan called The Contract with America. Very quickly, the new Republican "contract" plan devolved into congressional and presidential conflict. Partisan conflict over the role of government in American life, coupled to budgetary battles, led to governmental stalemate, and even shutdown, as congressional legislation met presidential vetoes. As the battle over the new Republican plan began to unfold, the Mikulski bill, along with the movement to reorganize FEMA, faded into the background.

The governmental stalemate and Senator Mikulski's loss of some of her leverage gave Witt the reprieve that he needed to reorganize FEMA without interference from either Congress or the president. In the political vacuum created by the changes in Congress and the stalemate between the Republican congress and the Democratic President Witt quickly moved to restructure both FEMA's mission, organization, and relations with others involved in emergency management at all levels of government and with those outside it.

VIII. FREE RIDERS AND MITIGATION: THE LEAST NOTICED AND UNDERSTOOD BUT MOST CRITICAL PROBLEM

Over the years of FEMA's existence, federal involvement in natural disasters had grown. Along with the growth in responding to natural disasters, the costs to the federal government had also increased. By the time that Witt assumed the directorship of FEMA, congressional concerns over the increasing costs had reached a point that many in Congress felt that some new type of financial arrangement was needed between the federal government and the State governments. At the bottom of this congressional concern was a growing reluctance to continue to bail out communities and states that suffered natural disasters, but who had taken no effective steps to institute preventive measures that would have decreased a disaster's impact.

Many states and local communities, on the other hand, felt that congressional criticism was either unwarranted or excessive. In the view of various states and local communities they recognized that they lay in "danger zones"—areas prone to flooding, earthquakes, tornadoes or hurricanes—but the probability of such a disaster occurring was "low." On the other hand, they also recognized that such high exposure would mean a huge number of costly claims in the event of a disaster.

Faced with a low probability but a high exposure, many of the danger-zone communities and states were reluctant to invest the millions of dollars necessary to change building codes, buy disaster insurance, or construct preventive barriers such as flood walls or reinforced buildings for earthquakes. Generally the feeling was that citizens were demanding services that met immediate needs, therefore, mitigation costs should be foregone in the expectation that the federal government would provide the funds avoided to repair much of the damage from a disaster. The result of this form of federal/state risk management game was that disaster impacts were not evenly distributed within even the same area under the same conditions.

A classic example of this problem arose during the 1993 midwestern flooding in Iowa. Two Iowa cities, Dubuque and Davenport, both located on the Mississippi River within a few hundred miles of each other, were impacted by the flooding in completely different ways. In the 1960s, Dubuque had spent a million dollars to construct a flood wall around the city. Davenport, in 1984, refused to construct a flood wall, estimated to cost $20 million, claiming that it not only did not have the funds but also that the flood wall would obstruct their view of the Mississippi. When the 1993 flooding hit Iowa, Dubuque remained dry and secure, but Davenport's downtown commercial area was completely flooded. After the flooding, Davenport, in spite of its past history of refusing to take preventive measures, received the federal funds to repair the flood damage.

The cost shifting process of risk assessment in which states and local communities assessed the costs of prevention versus the likelihood of federal aid after a disaster was not an issue the general public was aware of, let alone understood, but it had become a major point of contention within the emergency management relations between the federal and state governments. Witt was firmly convinced, as increasingly members of Congress were, that emergency management had to be able to do response and recovery well, but in the final analysis its emphasis had to be prevention or mitigation of disaster impacts. The free rider problem and mitigation were thus linked. The only politically feasible means of getting at the free rider problem was through mitigation. Political leaders were not going to deny people aid after a disaster has struck no matter how heedless they had been with regard to prevention.

Further aggravating this problem was FEMA's own involvement in both disaster relief and providing disaster insurance. While FEMA provided low cost flood insurance to home owners—in 1993 a $300 annual policy insured a house up to $185,000—and sought to use the insurance program to encourage communities to adopt tougher building codes, it also provided programs that negated the insurance program's intentions. FEMA's disaster relief program provided low-interest loans up to $120,000 for individuals and $500,000 for businesses. In essence, the Disaster Relief Loan Program undercut the intention of the Flooding Insurance Program and provided local communities and states with a way out of making tough decisions that would anger local developers and contractors. In essence, all of the incentive for disaster mitigation was nullified by the relief program.

The insurance industry, under the efforts of their Washington lobbying organization, the Natural Disaster Coalition, had been seeking ways to provide state governments with incentives to adopt tougher building code standards and emergency prevention systems. The coalition proposed that states be required to submit a comprehensive disaster relief plan to FEMA in order to be eligible for receiving the federal insurance and disaster relief. The submitted plans would detail specific steps the states would take to identify risk structures, their methods to improve building code enforcement, and the deployment of a comprehensive emergency response system. In addition, the coalition sought to link insurance premium levels to local building code standards. To support their case, the coalition pointed to Hurricane Andrew in Florida, and estimated that at least $4 billion in damages could have been prevented if just the existing building codes had been enforced.

Many legislators, especially those in ''danger zones'' frowned on the coalition's proposal, primarily because of fear of skyrocketing insurance costs. Still, the coalition's proposals did fit the mood of Congress, and the overall feeling that public willingness to aid those communities which refused to take preventive measures was waning or would if the issue received much exposure. But in order for FEMA to deal with the free rider/ mitigation conundrum, it first had to reach agreements with the states as to how their disaster preparedness plans would work within a national framework, and then what steps would be taken in relation to the national disaster response framework and then to deal with disaster prevention (Ward 1998). Only within such a comprehensive framework could FEMA effectively use its grant program to states in a way to get at the free rider/mitigation problem. But before such a comprehensive framework could evolve, federal and state relations would have to undergo extensive change.

IX. REINVENTING FEDERAL/STATE RELATIONS

Starting with President Jimmy Carter in the late 1970s, the process of reorganizing and downsizing the federal government had gained greater and greater emphasis with each succeeding Presidential Administration. While initially an executive initiative, over the years the effort had gained support from the general public, state governors, and congressional leaders. By the early 1990s, political leaders in both parties were rethinking the overall mission of the federal government, and seeking ways to both control rising costs for public services while increasing agency accountability to both political leaders and the general citizen.

President Clinton's capitalizing on this mood by championing ''reinventing government'' and the creation of the national performance review (NPR) provided Witt with an opportunity to reinvent FEMA's federal/state relations. The NPR report emphasized the necessity of the state governments entering into what were referred to as ''performance partnership agreements'' (PPAs) with the various federal agencies. The PPA concept proposed a radically new way of allocating federal funds to the various states, and in essence proposed that the state government's should have the flexibility of directing their own program development, while still being held ultimately accountable for their program performance by the federal agencies. The new approach recognized that each state had its own unique problems and resources and should be allowed to develop programs to maximize the use of federal funds while, at the same time, still being held accountable for the final level of program output achieved by the various program areas.

The new NPR approach—the performance partnership agreements—would give the states greater flexibility while still enabling FEMA to induce them to come up with outcomes that fit a comprehensive plan. FEMA recognized that many of the federal and state emergency management programs were duplicative and that in the past states had been reluctant to develop creative programs or partnerships in emergency management because of the lack of both financial incentives and flexibility. By utilizing the NPR approach concerning flexibility toward the state programs, FEMA hoped to restructure state and federal relations, improve the overall emergency management response capability, and yet by linking the receipt of both program grants and disaster funds to specific outcomes, to bring them into conformity with a national plan that could be the forerunner for an effort that focused on mitigation, and diminished the free rider problem (Ward 1998).

A task force composed of key officials from FEMA and several of the state emergency management programs developed a series of goals for the new partnership and subsequent funding programs for the partnership. Giving the states flexibility was risking it taking longer to negotiate agreements and meant that getting to the ultimate goal of mitigation would take longer to achieve, but the end result would be a nationally based comprehensive plan for emergency response that reflected the broad national goals, but achieved by individual state-specific objectives.

It is likely that Witt and those around him were confident that they would ultimately be able to get to an emphasis on mitigation simply because of their faith in the logic of mitigation as an idea that would attract support of powerful financial interests like the insurance industry and at the same time would make good sense to citizens once an educational campaign made clear its great potential to avoid human and financial loss. Witt's faith that mitigation was ''the answer'' and would prevail never wavered. At every opportunity, he would repeat his mitigation mantra: ''In the end, mitigation is the most effective form of emergency management'' (Wamsley 1993).

The final result of these PPA efforts was a FEMA strategic plan called ''Partnership for a Safer Future,'' which encompassed the PPA's at its core and extended them into a 5-year frame. Under the plan, FEMA laid out the overall objectives for national emergency management, and each state submitted a state-specific plan based on the PPA effort for achieving those ends. In order to assess each state's efforts toward meeting their goals, the program review process was changed.

In the past, state program managers had a checklist which they used to report on their success at meeting federal guidelines and standards. Under the new approach, FEMA allowed each state to determine how to improve the process, and worked with each state to establish state-specific measures of improvement. To ensure that each state ''stayed on target,'' the state-specific measures of improvement had to be collaterally set by each state and agency with the approval of FEMA. The process allowed the states to be responsible for establishing a response base, but with the expectation that it would improve disaster assistance within general national guidelines and structures.

Drawing upon the strategic plan, FEMA then entered into developing each of the states' formal agreements, called comprehensive agreements. FEMA regional staff were assigned to formally negotiate the agreements with each state's counterpart. In essence, the final negotiated agreement was then submitted to FEMA for final approval, and formed a contract between FEMA and the state agencies. In addition, the liaison staff of FEMA and their state counterparts would meet on a regular basis to review the agreement, and submit changes to FEMA when needed. The process thus became a continuous negotiating process, and a way to forge direct links between the federal government and each appropriate state agency.

Each PPA had allowed a state to develop it's own ''vision'' for emergency management, but in the Comprehensive Agreement this was framed within a five year plan which gave FEMA some assurance that a better response capability was emerging and would be constantly improved, and this enabled it to turn more of its attention to its ultimate goal of mitigation (Ward 1998).

X. ZEROING IN ON THE MITIGATION PROBLEM

By 1996, FEMA had negotiated comprehensive agreements with all 50 states. Immediately after the establishment of these, FEMA began to focus more directly on the mitigation issue, and proposed a new agreement called a Memorandum of Understanding (MOU) between the states and the federal government that would aim solely at mitigation efforts. The intention was that the MOUs would ensure that each state developed a statewide hazard mitigation plan, which included a priority list for mitigation projects within each state. Within FEMA, Witt established the Mitigation Directorate and charged it with implementing the MOUs.

Under the MOUs, Witt proposed establishing several incentives to encourage the states to develop comprehensive mitigation plans. One of these included the establishment of new disaster declaration criteria, which would reward pro-mitigation states by providing a higher cost sharing ratio for their next disaster.

In addition to providing a better cost sharing ratio, Witt began to lobby Congress for the establishment of a predisaster mitigation fund. The fund would have made money available to each state to create and implement innovative mitigation projects, revise building code standards, and underwrite insurance premiums for a wider range of types of disasters. Citing the 1993 midwestern floods, Witt emphasized the ''Volkmer bill,'' which allowed FEMA to buy out 10,000 properties within the various flood plains. While ambitious, the program was not well received by a Republican Congress more concerned with reducing federal costs and involvement in local and state affairs. Consequently the proposal stalled in Congress.

Recognizing the need for political and commercial support, Witt appealed directly to the Insurance industry to back his proposals, and to get involved in lobbying both the federal and state levels of government:

> The insurance industry has a valuable role in this. As leaders in the community . . . they can help bring the mitigation message to individual and corporate clients. Get to know local and state emergency management officials and get involved in emergency management activities. We have to continue to sit down together, you (insurers) and us, to help communities build safer. I know over the last three years we have made a difference and I know we can make even more of a difference in the next five years. Doesn't it make good sense for us to continue? I think it does, and I look forward to it. (Insurance Advocate 1996)

Witt's direct appeal to the insurance industry did not result in pressure on Congress to appropriate money for his mitigation plan. It did, however, win some respect from key congressional members who recognized that they were dealing with someone who understood how to find support from powerful people outside Congress if he felt forced to do so. More importantly perhaps his foray into Wall Street resulted in the emergence of a plan which eventually became known as ''Project Impact.''

A. Project Impact

In order to gain political and commercial support for funding a mitigation program, Witt had gone directly to Wall Street, and specifically to a very powerful and influential group within the insurance industry known as the Contingency Planning Exchange (CPE).

The CPE was established in 1985, and is composed of the United State's largest banks, most prominent legal and financial institutions, plus the biggest companies in manufacturing, trade, and advanced biological and mechanical technology. The CPE was initially developed under the Reagan Administration's Cold War/nuclear survival strategy, and was established to help the United States' largest corporations and financial institutions develop contingency plans for such a catastrophic event. The fall of the Soviet Union, like FEMA, had undermined the ''civil defense'' nature of the exchange's mission. The

CPE, like FEMA, was seeking a way to continue to exist within the new post-Cold War order. As Mark Harmowitz, CPE partnership coordinator and a member of the CPE executive board, put it: ''We at the CPE believe that we can no longer build contingency plans that only address the needs of our own companies. The impacts of disasters have far reaching consequences and demand that we plan our prevention, response and recovery efforts jointly with the communities where we operate. Avoiding damage from disasters is the key'' (Insurance Advocate 1998:4).

On the surface, the CPE's shift toward disaster mitigation might seem to be only an attempt by an organization to locate a new charter for existence after the demise of a previous charter. But in fact, the CPE's change in attitude was based on a more fundamental issue which was arising on Wall Street.

During the late 1980s and early 1990s a new type of investment had developed on Wall Street called the ''catastrophe bond,'' or ''cat'' bond for short. Such bonds were developed by investment bankers, who pooled insurance premiums, and repackaged them as securities. The development of the ''cat'' bond, had fueled a whole new area of investment called the ''reinsurance market,'' and spawned a new group of investment bankers and traders who specialized in this area. Aided by statisticians and meteorologists, these brokers analyzed the risks associated with catastrophes such as earthquakes and hurricanes, and then repackaged the reinsurance securities based on final profits after payouts for disaster claims. In terms of growth on Wall Street, the reinsurance market and Cat bonds were considered one of the prime future investment groups.

The key, of course, to making a profit in such a market was keeping the final payout schedule for disasters as low as possible. As in any insurance business, the major key to keeping pay-outs as low as possible is prevention prior to the catastrophe. CPE's new disaster contingency charter aligned with the profit concerns of the reinsurance market, and made it a prime candidate to work with various groups, such as FEMA, who were attempting to institute prevention and mitigation efforts before catastrophes struck.

Previously, FEMA had partially funded a project instituted by the New York State Emergency Management Office called the ''Joint Loss Reduction Project.'' Under the pilot project, both the New York State Emergency Management Office and the New York State insurance industry developed a shared mitigation program which promoted mitigation efforts tied to insurance premiums. It was this pilot program that became the basis for FEMA's ''Project Impact'' (Ward 1998).

Witt emphasized to the CPE and Wall Street that it was in the interest of the nation's business community to not only protect their own financial investments, but to also assist in protecting the communities in which they did business. Using the New York model, Witt proposed a joint public/private partnership to lead the nation in advancing a comprehensive mitigation program.

In order to bolster his case, Witt used the development of El Niño to put the ''fear of god'' into the reinsurance industry. For example, he told a gathering of the insurance industry: ''The impact of this year's El Niño continues to be felt across the country, We currently are handling 17 different disasters, all of them related to El Niño, according to the National Weather Service'' (Insurance Advocate 1998:4).

Witt went on to state that disaster figures did not take into account the loss from businesses closing and job loss, especially for small businesses—40% of which never reopened after a disaster. In the fall of 1997, FEMA held an ''El Niño Community Preparedness Summit'' in Santa Monica, California. President Clinton addressed the gathering of insurance industry representatives and emergency management leaders, and announced the establishment of a $50 million program which would be called Project Impact. Witt called on 500 businesses to join in a partnership with FEMA within 1 year to implement the program, and specifically called on the CPE to take the lead in representing the business and insurance industries in his efforts to have the program established permanently by Congress. ''The CPE is an important partner in FEMA's 'Project Impact.' Since disasters threaten the economic and commercial growth of entire communities, the comprehensive planning and solutions that the private sector can provide are essential'' (Insurance Advocate 1998:4).

Witt asked the CPE to persuade its membership to donate 12,000 hours of assistance to help small businesses prepare for natural disasters. In addition, he asked the CPE to request of its member companies a donation of $20 million in financial incentives to assist small businesses and communities in developing mitigation plans and implementing them.

Over the next 6 months, FEMA and CPE negotiated the general outlines of a joint program, and on March 25, 1998, they launched the program at a joint meeting in New York. Under ''Project Impact,'' seven pilot communities were to be selected to demonstrate the economic benefits of predisaster mitigation efforts. Each selected community would form ''teams'' to develop the local programs and would include representatives from the local business community, local government officials, and state emergency management departments.

Initially, seven pilot communities were selected for the program. Each of the communities received $1 million from FEMA as seed money to be used for disaster mitigation efforts such as installing hurricane straps in auditoriums, wind shutters on public buildings, and improved disaster shelters for victims. In order to receive the funds, each community had to pledge the cooperation of the local business community and local government officials in developing their mitigation plans. In addition, the communities were required to examine properties that were highly vulnerable, and to assess the cost of either replacing the property if damaged, versus outright purchase and demolition prior to a disaster.

Overall, the basic intention of Project Impact was to have communities assess and recognize the risks involved at the local level, and to take initiatives to address those risks. It was hoped that eventually, the process would lead to a recognition of the effect such an effort could have on the local communities bond ratings in the insurance market, and the impact that disasters had on the entire local community infrastructure.

The initial seven Project Impact pilot communities included a grant to Pascagoula, Mississippi—an area in which Senate Majority Leader Trent Lott held a significant investment in a chain of local pizza parlors.[9] Twenty more communities were expected to be added to the program within a year, and FEMA's eventual goal was to have at least one model community in each state.[10]

Project Impact was not, ultimately, the full-fledged Mitigation Program sought by FEMA. The failure of Congress to provide federal funds for property buyouts in high-risk areas significantly decreased its effectiveness. Nonetheless, Project Impact represented a major step toward FEMA's ultimate goal of designing an emergency management system which combined both emergency response and disaster prevention.

A framework for the development of a comprehensive response to natural disasters, one, which shifted essential resources to the state, and local levels of government, had finally been established. However, in order for such a comprehensive system to respond effectively, and to bring the necessary resources into play for both prevention and response, a support information system had to be developed. The development of such an information system seemed an overwhelming challenge.

In case of a disaster, one needs to know the types of resources that are available and their level of readiness. In addition, information about power and water/sewer lines in the affected areas, types of building structures, levels of building codes for property plats, and local chains of command for response are basic for effective response. The same information is also essential for assessing potential damage before an event occurring and for designating target area for prevention efforts.

Compounding the basic information problem is the fact that natural disasters occur in a non-deterministic manner. The direction and force of an earthquake, hurricane, tornado, or flood is constantly shifting based on factors beyond the limits of human cognition. Thus, monitoring the potential disaster must occur prior to the event, and while the disaster is at its full impact. This calls for an information system that must operate within a limitless number of probabilities.

Within FEMA, the development of such an advanced information system had been underway for many years before the appointment of Witt as head of the agency—especially under the ''black budget'' programs. Major breakthroughs in both computer and telecommunications technology, especially during the later 1980s and early 1990s, presented an opportunity for the creation of such a system. Unfortunately, the advanced telecommunications and computer assets needed for such a system existed but under control of the Department of Defense and they were highly classified. In order for FEMA to tap these assets for use in natural disasters, the issue of FEMA's role in civil defense and continuity of government, and its relationship with the Department of Defense, had to be resolved.

B. Settling the Issues Surrounding Civil Defense and Continuity of Government

FEMA's effectiveness in coping with natural disasters had long been hamstrung by the legacy of the Reagan Administration's obsession with nuclear attack survival. For years, as the country sought to cope with the effects of natural disasters, FEMA's National Preparedness Directorate, the directorate charged with civil defense and continuity of government, had necessarily kept large portions of the agency's capabilities behind a wall of secrecy. Fearful of revealing to the ''enemy'' ''top secrets,'' the directorate refused to deploy any of the advanced communications and technological systems that had been developed by the agency. These ''assets,'' while needed to aid disaster areas, were generally left immobilized during natural disasters.

The NAPA study had conservatively estimated that 27% of the agency's annual budget, about $100 million, had been directed into a ''black budget'' area devoted to national security preparedness. While some of the funds in the ''black budget'' would have been valuable in response to natural disaster, the national security and secrecy mentality of the operation had resulted in all of the advanced technological capacity being classified, and restricted in its use for response to natural disasters. By the time that Witt assumed the agency's directorship, no one was able to accurately estimate the total amount of funds that had been invested in the ''black budget'' operation. The end result was that FEMA had developed an advanced system for disaster response composed of underground installations, mobile units, ultrasophisticated and advanced communications systems, and probably the most advanced computer modeling systems in the world, but none of it was available for use in dealing with natural disasters.

Witt understood and was committed to lifting the secrecy shield, and deploying the civil defense assets in natural disaster operations. In order to alter the agency's mission emphasis, he quickly declassified a series of agency documents related to the ''black budget'' operation, and dismantled the national preparedness directorate. In addition, he established an open line item within the agency's budget for national preparedness, and allocated only $7.5 million for its annual operation. The number of employees with security clearances was sharply reduced and former classified projects were then redesignated as ''dual use'' for responding to both natural disasters and national security emergencies.

The first example of this dual-use declassification was the Mobile Emergency Response Support fleet (MERS) and the Mobile Air Transportable Telecommunications Systems (MATTS)—both under the direction of the Response and Recovery directorate's Mobile Operations Division (RR-MO). These state-of-the-art vehicles had previously been deployed at five sites across the United States. Their original intended use was to keep a sophisticated communications net mobile and invulnerable to disruption, and to locate designated senior government officials in the event of an attack or threat of attack and provide them with mobile communications and facilities to continue governmental operations. After the dual use classification, these units were first deployed in Des Moines, Iowa, for the midwestern flooding to provide communications backup, power units, and water-purification facilities.

While on the surface these efforts appeared to open the operation, in fact a large portion of the operation remained classified and subject to various restrictions. Because these assets were still related to the national security preparedness function, FEMA had only shared authority over them with the National Security Council, which was the ultimate overseer and coordinator of the national response to all-out war (Ward 1998).

But due to the collapse of the Soviet Union the political climate was changing rapidly and FEMA, the National Security Council and the Department of Defense were faced with increasing pressure from Congress in terms of budgets. All these agencies recognized that such pressures had to be addressed for the continued viability of all of them. In addition, the nature of national security was changing. While the fall of the Soviet Union had decreased the nuclear attack scenario, new threats were arising, especially in terms of terrorism.[5]

In order for FEMA to move toward a natural disaster emphasis within the agency's operations, and to improve the agency's natural disaster response capability by tapping these advanced systems, an agreement had to be reached between FEMA, the Department of Defense (DoD) and the National Security Council (NSC) regarding the national security preparedness assets in question.[6] Negotiations were entered into and a ''tiered'' system of access to the assets developed under the ''black budget.'' National security needs i.e., DoD and the NSC would continue to have first call on these assets in the event of an attack or threats to that effect. But barring such events, portions of the assets were to be available to FEMA for emergency management. Accordingly, many of the assets were declassified and designated for dual use operations. These included the emergency mobile fleet, computer modeling and projection of weather patterns, satellite camera and real-time video feeds for damage assessment, communication and computer linkages to DoD wide area network systems, and field computer and communications satellite uplinks and downlinks for use of on-site assessment and data feeds by personnel in the field. All of these dual use systems were available directly from the FEMA's natural disaster response center in the nation's capital. More advanced and classified systems were placed under DoD control and housed at DoD command centers. These advanced systems were integrated into the overall DoD defense and response systems, and access was restricted through formal authorization protocols. The secretary of defense was authorized to provide access to the various systems in support of natural disasters. Access to assets was defined within a set of defense priorities set within DoD directive 3025.1. The secretary of the army was designated the DoD executive agency for support of civil emergencies.

As envisioned the new arrangement would begin with the prediction of a natural disaster. As it unfolded, a liaison officer from FEMA would be assigned to the Network Management Operating Center of the National Communications System/Defense Information Systems Agency. That person would be linked, by both telecommunications and data lines, to the FEMA control center in Washington. As natural disaster preparations and response operations developed for each situation, FEMA could request access to more of the advanced system network's assets. Each request for additional assets would be passed from the liaison officer at Network Management Operating Center to DoD personnel for approval. Upon giving approval, DoD would release portions of the system's assets to FEMA's control center, and put in place a series of ''firewalls'' to other levels of the system. A DoD-designated representative would then monitor the system while it was accessed to ensure that use was limited to only the authorized areas and to sever the link if any unauthorized access attempt was made. Once the disaster was over, the system was reconfigured to its original access levels, and both centers would disconnect the temporary linkages (Ward 1998).

By releasing portions of the ''black budget'' assets to ''tiered access'' under DoD control and authorization, FEMA maintained a role in the civil defense ''force structure,'' which was an important matter of status and reputation, but at the same time enabled it to significantly move the agency's primary mission toward disaster response, and the development of the ''all hazards'' approach. In addition, while FEMA added a layer of authorization to its system for access, it was able to maintain access to the advanced systems that had been developed, and are still being developed, within the ''black budget'' operations (Ward 1998). Once the civil defense issue had been resolved, FEMA was better able to pursue its disaster response agenda, and to concentrate on developing a shared federal/state system for disaster preparedness and response, and ultimately, mitigation. The new system would be able to bring to bear formerly classified ''high value'' assets to dispatch resources and information promptly from a ''forward leaning posture'' and do so with much better understanding as to needs and priorities than ever before. That anguished dialogue over a barely functioning phone in the wake of Hurricane Andrew should never need to happen again, i.e., local EM office: ''*We need everything! Send us everything*! State EM office: ''We can't send *everything*! What do you *need*!!''

C. The Technological "Fix"

During the entire time that FEMA had been developing it's state and local efforts, its technical staff had been building an advanced system of assessment and response for natural disasters. They were aided in this by advances in both computer and telecommunications technology. Even before Witt's assumption of leadership, FEMA's technical staff had been working on using the advanced technological base, developed under the ''black budget,'' to supplement and improve its field response for natural disasters.

Shortly after Hurricane Andrew struck Southern Florida, Digital Matrix Services, Inc. (DMS), a Miami based Geographical Information System (GIS) software company contacted FEMA. DMS made available to FEMA its on-line digital database of Southern Florida, and the system was used by both FEMA and the Army's Special Forces transport division to assess damage, and to coordinate disaster relief into the hardest hit areas. Using the on-line maps in the DMS database, and satellite ground positioning systems, the relief efforts were able to navigate the devastated area in spite of the fact that all the street signs and land markers were destroyed. The system was also used to select sites for sanitation and debris removal, and the siting of field relief operations for food and water distribution.

After Andrew, FEMA continued to work with DMS on how to apply the GIS systems, and especially in terms of linking the systems to field efforts. The basic premise of the development project was to build a portable, ready-to-go database of geographical information that could be tapped as the need arose. The database of populated areas likely to suffer natural disasters would be constructed prior to a disaster, and then be configured and operationalized to deal with the specific area that suffered a natural disaster. Once the disaster was past, the system would then be reconfigured to a ''wait'' status, and continue to build its resource of information.

Using commercially available street network files, images in the database were rectified so that actual size and distance appeared in a true proportion to the ground structures. The structures could also then be linked to individual addresses and homeowner information to provide a direct match between structures and homeowners. Special vans equipped with the system would then drive down the devastated areas, feeding visual information on damaged buildings directly into the database through satellite links, and providing an immediate damage assessment of the affected areas. The system was also linked to the ''dual-purpose'' ''black budget'' computer modeling systems to provide ''what-if'' analysis for determining possible damage and prepositioning of resources in the event of an on-coming hurricane, or the aftershocks of an earthquake. After Witt assumed the leadership of the agency, he threw his full weight in behind these preliminary efforts (Ward 1998).

By June of 1993, just 3 months after Witt had taken over, FEMA tested an advanced system of field support, in cooperation with the Army Corps of Engineers, at Salt Lake City. The first trial of the proposed Disaster Management Information System (DMIS) involved the linking of laptop computers (running under Lotus Notes on-line conferencing capabilities) with microwave and satellite data links. The pilot system provided ''real-time'' conferencing capabilities between relief workers in the field and FEMA operational centers. Two-way wireless modems carried voice, data, and graphics to an earth station uplink that then bridged the communications gap to field offices. The laptop computers and desktop microcomputers were mounted in recreational vehicles, and provided relief workers with full access to power, water, and telephone grid maps, along with satellite assessment of fire and building damage in the affected areas. (American City & County 1993:38). The initial prototype DMIS was successful, and FEMA's technical staff began further development of the DMIS, with an especially heavy emphasis on the use of Geographic Information Systems (GIS). The Federal Geographic Data Committee supported FEMA's efforts.

As with most areas of computer and telecommunications development, the federal government has often been in the forefront of developing advanced geographical information systems. While almost every agency of the federal government has some capacity in terms of GIS, the most advanced systems have been developed by the Department of Defense, the U. S. Geological Survey, the Environmental Protection Agency, the Forest Service, and the Bureau of Land Management. While all agencies have some GIS capability, they are limited in their development of GIS by an Office of Management and Budget (OMB) Circular A-16, first written in 1967 and then revised in 1990. Under OMB Circular A-16, the Geographical Data Committee was established, and charged with coordinating data collection, establishment of standards, and the purchase of GIS systems. All federal

GIS systems must be capable of being linked, and form what is known as the National Spatial Data Infrastructure (NSDI). The Committee is chaired by the interior secretary and establishes the standards for technological platforms and software, policies for access, and control over the collection, storage, and distribution of spatial information. In essence, the committee is to develop a "shared vision" of data supporting multiple tasks, and held together by a common emphasis on geography.

Under the Geographical Data Committee's (GDC) direction, the computer modeling division of FEMA began to evaluate both the existing GIS systems available within the federal government, and the "black budget" modeling systems developed under the Reagan Administration. An assessment of the models showed that models originally developed to assess damage from a nuclear attack could easily be modified to assess damage from natural disasters, especially prior to the actual event occurring. The eventual system developed, called Consequences Analysis Tool Set (CATS) could use off-the-shelf GIS software and hardware, and link the system to remote sensing devices, resource databases, and demographic data plus land plats, to deliver assessment information. The system would have the capability of estimating damage prior to an actual event, provide direct support during a disaster, and, during normal times, be used for preparedness training and mitigation planning. The proposed CATS system could also be linked to the National Oceanic and Atmospheric Administration (NOAA) hurricane warning system to develop profiles of a hurricane's path and velocity, and to estimate potential damage assessments prior to landfall. The system, when linked to NOAA's system, could utilize the DMIS system to assess where damage was likely, the degree of damage that would result from wind, storm surges, waves, and flooding, and the number, and type, of both people and businesses that would be affected. Once the preassessment model was run, a second model would then determine the level of resources that would be needed, and the locations for prepositioning of the resources. The GDC gave FEMA authorization to develop the system, and by the summer of 1993 a prototype was in place and under testing.

The first test of the system was in August 1993 when Hurricane Emily hit the Outer Banks of North Carolina. CATS estimated that 674 homes would be destroyed, and the actual storm resulted in 683 claims being filed. The project was jointly funded by FEMA and the Defense Department's Nuclear Agency, which provided access to the U.S. Army Construction Engineering Research Laboratory's Geographical Resource Analysis and Support System (GRASS), which formed the base system for CATS. Using CATS as a base, further modeling was developed, and eventually models were constructed for floods, earthquakes, fires, and other less common disasters such as chemical spills. By 1995, both the DMIS and CATS were operational, and could be linked to a national disaster telecommunications network (Ward 1998).

The impetus for the telecommunications network had its foundation in 1989 during the San Francisco earthquake. Still mired in the cold war mentality, FEMA, up to that time, had remained a "paper based" organization when it came to natural disasters. As a result, the agency was inundated, after the San Francisco quake, with over 70,000 paper applications for relief. The warning signal from San Francisco was unheeded, however, and in the aftermath of Hurricane Andrew the agency was once again flooded with tens of thousands of written applications. This time the agency realized it needed to "modernize" the application system. It began to develop Local Area Networks and Wide Area Networks to speed up the processing of both disaster applications and checks. Utilizing the capacity of both the DMIS and CATS systems, the technical support division of FEMA modified the U.S. Army's GRASS system, and linked it to the mobile field vans operating with the DMIS. Field inspectors to assess damage used AST portable touchpad computers. The data from the damage assessment units was then fed, via Ethernet, into various servers located at FEMA regional offices. Each of FEMA's regional office servers were then linked to the other regional office servers. Using Cisco System routers, the sites could then distribute the workload on applications across the country (InfoWorld 1994:62).

At first the proposed new system was directed at decreasing the processing time for disaster applications, but as the system's effectiveness became apparent, the system was further modified to feed data directly into other state or federal agencies involved in the disaster response. It became apparent that the field agents, in place, were able to feed current information into the total system concerning the immediate level of damage on the ground. So the system was expanded to allow for the data assessment to be fed not only into the application system, but also into the Disaster Command Centers seeking to deal with response to the event. When the combination of DMIS, CATS, field vans, and field agents information was linked, the entire system was then linked, via satellite feed, from FEMA's Disaster Response Center in Washington, D.C., to field operations and command centers across the country. The final system provided a ''real time'' environment with direct feed from the disaster area, and all sharing the same level of information for coordinating the response effort (Ward 1998). With the final development of the telecommunications network, FEMA's transition into a network entity was complete.

XI. COMING OF AGE?

When one examines the history of FEMA, and the emergence of a network structure better suited for its role as national coordinator of response to natural disasters and emergencies, it becomes clear that FEMA has developed in two very distinct phases. The first phase, which represents the years of the Reagan and Bush Administrations, is one of seeking to model itself after a traditional hierarchical organization for management decisions, agency action, and technological implementation.

During this time the agency operated within a very set and rigid chain of command. It was heavily influenced by the civil defense portion of its mission, and tightly coupled to the overall federal response to a potential nuclear attack scenario and the continuation of government after such an attack. All other missions of the agency were considered secondary, and often either ignored or dismissed as irrelevant in light of the urgency of the primary mission. Decisions in relation to other levels of government, in particular state and local governments were framed within a traditional ''by-the-book'' mentality, with rigid adherence to regulations and rules. Pleas by local and state governments to allow them to exercise discretion and flexibility to fit local conditions were ignored, and in fact completely rejected as undermining ''efficiency.'' During this period of time, the agency tended to operate as a ''closed system,'' seeking to buffer the agency from outside influences, and often taking hostile actions toward individuals, groups, and even congressional actors, who were interested in the agency's decisions and methods of operation.

Information technology (IT) deployment within FEMA followed a classic systems design model premised on the assumptions that all operational linkages were definable, and had a set of limited boundaries and possibilities (Woodward 1958; Simon 1960). The agency also tended to apply technology within an organizational design structure that mirrored a top-down decision making process reflective of the existing agency decision premises and power structure.

In many ways, the agency, during this first cycle, exhibits many of the management/technology traits described by James March (1978, 1981, 1987). March's research findings tended to show that technologies perceived by management as increasing control, or creating stability of the organization under their control, will be more likely to be adopted than technologies management perceives as undermining or changing the organizations control systems or decision premises. Thus the agency, during this time, was willing to adopt and develop IT supportive of the continuity of government program, the agency's primary objective, but reluctant to develop a disaster assessment and response system which would have supported the agency's natural disaster program (a secondary, and minor, agency objective).

The first phase in FEMA's network development did not end abruptly, but rather was a period of four to five years during which the primary mission, civil defense and the continuation of government, was undermined and eroded. The cause of the erosion was the fall of the Soviet Union, and with it the reduced risk faced by the United States in terms of the nuclear war scenario. During this period of time, which roughly corresponded to the Bush Administration, FEMA, along with the entire military establishment, faced the issue of seeking to redefine their primary agency missions. In the case of FEMA, the mission redefinition was aided by the fact that the agency's original mission encompassed both a civil defense and a natural disaster response charter.

From a logical standpoint, it appeared relatively easy to shift the agency from a civil defense posture to a natural disaster posture. This was the position of Senator Mikulski and the congressional critics of the agency. But in actuality, the process of transition was not that easy to accomplish. Large portions of the agency budget were still committed to a joint continuation of government and Department of Defense response system, much of which was highly classified. In addition, the rigid hierarchy and chain of command mentality of the first phase was still in place, along with the individuals who had fostered the civil defense/continuation of government agenda of the agency. Thus while the agency's outside critics saw the transition as relatively easy, inside the agency and the policy subsystem was a remaining hard-core cadre who sought define a new "defense" posture for the agency, and to maintain the hierarchical and control organizational model.

The ultimate crisis for the agency, and the final destruction of the civil defense mentality, occurred shortly near the end of the Bush Administration when the agency was called upon to coordinate a "major" natural disaster—the landfall of Hurricane Andrew in South Florida. Unable to effectively respond to the disaster, the agency was pushed into a secondary role, thus fueling the congressional anger over the agency's inability to transition itself into a natural disaster response posture. It is at this point in time that the second phase of FEMA's network development emerged.

Fortunately, for FEMA, the crisis point occurred at a time when a different model for government reform was emerging—generally called "reinventing government"—adopted by and pushed throughout the federal government by Vice President Gore as the National Performance Review. The NPR philosophy combined several models from the private sector, and included concepts from total quality management (TQM), process reengineering, and organizational designs built around loosely coupled telecommunications networks. In essence, the NPR movement sought to place "citizen satisfaction" at the base of all program and agency evaluation. It was within this "reinvention" reform movement that James Lee Witt assumed the directorship of FEMA.

FEMA's "reinvention" efforts extended the NPR model in a significant way by expanding the agency's perspective to include those elements of the emergency management policy subsystem that existed outside both the agency and the federal government. Underlying this basic adoption of the NPR model was recognition by Witt, and others in positions of leadership, that the agency was not a ''mechanistic model, designed to achieve a specific, predefined output,'' and with everything outside the organization seen as mere context (Thompson 1967). Of course the agency prior to Witt did not see itself in quite such naïve and simplistic terms, but nonetheless it clearly tended in that direction. The agency's view of its world shifted under Witt so that it began to see itself as more of a social system, highly dependent on the agency personnel's interaction and relationships with other social agents (people) in other organizations in other branches and levels of government and outside the public sector as well—all of whom affected FEMA or who were directly affected by the agency's performance (Burns and Stalker 1961). In essence, the agency was no longer a closed system, as it was during its first phase of development, but rather had become an open system, in which the internal components and dimensions of the agency were linked to the external environment that encompassed all the agency's activities and relevant others, not only in its immediate task environment but also in its broader domain or political economy as well. (Thompson 1967; Wamsley and Zald 1976).

From the standpoint of the development of a network entity in the public sector, FEMA's experience has much to offer in terms of developing new strategies for governmental redesign efforts—especially in the deployment of IT in support of those efforts. FEMA could have elected to follow a path where technology was used to support predetermined management decisions. Or it could have elected to go for the technological ''fix,'' in which the capabilities of technology could have set the parameters of operations. Instead FEMA followed two parallel tracks for redesigning the organization.

On one track Witt, and the various department heads of FEMA, focused on creating formal and informal structures with other federal and state agencies necessary to foster cooperation and coordination prior to an actual disaster occurring. Undeniably it was aided in this by Witt's close relationship to the president. This gave FEMA officials the status that made people take them seriously. As one interviewee said, ''James Lee and his wife watch movies with the Clintons. Word gets around about that, and in this town that means people return your phone calls—and promptly too.''

Not only was the relationship to the president important, but so was the president's own perspective on emergency management. As a former governor and chairman of the National Governors' Conference, Bill Clinton was fully cognizant of how important emergency management could be to state and local government and therefore how important it could be to a president. Moreover, he had seen at first hand how important it had been to President Bush in 1992—indeed, he might well have owed his win over Bush in no small way to the debacle that surrounded Hurricane Andrew.

In all efforts to induce cooperation, FEMA recognized the constitutional ''rights of place'' held by other actors, and accepted the reality of a decentralized system of ''shared powers.'' There were no blustering claims of statutory powers or pointing to antiquated statutes that could conceivably give the agency awesome wartime emergency powers, as had occurred under Giuffrida. These negotiations, with relevant others ultimately, led to the creation of agreements on how various elements within a national disaster response system would interact in the event a disaster actually occurred.

On the second track, Witt supported the efforts of IT staff within FEMA to examine the possibilities of developing a new type of response system utilizing the network capabilities located both within the federal government, and outside federal control at both the state government and private sector levels. These efforts ultimately led to the creation of an advanced telecommunications and computer network system that was able to configure its response to an emerging situation rather than a predefined scenario.

The convergence of these two parallel tracks of development within FEMA ultimately led to the creation of a form of ''network'' entity, not an organization in the usual way the term is used but a social construct that spans levels of government and sectors of society. This new network operates under the recognition by all the members of the system that the resources and organization needed to respond to a natural disaster do not lie solely within the federal government or for that matter within government. And it operates by means of the technological capability of the most highly classified communications and computer platforms in the world. But in the process of creating this new network, Witt has also created a new policy subsystem that recognizes the shared power basis of our constitutional order and the cooperation necessary to achieve effective coordination in emergency management.

Have there been any rewards to FEMA, and Witt, for the agency's remarkable transition? In fact there has been some recognition of the hard work that went into the transformation. First, and not to be dismissed, was the self-satisfaction of those involved. After years of denigration and public humiliation, a favorable press is no small matter. Morale at FEMA has never been higher. There was formal recognition that it was an exemplar in the reinventing of government effort, and finally there was an unusual presidential honor bestowed upon the agency. On February 26, 1996 at the National Emergency Management Conference, President Clinton addressed the conference delegates, and announced a startling commitment to emergency management:

> I am very pleased with the progress that's been made. I also am more impressed than ever before about the importance, the integral importance of FEMA to the Nation's business. It now relates to the Transportation Department, the Department of Health and Human Services, the Labor Department, the Energy Department, right across the line because of all of us having to work with James Lee in the dealing with disasters. So today it's a pleasure for me to announce to all of you that I am extending Cabinet membership for the first time in history to FEMA and to James Lee Witt. (Weekly Compilation of Presidential Documents, 3/4/96, Vol. 32 Issue 9, p380, 2p.)

The successful development of any form of network entity, whether in the public or private sector, is highly dependent on the ''relationships'' that are established between key players in other organizations and the levels of trust held between the members of the partnership. (Chisholm 1996; Harari 1998; Holmlund and Tornross 1997; Sproull and Kiesler 1991) This trust development is usually based on two factors: how well the relationship benefits those involved, and the trustworthiness and competence of the leadership in the relationship. Witt has proved to all with whom the agency has developed relations that the relationship is valuable to them. They have received favorable attention for their roles in disaster response from the public, Congress and the president. Some may have been able to augment their budget appropriations with such attention. Witt has repeatedly shown himself and the agency competent. But questions remain about the future, one of these questions concerns what type of dependencies will the members of the new policy subsystem experience as they come to rely, even more than they have in the past, on this new network with its technological infrastructure?

It should be evident to the reader by now that there are two opposing views about the impact that technology has on an organization or other social constructs, i.e., a network.

One view, as expressed early in our discussion of James March's theories, holds that technology is used in organizations to reinforce hierarchy, control, and centralization. This body of research has a long history, with numerous supporters (Fleck 1984; Gotlieb and Borodin 1973; Mosco 1989; Orlikowski 1988; Simon 1960; Wiener 1950). The other view holds that technology leads to empowerment and liberation, and fosters decentralization of authority and control, especially IT. While it lacks the lengthy history of the first view, this latter position also has an abundance of supporters (Galbraith 1968; Naisbitt 1982; Roszak 1988; de Sola Pool 1983; Toffler 1980). The debate about whether IT and dependency upon it encourages centralizing or decentralizing—greater central control or greater autonomy throughout remains open. It is even conceivable that both possibilities exist, depending on how the network is used and who uses it.

Over time, the new network that FEMA has helped to create will undoubtedly expand. Its capabilities will become more sophisticated and powerful. As its functionality and utility increases, so will the dependency upon it of all the members of the policy subsystem (network). Yet ultimately the capability and efficacy of this new network hangs on the capability of the federal government's systems, especially the DoD's advanced systems, which are the "backbone" that links all the other systems together. Up to now, the DoD, FEMA, and the rest of the federal government, have been open to sharing this critical resource. But there is always the possibility that in the future access will become conditional. As it stands presently, a change in either the directorship of FEMA or a new presidential administration's position, could turn this network into a vehicle for even greater centralization and control. Only the future will tell what direction the network will take.

XII. CONCLUSION

When James Lee Witt was appointed to the directorship of FEMA, he was the first person to come to the position with significant experience as a state director of emergency management, having held such a position in Arkansas under then-Governor Clinton. Witt's challenges were daunting. He assumed the leadership of a thoroughly discredited and demoralized agency being threatened with extinction. Somehow, he had to bring the agency from the status of a "turkey-farm" to a professional, competent, high reliability agency capable of leading other government organizations and organizations outside of government in cooperative response to national emergencies and disasters. (At that point it would seem only Witt was thinking of eventually extending such cooperation to mitigation.) One would have been hard pressed to find anyone who believed he could meet those challenges. The best appraisal he might have received within the beltway was that "he couldn't do any worse than his predecessors." He quickly began to confound this pessimism, however, by quieting congressional critics, including some who had seemed implacable, moving quickly to turn around the abysmal morale of FEMA employees, and then reinterpreting the statutes so as to enable response capability to be set in motion *before* the declaration of a disaster by the president (Wamsley 1992–1993).

In addition, Witt proceeded to reorganize the agency in November of 1993 along the lines suggested by NAPA. Witt also set about institutionalizing the languishing Federal Response Plan (the interagency plan for coordinated response at the federal level) and improving relationships between FEMA and state- and local-level response organizations. It seems that it was realized early by Witt and those around him that FEMA's dismal reputation could only be changed with effective and highly publicized response to some emergencies that commanded national attention. Witt and his staff also clearly grasped that the states could no longer be left to fend for themselves until overwhelmed, with FEMA playing the role of responder of last resort.

To effectuate a more competent and integrated response, a better operational network had to be established encompassing federal, state, and local governments as well as nongovernmental entities. It has been in this realm of political relationship building that Witt has shown his greatest expertise. It is also in the establishment of this integrated emergency management system that we can see one of the clearest examples of a ''network organization'' or, better put, simply a network. That is, what has been established, more likely out of necessity than design and intuition more than conscious application of formal knowledge, is an interagency, intergovernmental, intersector response system that effectively coordinates all necessary resources needed in a response situation—regardless who ''owns'' them. Such a system would not have been possible without the leadership of Witt in establishing the necessary relationships for resource sharing, his relationship with a president aware of the importance of the emergency management function, and the great advances made in information technology in the last decade that have allowed such coordination to proceed without the need of a new centralized, coordinating agency (or a larger, more hegemonic FEMA).

Soon after these efforts began, Witt was required to lead the agency in its first responses to potential disaster (preparation for Hurricane Emily, which did not come ashore), a real if slowly developing disaster in the Mississippi Valley floods, a significant earthquake in California, floods in Texas and Georgia, and the Oklahoma City bombing. In these cases, Witt and the agency performed well and the press coverage was very positive (especially in comparison to previous press coverage). In fact, as of this writing, FEMA has been basking in its most extended and extensive public plaudits in its history. It appears that emergency management has become an acknowledged and accepted function of the federal government. Witt deserves a lot of credit for this accomplishment. Whether or not he is a great political executive, he is assuredly a very good one. Perhaps it should be sobering to think about how much difference a good political executive can make to an agency in a governmental system that operates with roughly 3000 senior political executives with little skill and experience and an average tenure of 2 years (Stokes, 1994).

Witt's many successes notwithstanding, the future of the network entity of which FEMA is the center faces many unanswered questions and a future that is as uncertain as it is promising. The number of emergencies and related costs of effective response continue to increase dramatically, while significant burden shifting from the states to the federal government (and from some states to others) continues. Additionally, public expectations of timely response by the national government are escalating at the same time that the emergency management policy subsystem and its focal agency, FEMA, are struggling to develop a network that can move forward with a comprehensive system under severe financial constraints.

As the Clinton Administration wound down, one other major question confronted Witt, FEMA the agency, and FEMA as the center of the emergency management network or policy subsystem. It is a question that has lain dormant now for several years. That is: What should be done about the inordinately high number of political appointee positions in FEMA? The NAPA panel, which included one state director of emergency management and one former deputy director of FEMA, believed strongly that as long as that many political appointee positions existed, the temptation to fill them with persons of dubious credentials would be too great for the White House Personnel Office to resist. The panel also believed that nine political appointees that required Senate confirmation would continue to foster ''stovepipes'' in FEMA.

The question dropped out of sight shortly after Witt used the positions to quickly bring in competent professionals in emergency management. Witt and those around him considered it a closed subject. When one of the authors pushed the NAPA case—that in the long run this question would arise again and the outcome might well be contrary to the public interest in another administration—one of Witt's closest associates acknowledged that, ''You might be right in the long run and with regard to other administrations, but we are concerned only with *this* administration.'' Such a statement is, of course, the final, bipartisan word on such matters from the desperately short time frame of American politics. But if there is any time when the public interest perspective on this matter can be raised and not buried as it was in 1993, it is in the waning days of an administration, when places in history and legacies loom a bit larger than partisan expediency. With the advent of a new administration, especially if there is a change in the party occupying the White House, negative potentialities will again spring to life.

If the American political system had a process for developing competent political executives with specialized, functional knowledge, one could say there is every reason to retain such a high number of political appointees. Sadly, such is not the case, and there is little prospect that such a process will develop in the foreseeable future. That is not to say that our system has not and can not produce such persons. James Lee Witt is proof to the contrary. It is to say rather that we have been luckier than we have any right to be. But the problem is even more complex because it involves not merely the political and administrative skills and functional competence of the person made FEMA director, but also the sensitivities and cognizance of the president regarding emergency management and his or her relationship with the FEMA director. Clearly that relationship has to be closer and built upon more than shared party and ideology. President Reagan and ''General'' Giuffrida or President Bush and Stickney are proof of that. The NAPA panel tried to finesse the problem by recommending the creation of an adviser to the president for crisis management in the White House Office to be the liaison with an effective FEMA director and a surrogate for an ineffective one. Witt of course would have none of that and said simply, ''That's what I am, and my office is at FEMA, not the White House'' (Wamsley, personal communication 1993).

But if seen through eyes other than those of the FEMA director, it is a bit more complex. Picture a president who comes to the office having served only as an ambassador or senator and who has almost no awareness or knowledge of emergency management. Picture a White House Personnel Office, beset, as always, with requests and pressures for appointments to office for deserving party faithful. And as always the more prominent and visible offices go to party faithful who are also prominent and visible. Offices like the directorship of FEMA, at least in the eyes of the White House Personnel Office, go to persons less well known. They are not of course, necessarily less competent, but the probability diminishes and luck becomes a more significant variable in the equation. Who will lobby or press for someone who is not only of the ''right'' party but also a skilled political executive who is knowledgeable about emergency management? The National Emergency Management Association (NEMA)? Perhaps, but there is little reason to believe that the association would have much influence. The National Governor's Association? They have more immediate and greater concerns. What we can easily see, then, is the disturbing prospect that the situation can be returned to the ''dark ages'' of emergency management virtually overnight.

In the best of all possible worlds, the directorship of FEMA would become an office seen as being largely above partisan politics, though still subject to presidential wishes and Senate confirmation, much as the FBI was in its early and middle years, or the CIA has been in most instances. But we clearly do not live in such a world. The NAPA study recommended elimination of most of the political appointees at FEMA. The Civil Service Reform Act of 1978 provides sufficient means to change a significant number of top positions if one needs to do that, as Witt did. As of this writing, information has appeared on the Internet suggesting that James Lee Witt is beginning to face up to this problem and has appointed a special advisory panel to advise him on what should be done. We can only hope this proves true.

From one perspective, the many accomplishments of James Lee Witt, of FEMA, and of the network entity of which it is the center are remarkable; yet from another perspective they are the necessary but still insufficient conditions for making this current phase in the evolution of emergency management in America the one that can be said to mark its ''coming of age.'' The necessary framework is in place for a comprehensive system not only for effective, cooperative response and recovery but also for mitigation. However, much remains to be done, many questions remain to be answered, and many issues are still to be resolved.

ENDNOTES

1. The Constitution provides an explicit federal role for suppressing civil disorders. Article I, Section 8 states that ''Congress Shall have Power to . . . provide for calling forth the Militia to execute the Laws of the Union, Suppress Insurrections, and repeal invasions.''
2. The Alaskan earthquake of 1964 set the stage by presenting the nation with the daunting task of completely rebuilding the physical infrastructure of one of our largest and most remote states. It was also a landmark in that the White House dramatically assumed direct responsibility for response and recovery in a way that previewed the evolving relationship between the presidency and disasters. The Alaska quake was followed by Hurricane Betsy in 1965, Hurricane Camille in 1969, the San Fernando Earthquake of 1971, and finally Hurricane Agnes in 1972.
3. The Civil Service Reform Act of 1978 allows up to 10% of the total Senior Executive Service to be political appointees.
4. For instance, in 1982, California, Maryland, Missouri, Alabama, and Washington all sought assistance because of flooding, but only California received aid.
5. Witt and his associates simply avoided dealing with the issue of political appointees and the recommendation that a Domestic Crisis Monitoring Unit be established in the White House. Their choice to avoid these items at that time made good sense from their perspective. Whether or not they should be reconsidered before a new administration assumes office is another matter and is addressed later in this chapter.
6. Wamsley has read all the statutes relevant to FEMA, and though he has no legal training, he sees no reason why FEMA lacks authority to operate from a proactive stance. There are so many statutes applicable to FEMA and the emergency powers that have been granted it or its predecessors over the years are so extensive, that it is hard to imagine what FEMA could not do. Some of FEMA's legal uncertainty seems to arise from the fact that managers in program areas, i.e. ''stovepipes,'' only looked at those statutes applicable to them. No one, including the legal staff, seemed to look at all the statutes from a comprehensive agencywide perspective.
7. FEMA officials clearly expected a report that was more enthusiastic, but the NAPA study team

and panel had good reason to be guarded in their assessment. There was a history of "new beginnings" that foundered to consider and there were still some outstanding disagreements between NAPA and FEMA, particularly the latter's refusal to do anything about the recommendation that political appointees be reduced.

8. The following is a list of the various responses and the level of funding appropriated for each disaster: Flooding: Minnesota, June 11, 1993: $72.5 million. Flooding: Wisconsin, July 2, 1993: $61.9 million. Flooding: Illinois, July 9, 1993: $243.5 million. Flooding: Iowa, July 9, 1993: $240 million: Flooding: Missouri, July 9, 1993: $262.5 million. Flooding: South Dakota, July 19, 1993: $34.4 million. Flooding: Nebraska, July 19, 1993: $53.7 million. Flooding: Kansas, July 22, 1993: $80.2 million. Hurrican Emily: North Carolina, Sept 10, 1993: $3.2 million. Wildland fires: California, Oct. 28, 1993: $83.2 million. Northridge earthquake: California, Jan. 17, 1994: $3.1 billion. Severe winter ice storms: Mississippi, Louisiana, Arkansas, Tennessee, Alabama, Feb. 28, 1994; $147.1 million. Severe winter storms: Pennsylvania, March 10, 1994; $75 million. Severe storms: Georgia, July 7, 1994; $210.8 million. Tropical storm Alberta: Florida, July 10, 1994: $29 million.
9. The other recipients were Deerfield Beach, Florida: Allegheny County, Maryland; Oakland, California; Seattle, Washington; Tucker and Randolph counties, West Virginia; and Wilmington, North Carolina.

REFERENCES

American City and County (1993). FEMA develops prototype disaster planning and response system. *American City and County* 108(*3*), 30.

American City and County (1993). Rethinking disaster assistance. *American City and County* 108(*10*), 12.

Bardach, Eugene (1974). *The Implementation Game*. Cambridge, MA: MIT Press.

Barrett, Susan and Colin Fudge (1981). *Policy and Action*. London: Methuen.

Barry, John M. (1997). *Rising Tide: The Great Mississippi Flood of 1927 and How It Change America*. New York: Simon & Schuster.

Borzel, Tanja (1998). Organizing Babylon: On the different conceptions of policy networks. *Public Administration* 76(*summer*), 253–273.

Burns, T. and Stalker, G. M. (1961). *The Management of Innovation*. New York: Barnes & Noble.

Chisholm, Rupert F. (1996). "On the Meaning of Networks," Groups & Organization Management, 21(2), 216–230.

Cigler, B. (1991). Cited in Thomas Drabek and Gerald Hoetmer (eds.), *Emergency Management: Principles and Practice for Local Government*. Washington, D.C.: International City Manager's Association.

Cohen, Susan G. and Don Mankin (1998). "The changing nature of work: managing the impact of information technology". In Susan Albers Mohrman, Jay R. Galbraith, Edward E. Lawler III, et al. (eds.), *Tomorrow's Organization: Crafting Winning Capabilities in a Dynamic World*. San Francisco: Jossey-Bass Publishers.

Congressional Quarterly (1992). Andrew is brutal blow for agency. *Congressional Quarterly Weekly Report* 50(*36*), 2703.

Cronin, Thomas (1980). *The State of the Presidency*, 2nd ed. Boston: Little, Brown.

De Sola Pool, I. (1983). *Technologies of Freedom*. Cambridge, MA: Harvard University Press.

Drabek, Thomas and Gerald Hoetmer, eds. (1990). *Emergency Management: Principles and Practice for Local Government*. Washington, D.C.: ICMA.

Elmore, Richard (1979). Backward mapping. *Political Science Quarterly*. 94(*winter*), 601–616.

Elmore Richard (1985). Forward and Backward Mapping: Reversible Logic in the Analysis of Public

Policy. In Kenneth Hanf and Theo A. J. Toonen (eds.), *Policy Implementation in Federal and Unitary Systems*, 33–70. Dordrecht: Martinus Nijhoff.

Fleck, J. (1984). Artificial intelligence and industrial robots. In E. Mendelshon, and H. Nowotny (eds.), *Nineteen Eighty-four: Science Between Utopia and Dystopia*. Vol. III. Dordrecht: Sociology of Sciences Yearbook. Vol. VIII.

Furstenhofer, Lt. Col. Norbert (1993). Correspondence with the author.

Galbraith, J. (1968). *The New Industrial State*. New York: New American Library.

Gilmour, Robert S. and Alexis A. Hailey (1994). *Who Makes Public Policy: The Struggle for Control Between Congress and the Executive*. Chatham, NJ: Chatham House Publishing.

Goodsell, Charles (1984). Political economy as a research focus. *Public Administration Quarterly*. 8(*3*), 288–301.

Gotlieb, C. C. and A. Borodin (1973). *Social Issues in Computing*. London: Academic Press.

Green, Richard (1987). Oracle of Weehawken: Alexander Hamilton and the Development of the Administrative State. Blacksburg, VA: Center for Public Administration and Policy, Virginia Polytechnic Institute. Unpublished Dissertation.

Hanf, Kenneth (1982). The implementation of regulatory policy: Enforcement as bargaining. *European Journal of Political Research*. 10(*June*), 159–172.

Hanf, Kenneth and Lawrence O' Toole, Jr. (1992). Revisiting old friends: Networks, implementation structures, and the management of inter-organizational relations. *European Journal of Political Research*. 121, 163–180.

Harari, Oren (1998). Transform your organization into a web of relationships. *Management Review* 81(*1*), 21–25.

Heaphey, James and Philip Kronenberg (1966). *Toward Theory Building in Comparative Public Administration*. Bloomington, IN: Comparative Administrative Group.

Hjern, Benny and Chris Hull (1982). Implementation research as empirical constitutionalism. *European Journal of Political Research* 10(*June*), 105–116.

Hjern, Benny, Chris Hull, and David Porter (1981). Implementation structures: A new unit of administrative analysis. *Organization Studies* 2(*3*), 211–227.

Holmlund, Maria and an-Ake Tornroos (1997). What are relationships in business networks? *Management Decision* 35(*March–April*), 304–310.

Hull, Chris (1985). The unit of analysis as a methodological problem. In Kenneth Hanf and Theo A.J. Toonen (eds.), *Policy Implementation in Federal and Unitary Systems*, 97–103. Dordrecht: Martinus Nijhoff.

InfoWorld (1994). FEMA Improves Disaster Relief with PC LAN/WAN. *InfoWorld* 16(*12*), 62.

Insurance Advocate (1996). FEMA director puts needs for mitigation of disaster costs as one of top priorities. *Insurance Advocate* 107(*19*), 19–20.

Insurance Advocate (1998). FEMA, Wall St. exchange join in 1st public/private disaster funding. *Insurance Advocate* 109(*13*), 4–6.

Kickert, Walter J. M., Erik, Hans Klijn, Joop, F. M. Koopenjan, eds. (1997). Managing Complex Networks: Strategies for the Public Sector. London: Sage.

Lane, Larry and Gary Wamsley (1998). Gulick and the American presidency: Vision, reality, and consequences. *International Journal of Public Administration* 21(*2*), 375–440.

Landau, Martin and Russell Stout, Jr. (1979). To manage is not to control: Or the folly of type II errors. *Public Administration Review*, March/April, 148–156.

Lasswell, Harold (1936). *Politics: Who Gets What, When, and How*? New York: McGraw Hill.

Light, Paul (1995). *Thickening Government: Federal Hierarchy and the Diffusion of Accountability*, 1–60. Washington, D.C.: Brookings Institution.

Long, Norton (1949). Power and administration. *Public Administration Review* 9(*autumn*), 257–264.

Majone, Giandomenico and Aaron Wildavsky (1984). Implementation as evolution, In Jeffery L. Pressman and Aaron Wildavsky, (eds), *Implementation*. Berkeley, CA: University of California Press.

March, James G. (1978). Bounded rationality, ambiguity, and the engineering of choice. *Bell Journal of Economics* 9, 587–608.

March, James G. (1981). Footnotes to organizational change. *Administrative Science Quarterly* 26, 563–577.

March, James G. (1987). ''Old Colleges, New Technology''. In S. B. Kiesler and L. S. Sproull (eds.), *Computing and Change on Campus.* New York: Cambridge University Press.

NAPA (1993). *Coping With Catastrophe: Building an Emergency Management System to Meet People's Needs in Natural and Manmade Disasters.* Washington, D.C.: National Academy of Public Administration.

National Governors' Association (1978). *1978 Emergency Preparedness Projects: Final Report.* Washington, D.C.: National Governor's Association.

New York Times (1982). ''Civil Defense Agency: Trying to do Something.'' *New York Times,* April 8.

Newland, C. A. (1987). Public Executives: Imperium, Sacerdotum, Collegium?: Bicentennial Leadership Challenges. *Public Administration Review* 47(*1*), 45–56.

Mosco, V. (1989). *The Pay-Per Society.* Toronto: Garamond Press.

O'Toole, Jr., Lawrence, Kenneth Hanf, and P. Hupe (1997). In Walter J.M. Kickert, Erik-Hans Klijn, and Joop F.M. Koppenjan (eds.), ''Managing Implementation Processes in Networks'' in *Managing Complex Networks: Strategies for the Public Sector,* 131–151. London: Sage.

Oleszek, Walter (1989). *Congressional Procedures and the Policy Process.* Washington, D.C.: Congressional Quarterly, Inc.

Orlikowski, W. (1988). Computer technology in organizations. In D. Knights and H. Willmott, (eds.), *New Technology and the Labour Process,* 20–49. London: Macmillan.

Perrow, Charles (1984). *Normal Accidents: Living With High Risk Technologies.* New York: Basic Books.

President of the United States (1978). New approaches to federal disaster preparedness and assistance. A Message from the President Transmitting a Report of the Same Title, May 14.

Pressman, Jeffery and Aaron Wildavsky (1973). *Implementation.* Berkeley, CA: University of California Press.

Roszak, T. (1988). *The Cult of Information.* London: Paladin.

Sabatier, Paul (1986). Top-down and bottom-up approaches to implementation research: A critical analysis and suggested synthesis. *Journal of Public Policy.* 6(*1*), 21–48.

Schneider, Saundra K. (1992). Governmental response to disasters: The conflict between bureaucratic procedures and emergent norms. *Public Administration Review* 52(*March–April*), 135–145.

Seidman, H and R. Gilmour (1986). *Politics, Position, and Power: From the Positive to the Regulatory State,* 4th ed. New York: Oxford University Press.

Simon, Herbert (1960). *The New Science of Management Decision.* New York: Harper & Row.

State Government News (1995). Taking a comprehensive approach to handling disasters. *State Government News* 38(*10*), 29–30.

Sproull, Lee and Sara Kiesler (1991). *New Ways of Working in the Networked Organization.* Cambridge, MA: MIT Press.

Thompson, James (1967). *Organizations in Action.* New York: McGraw-Hill Book Company.

Time (1992). ''Federal emergency management agency shreds list naming eight gay employees coerced from another gay employee.'' *Time,* June 1, p. 22.

U.S. Senate (1993). Report, Departments of Veterans Affairs and Housing and Urban Development and independent agencies Appropriation bill, 1993. pp. 102–355.

Wamsley, Gary L. (1992–1993). Interviews. Unpublished notes collected during original NAPA study conducted by FEMA for the U.S. Congress.

Wamsley, Gary L. (1985). Policy subsystems as a unit of analysis in implementation studies: A struggle for theoretical synthesis. In Kenneth Hanf and Theo A.J. Toonen, (eds.),

Policy Implementation in Federal and Unitary Systems, 71–96. Dordrecht: Martinus Nijhoff.

Wamsley, Gary L. and Mayer Zald (1973). The political economy of public organizations. *Public Administration Review* January/February, pp. 62–73.

Wamsley, Gary L. and Aaron Schroeder (1996). Escalating in a quagmire: The changing dynamics of the emergency management policy subsystem. *Public Administration Review* 56(*3*), 235–244.

Wamsley, Gary L., Aaron D Schroeder, and Larry M. Lane (1996). To politicize is not to control: The pathologies of control in federal emergency management. *American Review of Public Administration*. 26(*3*), 263–285.

Ward, Robert C. (1998). Interviews. Unpublished notes collected during research for this work.

Ward, Robert and David Robins (1998). The emergence of dissipative structures within information provider organizations. Paper, Annual Conference of the American Society for Information Science. Pittsburgh, October, 1998.

Washington Post (1982). ''After the disaster; FEMA rolls up its sleeves.'' *Washington Post*, March 22.

Washington Post (1983). ''Firing case on its way to trial.'' *Washington Post*, June 12.

Washington Post (1984). ''U.S. paid for FEMA chief's attendance at a fund-raiser.'' *Washington Post*, October 25, p. A1.

Washington Post (1984). ''Justice probes FEMA contracts.'' *Washington Post*, December 4.

Washington Post (1985). ''Retired military policemen troop into highly paid agency Jobs.'' *Washington Post*, February 3, p. A4.

Washington Post (1985). ''Disaster planners accused of rigging book Contract.'' *Washington Post*, March 29.

Washington Post (1985). ''Nuclear freeze leaves official in hot water.'' *Washington Post*, May 11.

Washington Post (1985). ''Top secret stamp busy at FEMA.'' *Washington Post*, June 15, p. F19.

Washington Post (1986). ''FEMA official resigns over a-plant report.'' *Washington Post*, April 15.

Weekly Compilation of Presidential Documents, 3/4/96, 32(9), 380.

Wee, Chow-Hou, Kakai-Sheany Hideajat, Wahyo Bam-Bang (1996). Suntzu on War & Management: Application to Strategic Management & Thinking. New York: Addison-Wesley.

Wiener, Norbert (1950). *The Human Use of Human Beings*. New York: Houghton Mifflin.

Willcocks, Leslie P., Wendy Currie, and Sylvie Jackson (1997). ''In pursuit of the re-engineering agenda in public administration. *Public Administration* 75(*winter*), 617–649.

25

Community Recovery and Reconstruction Following Disasters

Steven D. Stehr Department of Political Science, Washington State University, Pullman, Washington

I. INTRODUCTION

In this chapter I discuss a critical problem facing cities and towns in the aftermath of large-scale, natural disasters: once the immediate emergency response phase is over, how do the affected communities cope with the complex political, social, and economic activities that characterize the recovery and reconstruction phase of disaster management? The recent experiences of Los Angeles County (following the Northridge earthquake in 1994), the San Francisco Bay Area (the Loma Prieta earthquake in 1989), the South Carolina and South Florida coastal regions (Hurricanes Hugo and Andrew), and Grand Forks, North Dakota (massive flooding in the Spring of 1997), among others, have shown that natural disasters set into motion a bewildering array of intergovernmental and interorganizational processes. The costs associated with these processes are enormous. The recently concluded Second U.S. Assessment of Research and Applications for Natural Hazards conservatively estimates that between January 1, 1975, and December 31, 1994, natural hazards killed over 24,000 people (about 23 per week) and injured about 100,000 (about 385 per month) (Mileti 1997). The project staff also estimated that the United States sustained about $500 billion in damage during this period (about one-half billion dollars per week). Only about 17% of these losses were covered by private insurers. Responsibility for the remaining losses fell mainly on the public sector, with local governments playing the central role in acquiring the necessary resources (primarily from the federal government) and implementing recovery plans.

Local recovery and reconstruction after a disaster is primarily an organizational problem. The emergent organizational forms—both within the community and between the community and extracommunity actors such as state and federal governments—in the disaster recovery period appear to share many of the characteristics of those in the immediate-response phase, and many of the same problems associated with coordination, problem-solving capacity, political conflict, and information flows come to fore (Rubin and Barbee 1985). The important differences between the response and recovery periods related to intergovernmental and interorganizational behavior are the specific agencies and groups participating, the character of tasks undertaken, and the higher potential for goal conflict as the immediate crisis abates. Although there appears to be widespread agreement that the development of effective and durable intergovernmental and interorganizational relations is critically important to successful recovery efforts, relatively little is known about their creation, maintenance, and operational qualities. The management of these differentiated and loosely coupled networks must be viewed as a unique and legitimate problem for which most existing theories of private firms and public bureaucracies have only limited applicability.

The focus of this chapter is on how inter- and intracommunity linkages affect disaster recovery and reconstruction efforts and the strategies that community leaders adopt to manage the complex interdependencies that emerge in the aftermath of natural disasters. These strategies, I argue, are largely conditioned by the extent to which the afflicted community possesses (1) intracommunity social and political cohesion, or what I will refer to as horizontal integration, and (2) extracommunity political and social linkages to other governmental and non-governmental actors (or vertical integration) to secure various resources. Furthermore, I argue that the presence or absence of a central focal organization (or organizations) within the community is a critical feature of the recovery phase. The focal organization acts to maintain, monitor, and facilitate organizational network activities and is an important component in the implementation of recovery strategies.

The chapter proceeds as follows: First, I review some of the general problems typically associated with disaster recovery and reconstruction activities in the U.S. context. Second, I briefly discuss several variables that previous research has shown to be correlated to successful recovery efforts. The factors that influence local recovery highlight the importance of intergovernmental and intercommunity linkages. The literature related to these linkages is discussed in Section IV. Building on this discussion, Section V outlines a conceptual model of local disaster recovery, identifies a set of recovery strategies associated with this model, and presents several short case studies to illustrate the potential usefulness of the model. Finally, I suggest several lessons for local government policy makers who are concerned about preparing for the recovery and reconstruction phase of disaster management.

II. GENERAL PROBLEMS ASSOCIATED WITH DISASTER RECOVERY AND RECONSTRUCTION

The research findings on natural disasters indicate that a number of factors may influence the speed and effectiveness of community recovery. Some are specific to the disaster, such the size of the event and the scope of the damage. Others are related to antecedent conditions, including the availability of economic resources. From a practical standpoint, successful recovery from large-scale disasters is problematic for a variety of reasons. One set of problems relate to timing issues. Recovery decisions are often driven by pressures to rebuild quickly, and to ''return to normal''; this means that community safety or improvement goals such as modifying land use, retrofitting damaged buildings, creating new open space, or widening existing streets are often compromised or abandoned (Berke and Beatley 1991; May 1991; May and Bolton 1986). In addition, the long time frame of the typical recovery and reconstruction period allows political, social, and economic pressures to build as individual property owners and affected communities compete over differing perceptions of ''successful'' recovery and over scarce resources (Olson and Olson 1993; Wolensky and Wolensky 1991). In the aftermath of large-scale disasters, ''organizations have difficulty in developing and maintaining high levels of continuing coordination in tasks that are complex, uncertain, and extend over prolonged periods of time'' (Comfort 1988:181).

A second set of problems stem from what Peter May (1988) calls ''the implementation dilemma'' inherent in disaster recovery and reconstruction policy in the United States (cf. May 1986; May and Williams 1985). Simply stated, federal disaster policy administrators have a strong stake in promoting disaster mitigation and preparedness to lessen federal costs for disaster recovery, but they have little direct control over these efforts. Subnational governments and individuals owning property in hazardous areas to a large extent control decisions that determine the ultimate effectiveness of mitigation and preparedness measures adopted at the local level; in most cases these parties have few incentives to make these policies a high priority. A subset of this problem involves managing the complex intergovernmental linkages that a major disaster sets in motion. Local governments are often caught between the conflicting pressures of state and federal disaster officials on the one hand and demands from emergent citizen and business groups on the other. As Rubin and Barbee (1985) point out, ''intergovernmental relations in post-disaster settings often are characterized by limited coordination, uncertainty, problem complexity, and conflict among key actors'' (p. 58).

A third set of problems involve the capacity of local governments to respond to the demands of the recovery and reconstruction process. Regardless of the severity of a disaster or the level of assistance available from higher levels of government, primary responsibility for postdisaster recovery and reconstruction falls squarely on the shoulders of local governments (National Academy of Public Administration 1993; Wolensky and Wolensky 1991, 1990; Rubin 1991; Waugh 1990; LaPlante 1988).

Research undertaken to examine local governments' capacity to manage recovery activities has shown that their overall performance is, in the judgment of one study, ''inconsistent and problematic'' (Wolensky and Wolensky 1991:18). Among the problems identified in the literature are lack of resources and poor planning (Rubin, et al. 1985); the difficulty local officials sometimes have in shifting between pre and postdisaster roles (Wolensky and Miller 1981); increased resource dependence on the state government (Stallings and Shepart 1987); lack of adequate numbers of professionalized staff (Franvaviglia 1978); poor leadership and bureaucratic and legal constraints (Haas et al. 1977); and the emergence of powerful citizen and business groups that overshadow local government officials (Wolensky 1983). Berke and colleagues (1993) discuss other impediments to locally based reconstruction efforts, such as aid that does not meet the needs of the disadvantaged members of the community and the possibility that ''outside'' programs may exclude local involvement. On the basis of a study of the recovery processes following the earthquake in the City of Coalinga (California) in 1983, Tierney (1985) concluded ''The experience of Coalinga and other communities also indicates that government jurisdictions, especially local governments, have little guidance to direct their recovery activities following major damaging earthquakes'' (p. 47).

III. OVERCOMING RECOVERY IMPLEMENTATION PROBLEMS

Is it possible to overcome the ''problem'' of local government capacity to manage the disaster recovery process? Previous research has identified some predictors of successful local recovery. For example, Rubin and her associates studied 14 community recovery processes and found that the speed and quality of recovery appeared to be a function of three factors: (1) productive intergovernmental relationships, (2) effective competition for scarce resources, and (3) effective management of community-level decision making (Rubin 1991; Rubin and Barbee 1985). Topping (1997) advocates predisaster planning for postevent recovery, which he believes will help communities to organize processes for more timely and efficient action, clarify key recovery roles and responsibilities, identify and secure financing, and avoid repetition of other communities' mistakes. Although these prescriptions, as stated, would be difficult to implement, they do draw our attention to some important features of the recovery process. In particular, they highlight the importance of collective action involving multiple organizations—from both the public and private sectors—which cross governmental jurisdictions.

One promising finding from the recovery literature comes from an assessment of the City of Santa Cruz's (California) earthquake redevelopment process. Wilson (1991) found that the citizens and local officials improvised a successful ''adaptive strategy'' that was implemented outside of the city agency directly responsible for managing the recovery process. Berke and associates (1993) discuss the lessons of this case:

> The individuals involved in this learning process realized the limitations of the institutional arrangements in place and consequently altered their behavior. The key was not inflexible programs formulated in accordance with central administrative procedures, as evidenced by recovery studies in developing and developed countries. Success was explained by aid delivery systems with a capacity for embracing error, learning with people, and building new knowledge and institutional capacity through action. (p. 97)

If this finding is generalizable, then the challenge, as Berke et al. recognize, is to identify and develop institutional arrangements for disaster recovery processes that foster rather than constrain adaptive learning and flexible response.

IV. INTER- AND INTRACOMMUNITY NETWORKS AND THE LOCAL RECOVERY PROCESS

A number of researchers have found that the degree of integration among organizations that comprise the emergency response network prior to disasters is a reliable predictor of readiness and response effectiveness (Carley and Harrald 1997; Gillespie et al. 1993; Drabek 1992, 1986). In his review of a number of studies conducted by the Disaster Research Center, Quarantelli found that ''. . . the stronger and more well defined the inter-organizational linkages are prior to an event, the 'smoother' subsequent evacuation related activities will go'' (Quarantelli 1980:50–51). In their major study of community preparedness, Gillespie and his colleagues concluded that disaster preparedness predicts response effectiveness, and that the structure of interorganizational relations predicts disaster preparedness (1993:97–98).

In a body of research with a slightly different focus, Louise Comfort has written extensively about the role of ''self-evident natural networks'' and ''self-organization'' in emergency response (Comfort 1988, 1990, 1994a, 1994b). This view emphasizes the spontaneous emergence of order in networks of community organizations in the aftermath of natural or technological disasters. But research reported by Lindell and Meier (1994) and Kartez and Kelley (1988), among others, shows that communities vary considerably in their capacity to respond to emergencies. Although the value of emergent groups and organizations and the mobilization of community resources under the postimpact emergency conditions is well documented (but see Drabek 1986:154–157), emergent groups may complicate the recovery and redevelopment process.[1] This is a particularly important problem in the reconstruction and recovery phase, where competition over resources and community redevelopment goals often replaces the immediate postevent spirit of cooperation.

V. A CONCEPTUAL MODEL OF THE LOCAL RECOVERY PROCESS

Although the studies discussed in the previous section focus on the response phase of emergency management, some of the lessons learned in that context may be transferable to the recovery and reconstruction phases. Berke and colleagues summarize a variety of studies suggesting that ''the capacity of citizens and organizations involved in recovery to adapt to changing conditions is higher and inter-organizational aid delivery systems are more capable of meeting the needs and capacities of disaster stricken citizens when intra-community and inter-governmental ties are strong'' (1993:98). Earlier work related to social networks by Mileti and Sorensen (1987), Sorensen, et al. (1985), Granovetter (1973), Aiken and Hage (1968), and others support this view.

In particular, researchers have identified the importance of three key variables related to community problem-solving capacity: horizontal integration, vertical integration (Berke et al. 1993), and network centralization (Provan and Milward 1995). Horizontal integration refers to relations among the individuals and organizations within a community. Thus, a community with a high degree of horizontal integration is characterized by a tightly knit social network with relatively equal power distributions and features frequent, sustained interactions and communications. Conversely, communities with a low degree of horizontal integration have a weakly knit social fabric. Vertical integration describes a community's relations with extracommunity systems. A community's ties with larger political, social, and economic institutions may explain resource and information transfers and influence the extent to which these institutions are dependent on their environment.

Network centralization refers to ''the power and control structure of the network, and whether network links and activities are organized around any particular one or small group of organizations'' (Provan and Milward 1995:10). Integration and centralization are important complementary measures. *Integration* is a measure of the extent to which organizations in a system are interconnected; *centralization* describes the extent to which horizontal and vertical cohesion is organized around particular focal points.

A. Horizontal and Vertical Integration and the Role of Focal Organizations

Figure 1 shows the potential relationships between horizontal and vertical integration and depicts four types of communities. Also noted are the dominant recovery strategies that characterize each type of community. A type I community is ideally suited for an effective recovery effort. Communities of this type have well-developed ties to external resources and programs as well as viable horizontal networks that will enable it to exert influence over community recovery activities. Communities that can rely on preexisting stores of social capacity and cohesion are good candidates for the type of ''self-organizing'' behavior described by Louise Comfort.

		VERTICAL INTEGRATION	
		Strong	Weak
HORIZONTAL INTEGRATION	Strong	capacity and cohesion (self-organization) Type I	cooperation Type II
	Weak	Type III cooptation and coercion	Type IV conflict resolution

Figure 1 Community types by degree of horizontal and vertical integration and disaster recovery strategies. (From Berke et al. 1993.)

A type II community is an autonomous, relatively isolated community with few vertical ties. While these types of communities have viable horizontal social networks, they suffer from a lack of knowledge about and interaction with important external resources. Communities of this type will adopt a strategy of cooperation with potential resources providers, such as the state or federal government.

A type III community is in a classic state of dependency. Lacking a viable horizontal network, it is less likely to take into account local needs, concerns, or values in the recovery effort. A type III community does have the advantage of strong vertical ties and channels to facilitate the delivery external aid. This is an important advantage in the U.S. context, because a disproportionate share of disaster-related resources are allocated by the federal government. These types of communities will adopt a dual strategy of disaster recovery. Because horizontal cohesion is weak, local policy makers must engage in a strategy based on the cooptation of important constituencies within the community. However, owing to strong vertical linkages, these communities will be able to make claims on external resources. As the case of Los Angeles County after the Northridge earthquake demonstrates, politically powerful communities can bypass normal relief channels and, in effect, coerce the federal government into providing massive aid.

A type IV community faces significant obstacles in undertaking successful recovery efforts because it lacks access to external resources. Even if these vertical channels are activated, the lack of intracommunity integration severely limits the ability to manage the aid process or to influence the direction of recovery efforts. Community leaders in this situation will find their strategic options limited to attempting to mediate conflict.

The ability or inability of a community to activate horizontal and vertical networks to engage in reconstruction activities is likely related to the presence or absence of focal organizations in the community.[2] It should be emphasized that focal organizations need not be governmental entities. Indeed, as the experience of Santa Cruz County (California) (described below) demonstrates, cooperative community groups are perfectly capable of taking on this role.

The importance of centralized, coordinating mechanisms in disaster response networks was recognized early on by Anderson (1969) in his study of local civil defense offices and later by Drabek (1987) in his study of emergency managers. Both conclude that key actors at the focal points of emergency response networks tend to play a critical role in the formation and maintenance of interorganizational relationships. It is not yet known precisely what role centralized personnel play in the recovery and reconstruction processes.[3]

B. Case Studies

1. A Type I Community: Santa Cruz County (California)

Prior to the Loma Prieta earthquake in 1989, Santa Cruz County could be classified as a type I community (Berke et al. 1993; Rubin 1991). Horizontal integration was high owing to the high degree of interest in and experience with political activities on the part of the citizenry. Some of this activity was due to the fact that the county had experienced three presidentially declared disasters (floods, landslides, and wildfires) between 1982 and 1986. These disaster experiences induced the county government to develop new partnerships and capabilities with its citizens. Specifically, a cooperative association of households known as the Neighborhood Survival Network (NSN) was established to facilitate citizen self-help in future disasters. After the Loma Prieta earthquake, this high degree of horizontal integration played a vital role in aiding overlooked minority and low-income populations in rural mountain neighborhoods and in providing a basis for increasing vertical integration. The Federal Emergency Management Agency (FEMA) utilized the well-established ties developed by the NSN to assess needs and distribute assistance. In this case, Santa Cruz County moved from a type II community before the earthquake to a type I community after the event. In summary, earlier disaster experiences in the county stimulated local horizontal integration. Subsequently, local problem-solving capacity was expanded by vertical integration between federal relief efforts and local community organizations.

2. A Type II Community: Grand Forks, North Dakota

In the spring of 1997, the city of Grand Forks, North Dakota, suffered a devastating series of floods that inundated 80% of the city and forced almost total evacuation of its citizens. Despite the knowledge that Fargo, 70 miles upstream, had received the greatest snowfall in its recorded history (115 inches), and despite reports that soil in the Red River Valley was saturated from heavy moisture the year before, the National Weather Service predicted that the river's crest at Grand Forks would be 49 feet. The ultimate crest of 57 feet caught the citizens of the community off guard and unprepared for the intricacies of the recovery process to follow.

Grand Forks, like many medium-sized midwestern cities, has an extremely homogeneous population and a highly active network of churches, social clubs, and community groups. Owing to the high degree of horizontal integration, the community rapidly mobilized its limited resources to set up evacuation centers, provide food and safe drinking water, and establish communication channels to disseminate recovery information. But the scale of the disaster, coupled with the inexperience of local public officials with federal disaster aid programs and their lack of political clout in Washington, D.C., caused the recovery efforts to stall and exposed the weak extracommunity ties of the city. President Bill Clinton initially promised "100% assistance" for Grand Forks, and the city received assurances from FEMA that they would be helped ''every step of the way'' (Coleman 1997). But partisan bickering between the president and congressional leaders over pending legislation held up the federal relief package earmarked for Grand Forks. Despite the public pleadings of civic leaders, federal aid was delayed for several weeks. Meanwhile, city leaders discovered that the federal monies would cover only a small portion of the damages.

3. A Type III Community: Los Angeles County

At 4:31 a.m. on January 17, 1994, southern California was rocked by an earthquake measuring 6.8 on the Richter scale. Even though the Northridge earthquake—as the event would soon become widely known—was only a moderate earthquake in terms of duration and amount of ground-shaking, it would become recognized as the most expensive earthquake ever to strike the United States.[4] As of March 1997, public and private payments for residential rebuilding alone in the aftermath of the Northridge earthquake have totaled $12 to $13 billion, or 50 to 60% of the total recovery cost. Data collected by local building inspectors show that about 60,000 housing units were seriously damaged, the greatest majority of these being apartment buildings. Two years after the Northridge earthquake, only about 50% of the damage (in terms of dollars) to structures within the City of Los Angeles had been repaired. This represents repairs to only about 20% of the damaged buildings (Eguchi et al. 1996).

The County of Los Angeles encompasses over 90 separate cities and municipalities. It is estimated that over 100 different languages are spoken by children in the Los Angeles public schools. Although there are distinct neighborhoods and enclaves of ethnic groups, the county as a whole is exceptionally diverse. Owing to this diversity, overall horizontal integration in the county is low. However, because of its size (the county proper includes over 20 congressional districts) and the critical role that the state of California plays in presidential politics, Los Angeles County is politically very powerful. Thus, its vertical ties, particularly with respect to federal agencies, are quite strong. As a consequence, the county was able to bypass many of the intergovernmental aid hurdles that other jurisdictions find so difficult. Indeed, owing to congressional intervention and the high level of presidential interest, the FEMA teams mobilized with unprecedented speed, assisted by the department of Housing and Urban Development. The Los Angeles County Commissioners Legislative Analyst Office took the lead role in the postearthquake response and recovery activities. The main strategy employed was to ensure that large amounts of federal aid poured into the county and to placate affected groups in the communities by doling out this largesse. Despite the rapid federal response, weak horizontal linkages slowed reconstruction efforts as private property owners and local officials squabbled over the details of community recovery.

4. A Type IV Community: Saragosa, Texas

This small, isolated Mexican-American community in the southwest Texas desert was a type IV community before a devastating tornado hit it in 1987 (Berke et al. 1993; Pereau 1990). Indeed, Saragosa had a much lower capacity to cope with the demands of disaster recovery than the communities in the other three case studies. Before the tornado, the city had no locally incorporated government. Those official governance structures that existed were at the county level and were administered from the county seat more than 20 miles from Saragosa. A church was the only nongovernmental organization operating in the town before the disaster, but it had no administrative staff or clergy residing in the community.

The result of such a low degree of horizontal and vertical integration was that disaster recovery initiatives were, for the most part, organized outside of the community, with little input from the local people. A disaster recovery board was created to oversee recovery and reconstruction, but the committee was formed by a distant county judge with no mandate from the Saragosans. An obvious outcome of this process was that the committee encountered a great deal of internal politics and social resistance (Pereau 1990). The outcome of the recovery process was predictable. Compared to predisaster conditions, Saragosans considered themselves much worse off 2 years after the disaster (Pereau 1990). Thus, Saragosa became more firmly entrenched as a type IV community.

VI. CONCLUSION: LESSONS FOR LOCAL DECISION MAKERS

Studies of communities suffering through the aftermath of large-scale disasters consistently find that local government officials play the critical role in shaping the path of recovery and reconstruction. Strategic choices made by local decision makers both before and after an event determine the success of both the immediate and long-term recovery processes. Rubin and her colleagues, who studied the recovery processes in 15 communities, found that the effectiveness of local decision makers increased when they had the ability to act, reason to act, and knowledge of what to do (1985). These findings highlight the importance of training local government officials to cope with community needs in the disaster recovery phase.

Community leaders and local government officials can take steps before and after a catastrophic event to enhance the likelihood of achieving successful recovery and reconstruction outcomes should disaster strike. Several lessons stand out from the foregoing analysis.

1. Develop a recovery plan based on the strengths and weaknesses of your particular community.

Local officials in communities that are prone to natural disasters should develop disaster recovery plans that incorporate context specific information about the strengths and weaknesses of the community. Although emergency response plans are mandated in most jurisdictions, strategic choices in the recovery phase are often made without prior planning. The recovery plan should incorporate what Wildavsky has called "anticipation" and "resilience" (1988). Anticipation attempts to avoid hypothesized hazards before the fact (planning); resilience is concerned with dealing with events after they have occurred (learning). The recovery plan should be both realistic and flexible.

2. Utilize preexisting community organizations in the recovery process whenever possible.

As illustrated by the recovery model and the cases reviewed here, there are numerous local organizational and citizen capabilities that can be integrated into the recovery process. For instance, horizontal integration can involve organizational collaboration between community-based groups and local government (as in Santa Cruz County). Furthermore, the experience documented by the limited research on disaster recovery shows that vertical integration can be more effective at meeting local needs when activities that strengthen horizontal integration before and during recovery are present. Thus, communities need to know how to use the potentially relevant organizations and policy tools to avoid missed opportunities.

3. Designate a focal organization or create a recovery response team with representatives of the multiple organizations that will play a leadership role during the recovery process.

It is difficult to convince local governments to place a high priority on planning for low-probability events. However, studies have shown that the emergent recovery networks operate more effectively if they are managed by a central actor. The focal organization or the recovery team should not attempt to control resources or centralize decision making. Rather, their role will be to facilitate information processing for the other stakeholders in the process.

4. Develop and maintain intergovernmental relationships.

In most cases, successful recovery depends on the timely provision of resources from the state and federal governments. In large-scale disasters, a relatively large number of counties and cities are often competing for the same state and federal dollars and the attention of the same group of relief administrators. The ability to obtain the necessary resources without serious delays depends on the extent to which local officials understand the intergovernmental relationships in which the community is embedded. Nearly all communities have preexisting relationships with state and federal agencies. These relationships will be the starting point for developing intergovernmental partnerships in times of disaster.

5. Learn from other communities experiences.

Although each community is unique, there are lessons that can be learned by examining the successes and failures of other communities that have been visited by disaster. Local government officials should develop relationships with their counterparts in communities that have been through disasters to share information about the recovery process.

This chapter has highlighted the importance of the recovery phase of disaster planning and the need for local government officials to anticipate and respond to the complex set of demands that reconstruction will create. It has also focused on the importance of inter- and intracommunity linkages and the extent to which these factors present local decision makers with both opportunities and constraints. Thinking strategically about recovery requires that local officials and community leaders understand the interorganizational and intergovernmental networks that emerge after disasters. Successful community recovery depends in no small part on the utilization of both preexisting and emergent organizational relationships.

ENDNOTES

1. David Kirp's (1997) observations about the neighborhood rebuilding process following the Oakland hills fire of 1991 are revealing on this point.
2. In some cases, individual ''issue entrepreneurs'' may fill this role.
3. It should be noted that focal organizations and personnel need not be representatives of governmental bodies. It is possible that the coordinating function could be carried out by a volunteer organization or community group.

4. Estimates of the total cost of the Northridge earthquake vary from a low of about $25 billion to more than $35 billion. The low estimate includes losses to public and private property but neither inventory nor economic losses. The higher estimate includes business inventory, lost business, and traveler delay costs. Unless otherwise indicated, all of the cost and damage figures are derived from a study by Comerio et al. (1997).

REFERENCES

Aiken, M. and Hage, J. (1978). Organizational interdependence and intraorganizational structure. *American Sociological Review* 33, 912–930.

Anderson, W. A. (1969). *Local Civil Defense in Natural Disaster: From Office to Organization.* Columbus, Ohio: Disaster Research Center, The Ohio State University.

Berke, P. R., Kartez, J., and Wenger, D. (1993). Recovery after disaster: achieving sustainable development, mitigation, and equity. *Disasters* 17, 93–109.

Berke, P. R. and Beatley, T. (1992). *Planning for Earthquakes: Risk, Politics, and Policy.* Baltimore, MD: Johns Hopkins Press.

Carley, K. M. and Harrald, J. R. (1997). Organizational learning under fire: theory and practice. *American Behavioral Scientist* 40, 310–332.

Coleman, C. Y. (1997). "Grand Forks, N. D., finds its huge flood isn't a total disaster." *Wall Street Journal*, October 17, p. 1.

Comerio, M. C. (1997). Residential earthquake recovery: improving California's post-disaster rebuilding policies and programs. California Policy Seminar, Berkeley, CA, 1997.

Comfort, L. K. (1994a). Risk and resilience: inter-organizational learning following the Northridge earthquake of 17 January 1994. *Journal of Contingencies and Crisis Management* 2(*September*), 157–170.

Comfort, L. K. (1994b). Self-organization in complex systems. *Journal of Public Administration Research and Theory* 4, 393–410.

Comfort, L. K. (1990). Turning conflict into cooperation: organizational designs for community response in disasters. *International Journal of Mental Health* 19, 89–108.

Comfort, L. K. and Cahill, A. G. (1988). Increasing problem-solving capacity between organizations. In: Comfort, L. K. (ed). *Managing Disaster: Strategies and Policy Perspectives.* Durham, NC: Duke University Press.

Comfort, L. K. (1985). Action research: a Model for organizational learning. *Journal of Policy Analysis and Management.* 5, 100–118.

Drabek, T. E. (1992). *Microcomputers in Emergency Management: Implementation of Computer Technology.* Boulder, CO: Institute of Behavioral Science, University of Colorado.

Drabek, T. E. (1987). *The Professional Emergency Manager: Structures and Strategies for Success.* Boulder, CO: Institute of Behavioral Science, University of Colorado.

Drabek, T. E. (1986). *Human System Responses to Disaster: An Inventory of Sociological Findings.* New York: Springer-Verlag.

Drabek, T. E. (1985). Managing the emergency response. *Public Administration Review* 45, 85–92.

Drabek, T. E., Tamminga, H. L., Kilijanek, T. S., and Adams, C. R. (1981). *Managing Multiorganizational Emergency Responses: Emergent Search and Rescue Networks in Natural Disaster and Remote Area Settings.* Boulder, CO: Institute of Behavioral Science, University of Colorado.

Eguchi, R. T. et al. (1996). The Northridge earthquake as an economic event: direct capital losses. In *Proceedings: The Northridge Earthquake: Analyzing Economic Impacts and Recovery From Urban Earthquakes: Issues for Policy Makers.* October 10 and 11. Oakland, CA: Earthquake Engineering Research Institute.

Fischer, F. (1995). *Evaluating Public Policy*. New York: Harper-Collins.

Francaviglia, R. V. (1979). Xenia rebuilds: effects of predisaster conditioning on postdisaster redevelopment. *Journal of the American Institute of Planners* 44, 13–24.

Gillespie, D. et al. (1993). *Partnerships for Community Preparedness*. Boulder, CO: Institute of Behavioral Science, University of Colorado.

Goodman, P. S. and Pennings, J. M. (1977). *New Perspectives on Organizational Effectiveness*. San Francisco: Jossey-Bass.

Granovetter, M. S. (1973). The strength of weak ties. *American Journal of Sociology* 78, 1360–1380.

Haas, J. E. et al. (1977). *Reconstruction Following Disaster*. Cambridge, MA: MIT Press.

Kartez, J. D. and Kelley, H. (1988). Research-based disaster planning. In Comfort, L. K. (ed.). *Managing Disaster: Strategies and Policy Perspectives*. Durham, NC: Duke University Press.

Kartez, J. D. and Lindell, M. K. (1987). Planning for uncertainty. *Journal of the American Planning Association* 53, 487–498.

Kartez, J. D. (1984). Crisis Response planning: toward a contingent analysis. *Journal of the American Planning Association* 50, 9–21.

Kirp, D. L. (1997). "There goes the neighborhood." *Harper's Magazine* 294 (*March*), 45–53.

Kreps, G. (1991). Emergency management. In T. E. Drabek and G. J. Hoetmer (ed.). *Emergency Management: Principles and Practices for Local Government*. Washington, D.C.: International City Management Association.

LaPlante, J. M. (1988). Recovery issues following disaster: policy issues and dimensions. In L. K. Comfort (ed.): *Managing Disaster: Strategies and Policy Perspectives*. 217–235. Durham, NC: Duke University Press.

Lindell, M. K. and Meier, M. J. (1994). Planning effectiveness: effectiveness of community planning for toxic chemical emergencies. *Journal of the American Planning Association* 60, 222–234.

Lindell, M. K. and Perry, R. W. (1993). *Behavioral Foundations of Emergency Response Planning*. New York: Hemisphere.

May, P. J. (1991). Addressing public risks: federal earthquake policy design. *Journal of Policy Analysis and Management* 10, 263–285.

May, P. J. (1988). Disaster recovery and reconstruction. In Comfort, L. K. (ed.). *Managing Disaster: Strategies and Policy Perspectives*, 236–251. Durham, NC: Duke University Press.

May, P. J. and Williams, W. W. (1986). *Disaster Policy Implementation: Managing Programs Under Shared Governance*. New York: Plenum Press.

May, P. J. and Bolton, P. A. (1986). Reassessing earthquake hazard reduction measures. *Journal of the American Planning Association* 52, 443–451.

May, P. J. (1985). *Recovering from Catastrophes: Federal Disaster Relief Policy and Politics*. Westport, CT: Greenwood Press.

Mileti, D. S. (1997). *Second U.S. Assessment of Research and Applications for Natural Hazards*. Boulder, CO: The Natural Hazards Research and Applications Information Center. University of Colorado.

Mileti, D. S. and Sorensen, J. H. (1987). Determinants of organizational effectiveness in responding to low-probability catastrophic events. *Columbia Journal of World Business*, spring, 13–21.

National Academy of Public Administration (NAPA) (1993). *Coping with Catastrophe: Building an Emergency Management System to Meet People's Needs in Natural and Manmade Disasters: A Report by a Panel of the National Academy of Public Administration*. Washington, D.C.

Olson, R. S. and Olson, R. A. (1993). The rubble's still standing up in Oroville, California: The politics of building safety. *International Journal of Mass Emergencies and Disasters* 11, 163–186.

Pereau, J. (1990). *First World/Third World and Disasters in Context: A Study of the Saragosa and Wichita Falls, Texas, Tornados*. College Station, TX: Hazard Reduction and Recovery Center, Texas A & M University.

Provan, K. G. and Milward, H. B. (1995). A preliminary theory of interorganizational network effectiveness: A comparative study of four community mental health systems. *Administrative Science Quarterly* 40, 1–33.

Putnam, R. D. (1993). "The prosperous community: Social capital and public life." *The American Prospect*, spring, 35–42.

Przeworski, A. and Teune, H. (1970). *The Logic of Comparative Social Inquiry*, New York: Wiley-Interscience.

Quarantelli, E. L. (1980). *Evacuation Behavior and Problems: Findings from the Research Literature*. Columbus, OH: Disaster Research Center, The Ohio State University.

Rubin, C. B. (1991). Recovery from disaster. In T. E. Drabek and G. J. Hoetmer (eds.): *Emergency Management: Principles and Practices for Local Government*, 224–259. Washington, DC: International City Management Association.

Rubin, C. B. et al. (1985). *Community Recovery from a Major Natural Disaster*. Boulder, CO: Institute of Behavioral Science, University of Colorado.

Rubin, C. B. and Barbee, D. G. (1985). Disaster recovery and hazard mitigation: Bridging the intergovernmental gap. *Public Administration Review* 45, 85–92.

Schneider, S. K. (1995). *Flirting With Disaster: Public Management in Crisis Situations*. Armonk, NY: M. E. Sharpe.

Sorenson, J. H. et al. (1985). Inter and intraorganizational cohesion in emergencies. *International Journal of Mass Emergencies and Disasters* 3, 27–52.

Stallings, R. A. and Schepart, C. B. (1987). Contrasting local government responses to a tornado disaster in two communities. *Mass Emergencies and Disasters* 5, 265–284.

Waugh, W. L. Jr. (1990). Emergency management and state and local government capacity. In R. T. Sylves and W. L. Waugh Jr. (eds.). *Cities and Disaster: North American Studies in Emergency Management*. Springfield, IL: Charles C Thomas.

Wildavsky, A. (1988). *Searching For Safety*. New Brunswick, NJ: Transaction Books.

Wilson, R. (1991). *Rebuilding after the Loma Prieta Earthquake in Santa Cruz*. Washington, D.C.: International City Management Association.

Wolensky, R. P. and Wolensky, K. C. (1991). American local government and the disaster management problem. *Local Government Studies* March/April, 15–32.

Wolensky, R. P. and Wolensky, K. C. (1990). Local government's problem with disaster management: A literature review and structural analysis. *Policy Studies Review* 9, 703–725.

Wolensky, R. P. (1983). Power structure and group mobilizations following disaster: A case study. *Social Science Quarterly* 6, 96–110.

Wolensky, R. P. and Miller, E. J. (1981). The everyday versus the disaster role of local officials: citizen and official definitions. *Urban Affairs Quarterly* 16, 483–504.

Yin, R. K. (1984). *Case Study Research*. Beverly Hills, CA: Sage.

26

Potential for Disaster

Case Study of the Powell Duffryn Chemical Fire and Hazardous Material Spill

Jack Pinkowski Wayne Huizenga Graduate School of Business and Entrepreneurship, Nova Southeastern University, Fort Lauderdale, Florida

I. INTRODUCTION

At approximately 11:15 P.M. on Monday, April 10, 1995, a series of explosions occurred at the Powell Duffryn chemical storage facility in Savannah, Georgia. It caused a massive fire and chemical release onto the facility's grounds and into the adjacent marsh that garnered worldwide media coverage because of the imminent danger posed to the city, the environment, the adjacent navigable waterway, and the nearby population. It drew the serious attention of emergency response planners from all over the United States and internationally because the elements that were posed for disaster in Savannah are not unlike the existing scenario in many developed nations, as well as developing countries, that depend on the presence of dangerous industrial facilities near populated areas.

Government officials, private contractors, citizens, and nonprofit volunteers contributed to the crisis response. The breadth of official expertise in various elements of the emergency ranged from the rear admiral of the U.S. Coast Guard to the county dogcatcher. Fifty-one agencies, responsible government officials, and support groups eventually became involved in the crisis and themselves posed a challenge in way of the need for coordination and stress management. This case study examines the crisis from the personal perspectives of those who actually participated in the response based on personal interviews and a survey in the months following the incident. This case study includes the participants' evaluations of how well the incident was managed and their personal perceptions of the lessons learned from the experience.

II. PROLOGUE

To study this incident and the organization of the crisis and the emergency response to it is akin to the ancient Hindu fable of the blind men touching the elephant (Saxe, 1968). Although each of the blind men touched with his hands a different part of the elephant, there was a radical difference of opinion among them as to the nature of the beast, and although each was partly in the right, all were in the wrong. Different perspectives emerge in any multifaceted response. This is especially true in the tense atmosphere that requires critical judgment under difficult and stressful conditions that is typical of emergency crises. Sometimes opposing managerial, political, and legal opinions led analysts to different recommendations.

Each participant had their opinions about how well prepared their own unit was and also formed opinions about other governmental units as well as non-governmental respondents regarding their performance, preparation, and the appropriateness of their participation in the emergency response. This was especially significant if they were competing units. This study benefits from these multiple perspectives of their coordination in the Powell Duffryn disaster response. It is useful not only for the cadre of administrators who were involved in this incident but also useful for others in similar circumstances who may compare their own preparedness and conclude that they may also be in need of similar improvement in these focus areas.

As the reader will soon learn, the residents of Oaktree Townhomes, as the most at-risk potential victims of the disaster, have formed very strong opinions about government's responsibility for assuring them personal safety in the location of their homes. After this crisis, they demanded that someone prevent their industrial neighbors from rebuilding their plant (Ramsey, 1996). Even before the explosion, the residents had tried to have someone in authority listen to them to report their first-hand impressions, observations, and conclusions that something was just not right at the Powell Duffryn plant next door to their homes. They were not successful in their efforts to prevent disaster and near tragedy.

The other citizens of the City of Savannah and Chatham County, Georgia, now share with the townhouse apartments' residents heightened concerns regarding their own personal safety. They have become more aware of the substantial dangers inherent in living in a community where dangerous and hazardous industry, tourism, and family living are expected to coexist. As a result of the Powell Duffryn case, there has been a revelation of frequent threats to the citizens in the community represented by hazardous materials that are typically located throughout the area and very close to the residential population. Likewise, other citizens in other communities in the United States, and worldwide, may share a heightened awareness and fear of the potential for disaster in their own communities after having seen the widely distributed news accounts, photographs, and television video. Dramatic pictures make lasting memories.

Citizens in other jurisdictions may wonder how well their own local and national laws and regulations regarding hazardous materials will protect them. By studying the Powell Duffryn case, they may evaluate and compare their own community's preparation and the adequacy of its emergency response plans. In particular, this comparison should lead to concerns for the capacity of well-managed intergovernmental and interagency cooperation in any future disaster response scenario. The Powell Duffryn case points out the cooperative nature of a large-scale crisis response. This is especially apropos to coordination of government agencies at different levels of a federal system with nonprofit agencies, industrial firms, private contractors, special-interest groups, and private citizens.

III. TIMELINE OF THE POWELL DUFFRYN INCIDENT

A. Day 1

The Savannah Fire Department received a 9-1-1, emergency phone line, dispatch at 11:31 P.M. on April 10, 1995. The first of nine city firefighting units arrived on the scene at 11:33 P.M. They found six liquid chemical storage tanks on fire within a berm area at the Powell Duffryn tank farm. The berm, or earthen embankment, was intended to retain any spilled material but it contributed to the potential disaster because it provided a vessel in which the leaking chemicals could react with each other as well as the water applied to the tanks to cool them.

The Savannah Fire Department directed voluminous streams of water onto the tanks in an attempt to keep them cool while they evaluated the hazards that they were presented with. The first problem that they encountered was that details on the contents of the tanks that were on fire were not immediately available. Accordingly, the responding units could not know the consequences of the combustion byproducts from the burning material.

The city department requested specialized assistance from the Savannah International Airport Fire Department with training and experience especially relating to chemical fires and spills. The airport force, part of the State of Georgia National Guard, 165th Airlift Group, immediately dispatched a special foam unit, with hazardous material (hazmat) training, to the Powell Duffryn scene to help the city firefighters with chemical fire suppression techniques.

The U.S. Coast Guard (USCG)–Marine Safety Office (MSO) received notification at 11:34 P.M. from the Savannah Pilots of a fire at Powell Duffryn Terminals [this group captains commercial ships on the Savannah River—ed.]. The report from the river pilots indicated to the MSO that fuel tanks were on fire at Powell Duffryn and that the fire was being fought by the fire department (House, 1995).

B. Day 2

At 1:02 A.M. on April 11, 1995, the Georgia Environmental Protection Division (EPD) received their first call from the Chatham Emergency Management Agency (CEMA). Shortly afterward, at 1:08 A.M., the EPD received the initial report from the Savannah Fire Department advising that "An explosion had occurred at the Powell Duffryn Plant on President Street at Whalstrom Road, east of downtown Savannah" (House, 1995). They reported that how many tanks were involved, their capacity, and the nature of their contents were not initially known. They believed that at least one of the exploded tanks contained sulfate turpentine based on the familiarity of unnamed persons at the scene. An initial investigation into the nature of hazards relating to sulfate turpentine concluded that it was a stable, nonexplosive chemical. "They indicated that no records were immediately available as to what other hazmat may be on site" (House, 1995). The fire department advised the EPD that they "will allow the fire to burn itself out, and the Coast Guard will patrol the Savannah River for possible run-off" (House, 1995).

No injuries or fatalities were reported from the initial explosion. The city and county police departments evacuated the Oaktree apartment complex, next door to the chemical tank farm. The initial explosions affected no navigable waterways. A shelter was set up at Eli Whitney School that was just across the street from the apartments for the evacuees from the residential units. Those evacuees were clothed and fed by the Salvation Army who coordinated their efforts with the American Red Cross.

At 4:00 A.M. the manager in charge of the Powell Duffryn plant called the Environmental Protection Division (EPD) of the Department of Natural Resources to report that three of his tanks were burning and to provide technical details to the EPD. He reported that all the tanks contained crude sulfate turpentine. Tank #18 held 160,000 gallons, tank #22 contained 220,000 gallons, and tank #23 was partly filled with 220,000 gallons of the material.

However, he also advised that the burning tanks were 5 to 10 feet away from a tank containing sodium hydrogen sulfide (NaSH). He cautioned that it turns into a hazardous gas when heated. Furthermore, the chemical in tank #21 was Briquest, which has a pH of 2 and is therefore a strong acid, and tank #19 contained NaSH, which has a pH of 14, and accordingly is a strong base. He also indicated that tank #20 contained the chemical Antiblaze, which he said was a neutral solution. The pH number is a 14-point scale measure of alkalinity and acidity with a pH value of 7 representing neutrality. The lower the number, the more acidic is the solution with each unit change representing a 10-fold change in acidity or alkalinity. The significance of this information was that any mixture of a strong acid with a strong base would result in a violent chemical reaction.

On April 11, at 5:34 A.M., the MSO received a report from the Powell Duffryn representative that due to the large volume of fire fighting water, their earthen dike had partially collapsed and the chemicals could not be contained. The resulting chemical spill was a mixture composed of the leaking chemicals, the new chemicals formed by their interaction, the firefighting water, and the fire suppressant foam. It started to run off into the marsh and from there it would flow into the Savannah River.

This was a crucial determinant for the course of the emergency response. Once the navigable waterways of the United States became involved, the USCG entered into the response scenario and claimed controlling jurisdiction. The Coast Guard Marine Safety Office (MSO) established the Incident Command System (ICS) and designated their leader as the On-Scene Commander (OSC), an element of the Unified Command Structure (UCS). The USCG deployed containment booms in the marsh and in the Savannah River and fortified the earthen dike to limit the runoff to a 38-acre area of adjoining marsh. All of these measures were an attempt to keep the contaminated material out of the river (Benggio, 1995). Later that afternoon, at 3:15 P.M., the USCG deployed their Gulf Strike Team which specializes in chemical spills to participate in the now federal-level disaster response.

Based on the early-morning input from the Powell Duffryn manager regarding the chemical content and capacity of the tanks, the fire department initiated a chemical evaluation and developed a plan of attack based on the reported information. Foam application through a prepiped system that was in place on the tank farm finally commenced at 9:00 A.M. on April 11, the morning after the midnight explosions and commencement of the fire. The foam-and-water combination ''knocked the fire down,'' and the fire was reported out within a very short time. However, reignition occurred due to many ''hot spots and hidden fires'' (Horne and Phillips, 1996). At 10:30 A.M. on April 11, they made a crucial decision to let the fire burn (House, 1995). The decision of the leaders of the fire department response was based on the belief that they had only 70 gallons of foam left on hand. They reported consideration of the following facts: the smoke cloud was blowing to the north and not endangering the city or residential areas; foam resources were low; gases produced after the extinguished fire could be more dangerous than when the fire was burning; allowing the material to burn would allow more time to gather health information on the potential for the evolution of poisonous or noxious gases from the burning material; and additional time would allow for a better assessment of the appropriate extinguishing agents for whatever it is that would later be determined to be burning (Savannah Fire Department, 1995). Consequently, the fire raged for nearly two whole days.

C. Day 3

On April 12, the OSC made the decision to gather resources and extinguish the fire because the National Oceanic and Atmospheric Administration (NOAA) that provided on-site weather forecasts predicted a change in the wind direction (Benggio, 1995). The predicted new direction would blow the potential lethal fumes toward residential areas and possibly necessitate the evacuation of even greater numbers of citizens whose lives would be in danger from deadly gases.

The fact that it had become a federal-level response became significant. Although the tank farm was situated in the county, the predicted smoke and gas plume would be over the residential areas in the city subject to different jurisdictional command. The firefighters concurred in the decision to attempt to put out the fire. Based on the fact that the conflagration had lessened considerably after one tank had burned itself out, the firefighters believed they could now extinguish the inferno with the assets available to them. However, before proceeding they ordered additional foam from a military storage warehouse in Alabama that could not be delivered until 11:00 P.M. In the meantime, they tried to identify additional local resources for foam chemicals that could be made available to them. This included the Hunter Army Air Field Fire Department.

At 7:00 P.M. on April 12, the firefighters began their second attempt to extinguish the Powell Duffryn blaze. This time they had additional resources sent by Hunter Army Air Field. They provided three crash fire units (foam trucks), each with trained hazmat teams, to assist with the firefighting. Most important, they brought with them 2500 gallons of extra foam that they had on hand all along but that the Savannah Fire Department had been unaware of. At 9:00 P.M. the fire was declared out. However, foam application and water-cooling of the tanks continued through the next night and the next day.

D. Day 4

On Thursday, April 13, response leaders held meetings to evaluate environmental options for the marsh cleanup and the health risks to the emergency teams as well as the community. Many disparate interests were coordinated and participated in these decisions including: officials and representatives from the Agency for Toxic Substance and Disease Registry (ATSDR) of the Center for Disease Control, the Department of Natural Resources Environmental Protection Division (EPD), the Savannah City Manager, the Georgia Emergency Management Agency (GEMA), the Chatham County Manager, the Savannah Fire Department, the Chatham County Emergency Management Agency (CEMA), the USCG, and NOAA.

The Savannah Fire Department hazmat team members continued their deployment on the site until May 12, more than 30 days after the fire. They assisted the USCG and NOAA in air monitoring with an on-site weather station. At intervals of every half-hour throughout the period they produced computer-generated possible plume projections for the smoke clouds from the scene. They also performed decontamination of all exposed personnel from the investigation team of the Bureau of Alcohol, Tobacco and Firearms (ATF) who were called by officials to determine if the initial explosion and fire had involved a crime.

The Georgia State Fire Marshall and the Office of the Georgia Commissioner of Insurance served as officials in charge of the investigation of the fire. The federal ATF agents assisted the Chatham County Fire Inspector in making the investigation report to the state fire marshall. Together they concluded that the fire was accidental (Conway, 1995). They cited the circumstances of a new fire suppression system for the tanks that had been under construction as affording the possible opportunity for the disaster. They concluded that during the period of construction, random, uncontained vapors happened to leak from the incomplete piping system that was being installed. The vapors traveled along the ground to a source of ignition, where they ignited. The flame traveled back to the tanks containing crude sulfate turpentine and caused the explosion and fire in the storage tanks themselves (Conway, 1995).

After the fire was out, the emergency responders confirmed that the adjacent tanks were also leaking a caustic soda into the berm area. Now, leaking chemicals that had not been on fire were reacting together to produce new chemicals which the response had to deal with. Together with the other spilled chemicals, all of these formed a mixture that was flowing into the marsh that was already contaminated from the original chemicals and fire suppressant materials.

Due to a new wind shift on Thursday, April 13, the forward command center was moved upwind to a nearby baseball field as a precautionary measure. The continuing response activities had to be coordination only by radio because all of the land-based services had to be relocated with the move to the new command center location.

Based on another wind shift, on April 14, at 10:00 P.M., the ICS ordered a mandatory evacuation of 1800 additional citizens whose homes were within a one-half-mile radius of the site. The evolving atmospheric conditions led to a health assessment that the increasing menace of hydrogen sulfide gas exposure put them in jeopardy. The City of Savannah police and the Chatham County police canvassed neighborhoods door to door to communicate the new evacuation orders to all of the residents.

E. Day 5 Onward

Based on the evaluation of the abatement of any immediate health risks to the larger community, the mandatory evacuation was canceled the next day, April 15. However, the residents of the Oaktree Townhomes were still kept away from their apartments. For several additional weeks they experienced disruption to their daily lives, the hindrance of their ability to get to their jobs, even the difficulty for their children to go to school. In sum, it comprised substantial inconvenience as well as direct financial burdens for them as innocent bystanders.

The continuous health monitoring revealed on April 18 that the hydrogen sulfide gas danger had again reached a threatening level. At 1:00 P.M. on April 18, the Eli Whitney Elementary School that was across the street from the area of the tank farm and the town home apartments was evacuated. Regular public transit buses of the Chatham Area Transit (CAT) authority bused the children to the East Broad Elementary School two miles away. Public buses instead of school buses transported the children to the temporary school because of the possibility of imminent danger from toxic fumes. There was no time for parental notification or for calling up school bus drivers in the middle of the day that would allow for sending the children home. Their homes may also have been within the evacuation zone. For several weeks subsequently the school board scheduled all of the Eli Whitney students for classes at the old Savannah International Airport terminal building until all threats of hazardous gas exposure were eliminated from the area in proximity to their home school.

IV. EVALUATION

Chatham County is the most industrialized county in the state of Georgia. With three surrounding counties, Chatham, and the City of Savannah are home to nearly 350,000 people. A major port and industrial development have made possible a place where these people work, play, raise families, pursue higher education, retire, and enjoy a wonderful natural environment. But with that development comes a risk from industrial hazardous materials as well as potential disasters from their spills that pose serious threats to human life, property, and the environment.

In the words of a Savannah firefighter:

> We have two Interstates running through the county and a great deal of hazardous waste running up and down Interstate 95 and Interstate 16 . . . tons of hazardous material go up and down Bay Street every day, and that's not even mentioning the ports . . . there's a great deal that comes in on ships . . . Savannah's a railhead. There's a great deal of railroad traffic that comes in. There are literally tons and tons of hazardous material that come in and out of the city every single day (Daniels, 1995).

Although this individual is a member of the Savannah Fire Department Hazmat Team he functions in that specialized capacity only on a part-time basis. The hazmat team members, although specially trained, report to their primary jobs as regular firefighters.

The Chatham Emergency Management Agency has surveyed 61 permanent facilities in the county that they identified as hazardous material facilities. Their survey revealed that there are between 400 million and 12 billion pounds of hazardous materials at these permanent facilities at any given time during the year (CEMA, 1995). This quantity of hazardous material is in addition to the volume of material in transit daily across the county by ships, trains, and trucks that is ultimately destined elsewhere.

Many of these permanent facilities and transportation routes are adjacent to, or in close proximity to, what are described in the Chatham County Emergency Operations Plan as "vulnerable assets" (CEMA, 1995). Vulnerable assets include high-population residential areas, navigable waterways, sources of drinking water, government facilities, schools, hospitals, and nursing homes. Many communities in the United States face similar challenges. There is a lesson to be learned for developing nations as well in the juxtaposition of hazardous material storage sites placed next to where people live. Today, planners consider hazardous land use in their deliberations on the approval of building site plans in order to mitigate the dangers posed to residential areas by hazardous industrial manufacturing or storage facilities. However, Chatham County and the City of Savannah did not have any zoning ordinances before the 1960s (Brown, 1996).

The Powell Duffryn terminals fire and the subsequent hazardous-materials spill and the emergency management response to it resulted in a new awareness of the dangers of hazardous materials within the community and among many of those in responsible government positions. The inevitability of the real need for cooperation among the responding units to a disaster also came to be appreciated more. Different government units and agencies are essential to manage response objectives. In order to protect the public interest they must be prepared to cooperate and even cede management to another unit in the response matrix whether on the same government level or on another level of government organization. Intergovernmental cooperation is necessary to effectively respond to disasters as well as to achieve prevention through appropriate laws, regulations, and facilities management.

A. Coordination of the Intergovernmental Emergency Response

The coordination of the many different bureaucracies was successfully accomplished, in the Powell Duffryn response, through the utilization of the Incident Command System

(ICS) by the USCG. Upon the arrival on the scene of the USCG, a command center was established to embrace representatives of the various local emergency services. These included local government officials, state emergency services agencies, federal government agencies, and the representatives of the responsible private party—Powell Duffryn, Inc. Decisions made at the command center were implemented, not by level of government hierarchy, but instead by the unit that could best accomplish the function of the assignment. Figure 1 shows the division of the ICS into four functional areas. Advisory technical support also fed into the command center.

This ICS worked very well in the Powell Duffryn disaster response as assessed by those who were intimately involved with it (Pinkowski, 1996). The weaknesses that were expressed about the ICS addressed the need for more practical exercises within individual agencies. This was especially true for those who were new to the system. Interagency practice exercises were cited as very useful in making disparate entities more comfortable with the ICS. Collectively, the group in the Powell Duffryn response had previously worked together in joint emergency practice exercises. The Chatham Emergency Manage-

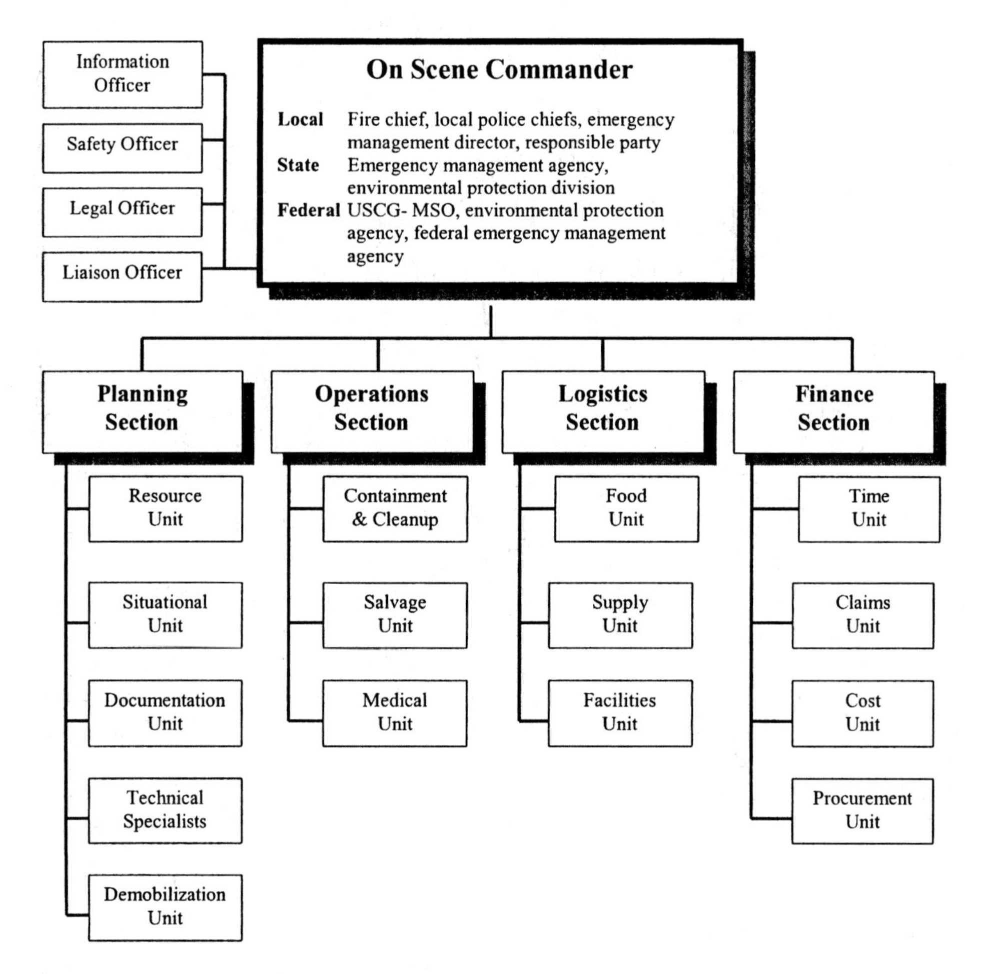

Figure 1 Incident command system unified command structure. (From ICMA, 1991; Monesmith, 1983; NWCG, 1981, 1983, 1985, 1991.)

ment Agency's coordination of a biannual exercise at the Savannah International Airport that simulates an aircraft landing disaster was mentioned in particular as a substantial contributor to their cooperative experience and familiarity with the ICS system. Federal government organizations and environmental agencies also regularly practice oil spills and recoveries through hazmat exercises. However, a shortcoming of this aspect of preparation was uncovered in the Powell Duffryn response. The police departments had not previously participated in the cooperative practice scenarios and therefore did not have practical experience with the ICS. Accordingly, they were the most unfamiliar with its chain of command (Tracy, 1996).

B. Management of the Fire Scene and Interagency Relations

When the fire department arrived on the scene, they did not know what was burning because there was no up-to-date record of what was stored in the various tanks at the Powell Duffryn compound (Horne and Phillips, 1996). The Superfund Amendments and Reauthorizations Act (SARA), Title III: Emergency Planning and Community Right-to-Know Act (1986) mandates the procedures and requirements for reporting hazardous materials that were followed. However, the act only requires a report annually on the kind and amounts of hazardous materials by private industrial firms and directs its submission to the state's Environmental Protection Division (EPD), not to local authorities. Another shortcoming of the existing procedures is that the annual report covers the hazardous materials that each industrial concern handled during the previous calendar year. Accordingly, details reported to the EPD that may be submitted in March, following the end of the year, may actually be 15 months old. The report may not even indicate the materials that are currently on a site. Therefore, the information provides very little utility for a fire response unit on the scene challenged with putting out a fire but not sure of what is burning. At Powell Duffryn the detailed, practical information from the terminal manager was not available to the firefighters until the fire had already been raging for five hours (House, 1995).

Once they found out definitively what was burning, the firefighters needed additional time to assess the best firefighting approach. This needs assessment included locating sufficient quantities of foam to do the job. Equipment to apply the foam was marshaled from various sources including other agencies and private industries. Until they had their assessment and staging details complete, the fire department chiefs decided they must just let the fire burn (Horne and Phillips, 1996). The Powell Duffryn fire burned for 9½ hours before the first attempt to extinguish it. In the meantime, fire department pump trucks applied huge volumes of water onto the adjoining tanks to lessen the possibility of their catching fire or exploding from the heat. This delay became the crux of a new problem and could have been substantially eliminated if detailed records were available on the scene. Those with the actual responsibility for addressing the emergency needed them.

The water used in this cooling, over the protracted period of time that the fire was allowed to burn, created an unforeseen outcome. Because the enormous volume of water accumulated beyond the capacity of the containment system around the tanks, the containment dike that was intended to localize any spill around the burning tanks was breached. Consequently, the water flowed into the adjoining marshlands and into the navigable waters of the Savannah River. That water eventually mixed with the firefighting foam and the spilled hazardous chemicals. Together they increased substantially the volume of hazardous material that had to be decontaminated.

Because of the extended period of time before attempts to extinguish the fire, the heat of the inferno, and the physical layout of the tanks, the pipes connecting the tanks as well as the tanks themselves began to leak hazardous material into the water-filled berm area. The USCG deployed floating booms in an effort to contain the environmental impact and mitigate against the pollution of the Savannah River. The result was a contaminated marsh covering 38 acres. NOAA estimated the total volume of the pollutants in the marsh to be 12 million gallons of hazardous product (Benggio, 1996). Including the material spilled on dry land, the total volume of pollutants that had to be processed and decontaminated after, and as a result of, the Powell Duffryn disaster came to 14 million gallons. To put the volume of contaminated hazardous material into perspective, consider that the crude oil spilled by the Exxon Valdez in March 1989 was only 10 million gallons. That spill had been the worst domestic hazardous material spill in U.S. history (Compton, 1996).

Another key element in the ''let it burn'' decision that allowed the delay in initial attempts to control the fire was the difficulty in the acquisition of an amount of firefighting foam adequate to put out the fire. The fire chiefs believed it to be fruitless to start applying the foam that they had available until adequate amounts were on hand to extinguish the blaze (Horne, 1996). They ordered alcohol based foam from the U.S. Army depot in Decatur, Alabama, but had to wait until 11:00 P.M. on Wednesday, April 12, for it to arrive on the scene (NOAA, 1995). In the interim, the Hunter Army Airfield Fire Department offered to assist in the response with its own foam trucks and trained hazmat firefighters, including their own supply of 2500 gallons of foam.

The army firefighters addressed the fire on Wednesday evening, April 12. According to those in charge of the Hunter Army Airfield Fire Department, ''the fire was out in 13 minutes'' (VanderArk, 1996). Actually, the army airfield fire chief said that he started calling the Savannah fire chief two days earlier to advise that his unit had materials and could help. The message did not get through as intended. He reported that he was told that it would be passed on to the command center and, if they needed his support, someone would get back to him.

Despite several phone calls offering support, he could not get through to the ones who actually could have used his information. From his location 10 miles away, he could see the black clouds filling the sky and he remained frustrated as he followed the continuous local and national news reports about the ongoing fire. Although he had the assets that the command center felt were missing, he could not get through to the command center in a timely manner because he did not have the proper access authority in the ICS.

V. LESSONS FROM THE POWELL DUFFRYN INCIDENT

The Powell Duffryn fire itself was spectacular and personally affected nearly 2000 people who were evacuated from their homes. The disaster represented a threat to the health and safety of the adjoining community for a protracted period of five weeks. Nevertheless, there was no loss of life directly from the fire or the initial explosions. Most of the participants involved in fighting the fire and in the emergency response rated their mutual effectiveness immediately afterward as ''good'' (Hobby, 1995).

Although the outcome of the Powell Duffryn incident did not result in human tragedy, it had the potential for a very different outcome. The storage tanks that were on fire were the smallest in the compound and held 220,000 gallons of flammable chemicals. Yet, close to those tanks were massive tanks with capacities of 1 million gallons each and four tanks that could hold 3 million gallons each (NOAA, 1995). The inventory of hazardous material storage sites in the county fuels speculation of what could have happened because hazardous sites in other locations also adjoin residential areas. Powell Duffryn is not even one of the larger operations with hazardous materials (Langley, 1996). Nor does Powell Duffryn even typically handle very hazardous materials. The chemicals that they normally store are generally considered to be not especially volatile. The National Fire Protection Association even rates crude sulfate turpentine, the material that caught fire, as a ''stable chemical'' (Benedetti, 1995). Yet, the combination of circumstances together represented the potential for a great human disaster.

A. Need For Up-to-Date and Immediately Available Details on Hazardous-Material Sites

When the fire department arrived on the scene, knowledge about the particular hazardous materials that were involved or the cause of the incident, i.e., what was on fire, were not available and would not be for over five hours. If the fire department had known soon after their arrival what they were dealing with, most of the problems encountered and the serious threats to the community that developed subsequently would never have matured.

Up-to-date information regarding storage of hazardous-material products, their amounts, and their specific locations within storage facilities can improve the management of an emergency response. In this case, existing legal reporting requirements proved to be inadequate for both firefighting safety and resource planning. The records that were filed in the state EPD offices were neither useful nor immediately available to the fire department commanders on the scene. In addition, because the reported information could be out-of-date, it may be obsolete. Current, contemporaneous databases that can be made immediately available to local emergency units would vastly improve emergency response and crisis risk assessment.

The presence of hazardous materials in close proximity to noncompatible hazardous chemicals also represents potential dangers if they should ever interact. The berm area intended for spilled material retention should be planned to prevent mixing of spilled product from adjacent storage vessels. Individual berms or retention walls for each tank would substantially reduce the potential for the creation of new products when spilled chemicals mix and interact.

In the case of Powell Duffryn, sodium hydrosulfide (NaSH), stored in one tank that was leaking, reacted with the chemical Briquest that was stored in a totally different, but adjacent, tank. The Briquest started to drip from a pipe attached to its tank that had been damaged by the initial explosion. The two chemicals reacted in the water that filled the berm enclosure that held all the liquid material coming from the several tanks as well as the external water applied to the tanks to cool them. Together the mixture generated toxic, and potentially lethal, hydrogen sulfide gas (NOAA, 1995). A member of the USCG Atlantic Strike Force described her surprise to discover the violent nature of the chemical activity in the berm enclosed pool: ''The reaction within the toxic pool was a surprise . . . unexpected . . . the reaction was so strong it felt like a whirlpool . . . that bubbly feeling . . . against your legs, through the containment suits'' (Woodson, 1995).

The delay that was believed to be prudent on the part of the fire department in the management of their response appears to have actually allowed for the creation of the situation wherein the stable chemicals came to be mixed resulting in violent, toxic effervescence. The delay was also partly the cause of the subsequent pollution of the marsh and waterways. For 9½ hours, massive amounts of firefighting water poured onto the tanks. It resulted in an enormous volume of liquid that had to be decontaminated because it was mixed with the leaking chemicals. When the firefighting suppressant foam was subsequently applied to the burning material, it also added to the volume of spilled chemicals and contaminants that polluted the environmentally sensitive marsh.

The time to extinguish the fire in the tanks, once efforts were commenced for the first time, took less than two hours. If this had been the case before the 9½-hour free-burn period, presumably the heat buildup and the damage to adjoining tanks would have been negligible. However, the delay created an opportunity for hazardous-material leaks that resulted in the generation of toxic gases. The potentially lethal gas proved to be the greatest threat to the public. If the hazards were known at the outset, the potential for disaster and environmental contamination most likely would have been eliminated.

B. Improved Communication and Preparation

The advanced preparation by the emergency management personnel both proved its utility and pointed out its weaknesses. In particular, mutual-aid agreements that are in place beforehand can help responders immediately call for the tools that they need from others who are prepared to help them by sharing assets in an emergency. Voluntary mutual-aid agreements between local hazmat industries can also make possible the sharing of safety technology as well as other resources and equipment in the event of a potentially disastrous situation. Private firms can help each other and develop beneficial relationships with responders at the same time. All of these benefits will facilitate emergency response and disaster prevention.

Because they are voluntary and organized by private firms, mutual-aid agreements are one way to protect the community at minimal public cost. In the wake of the Powell Duffryn incident, the Savannah Mutual Aid Resource Team (SMART) was formed with the encouragement of government leaders. The Chatham County Emergency Operations Plan refers to this network as being united by a voluntary agreement to assist each other. They commit to providing materials, equipment, and technical information needed to support the efforts of local responders in an attempt to ensure that effective disaster resources are available where needed in the event of an emergency (CEMA, 1995).

Channels of communication must always be available and open to such partners. After the Powell Duffryn fire was put out the first time, water was removed from the extinguished tanks and redirected to spot fires and adjoining tanks. This allowed the original tank that had been on fire to reignite from spontaneous combustion. The Savannah Fire Department leaders said: ''At the time we had 14 cans of foam left, about 70 gallons, we had to let it burn'' (Horne, 1996). Yet, due to the failure of communications, the fire response leaders did not know that only 10 miles away the Hunter Army Airfield fire department had three trucks with 2500 gallons of foam standing by willing to help. If they had this information, they could most likely have put the fire out again promptly with no further problems. Instead they ordered 8000 gallons of foam to be delivered by truck from nearly 500 miles away and the inferno was permitted to rage on for nearly 45 hours before it was finally declared out (NOAA, 1995).

Another shortcoming and need for improvements in communication and preparation that was discovered by the Powell Duffryn incident related to the coordination of the various police departments. Previously the police units had not participated in the county-sponsored emergency response drills. They were therefore the most unfamiliar with the

ICS that was implemented by the USCG to manage the scene. In addition, the county police, the city police, and the firefighting units were all on different radio frequencies and could not directly communicate with one another. Their radio equipment didn't even have the capacity to shift to the other emergency response units' frequencies. If every unit of a potential emergency response is included in practice drills, all will gain familiarity with the procedures that they will encounter and learn, in advance, if there are any basic incompatibilities that could inhibit their cooperative emergency response efforts.

C. Legal Perspectives on the Emergency Response

Realistically, relying on private industry to police itself and to provide for the good of the community is not, a priori, what anyone would expect from profit-driven, private corporations. Private-industry, mutual-aid associations are created to protect the assets of the industries, not the assets of the communities. After all, a hazardous-material disaster can be very expensive for the owner of the site of a disaster. The responsible party in the Powell Duffryn case, as in all hazardous-material spills, pays the bills for response, cleanup, and remediation. These financial responsibilities include reimbursing the governments for extraordinary expenses (Sechler, 1996), the costs of emergency services (Hall, 1996), and the expenses relating to other private contractors necessitated by the emergency response.

The costs of decontamination, cleanup, air monitoring, demolition, and rebuilding are substantial. But when you add the total of emergency reimbursement and the responsibility for decontamination of pollutants and soil remediation, the sum grows to a magnitude that any size business would want to avoid. At Powell Duffryn the federal government expenses alone amounted to nearly $1 million in only five weeks (NOAA, 1995).

In addition to responsibility for the immediate expenses related to the emergency response, there can be fines levied from several different levels of government. Industries also have to contend with liability lawsuits. In the Powell Duffryn case, 10 residents of Oaktree Townhomes sued for $5000 each, and many other residents settled with the company privately (Savannah News-Press, 1996). Powell Duffryn and its insurance company paid out more than $60 million (Saizer, 1996). Therefore, industrial concerns should be especially interested in joining together to share their resources and prevention expertise in emergencies because it is in the individual financial interests of each.

However, public safety certainly has to be one of the preeminent functions, objectives, and achievements of any government policy. Present-day awareness of possible impacts on our environment adds to public concerns regarding these resources: "Protecting the environment is so important that requirements and standards cannot be too high and continuing environmental improvements must be made regardless of cost" (Klaidman, 1991).

The obligation to protect the community and the environment requires strengthening the legal means that are already established as well as possibly drafting new laws and regulations. One of the changes needed after the Powell Duffryn incident involves the legal requirements for reporting hazardous materials because the outcomes of a disaster could affect both people and the environment. The existing reporting requirement, three months after the end of the calendar year, proved to be inadequate. Consideration should be given, at the very least, to making the information more up to date by changing to daily, monthly, or weekly reporting requirements. The timing of reports based on any significant changes in the products that are stored at hazardous-materials sites should also be considered in order to provide the most meaningful information when it is needed in an emergency. However, access to the information by those on the scene was shown to be the area of hazardous-material reporting that is most in need of improvement.

Although every alternative to more frequent and thorough reporting has associated with it additional costs to be absorbed by the firms that are required to report the information as well as the agencies charged with keeping it current, new computer and Internet technologies may facilitate compliance and be cost-effective. A low-tech solution that was originally introduced in New Jersey is the requirement for a lock box at the premise's entrance. Plant personnel are required to keep it updated indicating plant layouts and details of hazardous materials within its storage facilities and the fire department keeps a set of keys (Langley, 1996).

After Powell Duffryn, other topics that need legal review and reconsideration include zoning requirements, hazardous storage facility construction standards, and local-jurisdiction permits for the contents stored at hazardous-material facilities. Hazardous situations may exist today because zoning preplanning in the past did not prevent them. Retroactive zoning can turn back the clock at once but would entail great cost and face substantial political, popular, and corporate resistance. Changing zoning and construction standards for the future would play a part in eliminating potentially disastrous situations but will do little for situations that exist by virtue of the proximity of hazardous material industries to residential areas. Also at risk in the hazard scenario although sometimes overlooked are schools, nursing homes, government facilities, and drinking-water supplies. Many of these situations occur across government boundaries and may require intergovernmental cooperation and planning.

D. Political Perspective on the Powell Duffryn Incident

Complicating the response and primary responsibility in the Powell Duffryn case were several political issues. The chemical tank farm is on a tract of land that, although surrounded by city jurisdiction, is outside of the city. This makes the plant the primary responsibility of the county police while all roads and streets leading to and adjoining the plant are the responsibility of the city police force. This anomaly exists because in the past, in order to encourage industrial development that benefits the local economy and provides local jobs, the industrial tracts were favored by drawing them out of the city thereby eliminating the burden of city taxes.

However, regarding the potential industrial hazards that the industries represent, the county does not have a hazardous material firefighting unit. Accordingly, the city fire department is responsible for the Powell Duffryn plant that is actually in the county and outside of the city's jurisdiction. Even more convoluted regarding primary authority for disaster response, when the navigable waters of the United States became subject to pollution, the federal agencies claimed superior jurisdiction and the city, county, and state authorities acceded to the USCG command.

Another aspect to examine regarding the political perspective is the distribution of those citizens who are typically in jeopardy from potentially dangerous situations. The property manager described Oaktree Townhomes' residents as ''citizens with no place else to go'' (Ramsey, 1996). Many had no cars to get them to work and relied on public transportation. However, when the evacuated residents were relocated to a hotel, no public bus service was available and they could not even get to work. During the evacuation the 35 to 40 children who resided at the apartment complex also, for the same reasons, had a hard time getting to their temporary school from their temporary homes at the hotels. Many of the adults who lived at the Oaktree Townhomes were retired, but all of them were in low-income households. Realistically, they have few if any alternatives to living next to potential dangers because the rent is low. Comparable rent options in Savannah are very hard to find (Guyette, 1996).

When permitting the location of hazardous industries near residential areas, the special consideration for the possibility of disproportionate effects on the lower socio-economic levels of the population need to be included. By not prohibiting hazardous locations near residential areas, the economics of the market results in the appeal of the location to individuals who are resigned to accept the risk because they cannot afford a more costly alternative. During the response to an emergency, the special needs of this group of citizens may also be overlooked and not fully appreciated. Issues such as the evacuation to temporarily safe quarters may mean for them the inability to get to work or school because of the inaccessibility of affordable transportation.

VI. CONCLUSION

The Powell Duffryn Terminal, Inc., fire, hazardous material spill, and emergency response was a spectacular scene. Heavy black smoke filled the sky for days, there were 14 million gallons of hazardous pollutants that resulted, and hundreds of emergency management experts responded from all over the United States. It attracted the attention of worldwide media coverage. Over 50 government and private agencies were involved in the response efforts. Yet, fortunately, there was not one fatality attributable to the disaster. The intergovernmental response successfully handled various details very well with only limited environmental impact.

Even where the emergency management response avoids disastrous outcomes, analyzing the effectiveness of the response from political, managerial, and legal perspectives is worthwhile. In this case it has revealed areas from all three perspectives that require further thoughtful analysis.

If the lesson to be learned from this incident were to be reduced to one that is most important, perhaps it is that proper prior planning worked. Where the response was deemed to be inadequate, it can be attributed to the lack of adequate consideration and inclusion in prior practice and preparedness.

The Powell Duffryn case also points out the fundamental weakness of a part-time hazardous-material response unit in any community with a substantial, ongoing hazmat risk. A dedicated, full-time hazmat team within the Savannah Fire Department, or as a standalone unit for the county, would be one way to emphasize the importance of response readiness for these potential disasters. More important, it would contribute to the advanced preparation because they would have the equipment and supplies readily available, or in reserve, sufficient to meet potential emergency demands. If the specialized firefighters' only jobs were preparing for and responding to hazmat spills and emergencies, they could maintain inventories and practice diagnostics for various worst-case scenarios applicable to every site storing dangerous substances in the community. They could regularly survey storage sites and become familiar with operating procedures, personnel, and chemicals before they would have to deal with them under impending disaster conditions. The single most important shortcoming of the Powell Duffryn response was the lack of available information during the first half-day of response activity about the materials involved.

The observations, recommendations, and advice shared by a dedicated hazmat team with the industrial personnel can also augment the industries' own mutual aid agreements. They would come to know what questions to ask at a particular site and be the ones most familiar with alternatives regarding action decisions. This would be very beneficial in reducing the future potential for disaster.

REFERENCES

Benedetti, R.R. (1995). Senior flammable liquids engineer, Quincy, MA. Personal correspondence with State Fire Marshall's Office, Atlanta, June 29.

Benggio, B. (1995). *Powell Duffryn Storage Facility Incident Management Report, I.* Washington: National Oceanic and Atmospheric Administration (NOAA), Hazardous Materials Response and Assessment Division.

Brown, M. (1996). City Manager, City of Savannah, personal interview, Feb. 23.

CEMA. (1995). *Annex 17A—Hazardous Materials Emergency Response Plan.* Savannah, GA: Chatham Emergency Management Agency Compton's Learning Co.: Chicago.

Compton, F.E. (1996). *Compton's Living Encyclopedia.* America On Line.

Conway, R. (1995). *Investigation Report HMD-95-684-002.* Atlanta: Safety Fire Division, Commissioner of Insurance, State Fire Marshall, April 28.

Daniels, A.J. (1995). *The Powell Duffryn Incident.* Interview with Advanced Fire Fighter Mike McIlver, Savannah Fire Department HAZMAT Team, Savannah College of Art and Design Video Department.

EPD. (1995). *E.P.D./G.E.M.A. Report 041795-07.* Atlanta: Georgia Department of Natural Resources, Environmental Protection Division, April 11.

Guyette, D. (1996). Oaktree Townhomes resident, personal interview, Feb. 21.

Hall, D. (1996). Manager, MedStar E.M.S., personal interview, Feb. 15.

Hobby, J. (1995). Fire Chief, Savannah Fire Department, interview with Dawn Baker, WTOC television, April 13.

Horne, M.A. (1996). Assistant Fire Chief, Savannah Fire Department, personal interview, Feb. 16.

Horne, M.A., and Phillips, J.M. (1996). Assistant Fire Chief with Fire Battalion Chief, Savannah Fire Department Hazardous Material Coordinators, personal interview, Feb. 16.

House, A. Jr. (1995). *E.P.D. Report 041795-01.* Atlanta: Environmental Protection Division, Emergency Response Unit, Emergency Operations Center, message recorded April 11.

ICMA. (1991). Managing disaster response operations. In: *Emergency Management: Principles and Practice for Local Government.* Washington: International City Management Association.

Klaidman, S. (1991). "Muddling through." *Wilson Quarterly*, spring, p 73.

Langley, B. (1996). Director, Georgia Environmental Protection Division, personal interview, Feb. 9.

Monesmith, J., et al. (1983). "Unified command: A management concept." *Fire Management Notes*, 45(1).

NOAA. (1995). *Powell Duffryn Storage Facility Incident Management Report, I.* USCG POLREPS for Powell Duffryn Chemical Fire and Release, April 12. Washington: NOAA, Hazardous Materials Response and Assessment Division.

NWCG. (1981). *NIIMS ICS Operational System Description.* Boise, ID: National Wildfire Coordinating Group.

NWCG. (1983). *National Interagency Incident Management System—General Instructions, ICS Supervisory Personnel.* Boise, ID: National Wildfire Coordinating Group.

NWCG. (1985). *Unified Command, an Overview.* Boise, ID: National Wildfire Coordinating Group.

NWCG. (1991). *The National Interagency Incident Management System—Teamwork in Emergency Management.* Boise, ID: National Wildfire Coordinating Group.

Pinkowski, J. (1996). The Powell Duffryn spill: after action survey and report. In: 13th International Meeting on Prevention, Preparedness, and Response to Hazardous Material Spills, International Hazardous Material Spills Conference. New Orleans, June 26–29.

Ramsey, T. (1996). Property Manager, Oaktree Townhomes, personal interview, Feb. 21.

Saizer, J. (1996). ''Powell Duffryn pays state.'' *Savannah News-Press*, Jan. 23, p. 11A.

Savannah Fire Dept. (1995). *Report of Savannah Fire Department on Powell Duffryn Terminals, Inc., Fire*. Savannah: Savannah Fire Department, April 10.

Savannah News-Press. (1996). Editorial, Jan. 26, p. 14A.

Saxe, J.G. (1968). The blind men and the elephant. In F.C. Sillar and R.M. Meyler (eds.), *Elephants Ancient and Modern*. New York: Viking Press.

Sechler, B. (1996). ''Powell Duffryn: County should share in cleanup tab.'' *Savannah News-Press*, Feb. 13, p. 1-A.

Tracy, T.A. (1996). Captain, Chatham County Police Department, personal interview, Feb. 22.

VanderArk, K. (1996). Fire Chief, Hunter Army Airfield Fire Department, personal interview, Feb. 23.

Woodson, C. (1995). USCG, Atlantic Strike Force, broadcast interview by Leslie Trauba, WTOC Television, May 10.

27

American Presidential Crisis Management Under Kennedy

The Cuban Missile Crisis

Robert E. Dewhirst Department of Political Science, Northwest Missouri State University, Maryville, Missouri

I. INTRODUCTION

The Cuban Missile Crisis is one of the most extensively chronicled crises in American political history. Actions taken and decisions made during a 13-day period of October 16–28, 1962 have been discussed, studied, and analyzed by a generation of journalists, scholars, and even the participants themselves. Subsequent publication of the memoirs of many key antagonists, first the Americans in the 1960s and 1970s, followed by the Soviets in the two subsequent decades, filled in some information gaps found in early analyses. Moreover, key government documents were declassified in both the United States and Russia in the 1980s and 1990s. In addition to this abundance of information and speculation, widespread interest in the Cuban Missile Crisis also likely has been sparked by the spectacular drama of events occurring in each step of the affair. In many places, a simple account of the crisis's events reads like a best-selling thriller.

To be sure, the crisis, perhaps the seminal point in the history of the Cold War, marked one of the most dangerous brief periods in world history, with the confrontation of two nuclear superpowers, each with enough military firepower to destroy millions of lives.

II. THE HISTORIC AND POLITICAL SETTING

The Cuban Missile Crisis occurred at the peak of Cold War tensions. Throughout the nearly two decades following the end of the Second World War, the United States and the Soviet Union had faced off in one tense confrontation after another before Kennedy became president: the Berlin airlift, the establishment of Soviet puppet states in Eastern Europe, Mao's victory in mainland China, the shooting down of a U-2 spy plane over the Soviet Union, the Korean War, violent crushing of rebellions in Czechoslovakia and Hungary, or growing conflicts in Laos and South Vietnam.

As president, Kennedy had already endured such intense Cold War confrontations as his first (failed) summit conference with Nikita Khrushchev, the construction of the Berlin Wall, the unsuccessful Bay of Pigs invasion of Cuba, and budding Cold War conflicts in third-world countries and Africa and Southeast Asia. Kennedy seemed to move from one Cold War crisis to another. Moreover, the young president was especially burdened by fears of repeating the two public pratfalls of the unsuccessful summit conference and the Bay of Pigs debacle. On top of all this the president was enduring intense domestic crises as well—especially concerning the civil rights movement in states of the Deep South.

Yet the Kennedy Administration continued to focus on Castro and Cuba. Soon after the failed Bay of Pigs invasion, President Kennedy approved implementation of a Central Intelligence Agency (CIA) covert plan to overthrow Castro. Code named ''Operation Mongoose,'' the program had an annual operating budget of about $50 million and involved more than 2000 Americans and Cubans working from a base in the Miami area to initiate economic and political sabotage in Cuba (Giglio 1991:190–92)

In late summer 1962, the president ordered high-altitude flights over Cuba by U-2 spy planes. Initial surveillance flights produced photographs revealing Soviet surface-to-air missiles (SAMs) for antiaircraft defense of the island. However, on the evening of October 15, a pair of spy flights produced photographs indicating the construction of launch sites in western Cuba for Soviet intermediate- and medium-range intercontinental missiles. The weapons represented a ''first strike'' capability for the Soviets, placing the missiles within a few minutes' flight time to any spot on the heavily populated East Coast of the United States. Although the discovery marked a significant escalation in cold war tensions, the development also presented a possible avenue for resolution: construction of the launch sites and installation of the missiles had not yet been completed. After being notified immediately by his National Security Advisor McGeorge Bundy, President Kennedy began planning how to get the Soviets to remove their missiles before they completed their installation in Cuba.

III. KENNEDY'S CRISIS DECISION-MAKING APPARATUS

Eager to avoid repeating previous decision-making mistakes, especially those prevalent in the Bay of Pigs disaster, the president assembled a top-level task force to collect and study information and make recommendations of favored courses of action. The group, which later became known as the Executive Committee of the National Security Council (commonly abbreviated as the ExComm), met secretly throughout the 13-day crisis. Sessions were held at any of three sites: the cabinet room or the Oval Office itself in the White House or across Washington in a State Department conference room near the office of George Ball, undersecretary of state. Overall, the group advised the president both orally, through interaction during ExComm sessions, and in writing, through proposals explaining and defending favored courses of action or attacking rival positions (Blight et al. 1987; Kennedy 1969; Janis 1982).

Kennedy chose an eclectic group of 18 men whose advice he generally valued for either their ability to make intelligent decisions, possession of technical knowledge, or both. Over time, the unelected leaders of the group evolved into Robert Kennedy, the attorney general and the president's brother, and Robert McNamara, the secretary of defense. Others attending any or all of the sessions included Ball; Dean Rusk, secretary of state; Lyndon Johnson, the vice president; John McCone, director of the Central Intelligence Agency; Douglas Dillon, secretary of the treasury; Theodore Sorensen, the president's legal counsel; Alexis Johnson, deputy undersecretary of state; General Maxwell Taylor, chairman of the Joint Chiefs of Staff; Edward Martin, assistant secretary of state for Latin America; Llewellyn Thompson, a former ambassador to Russia; Roswell Gilpatrick, a deputy secretary of defense; Paul Nitze, assistant secretary of defense; Adli Stevenson, American ambassador to the United Nations; Kenneth O'Donnell, the president's appointments secretary; Dean Acheson, a former secretary of state, and McGeorge Bundy, the president's national security advisor (Blight et al. 1987; Allison 1971; Giglio 1991; Janis 1982).

Each member of the group, including the president himself, worked aggressively to maintain the secrecy of their deliberations. Each man, especially Kennedy and his cabinet members, did his best to honor previously made commitments for public appearances, fearing that a cancellation might ignite too many questions from either journalists or the public. The president even made congressional campaign appearances in Connecticut and Chicago, while the vice president went to Hawaii (Giglio 1991).

In marked contrast to the formal meetings of the full National Security Council, which so characterized the Eisenhower Administration, the pressure-packed sessions of Kennedy's ExComm were always informal and often highly argumentative. Both Kennedys strongly wanted to avoid the pitfalls characterizing the decision-making process leading up to the earlier Bay of Pigs debacle. They developed several methods to try to avoid repeating their previous errors. First, not every member attended each ExComm session. In fact, Robert Kennedy asked his brother to stay away from some meetings so as to assure a frank exchange of ideas and avoid the possibility of members voicing opinions that they thought might please the president. Conversely, few advisors or cabinet members would ever be willing to argue against a position he knew the president favored. Hence, when Kennedy did attend sessions, he would sometimes carefully hide his views so that others might feel freer to air their opinions. Robert Kennedy would also do this at times. In sum, the president wanted to make certain that each ExComm member felt free to give his best judgment (Janis 1982; Giglio 1991).

On the other hand, Robert Kennedy and Sorensen would at times assume the role of devil's advocate and challenge the positions and assumptions of the ExComm majority, thereby forcing members to defend their positions and possibly even view their positions from a different perspective. Furthering this effort, ExComm members at times divided into subgroups to develop position papers to be presented to the full group for critical analysis. Such practices often opened the door for subordinates to critique the analyses of their superiors and of generalists to challenge the work of subject experts. In addition, the president sought the counsel of experienced officials outside the ExComm, such Charles Bohlen and Robert Lovett, as two leaders in the Truman administration (Giglio 1991).

In sum, all of the participants writing their memoirs about the ExComm meetings agreed that the sessions tended to be lengthy and stressful, with members, including the president himself, loosing their poise more than once.

IV. PRESSURES AND LIMITATIONS CONFRONTING THE EXCOMM

Members of the group were working in response to powerful conflicting pressures. To begin with there was the obvious threat of making a decision that would ignite a thermonuclear war. This possible outcome constantly overshadowed deliberations, causing many members to lose both sleep and their composure during heated exchanges. Even the thought of contributing to decisions leading to such an outcome was a burden constantly weighing heavily on the thoughts of several members, especially McNamara and Rusk. The possibility of igniting a third world war and subsequently causing millions of casualties clearly seemed to pressure members to seek less forceful courses of action.

On the other hand, ExComm members felt overwhelming domestic political pressures to take any action necessary that would lead the Soviets to remove their missiles from Cuba. Most immediate were concerns over how the crisis might affect the midterm Congressional elections, to be held just the following month. On several occasions the president and others in the ExComm exclaimed that botched decision making would lead to Democratic congressional losses and possibly even a Republican takeover of Congress. Of course, longer-term effects were related directly to the president's ability to win reelection in 1964 and, ultimately, to his standing in history. Failure here could turn the tide of the Cold War struggle in favor of the Soviets.

In addition, the president and ExComm members were working under severe limitations. First, time limitations severely pressed ExComm's decision making. They had to work quickly to develop an effective plan leading to the removal of the missiles from Cuba before the Soviets completed installing the weapons. Such a delay could greatly strengthen Khrushchev's bargaining position. Second, members were limited in their knowledge of Soviet intentions and political and military capabilities. ExComm members spent much of their time speculating on likely Soviet responses to an array of possible American courses of action (Janis 1982; Allison 1971).

In sum, President Kennedy, advised by ExComm and working under unprecedented pressure, had to quickly develop a plan to compel the Soviets to remove their missiles from Cuba while also avoiding the ignition of a major war.

V. ALTERNATIVE COURSES OF ACTION ARE DEVELOPED

From the initial meeting on October 16 onward, ExComm members developed and debated eight possible options for responding to the Soviet action before eventually settling on two primary possible courses. Most members of the group quickly rejected any purely diplomatic solution, such as one focusing entirely on reaching a negotiated settlement through, for example, an arbitrator or mediator. On the other extreme, most in the group rejected a purely military solution, such as invading Cuba, unless other less drastic measures should fail.

Most ExComm members eventually came to favor one of two primary rival solutions. One option involved either a narrowly focused ''surgical'' air strike by the United States against the missile sites themselves or a broader attack that would also include nearby Soviet anti-aircraft installations. The proposal generated extensive debate in ExComm, with its advocates (termed ''hawks'' by some group members) maintaining that such action was the only certain way to remove the missiles quickly. Opponents of the plan countered by arguing that the attack would cause numerous Soviet and Cuban casualties and likely would ignite a counterattack, either from any surviving missiles in Cuba or from Soviet forces elsewhere, either in Europe or in Turkey, where the United States had its own missiles aimed at the heart of the Soviet Union. Finally, Robert Kennedy advocated an argument that proved effective against the air strike proposal—that America's moral tradition would never support a surprise attack by a more powerful nation against a smaller and weaker country (Gigilo 1991:197; Blight et al. 1987).

The second option, favored by a steadily increasing number of ExComm members during their lengthy sessions early in the crisis, featured the U.S. Navy's establishment of a blockade around Cuba. The blockade, which advocates euphemistically termed a ''quarantine,'' would prevent further shipment of missiles and associated military materials into the country. The action likely would not produce the casualties an air strike would, quarantine supporters argued. In addition, it would be a forceful yet limited, response. However, air-strike advocates noted that the quarantine was illegal by most interpretations of international law, would not prevent completion of the missile installation in Cuba, and would be so slow as to give Khrushchev valuable time to react elsewhere in the world. In sum, the blockade itself would not physically remove any missiles; its advocates simply hoped that it would force the Soviets to make a deal resulting in the missiles' removal.

Following lengthy debates spun throughout several meetings, the president called for a straw vote of the ExComm on Saturday October 20. The blockade won the vote, 11 to 6, over the air strike. The president agreed with the ExComm majority, although everyone agreed that the air strike could be made later should the blockade fail (Giglio 1991: 199–201). Although popular with a majority of the ExComm members, the blockade would never enjoy the unanimous support of the panel's members at any time during the crisis.

Several subsequently published reports assert that the president's thinking throughout the crisis was affected by his reading of historian Barbara Tuchman's *The Guns of August*, then newly published. This book chronicled how European leaders stumbled into the First World War through a series of mistaken decisions based upon misperceptions and unintended consequences. Hence Kennedy, determined to not make similar mistakes and lead the world into another world war, instinctively tended to side with the dove faction of the ExComm. However, he refrained from advertising these views during his appearances at ExComm sessions (Allison 1971; Blight et al. 1987; Janis 1982).

VI. THE CRISIS GOES PUBLIC

Throughout the early days of the crisis, the president had been overwhelmingly successful in maintaining secrecy, in order to give ExComm members sufficient time to prepare a response. Although several journalists, reporters from the *New York Times* and *Washington Post* in particular, knew fragments of the story—especially that it involved a Cold War military confrontation with the Soviet Union over Cuba—Kennedy succeeded in convincing journalists to censor themselves.

This enabled the president to gain maximum political leverage, both domestically and internationally, by dramatically announcing the crisis on national television the evening of Monday October 22. Earlier that day administration officials briefed the full cabinet, congressional leaders, and the chief executives of leading allies. An hour before the president's speech, Rusk gave a copy of the address to Anatoly Dobrynin, the Soviet ambassador to the United States. Kennedy's speech announced the discovery of the Soviet missiles, outlined the planned blockade of Cuba, and requested an immediate meeting of both the Organization of American States (OAS) and the United Nations Security Council. The president attacked the secret nature of the missiles' deployment, called for their immediate removal, and threatened massive retaliation should the weapons be used in a first strike (Giglio 1991).

Keeping the crisis secret until it could be announced dramatically—along with a proposed countermeasure—made for an important political victory for the president. That is, the drama and suddenness of the moment helped mute possible criticism from other political elites, as congressional leaders, newspaper and magazine editorials, and other chief executives largely supported the administration.

This approach undoubtedly also helped the administration win important international legal and political backing. The OAS voted 19 to 0 in favor of a resolution supporting the president's plan entirely. In addition, Stevenson had the Soviets dramatically on the defensive throughout the United Nations Security Council sessions on the crisis. Finally, early public opinion polls revealed that 84% of the American public supported the blockade and only 4% opposed it (Giglio 1991:203–207). The opening salvo of the public phase of the Cuban Missile Crisis clearly favored the Kennedy administration.

VII. EARLY ROUNDS OF THE PUBLIC CONFRONTATION

"Brinkmanship" now clearly dominated American management of the crisis. Kennedy was publicly confronting Khrushchev, as both national leaders stood on the brink of a nuclear war. By the evening of the day following Kennedy's dramatic announcement, the president and his ExComm completed final plans for implementing the blockade, particularly to determine which weapons were to be quarantined. The president now assumed detailed control over all matters concerning developing and implementing the blockade. In addition, he sought to win Khrushchev's approval for the plan. By the time the blockade was to begin—at 10 a.m. (East Coast time) on Wednesday October 24—the Americans had assembled a fleet of more than 160 vessels to handle the task. At the suggestion of an advisor, Kennedy shortened the blockade along the eastern side of the island from 800 to 500 miles, to allow Khrushchev more time to prepare a response to the American initiative (Allison 1971; Giglio 1991).

Throughout the night before, as 25 Soviet ships made their way across the Caribbean to Cuba, Khrushchev announced that his country would defend its rights. Then, at 10 a.m. on the day of the blockade, six Soviet ships near the blockade line had either stopped or turned back. Kennedy soon responded by ordering the Americans to follow closely any ships entering the blockade area, thus allowing those vessels additional time and space in which to turn around. As the blockade began taking effect, the two national leaders exchanged communications, both formally and informally. Of particular importance was Kennedy's letter to Khrushchev in which the president restated his previous public position, particularly the demand that the missiles be removed from Cuba. Also that day Stevenson had his dramatic confrontation with his Soviet counterpart before the U.N. Security Council. Yet Stevenson's forceful rhetoric, coupled with several enlarged photographs of Cuban missile sites taken earlier from the U-2 flights, were not enough to win official and public support from the United Nations.

Meanwhile that day, Kennedy maintained constant personal contact with the blockade forces, ordering that obvious non-weapons-bearing ships, such as tankers, be allowed to pass through. Finally, to demonstrate his resolve in maintaining the quarantine, the president ordered that Americans board and search a ship. However, he carefully selected non-Soviet ships initially, again working to give Khrushchev as much time to formulate a response as possible. The following day, the Soviets responded through informal links with an American television network executive that they would remove their missiles in exchange for an American pledge not to invade Cuba. The Soviets followed this contact with a letter from Khrushchev later that day, essentially restating the offer.

However, the following day, as ExComm members were analyzing the letter and preparing a response, the president received a second formal letter from Khrushchev. This message, transmitted over Moscow radio, contained a new proposal—that the Soviets would remove their missiles from Cuba if the Americans would remove theirs from Turkey. Making the ExComm session that day even more somber was a report from the Federal Bureau of Investigation (FBI) that Soviet officials in New York were preparing to destroy secret documents in their office (a practice normally only done at times of extreme emergency). During much of their session that day, Kennedy and the ''dove'' ExComm members considered strategies for persuading NATO members and recalcitrant Republican critics in Congress of the wisdom of removing the Jupiter missiles, outdated by then, from Turkey (Janis 1982; Blight et al. 1987).

More sobering news arrived early the next day, on October 27, when it was learned that a Soviet antiaircraft missile had shot down a U-2 spy plane over Cuba. Meanwhile, another U-2 spy plane inadvertently flew over Soviet airspace in eastern Siberia, nearly triggering an armed conflict as it scampered back to Alaska just in front of Soviet fighter planes, who nearly exchanged shots with American fighters who had scrambled to defend the returning U-2. The two incidents appeared to harden the positions of both the hawks and doves on ExComm. The hawks felt even more strongly that the United States should launch air strikes against Soviet installations in Cuba, while the doves argued that the incidents revealed the dangerous instability surrounding the crisis, and that accepting the Soviets' exchange offer would be the safest and sanest resolution of the confrontation (Blight et al., 1987).

The president at this time openly began moving more closely into the ExComm dove camp, fearing that a military response could lead to an uncontrolled escalation of armed responses and hence possibly a third world war.

These ExComm deliberations throughout October 27 led Kennedy to accept a now legendary strategy advocated by several group members, but especially his brother. Kennedy's counteroffer, contained in a letter sent to the Soviets that evening, accepted the basic proposal made in Khrushchev's *first* letter to the Americans and expanded upon in subsequent unofficial contacts. In essence, Kennedy ignored the Soviets' second proposal to mutually withdraw missiles from Cuba and Turkey and accepted Khrushchev's earlier offer to withdraw the weapons from Cuba in exchange for an American promise to end the blockade and not invade the island (Giglio 1991; Allison, 1971).

Soon after sending the letter, Kennedy initiated secret overtures to the Soviets reporting that he already had made plans to *later* (in 4 to 5 months) remove the American missiles from Turkey. To be sure, the president clearly was in an extremely delicate bargaining position. On one hand, he wanted to win Khrushchev's acceptance of the American offer, and the most likely way for that to happen would be if the Soviets would not appear to be dramatically backing down from a confrontation. On the other hand, Kennedy himself could not appear to be yielding to Soviet pressure. The president then would be open to outcries from congressional Republicans, his presidential challenger the next year, and a host of NATO allies. In sum, Kennedy needed to assure each side of ''saving face'' publicly (Giglio 1991; Allison 1971).

Waiting for a Soviet response to the American offer was almost unbearable for ExComm members, especially the president. Meeting that night, members considered their options should Khrushchev reject their offer. Hawks called for an immediate air strike followed by an invasion. Evidence revealed decades later suggested that Kennedy favored less drastic measures, such as possibly increasing the list of blockaded items to include petroleum products or asking the United Nations to request that the countries withdraw their missiles from Turkey and Cuba (Giglio 1991).

However, Khrushchev relieved the ExComm members' pressures early the following morning by accepting Kennedy's offer. The crisis had finally come to an end. Significantly, unstated in the public Soviet response was acceptance of the private pledge to remove the Jupiter missiles from Turkey.

VIII. ANALYSIS OF THE EXCOMM DECISION MAKING

One of the earliest analyses of the decision-making effort was written by Robert Kennedy and published in 1969, the year following his death. Of prime interest has been his explanations of the ''lessons learned'' from the crisis. Of particular note was his stressing the importance of empathy, or of ''placing ourselves in the other country's shoes'' when formulating offers and counteroffers. In addition, the attorney general urged that crisis decision makers such as presidents should take as much time as possible to formulate their plan, should seek out an array of opinions, should especially consult those with well developed expertise on the country(ies) in question, should always remember the aggressive eagerness of the military, should carefully monitor world opinion, should avoid humiliating other national leaders by furnishing them a face-saving mechanism, and should always avoid triggering an unanticipated chain of events escalating the crisis into a major conflict (as had occurred in the First World War) (Kennedy 1969).

The year Robert Kennedy's treatise was published, Graham Allison, a member of the Harvard faculty, published a journal article analyzing the administration's decision-making process during the crisis, followed 2 years later by the publication of a more thorough book-length treatment (*Essence of Decision: Explaining the Cuban Missile Crisis*). Allison produced one of the most widely discussed and influential analytical examinations of crisis decision making in American public life. The study was used extensively in university classes on policy making, bureaucracies, the presidency, foreign policy development, and institutional decision making to help educate a generation of scholars (Allison 1969, 1971).

A mainstay of Allison's effort was that he provided readers with *three* possible conceptual models (or ''cuts,'' as he termed them) for explaining and understanding decision making during that crisis. Readers then were free to compare and contrast the strengths and weaknesses of the explanations and, in turn, to learn from the unique contributions each offered to one's understanding of the decision-making process in that crisis. The first model, which viewed national leaders as rational actors seeking to attain specific policy objectives, was an approach traditionally taken in the analysis of foreign-policy decision making. Allison's second model was based on analyzing organizational processes and focused on decisions as ''outputs'' of governmental organizations. Here the emphasis was on understanding an organization's routine decision-making apparatus and appreciating its standard operating procedures. Finally, Allison developed a ''bureaucratic politics'' model that analyzes the behavior of either individuals or various branches of the bureaucracy. These are looked at based upon how they bargain and maneuver in relation to other power centers in the bureaucracy. A key factor here is determining how individuals and/

or bureaucracies maneuver to attain their personal or organizational goals (Allison 1969, 1971).

One of the many attractive aspects of Allison's analyses was his contention that the three models were essentially complementary and not rival explanations. For example, Allison notes that the "rational actor" approach viewed decision making from the perspective of the entire government, while the second approach looked at organizations within that government, and the "bureaucratic politics" approach examined the behavior of individuals within those organizations. Hence, analyses of decision making should look at *all* levels of behavior. The process of examining each level involved making a distinctive group of assumptions which, in turn, generated specific questions seeking to uncover information unique to that arena of analysis. The rational actor model saw the Soviets trying to strengthen their hand in Cold War nuclear deterrence by placing the missiles in Cuba. On the other hand, the Americans behaved rationally by employing a blockade as an interim step in exerting pressure, which ultimately rested upon the possibility of deploying the United States' massive nuclear arsenal. The organization theory and bureaucratic politics approaches focused on how those decisions were implemented by considering how the responses fit into the daily operation and policy goals of American government agencies and their leaders. In sum, the subsequent two models indicated that neither the United States (nor the Soviet side either, for that matter) was as rational or as monolithic in its decision-making processes as the rational actor model indicated (Allison 1971). For example, contrary to the president's orders, the U.S. Navy shadowed and forced to the surface several Soviet submarines in that region. And the Soviets, contrary to orders from Moscow, shot down a U-2 spy plane flying over Cuba.

Although the overwhelming bulk of the literature produced in reaction to Allison's analysis was complimentary and even laudatory, Jonathan Bendor and Thomas Hammond produced a sobering dissection of the original study. In sum, while Bendor and Hammond pay homage to the many contributions of Allison's analyses, they are critical of many of the details of his models. They maintain that Allison made several methodological errors in developing his models and that in several cases his assumptions simply are incorrect or, at least, significantly misleading (Bendor and Hammond 1992). Yet their critique notwithstanding, Allison's work remains important at minimum because it leads others to seek alternative and multiple-layered explanations for crisis decision making.

Another modern "classic" study of the ExComm crisis decision-making process was written by Irving L. Janis, a member of the Yale University faculty. His study, which defined and subsequently popularized his concept of "groupthink," was particularly useful for several reasons. First, his groupthink theory introduced elements of social psychology into the political, legal, and historic issues previously considered in studies of the Cuban Missile Crisis. In addition, Janis featured in both editions of his book case studies contrasting ExComm decision making in the Bay of Pigs debacle with the effort of nearly the same group of men later in the Cuban Missile Crisis. Readers were given an opportunity to see how ExComm members, especially the Kennedy brothers, learned from the mistakes made in the Bay of Pigs decision-making process (Janis 1982).

In sum, Janis's concept of groupthink is exemplified when members of a group, assigned to make a decision, work so hard at attaining unanimous agreement that they abandon efforts at seriously and objectively evaluating rival courses of action. Internal peer pressures to conform to the thoughts and goals of the group then become the overriding norm driving members' thought processes. Noteworthy symptoms of groupthink include the feeling of members that the group is invulnerable; a ready collective effort to rationalize and hence discard any effort to compel members to reconsider their assumptions, stereotyped negative views of rivals (as being either weak or incompetent, for example); overriding belief in their group's ''inherent morality''; the placing of immediate pressure on any group member seeking to dissent from the groups' prevailing views; a parallel ''self-censorship'' prohibiting members from expressing dissenting views; widespread pressures to agree with the group, creating ''a shared illusion of unanimity''; and the eventual appearance of ''self-appointed mindguards'' in the group, who block the flow of any information adverse to the group's assumptions (Janis 1982).

Janis's treatment of Cuban Missile Crisis decision making has been especially useful because of the efforts of ExComm members, particularly the Kennedy brothers, to identify and overcome the pitfalls of groupthink. They carefully sought out rival views or, when such views might not be available, played ''devil's advocate'' to attempt to create challenges to burgeoning majority views. Indeed, such efforts undoubtedly contributed to the lengthy and chaotic sessions that so dispirited some consensus-seeking members. The president avoided some meetings to assure that members would feel free to air their views without fear of possibly alienating him. In addition, his brother on several occasions would ask challenging questions, even confronting views he shared, to make sure that ExComm members considered as many perspectives as possible (Janis 1982). In sum, ExComm's decision-making process in the Bay of Pigs case was a classic example of ''groupthink,'' while the decision-making procedure in the Cuban Missile Crisis was a perfect example of overcoming the hazards of groupthink.

A broader analysis of the Cuban Missile Crisis decision-making effort has been provided by James Blight, Joseph Nye, and David Welch, some of Allison's Harvard colleagues. Writing more than two decades following the intense days of October 1962, the three men examined the proceedings of a seminar in March 1987 composed of a number of former ExComm members gathered with several scholars. The authors' bemoaned the fact that there was little agreement on the crisis management lessons that the Cuban Missile Crisis case study could offer decision makers today (Blight et al. 1987).

However, Blight and his colleagues praised the list of ''lessons learned'' presented by Robert Kennedy not long after the crisis. The three Harvard scholars then added their own—courtesy of two decades of hindsight—''updated'' list of five lessons learned from ExComm's crisis-management effort. First, they urged avoidance of similar superpower nuclear confrontations in the future, because another such crisis might lead to disaster. Second, they urged that decision makers avoid having ''rigidly preconceived world views,'' because these could possibly fatally damage their ability to analyze information gathered during a rapidly changing situation. Third, they emphasized the inadequacy of rational models of deterrence. Actors on either side of such a confrontation have rarely been found to be as ''rational'' as the model suggests they should be. Fourth, the authors urged that senior administration officials work hard ahead of time at preparing themselves to make crisis decisions that may be called for later. Finally, the scholars maintained that the crisis outcome revealed the importance of the United States having a nuclear deterrence capability. Blight and others maintained that fear of massive retaliation from the American nuclear arsenal helped compel the Soviets to end the crisis largely on the terms sought by President Kennedy (Blight et al. 1987).

Finally, Paul Anderson produced a distinctive analysis of administration decision making during the crisis. Examining primarily archival evidence of the decision-making process during the Cuban Missile Crisis, Anderson developed a theory of ''decision making by objection.'' He maintained that crisis decision makers were governed by three primary factors. First was an intense desire to avoid a failure (in terms of either igniting a nuclear war on one hand or of failing to get the missiles removed from Cuba on the other). In fact, their fear of failing was greater than their desire to attain a measurable success in the venture. In addition, throughout the crisis, decision makers were confronted with making a series of mostly dichotomous choices from among a number of nonrival options for action. These choices tended to be made in sequence, so that the process of selecting from among two alternatives would present decision makers with a new pair of alternatives—which, after a decision, was made—would present still another pair of alternative courses of action, etc. Finally, the process of making each of these decisions led decision makers to discover new goals as they went along. For example, ExComm initially only had the goal of showing America's commitment to removing the missiles from Cuba. But during the process of deliberation, ExComm uncovered other goals, such as avoiding being the aggressor in a Pearl Harbor–type attack and providing Khrushchev with a political face-saving ''out'' (Anderson 1983).

In sum, Anderson maintained that his model was better able than Allison and other efforts to explain this crisis decision making. His model ''captures the ambiguity and change in preferred courses of action'' in the crisis decision-making process. The Ex-Comm exhibited group decision making by ''argumentation and debate,'' as its members moved from selecting between one pair of choices to the next pair of choices. However, such a decision-making process is not foolish behavior, because to attempt to chose from among a larger array of choices could ''overwhelm the limited information-processing capacity'' of the ExComm members (Anderson 1983:218–220). Hence, their meetings, while appearing chaotic to some, could be said to be a productive approach to making important decisions under great pressure.

IX. CONCLUSIONS

There are at least two reasons why the decision-making processes of President Kennedy and ExComm likely will long endure as a prime example of performing well under intense pressure. First, the participants clearly attained their goal of forcing the removal of inter-continental missiles from Cuba while simultaneously avoiding escalating their confronta-tion with the Soviet Union into a third world war. For the American side at least, the story had a happy ending. Second, an abundance of information has since been made available, enabling scholars to study details of the event. There is an abundance of evi-dence (such as correspondence, official documents, and memoirs) for observers to sift through. Finally, the natural and intense drama inherent in the crisis has added something of a mystique to the events of October 1962.

REFERENCES

Allison, G. T. (1969). Conceptual models and the Cuban Missile Crisis. *American Political Science Review* 63, 389–718.

Allison, G. T. (1971). *The Essence of Decision: Explaining the Cuban Missile Crisis.* Boston: Little Brown.

Anderson, P. A. (1983). Decision making by objection and the Cuban Missile Crisis. *Administrative Science Quarterly* 28, 201–222.

Bendor, J. and Hammond, T. H. (1992). Rethinking Allison's models. *American Political Science Review* 86, 301–322.
Blight, JG, Nye, J. S. Jr., and Welch, D. A. (1987). The Cuban Missile Crisis revisited. *Foreign Affairs* 66, 170–188.
Giglio, J. N. (1991). *The Presidency of John F. Kennedy*. Lawrence, KS: University Press of Kansas.
Janis, I. L. (1982). *Groupthink*, 2nd ed. Boston: Houghton Mifflin.
Kennedy, R. F. (1989). *Thirteen Days: A Memoir of the Cuban Missile Crisis*. New York: W.W. Norton.

28

Emergency Management on a Grand Scale

A Bureaucrat's Analysis

John Carroll School of Public Administration, College of Architecture, Urban and Public Affairs, Florida Atlantic University, Fort Lauderdale, Florida

Situation Report: 1 September (all times are EST)
"The National Hurricane Center has released its latest advisory showing Hurricane Chanelle crossing the Florida peninsula. It has cleared Broward County and is impacting Collier County. Hurricane Chanelle is expected to enter the Gulf of Mexico in the next several hours. Hurricane Chanelle is continuing on its westerly heading, traveling at approximately 17 miles per hour. Maximum sustained winds are 135 miles per hour. The barometer reading is. . . ."

Chanelle was a category 4 hurricane covering a 150-mile front, with maximum sustained winds of 135 miles per hour on the north side of the eye wall. A ridge of high pressure turned the storm from the Atlantic Ocean west, making landfall in northern Broward County. The impact phase was initiated at 2100 hours. The storm surge was reported to be 15 feet from the center of the storm, gradually decreasing in height from the storm center north along the coastline. Areas south of the eye wall experienced an 8-foot storm surge. High tide at the Hillsboro Inlet, near the eye of the storm, was at about 2300 hours, worsening the storm surge conditions. Flood waters were expected to subside within 10 to 12 hours. Approximately 10 inches of rain fell across Broward County. Additional rain bands from the tail of the storm were expected over the next 24 hours. Heavy rainfall produced by the storm created severe flooding in all South Florida counties and widespread power outages throughout the state. As the storm moved inland, several major transportation routes were closed because of heavy rains.

The Broward County Emergency Management Division, through the County Emergency Operations Center, declared an "all clear" at 0900 hours. This meant this storm had dissipated sufficiently to begin recovery operations. The Florida governor requested a presidential emergency declaration. The governor also submitted a request for a major disaster declaration for individual and public assistance. A gradual movement north in the Gulf of Mexico was expected within 24 hours. Severe thunderstorm and tornado watches were in effect for the area impacted by Chanelle's passage. The president of the United States signed a disaster emergency declaration for the state of Florida for emergency assistance related to Hurricane Chanelle.

Disasters strike. Most of the time, they strike without adequate warning. The ability of the government to respond to the needs of people during a disaster has been tested on a number of recent occasions: i.e, the Loma Prieta (1989) and Northridge (1992) earthquakes in California; Hurricanes Hugo (1989), Andrew (1992), Iniki (1992), Opal (1996), and Mitch (1998); as well as flooding throughout the Midwest and tornadoes in the Midwest and SouthEast in 1998. Is the government ready to respond to the needs of its people? In the mythical Hurricane Chanelle, South Florida (which is home to over 4 million people) took the brunt. Landfall of the tropical cyclone ''eye,'' or center of the storm, was in Broward County. This county consists of the greater Fort Lauderdale area and is the geographic center of the population mass of South Florida. A direct hit by a major hurricane here would easily exceed the losses experienced in the 1992 Hurricane Andrew. Picture yourself as a high-ranking bureaucrat who might be in a similar situation and how you might respond to providing or restoring service.

I. INTRODUCTION

One of the tasks that truly tests the mettle of government is how it responds to emergencies and disasters. A growing body of emergency and disaster literature exists in both academic and government sources. This body largely points toward the ''rational/professional'' notion of public administration and thus the provision of emergency service. Another body of literature investigates the sociological aspects of dealing with emergencies and disasters. It is the intent of this chapter, through the lens of an experienced bureaucrat, to expand the body of knowledge by offering a model that takes rational and sociological thought into consideration. This chapter began with an example of an hypothetical disaster; what follows traces how government responds in emergency management. Definitions offered from the literature are amplified by the ''grand scale'' of a hurricane. The triad model is then explicated as a method for further developing emergency management policy. Each leg of the triad considers operational, administrative, and sociological concepts for the purpose of addressing proactive and reactive contingencies.

II. WHERE WE STAND: FEDERAL, STATE, AND LOCAL GOVERNMENT AND BUREAUCRACY

The ''bureaucratic administration'' movement, largely attributed to Woodrow Wilson from *The Study of Administration* and *Congressional Government* (Ostrom 1974), helped to give rise to professional government during the Progressive Era (1880–1920). At about the same time Wilson was calling for a science of management, Frederick W. Taylor was pioneering the development of time and motion studies. Premised upon the notion that there was ''one best way'' of accomplishing any given task, ''scientific management'' sought to increase output by discovering the fastest, most efficient, and least fatiguing production methods (Shafritz and Hyde 1992). Referred to as ''the world's first efficiency expert,'' (Kanigel 1997:18) Frederick Taylor produced a model of scientific management that gained wide acceptance in both the public and private sectors (Kelling and Coles 1996).

Other theories of the period would also help shape the direction and scope of the Progressive Era reforms. Henri Fayol's 14 principles of management would plainly lay out how organizations should be managed (Fayol 1916). Max Weber described the characteristics of bureaucracy, with the ''continental'' passion for order (Weber 1946). Following the Progressive Era, Luther Gulick (1937) called for the division of work and its coordination in the organization. His concepts included span of control, technical efficiency, how to construct organizations, and how to describe the functional elements of a chief executive. Classic organization theories would evolve from the ideas of these thinkers, among others (Shafritz and Hyde 1992).

Each of these contributions formed the basis of the ''rational'' notion of public administration, or the bureaucratic structure. American government largely continues to use these practices, with the occasional exception to practice the latest wave in leadership or management styles. Coupled with the rational notion is the presumption of ''professionalism'' on the part of the government employees at all levels. In a study that argues the subject of applying the term *professional* to public administration by Cigler (1990), an excellent overview of the demographics of government is offered. Cigler posits that as government programs grew and bureaucratic responsibilities expanded over the last 50 years, the professionalization of permanent career bureaucrats at all levels has also significantly increased.

Nearly one-third of today's public work force claims professional or technical expertise in an identifiable and specialized occupation that minimally requires a college degree and affords a lifetime career opportunity (Cigler 1990:637). Although employing only about one-sixth the number of persons found in the private sector, government at all levels employs almost three times as many professionals on a full-time basis (Reynolds 1995: 123). According to Stone (1990), ''the quality of executive management and administration in many states, numerous urban counties with elected executives and professional administrators, and most cities with managers is at a higher level than in the Federal Government'' (p. 18). This indicates that the notion of professionalism may be considered more important at the state and local levels. Gabris and Golembiewski (1997) argue that local government depends on ''functional bureaucratic design'' and ''hierarchical control'' (p. 71) for its operations, which may strengthen the ''rational/professional'' notion of public administration.

There are different types of county government structures, such as the commission (strong chair, coequal commissioner, supervisor, strong supporting elected official like a sheriff), council/manager, and elected executive. Municipalities have similar structures (Garnett 1985). The structure of government affects the patterns of influence and performance, because local government has only the powers and structure a state grants it (Garnett 1985). Reform efforts at the local level are pushing municipal and county governments further into the rational/professional corner. DeSantis and Renner (1994) analyzed how the political structures of counties in the United States affected public policy. They noted a recent increase in reform efforts at the county level in response to the increasing demands for service placed on local governments. They have also noted that reforms, at least at the county level, were aimed at providing a central executive leadership and increase the level of professionalism. The emphasis here appeared to be increasing control over managing the growing load of service demands (DeSantis and Renner 1994).

Gabris and Golembiewski (1997) would probably agree, because ''generally, local governments are the closest form of government to the people and the voters; this creates a special political demand for performance and results'' (p. 73). Additionally, ''career administrators are subject to more political pressure'' (p. 73) at the local level. With this in mind, it is local government that is the closest service provider, largest employer of government staff, and best suited to respond to emergencies. It is also firmly entrenched in the rational/professional mind set, which is how local government is structured toward emergency management.

III. GOVERNMENT TO THE RESCUE: WHAT IS EMERGENCY MANAGEMENT?

"Preparing for the worst," also known as emergency preparedness and response, is largely the responsibility of local governments and officials (Wolfe 1994:3). The states spent $1.6 billion in 1994 on emergency management (Nelson 1996). In the first 2 months of 1996, President Clinton declared 28 disasters. This represented three times as many declarations over the same period in any year during the last 20 years (Nelson 1996). When disasters threaten or strike a jurisdiction, people expect elected leaders to take immediate action to deal with the problem. Government is expected to marshal its resources, channel the efforts of voluntary agencies and private enterprise in the community, and solicit assistance from outside the jurisdiction if state and local resources are insufficient (Goss 1997).

But first, what is a "disaster"? The nature of a major emergency or disaster makes definitions difficult. To uses Crichlow's (1997) example, a train derailment that injures 15 people may be overwhelming for a smaller city or county but easily handled by a larger city or county with greater access to resources. In local government, an event or disturbance that occurs in one branch of government or jurisdiction does not necessarily affect any other (Gianikis and McCue 1997). However, a disaster will cross branches of government and even jurisdictions. According to Crichlow, "disasters are unique events of immense complexity" (p. 51).

Table 1 divides disasters into categories and types. While a number of them may not be considered disasters by some local government authorities (i.e., flood, structure fire, major road accident, or bomb threat), in other jurisdictions each may present a critical problem. Therefore, a definition of what constitutes a disaster could be considered subjective. This is especially true if you are the victim. You would consider it a disaster if your house burned down, but the government probably would not. Each of the above categories and types has the potential to become a disaster, even on the "grand scale" considered for this chapter. The intensity, size, location, complexity, and duration of the emergency

Table 1 Disaster Categories and Types

Weather	Man-Made	Transport and communication	Medical	Major disturbance	Energy
Floods	Structure fire	Telephone system	Epidemic	Civil disturbance	Fuel shortage
Tornadoes	Hazardous materials	EDP failure	Mass poisoning	Subversion/sabotage	Nuclear accident
Hurricanes	Building collapse	Major road accidents	Contaminated water supply	Labor unrest	Major power failure
Heavy snow	Power failure	Rail system/train crash	Major accidents	Bomb threats	
Earthquake	Explosions	Aircraft crash	Multiple victims	Disturbed people	
Forest fire	Terrorism				
Volcano					
Severe cold/heat					
Tidal wave					

Source: From Joint Committee on Information Technology Resources, Florida Legislature, 1993.

are all factors in determining if the emergency is a disaster. For the purposes of this chapter, a working definition is as follows: A disaster is an emergency considered severe enough by local government to warrant the response and dedication of resources beyond the normal scope of a single jurisdiction or branch of local government. Although state and federal government entities may classify categories of emergencies as warranting the label *disaster*, it is most often the local government that must make the determination.

In the late 1970s, a National Governors' Association study developed the current four-phase model of emergency management. Those phases are mitigation, preparedness, response, and recovery (Waugh 1994). Mitigation and preparedness are both considered proactive phases, or actions that are taken prior to the emergency. Mitigation is the assessment of the specific category and type of emergency and what the jurisdiction can do to reduce the risks associated with that emergency. For example, land-use policy that forbids building structures on a flood plain would reduce the risk of structures during a flood. In the 1990s, mitigation has been the focus of emergency managers from the federal through state to local governments. *Preparedness* refers to the actual planning, training, placement of resources, mutual-aid agreements across jurisdictions, and other coordination efforts before an emergency strikes. For example, a hazardous materials drill would test emergency plans and responses within jurisdictions.

Preparedness receives a great deal of attention in local government. Planning and attempting to forecast the future can play vital roles in preparedness. Poister and Strieb (1997) identify strategic management as a broader process or ''big picture'' approach to management. A bureaucrat can look for long- or short-term issues, but a disaster is likely to affect the long-term plan of local government. Disasters should be considered part of the strategic management picture. The following are important steps in developing effective preparedness strategies to deal with potential catastrophes: (1) create a detailed written emergency plan; (2) hold regular meetings to critique the plan; (3) invite businesses to participate in meetings; and (4) conduct a real-life walk-through of emergency responses (Burkhardt 1997:27).

Response and recovery are both reactive phases, or actions taken after the emergency has occurred. Response is the actual activation of disaster plans to meet an emergency. For example, an ''in flight'' emergency (meaning that a crash potential exists) is declared on an inbound passenger aircraft at a major airport. If the aircraft were actually to crash, the airport's plan would be activated and emergency forces would respond. Recovery consists of the actions taken by government to restore order and vital systems (such as electric, water, sewer, law enforcement, fire/rescue, etc.) and to provide assistance in the way of temporary housing, food, or medical attention (Waugh 1994; Nelson 1996; FEMA 1998).

Each level of government has an assigned role in our system of emergency management. Local government is the primary actor to first attend to the public's emergency needs. Depending on the nature and size of the emergency, state and federal assistance may be provided to the local jurisdiction. Local government is responsible for warning, emergency public information, evacuation, and shelter (FEMA 1996a). City and county emergency management offices are tasked with establishing and implementing strategies on the ways government would function in an emergency response environment (Crichlow 1997). According to Waugh (1994), ''county governments may in fact be the most logical and hospitable hosts for emergency management agencies because of their unique roles in state and local governance'' (p. 256). The state government offices are expected to fill roles. States assist local jurisdictions whose capabilities are overwhelmed by an emergency. State representatives may respond to certain emergencies to assist local officials. In addition, state emergency management offices work with their federal counterparts when federal assistance is deemed necessary (FEMA 1996a).

In 1979, President Jimmy Carter ordered the first major federal disaster strategy, dubbed the Comprehensive Emergency Management plan (Crichlow 1997). This strategy would help form the Federal Emergency Management Agency (FEMA) as the central hub for the national disaster response policy (Nelson 1996). FEMA adopted, as federal policy, the four-phase model for emergency management developed by the National Governor's Association. As an agency, FEMA has weathered its own share of criticisms over the years. Reorganization and a redefining of roles has placed FEMA in a better support role for the state and local governments.

Recently, FEMA was charged by the U.S. Senate Committee on Appropriations to develop national-level performance criteria to measure the capability of the states to effectively respond to disasters (Goss 1997). FEMA and the National Emergency Management Association (NEMA) jointly developed the Capability Assessment for Readiness (CAR) process. The central conclusion of this report is that the states do have the basic capabilities in place to effectively respond to disasters. In the vast majority of cases, the states can do this without federal assistance. The report made specific recommendations for improvement areas and set goals for reaching them (Goss 1997). The CAR is viewed in the government generated literature as a blueprint for future assessments of emergency management.

How does government actually respond in the face of a disaster? There are two types of responses in an emergency: one that is integrated and effective, and another one that is fragmented, in conflict, or duplicates efforts. In other words, one that works well and one that does not. Drabek and colleagues (1981) studied activities in various parts of the Unites States to determine if similarities in responses exist as well as to look for good or bad practices. One of the major points from this study is that most of those who manage disaster responses in general are surprised at the number and diversity of groups who will arrive to help with their special expertise.

In their study, as shown in Table 2, the ways government agencies that were studied responded to disasters had distinct similarities, differences, and general lessons that could be learned from those responses. The implications of this table are basic organizational behavior responses and not just emergency management issues. Each may play a role in the ways government responds to many routine issues as well as to disasters. The similarities, differences, and lesson learned, in and of themselves, are excellent recommendations to any government agency tasked with responding to disasters. This table, taken alone, can provide a solid outline for government.

IV. THE GRAND SCALE: HURRICANES

There are occurrences, in general terms, that may be classified ''disasters,'' which severely test the emergency management capabilities not only of local government but also of state and federal responses. In the earlier discussion of the categories and types of disasters, several may be presented as ''grand scale'' occurrences. In other words, when this emergency occurs, it is highly likely that all levels of government will have to implement emergency plans and commit resources. Those include, in the weather category, hurricanes, earthquakes (not tremors), volcanoes, and tidal waves; man-made category: terrorism, transportation and communications: aircraft (commercial passenger jet) crash; medi-

Table 2 Response to Disasters

Similarities	Differences	Lessons learned
1. Multiorganizational—more than one organization and resources must respond to participate.	1. Planning—organizations have different plans, some good, some not.	1. Communications—manage better.
2. Diversity—responding organizations will differ in size, complexity, authority, capabilities, etc.	2. Communications—not regulated, differing methods and equipment (radio frequencies, etc.)	2. Authority—who is in charge? Who is responsible for what?
3. Improvisation—necessary during response.	3. Decision and control—tended to be flat rather than hierarchiacal; less control.	3. Special resources—locate and use more effectively; keep a resource inventory.
4. Loose coupling—organizations loosely coupled before event and agency autonomies maintained.	4. Stable/unstable—if response is stable, it is effective; if it is unstable it is ineffective.	4. Media—work better with them throughout the response.
	5. Performance—perceptions vary widely.	

Source: From Drabek et al., 1981.

cal category: epidemic and mass poisoning; and energy category: nuclear accident (not incident). A grand-scale disaster does not alter the four-phase model of emergency response; rather, this type of disaster changes the response complexity. A grand-scale disaster will tend to overwhelm the resources of local government and probably those of the state government. It does not, however, lessen the need by government to take action to restore order after an occurrence.

What is a hurricane and why is it included for discussion in this chapter? Hurricanes are included because of the practical experience in this type of response brought by the author. It is the most frequent type of grand-scale disaster that can be expected anywhere along the Atlantic and Gulf coasts of the mainland United States. Despite the relative knowledge of when, where, and with what strength a hurricane will strike (sometimes known several days before it actually does, with advanced weather prediction models), even the smallest storm can be a multi-billion-dollar disaster. A hurricane, in nonmeteorological terms, is essentially a giant ''cyclone'' that forms in the tropical regions of the Atlantic, Indian, and Pacific Oceans as well as the Caribbean Sea. In the Atlantic, Gulf of Mexico, and eastern Pacific and Caribbean basins, this is a *hurricane*. In other parts of the world, it may be known as *typhoon*. This is a severe weather condition that brings high winds, rains, and unusual tidal conditions along the coastal regions. Table 3 depicts how hurricanes are categorized on the Saffir-Simpson scale.

Hurricanes, based on this system, are measured in terms of their intensity or strength. In each category, *wind* refers to sustained (or constant) speed, as opposed to gusts, which are sporadic. The still-water surge is the ''wall'' of water ahead of the actual cyclone. When a hurricane forms and moves, it pushes or displaces water in front of it, which is usually responsible for the widespread flooding when it comes ashore. For example, FEMA (1998) recommends evacuation of residents within 30 miles of the coastline during a category 4 or 5 storm, which may be a monumental task for many communities. An

Table 3 Hurricane Intensity Levels/Saffir-Simpson Scale

	Category 1	Category 2	Category 3	Category 4	Category 5
Sustained winds	74–95 mph	96–110 mph	111–130 mph	131–155 mph	>155 mph
Storm surge (+normal)	4–5 feet	6–8 feet	9–12 feet	13–18 feet	>18 feet
Wave action (over surge)	up to 8-foot waves	up to 12-foot waves	up to 18-foot waves	up to 25-foot waves	up to 25-foot waves

Source: From Broward Sheriff's Office, 1996 and FEMA, 1996a.

additional characteristic, wave action, involves the behavior of the surface water at the location where the storm comes ashore. Wave action is especially damaging to coastal areas because it is constant throughout the storm (up to 12 hours). It pounds structures and beach front along the coast at a height above the tide level. In the Atlantic/Gulf/Caribbean basins, hurricane season runs from June 1 through December 1 each year. The peaks of activity run from mid-August until mid-October (FEMA 1998). To demonstrate the level of disaster when a hurricane strikes the United States, Table 4 depicts the "top ten" costliest hurricanes in 1996 dollars.

As this table clearly demonstrates, hurricanes ranging in strength from categories 1 through 5 are included in the top ten. Tropical cyclones, when they strike the United States, are certainly grand-scale type disasters. This writer had the opportunity to respond to the locations of the top two storms (as of this writing), Andrew and Hugo, for varied assignments. The following cases illustrate those hurricanes in their relation to the grand scale.

A. Case 1: Hurricane Hugo, "The Big One"

Hurricane Hugo began as a tropical disturbance off the West African coast on September 9, 1989. It belongs to the class of hurricanes termed *Cape Verde storms*. Hugo gained in intensity as it crossed the Atlantic. Hugo affected the Caribbean islands of Guadeloupe

Table 4 Costliest United States Hurricanes (Tropical Cyclones): 1900–1996 (adjusted to 1996 U.S. dollars)

Rank	Name/Location	Year	Category	Damage
1	Andrew (SE FL/SE LA)	1992	4	$30,475,000,000
2	Hugo (SC)	1989	4	$8,491,561,181
3	Agnes (NE US)	1972	1	$7,500,000,000
4	Betsy (FL/LA)	1965	3	$7,425,340,909
5	Camille (MS/AL)	1969	5	$6,096,287,313
6	Diane (NE US)	1955	1	$4,830,580,808
7	Frederic (AL/MS)	1979	3	$4,328,968,903
8	Unnamed (New England)	1938	3	$4,140,000,000
9	Fran (NC)	1996	3	$3,200,000,000
10	Opal (NW FL/AL)	1995	3	$3,069,395,018

Note: Adjustment to 1996 on basis of U.S. Department of Commerce Implicit Price Deflator for Construction.
Source: From Maher and Beven, 1997.

and Montserrat, the U.S. Virgin Islands of St. Croix and St. Thomas, and Puerto Rico. Before it reached the islands, sustained winds of 190 miles per hour were recorded, making Hugo a category 5 storm. It was downgraded to a category 4 prior to striking the islands. After it passed over the islands, it headed out over open water and toward the mainland United States (National Research Council 1994:2).

Hugo struck just north of Charleston, South Carolina, before midnight on September 21. Sustained surface winds were estimated at 121 miles per hour. After 6 hours, Hugo reached Charlotte, North Carolina, with sustained tropical-force winds (54 miles per hour) and hurricane-strength gusts (87 miles per hour), causing major damage over 200 miles inland (National Research Council 1994:7). It should be noted that the National Hurricane Center issued a hurricane warning that extended from Fernadina Beach, Florida, to Cape Lookout, North Carolina (National Research Council 1994). This basically affected the entire southeastern coast of the United States.

It was estimated that between 4000 to 5000 historic buildings in South Carolina were damaged by Hugo. Rains following the passage of the hurricane caused additional severe water damage to buildings and their contents, which were already weakened by the wind and storm surge. As an example, the Poe and West Ashley branches of the Charleston County Library system lost approximately 20,000 books (National Research Council 1994).

B. Case 2: Hurricane Andrew, "The Bigger One"

It was not the actual hurricane but the response of government in the aftermath of Andrew that attracted so much attention. This disaster, almost alone, brought about the major reform of FEMA in the mid-1990s. Andrew was a category 4 hurricane that came ashore in south Dade (now Miami-Dade) County during the night of August 24 to 25, 1992. It would go on to strike again in the Louisiana, Mississippi, and Alabama regions after crossing the Florida Peninsula into the Gulf of Mexico.

Wamsley (1994) provided excellent insight into the way the emergency management function ran into trouble following Hurricane Andrew:

> Things were unfolding in the aftermath of the hurricane in a rather predictable fashion for the emergency management policy subsystem. Initially there was some confidence at FEMA, because a disaster declaration had been secured, and the agency had dispatched officials to the State (Florida) Emergency Operations Center (EOC) and communications equipment to Dade County even before Andrew's landfall. For Dade County and the State Emergency Management Organization, there was initially a sense of relief because the storm had missed the population center of Miami and loss of life was small, because warning and evacuation had been relatively effective.
>
> Things rapidly came unraveled. Neither the county nor the state emergency management systems were prepared for the destruction of a Class IV (Category 4) hurricane. Emergency management personnel, police and fire departments, power companies, and others who normally would have been the mainstays of disaster response were victims of Andrew themselves. No one was able to mount an effective assessment of the damage or of medical and life support needs. Officials in the State EOC at Tallahassee kept pleading with local officials to tell them what they needed, and frustrated and equally frantic local officials kept saying they did not know what they needed, "Send Everything." To which agonized state officials could only reply, "We can't send everything." (p. 240)

Table 5 Direct Hits by Hurricanes on United States Mainland, 1900–1996

Category 5	2
Category 4	15
Category 3	47
Category 2	37
Category 1	57
Total	158
Major Hurricanes (Categories 3, 4, and 5)	64

Source: From Maher and Beven, 1997.

What is the potential for a hurricane to strike somewhere along the eastern United States? Table 5 depicts the numbers of hurricanes that have hit the mainland United States and their respective categorical strengths.

This averages approximately 1.6 hurricanes per year making landfall somewhere along the U.S. Gulf or Atlantic coasts, or about five hurricanes every 3 years. For major hurricanes (category 3, 4, or 5), there are approximately two cyclones making landfall every 3 years (Maher and Beven 1997). This does not necessarily indicate a regular pattern of hurricanes or landfall locations. One year, there may be no activity directed at the U.S. mainland, while in 1996 North Carolina was struck by Hurricanes Fran (category 3) and Bertha (category 2) (Maher and Beven 1997). Hurricane Frederic struck the same Mississippi and Alabama region in September 1979 that Hurricane Camille had hit 10 years earlier. Frederic, as a category 3 (Maher and Beven 1997), had much less force than Camille's category 5. As a result of Hurricane Frederic, two-thirds of the structures in Jackson County, Mississippi, were damaged, as well as $500 million in damage to public property (Drabek et al. 1981). Yet both hurricanes made the ''top ten'' list in dollar damage. The ''scare'' of Hurricane Camille certainly helped save lives when Hurricane Frederic struck, but this is no indication that past activity can help predict the frequency or location of future storms.

There are some certainties: There will be hurricanes and some will make landfall on the United States mainland. Some of those (about 40%) will be considered major hurricanes. If you are a bureaucrat serving in local government along the Gulf and Atlantic coasts, it is only a matter of time until you will either be affected by a hurricane or directly impacted. According to a state-by-state comparison written by FEMA (1990), the state of Florida can expect to be affected in the following geographic pattern over a 50-year period: southeast and northwest Florida, over 30 times; central and north central Florida, 15 to 30 times; and northeast Florida, about 5 to 15 times. Hurricanes Hugo and Andrew resulted in losses in the tens of billions of dollars, but if their tracks had been only slightly different, damages could have approached $100 billion (Goss 1997). Therefore, hurricanes are indeed among the grand-scale disasters of emergency management.

V. THE TRIAD MODEL: A BUREAUCRAT'S ANALYSIS

A. An Overview

The three parts of the triad model are the operational, administrative, and sociological legs. Each should be a consideration by the bureaucrat/practitioner in formulating response

Figure 1 The Triad Model

to emergency management issues. ''Operational'' is generally an external function and concerns the actual service provided by the government entity. ''Administrative'' is generally internal and concerns how the government entity is run. Both are rational in their approach. The third leg, ''Sociological,'' may be either internal, external, or both in its functions. It concerns all of the other areas overlooked by operational and administrative needs. Those may include environment, politics, situation, relationships, structure, etc. It would also include the people who receive the service as well as those who provide it, because a disaster will impact both.

Why a ''triad model'' and how does it relate to emergency management, especially on the grand scale? As a public servant in the police service field for 20 years, this writer was trained and has progressed in the ''rational/professional'' notion. To a rationalist bureaucrat/practitioner, the operational response is primary to all others. In recent years, while developing methods to measure police service and emergency management, the administrative aspects of government itself became coequal to operations. Responding to Charleston for Hugo and Miami-Dade County for Andrew presented problems that were not immediately addressable by the traditional methods. The ''wild card'' in those grand-scale disasters, which should have been obvious during years in police service, was people. After all, people are what government service is all about, and people are not always going to react in ways that can be described as rational. Mix in a grand-scale disaster and rational behavior is out the window. This consideration paved the way for the sociological view as a key link between the other two legs.

For example, while we may consider him a rationalist, the author of the first recognized public administration textbook, Leonard D. White, offered this view, ''The objective of public administration is the most efficient utilization of the resources at the disposal of the employees. These resources include not only current appropriations and material equipment in the form of public buildings, machinery, highways, and canals, *but also the human resources bound up in the hundreds of thousands of men and women who work for the state*'' (italics added) (White 1926:58). This quote points well beyond what government does by making accountability of resources an important issue.

This example is strengthened by Waugh (1994):

> State and local government emergency management efforts are difficult, at best, because of the: (1) very diversity of hazards and disasters; (2) low salience of emergency management as an issue; (3) historic resistance to regulation and planning; (4) lack of

> strong political and administrative constituencies (advocates); (5) uncertain risk from hazards; (6) technical complexity of some regulatory, planning, and response efforts; (7) jurisdictional confusion; (8) economic and political milieu inhospitable to expanding governmental activities; and (9) questionable capacities of state and local government officials to design, implement, finance, maintain, and operate effective emergency management systems. (p. 257)

Further development of stepping beyond rationalism appears later in this section.

A triad model was adopted for two reasons. Aside from the comfortable fit each leg has in this model, there appears to be precedence for "threes" in the literature. Arnell (1990) offers a visual analysis of a three-legged stool for disaster/recovery planning. Although the thrust of his analysis was the protection of electronic data processing resources in the private sector, he does raise some excellent points. The legs of the stool are (1) off-site storage, (2) users, and a (3) backup site. The seat of the stool, supported by those legs, is an effective disaster recovery plan.

The concept of "C3" or "C-cubed" has been adapted from the military to civil police agencies. Command, communication, and control are viewed as a basis for functioning in an emergency or battlefield environment. The Federal Bureau of Investigation's Incident Command System was developed using this three-pronged concept for civil police agencies (Conner 1997). Another similar concept developed by FEMA as a critical emergency management function is direction, control, and coordination (DCC) (Goss 1997). Aside from the four-phase model of emergency management and within the DCC concept are additional sets of "threes." Emergency response management is subdivided into three phases: preresponse, transresponse (during), and postresponse. Analysis of the situation is centered on responding quickly, appropriately, and effectively (Goss 1997). Note the use of the term *control*, which should be considered strongly rational. The first two legs of the triad model are indeed rational in their orientation.

B. First Leg: Operational

Generally, operational issues are external to the agency: What is (are) the service(s) the agency is providing and how? The operational leg is part of the "rational/professional" notion. In an emergency management environment, the scope of service normally provided by a government may shift to other responsibilities. Bureaucrats should consider how to assign disaster services to branches of government or individuals within the organization. Operational issues may be covered in each of the four phases of the emergency management model. Mitigation issues may be part of an agency's regular operations mission (i.e., public works trimming trees before hurricane season to reduce loose branches and potential missiles in high winds).

Each branch of government should have its operational assignments committed from the preparedness stages. Plans should be periodically tested, evaluated, and amended as necessary. Relationships between agencies should be established and defined and regular contacts made to assure respective responsibilities. When a disaster strikes, whether with forewarning like a hurricane or with sudden impact like an earthquake, government must move into an operations mode to restore order and service, within both the response and recovery modes. Personnel, equipment, facilities, supplies, and other resources available (both within and outside the jurisdiction) should be identified for use in operations (FEMA 1996a). During a grand-scale disaster such as a hurricane, there will be a merging of varying disciplines, organizations, and agencies not accustomed to working together on a day-to-day basis (FEMA 1996a), not just at the local level but at all levels (local/state/federal) of government.

C. Second Leg: Administrative

The administrative leg, for this chapter, is generally considered to be an internal function of the government. How does the government agency or branch "engine" run? Items such as budgets and finance, personnel staffing, insurance, schedules, information systems, and the like are not considered the "service" an agency provides but are vital to that agency. Government is given an annual budget to provide a service. While the actual service falls under the operational leg of this model, it is how government goes about making this service happen that becomes the administrative leg. Without concerted attention to the administrative aspects, the operational ones would fail. The administrative leg can also be considered rational in its orientation.

Administrative functions also run the gamut of the four-phase emergency management model. Administrative procedures to support emergency measures before, during, and after disaster events and to preserve vital records (Goss 1997) are absolutely necessary to carry on during the response and recovery phases. Any hope for reimbursement from the state or federal level will rely entirely on the ability of the local government to keep thorough records of its activities and related costs. After a disaster has struck, especially one on a grand scale, is not the time to decide how emergency purchasing procedures will work. Methods have to be established for estimating damages and repairs to both public and private property. How will the government get access to its employees and make sure that they report to work where they are needed?

Arnell (1990) proposed establishing a "risk model," which estimates the consequences to the operation if it is "out of business" for 1, 2, 3, or more days and beyond. While he was addressing the information systems of businesses, the same question can be asked of government. How long will it take government to start up manually and then eventually get back to providing normal services? (Arnell 1990). For example, one of the important points noted in relation to Hurricane Hugo was how businesses were using the old-fashioned "cash drawer" approach because of to prolonged power failures. Items were either added by hand on paper or on a battery-/solar-charged calculator with handwritten receipts. Local government, in a grand-scale disaster, may have to resort to similar administrative methods.

D. Critique of the "Rational/Professional" Notion

Rationality, although the modus operandi of government, should not be considered the only way to do things. Our culture of modernity has as one of its chief constituents technical rationality. Technical rationality is the convergence of the scientific-analytical mind set and technological progress (Adams 1992:366). The critique of rationalism and the personal experiences of this writer in emergency management were combined with the work of Thomas Drabek to look beyond the "rational/professional" notion. The way people react, as opposed to the way they are expected to behave, leaves a giant gap in the rationalist approach. In his (1990) *Emergency Management: Strategies for Maintaining Organizational Integrity*, Drabek champions a social scientist's approach. He studied the nature of human response to large or grand-scale disasters. This is often overlooked by the mechanics of government. He notes that people and their government tend to be indifferent to disaster, with the exception of agency directors who might seek to increase the capability of emergency management. This is probably true of most government functions. Not only does the average person not display much interest in the inner workings of government, but various agencies within government display the same attitude. Public works does not care what is going on at the fire department, code enforcement does not care about personnel (unless they have a vacancy that needs to be filled). People are generally not concerned about a service, for self-interested reasons, until they require that service. People take for granted the most basic of services, such as water, sewer, and garbage, which are often provided by government. After a disaster, even those basic provisions may be unavailable.

Drabek notes the following elements may have an impact on response: size of jurisdiction, its wealth, stability, the type (city, county, region, or a combination), structure of the government (council, strong mayor, commission, etc.), and the strength of relationships at that level. American government is decentralized by design, but organizations must work together when an activity such as dealing with a disaster spans all the resources of a single agency or jurisdiction. The national four-phase model of emergency management, FEMA's model Emergency Operations Plan (EOP), the Capability Assessment Report (CAR), or many of the other approaches reviewed overlook Drabek's important points.

E. Third Leg: Sociological

This leg bridges the gap left open by the operational and administrative legs. It includes both the internal and external issues overlooked by rationalism: political issues, previous experiences of bureaucrats, personal and professional relationships, formal and informal policy networks, environment, morale, communications, employees and those served by the agency, behavior patterns, situations, economics demographics, culture, weather climate, complexity or intensity of the emergency, and a host of other intangibles. The items that should be considered for inclusion in this leg can be numerous and are only limited to the resources of the bureaucrat.

As an example, Vila (1996) studied the issue of how police officers perform under conditions of fatigue. He notes that, "the effects of fatigue on human behavior are well known. Excess fatigue causes sleep loss, circadian disruption, and other factors that tend to decrease alertness, impair performance, and health and safety . . ." (p. 51) These effects were observed among patrol officers in a typical urban setting. These will be the same conditions for all bureaucrats in a disaster setting, not just for emergency service workers.

The previous experiences of bureaucrats should not be excluded. Experience is cumulative, and there is strong likelihood that others have probably been through a similar situation in the past. The mistakes made in the past can be avoided by drawing upon the experiences of others. This was one of the key lessons learned by this writer in Hugo and Andrew. When Hurricane Andrew was taking aim at south Florida in 1992, a member of the Charleston County sheriff's office, who experienced Hurricane Hugo at first hand in 1989, was brought in as a member of the Broward Sheriff's Office Emergency Operations Center (EOC). His advice, grounded in practical experience, was invaluable. For example, one of the experiential items offered from Charleston centered on water. When hurricane conditions are anticipated, drinking water should be stockpiled for use during the recovery. Then there will be plenty of water on hand, and if not, it will be supplied from outside sources. However, there will not be any water pressure until this service is restored (which may be days or weeks). After the first flush, there will no longer be toilets. If you are a bureaucrat who must be on duty for days or weeks without a break, with your government agency in the response/recovery phases, you will consider this a very serious inconvenience.

Places where infrastructure, sense of community, and socioeconomic conditions are already weak before a disaster strikes may have amplified problems in the response and recovery phases. There are populations who depend on government service on a regular basis, or even a day-to-day basis, for basic subsistence. What happens when a segment of society that has little or nothing to begin with has that taken away by a disaster? Mitigation and planning, the proactive phases, may not be sufficient to address this demographic issue. Those who are already dependent on government service will not suddenly become self-sufficient after a disaster. This is where the sociological leg would complement the rationalistic legs of operational and administrative needs.

The Disaster Research Center (DRC), located at the University of Delaware, engages in various types of sociological and social science research involving individuals, communities, organizational preparations, responses, and recovery in natural and technological disaster situations (Disaster Research Center 1998). Previous research has examined legal aspects of governmental responses in disasters, the emergence and operation of rumor control centers, the functioning of relief and welfare groups in stress situation, the sociocultural aspects of mass fatality situations, community response to acute chemical hazards, mass media reporting of disasters, problems involved in mass evacuation and sheltering, and the organizational and public response to the 1985 Mexico City earthquake (Disaster Research Center 1998). The Disaster Research Center, among many others in the academy, should be considered sources of information for the third leg of the triad. The sociological aspect is the key link between operational and administrative issues in emergency management.

VI. CONCLUSION: IMPLICATIONS FOR PUBLIC POLICY

In the last decade, the United States has experienced numerous different types of disasters having great magnitude, affecting large numbers of our citizens, and incurring great financial losses. Disasters are also requiring more sophisticated and timely response than ever before in our history (Goss 1997). Emergency management in the United States is now a multi-billion-dollar-a-year endeavor (Goss 1997). Over the last decade, the overall cost of disaster to the United States has grown significantly. From 1989 to 1993, the annual losses from disasters were $3.3 billion. From 1994 to 1997, the average annual losses have increased to $13 billion. On the federal side alone, disasters have cost over $20 billion over the same period (FEMA 1998a).

Statistics show that emergencies are occurring with greater frequency and intensity—a trend that is expected to continue. Crichlow (1997) identifies this rise as being due to increasing population density, especially near coastal areas for hurricanes in the East and South and earthquakes in the West. Poor land-use policy and aging infrastructure are also factors. In his analysis, all cities and counties experience major emergencies, many of them more than once per decade. Local officials are expected to manage emergencies with the same professionalism and competence that typifies their routine performance (Crichlow 1997). Hurricanes Hugo, Andrew, and Iniki and the Loma Prieta earthquake are still having profound impacts on the national emergency management system (Waugh 1994).

The purpose of the triad model is to help bureaucrats think about additional ways to consider policy making for emergency management. Difficulties abound in the attempt to sort out the various forces that shape local policy. Planning requires executives to translate broad policies into more operational and specific objectives. Planning also requires monitoring the organizational environment to identify emerging problems (Moore and Stephens 1991:22). While this appeared in the police literature, it has applications across the public sector. It encompasses both the rational and sociological approaches. If all of the above policy implications could be considered, proactive and reactive contingencies could be drafted. FEMA is an excellent resource for written guidelines, such as their comprehensive all-hazard Emergency Operations Plan (EOP) (FEMA 1996a). Proactive contingencies would include the mitigation and preparedness phases of the emergency management model, and reactive contingencies would include the response and recovery after a disaster.

In a grand-scale disaster, each level of government would be tasked to respond. The agencies of the federal government, through FEMA, are the major players for relief on the grand scale. The state is the intervening level. County and local government bear the brunt of the problem, because they are first to respond and actually provide service. County and local government officials should also know that they have to do a good job, because it will be hard to live down the negative feelings of poor performance after the emergency has passed and recovery is completed. You the bureaucrat, grounded in the "rational/professional" notion, may not have resources enough on hand to deal with emergency management on the grand scale. Complicate your grand scale response further: the President of the United States and his entourage will be touring your disaster area. How will your resources respond to the additional strain?

The triad model may be adapted to address those contingencies. The triad model may offer another method for measuring how government can shape policy to respond to disasters. Not all disasters are on the grand scale. The triad model will still hold additional keys for your consideration and policy. Hurricane Chanelle, our hypothetical category 4 storm, is out there. Your county or city government may be in its path. You may be the recipient of a disaster on a grand scale. Are your plans sufficient? Are you ready?

REFERENCES

Arnell, A. (1990). *Handbook of Effective Disaster Recovery Planning*. New York: McGraw-Hill.

Broward Sheriff's Office (1996). *Unusual Occurrence Plan*. Cross City, FL: Pride of Florida.

Burkhardt, J. (1997). Planning, private sector support are keys to preparation. *American City & County* 112, 27.

Cigler, B.A. (1990). Public administration and the paradox of professionalization. *Public Administration Review* 50, 637–653.

Conner, T.W. (1997). Incident command systems for law enforcement. *FBI Law Enforcement Bulletin* 66, 14–17.

Cooksey, M.B. (1997). Emergency preparedness: A BOP follow-up report. *Corrections Today* 59, 34–36.

Crichlow, D. (1997). "Taking a comprehensive approach to handling disasters. *American City & County*, 112, 50–60.

DeSantis, V.S. and Renner, T. (1994). The impact of political structures on public policies in American counties. *Public Administration Review* 54, 291–295.

Disaster Research Center (1998). *The Disaster Research Center*. <http://www.udel.edu/DRC>.

Dow, E. (1997). County's emergency plan is no accident. *American City & County* 112, 32.

Drabek, T.E., Tamminga, H.L., Killijanek, T.S., and Adams, C.R. (1981). *Managing Multi Organizational Responses: Emergent Search and Rescue Networks in Natural Disaster and Remote Area Settings*. Boulder, CO: University of Colorado, Institute of Behavioral Science.

Drabek, T.E. (1990). *Emergency Management: Strategies for Maintaining Organizational Integrity*. New York: Springer-Verlag.

Fayol, H. (1916). General principles of management. In J. Shafritz and J. Ott (eds.) *Classics of Organization Theory*, 3rd ed. 56–68). Belmont, CA: Wadsworth Publishing.

Federal Emergency Management Agency (FEMA) (1990). *Risks & Hazards: A State by State Guide*. Washington, DC: U.S. Government Printing Office.

Federal Emergency Management Agency (FEMA) (1996). *Hurricane Erin Situation Report #6*. <http://www.fema.gov/hu95/sitrepe6.html>.

Federal Emergency Management Agency (FEMA) (1996a). *Guide for All-Hazard Emergency Operations Planning*. Washington D.C.: U.S. Government Printing Office.

Federal Emergency Management Agency (FEMA) (1998). *Atlantic Tropical Storm Formation, 1885–1996*. <http://www.fema.gov/library/strmfrom.htm>.

Federal Emergency Management Agency (FEMA) (1998a). *Report on Costs and Benefits of Natural Hazard Mitigation*. <http://www.fema.gov/MIT/cb_toc.htm>

Gabris, G.T., and Golembiewski, R.T. (1997). The practical application of organization development to local governments. In J. Gargan (ed.), *Handbook of Local Government Administration*. 71–100. New York: Marcel Dekker.

Garnett, J.L. (1985). Organizing and reorganizing state and local government. In J. Rabin and D. Dodd (eds.), *State and local government administration*. 3–32. New York: Marcel Dekker.

Gianakis, G.A., & McCue, C.P. (1997). Local government capacity building through performance measurement. In J. Gargan (ed.), *Handbook of Local Government Administration*. 239–262. New York: Marcel Dekker.

Goss, K.C. Federal Emergency Management Agency (FEMA) (1997). *Capability Assessment for Readiness: A Report to the United States Senate Committee on Appropriations*. Washington, D.C.: U.S. Government Printing Office.

Gulick, L.H. (1937). Notes on the theory of organization. In J. Shafritz and J. Ott (eds.), *Classics of Organization Theory*, 3rd ed. 87–95. Belmont, CA: Wadsworth Publishing.

Joint Committee on Information Technology Resources, Florida Legislature (1993). *Contingency planning and disaster recovery in Florida state government*. Tallahassee, FL: The Committee.

Kanigel, R. (1997). Taylor-made. *Sciences* 37, 19–23.

Maher, B. and Beven, J. (1997). The deadliest, costliest, and most intense United States hurricanes of this century. *NOAA Technical Memorandum NWS TPC-1* (on-line). <http://www.nhc.noaa.gov/pastcost.html>.

Moore, M.H. and Stephens, D.W. (1991). Organization and management. In W.A. Geller (ed.), *Local Government Police Management*. 22–58. Washington, D.C.: International City/County Management Association.

National Research Council (1994). *Natural Disaster Studies: Hurricane Hugo*. Washington, D.C.: National Academy of Sciences Press.

Nelson, L.H. (1996). When disaster strikes. *State Legislatures* 22, 28–33.

Ostrom, V. (1974). *The Intellectual Crisis in American Public Administration*. Tuscaloosa, AL: University of Alabama Press.

Poister, T.H. and Strieb, G. (1997). Strategic management: A core responsibility of local government administrators. In J. Gargan (ed.), *Handbook of Local Government Administration*. 101–128. New York: Marcel Dekker.

Quade, E.S. (1982). *Analysis for Public Decisions*. New York: North Holland.

Reynolds, H.W., Jr. (1995). Educating public administrators about ethics. *Annals of the American academy of political & social science* 537, 122–138.
Shafritz, J.M. and Hyde, A.C. (1992). Early voices. In J. Shafritz and A. Hyde (eds.), *Classics of Public Administration*. 1–10. Belmont, CA: Wadsworth Publishing Company.
Syles, R.T. (1994). Ferment at FEMA: Reforming emergency management. *Public Administration Review* 56, 303–307.
Ventriss, C. (1991). Contemporary issues in American public administration education: The search for the educational focus. *Public Administration Review* 51, 4–14.
Vila, B. (1996). Tired cops: Probable connections between fatigue and the performance, health, and safety of patrol officers. *American Journal of Police* 15(2), 51–92.
Wamsley, G.L. (1996). Escalating in a quagmire: The changing dynamics of the emergency management policy subsystem. *Public Administration Review* 56, 235–244.
Waugh, W.L. (1994). Regionalizing emergency management: Counties as state and local government. *Public Administration Review* 54, 253–258.
Weber, M. (1946). Bureaucracy. In J. Shafritz and J. Ott (eds.) *Classics of Organization Theory*, 3rd ed. 81–86. Belmont, CA: Wadsworth Publishing.
White, L.D. (1926). Introduction to the study of public administration. In Shafritz, J.M., & Hyde, A.C. (Eds.). (1992). *Classics of Public Administration*, 3rd ed. Belmont, CA: Wadsworth Publishing.
Wolfe, M. (1994). Managers need to get involved in the emergency planning process. *Public Management* 76, 3.

29

Lessons Learned from Three Mile Island and Chernobyl Reactor Accidents

Frances E. Winslow Office of Emergency Services, City of San José, San José, California

I. INTRODUCTION

Recent federal programs to assist cities in developing a response to potential terrorist acts have covered three principal types of potential attacks: chemical, biological, and nuclear. While all three types of potential attacks pose unique problems for local government agencies, there are existing systems and paradigms for managing chemical and biological attacks. Most large cities have an emergency response plan for hazardous materials accidents. Chemical attacks by terrorists bear a resemblance to hazardous materials accidents, providing a basic response plan which can be modified to include terrorist-caused releases of highly toxic substances in public places. Likewise, most communities have emergency response plans for medical events. Beginning with the multiple casualty incident plan, and moving into disaster medical health plans, most metropolitan areas have a basic response system in place that can be modified to assist and treat the victims of a terrorist-caused health emergency like a biological attack.

Few local governments have had experience in coping with accidents related to the release of nuclear materials. Most metropolitan areas have few potential sources of catastrophic nuclear release. Medical sources are typically small and well contained. Sterilizers in industrial facilities and research reactors at university research centers are typically small, with fuel rods safely sealed or submerged in water. Most major military facilities with nuclear materials have been located in remote areas rather than the metropolitan areas that are being prepared for potential terrorist activities.

There are nuclear reactors used to generate power in some metropolitan areas. Their emergency plans may provide some information useful in preparing an emergency response to a nuclear terrorist act. Moreover, two nuclear power reactors—Three Mile Island in Pennsylvania and Chernobyl in The Ukraine—have had actual emergencies, whose lessons inform the emergency planning effort. They provide a good model for the post–event recovery issues that must be addressed in an effective plan.

The exact location of a nuclear event, and the composition of the nuclear material will, of course, effect the specific response plan. For example, the radionuclides may differ between a reactor accident and a terrorist release of nuclear material. This will influence both the immediate and long-term effects on the victims, and the degree of damage to the physical plant of the community. Second, the size of the deposition population may be significantly larger or smaller in size than that in the reactor event. However, the basic issues for emergency planning remain the same, regardless of whether the source of the radioactive material is a nuclear power plant reactor or a terrorist device.

The common issues among unexpected releases of nuclear material provide the framework for this chapter. These issues are first-responder protection, victim care, public information, community protection, and psychological impact.

II. FIRST-RESPONDER PROTECTION

For 50 years the model of nuclear release impact on a human population was the Japanese experience at the end of World War II (Sokolov 1998). The bombs dropped over Hiroshima and Nagasaki resulted in specific epidemiology among the survivors, notably radiation burns and leukemia. Longitudinal studies of the survivors of these events suggested that the Japanese results would be replicated in any future nuclear releases in populated areas. Dr. Viktor Sokolov suggests that actual data from Chernobyl contradicts this assumption. He notes that actual epidemiology of Chernobyl survivors suggests, rather, that reactor accidents produce different results in the victim population. The National Radiation and Epidemiological Registry of the Medical Radiological Research Center in Obninsk has developed findings that the principal long-term exposure for the Chernobyl victims was an internal exposure from food at low dose rates (Sokolov 1998:103), a different exposure pattern than experienced by the Japanese bomb blast victims. This lower dosage and ground level deposition makes it a better model for planning for WMD/nuclear events.

Dr. Michael H. Momeni has noted that the expected leukemia rates have not been observed among the Chernobyl survivors. In reactor accidents, radiation risks are principally from ''chronic irradiation due to inhalation of contaminated airborne radionuclides, ingestion of contaminated food and water, and external exposure to contaminated ground.'' (Momeni 1998:150) On the other hand, the damage experienced by bomb blast survivors from plume shine appears not to be a problem with reactor accident victims, and by extrapolation, would not be a likely consequence of a weapons of mass destruction (WMD)/nuclear event.

The results from these effects instead have included thyroid cancer and specific types of tumors in higher than expected proportions, with less than anticipated levels of leukemia. Also, gastrointestinal damage and skin lesions are more important epidemiological findings in these events than previously anticipated. However, ''no consistent attributable increase has been confirmed either in the rate of leukemia or in the incidence of any malignancies other than thyroid carcinomas'' (Crick 1998:2).

Therefore, community emergency response plans must consider the appropriate prophylactic response to potential health risks. Initially, protection of first responders from exposure to damaging nuclear emissions and dose measurement of the exposed population are critical to minimize the health effects on the first-responder population. Lessons learned from Chernobyl include the importance of the management of bone marrow damage through the administration of hemopoietic growth factors rather than bone marrow transplant to counteract radiation damage to the blood creation system of the body (Crick 1998:1). Administration of potassium iodide (KI) to the general population of first responders in the affected areas may not be as beneficial as originally thought. There are portions of the population that suffer adverse reactions to iodides, and the benefits of KI are limited to those portions of the population with iodine-deficient diets or those who receive it immediately after the event (Momeni 1998:150) However, the Polish experience suggests that a single protective dose of KI would have only moderate and treatable unwanted side effects in the general population and would significantly lower the thyroid burden of radioactive iodine 131 over time (Nauman 1998:202).

Based on the findings of the significance of first-responder exposures, the importance of respiratory protection was reinforced. Inhalation of radioactive material promotes adverse health effects in first responders. At present it appears that any supplied air system provides adequate respiratory protection during acute exposure during an emergency response to a reactor site.

Some research suggests that first responders receiving more than 50 REM are suffering from a new form of radiation induced illness. Headaches, general disability and a lower overall immune response form a syndrome that is being referred to as ''Chernobyl AIDS'' (Allen 1998). Psychosomatic responses, including a higher incidence of stress-related illnesses were also related by first responders after Chernobyl. This suggests the importance of early psychological intervention, including critical incident stress defusings for all first responders after each shift.

Overall the anticipated effect on first responders provided with reasonable shielding is minimal. Of the 800,000 who were ''registered as helping to alleviate the consequences of the accident, . . . 237 were initially admitted to the hospital. Acute radiation syndrome was diagnosed in 134 cases, of whom 28 died from radiation injuries, all within the first three months'' (Crick 1998:1). These findings suggest that proper training of emergency responders regarding the deployment and use of protective measures and protective equipment is the key to minimizing health effects for that population.

III. GENERAL POPULATION AND VICTIM CARE

The general population in the area of the Chernobyl accident did not experience a measurable increase in any specific health affects. ''No consistent attributable increase has been confirmed either in the rate of leukemia or in the incidence of any malignancies'' in the general population (Crick 1998:1). A small increase in the reported incidences of some nonspecific health effects may be due to the intense monitoring of the potentially affected population rather than any increase in actual health-related effects. Small illnesses that might never have been reported to medical authorities are now being picked up in the target populations due to the longitudinal study being conducted.

One segment of the population did clearly demonstrate health effects after Chernobyl. There was a ''highly significant increase in the incidence of thyroid cancer in the affected areas among . . . the children'' (Crick 1998:1). The increase was most marked among those who were born less than 6 months after the accident and those who were less than 5 years old at the time. The papillary thyroid cancers in children were aggressive, but traditional treatment, including removal of the thyroid, was successful in most cases (Crick 1998:1). The International Federation of Red Cross and Red Crescent Societies has a long-term project of health screening for the at-risk age group of children. The project also provides pure milk powder and micronutrition in schools and children's institutions (Revel 1998:56).

Decontamination of the affected area is also critical for the long-term health of the general population. At Chernobyl the radioactive materials were dumped into the ruins and a containment structure was built around them. It is estimated that 50,500 square kilometers were polluted by the accidental release of radionuclides (Kholosha 1998).

An area of 1000 kilometers radius was checked for radiological emissions. It was discovered that dose rates followed the terrain. Roadways in these areas were washed, and fallen leaves and agricultural debris were destroyed. These actions lowered the radiation exposure by 30% (Kholosha 1998). Exposed foodstuffs, especially milk, were eliminated. Grazing lands and animal food were monitored, and soil modifiers were used to mitigate the radiation effects. Newly produced milk was ''filtered'' (sic) to remove radiation (Kholosha).

Outside of the Ukraine there were also significant areas of radiation deposition. For example, hot spots were found as far away as the mountain areas of Norway. Humans there were exposed through external radiation from deposited radionuclides, inhalation of radionuclides from the air, and ingestion of radionuclides through food. Initially, the principal exposure in areas remote from the accident was from these external sources. However, after the first few months, the principal route of exposure was ingestion of contaminated foodstuffs (Harbitz 1998:24).

Sheep and reindeer were affected, principally through grazing. Internal doses among the human population of those areas remained high because of the contamination of the food chain. The population ingested high levels of radioactive cesium through the consumption of reindeer meat, freshwater fish, and milk. (Harbitz 1998:23).

The government of Norway established intervention levels for contamination of the food supply. For example, ''about 35% of all lambs were contaminated at levels above the intervention levels at time of slaughter.'' Animals were treated to mitigate the affects of cesium ingestion from contaminated pasturage. These measures included the addition of Prussian Blue, a cesium binder, in salt lick, boli, and mixed in concentrate, and special feeding of lambs and sheep. For the 10 years following the accident, over ½ million lambs and sheep were included in the special feeding program at a cost of over $23 million. Thus, protection of the food stock is a major economic burden for the government in affected areas (Harbitz 1998:24).

Populations living more remotely, and with greater dependence on the natural resources of their areas, need special consideration. Many populations rely on hunting and fishing for their livelihoods. An example is the Laplanders, who rely on reindeer for most of their protein. In addition, the poor of many countries supplement their diets with wild game and fish. A careful review of the sources of foodstuffs must be undertaken. Since prohibiting hunting is unlikely to be successful among dependent populations, monitoring stations must be established where hunters and fishermen can have their game evaluated for safety (Drottz-Sjoberg 1998:72).

The population of Belarus experienced a 53% contamination rate. The Chernobyl plume moved unexpectedly, and the population received their initial dose of radiation through cloud shine and inhalation. It was 8 days after the accident before the first protective actions were taken for the general population. The principal measure was to end the consumption of contaminated foodstuffs, which had yielded high doses of iodine 131 (Buglova 1998:204).

IV. PUBLIC INFORMATION

Chernobyl generally yields negative lessons for public information. Little information was given to the affected populations in the first crucial hours. The government chose to surround the event with secrecy. It was 24 hours after the onset of the event when people were told that there had been an accident at the reactor. The only information given to them was to be ready to evacuate within 2 hours (Kholosha 1998). Therefore, individuals at most immediate risk were unable to take even minimal protective actions against immediate exposure. One Norwegian leader has characterized the silence as causing ''unnecessary harm to affected individuals, and a long, heartbreaking, and politically turbulent post-accidental situation'' (Drottz-Sjoberg 1998:71).

Early and honest information must be an integral part of the emergency response and recovery plan for weapons of mass destruction/nuclear, biological, chemical (WMD/NBC) events, including self-help recommendations. Social and cultural norms of the affected populations must be considered. For example, city dwellers can more easily conform to food regulation than can rural populations who live more directly off the land. Commercially prepared products can be evaluated by case lot and safe food rapidly restored to circulation in cities and towns. On the other hand, the population of animals available to hunters and fishermen can be evaluated only after the game have been caught. Unless evaluation stations are established in these remote areas, exposure through ingestion of contaminated game will continue for long periods of time, raising the health effects even in distant populations.

Honest public information may lead to some inappropriate actions. For example, during the Three Mile Island event, the governor of Pennsylvania broadcast a suggestion that pregnant women and children under 2 years of age within the immediate area of the reactor should leave as a precaution. The result was that people all over the state left for distant refuges in the homes of relatives or hotels (Behler 1998). This behavior reflects a further societal effect: those who can afford to leave and have the means do leave. Those left behind are the poor, less educated, and marginalized populations who need greater social and financial support to evacuate (Drottz-Sjoberg 1998:72).

The Chernobyl experience points out that short-term public information will come from the media. Emergency public information officers must be prepared to address detailed technical questions from the press. It is essential to have an expert with credibility and a ability to speak in simple terms who can provide briefings for media representatives.

In the long run, the best public information should be delivered one on one. Teachers, doctors, counselors, and health workers need to be given continuous factual information about ongoing environmental affects so they can calm community fears. Written materials for the general public must be cast in very simple terms. Numbers must be interpreted in easy-to-understand impact statements. Radiological measurements mean little to the average resident. Rather than quoting dosages and effects, public information pamphlets should list such facts as symptoms, lengths of exposure, and specific areas where the population might be affected.

Public education is essential in guiding self-protective action of the general population. When information was released that said people were being given Kl as protection against radiation affects, some parents administered tincture of iodine to their children, even though the label clearly states ''poison.'' Any public information about medical care must detail not only the steps to take but also any obvious steps to avoid (Nauman 1998:200).

Special populations must be considered the in development of long-term public information materials. The Canadian government developed a coloring book for children to help them understand nuclear and chemical accidents and their potential effects on themselves and their communities (Becker 1998).

Appropriate public information can be a critical link in community recovery. There must be no conflicting information. The representatives delivering information to the media must have high credibility with the public. All public information must be delivered in a culturally sensitive way, including appropriate language, reading level, and respect for local traditions. Information on where to get help should be featured prominently. Specific and practical information should be repeated frequently as public service announcements in electronic media and as advertisements in the press.

Civic leaders need to make an honest estimate of the population's view of the government after the accident. The general population may blame government agencies for the accident, believing that the accident was related to their failure to do their jobs. In that case, other spokespersons with more credibility should be selected. A generalized hostile view of government may impact the ability of members of the public to ''hear'' the message about radiation and its effects (Flynn 1998:67).

V. COMMUNITY PROTECTION

Community protection can take several forms. The most obvious is direct site remediation. In Chernobyl the debris was placed in the ruins of the reactor and encased in a protective structure referred to as the ''shelter object'' (Rudenko 1998). This may not prove to be a useful strategy. The result is a permanent reminder of the event and a monument to the contamination that remains in the area.

In addition, there is a concern that ground-water contamination may result from the way the reactor building was constructed and then damaged. Experts from the National Academy of Sciences of the Ukraine have reviewed the threat to the region's ground water, noting that 200 tons of fuel remain in the ruined rector with coolant water that is still reactive. Studies show that the local river is the drain where reactor water and ground water intermingle. Strontium, cesium, and plutonium are all found in the area's ground water, along with some tritium and americium. This suggests that internal shelter water is leeching out (Rudenko 1998). The long-term health effect could be devastating to consumers of the ground water, especially if it is used to irrigate field crops or for community drinking water supplies through wells.

The Chernobyl experience points to the importance of developing a community protective plan that includes meaningful remediation. A sealed environment that does not include a ground barrier is not fully effective in protecting the community from long-term effects of radiation. The experience in Slovakia with contamination from an early nuclear reactor provides some useful guidelines. Remediation must include the acknowledgment of the facts of current health physics. The environment should be cleaned up to background levels if possible but to below levels of concern as a minimum. Some combination of remediation steps will be needed to achieve this goal. Fencing off highly contaminated areas to limit population exposure is essential. Affected soil should be removed and remediated through the addition of binders or modifiers (Slavik 1998).

Evacuation was also used as a protective measure, both in Belarus and in the Chemobyl area. Evacuation of pregnant women and young children was very effective in lessening their exposure to iodine 131 (Buglova 1998:204). However, since radiation effects are long term in a community, meaningful evacuation will have to continue over weeks or months while community cleanup proceeds. Populations must be properly prepared to bring along appropriate personal items, including records and personal papers, when they leave their homes. The government must also be prepared to provide immediate emergency shelter as well as long-term relocation for many of the evacuated. In the Chemobyl area, people were evacuated the day after the event, but they were not offered shelter, which created new social and psychological problems for the victims (Kholosha 1998).

In the United States, the Environmental Protection Agency has established recommended intervention levels for various actions. Exposures of 5 REM should lead to sheltering in place. Exposures of 50 REM require a 1-week evacuation to allow for remediation and dissipation. Levels over 100 REM require long-term relocation of the population at risk (Meinhold 1998:212).

The decision to evacuation brings with it some inherently negative results. Experts must monitor the community for the time when REM levels drop and return is safe. What standards can be used when contamination will be long term? Meinhold suggests that emergency response behavior should be based on the criteria, ''do more good than harm'' (Meinhold 1998:210), but this is a subjective criterion that could be difficult to apply. The principal public policy problem is to determine ''How safe is safe?'' Standards established by the International Council on Radiation Protection and the National Council on Radiation Protection may provide some protection in political and legal arenas, but in the mind of the general public, will the community ever be really safe?

VI. PSYCHOLOGICAL IMPACTS

At the 10th anniversary of the Chernobyl accident, experts concluded that ''social and psychological effects were among the most prominent and lasting consequences'' of the nuclear reactor accident (Drottz-Sjoberg 1998:73). People fear radiation, partly because they do not know much about it and partly because of what they do know about it. The bombing of two Japanese cities at the end of World War II remains the image of nuclear exposure for most people. One important part of emergency planning for response and recovery to nuclear WMD events is the acknowledgement that the public's reaction to a nuclear event will not be logical or knowledgeable.

Most people have had some exposure to a hazardous chemical in their home (bleach, paint thinner, ammonia, pesticides), so they understand that although dangerous, such chemicals can be handled safely. Most people have been around infectious and contagious disease (chickenpox, measles, annual flu outbreaks), and they believe that medical science can protect or cure them. Therefore, managing chemical or biological WMD events offers the planner a public with some useful basic information. Analogies can be used to describe the event and the protective actions needed.

Planners should assume that the public response to a WMD/nuclear event will be ill informed and panic prone. Experts agree that any action on the part of a public agency will result in anxiety among the affected population (Meinhold 1998:210). Planners must seriously consider what countermeasure policies can really work to ameliorate panic and psychosocial effects in the general public (Allen 1998:60).

The first cause of psychological stress is that most health effects take at least 5 years to appear (Reveal 1998:57). In addition, the stress of the experience itself induces psychological illness. These illnesses can take the form of psychosomatic illness and the ''induction of anxiety, depression and helplessness. . . . An apprehension about risks of unknown events and lack of control, fed by misinformation and poor comprehension of reality, increases anxiety and its consequences'' (Momeni 1998:151). The protective actions taken by public agencies, notably evacuations, actually had economic and psychological costs that must be taken into account in planning.

First responders will have anxiety about their own health and the risks they are assuming in responding to the event. Training on nuclear scenarios in advance of an event is a helpful mitigation tool. In addition, provision of appropriate protective equipment and enforcement of safe use of that equipment will aid in lessening responder stress. Finally, critical incident stress debriefings and long term counseling for first responders should be built into any plan.

Victims will experience psychological effects from several sources. First, they will not understand the event and its implications well. They will be afraid for themselves and their children, both their short- and longer-term health risks. They will also fear the loss of their homes and communities and the economic upheaval that accompanies such events. There will also be fear and blame in a nuclear WMD event, with scapegoating common. All of these behaviors enhance psychological stress. This stress may manifest itself as illness, or may exacerbate physical illness.

The emergency response and recovery plan needs to include a psychological/mental health component. Resources available within the community and from other sources need to be preidentified. Potential counselors need to receive pre-event training on WMD/NBC awareness, and a briefing on potential responses. They must be prepared to evacuate with the effected population, and offer their services in the shelters. Defusings and debriefings for community groups begin the process of psychological care. Long-term counseling will be needed for those who are permanently displaced, those who are bereaved through the event, and those who become ill or have a close relative who becomes ill. The counsellors may become a critical source of the one-on-one public information discussed earlier.

The community at large will also be disrupted and psychologically affected. Even those too far away to be affected may believe that they and their families are at risk. The Three Mile Island experience in Pennsylvania showed that unaffected people self-evacuated to distant points because of fear (Drottz-Sjoberg 1998:73). Psychological counseling and aggressive public information campaigns must be directed at the unaffected portions of the community as well as the victims. Active intervention in the management and remediation of the WMD/NBC event is also critical to the recovery of the general community. The perceived failure of the government to act in a timely fashion in the Three Mile Island event resulted in high anxiety among the unaffected general public (Drottz-Sjoberg, 1998:73).

Terrorist events using nuclear devices are likely to generate low exposure levels for relatively short periods of time. It is critical that the emergency response be an appropriate reaction to the actual threat. Terrorists are anxious for their actions to be as disruptive as possible. Therefore, it is incumbent on the public officials to critically evaluate the actual threat to the population and draw the lines for evacuation and medical evaluation as narrowly as possible. Guidelines like the International Council on Radiation Protection Publication 63, *Principles for Intervention for Protection of the Public in a Radiological Emergency* can provide guidance for incident commanders and public officials. Such guidelines document what is prudent while protecting the public officials from overreacting in response to political pressure.

VII. CONCLUSION

Nuclear reactor accidents in the Ukraine and Pennsylvania demonstrate the results of too little government action and delayed government action. Public officials planning for the response to, and recovery from, WMD/nuclear events can benefit from the lessons of these two events. Illness and injury is most likely to be localized and generally limited to those in immediate proximity to the device. Most injuries can be ameliorated with rapid medical intervention. Medical impacts on the wider community should be minimal and amenable to relatively simple medical procedures. Communitywide impacts will be effected mostly by environmental factors: the wind speed and direction, whether the release is contained in a building or in the outdoors, whether ground water is contaminated, whether the event occurs in a metropolitan area with little agriculture, or in an area with animal agriculture or hunting/fishing resources. The socioeconomic factors in the community may make the response and cleanup easy because people trust the government and understand the information they are given. On the other hand, the situation may be made worse through low educational level, lack of English literacy, or monolingual, non-English language barriers; or an overall distrust of government.

As with any emergency, scenario-based advance planning will make a response more effective and efficient. Some of the lessons learned from Chernobyl and Three Mile Island can aid the planner in the quest for a workable and effective plan.

REFERENCES

Allen, Peter T. (1998). Modelling social psychological factors after an accident. Presented at the International Radiological Post–Emergency Response Issues Conference, Washington, D.C., September 9.

Becker, Dr. Steven M. (1998). Constructing more effective post–emergency responses: The human services component. Presented at the International Radiological Post-Emergency Response Issues Conference, Washington, D.C., September 9.

Behler, G.T. Jr. (1998). *The Nuclear Accident at Three Mile Island: Its Effects on a Local Community*. Historical and comparative disaster series, No. 7. Newark, DE: University of Delaware, Disaster Research Center.

Buglova, E. and Kenigsberg, J. (1998). Emergency response after the Chernobyl accident in Belarus: Lessons learned. In *International Radiological Post-Emergency Response Issues Conference Meeting Proceedings*. Washington, D.C.: EPA.

Crick, Malcolm J. (1998). EC/IAEA/WHO 1996 Conference one decade after Chernobyl: Implications for post-emergency response. Paper presented at the International Radiological Post–Emergency Response Issues Conference, Washington, D.C., September 9.

Drottz-Sjoberg, B.-M. (1998). Public reactions following the Chernobyl accident: Implications for emergency procedures. In *International Radiological Post-Emergency Response Issues Conference Meeting Proceedings*. Washington, D.C.: EPA.

Flynn, Brian W. (1998). Emergency events involving radiation exposure: issues impacting mental health sequelae. In *International Radiological Post-Emergency Response Issues Conference Meeting Proceedings*. Washington, D.C.: EPA.

Harbitz, Ol. (1998). Consequences of the Chernobyl accident and emergency preparedness in Norway. In *International Radiological Post-Emergency Response Issues Conference Meeting Proceedings*. Washington, D.C.: EPA.

Kholosha, Volodymyr I. (1998). Managing the immediate and long term response to the Chernobyl accident—Problems and perspectives. Presented at the International Radiological Post-Emergency Response Issues Conference, Washington, D.C., September 9.

Meinhold, Charles B. (1998) Philosophical challenges to the establishment of reasonable clean-up levels. In *International Radiological Post-Emergency Response Issues Conference Meeting Proceedings*. Washington, D.C.: EPA.

Momeni, Michael H. (1998) A discussion of public health issues from a severe nuclear teactor accident. In *International Radiological Post-Emergency Response Issues Conference Meeting Proceedings*. Washington, D.C.: EPA.

Nauman, Janusz A. (1998) Potassium iodine prophylaxis in case of nuclear accident; Polish experience. In *International Radiological Post-Emergency Response Issues Conference Meeting Proceedings*. Washington, D.C.: EPA.

Revel, Dr. Jean-Pierre. (1998). Red Cross programme responding to humanitarian needs in nuclear disaster. In *International Radiological Post-Emergency Response Issues Conference Meeting Proceedings*. Washington, D.C.: EPA.

Rudenko, Dr. Yuriy F. (1998). Radio-hydrogeochemical monitoring of area adjacent to the ''Shelter'' object. Presented at the International Radiological Post-Emergency Response Issues Conference, Washington, D.C., September 9.

Slavik, Dr. Ondrej. (1998). Clean-up criteria and technologies for a Cs-contaminated site recovery. Presented at the International Radiological Post-Emergency Response Issues Conference, Washington, D.C., September 9.

Sokolov, V.A., Khoptynskaya, S.K., and Ivanov, V.K. (1998). Five years' experience in publishing the bulletin ''Radiation and Risk.'' In *International Radiological Post-Emergency Response Issues Conference Meeting Proceedings*. Washington, D.C.: EPA.

30

The 1989 Rail Disaster at Clapham in South London

Francis R. Terry Interdisciplinary Institute of Management, London School of Economics and Politics, London, England

I. SAFETY-CRITICAL INDUSTRIES

Passenger transport industries, by their nature, are potentially dangerous to users as well as to the employees. Movement at speed, through the air or on the surface carries with it the perpetual risk, however small, of a collision or impact that is harmful or threatening to the lives of those concerned. Yet the demand for travel has never been greater (Department of Transport 1993; Kinnock 1997), and the standards of safety expected are consistently rising (UK Health and Safety Commission 1993). The boundary between risks that individuals are presumed to be voluntarily incurring by embarking on a journey and the risks that it is the responsibility of the transport operator to minimize or eliminate is continuously shifting in favour of the passenger. In the eighteenth century, the traveler by ship or stagecoach placed his life in the hands of the pilot or coachman and could only pray for safe deliverance; today, an ever-extending panoply of regulation and legal rights is aimed at providing reassurance to travellers.

Modes of transport differ greatly, of course, in the levels of risk which are characteristic of them: travel by motorcycle carries far higher risks than travel by rail or air. There is also considerable variance in the degree to which levels of risk are tolerated by members of society. Most of us have long ago accepted the trade-off between the convenience of the automobile and its relative lack of safety, in statistical terms, compared to other modes. That does not diminish, however, the constant pressure from consumer bodies and regulators to contain risks and protect transport users. The campaign to increase safety may rest from time to time, but with each new disaster it takes another push forward.

Passenger transport industries are thus essentially different from many other manufacturing or service industries. Where the object of a particular industry is the creation of consumer durables, for example, concern for safety is met by effective research and development, by supervision of the production processes, and by regulatory control imposed from without. In the case of the passenger railroad, however, participation by members of the public is a necessary element of what the production process is seeking to achieve. Consequently, public expectations of safety demand completely different standards and practices from other industries where safety is a largely internal matter for management and workers, overseen by external regulators. I describe industries like the passenger railroad as being ''safety-critical,'' meaning that if the standards of performance by management, staff *and customers* are not consistently maintained above certain levels, injury or death will result.

While there is a well-known literature on the causes and consequences of industrial accidents, much of this is essentially plant-focused. It deals with relationships between management and workers in the context of manufacturing organizations and it seeks broad explanations in terms of the psychology and sociology of work in society (Gouldner 1954; Nichols 1975). In this chapter, an attempt is made to explore how accidents occur that do not have any immediate physical consequences for members of the work force themselves and which workers, as a result, may have less direct (or at any rate different) incentives to avoid. How should safety-critical industries seek to avoid accidents and what happens when they fail?

II. BACKGROUND TO THE CLAPHAM DISASTER

The long-term trend of safety on Britain's railroads had been steadily improving during the 30 years up to 1987 (Department of Transport 1995). Prior to that, two very serious accidents had occurred in 1952 and 1957, at Harrow and Lewisham (both in the London suburbs), involving antiquated rolling stock and human error (Rolt 1966). Major changes in signaling and working practices had followed. Then, on December 12, 1988, at the height of the morning peak hour, a disastrous collision occurred close to one of the world's busiest railroad junctions, at Clapham in south London. Thirty-five people died and nearly 500 were injured, 69 of them seriously. The Clapham crash has been selected for discussion in this chapter because it illustrates a series of lessons about how crises occur in safety-critical industries as a result of flaws in organizational and individual behavior, often far removed from the immediate event.

The causes of the Clapham accident were, on the face of it, clear enough but the British secretary of state, Paul Channon, MP, decided to set up a special court of inquiry under an eminent lawyer, Anthony Hidden, QC. The appointment of a special court was an unusual step, because railroad accidents are normally investigated by the UK Railway Inspectorate. The inspectorate has been in existence since the passing of the Regulation of Railways Act 1871 and had previously handled investigations equally serious or involving greater loss of life. The style of the inspectorate, traditionally, had been to examine the facts of an accident, hear testimony of those concerned, identify the cause, and attribute responsibility. It often made recommendations for changes in equipment and working practices, which railroads were not necessarily obliged to follow, though in the end they usually did. Sometimes, reluctance on the part of railroads led to new legislation designed to prevent a recurrence of a particular type of accident.

The scope and tone of the Hidden inquiry was different in a number of respects. Although it ranged over many of the issues that a Railway Inspectorate inquiry would have done (and indeed had the cooperation of the inspectorate in its work) it also examined the deeper institutional and behavioural factors connected with what proved to be a crisis in railroad safety management. To understand this crisis, we need first to look at the circumstances of the Clapham accident.

III. THE CIRCUMSTANCES OF THE ACCIDENT

There are four rail tracks approaching Clapham Junction from the direction of Wimbledon, on the southern edge of London. They run in a cutting, on a curving alignment, with trains passing at intervals of less than 2 minutes in the peak periods. The signaling equipment is designed to ensure that these intervals can be maintained with complete safety. A train, for example, that is stationary in the platform at Clapham Junction station is automatically protected by a red signal light some distance behind it and by an audible warning system sounded inside the driving cab of any other train that might inadvertently try to pass such a signal.

On the morning of Monday December 12, 1988, just after 8:00 a.m., three trains were running toward the cutting in accordance with their normal timetables. Two passenger trains, packed with commuters, were heading into London one behind the other; a third train was running empty in the opposite direction on an adjacent line. The first of these trains, driven by driver (engineer) H, received an unexpected and very abnormal warning when the signal closest to Clapham Junction station suddenly changed from green to red at the moment he was about to pass it. He had thus unwillingly become involved in an incident known in railroad parlance as SPAD, or Signal Passed At Danger. He reacted in accordance with the *British Railway Rule Book*, section C, which says that: "If the train inadvertently passes a signal at Danger, the Driver must stop immediately. He must not then proceed until authorised. . . ."

He applied his brakes immediately, bringing the train to a stand beside the next signal post, from where he was able to speak by telephone about the irregularity to the signals controller. He had stopped his train confident in the knowledge that the automatic signaling system would protect his own train in the rear by detecting its presence on the track and showing a red aspect to the following train. The engineer of the following train, having passed a succession of clear signals, entered the cutting on the approach to Clapham Junction and, rounding the curve, saw immediately ahead of him the rear of H's train. It was on the same track, stationary, and within a distance in which he could not possibly stop. Despite full emergency braking, this second train collided heavily with H's train before forcing it out to the off-side, where it struck the third train running out from London in the opposite direction. A fourth train, also approaching Clapham from the south, managed to stop only 20 yards from the wreck. An appalling accident had occurred.

The telephone calls of people nearby brought a response from the emergency services, which the inquiry inspector commended for its speed and efficiency, though there was a difference of view subsequently about whether the fire brigade were correct in assuming overall command of the incident, rather than the police (Flin 1996). The first fire engine was on the scene within 5 minutes of the accident, just as local police were arriving. The first ambulance came 4 minutes later. An intensive rescue operation then began, to locate and evacuate those who were injured, trapped or shocked as well as those who were unscathed, and to remove the fatalities. The rescue work was hindered by the steep walls of the cutting, and it was many hours before some semblance of normality was restored.

IV. TERMS OF THE INQUIRY

In investigating what had gone wrong, Mr Hidden focused on three questions (Hidden 1989). First, how had the accident happened? His conclusion was, simply stated, that the signaling system designed to be totally safe had in fact failed. How had it failed? The answer to this second question was that during technical alterations to the signaling system, a wire should have been removed. In error, it was not. Instead, the wire continued to feed current into a circuit; this had the effect of preventing the signal to the rear of H's train from showing red and thereby protecting it from a collision.

The third question was the most interesting from the point of view of our wider understanding, namely: How had the situation been allowed to happen? To find the answer, we need to consider the following factors as they apply in a safety-critical context:

The organization and planning of maintenance work among the signal engineering personnel
The practice of supervision
Management, communications, and information

V. ORGANIZATION AND PLANNING

Over the weekends before the accident, a program of major renovation and improvements to the signaling system had been under way to replace signaling installed in the late 1930s. In the Clapham area, some of this work was carried out by a senior technician, Mr. M. During a Sunday morning 2 weeks before the accident, M had correctly installed some new wiring, but he had left an old wire still connected at the fuse end; at its other end, he did disconnect it, but left it close to and in a position where it was in imminent danger of making contact with its old terminal. He should, of course, have disconnected both ends, and in addition cut the wire back so that it could never make a false contact. The conclusion of the inquiry was that M had been interrupted in the course of his work, and although he had intended to complete the task properly, he had subsequently omitted to do so. Further work nearby, 2 weeks later, had the effect of nudging the redundant wiring back into contact with the terminal, leading directly to the signal indications that caused the accident.

M had worked for British Railways for 16 years, including work on large resignaling schemes. He was held in high regard by his colleagues and superiors, believed in his own professional competence, and was partly instrumental in translating the intentions of the railroad design office into electrical wiring layouts that were entirely satisfactory from a conceptual point of view. He felt fit and ready for work on the Sunday morning before the accident and did not feel under pressure in discharging a series of straightforward tasks. Nevertheless, M had been in the habit of voluntarily working 7 days per week in order to maximize his income through overtime payments. Although M was not prone to lapses of concentration, the inquiry found that constant work without any refreshing break had probably blunted M's attention to detail at a crucial moment.

The situation was part of a wider organizational problem. Plans for the resignaling scheme had been drawn up 2 years previously, when staffing levels were higher. The reduction in staff by 1988 meant that weekend work had to be carried out by volunteers who were prepared to put in extra hours. They came from various grades and levels of experience, and no attempt was made by management to relate the size and composition of the work force to a work program that had been decided somewhat arbitrarily 2 years before and not reviewed since. During Mondays to Fridays, signaling staff worked in regular teams and knew the abilities of their colleagues; at the weekend, no teams existed.

As a result bonds of trust, as well as the mutual understanding of colleagues' competences and limitations, were not present. Work became slower and less efficient.

For working at weekends, staff were paid premium rates. A man such as M could double his salary by continuous voluntary weekend work. In the 13 weeks prior to the accident, 28% of the work force had worked 7 days in every week and another 34% had worked 13 days out of every 14 (Hidden 1989). The pay system, therefore, gave perverse incentives in a safety-critical context. It is clear (with hindsight) that such sustained periods of work were not good for morale, for enthusiasm for the task, nor for clearness of thought and sharpness of action.

VI. THE PRACTICE OF SUPERVISION

Good practice demanded that on such a job as M was engaged, an independent check—known as a wire count—should take place. The wire count should first have been made by M himself at the conclusion of the job and again by his supervisor or the engineer responsible for testing and commissioning the modified signals installation. M, however, had never been taught the importance of a wire count, while his supervisor, Mr. B, had spent his time out on the tracks, leading a gang doing manual work. B had worked long and hard over the weekends before the accident, often carrying out tasks alongside other members of his gang; but he was acting like a technician rather than a supervisor and consequently had neglected crucial aspects of his duties.

It appears then, that although B was energetic and well intentioned, his effort was pointed in the wrong direction. As a result of the limited numbers available to work on the tracks and his good opinion generally of M's work, B had never even entered the relay room where M had been working, let alone checked out his technical work. B's style of leadership may have helped to motivate the track gang, but it had distorted his view of his own role and his priorities. He had had no instructions as to the importance of wire counts during the progress of the resignaling project and had never known one to be carried out prior to testing of a modified installation.

There had in fact been a departmental instruction entitled *Testing New and Altered Signalling*, drawn up some months previously, which should have been circulated to all staff down to supervisor level, including B. One of its internal testing requirements stated: "Carry out a wire count on all free-wired safety relays and terminations. . . ."

B, like a number of other supervisors, had not received a copy of this instruction. That did not of course exonerate him from carrying out the quality check, which, as a supervisor, he should have made; but it removed another line of defense against fatal or injurious accidents.

Similar deficiencies affected the work of the testing and commissioning engineer, Mr. J. He had reluctantly been moved to his present post after his existing job was abolished. He did not like his new job and tackled it with low motivation; he had received no induction training and little advice from his predecessor. Although he had seen the new departmental instruction (*Testing New and Altered Signalling*), he believed it to be a consultation draft and was not aware that it was in force. Had he studied and implemented that document, he would have realized that a wire count (together with other tests) was mandatory. Similar misapprehensions and ignorance affected J's two colleagues, who might have drawn his attention to the departmental instruction but who had not read it or at any rate not understood its significance.

This omission was all the more remarkable because there had been a series of ''wrong side'' failures of signaling equipment in other parts of the railroad system over the preceding 3 years, which had arisen from similar causes. Fortunately no injury or loss of life had resulted. The internal inquiries undertaken by the railroad had recognized that a revision of testing procedures was urgent, and this had led to the decision to issue the new departmental instruction. There was also a recognition of the importance of staff training. In practice, however, these good intentions did not translate into effective action.

VII. MANAGEMENT, COMMUNICATION, AND INFORMATION

In a safety-critical context, management must set up lines of communication that are reliable and robust. It must not only issue instructions but also ensure that information actually reaches staff; for their part, staff must be taught how to interpret information received and how to put it into effect. These three aspects—clear definition of instructions, effective communication, and comprehensive training—enable management to ensure that the work force performs as intended.

The contrast with the actual situation leading up to the Clapham accident is striking. Toward the end of 1982, the need for instructions on testing procedures for new and altered signaling was recognized; in July 1984, the issue of a possible interim instruction was considered at a management team conference but not proceeded with. A year later, it was agreed that provisional copies of the draft instruction should be issued on an advisory basis to staff carrying out testing, and following a number of ''wrong side'' failures, the instruction was given official authority. It was recorded by the management team that the ''. . . need for a full testing procedural document was more urgent than ever, but the resource difficulty is recognised.'' It was not until May 1987 that the full document was actually issued. Over the same period, not one single training course was carried out, despite the need identified by the internal inquiries into ''wrong side'' failures.

The impression gained is that while registering the importance of safety-related documents, management failed to give them the necessary priority or adequate resources. There was no monitoring of progress, the distribution of copies was haphazard, and their importance was not understood by the work force. Supplementary checklists to enable the instructions to be carried out were never produced. Yet management continued in the false belief that their commands were being implemented, at least in spirit.

There was a second important area in which management was defective, and that was the planning and control of the whole resignaling project. As previously explained, the schedule of works had been drawn up 2 years before works in the Clapham area were actually undertaken. In the meantime, there had been staff reductions, including the loss of technicians in particular categories of skills. This was a result of expansion in the electronic communications industry more widely, with a number of potential employers able to offer higher rates of pay and more sociable working hours in competition to the railroad. The program for carrying out resignaling works was very tight, requiring continuous weekend working, and no individual manager wanted to be the first to admit that targets could not be met.

If one looks at the major aspects of a resignaling scheme, they break down into:

Control of finances
Control of design work

Control of installation work by railroad employees
Control of work carried out by external contractors

The correct model would have been to appoint a project manager to co-ordinate the four aspects through an overall plan of works and to take the strategic decisions. Such a person would have ensured that deadlines were realistic and progress was regularly reviewed. He could also have considered the competing claims of the drawing office which was under pressure to produce modified drawings and the requirements of the installation staff to have accurate specifications of work to be done. In reality, responsibility was diffused and divided at the start of the scheme and was complicated further by a succession of reorganisations which took place through the 1980s on British Railways.

VIII. TRUST, HABIT, AND CONFIDENCE

Why did such obvious organizational flaws and failures of management persist in the British railroad industry? The explanations developed in the remainder of this chapter are partly at the corporate level and partly at the interpersonal level. They draw on the work of industrial sociologists such as Nichols (1975), Gouldner (1954), and others. At the corporate level, British Rail was subject to strong financial pressures from government, which had imposed tight ceilings on investment and tough performance targets (Harman et al. 1995). Although these pressures made the planning of resignaling schemes difficult, they do not in themselves explain the failure to review programs regularly and ensure that they could still be achieved with reduced numbers of staff.

On the other hand, the emphasis given by government to cutting public subsidy for railroads had led senior management to raise commercial objectives much higher in their list of priorities during the 1980s (Green 1993). This switch in emphasis represents a sharp contrast with the situation in many European railroads, where public service and the protection of employment tend to be valued more highly than commercial objectives. The switch had status implications for the British railroad work force, in that engineers and technicians no longer enjoyed the traditional widespread respect they were accustomed to. In consequence, the culture of the signaling department became fatalistic and demotivated. The perpetual demands from top management and from the business side of the organization to hasten forward with the Clapham area resignaling had blunted the technicians' attention to detail and led to "cutting corners," as we have seen, in both work and supervision.

This malaise was compounded by a collective belief that the signaling department was actually behaving in a safety-conscious way, even when it was not. The series of incidents (SPADs) in which signals were passed at danger was being investigated internally and efforts being made to prevent them. Unfortunately, the same attention was not being paid to "wrong side" failures, which were almost as prevalent and potentially just as dangerous. The focus of safety efforts was thus misplaced—a familiar factor in understanding the causes of disaster in safety-critical industries.

At the working level, the ability of technicians and supervisors to perform at their best and most vigilant was undercut by the corporate pay policy, which overrewarded weekend work and discouraged staff from taking necessary rest days. It also led to the creation of ad hoc teams at weekends who had not worked together before and did not know each other's professional competences at first hand. This drawback was concealed by the strong sense of mutual trust amongst technicians from similar backgrounds and with similar experience behind them. It led to an assumption that ''people who know what they are doing should be left alone to get on with the job,'' thus undermining the importance of ensuring that designs were properly worked out and new installations thoroughly checked.

Faith in experienced colleagues was no safeguard against procedures that were incorrect. As we have seen, M had never been properly trained in the first place, he had not read official instructions, and his mistakes had never been pointed out to him. In the signaling department there was instead a powerful sense of trust between fellow professionals and a pride in long-established ways of working. Many signaling technicians identified themselves as experts in signaling first and foremost and only secondarily as workers in a safety-critical industry. Supervision and strict application of instructions from railroad management were forms of social action that tended to cut across the technicians' belief in themselves and in each others' professional competence; consequently instructions from above were given less weight than they should have been.

Pressure on resources and failures at management level had also prevented regular training for technicians in safety-relevant areas. The management's intentions were clear enough: they recognized the importance of training, but meetings and proposals were not transformed into action on the ground. By using the rhetoric of ''absolute safety'' and ''zero accidents,'' management had generated a completely false sense of self-confidence in current methods of working. In parallel, frequent reorganizations had sought to produce more rational and efficient structures, but within these, roles and responsibilities were left poorly defined. One consequence of this was that individual managers and supervisors, unsure of their positions and lacking in morale, were reluctant to speak out when they thought that project time scales were no longer realistic and training was inadequate.

In particular, it was crucial for the stages of design, installation and testing to be separately carried out. M, as an installer, had adjusted and interpreted the overall design of the wiring scheme as he had gone along; this in itself was liable to cause errors and uncertainties for those who came after him. But his work had not been rigorously examined by B or tested in the prescribed way by J either. As the testing and commissioning engineer, J had trusted M's professional competence and abbreviated the process of checking out the signaling modifications. Thus a multilevel system of design, installation, supervision, and testing had degenerated into a series of individual errors, producing ultimate disaster.

IX. CONCLUSION

In safety-critical organizations there is an almost impossible balance to be struck between slavish adherence to the rule book and reliance on individual initiative and judgment. An overbureaucratized organization is prey to inefficiency and stagnation; on the other hand, too much reliance on individuals' own choice of design, method, and procedure introduces unacceptable risks. It is clear from the Clapham accident that under the burden of poor management, repeated reorganization, and professional complacency, the balance had shifted too far in favor of the individual. The aftermath of the Hidden inquiry was a radical overhaul of virtually every aspect of railroad safety in Britain. New technology, new working procedures, fresh training, and strong leadership from the top were all introduced to prevent a recurrence of Clapham.

Even so, anxieties about safety have not disappeared. The privatization of British Rail has involved a separation of responsibility for the infrastructure of track, signaling, and power supplies from the provision of rolling stock and the operation of train services. Yet railroads are integral systems: the relationship of train to track and signals to train are but two obvious examples of how the system needs to be treated as a whole. The implications of privatisation for safety management became the subject of major report by the UK Health & Safety Executive (1993), and it is by no means clear that all the issues have been satisfactorily resolved in the view of the regulators. One thing is certain however: as a result of the Clapham accident, our understanding of the wider ramifications of running a safe railroad—beyond the performance of the front-line technicians—has been greatly improved. But it has been at a terrible cost.

REFERENCES

Department of Transport (1988). *Investigation into the King's Cross Underground Fire* (the Fennell Inquiry). London: HMSO.

Department of Transport (1989). *Investigation into the Clapham Junction Railway Accident* (the Hidden Inquiry). London: HMSO.

Department of Transport (1993). *National Travel Survey 1989/91*. London: HMSO.

Department of Transport (1995). *Transport Statistics Great Britain 1995*. London: HMSO.

Flin, R. (1996). *Sitting in the Hot Seat*. Chichester, U.K.: John Wiley & Sons.

Gouldner, A.W. (1954). *Patterns of Industrial Bureaucracy*. Glencoe, IL: The Free Press.

Green, C. (1993). *Sweating Assets*. London: British Railways Board.

Harman, R., G. Sanderson, G. Ferguson, and B. Atkin (1995). *Investing in Britain's Railways*. Reading, U.K.: Atkin Research & Development Ltd.

(UK) Health and Safety Commission (1993). *Ensuring Safety on Britain's Railways*. London: Department of Transport.

Kinnock, N. (1997). "A fresh look at transport policy." *Public Money & Management* 17(3), 4–7.

Nichols, T. (1975). "The sociology of accidents." In Esland, Salaman, and Speakman (eds.), *People and Work*. Edinburgh, U.K.: Holmes McDougall.

Rolt, L.T.C. (1966). *Red for Danger*, 2nd ed. London: Pan Books.

31

Emergency Management in Korea

Mourning over Tragic Deaths

Pan Suk Kim Department of Public Administration, Yonsei University, Wonju, Kangwon-do, South Korea

Jae Eun Lee Department of Public Administration, Chungbuk National University, Cheongju, Chungbuk, South Korea

I. INTRODUCTION

Life is filled with the uncertainty and the complexity of turbulent environments. Most nations in the world have been affected by numerous crises, such as earthquakes, hurricanes, floods, chemical spills, collapsing buildings, and so on. Society would pay a heavy price during times of crisis if there was not an organization prepared to deal with such an event. This is why more people demand that the government, which is responsible for protecting the life and safety of citizens, prepare to respond to crisis proactively and effectively.

Traditionally, crisis management in Korea has been related to natural disasters, such as damage from storms or floods, rather than man-made disasters. The Korean government, like other developing countries, has accelerated its economic development at a much faster rate than is the norm in the process of societal evolution and adaptation. Up until recently, man-made disasters had not been fully realized nor prepared for by the government in Korea. As a matter of fact, over the past few years, a series of major man-made disasters have stricken Korea. During these times of crisis, the government has shown itself to be lacking a system to deal effectively and efficiently with a crisis situation. Consequently, the question of how to deal with the matter of the man-made disaster management is a timely subject in Korean society.

II. CONCEPTUAL FRAMEWORKS

A. Definition of Crisis

Throughout human history, crisis has been an inherent part of human existence. All human beings experience crisis, uncertainty, and environmental threats. Even though a society might initially appear to be safe, the potential for crisis does exist. It is necessary to recognize that crisis is a subjective concept: what is considered as a crisis for one party may not be a crisis for another, as crises are part of human life. It is, therefore, no surprise to discover that various definitions of *crisis* exist.

Crisis, with its varying definitions also has varying effects, not only for different cultures, situations, times but also for researchers. As such, it is possible for researchers to have a subjective view of crisis.[1] For example, while natural disasters may be viewed as acts of God within determinism or creationism, they may be seen as objects to be overcome by society within evolutionism or volunteerism (Wenger 1978:20).

According to the Webster's dictionary, crisis is defined as ''a decisive moment or a turning point, the point in time when it is decided whether an affair or course of action shall proceed, be modified, or terminate'' (*Webster's* 1966:537–538). By other accounts, it is defined as an event or a series of events which occur in a system (Jackson 1976: 210–211).

But the above definitions are so general and broad that they are difficult to apply to crisis management in policy studies. It is possible to investigate the specific meanings of crisis in terms of an organization's survival in external and internal environments. D'Aveni and MacMillan (1990:635) define a crisis as any event or condition that threatens the survival of the organization. Charles F. Hermann (1963:63–65) has suggested a working definition, formulated along three dimensions. An organizational crisis (1) threatens high-priority values of the organization, (2) presents a restricted amount of time in which a response can be made, and (3) is unexpected or unanticipated by the organization.[2]

Finally, observing the consequences and effects of crisis, Barton (1993:2–3) has argued that a crisis is a major, unpredictable event that has potentially negative results. So, the event and its aftermath may significantly damage an organization and its employees, products, services, financial condition, and reputation.

The operative definition of *crisis* in this discussion will be an event and/or a situation which endangers the established system, the health, life, and property of its members. Assuming that the forecast, preparedness, and response to crisis depend on management efforts, effective crisis management must be rooted in prevention, a refusal to allow past crises to recur, and a commitment to be prepared for any and every eventuality.

In short, when crisis prevention and response are the policy objectives of crisis management, it is then possible to prepare for crisis. This is based on the definition that crisis is an event and/or a situation which threatens the existence of a system, including the state, social community, government, organization, natural environment, an ecosystem, and so on. Until now, little distinction has been made between the concepts of crisis and a number of related terms such as: disaster, hazard, danger, calamity, catastrophe, emergency, risk, threat, incident, accident, etc. It is possible, of course, for a researcher to make an operational definition, or redefinition for his work. In this paper, the term ''crisis'' is treated as being separated from some of these other concepts based on the intensity and scope of influence. The terms *disaster, hazard, accident*, etc., refer to only one event and/or situation, while *crisis* includes the concepts of natural disasters, man-made/technological disasters, and social disasters.

B. Types of Crisis

Crisis may be classified systematically. That is, crisis may effect political, economic-technological, social, and/or natural systems. First, crises which occur in political systems may be: war, armed strife, coup d'etat, terror (Rapoport 1992:1070), subversive activities, hijacking (Waugh and Sweeney 1988:131). Second, crises occurring in economic-techno-

Table 1 Various Types of Crises in Systems

System	Crisis (Disaster)
Political	War, armed strife, coup d'etat, terror, subversive activities, hijacking
Economic-technological	Architectural collapses, flammable chemical explosions, radioactive or toxic chemical spills, and progressive environmental pollution.
Social	Rioting, disease, violent labor strike
Natural	Flood, typhoon, earthquake, drought, cold-weather damage, storm

logical systems may be hazardous waste spills (Zimmerman 1985:30), radioactive contamination, oil spills, destruction of ozone layer, etc. The form and frequency of man-made disasters depends heavily on the level of technological development. Not only do disastrous events increase in frequency with increased technological sophistication, they also intensify or worsen (Fowlkes and Miller 1988:23). Third, crises such as the emergence of contagious disease or an unidentified epidemic, and violent protest or rioting, are socially derived. Finally, there are many natural disasters or crises—such as floods, typhoons, earthquakes, droughts, cold-weather damage, and storms. The stereotypical crisis is a natural disaster that originates from the unbridled play of the forces of nature (Fowlkes and Miller 1988:23).

Traditionally, crisis and emergency management has emphasized natural hazards rather than man-made technological hazards (Zimmerman 1985:29). While natural disasters (floods, earthquakes, droughts, etc.) are caused by natural phenomena and affect the physical and financial health of human beings, man-made or technological disasters caused by human error also have a baneful influence upon human beings. Technology and its consequences have emerged as a major hazard for modern society (Kasperson and Pijawka 1985:7).

Natural disasters have always been considered a grave occurrence, but they were part of nature's order, something that had to be accepted as part of life (Clary 1985:20). Nonnatural disasters, however, are a modern occurrence whose effects are similarly grave. In this paper the nonnatural disasters are divided into two categories, man-made technological disaster/crisis and social disaster/crisis, for appropriate crisis management.[3] The two areas, man-made technological disasters and social crisis, differ substantially in terms of their nature and a management style of emergency management. This paper expands on the importance of emergency management for social disasters.[4]

C. The Importance of Crisis Management

Every year, numerous natural, man-made, and social disasters occur in the world. But, before the mid-1980s, there was little research on proper policy and administration in the area of crisis and emergency management (Mushkatel and Weschler 1985:45). Since that time, in the United States, significant progress has been made in terms of emergency management to deal with various disasters. Before the 1990s, most public officials in Korea were not fully familiar with processes for recovering heavy losses in the event of natural disasters. In those days, preventative methods for man-made disasters were not fully developed.

Supposing that the primary function of government—any government in any country—is to protect the lives and property of its citizens (Giuffrida 1985:2), crisis and emergency management need to be regarded as an important part of government's responsibilities to preserve and protect its people. Therefore, crisis and emergency management, which is the process of developing and implementing policies and programs to avoid and cope with the risks to people and property from natural and man-made hazards, has to be considered as a national policy objective, or an administrative process (Cigler 1988).[5]

Technological malfunction has emerged as a major source of hazard for modern society. With urban public services and facilities multiplying, man-made technological disasters in modern cities have a greater likelihood of occurring than in the past. Also, in modern society, property damage and injury caused by conflicts among various groups—ethnic, religious, or political—are on a larger scale than other disasters.[6]

D. The Climax of an Interdisciplinary Approach to Crisis Management

Because the scope, range, and extent of crisis/emergency management are very broad, it is impossible for students of a single discipline to manage disaster and crisis situations thoroughly. On the contrary, many professionals in diverse academic fields must intervene to manage a crisis. For example, Pauchant and Mitroff (1990:122–127) discovered that the Bhopal crisis, December 2, 1984, a leak of a highly toxic gas that originated in Union Carbide (India) Ltd. (UCIL), began as an ''incident'' at the unit level, quickly accelerated into an ''accident'' that then affected the total system, finally turning into a full-blown crisis.[7] According to reports, the issues relating to the Bhopal crisis are inordinately complex. They involve a web of financial, legal, medical, technical, managerial, political, communicational, and therapeutic factors. The qualified professions required to deal with all of these factors cover a range of disciplines including sociology, psychology, management science, engineering, political science, law, economics, anthropology, ethics, health science, religion, and theology.

Above all, as modern scientific technology's development is accelerated, more human knowledge is required to meet the demands of crisis management. With hundreds of corporate calamities and/or industrial crises in international and multinational businesses (Gladwin and Kumar 1987:23) being added to the list for crises, the need of interdisciplinary approaches becomes absolutely necessary.[8]

III. THE AREA OF CRISIS MANAGEMENT AS A POLICY OBJECT

Different types of crisis events, including natural and technological disasters, civil disturbances, terrorist actions, acute international conflicts, and nuclear threats are all serious threats to basic social, institutional and organizational interests and structures (Rosenthal et al. 1991:212). Thus, the time to deal with emergencies is before they happen (McLoughlin 1985:165). For that reason, it is necessary for us to examine the areas of crisis and emergency management as a policy object.

A. The Crisis Area As a Policy Object

Existing crisis management research, involving crisis and/or emergency management functions, has generally been lacking a discussion of the issues regarding crisis as a policy object, focusing instead on the governmental response to disasters. Without fully discussing the area of crisis as a policy object, governmental preparedness and/or response to various crises may be ineffectual.

While every person has the same propensity to abhor, and/or avoid the large or small crises—which may intimidate them and pose threats to their property, family, or organization — each person has his or her own peculiar response to a crisis. Kharbanda and Stallworthy (1989:86–87) have argued that, depending on their background and upbringing, people react differently even to the same factor. Accordingly, there is a very wide gap between the real risk and the perceived risk as far as the general public is concerned. Even though human beings experience the same crisis, perception and response modes differ within one's sociocultural contexts. The first step in the process of defining a situation as a crisis involves perceiving an event in the environment that triggers the crisis (Billings et al. 1980:302). This, therefore, allows one to consider crisis within a sociocultural category as well as a scientific technological category (Young Kim et al. 1995:952–953). The basic question is: What are the responsibilities for public management to deal with various accidents, events, and situations? For example, in Korea, more than 10,000 people die from traffic accidents each year. These accidents are seen as crisis involving a threat to personal life and happiness. Traffic accidents are not only the biggest cause of death for travelers but are also one of the major causes of death per se.[9] However, most traffic accidents are not considered crises in governmental crisis management policy.

Based on Wenger's thesis that there are two dimensions of crises, intensity and scope, figure 1 shows that crisis can be divided into six groups which are useful in formulating crisis management policy. Figure 1 shows three implications for a crisis management policy. First, the crisis must have high intensity for the social community. If the intensity of crisis is not perceived as high, public servants and community members will not need to respond seriously. Government responsibility for planning and preparing for the uncontrollable is necessary to prevent catastrophe; therefore, the intensity of crisis must be great. Second, although the crisis intensity may be perceived by

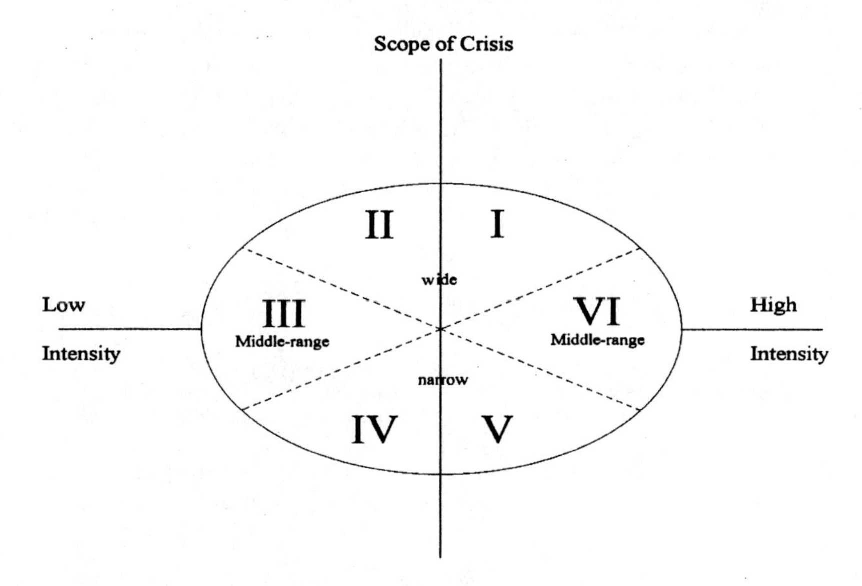

Figure 1 The areas of crisis as a policy object.

Table 2 Compositions of Crisis Area As a Policy Object

Composition Order	Scope and Intensity
Composition I	Wide scope + high intensity
Composition II	Wide scope + low intensity
Composition III	Middle-range scope + low intensity
Composition IV	Narrow scope + low intensity
Composition V	Narrow scope + high intensity
Composition VI	Middle-range scope + high intensity

some to be high, it must be noted that crises in a narrow scope it may not be a policy object of crisis management. A crisis of narrow scope may affect an individual, family, informal group, and organization, but the condition is not thought of as a crisis by those outside the scope of the crisis. These smaller groups, however, often do not possess adequate crisis management mechanisms (Wenger 1978:28). So, crises that occur in narrow scopes may be managed by private agents and established government institutions, such as insurance agencies, fire rescue officials, police, etc., not by crisis management organizations. Third, crises meriting a policy object for crisis management represent a crisis of relatively high intensity within middle-range or wide scopes, such as the community and society.[10]

Among the six groups of crisis scope and intensity, compositions I and VI in Table 2 illustrate the areas of crisis deserving of a crisis management policy object. The distinctions in areas and nature of crisis embodied in these six modes help to distinguish the differing roles that governmental agencies have assumed in crisis and emergency management. The type and extent of activity for any governmental agency depends in part upon the crisis areas that are defined in Table 2. The types of crises within compositions I and VI are shown in Table 3.

Within the category of crisis deserving a policy object, one must raise the question: What is the dividing line between high and low intensity? Or: How are we drawing a distinction between the two intensities? The answers to these questions originate from the ambiguities of the social perception of crisis. The essence of a disaster lies in its social, not physical, consequences; no physical agent or event has a social meaning outside of a social context (Wenger 1978:25–26). That is, only when an accident or event negatively

Table 3 Crisis As a Policy Object

Composition Order	Scope & Intensity	Cases of Crisis
Composition I	Wide and high	War, armed strife, coup d'etat, rioting, destruction of ozone layer, subversive activities, hijacking
Composition VI	Middle-range and high	Architectural collapse, gas explosions, terrorism, radioactive contamination, acid rain, hazardous waste spills, emergence of contagion or unidentified epidemic, floods, typhoons, droughts, earthquakes, cold weather damage, storms, violent protest

effects society may one regard it as a crisis. And then, when the existing governmental, traditional, and social institutions are not equal to the crisis condition, it may well be said that the intensity of an event is great. For example, unless the established organizations for emergency management within a community, such as fire rescue departments or police departments, manage the demands in a crisis situation, a crisis is defined as having a high intensity (Lim 1996:13). So, the existing social system for managing such events is a relative criterion for distinction between the high and low intensity of a crisis.

Given these studies, the ''Sampoong disaster'' in Korea can now be examined. The Sampoong disaster is classified as a composition VI event with middle-range scope and high intensity. This paper documents the crisis and emergency management system and the societal response to this major man-made disaster in Korea.

IV. EMERGENCY MANAGEMENT IN KOREA: MANAGING THE SAMPOONG DISASTER

The Sampoong disaster is significant for two reasons: first of all, it is considered the worst crisis in modern Korea. Second, it has been a turning point, changing the emergency management system in Korea. With this event as momentum, public attention to man-made disaster management has been growing significantly.[11]

What shocked the public is that the above disaster could easily have been avoided if proper maintenance and care was taken. The cause of the Sampoong collapse was reported as poor maintenance of the building, therefore making it a man-made disaster.

A. The Sampoong Building

The Sampoong building had two wings, with one housing the department store and the other sports and leisure facilities. The wing that collapsed was the one housing the department store. It was built by Sampoong Construction and Industry Co. and completed in November 1989. An addition to the building was completed in October 1994. The building housed 556 departments with 681 employees. It stood 27.6 meters high and sat on a 29,008-square-meter lot. The four underground floors consisted of a parking lot and an electricity control room. Three of the collapsed building's floors comprised the department stores and the upper two floors physical fitness facilities and restaurants. The department store was operated by Sampoong Construction Co., whose engineering ranks 858th among the nation's construction firms.

B. Warning Signs of Architectural Collapse

The warning signs that, if heeded, could have prevented the collapse of the Sampoong Department Store came as early as 15 days prior to the accident. At that time, a restaurateur on the fifth floor reported a fissure on the ceiling of the building to management. But management's response was lukewarm, and management took no action. Then, 5 days before, a housewife, who had entered the same restaurant to get something to eat after some routine weekend shopping, was showered with a water leak from the ceiling of the restaurant. Three days before the collapse, a report of a gas leak again went unheeded by the department store management.

On the very day of the collapse, June 29, the signs that should have set off alarm bells appeared before opening hours, in the restaurants on the fifth floor. Around 9:30 a.m., the floor of the restaurant cracked open slightly. An environmental technician reported the incident to the management. Top executives of the department store stopped by an hour later, mumbling something about seeking professional assessment. Between 11:00 and 12:00, neighboring restaurants were experiencing water leaks from ceilings and cracks in the floors. Only at this point did the management close off the fifth floor, while the other floors continued with business as usual. Sometime after 1:00 p.m., a breakdown of air conditioning and gas services as well as a power failure occurred throughout the department store. The management met around 3:00 p.m. for an emergency meeting without notifying the employees and shoppers of the situation. When things were at their worst, the executives of the department management left the building, consequently leaving many employees and shoppers still inside.

C. The Collapse

The Sampoong Department Store, one of the nation's biggest, in Sochodong, southern-Seoul, collapsed from the top down at about 5:55 p.m., on June 29, 1995, trapping hundreds of shoppers and store employees in the rubble. It took only 5 seconds for half of the huge five-story building to fall into the basement, becoming nothing more than a pile of rubble and a tomb for hundreds of shoppers and store employees. Ambulances and fire engines from across Seoul rushed to the scene, but rescue workers were overwhelmed by the number of casualties. The adjacent streets were clogged with rescue vehicles, large personnel cranes, and equipment trucks. Firefighters proceeded to hose down the debris to settle the rising dust and put out fires.

The evening rush hour traffic around the area hindered rescuers' efforts. Private cars and taxis were mobilized to transport the injured to nearby hospitals. Hospitals ran short of blood due to the large number of casualties. People who escaped the collapse were left in shock on the street.

Gas lines in the immediate area were shut off to prevent possible explosions. Luckily a safety supervisor at the department store found problems in the building structure on the morning of June 29, and closed the main gas valve, preventing an even greater disaster.

D. The Causes

So what really went wrong? First, unsound business practices were rampant in the Korean domestic construction industry. One is the extensive pyramid-style subcontracting system, which ultimately serves to put a squeeze on construction budgets and consequently run the risk of accidents. The construction of Sampoong was atypical in that the structure was built by the store's parent company. As then Justice Minister Woo-Mahn Ahn said, the disaster was thought to have been caused by shoddy construction and the motive of tight budgeting may still have been the most important factor causing the disaster.

Second, further encouraging the faulty construction was a virtual absence of construction management and supervision by a third party, despite construction legislation requiring a watchdog for all construction projects, public or private.

The third and possibly the most frustrating reason for the disaster was the lack of appropriate governmental supervision of safety. After a couple of gas explosions and bridge collapses, governmental officials were prompted to broaden their safety check to public works such as subways, gas pipelines, and large-scale government construction projects. However, privately built structures were left out. This had left private owners or management companies responsible for the safety of their own buildings. But this system, based on self-interest, revealed its all too fatal flaws in the Sampoong case.

Finally, a thorough examination of the department store structure could have brought about reinforcement measures. The department store failed to fulfill its responsibility of supervising its own premises. The extreme case is that during an emergency meeting at 4:00 p.m. Thursday, just 2 hours before the collapse of one wing of the two-wing shopping mall, management decided to go ahead with store business, spurning a suggestion to evacuate the shoppers and employees and launch immediate repairs.

Consequently, the weak concrete columns and steel beams of the seemingly sound building failed to support the weight of the structure. And this tragic disaster, as was the case with other disasters, was attributed to the lack of conscience, business morality, and unscrupulousness in the construction industry.

E. Governmental Responses to Disaster

At 5:56 p.m., 1 minute after the building collapsed, witnesses and fire officers of the nearby fire department reported the collapse of Sampoong Department Store to the consolidated alarm office of the fire station in Seoul. By virtue of the Emergency Communications System shown in Figure 2, thousands of police and military troops equipped with excava-

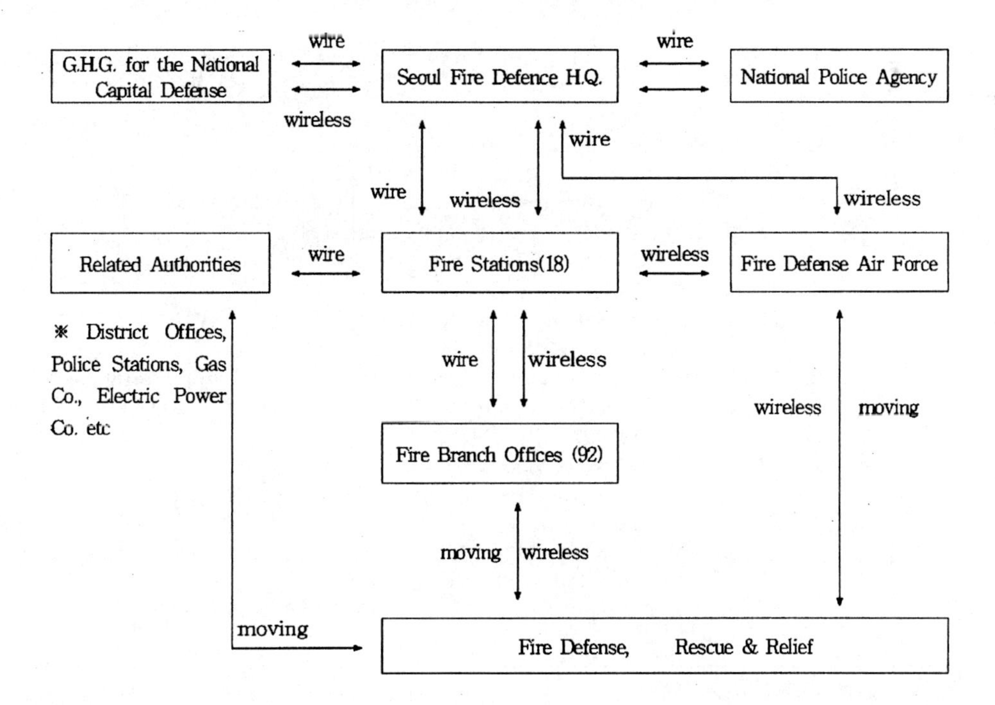

Figure 2 Emergency communications system. (From Seoul Fire Defense Headquarters 1993).

tors, cranes, fire engines, and other rescue equipment rushed to the scene. Most of the manpower and equipment, however, could not be used immediately, as experts warned of the possibility of further collapse of the remaining part of the department store, which already leaned about 5 degrees northward. Steel structures, concrete, and other piles of heavy rubble also prevented rescue teams from getting easy access to those trapped underground in the basement levels.

The Defense Ministry committed more than 1500 military rescuers, four cranes, 32 trucks, and other equipment to the rescue effort, and the U.S. Forces Korea (USFK) sent 40 rescue workers, six fire engines, a medical support team, and metal cutting teams with two large metal cutters to the scene of the disaster Thursday night, shortly after the building collapse.

The disaster headquarters were established at 6:00 p.m., and a field command office at 6:20 p.m. In Table 4, the government's main response to the Sampoong disaster is outlined.

At the same time, the Korea National Red Cross (KNRC) sent hundreds of rescue officials and two large vehicles for cooking to the scene along with emergency relief supplies like blankets, bottled water, food, gas masks, and gloves. To meet the increasing demand for blood transfusions for the casualties, the KNRC supplied its stored blood to the hospitals that took in casualties of the disaster. Other citizens and volunteers who made search-and-rescue efforts during the initial stage, provided food and water to

Table 4 A Governmental Control Measure of the Sampoong Disaster

Time phase	Period	Contents of Control Measure
Initial stage	June 29–30 1995	Operating the disaster headquarters
		Establishing the field command office
		Committing 13,175 men, 1,525 types of equipment to the scene
		Recovering the victims (dead 66, injured 844), and 79 hospitalized
Middle stage	July 1–19 1995	Operating the field headquarters
		Proclaiming the Special Disaster Area
		Supporting the expenditure: ₩ 13,899,000,000 ($17,373,7500) (national funds 50%, local funds 50%)
		Committing 77,066 men, 8670 types of equipment to the scene
		Recovering the victims (dead 459, injured 932)
Late stage	July 20–Sept. 16 1995	Finishing the rescue operation (withdrawal)
		Completing removal of debris (34,000 tons)
		Grants for funeral expenses: ₩ 1,686,550,000 ($2,108,187,000)
		A special reward for the bereaved families: ₩ 135,600,000 ($169,500)
		Reward for victims: ₩ 144,200,000 ($142,750)
		Medical treatment cost for the injured: ₩ 180,000,000 ($225,000)
		Financial support: 135 cases (enterprise 122, personal 13): ₩ 8,616,000,000 ($10,770,000)
		Tax support, 1245 cases: ₩ 6,868,000,000 ($8,585,000)

Source: From Lim 1996.

emergency workers and supported the field emergency operations during the response period.

On Friday, June 30, U.S. high-tech gear arrived at the scene of the collapsed Sampoong Department Store and quickly located at least six survivors in the rubble. A U.S. team that had aided in the rescue at the Oklahoma City Federal Building, arrived at the scene with system to locate survivors (STOLS) and a seismic radio locator designed to detect any vibration from trapped survivors in the debris. They worked with the STOLS device from 8:00 p.m. to 9:00 p.m. But it was not as successful as had been hoped. One member of the STOLS team said that the device was hindered by the many rescue officials and other rescue equipment that created noises at that time. A special rescue team from a coal mine in Taebaek, Kangwon Province, Korea, arrived to join the rescue operation. In the afternoon, President Young-sam Kim visited the accident site and called on officials to speed up rescue efforts to make sure that anyone alive in the wreckage would be saved.

F. Rescue Operations and Casualties

On the night of July 1, a total of 24 people, 14 of them women, were rescued after being buried together for about 52 hours in the basement of the collapsed Sampoong Department Store. The 24 rescued were among about 130 people pulled out of the rubble alive. They were carried out at intervals of 2 to 3 minutes, and it took about 50 minutes to get them all out. A rescue team found the 24 survivors on a third basement floor around 11 a.m., when they were climbing down an underground stairway into the remaining section of the building. Workers reached them by cutting through concrete slabs with drills, iron cutters, and hammers.[12]

On July 19, President Kim Young Sam designated the site of the collapsed Sampoong Department Store and its vicinity (about 67,000 square meters of area in and around the accident site) a ''special disaster area (SDA)'' in accordance with the Disaster Management Act, which passed in the National Assembly on July 15, 1995. In a special statement, Kim said that the government would provide the special administrative, financial, and tax supports needed for rescue, relief, and restoration of the disaster area. President Kim also vowed that the government would root out corruption in the industry and the source of faulty construction practices.

Victims' condition data are presented in Table 5. The death toll from the collapse reached a total of 459, including shoppers and employees. Some 62 of the 459 bodies

Table 5 Summary of Victims Condition

	Dead		Injured			Missing	
Types	Identified	Unidentified	Serious	Slight	Returned Home	Men	Women
Victim No.	397	62	187	196	549	41	128
Subtotal	459			932		169	
Total				1391			

Source: From Socho-gu 1995.

remained unidentified, as they were badly mangled and decomposed. Approximately 930 persons were injured, 169 were missing in the collapse.

V. IMPROVING CRISIS AND EMERGENCY MANAGEMENT SYSTEM IN KOREA

The practice of crisis and emergency management in Korea has undergone a significant transition since the collapse of the Sampoong Department Store in southern Seoul. Emergency management's scope has expanded from an earlier emphasis on natural hazards to today's all-disaster approach, which addresses natural, man-made, and civil defense disasters. Disasters and crises themselves often serve as the impetus for institution-led change. The Sampoong disaster, for example, prompted the National Assembly to enact the Disaster Management Act. The national government created the Disaster Management Bureau to respond to man-made disasters, which often occur in Korea (Sang Lee 1996:124). The Korean disaster management system has been reestablished through the enactment of the Disaster Management Act of 1995 and the full revision of Natural Hazards Management Act of 1995 after a series of catastrophic man-made disasters since 1993 (Seong Lee 1996: x).[13] In this context, this section examines the emergency management system of the central and the local Korean governments.

Only government has the technical capability, the appropriate resources, and the authority to coordinate a range of disaster-related responses. Thus, natural disasters inevitably pose problems that cannot be adequately addressed by private-market activities (Schneider 1995:17). The same may be said of man-made technological disasters. According to the Constitution of the Republic of Korea, government has the responsibility to manage all the disasters and to protect its citizens.[14] The central government has served as the pivot in emergency management in Korea. First of all, the Central Safety Committee within the Office of the Prime Minister executed a plan in which there were measures for disaster prevention, control, management, coordination, and so on. In its early years, the Civil Defense and Disaster Control Headquarters (CDDCH), within the Ministry of Home Affairs, had failed to provide a coordinated national response to natural and man-made disasters. Since the enactment of Disaster Management Act, CDDCH has more responsibility in emergency management. As illustrated in Figure 3, the Civil Defense Headquarters (CDH) became the CDDCH. This newly formed body includes four bureaus: the Civil Defense Bureau (CDB), the Disaster Management Bureau (DMB), the Hazard Prevention Bureau (HPB), and the Fire Service Bureau (FSB). Further, the Disaster Management Bureau (DMB) includes three divisions: the Overall Disaster Control Division (ODCD), the Disaster Management Division (DMD), and the Safety Guide Division (SGD); these three were added to the existing organizations. (See also Table 6.)

In addition to the disaster management organizations within the Ministry of Home Affairs, the disaster-related central departments have a responsibility to support emergency management. For example, the Regional Construction and Management Office (RCMO); and the Flood Control Office (FCO) within the Ministry of Construction and Transportation as well as Hazard Prevention Bureau (HPB) within the Ministry of Home Affairs have charge of natural hazards management. The Ministry of Construction and Transportation covers the field of engineering safety in man-made disaster management. The Ministry of International Trade and Industry and the Ministry of Construction and Transportation are in charge of industrial safety; and the Ministry of Construction and Transportation,

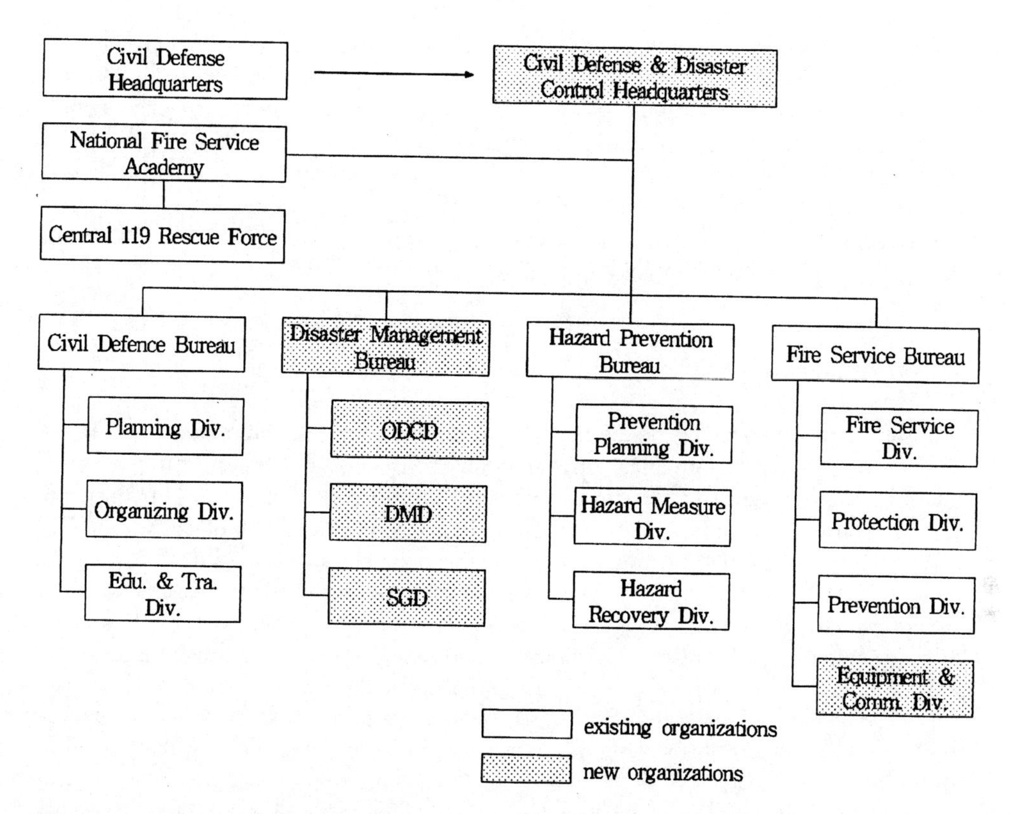

Figure 3 Change in disaster management organizations. [Modified by the authors from materials from Ministry of Home Affairs (1996:36).]

the National Police Office, the National Railroad Administration, and the Maritime and Port Administration assume responsibility for transportation safety.

When a disaster strikes, it does so in one or more local jurisdictions. As local government has the first line of official public responsibility, local government has to develop and maintain a program of emergency management to meet the responsibility of providing

Table 6 Disaster Management Organizations

Organizations	Characteristics
Civil Defense Bureau (CDB)	Organizing, operating, mobilizing, and training/educating the Civil Defense Crops Unit of provision against war and various disasters
Disaster Management Bureau (DMB)	The general management of man-made disasters, including in its responsibilities conflagrations, architectural collapse, explosions, etc. It mobilizes the manpower, equipment, and various resources
Hazard Prevention Bureau (HPB)	Managing, measuring, planning for, and researching the prevention of natural hazards, including typhoons, floods, snowstorms, earthquakes, etc.
Fire Service Bureau (HSB)	Planning, responding, preventing, and extinguishing fires and efforts to rescue and relieve victims.

Source: Modified Ministry of Home Affairs (1996).

protection and safety for the public (McLoughlin 1985:165). Before the collapse of Sampoong Department Store, each office or agency had responded separately to the disasters, because of the lack of coordination within the local government. Since the enactment of the Disaster Management Act, emergency management organizations in local government have more authority, responsibility, and ability to act in emergency situations. Thus, it can be said that through the enactment of the Disaster Management Act of 1995, local governments were given a mandate to prevent disasters to the best of their ability or, failing that, to deal effectively with any disaster that should occur.

VI. CONCLUSIONS

Worldwide, disasters are becoming more frequent, more serious, and more deadly. In less developed countries in particular, growing populations and economic pressures are pushing increasing numbers of people to live in more hazardous locations, usually major urban centers (Durham and Suiter 1991:124). The primary economic policy objective of developing countries, especially Korea, has been to pursue a sustained, high rate of economic growth. In the maze of capitalistic competition, there have been bad practices in individual entrepreneurs' scramble to get ahead. The emphasis on speed has resulted in violations of acceptable or safe standards. Examples of poor workmanship and structural weakness in apartments, hotels, and other buildings spring up by the dozen every month.

The collapse of the Sampoong Department Store in Seoul was just one in a series of disastrous accidents. It was the result of various immoral actions taken by the executives of the company. The disaster of Sampoong might have been prevented if legislation, strict government control, and protection had been implemented prior to this disaster. However, it serves as a major turning point in the prevention of disasters in Korea.

Because of the Sampoong collapse, the Disaster Management Act was instituted. This act enables the central government to take responsibility for emergency rescue operations, medical treatment, relief work, and rehabilitation of the damaged facilities. Korean crisis and emergency management is now in a transitional period because the government learned its lesson the hard way. The Sampoong catastrophe has awakened people to the ugly realities of corrupt business practices and their consequences.

Ultimately, it should be noted that the primary goal of crisis management is to prevent the occurrence of disasters, particularly man-made and social. It is also important to emphasize that although much headway has been made, this progress should not halt. The devastating effects of a few recent incidents illuminate the fact that all Korean citizens have an obligation to themselves and to humanity to push for the further improvement of policies regarding the prevention and management of crises. In short, every single Korean must do everything possible to avoid another Sampoong disaster.

ENDNOTES

1. According to Robinson (1974:510–513), because of its varied meanings, the term *crisis* has not been useful in building ''systematic knowledge'' about social phenomena. So crisis will become a useful concept when it plays a part in theoretical formulations.
2. Hyung-Yul Kim (1987:67) defines crisis as a state that makes goal achievement difficult under certain conditions which incur a loss and danger to a system. Pauchant and Mitroff (1990:

121) define a crisis as a disruption that either affects or has the potential to affect a whole system, thus threatening the very core of its social identity.

3. Hoetmer (1991:xxi) identified four types of disasters: natural, technological, civil, and ecological. According to him, violent natural events (for example, earthquakes, floods, tornadoes) that have an extreme impact on human beings are natural disasters. And events that have an extreme impact on human beings but are caused by human omission or error are technological disasters. Deliberate human acts, such as wars, that cause extensive harm are categorized as civil disasters. Finally, ecological disasters, a fourth type of disaster, are caused principally by human beings, and initially affect, in a major way, the earth, its atmosphere, and its flora and fauna, rather than human beings. He has said that ecological disasters, unlike other types of disaster, are usually insidious rather than dramatic, but ultimately they are just as deadly.
4. Social crisis is an criminal event and/or a situation where a certain group or persons try to achieve their illegal, political, ideological, ethnical, religious, or secular, goals. For example, on March 20, 1995, a total of 12 people died and approximately 5000 were injured when terrorists released sarin, a nerve gas, in the Tokyo subway (*Newsweek*, April 3, 1995:11–16). On April, 19, 1995, approximately 150 deaths and more than 500 injuries occurred when a truck bomb exploded, destroying the federal building in Oklahoma City, U.S.A., in what was thought to be a terrorist act (*Time*, May 1, 1995:27–34). It is well known that these criminal events may well be examples of social crisis. According to Weinberg and Davis (1989:6–13), terrorism is politically motivated crime intended to modify the behavior of a target audience and also has been used by groups pursuing ethnic-separatist or nationalist aims.
5. Rosenthal and Pijnenburg (1991:3) have argued that crisis management involves efforts to prevent crises from occurring, to prepare for a better protection against the impact of a crisis agent, to make for an effective response to an actual crisis, and to provide plans and resources for recovery and rehabilitation in the aftermath of a crisis.
6. In building an effective emergency management system, one should think over the following eight variables: time, space, culture, environmental uncertainty, information, types of crisis, financial conditions, and actors (Jae-Eun Lee, 1992:48–55).
7. Sethi (1987:103) has said that it is reasonable to conclude that the Bhopal accident was not a natural disaster, which could not be foreseen or prevented. It was not the price of progress that must be paid. It was instead a combination of small errors, postponed maintenance, and poorly trained personnel whose cumulative effect resulted in the ensuing catastrophe.
8. In contradiction to this theory, Quarantelli and Dynes (1977:43–45) have argued that the history of interdisciplinary research, including efforts in the area of disaster, does not support the ideas that better research results are obtained or that applications of findings are more easily accomplished by taking an interdisciplinary stance. They feel that in such an approach, contributions of different disciplines are often reduced to the lowest common denominator, which is sometimes only slightly, if at all, above a common-sense level. Quarantelli and Dynes further state that research findings in an interdisciplinary setting are often even more difficult to translate into practical terms.
9. Hodgkinson and Stewart (1991:48) have said that traffic accidents are so common that they are not viewed as "disasters" except when a number of individuals die together and media attention is excited. Death or injury in a traffic accident is most certainly a "personal disaster." The same may be said of fire, which is usually caused by a family member's error or employee's indifference. Solutions to these problems belong to the private sector (automobile insurance, fire insurance), not to the public sector.
10. According to Kunreuther (1973:27), insurance is the normal way for an individuals to protect themselves against the risk of loss from natural hazards. Yet the evidence is fairly strong that people do not take out insurance against disasters unless they are required to do so. Most homeowners in the United States are insured against damage from windstorms and hail because these hazards are included in the comprehensive homeowners' policy that property owners are usually required to purchase as a condition for a mortgage.

11. An architectural disaster collapse came after the series of similar man-made disasters in the 1990s. On March 28, 1993, a railroad disaster involving the ''Mugunghwa'' passenger train carrying about 600 passengers derailed due to land erosion north of Kupo Station along the Seoul-Pusan line. Casualties from the accident marked it as the worst recorded railway mishap, 78 people died and 163 were injured. On July 26, 1993, an Asiana 737-500 airliner, en route to Mokpo from Seoul carrying 110 passengers and crew, crashed while trying to land at Mokpo, Korea; 66 of those aboard were killed and 44 others injured. On October 10, 1993, the Sohae Ferry with 400 crewmen and passengers aboard, sank in a matter of minutes near Wi-do (island) in the West Sea, North Cholla Province. The causes of the ''Sohae Ferry'' disaster, which claimed the lives of 292, were overloading and improper maintenance. On October 21, 1994, a section of the Songsu bridge, one of the busiest bridges that cross the Han River in Seoul, collapsed during morning rush hour. Thirty-two people were killed in that disaster. On October 24, 1994, a fire engulfed a pleasure boat on the Chungju Lake near Chungju, North Chungchong Province, with 29 killed, 33 injured. On December 8, 1994, in the city-gas explosion at Ahyon-Dong, Mapo-gu, Seoul, 12 people were killed. On April 28, 1995, in Taegu, a construction worker accidently broke a gas main at a subway construction site. An explosion fueled by a city gas leak rocked the entire city killing 101 morning commuters and injured 270 others.
12. Removal of iron beams and other debris from the five-story department store started July 3, together with the search for survivors after consultation with the bereaved family members. ''There is a possibility that there are people still alive trapped in the rubble of the Sampoong Department Store,'' said an official at the Relief and Rescue Center based at City Hall. Many bereaved family members, consequently, agreed to help with the removal work and the hunt for survivors. One survivor, Myong-sok Choi, was pulled out of the wreckage 8:20 a.m., Sunday, July 9. He was discovered in what had been the first basement. The rescue of the 20-year-old man, who worked as a part-time sales clerk at the store, raised hopes of finding more survivors, He said, ''When I knocked on the wall, there was a response. I thought there were still people alive.'' He said, ''there was nothing to drink but a trickle of rainwater.'' For sustenance, he ate bits of cardboard boxes. At 3:30 p.m., July 11, an 18-year-old female sales assistant, Ji-hwan Yoo, was lifted from the rubble, after lying buried for 12 days, more than 285 hours, in a small pocket under the collapsed building. Encouraged by the miraculous discovery of the two survivors, rescue workers stepped up their last-ditch search for more survivors. Survivor-locating devices such as vibration and sonar detectors as well as endoscope cameras were brought in to search for signs of life, and more rescuers and heavy equipment were stepped up. The rescue operation focused on the central basement area of the disaster site of about 1 square kilometer, with cranes carefully removing debris and concrete slabs. At 11:20 a.m., July 15, on the second basement level, rescue workers pulled out another survivor from the rubble of the Sampoong Department Store. Sung-hyon Park, 19, miraculously alive after being trapped 377 hours and 20 minutes. Park, an employee in the children's clothing section, said that she had not eaten or drunk anything while she was trapped in a small pocket under the rubble for 15 days and 17 hours. In 1969, a coal miner, Chang-son Yang, was trapped in a mine in South Chungchong, Korea, for 368 hours, or 15 days and 8 hours. Park's survival was 9 hours longer than Yang's. After she was pulled out, she said that there were more survivors in the rubble. The rescuers therefore conducted searches near the place where she was found, but they failed to locate more survivors.
13. According to Disaster Management Act, Article 2, *disaster* refers mainly to man-made technological disasters, including fires, architectural collapse, massive explosions, traffic accidents, CBR (chemical, biological, and radiological) accidents, environmental pollution, etc. It excludes natural hazards.
14. Article 34 of the Constitution stipulates: (1) All citizens shall be equally valued as human beings. (2) The state shall have the duty to endeavor to promote social security and welfare. (3) The state shall endeavor to promote the welfare and rights of women. (4) The state shall

have the duty to implement policies for enhancing the welfare of senior citizens and the young. (5) Citizens who are incapable of earning a livelihood due to a physical disability, disease, old age or other reasons shall be protected by the state under the conditions as prescribed by law. (6) The state shall endeavor to prevent disasters and to protect citizens from harm therefrom.

REFERENCES

Barton, Laurence. (1993). *Crisis in Organizations: Managing and Communicating in the Heat of Chaos*. Cincinnati, OH: South-Western Publishing.

Billings, Robert S., Thomas W. Milburn, and Mary Lou Schaalman (1980). A model of crisis perception: A theoretical and empirical analysis. *Administrative Science Quarterly* 25, 300–316.

Cigler, Beverly A. (1988). Emergency management and public administration. In Michael T. Charles and John Choon K. Kim (eds.), *Crisis Management: A Casebook*. 5–19. Springfield, IL: Charles C Thomas Publisher.

Clary, Bruce B. (1985). The evolution and structure of natural hazard policies. *Public Administration Review* 45 (special Issue), 20–28.

D'Aveni, Richard A. and Ian C. MacMillan (1990). Crisis and the content of managerial communications: A study of the focus of attention of top managers in surviving and failing firms. *Administrative Science Quarterly* 35, 634–657.

Durham, Tom and Lacy E. Suiter (1991). Perspectives and roles of the state and federal governments. In Thomas E. Drabek and Gerard J. Hoetmer. (eds.), *Emergency Management: Principles and Practice for Local Government*. 101–127. Washington, D.C.: International City Management Association.

Fowlkes, Martha R. and Patricia Y. Miller (1988). Unnatural disaster at Love Canal. In Michael T. Charles and John Choon K. Kim (eds), *Crisis Management: A Casebook*. Springfield, IL: Charles C Thomas Publisher.

Giuffrida, Louis O. (1985). FEMA: Its mission its partner. *Public Administration Review* 45 (special issue).

Gladwin, Thomas N. and Rajesh Kumar (1987). The social psychology of crisis bargaining: Toward a contingency model. *Columbia Journal of World Business* 22(*1*), 23–31.

Herman, Charles F. (1963). Some consequences of crisis which limit the viability of organizations. *Administrative Science Quarterly* 8(1), 61–82.

Hoetmer, Gerard J. (1991). Introduction. In Thomas E. Drabek and Gerard J. Hoetmer (eds.), *Emergency Management: Principles and Practice for Local Government*. Washington, D.C.: International City Management Association. pp. xvii–xxxiv.

Hodgkinson, Peter E. and Michael Stewart (1991). *Coping with Catastrophe: A Handbook of Disaster Management*. New York: Routledge.

Jackson, Robert J. (1976). Crisis management and policy-making: An exploration of theory and research. In Richard Rose (ed.), *The Dynamics of Public Policy*. Beverly Hills, CA: Sage Publications, pp. 209–235.

Kasperson, Roger E. and K. David Pijawka (1985). Societal response to hazards and major hazard events: Comparing natural and technological hazards. *Public Administration Review* 45(special Issue), 7–18.

Kharbanda, Om P., and Ernest A. Stallworthy (1989). Planning for emergencies: Lessons from the chemical industry. *Long Range Planning* 22(*1*), 83–89.

Kim, Hyung-Yul (1987). A study on emergency management in the process of policy implementation. *Social Science Review* (Yonsei U., Korea) 18, 65–87.

Kim, Hyung-Yul (1997). *Policy-Making*. Seoul, Korea: Dae-Young Munhwasa.

Kim, Young-Pyoung, Byung-Sun Choi, Young-Jin Soh, and Ik-Jae Chung (1995). Risk perception in Korea and policy implications. *Korean Public Administration Review* 29(3), 935–954.

Kunreuther, Howard (1973). *Recovery from Natural Disasters: Insurance or Federal Aid?* Washington, D.C.: American Enterprise Institute for Public Policy Research.

Lee, Jae-Eun (1992). A Study of the General Model for Crisis Management in Policy Implementation Process. Master's thesis in public administration, Yonsei University, Seoul, Korea.

Lee, Sang-Pal (1996). An evaluation of disaster management system by intelligent failure learning: A case study on institutional change before and after Sampoong building collapse. *Korean Public Administration Review* 30(2), 113–127.

Lee, Seong-uh (1996). *A Study on the Establishment of an Effective Disaster Management System in Korea*. Seoul, Korea: Korea Institute of Public Administration.

Lim, Song-Tae (1996). *A Study of Comprehensive Disaster Management in Korea*. Seoul, Korea: KRILA (Korea Research Institute for Local Administration).

McLoughlin, David (1985). A framework for integrated emergency management. *Public Administration Review* 45(special Issue), 165–172.

Ministry of Home Affairs (1996). *A Disaster Yearbook*. Seoul, Korea: Ministry of Home Affairs.

Mushkatel, Alvin H. and Louis F. Weschler (1985). Emergency management and the intergovernmental system. *Public Administration Review* 45(special Issue), 49–56.

Namkoong, Keun (1995). Comparative study on disaster management system: The case of the USA and Korea. *Korean Public Administration Review* 29(3), 957–981.

Pauchant, Thierry C. and Ian I. Mitroff (1990). Crisis management: Managing paradox in a chaotic world. *Technological Forecasting and Social Change* 38(2), 117–134.

Perry, Ronald W. (1985). *Comprehensive Emergency Management: Evacuating Threatened Populations*. Greenwich, CT: JAI Press.

Petak, William J. (1985). Emergency management: A challenge for public administration. *Public Administration Review* 45(special Issue), 3–7.

Quarantelli, E.L. and Russell R. Dynes (1977). Response to social crisis and disaster. *Annual Review of Sociology* 3, 23–49.

Rapoport, David C. (1992). Terrorism. In Mary Hawkesworth and Maurice Kogan (eds.), *Encyclopedia of Government and Politics*. 2:1061–1079. London and New York: Routledge.

Reilly, Anne H. (1987). Are organizations ready for crisis? A managerial scorecard. *Columbia Journal of World Business* 22(*1*), 79–88.

Robinson, James A. (1974). Crisis. *International Encyclopedia of the Social Sciences*. 3:510–514. New York: The Macmillan Company.

Rosenthal, Uriel, Paul Hart, and Alexander Kouzmin (1991). The bureau-politics of crisis management. *Public Administration* 69(2), 211–233.

Rosenthal, Uriel and Bert Pijnenburg (eds.) (1991). *Crisis Management and Decision Making: Simulation Oriented Scenarios*. London: Kluwer Academic Publishers.

Schneider, Saundra K. (1995). *Flirting with Disaster: Public Management in Crisis Situations*. Armonk, NY: M. E. Sharpe.

Seoul Fire Defense Headquarters (1995). *A Report to the Special Investigation Committee of the National Assembly*. Seoul: Seoul Fire Defense HQ.

Sethi, S. Prakash (1987). Inhuman errors and industrial crises. *Columbia Journal of World Business* 22(1), 101–110.

Socho-gu (1995). *A Report on the Collapse of the Sampoong Department Store to the Special Investigation Committee of the National Assembly* (Rec. No. 20950180). Seoul, Korea: Socho-gu.

Waldo, Dwight (1980). *The Enterprise of Public Administration*. Novato, CA: Chandler & Sharp Publishers.

Waugh, William L. Jr. (1994). Regionalizing emergency management: Counties as state and local government. *Public Administration Review* 54(3), 253–258.

Waugh, William L. Jr. and Jane P. Sweeney (1988). International Law and the 1985 TWA Hijacking.

In Michael T. Charles and John Choon K. Kim (eds), *Crisis Management: A Casebook*. Springfield, IL: Charles C Thomas Publisher.

Webster's Third New International Dictionary (1966). Springfield, MA: G. & C. Merriam Co.

Weinberg, Leonard, and Paul Davis (1989). *Introduction to Political Terrorism*. New York: McGraw-Hill Publishing Company.

Wenger, Dennis E. (1978). Community response to disaster: Functional and structural alterations. In E. L. Quarantelli (ed.), *Disasters: Theory and Research*. 17–47. Beverly Hills, CA: SAGE Publications.

Zimmerman, Rae (1985). The relationship of emergency management to governmental policies on man-made technological disasters. *Public Administration Review* 45(special Issue), 29–39.

32

The 1994 Plague Outbreak in Surat, India

Social Networks and Disaster Management

Rita Kabra Open University Kanpur, India

Renu Khator Environmental Science and Policy Program, University of South Florida, Tampa, Florida

I. INTRODUCTION

One day in September 1994, the news spread like wildfire that an instant-killing strand of plague has taken Surat, the "dirtiest city" in India, in its grip. A mass exodus of several thousand, including public officials, municipal workers, doctors, nurses and even patients from hospitals' death wards, followed within hours. Within a few days, the panic spread to other parts of India, where people worried about the spread of the disease resulting from the fleeing population. On the governmental front, another disaster was unfolding: local officials were struck with panic, public employees were fleeing faster than the population, and no assistance was coming from state and federal officials. Clearly, the city had been traumatized by the fear of death and collective stress had immobilized the governmental machinery.

This incident—against the backdrop of the mushrooming literature on disaster and emergency management following the Hurricane Andrew, the Northridge Earthquake, the 1993 Great Midwestern Flood, the New York Twin Towers bombing and the Oklahoma City Murrah Federal Office Building bombing in the United States—affords us the opportunity to raise some cross-cultural comparative issues: is disaster management different in different political settings and does culture—social and political—play a role in disaster management? The following case study of Surat's plague is intended to identify the nature and scope of disaster management in a developing country setting. It is hoped that this case study, when compared with the case studies completed in the American setting (Comfort 1988; May and Williams 1986; Sylves and Waugh 1990; Sylves and Waugh 1996; Waugh and Hy 1990) will help us understand the appropriateness or lack thereof of western disaster management strategies for non-western settings.

II. INDIA'S ENCOUNTER WITH PLAGUE

Plague is primarily and basically a zoonosis caused by bacillus *Yersinia pestis*, involving rodents and fleas. It exists in natural foci and is transmitted by infected flea bites to humans living in or intruding into the same ecological environment. There are three clinical forms of plague: (1) bubonic plague, caused by infected flea bites where lymph glands are swollen and painful and the person develops fever; (2) pneumonic plague, a highly infectious strand, where the lungs are extensively involved and the disease spreads from person to person; and (3) septicemic plague, where the bloodstream is invaded by bacteria due to heavy infection.

Plague has been one of the greatest scourges of the human race. The association of plague with rats was known to the ancients. Epidemics of plague are mentioned in Bible. *Bhagwat Puran*, an ancient Indian text written about 1500 to 800 B.C., specifies that as soon as the dead rats are seen, the residences should be immediately abandoned. Down the ages, plague was known as *mahamari*, the great death.

Since the dawn of Christian era, there have been three great pandemics. The first began in A.D. 542 (the Justinian plague) and is estimated to have caused 100 million deaths. The second began in Year 1346 and lasted for three centuries; it claimed 25 million lives. The last began in 1894 and continued until the 1930s. As a result of the last pandemic, natural foci of infection apart from humans were established in many countries and regions such as Central Asia, Iranian Kurdistan, Arabia, Central and South Africa, Myanmar, Vietnam, Indonesia, South America and the western United States. The danger still exists that plague may spill over into the human population, as happened in India, where plague reappeared in 1994 after a silent period of 28 years.

The first recorded outbreak of plague in India occurred in A.D. 1031–1032. Plague reached India from Central Asia, following invasion by the Sultan Mohammad (Arabian chronicles). The next outbreak was in 1325, when plague spread in Malabar following the invasion of Mohammad Tuglaq, and again after Taimur in 1403, when Sultan Ahmad's army was destroyed in Malwa. In 1617, plague was reported during the Mughal Emperor Jehangir's reign from Punjab, Ahmedabad, Surat, and Deccan. In 1812–1821, plague hit Kathiawar, Gujrat, and Kutch; it was supposed to have been imported from Persia. In recent history, India got involved in the pandemic of 1895–1896 in Calcutta, Bombay, and other cities. Plague reached its peak in India in 1907 and continued thereafter for another 11 years till 1918. The annual mortality was over 500,000 deaths between 1898 and 1908. The disease continued to be a major public health problem until the mid-1940s. Thereafter, it began to decline speedily as a result of large-scale application of DDT for malaria control. The trend of plague mortality in India is as shown in Table 1.

Since the last reported cases in 1966, there had been no laboratory-confirmed cases of human plague in India until its reappearance in September 1994, when four persons tested positive for bubonic plague in Beed (Maharashtra), followed by an outbreak of pneumonic plague in Surat. Cases were also reported in Delhi, Bombay, Calcutta, and other cities. A total of 4780 cases were reported, of which 167 tested positive for plague, resulting into 53 deaths (Park 1995).

III. THE SURAT PLAGUE CRISIS

Surat a metropolis that has grown very rapidly, is a major center of industrial growth in western India. Surat has a tradition of business, and it was here that the British established

Table 1 Plague Mortality in India

Period/Years	Annual Mortality
1898–1908	5,48,427
1909–1918	4,22,153
1919–1928	1,70,272
1929–1938	42,288
1939–1948	21,797
1950	18,813
1952	3,894
1954	705
1956	195
1958	206
1960	108
1962	200
1964	15
1966	8
1968	Nil
1970	Nil
1994	53

Source: From Seal (1960), World Health Organization (1967), Ghosh (1962).

their first trading post in 1813 and the Dutch in 1820. Though the city is one of the oldest municipalities, set up in 1852 and made a corporation in 1966, it had become unmanageable in recent years. The textile factories and the diamond cutting industry had attracted a large number of migrant workers from other Indian states.

The growth of Surat's population has been extraordinary, increasing from 317,519 in 1961 to an estimated 1.7 million at the beginning of 1993. Today, 28% of the population lives in slums while migrant labor makes up 75% of the numbers. Jan Breman of the Centre for Asian Studies, Amsterdam, describes Surat as "one big transit camp" of workers. The growth of urban living facilities and civic amenities remains far behind the growth of Surat's population. The city has become notorious for its filthy appearance, allowing the media to label it as the "filthiest city in India" (Blank 1994). Describing the hygienic conditions during the months preceding the outbreak of plague, a news report reads: "Waterlogged carcasses of nearly 1,000 cattle, victims of a heavy monsoon season, have littered streets since August" (Blank 1994). Another report says: "Surat is an unhealthy place at the best of times, with a high incidence of malaria, typhoid, cholera and all the other diseases of overcrowding and poverty...labourers who have flooded in from Maharashtra, Punjab, Uttar Pradesh, Orissa and elsewhere usually settle in unplanned areas on the edge of the city, without proper water or sewage systems. Diseases fester in these slums" (Economist 1994).

The epidemic of plague in 1994 may not have started in Surat but rather in the neighboring Beed District of Maharashtra. There were tremors in the district during earthquake in Latur, Osmanabad region, in 1993. Outside the main earthquake area, many people left their homes and many of these old houses were used to store food grains. The storage places became infested with rats as wild rodents, disturbed by the earthquake, migrated to human habitat and infected domestic rodents. When the storage houses were opened after a long time, fleas came out and attacked human beings and bubonic plague started. By September's end, 325 cases of bubonic plague were identified in Beed District. On September 22, 1994, an epidemic of pneumonic plague spread rapidly in the city of Surat. Plague could have been brought to Surat by migrant workers from Maharashtra, where it started as bubonic plague (as a result of transmission from natural foci, i.e., rodents to domestic rodents and then through rat fleas to human beings). The possibility of it having originated in Surat itself has not been totally discarded by scientists (Hazarika 1995). From Surat, the disease spread to Maharashtra, West Bengal, Delhi, Varanasi, Haryana, Pubjab, and Kerala.

The plague epidemic led to a large-scale exodus of people from Surat: approximately 270,000 people left Surat by air, rail, and road in first 3 days, and half of the population had gone by September's end. A large number of private doctors and nurses fled the city too, creating a more intense panic than necessary (Penberthy 1994). Municipal workers followed the suit, making the initial cleanup a nightmare. Speaking of the challenge at hand, P.R. Deobhankar, the head of rat patrol in Bombay, said, "our employees are only 115 while our enemy numbers over 50 million" (Blank 1994). The coordination between public health authorities and hospital health personnel was poor. A fear-stricken population had little faith in the public health system and the task of isolating patients became difficult. More than 100 plague patients ran away from hospitals in Surat to other cities, causing the spread of the disease outside of city boundaries.

Interestingly, Surat's people had experienced crises in the past and were used to responding to any crisis by their feet. In 1992, approximately 300,000 people had been reported to flee following a Hindu-Muslim confrontation. Earlier in 1994, thousands had fled when a local astrologer predicted that a dam up river would burst. These behavioral responses in the past were again replayed during the plague crisis and city officials could do little to control it. Following the news of the outbreak, people resorted to panic buying of tetracycline capsules that resulted in shortage of drugs and black marketing.

IV. RESPONSE AND MANAGEMENT IN SURAT

In India, there is no epidemic control or disaster management master plan. Situations are tackled as and when they emerge (Frontline 1994). For first 3 days (September 22 to 24), not much was done to control the plague, as health and general administration in Surat were in chaos. On September 25, the Rapid Action Force was deployed in Surat and the government announced an eight-point action plan. When, K.V. Bhanujan, the disaster manager, was deputed from the state capital to direct the plan, he found the local management in shambles. As part of the patched together master plan, the following measures were adopted to control the epidemic in Surat:

- Blood samples of patients were sent for laboratory tests.
- An education campaign was launched to inform the public that pneumonic plague was curable and people were advised not to leave Surat.
- Efforts were made to isolate close contacts of patients and administer chemoprophylaxis.
- Spraying of DDT in vulnerable areas like slums was started to control fleas.
- As a part of antirodent measures, regular garbage removal was instituted. Some nongovernmental organizations also joined government efforts to clean up the city.

Corresponding to the spread of the epidemic to other cities, the following actions were agreed upon:

- Medical teams were deployed at railway stations/bus stands/airports to screen people coming from Surat and Maharashtra to detect plague and treat it.
- Newspapers, radio, and television were used aggressively to educate the public.
- All trucks/buses entering the city were fumigated.
- Hospitals were directed to identify plague patients and organize hospital beds and treatment.
- Availability of antibiotics to treat patients/prophylaxis was ensured.
- Additional arrangements were made to dispose of the garbage immediately.
- An aggressive approach to kill rodents was also undertaken and pleas were made for the people to implement it immediately.

Despite these efforts, the plague panic intensified and the disease spread to other cities. Many factors were responsible for the plague's spread, including the delay in diagnosing the disease, lack of health education among the people, large-scale exodus of people, lack of personnel in the public health system, and absence of a management plan. The bottom line is that people started to take individual measures before even giving government a chance. They had low level of trust in the government and used social networks to obtain treatment and shelter. They followed whatever measures they considered to suit their individual interests, including hoarding of medicine, running away, and not reporting symptoms. On the positive side, they eagerly participated in rodent removal and garbage disposal exercises.

As the number of plague cases started to increase in India, several countries responded with alarm. From September 25, 1994, airplanes from India were fumigated on arrival at airports in Rome and Milan and passengers were subjected to special health checks. In Frankfurt, passengers were checked by doctors upon arrival. Similar restrictions were applied in Bangladesh. On September 28, an international alert was declared against air passengers from India. Saudi Arabia, Kuwait, Bahrain, Oman, and Quatar suspended all flights between their countries and India. One Air India flight to Jeddah with 240 passengers on board had to be recalled after takeoff, and pandemonium resulted at the international airports when thousands of passengers were told that their flights had been canceled. Dubai, Abu Dhabi, and Pakistan soon followed suit. Malaysian Airline stopped operations to India. In Delhi, foreign tourists started using surgical masks outdoors. One major tour operator from Germany canceled a tour of India and major British tour operators like Thomas Cook and Lunn Polly also started to offer refunds to anxious travelers. On September 29, the United Arab Emirates decided to suspend all cargo transshipment from India, and that put trade in jeopardy. Air India, India's primary international airline, alone was losing 20 million rupees per day.

Plague surveillance in India exists only in its rudimentary form. The country's only surveillance unit is in Bangalore. Established in 1975, it works under the National Institute of Communicable Diseases, New Delhi—India's central plague laboratory and nerve center for the control of diseases. This unit carries out research in epidemiology and detection of plague and other rodent-borne diseases like leptospirosis. Maharashtra shut down its plague monitoring facility in 1987.

Government's lack of attention to preventive funding is another drawback. The real per capita expenditure on public health and disease-control programs has been cut back

Table 2 Index of Real per Capita Public Health Expenditures

Year	Index of Expenditure on Public Health (1984–85 = 100)	Index of Expenditure on Prevention and Control of Disease (1984–85 = 100)
1984–85 (base year)	100	100
1985–86	101	94
1986–87	100	94
1987–88	95	98
1988–89	97	100
1989–90	103	103
1990–91	100	94
1991–92	95	87
1992–93	94	83

in recent years (Table 2). V.B. Tulasidhar, an economist at the National Institute of Public Finance and Policy, has noted that ''real expenditure on disease control program remained virtually stagnant during 1985–91 and fell steeply during adjustment period'' (1993). In 1989, the government-operated Haffkin Bio Pharmaceutical Corporation, Bombay, ceased production of antiplague vaccine. However, after the outbreak, it restarted production.

V. ANALYSIS AND CONCLUSION

The experience of India contrasts sharply with the experience of the United States when Hurricane Andrew hit the shores of Florida in 1992 or when the Murrah Federal Building blew up following a targeted bombing in 1995. While the American experience centered on a planned, comprehensive institutional response, at the core of the Indian experience were individual responses by individual citizens acting in their own individual interests. Arguably, both governments—American and Indian—faced harsh criticism following the disasters, irrespective of the level of effort they had put forth. Both were labeled as insensitive and incompetent by their respective media. The Indian experience, however, portrays people taking charge of their own destiny and relying more on their social networks than on the governmental organization. The American notion of ''providing for the citizens'' was not evident in India and citizens affected by the Surat plague did not rely on the government to evacuate them to safer areas or to provide them with shelter and food. They called up their relatives, made their own arrangements for temporary shelter, found their own medication in the pharmacies of friends and relatives, and interpreted their own symptoms and the dangers of plague. In a clearly manifested expression of low trust toward government's response capacity, people relied on family, friends and well-wishers to deal with the crisis. Evidence show that they also readily used practices of bribery and corruption to find a safer haven. This is not to say that the government did not do its best; however, what India experienced was the unwilling partnership between political institutions and social networks that fanned the crisis by letting people engage in disruptive practices (such as fleeing from the city and hoarding medicine) but that, in the end, also helped in managing the disaster.

The unwilling partnership between political and social networks—where social networks (such as family and friends) assumed the responsibility of providing transportation, shelter and medical treatment while political networks (government agencies, hospitals and media) undertook the charge of information dissemination— resulted from the confusion caused by collective stress rather than a planned institutional strategy. People accepted instructions and guidelines from the government, but only to the extent that these did not inhibit them from taking individual actions. They, for instance, rejected the order of not hoarding the medicine but aggressively joined in the campaign to burn garbage and kill rodents. Instead of lining up in front of government clinics that, to begin with, were unprepared to respond to the emergency, people turned to their own physician friends to obtain instructions and medicine. Instead of relying on the government to transport them to temporary shelters, an act that would have taken a massive amount of coordination among various governmental units, people turned to their relatives in other cities for shelter. Amid chaos, the system of transportation also held on to the needs of the disaster-stricken population because there were people willing to offer bribery to obtain tickets, and there were others willing to make extra money by serving as temporary transporters. The government's role, in most instances, was dwarfed by the role that social networks played in disaster management. The eight-point plan put forward by the government acknowledged these limitations and, unlike disaster plans in the United States, limited its own role to either scientific or rudimentary tasks such as testing of blood samples, advising people not to leave the city, spraying of DDT, fumigating trucks and buses, and killing rodents. These were the acts that individuals could not have undertaken on their own because their social networks did not have the historical experience of engaging in them.

The engagement of social networks in disaster management is not always positive. In Surat, they were a nightmare for the medical personnel, who needed to identify and isolate patients. The availability and appropriate application of medicine could also not be ensured because of hoarding and self-treatment. People's interpretations of the causes and symptoms of plague also created serious barriers in governmental efforts to offer accurate information and preventing the crisis from taking on a bigger than necessary dimension.

Considering that social networks played such a pivotal role, it would be a mistake for India to ignore their potential contribution in disaster management and to follow the U.S. model of disaster management that is based on institutional response, government preparedness, and civic responsibility. It is clear that political institutions alone could not have managed the plague disaster in India; nonetheless, it is also clear that some form of cohesive governmental response was needed. Social networks working as solitary units to manage disasters do not offer a comforting feeling either to planners or to citizens. The first challenge for the Indian government is to harness the energy of social networks and incorporate them as constructive partners in the design and implementation of disaster management plans.

According to Allan H. Barton, disasters are situations characterized by collective stress (Barton 1970). Sometimes, collective stress can produce aversion to organized relief efforts, especially in those settings where legal and formalistic frameworks are already weak. People tend to find alternative means of dealing with their stress rather than looking up to the government as their savior. Establishing an ongoing networking relationship and partnerships with sociologists, civic groups, and neighborhood associations is useful in finding a collective response.

The second challenge for India is to institutionalize some form of disaster response. This institutional response should compliment rather than compete with the social response mechanisms that are already in place. While it is clear that India needs a better-coordinated institutional mechanism to deal with disasters, whether it needs an agency like the United States' Federal Emergency Management Agency (FEMA) is strongly debatable. FEMA, irrespective of its authority base, does not enjoy full confidence of either the public or the government. In fact, it faces harsh criticism every time a disaster strikes in America. After the Hurricane Andrew disaster in 1992, the criticism of FEMA was so intense that it felt forced to reorganize itself (Sylves and Waugh 1996) to become a more professionally managed, increasingly responsive, and better coordinating organization. The thrust of FEMA's reorganization was to make it more open to other federal, state, and local agencies that also play a role in disaster management. The role of federal, state, and local governments and coordination among them are some of the most critical policy implementation issues in disaster management (May and Williams 1986). Two decision dilemmas deserve particular attention: (1) how active the federal government should be in policy making and (2) how federal programs can alter local and state actor behavior in regard to their management practices. In the United States, the federal government actively participates in policy making as well as implementation by offering fiscal incentives and passing action-forcing legislation. The Canadian federal government, on the other hand, takes a more "backdrop" approach, for it considers disaster management to be primarily a local responsibility. In many provinces of Canada, the provincial government is required to set up a Provincial Field Response Centre (PFRC) to provide coordination and policy guidelines; but in others, a decentralized and coordinated local system is all that is considered necessary.

While no universal implementation model exists, the concept of shared governance colors most of the literature today. It is important that governments focus on the outcome (quick and efficient coordination of all governmental efforts) rather than the process (whether to achieve it through a centralized or a decentralized model). Countries should adopt the process based on their cultural and institutional strengths and weaknesses. Uriel Rosenthal in his study of disaster management in the Netherlands, finds that cultures, social and political, play a very important role in defining the nature and scope of disaster management and he cautions us against transplanting the American model to other settings (1988). Considering the strength of India's social networks and the absence of a federal program, it is best to nurture the role of those networks, albeit in a systematic manner. Furthermore, disaster management should be considered a dynamic and evolving process in which frequent reviews and alterations are necessary.

Availability of resources, or lack thereof, forms the third area of challenge for disaster managers. While lack of resources certainly inhibits a government's ability to respond to disasters, their availability does not necessarily guarantee effective disaster management mitigation and response. In 1999, the British government was harshly criticized for its management of the Soufriere Hills volcano eruption on September 22, 1998, in the British-dependent territory of the tiny Caribbean Island of Montserrat even though it had pledged $60 million over 2 years to the island's relief efforts (Lennard 1998). Clearly, India faces an acute shortage of resources, particularly of resources that can be dedicated to preventive measures. In the case of Surat, rat infestation was known to the government; its eradication before the outbreak could have been possible given the availability of resources. But faced with resource scarcity, India and other countries with similar constraints will have to rely on engaging social networks and altering cultural belief systems and social habits as preventive measures. The strategy of creating a comprehensive institution-based American-style response system is not a feasible one.

As disaster management enters the new millenium, countries like India will have to acknowledge their unique cultural and social strengths and rely upon them for disaster management. Undoubtedly, a coordinated approach between government agencies at all levels and between the government and social networks will have to complement the role that individuals alone or as groups already play.

ACKNOWLEDGMENT

The authors wish to thank Dr. Suresh Kabra for his assistance with medical terminology and research for this paper.

REFERENCES

Barrier, Michael (1998). ''Planning for a disaster.'' *Nation's Business* 86(5), 51–52.

Barton, Allan H. (1970). Communities in Disaster: *A Sociological Analysis of Collective Stress Situation*. Garden City, NY: Doubleday.

Blank, Jonah (1994). ''Bombay's rat patrol takes on the plague.'' *U.S. News and World Report*.

Burns, John F. (1994). ''Calm returns to Indian city hit by plague.'' *New York Times*, September 26.

Cover Story (1994). *Frontline*, Madras. 8–21. October, pp. 12–13.

Economist (1994) ''The old enemy.'' *Economist* 1994.

Ghosh, B.N. (1962). *A Treatise on Hygiene and Public Health*, 15th ed. Scientific Publication House, Calcutta.

Hazarika, Sanjoy (1995). ''Plague's origin a mystery,'' *New York Times*. March 14.

Jayaraman, K.S. (1994). ''Indian plague poses enigma to investigators.'' *Nature* October 13, 547.

Lennard, Jeremy, (1998). ''Grumbling from an ashen island.'' *Americas*.

Luis K. Comfort (ed.) (1988). *Managing Disaster: Strategies and Policy Perspectives*, Durham, NC: Duke University Press.

May, Peter J. and Walter Williams (1986). *Disaster Policy Implementation*. New York: Plenum Press.

Park, K. (1995). *Preventive and Social Medicine*, 14th ed. Jabalpur, India: Banarsidas Bhanot Publishers.

Penberthy, Jefferson (1994). ''One man against the plague,'' Time.

Rosenthal, Uriel (1988). Disaster Management in the Netherlands: Planning for real events. Luis K. Comfort (ed.), *Managing Disaster*. 274–295.

Seal, S.C. (1960). *Bulletin of the World Health Organization* 23, 286.

Sylves, Richard T. and William L. Waugh, Jr. (eds.) (1990). *Cities and Disasters: North American Studies in Emergency Management*. Springfield, IL: Charles C Thomas.

Sylves, Richard T. and William L. Waugh, Jr. (eds.) (1996). *Disaster Management in the U.S. and Canada*, Springfield, IL: Charles C Thomas.

The Times of India (1994). New Delhi, October 6.

Waugh, William L. and Ronald John Hy (eds.) (1990). *Handbook of Emergency Management*. Westport, CT: Greenwood Press, 1990.

World Health Organization (1967). *Epidemic and Vital Statistics Report* 20, 380.

33
Disaster Management in Hong Kong

Ahmed Shafiqul Huque Department of Public and Social Administration, City University of Hong Kong, Hong Kong, China

I. INTRODUCTION

Management in the public sector is a complicated process, and it is compounded in the case of crises and emergencies.[1] A large number of public agencies are brought together to deal with emergencies and provide a vast range of services. The tasks range from maintenance of order and security (restrictive role) to search and rescue (proactive role) to provision of shelter, comfort, and rehabilitation (compassionate/encouraging role). In short, emergencies require officials to perform a wide range of services within a short period of time under extremely difficult circumstances. The tasks have to be accomplished often without the usual support available from their own or other agencies.

Emergency management entails a number of activities that range from adequate planning and preparation to subsequent support and mitigation. Most governments prepare themselves with a comprehensive plan that covers the various possibilities of disasters and lay out a series of actions to deal with them. It is often found that organizations oriented in routine and regular patterns of operation are unable to cope with the complex and challenging tasks of emergency management. This chapter seeks to examine the planning process for dealing with emergencies in general and the case of Hong Kong in particular to shed light on the difficulties encountered in preparing for emergencies in a comprehensive manner and dealing with them. Such an investigation is expected to provide insight into the nature of the problem and lead to recommendations on alternative arrangements for the management of disasters.

Modern states are exposed to devastation from a wide variety of natural disasters. Hong Kong is no exception, as the territory experiences a substantial amount of rainfall and is frequently hit by tornadoes and thunderstorms. ''Cyclone, flood and landslide occur one or more times a year. Storm surge happens every 2 to 3 years and drought every 5 to 10 years'' (ESCAP 1990b:149). This list indicates the range and diversity of calamities that Hong Kong can expect to face throughout the year. In June 1972, ''147 people were killed and 102 injured'' during a rainstorm (GEO 1982:6). Various reports by the GEO indicate numerous cases of heavy rainfall, landslides, and flooding over the years. The small land area interspersed with hills and slopes, limited road space and overcrowding of vehicles, and the limited capacity of the public transportation system combine to present a formidable challenge to the assurance of safety of the citizens during natural disasters. Moreover, the density of the population and high-rise buildings have grave implications for fire safety and crowd control. Additionally, the establishment of a nuclear power plant in an adjacent province of China has given rise to further concern about the potentials for calamities.

The above-mentioned factors underline the need for Hong Kong to have a definite plan for dealing with disasters and emergencies. Administrative arrangements adopted by the government of Hong Kong are simple in nature and operate at a high level of efficiency. Over the years under British colonial rule, various changes have been introduced to improve the process, and the manageable size of the territory, minimal intervention by the government in the private sector, small size of the public service, and the nonpolitical character of administration have combined to maintain the simplicity of the system. Advanced technological developments and a healthy fiscal reserve have added to the efficiency of public organizations. It has been possible to make quick decisions and act on them in times of emergencies. Various methods and mechanisms are in place for forecasting inclement weather and broadcasting warnings. During major holidays, elaborate arrangements are made to divert traffic and effective crowd-control measures are taken. In spite of a range of arrangements to be followed when disasters strike, the need for developing a comprehensive plan for dealing with emergencies was felt.

This chapter examines the existing systems and procedures in Hong Kong for dealing with emergencies and ensuring the safety of the citizens. The focus of inquiry is the *Hong Kong Disaster Plan* (HKDP) prepared by the Security Branch of the Hong Kong Government and published in 1994. Although various government departments have their own plans and programs for dealing with emergencies, this was the first attempt to develop a comprehensive plan to detail the nature of tasks and responsibilities for the agencies involved. The document is reviewed and analyzed with reference to the ideas prevalent in the general literature on emergency management. The overall purpose is to highlight the need for transforming the role of public agencies and strengthening the relationships between the governmental and nongovernmental organizations to deal with emergencies.

II. EMERGENCY PLAN AND MANAGEMENT

A community may be vulnerable to disasters from a number of sources, and each of these may require different kinds of preparation and response. At the same time, it should be pointed out that the basic principles, policies, arrangements, and techniques for emergency management are universal. Depending on the location and physical features, the nature of disasters may vary; distinctions must be made on the basis of the type of crisis and modifications in the actions made to suit the needs of particular cases. However, disasters involve risk and uncertainty, placing communities in unexpected difficulties. They should be met with carefully planned responses.

Disasters lead to severe disruptions—which may be sudden, unexpected and widespread—to normal patterns of life. There are human effects such as loss of life, injury, hardship, and adverse effects on health; effects on social structure such as destruction of or damage to governmental systems, buildings, communications, and essential services. Because of such disruptions, community needs—as for shelter, food, clothing, medical assistance, and social care—must somehow be met (Carter 1991:xxiii). Carter considered the combined effects of such consequences to define a disaster as "An event, natural or man-made, sudden or progressive, which impacts with such severity that the affected community has to respond by taking exceptional measures" (Carter 1991).

Nature does not always win over human endeavors, and there are instances of successful management of emergencies. Most frequently they are related to particular aspects of the task, and it is difficult to locate studies that detail a comprehensive plan for dealing with disasters. For example, the public health service's response to hurricane Andrew in the United States in 1992 was considered effective (Ginzburg et al., 1993), and Carney (1993) recorded the success of a community in Des Moines, Iowa, in coping with flood. On the other hand, there are more examples of ineffective management. There are numerous journalistic reports of severe damage to life and property in various parts of the world. Gillepsie and Murty (1994) discussed "cracks" in postdisaster service delivery in describing the failure of organizations "to work together effectively and to reach shared community goals."

The impact of a disaster can be considerably contained with a high level of preparedness and an effective plan. There are differences of opinion on this issue. On the one hand, disasters cannot be prevented; therefore planning cannot be effective in warding them off. On the other hand, it can be said that numerous deaths and injuries can be related to deficiencies in or the lack of an emergency plan. In case of emergencies, there is an urgent need to make quick decisions and carry them out, although there is generally a lack of competent manpower, resources, or time, particularly in developing countries. Carter listed a number of advantages in having a ready plan to deal with emergencies. The plan indicates a clear and coherent approach for dealing with the emergency and provides a basis for coordinated action. Responsibilities are allocated clearly and the agencies and departments involved have a common reference point for their role in its implementation (Carter 1991:41).

Since the nature of emergencies and the style of administration may vary from one country to another, it is difficult to present an ideal emergency plan. Foster (1980:213–234) developed a list of items that are important for formulating effective emergency plans. He suggested that considering the circumstances under which emergency plans have to be implemented, it is imperative to formulate, legitimize, publicize, and test the system before disaster strikes. Effective emergency plans should be backed up by appropriate authority, and it should clearly describe "the purpose of the document as well as the conditions under which it becomes operative" (Foster 1980:217). There should be a sound assessment of the hazards that are likely to affect the community. The most likely sources of disasters need to be identified and preparation made for tackling them.

It is necessary to obtain detailed information about the probable locations and scale of expected damage and casualties "if the demands likely to be placed on personnel and equipment are to be predicted and accommodated" (Foster 1980:220). It is also important "to designate a legitimate source of overall control of disaster activities" to indicate "which official, agency or organization has the authority to make crucial decisions during a crisis" (Parr 1969). Foster suggests that all emergency plans "should include a detailed listing of all emergency-related personnel, their addresses, and business and private telephone numbers" (1980:224). An effective warning system should be developed to provide "an optimum preimpact response so that potential life and property losses can be detected prior to impact," and Foster details the requirements of preimpact preparations as well as disaster evacuation measures (1980:226–227).

An emergency plan should provide for shelters for evacuees as well as the setting up of centers for coordinating the rescue, evacuation, and recovery process. There is a need to obtain and transmit accurate information on a variety of aspects, and this highlights the importance of effective communication. Information relating to the disaster should be promptly disseminated to ''community organization, the mass media, and to the public'' (1980:230). In searching for and rescuing victims of a disaster, ''specialized equipment such as boats, planes, helicopters, mobile hospitals, bulldozers, and other technology together with the qualified personnel to operate and maintain them'' must be ensured. It will also be necessary to maintain order and discipline in the community as well as to provide medical facilities and even morgues for the more unfortunate victims. Foster proceeds to list the restoration of community services, protection against continuing threat, and continuing assessment of the overall situation as other essential tasks during an emergency and recommends their inclusion in a comprehensive plan.

''Following a natural disaster, the emergency plan should be implemented by territorial departmentalization, led by one specifically appointed business unit'' (Kaplan 1996: 79). The organizational structure of headquarters is significant, since it has implications for the direction, decisions, control, communication, level of efficiency and safety. The administrative organization serves as the ''foundation'' of the plan since it ''supports the paperwork and resource assignments for the entire restoration effort'' (1996:84). Kaplan goes on to emphasize the need for a clearly defined chain of command, firm policies on authority, a well-organized communication headquarters, and availability of information at short notice. He also stressed the need for regular rehearsal of the plan and refresher training to build a team of disaster managers and ensure the uniformity and standardization of policies and procedures. The plan should take into consideration the need to restore utility and other essential services and hence be equipped with technical competence. Kaplan's study underlines the need to adopt a through approach, which should begin with the acquisition of information and knowledge about the nature, type, and impact of disasters and help take a community through the challenge and restore normalcy as quickly as possible.

For the purpose of developing an adequate emergency plan, Kaplan has identified eight key areas. These cover a wide range of activities and can be made effective by the establishment of organizations with specific responsibilities. Organization and planning must be followed up by ''employee services'' to ensure that affected personnel are able to report for duty while arrangements are made to ensure safety and return to normalcy for their families (Kaplan 1996:137). Efforts must be undertaken as soon as possible to restore services disrupted by disasters, and this can be facilitated by ensuring ''the availability of the right type of materials, at the right quantity, at the right place, at the right time'' by the ''inventory services coordinator'' (1996:213). ''The external services organization coordinates and facilitates the flow of information with government agencies and media and assists in the expeditious and safe restoration of services in the aftermath of a disaster'' (1996:222). In service-providing organizations, a check for field-related problems after disaster strikes is essential to ''to ensure that a clear line of communication exists between the communications headquarters and customers'' (1996:269).

While Foster has developed a comprehensive plan for disaster management, taking into consideration every detail, Kaplan's subsequent study focused on a specific type of service provision after natural disasters had struck. However, it should be borne in mind that governmental style and emphasis on plans may vary to a considerable extent from the prescribed model, and their implementation is subject to various constraints. It is desirable for such plans to seek to combine the advantages of both models and consider arrangements for dealing with the emergency itself as well as ensure the continuity of routine administrative activities by restoring services as quickly as possible. The following section provides an overview of the Hong Kong Disaster Plan and assesses it on the basis of these requirements.

III. THE HONG KONG DISASTER PLAN (HKDP)

The structure of government is simple in Hong Kong, and a highly centralized system of administration has been established in which activities are grouped and assigned to various departments of the government. The central secretariat at the top exercises effective control, while regional councils and district boards at the lower levels provide a limited amount of support. Due to the centralized nature of administration and the small size of the territory, it has been possible to deal with emergencies through joint efforts undertaken by a number of government departments.

However, there have been occasions when the need for a plan to deal with disasters has been felt, and a system of emergency management has evolved slowly in Hong Kong. The territory has been hit frequently by natural disasters, but a new storm warning system was introduced only in 1993 after a public outcry over chaos at schools in the territory in May 1992. Although it was reported to be a ''marked improvement on the chaos'' caused in the previous year, ''unionists claimed the system had prompted confusion among workers not sure whether to go home or stay where they were'' (*South China Morning Post*, June 17, 1993). Similarly, the government was severely criticized in June 1997 after a late broadcast of a rainstorm warning led to confusion and tension among parents and students in Hong Kong. None of these cases resulted in massive damage, but it is clear that efforts have to be made to effect improvements in the system of emergency management. Incremental steps were no longer considered to be adequate in dealing with the problem, and dissatisfaction has often been expressed by the community over the management of various types of emergencies, including heavy rain, typhoon, landslide, fire, and overcrowding. Eventually in 1994, the Security Branch of the Hong Kong Government issued a disaster plan for dealing with all kinds of emergencies.

The HKDP covers a wide range of activities including the alert and warning system; procedures for managing the rescue, recovery, and restoration; as well as the respective roles and responsibilities of departments and agencies. According to the plan, the Royal Hong Kong Police Force (RHKPF) and Fire Services Department (FSD) will be the first to be called during an emergency. They will confirm the information and initiate the alert system by calling the Security Branch duty officer (SBDO). The SBDO will secure approval from the secretary of security and activate the Government Secretariat Emergency Coordination Centre (GSECC), and this body will coordinate the response to the emergency. As the situation requires, ''each responding organization will immediately take all necessary action . . .'' (Security Branch 1994:6).

The section on rescue management specifies that the responsibilities will rest with the FSD on land and the Marine Department (MD) at sea, while the RHKP will carry out a supporting role for both. The document recognizes that it is ''necessary to exercise strict control over access to the disaster site, in order to ensure that the emergency services are not deflected from their task of saving lives, protecting property and safeguarding the disaster site for subsequent expert investigation'' (Security Branch 1994:7). The Government Flying Services provide assistance ''in support of various government department and agencies as well as a round-the-clock emergency air ambulance and search-and-rescue services'' (*Hong Kong 1997*:308). The roles and responsibilities of various departments, such as the Civil Aviation Department (in case of an air crash), FSD, and RHKP in effecting rescue operations are outlined. In short, the HKDP provides ''for on site command and control, and off-site command and coordination in the event of a disaster'' (Ying 1995:115).

The plan provides specific guidelines for dealing with disasters by outlining the roles of the City and New Territories Administration (CNTA), the Information Services Department (ISD), and the Hospital Authority (HA). The first two bodies are given the task of overseeing press activities and arranging briefings to the media, while the HA provides hospital services for the victims. The GSECC is responsible for obtaining and issuing policy directives on behalf of the Governor's Security Committee (GSC, now to be referred as the chief executive's Security Committee), Chief Secretary (CS),[2] and Secretary for Security (SforS); advising GSC on the need for enactment of emergency legislation for dealing with the disaster; providing a permanent link with the SforS through which decisions on policy matters can be made by the departments concerned; coordinating the acquisition and mobilization of civil and military resources and those of outside agencies; liaising with departments for obtaining and collating information on the overall situation as it develops; acting as a link through which urgent public messages could be issued from the government secretariat for publication or broadcast; briefing senior public officials on the situation; and ''performing any other duties set out in the GSECC Guide, the Internal Security Guide, contingency plans or as may be required by GSC, CS and/or SforS at the time'' (Security Branch 1994:9). Liaison officers from various departments will perform specific tasks related to their own organizations. For example, the Transport Department (TD) duty officer ''will establish contact with public transport operators and keep GSECC informed of the situation'' (1994:9), and other departments will fulfill their part in contributing to the rescue process.

The HKDP devotes considerable attention to recovery management following the control of disasters ''to return the community to a condition acceptable by that community.'' The physical, psychological, and social needs of the community can be satisfied by providing accommodation, food, clothing, and relief funds; responding to inquiries from the public; and following up with an inquiry into the causes and effects of the disaster.

''The relevant District Officer[3] from City and New Territories Administration will set up his own emergency co-ordination centre and co-ordinate relief measures to be provided by Social Welfare Department, Housing Department and other agencies (Ying 1995: 115). Temporary shelters are to be arranged, and the Social Welfare Department (SWD) is responsible for providing essential relief items to the victims. The district officer (DO) ''will assist the Police in dealing with inquiries at the scene from members of the public, while the Director of Information Services ''will be responsible for disseminating information on the situation to the public through the media and government departments concerned . . .''; and the ''SWD will be responsible, in conjunction with the Housing department, for establishing a combined registration Centre for disaster victims'' (Security Branch 1994:11–12). This will be followed by restoration management in order ''to release the disaster site as soon as possible.''

The plan indicates the respective roles and responsibilities of the relevant agencies and also reiterates that government departments should carry out their normal functions as far as possible. This is a tall order, as public agencies are usually burdened with a heavy workload. It has been suggested that military units may be called upon to help, but with the departure of the British armed forces personnel prior to the handover of Hong

Kong to China, there is a vacuum in this area. Although the People's Liberation Army (PLA) has a small contingent stationed in Hong Kong, their involvement in the rescue and relief operations during an emergency has not been made clear yet. A few nongovernmental organizations (NGOs) have been listed in the plan, and these can be called upon for providing assistance with a variety of tasks.

Emphasis has been placed on communications and an appendix to the plan includes a directory of relevant telephone numbers of departments involved in the HKDP. Interestingly, appendix C is not included in the document available to the public. Several technologically advanced devices are to be used to facilitate conference calls and ensure privacy, while a back-up system has been planned in the event of disruptions in the system of communications.

Dissemination of information is crucial in managing emergencies, preventing outbreaks of panic, and reducing the impact of hazards. The ISD will coordinate the collection and dissemination of information. The GSECC "will provide ISD with bulletins and advice for the public." The CNTA will deal "with technical and operational enquiries from the media and public on site" as well as monitor public reaction to keep GSECC informed. The GSECC will coordinate the decision-making process and provide information to the ISD for broadcast to the public. In fact the HKDP "provides details to ensure effective and efficient communication, both in respect of interdepartmental and internal departmental communications" (Ying 1995:117).

The HKDP includes two appendixes. Appendix A specifies the roles of the Agriculture and Fisheries Department, Architectural Services Department, Auxiliary Medical Services, Buildings Department, CNTA, Civil Aid Services, Civil Aviation Department, Civil Engineering Department, Drainage Services Department, Education Department, Electrical and Mechanical Services Department, FSD, Government Flying Service, Government Land Transport Agency, Government Supplies Department, Department of Health, High ways Department, HA, Housing Department, ISD, Lands Department, MD, Regional Services Department, RHKP, Royal Observatory, Security Branch, SWD, TD, and Urban Services Department. Appendix B provides a list of NGOs that are expected to assist with dissemination of information and public broadcast, operation of cargo terminals, public transportation, and power supply. The long list of departments, public agencies, and NGOs gives rise to concern over the prospect of cooperation among them, especially since some of these have no interaction in the course of regular administrative activities. The last page of the document includes a "Record of Amendments," although its purpose is not clear in the layout.

The HKDP strives to cover all aspects of emergency management. Beginning with the recognition of an emergency, there are systematic procedures for notifying relevant agencies, providing accurate information to the victims and the public, searching and rescuing survivors, providing them with the required support and comfort, and rehabilitating them, followed by an investigation to identify the causes and developing strategies for future reference. There is a cycle of activities beginning with prevention and moving through the stages of amelioration and rehabilitation, with follow-up action designed to keep an eye on strengthening the preventive aspect. It appears that the HKDP strives to be effective by "bringing together the involved parties, defining their respective functions as well as those of the co-ordinating departments in conducting and controlling the rescue functions" (Ying 1995:117).

On some occasions, the plan has not been completely effective in handling emergencies in Hong Kong in recent years. "Factory owners and a church hit out at the government yesterday for failing to coordinate its contingency plan when the red rainstorm signal was hoisted'' (*Hong Kong Standard*: May 1, 1996). In another case, a fire that killed 40 people in November 1996 could not be contained due to violations of fire safety procedures, the illegal alteration of fire doors and exits, as well as the lack of adequate number of ladders of the required capacity (*South China Morning Post*: December 13, 1996). Each case of disaster illustrates the inadequacy of one single set of emergency management measures and draws attention to the need for constant revision of the plan.

Considering the tasks and responsibilities assigned to the various agencies and institutions in managing disasters, some comments can be made on the HKPD. From the activities of the Hong Kong government, it is clear that efforts are frequently undertaken to improve the capability to deal with emergencies. For example, school principals were invited to an exhibition and seminar at the Royal Observatory to ensure that they ''knew what to do in typhoons or rainstorms'' (*Hong Kong Standard*: October 14, 1993). ''A typhoon contingency plan has been established to direct traffic in the event of bad weather during one phase of construction'' of a bridge connecting the new airport with the city (*South China Morning Post*: May 12, 1995).

Media briefing and public relations activities have been correctly identified as major tasks for emergency management in the HKDP. In fact, keeping the public and the media informed of disasters and actions to deal with them constitutes part of the management. This aspect of emergency management can be helpful in coping with losses and the impact of disasters as well as future tribulations.

The HKDP seeks to provide a detailed description of the functions and responsibilities of various agencies in cases of emergencies. The plan appears to be designed with the assumption that emergencies can be tackled with a number of steps arranged in a proposed sequence. A series of activities is suggested to respond to the needs for detecting a disaster, rescuing the victims, recovering the survivors, and rehabilitating them. It gives the impression that emergencies can be completely and competently dealt with by following the prescribed steps.

Tasks and responsibilities for various departments and agencies have been assigned on the basis of their specified roles. For example, the Drainage Services Department ''is responsible for clearing and repairing blocked and damaged sewers and storm-drains,'' while the Highways Department is ''responsible for clearing and repairing blocked or damaged public roads, removing dangerous and fallen boulders and dealing with landslides on Government land, answering requests for assistance in the saving of life, protection of property and miscellaneous calls for action or assistance within the resources'' of the Department (Security Branch 1994:20–21). All agencies that could be conceived to be of some use during an emergency have been listed and their functions briefly described. The task of determining an effective way of coordinating their activities appears to be left to the concerned departments and officials.

The designers of the HKDP appear to be confident of the existence of an effective system of communication among the agencies involved. Obviously, the successful implementation of the plan will depend on smooth communication and cooperation among the actors and agencies, but it is also necessary to recognize the possible conflicts and rivalry as well as jurisdictional disputes that are common in modern organizations. The highly developed system of communication technology in Hong Kong can help to overcome potential problems in this area.

In a nutshell,

> Emergency measures for cyclone, flood, storm surges and landslide include: warning dissemination and collation of information by the Information and Services Department; search and rescue, crowd control and evacuation by the Civil Aid Services and the Royal Hong Kong Auxiliary Air Force; protection of life and property, emergency rescue works by the Fire Service; ambulance and medical assistance by the Hospital Service Department; anti-flood measures by the Drainage Service Department; damaged building, building works and landslips[4] and slope control by the Building Ordinance Office; traffic control and area security, coordination of traffic and transport operation by the Hong Kong Royal Police; removal of roads obstruction, removal of dead bodies and animal carcasses by the Urban Services Department and closure of schools by the Education Department. These measures are coordinated and supervised by the Central Coordination Centre (ESCAP 1990b:150).[5]

It is important to realize that one of the features of disasters is that they are unpredictable in terms of the time, place or velocity with which they will strike. Emergency plans should be more flexible in terms of deciding which steps should be taken immediately and how the subsequent activities are to be organized. For example, there may be a need to initiate recovery even before the disaster has been controlled. But the HKPD recommends that "After a disaster has been controlled, recovery operations are to be conducted to assist the victims" (Security Branch 1994:11).

In planning emergency management, special bodies may be delegated authority for directing relevant activities. Turner (1995:535) feels that "it is important to be able to rely on people and organizations with good local knowledge, with an intimate knowledge which permits them to deal swiftly and flexibly with unique local uncertainties." A limited number of NGOs are listed in the HKPD for providing assistance to the task of emergency management. These include a number of commercial organizations that provide services in the communications sector through telecommunications services, radio and television broadcasts, and management of marine terminals. The others are involved in providing transportation services and public utilities. While these NGOs certainly have a useful role to play, a vast number of NGOs specializing in rescue and recovery have been left out of the formal plan. This does not mean that other NGOs do not participate in rescue and rehabilitation operations. But it would be more productive to allow provisions for sharing the responsibilities and tasks entrusted to the Social Welfare Department by a number of NGOs which are engaged in the provision of care, relief, and assistance to the disaster victims. Rehabilitation of such victims is often a huge responsibility that few governments are able to handle on their own.

With reference to the ideas and contents for developing emergency plans proposed by Foster (1980) and Kaplan (1996), comments can be made on the inadequacy of the HKDP. It does not spell out clearly the conditions under which the plan becomes operative but vaguely refers to the incidence of disaster. There is no reference to particular type of hazard to which the agencies should respond but a general assumption that specific agencies will be activated as the need arises. The GSECC is presented as the coordinating body, but its nature of authority has not been spelled out.

The plan does not provide detailed guidelines on the process of mitigation. The conventional method of mitigation has been followed and the emphasis has been on the construction of facilities and ensuring that they remain operational. Over the years, a number of steps have been taken to mitigate flood losses, such as the gradual resolution of the squatter problem, improvements in the maintenance of storm water drainage and foul-water sewerage systems, and reclamation of land in the waterfront followed by construction of concrete seawalls. A new legislation to ''enable the Government to implement effective drainage maintenance and management under a comprehensive strategy'' is under consideration (ESCAP 1990b:28).

Disaster mitigation cannot be attempted with a casual approach and involves careful consideration of a number of factors. The United Nations Development Program (UNDP 1994) suggests that the measures should be a combination of actions related to engineering and construction, physical planning, economic development, management and institutional measures, as well as societal disposition in which a ''safety culture'' can take root. Hong Kong has not taken such a comprehensive approach to disaster mitigation, but it appears that awareness is growing and the community and government appear to be moving slowly in that direction.

IV. ISSUES IN EMERGENCY MANAGEMENT IN HONG KONG

Emergency management has received attention rather late in Hong Kong in spite of frequent assaults by natural disasters whose effects are becoming increasingly strong. The other reason could be the hands-off approach adopted by the government, which tended to leave the mitigation tasks to the family and community. But major changes in the social, economic, and political systems in the past few decades have made the public more conscious of their rights, and arrangements for emergency management had to be streamlined.

The problems revealed by an examination of the HKDP can be expected to arise in any society. The nonavailability of human and material resources is a major handicap in many developing nations. The experience of Hong Kong may be useful in drawing lessons for managing emergencies in small geographical units. However, a number of points can be suggested for improving the system of emergency management, and these are related to organizational arrangements, coordination of activities, and the political will to view emergency management as an integral part of governance in modern states.

Emergency management entails a diverse range of functions by public organizations. Law and order have to be upheld and discipline has to be strictly maintained, since the lives and property of a large number of people and the community are at stake. At the same time, it is necessary to bring the disaster under control, contain its impact, and rescue the victims. They have to be provided with proper shelters, and relief materials have to be distributed among them. Simultaneously, efforts have to be initiated to rehabilitate the victims of the disaster. All these functions have to be performed within a short period of time, and the concerned agencies are also expected to continue performing their normal duties. In short, emergency management calls for performing most functions a government performs with fewer agencies and staff and within a shorter time span.

The success of emergency management depends to a great extent on the quality and operation of communication facilities, shelters, and planned development of a community. Hong Kong has the advantages of small size and complete administrative autonomy, which are extremely conducive to the development of an effective system of emergency management. ''Huge investments are committed to the rapid development of communication and transportation network, setting up of towns and settlements, and establishment of facilities to assist in trade and commerce'' (Huque 1997:6–7). A high percentage of mitigation and recovery activities require the support of effective public works. Unfortunately, the current infrastructural projects in Hong Kong appear to neglect facilities that could be useful in emergency management, and the HKDP concerns itself entirely with organizational and personnel arrangements. This trend can be expected to change after the completion of the huge airport and port development projects in Hong Kong.

In managing emergencies, organizations require a high degree of flexibility to decide on actions on the basis of needs of the moment. This is one area that emerges as a challenge to traditional organizational arrangements where regularity of procedures serves a useful purpose. For example, in many countries, the police perform a number of functions unrelated to crime control and law enforcement, such as emergency medical services or mediation of family disputes (Moore 1990:78–79). In the same way, emergency management requires the performance of multiple functions, and organizational flexibility is an essential trait. The closely knit administrative structure of Hong Kong has been able to deal with this issue due to the proximity of officials and an effective network for communication. The cohesive nature of the Hong Kong civil service contributes to the effectiveness of cooperative efforts.

A related requirement is the need for innovation in management. Innovation is advocated in all types of situations but cannot be pursued in rigid and inflexible organizations. Emergencies call for dealing with problems as soon as they arise, and require administrators to utilize innovative measures to reduce human suffering and to deal with urgent matters. Kiel (1994:14–16) advocates dynamism in organizations that will face complex tasks: ''surprises are expected as work processes are transformed but they are seen as part of the risk, uncertainty, and reward of creation and innovation''. A note of caution should be added to underline the risks involved in tampering with existing practices and procedures, and innovation must be applied with extreme caution.

Activities related to weather forecasting and other geophysical services have been vested in the Hong Kong Observatory, while functions related to drainage and sewerage are performed by the Drainage Services Department. The Agriculture and Fisheries Department and the Territory Development Department complete the list of mitigation agencies in Hong Kong (ESCAP 1990a:29–30). Moreover, in drawing upon the leadership of several agencies with specialized capabilities, it is possible to overlook the potential sources of conflict that may arise. In managing emergencies, it may not be desirable to bring together organizations that may be competing with one another for governmental funds or power. In decentralized administrative organizations, the situation also carries the danger of jurisdictional conflicts and the risk of disagreements over the chain of command. It is advisable to establish a clear structure of authority to allow agencies and officials to work under a common framework of organization. The centralized nature of public administration in Hong Kong helps avoid much of this risk.

Emergency management may be carried out by public as well as nonpublic organizations. The public nature of agencies imposes a number of constraints and limitations on them. In cases of emergencies, it may be prudent to grant exemptions from some of the requirements of openness, access to information and officials, and strict vigilance in order to allow the organizations more time, freedom, and flexibility to complete the urgent task of emergency management. The current constitutional and administrative arrangements in Hong Kong do not appear to impose additional constraints on public organizations. Increased participation of nongovernmental organizations in emergency management could help overcome this constraint.

A final point worth noting is the perception of emergency management held by governments. In many countries, it has been viewed as a sporadic problem that should be dealt with as and when necessary, while governments prefer to concentrate on routine administrative activities. It is essential for governments to integrate emergency management into the framework of routine administrative activities. Emergency management should be treated as an ongoing process and activities of preparation, mitigation, and rehabilitation should be viewed as a continuous process and be recognized as one of the core functions of the government. Total commitment to the establishment of an effective emergency management system by the Hong Kong SAR government as well as the national government in Beijing is extremely important in this respect.

The HKPD does not appear to have a clear organizational framework for operationalizing the plan. It would be helpful to supplement the definition of the respective roles of the various departments/agencies with an organizational structure for bringing together and ensuring better coordination of their efforts. Information could be collected on the expertise, services, and resources of nongovernmental organizations, and these could then be incorporated in the HKDP.

V. CONCLUDING OBSERVATIONS

Hong Kong has an efficient system of administration, which has been instrumental in developing the territory into one of the leading trading and financial centers in the world. Although natural disasters are quite common in Hong Kong, it has been possible to avoid major losses through an effective warning system and adequate services provided by a variety of organizations. Emergency management does not pose a major challenge to Hong Kong, which has a cohesive and centralized civil service, an excellent technological support system, and a healthy economy and financial capability of the government can afford to allocate adequate resources for dealing with disasters. While developments in the area of subsequent rehabilitation and mitigation have been slow, there has been progress in recent years, as social services are now receiving increased allocations from the government.

As Hong Kong has finally been reintegrated with the People's Republic of China, a number of changes may be ushered in the area of emergency management. Like Hong Kong, China is frequently affected by natural disasters, and it is expected that Hong Kong's experience and expertise could be used to facilitate mitigation work on the mainland. According to *The Basic Law of Hong Kong Special Administrative Region of the People's Republic of China* (1990), Hong Kong will become an autonomous region of China and will continue to enjoy a high degree of autonomy for at least the next 50 years. There is no suggestion to replace or reject the Hong Kong Disaster Plan, and the current arrangements will continue to be in place for managing emergencies in Hong Kong. Moreover, it is expected that special administrative and economic zones in China with small areas similar to Hong Kong may choose to develop their own emergency plans.

Increased interaction can be expected between emergency managers in Hong Kong and China. While the official policy will continue to be a separation of administrative machinery and personnel, it is obvious that policies and considerations on emergency management in Hong Kong and China will have an impact on one another. In terms of emergency management, this might result in a desirable fusion of the high level of technical expertise available in China and the modern managerial techniques prevalent in Hong Kong.

Some natural calamities are inevitable, but many (including man-made disasters) can be avoided with careful management and development of sound policies. With adequate allocation of resources, floods or land slippage problems can be mitigated, but the resources may greatly exceed the periodic response and recovery after calamities strike. Disasters will most likely continue to affect lives and properties in the tiny Hong Kong Special Administrative Region, but the system of management can be improved considerably with the available resources and facilities. Hong Kong should be able to serve as a laboratory for experimenting with ideas to deal with emergency in small, self-contained communities.

ENDNOTES

1. In this chapter, the terms *disaster* and *emergency* are used interchangeably. The document released by the Hong Kong government has been titled *Hong Kong Disaster Plan*; it provides guidelines for dealing with all types of emergencies.
2. From July 1, 1997, the designation for the Chief Secretary has been amplified, and the current title is Chief Secretary for Administration.
3. The district officer is a member of the civil service, and is placed in charge of the various districts.
4. The term *landslips* is used for *landslides* in Hong Kong Government documents, perhaps to indicate incidents of smaller magnitude.
5. The titles of some government departments in this excerpt from the ESCAP document are not accurate, but they are close enough to the actual titles and can be identified.

REFERENCES

Basic Law of Hong Kong Special Administrative Region of the People's Republic of China, The (1990). Consultative Committee of the National People's Congress.

Carney, C. (1993). Community and organization capacity: The key to emergency response and recovery. *Public Management*, December, pp. 11–14.

Carter, W.N. (1991). *Emergency Management: An Emergency Manager's Handbook*. Manila, Asian Development Bank.

ESCAP, Economic and Social Commission for Asia and the Pacific (1990a). *Urban Flood Loss Prevention and Mitigation*. Bangkok, Water Resources Series No. 68.

ESCAP, Economic and Social Commission for Asia and the Pacific (1990b). *Preparedness and Other Operational Measures for Water-Related Natural Emergency Reduction in Asia and the Pacific*. Bangkok, Water Resources Series No. 69.

Foster, H.D. (1980). *Emergency Planning, The Preservation of Life and Property*. New York: Springer-Verlag.

GEO, Geotechnical Engineering Office (1982). *Report on the Rainstorm of May 1982*. GEO Report No. 25. Hong Kong: Civil Engineering Department, Hong Kong Government.

Gillepsie, D.F. and Murty, S.A. (1994). Cracks in a postemergency service delivery network. *American Journal of Community Psychology* 22(5), 639–660.

Ginzburg, H.M., Jevec, R.J., and Reutershan, T. (1993). The Public Health Service's response to Hurricane Andrew. *Public Health Reports* 108(2), 241–44.

Hong Kong Standard.

Hong Kong 1997. Hong Kong: Government Printer.

Huque, A.S. (1997). ''Public administration and infrastructure development.'' *Hong Kong Public Administration* 6(*1*), 1–9.
Kaplan, L.G. (1996). *Emergency and Emergency Planning Manual*. New York: McGraw-Hill.
Kiel, L.D. (1994). *Managing Chaos and Complexity in Government, A New Paradigm for Managing Change, Innovation, and Organizational Renewal*. San Francisco, Jossey-Bass.
Moore, M.H. (1990). Police leadership: The impossible dream? In E.C. Hargrove and J.C. Gildwell (eds.), *Impossible Jobs in Public Management*, Lawrence, KS: University Press of Kansas.
Parr, A.R. (1969). A brief on emergency plans. *EMO Digest* 9(*4*), 13–15.
Security Branch, Hong Kong Government (1994). *Hong Kong Emergency Plan*. November.
South China Morning Post.
Turner, B.A. (1995). A perspective from the social sciences. In T. Horlick-Jones, A. Amendola and R. Casale (eds.), *Natural Risk and Civil Protection*. London: E & FN Spon, pp. 535–537.
UNDP, United Nations Development Program (1994). *Emergency Mitigation*, eds. Second Edition, Emergency Management Training Program, Geneva.
Ying, D.L.C.C. (1995). A Study of the Lan Kwai Fong Emergency in the context of Emergency Management, unpublished Masters Dissertation, City University of Hong Kong.

34

Coping with Calamities

Disaster Management in Bangladesh

Habib Zafarullah School of Social Science, University of New England, Armidale, New South Wales, Australia

Mohammad Habibur Rahman and Mohammad Mohabbat Khan
Department of Public Administration, University of Dhaka, Dhaka, Bangladesh

I. INTRODUCTION

Bangladesh is a disaster-prone area. It has, since time immemorial, experienced natural calamities of immense magnitude, leaving in their wake death, destruction, and misery—with profound implications for human welfare, the environment, and the management of relief and rehabilitation. Some of these calamities, like cyclones, tornadoes, and tidal bores, have occurred sporadically, abruptly catching the people unaware; others, like floods, river erosion, and drought, have been perennial events, their occurrence often prognosticated in advance. In every case, however, the effects of human misery have been massive, environmental degradation extensive, and the pressure on the government to provide support to victims and reconstruct calamity-torn areas stupendous. Disaster preparedness programs and postdisaster relief operations are the two key components of disaster management in the public and nongovernmental sectors.

Both sporadic (cyclones, tidal waves) and perennial (flood, drought, and river erosion) natural disasters are prevalent in Bangladesh. The impact of the former is sudden and intense, while that of the latter is not immediately felt by those affected and in the areas these occur. The long-term consequence of both, however, may be severe, requiring concrete and comprehensively designed plans of action for both governmental and nongovernmental intervention. However, disaster management, in its contemporary sense, has only been a recent addition to the range of functions performed by the government in Bangladesh, although a ministerial department specializing on relief administration has been in existence since independence. Specifics of disaster management—like risk assessment, establishing the baseline for planning and decision making, developing broad-based risk evaluation criteria, designing preparedness and mitigation strategies, accessing resources to cope with hazards, creating networks for postdisaster relief and rehabilitation, public education and training, and, last but not least, formal community involvement in coping with disasters—are still being adapted for the peculiar Bangladesh situation and partially applied in practice.

This chapter examines the existing initiatives of the Bangladesh government in managing disasters, assesses the institutional arrangements in both the public and nongovernmental sectors, reviews international interventions, and identifies some of the major problems and constraints in the existing disaster preparedness and mitigation framework.

II. THE NATURE OF DISASTERS IN BANGLADESH

Bangladesh lies on a deltaic plain fed by mighty rivers, which originate in the Himalayas and run across Nepal and India. Over 120 million people cram a land area of a little over 55,000 square miles. This makes the population highly vulnerable to natural hazards. While landlocked on three sides, in the south the country faces the Bay of Bengal, notorious for serving as the breeding ground for frequent cyclonic depressions. The coastal regions of the country are thus susceptible to cyclones, which can be fierce, with wind velocity reaching 145 miles per hour, as happened in 1991, and these are accompanied by tidal waves as high as 20 feet. Since the 1960s, nearly a million people have perished in several cyclones; the worst, which hit in 1970, claimed nearly 700,000 lives (Burton et al. 1978; see also Hanson 1967:12–18; Milne 1986:74; Bilski 1991).

Heavy monsoonal rains during midyear is the prime cause of floods in Bangladesh. Intense siltation has raised riverbeds to such a height that even mighty rivers like the Padma (the extension of the Ganges) overflow. Deforestation in the higher catchment area is another cause of flooding in the lower riparian country. The control of peak flows of the Ganges river by the Farakka Barrage in India has also had some influence in diverting the flood waters from that country into Bangladesh (Monan 1989:27). Arguably, the Barrage is rendering the Ganges River management regime ineffective. While floods, known to have both a beneficial and a destructive effect, are "an essential component of the social and ecological system" of a country (Blaikie et al. 1994:124), in Bangladesh the frequent occurrence of high-intensity floods has had a profoundly injurious impact on the lives of the common people. In the 1987 and 1988 floods, over 4000 people and nearly 237,000 cattle perished, 29,630 kilometers of roads and almost 2000 kilometers of railway embankment were damaged, 2000 culverts and 436 bridges were destroyed, and several thousands of industrial, educational, and health care infrastructures were affected (Asian Development Bank 1991:90). The floods of 1998, however, have been recorded as the worst in history. Two-thirds of the country was inundated, 30 million people were affected, and more than 1100 lost their lives. The economy was hard hit; the growth rate of the gross domestic product (GDP) was at risk of dropping significantly, the budget deficit was likely to increase, and country's balance of payments negatively affected (World Bank 1998).

While safety measures may have been improved over the years since the 1970 catastrophe, managing disasters from a holistic standpoint remains problematic in Bangladesh. Government efforts at improving warning systems, constructing storm shelters, and building embankments to prevent tidal waves have been meager compared to the requirements of effectively countering the severity of cyclones that strike the country at almost regular intervals (Blaikie et al. 1994:163).

III. MANAGING DISASTERS: THE PUBLIC SECTOR

The construction of the policy framework for managing disasters was initiated in the late 1980s, after several natural disasters (floods, cyclones, droughts, etc.) struck the country and forced the government to reconsider its options regarding the problem. Apart from pressures from within the government and the people at risk, external stimuli from international agencies (for example, the United Nations Development Program and the World Health Organization) also served to rearrange existing postdisaster relief and health care measures and to create new structures for reducing the impact of these phenomena. While planning and decision making are restricted to centralized organizations and specialized committees at the ministerial level, risks and hazards assessments and vulnerability analyses, even if imperfect, are shared by both governmental and nongovernmental agencies.

A. Network of Agencies

The management of natural disasters in Bangladesh is the responsibility of several public agencies, the foremost among them being the Ministry of Disaster Management and Relief (hereafter the ministry), which is the specialized structure to oversee both disaster mitigation initiatives and postdisaster relief and rehabilitation. It is supported by several other agencies and advisory bodies at several levels in the machinery of government (see Figure 1). The institutional arrangements for effective disaster preparedness planning and risk reduction involve linkages and transactions between the disaster-management structures both at the pre- and postdisaster phases of the disaster cycle as well as during disaster-free periods, when long-term policy initiatives and program evaluation become imperative.

The National Disaster Management Council (hereafter the national council), formed after the severe floods of 1988, is a high-powered body with the prime minister presiding over it. This 29-person body has representation from all relevant ministries[1] and the three armed services. It meets at least twice a year and is responsible for formulating or approving policies relating to disasters on the basis of the recommendations of the Interministrial Disaster Management Coordination Committee (hereafter the coordination committee) and the National Disaster Management Advisory Committee (hereafter the advisory committee). It provides guidance and direction toward policy implementation, making laws and rules directed at mitigating the effect of disasters, setting guidelines for activities throughout the disaster cycle, and coordinating the activities of the civil administration, defense forces and nongovernmental organizations (NGOs) (GOB 1997:4). Being at the center of political power, it wields enormous control over resources necessary for the building of the physical infrastructure to confront disasters and to assist victims in rehabilitation.

The coordination committee is led by the disaster management minister and supported by the administrative chiefs of several other ministries and officials of some public agencies and the Bangladesh Red Crescent Society (BRCS). Representatives of executive bureaus and NGOs are often invited for consultation and advice. The main purposes of this committee are to oversee the implementation of the policies, decisions, and directives of the national council and keep it informed of developments, coordinate the activities of all disaster-related government agencies, review the disaster preparedness initiatives of all ministries/agencies twice a year, and direct relief operations in the aftermath of disasters (GOB 1997:7).

The advisory committee represents a cross-section of the community. It is a large body composed of legislators from disaster-prone areas, civil society representatives, and specialists in water resource management, meteorology, seismology, infrastructure planning, social anthropology, education and training, and disaster matters. The prime minister nominates an expert on disaster management as the chairperson of this committee, which, among other things, provides technical and managerial advice on disaster mitigation, pre-

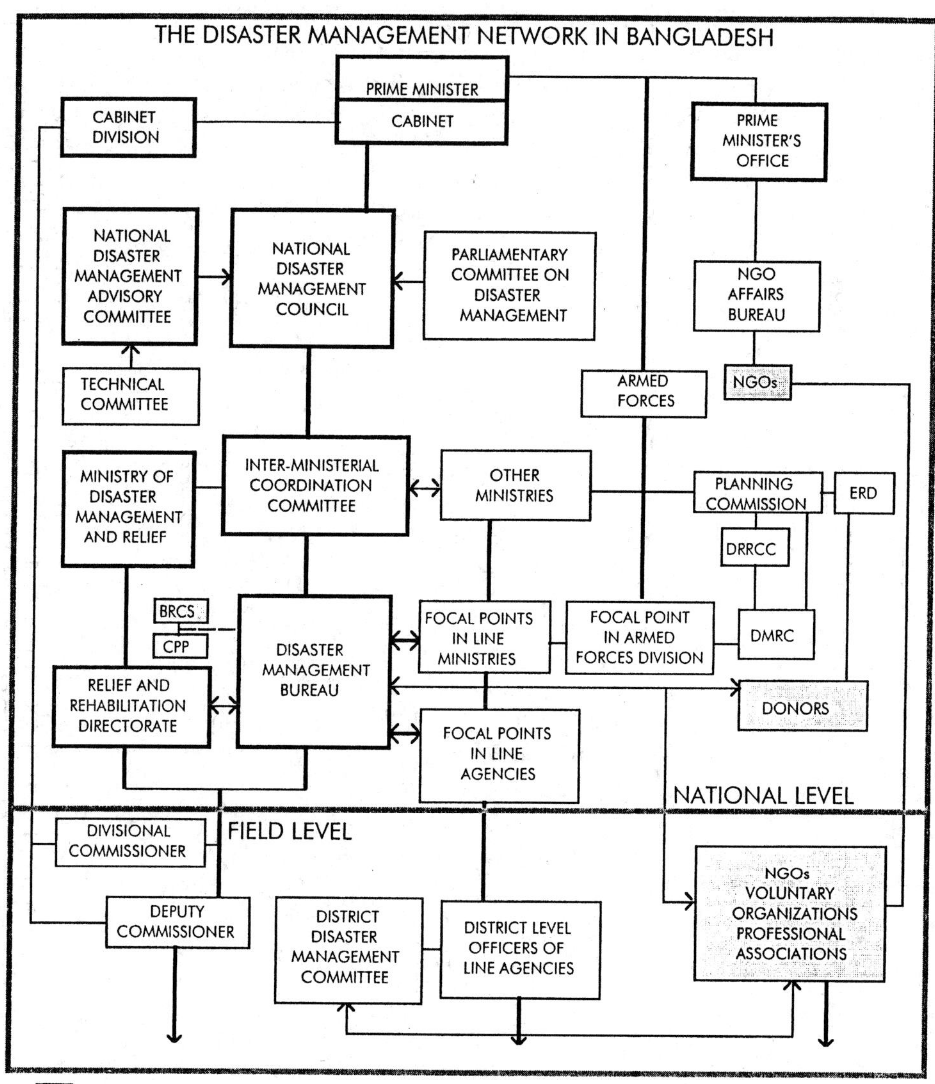

Figure 1 The disaster management network in Bangladesh. (From DMB 1993.)

paredness, emergency services, rehabilitation, and reconstruction. Postcalamity evaluation of disaster mitigation programs and propositions for long-term rehabilitation plans are key aspects of its operational agenda.

The ministry has been designated as the focal point of all disaster management initiatives of the government. Information and data on all phases of the disaster cycle supplied by the Disaster Management Bureau (hereafter the bureau) are utilized by the ministry in making decisions and feeding the national council and the coordination committee in their policy-making pursuits. Once every quarter it reviews its own action plan, identifies disaster-risk zones, distributes relief materials, undertakes rehabilitation programs, provides logistical support, and transmits information to local officials on impending disasters and ways to encounter them. Its chief executive officer directly supervises and controls emergency relief operations in the postdisaster phase (GOB 1997: 10–11).

The principal objective of the bureau, established in 1992, "is to reduce the human, economic and environmental costs of disasters" by (1) enhancing the capacity to plan and prepare for disasters and to cope with their consequences; (2) increasing the capacities of households and local communities in the highly disaster-prone areas to cope with cyclones, floods and other potentially disastrous situations; (3) increasing the efficiency and the effectiveness of response to emergencies; and (4) ensuring that measures are taken to reduce disaster risks as much as possible and that such risks are properly considered in general development planning (DMB, 1993).

Operating under the direct supervision of the ministry and responsible to the coordination committee, the bureau enjoys some degree of operational autonomy in the disaster management framework of the government. It provides informational inputs to the government on disaster policy matters and liaises with all organizations in both the public and voluntary sectors involved in the prevention and mitigation of disasters. Its activities include hazard mapping and vulnerability analysis, planning and construction of embankments and related water control structures to contain floods and cyclone-proof shelters, developing and enforcing of building code, forecasting/warning dissemination, contingency planning for response, rescue operations, damage and needs assessments, procurement and distribution of relief, and reconstruction and rehabilitation (DMB 1993:24–25).

The bureau is responsible for integrating the planning and implementation of non structural mitigation measures of all participating ministries in disaster prevention and mitigation. It has prepared guidelines to assist local councils in formulating their own action plans to prevent and mitigate disasters and has published booklets on cyclones, tidal surges, and floods to help local administrators save life and property; occasionally it disseminates information to the public on disaster preparedness and mitigation.

The training programs conducted by the bureau are designed to (1) increase awareness at all levels of society concerning the practical ways of reducing disaster risks and losses; (2) strengthen national institutional capacity for disaster management, with emphasis on preparedness and support to the disaster management committee at the local level; (3) enhance the knowledge and skills of key personnel with disaster management responsibilities, develop disaster management training capabilities, and provide relevant operational guidelines; (4) establish disaster action plans in the most disaster-prone areas and mobilize local communities to prepare and protect themselves and to increase their own capacities to cope with and recover from disasters; (5) promote proven local-level risk reduction measures and develop postdisaster assistance strategies to maximize recovery benefits; and (6) improve the effectiveness of warnings and warning dissemination systems, and the facilities at shelters and evacuation sites in high-risk areas (DMB 1993:28–31).

Clearly, such a broad range of functions requires the bureau to establish and maintain linkages with a host of agencies at various levels in government and the community. Indeed, it serves as a link between the upper echelons of the disaster management hierarchy and the local administration and NGOs at the point where disasters occur. Its horizontal linkages are with the Relief and Rehabilitation Directorate (hereafter the directorate), disaster management focal points in several line ministries and the armed forces, and the international donor community.

Apart from performing its normal duties as the premier administrative organization in relief and rehabilitation, the directorate, during normal (disaster-free) times, transports food and relief materials to areas predisposed to frequent disasters and maintain stockpiles for distribution whenever required. It also builds road links to disaster shelters or relief and recovery camps and organizes and oversees tree planting and levy bank development programs to facilitate the prevention and deintensification of cyclones, tidal bores, floods, and river erosion.

B. Encountering Disasters

The disaster cycle in Bangladesh is partitioned into four discrete but overlapping phases: predisaster planning, preparedness, disaster and postdisaster response, recovery and reconstruction (GOB 1997:2). The predisaster phase is described as one in which there is no imminent possibility of a natural calamity; but—in anticipation of likely disasters—it is concerned with long-term planning to prevent or mitigate the catastrophic consequences in their wake. During the disaster-preparedness phase, efforts are directed at warning the people of impending disasters, informing them about their force and magnitude, and outlining the means with which to face them. The third phase is one when disasters actually strike and cause human casualties and physical destruction. This phase can be either short (in the case of cyclones, tornadoes, tidal waves, and flash floods), with the impact felt immediately or long after (e.g., prolonged floods, river erosion, drought), when consequences may be experienced gradually over a protracted period of time. In the postdisaster phase, where the focus is on rehabilitation and reconstruction, both government and NGOs are involved in normalizing community life, alleviating the economic plight of disaster victims, and rebuilding infrastructures.

In each of these phases, several public agencies are actively involved, either in concert or on their own, but not entirely insulated from the rest of the disaster management community. The national council is more active during the pre and postdisaster phases, while the coordination committee, the ministry, the bureau and the directorate remain operative during all phases of the disaster cycle.

Prioritization of disaster preparedness and mitigation (DPM) projects and their incorporation into national development plans is expected to be made by the national council on the recommendations of the coordination committee, which also spells out the methodology of disaster impact assessments (DIA) applicable to large projects and oversees project design and implementation. Other public agencies and NGOs utilize data and inputs emanating from the Emergency Operations Center (EOC) run by the bureau in conjunction with the ministry in their DPM activities and programs.

The Cyclone Preparedness Program (CPP) involves the organization of semiannual drills to test the disaster preparedness status of public organizations active in DPM operations. Volunteers are recruited early in the year and trained in disaster preparedness activities, especially in the use of warning systems. The central headquarters of the CPP liases with local councils and preparedness committees in facilitating the broadcast of predisaster warnings, selecting sites for shelters, and evacuating the people from areas threatened by impending disasters.

IV. COPING WITH DISASTERS: THE NONGOVERNMENTAL SECTOR

The nongovernmental sector in Bangladesh has made tremendous inroads in mitigating disasters, rehabilitating victims, and in providing them with relief. A large number of NGOs and voluntary organizations are involved in undertaking and managing projects to lessen the ravages of disasters and contribute to the disaster management operations of the government. In this section, we review some of the nongovernmental projects relating to cyclones, floods, and droughts.

A. Predisaster Activities

The construction of cyclone shelters has been an important operational activity of some large NGOs, complementing the efforts of the government. The BRCS and Caritas International have led the way in the construction of cyclone shelters along the country's coastal belt. These shelters have proved to be effective lifesaving utilities during cyclonic storms in high-risk zones (HRZs), which are susceptible to overwhelming tidal waves. The BRCS and Caritas's cyclone preparedness programs are geared to disseminate cyclone warnings to those living in HRZs by using an extensive radio system and looking after the people taking refuge in shelters (BRCS ND; Caritas 1995:5,16). Both programs have served to reduce human casualties during the 1991 and 1994 cyclones that hit the southern districts of the country.

Another local NGO, Proshika, has its own Disaster Management and Preparedness Program (DMPP). It has an infrastructure development component (construction of cyclone shelters, cluster settlements, upgrading schools for flood shelter, tiles houses, afforestation) and a noninfrastructure component (awareness building through training, providing equipment, etc.) (Proshika 1998a). Its personnel undergo continuous training in disaster management and its awareness-building programs consist of dissemination of information on the impact of disasters upon health, agriculture, and livestock through leaflets and radio and television messages (Proshika 1998b).

B. Postdisaster Activities

During the postdisaster phase, NGOs provide relief and rehabilitate disaster victims. For instance, BRAC, one of the largest NGOs in the country, undertook a massive program of rehabilitation after the devastating floods of 1998. Immediate action involved the distribution of foodstuffs, water containers, water-purifying tablets, oral rehydration saline to prevent or cure diarrhea and other water-borne diseases, clothing, essential commodities and medicines, and the construction of temporary shelters. Long-term programs include relaxing the terms of loans provided to its members, helping affected farmers with agricultural inputs, assisting individual families in rebuilding forests on public lands, assessing the extent of damage caused by flood waters to horticulture, helping nursery growers replace their seeds and saplings, and undertaking roadside tree plantings to prevent future erosion by floods. BRAC has also helped to restore ravaged poultry farms and fisheries, rebuild damaged houses and community schools, and improve sanitation (BRAC 1998). Other NGOs have adopted similar postdisaster programs that have supplemented governmental initiatives in providing succour to the flood victims.

V. RESPONDING TO DISASTERS: INTERNATIONAL INTERVENTIONS

The disaster management program in Bangladesh has had consistent international support during both normal and disaster periods. This support has come in the form of technical assistance in designing disaster management projects, postdisaster relief, medical teams, commodity relief, humanitarian aid, and infrastructure reconstruction.

The UNDP, WHO, UNICEF, World Bank, Asian Development Bank (ADB), and other international development agencies have in recent years geared their efforts to financing disaster recovery projects. The UNDP regularly reviews ongoing national relief operations and previews the task of confronting future disasters. Inputs from government organizations, United Nations field agencies, major donors, and the apex body of NGOs assist in designing strategies for future action. A UNDP task force works closely with the government in determining areas and segments of the population most vulnerable to a ''third wave'' of floods (see UNDP 1995).

Apart from a fast-track emergency recovery project designed to maintain macroeconomic stability and restore damaged infrastructure in the wake of the 1998 floods, the World Bank is committed to ''long-term strengthening of the country's capacity for disaster preparedness and management'' (World Bank 1998).

Several international donor agencies and western governments have, since the 1988 floods, prescribed different strategies to grapple with recurrent floods. Four major studies were initiated by bilateral and multilateral agencies to examine options for flood mitigation. A UNDP-Bangladesh team carried out a flood policy study, a team from Bangladesh and France prepared a prefeasibility study of flood control, USAID sponsored the Eastern Waters Study, and a team from Japan reviewed options for flood management. The nature of recommended options varied. The French proposal was for ''high-tech'' interventions, while the United States was for a more practicable ''living with floods'' approach (Blaike et al 1994:138). The initial studies provided the base for a major project—the Flood Action Plan (FAP). It has been coordinated by the World Bank and endorsed and supported by the G-7, which committed about $150 million to formulate a long-term flood management program, later transformed into an integrated water management program. This shift in strategy was a response to the concerns of civil society and the international donor community regarding potential impact of the FAP interventions on poverty (land, assets, and income) and the environment (RDRS 1996; Blaike et al. 1994:139).

A set of guiding principles formulated by the UNDP formed the basis of FAP. These were as follows:

- Phased implementation of a comprehensive flood plan
- Effective land and water management of protected and unprotected areas
- Strengthening and equipping the disaster management machinery
- Improvement of the flood forecasting system and establishment of a reliable and comprehensive flood warning system
- Safe conveyance of the large cross-boundary flow to the Bay of Bengal by channeling in through the major rivers
- Effective river training works for the protection of embankments, infrastructure, and population centers
- Reduction or distribution of load on the main rivers through diversion of flows into major distributaries and major tributaries or special diversions

Improvement of the conveyance capacity of the river networks
Development of flood-plain zoning
Coordinated planning and construction of all rural roads, highways, and railway embankments with provision for unimpeded drainage
Encouraging maximum possible popular participation by beneficiaries

FAP consists of 26 components (feasibility studies and pilot projects), each of which has direct relevance to disaster management. The donors for these studies/projects include the International Development Association; the Asian Development Bank; the European Economic Community; UNDP; and Canadian, Danish, Japanese, French, United States, Swedish, Swiss, Finnish, German, and British governments.

The external interventions in disaster management have generally taken the form of financial assistance in response to the Bangladesh government's scheme both to undertake short-term postdisaster relief operations and reconstruction and to develop action programs for the longer term. However, some international agencies—like the World Bank, UNDP, and development agencies representing western governments—on their own initiative, are involved in monitoring and evaluating disaster management projects and constantly advising the government on strategies for improvement.

While external intervention in disaster mitigation and postdisaster relief support has always been welcome in hazard-prone Bangladesh, there has been an apparent reluctance on the part of the government in recent times to approach foreign governments and international aid-giving agencies for assistance. This was evident during the 1998 floods, and some western countries, noting the government's restraint in approaching them, made their own assessment of the flood situation for providing emergency relief to affected areas. This ''self-restraint,'' if repeated in future, will prove disastrous to the government's disaster mitigation initiatives.

VI. PROBLEMS AND CONSTRAINTS

The disaster management system, as noted above, is still evolving in Bangladesh. However, certain systemic and procedural constraints are impinging upon the development of an effective modus operandi to cope with natural calamities. These will need to be removed and a more sophisticated apparatus created to reduce the ravages on life and property.

A. Lack of Coherent Policies

Apart from a manual (*Disaster Related Directives*), published by the Ministry, there is no statute or policy to guide action. No definite physical planning regulations exist to manage the physical or infrastructural component of the program. Consequently, linkages between hardware (construction of cyclone/flood shelter, signal system, etc.) and software (training, awareness, community participation) approaches are not established. Although some NGOs have recently included disaster management in their agendas, many still do not have a clear policy vision or strategic approach to appropriately address disaster issues and problems. In practice, in the absence of a coherent national policy, governmental and nongovernmental agencies operate unsystematically and in their own idiosyncratic ways without coordinating their activities. However, consultants, working under a UNDP-UNICEF–funded project (1995–99), are in the process of drafting a Disaster Management Act, which may later be adopted by the government as a policy framework. But in the meantime, disaster management in the environment of a policy vacuum is experiencing immense difficulties in weathering frequent storms.

B. Institutional Constraints

The structure of linkages and the transaction procedures in the disaster management framework are convoluted and obscure, often leaving participating agencies in a quandary and unsure of their proper roles in the disaster management phenomenon. DPM operations, in fact, involve a complex web of interactions among several national and subnational public agencies and organizations in the nongovernmental/voluntary sector. The lines of communication between the national headquarters of government agencies and their field offices frequently break down during the disaster phase, especially if the magnitude of a calamity is intense (e.g., cyclones, tornadoes, tidal waves). Disaster management itself then turns out to be a disaster. Although the government has outlined the role of several public organizations in each of the four disaster phases, this is inadequate in reducing the primary, secondary, and tertiary effects of disasters. The several public agencies having relevance to DPM operations are not always brought within the fold of a total disaster management program.

The institutional capacities of the ministry, the bureau, and other agencies have not been strengthened despite the occurrence of severe disasters in the recent past. Their existing organizational structures resemble, to some extent, obsolete perceptions and ideas about disaster management. This produces inefficiency and ineffectiveness. Information networking and other sophisticated technology are yet to be introduced. Technical weakness and managerial incompetence hinder smooth conduct of disaster operations. Although some government officials periodically receive appropriate training, in many cases, if they are frequently transferred from one agency to another, their skills remain underutilized.

Another serious capacity constraint for the bureau is its lack of an organized field corps. In implementing decisions of the ministry, it must, therefore, rely on the administrative heads and relief officials of districts and subdistricts to implement some of its programs, which may be of lesser priority for these local people. Furthermore, the district relief officers, field personnel of the ministry, mainly remain preoccupied with their own routine work, like food-assisted rural development programs. This severely reduces the capacity of the bureau to execute its responsibilities in the field.

The existence of bureau itself is threatened. Still working as a project with financial assistance from UNDP-UNICEF, it is facing termination and the government has no definite plan to continue and expand its activities. This governmental apathy toward designing a long-term strategy and creating a permanent coordinative point in disaster management will be counterproductive, as all other initiatives will falter in the absence of an anchor at the center.

C. Staffing Problems

Problems relating to personnel management impair efficiency in the delivery of appropriate services to the community. As in the case of other projects, civil servants are deputed to positions in DMB and, more often than not, they belong to the administrative cadre of the Bangladesh Civil Service and are not responsible to the ministry; rather, their loyalty is toward their own line ministry—the Ministry of Establishment (MoE). There is an apparent lack of commitment among these officials, as their training/orientation is not in a specialized task like disaster management and, being generalists, they are often moved to other agencies before they can settle in and learn to adapt themselves to unfamiliar jobs. Consequently, officials do not develop a sense of belonging and thus cannot wholly entrust themselves to their work. The government appears to be unconcerned about creating a well-trained and specialized corps of permanent personnel either for the Ministry or the DMB.

D. Ineffective Coordination and Collaboration

DPM activities often require routine consultations and continuous exchanges of information among several agencies as well as mutual support in each other's programs and projects. Lack of cooperation and coordination between governmental agencies, particularly those on the coordination committees at the national, subnational, and local levels, is a major institutional problem. This is particularly evident in the interface between different line agencies, which are more concerned with their specific agency objectives than with contributing to disaster preparedness and mitigation initiatives. Often parleys of the National Council and Coordination Committee are unattended by agency chiefs; they may be represented by junior officials who may not have the authority to make decisions on certain matters. Also critical is the inadequacy of the coordinative and consultative mechanism between government agencies and NGOs. Coordination committees at the local level have NGO representation, but there appears to be little government-NGO coordination in DPM projects like the selection of site for cyclone shelters (Caritas 1995:6). Through coordination of the government and ADAB (association of NGOs) overlapping problems can be eliminated.

NGOs have burgeoned considerably over the years, but very few cooperate with one another, let alone reinforcing the efforts of established NGOs working in postdisaster relief operations. Some NGOs have also shown a tendency to adopt dishonest tactics in utilizing inappropriate materials in the construction of shelters thereby leaving them susceptible to cyclones and tornadoes (Sattaur 1991:23).

E. Bureaucratized Response to Disasters

The usual bureaucratic obstacles, not uncommon in Bangladesh, frequently involve the postponement of decision making and affect the delivery of service at the point where disasters occur. The bureaucracy goes through the routine rigmarole of allocating goods and services to disaster victims; organizing logistics for distribution of food, clothing, and other essential commodities; providing temporary shelters and health care facilities; and managing other emergency services. The bureaucratic response to disasters is often so belated and heedless that by the time it matures, its basic intent is lost. Western donors have been cynical about the bureaucracy's ability to undertake relief operations efficiently and its failure to implement flood control projects (*Holiday*, August 26, 1998; *Economist*, September 12, 1998). The voluntary sector has often been critical of the administration's failure to support its DPM operations.

F. Inadequate Research and Evaluation

The capacity to continuously research, evaluate, and monitor disaster management initiatives in both public agencies and NGOs is rather weak. The reluctance of public, nongovernmental, and international agencies to share information on disaster matters obviates genuine cooperation and hampers concerted efforts during both pre- and postdisaster phases. The government agencies are averse to the notion of engaging professionals and specialized academic/research institutions to take on research and evaluative studies for improving disaster management programs.

G. Perversion of Relief Operations

The relief operations of the government are open to corruption by unscrupulous functionaries at the local level, and the mechanism to hold them accountable are ineffective. Misappropriation of relief materials is not uncommon. Local bureaucrats are often charged for being partisan in the distribution of relief goods. The ''vulnerable group feeding'' program of the government launched after the 1998 floods was politicized by officials supportive of the ruling party, and flood victims not known to tread party lines were discriminated against (Kabir 1998; see also *Independent*, September 23, 1998). On the other hand, NGOs keen to lend their hands to distributing relief were asked ''to leave the task to the authorities lest they add to the confusion'' (*Economist*, September 12, 1998). Pilferage and waste in storing and distributing relief goods are common occurrences that remain unaccounted for.

H. Lack of a Participatory Approach

While community participation is a central component in any effective disaster management program, it has not been fully incorporated in the planning, implementation, evaluation, and monitoring phases of such programs in Bangladesh. Most of the schemes in the past were based on a centralized decision-making process without sufficient inputs from communities most vulnerable to disasters. NGOs, however, have benefited from feedback from the constituencies they serve and their programs and services have been refined and enlarged as a result. There is, therefore, greater need for a more active participatory approach by the government to make its disaster management regime useful to the community. There must be a shift from ''planning for communities to planning with communities'' and from ''communicating to communities to communicating with communities'' (Anonymous 1997).

VII. CONCLUDING OBSERVATIONS

Disaster management is not only about providing relief but rather ramifies the entire fabric of social and economic life of the nation. Thus, it has to have wide coverage. Apart from causing death and destruction, disasters also have a marked effect on the natural environment, including forestry resources as well as plant and animal life. To protect these, disaster management obligates interagency engagements beyond those of immediate relief and rehabilitation. Ravages to agricultural crops and vegetation, destruction of communications and transportation facilities, disruptions to utility services, and the spread of epidemic diseases in the wake of disasters call for a comprehensive approach to disaster management.

In Bangladesh, the wide and generally complex network of organizations makes disaster management cumbersome. Malcoordination between public agencies themselves and those in the nonpublic sector often miscarries programs to provide succour to disaster-affected zones and their inhabitants. In the absence of coherent national policies, different sections within the disaster management community seem to operate according to their own dictates and do not follow a consistent or harmonized pattern in helping affected people. The entire system seems to operate on the bases of interim and often conflicting measures. Thus, postdisaster relief efforts are often duplicated and rehabilitation programs overlap.

A nexus between the administrative and technical dimensions of disaster management will produce better results than can a system that is skewed to either of the two. Any strategy for creating protective measures cannot be divorced from the environmental and socioeconomic imperatives of society. The long-term effects of deforestation in the coastal regions exposed to cyclones and tidal waves, and of flood-control schemes on agriculture, land settlement, health, habitat, etc., require periodic assessment. Spatial inaccessibility to resources (shelter, relief, drinking water, health care) both during and after disasters has the potential to displace people, even if only temporarily, from their habitats to get more immediate aid or even shelter, employment, and access to basic services (Khan 1991:340). Improper flood control systems may also result in progressive silting up of the coastal rivers and creeks, drainage congestion in the polder areas, stoppage of land formation, and increased levels of water and soil salinity. The impact of all these phenomena must be carefully assessed. Therefore, during normal times, disaster management agencies, both in the public and nongovernment sectors, can apply themselves to understanding them and prescribing options and strategies for mitigation policy initiatives. The common people must be sensitized to the DPM factor through education and training in facing emergencies.

The government must take the entire nation into its confidence in developing policies and strategies for facing natural calamities. Extensive consultations with civil society, the international donor community, and those who are directly exposed to dangers from extreme natural events have the potential to provide the foundation for an integrated approach to disaster management. A genuine practical partnership between public and nongovernmental organizations with the support of the international community will attain more than is possible by approaches that are piecemeal in scope and fragmented in nature. Most importantly, the disaster management system will work well if it is integrated with mainstream development and nation-building strategies.

ENDNOTE

1. The following ministries are represented by their ministers: Water Resources; Finance; Local Government, Rural Development and Cooperatives; Communications; Health and Family Welfare; Food; Home (Internal Security); Disaster Management and Relief; Agriculture; and Inland Water Transport (GOB 1997: 3–4).

REFERENCES

Anonymous (1997). Applying risk management to disaster management: The benefits from focusing on the vulnerability, not just the hazard. <www.geocities.com/CapitolHill/5487/dis2.htm>

Asian Development Bank (1991). *Disaster Mitigation in Asia and the Pacific*. Manila: Asian Development Bank.

Bilski, A. (1991). ''Winds of death.'' *Maclean's* 104(*19*), 22–23.

Blaikie, P., Cannon, T., Davis, I., Wisner, B. (1994). *At Risk: Natural Hazards, People's Vulnerability, and Disasters.* London: Routledge, 1994.

BRAC (1998). 1998 Flood Relief and Rehabilitation Programme. <http://www.brac.net/flood98.htm>

BRCS. Bangladesh Red Crescent Society. <http://203.85.170.66/BangladeshP.htm>

Burton, I., Kates, R., White, G. (1978). *The Environment as Hazard.* New York: Oxford University Press.

Caritas (1995). *Use and Impact of Cyclone Shelters and School Buildings of Caritas.* Dhaka: Caritas Development Institute.

DMB (1993). *The Disaster Management Bureau.* Dhaka: DMB.

Economist. News weekly published in London.

GOB (Government of Bangladesh) (1997). *Durjog Bishayak Sthahi Aadeshaboli* (in Bangla). Dhaka: Ministry of Disaster Management and Relief.

Hanson W.J. (1967). *East Pakistan in the Wake of the Cyclone.* London: Longman.

Holiday. National weekly published in Dhaka.

Independent. National daily published in Dhaka.

Kabir, N. (1998). ''DCs under fire from opposition MPs.'' *The Daily Star.* October 26.

Khan, M.I. (1991). The impact of local elites on disaster preparedness planning: the location of flood shelters in northern Bangladesh. *Disasters*, 15(*4*), 340–354.

Milne, A. (1986). *Floodshock: The Drowning of Planet Earth.* Gloucester: Alan Sutton.

Monan, J. (1989). *Bangladesh: The Strength to Succeed.* Oxford: Oxfam.

Proshika (1998a). Disaster Management and Preparedness Programme (DMPP). <http://bangladeshonline.com/proshika/DMPP.htm>.

Proshika (1998b). What Proshika is doing for victims of flood 1998. <http://bangladeshonline.com/proshika/proshika_doing.htm>

RDRS (1996). *RDRS Position Paper on Flood Action Plan.* Dhaka: Rangpur-Dinajpur Rural Service.

Sattaur O. (1991). ''Counting the cost of catastrophe.'' *New Scientist.* June 29. pp. 21–23.

UNDP (1995). *Report by the Independent Flood Action Plan Review Mission.* Dhaka: UNDP.

World Bank (1998). Press release no. 99/2019/SAS. Dhaka: World Bank.

35

Crisis Management in Japan

Lessons from the Great Hanshin-Awaji Earthquake of 1995

Masaru Sakamoto Faculty of Law, Ryukoku University, Kyoto, Japan

I. INTRODUCTION

Generally, the issue of crisis management can be related to various emergency situations. Some emergencies are related to natural disasters, such as earthquakes, typhoons, and volcanic eruptions. Other emergencies are related to human-made disasters, such as environmental pollution, fires, and food poisoning. Another type of emergency is related to the administrative crises involving such things as financial failures, corruption, privacy information leaks, or social crises involving population outflows, urban riots, or poverty.

In recent years, Japan has experienced a number of tragic disasters. They include the great Hanshin-Awaji earthquake of January 1995, the sarin nerve gas attack on the Tokyo subway system of March 1995, the massive outbreak of food poisoning from 0–157 *Escherichia coli* bacteria of May 1996, and the Tokaimura nuclear accident at a uranium processing plant of September 1999.

The experience of these four disasters has given us an opportunity to enhance our awareness of the need for emergency preparedness and crisis management. Although the term *crisis management* has become popular in Japan, its significance has not necessarily been well understood.

Focusing on the great Hanshin-Awaji earthquake of 1995, this chapter describes the following two points: first, the conditions and problems of Japan's crisis management system and, second, the recent developments in the reform of Japan's crisis management system.

II. THE GREAT HANSHIN-AWAJI EARTHQUAKE OF 1995

At 5:46 a.m. on January 17th, 1995, the great Hanshin-Awaji earthquake hit Kobe and its surrounding areas, including Nishinomiya, Ashiya, Takarazuka, Awajishima Island, Amagasaki, Itami, Akashi, Kawanishi, and parts of Osaka and Kyoto prefectures (see Figures 1 and 2). On January 21, Japan's Meteorological Agency upgraded the intensities of the quake at Sannomiya (business center of Kobe) and Northern Awajishima Island to 7 on the Japanese scale (corresponding to at least 11 on the modified Mercalli scale), making these the highest intensities ever experienced in Japan. According to the Japan's Meterological Agency, the hypocenter (7.2 on the Richter scale) was located just below Awajishima Island; the quake was caused by a movement of a fault which runs below Awajishima Island and Kobe. Among its unique characteristics, the vertical and horizontal shaking occurred simultaneously.

The quake caught the residents of the Kansai region off guard and killed more than 5300; including those who died from shock after the calamity, the death toll was estimated at 6308. Unfortunately, almost half of the victims were aged 60 or older, and the majority were either crushed or suffocated to death in collapsing buildings—usually their homes. The quake caused especially serious damage to old, flimsy wooden houses with heavy tiled roofs—the sort of structures least likely to withstand a major tremor.

Before the earthquake, it was assumed that in the Hanshin-Awaji areas there would be no earthquake. In addition, the master plans for disaster prevention in Kobe and other municipalities were designed to prevent only magnitude 5 earthquakes, not those of magnitude 6 and higher. Therefore, preparations for a large-scale vertical-thrust earthquake in major urban areas were undeniably inadequate.

According to the report of the Ministry of Construction, the gravity measurement registered in the temblor in Kobe was more than twice that of the great Kanto Earthquake of 1923. In terms of magnitude on the Richter scale, the January 17 quake was a high 833 gals in Chuo Ku (ward), Kobe, compared with an estimated 300 to 400 gals in the case of hardest-hit areas in the 1923 quake. The gal is a unit of acceleration equivalent to 1 cm/sec^2.

As Table 1 shows, the great Kanto Earthquake of 1923 caused destructive damage to Tokyo and its surrounding areas (as for the location, see Figure 2). As this quake occurred just around noon, when meals were being prepared, the majority of the victims were killed not by the collapsing buildings themselves but rather by the ensuing fires. Since, at that time, most of the houses were built of wood, those that burned down completely numbered 447,128; the victims numbered 99,331 dead, 43,476 missing, and 103,733 injured. The other damages were 128,266 fully collapsed structures, 126,233 half collapsed structures, and 868 washed away by tsunami. The total amount of damage was estimated at about 5.5638 billion yen.

Despite the fact that the death toll from the Hanshin-Awaji earthquake was the worst in Japan's postwar history, the effect would have been considerably more horrific if the tremors had occurred later in the day. At 5:46 a.m., not many automobiles were on the roads, and the first Shinkansen (bullet train) of the day had been set to start running at 6 a.m. Had the quake occurred a few hours later, when the trains were running (with an average capacity of about 1600 passengers), the casualty rate would have been much higher.

Further, because many people were still asleep and most of those who were awake had yet to begin preparing meals on that fateful morning of January 17, the number of heating and cooking fires lit at that time was considerably lower than what would have been the case if the quake had struck an hour or even half an hour later.

In addition, it was a blessing that the quake occurred on Tuesday, after three consecutive holidays, as all cabinet ministers were in Tokyo and they were able to attend a cabinet meeting to discuss emergency measures. However, the cabinet failed to take quick and appropriate action in the wake of the earthquake, as shown below.

Table 1 Japan's Major Earthquakes Since the Meiji Era (1891–1995)

Date	Location	Magnitude	Death toll/damage
10/28/1891	Kanto[a]	8.0	7273 (dead); about 14,000 (full collapses)
9/1/1923	Kanto	7.9	99,331 (dead); 43,476 (missing) 128,266 (full collapses); 447,128 (burned)
5/23/1925	Kansai[b]	6.8	428 (dead)
3/7/1927	Kansai	7.3	2925 (dead); 12,584 (full collapses)
11/26/1930	Shizuoka	7.3	272 (dead); 2165 (full collapses)
3/3/1933	N. E. Honshu	8.1	3064 (dead); 1817 (full collapses); 4034 (flooded)
9/10/1943	Tottori	7.2	1083 (dead); 7485 (full collapses)
12/7/1944	C. Honshu	7.9	1223 (dead); 17,599 (full collapses); 3129 (flooded)
1/13/1945	C. Honsyu	6.8	2306 (dead)
12/21/1946	Shikoku	8.0	1432 (dead); 11,591 (full collapses); 1451 (flooded); 2,598 (burned)
6/8/1948	Fukui	7.1	3769 (dead); 36,184 (full collapses); 3851 (burned)
3/4/1952	Hokkaido	8.2	28 (dead)
6/16/1964	Niigata	7.5	26 (dead); 1960 (full collapses)
5/16/1968	S. Hokkaido	7.9	52 (dead); 673 (full collapses)
5/9/1974	Shizuoka	6.9	30 (dead); 134 (full collapses); 5 (burned)
1/14/1978	Shizuoka	7.0	26 (dead)
6/12/1978	Sendai	7.4	28 (dead); 1183 (full collapses)
3/21/1982	E. Hokkaido	7.1	0 (dead)
5/26/1983	Akita	7.7	104 (dead); 934 (full collapses)
9/14/1984	Nagano	6.8	29 (dead); 14 (full collapses)
12/17/1987	Chiba	6.7	2 (dead)
1/15/1993	E. Hokkaido	7.8	2 (dead)
7/12/1993	E. Hokkaido	7.8	231 (dead)
10/4/1994	E. Hokkaido	8.1	0 (dead)
12/28/1994	Aomori	7.5	2 (dead)
1/17/1995	Kansai	7.2	6308 (dead); 106,247 (full collapses); 7050 (burned)

[a] Kanto includes Tokyo and its surrounding areas.
[b] Kansai includes Osaka, Kobe, and Kyoto and its surrounding areas.

The great Hanshin-Awaji earthquake has taught us many lessons. It exposed the wretched fragility of highly advanced urban infrastructures, and its occurrence highlighted the inadequacies of lifesaving efforts: highways were blocked by rubble and traffic, firefighters were incapacitated by the cutoff of water pipes, and rescue teams had no equipment to remove debris to save those buried underneath. While recent buildings built according to the latest codes appeared to have withstood the impact, a large number of reinforced concrete structures were completely destroyed.

Lifeline facilities were severely damaged over large areas. Because of the fierce vibrations, which lasted a mere 20 seconds, 900,000 households were left without power, 850,000 households were without gas, and water supply cuts affected about 2.5 million people.

The myth of Japan as a safe country—which had been built up over the 50 years since the World War II—had collapsed. The quake caused especially destructive damage to Kobe. The details of damage in Kobe are as follows.

A. Damage in Kobe City

The toll in Kobe city (population: 1,468,208) was 4484 dead, 1 missing, and 14,679 injured. Damage to buildings was 67,471 fully collapsed structures, 55,145 partially collapsed structures, 6975 completely burned down, and 413 partly burned. Of those who died, 58% were 60 years old or older. Many people died of crush injuries or suffocation (73%) or were found injured under the ruins. In relation to the damage in Kobe, damage to the surrounding areas was as follows (see Figure 1):

Nishinomiya city (population 412,463): 1107 dead, 1 missing, 6386 injured, 19,500 fully collapsed structures, 16,300 partially collapsed, 50 completely burned, and 2 partially burned.

Ashiya city (population 85,736): 433 dead, 2759 injured, 4661 fully collapsed structures, 3943 were partially collapsed, 11 completely burned, and 1 partially burned.

Takarazuka city (population 202,456): 116 dead, 1100 injured, 1339 fully collapsed structures, 3718 partially collapsed, 2 completely burned.

Awajishima Island (population 161,000): 59 dead, 1173 injured, 3407 fully collapsed structures, 5294 partially collapsed, 1 completely burned, 1 partially burned.

Amagasaki city (population 488,606): 48 dead, 3786 injured, 4880 fully collapsed structures, 2520 partially collapsed, 8 completely burned.

Itami city (population 184,319): 19 dead, 2581 injured, 1369 fully collapsed structures, 7200 partially collapsed, 1 completely burned.

Akashi city (population: 278,307): 8 dead, 1884 injured, 2210 fully collapsed structures, 3380 partially collapsed.

Kawanishi city (population 142,792): 2 dead, 485 injured, 536 fully collapsed structures, 2583 partially collapsed.

Osaka Prefecture (population 8,630,000): 28 dead, 3546 injured, 896 fully collapsed structures, 7138 partially collapsed, 1 completely burned, 7 partially burned.

Kyoto Prefecture (population 2,585,000): 1 dead, 49 injured, 2 fully collapsed structures, 5 partially collapsed, 1 completely burned.

The total was 6308 dead, 2 missing, 38,495 injured, 106,247 fully collapsed structures, 130,334 partially collapsed, 7050 completely burned, and 424 partially burned. The total cost of the damage was estimated to be about 9.9268 trillion yen in the case of Hyogo Prefecture, about 288 billion yen in the case of Osaka Prefecture, and 2.7 billion yen in the case of Kyoto Prefecture.

On January 23, 1995, a total of 319,638 evacuees were living in shelters, and 1239 shelters were operating. In Kobe city, 222,127 evacuees were living in shelters as of January 18, 1995 and 236,899 persons were using shelter services on January 24, 1995 (peak); 599 shelters were operating as of January 26, 1995 (peak). With the completion of enough temporary houses, evacuation shelters were removed in August 1995.

Many important public facilities including the city hall and some hospitals were either damaged or collapsed entirely, and 80% of schools were damaged. Museums, the central library's older buildings, the Port Island sports center, sake breweries, and the Ijinkan (historic foreign residences) were also severely damaged.

Road and railway networks were cut into pieces with the collapse of bridge girders supporting the Hanshin expressways, the main artery connecting Osaka and Kobe, as well as those of the JR-Sanyo Shinkansen (see Figure 1). Traffic was interrupted due to sinking ground, cracks, and collapsed buildings. The access to Port Island and Rokko Island—these are reclamation islands—was interrupted.

The main roads in the harbor area were cut off. Almost all container berths and wharves were unusable. Liquefication of land occurred throughout the Bayside area, as on Port Island.

About one-third of the parks were damaged (collapsed structures, cracks, etc.). About 110 sections of grade rivers and 23 sections of regular rivers were damaged; 162 places needed to be reinforced immediately after the earthquake. Furthermore, electricity, gas, and water supplies were cut off over an extensive area, and telephone lines were interrupted, causing major chaos in the affected area.

As for the damage to big manufacturing and local business, many of the big manufacturers in Kobe suffered damage to their main factories, and their production lines were interrupted. About 80% of the shoe factories were damaged and 7 of the 31 sake breweries were seriously damaged. One-third of Kobe's shopping districts and half of the markets were heavily damaged. Many facilities used for tourism, accommodations, and conventions were damaged, in addition to many harbors for fishing vessels, farms, and other agricultural facilities.

The gross production in Kobe city has decreased because companies transferred from Kobe or reduced their production. Many container cargoes were shifted to other ports due to the severe damage to Kobe Port. The interruption of Hanshin expressways has detrimentally affected not only Kobe's economy but also Japan's economy as a whole.

B. Restoring the Infrastructure in Kobe

Evacuee shelters were removed on August 20, 1995, but 145 people were still living in former shelters as of October 1, 1997. Even though infrastructure has been restored in most areas that were affected by the quake, about 27,517 families were still living in makeshift shelters as of October 1, 1997.

Housing starts in Hyogo Prefecture in fiscal 1996 totaled 125,623. Of this figure, 100,738 were in the 20 municipalities that were devastated by the quake. In case of Kobe, 33,823 temporary shelters were built (newly built—29,178 in Kobe, 3168 outside of Kobe; 1477 units of public housing are also being used as temporary shelters).

More than 10 million cubic meters of disaster waste was created by the quake. Removal of buildings that suffered damage in the quake was paid for by Kobe city if the owner applied to the city government. By April 30, 1996, a total of 64,300 of 68,500 buildings had been removed. All of them were removed by the end of fiscal 1995, and the debris was burnt or buried by the end of fiscal 1996.

The Kobe city government has created a "Three Year Plan for the Restoring Houses after the Earthquake," and 72,000 houses were planned to be built after the quake. A total of 45,000 were built by the public sector and 27,000 by the private sector. 6000 units of public housing for the quake victims were built, and 1500 units of public housing, damaged by the quake, were rebuilt.

Land Readjustment Projects were also planned in 30 areas. At the end of 1996, some 45 local conferences for urban readjustments had been established. Urban Redevelopment Projects had been planned in 11 areas, including 2 stricken areas. At the end of 1996, 11 local conferences for urban redevelopment had been established. The concrete plans were decided by the end of fiscal 1995. The redevelopment has been proceeding at a steady pace in 11 designated districts, although a rezoning plan had not been finalized for MoriMinami in Higashi-Nada Ku(ward) until October 1999.

As for the situation in industries, big manufacturing companies have been restored almost completely, but functions have decreased. Shoe manufacturing, however—a key local industry—had achieved only a 60% recovery as of October 1997, while department stores in downtown Kobe were fighting an uphill battle, with their proceeds hovering just above 80% of preearthquake figures.

Some 90% of Kobe's hotels and sightseeing facilities had reopened by the end of March 1996, but the number of tourists visiting Kobe reached only 60% of the preearthquake level. In May and June 1997, Kobe hotels enjoyed a combined room occupancy rate greater than before January 1995. In order to support local businesses and secure enough employment, the city government has put several projects into effect, such as special financing (139.3 billion yen in total).

As for the railway and road networks (see Figure 1), the JR line recovered most rapidly. The JR Shinkansen line between Shin-Osaka and Himeji was out of service, but full service resumed in April 1995, so that Kobe and Osaka were directly connected.

The Hankyu private railway line's full service connecting Kobe with Osaka and Kyoto resumed on June 12, 1995. The Sanyo private railway line's full service connecting Kobe with Akashi and Himeji resumed on June 18, 1995. The Hanshin private railway line's full service connecting Kobe with Osaka resumed on June 26, 1995. Operation of the entire municipal subway system resumed on February 16, 1995, with some stations remaining closed. Full service resumed on March 31, 1995. The train connecting Port Island to the mainland was fully restored on July 31, 1995, and the train connecting Rokko

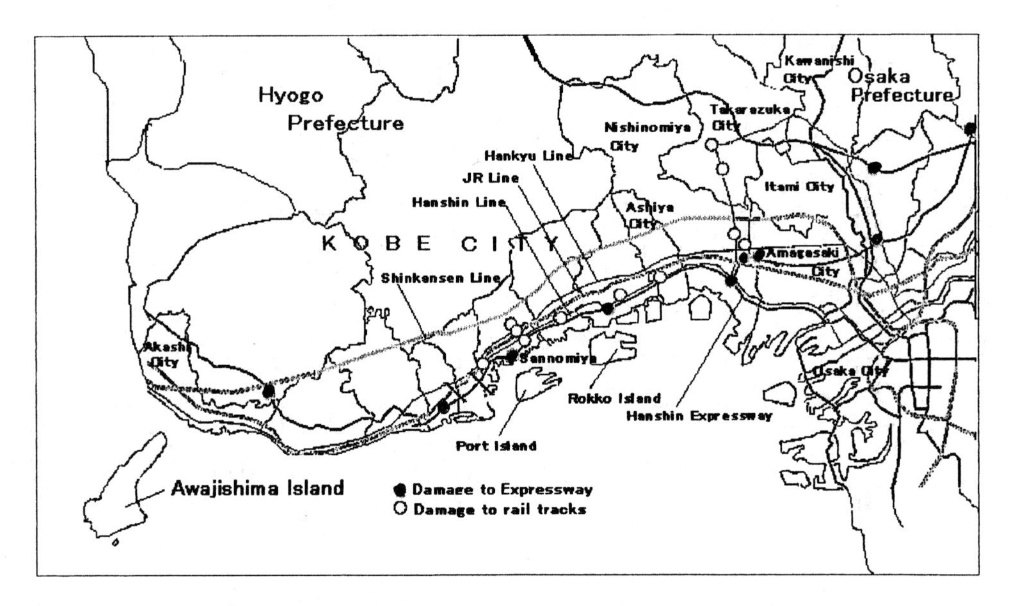

Figure 1 The location map of damage to transport lines in Kobe and its surrounding areas affected by 1995 earthquake.

Island to the mainland was fully restored on August 23, 1995. All of the municipal buses (73 routes) resumed on June 22, 1995.

The Kobe route of Hanshin expressways connecting Kobe and Osaka was opened on October 1996. Its Wangan route, running along the bay area between Osaka and east side of Kobe, was fully reopened on September 1, 1995. The harbor highway connecting Port Island with Rokko Island was fully reopened in July 1996. All lanes of the Kobe Bridge, connecting Port Island with the mainland, reopened in July 1996. Rokko Bridge connecting Rokko Island with the mainland reopened on September 28, 1995.

As for the port facilities, 93 out of 170 berths are available as of May 1996. Container berths were used 24 hours a day as a temporary measure. Of 201 shipping routes, 160 were reopened as of May 1, 1996. 82.3% of container cargo and 89.5% of the number of container ships were back in service of April 1996.

C. The Government's Responses to the Earthquake

As mentioned above, the quake caused destructive damage to the Hanshin-Awaji areas. What has been the government's response to the quake?

1. The Initial Responses of Government Leaders

The nation was appalled by Tokyo's lack of leadership and absence of crisis management in the initial hours after the quake, while local governments fell into chaos, with many officials themselves becoming victims. The government leaders' initial responses to the quake were very slow.

In an interview dated January 25, 1996, former Prime Minister Tomiichi Murayama was asked "What did you do after you received the first reports on the quake?" He replied as follows:

I learned of the quake on the 6 a.m. TV news. The newscaster said the [quake's] intensity was 6 on the Japanese scale of 7 in Kyoto, but said nothing about Kobe. Kobe was so severely damaged that no reports were reaching TV stations then. So I called someone in Kyoto right away and asked, "The TV news reported the quake, but how is the situation in Kyoto?" He answered, "There were big tremors, but we did not suffer any damage." So my first impression was that the quake was not serious. Then, at around 7:30 a.m., my secretary called me and said damage was likely to be widespread. So I decided to go to my office earlier than usual. (*Yomiuri*, Jan. 25, 1996) The arrival time of prime minister to his office was about 8:30 a.m.

It was an incredible surprise that a prime minister's official residence not only received initial information about the temblor from TV broadcasts but also that he had to rely on such sources in his initial effort to gauge the scale of the disaster.

Meanwhile, the governor of Hyogo prefecture, comprising Kobe and its surrounding areas, was also slow in compiling information. The governor arrived at his office at 8:20 a.m. by car, but 2½ hours had passed since the quake. Although he tried to take the necessary emergency measures in order to prevent the disaster from worsening, it was too late to seek help from the Self-Defense Forces (SDF). Unfortunately, he did not get enough information to seek help from the SDF until 10 a.m.

In relation to the initial response of the mayors, the arrival time to their offices ranged between 6:35 a.m. (mayor of Kobe city) and 10:30 a.m. (mayor of Nishinomiya city). The differences were due their varying knowledge of the crisis.

Table 2 Jobs Created by Officials in the 7 Days After the Quake

	Hyogo prefecture	Kobe	Cities	Towns	Total
Same as before the quake	2.9	0.8	1.3	10.9	2.3
Same, but job quantity increased	2.2	6.3	4.4	8.8	5.1
Changed to the disaster-related jobs	46.7	65.0	42.7	16.3	45.7
Added disaster-related jobs to regular jobs	47.4	28.0	51.6	61.9	45.3

Source: Kume 1997:687.

2. Responses of Administrative Organizations

Despite the differences in the initial response of the chief executives, the administrative organizations in the areas affected by the quake managed to respond to the emergencies. The recent survey research for the section chiefs and upper-level officials in affected areas (Hyogo prefectural government, Kobe municipal government, and another 9 cities and 10 towns) suggests the conditions of the organizational responses of each government to the emergencies. Table 2 shows the kinds of jobs they created during the 7 days after the quake, while Table 3 shows the degree of the similarities to their regular jobs in ordinary times.

Based on the organization theory proposed by H. Simon and J. March, the study points out that the responses of the administrative organizations to emergencies at affected local governments tend to depend on the ''coordination by feedback'' in addition to the ''coordination by disaster prevention plan,'' but the degree of its dependence is different from the levels of governments (see Kume 1997: tables 2 and 3).

According to Table 2, the ratio of disaster-related jobs created through the mobilization of the employees from the existing organizations tended to increase at rising levels of government. According to Table 3, the ratio of the job similarities to the regular jobs in ordinary times also tended to increase at rising levels of government. These tables show that the larger the administrative organizations, such as prefecture and city, compared to the smaller ones, such as the town, were better able to respond to the emergencies through coordination of existing personnel resources. Although the disaster prevention plans at the local level were not able to respond to emergencies effectively, the administrative organizations of the affected local governments attempted to respond to the emergencies through coordination by feedback.

Despite the organizational responses to the emergencies the local level, the people

Table 3 Similarities Between Disaster-Related Jobs and Regular Jobs

	Hyogo prefecture	Kobe	Cities	Towns	Total
All are related jobs	36.2	34.6	22.5	19.0	26.9
Most are related jobs	35.4	23.8	27.1	28.4	27.2
Parts are related jobs	15.0	21.5	26.5	31.0	24.4
None are related jobs	13.4	20.1	23.8	21.6	21.5

Source: Kume 1997:688.

living in Japan have been forced to recognize that the nation does not have a reliable crisis management system.

III. THE CRISIS MANAGEMENT SYSTEM IN JAPAN

The massive death toll and property damage caused by the quake could have been reduced substantially if the government had been more prompt in launching search-and-rescue and firefighting operations involving large numbers of SDF members and if traffic had been better controlled to allow the entry of emergency vehicles. Many emergency vehicles were caught in huge traffic jams involving private automobiles. The Murayama cabinet seems to have failed to correct what is seen as weak leadership, an absence of centralized coordination, and a shortage of information, which underlie the sorry state of the nation's crisis management system.

Unfortunately, the nation has not learned how to deal with national emergencies effectively, despite its history of disasters such as earthquakes, typhoons, and volcanic eruptions (see Table 1 and Figure 2). The government's main mistake was that it failed to grasp, in the initial hours, the full extent of the quake's damage. Why, then, did the

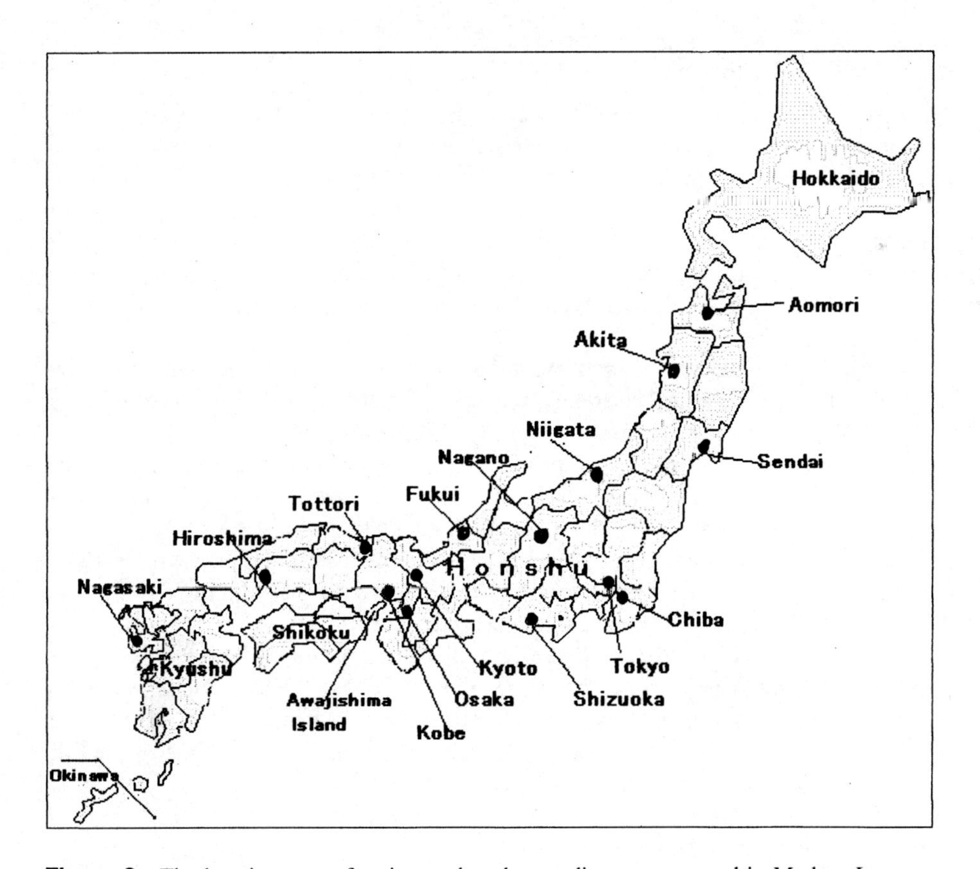

Figure 2 The location map of major earthquakes or disasters occurred in Modern Japan.

governments fail to respond swiftly? The reasons can be considered from the following viewpoints.

A. Inadequacy of Japan's Legal System

The primary purpose of a state is to protect the lives and property of its people. Therefore the state must have a crisis management system established in law to respond to emergencies such as disasters, terrorism, and crime. A number of nations have included provisions in their constitutions for dealing with emergencies. However, Japan has lacked such laws and regulations for emergencies. In contrast, Germany included emergency provisions in its Constitution in 1968, which temporarily restrict people's rights and abrogate standing rules.

According to these provisions, a joint committee comprising members of the lower and upper houses of the German legislature will be set up in case of an emergency in order to provide emergency legislation. However, the provisions stipulates that those laws will be valid for only 6 months, and if the parliament rejects the laws during that period, they will be rescinded. It must be examined whether Japan should legislate an emergency law similar to that of Germany.

B. Defects in Japan's Security System

Generally, the situation of emergencies can be divided into three types. A state of emergency in terms of national defense may be defined as a situation in which an external armed attack has occurred or is imminent. A state of emergency in terms of public order may refer to a situation in which the society is thrown into chaos as a result of a large-scale disaster or civil disturbance, acts of terrorism, or hijacking. A state of emergency in terms of disasters may refer to massive earthquakes and other natural disasters, accidents at nuclear power plants, and major accidents involving oil spills caused by tankers and trains as well as ships.

In case of emergencies, the existing three offices (the Cabinet Security Affairs Office, the Cabinet Information Research Office, and the Cabinet Councilors' Office) under the control of the Cabinet Secretariat that respond to crises has not functioned as a control tower (see Appendix 2). In Japan, the prime minister, the head of the executive branch, shall determine and declare a state of emergency. Under the current system, a countermeasures headquarters is established within the government based on the Basic Law on Disaster Countermeasures in times of disaster, but in a state of emergency involving national defense or public order, there are no provisions provided in laws relating to the SDF and police concerning the establishment of a command center.

Therefore, the nation should create a centralized organization for dealing with three types of national emergencies under the prime minister's direct command that can oversee relief and reconstruction operations. It is urgently important that a system be set up in which a single organization can make swift decisions by taking over, if necessary, the responsibilities usually reserved for ministries or local governments during national emergencies. In this sense, the U.S. Federal Emergency Management Agency (FEMA) would be effective as such an organization model.

FEMA was created in 1979 to deal with a nuclear attack under presidential command, but it was reorganized later to deal with natural disasters as well. FEMA is staffed with about 2700 experts has centralized authority to coordinate rescue operations, provide aerial surveillance of disaster areas, and arrange financial assistance to survivors.

Under the Japanese version of FEMA, it would be necessary to develop and train specialists in crisis control and to provide the necessary background for officials. However, against the recent government drive for the administrative and financial reform, it is expected to be difficult to create a new organization similar to FEMA. Therefore it might be more realistic to reorganize the three Offices of the Cabinet Secretariat as a comprehensive organization for dealing with emergencies.

C. Absence of Swift Decision-Making Mechanisms

Crisis management requires strengthening the prime minister's power and eliminating the harmful effects of factionalism in government ministries and agencies. Under the Constitution, the prime minister is head of government—equivalent to a president with representative right in a company. Furthermore, the Cabinet Law restricts the prime minister's power to something like that of a chairman; also, the National Government Organization Law concerning national administrative organizations makes the prime minister head of the Prime Minister's Office—a position equal to that of other ministry heads.

The prime minister, therefore, does not have the power to give binding directives to ministers even in cases of emergency. The prime minister is able to instruct and supervise ministers only by following decisions made at a cabinet meeting (Article 6, Cabinet Law; see Appendix 1).

It is necessary to revise the cabinet law to create a responsible and flexible mechanism to deal with emergencies. The law should allow the prime minister to take command in such cases of emergency, for instance, by establishing a disaster headquarters and implementing minimum emergency measures. His decisions could be approved later at a cabinet meeting.

In terms of the prime minister's powers, Article 78 of the existing Self-Defense Law provides that a prime minister will be granted special power to mobilize the SDF without Diet approval when Japan is attacked by a foreign country and he needs to take immediate action to defend the country, that he must get Diet approval as soon as the state of emergency vanishes, and that, if he fails to win Diet approval, he must order the SDF to withdraw immediately. These article will be helpful in examining the emergency provisions.

D. Confused Government Information System

The government information system—collection, analysis, assessment, and dissemination—is not organized adequately to deal with large-scale emergencies. In Japan, it is often said that important information is not flowing into the prime minister's office. The government ministries and agencies tend to monopolize the information they obtain and do not share it with outsiders. Under the current system, information on natural disasters collected by local authorities, police, firefighters, and the SDF is not directly reported to the prime minister's official residence. Instead, it flows to the National Land Agency, which supervises and coordinates government rescue operations in natural disasters.

The agency's disaster prevention bureau, which is primarily responsible for relief, is the smallest bureau in terms of personnel, with only 36 staff members. Many of the agency's officials are also on loan from other ministries, such as Finance and Construction.

The agency failed to grasp the magnitude of the disaster because telephone lines in the Kobe area were disrupted, making it difficult to contact prefectural authorities, and because those officials themselves suffered damage in the quake. The agency's disaster prevention wireless network does not have a linkup with prefectural authorities.

Not knowing the extent of the damage, the prime minister and top officials at first seemed to let the agency take the initiative in the quake response, despite the fact that the agency did not have its own information gathering network or authority to issue instructions to other organizations, including police and the SDF. Therefore it is necessary to reorganize the government information system, enabling it to collect all the relevant information in the prime minister's official residence.

E. Legal Problems in Intergovernmental Relations

The first 48 hours of a disaster are considered crucial for rescue operations. In the Hanshin-Awaji earthquake, the SDF's delay in joining relief activities in the initial hours after the quake was criticized. On January 17, it was not until 10 a.m., or more than 4 hours after the quake struck, that the governor of *Hyogo* prefecture asked the SDF to help. Then, shortly after 1 p.m., about 150 SDF members began official operations in Kobe, arriving from Himeji, where ground SDF troops are stationed.

Why did the SDF delay in taking action for rescue? Under Article 83 of the SDF law regulating SDF operations, SDF members may be dispatched to a disaster area, in principle, only at the request of governors concerned. Under the law, this authority had been granted only to governors. Unfortunately, mayors of Kobe and the heads of surrounding cities and towns were unable, for long hours, to contact the governor of Hyogo prefecture to request the dispatch of SDF troops.

In addition, based on Article 94 of the SDF law, SDF members are allowed to give evacuation orders to disaster victims or enter private property only when police officers are not available. Only police officers and Maritime Safety Agency officers are allowed to enter private property and remove objects from disaster areas. The SDF members constitute a core of crisis management, but they cannot, for example, remove wreckage from roads if police officers from the area are not present.

The quake brought to light the legal problems of inter-governmental relations and the lack of rudimentary crisis management in relation to the dispatch of the SDF and its function.

F. Bureaucratic Red Tape

While thousands of people had contacted the Kobe municipal government to offer their services as volunteers on 4 days after the quake, human resources were wasted by a government system unused to harnessing the efforts of individuals in an emergency.

Despite the inadequacies of traditional bureaucratic responses in an emergency, the government officials tended to stick to paperwork for volunteer help by demanding volunteers' registration or asking for their requests in writing. This is one example of the bureaucratic way of doing things despite the urgent need for volunteer services.

In addition, Japan's national government was also slow to accept offers of help from other countries. Bureaucratic rigidity was blamed for the slow governmental response, including critical delays in responding to international offers of aid. Before accepting a specially trained tracker-dog team from Switzerland, the Health and Welfare Ministry reportedly insisted that the animals be quarantined for a certain time, as generally required. Although this was later retracted, the team's arrival was substantially delayed. Unfortunately, such aspects of bureaucratic factionalism and red tape were exposed in the response to the quake.

IV. REFORM OF CRISIS MANAGEMENT SYSTEM

The great Hanshin-Awaji earthquake forced us to recognize the conditions of Japan's crisis management. It exposed the problems of Japan's organizations, systems, and laws in dealing with emergency situations. How is the conditions of Japan's crisis management following the quake?

A. Organizational Reform

At that time, there were three offices that fall under the control of the cabinet secretariat that respond to crises: the Cabinet Security Affairs Office, the Cabinet Information Research Office and the Cabinet Councilors' Office on Internal Affairs (see Appendix 2). The crisis management system under the Prime Minister's Official Residence has been criticized for its lack of competency in collecting information and for its poor interministry liaison/coordination capabilities.

In order to strengthen the control of the Prime Minister's Official Residence over natural disasters and contingencies, the government planned to strengthen the Cabinet Security Affairs Office so that the prime minister will be able to provide more effective leadership in case of crises. The plan, part of the government's drive for administrative reform, was draw up on the assumption that the prime minister should take direct control of handling emergencies.

The Administrative Reform Council, which was under the direct control of former Prime Minister Ryutaro Hashimoto, had been expected for drawing up detailed proposals to beef up the Cabinet Security Affairs Office. The office, which comprises senior bureaucrats of the Defense Agency, the Foreign Ministry, the National Police Agency and four other government bodies, was accused of being ineffective during the Gulf War and in the aftermath of the great Hanshin-Awaji earthquake. In recent cases of the hostage taking at the Japanese ambassador's residence in Lima by Peruvian rebels and the oil spill caused by the Russian tanker *Nakhodka*, the prime minister's executive office exposed the defects again in gathering information about it.

Based on the recommendation of Administrative Reform Council, Hashimoto's cabinet decided to form an organization to oversee crisis management. The organization formed in fiscal 1998 has been headed by a ''crisis management specialist'' who has the same status as the deputy chief cabinet secretary and maintain a staff to plan ahead for crisis. The head of the office, who would probably be recruited from outside the government would also serve as one of the prime minister's senior aides. To this end, the government submitted a bill to revise the cabinet law to an extraordinary Diet session in autumn of 1997.

The new organization was formed by partially restructuring and integrating the above mentioned three offices and was given powers to secure information and initiate measures to deal with crisis management issues from a wide-ranging perspective to be supervised by the crisis management specialist.

B. Legal Reform

Nations can take two main legal approaches in dealing with emergencies. One is to invest the leader of the nation with full power. The French Constitution provides the president with power to take ''any necessary measures'' to deal with emergencies. This approach is common in countries with a presidential system. The other is to deal with emergencies based on law. Germany, for example, has specific provisions in its Basic Law (constitution) to deal with emergencies, as mentioned above. It overhauled the Basic Law in 1968 to create a systematic legal framework to deal with emergencies.

Following the quake, the Japan's government has revised its Basic Law on Disaster Countermeasures, beefed up the prime minister's office's ability to gather information and established a system that allowed the prime minister to have prime ministerial aides. But no sweeping review involving the Constitution has been conducted.

In the quake, the SDF's delay in joining relief activities in the initial hours after the quake was criticized. Criticism has been focused on the legal problem attached to dispatching troops. Under Japan's SDF law, SDF troops are to be deployed for disaster relief and rescue work at the request of the prefectural governor. This authority had been granted only to governors. Thus, in cases where the municipal governments heads are unable to contact with a governor concerned, municipal governments cannot directly request the dispatch of SDF troops for rescue operations. Unfortunately, this was the case in the great Hanshin-Awaji earthquake.

The revised Anti-Disaster Basic Law of December 1995, however, allows municipal governments heads to request the SDF to dispatch troops for relief efforts. This is very important reform of intergovernmental relations, making it easier for the SDF to act swiftly.

Also, under the previous Anti-Disaster Basic Law and Large Scale Earthquake Special Measures Law, the government was unable to set up a disaster countermeasure headquarters comprising all cabinet ministers unless an emergency disaster proclamation calling for economic control was issued first. With the revision, no such proclamation is required in extreme disaster scenarios such as the quake.

Further, SDF's dispatches for disaster rescue operations are authorized to demarcate areas where people are banned from entering in times when policemen and Maritime Safety Agency personnel are not available. In addition, the revised law require the national and local governments to make efforts to promote mutual assistance pacts among local entities for emergency situations, register and train volunteers, and consolidate for volunteer activities. These revisions of two disaster laws are expected to strengthen crisis management functions of the prime minister's office and local governments heads.

V. CONCLUSION: LESSONS FROM THE GREAT HANSHIN-AWAJI EARTHQUAKE

The great Hanshin-Awaji earthquake exposed the problems of Japan's crisis management system. These problems can be summarized from the following points.

A. Master Plan for Disaster Prevention

The Central Disaster Prevention Council, a panel chaired by the former Prime Minister Tomiichi Murayama, finalized a new master plan for disaster prevention on July 18, 1995, some 6 months after the great earthquake. It was the first major revision to the plan in the 24 years since it was drafted. Although the revision was too late, it details steps to minimize damage arising from earthquakes, volcanic eruptions, typhoons, and other disasters. In addition, it details emergency measures to be taken immediately after such disasters as well as the roles that the national and local governments and residents should play in the restoring stricken areas. This is a step forward for effective crisis management.

However, this plan does not tell how the local governments should create the organization responsible for crisis management and draw up their own master plan for disaster prevention. Also, it does not define where each organizational structure should stand in relation to the national government and local governments or the relationship between prefectural government and municipal governments. Therefore, the new master plan will be inadequate as compared with the FEMA's manual in the United States, directing the organizational structures in relation to the intergovernmental relations.

B. Organizational and Legal System

The Administrative Reform Council, chaired by former Prime Minister Ryutaro Hashimoto, issued an interim report on September 3, 1997, setting the agenda for political debate on how to make the government smaller and more efficient. In the report, the Administrative Reform Council called for a drastic reorganization of central government offices and a stronger role for the cabinet to boost the cabinet's crisis management function.

The report proposed that the current 22 ministries and agencies—the prime minister's office, 12 ministries, 8 agencies and one commission)—should be condensed into a much strengthened cabinet office, 10 ministries, one agency and one commission responsible for defense (see Appendix 2). Historically, the modern day cabinet arrangement started in 1885 with nine ministries: foreign, finance, justice, education, army, naval, interior, agriculture and commerce, and communication. Over the past 115 years, that number has grown to 22. The only great reduction in the number of ministries came during the Allied occupation of Japan after World War II.

There have been many small-scale attempts to reform the governments, but they have failed under pressure from bureaucrats. In addition, legislators have not acted to slim down the system. Against that historical background, the current reform plan can be seen as the first large-scale attempt at peacetime reorganization since the Meiji era (1868–1912).

The report also called for a system that would allow the prime minister to exercise stronger leadership enable the government to engage in unified policy making and effective crisis management. Based on its recommendation, the Hashimoto cabinet decided to create the new post of a "crisis management specialist" rather than a new organization similar to the U.S. FEMA.

This decision is partly effective under the government's recent drive for administrative and financial reform, but it is not effective as an organization of crisis management. We do not agree with the logic that costs should be more important than public safety and democracy. The costs must be considered as necessary expenses for maintaining public safety and democracy. This is an essential concept of government.

The council issued a final report in December of 1997, taking into consideration the views of the ruling three-party alliance—the Liberal Democratic Party, Social Democratic Party, and New Party Sakigake (Pioneers). Then, the government drafted reform bills based on the final report and submitted them to the ordinary Diet session in 1998. The target for implementation is 2001.

C. Prime Minister's Powers

At the time of earthquake, the prime minister of Japan could not take direct command or supervise officials of ministries and agencies; instead he had to follow cabinet decisions in directing ministries. Because of these limitations, it was difficult for the prime minister to exercise strong political leadership.

The Reform Council intended to strengthen the prime minister's powers, but the cabinet Legislation Bureau and others opposed to granting the prime minister's powers that might violate the Constitution, which reads, ''The Cabinet, in the exercise of executive power, shall be collectively responsible to the Diet.'' Therefore, the reform council compromised in proposing that the cabinet approve in advance the system whereby the prime minister would make decisions.

However, the council's proposals are inadequate, especially when compared to the situation in Germany. As mentioned above, Germany amended its constitution to incorporate detailed provisions for dealing with emergencies. If the government seek the creation of effective crisis management system under the prime minister's leadership, it will be necessary not only to revise the cabinet law, but also to legislate an emergency law similar to that of Germany.

D. SDF's Function

There is a popular view that the SDF should constitute the core of national crisis management system. However, constitutional questions have been raised concerning the SDF. Discussion of the SDF has long been regarded as taboo. There has been deep concern among some political parties, labor groups, and scholars that the establishment of provisions for an emergency could lead to militarism.

Also, there has been a lack of thorough discussion on the issue because, in addition to having relied entirely on the United States for its security, the nation has not experienced the serious emergencies until the great Hanshin earthquake of January 1995.

During the emergencies of the quake, SDF members were unable to take part in the rescue operations swiftly, because of the delay of the request by a prefectural governor. The delay of request for SDF's dispatch resulted in worsening the disaster. Following the quake, the function of the SDF in case of crises became more effective through the revision of related laws, as mentioned above.

E. Training of Crisis Skills and Volunteer Activities

Organizations can be effective when their personnel can work together. What is most important for crisis management is how to mobilize personnel and systems in case of crises. It is important to establish procedures or manuals stipulating how to respond to the crises, to develop crisis control skills and knowledge, and to train officials accordingly. However, there are limited numbers of officials dealing with crisis management in public organizations. In addition, if officials have themselves been hurt in disasters, they cannot function. Therefore, volunteers' activities are essential to make a crisis management system more effective.

In the quake, over 1.3 million volunteers conducted a variety of relief activities. As a result of their invaluable help during the quake, 1995 is called the original year of volunteer activity in Japan. In the earthquake, volunteer activities with specific targets and skills were especially evaluated.

Furthermore, it is essential to systematize volunteering in disasters and to create a structure to coordinate volunteer activities. Therefore, the local governments must take a leadership role in establishing a system for registering and dispatching disaster relief volunteers with specialized skills.

F. Creation of a Safe Society and Protection Against Disasters

In the quake, the concentration of urban functions in a small region exacerbated the damages incurred. In city planning, urban functions should be dispersed, and spaces such as parks, green space, and rivers should be adapted for possible emergency use. In addition, systems with backup capabilities for transportation, communication, and essential services must be created.

Most of the deaths in the quake were caused by the collapse of old structures, while recent structures built according to latest codes could withstand its impact. Increasing the earthquake resistance of old constructions is a major issue. Given a lesson that the ''retrofit'' type of construction proved resistant to the North Ridge Earthquake of 1994, it is important to promote the construction of that type of structure and to create urban communities capable of resisting earthquakes.

Japan's national and local governments have too much believed in the myth of Japan as a safe country and have neglected to take adequate measures for disasters, despite its history of disasters—such as earthquakes, typhoons, and volcanic eruptions.

In the case of Kobe and other municipal governments, their master plans for disaster prevention have not been designed to prevent magnitude 6 and higher-level earthquakes. But, the prevention plans for magnitude 6 and higher-level earthquakes would impose a heavy financial burden on the local governments. Therefore, if the local governments were to face a financial crisis, it might be difficult for them to pay for the necessary expenses for preventive measures.

However, governments should learn that the most important task is to protect the lives and property of their people. The governments should establish strong disaster prevention communities that people can depend on. This is a mission of governments and part of their mourning for the 6308 victims of the great Hanshin-Awaji earthquake of 1995.

For a swift response to disasters such as the quake, it is necessary to enhance our awareness of need of emergency preparedness. It is a matter of course that we need to store such necessities as food, water, flashlights, and radios in anticipation of disasters.

In the great Hanshin-Awaji earthquake, many people were rescued from the rubble of collapsed structures by family and neighbors. In the earthquake, the effectiveness of rescue and relief activities through the cooperation between firefighters and neighbors was proven. It is important for local governments and residents to cooperate in resisting disasters. Furthermore, the national and local governments should reexamine their master plans for disaster prevention and revise them as needed.

G. Aftereffects of the Earthquake

Many victims of the earthquake suffered serious injury both mentally and physically and lost their dreams and hopes for the future. The earthquake struck a region with a rapidly aging population. When wooden houses collapsed, many senior citizens died under the ruins of their houses or furniture.

The victims who had lost their homes were forced to take refuge in schools and parks, shivering both from the bitter cold and the fear of aftershocks. At the emergency's peak, the number of evacuees amounted to 320,000, among whom the elderly in particular were forced to live with great difficulty in unfamiliar surroundings. The long period of residence in evacuee shelters caused mental fatigue or psychological stress, especially among children, the handicapped, and the elderly. Therefore, systematic care and counseling for the psychological stress that they have suffered from the earthquake must be provided over long periods.

According to recent survey research involving firefighters and rescue team members who engaged in fire and rescue activities after the quake, they tended to feel stress or fatigue as a result of their work during the quake. The survey found that these symptoms had been caused by their feelings, accusing themselves for failing in fire and rescue missions. Given their feelings, it is essential to give them mental care and counseling to help them deal with the trauma resulting from the earthquake.

Finally, We should always remind ourselves that Japan is extremely vulnerable to earthquakes, typhoons, and volcanic eruptions. Bearing in mind that over 6000 victims were killed by the earthquake, national and local governments should seek to establish the reliable crisis management systems in order to create a safer society. This tragedy has taught us many lessons about the prime minister's leadership, the effective crisis management system, effective information gathering strategies, care for those especially susceptible to disasters, the elderly, the handicapped and foreign residents and measures for protecting the livelihood of disaster victims.

The Japanese saying that ''Natural disaster visits us at times when people least expect it'' is surely true. The proverb that ''Preparing for the worst is the best prevention'' is also true. We can never forget the lessons from the Great Hanshin-Awaji Earthquake of 1995 and should be better prepared for the possibility of another major disaster in the future.

APPENDIX 1

THE CABINET LAW (Law No. 5 of 1947, as Amended)

Article 1. The Cabinet shall perform functions provided for in Article 73 and other articles of the Constitution of Japan.

Article 2. (1) The Cabinet shall be composed of the Prime Minister, who shall be its head, and twenty Ministers of State.

(2) The Cabinet, in the exercise of executive power, shall be collectively responsible to the Diet.

Article 3. (1) The Ministers shall divide among themselves administrative affairs and be in charge of their respective share thereof as the competent Minister, as provided for by other law.

(2) The provision of the preceding paragraph does not preclude the appointment of Ministers who have no specific share of administrative affairs under their charge.

Article 4. (1) The Cabinet shall perform its functions through Cabinet Meetings.

(2) The Prime Minister shall preside over Cabinet Meetings.

(3) Each Minister may submit to the Prime Minister any question or matter and ask for a Cabinet Meeting therefore.

Article 5. The Prime Minister, representing the Cabinet, shall submit Cabinet bills, budgets and other proposals to the Diet, and shall report to the Diet on general national affairs and, foreign relations.

Article 6. The Prime Minister shall exercise control and supervision over the administrative branches in accordance with the policies to be decided upon at Cabinet Meetings.

Article 7. The Prime Minister shall, following consultation at Cabinet Meetings, decide on any point of doubt relating to jurisdiction between the competent Ministers.

Article 8. The Prime Minister may suspend the official measures or orders of any administrative office, pending action by the Cabinet.

Article 9. In case the Prime Minister is prevented from discharging his functions, or the post of the Prime Minister is vacant, the Minister of State designated by him in advance shall perform temporarily the functions of the Prime Minister.

Article 10. In case a competent Minister of State is prevented from discharging his functions, or the post of such Minister is vacant, the Prime Minister, or the Minister of State designated by him, shall perform temporarily the functions of the said competent Minister of State.

Article 11. No provisions imposing obligations or restricting rights can be made in a Cabinet Order unless authorized by law.

Article 12. (1) There shall be set up in the Cabinet a Secretariat.

(2) The Cabinet Secretariat shall be in charge of general affairs such as arrangement of the agenda of Cabinet Meetings, be in charge of the coordination necessary for keeping integration of the policies of administrative offices such as the coordination of important matters for decision by Cabinet Meetings, and be in charge of the collection and researches of information concerning important policies of the Cabinet.

(3) Besides the matters mentioned in the preceding paragraph, the Cabinet Secretariat shall assist the work of the Cabinet as provided for by a Cabinet Order.

(4) Besides the Secretariat there shall be set up in the Cabinet necessary offices which shall assist the work of the Cabinet, as provided for by law.

Article 13. (1) The Cabinet Secretariat shall have one Chief Cabinet Secretary.

(2) The post of the Chief Cabinet Secretary shall be filled by a Minister of State.

(3) The Chief Cabinet Secretary shall preside over the affairs of the Cabinet Secretariat and shall control and supervise the personnel thereof in regard to the performance of their duties.

Article 14. (1) The Cabinet Secretariat shall have two Deputy Chief Cabinet Secretaries.

(2) The Deputy Chief Cabinet Secretaries shall assist the Chief Cabinet Secretary.

Article 14-2. (1) The Cabinet Secretariat shall have Cabinet Councillors, Cabinet Deliberators, Cabinet Researchers, Cabinet Officials and other necessary personnel.

(2) The Cabinet Councillors shall, by order, be in charge of general affairs such as arrangement of the agenda of Cabinet Meetings.

(3) The Cabinet Deliberators shall, by order, be in charge of the coordination

necessary for keeping integration of the policies of administrative offices such as the coordination of important matters for decision by Cabinet Meetings.

(4) The Cabinet Researchers shall, by order, be in charge of the collection and researches of information relating to important policies of the Cabinet.

(5) The Cabinet Officials shall, by order, perform the affairs of the Cabinet Secretariat.

(6) The fixed number of the Cabinet Councillors, Cabinet Deliberators and Cabinet Researchers shall be prescribed by a Cabinet Order.

Article 15. (1) In the Cabinet Secretariat there shall be three Confidential Secretaries assigned to the Prime Minister, and one Confidential Secretary each assigned to the Ministers of State other than the Prime Minister and the competent Ministers.

(2) The Confidential Secretaries mentioned in the preceding paragraph shall, by order of the Prime Minister or of the Minister of State to whom they are respectively assigned, take charge of confidential matters or shall assist temporarily in the affairs of the administrative organs concerned including the Cabinet Secretariat.

Article 16. Deleted

Article 17. The internal organization necessary for the discharge of the affairs coming under the charge of the Cabinet Secretariat shall be prescribed by a Cabinet Order.

Article 18. So far as the affairs coming under the jurisdiction of the Cabinet Secretariat are concerned, the competent Minister as referred to in this Law shall be the Prime Minister.

Appendix 2 The National Government Organization of Japan

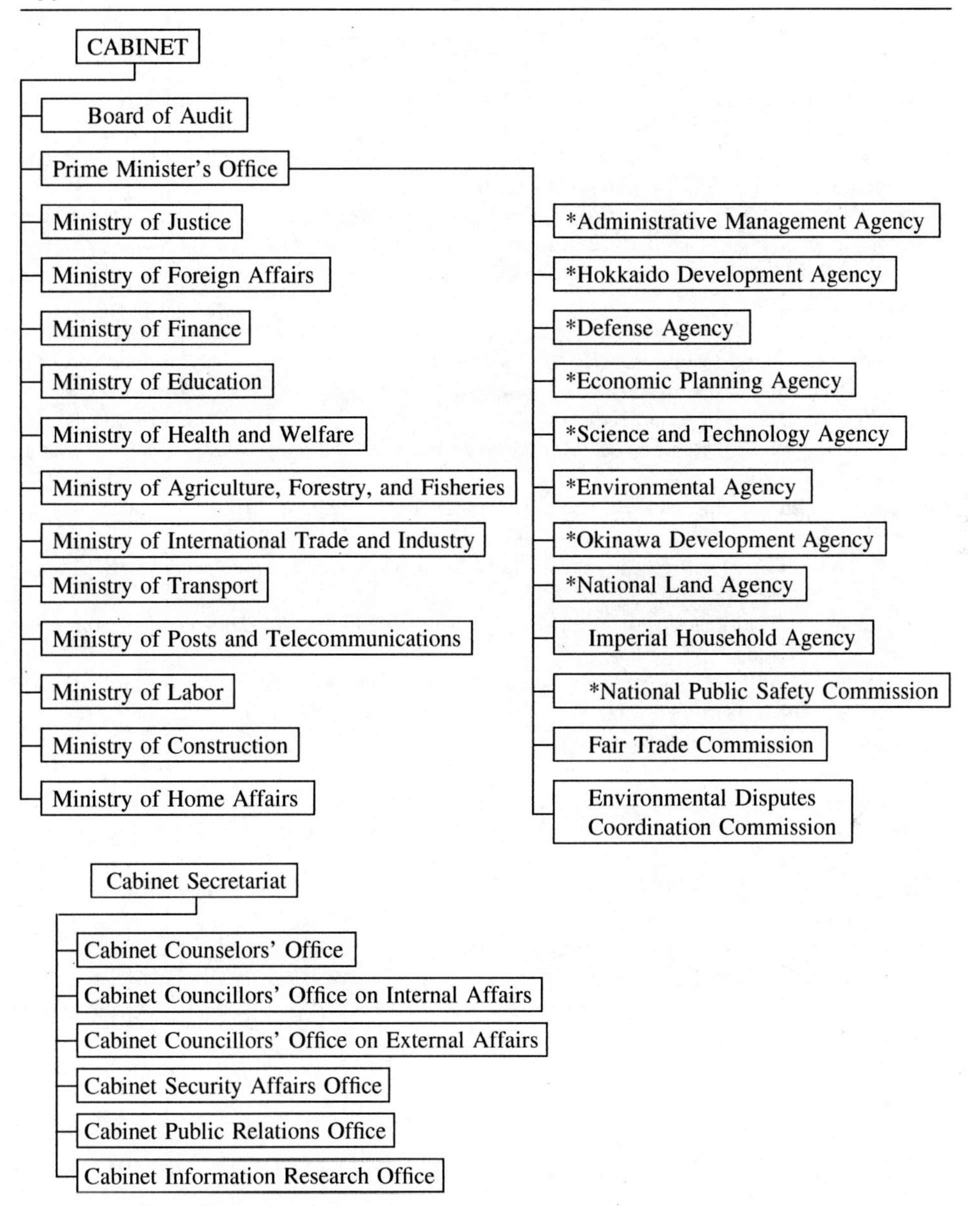

* Agencies and Commision marked with asterisk (*) are external organs of the Prime Minister's Office headed by a Minister of State. (as of November 1, 1997)

REFERENCES

Abe, Yasutaka (1995). ''Hanshin Chiiki no Shinsai Fukko'' (Restoration in Hanshin areas). *Toshi Mondai* 86(*8*), 3–14.

Aoyama, Kozo and Suzuki, Ranko (1995). ''Amerika ni okeru Shinsai ji no Okyu Taisei'' (U.S. Federal Emergency System in times of Earthquake). *Toshi Seisaku* 80.

Iokibe, Makoto (1996). ''Kiki Kanri-Gyosei no Taio'' (Crisis management: administrative responses). In *Hanshin Dai Shinsai* (Great Hanshin Earthquake).

Kawata, Yoshiaki (1997). ''Hanshin-Awaji Dai Shinsai no Kyokun no Sogoka'' (Integrated lessons of the Great Hanshin-Awaji earthquake). *Toshi Mondai Kenkyu* 49(*1*), 14–32.

Kobe News (1995). ''Dai Shinsai so no toki Waga Machi wa'' (Our town's situations in times of the Great Earthquake).

Kume, Ikuo (1997). ''Shinsai to Gyosei Soshiki Kanri'' (Earthquake and management of administrative organization). *Kobe Hogaku* 46(*4*), 675–692.

Kurata, Washio (1997). ''Bosai Katsudo to Community'' (Disaster prevention activities and community). *Toshi Mondai Kenkyu* 49(*11*), 42–57.

Mainichi News (1995). ''Hanshin Dai Shinsai no Zen Kiroku'' (Document of the Great Hanshin-Awaji Earthquake), 1–226.

Mayama, Tatsushi (1997). ''Kiki Hassei ji ni okeru Gyosei Shisutemu no Kadai'' (Problems of the administrative system in times of crisis). *Toshi Mondai Kenkyu* 49(*1*), 45–58.

Mayama, Tatsushi (1997). ''Bosai Gyosei no Kadai'' (Problems of disaster prevention plans). *Nenpo Gyosei Kenkyu* 32, 115–134.

Management and Coordination Agency, Prime Minister's Office (1996). *Organization of the Government of Japan*, pp. 1–144.

Oku, Mami (1996). ''Amerika ni okeru Jyutaku Fukko Shien'' (Lessons learned from the Loma Prieta and North Ridge earthquakes). *Toshi Mondai* 87(*4*), 27.

Sumitomo Kaijo Risuku Kenkyusyo (translation) (1995). FEMA. Nihon Kikaku Kyokai.

Takayose, Shozo (1997). ''Shinsai to Chiho Gyosei'' (Earthquake and local administration). *Nenpo Gyosei Kenkyu* 32, 85–103.

Takayose, Shozo (1997). ''Hanshin Dai Shinsai to Chiho Bunken'' (Great Hanshin Earthquake and local decentralization). *Jichi Forum*. January, pp. 19–26.

Uotani, Masuo (1995). ''Chiho Jichitai no Shinsai ji no Kiki Kanri'' (Crisis management in times of earthquake of local entities). *Jichi Kenkyu* 71(*7*), 70–86, and 71(*9*), 81–95.

Yamakawa, Katsumi (1996). ''California no Jishin Kiki Kanri Shisutemu'' (Crisis management system for the earthquake in California State). *Kandai Hogaku* 46(*4–6*), 569–609.

Yoda, Hiroshi (1996). ''Hanshin Awaji Dai Shinsai to Gyosei Kaikaku'' (Great Hanshin-Awaji earthquake and administrative reform). *Toshi Mondai* 87(*3*), 27–37.

Yomiuri News (1995). ''Hanshin Dai Shinsai'' (Great Hanshin Earthquake).

36

Integrating Public Administration, Science, and Community Action

A Case of Early-Warning Success in Qinglong County for the Magnitude 7.8 Tangshan Earthquake

Jeanne-Marie Col Department of Economic and Social Affairs, The United Nations, New York, New York

Jean J. Chu Institute of Geology and Geophysics, Chinese Academy of Sciences, Beijing, People's Republic of China

I. INTRODUCTION

Public administrators of Qinglong County were able to combine scientific information, public education, extensive preparation, and speedy countywide communications to prevent human tragedy during the Great Tangshan Earthquake (GTE) of 1976. Many of the 470,000 residents of Qinglong County evacuated from their homes just before the magnitude-7.8 Tangshan earthquake hit (United Nations, 1996; Li and Mervis, 1996; Wang, 1991; Qian, 1986, 1989). No one in that county died from the destruction caused by GTE. In the counties surrounding Qinglong, however, nearly a quarter of a million people were crushed to death (Wang, 1998; Qian, 1986, 1989; Chen et al., 1988).

The remarkable experience of Qinglong County, unknown to the world and China for over 20 years, was discovered through a cooperative effort between the United Nations and the government of China in the last few years. An examination of the devastation of and response to the GTE (Qian, 1986, 1989) led to the discovery that one county in the area had successfully prepared for and mitigated the impact of the earthquake. Qinglong County utilized its extensive scientific citizen-based precursor monitoring system, along with exemplary administrative procedures and community spirit, to prepare for the possibility of a major earthquake. Qinglong County established an earthquake office, organized procedures for preparation and response, trained officials, set up a precursor-monitoring network that involved communities and neighbors, and, in July 1976, activated their county earthquake plan to maximize citizen safety. In 1995, UN and Chinese government officials visited the county, found documents that confirmed the historic action, and interviewed officials and villagers who explained the July 1976 events.

The Qinglong County experience shows how collaboration and coordination among public administrators, citizens, and scientists led to the identification of natural disaster risk and effective mitigation. Specifically, [1] public administrators not only had sound public policy but also followed the policy guidelines; [2] citizens were not only knowledgeable but also felt empowered to act; and [3] scientists, cooperating with public administrators and citizens, collected, shared, and disseminated their multidisciplinary data to make joint predictions. When public administrators, citizens, and scientists all work together, they strengthen the ability of their communities to survive disastrous earthquakes and other large and destructive natural events.

The successful early-warning experience of Qinglong County for the 20th century's most destructive natural disaster in terms of loss of life, provides useful clues as to how large communities can reduce the impact of catastrophic natural disasters. This chapter analyzes the lessons learned from data gathered over the last few years, which are presented in the case study summary and the events chronology of Appendix 1.

II. CASE STUDY SUMMARY

More than 20 years ago, on July 28, 1976, a magnitude (M) 7.8 earthquake destroyed the city of Tangshan in Hebei Province, China, killing 240,000 people. Two weeks prior to this large earthquake, Chunqing Wang, the official in charge of earthquake disaster management for Qinglong County (located 115 km from the city of Tangshan), had attended a regional conference organized by the State Seismological Bureau (SSB in 1976; now CSB, China Seismological Bureau, as of 1998). During that five-day conference that began on July 14, 1976, the Qinglong official listened carefully to the speakers at the seminars, panel discussions, and exhibitions. He took detailed notes on techniques of earthquake monitoring by the lay public and precautionary work for large earthquakes.

On the evening of July 16, 1976, scientist Chengmin Wang of the SSB's Analysis and Prediction Department, speaking to a session of 60 attendees, explained that professional earthquake monitoring groups and lay detection centers had reported abnormal signals for the Beijing-Tianjin-Tangshan-Bohai-Zhangjiakou region relating to a possible earthquake. The analysis of scientific data acquired by seven major techniques, including crustal stress and electrical measurements, indicated that there was a good possibility that this region would be struck by a significant earthquake between July 22 and August 5, 1976. Session attendees listened to preliminary cautionary advice, and were encouraged to examine readings of county level earthquake precursor monitoring equipment managed by the lay public. Furthermore, the officials were encouraged to enhance earthquake preparation measures such as examining buildings in critical condition, intensifying public education, and promoting general awareness of possible approaching earthquakes.

Qinglong official Chunqing Wang returned to his county. He reported on the Tangshan conference, particularly on the talk given by scientist Chengmin Wang of the SSB, and included updated information from the county's lay monitoring stations. The county committee took the report very seriously. More than 800 officials of Qinglong County's administrative system listened to Chunqing Wang's report. A flood was also predicted at the time. It was decided that the associate secretaries of each community in the county should return, with a county-level official, to their communities immediately, without seeing their families first, to teach the people about earthquake and flood preparation. In

Qinglong County Administrators Issue Early Warning Four Days Before Earthquake

Meeting of the Chinese Communist Party (CCP) Committee of Qinglong County

Attending members:	Zhang Pingyi, Yu Shen, Chen Yongfu, Ma Gang
Other attendee(s):	Sun You
Chairperson:	Zhang Pingyi
Meeting date and time:	July 24, 1976; 20:30 PM (8:30 PM)
Minutes by:	Chai Wanhui
Meeting place:	Small Conference Room at the County Committee

Meeting notes:

Wang Chunqing, of the Science Committee, reports on the main points of the earthquake conference.

There may be, from July 22 to August 5, a magnitude 5 earthquake, location is the Beijing-Tianjin-Tangshan-Bohai-Zhangjiakou region; from the second half of this year to the beginning of next year, a magnitude 8-9 earthquake may occur.

Our county has a total of 16 monitoring sites, of which 6 sites are equipped with instruments.

The Earthquake Office should write up information on earthquakes and send it to the broadcasting station for dissemination. The Office should emphasize that there may soon be an earthquake, and that its effects can be mitigated. Pay attention to the following tasks: auditoriums, movie theatres, and other places where people gather, should receive special attention; also pass down instructions that each monitoring station should report in a timely manner relevant observations; people on duty must be on alert. Pay attention to safety measures at schools.

Assign people to special duty at the monitoring sites, for this period of time; the county Earthquake Office should receive daily reports from these sites.

1. Strengthen leadership at all levels to complete the tasks ahead.

2. Promote dissemination of information and education on earthquakes.

3. Strengthen work at the monitoring sites; improve timely communication and reports.

Earthquake equipment should be placed in suitable air-raid resistant shelters.

Earthquake Office location: for now in the previous office space of the Science Committee; re-establish telephone communications, with overnight duty personnel.

Figure 1 Early-warning document sent out on 24 July 1976 by Qinglong County public administrators. (United Nations, 1996; UNGP-IPASD Website: http://www.globalwatch.org/ungp/).

a countywide telephone conference on July 24, 1976, County Secretary Guangqi Ran discussed earthquake and flood preparations.

During the days of July 25 and 26, 1976, each community in Qinglong County held an emergency meeting to prepare and instruct villagers in disaster damage reduction. Examinations of buildings in critical condition were made. Special attention was given to prepare reservoirs. Most villages had overnight watch guards on duty. County and village broadcasts instructed people not to close their doors and windows at night so that they could leave their houses immediately as soon as they felt shaking at the beginning of an earthquake. They were also told to avoid being close to tall buildings and power lines. On July 27, 1976, a leading county official gave a major talk at the county's agricultural meeting on the earthquake situation and on mitigation measures for the area. At 3:42 AM on July 28, 1976, the Great Tangshan Earthquake (GTE) struck.

More than 180,000 buildings in the county were destroyed by the GTE; over 7000 of these totally collapsed. However, only one person died, and he died of a heart attack. Meanwhile, in the city of Tangshan and in all of its other surrounding counties, at least 240,000 people were crushed to death and 600,000 were seriously injured.

Five hours after the earthquake, Qinglong County dispatched the first medical team to the disaster zone. Within a few more hours, the county organized and sent relief teams to Tangshan to help with rescue work and the transport of the injured.

Dr. Wu Dong of Qinglong's Dazhangzi Hospital happened to travel to Tangshan City on the day of July 27, 1976. That night, lodging in his relatives' house, Dr. Wu told them that Qinglong County was preparing for the possibility of an earthquake, kept his clothes by his bedside, and deliberately opened the windows and doors. When the earthquake struck, he left the building after arousing his relatives' family of four. Except for one injury from a falling object, the whole family escaped unhurt, although they were only a few kilometers away from the M7.8 earthquake epicenter in the heart of Tangshan City. Families in surrounding houses suffered enormous numbers of deaths and casualties.

The difference between preparedness and lack of preparedness in the GTE is measured in life and death. The official early-warning document alerting Qinglong County residents of a possible large earthquake was issued by the county's top administrators four days before the GTE (Fig. 1) (United Nations, 1996; UNGP-IPASD Website). This early-warning document came to light during a UN research mission to Qinglong County in September 1995 to verify the facts surrounding the county's historic actions. The United Nations has subsequently compiled, based on numerous documentation obtained during its research effort, a detailed reconstruction of the Qinglong County experience during the 1976 Tangshan earthquake (United Nations, 1996). This account details a dramatic example of a "best practice in public administration" and is attached as Appendix 1.

III. EARTHQUAKE EARLY WARNING: THE QINGLONG COUNTY EXPERIENCE

The discovery of the early-warning success of Qinglong County galvanized the United Nations to establish a Global Programme for the Integration of Public Administration and the Science of Disasters (UNGP-IPASD) (Appendix 2). Since 1996, this UN Global Programme has researched several Chinese early warning successes for large earthquakes [M7.3 Haicheng in 1975 and M7.3 Menglian in 1995 (Li and Mervis, 1996); M6.3 to M6.6 Jiashi in 1997 (Li and Kerr, 1997)], all of which share common elements of success.

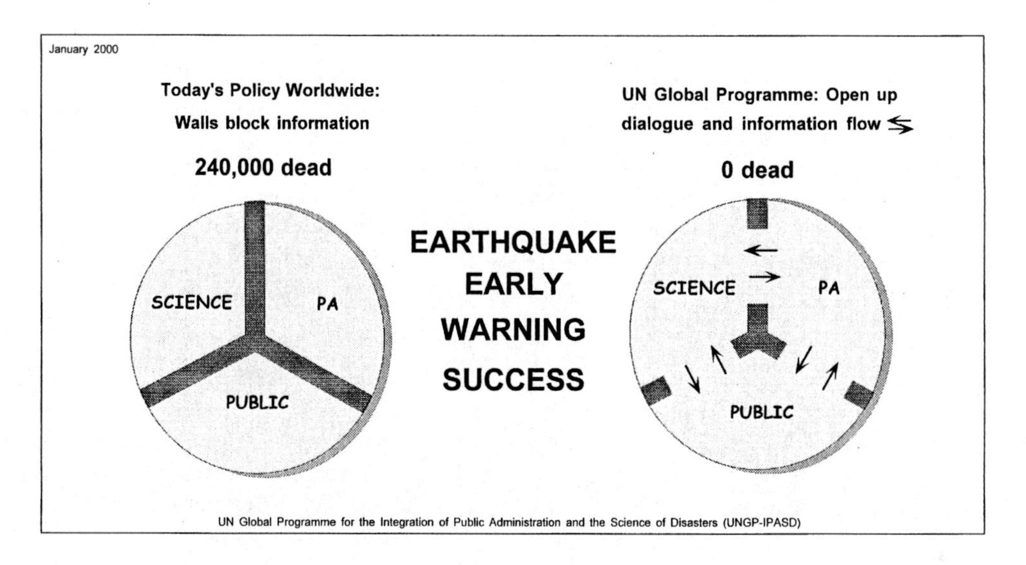

Figure 2 *Past Success Offers Model for Future Quake Early Warning*: Scientists, public administrators (PA), and lay public shared information in early warning success for Qinglong County, China, during 1976 magnitude M7.8 Tangshan earthquake. While there were 240,000 deaths in the surrounding region, no one died from the destruction of 180,000 buildings in Qinglong County, located 115 km from the M7.8 epicenter (http://www.globalwatch.org/ungp/).

The experience of Qinglong County, however, is especially useful, for it is in the marked contrast of the Qinglong County experience to that of its surrounding neighbors that we discover clues on how modern urban communities can better protect themselves against large and sudden disasters such as earthquakes. Figure 2 illustrates some basic concepts that arise from these clues, with expanding details in the text below.

A. Public Administrators Take Initiative

What brought about the proactive strategies of the Qinglong County administrators for the catastrophic Tangshan earthquake? The events analysis (Appendix 1) points out that the county benefited from a unique combination of good public policy, a countywide public-awareness campaign, establishment of responsible offices, leaders who trained themselves to be both sensitive and efficient, deployment of earthquake precursor equipment, and training of citizen monitors. Not one of these elements, in isolation, could have led to the complete success of Qinglong County. The key elements of ''science policy,'' citizen awareness, public administration alert, and citizen participation in scientific monitoring combined to create a compelling dynamism that moved the county along the continuum of mitigation success.

1. Science Policy

The national State Council policy Document 69 (Appendix 4) announced to seven municipalities and provinces in Northeast China that a major earthquake was likely and that preparation and mitigation were advisable. This policy document outlined actions to be taken by public administrators and citizens in response to an intermediate-term warning of anticipated earthquake activity as outlined by national-level scientists, based on precursor activity measured through professional and lay monitoring. The policy document warned of the likelihood of an M6 earthquake and the possibility of an M7–8 earthquake.

2. Implementation: Medium-Term Preparedness

The Qinglong County public administrators implemented this national policy in the cities and rural areas of the county. Like many similar jurisdictions, the public officials set up an earthquake office for earthquake preparedness activities, including precursor monitoring, public education, and strengthening of physical structures such as buildings and water reservoirs.

3. Preparation for Decision Making in an Emergency Situation

The head of the Qinglong County Communist Party leadership strengthened his ability to interpret data for declaring earthquake alerts, without knowing if he would ever need to use this skill. Lacking access to sophisticated geological materials in the county, the head of Qinglong travelled to Beijing where he bought an academic book on earthquake dynamics. His reading of this book helped him to understand the relevance of various precursor events, thus improving his ability to interpret data related to earthquakes.

4. Delegation, Initiative, and Communications for Speedy Action

When Qinglong County established its earthquake office in June 1976, the leadership appointed a 21-year-old recent graduate as head, delegating to him responsibility for preparatory activities. Based on the suggestions of Document 69, the young administrator increased the number of precursor monitoring stations from six to 16, with nine of these lay monitoring stations at schools. Further, he intensified public education, distributing thousands of copies of booklets and posters, and presenting slide shows and movies in villages, towns, and cities.

When he attended a meeting in Chengde in July 1976, he heard about a larger, regional meeting about to take place in Tangshan, and proceeded to Tangshan immediately. At the Tangshan meeting, he learned that some precursor data indicated a M5–6 earthquake soon and an M7–8 within one or two years (major points of the scientific presentation in Appendix 1 for 16 July 1976).

On returning to Qinglong County, he discovered that the latest county-based precursor data indicated a possible imminent earthquake. Informally, he checked with earthquake precursor monitoring stations in neighboring counties and learned that they were also recording significant anomalies. He quickly prepared a report to the county's science committee. The deputy director of the science committee, who had been empowered by his director to take action when the director was away, realized the relevance and importance of the report and arranged for a meeting with the county's top leadership.

5. Teamwork and Responsibility for "Action and Inaction"

Realizing the relevance of the data and the importance of rapid and comprehensive mobilization, the county head decided that the report should be made not only to him but also to the entire CCP Standing Committee of Qinglong County. This act of inclusion brought the main implementation team into the decision-making situation, thereby facilitating timely and effective teamwork. When the head of the earthquake office reported on the strong possibility of an M5 earthquake between 22 July and 5 August, the county CCP adopted and promulgated an action plan (details in Appendix 1 for 24 July 1976). Although the CCP realized that their county's plan might be considered controversial, they concluded that the national State Council Document 69 contained sufficient instruction to cover their action plan. Thus, Qinglong County issued an earthquake alert on 24 July 1976 at 20:30 p.m. (Fig. 1). Immediately, institutions were notified by telephone and the earthquake office worked 24 hours nonstop on detailed instructions to county officials and the general public on the earthquake situation and preparation measures. The county officials used an already-planned conference on agricultural issues to publicize the urgent earthquake situation. The county officials emphasised that every official would be responsible for preparing people in their areas and held accountable for their actions or inactions (details in Appendix 1 for 24 July 1976).

6. Developing Shared Perception of Risk

Meetings were held at town and village levels, as well as in all institutions. The head of the county CCP took up residence in a makeshift tent made of poles and a plastic sheet in order to communicate the seriousness of the situation. The associate head of the CCP visited 23 towns, examining earthquake preparations. County engineers and other officials maintained a 24-hour watch at ''lifeline'' services, such as reservoirs and power generation sites. The earthquake alert and follow-up actions created a shared perception of the emergency (Comfort, 1999).

B. Citizens Self-Mobilize

Citizens in the towns and villages of Qinglong County were active participants in the preparatory and mitigation activities for the possible earthquake in 1976. While it is normal for citizens to be motivated to help neighbors and victims' in the aftermath of a major disaster, it is unusual for citizens to participate directly in preparatory activities. Some recent and successful examples include evacuations from volcanoes that are beginning to erupt (Mount Pinatubo in 1991) and from coastal areas that are apparently in the path of typhoons (Hurricane Floyd in 1999). Even with these more visible signs of approaching disaster, observers often note considerable panic among some citizens. But in the case of Qinglong County in 1976, while precursors for the approaching disaster were more subtle, local citizens enthusiastically engaged in preparations with little sign of panic. What explains this quiet vigilance and determination?

1. Community Awareness Through Widespread and Intensive Public Campaign

From 1974, when the county was first notified about the possibility of earthquake(s) over the next few years, the citizens of Qinglong County received pamphlets, watched movies, observed posters, participated in drills, and held community discussions about earthquake dynamics. People in the cities, towns, and rural areas learned about ways to watch for earthquake precursors, and accepted the responsibility and challenge to heighten their awareness of their environment over the coming years. They created measured response plans geared to prepare the community for possible disaster(s) while minimizing the economic impact of such preparations.

2. Lay Monitoring of Earthquake Precursors by Ordinary Citizens

When the Qinglong County earthquake office promoted the monitoring of earthquake precursors, many institutions became involved. Employees in factories and mines were trained to monitor for earthquake precursors using instrument readings or observational data. Likewise, students in schools became involved in operating simple scientific equipment and in interviewing neighbors on observable earthquake-related phenomena.

3. Response to Earthquake Alert on 24 July 1976

Local residents remained calm and focused as they organized themselves to carry on their daily lives under the earthquake alert:

Schools moved furniture outside and held classes in the open air.
Merchants quickly constructed shelving outdoors under plastic sheets, and continued selling their goods.
Where land was available, people built makeshift tents and camped outdoors.
In the more densely populated areas, people practiced exiting their homes and offices quickly, and slept near exits during the night.
Citizen assemblies to share earthquake preparedness strategies were held in all institutions and communities.
During the days before the earthquake, communities established patrols to monitor preparatory activities.

4. Confirmation of Sense Data Observations

Local people in their communities combined the official earthquake warning with sense data perceived in their local neighborhoods, to conclude that the warning was legitimate and should be heeded. In the cities, towns, and villages, people noticed changes in water, weather, and animal behavior.

Despite the lack of foreshocks, every single person in Qinglong County was prepared for the earthquake and escaped death from the ensuing destruction. During the preparatory period, people had secured their families and their livestock. Even their animals escaped death from the earthquake.

Official county documents and personal written testimonies (translated from Chinese into English) describe the preparations at county, town, and village levels. Based at 16 monitoring stations, the county's lay methods of detecting precursors included anomalies in the level, color, temperature, chemistry, and quality of the water, release of gases, strange animal behavior, and changing weather. Depending on data from a wide variety of methods, the county administrator combined information from several methods, all indicating unusual tendencies. In each and every neighborhood and village, all county residents had taken precautions against a possible earthquake.

C. Scientists Share Information

There were more than seven methods used by professional earth scientists in China to monitor for earthquake precursors at the time (Wang, 1991; Mei, 1982; Chen, 1988; Qian, 1989). At the SSB Conference held in Tangshan two weeks before the great earthquake, a government scientist informally shared with the administrators attending the meeting the most recent update on the regional earthquake situation based on information from professional and lay observers (Li and Mervis, 1996). It was at this session that public administrator Wang Chunqing noted the work of two methods in particular—crustal stress and geoelectric (United Nations, 1996). Chu et al. (1996) discuss geoelectric, geologic, seismic, meteorologic, and hydrologic data related to the 1976 Tangshan earthquake. The crustal stress method is introduced here.

In the 1960s, Chinese earth scientists developed a method to monitor variations in crustal stress over time (Huang et al., 1982, 1991). This method was based on a concept proposed by Swedish scientist Nils Hast (1958). The physical principle underlying the method is inverse magnetostriction: the dependence of magnetization (susceptibility or remanence) on applied stress (Sheriff, 1984), or, equivalently, changes in magnetization caused by an application of mechanical stress (Chikazumi and Charap, 1964; Tremolet de Lacheisserie, 1993). Many ferromagnetic materials have magnetic properties that are highly sensitive to applied stress; in fact, stress may be ranked with field strength and temperature as a primary factor affecting magnetic change (Tremolet de Lachesserie, 1993). Chinese earthquake scientists use ferromagnetic sensors to measure changes in crustal stress via changes in magnetization.

By 1972, the Seismo-Geological Brigade (Beijing Sanhe team) of the SSB had established a national network of more than 100 professional crustal stress-monitoring stations, of which 24 were located in North China. Each station was equipped with three crustal stress sensors oriented horizontally in three different directions (Huang et al., 1982). The depth of placement of these three sensors was no less than 20 m, to avoid the effects of seasonal changes in temperature, and no greater than 100 m owing to technical costs; the average depth was 50 to 60 m. Crustal stress measurements were taken every two hours and the averages of the 12 readings per day per sensor were transmitted daily, by telephone or telegraph, for official record at the Office of Analysis and Prediction of the Seismogeological Brigade in Beijing. For further details on the crustal stress method, see Huang et al. (1982) and Huang et al. (1991).

Crustal stress data taken before, during, and after the 1976 Great Tangshan Earthquake came from stations that were separated by distances of as much as 1000 km. The

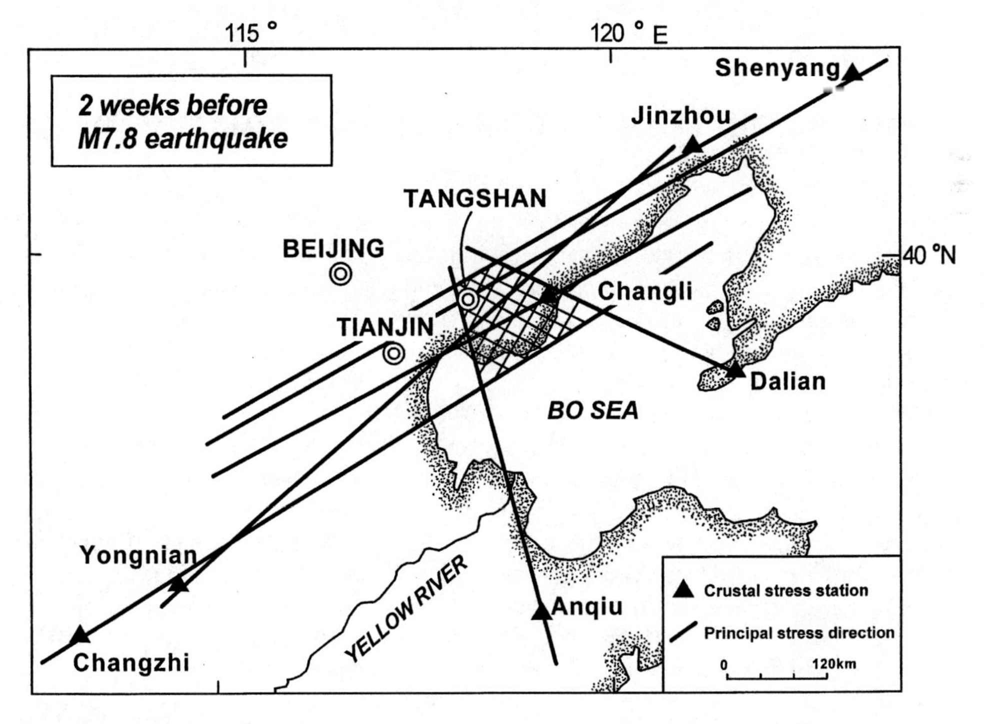

Figure 3 Map of crustal stress lines that intersect in the Tangshan region. A similar map was submitted to the SSB by the crustal stress team two weeks before the Tangshan earthquake devastated the city.

early-warning document of 24 July 1976 cites the period of 22 July to 5 August 1976 for a possible earthquake in the Tangshan region. These dates, carefully noted by public administrator Wang Chunqing, were given at the SSB Tangshan Conference during an informal science lecture 12 days before the GTE (United Nations, 1996). Set by the Beijing Sanhe team, these dates were established using imminent precursory signals from a total of sixteen crustal stress stations in the North China region.

Imminent signals from twelve crustal stress stations in the North China network were used to compile the map of Figure 3. This figure shows the principal stress (σ_1) directions (straight lines) of those stations with accelerated changes in anomalous stress just before the 28 July 1976, M7.8 Tangshan earthquake (Huang et al., 1982).

Note that the intersection of these lines includes the city of Tangshan and much of the eventual rupture region (cross-hatched area) (Chen et al., 1988; Chu et al., 1996). It is indeed by the intersection of such lines that the crustal stress method is able to locate where an earthquake may eventually strike. A map similar to Figure 3, based on precursory signals from seven stations, located Haicheng as a site for a possible earthquake several weeks before the 1975 M7.3 Haicheng earthquake (Huang et al., 1991).

Though the crustal stress team was successful in determining the location and timing of the 1975 Haicheng and 1976 Tangshan earthquakes, lack of familiarity with some important aspects of precursory signals (e.g., amplitude vs. length of time of signal) resulted in earthquake predictions of M5.

Through its 30 years of applied research, over 175 earthquake predictions have been officially recorded using the crustal stress method. The accuracy of these predictions has been evaluated using ESTAPE (Appendix 3).

IV. THE PRESENT GLOBAL SITUATION AND SUSTAINABLE HUMAN DEVELOPMENT

The present world view assumes that scientists are responsible for disaster forecasting, and that the role of public administrators is to take the conclusion of scientists and then mobilize their communities appropriately. Everything is compartmentalized and there is no flow of information until a firm assessment is made. This sequence of actions would be fine if disaster prediction were a mature science and predictions were 100% accurate. However, as is generally known, even the prediction of weather is not totally accurate, and prediction of earthquakes lags most seriously behind. In fact, it is generally believed that earthquake prediction is not possible, at least in the near future (*Economist,* 1997).

Meanwhile, what can communities do to protect themselves from the tragic consequences of earthquakes? While it may be a long time yet before the regularities common to each earthquake are discovered and universally accepted, the experience of Qinglong County provides us with directions of action that can strengthen the mitigation capacity of today's ever expanding urban settlements.

It is clear from the description above and in the chronology of events outlined in Appendix 1 that the open flow and exchange of disaster-related knowledge and information through all levels of society promotes disaster mitigation. Of equal importance is the active participation of every sector of society in preparing communities for possible natural hazards. Figure 4 analyzes in tabular form the actions various sectors of society can choose to take to bring about the consequent protection against natural disasters.

CITIZENS, PUBLIC ADMINISTRATORS & SCIENTISTS MITIGATE NATURAL DISASTERS FOR SUSTAINABLE HUMAN DEVELOPMENT

When citizens, administrators and scientists share perspectives with each other, they establish basis for taking joint action and create action networks throughout their communities. Intensified action enhances not only self-reliance, well being and orientation to the future, but also community survival and development.

Attitude / Consequent Level of Participation	Citizens	Public Administrators	Scientists	Natural Disaster Outcomes
Unaware / little or no participation	It will not happen here and not to me, my family and my community; citizens ignore disaster warnings, or they panic	Doing just enough work to hold the job; too busy with immediate priorities every day to consider the likelihood of natural disasters	Studying phenomena without considering their possible relationship to natural disasters and people	Total tragedy
Educated / moderate level of participation	It might happen; but when it does, someone else will take care of necessary preparations / relief	Gathering and cataloging of information; developing natural disaster management plans; gathering statistics on the community, its vulnerabilities and its disaster relief needs; lack of standards for evaluating accuracy of predictions; who can take responsibility for deciding accuracy or usefulness of predictions	Scientists can notice and record correlation between natural phenomena and disasters; scientists could produce predictions with a degree of probability, but administrators and the public usually demand absolute accuracy	Tragedy; massive relief; major impact on social and economic development
Aware and alert / high level of participation	Citizens accept possibility of natural disaster occurrences; citizens educate themselves and prepare community-based plans; citizens organize regular drills; circulate posters, pamphlets, school materials, videos, etc.; citizens participate in lay monitoring of disaster precursors; school children participate in lay monitoring as part of science curriculum and community work . ***Citizens become aware of their immediate natural environment & its subtle shifts***	Organizing practice drills; establishing real-time information sharing; promoting disaster-related public education; involving mass media in dissemination of disaster-related information; reaching out to community groups, private sector, NGOs, etc. for integrated public education, disaster preparedness and response ***Public administrators understand some basic dynamics of the Earth***	Scientists share and discuss recorded precursor signals with scientists of other disciplines, among lay persons and citizens, and especially among public administrators, who can translate scientific observations into programmes and actions likely to protect communities from natural disasters ***Scientists share their observations in ways that are comprehensible to administrators and the public***	Early warning success; evacuations of communities where necessary; safeguarding lives and property; minimize deaths and relief costs; more resources still available for sustainable human development

UN Global Programme for the Integration of Public Administration and the Science of Disasters (UNGP-IPASD) Web Site: *http:/www.globalwatch.org/ungp/*
J.-M. Col, Senior Interregional Adviser, UNDESA/New York, and Coordinator, UNGP-IPASD col@un.org Tel: (1-212) 963 8377 FAX: (1-212) 963 2916
J.J. Chu, Chinese Academy of Sciences, and Consultant, UNDESA jean.chu@undp.org Tel: (86-10) 6532 3731 ext. 339 FAX/Tel: (86-10) 6237 5167
Liu Xiaohan, Director, Coordination Unit / Beijing, UNGP-IPASD wendyxu@public3.bta.net.cn Tel: (86-10) 6237 5165 FAX: (86-10) 6237 5167

Figure 4 Citizens, public administrators, and scientists mitigate natural disasters for sustainable human development.

Key elements for success lie in the attitude and level of participation of community members to protect their community against the impact of natural disasters. For such disasters, the degree of environmental and social awareness and willingness of individuals to participate and communicate can make the difference between tragedy and survival. From the natural disaster mitigation perspective, communities are composed of three broad categories of individuals: citizens, public administrators and scientists. For each category, there can be a continuum of involvement. Indeed, this continuum represents a differentiation among levels of participation, from passive to active (Almond and Verba, 1989):

1. Where community members are mostly passive and only occasionally read about disasters and what to do to keep safe for such events, they are ill-prepared to take action against the evolving natural phenomenon and are subject to rumors and panic.

2. Partial citizen action involves those who read about natural disasters and respond to warnings. Such citizens are aware that natural disasters can be anticipated and even forecast. Indeed, these individuals are aware of the community's interest in being protected, and expect the government to warn them of danger from natural disasters.

3. At the most active end of the continuum is the "participant" who is attuned to risk and vulnerability to natural disasters and also participates in disaster mitigation activities. In the case of earthquake prediction, the participant may even be a "lay monitor"; that is, he or she may be responsible for recording the readings of one or more

instruments that are designed to record evidence of earthquake precursors. The ''participant'' political culture characterizes the people of Qinglong County, where they participated in lay monitoring, were sensitized to noticing local, microprecursors, and launched preparatory mitigation activities upon their own confirmation of the early warning.

Although these levels of involvement represent three points on an ''activism'' continuum, the categories are not static. People can learn to be more active through experience of natural disasters and through focused learning, e.g., public disaster education campaigns during a warning (prepare) or an alert (evacuate or take cover) period. The occurrence of dramatic natural disasters can make a lasting impression on community members. If such experiences are also shared via media with others in regions of potential danger, even more people can be educated to safeguard themselves during a destructive earthquake. With the sharing of experiences and perspectives, learning can be not only comprehensive and coordinated but also effective.

Natural disasters also present opportunities for public administrators to be more or less active on behalf of their communities. At their most passive, officials provide assistance to victims: food, shelter, loans, raw materials, etc. A moderate level of activity would involve developing a disaster management plan and gathering various statistics on the community and its disaster relief needs. A high level of activity would involve disaster education programs for the public, upgrading and enforcing building codes (Survivors, 1999; Shaking, 1995), practice drills to simulate natural disaster situations, and investment to install precursor-monitoring equipment and to organize some staff and/or citizens to record the readings of these instruments.

Among scientists, the various levels of activity can be described as first, studying phenomena without considering the possible consequences for natural disasters. On a higher level, a scientist can notice and record correlation between natural disasters and certain natural phenomena. Most actively, a scientist can discuss the phenomena with scientists of other disciplines, among lay persons and citizens, and especially among public administrators who can translate scientific observations into programs and actions likely to protect communities from natural disasters.

For each category—administrator, scientist, and citizen—there are degrees of commitment and activity. When they explain their specialties and perspectives to each other, they establish a basis for taking joint action. When all three types of people are participating actively, strong synergies can grow among the three types and can weave action networks throughout their communities. Participants sensitize their partners to the nuances of their own specialties. Public officials come to understand some dynamics of the Earth. Scientists discover actions relevant to various population groups. Citizens become more aware of their immediate natural environments and its subtle shifts. When all three groups intensify their activities, the pulse of the community quickens and the sense of self-reliance, well-being, and future orientation are all enhanced. Indeed, the chances of community survival and even thriving are enhanced when the categories of individuals are in tune with each other and also with shifts in the natural environment.

V. ANALYSIS

A. From Social Dilemma to Social Change

The world is in a quandary where earthquake disasters are concerned. There is no consensus among scientists that earthquake prediction is possible. Public administrators demand that scientists give them a clear signal when a disaster will happen, a demand that scientists cannot fulfill (Normile, 1996). The public expects that scientists will tell community officials when a disaster will hit and these same officials will then act to protect their respective communities. Reality tells us otherwise, as things are not so simple and straightforward.

Earthquake tragedies such as Tangshan in 1976, Kobe in 1995, and Turkey and Taiwan in 1999 point to a social dilemma that, until recognized for its immense danger and addressed, will continue to produce huge human and economic tolls in our megacities. The social message of the Tangshan tragedy and the Qinglong County success is that where large metropolises are concerned, there will hardly ever be consensus among scientists and/or public administrators to mobilize for devastating earthquakes.

The challenge that humanity now faces is to rethink, along the lines of the Qinglong County experience, how we can reorganize ourselves and our communities, in light of Figure 4, to strengthen our disaster mitigation capacities. By educating ourselves and creating new avenues of information sharing and networking for disaster mitigation, we may find that, as Qinglong County did, the economic, social, and psychological concerns usually associated with disaster preparedness are minimized and even transformed.

B. Multidisciplinary Approach

The prediction of earthquakes is a multifaceted process. For three decades, Chinese earthquake scientists have based their prediction work on intense monitoring and analysis with a spectrum of multidisciplinary methods (Chu et al., 1996). They have found that, while no single method records precursory signals for all events, a multidisciplinary approach will often yield some precursory signals for most, especially large, earthquakes. The interlinking of professional and lay observation methodologies has also helped to define the location and timing of earthquakes.

C. Shared Risk and Shared Responsibility

Given the uncertainties associated with earthquake prediction, anticipation and preparation for an earthquake are possible provided that information on the potential disaster is shared with the public at large, preferably through public administrators with training in disaster management. Successful warning for earthquakes will become possible when information from earthquake scientists is openly communicated to local public administrators who then, understanding and accepting the uncertainties involved, can choose to act upon the information and to educate and empower their local communities to mitigate the potential disaster. The ultimate decision for taking any action based on available information rests first with the public administrators, and then with each individual. Hence the consequences of such action involves responsibility at the most fundamental level, i.e., shared risk and shared responsibility taken on by the community's citizens. Successful early warning can best be achieved through avenues of disaster-related communications that are open and transparent.

D. Concept of Probability

One difficulty of using earthquake prediction information within a community involves the need to widely cultivate an appreciation for the concept of probability. Both public administrators and citizens need to understand that, like hurricanes and typhoons, earthquakes occur occasionally. It is difficult to predict the three main aspects of earthquakes—time, location, and magnitude. Various cultures have differing tolerances for uncertainty (Hofstede, 1984). But just as communities can prepare for the possibility of hurricanes, they can prepare for the possibility of earthquakes. In line with the concept of probability, a community can plan a range of preparedness responses taking into account the likelihood of the earthquake's occurrence as well as the economic impact of a particular preparedness activity. For example, if individual householders know that an earthquake is probable over the next two weeks, and they have direct access to their gas lines, they can choose to shut off their lines when they retire to bed, thus reducing their injury from fires which are often associated with earthquakes. Acceptance of uncertainty makes possible the planning of ''measured'' responses. Willingness to work with uncertainties allows communities to prepare for potential disaster with the minimum of psychological, social and economic impact on the community's daily routine. As difficult as it is psychologically to prepare for an earthquake, the possibility of earthquakes requires calm preparation.

E. Multiple Communication Pathways

Although engineering solutions are practical in countries that can afford to construct very strong and resilient buildings, highways, and bridges, poorer countries need to include evacuation measures within their range of options. These evacuation measures can be set to correspond to a variety of earthquake strengths, with procedures for activating each degree of response before the earthquake hits. Speed, accuracy, efficiency, and complex coordination are often required, especially to prevent earthquakes from developing secondary and tertiary impacts, such as gas leaks and fires. Optimally, all levels of governments, scientific institutes, nongovernmental organizations, and relevant private-sector units would be networked together, sharing data and information accurately and with minimum delay. Unfortunately, agencies seldom have multiple communication pathways, and those that do exist are generally fragile rather than robust. The few scientists in each disaster-prone country, challenged by the difficult demands of public administrators and citizens to issue accurate predictions (Normile, 1996), are usually unable to serve their publics as they face heavy consequences and responsibility from any decision that they make regarding earthquake prediction/early warning.

VI. CONCLUSION

Just as microfinance is important to the economic health of a developing community, so is micropreparedness essential in the reduction of natural disasters. As each individual actively prepares, the family, community and urban metropolis become better protected against the devastation of natural disasters. The Qinglong County experience shows us that tragedies even from great earthquake disasters can be successfully prepared for. The main ingredient is awareness that [1] large earthquakes are preceded by numerous precursors; [2] there are a variety of disaster mitigation methodologies available to monitor for changes in the natural environment related to earthquakes; and [3] while today's urban metropolises are physically more than ever vulnerable to the devastation of natural events, it is through the networking of all levels of society and the open communication of disaster information that these megacommunities will achieve earthquake early warning successes.

APPENDIX 1

Qinglong County and the 1976 Tangshan Earthquake: A Model Integrating Public Administration and the Science of Disasters

Public administration lessons	Events Analysis			
	When	Who	What	Impact
Policy statements are essential. National earthquake (EQ) policy statement sets operational framework for later specific EQ disaster mitigation measures.	29 June 1974	State Council, People's Republic of China	State Council orders Document No. 69 sent to seven municipalties and provinces: Beijing, Tianjin, Hebei, Shanxi, Inner Mongolia, Liaoning, Shandong. Document No. 69 alerts public officials to the serious earthquake (EQ) situation; informs them of risk and advises region to prepare for EQs of magnitude greater than six (M>6); M7–8 also possible.	Document No. 69 alerts northeast China to the possibility of large earthquakes (EQs) within two years. Scientific information is shared openly with leading public administrators in the seven risk areas of North China and the Bohai Sea. EQ management offices are established and top priority is places on EQ preparedness. Cooperation between professional and lay detection teams is emphasized, and detection networks at regional, county, and village levels are set up and strengthened. Public education and EQ monitoring programs are intensified.
Counties intensify efforts in EQ preparedness—detection of precursors, public education and review of infrastructure.	From 1974	Counties in the region affected by Document No. 69	EQ preparedness programme is implemented, including monitoring, public education, and strengthening of structures. Lay monitoring in factories, mines and schools is encouraged. EQ office for EQ preparedness activities set up in most counties by 1976.	Public learns about EQs, the lay detection of precursors (anomalies in water level, color, temperature, chemistry, and quality; release of gases; animal behavior; weather changes), methods of preparing for disasters, and the need for heightened awareness.

APPENDIX 1 Continued

Public administration lessons	Events Analysis			
	When	Who	What	Impact
Experience, interest and responsibility spurs top public administrator to strengthen scientific background.	From 1974	Ran Guangqi, Head of Chinese Communist Party (CCP) in Qinglong County	Alerted by Document No. 69, and recalling the experience of the 1966 magnitude (M7.3) Xingtai EQ, Ran decides to learn about EQs from the County's Science Committee office and from textbook by Chinese geologist, Li Siguang (in English J.S. Lee).	Through gradual self training, the head of Qinglong County strengthens his disaster decision-making ability.
Energetic administrator increases county's EQ awareness and preparedness.	From November 1975	Wang Chunqing, a 21-year-old Qinglong County administrator	Placed in charge of Qinglong County's Science Committee's EQ disaster management program. Appointed in June 1976 as head of County's newly established EQ office.	Increases County's EQ monitoring stations (sites) from 6 to 16 (9 of these lay monitoring sites are at schools). Intensifies public education, distributing thousands of copies of booklets and posters; presenting slide shows and movies in villages, towns and city, including short EQ preparedness film before every cinema presentation, with materials provided by the State Seismological Bureau (SSB).
Delegation of authority creates conditions for greater efficiency.	Just before 8 July 1976	Wang Jinzhi, Head of Qinglong County Science Committee, before leaving town for a meeting	Gives his deputy Zhang Hongjiu instruction to process urgent matters without waiting for his return.	County officials are able to take action quickly.
Open channels increase information sharing	8 July 1976	Wang Chunqing	Attends Chengde District meeting on EQs.	Learns of the larger, regional meeting on EQs in Tangshan and proceeds there by 14 July 1976.
Administrators are trained to educate the public	14–19 July	State Seismological Bureau (SSB)	SSB holds regional conference in Tangshan City.	Trains administrators to educate public on measures for EQ preparedness.

Conference organizers quietly supportive of unplanned scientific presentation	16 and 18 July	Wang Chengmin, Head of Beijing-Tianjin section of the SSB Analysis and Prediction Department.	During Tangshan conference, holds two informal evening meetings (with only 2 hours prior notice) on intermediate- and short-term predictions of EQ.	Shows and discusses data of precursory signals, allowing participants to draw their own conclusions, and to integrate these conclusions with past plus recent data and empirical trends.
Local administrators share EQ information development of interdisciplinary network of professionals who are knowledgeable about EQ preparedness and mitigation.	16 July 1976	Wang Chunqing, administrator, attends scientist Wang Chengmin's presentation.	Takes detailed notes on presentation by Wang Chengmin.	Major points of scientific presentation are 1. Many EQs of $M > 7$ have recently occurred throughout the world. 2. Professional EQ monitoring teams and lay detection centers are reporting abnormal signals for Beijing-Tianjin-Tangshan-Bohai-Zhangjiakou region, which may relate to a possible EQ. 3. Analysis of scientific data acquired by seven major techniques, including stress and electrical measurements, indicate there is a good possibility this region will be struck by a significant EQ. Data include (i) the Sanhe monitoring team's prediction of an EQ of M5, between 22 July and 5 August 1976; (ii) synthesis of data from several field teams regarding dates, locations, and assessments of the situation, plus comments on various EQs in northeast China and in Inner Mongolia: *"From all the data and trends, we conclude that this area, within 1–2 years, may have a M8 EQ; the area should therefore actively prepare, widely circulate this EQ knowledge (especially to big factories and mines) and make plans and proper measures for EQ preparation."*

APPENDIX 1 Continued

Public administration lessons	Events Analysis			
	When	Who	What	Impact
Report recent developments in a timely manner to county officials.	Conference ends 19 July; return to county headquarters 21 July.	Wang Chunqing.	Returns to Qinglong County and reports immediately to Zhang Hongjiu, Deputy Head of Science Committee on EQ situation.	Zhang Hongjiu takes information very seriously and recommends county-wide preparations and education. They go together to report to Yu Shen, the County's Associate Director in charge of supervising the County's Science Committee.
Busy, senior officials recognize significance of information reported by junior official; increasing leadership awareness of EQ risk.	21 July	Wang Chunqing and Zhang Hongjiu	Together, they report to Yu Shen.	Tell Yu Shen of danger of impending disasters (predicted EQ and possible flood). Yu Shen recommends they make appointment to report to leadership as soon as possible. He instructs Wang Chunqing to contact Ma Gang, county office administrator, to arrange appointment with Ran Guangqi, head of CCP in Qinglong County.
Science and administrative tasks are coordinated and integrated.	21–24 July	Wang Chunqing	Participates in alerting top county administrators of EQ situation, while also checking (over a three-day period) with county's 16 lay monitoring sites for latest readings. (All 16 sites are linked by telephone to county's EQ office.)	Activities include: 1. Meets with Ma Gang on 22 July 1976, who recognizes significance of EQ situation and urgency of notifying county head Ran Guangqi. 2. Contacts lay monitoring sites for record updates to assess immediate EQ situation in county; unusual changes noted at four sites. Integrates lay monitoring findings into report to county leadership.

Topmost official takes report seriously; crystallization of priority on EQ risk.	23 July	Ran Guangqi, head of CCP in Qinglong County	Says the report should be made not only to him, but also to the entire CCP standing committee of Qinglong County.	Calls special meeting of the CCP Standing Committee to meet at 8:30 pm on 24 July, to hear Wang Chunqing report on EQ situation (even though the CCP and government officials were busy preparing for a major agricultural conference).
Develop communicative and informative mechanism to support mutual activities: incoming information flows both vertically and horizontally into EQ Office; protocols for speedy communication are set. *Integrated past and current, EQ and flood, data in decisionmaking.* *Senior officials take report by junior official seriously. Focused attention on EQ by strengthening power of responsible officials to act without delay or further reference to the top leaders.*	24 July 1976	Zhang Pingyi, Yu Shen, Chen Yongfu, Ma Gang (also Sun You): *At the CCP Standing Committee meeting, there is a difference of opinion concerning the appropriate response to the EQ situation, the possibility of creating panic and loss of credibility, and the degree of popular knowledge and/or presence of superstitutions about EQs.* *Ran Guangqi (absent at another meeting, but kept fully informed) and Yu Shen, both of whom hold important posts, assert the wisdom of community preparation in view of Document No. 69 and information from the Tangshan conference.*	Wang Chunqing reports on EQ situation: Notes strong possibility of EQ M5 between 22 July and 5 August in Beijing-Tianjin-Tangshan-Bohai-Zhangjiakou area; and M8 likely from second half of 1976 to beginning of following year. (Of the county's 16 monitoring stations, six have monitoring equipment installed.)	Action plan includes: 1. Strengthen leadership at all levels. 2. Establish EQ Command Office: Head, Ran Guangqi, Executive Head, Yu Shen; Associate Head, Wang Chunqing; staffed for 24-hour communication; location, for now, in Science Committee's office area. 3. Strengthen monitoring stations, by assigning people to special 24-hour duty, and by scheduling daily reports to EQ office. 4. Place EQ equipment in air-raid resistant structures (built for air defense). 5. Promote education on EQ detection and preparation. 6. Instruct EQ office to write up EQ preparation measures for county officials and the general public. Disseminate information county-wide by telephone and by public address system. 7. Emphasize that there may soon be an EQ, and that its effects can be mitigated. Give special attention to auditoriums, cinemas and theaters. Strengthen school safety measures. 8. Instruct officials, civil workers and citizens to be on alert. (Key officials go without sleep for three days.)

APPENDIX 1 Continued

Public administration lessons	Events Analysis			
	When	Who	What	Impact
County alerts government officials at town and village levels.	24 July 1976	Ran Guangqi, head of Qinglong County CCP.	Immediately after meeting, notifies by telephone conference the leading officials of all 43 towns in Qinglong County of possible disaster(s). *County is composed of towns and surrounding villages, known respectively in 1976 as communes and brigades.*	Discusses and arranges preparations for EQ (and flood). Likens urgent disaster situation to that of fire alarm. Emphasizes that every official is responsible for preparing people in their areas and is accountable for their actions or inactions.
Communication channel between counties is utilized; communication network activated	From 24 July onward	Wang Chunqing	Contacts surrounding counties	Requests information on any anomalies recorded in neighboring counties, in accordance with periodic practice.
Public EQ announcement prepared for countywide dissemination; anticipation of EQ risk.	Through night of 24 July and the day of 25 July	Wang Chunqing and staff	Work 24 hours nonstop, on detailed instructions to county officials and general public on the EQ situation and preparation measures.	Activate countywide information network; public informed of EQ risk and of potential losses. Preparation measures include: 1. Broadcast lectures on EQs. 2. Alert EQ monitoring stations to pay particular attention, with overnight watch duty, between 22 July and 5 August 1976. 3. Assign officers to EQ preparation work on county, district, town and village levels. 4. Inform by telephone the 22 factories, mines, schools, post offices, reservoirs, cinemas, auditoriums, etc., to prepare for a possible EQ.

County officials show flexibility by using an already-planned conference on another topic as the occasion to publicize the urgent EQ situation; adoption of adaptive organizational behavior.	Morning of 25 July	County leadership has Wang Jinzhi report on EQ situation at county-level agricultural meeting of more than 800 county and town officials. *County has 43 towns, each composed of a cluster of contiguous villages (a total of 404 organized villages, and 27,000 native places where government supervision is less)*	Use event of agricultural meeting to discuss impending EQ (and flood) situation.	At the agricultural meeting, a decision was made to send two officials (one county level and one local community) to each town, with the following instructions: 1. Everyone must be informed by the end of 26 July! 2. Officials must travel straight to the office and begin work, without stopping at home or for personal business (anyone negligent will be held accountable). 3. Immediately begin EQ and flood preparations and public education campaign. 4. Each town and each village should have an EQ command office to transmit information down and across to neighboring towns and cities. 5. Set up 24-hour communications; reports, patrols, and links with nearby counties, to know every detail of trends in surrounding areas. 6. Use various means for education of people: broadcasting, workshops, telephone calls to village offices, blackboards, night schools, and neighbors informing neighbors. 7. Keep windows and doors open; neither cook nor eat inside; and where feasible, stay in sheds in the fields.

APPENDIX 1 Continued

Public administration lessons	Events Analysis			
	When	Who	What	Impact
County government reaches out to entire population; alerts community.	Evening of 25 July	Broadcast Bureau	Begins broadcasting EQ information 3 times a day using public announcement system that reaches all rural, residential, and business areas in the county.	The population is alerted to the most recent EQ situation, on the dangers of EQs, and of how to make themselves safer before, during and after an EQ.
Shared perception of emergency	From 25 July	Towns and villages	Emergency meetings at town and village levels	Ability to spread the word is enhanced through this community-based network.
Leading public administrator sets example.	From 25 July	Ran Guangqi, head of Qinglong County	Takes up residence in makeshift tent made of poles and a plastic sheet.	Encourages all county officials and residents to heed warnings to stay away from buildings.
Officials do not rest during the emergency preparations, working day and night; intensify investment of resources in preparedness.	24–27 July	Secretary of Dazhangzi Town (also a member of the Qinglong County's CCP Standing Committee)	Personally participates in town's EQ preparation activities: remains at town's reservoir for 7 days; does not sleep for 3 days; eats only rice with salt.	Instructs villages to set up own EQ offices with 24-hour monitoring. (Pre-EQ situation: hot weather, rains, humidity, awareness of 1975 M7.3 Haicheng EQ.) Emergency broadcast on night of 27 July requests village officials to examine all buildings; every home is to have one person on watch (in shifts) throughout the night.
Top official integrates past and current information and goes to the people to assess EQ preparations.	From 25 July	Zhang Pingyi, associate head of CCP in Qinglong County	Visits 23 towns, examining EQ preparations	Emphasizes EQ preparation, because he remembers in a previous provincial meeting the discussion of large disasters caused by EQs in Japan.
Responsible officials work day and night; intensive engagement in preparedness efforts.	From 25 July	County engineer	Sleeps outside for a month; maintains 24-hour watch before, during and after EQ mainshock and aftershocks.	Stays on alert to shut off power as soon as an EQ occurs; equipment guarded 24 hours a day.

VILLAGE 1		Xia Dahudian		
Public behavior changes in response to reliable data concerning EQ risk (scientific data from county level seen within context of earlier observations at grass-roots level). *Villagers see county prediction as providing a framework for understanding already perceived sensory data.*	From 25 July	Village CCP and civil defense members are most responsible for carrying out EQ preparations. *Xia Dahudian village of Qinglong County is 90 km from Tangshan.*	Actions: 1. Broadcast EQ situation through loudspeaker at every home, factory, harvest field and street corner. 2. Alert people to build sheds in fields, move from homes into sheds, and avoid structures including walls and power lines. 3. Carry elderly out to sheds. *Note: by evening of 26 July 1976, everyone is relocated to sheds.*	Results: 1. Most villagers believe the EQ broadcast because county officials base their report on data from scientists. 2. EQ warning corroborates lay monitoring evidence from two local sites; strange animal behavior and changes in water level, color, chemistry, and gas release observed. *NOTE: from 20 July 1976, villagers noticed domestic animals behaving very strangely: pigs ran in circles and would not stay in pens; chickens refused to stay in chicken coops; and yellow weasels left their hiding places and ran around unafraid of the villagers.* 3. Village patrols (twice daily) are set up to prevent people from sneaking back into their houses (able-bodied people are fined if caught inside houses). 4. Villagers learn lay techniques to sense EQs, e.g., overturning empty glass bottles and balance in metal wash basin, so as to hear the bottle tip over in an EQ.

APPENDIX 1 Continued

Public administration lessons	Events Analysis			
	When	Who	What	Impact
VILLAGE 2		Xia Baoyuhuai		
Grass roots respond to report by county officials. *Note: Every family is taught to take responsibility for themselves*	From 25 July	Village CCP and civil defense members are most responsible for carrying out EQ preparations. *Xia Baoyuhuai village of Qinglong County is 75 km from Tangshan.*	Actions: 1. Emergency meeting of leading officials and heads of production teams. 2. Mass meetings of more than 300 people to inform villagers of possible EQ and of preparatory strategies. 3. Build sheds for shelter of people leaving homes; by late 26 July, everyone is out of homes and buildings. 4. Intensify watch for precursors.	Results: 1. People note that chickens are flying high, and pigs are running into walls; well water is muddy and colder than normal on 26–27 July; at a hot spring nearby, used for washing clothes and usually 40°C, water becomes cold 4–5 days before EQ; weather is extremely hot and humid, starting 18 July. 2. Elementary school students put bottles upside down to sense earth shaking. 3. Every family assigns one person to NOT sleep (in shifts), families are instructed to take responsibility for their own survival and safety.
VILLAGE 3		Wen Quan		
Delegation and division of labor; diligence is maintained.	From 25 July	Village CCP and civil defense members are most responsible for carrying out EQ preparations. Wen Quan Village in Qinglong County is 70 km from Tangshan.	Actions: 1. Divide tasks into building sheds, having people leave their buildings, and public education.	Results: 1. Build tents and sheds from locally available materials. 2. Villagers observe large numbers of yellow weasels; nocturnal animals that normally hide and are afraid of people; residents had not realized the significance of this and other strange animal behavior (observed 10–20 days before the EQ) until county EQ announcement.

Intensify EQ alert.	25–26 July	Town officials	Broadcast information widely into all levels to intensify EQ monitoring and preparation.	Heightened awareness that EQ could "happen any day now"!! Widespread dissemination of information on precursors.
		DAY BEFORE THE EARTHQUAKE		
Educate lay public both in Qinglong City and throughout the county	27 July	Wang Jinzhi, head of County Science Committee	At the request of county leaders, gives special talk on EQ situation and mitigation measures to more than 800 officials attending the agricultural meeting.	Attendees are informed on the EQ situation, advised to keep doors and windows open, and instructed on how to get out and run away from buildings should an EQ strike.
School children participate in EQ science and public administration preparedness. *Students are a major resource in preparedness activities.*	From 24–27 July	Local middle school in Qinglong City: 3 physics teachers and small study group of students (This school lay monitoring site, one of 9 in the county, was set up in December 1975.)	Collect data from local people and record precursors; students note changes in water, and that normally nocturnal yellow weasels are running around in large numbers and in broad daylight (with an especially large increase noted 27 July 1976).	Symposium planned for 28 July is moved to 27 July at the insistence of students who see large increase of yellow weasels running around in daylight. By evening of 27 July, school buildings are declared off-limits to everyone; students are not allowed to be inside buildings.
Informal transmission of information across county boundaries	27 July	Dong Wu, a doctor at the hospital in Qinglong County	Goes to Tangshan on night of 27 July and stays with relatives	Informs his relatives that Qinglong County is prepared for an EQ and warns them to also prepare; they listen in disbelief, and tell him not to tell others in order to avoid panic; he puts his clothes by his bedside to leave house quickly should EQ begin. Relatives accept his advice to leave doors and windows open, sleep lightly and stand an empty bottle upside down on edge of table.

APPENDIX 1 Continued

Public administration lessons	Events Analysis			
	When	Who	What	Impact
		DAY BEFORE THE EARTHQUAKE		
Witnesses' accounts of EQ warning data and actual experiences	28 July (just before EQ)	Residents of Qinglong County	Precursors appear immediately before EQ	1. Eye witnesses from villages of Xia Dahudian and XiaBaoyuhuai report: "Sky brightens momentarily with white light in direction of Tangshan City; ominous rumbling heard; ground vibrations begin." 2. Dr. Dong Wu in Tangshan sees flash of white light and hears sound of ominous rumbling.
		THE EARTHQUAKE'S IMPACT IN TANGSHAN		
Lack of communication between public administrators and scientists leads to an unprepared public; great human suffering results. *Generalized breakdown of sociotechnical connections*	28 July 1976, at 3:42 am	M7.8 Tangshan EQ	The Great Tangshan EQ (GTE); Intensity XI (11) in area with maximum damage; trees lining the EQ fault surface rupture are burnt on the side closest to the fault.	1. 242,469 people die, almost 1/4 of Tangshan's 1 million population. 2. 600,000 were seriously injured. 3. 7000 families were completely obliterated. 4. 10,000 Tangshan residents lost their spouses. 5. 2652 children became orphans.

				6. 3800 people were left as paraplegics or amputees. *"On 28 July 1976 at 3:42 a.m. an EQ of a magnitude of 7.8 occurred in Tangshan in the northeastern part of China. The hypocenter was directly under the city of Tangshan at a depth of 11 km. The seismic intensity at the epicenter measured XI. People were fast asleep when the EQ struck. Lightning flashed across the sky and the earth rumbled ominously seconds before the earth began to shake. In a matter of seconds an industrial city of a million people was reduced to rubble. About 240,000 people perished, and some 7000 families were completely obliterated. This catastrophe not only shook China but stunned the world."*
Knowledge and preparation reduce loss of life; officials can empower the public to save their own lives.	28 July, 3:42 am	Qinglong County	County residents are aware and prepared by the time GTE strikes. (Note: Qinglong County is located 115 km from Tangshan.)	1. Only 1 death (due to heart condition) occurred. 2. Animals are safe. 3. County sustains maximum damage of intensity 8. Residents at Wen Quan village hear and experience the destructive power of the EQ, as large sections of the 1000 year old Great Wall split and crash down from nearby hilltops. 4. 7000 buildings collapse totally. 5. 180,000 buildings are damaged. 6. At county middle school, roof shifts and walls collapse, but no loss of life occurs.

APPENDIX 1 Continued

Public administration lessons	Events Analysis			
	When	Who	What	Impact
THE EARTHQUAKE'S IMPACT IN TANGSHAN				
				7. Some residents want to return to homes to escape heavy rains but the civil defense insists that people stay in tents during the aftershock period.
Relevant knowledge supports mitigation of disasters	28 July, 3:42 am	Agricultural meeting in Qinglong City	More than 800 meeting attendees are able to exit urban building complex, avoiding serious injury.	One attendee misses the lecture on EQ safety held at county headquarters on the evening of 27 July and hence does not leave the building in the safest manner; he is cut by breaking glass.
Survivors of disasters can play a significant role as rescuers.	28 July, 3:42 am	Dr. Dong Wu	Wakes relatives at first sound of the rumbling, and runs outside; lifts two relatives out of their home through an open window before the building collapses.	Saves himself and his relative's entire family. Drives 180 km to find a functioning hospital for one injured relative; Stays to help injured at the hospital for four days. Qinglong County officials, who had sent Dr. Dong to Tangshan on medical business, dispatch a search car, which finds him on day 7; they bring him back to his much relieved family in Qinglong.
Well-prepared local survivors can be the first to assist others during a disaster.	28 July	Qinglong County	Immediately organizes a rescue effort: within 5 hours after EQ, sends first medical team to the disaster zone.	Sends the first rescue team that reaches Tangshan after the M7.8 (mainshock) EQ. In total, three rescue teams are sent. Supplies, water and food also are sent to Tangshan. Production is maintained. Receives injured at county hospital.

AFTERSHOCKS				
EQs continue to create havoc after mainshock; close cooperation between public administrators, scientists and lay public is essential to minimize damage and loss of life. *Limiting damage requires collaborative action.*	28 July onward, for 6 months	Area in and around Tangshan	1. Large aftershocks, M6.2 and M7.1, occur on 28 July; many significant EQs occur for months after the M7.8 mainshock. 2. Aftershocks define EQ rupture zone; region of damage is centered on Tangshan and stretches radially for 200 km. 3. Heavy rains follow mainshock.	1. M7.1 aftershock destroys almost all of the remaining buildings left standing after the mainshock. Survivors rebuild four times, with efforts often destroyed by aftershocks. 2. Aftershock activity causes many more deaths and injuries. 3. Heavy rains impede rescue efforts, adding to the death toll. 4. As many as 400,000 people live outdoors. 5. Careful questioning of lay public by teams of scientists after M7.8 mainshock provides invaluable data on EQ precursors, enabling rescuers to organize their efforts around the aftershocks. (In the village of Yangguanlin, the observations of children lead scientist to predict the Ninghe M6.9 aftershock in November 1976.)
RECOVERY				
From EQ ashes, a new city arises; public administrators, scientists and lay public continue to learn from GTE. *Crisis provides opportunity for learning.*	From 1976 to 1986	Area in and around Tangshan	1. Rebuilding begins in damaged region almost immediately. 2. New building codes protect to EQ intensity level of VIII (8). 3. Historic sites designated to educate officials, scientists and lay public on EQs. 4. Monument and museum built by Tangshan city in memory of GTE victims.	1. Some schools open in the streets after one month; some factories begin production within 2 weeks. 2. One million sheds house survivors for six months after the EQ. 3. After 7 years, people return to normal housing. 4. After 10 years, all buildings are reconstructed, except for 7 historical sites, which are preserved as examples of the destructive power of EQs.

APPENDIX 2

United Nations Global Programme for the Integration of Public Administration and the Science of Disasters (UNGP-IPASD)

Established in January 1996 by the United Nations Secretariat and directed by the Department of Economic and Social Affairs (UNDESA), the United Nations Global Programme for the Integration of Public Administration and the Science of Disasters (UNGP-IPASD) facilitates the sharing of information, data and experiences among scientists and administrators. The program builds on three pillars: [1] improvements in coordination and cooperation in government operations; [2] advances in anticipating the occurrence of natural disasters; and [3] public education and participation in disaster awareness and preparedness.

While its goal is to reduce human suffering related to the incidence of natural disasters, the Global Programme also serves to improve the effectiveness and efficiency of public administration so that everyday routine, as well as disaster management functions are performed optimally. Both anticipation and management aspects are integrated in this program, in order to take advantage of scientific information on disasters and public administration capacity to respond to such information with measured, effective strategies.

The UNGP-IPASD encourages the integration of applied natural sciences and public administration in order to strengthen significantly the capacity of local communities to assess and mitigate their immediate risk from natural disasters, particularly from earthquakes. Although natural events are often global in scope, it is said, "all disasters are local". By integrating international and local networks of scientists and administrators, a global monitoring network for disasters can be linked to the most operational level, that is, any community, especially those linked to the Internet.

Since its inception, the UNGP-IPASD has involved participants from Armenia, Brazil, China, Ecuador, India, Iran, Japan, Mexico, Mongolia, Peru, Philippines, Russia, Slovakia, Trinidad and Tobago, Turkey, Ukraine, and the United States. Financial support has come from the United Nations Development Programme (UNDP), and the Foundation for Research and International Education relating to Natural Disasters (FRIEND), a not-for-profit NGO (nongovernmental organization) set up to fund program activities. The Programme's accomplishments and ongoing activities include community pilot projects, regional conferences, publications and information-sharing activities. Particularly noteworthy achievements are: [1] the UNGP-IPASD's facilitation in the early warning successes for the 1997 large earthquakes in Jiashi County, China (Li and Kerr, 1997) and for the 1998 catastrophic floods in southern China; [2] research on best practices in public administration in natural disasters; [3] publications, including a practical handbook for communities seeking ways to reduce their vulnerability to large and sudden disasters; and [4] information sharing through national and international workshops, as well as through the UNGP-IPASD Website (http://www.globalwatch.org/ungp/).

The global program held its first United Nations Interregional Technical Conference in January 1997 to bring together public administrators and scientists for the rapid development of global networks for early warning research and communication. In February 1998, a workshop was held to launch a practical international network to collect and share scientific data relating to precursors of earthquakes and weather disasters as monitored by geomagnetic methods.

UNGP-IPASD represents a contribution of the Department of Economic and Social Affairs (DESA) to the International Decade for Natural Disaster Reduction (IDNDR). The Global Programme used an initial donation of US$150,000 to the UN Trust Fund UNEPPA

(United Nations Fund for Integrating Public Administration and the Science of Earthquakes in Prediction) to support research related to Qinglong County and to hold the first international conference of the UNGP-IPASD in Beijing, China, in January 1997.

APPENDIX 3

Evaluation of Short-Term and Annual Prediction of Earthquakes (ESTAPE)

To evaluate the practical results of prediction research, the UN Global Programme UN Global Programme-IPASD developed ESTAPE, the Evaluation of Short-Term and Annual Prediction of Earthquakes. ESTAPE provides city administrators and public safety officials with a simple tool to evaluate earthquake predictions so as to distinguish which information should be taken into account in preparing their communities for natural disasters.

How ESTAPE Works

Fundamental Premise: Any prediction, to be evaluated by ESTAPE, must have been made before the predicted event. In order to ensure the soundness of an ESTAPE evaluation score, the following information needs to be on record: [1] the date on which and [2] the agency to which the prediction is submitted and/or accepted; [3] a listing of the method(s) used to generate the prediction; and [4] the name of the individual or group that calculates the ESTAPE score. Adherence to these procedural pre-requisites assures a level of confidence in the ESTAPE score.

Key Inputs: ESTAPE is based on three key parameters that are typically used to describe earthquakes: magnitude, time, and location. ESTAPE looks at the error (misfit) in the parameter values between the predicted natural event and the actual earthquake.

Scoring of Predictions: If the prediction is completely accurate, i.e., the magnitude, time, and location of the actual earthquake have values that match those predicted, a 100% score is attributed to each parameter, giving an overall combined score of 100%. Anything less than a perfect match in any of the parameters is scored according to the degree of "error" or "misfit" using the tables ESTAPE-S and ESTAPE-A.

ESTAPE-S (Table 1 of Chu and Col, 1998) is used to evaluate short-term predictions of earthquakes. Short-term typically implies several weeks to several days before an event. ESTAPE-A (Table 2 of Chu and Col, 1998) is used to evaluate annual predictions. As long as the forecasted seismic event occurs within one year of the date of submission of the prediction, the score for the time parameter of an annual prediction is 100%. We note here that ESTAPE scores for short-term predictions are very time sensitive, whereas by comparison, the scoring of annual predictions is much less time-sensitive. For this reason, overall scores for the two types of prediction categories (short-term and annual) are not comparable.

The Internet: The ESTAPE evaluation approach is currently available on the Internet at <http://www.globalwatch.org/ungp/>. Listings of official predictions made over the last 30 years are posted on this UNGP-IPASD Web site. For references that describe ESTAPE in detail, please refer to Chu and Col, 1999, and United Nations, 1998.

The Strengths of ESTAPE

The ESTAPE approach creates an open environment where any individual can independently evaluate the practical results of prediction research. ESTAPE focuses on providing scientific information in a format that is easy to understand and which can then be used by public officials and members of civil society. In its essence, ESTAPE provides a "yardstick" to measure earthquake prediction reports.

For example, the information contained in the short-term prediction that contributed to the successful early warning for the Qinglong County community of nearly a half-million people during the magnitude M7.8 Tangshan earthquake has an overall ESTAPE score of just over 60%. Thus, information associated with scores of 60% or greater is socially useful.

In the more recent successful early warning for a series of larger than magnitude 6 earthquakes in Jiashi County in western China (Li and Kerr, 1997), the overall ESTAPE score for the multidisciplinary prediction effort by UNGP-IPASD scientists is 88%. This result is encouraging, for it indicates that by combining a number of different approaches to earthquake prediction, the resulting forecast is more likely to reflect the real situation.

Single predictions can be assessed by ESTAPE for accuracy. Even more potent and revealing is the comprehensive analysis of prediction records that span years of forecasting work using different methodologies. Public administrators can assess these catalogues of past predictions using ESTAPE to see which forecasting technologies have the best "batting record" for anticipating earthquakes. The practical benefits of such a screening is that officials and individuals can then chose to act on the information provided by the more reliable of methodologies.

As an example of a prediction catalogue, crustal stress experts in China have officially submitted their predictions to the Chinese Seismological Bureau during the last three decades. A UNGP-IPASD evaluation using ESTAPE of their more than 175 short-term earthquake predictions made over these years shows that their method was socially useful (overall ESTAPE-S scores of 60% or more) for one out of every three earthquakes. For a detailed listing of the 175 predictions, see <http://www.globalwatch.org/ungp/>. For an evaluation of an annual prediction catalog using ESTAPE-A, please refer to Chu and Col, 1999, and United Nations, 1998.

For public administrators, annual forecast(s) from methodologies screened by ESTAPE can provide these officials with lead-time to set up local earthquake offices, conduct disaster education campaigns and raise public awareness to the importance of networking and communicating changes in the natural environment. Short-term forecasting technologies would also be implemented in the region of concern and lay-monitoring equipment installed with the training of local observers. All of the information gathered through these activities, when integrated into a comprehensive disaster plan, can play a significant role in mitigating the impact of large and sudden natural disasters such as earthquakes.

APPENDIX 4

State Council Document No. 69: Successful Medium-Term Forecast and Fundamental Policy for Multisectoral Participation

The background for the early warning success of Qinglong County was set in the early seventies, when top Chinese policy makers asked earthquake scientists to assess the disaster situation for North China. Their request resulted in State Council Document No. 69 (United Nations, 1996; http://www.globalwatch.org/ungp/). This document, a national policy statement issued in June 1974, directed disaster managers to prepare for a possible natural disaster of devastating magnitude within the ensuing two years. This forecast was later confirmed by the occurrence of the North China M7.3 Haicheng earthquake in 1975 and the M7.8 Tangshan earthquake in 1976.

Though successful in its medium-term assessment, the major social effect of Document No. 69 (see the first and last sections below) was to encourage multisectoral participation in disaster monitoring and preparedness. National policy makers recognized that public education and combining the efforts of citizens, public administrators and scientists in disaster monitoring could increase the probability of recognizing precursors of destructive imminent earthquakes, as well as reduce public panic.

With the existence of Document No. 69, public administrators were encouraged to take initiatives in expanding their disaster mitigation efforts. The public officials of Qinglong County took the challenge of this document seriously. A review of the activities in the *Events Analysis* (Appendix 1) reveals that public administrators went beyond the expectations of their job descriptions to create the disaster mitigation success of Qinglong County. When interviewed, each of these officials said, "I was just doing my job." But in several key cases, the individuals performed in exemplary manner, and taken as a whole, the institutions in the community worked in a coordinated manner to bring about an integrated success.

STATE COUNCIL DOCUMENT NO. 69
PEOPLE'S REPUBLIC OF CHINA
29 JUNE 1974

STATE COUNCIL ENDORSES CHINESE ACADEMY OF SCIENCES' REPORT ON THE EARTHQUAKE SITUATION IN NORTH CHINA AND THE BOHAI SEA AREA

To the leading public administrators of Beijing, Tianjin, the provinces of Hebei, Shanxi, Shandong, and Liaoning, and the autonomous region of Inner Mongolia:

Please pay close attention to the information and implement the recommendations in the attached Chinese Academy of Sciences "Report on the Earthquake Situation in North China and the Bohai Sea Area."

Earthquake work is an important mission that concerns the preservation of lives and property. We look to you to build and strengthen earthquake management offices by implementing the national policy; that is, place top priority on earthquake preparedness, integrate the efforts of professionals and the lay public, and combine Chinese and Western methods. Intensify earthquake preparedness and mitigation efforts by mobilizing professional teams and organizing lay public monitoring and preparation.

At present, the science and technologies to monitor and predict earthquakes are still in their early stages. Therefore, the large earthquakes forecast in this report for this year and next year are estimates only; they may or may not occur. However, we should operate on the assumption that there will be a large earthquake and should therefore make preparations.

At the same time, you must minimize the potential for public panic and social disarray that this alert may cause.

"REPORT ON THE EARTHQUAKE SITUATION IN NORTH CHINA AND THE BOHAI SEA AREA"

CHINESE ACADEMY OF SCIENCES, 15 JUNE 1974

TO THE STATE COUNCIL:

From 7–9 June 1974, the State Seismological Bureau (SSB) held a conference on the earthquake situation in the North China and Bohai Sea area. Representatives came from twenty units of earthquake disaster management and research institutions of Beijing, Tianjin, Hebei, Shanxi, Inner Mongolia, Shandong, and Liaoning.

The conference analyzed the earthquake situation of the above-mentioned areas. The majority opinion is that, within this year or next year, earthquakes of magnitude 5 to 6 may occur in: the Beijing-Tianjin area; north part of the Bohai Sea; Handan and Anyang in the border area between Shanxi, Hebei, and Henan; the Linfen basin in Shanxi; the Linyi area in Shandong; and the central part of the Yellow Sea. Earthquakes of around magnitude 5 may occur in Inner Mongolia in the area around Baotou and Wuyuan.

THE PRINCIPLE EVIDENCE FOR THE ABOVE IS:

Beijing-Tianjin area

- Recent frequent occurrences of small earthquakes
- Abnormal readings of crustal deformation
- Anomalous gravity measurements
- Unusual changes in radon content in groundwater

Northern Bohai Sea area

- Changes in water level in Jinxian County had been gradual over the past few years, with a rate of 0.11 mm/year. However, the cumulative change in water level has already reached 2.5 mm (in 9 months).
- Geomagnetic anomaly of 22-gamma recorded in the Dailian area.
- Six tide-monitoring stations in the northern Bohai Sea area all reported increases of 10–20 cm in sea level in 1973, a phenomenon that has not been seen for the past 10–20 years.
- Marked increase in microseismicity.

Linfen Basin in southern Shanxi

- Anomalies in seismic velocity in recent years

Shanxi, Henan, Hebei border area, and the central part of the Yellow Sea

- Increase in microseismicity

Linyi area in southern Shandong

- A pattern of high seismicity in the area peripheral to Linyi has emerged in the past few years. This pattern is similar to the one that formed before the historic 1668 M8.5 earthquake in the same area.

In addition, based on the historical pattern of major earthquake activity, the study of regional seismicity, the influence of the Western Pacific seismic belt and those earthquakes with focal depths of 400–500 km on North China, some colleagues believe that North China has accumulated enough seismic energy for an earthquake of M7–8.

Furthermore, prolonged drought in the northern part of North China, and abnormal meteorological conditions rarely seen since 1949—a warm winter, a cold spring, and imbalance in humidity during the past year—indicate the possibility of a major earthquake of around M7 in North China.

In contrast, some colleagues have observed an increase in the Earth's rate of rotation over the last year, which from past experience indicates that large earthquakes are unlikely. An additional observation is that there is usually a long time period between large earthquakes in this region. They therefore believe that no earthquake greater than magnitude 5.5 will occur in North China in the next few years.

Learning from the lessons of the successive devastating earthquakes in Liyang County in Jiangsu Province and Zhaotong County in Yunnan Province, the conference participants recommend that we should operate on the assumption that there will be a large earthquake despite the inconclusive analysis. Therefore we should heighten our alertness and prepare for the sudden strike of an earthquake of M>6.

OUR RECOMENDATIONS FOR STRENGTHENING EARTHQUAKE WORK IN THE RISK AREAS ARE:

1. Strengthen leadership in earthquake work. Appoint at least one public official in each of the seven risk areas (Beijing, Tianjin, etc.) to take charge. Strengthen existing seismological bureau and earthquake offices in Beijing, Tianjin, Hebei, Inner Mongolia, and Liaoning. In Shanxi and Shandong, where there are no established earthquake offices or lay monitoring stations, such facilities should be set up immediately. Initiate earthquake preparedness work at all regional and county levels and integrate the management of professional and amateur (lay public) monitoring teams.
2. Develop lay public monitoring and preparation networks and mobilize the public in earnest. In the seven risk areas, there are currently about 5000 people who participate in amateur monitoring teams, which is still inadequate. Experience has shown that in areas where good lay monitoring and preparation are implemented, it is possible to capture imminent precursors thereby mitigating losses. Factories and major mining enterprises should take steps to organize amateur monitoring teams and train volunteers. Villages should establish public education and monitoring programs, and make effective use of meteorological stations, schools, and amateur science groups. At the same time, avoic panic by preparing the public psychologically for potential calamity.
3. Professional teams should investigate fully all the areas in which anomalies have occurred, provide comprehensive analysis, and continue to monitor the earthquake situation. Raise the level of earthquake prediction and strive for timely early warning. Assure the normal functioning of the 109 professional monitoring centers in the risk areas. New centers should be considered if necessary. Professionals should also work with the public and draw from their valuable experiences, and consider development of lay monitoring and preparation a personal goal.
4. Establish two regional groups. One group, Beijing-Tianjin-Tangshan-Zhangjiakou, headed by the State Seismological Bureau (SSB), should include earthquake offices in Beijing, Tianjin, and Hebei, the Geophysics Institute, the Seismic Geology Group, and the Seismic Measurement Team. The second, the Bohai Group, should comprise of the Liaoning, Tianjin, and Shandong earthquake offices, headed by the Liaoning office. These two groups should cooperate closely and share all monitoring data in a timely manner.

REFERENCES

Almond G., Verba S. (1989). *The Civic Culture*. Newbury Park, California: Sage Publications. Original edition published in 1963 by Princeton Press; revised in 1986 by Sage Publications.

Chikazumi S., Charap S. H. (1964). *Physics of Magnetism*. New York: John Wiley and Sons, Inc.

Chen Y., Kam-ling T., Chen F., Gao Z., Zou Q., Chen Z. (1988). *The Great Tangshan Earthquake of 1976: An Anatomy of Disaster*. Pergamon Press.

Chu J. J., Gui X., Dai J., Marone C., Spiegelman M. W., Seeber L., Armbruster J. G. (1996). Geoelectric signals in China and the earthquake generation process. *Journal of Geophysical Research* 101, 13,869–13,882.

Chu, J. J., Col J.-M. (1999). Evaluation for Short-Term and Annual Prediction of Earthquakes (ESTAPE), in M. Hayakawa (ed.) *Atmospheric and Ionospheric Electromagnetic Phenomena Associated with Earthquakes*. Tokyo, Japan: Terra Scientific Publishing Company (TERRAPUB), 919–929.

Comfort, L. (1999). *Shared Risk: Complex Systems in Seismic Response*. Amsterdam, The Netherlands: Pergamon.

Hast, N. (1958). The Measurement of Rock Pressure in Mines. Sveriges Geologiska Undersokning, Ser. C. (Avhandlingar och uppsatser, No. 560), Arsbok 52, No. 3, Stockholm.

Hofstede, G. (1984). *Culture's Consequences*. Beverly Hills, California: Sage Publications.

Huang X., Li J., Zhao S. (1982). The results and analysis of crustal stress measurements, in S. Mei (ed.) *The 1976 Tangshan Earthquake*. Beijing, China: Seismological Press, 296–314.

Huang X., Li J., Ge L., Jiang H., Mo H., Jin N., Gu X. (1991). Characteristics of the crustal stress precursory signals and stress field analysis for the (1975) Haicheng M 7.3 earthquake, in *Methods of Earthquake Prediction—Collected Works of Applied Research: Monograph on Deformation, Gravity, Strain*. Beijing, China: Seismological Press, 488–502.

Li H., Kerr R. (1997). Warnings precede Chinese temblors. *Science* 276, 526.

Li H., Mervis J. (1996). China's campaign to predict quakes. *Science* 273, 1484–1486.

Ma Z., Fu Z., Zhang Y., Wang C., Zhang G., Liu D. (1989). *Earthquake Prediction: Nine Major Earthquakes in China (1966–1976)*. New York: Springer-Verlag.

Mei S. (ed.). (1982). *The 1976 Tangshan Earthquake*. Beijing, China: Seismological Press.

"Nature rarely repeats itself." *The Economist*. 2 August 1997, 63–64.

Normile D. (1996). Chair quits Japan panel in protest. *Science* 271, 1799.

Qian G. (1986). *The Great Tangshan Earthquake*. China: Liberation Army Literature and Art Publishing House.

Qian G. (1989). *The Great China Earthquake*. Beijing, China: Foreign Languages Press.

"Shaking all over." *New York*. December 1995.

Sheriff R. E. (1984). *Encyclopedic Dictionary of Exploration Geophysics*. Tulsa, Oklahoma: Society of Exploration Geophysicists.

"Survivors lead a chorus of demands to punish builders." (Dateline: Istanbul, Turkey). *New York Times*. September 1999.

Tremolet de Lacheisserie E. du. (1993.) *Magnetostriction: Theory and Applications of Magnetoelasticity*. Boca Raton, Florida: CRC Press, Inc.

United Nations. (1996). *Guidelines on Capacity Building for Disaster Management*. New York: UN Publication ST/TCD/SER.E/32.

United Nations. (1998). *Manual on the Forecasting of Natural Disasters: Geomagnetic Methods*. New York: UN Publication ST/TCD/SER. E/65.

Wang C. "Recollections of the great Tangshan earthquake." Disasters and Society section, *China Earthquake News*, 25 July 1991, 3.

Wang J. "Our Qinglong County did prepare for the great Tangshan earthquake." Disasters and Society section, *China Earthquake News*, 25 July 1991, 3.

Wang Y. "Preparedness cuts loss." Science section, *China Daily*, 28 April 1998, 9.

37

Public Management and Natural Disasters

A Case Study of Earthquake Management in Iran

Behrooz Kalantari Savannah State University, Savannah, Georgia

I. INTRODUCTION

With crises occurring every day throughout the world, there is a growing interest and urgency in studying them and preparing for their devastating consequences. This need is more evident in the public sector owing to its commitment to and responsibility for the protection of the lives and property of its citizens.

The perception of crisis management has changed throughout history. For example, until not very long ago, people perceived natural disasters as inevitable phenomena and accepted them with all their consequences, attaching supernatural values to them. Some cultures believed that they deserved the negative consequences of disasters and saw them as punishment for their sins. Therefore there was no systematic effort to mitigate the dangers.

There is not much documented research or the systematic study of the subject available; most of the literature deals with the behavioral aspect of emergency management (Drabek 1991:20). The most frequently documented event concerning the management of crisis is the collision of a French ship with a Belgian ship in 1917 (documented by Samuel Henry Prince). Prince is considered a pioneer in studying the practical methods of dealing with disasters (Drabek 1991:20). His work opened up new areas of research in dealing with human behavior during crises. Crisis management can be defined as ''the discipline and profession of applying science, technology, planning, and management to deal with extreme events that can injure or kill many people, do extensive damage to property, and/or disrupt community life'' (Drabek 1991:1). Some define crisis management in relation to emergencies that are considered routine and do not have community-wide impact or do not require extraordinary use of resources or procedures (Drabek 1991: 4). However, when situations are ''unexpectedly torn from their standard operating procedures or are required to obtain resources outside their standard operating procedures or are required to obtain resources outside their normal authority, they move beyond the emergency level of operation, and become crisis or disaster'' (Drabek 1991:5).

A crisis develops when a situation reaches its critical phase. Therefore, at an individual level, crisis management can be defined as ''removing the risk and uncertainty to allow one to achieve more control over one's own destiny'' (Fink 1985:15). There are different categories of crisis, depending on the context of the situation. Disasters can be a result of natural phenomena, or they can be a direct result of intentional actions taken by individuals or groups (Nudell and Antokal 1988:34). In addition, crises are usually differentiated based on the extent of time that is involved. They can be short-fused (unanticipated), or long-fused (anticipated) (Nudell and Antokel 1988:2).

II. STEPS IN CRISIS MANAGEMENT

Crises are divided into several stages. They include a ''prodromal stage'' which is referred to as the warning stage. Recognition of the prodromal stage is very critical, because if this stage is recognized or identified, it is much easier to manage a crisis. In other words, managing a crisis is much easier before it becomes ''acute.'' In some situations, this stage is identifiable. The second stage is the ''acute crisis stage'' (Fink 1986:21), which in reality is the damage-control stage: ''avalanche-like speed and intensity accompanies and characterizes this stage'' (Fink 1986:22). In the acute crisis stage, the ability to control flow, speed, and direction, seriously influences the duration and resolution of the crisis situation. The key to success is to control as much of the crisis as is possible.

The next stage is the ''chronic crisis stage,'' which is the cleanup stage or when the crisis is nearly under control and one deals with the aftermath: recovery, self analysis, and public relations (Fink 1986:23–24). The final stage is called the ''crisis resolution'' stage, when the situation is under control (Fink 1986:25–26).

These stages can be operationalized into several generic steps and be adopted to every new and unique situation. The steps can be summarized as:

1. Assessing the threat on hand
2. Identifying resources available
3. Selecting crisis team personnel
4. Locating the crisis management center
5. Training crisis team
6. Testing contingency plans and emergency procedures
7. Dealing with the media (Nudell and Antokol 1988:4)

A successful crisis management process requires the coordinated and combined effort of a number of public or volunteer agencies in order to bring about resolution.

The main element in crisis management is preparation and planning. It is important that plans be updated frequently to deal with the changing environment. In addition, planning should emphasize training and educating those who are involved with implementation. Planning should be based on facts and the experience of those who have been involved with previous crisis. In the planning stage, it is also important that the planner remain flexible. This is because it is not practical to plan for every emergency, and situations and circumstances are always unique. In addition, complicated plans are often not properly implemented because they are intimidating to those who execute them (Drabek 1991:36).

In addition, crisis management operations should be prioritized during the planning process. For example, in every crisis, restoring community functions should be a high priority. This has to take place when the disaster is over (Drabek 1991:43). It is also important that planners deal with public information by consistently releasing information to the public. Keeping accurate record of what is occurring during the crisis is also very useful in dealing with future disasters.

One of the frequency used models of emergency management is the "emergency resource coordination model" (Drabek 1991:45). This model advocates a hierarchical approach to the structure of the decision-making process because there must be a center to coordinate emergency management activities. These centers are usually called "emergency operation centers." Their role is as information clearinghouses and decision-making centers that coordinate activities and pass the information throughout the organizational structure.

It is important to realize that one major problem with a crisis management situation is that crises usually create great deal of confusion, chaos, and conflict. Therefore, a single command center will assure that efforts are directed to the needed area. In most plans, public officials and public organizations are offered certain roles to play. They must identify a single agency responsible for coordination and control of different activities (Drabek 1991:VIII). The role of emergency managers is very crucial in the management of crisis. Dictatorial styles of management should be avoided. Managers must possess communication skills, organizational ability, human relations skills, and control under stress.

The most critical objective in any crisis is to contain damages as much is possible and prevent the loss of life and property. In cases of natural disasters, only limited actions can take place. However, in man-made crisis, the possibility of containing the incident is more attainable. In any case, there are two critical points to remember: the primary objective is to establish a mission plan, and next, to establish a process of dealing with the crisis. The most critical aspect of the mission, as well as the process, is to remain focused on the goals.

The process contains detailed analysis of the actions that can be taken and formulation of a plan of action. Each step of the plan is determined by the circumstances present and their relationship to the objectives of mission and safety priorities. In designing the plan of action, It is important that flexibility in the implementation process be maintained. There are always elements of surprise during the implementation of a plan. Training and quick decision making are crucial in every situation, especially for those who are in the front line facing the crisis. In other words, the best plans will not work if the initial response is not effective. The main goal of crisis management is to avoid the disasterous circumstances of crisis and reduce damages by bringing the situation back to normal.

III. EARTHQUAKE CRISIS

Comparing the scope of natural or man-made disasters is difficult. However, it can be argued that among natural disasters earthquakes rank first in severity. Since 1905, earthquakes have claimed the lives of over 1 million people and have cost millions of dollars in material damages. The magnitude of the loss of life due to earthquakes is unmatched by any other natural or man-made disaster throughout history.

Earthquakes are caused primarily by the movement of plates that separate the earth's crust. These movements cause a range of vibrations that send shock waves to the surface. Moving plates' seismic waves begin when a large section of rock suddenly shifts. Those waves are measured by the Richter scale with a rating of 1 being the weakest and a rating of 9 the strongest. The Richter scale measures energy release at the focus of a quake. The strongest shocks occur where earth's plates meet each other. There are two primary faults where the earth's plates meet. One fault goes through the Mediterranean and Caspian Seas, passing through Iran toward southern Asia. The other fault passes the Pacific Ocean and goes through Japan and New Zealand and continues toward North and South America. Among the countries that have had major earthquakes during the past century, Iran ranks at the top of the list.

IV. THE KHORASAN EARTHQUAKE

The following analysis concentrates on the latest major earthquake (1997) in Iran, which was responsible for the death of 2400 residents and the loss of $223 million in 1997. The strength of this earthquake was 7.1 and the location was in the southeastern province of Khorasan, around the cities of Qaen and Birjand with a 600-km radius.

During the last 90 years, 80 earthquakes with the strength of at least 6.0 on the Richter and 11 with the strength of more than 7.0 on the Richter have occurred in Iran (Table 1).

In 1991, a total of 60 earthquakes occurred in Iran, of which eight were rated over 5.0 on the Richter (NETF 1998:12–13). During the last 25 years, 60,000 people have lost their lives in the earthquakes. There have been millions of dollars in material losses (NETF 1998:5). In 1990, an earthquake rated 7.2 on the Richter scale hit the northern provinces of Iran and killed 50,000 residents in several cities. It was the most destructive earthquake of the last two decades. The 1990 earthquake also caused severe fiscal damages equal to 7.2% of the gross national product (GNP) of the country (NETF 1998:1).

In 1907, for the first time, the parliament passed a law delegating the authority to the Ministry of Interior in order to deal with natural disasters. However, it was not until 1970 that this ministry initiated systematic efforts in dealing with the problem of natural disasters. In 1991 an act of parliament created the "High Council for Prevention and Reduction of the Injuries Caused by Catastrophic Events & Reconstruction of Damaged Areas" to deal with the problem of emergencies (NETF 1998:21). Article (3) of the regula-

Table 1 Distribution of Earthquakes (over 7.0 on the Richter Scale), in the Last Century in Iran

Date	Place	Strength
October 1909	Darood	7.4
October 1929	N. Khorasan	7.2
April 1930	Deylaman & Salmas	7.4
October 1948	N. Khorasan	7.2
July 1957	Larijan	7.4
August 1968	Dasht-e-Bayaz	7.3
September 1978	Tabas (Khorasan)	7.7
November 1979	Qaen (Khorasan)	7.3
June 1983	Daylaman	7.3
June 1990	Gilan & Zanjan	7.3
May 1997	Qaen (Khorasan)	7.1

Source: Kayhan May 19, 1997, p. 5.

tions of this act indicates that the minister of the interior is the chair for this high council and several other ministries are members; they include Agriculture, Power, Construction Jihad, Roads and Transportation, Housing and Urban Development, Business, Health and Medicine, Defense and Logistics, Red Crescent Organization, Office of Budget Planning. Section 1 of the same article indicates that headquarters of the council will be located at the Ministry of Interior in the capital city (Tehran) (NETF 1998:21). According to section 2, in every province a similar organization called the Province Council will be formed. According to article 3, the High Council meets regularly every 3 months, and/or upon the request of members in times of crisis. It also has a secretarial office in operation 24 hours a day.

V. SPECIFIC FUNCTIONS OF THE COUNCIL

According to article 5-2, this council is the primary decision maker in managing disasters but also is responsible for disaster prevention and reconstruction of damaged areas (NETF 1998:22). The high council, along with the province councils, is allocated specific budget and functions continuously, collecting information and sharing it (NETF 1998:23).

According to article 7, the governor-general of each province chairs the province council with representatives of various public officials. Their functions include:

1. Prevention and reduction of the effects of crisis
2. Relief and lifesaving in times of crisis
3. Reconstruction of the damaged areas (NETF 1998:23)

Article 7-1 indicates that each province council has to establish two task forces: first, "prevention and reconstruction," chaired by the deputy governor for development. This task force includes the representatives of different government agencies such as, the Planning and Budget Office, Construction Jihad, Agriculture, Roads and Transportation, Housing & Urban Development, Health, Water & Electricity. The second task force is called, "Relief and Lifesaving," chaired by the governor-general's deputy. Other high officials representing different departments in this task force include Agriculture, Roads and Transportation, Business, Housing and Urban Development, Construction Jihad, Armed Forces; Basij (a volunteer organization), Health, Red Crescent Society, and Water & Electricity. Membership is not limited to these representatives and representatives from other organizations can be invited to participate. (NETF 1998:24).

Province Councils are headquartered in the office of the governor-general of each province. According to article 7-6, the councils have to meet at least every 2 months to make decisions concerning prevention, assistance, prediction, and preparation for future natural disasters or reconstruction of damaged areas. (NETF 1998:24). The other significant function of the province councils is coordinating the functions of different executive organizations (NETF 1998:24). The councils also have to evaluate their past performance and provide feedback for consideration in future projects. Finally, the councils are responsible for the development of their own yearly budget and its submission to the Ministry of Interior. The city councils are patterned after the province councils and function similarly, only on a smaller scale (NETF 1998:25). The councils' executive arm is called the Emergency Task Force (ETF), which is chaired by the deputy to the interior minister. At the province levels, the councils are also called (ETF) during the crises and chaired by the governor-general of each province.

VI. THE RED CRESCENT SOCIETY

The Red Crescent Organization was created in 1924 by an act of parliament and in 1929 became a member of the International Federation of Red Crescent and Red Cross Organizations. After the Islamic Revolution, its name was changed from the Lion & Sun Society of Iran, to the Red Crescent Society of the Islamic Republic of Iran (Nudell and Antokol 1998:1–2).

Its overall orientation is very similar to the Red Cross organization in the West. It has 277 offices around the country with 315 youth organizations. This organization is the most effective in the country during crises. The society's major strength lies in its reliance on 125,000 youth members and 400,000 trained volunteers who are spread out all over the country and can deliver services at any time during the crises (Nudell and Antokol 1998:3). They have a variety of responsibilities including service delivery, training, and research. Their financial support mostly comes from philanthropic donations, investments, fund raising activities, and government assistance. The earthquake operation of the society is composed of a well-developed process which is ready to deliver trained volunteers who are equipped and prepared to address essential needs of victims.

Their "find and rescue" phase is part of the first stage operation that deals with the activities during the first phase crisis. It concentrates on transfer of the injured to the medical centers, temporary settlement of victims, and transfer and burial of the dead (Nudell and Antokol 1998:4). In addition to their immediate rescue operations and dealing with victims, the society provides temporary settlement for survivors. The length of time that these settlements are in operation depends on the severity of the crisis (from 15 to 45 days). They provide the basic living necessities to survivors including food, cooking facilities, tents, blankets, mattresses, electricity, clothing, and health care (Nudell and Antokol 1998:5).

In order to train volunteers for crises, the society has nine major headquarters around the country. It has short and long term training sessions for public or private organizations that are interested in receiving the training (Nudell and Antokol 1998:12). The Society is also a center for delivering medical services including doctors, hospitals, and medicine. Their health care operation includes 17 hospitals in Iran and in several other countries including The Emirates, Bosnia, Afghanistan, Ghana, and Mali (Nudell and Antokol 1998: 15).

VII. KHORASAN EARTHQUAKE OF 1997

The most recent and major earthquake in Iran was the Khorasan earthquake of 1997, rated 7.1 on the Richter scale. It shook the eastern part of Iran in the southeast of the province of Khorrasan on in the midafternoon May 10, 1997 (*Kayhan* 1997: May 10, p. 1). The center of the quake was in the suburbs of the city of Qaen; it had an approximately 600-km radius covering several small villages between Qaen and the Birjand area. This earthquake was the fourth worst earthquake that had shaken the area since 1968 (*Quds* 1997: May 13, p. 2). This quake claimed the lives of 2400 people and damaged 200 villages, with 70 to 100% losses (*Hamshahri* 1997: May 12, p. 14). The quake injured 13,000 residents of the 60,000 population and destroyed over 100 educational units. Most of the victims were students and teachers who were attending schools, because the earthquake happened in the midafternoon (*Kayhan* 1997: May 13, p. 14). Due to the strength of the quake, 23 hours after its occurrence, the area was still receiving 130 aftershocks of between 2.8 and 5.5 on the Richter (*Khorasan* 1997: May 12, p.4). Besides human loss, nearly 30,000 domesticated animals, including cows and sheep, died (*Keyhan* 1997: May 12, p. 14).

VIII. DEALING WITH THE AFTERMATH OF THE QUAKE

The two major organizations involved with controlling the crisis were the National Emergency Task Force (NETF) and the Red Crescent Society. The NETF was responsible for the planning and coordination of the rescue operation while the Red Crescent, due to its experience and supplies, was very effective in delivering assistance immediately after the incident. The overall plan of the operation and activities of the NETF and the Red Crescent revolved around three phases. They included the following:

1. Relief and life saving (Nejat and Emdad), which included the rescue operations and transfer of the injured to the medical centers
2. Temporary settlement (Eskan) of the survivors
3. Permanent settlement, which involved the long-term plan of reconstruction of the residential areas (*Khorasan* 1997: May 13, p. 3).

The NETF unit in Qaen was the closest center to the earthquake-stricken area. Therefore, it met immediately after the incident to plan for the coordination of assistance activities. It communicated the information to the NETF center in Mashhad, the capital of the province, and the main headquarters in Tehran (*Kar Va Kargar* 1997: May 11, p. 2). Therefore, several committees were set up at the main quarters of NETF in Tehran. They included Health and Recovery, Transportation, Logistics & Support, Information & Statistics (Quds, 1997, May 12, p. 2). The Deputy Minister of Interior headed the coordination of efforts (*Kar Va Kargar* 1997: May 11, p. 2). With coordination with the NETF unit in Qaen, the governor of Khorasan (who chaired the province's NETF in Mashhad) announced the immediate need for blood, food, medicine, ambulances, medical doctors, tents, water, and bulldozers to recover and rescue the victims (*Resalat* 1997: May 11, p. 1). Meanwhile, the central office of UNDF sent four helicopters from Tehran to transfer the injured to medical facilities and four C-130 planes to transfer food items and other medical necessities to the area (*Resalat* 1997: May 11, p. 1).

The Red Crescent Society was the first organization to enter the area for the rescue operation. The early hours of the incident were very critical because many lives could be saved if survivors could be found quickly and the injured received proper medical attention. The Red Crescent's operation was facilitated by the help of trained volunteers, as well as staff members and medical facilities. The injured were transported by Red Cross ambulances and the help of private pickup trucks and passenger cars to medical centres in Qaen. However, due to the limitations of medical facilities in Qaen, every public facility including a sports center and educational area were used to care for the injured (*Resalat* 1997: May 11, p. 1). In order to expedite the work, Red Crescent transferred 2000 volunteers to the area within 2 days and provided medical care at the early stage of the operation, in addition to survivor search equipment, bulldozers; food, and clothing (*Keyhan* 1997: May 12, p. 1). Permanent and temporary blood transfusion centers were set up by the Red Crescent Society and 1800 units of blood were delivered to the medical centers in the area. (*Keyhan* 1997: May 12, p. 1). In addition, the Blood Transfusion Organization collected 2000 units of blood and delivered them to the area (*Hamshahri* 1997: May 12, p. 14). Within 2 days after the incident, the Blood Transfusion Organization in Mashhad collected 3700 units of blood, which was adequate to meet the needs of the operation. (*Kayhan* 1997: May 14, p. 14).

The total number of rescue workers involved in the operation, including the Red Crescent, Army, and Basij, reached the 4300 by day 2 of the operation. Also, the Basij Organization of Khorasan alone delivered 800 volunteers with 20 buses and pickup trucks and ambulances to the area (*Kayhan* 1997: May 12, p. 14). Red Crescent set up 4000 tents for the temporary settlement of the survivors on the first day of operation and rescue workers were active in 180 villages (*Kar Va Kargar* 1997: May 12, p. 1). New settlers were provided with basic living necessities, including food, cooking facilities, kerosene lamps, and blankets (*Kayhan* 1997: May 12, p. 14). Some of the seriously injured were ransferred to Mashhad or Tehran through special arrangements made by The Iranian Aviation Organization (*Kayhan* 1997: May 12, p. 14). Participation in the overall operation was very impressive. Help came from neighboring cities, towns, and faraway provinces. They provided not only monetary donations but also volunteers and medical necessities and items such as tents, blankets, food, transportation, and cooking equipment (*Khorasan* 1997: May 12, p. 4). Assistance and donations were widely received from all aspects of society including private citizens, corporations, public employees, students, and the medical schools at different universities (*Hamshahri* 1997: May 12, p. 14). The Red Crescent was the main organization to collect private donations. International help included survivor search equipment, tents, and food items were flown in from 38 countries as well (*Ettelaat* 1997: May 13, p. 13).

Three days of national mourning were announced and arrangements for the burial of the dead were made. Operation of the temporary settlement ended on the third day of the earthquake. (*Ettelaat* 1997: May 13, p. 13). In the two phases of the operation, rescue workers were able to rescue 6000 residents from the rubble and transfer them to medical centers as well as settlement of 10,000 residents from 170 seriously damaged villages (*Kayhan* 1997: May 12, p. 14). In order to care for orphans, a special committee was set up by the Ministry of Interior and 40 social workers tended the children while construction began on an orphanage house in the area (*Keyhan* 1997: May 14, p. 14).

IX. RECONSTRUCTION

The third phase of the operation started 1 month after the incident. Using their previous experiences from the Mangil and Roodbar earthquake, which occurred in the northern province of Gilan in 1990, the rebuilding of the residential areas was transferred or given over to the residents themselves. They formed special temporary committees to facilitate the construction of residential areas. The government committed to giving 8 million rials (400 rials = $1) on loan to each resident, loans of 3 million rials for animal losses, and 2 million rials of nonrefundable grants to each damaged household in the area. In addition, those families that suffered a human loss during the incident received 500,000 rials extra in not repayable help (*Ettelaat* 1997: May 13, p. 13). The Ministry of Housing and Urban Development undertook the responsibility of facilitating the construction of the residential buildings and rebuilding the infrastructure of the villages (Khorasan 1997: May 13, p. 16). Also, the ministry of interior provided building material for the construction of homes

(*Ettelaat* 1997: May 13, p. 13). In addition, a committee of agricultural specialist was set up to study the effects of the earthquake on the agriculture of the areas and the reconstruction of the irrigation facilities and other agricultural matters (*Ettelaat* 1997: May 13, p. 13). The Maskan Foundation supervised loan acquisition and facilitated the construction of the buildings by providing some construction material (*Kayhan* 1997: May 20, p. 5). The Mustasafan and Janbazan Foundations also provided cement for the construction of the residential buildings (*Kayhan* 1997: May 19, p. 24).

X. CONCLUSION

Earthquakes are among the most dangerous and costly natural disasters. They usually occur in vulnerable parts of the world (due to their geographical locations). Iran is considered one of the most countries vulnerable to earthquakes. During the last 25 years, 60,000 Iranians have lost their lives to earthquakes. With millions of dollars in material damages. In 1990, the Mangil and Roodbar earthquake killed 50,000 and caused damages equal to 7.2 percent of the GNP.

This study focuses on management of crisis during the 1997 earthquake occured in the Khorasan provience. The quake was managed by the NETF, which is responsible for planning and coordinating the activities of several public organizations during emergencies.

Although the overall management of crisis was successful in controlling the extent of damages, their operations can be improved immensely. It can be argued that the Red Crescent Society was the major contributor to the reduction of human and material losses. This was due to experience, and proper preparation and evolution of their capabilities in dealing with previous crisis. Taking into consideration that the 1997 earthquake in the Qaen area was the fourth worst in 25 years, the extent of damages was too high. The most important aspect of crisis management is the "prodormal stage," in which the crises are prevented either by taking actions or by prediction of occurrence. One critical function of organizations such as NETF is to predict the timing of crisis. At present, several countries including Russia, China, and the United States are active in conducting research in earthquake prediction. In 1975, China successfully predicted a 7.3-magnitude earthquake and evacuated the 90,000 residents of Hatcheng 2 days before its occurence.

Besides prediction of crises, a major cause of death in the Qaen earthquake was the condition of residential buildings with low resistance to high-magnitude earthquakes. Factors that contributed to this extreme damage included construction material, unstable traditional structure, and construction techniques. Some of the buildings which were built after the previous earthquakes were destroyed again by recent earthquake (*Ettelaat* 1997: May 13, p. 13). In general, crisis management in Iran is in need of improvement in the following areas:

1. Essential scientific research to enhance capabilities to predict future events
2. Construction and inspection of present residential buildings in the areas that are susceptible to earthquakes in order to increase resistance against future quakes
3. Collection, maintenance, and systematic analysis of relevant data that can be utilized to improve the management of crisis in the future

REFERENCES

Abrar (1997). ''The leader asked Astan Qhods Razvi to help.'' May 11, p. 1.
Drabek, Thomas E. (1991). *Emergency Management Principles and Practice*. Washington, D.C.: International City Management Association.
Effective Emergency and Crisis Management (1995). Lexington, MA: Lexington Books.
Ettelaat (1997). ''Damage estimates in the earthquake-stricken areas.'' May 13, p. 13.
Fink, Steven (1986). *Crisis Management: Planning for the Inevitable*. New York: AMACOM.
Kayhan (1997). ''Help delivery is continuing to Qaen.'' May 13, p. 1.
Kar Va Kargar (1997). ''Authorities visit the earthquake-stricken area.'' May 11, p. 2.
Kar Va Gargar (1997). ''Red crescent of Khorasan's continuous operation.'' May 12, p. 1.
Kayhan (1997). ''Earthquake in Qaen.'' May 10, p. 1.
Kayhan (1997). ''Government will help the survivors.'' May 13, p. 14.
Kayhan (1997). ''More help is needed for the earthquake-stricken area.'' May 12, p. 2.
Kayhan (1997). ''Reconstruction and help is under way.'' May 19, p. 5.
Kayhan (1997). ''Reconstruction has started in the damaged areas.'' May 20, p. 5.
Kayhan (1997). ''Red Crescent's operations in the earthquake-stricken area.'' May 11, p. 1.
Kayhan (1997). ''Temporary settlement of victims is completed.'' May 14, p. 14.
Khorasan (1997). ''Reconstruction will start in one month.'' May 13, p. 16.
Khorasan (1997). ''Spirit of Volunteerism is Great.'' May 12, p. 15.
NETF (National Emergency Task Force). (1998). *National Emergency Handbook*. Tehran: Ministry of Interior Publications.
Nudell, Mayor and Antokol, Norman (1988). Introduction to the functions of the Red Crescent of the Islamic Republic of Iran. In *The Handbook for the Red Crescent Society of Iran*. Tehran: Red Cresent Publications.
Qouds (1997). ''Damage estimates in the earthquake-stricken area.'' May 13, p. 5.
Qouds (1997). ''Donations are forthcoming.'' May 13, p. 3.
Qouds (1997). ''Extent of the Damage and Operation Problems.'' May 12, p. 2.
Qouds (1997). ''History of earthquakes in the Qaen area.'' May 13, p. 2.
Resalat (1997). ''Recovery operations for the earthquake in Qaen.'' May 11, p. 1.

38

Lebanon: Culture and Crisis

Gil Gunderson Graduate School of International Policy Analysis, Monterey Institute of International Studies, Monterey, California

I. INTRODUCTION

Legend has it that Egypt's President Nasser once remarked that if Lebanon did not exist, the Arabs would be wise to create it. For Lebanon was a vital link between the Arab peoples and the growing global order, especially for Europe and the Americas. It was a center for finance and trade, transportation and tourism, as well as diplomacy and education. Lebanon was a crossroads in the full sense of the term, where westerners learned the manners of the Middle East and middle easterners experimented with western ways. Many citizens of this small country enjoyed a high level of economic prosperity and a modicum of political democracy. Lebanon's capital city, Beirut, savored the sobriquet "Paris of the Middle East." And the peaceful though tenuous coexistence of its diverse religious communities earned it another compliment, "Switzerland of the Middle East." Not all Lebanese were pleased with these references, which pointed toward the country's western inclinations, and the root of Lebanon's recent crises has been the continuing tension between its "Western exterior and its Arab soul," as one writer has expressed it (Mackey 1989:132) This strain has stemmed from Lebanon's enduring crisis of cultural identity, which has caused an almost total lack of cultivation of a cohesive nationalism. Neither Paris nor Switzerland has suffered through the death and destruction that the inhabitants of Beirut and Lebanon have endured throughout this cultural crisis.

A. Lebanon's Cultures

Lebanon has always been a territorial state, never a nation state. Its cultural crisis began with the eras of Roman, Ottoman, and French mandate when the idea of a separate country dominated by Christians and autonomous from neighboring Moslem Syria was conceived. Religious identity has been the foundation of existence for the Lebanese, whether their affinity be Maronite Christian, Greek Orthodox, Orthodox Christian, Sunni Moslem, Shia Moslem, Druze or other sects among the official list of 16 religious faiths. Under the Ottoman Empire, religious sects carved out small feudal societies inhabiting exclusive and remote geographical enclaves, which have remained to this day (Salibi 1988:12–18). The Ottoman colonial administration gave local leaders a degree of autonomy within a framework of indirect rule in exchange for collection of taxes and at times conscription. Each religious sect had a strong tradition of family status bounded by common religious affiliation. Each religious community developed its own power structure based on family inheritance, its own laws governing marriage, and its own courts to adjudicate civil disputes. Most important, there was little commitment to the spirit and practice of individualism. The religious sect was for its members the highest good, and the individual was secondary to the community as a whole (Petran 1987:13–16). Major religious communities dominated large sections of the territorial state with great pride in their respective religious beliefs and immense fear that other faiths would like nothing better than to see them crushed into submission. Each sect viewed itself as a superior religion but a minority faith. Central to this cultural conflict was the fact that Christians have especially dreaded being subsumed in an Islamic Lebanon, whereas Moslems have resented being dominated by the Christian minority oriented toward the West. Such a combination of hubris and suspicion resulted in a failure to cultivate a political culture based on secular norms.

Culture utilized in the present interpretation follows Geertz, who writes that individuals are "suspended in webs of significance" and these "webs of beliefs" constitute a culture (Geertz 1973:5, 311). Cultural behavior rests with standards of moral behavior located "in the minds and hearts of men" (Geertz 1973:11). Thus cultural norms are mental and unavailable for direct observation. Nonetheless outside inquiry can grasp cultural existence in the form of existential social associations that people practice. For Geertz "Society's forms are culture's substance" (Geertz 1973:28). It is these action patterns and social forms which the observer can perceive from his or her subjective interpretive stance. As such, cultural inquiry is always incomplete, uncertain, and contestable, but culture expressed in organizations and institutions begins to uncover meaning and significance about a people and their valuations. For Lebanon the identification of existing political forms offers clues toward understanding this country's cultures and what they mean to its members.

When our focus turns more specifically to political culture, we concentrate on those public institutions that Lebanon's sectarian groups have designed for themselves. Political institutional forms are an expression of culture and, in turn, they reinforce cultural beliefs. A country's existing political institutions and public policy process reflect the essence of those inherent beliefs about correct relationships between the rulers and the ruled which we call political culture. Unfortunately, the Lebanese have only been able to agree upon fragile centralized political institutions, with true power for policy retained within religious communities. Lebanon's crisis begins with this fact.

In Lebanon, history taught that those outside one's family and religious sphere were never to be trusted:

> The Lebanese individual traditionally derived his social identity and psychological support from his primordial affiliations—family, neighborhood, or religious community, but rarely from the nation as a whole. He was always a member of the Arslan or Junblatt Druze clans before he was a Druze, or a member of the Gemayel or Franjieh Maronite clans before he was a Maronite. The civil war and the Israeli invasion only reinforced this trend, dividing Lebanese into tighter-knit micro-families, or village and religious communities, but pulling them farther apart as a nation. (Friedman 1989:46)

To outsiders one identified oneself as a Maronite or Greek Orthodox Christian, a Sunni or Shia Moslem, or a Druze, to name only the largest religious sects. Family ties within religious clans provided a hierarchy of authority and power. Inheritance was a strong traditional value. Religious sects, Christian or Moslem, deeply believed that they were the Almighty's cherished. Each group presumed that they were agents of God and that their behavior involved acting out His will on earth. Revenge was a moral right and responsibility. Everything is permissible and possible because whatever befalls, for good or bad, was the will of God. Finally, each Lebanese religious sect believes that it is a minority and a persecuted victim. No contemporary Lebanese religious sect can claim a majority of the total population, although Moslems outnumber Christians at least two to one. Writing about the Maronites, but in words applicable to Moslems and other Christians as well, Fisk summarizes: "They (Maronites) were a pragmatic, brave, distrustful people who learned that responsibility for the continued existence lay exclusively in their own hands, that their ultimate fate depended solely upon their own determination and resources. It was a characteristic that they were to share with all the minorities of Lebanon; and later with the Israelis" (Fisk 1990:55). An "eye for an eye" type of revenge for wrongs committed against one's people is prevalent throughout each religious community. Vengeance is directed against the offending sect, not necessarily those individuals guilty in what might be called the "myth" of group responsibility.

It has been the cultural tradition in Lebanon that "political loyalty belongs to individuals rather than organizations" (Mackey 1989:97). Most important is one's relationship with the religious community's *zaim*, who functions much like the "boss" in large American cities at the turn of the century. The *zaim* was the principal cultural form for political authority. It is a traditional position passed from father to son. The local *zaim* served as a protector and agent for his co-religionist in both rural villages and municipal districts. More recently, a *zaim* was the key link between Lebanon's traditional culture and modern parliamentary government. He served as a patron who secured political patronage and other favors in exchange for votes at election time. Lebanon's executive and legislative institutions were made up of *zuama* (political bosses) competing against one another for resources but standing together to protect the confessional system of rule which they controlled (Mackey 1989:98) Often *zuama* competed within religious sects, with several leading families providing *zuama*, such as Salem and Karami for the Sunni and the Chamoun, Gemyal, and Franjieh for the Maronites. Each *zaim* had his own bodyguards or militia, and when political compromise was not forthcoming, violent brawls between and within religious sects were not uncommon. When Lebanon became a state with western-style parliamentary institutions, the *zaim* form was perpetuated as it continued to dominate the relationships between rulers and ruled. Only now the *zaim* was elected and representation of his constituents was centralized in political competition with *zuama* from other religious sects. Fisk captures the deep respect for traditional authority that the Lebanese continue to hold: "Every community, every tribe, had produced its leaders whose pronouncements, conspicuous wealth, bodyguards, cruelty, education and private armies proved more efficacious than any electoral appeal. Their principal characteristics were a declared love of Lebanon, a publicly expressed desire to respect the National Covenant and a ruthless determination to ensure that their power was passed on to their sons" (Fisk 1990:75). Lebanon developed its own "ism," popularly called confessionalism, meaning the institutionalized religious basis of public organizations, to designate its peculiar form of democracy.

In Lebanon economic conditions were framed by culture. Demographic and economic changes stimulated Lebanon's cultural crisis, bringing it to a head. Sectarian fidelity insured that in Lebanon "from generation to generation, prestige and political power were maintained and transmitted independently of economic power, through the channel of familial lineage" (Picard 1997:4). Confessionalism and family ties provided the legitimacy for a political system that was oriented to a service economy which, by design, was virtually unregulated, resulting from an immobile public policy toward industrial or agricultural production because of possible political consequences. The confessional political cultural provided a platform for economic elites to influence public policy. Yet "No ruling class dedicated to national concerns ever developed" (Petran 1988:12). Common commercial activity involved a modicum of cooperation between economic elites, notably between Maronites and Sunnis, but these relationships, transcending religious parochialism, underwent serious strains when confessional politics turned to sectarian violence. Lebanese economic interests manipulated the confessional system, but at bottom cultural commitments subsumed economics in this society based on a service economy combined with family farm agriculture and very little industry. Lebanon's merchant elites, whatever their religious persuasion, did not wish to change the confessional way of making public policy. In fact their political clout was largely expressed directly through the presidency and was dependent for its success on a divided parliament geared to local, not national, well-being. The absence of credible national cohesion in Lebanon facilitated secular material interests of its merchant and commercial class which was "Disdainful of democracy, hostile to populism, they were the natural antagonists of nationalist as well as pan-Arab or pan-Islamic movements.... Cosmopolitan and secular, they remained wedded to the confessional system as a guarantor of the status quo" (Gendzier 1997:55). Confessionalism and clan connections provided legitimacy for a public policy that was oriented to an economy that was itself a product of politics and that placed protection of respective religious cultures above all else.

Lebanon's cultural complex was reflected in the design of its governmental forms. In 1943 the Free French under General de Gaulle restored the Lebanese Republican Constitution, which had been suspended under the Vichy government (Hiro 1992:5) But it was the unwritten National Pact (1943) that sought to design Lebanon's political system according to its cultural mosaic. The National Pact was a compromise between Christian, primarily Maronite, and Moslem, mainly Sunni, elites to divide the state's political, administrative, military, and security forces offices on a religious basis. A popularly elected parliament was to appoint a president who then selected the prime minister, who, in turn, selected his cabinet. Elections were unique in that every voter was required to return to the village or city of his or her birth to cast a ballot. Candidate "lists" designated candidates for a district by religion: for example, three Maronites and two Sunnis on a list would oppose another three Maronites and two Sunnis, meaning that voters were encouraged to support candidates from their own and other religions. The president was always to be a Maronite Christian, the prime minister a Sunni Moslem, and the speaker of Parliament a Shia Moslem. Cabinet seats were allotted on the basis of a religious formula. Parliament was to be divided on a 6:5 basis in favor of the Christians, who, in a 1932 census, made up 54% of the total population. The first parliament was composed of 42 Christians and 35 Moslems, including the Druze (a religious sect that had severed itself from Islam proper). The bureaucracy and military officer corps were also divided according to religious affiliation by Article 95 of the constitution, which stated that sectarian communities would be equally represented in government employment. Most crucial was a side agreement to the National Pact. Lebanon's Moslems pledged loyalty to an independent Lebanon and Christians agreed that Lebanon should present an Arab, not western, face to the world: "The Muslim political establishment recognized the legitimacy of a sovereign Lebanese entity in return for the Christian communities' willingness to share power and recognition of at least partial Arab character of this entity" (Rabinovich 1984:24).

The contradictions in the National Pact reflect the core of Lebanon's cultural crisis.

Christians who dominated Lebanon did not wish to share political power and the benefits it brought with Moslems on an equal basis because it would compromise their autonomy, if not their survival. In domestic affairs this led to public policy that neglected social and economic development, chiefly in the southern part of the country inhabited by Shia Moslems. For foreign affairs, the Christians tended to emulate and to depend upon western countries, first France, then the United States, and ultimately on Israel. The combined Moslem majority, however, was inclined by religion, language, and ethnic regard to champion the Arab consensus and the Palestinian cause against Israel. These culturally based tensions inherent in the National Pact activated the turning point in Lebanon's crisis and the threat to regional stability that it posed.

B. Crisis Situations

A crisis in international affairs has been defined as a decisive point in an evolving situation; it is an unstable condition in political, social, or economic affairs involving an impending pivotal change. Crises are highly volatile, dangerous situations requiring immediate remedial action. A crisis involves challenge and opposition between two or more actors: "Once a crisis is set into motion, each side feels impelled to do what is needed to protect or advance its most important interests; at the same time, however, it recognizes that it must avoid utilizing options and actions for this purpose that could trigger unwanted escalation of the crisis" (George 1991:23). Simply put, a crisis is an emergency, a turning point in a "sequence of interactions . . . involving the perception of a dangerously high probability of war" (Snyder and Diesing 1977:6). There is something vital, real or imagined, at stake in a crisis situation, and there is a perceived short time horizon for coping with it. The turning point can be considered an "intermediate zone" between peace and war, between abeyance and violence (Snyder and Diesing 1977:10). Bell's definition corresponds closely to the Lebanese case: "the essence of true crisis in any given relationship is that the conflicts within it rise on a level which threatens to transform the nature of the relationship" (Bell 1971:9–15). Christians were determined to preserve the status quo of the National Pact because it preserved their political domination. Moslems desired to change the National Pact toward equal representation in political and security offices; they wanted a Lebanon that was oriented toward the Arab consensus in the region, whereas the Christians were inclined toward a Lebanon within western designs for the Middle East. These sought-after changes by the Moslems and the conservative position of the Christians brought the situation to crisis; they were the gist of possible transformation in the nature of political relationships between the religious sects.

The chief difficulty involved in the study of international crisis, as George conveys, is that "crisis management tends to be highly context-dependent" (George 1991:23). A complex crisis involves many actors, and each participant has its own objectives and means to preserve or transform the situation. Seldom is there a single crisis, but rather each crisis situation comprises various crises, each one conceived from a different perspective depending upon the participants' perspectives. This renders a unified theory of crisis management highly problematic. As such the growing literature on international crisis and its management is diverse. One assessment offers 28 variables for the critique of an international crisis and its management (Brecher et al. 1988:59). Even the term *crisis management* is fraught with danger because it suggests that "rational management" is the means to resolve a crisis. But rational management is an highly organized technical approach to normal administrative matters. A crisis situation is imbued with uncertainty and unpredictability. A crisis is boundless, no one knows at the outset its direction and duration, hardly the task for the bureaucratic canon. Crisis ''management'' theory and practice undoubtedly will continue to offer multiple modes and prescriptions. In the present inquiry we rely on the term *crisis resolution*, which is eclectic; it can only be universalized at high levels of generality; thus we limit our discussion to the broad categories of military and political means toward crisis resolution.

II. LEBANON'S 1958 CRISIS SITUATION

Lebanon's 1958 domestic crisis was a matter of the Lebanese government led by its Christian President Camille Chamoun and his principal advisor Charles Malik, seeking to extend Chamoun's presidential mandate beyond the stipulated 6-year term. Lebanon, so they argued, was threatened by the rising tide of Nasserism, a radical form of Arabism and socialism and anathema to Lebanon's Christian political and commercial elites. President Nasser's eloquent rhetoric urging radical nationalism throughout the Arab world gained sweeping support among ordinary citizens who had been subjugated first by colonialism and then by conservative Arab regimes. Chamoun and Malik interpreted *Arabism* as another term for *Islam*. President Eisenhower and Secretary of State Dulles believed Nasser was a threat to American oil interests in the Gulf, and they sought to enlist moderate Arab regimes in the ''Eisenhower doctrine,'' directed against revolutionary Arab nationalism and communism. Egypt's Nasser was no threat to Lebanon. He was unenthusiastically, as it turns out, involved in a merger with Syria into the United Arab Republic; he did not trust the Syrians and they, in turn, were resentful of Nasser's Egypt-first priorities. In contrast to the diabolical picture of Nasser that many Americans held at the time, he desired distance from the Soviet Union and accommodation with the United States over Lebanon and elsewhere. The United States, fearful of Nasser's growing dependence on the U.S.S.R. for arms and aid, rejected the Egyptian's overtures out of hand (Gendzier 1997:257–263).

Chamoun and Malik used the supposed threat of Nasser to cajole the United States into military assistance and outright protection against foreign aggression. Chamoun and Malik were Lebanese Christian nationalists with a definite prowestern political and economic orientation. As such they were passionate believers in Lebanon's confessional political institutions that guaranteed Christian dominance. They desired a Lebanon with a strong domestic military and a willing external benefactor to buttress the country's sovereignty together with their own political fortunes. But in the long term they miscalculated because the United States had different objectives. Lebanon, in American eyes, was little more than an ancillary element toward its main concerns of oil, Israel, and Soviet aspirations in the Middle East.

Inside Lebanon the 1958 intramural crisis continued to boil. Moslem leaders mobilized their sects to revolt against the Chamoun regime; they rejected another presidential term for Chamoun and viewed with disdain his pro-American and anti-Nasser postures. Outnumbering Christians by at least 2:1, the Druze and Shia sects, with some Sunni support, demanded greater access to institutionalized political power which, in turn, would enhance their influence on the distribution of Lebanon's growing economic wealth. They sought to deconfessionalize Lebanon's political system and force Chamoun out of office. However, although there were demands about a genuine nonconfessional democracy for Lebanon, the United National Front (UNF), as the opposition called themselves, was ''led by a largely conservative coalition of political leaders bent on the restoration of their own power rather than its dissemination'' (Gendzier 1997:4). They insisted that the national parliament be expanded to 88 members, divided equally between Moslems and Christians, and that the regime cease making prowestern foreign accords prior to the June 1957 elections, when a new parliament would be chosen (parliament elects the Lebanese president). They sought to deter Chamoun and Malik by changing the players but not the confessional system upon which their own political status was based. The 1958 civil war in Lebanon was fought between those in power, mostly Maronite Christians and those who wished a larger share of political authority and ensuing economic privilege, mostly Shia and Druze. Also, at issue was the status quo of the Lebanese state. ''The 'weak state,' it emerged, represented the interests of those with political and economic influence who were committed to minimalist government. 'Weakness,' in this instance, was a deliberate function of power, not its absence'' (Gendzier 1997:54–55) The domestic crisis amounted to a question of who would dominate Lebanese public and foreign policy: Maronite Christians or a secular Moslem alliance. The crisis situation played into the hand of the United States efforts to promulgate its foreign policy in the Middle East.

A. American Intervention

President Eisenhower, ostensibly responding to a plea from Chamoun, sent the Marines to terminate the civil war. Lebanon's major players, Chamoun, United Lebanese Front, commercial elites, and the impotent military, played right into the hands of American policy makers, who long recognized that ''any change in confessionalism to be disadvantageous to U.S. interests'' (Gendzier 1997:177). American military intervention in this civil war was difficult; there was no enemy to destroy. The United States landed on Beirut's beaches to provide law and order for the purpose of reestablishment of the Lebanese state and its traditional political, administrative, and security apparatus. Lebanon was ''saved'' from Arabism, Nasserism and communism. But for the Lebanese, American intercession amounted to little more than a confessional ''truce,'' a pause in the enduring cultural-political crisis There were neither American efforts nor domestic demands for change away from the existing state of domestic political affairs. The violence was suppressed by the presence of the Marines. The United States emerged from the 1958 Lebanese crisis as ''the uncontested Western power in the region with the foundations of its policy objectives unchanged'' (Gendzier 1997:367). Crisis resolution was for the sake of the manager, not the managed.

American intervention reestablished the ''weak but stable'' state formula for Lebanon. Every democracy must be able to defend itself. But the tragic catch in Lebanon is that when the fragile institutions of government can no longer reach compromises on sectarian differences, civil violence raises its ugly head. Due to the confessional stipulations for the Lebanese army, the Lebanese state cannot defend itself. General Shihab, Lebanon's military chief, opposed his fellow Maronite Chamoun, but he also did not have much faith in the opposition. Shihab may have had presidential ambitions, and as it turned out he was the successful compromise candidate who succeeded Chamoun. As military chief he knew all too well that to commit the army to sectarian conflict resolution was its death knell. The primarily Moslem enlisted ranks and the overwhelming Christian, with some Druze, officer ranks would divide and leave the barracks with their weapons and join their own religious persuasions in any all out civil war. Such is the security situation of the ''weak'' confessional state; it can neither provide the state protection from outside aggression nor maintain law and order in a context of domestic violence. The military has only been effective in Lebanon when there is a political balance of power between Moslems and Christians. The manifest aspects of the 1958 Lebanese crisis were suppressed by American intervention, but the latent culture core of the crisis remained in placed. Indeed, sectarian animosity intensified, to break into violence again in 1975.

III. LEBANON'S 1975–1989 CRISIS SITUATION

Lebanon's long 1975–1989 crisis chronicles the tragic story of Lebanon's fall from a sovereign state to a people dominated by foreign powers and reduced to being a pawn in the smoldering violence that continues to plague the Middle East. Lebanon's tragedy once again centers on its religious pluralism, public institutional failure, and the exploitation of these fragile circumstances by more powerful regional and international nation-states. The 1975–1989 crisis emulated that of 1958, but it was much more complex, with added internal and external participants and with considerable carnage inflicted on the civilian population. The Lebanese state was reduced to a empty shell beholden to domestic militias and external armies. Inside Lebanon the interaction of sectarianism and material deprivation was at the bottom of Lebanon's "troubles," as the most recent sectarian conflict was called (Harris 1997:63). Again in 1975 as in 1958, the chief difficulty was that Lebanon's religious sects never were able to sustain public institutions which were capable of responding to changing economic, demographic, and regional political realities. By 1975 the notion of "public" had limited significance for the Lebanese. More and more political and economic rewards were fulfilled through one's connections within a family-sect and patron-client system based on the *zaim*. The Lebanese state was little more than a holding company wherein representatives from each religious sect gathered to make public policy that protected their religious community's self-defined interest. Disadvantaged sects, mainly Shia and Druze, desired a greater share of the political power and economic prosperity, but the Christian dominated state was not forthcoming. The anti-Christian coalition withdrew their legitimacy, and the crisis turned violent. Christian sects, Maronites in particular, who enjoyed political power and economic prosperity were willing to engage in violence to protect their economic privileges. Throughout this long crisis period the Lebanese were willing to sacrifice material well being to protect their sectarian autonomy. Moslems and other progressive forces including small communist parties, referred to as leftist which meant in this context against Christian political domination, were also willing to take to the streets to change the status quo. At bottom both those in power and those challenging it were willing to protect the very being of their respective religious sects through unbelievable acts of brutality against their challengers. In April of 1975 Lebanon's cultural crisis took to the barricades, and a devastating civil war began. The key intramural issue centered on the distribution of power. Shia and Druze leaders, as well as Sunni, desired a greater share of political power which would lead, so they believed, to a greater share of Lebanon's economic pie for their religious communities. They called for deconfessionalization. Furthermore, the Moslem-leftist alliance desired Lebanon to become an active participant in the Arab-Israel dispute, especially in support of the Palestinians. The Christians viewed this as a threat to their hegemonic prosperity.

But to designate this war as Christian versus Moslem, right versus left, reactionary versus progressive, or "haves" versus "have nots" is to oversimplify. Basically Lebanese antagonists were separated by a religion-oriented political culture, but there were exceptions to this and participation across religious lines was frequent, especially among intellectuals and others emancipated from communal constraint. Moreover, as the crisis developed and participants increased there was significant changing of alliances. Lastly, there was significant infighting amid Christian elements and within the Moslem-leftist militias. External participants also shifted their guns toward one or another group as the crisis evolved. Syria switched its support from one side to the other to suit its objectives. Israel and the United States did likewise. The war lasted for almost 15 years, with an enormous amount of physical destruction and estimates of 100,000 people killed, most of whom were civilians.

A. Palestine Liberation Organization Intervention

In 1975 the tension between a Christian-oriented Lebanese political and economic system clashed with Arab nationalism over the issue of the presence Palestinian armed units. Since the establishment of Israel in 1948, Lebanon had been a refuge for hundreds of thousands of Palestinian refugees. Neither the Lebanese nor the Palestinians were eager to assimilate. The Lebanese considered the refugees a heavy burden on their social and economic system. In turn, the Palestinians endeavored to create a distinct Palestinian nationalism, separate from other Arabs, in the hope that such identity would facilitate their eventual return to Palestine. In 1971 the situation grew uneasy when King Hussein of Jordan in a bloody civil war pushed Yassir Arafat's Palestine Liberation Organization (PLO) militias out of his Hashimite Kingdom. The PLO militias entered Lebanon, and reorganized themselves in the southern part of the country, building bases and supply depots in an area which came to be known as "Fatahland" after Yassir Arafat's mainstream Palestinian unit, Fatah. The PLO's headquarters and research center were located in Beirut. Lebanon was the last refuge for the PLO as a militant force. Syria and Egypt held their Palestinians on very tight leashes, integrating armed elements into their own military forces. The PLO began to make incursions from Lebanon into Israel, attacking both military and civilian targets in Israel and inflicting casualties on civilians and military targets alike. Israel, in turn, sent its air force and commandos to counterattack at both Palestinian armed detachments and civilian camps as well as Lebanese targets across southern Lebanon, bringing terror and ruin to the residents who fled from their homes and farms to Beirut. A most notable incident was the destruction in 1968 of 16 of Lebanon's Middle East Air Line planes, which were parked overnight at the Beirut International Airport. The Lebanese government and army came under hostile criticism for not defending the country against continued Israeli incursions. Lebanese, not only the Christians but also Shia and other Moslems, began to express resentment over the presence of the Palestinians, who often behaved with disclaim toward their hosts. The Maronites grew uneasy about the PLO's growing "state within a state." The Lebanese Army and the PLO engaged in skirmishes. This infuriated those who maintained that the Lebanese state was unwilling to engage the Israelis but able to punish the Palestinians. But to assault the PLO was considered anti-Arab by Moslems in Lebanon, who believed that the Palestinians were an integral part of the Arab nation and that Israel was its enemy.

By 1975 the Christians, led by Maronites, were pitted against the Lebanese National Movement (LNM), which was mostly Moslem, Druze, and progressive secular militias, all of whom supported the Palestinians. The LNM and the PLO were both pitted against the Christians, but for different reasons. The PLO, which believed that Lebanon was their last refuge to strike against Israel, supplied many of the arms and fighters to the LNM, which was lead by the Druze *zaim* Kamal Junblatt, whose main objective was greater democracy as well as social and economic reform in an independent Lebanon. The LNM required the military support of Palestinian fighting forces to defeat the Maronites. Lebanon's Army was smaller and less well equipped than either the Christian militias or the LNM-PLO alliance and remained on the sidelines except for those troops who deserted to fight on one sectarian side or another. Christian militias battled the Palestinians and Lebanese Moslems as well as smaller ''leftist'' armed combatants. The strain between a Christian dominated Lebanese state and a Lebanon pledged to Arab nationalism raised its ugly head once again, and the weak Lebanese state with its inept security forces was unable to contain the crisis as the violence increased.

B. Syria's Intervention

The civil war was savage and bloody; few prisoners were taken by either side. Little distinction was made between military targets and civilian population. In the beginning Syria supplied and supported the LNM-PLO alliance, sending its own tightly monitored Palestinian armed units into action. After several vicious battles, the LNM-PLO beat down the Maronites. The Christians hinted at partitioning themselves into a ministate, leaving the rest of Lebanon to Moslems and Palestinians. Maronite leaders appealed to western nations and to the Vatican for assistance. With the LNM-PLO on the offensive, regional implications of the Lebanese crisis grew more tense. Neither Israel nor Syria wished a radical LNM-PLO to rule Lebanon because they both feared that such a regime could very well drag them into a war they did not want. Saudi Arabia's royal family was also apprehensive about possible regional consequences of a radical regime ruling in Lebanon. The United States worried that either a partitioned Lebanon or revolutionary LNM-PLO rule would destabilize the region, allowing the Soviets to benefit. Although throughout the Lebanese crisis, the USSR as a rule positioned itself on the sidelines and in the latter stages of the crisis was too involved in its own domestic degeneration to be a major player. Besides the USSR was caught between the animosity of its two clients, Syria and the PLO. External regional states were joined in a belief that a return to status quo in Lebanon was in their vital interest. In 1976 with American encouragement, Saudi financial support, and Israel's tacit concurrence, Syrian troops intervened on the side of the Maronites, expelling the LNM-PLO forces from Christian areas. Syrian military forces now prevailed in the form of 30,000 troops, an amount far superior to anything Lebanese militias or Palestinian commandos could bring into action.

Saudi Arabia organized an emergency meeting in Riyadh to legitimize Syrian intervention in sovereign Lebanon. An Arab League–sponsored peacekeeping force, called the Arab Deterrent Force (ADF), was sent to Lebanon. This force of 30,000 comprised 25,000 Syrian troops, already in position, and a token of 5000 from other Arab states. Syrian military occupation was quickly followed by political intercession. In one observer's words, ''Following his visit to Damascus in early February, President Sarkis (Lebanon) joined President Assad (Syria) in issuing a communique which conferred the importance of co-ordination between the two countries in matters related to their interests, and instructed presidential assistants to 'formulate a joint working plan inspired by the need for co-ordination between the two countries' (Hiro 1992:45). Syrian military and political hegemony in Lebanon was secured, supported by the Arab League with the blessing of the United States and compliance of Israel. Syrian dreams of regaining its lost territory which French imperialism had appropriated had been partially achieved. Syria had never recognized the sovereign Lebanese state, and it was content with a weak Christian Lebanese government that was beholden to it. Syria's superior troop and arms strength imposed order on Christians and Muslims alike. Lebanon's cultural differences and its governmental institutions were subsumed but not rectified by Syrian intervention. The crisis was defused, but not resolved, by agreement among external players that Syria should "manage" the crisis through military intervention and political guidance.

C. Israel's Intervention

Israel invaded Lebanon in early 1978, though throughout the years it had mounted numerous air and ground incursions in search of the PLO. The Israeli Defense Forces (IDF) raced to a zone just below the Litani river in the southern portion of Lebanon. It succeed in driving out both PLO forces and Palestinian and Lebanese civilians from the area. Thousands of refugees fled north into the Beirut area, seeking to escape the advancing IDF, which met little armed resistance. Israel was uncertain about Syria's new role in Lebanon, and it sought to establish its own mastery over southern Lebanon, restricting Syrian influence to the northern section of the country. The Litani river marked the "red" line between Israel's and Syria's spheres of armed presence. Some in Israel coveted southern Lebanon's water resources. Yet the immediate motivation for Israel's invasion was that it sought to secure its northern border from Palestinian commando infiltration and rocket attacks. Israel and Syria committed a significant portion of their armies to Lebanon. This enlarged Lebanon's crisis situation. Lebanese religious sects and militias turned to either Syria or Israel, sometimes both, for support in their intramural crisis. External intervention multiplied the clutter of devastation, only to invigorate sectarian conflict among the Lebanese. The Maronites, wary of Syrian intentions, tilted toward Israel which intensified its military support of the Christians. The LNM-PLO reverted to collaboration with Syria, which resulted in increased assistance for the Moslem-Progressive-Palestinian militias. The Lebanese government remained helpless, caught between Syria and Israel, Christians and the Moslem-PLO alliance and its own inept legitimacy and security. Lebanon's internal cultural crisis became submerged by regional security circumstances.

United Nations Security Council Resolution 425 called for Israel's withdrawal from Lebanon. It also authorized the United Nations Interim Force in Lebanon (UNIFIL) which was to assist the Lebanese Army in establishing law and order in the area south of the Litani River after the IDF withdrawal. UNIFIL quickly moved into the area when Israel withdrew. Yet the Israelis did not leave empty handed. They organized a militia, headed by renegade Lebanese Army major, Said Haddad, with Maronite leadership and Shia participation. Israel armed, trained and financed this force of 2000 to 3000 fighters, called the South Lebanese Army (SLA). Israeli officers were seconded to Haddad's Army. The purpose of the SLA was to keep Palestinian commandos out of border areas so that they would be unable to mount rocket or other forms of firepower on Israeli. UNIFIL was to prohibit both Palestinians from moving south to raid Israel and the SLA from stalking the Palestinians. But the enfeebled UNIFIL did not deter anyone. The UN could only use light weapons in defense; this provided little restraint and less respect from Israel and the SLA as well as the PLO which begin to return to the area in small numbers. Israel also demanded that Syrian forces remain north of the Litani, and it demanded that the Lebanese Army be prohibited from sending its own forces to police the area in conjunction with

UNIFIL. Israel also claimed rights to Lebanese air space (Hiro 1992:54). With the Israeli sponsored SLA and UNIFIL two new armed elements were now involved in the spreading Lebanese crisis situation.

Israel's invasion presented fresh complications to Lebanon's crisis. Through the SLA Israel also established itself as a major presence in the Lebanese crisis situation, and at the same time it began to build an alliance with Christian Maronite forces, now principally the Phalangists lead by the Gemayel family. Lebanon now became a pawn in Israel's conflict with the Palestinians and Syrians. By so doing it drove a deeper wedge into Christian-Moslem strains, escalating sectarian differences between Maronite Christians and the LNM-PLO alliance. Like the United States in 1958, the Palestinians in 1975, and Syria in 1976, Israel's 1978 intervention did nothing to alleviate the crisis. Multiple external military interventions in Lebanon's intramural crisis intensified the violence which in turn drove the Lebanese deeper into sectarian conflict and circumvented political resolution. As long as external intervention was provided on a divide and rule basis, violence only expanded as religious sects increased their suspicions of each other.

Israel's partial military withdrawal was followed by an extension of its influence in Lebanon's intramural crisis. Israeli and Maronite Phalangists Christian contacts and arms aid became a regular occurrence. (Rabinovich 1984:60–88) As the Israel-Maronite alliance escalated, Syria once again moved closer to the LNM-PLO forces. From Christian areas in East Beirut through Mount Lebanon, the Maronites consolidated their political control as well as their military forces, although not without bloody Christian versus Christian battles over leadership within the Maronite community. Bashir Gemayel's Kateb party was victorious and established their own "state within a state," with schools, clinics, taxes, amounting to an almost de facto partition with Israel looking approvingly over its shoulders. The Lebanese Front, as the loosely united Christian forces were now called, threatened to partition Lebanon establishing a ministate, an idea which Moslems and foreign governments found unacceptable. The Lebanese government and what was left of its Army were a nonfactor at this time.

Increasingly Syria began to endorse and empower Amal, a secular Shia militia and political unit which cooperated with the LNM but maintained its organizational independence. The Druze leader of the LNM, Kamal Junblatt, was assassinated, most claim by the Syrians because he resisted growing Syrian influence in Lebanese affairs. With his demise, Syrian influence over the LNM increased. Also, the PLO and Syria enjoyed a reapproachment because of their joint opposition to Israel's tactics in Lebanon. Syria withdrew some of its forces from Beirut, moving them into the Bekka valley. The Syrians defeated the Labanese Front in a large battle at Zhale. Israel gave token support to the Maronites, but its modest effort only signaled to the Syrians that it was not willing to go to war on behalf of its Christian allies. On its part, Syria made no move to cross the line which divided Israeli and Syrian spheres in Lebanon. Each could restrain their respective clients so that the intramural crisis would not explode into an all out war between the two major antagonists. Regional affairs subsumed Lebanon's crisis, perpetuating domestic turmoil for the sake of area security.

By early 1982 there was some movement between the LF and the LNM on national reconciliation. Both sides felt threatened by their patrons, Syria and Israel, because interventions looked more and more like permanent occupations. Moreover the Phalangists and several elements within the Moslem community were disturbed with continued PLO operations in Lebanon. Throughout the entire Lebanese crisis situation there were warnings of partition on behalf of the Christians and calls for deconfessionalization and economic reform coming from the Moslem side; these threats appear to have intensified with full scale external intercession. At bottom, however, most Christians maintained an allegiance to a united Lebanon, whereas most Moslems were willing to live under a confessional political system, if it guaranteed equality of political power divided between the Moslem majority the Christian minority. Both Christians and Moslems resented a Lebanon divided and occupied by foreign forces. Curiously, it was as if the Lebanese intramural conflict was taken out of their hands by superior external states. On one hand, external interference motivated a modicum of unity among the Lebanese who jointly lost control of their civil conflict. But their efforts at national consolidation continued to falter on the old cultural bugaboos, which had plagued Lebanon from its outset as a territorial state. The Christians demanded Syrian, Israeli and PLO withdrawal from Lebanon before serious talks at domestic reform began. While the Moslems wanted to discuss reform with Israel out of the picture; they were willing to tolerate a Syrian and Palestinian presence until Lebanon regained its stability. All the while the Phalangists and the Israeli government intensified their joint preparation for the objective that joined them: destruction of the PLO's military and political capacity.

D. Israel's Invasion

In 1982 Israel invaded Lebanon for the second time. Specifically, after signing its peace treaty with Egypt, Israel shifted to destruction of the PLO as a military and political force. Although Israel's northern border with Lebanon had been quiet in 1981 due to an agreement between Israel and the PLO, Prime Minister Begin and Defense Minister Sharon aspired to eliminate the PLO once and for all. As it turned out Israel's Defense Forces had little trouble pushing through Lebanon to the outskirts of Beirut in their effort to smash the PLO's armed elements and political infrastructure. Begin and Sharon believed that Palestinian nationalism could be quashed with planes, tanks, and massive numbers of troops. The PLO, Syria, and the various Moslem Lebanese militias were no match for the IDF, although the Palestinians proved to be courageous and valiant fighters. After an initial engagement between Syrian and Israeli armies, Syria backed away from direct combat. President Assad of Syria decided to not hinder Israel's destruction of the PLO because he had long desired to supervise the Palestinian movement and its interaction with Israel. A weaker PLO suited Syrian regional ambitions. No other Arab state came to the aid of the Palestinians.

Israel's military designs were coupled with political objectives. In addition to elimination of the Palestinians as a factor in the Middle East equation, Begin and Sharon desired to promote the Phalangists' Gemayel as the next president of Lebanon. Israel's political objective was to create in Lebanon a friendly regime under its influence. Gemayel requested and received Israel's military assistance during the Lebanese civil war. In turn, Israel coordinated its military invasion with Gemayel's Phalangists forces. Israel was to push the Palestinians from the south into Beirut, and Gemayel forces were to finish them off in the capital city. But Gemayel reneged on the deal; he refused to send his troops into Beirut to engage the Palestinians in door to door, hand to hand, combat. Gemayel knew that Israel was too weak economically, if not militarily, to protect him from the vengeance of the Arab states if he joined them in crushing the Palestinians. Moreover, it was also questionable if the Phalangists militias could get the job done. Israel itself feared loosing too many of its soldiers fighting the Palestinians in the streets of Beirut, but this did not stop Sharon from horrendous bombing and continuous shelling of west Beirut (Fisk

1990:282–308) In Israel the Lebanon war grew unpopular, and the Began government was on the defensive against an increasing wall of public opinion. President Assad's authoritarian regime, allowing few public liberties, withstood adverse public opinion. Israel had the PLO surrounded and trapped in Beirut, but the Palestinians did not surrender. The PLO won immense international support for their courageous stand in Beirut against the siege of the IDF. Lebanese and Palestinian civilians, who were the main victims of the IDF's onslaught of Beirut, rallied to the PLO (Chomsky 1983:359–375).

E. American Intervention

In 1982 President Reagan stepped in to negotiate an end to Israel's blockade of Beirut. He sent Ambassador Habib to arrange a deal between the IDF and the PLO. Once again the United States became involved in the Lebanese crisis, at first politically, then followed by U.S. Marines as part of the Multi-National Force (UNF) which included French, Italian and British troops. Another external armed element was added to Lebanon's crisis, and subsequently this additional armed element added not to the resolution, but to the escalation of violence. The essence of Habib's negotiated agreement between the PLO and Israel was that the latter was not to invade Beirut, and, in exchange, the PLO armed forces were to leave Lebanon altogether for hastily arranged sanctuaries in Arab countries. Both sides eventually broke the agreement, but in the short run it looked as if Habib's mediation would be successful. American, French and Italian troops entered Lebanon to police the exit of the PLO and to establish a security line between the IDF and Moslem West Beirut. With great pomp and ceremony that appeared to be designed more for victors than vanquished, the PLO left Beirut.

Bashir Gemayel was elected Lebanon's president in 1982 with Israel's blessing, but he was assassinated before taking office. Subsequently, his older brother, Amin, was elected by Parliament with American backing. Bashir Gemayel had grown close to Israel, but he let them down for failing to move his armed forces into West Beirut. Amin Gemayel did not carry the burden of being Israel's puppet. The Multi-National Forces forces left Lebanon following the PLO's departure. The IDF entered the security vacuum generated by the PLO's evacuation and established itself as police and protector, claiming that Palestinian armed elements remained hidden in West Beirut. This did not quiet various Lebanese militias, fighting among themselves for turf in the city and surrounding suburbs and mountains, and at the same time harassing the Israelis with hit and run tactics. Then the sheer horror of Shabra and Shatila was felt around the world. Phalangists entered the refugee camps and slaughtered Palestinian men, women, and children in a massacre too horrendous for human understanding (Fisk 1990:359–400). The IDF was implicated because the camps were under its immediate jurisdiction and protection. Indeed, some suggest direct collaboration between Israel and the Phalangists. The tragedy at Sabra and Shitila combined with the assassination of Bashir Gemayel was the beginning of the end of Israel's invasion of Lebanon. Over 300,000 Israelis protested the war and massacre in the streets of Tel Aviv. Israel's war in Lebanon was over.

The IDF diminished the armed Palestinian pretense in Southern Lebanon, although the guerrillas soon began to reinfiltrate the area. The Israelis continued to arm and command the SLA. The IDF's pullback was not effortless, as Shia and progressive militias harassed the retreating forces with hit and run tactics. The IDF evacuated southward, leaving empty territory for the Lebanese militias to battle over. This was especially true in the Chauf region where the Druze and the Maronites renewed their centuries old bloody battles. The Lebanese Army, rebuilt and resupplied by the United States, entered the battle on the side of the Lebanese forces, but in the end the Druze fighters prevailed. Syria had removed its armed elements into the Bakaa Valley, and now, in light of the Christian-Israeli alliance, renewed its sustenance and support of those battling against the Maronites. With the IDF moving south, Syria chose to reenter the forefront of the Lebanese crisis situation. Now that the PLO was subjugated and Israel withdrawing, Syria once again became the most powerful external player in Lebanon. Its overall objective was to secure a balance among the Lebanese religious sects and other militias so that it could rebuild Lebanon's institutions in a way that suited Syrian vital interests.

The United States tried to devise a peace treaty between Israel and the Lebanese government of Amin Gemayel. The May 17, 1983 agreement, fixed by the United States and signed by Israel and Lebanon, proposed to eliminate Israel's presence in the South of Lebanon and in exchange for a ''peace treaty'' with Lebanon. In the agreement Israel was granted certain security guarantees in southern Lebanon. But Israel additionally insisted that it would not leave Lebanon before Syria extracted its military forces. Syria was not involved in the May 17 agreement. For some unexplained reason the Americans believed that they could negotiate the withdrawal of Israel and Syria from Lebanon without Syrian involvement in the negotiations. To no one's surprise, President Assad dismissed May 17, saying Syria would not leave Lebanon until Israel had done so. Later when the Lebanese government opted for a Syrian solution to its crisis, it abrogated this agreement with Israel. Nonetheless by virtue of the the SLA and its own military resources, the IDF retained influence over a great deal of southern Lebanon.

The UNF returned to Beirut after the Sabra-Shatila massacres. The United States was especially dismayed because Ambassador Habib pledged safety for Palestinians civilians after their armed defenders left Lebanon. Yet the United States made a drastic error. U.S. Marines, along with French Legionnaires and Italian forces, were sent to police a truce between Christians, now reorganized into the Lebanese Forces (LF), and the newly formed Lebanese Salvation Front (LSF), comprising mainly Shia and Druze with some Maronite complicity. At the same time the United States Army was arming and training the new Lebanese Army. For the LSF, the Lebanese Army represented the Christian regime and Christians in general. From their view there was no difference between U.S. Marine peacekeepers and U.S. Army under-pinning of Lebanese government security forces. The Americans and French peace keepers became targets for the anti-Christian elements. The U.S. fleet in the Mediterranean and U.S. fighter planes entered the fray, shelling Druze and Shia positions in the mountains. The Marine barracks at the Beirut international airport, a virtual target waiting for disaster, and a French contingent in Beirut were blown up by suicide trucks on a Sunday morning, killing over 300 peacekeepers. The United States missed out on crisis resolution through diplomacy because it did not include Syria in the May 17 agreement. American intervention failed in its military efforts because it provided only two token forces which had contrary objectives. President Reagan ''redeployed'' the Marines to offshore naval vessels. Israel had failed to impose its military and political desires for the Lebanese crisis. The United States had failed to rectify the military situation with its token Marine force and army technical and material assistance to the Lebanese government. The United States, with Israel's acquiescence, reverted to Syria as the one external force that was able to impose order on Lebanon.

After Israel's withdrawal, the secular Shia group, Amal, became Syria's primary agent in Lebanon. Amal, like its Syrian guarantor, had no quarter for the PLO. In the southern areas of Lebanon the Shia had too long suffered from both PLO, SLA, and IDF battles, loosing their homes, fields, and lives to never ending cycle of death and destruction. Lebanon's Shia population was by then the largest and the poorest among its many religious sects. Inhabiting rural agricultural areas in the south of Lebanon as well as the Bekka valley, they were disenfranchised at the outset of the Lebanese crisis, second class citizens in relation to the political and economic power that many Christians and Sunni Moslems enjoyed. Amal's main objective was a sovereign and democratic Lebanese regime based on a deconfessionalized polity in which the Shia would hold a political majority. Another occurrence of deconfessionalism for the sake of confessional aggrandizement. Nonetheless a new force appeared in the wake of the vacuum created by the departure of the PLO and IDF. A break away Islamic Shia force called Hizb'allah, or the party of God, began to contest secular Amal for the hearts and minds of the Shia in Lebanon.

F. Iran's Intervention

Hizb'allah's historical, religious and financial ties to the Shia Islamic regime in Iran emanated from that country's objective of exporting its successful 1979 Islamic revolution (Jaber 1997: 31; Ranstorp 1997: 119). Iran targeted Lebanon for its extension of political Islam. Yet the situation was delicate because Iran was caught between Hizb'allah and Syria. The latter had been the only Arab state to support Persian Iran in its long war during the 1980s against Arab Iraq. Thus Hizb'allah's activities in Lebanon have been linked with Syria and Iran in a triangle of cooperation and conflict. Hizb'allah origins began as a Shia response to the 1975–1988 Lebanese civil war, a reaction to growing dissatisfaction with Maronite and Sunni public policy which left this Islamic sect outside political power and economic privilege. It gained its impetus and established itself as a military-political force in the context of the Israeli invasion and occupation of Lebanon in 1982. Hizb'allah's guerrilla actions against Israel's occupation were instrumental in Israel's retreat from Lebanon. This was the first time that Israel gave up captured Arab lands without achieving anything in return. Israel's routing of the PLO provided an opportunity for Hizb'allah. The geographic vacuity left by the departure of the PLO and IDF was in large part filled by Hizb'allah, which was never close to the secular and Sunni PLO, but, on the other hand, this sacred Shia force was publicly pledged to regain Palestine and Jerusalem's Islamic Holy shrines. Israel's IDF provided a easy target for Hizb'allah's carefully planned hit and run guerrilla tactics, loosing on one occasion 75 soldiers in a single explosion the southern city of Tyre. As previously indicated, American and French UNF contingents were also victims of Hizb'allah's suicide bombings. Hizb'allah and Amal fought an intramural turf battle, with the former gaining the upper hand until Syria halted the fighting. The success of Hizb'allah's actions against Israel, PLO, French, Americans and even its secular counterparts in Lebanon, attracted many young Shia men and other supporters to its organizational discipline and religious fervor. Hizb'allah also achieved public support through operation of schools, clinics, and other welfare services for the Shia population. In the minds of many, Shia and otherwise, it was Hizb'allah which hastened the departure from Lebanon of western military and political influence. Later, kidnappings of western citizens all but eliminated Americans and western Europeans from Lebanon. Hizb'allah was an indigenous entity, pledging hope and dignity for a people so long subjugated under imperialism. Close personal relationships between Shia and Iranian clerics, stimulated by the success of the Iranian revolution, sparked the organization of a tight knit and secret hierarchical elite Hizb'allah. Iran sent money, arms, and cadres to train Hizb'allah's militia. Two-thousand Pasardan, or Iranian revolutionary guards, were transport through Syria to Lebanon to safeguard Hizb'allah.

Hizb'allah operated within a Lebanon over which Syria maintained military and political hegemony. Syria was the third party in a triangle of power determining Hizb'allah's ideological quest and political domination. Just as Iran's foreign policy objectives differ from Hizb'allah's, Syria has endeavored to establish its mastery over all Lebanese religious militias, including Hizb'allah. But Syria has treated Hizb'allah with a velvet glove, and its has labored to prevent Hizb'allah from offsetting its relationship with Iran. Syria has continued to sponsor Amal, Lebanon's secular Shia political and military force, as a means to divide the Shia community and counterbalance Hizb'allah. Syria cannot deal harshly with Hizb'allah which enjoys a continued close relationship with Iran and a militant stance against Israel. Iran urged Lebanese Moslems to establish an Islamic republic in Lebanon through Hizb'allah. Iran and Syria had altogether different policy objectives, and there was always tension between the two over Hizb'allah. Syria feared that a sacred regime in Lebanon would possibly spread its influence throughout the region. In the early 1980s President Assad had crushed in a brutal manner the resurgent Islamic (Sunni) Moslem Brotherhood in Syria. Iran, although on the surface supporting Hizb'allah political ambitions, has since the death of Khomeini placed its foreign investment, trade and diplomatic ties to the western Europe and Asia on a higher priority than export of its Islamic revolution. This turn of events placed Syria in a stronger position in regard to Hizb'allah's political initiatives. Moreover, it eased tension among Lebanon's Moslem and Christian sects both of whom felt their own political fortunes threatened by the rise of radical Islam.

G. Crisis Resolution: The Ta'If Agreements

The Lebanese crisis situation turned from violence to the signing of the National Conciliation Document, better known as the Ta'if Agreements, after the city in Saudi Arabia were the document was promulgated. Syria could not altogether disarm the militias and the intramural fighting continued. Skirmishes were fought not only between the Christian Lebanese Front and the Druze-Shia forces, but also within the Maronite community, between Amal and Hizb'allah, between Amal and the Palestinian camps. In the Lebanese crisis the pattern has been that when a truce is on the horizon, fighting escalates as each sect seeks to better its position on the ground for negotiation purposes. But Syria was able to establish a modicum of security in West Beirut, although its grip over the rest of the country was tenuous.

After the term of President Amin Gemayel ended in 1988, the Lebanese state underwent further stress. When the President's tenure was completed, Parliament failed to select a successor. Lebanon actually had two governments one headed by the Sunni Prime Minister Salim al-Hoss, who refused to resign, and the Maronite General Aoun, who was appointed as prime minister to head an interim government by the outgoing president. Aoun believed he could unite the Lebanese against the Syrians prior to domestic political reform. But subsequently Syria crushed Aoun, who fled to France. The PLO militias had been reduced to a minor presence, and, in addition the Palestinians were caught up with the Intifada on the West Bank and Gaza. Ultimately Syria once again established a modicum of security in both Christian and Moslem sections of the country, and attention was turned to political reconciliation. Amal followed Syria's lead, as did the remnants of the LNF and LSF. The Lebanese population was exhausted from warfare and the economy in ruins. The Christians were uneasy with the Syrian pretense, but they were somewhat placated that there was no voice from Damascus calling for a total end to the confessional system. Moslems, too, were uneasy about Syria's growing power over Lebanese affairs, but there was no longer an alternative to President Assad. The PLO had been reduced to a shadow of its former strength and weight in Lebanese affairs. Israel and the United States were no longer visible players, but their ever watchful eyes and communication with both Syrian and Lebanese leaders was preserved. Under the guise of the Arab League, Saudi Arabia offered to host a meeting of Syrian and Lebanese officials in the hope that agreement could be attained on national political consolidation. Lebanon reached a truce period which was welcomed by religious sects and militia fighters. Thanks to the superiority of the Syrian military, external players turned the crisis situation from violence to reform of political institutions.

Under Syrian guidance, with the behind the scenes approval of the United States, Lebanon's multifarious religious sects begin to design a new way to govern themselves. The warlords, as the old-line *zaims* were now called, from the various religious communities, and Syrian officials met in Geneva (1984) and Lausanne (1985) without coming to an agreement. Syria then turned away from established religious community elders, and designed in 1985 a "tripartite agreement" between younger leaders of Christian and Moslem militias. This too failed. Yet according to one participant in the process, these conferences and agreements, failures as they were, "all found their way into the National Conciliation Document reached in Ta'if, Saudi Arabia, in October 1989" (Salem 1995:241). American and Syrian cooperation grew closer because they shared a mutual objective in perpetuating a weak but stable Lebanon. Washington and Damascus collaborated to select Lebanon's next President, Rene Muawwad, but he was soon assassinated. Another Maronite, Elias Harawi, with Syrian and American sponsorship, was chosen to replace him. A billionaire Saudi-Lebanese businessman, Rafiq Hariri, was vetted by the external powers as prime minister. Amal's leader and Syria's partner, Nabil Berri, assumed the post of speaker of the Chamber of Deputies. Syria was placated by its accommodation with the Americans over Lebanon because now the superpower found itself endorsing Syrian objectives. The single most important basis for this turn of events, especially for the ensuing Ta'if agreements, remains that Syria and the United States both feared the rise of Islam as a political force in Lebanon.

Lebanese religious communities found a modicum of unity among themselves and external powers during the crisis end game. All parties to the Lebanese crisis situation hoped to control the rise of Hizb'allah "before a resurgent fundamentalism rendered Christian-Muslim dialogue impossible" (Salem 1995:217; see also pp. 227 and 233). Everyone involved in Lebanon's crisis resolution phase from Syria and the United States, Israel and the PLO, the Maronites, Sunni, Druze and secular Shia, faced with trepidation a turning point that held the possibility of destroying their respective objectives in Lebanon: the rise to power of a Hizb'allah with its strong ties to Iran. The Islamic challenge transformed the Lebanese crisis by bringing a curious unity to intramural and external players who heretofore had significantly contrary ambitions. But all these drastic differences became subordinated to a common danger. Now everyone inclined toward political negotiation to defuse the fire of Hizb'allah and to salvage a peaceful resolution to the Lebanese crisis.

Syria—with the backing of Saudi Arabia, the approval of the United States, and the concurrence of Egypt and Israel—produced a National Reconciliation Document for the Lebanese. None of Lebanon's sectarian leaders was overjoyed with Ta'if. The Maronite Christians retained the office of the president but with reduced powers in favor of the Sunni prime minister, who was now chosen by parliament, not the president. The Shia speaker of the parliament was granted enhanced authority to the point where he shared executive authority with the president and prime minister in an ambiguous troika (Hanf 1993:583–590). Parliament was equally divided into Christian and Moslem seats, and eleven seats were added to the total so that no religious sect would loose a designated seat. Pressured by Syria, Amal and the Druze acquiesced in Ta'if as did the Maronites and Sunnis. Confessional arrangements for the governing of Lebanon were modified but at bottom the designation of executive and legislative offices by religious conviction was perpetuated, if not enhanced amidst vague indications that deconfessionalization was for the future. Lebanon's National Pact remained the basis of its state machinery. Syria was the real winner, for Ta'if legitimized its military and political domination of Lebanon. Iran and Hizb'allah were opposed to the agreement (Ranstorp 1997:51). Syria was careful, nonetheless, not to push Hizb'allah into a violent reaction against Ta'if. Interestingly while Ta'if called for the disarmament of all sacred and secular militias in Lebanon, Syria made an exception for Hizb'allah: it alone was designated a revolutionary force designed to battle Israel and thus was allowed to retain its military forces. Iran's Pasardan were also permitted to remain in Lebanon. For its part, Hizb'allah ceased its call for the overthrow of sectarian government in Lebanon, and it participated in the next parliamentary elections. The lengthy violent stage of the crisis ended. Syrian hegemony reigned over Lebanon, and the Lebanese essentially returned to the confessional political forms with which they began their destructive crisis.

IV. CULTURE AND CRISIS RESOLUTION

Lebanon's 15-year crisis, actually a series of interrelated crises, was grounded in cultural differences between its 16 religious sects. It was impossible for either domestic or foreign participants to unravel Lebanon's crisis because it evolved from deep cultural roots. When an international crisis is launched from extreme cultural relativism, it can not be resolved—as opposed to interrupted—by any factor other than the involved cultures themselves. Cultural crises might be suppressed, but only changing the causes will begin resolution. Cultures are based on primordial beliefs; still, these are not immutable. Culture is learned and can be unlearned, replaced by other norms. Cultures are continuously becoming, cultivating themselves, but they do not, cannot, change on demand. Reform of political institutional forms, such as Ta'if proposes, does not reach into the fundamental causes of the original crisis. As such, Lebanon's cultural crisis can only be resolved by its religious communities, not by the imposition of formulas imposed by external agents for their own purposes. Ta'if is little more than a pause.

In Lebanon's crisis it was demonstrated that external violence against religious sects only intensifies their parochialism. Cultures withdraw into a defensive mode when an external factor seeks to command them. Overall, militias were much better at defending their communities than attacking their opponents. Lebanon's long experience of sectarian fighting, however, provoked a revulsion against bloodletting. Recent postconflict research claims that "The overwhelming majority of Lebanese want peace, coexistence and national unity. They have expressed this not only as individuals in anonymous interviews, but also as groups in mass demonstrations over the years of war, repeatedly, whenever they had the opportunity" (Hanf 1993:638). Lebanese of all religious faiths have expressed their animosity against militias and their leaders. They appear to be especially unhappy about continued Syrian and Israel occupation of their country. There is some indication individuals wish to break out of the shackles of confessionalism. Where these trends will eventually lead is unknown. They indicate not a revulsion against religion, but they do point toward a wish for a secular polity beyond the confines of confessionalism. Perhaps the long and difficult crisis has reached that stage in a political crisis that the late Hannah Arendt wrote prophetically: "The disappearance of common sense in the present day is the surest sign of the present-day crisis. In every crisis a piece of the world, something common to us all, is destroyed. The failure of common sense, like a diving rod, points to the place where such a cave-in has occurred" (Arendt, 1977:178). If a turn toward sense-in-common about governance be the case in Lebanon, a formidable step toward reconciliation has been achieved.

Crisis intervention, or management if one wishes, by external armies, served to escalate not contain the violence covering Lebanon. External military intervention failed when it entered the crisis on a one-track basis for its own purposes supporting one intramural side or another. Every domestic participant appealed to particular external support for arms and diplomatic leverage, but the all-too-willing responses only served to tip the balance between the warring Lebanese sects and intensify sectarian suspicions and hatreds that lead to so much bloodletting. External intervention fed upon and intensified the contradictions of Lebanon's National Pact. Each external player sought to capitalize on the crisis rather than end the conflagration. It was as if each external intervention pushed brutality to new and higher levels in a never-ending cycle of fury, engulfing both Lebanese and those that dared to intervene. Syria, PLO, Israel, the United Nations, France, and the United States, to mention only the most consequential external forces, all learned that piecemeal military entry into the Lebanese quagmire would result in failure and humiliation, if not defeat. Only when the major players agreed that Syria alone should establish total military jurisdiction over the intramural parties was the fighting suspended. Syria, then, of all the external intercessions, possessed the will and patience and committed the quantity of resources to sustain the military mastery that was needed to repress Lebanese militias from the Maronites, Druze and Shia to Hizb'allah. It was not until every major external and intramural participant yielded to Syria's hegemony that a political resolution to the crisis was able to begin. Every intramural and external participant held a veto over crisis resolution, and it was not until the common threat of an Islamic resurgence in Lebanon became recognized that each party convinced itself that the time had come to reach a nonviolent settlement. Military crisis intervention was not successful until it was unified and comprehensive.

Lastly, attempts to understand the Lebanese case demonstrate that there was in fact no such thing as a "Lebanese crisis." An international crisis is like the proverbial elephant, it depends from what side one observes the beast to realize what the crisis is all about and what how it might be unraveled. Curiously, the Lebanese case shows that no major intramural or external participant actually desired resolution or even serious management of the crisis's cultural core. Each contestant's understanding of the crisis produced a distinct interpretation, a different conceptualization of the meaning of the situation. In the Lebanese experience there were as many different crises as participants, including those who after the fact pursue understanding through inquiry. We return full circle to George's statement that an international crisis is "context-dependent," and this insight stands as a step toward greater understanding of international crisis situations and efforts toward their resolution.

REFERENCES

Arendt, Hannah (1977). *Between Past and Future*, enlarged edition. New York: Penguin Books.
Bell, Coral (1971). *The Conventions of Crisis*. London: Oxford University Press.
Brecher, Michael, Wilkenfled, Jonathan, and Moser, Shella (1988). *Crisis in the Twentieth Century*: Vol 1. *Handbook of International Crises*. New York: Pergamon Press.
Chomsky, Noam (1983). *The Fateful Triangle*. Boston: South End Press.
Fisk, Robert (1990). *Pity the Nation*. New York: Atheneum.
Friedman, Thomas L. (1989). *From Beirut to Jerusalem*. New York: Doubleday.
Geertz, Clifford (1973). *The Interpretation of Cultures*. New York: Basic Books.
Gendzier, Irene L. (1997). *Notes From the Minefield*. New York: Columbia University Press.
George, Alexandar L., ed. (1991). *Avoiding War: Problems of Crisis Management*. Boulder, CO: Westview Press.
Gilmour, David (1983). *Lebanon: The Fractured Country*. New York: St. Martin's Press.
Hanf, Theodor (1993). *Coexistence in Wartime Lebanon*. London: I.B. Tauris & Co. Ltd.
Harris, William W. (1997). Faces of Lebanon. Princeton, NJ: Markus Wiener Publishers.
Hiro, Dilip (1992). *Lebanon: Fire and Embers*. New York: St. Martin's Press.
Jaber, Hala (1997). *Hezballah, Born with a Vengeance*. New York, Columbia University Press.
Mackey, Sandra (1989). *Lebanon, Death of a Nation*. New York: Congdon & Weed, Inc.
Petran, Tabitha (1987). *The Struggle for Lebanon*. New York: Monthly Review Press.
Picard, Elizabeth (1996). *LEBANON: A Shattered Country*. New York/London: Holmes & Meier.
Rabinovich, Itamar (1984). *The War for Lebanon 1970–1983*. Ithaca and London: Cornell University Press.
Randal, Johnathan (1983). *Going All the Way*. New York: Viking Press.
Ranstorp, Mangus (1997). *Hizb'Allah in Lebanon*. New York: St. Martin's Press.
Salem, Elie A., *Violence and Diplomacy in Lebanon*, (1995), London: I.B. Tauris.
Salibi, Kamal S. (1976). *Cross Roads to Civil War*. Delmar, NY: Caravan Books.
Salibi, Kamal (1988). *A House of Many Mansions*, Berkeley, CA: University of California Press.
Schiff, Ze'ev and Ya'ari, Ehud (1984). *Israel's Lebanon War*. New York: Simon & Schuster.
Shehadi, Nadim and Mills, Dana Haffar, eds. (1988). *Lebanon: A History of Conflict and Consensus*. London: I.B. Tauris & Co. Ltd.
Snyder, Glenn H. and Diesing, Paul (1977). *Conflict Among Nations*. Princeton, NJ: Princeton University Press.

39

Transforming Danger into Opportunity

Jordan and the Refugee Crisis of 1990

Emad Mruwat, Yaser Adwan, and Robert Cunningham Department of Political Science, University of Tennessee, Knoxville, Tennessee

I. INTRODUCTION

This chapter reviews Jordan's internal and external situation at the onset of the Persian Gulf crisis of 1990, narrates the refugee flow, and describes Jordan's strategy for handling that crisis. The conclusions arising from analyzing this Jordanian case suggest that an effective crisis management strategy for small or poor countries may differ from crisis management strategies for large, affluent nations.

II. JORDAN'S POLITICOMILITARY SITUATION

The Hashemite Kingdom of Jordan occupies a hazardous geopolitical location. To the north is Syria, an Arab socialist state with no love of monarchy. To the east lies the unpredictable Saddam Hussain's Iraq. To the south is Saudi Arabia, a monarchy traditionally supportive of Jordan but threatened by Saddam Hussain's conquest of Kuwait and concerned about a possible Jordan-Iraq connection. The Saudis fear that their huge oil reserves might tempt Saddam to march south. To Jordan's west is Israel, which fought wars against Jordan in 1948 and 1967. Jordan fears that Israel will use any pretext to solve its ''Palestine problem'' by attacking the Jordanian army, driving Palestinian citizens over the border into Jordan, installing a puppet Palestinian regime, and then defining Jordan as the Palestine homeland. This fear has been tempered by the creation of a Palestine Authority on the West Bank of the Jordan River. However, given the ideology of Likud Party supporters and coalition partners that all the land of Palestine belongs to Israel, security on Jordan's western boundary remains a latent issue. Potential aggressors lie East, North, and West, and Jordan's 4.5 million population is less than that of any of its neighbors.

Jordan has been ruled by the Hashemites since the 1920s, and despite internal opposition has supported the West throughout the Cold War (Salloukh 1996). However, as a result of the Iraqi invasion of Kuwait in 1990, and King Hussain's neutral posture toward that conflict (seen by members of the anti-Iraq coalition as a pro-Iraq stance), the West withdrew its financial and military aid from Jordan, and threatened to blockade Aqaba, Jordan's only sea outlet.

III. POLITICOECONOMIC SITUATION IN JORDAN PRIOR TO THE CRISIS

In the summer of 1990 Jordan faced several difficult challenges: heavy international indebtedness, a new, freely elected Parliament with a substantial Islamic element, and uncertainties about having cut itself loose from its Palestinian territory on the West Bank of the Jordan River.

Over the 20 years prior to 1990 the Jordanian economy had undergone a series of fluctuations. The economy performed well in the 1970s, when the elevated oil prices attracted many Jordanians to work in Saudi Arabia, Iraq, Kuwait, and the United Arab Emirates. The remittances from family members abroad provided a strong injection of capital into the Jordanian economy. The economic situation began to decline with the drop in oil prices commencing in the early 1980s. Jordan's gross domestic product (GDP) increase dropped from 10% during 1979–1980 to 8.7% in 1981, to 5.5% in 1982, and to 0.2% in 1983 (United Nations Economic and Social Commission for Western Asia 1991: 10). As this trend continued in the succeeding years, Jordan began sinking deep into debt.

To remedy the situation the Jordanian government sought the assistance of the International Monetary Fund (IMF) and the World Bank. An economic structural adjustment program (EAP) was agreed upon which covered the 1989–1993 period (United Nations Economic and Social Commission for Western Asia 1992). To comply with the structural adjustment program that these international entities impose on requesting states, Jordan implemented two of the major recommendations: reducing government expenditures and providing incentives to the private sector. Lowering government expenditures meant a reduced standard of living for Jordanians, a policy particularly threatening to those who already had difficulty making ends meet.

In the political realm, Jordanian parliamentary elections took place in November 1989; they were substantially free of governmental interference. Of the 80 seats in Parliament, the Islamic Front won 23 seats, and independent Islamists won an additional 11 seats. Together, they constituted the strongest force in Parliament. The significance of Parliament substantially increased, and a parliamentary committee began pushing to abolish the martial law under which individual rights and freedom of expression had been curbed. This was a significant move, for government employment had long depended on getting a work permit, which required security clearance. Individuals who were seen as a threat to the stability and survival of the regime were denied a security clearance.[1] This increased political freedom was seen as a potential risk to the King. Fear of losing the opportunity to obtain a work permit was considered a substantial deterrent to antiregime activities.

In July 1988 Jordan relinquished its claim to the West Bank, which reduced tension between King Hussain and some nationalistic Palestinian groups who saw the King as an impediment to their freedom. Giving up the West Bank also eased pressure on the national budget, as Jordan from the occupation of the West Bank by Israel in 1967 until 1988 had continued to pay the salaries of government employees living on the West Bank. Ceding authority meant that Jordan would no longer hold itself responsible for underwriting those salaries. However, in the minds of some nationalistic East Bank Jordanians, excising the West Bank removed the justification for Palestinian involvement in Jordanian politics. "They have their own country; let them go and live there," represents an attitude which brought to the surface latent tensions between Palestinians and East Jordanians.

Economic hardship, political uncertainty, and narrow nationalism were three potentially destabilizing factors facing Jordan in the summer of 1990.

IV. THE ECONOMIC IMPACT OF POLITICAL NEUTRALITY

The structural adjustment plan imposed by the World Bank and IMF was having its anticipated effect of lowering inflation and retarding the foreign debt increase, but the Iraqi invasion of Kuwait created the potential for a severe downward economic spiral. As a result of its unwillingness to join the coalition against Iraq, Jordan lost both revenue and markets for its products. In 1989, the year prior to the invasion of Kuwait, Jordan received $616.1 million in financial aid and governmental assistance from Arab oil-producing countries, which amounted to 80% of the Jordanian government's external receipts. That assistance stopped cold. Foreign direct investment from the Persian Gulf states, totaling $185 million in 1989 (United Nations Economic and Social Commission for Western Asia 1991: 10) came to a halt. Jordan had been receiving its oil from Kuwait, Saudi Arabia, and Iraq at an average of $8 per barrel, which was about half the market price at that time. Remittances by Jordanians working abroad coming through official channels averaged $872 million from 1986 to 1989 (United Nations Economic and Social Commission for Western Asia 1991:6). Additional wealth to the nation accrued from private exchanges through money changers or in the form of consumer and capital goods from abroad.

Regarding trade, Jordan lost markets in Saudi Arabia and throughout the Persian Gulf. Iraq, which purchased 24% of Jordan's exports in 1989 (United Nations Economic and Social Commission for Western Asia 1991:3) was subject to embargo by the alliance, which meant that such trade was highly uncertain, and subject to elimination at the whim of the alliance. The transport sector accounted for more than 12% of the Jordanian GNP in 1989. Revenues from the transport fleet, which operated with Iraq and Kuwait, were estimated at $425 million for 1990 (Central Bank of Jordan 1990:66). Estimated losses in manufacturing for 1990 amount to $253 million (United Nations Economic and Social Commission for Western Asia 1992). In the last half of 1990, real domestic product declined 9%, unemployment was 20%, and the cost of living rose 8.5% (Ministry of Planning 1991). Enforcing an embargo on the port of Aqaba would prevent both imports and exports from the country. The embargo on Iraq had a severe impact on the port of Aqaba, for approximately 70% of the goods unloaded there were destined for Iraq. Shipping companies began to charge beneficiaries $25,000 per week for each ship coming to the port of Aqaba; this naturally prompted insurance fees to rise and caused some ships to seek other ports (Central Bank of Jordan 1990:66). With the cessation of oil from Kuwait and Saudi Arabia, Iraq provided Jordan with 82.5 percent of the latter's needed petroleum (Brand 1994:286). In sum, the revenue streams of direct government aid, expatriate remittances and their investment impact, investment from the Persian Gulf area, revenues from trucking and transit, and traditional agriculture and mineral markets were all terminated or at risk of closure at any moment.

In its Twenty-Seventh Annual Report (1990:64–65), the Jordanian Central Bank estimated Jordan's losses from the crisis as follows: $728 million in foreign exchange, $568 million in budgetary support from Arab countries, $229 million in commodity exports, $213 million in lost remittances from Jordanians working in Iraq, Kuwait, and other Persian Gulf countries, and a $274 million loss in tourism. Jordan's independent political stance in the run-up to the 1991 war between Iraq and the coalition created a large economic problem for the country.

V. JORDAN'S RESOURCES: EXTERNAL FACTORS

Every threat carries the seeds of opportunity. Jordan's strategic location and neutral stance received public condemnation in the Western popular press; however, its location and behavior remained important to both Iraq and the Anti-Iraq alliance. Lying geographically in the center of Egypt, Israel, Syria, Iraq, and Saudi Arabia, Jordan is a keystone which, if it imploded, might not only undercut the alliance but also ignite a conflict between Israel and its neighbors, jeopardizing the continued flow of Middle Eastern oil to both the West and the Far East. The West did not want Jordan to join Iraq, but a war in or involving Jordan would unleash unpredictable forces which might rip apart the fragile alliance against Iraq.

If Jordan became embroiled in a civil war, or was drawn into conflict with any neighbor, Syria, Iraq, or Israel might intervene as a preemptive act of self-defense. That action would have undermined the ability of the West to hold the alliance together, for among Jordan's neighbors the Arab-Israel conflict had a higher salience than the Iraq issue. Only the Persian Gulf nations and the West saw the Iraq issue as primary.

A viable Jordan was also important to Iraq. All Iraq's external trade came overland from Jordan. A Jordan in the hands of the alliance would reduce Iraq's ability to obtain goods from abroad. The diplomatic relations that both Iraq and the alliance had with Jordan made King Hussain the natural mediator in the conflict, a role which was useful to both Iraq and the alliance.

VI. JORDAN'S RESOURCES: INTERNAL FACTORS

In addition to the international benefits, Jordan's location in the eye of the conflict could provide an opportunity to ease its domestic problems: the internal cleavage between East Bank and West Bank Jordanians, the structural readjustment imposed by the IMF, and the paucity of foreign exchange holdings. With the survival of the nation at stake, the King could extract sacrifices from the people for the benefit of the nation with minimal dissent.

While East Bank and Palestinian Jordanians each had mutual suspicions of the other's intentions, they were united in resenting the wealth of the Kuwait, Saudi Arabia, and the Emirates, wealth they felt should be shared more widely among all Arabs. They saw Saudi and Kuwaiti oil as Arab oil. Images of Kuwaitis with gold-plated bathtubs while Arabs in Cairo, Amman, and Damascus were in poverty did not sit well with Arab public opinion. Saddam Hussain's willingness to take on these presumed Kuwaiti plutocrats and to risk a battle with the West struck a responsive chord in Jordan and among ordinary Arabs everywhere in the Middle East. For King Hussain to go counter to strongly felt

Jordanian public opinion supporting Iraq when the Jordanian economy was in such a weakened position would have been a risky political act. Taking a middle position calling for Iraqi withdrawal from Kuwait while opposing the western military presence in the Middle East drew popular support from every quarter of the Arab world except Saudi Arabia and Kuwait.

This domestic cohesiveness and perception of an embattled small country strengthened the hand of the Jordanian government in imposing the IMF/World Bank structural readjustment plans, which caused economic hardship for Jordanians by eliminating subsidies on key products such as sugar, powdered milk, and rice. In addition, the embargo legitimized the government's restrictions on the importation of luxury consumer goods, thereby conserving foreign exchange.

Jordan also had internal resources for dealing with the impending refugee crisis. The nation had experienced refugee in-migrations in 1948 and 1967, as Palestinians were driven from their homes. While the Jordanian personnel involved in handling refugee operations changed over the 1948–1967–1990 period, sufficient institutional memory remained to be able to respond effectively to the 1990 crisis. On both previous occasions, Jordan had been flooded with refugees, and the Jordanian government had attempted to alleviate the sufferings of the Palestinian refugees. In 1948 the Arab League provided some assistance, but witnessing the gravity of the situation King Abdullah had pleaded for western assistance as well (Plascov 1981:42).

Foreign assistance, and in particular UNRWA's work during the 1967 crisis, greatly facilitated Jordan's ability to cope, so as not to threaten the stability and survival of the kingdom. Jordan had in place a working relationship with international relief and welfare organizations.

Such was Jordan's situation as 1.1 million people—Jordanian citizens as well as Egyptians, Yemenis, Sri Lankans, Indians, Pakistanis, Bangladeshis, Thais, Malaysians, Filipinos, Indonesians, and others, trapped in Iraq and Kuwait—headed overland toward Jordan in the period of August to November 1990, creating a refugee crisis with which Jordan had to cope.

VII. INFLUX OF REFUGEES AND RETURNEES

The *New York Times* reported on August 13, 1990, that 2 million people were near the Jordanian border; yet Jordan appeared to ignore this grave situation. Despite the closure of the Turkish border with Iraq and other publicly available information that large numbers of refugees were heading toward Iraq's border with Jordan, Jordan continued business as usual. No extraordinary preparations were made to face the returnees' crisis. Was it done purposefully? Since Jordan had few resources to commit to dealing with this emergency situation, perhaps they deliberately allowed the situation to reach crisis proportions.

It appears that the government of Jordan decided that by doing nothing, the international community would offer aid to help those in need. If Jordan solved the problem on its own, Jordan would gain few resources from abroad and probably little sympathy or good will for its sacrifice. Jordanian policy makers played the issue of the refugees skillfully for the benefit of the country in terms of gaining both international resources and sympathy. At one point, when the international community showed little sensitivity toward Jordan's concerns, Jordan closed its border, thereby shutting down the evacuees' only exit from Iraq. Jordan would not be taken for granted. Implicitly, Jordan demanded that the international community understand Jordan's position, and give Jordan resources to deal with the refugees.

Once the international community made a financial commitment to assist Jordan in dealing with the refugee problem, the Jordanian system sprang into action. The Jordanian government abolished normal entry requirements at all its borders to allow easy entrance of refugees and to meet the pressure of the massive exodus of people crossing into Jordan from Iraq. Visas, paperwork, security checks, and other requirements were abolished. Jordan opted for a strategy that primarily focused on registering name, country of residence, and home country, concentrating only on information needed to identify and transport refugees. For those whose final destination was not Jordan, transit camps were set up along a route from the Iraqi border to the airport south of Amman and to the port of Aqaba. People were moved quickly and effectively through this pipeline by the government of Jordan in cooperation with non-governmental organization (NGO) employees. The average time spent by an individual in the pipeline was 2 weeks. By mid-December 1990, the refugee transit crisis was over.

Approximately 350,000 of these 1.1 million travelers stayed permanently in Jordan. The cost of caring for these people was estimated at $48 million, which covered their food, shelter, transport, and adequate medical and human assistance (Central Bank of Jordan 1990:67).

VIII. MANAGING THE CRISIS

According to Littlejohn, crisis management is ''a technique both for avoiding emergencies and planning for the unavoidable ones, as well as a method for dealing with them when they occur, in order to mitigate their disastrous consequences....Crisis management provides an organization with a systematic, orderly response to crisis situations'' (Littlejohn 1983:10–11).

Jordan's handling of the crisis can be conceptualized as operating at three arenas or levels: external strategic, internal strategic, and internal operational. A team focused primarily on a specific arena but was sensitive to events occurring in each other arena. Failure in any arena could spill over into another area, potentially destabilizing the nation and the entire region.

The Palace (King and Crown Prince) dealt primarily at the external strategic level. They had to decide how to position the country in inter-Arab and international affairs. Pressured by the alliance of Saudi Arabia, Egypt, Syria, the United States, and western Europe on the one hand to join against Iraq, and on the other side by heavy trade and transit with Iraq and a vocal and increasingly restive population which strongly supported Iraq, the Palace sought an Arab solution to the conflict but was sharply rebuffed by members of the alliance. Throughout the August–December period, the Palace initiated and responded to challenges in attempting to expand its decision-making latitude and furthering the national interest. The response in this arena fits the political/strategic requirement for crisis management: limitation of objectives pursued in the crisis, and limitation of means employed on behalf of those objectives; see George (1991:24).

The internal strategic (middle-level) team was headed by the prime minister and composed of the following ministries: Finance, Social Development, Foreign Affairs, Planning, Health, Information, and Interior. These ministries linked the operational refugee crisis to the international arena. Internally, they set policies on health, customs, and transportation—significant matters touching perhaps on inter-Arab politics but often driven by operational issues bubbling up from below and affecting the refugee stream. They also dealt with international agencies in renegotiating Jordan's debt, with donor countries supplying aid to the refugees, with general budget support, and with NGOs involved in the refugee relief effort. Domestically, they worked closely with parliamentary and party leaders on local issues and legislation to ensure the legality of administrative actions. Although cabinet members are the chief decision makers for issues within their jurisdiction, in this case they play the middle manager role because, although they offer information and suggestions, the primary policy determination comes from the Palace.

The third arena involves the refugees streaming out of Iraq. A subministerial team, headed by the undersecretary of the interior, with similar-level representation from the departments of finance, transportation, information, social development, health, army, and public security, addressed this situation. A representative from each department provided the link for meeting quickly specific operational needs. For example, if five doctors were needed at a specific location, the representative from the Ministry of Health would respond to this need.

This multilevel matrix structure worked to reduce the impact of surprises, to provide information quickly to those who needed it, and to rush the information or services to the appropriate spot. The chair of the operations arena team, the undersecretary of the Interior Ministry, is fluent in several languages and had experience dealing with the international media. Each member of the team was picked for the assigned role based upon both competence and suitability for working effectively with others. The importance of using a matrix-type organization for handling crises, an organizational structure characteristic reflected in the linkage among the three Jordanian refugee crisis management teams, is the main theme of Littlejohn (1993).

Many international NGOs were allowed to operate in the country and provide services to the evacuees and to use the media in requesting further donations from their home base. UN Resolution 664, which called on Iraq to allow all foreign citizens to leave its territory, gave Jordan the leverage to press for certain conditions to be met before Amman could allow these foreign citizens onto its soil. These preconditions included participation by the expatriates' home countries in repatriating their own citizens. Jordan did not want to get stuck with the responsibility for transporting Sri Lankans, Filipinos, or Thais to their home countries.

This structure—interconnected teams operating at executive, middle, and operational levels—is more complex than that envisioned by Littlejohn (1993) and resembles the structure of highly effective organizations.[2] The clearly defined, mutually agreed mission has highest priority. Resources are readily available. The siege environment generated domestic anxiety and allowed decision latitude to the leaders—which they quickly devolved, when appropriate, to the operational level. Even the Islamists, whom some might suspect of having their own agenda of undermining the King, were heavily involved and completely cooperative in providing goods and services to evacuees. Three important ministries—Education, Social Welfare, and Labor—were held by members of Islamic movements, and these ministries were fully committed to the goals and means devised to meet this crisis.

Skillfully addressing the international political, international technical, local political, and local technical arenas, the country was able to deal effectively with the refugee crisis, strengthen its international stance, and attract new resources to Jordan—a country under siege.

IX. THE AFTERMATH OF THE CRISIS

Jordan entered the crisis in the spring and summer of 1990 facing economic and political difficulties. The financial picture was deteriorating, severely threatening the stability of the currency, and traditional regional and western allies abruptly withdrew their support. Internal conflicts between West Bankers and East Jordanians, and between Islamists and moderates, lay just below the surface.

The spring of 1991 smiled on Jordan. Financial support flowed in from Japan, Germany, and the European Union. These sources provided $140 million in aid and $212 million in loans. The United States had written off $324 million of Jordanian debts, and rescheduled $645 million of other American loans (Central Bank of Jordan 1990:67–68). The inflow of private capital from returnees was estimated at $1.2 billion (Van Hear 1995).

With political skill and good fortune, the Jordanian leadership strengthened the Islamic parties' bonding to the political system, gained credibility as an independent voice in the Arab world, obtained low-cost oil from Iraq, developed an Iraqi market for Jordanian-manufactured pharmaceuticals and other items urgently needed by a distressed nation, relieved Jordan of substantial debt obligation to the United States, and obtained new loans and grants from Japan and the European Union. A dangerous situation had turned into a political and economic windfall.

X. CONCLUSIONS AND IMPLICATIONS FOR CRISIS MANAGEMENT THEORY

In August 1990, Jordan appeared to approach the impeding refugee crisis with a reactive stance, for the country was seemingly oblivious to the mass of humanity heading its way. Any casual observer could anticipate that Jordan would be an escape route from the conflict for the large numbers of expatriates working in Iraq and Kuwait. Iran and Iraq had just ended a war and that border was closed; Saudi Arabia and Turkey were closed because they had joined the alliance against Iraq. Only Jordan had an open border. However, Jordan seemingly took no action to prepare for the impending refugee avalanche.

The scholarly literature—as well as common sense—would dictate that a nation should plan and prepare for the imminent crisis. However, to have taken anticipatory action prior to an actual crisis would have absorbed significant Jordanian resources, resources that were needed by Jordanian citizens. Jordan waited to act until the crisis exploded—when the refugees overwhelmed the facilities at the Iraq-Jordan border, an event attended by the international media. In full view of the world Jordan used a combination of threats to stall the movement of refugees (which could embarass the western alliance) to support its requests for resources and concessions. At the same time, Jordanian ministries coordinated among themselves and with NGOs for expert management of the refugee flow.

Perhaps the lesson for small nations managing crises is to adopt the paradoxical posture of preparedness to act, yet holding back and attempting to leverage the resources of larger nations to assist in the effort. Be the manager of the crisis rather than the provider of the relief goods. Preemptive action in crisis situations may be appropriate for economically self-sufficient nations. Poor nations may be better served by emphasizing planning and preparation, but withholding action, a strategy which appears more reactive than proactive. Poor nations can exploit their weakness by calling for financial help from the more advantaged countries and international organizations, then allocating their own resources flexibly in pursuing own agendas.

Political controls can be relaxed without serious risk of antiregime activity by citizens. At times of natural disaster or externally generated crisis, dissidents are less likely to seek political advantage, more willing to postpone their agenda to serve the greater national good, and are more easily coopted into the well-defined, consensually agreed mission of the regime. Devolving administrative authority carries minimal risk because behaviors are publicly visible and constrained by the narrowly defined, humanitarian goals. The wise leader of a small or poor nation which publicizes its plight and acts efficiently to solve the problem can turn crises into significant advances toward nation building.

ENDNOTES

1. For stories describing such situations, see Cunningham and Sarayrah (1993:85–86,156–157).
2. For example, Kanter (1989) is typical of the current thinking on desirable management structure.

REFERENCES

Brand, Laurie A. (1994). *Jordan's Inter-Arab Relations: The Political Economy of Alliance Making*. New York: Columbia University Press.

Central Bank of Jordan (1990). *Twenty Seventh Annual Report*. Amman: Department of Research and Studies.

Cunningham, Robert and Yasin Sarayrah (1993) *WASTA; The Hidden Force in Middle Eastern Society*. Westport, CT: Praeger.

George, Alexander L. (1991) A Provisional Theory of Crisis Management; in Alexander L. George, ed. *Avoiding War: Problems of Crisis Management*. Boulder, CO: Westview Press, 22–27.

Kanter, Rosabeth (1989). The New Managerial Work. *Harvard Business Review* 67(6), 85–92.

Littlejohn, Robert F. (1983). *Crisis Management: A Team Approach*. New York: American Management Association.

Ministry of Planning (1991). "The financial burden of the Jordanian returnees on the economy" (preliminary report). Amman, September 7.

Plascov Avi (1981). *The Palestinian Refugees in Jordan 1948–1957*. London: Frank Cass and Company Limited.

Salloukh, Bassel F. (1996). State strength, permeability, and foreign policy behavior: Jordan in theoretical perspective. *Arab Studies Quarterly* 18(2), 39–65.

United Nations Economic and Social Commission for Western Asia (1992). *The Impact of the Gulf Crisis on the Jordanian Economy*. Amman, June.

United Nations Economic and Social Commission for Western Asia. (1991). *The Return of Jordanian/Palestinian Nationals from Kuwait: Economic and Social Implications for Jordan*. Amman.

Van Hear, Nicholas (1995). The impact of the involuntary mass "return" to Jordan in the wake of the Gulf crisis. *International Migration Review*. 29 (summer), 352–374.

40

Managing Terrorism as an Environmental Hazard

William Lee Waugh, Jr. Department of Public Administration and Urban Studies, Georgia State University, Atlanta, Georgia

I. INTRODUCTION

A few years ago it might be said with some confidence that most Americans were in greater danger of severe injury or even death from a fall in the bathtub, shark attack, or being hit by lightning than they were from a terrorist attack. That observation is still true in the sense that terrorist events are relatively infrequent in comparison with other threats to life and limb and property. However, the risk posed by terrorist violence is far greater today than it was only a decade ago. The increasing destructiveness of terrorist weapons, the apparent willingness of terrorists to kill large numbers of people, and the increasing fragility of modern society have fundamentally changed the nature of the threat. As a consequence, terrorism has become a significant environmental hazard for all modern societies and, therefore, should be managed like other hazards in order to minimize the risk.

The means to mass destruction are available to anyone with access to a large library or the Internet. Quite apart from the availability of automatic weapons and even more destructive military technologies, relatively unsophisticated weapons manufactured in a kitchen or garage can have a devastating impact. The bombs used in the World Trade Center and Murrah Federal Office Building attacks were large but relatively unsophisticated. As the July 1996 bombing in Atlanta's Centennial Olympic Park may have demonstrated, an individual or group with minimal technical skill can kill, maim, and disrupt society. The park bomb could have killed many more than it did. It was sheer luck that only one death resulted from the shrapnel. Fortunately, there have been few cases outside of war and international conflict that have resulted in mass destruction and mass casualties for Americans. Notwithstanding our experiences in Lebanon and Saudi Arabia, we have had few major disasters caused by terrorist events. However, the recent World Trade Center and Oklahoma City bombings suggest that that good fortune may be short-lived and that we should be prepared for similar and perhaps more destructive events. The fragility of modern power, transportation, communications, and water networks and the damage that would result from their interruption demands preparation to respond to the possibility of terrorist violence.

The thesis of this analysis is that terrorism cannot be prevented and it poses sufficient threat to individuals and communities in the United States that we need a broad strategy to manage the hazard that it presents. We should adopt a comprehensive emergency management program to prepare for, mitigate the effects of, respond to, and recover from terrorist events, in other words. There is still a tendency to think of antiterrorism policies as response policies, much as we tend to do with disaster policies of other kinds, but a more comprehensive approach is needed. An approach that recognizes that local authorities, rather than federal agencies or military forces, are likely to be the first responders is also critical. While exposure to the risk of terrorist violence is increasing, the design of antiterrorism policies has been difficult and has tended to reflect piecemeal solutions to a few aspects of the hazard. In effect, we tend to address the symptoms rather than the root problem. The nature of the violent phenomena, the complexities of the intergovernmental and multiorganizational responses, and the practical problems of designing and implementing effective programs to prevent or minimize the effects of terrorism suggest that an all-hazards emergency management strategy would be most appropriate. In short, we have mechanisms for dealing with large-scale threats to life and property from natural and technological hazards, and those mechanisms should be used to deal with the hazard of terrorism.

This analysis examines the nature of terrorist violence and how assumptions about its nature shape antiterrorism policies and programs, outlines a comprehensive emergency management approach to the problem, describes briefly how American antiterrorism policy can be adapted to that approach, and concludes with recommendations for a broader antiterrorism policy to address the potential for large-scale events.

II. THE NATURE AND PROCESS OF TERRORISM

Terrorism is a highly political and emotional issue. The observation that ''one man's terrorist is another man's freedom fighter'' is a cliché, but it is also an explanation of why terrorist violence confounds policy makers. A wide variety of acts may be termed ''terroristic,'' including the dumping of British tea into Boston Harbor by the ''Sons of Liberty'' during the American Revolution and the bombing of civilian populations by both sides during World War II. The most common shapers of public perceptions of terrorism, however, have been the national liberation struggles of the postwar era, the international conflicts of the Cold War, antigovernment violence by leftists during the 1960s and early 1970s, racist and nativist violence that has persisted for most of American history, and, more recently, antigovernment, antitax, antiabortion, and other violence by groups against government offices, women's clinics, law enforcement officers, and other targets. While those manifestations of terrorism are similar, there are rather fundamental differences that have to be accommodated in a comprehensive antiterrorism policy. The six basic models of terrorist violence with which Americans have had to contend are as follows:

1. The revolution or national liberation model
2. The civil disorder model
3. The law enforcement model
4. The international conflict or surrogate warfare model
5. The human rights or repressive government model
6. The vigilante model

The models reflect important differences in the nature of the violence or at least different assumptions about its origins and purposes. Clearly, perspective is critical to an understanding of both the nature of the violence and how governments respond. For example, the ''official'' interpretation of the violence determines the lead agency in managing the events, although others may interpret the nature of the violence differently. When the bombing in Atlanta's Centennial Olympic Park was judged to be terrorism, the FBI became the lead agency for the investigation and for maintaining security against other potential attacks. While the use of a bomb triggered the federal lead, the designation of the act as terrorism triggered a shift in security agency leadership. The declaration that it was an act of terrorism solved a great many jurisdictional and functional issues.

The *revolution model* is a product of the national liberation war experience. That model reflects the assumptions that the terrorists have military as well as political objectives and that the violence will escalate if not countered. The latter assumption is that terrorism leads to guerrilla warfare and ultimately civil war, unless the authorities can effectively reduce the level of violence. The *civil disorder model* is a product of the political turmoil of the 1960s and reflects the notion that terrorism is simply an extension of legitimate dissent or an expression of extreme anger or frustration, while the *law enforcement model* offers the counterview that the violence is a challenge to government authority. Law enforcement officials typically recognize the challenge to authority but not the political nature of the acts (Waugh 1982, 1989b, 1990).

The *international conflict model* generally reflects a more ideological perspective on terrorist violence. It is generally assumed that the violence is sponsored by a nation or its supporters against a foreign government, business, or group. The assumption is that the violence is being perpetrated by others for ideological, economic, or other ''international'' reasons. The *human rights or repressive violence model* has generally been applied to violence used by government authorities or their agents against their own citizens. While we typically do not think of our government as terroristic, the antigovernment literature of many of the militia groups certainly suggests that they do perceive the national government in that way. Indeed, the violence by federal law enforcement agents against the Branch Davidians in Waco has become such a symbol for many extremist groups. Lastly, the *vigilante model* is a product of recent American and European experience with violence by ultra-conservative groups. Vigilanteeism presents an additional problem in that law enforcement officials and military personnel may also be associated with the violent groups or supportive of their objectives. The six models represent some of the interpretations of the violence that may influence actions.

The perspective of government officials—i.e., which model is chosen—has a profound impact on the design of antiterrorism policies and programs (Waugh 1982, 1989b, 1990). However, we should not assume that all terrorists are sponsored by foreign governments, desire to overthrow the government, or even intend long campaigns of violence. The fact that the terrorists may have legitimate political grievances should also be considered, because it may affect their internal and external resources, their persistence, and options to stop or reduce the violence.

A. Definitions of Terrorism

Notwithstanding differences in perspective, there are common elements in the definitions of terrorism used by most scholars, analysts, and policy makers. In general terms, the definitions usually suggest that terrorism involves:

1. The use or threat of extraordinary violence
2. Goal-directed (or rational) behavior
3. The intention to have a psychological impact beyond the immediate victims
4. The choice of victims for their symbolic value

That is, political ''terrorism is the use or credible threat of violence that is out of the ordinary, for political objectives, with an intended impact broader than the immediate victims (human or otherwise) who were chosen for their symbolic value'' (Waugh 1982: 27). A credible threat of violence is sufficient. More importantly, terrorism is goal-directed and hence rational behavior. While violent acts perpetrated by psychotic persons may appear terroristic, there has to be some intent to ''terrorize'' if it is to fit the definition. The choice of victims for their symbolic value establishes the underlying the rationality of the violent acts. Political terrorism is intended to communicate a threat of violence and a political message to influence the behavior of a target group, whether government officials, business persons, or members of minority groups. When victims are killed, they are not terrorized. Their deaths are meant to send a political message to the target group. Given those criteria, the nature of the Unabomber's campaign of violence might present some definitional confusion. The crucial question may be whether there was a target group that was terrorized in some manner by the threat of a bombing. The lack of a clear objective, i.e., the seeming irrationality, in the attacks clearly made it more difficult for law enforcement authorities to identify the bomber and made it unlikely that many potential targets actually felt threatened.

B. The Process of Terrorism

The general process of terrorism is illustrated in Figure 1. The process is essentially the same for kind of violence in each of the six models. There are three primary actors or sets of actors:

1. The terrorists
2. The victims (people, animals, buildings or other inanimate objects)
3. The targets of the threat and the political message

There are also three secondary actors or sets of actors:

1. The nontargeted domestic audience
2. The nontargeted international audience
3. The government or governments responsible for responding to the violence (whether they do or not)

One or more governments may have responsibility for responding based upon territorial jurisdiction over the events, nationality of the victims, legal jurisdiction based on something other than territory, or involvement in the event as a target, terrorist, or victim.

The process of terrorism has six elements:

1. The use or threat of violence
2. The threat of violence against the target group
3. The political message or action sought from the target group
4. The broader communication of the threat and political message to domestic and international audiences and to responsible governments
5. The reaction of the target group to the threat and the political message (e.g.,

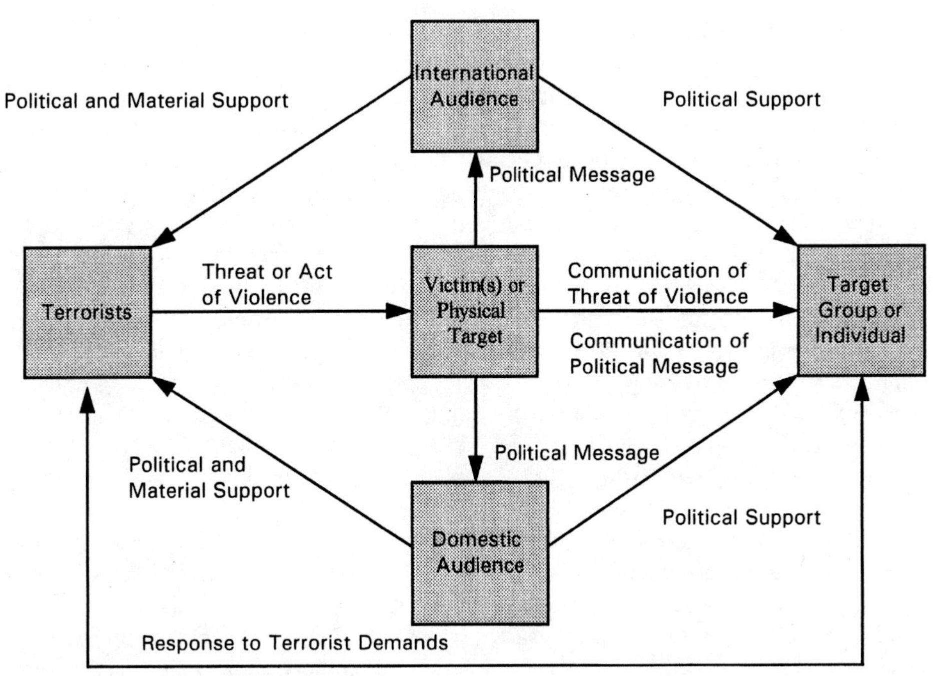

Note: Adapted from Waugh, 1982, 1990.

Figure 1 The Process of Terrorism

compliance with the terrorists' demands, change in policy, or change in personnel)

6. The reaction of the responsible government to the conflict between the terrorists and the targets (e.g., expressions of support for one side or the other, apathy, or interventions in the conflict)

C. Theories of Response

Prescriptions for how to deal with terrorist violence can generally be categorized as recommendations to:

1. Eliminate the causes of the violence
2. Increase the costs of using terrorism
3. Deny terrorists the benefits they seek

Addressing terrorists' legitimate grievances, i.e., alleviating economic or political or social conditions that cause frustration and violence, is seldom mentioned as a policy alternative. However, logic suggests that authorities should be aware of and responsive to the precipitants of terrorist violence, including the validity of the terrorists' complaints. While terrorism is generally considered an illegitimate practice, the political objectives of terrorists may be legitimate. As a practical matter, it may be easier to address the causes of terrorism than it is to eliminate the terrorists forcibly. In fact, terrorists with clearly legitimate causes are more likely to receive support from international and domestic sources and therefore should be more difficult to apprehend. Also, not all terrorists seek to overthrow the government. The common wisdom has generally been to separate the achievement of political objectives from the violence, so that the terrorists are not seen as winning concessions through their acts.

Perhaps because of the dominance of the law enforcement and military or "national liberation" perspectives, the most frequently chosen policy option is to increase the costs of using terrorism. The first priority is to deny terrorists the opportunity to commit acts of violence against their targets. While it is impossible to secure all possible targets, the most probable targets or victims can usually be identified if the terrorists' objectives can be determined. The second priority is to increase the costs of committing acts of terrorism by forcing terrorists to choose more risky and more resource intensive tactics. Strong security procedures increase the danger to terrorists, for example. Reducing access to automatic weapons, reducing availability of bomb-making materials, inhibiting transfers of money and other resources, and restricting travel can increase the logistical costs to terrorist organizations. But, there may be other tradeoffs that are more disruptive than the terrorists acts themselves. Strict security measures may well interfere with the freedoms of the other members of society.

One way to increase the costs of using terrorism is to assure that terrorists are punished. Effective law enforcement—i.e., the apprehension of terrorists and their supporters—reduces the scarce human resources in terrorist organizations. However, apprehending terrorists is not easy. Terrorists often, although not always, find support among those with similar views. Mechanisms for international apprehension of terrorists are often lacking. Indeed, extradition treaties are generally bilateral and many nations have very strong traditions of granting political asylum to those branded as terrorists by other nations. The principle of *aut punire aut dedere*, that all nations should try terrorists or extradite them to a nation that will, is not as widely supported as U.S. officials would like. Moreover, the likelihood of concerted international action to assure the punishment of terrorists is not promising given the differences in how terrorism may be defined. Much more success has been realized when there has been general agreement on the outlawing of particular tactics, such as attacks against international aviation or diplomatic personnel and facilities. Recent captures of international terrorists have essentially been accomplished through kidnapping, although there have seldom been complaints by the governments with jurisdiction. It should also be noted that such "arrests" can become sensitive diplomatic issues. Few nations will officially tolerate trespassing by foreign law enforcement, military, or intelligence officials.

The third priority or option is to deny terrorists the benefits of their violence. U.S. and Israeli policies of "no negotiation, no compromise" are based upon this idea, although compromises have been made, particularly by the U.S. government, when the compromise could be made without publicity. Ransoms have been paid and other demands have been met in some cases. The denial of benefits is perhaps most often associated with responses to international terrorism. Because the "unit of analysis" in international affairs is nations, individual human lives are not given as much weight in the calculus of foreign policy as they are in domestic antiterrorist policy. Therefore, it is far easier for national officials to argue against making concessions than it is for local officials to do so (although it is generally easier to make concessions during international terrorist events when they are not made public).

To deny terrorists the benefits they seek also presupposes that their objectives can be identified. Denial of the tactical objectives—usually money, prisoner releases, publicity, and/or safe passage/asylum—can reduce the ability of the organization to operate.

Denial of the strategic objectives (publicity, punishment, organizational imperatives, provocation, disruption, and/or instrumental gains) can reduce the effectiveness of the organization. And denial of the ideological or ultimate objectives of the terrorists can undermine the groups' political reason for being (Waugh 1982, 1983).

In some measure, the descriptions of the theories of response are oversimplifications, and there are certainly many more policy options associated with each. But the brief descriptions provide some background for understanding how governments and other agencies can intervene in the process of terrorism to eliminate the causes of the violence, increase the costs of using terrorism, and deny terrorists the benefits they seek. It should also be noted that more than one approach may be necessary to provide an effective response to terrorism.

D. Intervening in the Process of Terrorism

The six models of terrorism offer a variety of alternative policy options to intervene in the process and alter the effect sought by the terrorists. The intervention model in Figure 2 suggests that the process of terrorism can be interrupted and, perhaps, disrupted by effective antiterrorism policies. Governments might adopt some or all of the intervention strategies, depending upon the level of the threat, legal and political factors, and resource constraints. Other options are also possible.

The risk that terrorism poses must be assessed as it would be for other types of hazards, focusing on the probability of a disaster and its potential intensity. Risk assessment has to take into consideration whether the political milieu is supportive of terrorists,

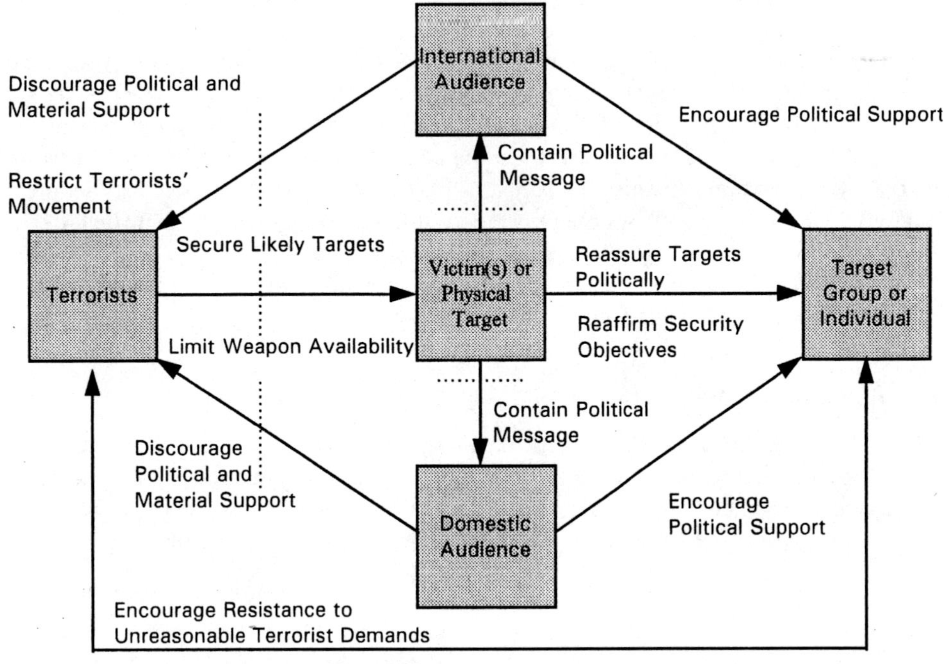

Note: Adapted from Waugh, 1982,1990.

Figure 2 Intervening in the Process of Terrorism

the opportunities for terrorists to access potential targets, indicators of increased terrorist activity (e.g., bank robberies, thefts of weapons, etc.), and so on. As with natural and technological hazards, the risk to a particular community may be so low that little investment in emergency management programs or increased investment in basic law enforcement programs is warranted. Expense is a practical concern that cannot be ignored in the design of antiterrorism policies and programs. For that reason, programs that can be used for other kinds of environmental hazards would be most appropriate at the local and regional levels. Most communities will have little use for a stand-alone, dedicated antiterrorism program unless the resources can be brought to bear in other kinds of disasters.

III. INTEGRATING EMERGENCY MANAGEMENT AND ANTITERRORISM POLICY MODELS

The application of the comprehensive emergency management models to terrorism-related hazards and disasters is somewhat complicated by the ambiguous nature of the phenomenon of terrorism. Perspective is all important. Nonetheless, if the risk of large-scale terrorist events justifies significant investment in antiterrorism programs, attention must be given to investments in preparedness, mitigation, response, and recovery as well as in law enforcement or military response. By their very nature, large-scale, mass casualty events can become much more than law enforcement problems. Concerns with minimizing secondary damage, restoring lifelines, reducing the likelihood of future damage, and helping communities recover may well overshadow the pursuit of the terrorists. To the extent that law enforcement agencies may be designated as the lead agencies in such events, there may be serious problems getting officials to focus on the broader issues of response and recovery and to assure attention to the need to implement mitigation programs following the disasters. The criticism directed against the Federal Aviation Administration (FAA) and other federal agencies involved in the investigation of the TWA Flight 800 tragedy off Long Island is a case in point. The slow recovery of bodies angered family members, drew political criticism, and demonstrated the conflicts that may arise between response and recovery functions. Even in the preparedness phase, security priorities may interfere with safety and emergency response priorities. Indeed, studies of security in nuclear facilities by the U.S. General Accounting Office have found that security procedures often prove to be impediments to effective firefighting and other emergency responses. Sorting out the priorities is a central concern for emergency managers.

A. A Comprehensive Emergency Management Model for Terrorism

The outline of a comprehensive emergency management system based on the four-phase model and the policy intervention model follows. The outline is tentative in that more programmatic elements can certainly be added within each phase depending upon the assessment of risk, the kinds of terrorism that might reasonably be expected, and the available resources.

B. Mitigation of Terrorist Violence

Mitigating terrorist violence is no small task because such violence may occur almost anywhere and at any time. However, to the extent that terrorist objectives are known, many potential targets can be anticipated. As a practical matter, terrorist organizations tend to have a limited repertoire of techniques—e.g., bombing or assassination or hijacking—and those limitations help identify possible or likely targets.

Responsibility for antiterrorism programs rests with a variety of federal, state, and local government agencies as well as a with a number of quasi-governmental and nongovernmental entities. A comprehensive antiterrorism program necessarily would involve participants drawn from organizations ranging from general-purpose governments to independent government agencies and from international organizations to business firms and private humanitarian organizations. Each may interpret the violent events differently and respond according to their own perceptions of the violence.

The initial goal in mitigation programs is generally to prevent disaster from occurring. Few analysts and officials suggest letting terrorists achieve their objectives, because it is felt that that this might only encourage further violence. Nonetheless, eliminating the precipitants of terrorist violence, particularly when the goals are legitimate, may be the easiest and most effective course of action (Waugh 1982, 1983, 1990). That is certainly an underlying assumption of the "civil disorder" model of terrorism (Waugh, 1989). In fact, the principal impediment to concerted international action to reduce the hazard of terrorism has been the opinion of many members of the U.N. General Assembly that it is legitimate to use violence to combat racism, colonialism, imperialism, and other forms of oppression and domination. They argue that those conditions themselves constitute acts of terrorism. Some nations, such as France and Mexico, have strong traditions of support for revolutionaries. National mythology, ideological sympathy, and romantic images encourage tolerance if not support for terrorists. That is no less true in the United States. Patriotic themes and romantic views of American history are certainly common in the extremist literature. Consequently, while agreement on a definition of terrorism may yet be elusive, some attention to the legitimacy of political demands is necessary.

With that caveat in mind, mitigation programs can also focus on cultivating a climate hostile to terrorists. International treaties can:

1. Interfere with the transfer of arms, munitions, moneys, and other critical materials to terrorist organizations
2. Deny terrorists safe staging areas outside of the target nation
3. Discourage active governmental and private support for terrorist organizations
4. Provide for the trial or extradition of terrorists (the principle of *aut punire aut dedere*)

Domestically, interventions can utilize structural or engineering approaches and/or regulatory and planning approaches, including programs to:

1. Identify terrorists and their likely targets so that antiterrorism resources can be better targeted
2. Assess the vulnerability of potential targets and facilitate preparedness and mitigation programs
3. Provide technical assistance to improve the response and recovery capabilities of responsible agencies (FEMA 1987)
4. Cultivate strong working relationships with individuals, agencies, and governments involved in antiterrorism efforts (FEMA 1987)
5. Lessen the availability of arms, explosive, and other materials that may be used by terrorists

6. Monitor and control the movement of people across national borders, particularly when they are suspected terrorists or are traveling to locales that might be targeted by terrorists
7. Monitor large transfers of money and thefts of weapons and other supplies that may presage terrorist violence or be used to support terrorist organizations
8. Secure the most likely targets and reduce the opportunity to attack other potential targets

This list is certainly not exhaustive. Infiltration of terrorist groups, close surveillance of suspected terrorists, preventive detention as used in Great Britain against the IRA in the 1970s (Wilkinson 1977:194), preemptive strikes against terrorists and their bases as used in Lebanon by the Israelis, and other actions may be necessary if the risk is sufficiently great. Structural approaches, including designing buildings to facilitate surveillance and to restrict access, are gaining in popularity. Bomb threats in airports were reduced significantly when luggage lockers were moved to less crowded areas or removed altogether. Some policy options may be that logical and simple.

C. The Reality of Mitigation Programs

As with emergency management programs for other kinds of hazards, mitigation efforts will likely be of little concern to communities that either have little risk or do not perceive a significant risk of terrorism. Like other emergency management programs, antiterrorism programs generally lack strong administrative and political constituencies. As the memory of disaster fades, so does the public's willingness to invest tax dollars in programs to address the problem. In other words, although some police departments may be willing to invest scarce resources in training and maintaining specialized antiterrorist units, the community and its officials may not be willing to do so.

Resistance to terrorism hazard mitigation programs may be greatest among those concerned about the political, social, economic, and legal implications of such programs. The current debate over the accessibility of military assault rifles and the opposition to tagging explosives and their components to help identify manufacturers are illustrative of the resistance to regulations in the United States. Restrictions on freedom of movement and other behaviors that may help terrorist organizations are similarly resisted. Structural mitigation programs may be more easily implemented, but they can also be quite expensive. Fortunately, as in the case of airport security measures, although the public may object to the inconvenience at first, they eventually get used to it. At some point, however, the cure can become worse than the disease. In the absence of a serious terrorism problem, strong security measures are difficult to justify.

Terrorism may present technical problems for responding authorities as well. The kinds of antiterrorism expertise that are needed depend upon the kinds of acts that may occur. Nuclear, biological, and chemical threats would present major problems for all concerned, but most especially the emergency medical system personnel. Less sophisticated bombs and other armed attacks would be far easier to handle by current emergency medical systems. While a range of capabilities, an all-hazards approach, is logical, the capacities of the "first responders" are critical.

There is also considerable expertise for hire, to develop preparedness and mitigation programs, and to staff antiterrorism units. But, it is important to be sensitive to the nature of the antiterrorism industry and its vested interests in both the definition of the problem and the policy options considered. Former military and law enforcement officers, as well as entrepreneurs of other persuasions, offer programs that may or may not address the kinds of hazards that terrorism poses. Experience with the kind of violence that may be anticipated is critical, as is broad civilian emergency management experience.

D. Preparedness for Terrorist Violence and Disasters

The required level of preparedness is dependent upon the level of risk. Once the hazard is known, the process of developing capability assessments, including resource inventories and testing plans, is much the same as it might be for a natural disaster. Terrorists typically choose targets that offer minimal hazard to themselves and prefer locales in which they will not be conspicuous. Airports, large cities, major events, resorts, large buildings, and busy venues are inviting targets. Crowds, particularly crowds of tourists, can camouflage terrorist activity (see, e.g., Richter and Waugh 1986). Fragile and critical life support systems—such as power, water, communication, and transportation networks—are also inviting. Intelligence gathering may further focus the security effort and help anticipate the nature and intensity of possible terrorist attacks.

After the identification of hazards, a comprehensive preparedness program for terrorism-related risks or hazards would include the development of the following:

1. Operation plans for the emergency response by police (and/or military) and other public safety and emergency management personnel, including plans for the utilization of volunteer groups that may also respond to the emergency
2. An emergency management organization with designated lead agencies, cooperative agreements, and mechanisms for liaison and coordination to carry out the plans
3. A resource inventory and management plan to utilize the full range of public, private, and nonprofit sector resources
4. An administrative structure to manage the law enforcement response (likely directed by the lead law enforcement agency)
5. An administrative structure to coordinate the broader emergency management effort (likely directed by the responsible emergency management agency)
6. An emergency communications network to tie together the emergency management organization
7. Alert and warning systems
8. A public information mechanism
9. A plan for the continuity of government, to assure consistent and continuing control of the emergency management efforts, as well as to assure the performance of other necessary governmental functions
10. An appropriate evacuation plan
11. Training and education programs to assure that emergency personnel are adequately prepared to respond to a potential disaster
12. Exercises and drills so that the plans and organizational arrangements can be tested and changed when necessary (Adapted from McLoughlin 1985; Waugh 1990.)

E. The Reality of Disaster Preparedness

Planning for emergency response involves a variety of agencies and jurisdictions; therefore planners must anticipate coordination problems. As with other kinds of disasters, local authorities are generally the first responders and should have central roles in the response plan. The coordination of multiorganizational and intergovernmental responses may be the single most difficult task for emergency managers. The experience with the Atlanta Olympic Games demonstrated that it was more difficult to coordinate the larger military and police effort with the private security and volunteer security organizations than it was to secure facilities and protect VIPs.

Here, too, there are no strong administrative and political constituencies to lobby for preparedness efforts. An adequate operational capability will be dependent upon federal and state funding and technical assistance. Local self-reliance is not a realistic option and new technologies and tactics are only slowly transferred to the front-line agencies. Local officials in the United States simply do not see terrorism as a major threat to their communities (Waugh and Nigro 1998; Nigro and Waugh 1999). The adaptation of other emergency management programs to the management of the hazard of terrorism, therefore, is all the more important.

F. Responding to Terrorist Events

Just as much of the public sees the function of emergency management largely as disaster response, without considering the efforts that should precede and follow that effort, the view of antiterrorist programs tends to focus on the police or military response to the terrorists themselves. Comparatively little attention is paid to the need for a more comprehensive response, including resolving the crisis if it is continuing, reducing the impact of the violence on the targets and other audiences, reducing the danger to public health and safety, and providing immediate care to those injured. The full range of response programs, from evacuation of threatened populations to provision of temporary shelter, may be necessary in large-scale terrorist events. Generally speaking, the lead law enforcement agencies are ill prepared to coordinate those operations and may not appreciate the importance of actions that emergency managers recommend.

G. The Reality of Emergency Response

Terrorism gets the public's attention. As a rule, overreaction is a bigger problem than apathy. Political and administrative constituencies for disaster response are not hard to find once the terrorists have struck. Indeed, terrorist organizations often attempt to provoke an overreaction as a means of discrediting the government and causing a public panic (Waugh 1983). Governments, too, may use the threat of terrorism as an excuse to abridge civil liberties and to silence political opponents (Waugh 1982). As in the case of natural hazards, the public is more supportive of regulatory actions that are credible responses to identifiable hazards. Scientific evidence is more credible than political rhetoric, but the latter can provoke public hysteria if not well considered. Accurate communication of the threat to the public is all important. This is no less true in responses to terrorism than it is in responses to hurricanes, earthquakes, and other disasters.

Here, too, multiorganizational and intergovernmental responses may be the largest problem for emergency managers. Terrorist violence poses particular problems because of the legally mandated lead role for federal agencies. The 1996 Antiterrorism Act makes the FBI the lead agency once the violence is judged to be terrorism. In some measure that clarifies federal agency roles, but the determination itself can complicate the roles of other government agencies. The Atlanta Centennial Park bombing is a case in point. Federal jurisdiction was assured by virtue of it being a bombing, but the relationships among the lead agency and the supporting cast was based upon the newly mandated structure for dealing with terrorist events. Actions to secure the park, preserve evidence, and investigate the bombing had broad implications for the games themselves. A decade earlier, the British government was heavily criticized for using military forces to secure Heathrow Airport from IRA attacks because of the potential damage to the tourism industry.

It is far easier to assign responsibility for hazards or disasters on the basis of geography. While terrorists may cross borders and acts of terrorism may affect a large number of jurisdictions, the American legal system still largely assigns jurisdiction to local authorities unless the case involves a kidnapping, bombing, or bank robbery. However, as first responders, small community public safety offices may have to handle cases of terrorism until help arrives. It cannot be assumed that trained and experienced antiterrorism units and national and regional or state emergency management officials can be mobilized quickly enough to intervene before critical decisions have to be made. The success or failure of the response may well rest with local authorities and be dependent upon their capacities to handle crisis events. In effect, to the extent that small communities are prepared for disasters of any kind, they need and likely have some capacity to respond to terrorism-related disasters. Local authorities need to be prepared to respond to a wide range of possible disasters and, although nuclear, biological and chemical disasters (or similarly exotic or large-scale disasters) may quickly outstrip their resources and capabilities, they will have at least some procedures that can be adapted to the demands of the terrorist event.

The key may be in separating the law enforcement function of dealing directly with the terrorists from the emergency management function of dealing with the disaster. Once a large-scale, mass-casualty event has occurred, the disaster response should take precedence over the issue of dealing with the terrorists. Indeed, if a nuclear device is set off, the medical response should necessarily guide all other efforts.

H. Recovering from Terrorist-Sponsored Disasters

Recovery is seldom a topic in the discussion of antiterrorism policies. There is a small literature on the emergency medical aspects of terrorist violence, but it is uncertain how that might differ from medical responses to other kinds of disasters (except in terms of scale). Fortunately, there have been relatively few large-scale, mass-casualty terrorist events in the United States. The response and recovery efforts following the Murrah Federal Office Building bombing are testament to the adaptability of normal emergency management procedures to terrorist events. In large measure, the response was similar to that of a structural failure. The nature of the injuries and the number of deaths were similar. The need for psychological counseling for victims and their families and for responders, employment assistance for survivors, and other longer-term recovery programs was similar. Nonetheless, there are striking differences in how victims, emergency responders, and the general public feel about the tragedy. Being bombed by other Americans is not the same as being victimized by seismic forces or meteorological phenomena, even if the casualty rate is the same. The psychological impact of the Oklahoma City bombing has not yet been fully realized.

Without speculating too much about the hazard that terrorism poses, we are almost certain to experience terrorist events with more casualties and even a broader geographic impact than the World Trade Center and Murrah Office Building bombings. Recovery efforts may require sheltering, feeding, and caring for thousands or even hundreds of thousands of victims. The scale of such scenarios may well be similar to our experiences with hurricanes and earthquakes. While our current capabilities can certainly be brought to bear in such events, continuing violence, nuclear or biological or chemical contamination, or severely damaged lifelines may complicate the recovery process. However, as with any other catastrophic disaster, ad hoc programs are implemented, procedures are adapted, and national or even international assistance is sought. Emergency management, by its nature, is adaptive.

I. The Reality of Disaster Recovery

One of the truisms of emergency management is that recovery programs enjoy the public support that mitigation and preparedness programs do not. Conflict over how to recover is common, however. Financial gain is the usual motivation, but terrorist violence can provide partisan gain for those desiring change. Emergency managers have to get used to charges that evacuations were made too soon or not soon enough, that mitigation programs are too expensive or too difficult to implement, and so on. Terrorism is an intensely political phenomenon. Racially motivated violence has been tolerated, even condoned, by authorities in some communities. Antiabortion violence has been tolerated and even condoned by some. Violence of the right and the left has been tolerated at one time or another in the United States. There is also very strong pressure to respond with force. The hard-line "no negotiation, no compromise" policy, for example, can complicate response and recovery efforts and may well interfere with the resolution of hostage events and cost lives (Waugh 1990).

Recovery efforts can overwhelm the capacities of local authorities, and that is no less true of programs that follow terrorist-sponsored disasters. Fragmented government responsibility complicates recovery. The fact that recovery programs are often designed in response to specific disasters, rather than in anticipation of the next (May and Williams 1986), also complicates recovery efforts. Fortunately, the images or memories of disaster give the programs credibility and salience. It is very difficult to deny aid to a stricken community. All of this is to say that we probably do not need specially designed recovery programs for terrorist events unless nuclear, biological, or chemical threats are expected. We have scenarios that range from relatively minor calamities to society-disrupting cataclysms, so we already have a broad range of capabilities and resources.

IV. THE NEED FOR A COMPREHENSIVE EMERGENCY MANAGEMENT APPROACH TO THE HAZARD OF TERRORISM

The thesis of this analysis has been that an emergency management approach to the problem of terrorism may provide a framework for a more comprehensive and effective policy. Framing the problem of terrorism in terms of its broader potential impact does suggest that the design of policy and the structures of response should be significantly different than those common today. There have been a number of major impediments to the design of effective policy. First, emergency management, including management of the hazard of terrorism, has been perceived largely as a response process. Second, the function of emergency management has suffered from its association with civil defense programs and, similarly, antiterrorism programs have been defined by their association with the military and law enforcement activities designed to resolve the incidents. In both cases, public officials and the public at large have been slow to see the functions in terms of their broader implications and impacts, and that predisposition to define the problem in limited terms has led them to believe that simple, limited responses will be adequate.

An assumption in the analysis has also been that the organizational context of our antiterrorism policies and programs limits their flexibility and predisposes us to certain kinds of responses. In short, we may have institutionalized solutions that are both ineffective and inappropriate given the level of threat posed by terrorists. The emergency management framework is offered as a vehicle for redefining the policy problem and the models of terrorism are offered to suggest that we need different policies based on the kinds of hazard that the violence presents. The problem of terrorism should be disassembled, in other words, and we should design policy to fit each kind of terrorist violence.

A. Terrorism and the Emergency Management Perspective

The emergency management perspective is valuable for several reasons. Terrorism is somewhat unpredictable and may vary considerably in intensity. The level of preparation necessarily should address worst-case scenarios, within reason, that are more comparable to our experience with natural hazards. The all-hazards emergency management model focuses on a broad range of activities that may be required to mitigate, prepare for, respond to, and recover from the effects of a catastrophic terrorist incident, rather than only on the resolution of the conflict with the terrorists. Application of the model also requires attention to the need to assess both the hazard and organizational capabilities in order to address the hazard effectively. Moreover, the routinization of antiterrorism programs would help resolve some of the jurisdictional issues and coordinate multiorganizational and intergovernmental efforts. Most importantly, the agencies responsible for antiterrorist responses should also be required to consider the implications of their actions for hazard mitigation and recovery.

The emergency management perspective may also suggest other solutions to the problem of terrorism. To the extent that terrorists seem more willing today to kill and maim large numbers of people, emergency managers may become the last line of defense. More attention to mitigation programs, such as security-sensitive construction and attention to grievances that may lead to violence, would also be beneficial. The approach may also offer a clearer set of policy objectives. Certainly shifting organizational control from military and law enforcement agencies to civilian agencies may have a significant impact on policy and new organizational arrangements may suggest new solutions. Diplomacy, rather than authoritarian leadership, is associated with effective emergency management (Drabek 1987; Waugh 1993).

B. The Models of Terrorism and Policymaking

It is also suggested that the perspective that one has on terrorism reflects fundamental assumptions about the nature and course of the violence. The assumptions may be accurate or not. We should be very certain that we have an accurate assessment of the threat that terrorism poses to the United States. The very existence of some regimes and nations is threatened by terrorism. That is not the case in the United States. Our government is less vulnerable to disruption and our society is more resilient. Also, to respond militarily to terrorist violence elevates the status of the terrorists. To respond by using law enforcement agencies alone defines the problem as a police matter. An appropriate response is essential.

C. An Emergency Management Framework for Antiterrorism Programs

An initial conclusion is that we should consider the need for disaster preparedness, hazard or risk mitigation, and disaster recovery as well as emergency response in the design of our antiterrorism policies. The all-hazards model provides ample framework for a comprehensive policy, including provisions to assess, maintain, and upgrade capabilities. The major problems are coordinating the multiorganizational and intergovernmental efforts and assuring an adequate capability among the potential first responders—the local agencies.

Overcoming the obstacles to effective action will not be easy. While terrorism has had considerable salience as an issue over the past three decades, that public interest has tended to wane during periods of relative inactivity. The public has apparently adjusted to the security programs at airports and in public buildings, albeit with only occasional demonstrations of frustration. That familiarity, however, breeds complacency and educational campaigns are necessary to renew understanding of the danger of terrorism and the nature of antiterrorism technologies. The level of public interest in antiterrorism programs, too, may wane as the salience of national security issues wane. Recent changes in the relations between East and West are leading to debates in western Europe and the United States, as well as elsewhere, concerning levels of defense spending. Tying antiterrorism programs to broader emergency management programs may well increase the salience of all the programs.

Another reason that the emergency management approach may be helpful is that it broadens the political and administrative constituencies for antiterrorism programs. If terrorism is viewed as a common environmental hazard involving political leaders and professional emergency managers at all levels of government rather than as a federal problem, antiterrorism programs will rest on a firmer political base. A broader intergovernmental effort may also reduce friction among the responsible agencies and increase state and local capacities to address the hazard. Coupled with adequate technical assistance, training, and fiscal transfers, capacity-building can also benefit other emergency management functions.

None of this is to say that terrorism does not pose unique emergency management problems. Hazard reduction may well require addressing problems of poverty, political frustration, and simply anger. In that regard, viewing the hazard reduction effort in the context of federal, state, and local social and economic programs may be helpful. Just as emergency managers should be at least consulted as part of a community's land-use planning and building code administration efforts, they might also be kept apprised of policies and programs that affect the social well-being of the community. When factory closings and reductions-in-force in local government agencies can create potentially violent situations, a broad understanding of social and economic forces is necessary.

The political nature of terrorism also poses problems. Natural and man-made disasters attract political figures seeking to enhance their images as decisive, effective, and even brave leaders. That does not make terrorist events unique, but the actions of political leaders and the media may exacerbate the problems of response and recovery to a greater extent than they might in other kinds of disasters. Presidents have generally learned to delegate crisis management responsibility to appropriate professionals, but governors and mayors have been slow to learn that lesson. The attention of political leaders may be exactly what the terrorists seek. While there is a political imperative for leaders to appear strong and decisive and the public may wish to see its leaders out front despite the costs, officials have to understand the nature of the hazard and the risks involved.

The principal recommendation is that emergency management officials be given the lead responsibility for managing the hazard of terrorism, if the scope of the hazard warrants, and that the law enforcement and national security authorities be responsible for resolving immediate crises. In essence, the recommendation is to separate the emergency management coordination function from the law enforcement or military response. The challenge is to design a mechanism that permits the emergency management agency to coordinate the programs without necessarily controlling the direct response to the terrorists. Law enforcement is one of several response agencies, in other words.

V. SUMMARY

In summary, terrorism is a growing environmental hazard. While terrorist incidences have tended to be cyclic and the motivations of terrorists have changed over the past 50 years, the utility of terrorism is easy to understand. It works or, at least, it has worked for some groups. For policy makers, some of the causes are understood, such as frustrations over social change and economic suffering and anger associated with political intolerance and racism, but there may be no solutions for those problems. To the extent that it is a natural political hazard, it has to be understood. To the extent that it is a social and political phenomenon, it has to be addressed broadly. To the extent that it poses a potentially catastrophic risk to large segments of our society, it has to be managed comprehensively.

REFERENCES

Comfort, L.K., ed. (1988). *Managing Disaster: Strategies and Policy Perspectives.* Durham, NC: Duke University Press.

Dery D. (1984). *Problem Definition in Policy Analysis*, with an Introduction by A Wildavsky. Lawrence, KS: University of Kansas Press.

Drabek T.E. (1987). *The Professional Emergency Manager: Structures and Strategies for Success.* Program on Environment and Behavior Monograph No. 44. Boulder, CO: University of Colorado, Institute of Behavioral Science.

Drabek T.E., Tansminga H., Kilijanik T., Adams C. (1981). *Managing Multiorganizational Emergency Responses.* Publication No. 6. Boulder, CO: University of Colorado, Institute of Behavioral Science.

May P.J., Williams W. (1986). *Disaster Policy Implementation: Managing Programs Under Shared Governance.* New York: Plenum Press.

Nigro L.G., Waugh W.L. Jr. (1998). *Workplace Violence in American City and County Governments: Municipal Yearbook 1998.* Washington, DC: International City/County Management Association.

Richter L.K., Waugh W.L. Jr. (1986). Terrorism and tourism as logical companions. *Tourism Mgt.* December, 230–238.

Sylves R.T., Waugh W.L. Jr., eds. (1990). *Cities and Disaster: North American Studies in Emergency Management.* Springfield, IL: Charles C. Thomas Publishers.

Waugh W.L. Jr. (1982). *International Terrorism: How Nations Respond to Terrorists.* Chapel Hill, NC: Documentary Publications.

Waugh W.L. Jr. (1983). The values in violence: Organizational and political objectives of terrorist groups. *Conflict Q* 3(4), Summer, 1–19.

Waugh W.L. Jr. (1989a). Integrating the policy models of terrorism and emergency management. *Policy Studies Review* 12(3), Fall, 287–300.

Waugh W.L. Jr. (1989b). Informing policy and administration: A comparative perspective on terrorism. *Int J Public Admin* 2(4), 12.

Waugh W.L. Jr. (1993). Co-ordination or control: Organizational design and the emergency management function. *Int J Disaster Prev Mgt* 2(*December*), 17–31.

Waugh W.L. Jr. (1996). Emergency management for the new millennium. In: R.T. Sylves, W.L. Waugh, eds. *Disaster Management in the US and Canada*, 2nd ed. Springfield, IL: Charles C. Thomas Publishers.

Waugh W.L. Jr., Nigro L.G. (1999). Dealing with workplace violence in georgia's cities and counties. *Public Admin Mgt* Vol. 4, No. 3 <http://www.pamij.com/99_4_3_Waugh.html>

Waugh W.L. Jr., Hy R.J., eds. (1990). *Handbook of Emergency Management.* Westport, CT: Greenwood Press.

41

Planning for Weapons of Mass Destruction/Nuclear, Biological, and Chemical Agents

A Local/Federal Partnership

Frances E. Winslow Office of Emergency Services, City of San José, San José, California

I. THE SETTING

For many years Americans have considered terrorism an activity that takes place abroad, typified by events like the IRA bombings in London. However, changes in domestic politics have made it clear that terrorist events can occur within the United States. The Federal Bureau of Investigation (FBI) defines terrorism as ''the unlawful use of force against persons or property to intimidate or coerce a government, the civilian population, or any segment thereof, in furtherance of political or social objectives'' (FEMA 1996). Events such as the bombing of the World Trade Center in New York and the Murrah Federal Building in Oklahoma City demonstrate that domestic terrorism is a real probability.

While the use of explosives has been a typical terrorist activity, both in the United States and in other countries, the use of Sarin gas, a military weapon, in a Tokyo subway terrorist event, has demonstrated the need to also consider the possibility of civilian authorities having to response to terrorist events that involve the use of ''weapons of mass destruction,'' military chemicals, and weaponized biological agents with the power to affect thousands of people. Within the category of weapons of mass destruction (WMD) are three broad categories: nuclear, biological, and chemical, referred to as NBC agents. These WMD/NBC agents have the potential to create chaos within the civilian community, disable large numbers of police, fire and emergency medical personnel (first responders), and engender a major media event, thus highlighting the terrorist's ''cause'' (Nunn 1996).

II. FEDERAL RESPONSE: LEGISLATION AND DIRECTIVE

Recognizing that the former Soviet Union had control of numerous WMD/NBC agents and weapons, the House and Senate passed legislation in 1991 that was designed to ''support the destruction and deactivation of much of the former Soviet Union's nuclear arsenal. [At a cost of $400 million per year] . . . missiles . . . have been dismantled and stored . . . thousands of weapon scientists are now employed on civilian projects, and key nuclear facilities . . . have been made more secure'' (Selden, no date). This legislation was called the Nunn-Lugar program after the bill's co-sponsors: Senator Sam Nunn (D) of Georgia and Senator Richard Lugar (R) of Indiana. As a result of the success of this program, the threat of the proliferation of nuclear material from the former Soviet Union into the hands of terrorists or unfriendly nations was greatly reduced.

As a result of the government's analysis of the potential for terrorist events within the United States, Presidential Decision Directive (PDD) 39 was issued by President Bill Clinton on June 21, 1995. Its formal title is ''U.S. Policy on Counterterrorism.'' One segment, entitled ''Reducing Our Vulnerabilities,'' detailed the responsibilities of a variety of federal departments and agencies in the domestic counterterrorism effort. The FBI was mandated to be the lead agency for crisis management, and FEMA is the lead agency for consequence management. These agencies are directed to work with states to assure that their plans are adequate.

The last unclassified portion of PDD-39 focuses on weapons of mass destruction. It states, ''The United States shall give the highest priority to developing effective capabilities to detect, prevent, defeat and manage the consequences of nuclear, biological or chemical (NBC) materials or weapons use by terrorists.'' Funding for these activities was to come from agency budgets. Congressional budgetary processes apportioned the new support among 40 federal agencies ''eager for part of the billions of dollars that Congress began appropriating for anti-terrorism programs'' (Miller and Broad 1998). At this point the counterterrorism effort was a congressionally sponsored and managed program.

Under the Federal Fiscal Year 1997 Defense Authorization Bill (Public Law 104–201, September 23, 1996), funding was provided for the Department of Defense ''to enhance the capability of federal, state and local emergency responders in incidents involving nuclear, biological and chemical terrorism'' (Chemical Biological Defense Command, no date). This legislation is generally referred to as the Nunn-Lugar-Domenici Domestic Preparedness program, after its principal sponsors: Senators Nunn and Lugar and Senator Domenici of New Mexico. This legislation charges the army's Chemical Biological Defense Command (CBDCOM) with ''enhancing existing metropolitan response capabilities to include nuclear, chemical and biological incidents'' (Chemical Biological Defense Command, no date). This legislation, whose formal title is ''Defense Against Weapons of Mass Destruction Act of 1996,'' contains five subtitles: (1) Domestic Preparedness, (2) Interdiction of Weapons of Mass Destruction and Related Materials, (3) Control and Disposition of Weapons of Mass Destruction and Related Materials and Technologies Outside the United States, (4) Coordination of Policy and Countermeasures Against Proliferation of Weapons of Mass Destruction and Related Materials and Technologies, and (5) Miscellaneous. The descriptive portion of this paper will focus on the domestic preparedness initiative.

On April 10, 1998 President Clinton participated in discussions with seven scientists and cabinet members about the threats of bioterrorism. His interest in the subject was peaked by the book *The Cobra Event*, a fictional account of a biological attack against the United States. Informed sources stated that the panel urged the president to develop better response capacity for antidotes, vaccines and antibiotics; and a stronger medical surveillance system (Miller and Broad 1998). At this point the initiative in counterterrorism returned to the executive branch.

On May 22, 1998 President Clinton issued two additional presidential directives on counterterrorism topics: PDD 62 and 63. On the same day he articulated a new role for the National Guard, and he highlighted the defense against biological weapons in his commencement speech at the Naval Academy. The two new PDDs provide for two new approaches to counterterrorism.

PDD-62,the "Combating Terrorism" directive, according to a White House press release, "creates a new and more systematic approach to fighting the terrorist threat. . .." It addresses many agencies in the executive branch of government, bringing them into the program to apprehend and prosecute terrorists, increase transportation security, enhance response capabilities, and protect the computers "that lie at the heart of America's economy" (White House a 1998). Specifically, it establishes the Office of the National Coordinator for Security, Infrastructure Protection and Counter-Terrorism, to oversee "counter-terrorism, protection of critical infrastructure, preparedness and consequence management" for WMD events (White House a 1998). The office will also lead in the development of guidelines that might be needed for crisis management.

PDD-63 follows recommendations made by a Commission on Critical Infrastructure Protection that was convened in 1997. It "sets a goal of reliable, interconnected, and secure information system infrastructure by the year 2003, and significantly increased security to government systems by the year 2000 . . ." (White House b 1998). New initiatives include a National Infrastructure Protection Center in the FBI, and public-private partnerships for infrastructure security. Essential government services are included for development of heightened security.

As the Cold War wanes, National Guard units are seeking peacetime missions. On May 22, 1998, President Clinton delivered the commencement address at the Naval Academy, announcing that 10 states would get specially trained National Guard units "to help local and state officials respond to potential terrorist attacks with chemical, biological or even nuclear weapons" (USA Today 1998). Each unit will have 10 full-time and 10 reserve members, with a $49.2 million budget for their salaries, training, and equipment. According to Defense Secretary William Cohen, "The teams. . .will be able to deploy rapidly, assist local first responders in determining the nature of an attack, provide medical and technical advice, and pave the way" for other federal resources. Other reserve units will be trained to assist these 10 teams in reconnaissance and decontamination. Because of legal restrictions on the domestic role of military units, the Guard will be in a support role with local resources (USA Today 1998). Furthermore, the length of time required for deployment and employment of a Guard unit precludes a "first responder" role, as NBC agents wreak irreversible havoc within the first hour after an attack, a period when local officials may not yet have analyzed the evidence leading to a conclusion that the event is a WMD/NBC event. By the time a WMD/NBC event is confirmed, and a request for state resources is placed, assembly and travel time would place the Guard's arrival too late for its stated mission of providing analysis and advice.

In the same Naval Academy commencement speech the president announced that "we will undertake a concerted effort to prevent the spread and use of biological weapons," and that we will "pursue the fight against biological weapons on many fronts," including improvement of national medical surveillance, a widening of the initiative to prepare local first responders, and "the creation of stockpiles of medicines and vaccines to protect our civilian population against the kind of biological agents our adversaries are most likely to obtain or develop" (White House c 1998).

The two new PDD's, along with the new mission for the National Guard, provide additional support for the local first responder partnership, known as the Metropolitan Medical Strike Team/Metropolitan Medical Strike Team System, being developed under the Nunn-Lugar-Domenici Domestic Preparedness initiative.

III. DOMESTIC PREPAREDNESS PROGRAM

In order to create the capability to respond to WMD/NBC events at the local level, six federal agencies were designated to participate in the Nunn-Lugar-Domenici program. The Department of Defense, in conjunction with FEMA and the Department of Energy (DOE), is required by the Defense Against Weapons of Mass Destruction Act of 1996 to "establish a program to provide training and advice to federal, state and local officials

Table 1 Domestic Preparedness Initiative Cities

New York, NY	Minneapolis, MN	Grand Rapids, MI
Los Angeles, CA	Tulsa, OK	Yonkers, NY
Chicago, IL	Honolulu, HI	Hialeah, FL
Houston, TX	Cincinnati, OH	Montgomery, AL
Philadelphia, PA	Miami, FL	Lubbock, TX
San Diego, CA	Fresno, CA	Greensboro, NC
Detroit, MI	Omaha, NE	Dayton, OH
Dallas, TX	Toledo, OH	Huntington Beach, CA
Phoenix, AZ	Buffalo, NY	Garland, TX
San Antonio, TX	Wichita, KS	Glendale, CA
San Jose, CA	Santa Ana, CA	Columbus, OH
Baltimore, MD	Mesa, AZ	Spokane, WA
Indianapolis, IN	Colorado Springs, CO	Tacoma, WA
San Francisco, CA	Tampa, FL	Little Rock, AR
Jacksonville, FL	Newark, NJ	Bakersfield, CA
Columbus, GA	St. Paul, MN	Fremont, CA
Milwaukee, WI	Louisville, KY	Fort Wayne, IN
Memphis, TN	Anaheim, CA	Newport News, VA
Washington, DC	Birmingham, AL	Arlington, VA
Boston, MA	Arlington, TX	Worchester, MA
Seattle, WA	Norfolk, VA	Knoxville, TN
El Paso, TX	Las Vegas, NV	Modesto, CA
Cleveland, OH New	Corpus Christie, TX	Orlando, FL
Orleans, LA	St. Petersburg, FL	San Bernardino, CA
Nashville, TN	Rochester, NY	Syracuse, NY
Denver, CO	Jersey City, NJ	Providence, RI
Austin, TX	Riverside, CA	Salt Lake City, UT
Fort Worth, TX	Anchorage, AK	Huntsville, AL
Oklahoma City, OK	Lexington-Fayette, KY	Amarillo, TX
Portland, OR	Akron, OH	Springfield, MA
Kansas City, MO	Aurora, CO	Irving, TX
Long Beach, CA	Baton Rouge, LA	Chattanooga, TN
Tucson, AZ	Raleigh, NC	Chesapeake, VA
St. Louis, MO	Stockton, CA	Kansas City, KS
Charlotte, NC	Richmond, VA	Metaire, LA
Atlanta, GA	Shreveport, LA	Fort Lauderdale, FL
Virginia Beach, VA	Jackson, MS	Glendale, AZ
Albuquerque, NM	Mobile, AL	Warren, MI
Oakland, CA	Des Moines, IA	
Pittsburgh, PA	Lincoln, NE	
Sacramento, CA	Madison, WI	

responsible for crisis and consequence management in a nuclear, radiological, chemical or biological emergency. . . . Of the funds authorized for this purpose, a portion is to be transferred to the Public Health Service for medical response teams'' (Subtitle A, Section 1311). Thus, a new program was begun that created a partnership among six federal departments/agencies and local emergency responders and emergency managers. The federal partners are the Department of Defense (DoD), Department of Energy (DoE), Federal Bureau of Investigation (FBI), Public Health Service (PHS), Environmental Protection Agency (EPA), and Federal Emergency Management Agency (FEMA).

Twenty seven cities were selected to be part of this initial program. Unlike most federal programs, which require grant applications or some request to participate, the cities were selected at the federal level, and contacted in the spring of 1997 with the information that they were on the list. In April 1997 a meeting was held at Dulles International Airport in the suburbs of Washington, D.C., to announce this program to the participating cities. The notices were sent out less than 1 week in advance of the meeting date, resulting in a low level of participation by cities outside the eastern seaboard.

Faxes were sent to the mayors of the 27 cities, asking them to designate the principal point of contact for the program immediately. This procedure ignored the reality that many of the cities function under a city manager form of government. There was also no provision made for regional or state level coordination, even though several states had multiple cities in the first 27. For example, California has four: Los Angeles, San Diego, San Jose, and San Francisco. Later in Federal Fiscal Year 1998, a total of 120 cities were placed in the program (Table 1).

IV. FINANCIAL SUPPORT FOR COUNTERTERRORISM

Federal funds to support this domestic preparedness effort come from three sources, DoD, DHHS, and FBI, each with a slightly different set of goals and rules. Although the 120 cities are the same for the DoD and DHHS efforts, the FBI's program varies by region. The FBI is providing training and tabletop exercises to communities based on its intelligence about potential threats in a given region. Furthermore, the Office of Justice Programs grant program uses 120 entities, including counties as population entities, significantly changing the list of eligible communities.

The DoD had funding to create and deliver a set of ''train the trainer'' courses, written by consultants, to bring DoD training materials to the civilian level. These courses are designed to equip local government ''first responders'' with the tools to respond safely and to save the maximum number of victims of a WMD/NBC event. Courses include First Responder Awareness, Operations, Incident Command, Hazardous Materials Technician, Emergency Medical Technician, and Hospital Provider. These six courses are intended to be delivered to police, fire, and medical personnel, and emergency operations center staff. In addition, a course is being developed for the executive management of a community.

Before a city receives training, there is a 2-day meeting with representatives of the six federal partner agencies. Each agency outlines its responsibilities and its counterterrorism assets available to local government. The local government then outlines its current strengths and training needs. This meeting theoretically forms the basis for the week of train-the-trainer courses. There are 4 days of repeated delivery of the six courses. On the last day there is a tabletop exercise/facilitated discussion that includes all levels of WMD/

NBC response. Work groups for the breakout sessions include an incident site team, emergency operations center team, operational area team, regional/state team, and federal team. A scenario forms the basis for this last class, providing a learning model for all the participants.

The DoD recruits, trains, and pays for all the instructors and instructional materials for the train-the-trainer courses. In addition, there is $300,000 worth of instructional support material that is provided to the selected cities. The Standard Training Equipment Set of training aids includes audiovisual and written materials to support the six courses, simulators to train personnel to use various detection devices, a set of personal protective equipment, decontamination equipment, and detection equipment.

DoD has also created new resources to support the local counter-terrorism response: a web site, a specialized team and a helpline. There is a web site which outlines the resources, training, and future plans for local assistance in counter-terrorism: www.cbdcom.apgea.army.mil/Missions/dp/index.html.

Also supporting a local government's response is C/B-RRT: Chemical/Biological Rapid Response Team located on the East Coast. C/B-RRT is deployed to support the FBI and assist state and local responders "in the detection, neutralization, containment, dismantlement and disposal of weapons of mass destruction containing chemical, biological or related hazardous materials." (CBDCOM 1998) The basis of the team is the Army's Technical Escort Unit's Chemical Biological Response Teams. Tech Escort is deployed within 4 hours. Additional resources include U.S. Army Chemical Biological Defense Command, Aberdeen Proving Ground, Maryland; U.S. Army 52nd Ordnance Group; U.S. Army Medical research Institute for Infectious Diseases, Fort Detrick, Maryland; U.S. Army Medical Research Institute for Chemical Defense, Aberdeen Proving Ground, Maryland; U.S. Army Material Command Treaty Lab, CBDCOM, Aberdeen Proving Ground, Maryland; U.S. Navy Medical Research Institute, Bethesda, Maryland; U.S. Navy Environmental and Preventive Medicine Unit; and U.S. Naval Research Laboratory.

Another resource is a toll free Chemical/Biological HelpLine run by CBDCOM at Aberdeen Proving Ground. The number is available for first responders such as police, fire, hazardous materials technicians, emergency medical technicians, and emergency management officials. In addition, bomb squad members, dispatchers, and other support personnel may use the information line. Security of the information is assured through a call screening process. Information is available during nonemergency periods on preparedness. It is also available to support emergency personnel during a response. Toll-free phone lines, fax, e-mail and internet sites all support this effort (CBDCOM's web site).

The second source of funding for local government WMD/NBC preparedness is the Department of Health and Human Services (DHHS), managed by United States Public Health Service (PHS) officers. Recognizing that a major impact on medical facilities from victims of a WMD/NBC event would require assets with specialized training and equipment, DHHS was given funds to contract with 27 cities to create Metropolitan Medical Strike Teams (MMST) and the wider Metropolitan Medical Strike Team System (MMSTS). The contracts were made for an average of $350,000, with a planning standard of up to 1000 victims. The funds are designated for specific activities that will result in the creation of a local WMD/NBC emergency response capability. The MMST includes police personnel tasked with a search for secondary devices, security, crowd and traffic control, and evidence collection. It includes fire department personnel who are emergency medical technicians (EMTs), paramedics, hazardous materials technicians, and incident commanders. It also includes medical specialists who will research the signs and symptoms to determine the particular agent and the best antidotes/countermeasures. The wider system includes emergency medical transportation personnel, emergency medical care providers in hospitals, police and fire dispatchers, emergency public information officers, and emergency operations center leaders. The DoD courses provide the backbone of the training for this team.

In addition to the materials provided as part of the DoD training cache, the PHS funds will purchase specific types of support equipment, such as personnel protective equipment for first responders, detection equipment, decontamination equipment, specialized communication equipment, medical equipment, and pharmaceuticals. A PHS Project Officer is assigned to each of the 27 cities, to oversee the development of the MMST, its supporting plans, and the lists of goods to be purchased with DHHS funds. The allocation is roughly $100,000 for pharmaceuticals and $250,000 for equipment. No vehicles may be included.

In support of this system, a series of plan documents is required to be developed by the MMST. First there is a planning process, then a training plan, which includes the DoD training, but also covers ongoing training and refresher training. Third is a MMST/MMST System Plan which outlines the relationships among the various jurisdictions and occupational specialties within the community. Finally, specific lists of pharmaceuticals and equipment must be approved by the PHS Project Officer, along with custody plans for each group of equipment.

The third partner offering financial support to the counterterrorism effort is the FBI. They are offering competitive grants for an average of $250,000 per eligible jurisdiction (cities and counties), depending on the population size, for assets to support the multijurisdictional/multitask activities of the community in counterterrorism. Competitive grant applications for these funds may include a variety of goods not covered by the DHHS funds, such as law enforcement resources. One major city applied for funding to purchase personal protective equipment for the bomb squad that provides splash protection, inhalation protection and protection against explosives.

The FBI's primary role within the Nunn-Lugar-Domenici program's local preparedness element is as the principal trainer for the terrorism awareness portions of the courses. In addition to participating in the DoD training modules, the FBI provides its own briefings, and conducts tabletop exercises to develop integrated terrorism response plans. The issue of turn over of responsibility for the investigation and evidence collection at a terrorist event has been subject to some controversy in the past. However, the FBI's counter-terrorism plan includes a complementary role for local law enforcement, and the development of a Joint Operations Center that includes local participation (FBI).

V. DOMESTIC PREPAREDNESS PARTNER AGENCIES

The Department of Energy is a training partner. As the experts on nuclear materials, they offer specialized courses on managing both the victims and the community consequences of radiological or nuclear events. They presented a free conference in Washington, D.C. in September 1998 that covered a variety of planning, preparedness, and response skills.

The principal consequence management agency is FEMA. Originally it was envisioned that FEMA would manage a WMD event as it manages natural disasters. However, early in the planning stages it became clear that there may be a need to enhance FEMA's legal authority to spend funds for WMD/NBC consequence management. Currently, the Stafford Act provides the basis for most disaster assistance to affected communities. However, the Stafford Act does not provide for assistance in terrorist events, and it does not cover law enforcement activities. This is a dilemma that will require some consideration and legislative intervention, to assure that communities suffering a WMD/NBC event receive federal financial assistance for their response and recovery costs.

A. The Future of Sustained Response

The philosophy behind the Nunn-Lugar-Domenici program was the development of a permanent counterterrorism capability at the local level. In order to create this at the least cost, the ''delta'' concept was created for the delivery of training and equipment. The concept is that the federal partners will use their expertise and federal funds to enhance existing hazardous materials response capabilities, emphasizing only the delta information where the standard hazardous materials response branches off into the specialized fields of chemical and biological weapons. Many of the techniques and considerations are the same for the management of a hazardous materials event and the management of a WMD/NBC event. The delta comes in two major areas: equipment, more sophisticated detectors and more stringent personal protective equipment requirements of a WMD/NBC event; and victims, many more severely injured people needing decontamination and unusual definitive medical care. These victims may also require extensive applications of medical technology and large quantities of pharmaceuticals.

While a large cadre of trainers was trained by DoD in each selected community, over time these people will have to be replaced by additional local trainers. The addition of counterterrorism course work to fire and police academies, and the delivery of this training to other public employees, such as airport and stadium workers, will drain local training budgets. No money was provided through any federal funding process to pay for the overtime costs of delivering the DoD classes to public employees. No money was provided for the ongoing costs of training supplies, once the DoD ''loaned training equipment'' is used up or becomes out dated. At a cost of $4000 each, Level A hazardous materials suits are unlikely to be stockpiled in sufficient quantities to protect the public safety staff needed to respond to 1000 victims. City budgets are already strained by current community needs and demands. Youth gangs, homeless people, provision of affordable housing, and other immediate social problems compete for scarce public resources with disaster preparedness. Expensive terrorism counter measures are unlikely to be sustainable over the long term without additional federal support.

The initial federal funds were not sufficient to completely prepare a community for a WMD/NBC response, even as an enhancement of existing hazardous materials and emergency medical response capabilities. Exotic pharmaceuticals for up to 1000 victims would have overwhelmed the funding, without any other purchases. Local staffs were forced to set priorities for the use of the $350,000 DHHS MMST funds that promised the greatest benefit to the community in the event of a terrorist attack. Rather than purchase a cache of expensive drugs that would become outdated in 5 years, communities allocated their funds for commonly used but necessary drugs, like atropine and antibiotics, that might be able to be cycled through the normal medical system. This could result in a sustainable cache. However, in order to assure the timely delivery of treatment, caches may have to be maintained within MMST resources, where they would not be used routinely. A

WMD/chemical event could require such large quantities of atropine that all WMD cached supplies as well as local supplies with the approval of the Food and Drug Administration (FDA) would be exhausted. Access to veterinary resources is being investigated to boost local capabilities.

Some cities have considered stockpiling their pharmaceutical caches within the county hospital system as an oversupply. FDA guidelines on supply limits may make this difficult. Even when it is possible, using a 1000-patient single event cache of antidotes and antibiotics may not occur within the shelf life of the products, except in the largest metropolitan areas. For-profit institutions do not want to allocate the storage space for portions of the MMST drug cache, even if the drugs are originally purchased through federal funds.

Others have considered having the Veterans Administration hospitals serve as the cache location. However, they are not strategically located to serve all of the 27 selected cities, and even less so to care for the 120 cities on the final list. Finally, some cities proposed having military medical facilities stockpile the expensive, exotic drugs and pharmaceuticals, notably vaccines and antitoxins. The drawback for most areas is the time to deliver from the nearest military facility. In many cases these items must be administered to the patients within 1 to 2 hours to be effective, and it is unlikely that a stockpiled cache from a military base could be mobilized that quickly. Considering that it will take about an hour before the first contaminated victim can receive definitive care (following extrication and decontamination), it may not be realistic to plan to use this type of storage.

Funds allocated for equipment that has multiple uses is a better investment. For example, equipment like decontamination tents can be used for hazardous materials responses. Such use would be more frequent than a counterterrorism employment, guaranteeing that staff continue to be familiar with the procedures for locating and setting up the equipment. Multipurpose items would be more likely to be inspected periodically. An unmet challenge is how to respond to the need to stockpile expensive and fragile medical equipment, like ventilators.

Maintaining the training of the medical community will be a harder task than for public employees. While emergency medical technicians and paramedics in fire departments may be able to be included in departmentwide refresher training, it will be difficult to keep other medical personnel up to date, even if they are initially trained. Emergency medical transportation and hospital services are typically provided by for-profit organizations, who see no financial benefit in investing staff time in counterterrorism training. Alternatives to the 8-hour DoD course will have to be developed, in modules that can be included in standard medical staff meetings. The need for awareness and decontamination training classes is especially important in medical facilities, but without financial support or some other incentive, it is unlikely to be sustained. Reaching physicians is especially difficult.

While the medical community plays an important part in a chemical weapon response, it is an even more critical key to saving lives in a biological event. It is the medical community whose epidemiology and disease reporting systems will most likely give the first hint of a biological attack. PDD-62 postulates the improvement of medical surveillance. A national computer-based system for infectious disease reporting in real time should be developed if there is to be any hope of detecting the use of a biological weapon in time to benefit any of the victims. Reports of multiple cases of unusual diseases in one area, such as smallpox or anthrax, may be the first warning that an attack has occurred.

Mass vaccination of the public, and definitive care for the victims, will only result from good medical surveillance in a non-threat environment.

While the MMST/MMST System contract requires the city to make a long-term training plan, the city has little or no control over many of its MMST System partners, especially those in private practice and for-profit institutions. Incentives like continuing education units (CEU's) may draw some practitioners to training over time, but more funding would be needed to increase the probability of sustained system capability.

B. Nunn-Lugar-Domenici: Development or Devolution

The federal programs to create a domestic counterterrorist capability at the local government level represent an interesting exercise of federal power. While the federal government has been distributing federal funds to support specific local government programs since the New Deal, in the past most of these programs were managed as grants. While the ability to apply might have been offered, the elected officials of a community usually had to make a decision to apply for the grant or program. This decision process allowed the local government's professional staff to analyze the costs to the community of participation in the federal program. They could advise the elected officials on the overall cost-benefit to the community and of the budgetary impact in each year of participation in the grant. While it is true that few federal grants cover all of the costs to a community of participation, they generally made a conscious decision to accept the federal program and its package of costs and revenues.

Prior to the Nunn-Lugar-Domenici legislation, acts of terrorism were handled as either local crimes, managed as a law enforcement response, or as a national problem, managed by the FBI. This new program creates a new responsibility for local governments while providing no ongoing financial support for it. Cities were selected for participation in the program and generally reacted toward the notification as if it were a mandate. Most cities simply added the creation of the MMST to the existing workload of a senior city administrator, who had to engender support for the program from the most impacted departments: police, fire, and medical resources. In general, department heads felt compelled to cooperate while decrying the impact on budgets that are already minimal. Federal funding was strictly limited to the acquisition of a specific list of supplies and equipment, in most cases items that the local government did not previously intend to purchase. These goods are now the responsibility of the local governments, who must provide ongoing storage and maintenance, and replacement if the material is damaged or destroyed.

This program has created a new duty at the local government level: the duty to be prepared to respond to a weapon of mass destruction/nuclear, biological, or chemical attack on the community. In the past such attacks were considered acts of war, and it was anticipated that military resources would be deployed to manage the response and recovery. Now local governments have been "empowered," without prior consultation, to take over this technical and dangerous role. Police and fire employee unions in some cities have questioned whether this is a meet-and-confer issue because they think it may change working conditions, as they have never before been expected to deal with weapons of mass destruction. Exposure to Sarin gas during an emergency response is quite different from exposure to a methamphetamine lab or an industrial chemical release.

Federal leaders view the development of the local response capabilities as empowering local government to provide effective service to their communities. Local governments often view the program as a transfer of responsibility from the federal government to the local government. Local governments now face a limitless future of maintaining a new capacity that is unlikely to be used. As FBI Director Louis J. Freeh noted in his Senate hearing testimony on April 23, 1998, WMD/NBC events are "a phenomenon which is of low probability, based on the cases that we know about, but extremely catastrophic consequence" (Weiner 1998). Given the demands on local government to develop emergency response capabilities to high-probability events, the development of an MMST may not appear to be a good application of scarce resources.

Therefore, many communities are attempting to make the MMST a multiuse group, whose equipment and skills may be applied in industrial chemical accidents, multiple-casualty accidents, and similar more frequent events. This approach benefits all parties, as skills and familiarity with equipment are maintained when the team and its supplies are multipurpose and have actual response experiences.

The financial issue is a second problem created by the federal selection of communities for Nunn-Lugar-Domenici funding. The program became an unfunded mandate for training. Federal contractors provided information to the selected cities about the "free" training. In fact, the cost to a city to receive the training is very high. The federal program developers did not factor into the development process the cost of the time for local government employees to sit in classrooms to receive the training. Some employees might be able to be trained during on-duty time. However, the DoD-developed courses last 4, 8, or 12 hours. It is unlikely that so much time could be provided during the normal work day for most public safety personnel, who typically spend most of their time in the field. Therefore, most police and fire personnel taking the DoD training courses are either on overtime or are being back-filled in the field with someone else on overtime. The cost to the city of San Jose Fire Department to receive the train-the-trainer courses exceeded $65,000. This does not include the personnel time cost to the Office of Emergency Services, public information officers, Police Department, or the partner County Public Health Department and private sector hospital and ambulance personnel. These trainers now have to train the rest of their departments, at a further cost in personnel time, and significant expense for copying and binding the training materials for the students. With overtime budgets stretched thin by natural hazards responses, this additional expense has a significant budgetary impact. Since the MMST is expected to use unique equipment (notably the military warfare chemical detectors), ongoing training to maintain proficiency means that the training costs will continue indefinitely.

Furthermore, the MMST process required the development of a series of plans: plans to write the plans, plans for emergency response, training plans. All of these had to be coordinated with the local MMST development oversight committee. The cost of staff time to undertake this planning and plan writing process was not included in any budget, nor in any presentation on the process. The $350,000 in equipment was seen as a quid pro quo that should have been acceptable. Considering that most of that equipment is single-use and nothing the local government was anxious to possess, the local government was forced to make an investment in personnel effort for which they may see little overall value added to the city's response capabilities. The same amount of planning time invested in a higher-consequence natural disaster event could have had more immediate benefit to the community.

In most local governments the extra work of the MMST development was absorbed by senior and executive staff in the affected departments—people on salary. Staff at this level typically have little time that is not programmed for specific projects. This federal project was not announced until April, too late in the local governments' annual budget cycle to be included in personnel resource planning. Therefore, much of the MMST development work is actually being paid for with ''volunteer'' time ''donated'' by these salaried people after normal working hours, or through lost opportunity costs as other work is deferred.

Finally, the federal program developers appear not to have considered the political ramifications at the local level of participation in the program. After reviewing the requirements for participation in the MMST, the city of San Diego chose not to participate. Citing the lack of financial and staff capacity to support a new program, they deferred the effort to the county's health department. For the purposes of developing a MMST within San Diego County, the law enforcement and fire roles are being filled by federal employees in the Department of the Navy's fire and security services.

Other communities have found that smaller surrounding jurisdictions assume that because they received funding for the development of the MMST, the receiving community is now a regional resource, and has some obligation for training and response in other communities. The federal documents specifically state that local MMSTs are not deployable. However, because the state was left out of the planning and development process, issues related to mutual aid and regional responsibilities are murky. Small communities think that the larger ones received the DoD courses on a train-the-trainer basis to become a training resource for the whole region.

The relationship among MMST's is also unclear. Is one MMST expected to go to the aid of another in a WMD/NBC event? Clearly the 49-person team would be overwhelmed by the 1000 victims postulated by the planning parameters. Could team members be spared from their own community if a MMST city in the regional had been the subject of attack? National, deployable teams exist in Los Angeles, Denver, and North Carolina, but their response times for most of the first 27 cities would not be rapid enough to make a difference to the victims.

Further, the postulated involvement of the National Guard poses yet another intergovernmental dilemma. The National Guard is a state asset, deployed by the governor. Except when federalized they are not part of the United States military. Yet the WMD/NBC mission was announced by federal authorities without consultation with state organizations responsible for the Guard. While Guard units are actively seeking missions in the post–Cold War era, the WMD/NBC mission may not be a good use of the $49 million being assigned. What is the cost-benefit of such a resource, when it would be hours, or days, before the unit could be mustered and deployed to the site of the attack? When questioned about the statement that the National Guard would become first responders, one law enforcement executive who is also a National Guard officer said, ''Well, they would be the first *military* responders.''

The role assigned in the president's announcement was reconnaissance and decontamination (*USA Today* 1998). Is this reconnaissance of the crime scene? The local FBI and local government law enforcement personnel will have long since completed scene reconnaissance, and probably have begun evidence collection. What are they going to decontaminate? The scene of the event? All of the victims will have been decontaminated, triaged, and treated within the first few hours. The untreated will no longer be salvageable victims but will be deceased. What use are these reconnaissance and decontamination activities 24 to 48 hours after the event? By then the role is recovery and consequence management, a role more suited to psychologists and environmental specialists than to a military unit.

C. Lessons Learned

The Nunn-Lugar-Domenici Domestic Preparedness program is a good example of an idea that was released before it was fully developed. A variety of unresolved problems plague the program.

First, what does the "direct to the cities" approach say about federalism in 1998? The federal government, in the guise of two senators and their staffs and committees, arbitrarily selected 27 communities, based principally on population, to participate in a new counterterrorism initiative. There was no consultation with the states about the communities within their jurisdiction that were selected, nor about the relationship between the federally formed MMSTs and the state's own internal resource management system. There was no needs assessment by the states or local governments. A "one size fits all" approach to "boilerplate" training resulted in sophisticated fire departments with hazardous materials response teams receiving the same training as departments with limited or single industry focused hazardous materials response capabilities. Departments with public ambulances and those with private contractors received the same guidelines for team development. Communities that tried to use the MMST funds to bolster existing capabilities often found that contractors hired for the nationwide list review balked at their equipment selection, insisting that they "lacked" some critical capability simply because they had not bought it from federal funds. Some items, like cyanide kits and biological "smart tickets" became "required" items, even when communities questioned their usefulness in an actual event.

Second, the implications of deploying a MMST within a community, county, region, state were not considered before the program was announced and the contractual deadlines set. Cities were notified in April 1997 with contractual deadlines established to meet the needs of federal budget cycles rather than local planning cycles.

DoD contractors presented a schedule of training classes followed by a full-scale field exercise in 6 months. Yet the training equipment had not been delivered to most cities as long as 8 months after the training was received. Rather than ordering the training equipment on which there was no disagreement, DoD reviewers held up the entire list while a community justified its need for a particular item. Even delaying the full-scale exercise until 9 months after the training has resulted in training equipment coming barely in time to be used in the exercises.

When significant new programs requiring large commitments of unfunded resources by local governments are proposed, they should be offered on a grant basis, and time should be built into the schedule for a thorough analysis of the investment required by the recipient community. The imperative for this program was the three pronged "wakeup call" embodied in the World Trade Center bombing, Tokyo subway Sarin attack, and Murrah Building explosion, according to Senator Nunn (Nunn 1998). Impelled by these events, Congress used the budget to propel the MMST and DoD training programs into the local communities.

Staff assigned to manage the programs have had a struggle to rationalize the process, and try to create a manageable program. Los Angeles County already had a counterterrorism task force working on countywide planning issues, so they were more prepared than most to develop the new initiatives. Their existing committee formed a nucleus to develop the MMST and receive the DoD training across the 88 cities that make up Los Angeles County's 10 million population base. Most communities started from nothing to create a MMST/MMST system that meets federal mandates and local needs. While the experience generated beneficial relationships across professional lines that will be useful in other responses, the cost in time and lost opportunities to complete other pressing work has yet to be counted.

Third, although the federal government articulated a position that the local government would guide the MMST development process in each community (local control), this control is actually very carefully circumscribed by both DoD and DHHS headquarters units. Local requests for multiuse equipment and multipurpose teams have met with resistance at the national level. There is a clear message that the Nunn-Lugar-Domenici funds are not to be used for "everyday" events that are seen as the local government's responsibility. However, multiuse training and equipment is a more efficient use of time and money, guaranteeing ongoing proficiency and frequent capability exercising. Repeated iteration of this message has had only a moderate effect on the national level responses to local requests.

VI. CONCLUSION

The current effort to provide counterterrorism capabilities at the local government level is an worthwhile start on an important mission. Without a permanent stream of federal funding to support the training of the participants and the maintenance of supplies and equipment, however, this program will fail, like the civil defense efforts of earlier times. If the country truly considers domestic terrorism a potential threat that deserves countermeasures, a financial commitment to maintain local preparedness is essential. Without an ongoing commitment, communities will be left with a false sense of preparedness and an outmoded cache of response materials. The domestic counterterrorism effort deserves the serious consideration of the Congress and a federal financial commitment into the future based on realistic funding at the local level, a realistic analysis of costs and benefits to local governments, and the intelligent application of federal stockpiling capabilities nationally.

REFERENCES

Chemical Biological Defense Command (no date). *Domestic Preparedness Fact Sheets*. Aberdeen Proving Ground, MD: Chemical Biological Defense Command Public Affairs Office.

Chemical Biological Defense Command (no date). ⟨http://www.cdbcom.apgea.army.mil/Missions/dp/dp_cbrrt.html⟩

Defense Against Weapons of Mass Destruction Act of 1996, Subtitle A, Section 1311.

Federal Bureau of Investigation (1998). "Unified Command," 1998.

FEMA (1996). *Emergency Response to a Criminal/Terrorist Incident: Participant Handbook*, October, p. PH2.11.

Miller, Judith and Broad, William J. (1998). "U.S. Fails secret exercise simulating germ-weapon attack." *The New York Times*, April 26.

Nunn, Senator Sam (1996). The Nuclear Roundtable, July 18. ⟨http://www.stimson.org/rd-table/nunnrtbl.htm⟩.

Selden, Zachary (no date). "Nunn-Lugar: New solutions for today's nuclear threats." Business Executive for National Security Special Report. ⟨http://www.bens.org/pubs/nunnlugar.html⟩
USA Today, "10 states gets(sic) N. Guard anti-terror teams," May 22, 1998. ⟨usatoday.com.⟩.
Weiner, Tim (1998). "Reno says U.S. may stockpile medicine for terrorist attacks." *New York Times*, April 23.
White House (1998). "Combating terrorism: Presidential decision directive 62." Office of the Press Secretary, May 22.
White House (1998). "Protecting America's critical infrastructures: Presidential decision directive 63." Office of the Press Secretary, May 22.
White House (1998). "Remarks by the president at the United States Naval Academy commencement." Annapolis, Maryland, May 22.

ADDITIONAL RESOURCES

"A bottom line in war on terrorism: How to best spend the money." *USA Today*, May 4, 1998.
"A drill finds U.S. unable to cope with germ war." *New York Times*, April 26, 1998.
"A growing fear of toxic terrorism." *Los Angeles Times*, February 24, 1998.
"Anniversary stirs painful thoughts." *San Jose Mercury News*, April 19, 1998.
Anti-terror 'czar' to coordinate $7B effort." *USA Today*, May 4, 1998.
Barnes, Cecily. "Big bang theory." *Metro: Silicon Valley's Weekly Newspaper*, August 20–26, 1998.
Broad, William J., WuDunn, Sheryl, Miller, Judith. "Scope of cult attacks revealed." *San Jose Mercury News*, May 26, 1998.
"Domestic prep. program on target despite military oversight: Experts." *Emergency Preparedness News*, December 10, 1997.
"FBI Director Freeh's statement to the U.S. Senate on counterterrorism." ⟨http://www.fbi.gov/congress/counter/terror.htm⟩
"FBI's role in the federal response to the use of weapons of mass destruction." ⟨http://www.fbi.gov/congress/wmd/wmd.htm⟩
Gillert, John. "Combatting terrorism at Home: The 'NBC' difference." *Journal of Civil Defense*, Winter 1997–98.
Graham, Bradley. "Standing guard for toxic attacks." *San Jose Mercury News*, December 14, 1997.
Hicks, Victoria Loe. "One faithful man's descent into cult terrorism." *San Jose Mercury News*, June 6, 1998.
Johnston, David, Sack, Kevin. "Blasts connected." *San Jose Mercury News*, February 27, 1998.
"Marines to be trained in warfare amid skyscrapers." *New York Times*, May 2, 1998.
Miller, Judith, Broad, William J. "Clinton set to OK anti-terror plan." *San Jose Mercury News*, April 26, 1998.
Morris, Ralph. "Bio-terrorism threat is real." *San Jose Mercury News*, August 11, 1998.
"On Language: Weapons of Mass Destruction." *New York Times*, April 19, 1998.
"Postscript: Chemical Terrorism in Japan." ⟨http://www.csis-scrs.gc.ca⟩
"Presidential Decision Directive (PDD) 39, U.S. Policy on Counterterrorism (unclassified)." ⟨http://www.fas.org:80/irp/offdocs/pdd39.htm⟩
Proceedings of the Seninar on Responding to the Consequences of Chemical and Biological Terrorism, July 11–14, 1995. Washington, DC: U.S. Public Health Service.
"Reno says U.S. may stockpile medicine for terrorist attacks." *New York Times*, April 23, 1998.
Salmon, Jacqueline L. "Preparing for the worst: Pentagon drill tests local, federal response to a terrorist attack." *Washington Post*, May 31, 1998.
Sidell, Fredrick R, M.D., Patrick, William C. III, Dashiell, Thomas R. *Jane's Chem-Bio Handbook*, 1998. Janes Information Group, Alexandria, VA.

Statement of Attorney General Janet Reno before the Subcommittee on Technology, Terrorism and Government Information, Committee on the Judiciary and Select Committee on Intelligence, United States Senate, concerning the Threat of Chemical and Biological Weapons, April 22, 1998.

''Taking the terror out of bioterrorism'' *New York Times*, April 8, 1998.

Terrorism Incident Annex, Federal Emergency Response Plan. ⟨http://www.fas.org/irp/offdocs/pdd39_frp.htm.⟩

The Journal of the American Medical Association, August 6, 1997.

''U.S. fails secret exercise simulating a germ-weapon attack.'' *New York Times*, April 26, 1998.

Winik, Lyric Wallwork. ''We live in a dangerous world.'' *Parade Magazine*, April 5, 1998.

''Word for word/Jane's fighting germs: The grim do's and deadly don'ts of handling chemical attacks.'' *New York Times*, March 8, 1998.

42

Emergency Managers for the New Millennium

Ellis M. Stanley, Sr. Emergency Preparedness Department, City of Los Angeles, Los Angeles, California

William Lee Waugh, Jr. Department of Public Administration and Urban Studies, Georgia State University, Atlanta, Georgia

I. INTRODUCTION

The history of humanity is inexorably linked to scientific advances, each one built upon the advances of the past, like the levels of a pyramid, with each new discovery spurring a new round of societal growth. However, while technological advances can improve the quality of life, they also create new problems. Just in our lifetimes, we have seen many scientific and technological marvels become commonplace—from polio vaccine to jet aircraft and from cellular phones to the desktop computer. Such developments have enhanced both the length and the quality of our lives. In not too many years, we will see cures for some of humanity's most pernicious diseases; communications on a scale and at a speed almost beyond imagination; a new generation of tough, versatile materials; and intelligent transportation systems, including efficient cars that direct themselves along "smart" highways. To some extent, the forms that these changes will take can be surmised by evaluating trends in telecommunications, computing, cybernetics, government, industry, education, emergency management, and other fields. But, there will always be surprises inherent in the adoption of new technologies, as well as surprises resulting from the directions new developments take.

It can be expected that technological advances will introduce new hazards. Complex systems are fragile and, to the extent that we become dependent upon them and are willing to entrust our health and safety to them, failure can result in devastating loss of life and property. This is not a pessimistic view; rather, it is a realistic one. As Charles Perrow has pointed out (1984), failures in complex systems are inevitable, regardless of the care of operation and the redundancy of safety mechanisms. Conversely, there will be new technologies for the management of environmental hazards and to aid in disaster response. In essence, even as we develop more and better tools to reduce the risks to society, there will be far more hazards to address. The role of the emergency manager in the new millennium is to ensure that risk will be effectively managed and that public health and safety will be enhanced rather than weakened by the coming changes.

As more and more is known about hazards, the risks that they pose can be better addressed. Clearly, recent disasters have provided important lessons concerning natural phenomena and technological failures that are helping shape environmental and emergency management policies. The causes and implications of weather phenomena such as El Niño still challenge scientists, but explanations and solutions are slowly being found. However, the risk to society is increasing. Old hazards are made more risky by the increased exposure of people and property to their potential effects. El Niño storms along the Oregon coast have uncovered the remains of ancient forests buried after cataclysmic earthquakes. The evidence suggests that cycles of earthquakes every 350 to 500 years wreak havoc on coastal communities from the Pacific Coast of North America to Japan and elsewhere on the Pacific Rim (Cain 1998). During the last cycle, much of the coastline was only sparsely populated, but now, large population centers, including Portland, may be vulnerable if the pattern continues. The 1998 prediction of a near miss of Earth by Asteroid 1997 XF11 in 2028 also pointed out dangers that we may face in the future. While the asteroid is only expected to come within 600,000 miles of Earth, rather than the 26,000 originally predicted, the potential for disaster is manifest. Scientists estimate that ''house size'' asteroids have struck Earth approximately every 100,000 years, with dire effects on animal and plant life (Nesmith 1998). The probability of a major asteroid strike is relatively low compared to a 100-year flood or even a 1000-year volcanic cycle, but such a strike could wipe out human life on the planet. A smaller asteroid hitting the ocean would cause tsunamis that would destroy communities far inland. Speculation about such dangers should serve to sensitize governments and individuals to the need to prepare and to be flexible in the design of disaster programs.

We will also encounter new hazards wrought by humans as well as those resulting from the adoption of new technologies or from ignorance of past cataclysms. Nuclear terrorism may take new forms as fissionable materials from the former Soviet states are bought by ''rogue states'' to enhance their international positions, international and domestic terrorists to advance their political agendas, criminals to extort money, and/or crackpots to vent their delusions. Biochemical terrorism poses similar dangers, complicated by the relatively ''low-tech'' capabilities needed to produce sarin gas, anthrax spores, and other lethal agents. Cyberterrorism, too, is an increasing threat as complex computer systems run communications, transportation, and other networks. Data-driven decision support systems are vulnerable to disruption and lives may be at risk when air traffic–control, subway, hospital, and other computer systems are violated by terrorists for political purposes or even hackers intent only on vandalism. Bombs and lesser weapons of destruction also pose significant risks, particularly given the evident willingness of terrorists and criminals to kill large numbers of people. The bombing of the Murrah Federal Office Building in Oklahoma City demonstrated that seemingly unthinkable crimes are possible and security precautions are becoming a familiar aspect of public and private workplaces.

As we move into the new millennium, progress poses two significant challenges. The first is the unknown itself; the second is fear of the unknown. The second challenge usually proves to be the greater obstacle. Progress in addressing known hazards, including expanding capacities to adapt to new challenges, should encourage confidence and reduce fear. While there are ''wicked problems'' that may defy solution, societies can develop resilience that will assure survival. Fear can be healthy if it encourages appropriate caution and preparedness, but it should not engender fatalistic attitudes about the future. Capable emergency management agencies and an educated public provide the tools for survival. In response to the changing imperatives, the field of emergency management is finding new tools to manage hazards and to deal with disasters; it is professionalizing and promises to become one of the most challenging occupations in government. This chapter examines the major changes taking place in emergency management and how they will help shape the present millennium.

II. TECHNOLOGICAL CHANGE

Christian E. Stalberg wrote in 1994; "The emergence of the intelligent city in the 21st century will radically transform emergency management as we know it today." Computing and telecommunications technologies, once separate and well-defined, will merge and their distinctiveness will blur. Mobile wireless and Metropolitan Area Networks (MANs) will serve as the telecommunications backbone over which municipal management information systems will synchronize the various functions of government agencies and departments. Traditional organization and separation of municipal departments and agencies will undergo significant change as the intelligent city makes interdependent relationships more concrete and dynamic. Resource allocation will become more efficient as a separate and distinct function which is called upon during times of crisis, as it is today. Emergency management, like other government responsibilities, will become integrated into every facet of municipal planning and operations. The intelligent city will incorporate each of the elements of emergency management (preparedness, response, recovery, and mitigation) into its overall planning and operational matrix.

Emergency management professionals have to be prepared to meet the challenges brought by technological and social change. The intelligent city will, in many respects, operate very much like an organism, monitoring its various component systems and responding accordingly to potential or actual changes of state in order to maintain equilibrium. This sensitivity to potential or actual changes affecting the equilibrium of the city will have important ramifications for emergency management. As conditions favoring disaster are detected, the intelligent city will respond accordingly, heightening readiness as appropriate. The intelligent city will assimilate knowledge of hazards and implement hazard mitigation as an integral component of its overall functionality.

Who will be responsible for this "intelligent city"? Well, everyone, of course, but it will be the primary responsibility of the emergency manager. It also depends on the assumption that *everyone* (local government, the community, the private sector, etc.) will be involved in the process. When a city is threatened by a impending or actual hazard that puts lives and/or property at risk, emergency managers interact with different departments and agencies in anticipation of changes that must be made to reduce losses or avoid them altogether. Emergency management is basically all about managing and coordinating a complex system.

Hewlett Packard, in its 1994 corporate vision video *Synergies*, portrayed how a range of information tools could benefit a community in a time of crisis. The tools included hand-held translation devices to facilitate oral communication with an ethnically diverse population during emergencies, decision support systems to aid in disaster operations, and a plethora of other high-tech tools to assure that the emergency management system is seamless and effective. The video is part of a broad vision of how information technologies will serve people at the beginning of the next century. It focuses on HP's unique "MC^2" strengths in Measurement, Computing and Communications and what we might achieve with them in the years ahead. Predicting technological advances more than a few years into the future is difficult at best. Undoubtedly HP's 1994 vision is already outdated, as some of the technologies have already been introduced and refined, some have been superseded before they even left the R&D facilities, and some have been tested and rejected for one reason or another. Societal needs and markets are moving targets and technological advance is not a linear process.

In terms of the tools of emergency management, it is already difficult to keep up with the changing technology. We are seeing telecommunications and computers merging, becoming nearly indistinct, and they are linking the various subsystems of the cities—e.g., transportation, energy, waste, etc.—through metropolitan area networks into an overall system imbued with intelligence. Imagine a single knowledge base, feeding and being fed by numerous subsystems that will serve as the ''brain'' of the intelligent city. For example, in the event of an emergency, traffic patterns will be changed automatically to permit orderly evacuation and/or rendering of aid. Spatial intelligence, combining information provided by next-generation GPS and GIS, will drive radio-direction, radio-location, and navigational guidance systems to plot vehicles and regulate and disperse traffic flows. Technology for storm prediction and tracking will improve, increasing the reliability and accuracy of preparedness activities (e.g., warning and evacuation). Automated forecasts and historical data will be matched and likely scenarios will be plotted. Computer-aided education and simulations using virtual reality will be used for training exercises. Emergency warning and notification systems will extend into the home and the workplace, taking advantage of the ''anytime, anywhere'' model of connectivity. These tools and technologies are being used today. All of this technology was in use at the 1996 Centennial Games in Atlanta and are being used in other cities like Los Angeles,and Chicago.

III. THE HUMAN DIMENSION

The greatest opportunity for change in emergency management is in the human dimension, including the emergency manager and the public. It is fairly certain that in the future, public debt, insurance industry losses, and the trend toward greater societal equity will result in an increase in the responsibility the individual bears for his or her own actions and how they affect society. Institutions that currently absorb and then spread losses (government and insurance) across society will undergo a transformation as society systematically goes about the business of mitigating hazards rather than creating or aggravating them. As the impact of control and communications systems become widespread, there is a fear of their misuse. The dangers of control and conditioning have been amply described in George Orwell's *1984* and Aldous Huxley's *Brave New World.* Advances in information gathering and processing are raising very important issues about individual privacy and proprietorship of data. Decision making by community, regional, national, and international agencies raises very important issues relative to individual rights (particularly property rights), public participation in policy making, and other individual and group prerogatives.

The education and training of emergency managers, as well as the education of other public officials and private citizens, is also expanding. Many universities have accepted the challenge by including emergency management as a subject in undergraduate and graduate curricula. The courses are being offered as part of degree and/or certificate programs or as separate classes in public administration, sociology, geography, civil engineering, and other departments (Stanley 1992). The integration of disaster research, education, and practice is expanding rapidly as emergency managers, researchers, and educators are being brought together by such organizations as the Natural Hazards Research and

Applications Information Center at the University of Colorado. It is a challenge for researchers to keep abreast of the issues that are raised in hazard management and disaster operations and it is a challenge for emergency managers to keep up with the growing body of knowledge.

The impact of the changes upon emergency managers themselves will be profound. The image of emergency managers as ''air raid warden-type'' officials with little natural disaster experience has taken decades to dispel. Now, few communities can afford to entrust their safety and property to untrained, inexperienced administrators. The social and economic risks are too high and the political risks can prove costly for elected officials. The profession has also advanced past the Civil Defense era's models of ''command and control,'' opening up the communication process and involving more public, private, and nonprofit organizations in decision making. Emergency operations are cross-sector, intergovernmental, multi-organizational efforts, requiring political skill as well as technical expertise. Officials are at least talking to one another. But the challenge yet to be faced is how to manage the vast amounts of information that technology has put at their fingertips.

The changes in the field of emergency management signal the development of a distinct profession. A ''profession'' emerges as occupational groupings mature and there is an identifiable body of technical knowledge. Members begin to identify with colleagues in other jurisdictions or even nations, develop standards of conduct and professional practice, and establish minimum professional qualifications and experience. That process is well under way in the field of emergency management and, in the twenty-first century, emergency management agencies and policy making will increasingly be guided by professionally trained and educated officials.

Professionalization of the field will also reduce the unevenness in agency capacities and encourage communities to recognize and address hazards. Emergency management has been an administrative ''backwater'' in many jurisdictions. Offices have been staffed by persons with few technical skills relating to environmental hazards or disaster operations. Thomas Drabek's 1987 study of professional emergency managers found that, while some communities had highly capable officials and offices with considerable technical and administrative capacity, many had poorly trained, inexperienced officials with little or no administrative and political support. Indeed, local offices often had only one emergency manager, who sometimes was part-time and sometimes was unpaid. The very unevenness of capabilities made it difficult to develop effective regional, state, and national emergency management systems. The early experience of the Federal Emergency Management Agency was much the same. The national system was made all the more complex by conflicts in agency missions and organizational cultures (Waugh 1993, 1996).

Just as in other areas of government administration, the need for officials to have technical skills, appropriate education, and relevant experience grows as jurisdictions grow. Rural communities generally find it easier to adjust to known hazards and to reduce the risk to life and property. People learn to live with the risks, often at their own peril. However, as population grows and concentrates in urban areas, the exposure to risk grows. Complex transportation, communication, and power systems, the lifelines of communities, are fragile and the costs of disruptions increase as dependence upon them grows. Individuals can afford to live with risks that communities cannot.

California and Florida exemplify the problem of risk exposure. Tremendous population growth in both states particularly in hazardous coastal areas, coupled with the infrequent albeit inevitable major disasters, has created the potential for catastrophe. Both states have populations concentrated in areas subject to periodic disaster and both have populations that are unusually diverse, thus complicating the processes of communication and often increasing the vulnerability of residents. Nonetheless, emergency management officials have to assess risk as accurately as possible, communicate the danger to residents who may have little or no disaster experience and may not even believe or understand official estimates of probability, educate residents on how to reduce the risk to themselves and their property, and make sure that public resources are brought to bear to reduce hazards, prepare for and respond to disasters, and recover from disasters once they occur. Mitigation strategies have to be devised and implemented and an effective emergency management system has to be cultivated. Those tasks go far beyond the capabilities and authority of the emergency management agencies themselves. Complex networks of public agencies, nonprofit organizations, and for-profit companies provide capabilities ranging from emergency planning, temporary shelter, emergency medical services, and unemployment benefits to psychological counseling of both victims and responders, risk assessment, evacuation, and search and rescue. The network is highly professional in California and increasingly professional in Florida. There is also an increasing linkage of disaster management to other programs, e.g., homeless shelters, HIV/AIDS hospices, children's services, veterinarian services, food banks, social services for non-English-speaking groups, crisis counseling, employment services, and charitable organizations. Guiding emergency management agencies through the intergovernmental and multiorganizational maze requires administrative and political experience and skill, as well as personal qualities that facilitate communication and encourage cooperation.

Failure of local officials in fulfilling their tasks can result in significant legal liability, particularly if the failure was in one of their areas of discretion. Federal and state officials enjoy the protection of sovereign immunity, meaning they cannot be sued unless their government agrees to permit it. Local officials are protected by the same principle of sovereignty as long as they are exercising authority or implementing policies and programs mandated by state or federal officials. However, much of the business of emergency management is discretionary on the part of local officials. Land-use regulation, building codes, and other hazard reduction mechanisms typically are local responsibilities. Local officials may also be held liable for evacuation orders that prove unnecessary, loss of property value when development is restricted, loss of property value when hazards are identified and the risk is publicized, and other decisions. The potential legal costs of poor decision making are strong arguments for effective, professional emergency managers. Political skill is also needed as the reliance on nonstructural mitigation increases. Land-use regulation and building codes, in particular, are intensely political issues in local government and often involve groups, such as developers, who are very influential in community affairs.

As President Bush almost found in south Florida in the aftermath of Hurricane Andrew, there can be significant political costs if officials do not prepare reasonably and respond decisively to a major disaster. The poor showing of officials of the Federal Emergency Management Agency (FEMA) almost cost President Bush the state's electoral votes in the 1992 election. That lesson has not been lost on President Clinton, governors, mayors, and other elected officials. None would wish to entrust their political careers to ineffective emergency management officials. FEMA and its state counterparts, in particular, have benefited from the attention to professional competence in the selection of agency directors and other officials.

The process of professionalization began decades ago in many larger communities. In some cases, the level of risk or frequency of disaster was so high that officials necessarily hired experienced and capable emergency managers. In some cases, highly capable administrators helped design and staff their own agencies to assure effectiveness. While ''bottom-up'' organizational designs were common in some communities, appropriate training and experience were mandated by state officials in other states. The dilemma of emergency management is not that local officials and agencies are incapable of addressing hazards and responding to disasters, it is the unevenness of capabilities. Some agencies are well organized and capable and others are not. Disaster experience, public attention, investments of resources, and good leadership encourage capacity building. The challenge for state and federal officials is to raise the capabilities of all agencies and officials to at least minimal acceptable levels of competence so that the system can function effectively regionally and locally.

Another challenge is to increase the capacities of local officials and agencies so that they can function effectively and coordinate with their counterparts in neighboring communities. Local officials are typically the ''first responders'' to disaster and, as such, can determine the overall success of disaster operations and recovery efforts. Capacity building necessarily has to begin at the local level. Local officials, too, have principal legal responsibility for mitigation, such as land use and building regulation, as well as for response and recovery efforts. Unless state officials assume responsibility for disaster operations or ask federal officials to do so, locals are in legal control. Moreover, while environmental hazards may be regional, such as the hazards posed by seismic fault lines or large coastal storms, risk is more often localized. Population centers, hazardous soil conditions, floodplains, and such require local attention. To some extent, state and federal authorities can help local agencies with their preparedness, mitigation, response, and recovery efforts, but local officials have to tailor their efforts to the specific hazards and capabilities within their own communities. As in other program areas, there have been historical targeting problems when programs are mandated from the federal, or even the state, level. While FEMA has emphasized ''all-hazards'' programs since the 1980s, that generally does not literally mean addressing all conceivable hazards. For local officials, it usually means addressing the range of hazards that may reasonably occur in their community (Waugh 1996).

Professionalism was one of the three themes Thomas Drabek identified in his landmark study of successful emergency managers in 1987. He sought characteristics associated with the perception of success and the responses of agency representatives indicated that the success of emergency managers was related to:

1. Professionalism, including the exercise of the coordinator role, knowledge, commitment, and external recognition
2. Individual qualities, including ''people skills,'' or personality, communication skills, unique personal qualities, and disaster experience
3. Specific emergency management activities, including an all-hazards approach to emergency management (rather than a civil defense approach alone), agency or individual visibility in the community that encourages linkages, and task-related activities

In short, success was associated with technical skill, interpersonal skills, relevant experience, professional and administrative visibility, and an orientation toward cooperation and collaboration, rather than an authoritarian or ''command-and-control'' approach (also see Waugh 1993).

Institutions of higher education, as well as the International Association of Emergency Managers' (formerly the National Coordinating Council on Emergency Management) CEM (certified emergency manager) Certification Commission recognized that continued learning is necessary. The lag time between gaining of new knowledge through experience and the dissemination of that knowledge in ways to effect change will be reduced considerably by improved information capture, processing, and distribution. Maintenance learning—i.e., maintaining the status quo, will give way to innovative learning. The separation of education and work will end and the two will become almost indistinguishable from one another. This will occur for three reasons: (1) real learning is experiential, i.e., on the job; (2) the time lag between gaining new knowledge and its implementation is wasting valuable resources; and (3) a measurable return on investment in creating new knowledge must be gained if further investment is to take place. This has important implications for emergency management in extending hazards reduction into all phases and aspects of society.

The development of the CEM program addressed the technical and administrative aspects of the emergency manager role as well as the need for relevant experience and training. CEM is administered under the auspices of the International Association of Emergency Managers, a professional organization largely made up of local government emergency managers. The program was created in cooperation with FEMA, the National Emergency Management Association (NEMA), and other national and state professional organizations with related interests. Certification requires that applicants possess a 4-year degree in an appropriate area of study, at least 3 years of emergency management experience, at least 100 hours of emergency management classroom training within the last 5 years, at least 100 hours of general management training within the last 5 years, and three references to substantiate the training and experience. Experience in emergency planning, exercises, disasters, budgeting, and related functions is also assessed. Once certified, managers must pass a written test every 5 years.

Up until 1994, the education requirement was waived and, until 1996, equivalent coursework was accepted. If the normal course of professional development continues, standards will be raised periodically and equivalent education, training, and experience will become less acceptable. Education, training, and experience requirements may also become more specific and longer. To date, job announcements do not always mention CEM credentials as a minimum qualification, although that will change as more receive the credential and they advance into executive positions with responsibility for new hires. It might be expected that additional skills and competencies, beyond the CEM credential, will include broad experience with natural and technological hazards and disasters, expertise in new information technologies, knowledge of the more technical aspects of hazards and their mitigation, and people skills. Political acumen will be a valued skill as well.

IV. CONCLUSION

The future of state and local government in the United States will be shaped by a combination of forces, including technology, politics, economics, demographics and environmental change. As futurist Alvin Toffler has indicated in *The Third Wave*, strong leadership will be replaced by local and individual action. Government will provide the resources, especially the learning mechanisms, to equip individuals for their increased responsibilities. Government will encourage self-sufficiency in preparedness, response, recovery and hazard mitigation within individual neighborhoods and communities. Governments will partner more with the private sector to maximize the greater potential of resource utilization within the community. Government will become less topheavy, more flat and decentralized, following similar trends in the business sector. Continued decreases in federal aid will demand that local governments realize greater efficiency and look for economies of scale in service delivery. This will be accomplished by increased privatization of public services and government stimulation of local self-sufficiency. Geologic, fire, wind, and flood hazard districts will be created to raise funds for hazard mitigation. Citizens will have more control over the activities of government which affect them. Citizen access to government will increase through direct participation in decision-making via telecommunications, making most, if not all, representative forms of government obsolete. Governments primary job will be to inform and educate. Local government has become more complex and fragmented. At best departments do not work in concert; at worst their objectives are at complete odds with one another. The emergency manager of tomorrow will be the catalyst to eliminate the incongruities between government agencies, operating not in isolation but in relation to all other departments and agencies within government.

Hazard identification will be incorporated into the fabric of infrastructure design, planning, and operations. Agency actions will be in concert with one another throughout the municipality as decision-making and plan "checks" will occur with every other agency in the municipality. Within this matrix, planning and operations are a continuum, feedback and corrections are immediate, and accommodation or rejection of innumerable actions take place. The relationship between risk and cost will be better understood and individualized. Mechanism for mutual aid will improve, as cities and states will be linked through what in now taking shape under the guise of the "national information superhighway," the deployment of LEOS (Low Earth Orbital Satellites) and the like. Through these interconnections, cities will compare experiences and learn from one another. Vulnerable infrastructure in high hazard areas will be identified and systematically retired.

In the new millennium, emergency management will become more *proactive*, rather than *reactive*, as it is today. Emergencies will occur with less frequency as "unexpected situations" or "sudden occurrences" decrease with applied cybernetics. There should be fewer surprises and more lead time in which to prepare, in other words. Virtually all of the technologies necessary to construct the intelligent city have already been introduced, albeit some in rudimentary form. Technological forces in computing and telecommunications have already precipitated dramatic changes in the manner and style in which cities operate. While we are in the infancy of consciously merging the various components, the groundwork for the intelligent city is already being laid, changing the municipal landscape and transforming both the theory and practice of emergency management forever.

Emergency managers need to heed the words of Socrates: "Let him who would move the world first move himself." There is strong momentum for the continued professionalization of emergency managers. The process is reaching maturity—the focus is changing from minimum qualifications to more rigorous requirements for continuing education and technical training. To be effective, emergency managers will have to understand the intergovernmental and organizational environments in which they work, as well as be proficient with the available tools and knowledgeable about the hazards that they will have to address. Political skills are more important than technical skills if emergency management is to be integrated into the fabric of society and emergency managers are to be effective advisors for elected officials and the public at large and as administrators of their programs.

The key is to look to the future with hope, with optimism, and—above all without fear.

REFERENCES

Bidgoli, Hossein (1989). *Decision Support Systems: Principles & Practice.* San Francisco: West Publishing, p. 368.

Burgess, John H. (1978). *System Design Approaches to Public Services.* Rutherford, NJ: Fairleigh Dickinson University Press.

Cain, Brad (1998). "El Niño exposes Oregon coast's lush, violent past." *Atlanta Journal-Constitution*, March 12, p. A4.

Comfort, Louise K. (1988). *Managing Disaster: Strategies and Policy Perspectives.* Duke Press Policy Studies. Durham, NC: Duke University Press.

Drabek, Thomas J. (1987). *The Professional Emergency Manager: Structures and Strategies.* Monograph #44. *for Success.* Boulder, CO: University of Colorado, Institute of Behavioral Science.

Hewlett-Packard Company (1994). *Synergies* (video).

Hitchcock, H. Coates, J. (1985). The Future of State and Local Government as Seen in the Futures Literature. The Academy of State and Local Government, March 14, p. 122.

National Research Council (1994). *Facing the Challenge: The U.S. National Report to the IDNDR World Conference on Natural Disaster Reduction, Yokohama, Japan, May 23–27, 1994*, Washington, D.C.: National Academy Press.

National Science and Technology Council (1994). *Technology For a Sustainable Future: A Framework for Action.* Washington, D.C.: NSTC.

Nesmith, Jeff (1998). Pondering paths of those asteroids. *Atlanta Journal-Constitution*, March 15, p. A15.

Perrow, Charles (1984). *Normal Accidents: Living with High Risk Technologies.* New York: Basic Books.

Schriesheim, Alan (1996). Obstacles to 21st Century Technology. Presentation at Mid-America Regulatory Commissioners Conference, Chicago, Sponsored by the Argonne National Laboratory, June 17.

Stalberg, Christian E. (1987). Digital Telematics: Present and Future. *Informatics*, 4(*3*), 221–232.

Stanley, Sr., Ellis M., "Education: The Foundation of Professionalism," Building Bridges, A Special Edition of the *NCCEM Bulletin*, October, p. 9.

Stanley, Ellis M. Sr. (1995). "Risky business." *ASPEP Journal.*

Sutphen, Sandra, and Waugh William L. Jr. (1998). Reform and innovation in emergency Management. *International Journal of Mass Emergencies and Disasters*, March.

Toffler, Alvin (1981). *The Third Wave.* Toronto: Bantam Books.

Waugh, William L. Jr. (1996). Disaster management for the new millennium. In Richard T. Sylves and William L. Waugh Jr. (eds.), *Disaster Management in the U.S. and Canada.* Springfield, IL: Charles C Thomas Publishers.

Waugh, William L. Jr. (1993). Co-ordination or control: Organizational design and the emergency management function. *Disaster Management and Prevention: An International Journal* 2(*December*) pp. 17–31.

43
Coastal Hazard Mitigation in Florida

Patricia M. Schapley and Lorena Schwartz Joint Center for Environmental and Urban Problems, Florida Atlantic University, Fort Lauderdale, Florida

I. INTRODUCTION

Preventive medicine is to health care what hazard mitigation is to emergency management. Both concepts are based on the belief that reliable information, adequate resources, and rational decision making can reduce the risks associated with living in an environment that is not entirely predictable or controllable. Just as one may practice preventive medicine to reduce the chances of needing more expensive treatment in the future, public officials may invest in hazard mitigation programs to minimize the costs of recovering from the impacts of a major disaster.

For several reasons, natural hazard mitigation increasingly is becoming a policy priority for public officials and managers, particularly in coastal areas. This concern arises primarily from the recent sequence of major and costly disasters in the United States (Hurricanes Hugo, Iniki, Opal, and Andrew; the Northridge earthquake; and the Midwest floods) and the skyrocketing public and private costs associated with disaster recovery. In particular, sustained population growth in the coastal areas from Texas to Maine means that more lives are vulnerable to natural hazards and require protection from the potentially deadly effects of flooding, hurricanes, and other coast-related storm events. Urban development in these coastal areas also means that a larger number of private and public properties are at risk.

With nearly 1200 miles of coastline and a coastal population approaching 12 million, the state of Florida serves as an excellent case for analyzing the components of a coastal hazard mitigation program. The purpose of this chapter is to describe Florida's approach to mitigating the impacts of natural hazards in its coastal zone. It begins with an explanation of the purpose of hazard mitigation and its connection to the broader objectives of emergency management. It continues with an overview of hazard mitigation policies and programs at the federal level that are the context for Florida's approach. The main section of this chapter then presents the policy framework used in Florida to manage the impacts of growth in coastal areas and mitigate hazards associated with coastal development. It includes details on the events and factors that shaped Florida's approach into what it is today. The chapter concludes with the authors' assessment of the strengths and shortcomings of this approach.

A. Definition of Hazard Mitigation

Godschalk et al. (1999) define natural hazard mitigation as ''advance action taken to reduce or eliminate the long-term risk to human life and property from natural hazards'' (p. 5), such as hurricanes, floods, earthquakes, and landslides. Examples of natural hazard mitigation include adoption of stricter building codes and design standards; land use restrictions in hazardous areas; construction of flood- and erosion-control devices; relocation of structures from hazardous to safer areas; and educational programs for public officials and the community about risks associated with living in hazardous areas and the benefits of hazard mitigation activities. Hazard mitigation is considered a phase of emergency management, which also includes disaster preparedness, response, and recovery (Godschalk 1991). Until recently, most communities emphasized these three phases of emergency management and undervalued the importance of mitigation.

Hazard mitigation may occur before or after the effects of a natural hazard. The intent of ''predisaster'' mitigation is to reduce the physical impacts of a hazard by taking steps to either avoid the hazard or reduce or eliminate the potential for damage. An example includes adoption of land-use controls that prohibit development in areas identified as hazardous. ''Postdisaster'' mitigation takes place in response to the impacts of an actual disaster. For example, local officials may institute stricter building codes following a major hurricane and require that damaged structures be rebuilt in accordance with these regulations.

Mitigation measures can provide many benefits to states and communities with hazard-prone areas. These benefits include saving lives and reducing injuries; preventing or reducing property damage; protecting critical facilities such as hospitals, police stations, roadways, and utilities; reducing economic losses; minimizing agricultural losses; minimizing social dislocation; and lessening legal liability of government and public officials (National Research Council 1989; Godschalk 1991). It is now widely accepted that hazard mitigation measures will reduce long-term costs to the public and property owners by reducing expenditures on disaster recovery and assistance.

B. The Need for Natural Hazard Mitigation

Interest in hazard mitigation has grown as public officials have come to acknowledge that conventional emergency management measures such as early warning systems and evacuation plans are not enough to protect communities from the long-term economic and social losses associated with natural disasters. In 1989, the National Research Council reported that disaster preparedness and evacuation are effective strategies to reduce death and injuries, ''but do little to prevent property damage and the sometimes devastating economic impacts associated with disasters'' (p. 7). Furthermore, a sequence of major and costly natural disasters in the late 1980s and early 1990s (including Hurricanes Hugo, Andrew, and Iniki, the Northridge earthquake, and the Midwest floods) reinforced the council's message and prompted several in-depth reviews of the nation's emergency management and disaster relief programs, leading to reforms at the federal level that place greater emphasis on hazard mitigation. Federal officials and the private sector now extol the benefits of hazard mitigation and promote the adoption of mitigation measures by state and local agencies, businesses, and homeowners.

II. DESCRIPTION OF COASTAL HAZARDS AND EXPOSURE IN FLORIDA

Florida is a 447-mile-long peninsula with 1197 miles of coastline and 2276 miles of tidal shoreline (Florida State University 1992). Due to its geography, topography, and climate, it is vulnerable to a variety of natural hazards, namely hurricanes and tropical storm events, coastal flooding, storm surges, and coastal erosion. Florida has the dubious distinction of being the target of more hurricane strikes than any other state. From 1891 to 1996, a total of 74 hurricanes and 79 tropical storms hit the state. These storms caused at least 3800 deaths and $40 billion in property damage (Williams and Duedall 1997). Florida also has experienced coastal flooding and tornados associated with tropical and other storm events.

Coastal shoreline erosion is another common hazard in Florida. Although erosion is a natural, ongoing process, it constitutes a hazard in places where the shoreline is developed for private or public purposes. Florida's Department of Environmental Protection has classified 233 miles of sandy beaches as ''critical erosion areas'' where substantial development or recreational interests are threatened (Florida Department of Environmental Protection 1993). Complicating this problem is a predicted rise in sea level over the next century, which could increase beach erosion. State and local officials must determine how to diminish the threat of erosion to affected coastal communities through structural and nonstructural shoreline stabilization methods and through regulation of future land use and construction. Any of these choices presents high costs, both economically and politically.

In Florida, natural hazard mitigation has become a priority largely due to population growth in its hazard-prone coastal areas. In 1940, Florida was the 27th largest state in the nation; but by 1990, it had become the fourth largest, with a population of nearly 13 million people (Florida State University 1992). By 1997, its population had increased to 14.7 million (University of Florida 1998). This growth has concentrated for the most part in the state's 35 coastal counties, and this trend is expected to continue. As of 1996, some 11 million people, or 77 percent of the state's population, lived in coastal counties (University of Florida 1997). By the year 2020, analysts project that population in the coastal counties will increase by 50 percent to about 15.4 million people, or nearly 76 percent of the statewide population (Florida Center for Public Management 1997).

It is also important to point out that some of this growth has occurred in or near areas that are the most highly vulnerable to coastal hazards, such as barrier islands, beachfronts, estuarine shorelines, and flood zones. Consequently, it has become increasingly difficult to evacuate residents from areas that are in the path of a hurricane. This problem is particularly acute in Florida's urbanized coastal areas, where it could take more than 80 hours to evacuate threatened areas in the event of an approaching hurricane (Sheets 1995).

Another consequence of Florida's coastal development is increased exposure to property damage. In 1980, the state's total value of insured coastal property exposure was nearly $333 billion. By 1993, that figure had grown by 162 percent to $871.7 billion. This figure represents about 28 percent of the total value of insured coastal property exposure in the 18 states along the Atlantic Ocean and Gulf of Mexico (Insurance Institute for Property Loss Reduction 1995). In 1996, the National Flood Insurance Program (NFIP) held over 1.5 million policies in Florida's coastal counties, providing nearly $149 billion worth of coverage (Florida Center for Public Management 1997). In addition, the Florida Hurricane Catastrophe Fund, which the 1993 Legislature established to provide reinsurance for catastrophic losses due to hurricanes, had a total exposure of more than $632 billion in residential and commercial properties throughout the coastal counties (Florida Center for Public Management 1997). Since Hurricane Andrew hit Dade County in 1992 and produced more than $15.5 billion in insured claims, property insurance has become more expensive and harder to obtain, particularly in coastal counties (Ayscue 1996).

In spite of the risks, Florida's population, especially in coastal areas, continues to grow at high rates. Coastal hazard mitigation has been and will remain a major policy issue in Florida due to the number of lives at risk and the value of private and public property at risk along its extensive shoreline. Since the 1970s the state of Florida has taken significant steps toward the development of a statewide comprehensive approach to hazard mitigation involving actors at the state and local levels. Before looking at this approach, a description of the federal approach to hazard mitigation is provided as context for Florida's program.

III. THE FEDERAL GOVERNMENT'S ROLE IN HAZARD MITIGATION

Since the federal government plays an important role in shaping and supplementing state and local hazard mitigation programs in Florida, it is important to understand how the federal approach to hazard mitigation has evolved and how it currently operates. The federal role in natural hazard mitigation began in the early 1900s as ad hoc efforts to provide disaster relief and build flood control structures (Congressional Research Service 1992). It has expanded to include a multifaceted, all-hazards approach that focuses on emergency preparedness, disaster relief, flood insurance, and mitigation. Four pieces of legislation provide the basis for federal involvement in coastal hazard mitigation: the National Flood Insurance Act, the Coastal Zone Management Act, the Coastal Barrier Resources Act, and the Robert T. Stafford Act Disaster Relief and Emergency Assistance Act. Two agencies, the Federal Emergency Management Agency (FEMA) and the National Oceanic and Atmospheric Administration (NOAA), are largely responsible for administering the provisions of these acts. FEMA retains the majority of this responsibility as it administers disaster assistance, implements the National Mitigation Strategy, and houses the Flood Insurance Administration (FIA), which administers the National Flood Insurance Program and Community Rating System. NOAA oversees the National Coastal Zone Management Program, which covers a variety of coastal issues including coastal hazard mitigation and coastal development.

The federal government's initial role in emergency management was narrow and limited. The various disasters that occurred in the United States between the years of 1803 and 1950 were handled through a series of ad hoc federal actions, which provided financial and technical resources to stricken areas. However, in 1950 the Federal Disaster Act was passed which provided for the first time a continuing federal role in disaster relief (Drabek 1991). This role expanded in the 1960s as the federal government began to institute a series of financial incentives and disincentives to encourage states and communities to adopt hazard reduction measures. There was no centralized federal program for emergency management until 1979 when President Carter created FEMA.

A. National Flood Insurance Program

Hazard mitigation first became a part of federal emergency management activities in 1968 with the National Flood Insurance Act. The act made federally subsidized flood insurance available to properties in communities that enforced land use and control measures designed to reduce vulnerability of structures to damage from flooding. These measures included restrictions on new construction and substantial improvements to existing structures. Its intent is to limit inappropriate development in floodplains and provide insurance for structures in flood-prone areas. Today, more than 18,000 communities currently participate in the NFIP (FEMA 1998). In effect, the NFIP serves as an incentive to communities to adopt mitigation measures in return for insurance that otherwise would not be affordable to the average homeowner. Its creation signified a switch from structural (such as dams and levees) to nonstructural solutions (such as land use and structural elevation) to mitigating flood damages (Burby and French 1985).

In 1990, FEMA initiated the Community Rating System, which rewards communities with mitigation programs by reducing flood insurance premiums. Following the 1993 Midwest floods, Congress reformed the NFIP to increase the amount of funding available for mitigation activities. The National Flood Insurance Reform Act of 1994 authorized the annual transfer of $20 million into the newly created National Flood Mitigation Fund to provide grants to states and localities for planning and implementing mitigation projects such as elevation, acquisition, and relocation (''Flood Insurance Revamped'' 1994). Although there were attempts to amend the NFIP to require coastal shoreline setbacks for structures, none succeeded.

B. Disaster Relief

By the 1970s, the federal government began to condition the provision of disaster assistance on state and local commitment to mitigate the impacts of future natural disasters. In 1974, the Disaster Relief Act required that state and local governments evaluate hazards in affected areas and take action to mitigate the hazards, including land use and building standards, in order to receive federal disaster aid (Congressional Research Service 1992). In 1988, Congress passed the Robert T. Stafford Disaster Relief and Emergency Assistance Act [42 U.S.C. s. 5121 (1996)], the nation's first significant piece of hazard mitigation legislation. It provided for federal financial support of state and local hazard mitigation activities, including planning and projects. Specifically, Section 409 of the act authorized FEMA to condition the provision of disaster assistance on state and local actions to mitigate hazards, including preparation of a state hazard mitigation plan. The purpose of the ''409'' plans is to ensure that states and local governments evaluate natural hazards in the area designated to receive federal disaster funds and identify projects and actions in order to reduce vulnerability to hazards [44 C.F.R s. 206.405 (1998)].

Thus, many states and local governments have undertaken hazard mitigation programs in response to federal requirements for disaster assistance, as well as participation in the National Flood Insurance Program. The Stafford Act instituted an approach to hazard mitigation that placed an increased responsibility on state and local governments to plan for hazards and implement mitigation measures. However, some have criticized the Stafford Act for encouraging state and local governments to mitigate hazards in the wake of a disaster rather than in anticipation of future ones (Godschalk, et al. 1999).

A series of major natural disasters from the late 1980s (Hurricane Hugo and the Loma Prieta earthquake) to the early 1990s (Hurricanes Andrew and Iniki), plus concern over the federal budget deficit, prompted the federal government to assess its emergency management program and identify ways to contain rising costs associated with disaster recovery (Congressional Research Service 1992). In 1993, FEMA adopted a new mission to reduce the loss of life and property by promoting the use of comprehensive risk-based emergency management programs. The main focus of the mission was to create an emergency management system that stressed mitigation rather than response and partnerships with local, state, and federal governments, voluntary agencies, business and industry, and individual citizens. In an effort to support this mission, FEMA initiated in 1994 development of a National Mitigation Strategy, which contains two long-range goals: to increase substantially public awareness of natural hazard risk so that the public demands safer communities in which to live and work; and to reduce significantly the risk of death, injuries, economic costs, and destruction of natural and cultural resources that result from natural hazards (FEMA 1997). It declares mitigation as the ''cornerstone'' of the federal emergency management program.

The National Mitigation Strategy proposes a list of responsibilities for FEMA, all federal agencies, state and local governments, the private sector, and citizens, and prefaces it with the statement that the ''ongoing role of the federal government will be significant, but limited'' (FEMA 1996). FEMA's responsibilities include providing technical assistance to federal agencies and state and local governments on mitigation and making mitigation ''the highest priority in recovery efforts following all disasters'' (FEMA 1997). The strategy defines state and local government responsibilities as developing strategic mitigation plans and identifying funding sources to support them; adopting and enforcing all-hazards building codes; adopting incentives and disincentives; incorporating mitigation of natural hazards into land use management plans and programs; and lastly, developing, supporting, and conducting ongoing public information campaigns on natural hazard mitigation (FEMA 1996).

However, the strategy emphasizes that mitigation occurs at the local level and that FEMA should promote partnerships between state and local agencies to build consensus on mitigation issues and needs. Thus, the expectation is that state and local governments will become the primary actors in this intergovernmental system and institute appropriate policies and programs to mitigate hazards. To qualify for federal assistance, states and local governments increasingly will have to demonstrate their intent to adopt and enforce hazard mitigation measures. Some critics predict that the goals of the National Mitigation Strategy will conflict with political unwillingness among elected federal officials to exercise restraint when providing disaster assistance to state and local governments and to exact meaningful mitigation actions, such as land use and building regulations, in exchange for funding (Platt 1996).

C. Coastal Management

Two pieces of legislation authorize the federal government to mitigate hazards in coastal areas: the Coastal Zone Management Act [16 U.S.C. ss. 1451–1465 (1998)] and the Coastal Barrier Resources Act [16 U.S.C. s. 3501 (1998)]. In 1972, the Coastal Zone Management Act was adopted to encourage states to undertake coastal planning. It authorized creation of the national Coastal Zone Management Program to provide policy guidance and financial and technical assistance to states that adopt coastal management programs in accordance with federal criteria. NOAA's Office of Ocean and Coastal Resource Management administers these provisions. To qualify for federal assistance, state coastal management programs must include (among other things) policies to reduce risks of flood loss, minimize the impact of floods on human safety, health, and welfare, and preserve floodplains. In addition, the management programs must identify, and indicate special policies for, "areas of particular concern" which may include areas subject to significant hazards due to storms, floods, erosion, and sea level rise. Finally, the management program must establish a process for assessing and reducing the impacts of shoreline erosion [15 C.F.R. s. 923 (1998)].

In recognition of the protective functions of coastal barriers, Congress passed the Coastal Barrier Resources Act (CBRA) in 1982 to guard these resources from inappropriate development. Coastal barriers, found along the shores of the Atlantic Ocean and Gulf of Mexico, are considered unsuitable for development because they are vulnerable to hurricanes, flooding, wind damage, natural shoreline recession, and significant sand movement during storms. Development of coastal barriers and alterations to these systems exacerbate coastal hazards (Bush et al. 1996). CBRA was enacted to identify remaining undeveloped coastal barrier resources and to restrict expenditure of federal funds that facilitate their development. The CBRA withdrew federal flood insurance and the use of federal monies for infrastructure from undeveloped coastal barrier islands identified in the Coastal Barrier Resource System. It originally affected 186 undeveloped barrier islands, which totaled 453,000 acres and 666 miles of shoreline (Beatley et al. 1994). In 1990, the Coastal Barrier Improvement Act added to the Coastal Barriers Resource System areas in Puerto Rico, the U.S. Virgin Islands, the Great Lakes, the Florida Keys, and additional areas along the Atlantic and Gulf coasts (Public Law 101-591, Nov. 16, 1990).

IV. FLORIDA'S APPROACH TO COASTAL HAZARD MITIGATION

Although the federal government's programs and policies have shaped the approach taken in Florida to mitigate hazards in coastal areas, the desire of Florida's citizens to manage the impacts of growth on its coastal areas, including natural and cultural resources, has been the primary force behind initiatives to adopt and implement mitigation actions. Since the late 1960s, growth and new development have been major concerns underlying the state's public policy agenda. A large and steady influx of new residents raised concerns about the state's ability to manage growth in a way that minimized its impacts on natural systems, cultural and historic resources, capacity of roadways and other public facilities, and quality of life in general. These concerns were particularly acute in the coastal areas, the destination of most of new growth as well as many tourists.

The state's formal commitment to protecting coastal areas began in 1968 with adoption of a new state constitution. It included an article that set forth natural resource conservation and protection as a policy of the state. Article II, Section 7 has become the foundation for many important laws passed in the following decades to protect coastal resources. The Environmental Land and Water Management Act (ELWMA) [Fla. Stat. ss. 380.012-.12 (1998)], passed in 1972, contained provisions authorizing the state to designate "areas of critical state concern" and adopt specific principles for guiding development in the area. Of the 12 critical areas either designated or considered for state designation, nine have been coastal sites, including the Florida Keys, Apalachicola Bay, and the Northwest Florida Coast. The Local Government Comprehensive Planning Act (LGCPA)

[Fla. Stat. ss. 163.3161-.3425 (1998)], passed in 1975, mandated the adoption of local comprehensive plans that contained coastal management elements. The legislature strengthened this mandate in 1985 by authorizing the state land planning agency to adopt minimum requirements for the content of local plans and to review and approve all local plans as compliant with these requirements.

Florida's hazard mitigation initiatives have been an outgrowth of these and other state laws designed to protect coastal areas from the impacts of growth. Closely related to concerns about protecting coastal resources from growth were concerns about the escalating number of lives and properties at risk in coastal areas and the state's ability to respond to natural disasters. Consequently, the ELWMA, the LGCPA, and other legislation sought to guide growth in coastal areas to protect estuaries, dune systems, and barrier islands from development impacts and to minimize the potential impacts of natural hazards on these areas.

Florida uses several methods to carry out its hazard mitigation objectives: (1) state planning mandates that require local governments to mitigate hazards in coastal areas using land use and development controls and counties to prepare emergency management plans; (2) state regulation of construction in coastal areas; and (3) funding and technical assistance for local mitigation activities. Two state agencies, the Department of Community Affairs (DCA) and the Department of Environmental Protection (DEP), are responsible for implementing mitigation programs in accordance with several different statutory authorities. The remainder of this section focuses on applications and outcomes of these methods.

A. State Planning Mandates

Florida is one of several states that has adopted planning mandates to accomplish statewide objectives for hazard mitigation as well as other purposes, such as natural resource protection, housing, and infrastructure. Specifically, the ELWMA and the LGCPA (discussed above) set forth state objectives for land use and resource protection to be accomplished through local planning and development regulations. These laws provide a statewide policy framework for managing the impacts of growth and development in coastal areas and require local governments to mitigate hazards in the coastal zone through comprehensive planning and regulation of land use and development. In fact, Florida's planning mandates emphasize land use and development controls as tools for local hazard mitigation. Local governments must prepare comprehensive plans that are consistent with goals outlined in the State Comprehensive Plan [Fla. Stat. s. 187.201 (1998)] and in regional policy plans. Furthermore, local land use and zoning decisions must be consistent with the goals and policies laid out in the local comprehensive plan. In this top-down policy framework, local comprehensive plans serve as the vehicles for carrying out state land use policies in the coastal areas.

The LGCPA includes provisions that apply specifically to coastal areas. They require each city and county with coastal territory to develop a local comprehensive plan that contains a separate coastal management element. The purpose of the coastal management element is twofold: to "restrict development activities where such activities would damage or destroy coastal resources" and to "protect human life and limit public expenditure in areas that are subject to destruction by natural disaster" [Fla. Stat. s. 163.3178(1) (1998)]. A total of 35 counties and 162 cities in Florida are required to prepare coastal management elements.

State requirements for the coastal management elements are comprehensive and detailed, causing the element to resemble a ''plan within a plan'' (DeGrove and Stroud 1988). The coastal management element must include a map of existing land uses; an inventory of natural disaster planning concerns including measures to reduce hurricane evacuation times, structures with a history of repeated damage from coastal storms, and identification of coastal high hazard areas and infrastructure within them; and policies and management techniques for limiting development in coastal high-hazard areas and areas of repeated damage and for regulating building practices and alterations to floodplains, beaches and dunes [Fla. Admin. Code 9J-5.012(3)]. In addition, the state requires that the coastal management element contain policies that address protection and conservation of coastal wetlands, marine resources, and habitat; priorities for shoreline land uses; public access to beaches and shorelines; historic resource protection; orderly development and use of deepwater ports; and protection of estuaries. These requirements resemble those of the federal government for state coastal management programs under the National Coastal Zone Management program.

The ELWMA also has been an important piece of legislation in the state's hazard mitigation program, though its application is limited to only 5 percent of the lands within the state. Since 1972, the state has applied the critical areas provision of the ELWMA to several coastal areas in order to address potential problems arising from overdevelopment, including hurricane evacuation. These areas include the Florida Keys, the Northwest Florida Coast, the Escambia-Santa Rosa Coast (two coastal counties also in Northwest Florida), and Hutchinson Island (a barrier island in Southeast Florida). Although only the Florida Keys officially were designated as an area of critical state concern, the statute was used in the other three areas to form Resource Management and Planning Committees composed of representatives of state and local agency interests, citizens, and the private sector. Their purpose was to prepare and adopt a long-term management plan for the area and seek approval for the plan from the state Administration Commission (i.e., the governor and cabinet). If an acceptable plan was not adopted, then the state was authorized to designate the area as an area of critical state concern and development decisions would have to undergo direct state review (DeGrove 1988).

Florida's state planning mandates have undergone critical review several times since their initial adoption in the early 1970s, leading to several revisions. A year-long, intensive review in 1992 of the state's growth management statutes emphasized the importance of post-disaster redevelopment plans for coastal communities. During the tenure of the third Environmental Land Management Study Committee (''ELMS III''), the impacts of Hurricane Andrew on Dade County revealed the deficiencies in local planning for postdisaster redevelopment. No community had developed specific plans addressing how the period following a disaster would be used as an opportunity to mitigate hazards (ELMS III, 1992). In most cases, local comprehensive plans contain policies indicating that the local government will enforce existing building codes and state regulations pertaining to construction seaward of Coastal Construction Control Lines (discussed below). ELMS III concluded the following: ''Little has been done to implement existing State policies intended to direct population growth away from Florida's most vulnerable coastal areas, and to limit public expenditures which subsidize growth in such areas. It is difficult to determine if the problem rests with the policies or the definition of the coastal high-hazard area'' (ELMS III 1992:90). Its recommendations led to a uniform definition of coastal high hazard area, now defined for planning purposes as the area within Category 1 hurricane evacuation zones.

Although Florida has adopted one of the strongest planning mandates in the nation (DeGrove 1992), a weakness has been the implementation of hazard mitigation and postdisaster redevelopment goals via the coastal management elements of local comprehensive plans. Based on a review of a sample of local comprehensive plans, Deyle and Smith (1998) found the content of coastal management elements generally weak and void of hazard mitigation policies other than those dealing with construction and site use regulation. They attributed this finding in part to the apparently low priority given to this issue by the state relative to other issues, such as urban sprawl, affordable housing, and adequate public facilities requirements. In addition, they found that local officials are generally unaware of the policies in their comprehensive plans that relate to hazard mitigation.

In general, the state's ability to accomplish hazard mitigation through local land use planning is limited. Local officials often are reluctant to restrict development in areas that offer ocean views and proximity to beaches and that contribute significantly to the tax base. Furthermore, it is extremely difficult to apply restrictive land use controls to areas that are developed already. Most coastal communities simply propose in their comprehensive plans to prevent an intensification of land uses in coastal high hazard areas rather than implement policies to reduce densities and relocate structures. However, as awareness about the vulnerabilities in the coastal areas grows, so too may the number of communities that opt to mitigate hazards through land use restrictions in the high hazard areas.

B. County Emergency Management Plans

The state's emergency management statute [Fla. Stat. ss. 252.31-.62 (1998)] also requires local governments to plan for the effects of natural hazards. Florida Statute 252 states that it is a responsibility of the state "to provide the means to assist in the prevention or mitigation of emergencies which may be caused or aggravated by inadequate planning for, and regulation of, public and private facilities and land use." Each county in Florida must prepare and adopt a comprehensive emergency management plan that is in compliance with state standards and that is consistent with the state comprehensive emergency management plan. Each county emergency management plan must include an evacuation component, a shelter component, and a post-disaster and recovery component and address preparedness, response, recovery, and mitigation [Fla. Admin. Code 9G-7.003(2)]. Specifically, the county emergency management plan must identify strategies for rectifying hazard-related problems, address state priorities for spending state and federal pre- and postdisaster mitigation funds, and establish procedures for updating local post-disaster redevelopment plans.

Counties must have an emergency management plan approved by the state in order to qualify for matching funds. In addition they must have a part-time or, in counties with a population of 50,000 or more, a full-time emergency management director (Florida Administrative Code, Chapter 9G-11.004). Municipalities are encouraged, but not required, to adopt an emergency management plan. However, municipal plans must be consistent with the applicable county emergency management plan.

The 1993 Legislature enacted these planning requirements following Hurricane Andrew. Legislators had filed bills in previous legislative sessions to authorize improvements to the state's emergency management program but none succeeded. Hurricane Andrew and the "storm of the century" that struck northern Florida in the winter of 1993 revealed the inadequacies in the state's response to emergencies and demonstrated that all parts of the state, not just southern Florida, are susceptible to natural disasters (Mittler 1997). In a related action, the 1993 Legislature also approved creation of the Emergency Management Preparedness and Assistance Trust Fund (discussed under ''Funding and Technical Assistance''), which provided a dedicated funding source to support implementation and administration of local emergency management programs.

The process requirements for local emergency management plans closely parallel those for local comprehensive plans. Both types of plans must meet state standards, must be consistent with a statewide planning framework, and must be approved by the state. However, their approaches to hazard mitigation differ in that county emergency management plans are operations-oriented and the local comprehensive plans are policy-oriented. The county emergency management plans address roles and responsibilities of various agencies and organizations in emergency management and indicate how the county will proceed before, during, and after an emergency. On the other hand, the local comprehensive plans must establish the policies that will govern local efforts to mitigate hazards either in response to a disaster or as part of day-to-day decision making.

C. Regulation of Construction and Development in Coastal Areas

In addition to mandates for planning in coastal areas, Florida law also includes regulations for construction in the most vulnerable portions of the coastal areas—beaches, barrier islands, and flood velocity zones (''V-zones''). To protect its beaches from the negative impacts of development, Florida adopted in 1965 the Beach and Shore Preservation Act [Fla. Stat. ss. 161.011-.45 (1998)]. This statute contains provisions addressing regulation of construction and reconstruction within areas located seaward of ''coastal construction control lines'' (CCCLs). These lines are located and mapped by the state's Department of Environmental Protection and adopted by administrative rule. The CCCL defines ''that portion of the beach-dune system which is subject to severe fluctuations based on a 100-year storm surge, storm waves, or other predictable weather conditions'' [Fla. Stat. s. 161.053(1)(a) (1998)].

New construction or reconstruction located seaward of the CCCL requires permit approval from the DEP and must comply with stringent standards applying to design and placement of structures. These standards are intended to protect the beach-dune system from development impacts and structures from the impacts of erosion and coastal storms. In addition, all new construction and reconstruction must be located behind the 30-year seasonal high-water line. However, state law allows for limited exceptions to this requirement if its application precludes a property owner from building a structure. These standards have the general effect of keeping structures as far as possible from the shoreline, elevating them above a destructive storm surge, and strengthening them to withstand hurricane-force winds. They resemble the requirements of the National Flood Insurance Program for new construction and reconstruction in communities participating in the program, with the key difference being the setback for new construction from the 30-year seasonal high-water line.

Florida's Beach and Shore Preservation statute also includes regulations pertaining to new construction in areas defined as the ''Coastal Building Zone.'' The Coastal Zone Protection Act [Fla. Stat. ss. 161.52-.58 (1998)], passed in 1985 along with revisions to the LGCPA, amended the Beach and Shore Preservation statute to ensure that growth and development in the Coastal Building Zone ''shall be managed through the imposition of strict construction standards in order to minimize damage to the natural environment, private property,and life'' [Fla. Stat. s. 161.53 (1998)]. Part of the intent underlying the requirements for the Coastal Building Zone is to minimize costs to the state for postdisaster redevelopment and ensure that preventive measures are taken to reduce the harmful consequences of natural disasters or emergencies.

The Coastal Building Zone is defined accordingly: (1) the land area from the seasonal high-water line landward to a line 1,500 feet landward from the CCCL; (2) in areas with no CCCL, the land area seaward of the most landward velocity zone (V-zone) line as shown on flood insurance rate maps [Fla. Stat. s. 161.54 (1998)]; (3) on coastal barrier islands, the land area from the seasonal high-water line to a line 5000 feet landward from the CCCL or the entire island, whichever is less; and (4) all land area in the Florida Keys located within Monroe County. In no case, however, shall the coastal building zone be less than 2500 feet landward of the CCCL [Fla. Stat. ss. 161.51 and .55 (1998)]. Designation of the Coastal Building Zone indicates that hazardous coastal areas extend beyond those defined by CCCLs and that these areas, while not vulnerable to storm surges and erosion, are also vulnerable to high winds and flooding associated with coastal storms.

Local governments in the coastal building zone are required to incorporate the standards set forth in the Coastal Zone Protection Act into local building codes and to enforce them. These standards pertain to structural requirements for major, major non-habitable, and minor structures. Major structures in the Coastal Building Zone must conform to the state minimum building code, NFIP standards for design, construction, and location, minimum wind load requirements of 110 miles per hour (115 mph in the Florida Keys), and design requirements for foundations (i.e., all anticipated loads resulting from a 100-year storm event). Of course, local governments are permitted to adopt standards that are more restrictive than those identified in the Coastal Zone Protection Act.

Although not a direct regulation of development in coastal areas, Florida's Coastal Infrastructure Policy [Fla. Stat. s. 380.27 (1998)] serves as a limitation to new development on barrier islands. An executive order issued in 1981 called for a reduction of state investment in infrastructure on coastal barriers. This policy was adopted as law in 1985 and now provides that no state funds shall be used to construct bridges or causeways to coastal barrier islands that were not accessible by bridges or causeways on October 1, 1985. Additionally, no state funds are to be used for planning, designing, or constructing projects which increase the capacity of infrastructure (such as roads and bridges, sewage treatment facilities, potable water facilities, utilities, and shoreline stabilization structures) unless consistent with the approved coastal management element. This policy parallels the federal government's Coastal Barrier Resource Act, discussed above.

D. Funding and Technical Assistance

Ensuring effective implementation of Florida's hazard mitigation policies requires substantial investments in funding and technical resources. In particular, the outcomes of the state's planning mandates pertaining to hazard mitigation are contingent on the state's commitment to helping local governments carry out these mandates and providing adequate support. The state currently provides several means of support related to its hazard mitigation policies: (1) programs for land acquisition, including hazard-prone properties; (2) funds for preparation of emergency management plans; (3) grants and technical assistance to local governments for preparation of mitigation strategies; and (4) grants to local governments for coastal management projects. These are described below.

1. Land Acquisition

Perhaps the most effective hazard mitigation strategy is government acquisition of hazard-prone properties and elimination of the possibility of their development. Since the 1970s, Florida has acquired numerous tracts of land for a variety of purposes, such as environmental protection, historic preservation, recreation and open space, and access to scenic views. When these purchases included hazard-prone areas, these actions have had the additional effect of removing these properties from the supply of developable land and reducing the threat of hazards to lives and property. Although the state's land acquisition programs do not operate primarily to serve the purposes of hazard mitigation, they represent an important tool for accomplishing this goal in coastal areas. The state considers acquisition of coastal lands as an important element of its coastal management programs [Fla. Stat. s. 380.21(4) (1998)].

One of the state's most significant attempts to acquire hazard-prone properties was made through the Save Our Coast initiative in the 1980s. Under this program, the state has acquired 73,000 acres of beaches, barrier islands, coastal marshlands, and beach access points (Deyle and Smith 1994). The state legislature issued $200 million in bonds to finance the initiative. In addition, the state's Conservation and Recreational Lands (CARL) program is directed to consider "the value of acquiring coastal high-hazard parcels, consistent with hazard mitigation and postdisaster redevelopment policies, in order to minimize the risk to life and property and to reduce the need for future disaster assistance" [Fla. Stat. s. 259.101(4)(d)1 (1998)] when using funds from Preservation 2000, Florida's $3 billion land and water conservation program. This language was added to the state's land acquisition statute in 1993 to ensure that state land acquisition programs used "hazard mitigation potential" as a criterion for selection of properties. Finally, the state established in 1991 the Florida Communities Trust (FCT) to assist local governments in implementing the coastal, conservation, recreation, and open space elements required as part of the comprehensive plans. The FCT administers a grants program that makes available $30 million to local governments on an annual basis for the purposes of furthering the coastal management, conservation, and recreation goals of the local comprehensive plan, conserving natural resources, and resolving land use conflicts.

Currently, the state's objective in coastal land acquisition is to support locally based processes, which recognize hazard mitigation, for identifying and prioritizing coastal properties that may be acquired as part of the state's programs [Fla. Stat. s. 163.3178(8) (1998)]. With a definitive acquisition list in hand, coastal communities would be ready to pursue land acquisition opportunities as they arise, particularly in a post-storm situation when federal disaster funds may be available. Coastal advocates have criticized the state land acquisition selection criteria and processes for overlooking hazard mitigation and other coastal objectives (ELMS III 1992).

2. Local Mitigation Strategies

In 1997, DCA launched a $20 million program called Breaking the Cycle. Its purpose is to provide incentives to local governments to increase their mitigation efforts and to incorporate mitigation into local comprehensive planning, building, and emergency management programs. Through this program, the DCA awards to cities and counties funds that can be used to assemble an intergovernmental, interdisciplinary team that analyzes vulnerability to hazards, outlines mitigation goals, and selects and prioritizes specific projects to fulfill these goals (Florida DCA 1997). A stipulation of the funds is that mitigation strategy development involve not only emergency management officials, but also local planners and building officials. The intent is to improve coordination on mitigation activities within each county and integrate hazard mitigation planning with the land use element of the local comprehensive plans, the comprehensive emergency management plans, and related codes and ordinances.

Local mitigation strategies are expected to streamline the process of requesting and receiving financial assistance from state and federal agencies for mitigation projects, either predisaster or postdisaster. According to DCA, "Communities that implement disaster-resistant planning techniques and strategies stand to receive more money after a disaster, and these communities will be given priority over those who have not implemented a mitigation strategy" (Florida DCA 1999:15). In addition, the DCA hopes that the local mitigation strategies will guide ongoing investments in mitigation projects and function like a long-term capital improvements plan for mitigation (D. Smith, personal communication, 1999). Presently, all 67 counties in Florida are under contract with DCA to prepare local mitigation strategies in cooperation with the municipalities within each county.

Several other programs designed to supplement the local mitigation strategies also exist under DCA's Breaking the Cycle umbrella program. The Resource Identification Strategy (RIS) provides data to local officials on available funds for mitigation and long-term redevelopment projects. The Residential Construction Mitigation Program makes low-interest loans to eligible homeowners for retrofits to strengthen their homes' resistance to wind. Its structural evaluation model is designed to satisfy the actuarial concerns of the insurance industry (D. Smith, personal communication, 1999). To understand how the programs of the "Breaking the Cycle" initiative interrelate with mitigation programs of other entities (such as FEMA, Red Cross, and local agencies), DCA created the Florida Showcase Community Project. The state selected two coastal communities as mitigation demonstration sites and, in cooperation with the State University System, will monitor and evaluate implementation of mitigation initiatives (Florida DCA 1999).

3. Emergency Preparedness and Assistance Trust Fund (EMPATF)

As described above, the Florida Legislature created in 1993 the EMPATF to provide a dedicated funding source for emergency management. Revenues for this fund come from a surcharge on private and commercial property's insurance premiums. Moneys from this trust fund support the development and implementation of state and local agency emergency management programs. At the same time, the legislature established the Florida Hurricane Catastrophe Fund to provide reimbursement to insurers for a portion of their losses due to catastrophic hurricanes. Beginning in 1997, the legislature annually appropriates a minimum of $10 million from this fund to state and local agencies for loss reduction programs and efforts to protect infrastructure [Fla. Stat. s. 215.555(7)(c) (1998)].

4. Grants for Local Coastal Management Programs

The state legislature passed in 1978 the Florida Coastal Management Act [Fla. Stat. ss. 380.205-.24 (1998)] in recognition that "the coastal zone is rich in a variety of natural, commercial, recreational, ecological, industrial, and aesthetic resources of immediate and potential value to the present and future well-being of the residents of this state which will be irretrievably lost or damaged if not properly managed" [Fla. Stat. s. 380.21(3)(a) (1998)]. The Coastal Management Act authorized the state to submit a coastal management program to the federal government for approval and directed that this program be based on existing state laws pertaining to land use, comprehensive planning, and other relevant areas. Florida's coastal program received federal approval in 1981.

This program is based on several existing state authorities pertaining to coastal issues, such as beach and shore preservation, comprehensive planning, environmental control, and emergency management. Participation in the Coastal Management Program qualifies the state for federal matching dollars to enhance efforts to implement these laws and programs. State and local agencies are eligible to apply for these funds to accomplish hazard mitigation objectives, such as development of a postdisaster redevelopment plan. A primary objective of the state's coastal program is to mitigate hazards and the program provides funds to local governments and state agencies to support planning for hazard mitigation.

The state also provides matching funds to local governments for eligible beach management projects to reduce the impacts of erosion on beaches. The Beach and Shore Preservation Act directs the state to develop a long-term plan for restoration of critically eroding beaches based on several criteria, including the extent of existing and potential damage to beachfront property. In 1998, the legislature established a dedicated funding source for erosion control projects by earmarking a portion of state revenues from documentary stamp taxes for this purpose. Up to this point, funds for erosion control were appropriated annually from general revenue on an ad hoc basis, complicating long-term planning.

E. The Insurance Issue

Apart from the mandates, regulations, and incentives that Florida uses to compel hazard mitigation in its coastal communities, the rising cost of property insurance is becoming one of the primary reasons why communities and property owners undertake hazard mitigation. The insurance crisis also has introduced the insurance industry as a major advocate for expansion of hazard mitigation programs. The purpose of this section is to describe the mechanisms created in Florida to ensure the availability of property insurance in coastal areas.

The destruction left from Hurricane Andrew in 1992 brought many changes to the insurance market in Florida. Prior to this disaster, the insurance industry was lulled by years of relatively low losses. The hurricane activity between 1982 and 1991 was one of the lowest on record for Florida. A 1986 study by the All-Industry Research Advisory Council, an advisory organization for the insurance industry, released a study of the potential worst-case losses that the industry might face from hurricanes. The study predicted that two $7 billion hurricanes could occur in the same year (Ayscue 1996). However, Hurricane Andrew shattered that estimate by causing an estimated $15.5 billion in damages to insured property. The 1980s was a time of unbounded competition for homeowners' policies throughout Florida and insurance companies lowered rates to gain a larger share of the insurance market in Florida. Often the rates given were even lower than what the insurance company's own actuaries felt were necessary to cover any future claims. But what the insurance industry did not count on was a hurricane such as Andrew to expose their overexposure.

Adding to this environment of complacency was the fact that during these years Florida experienced relatively few and mild hurricanes. Hurricane Andrew brought the realization to insurance actuaries that their methodology for calculating risk was primitive and did not properly account for the full cost of possible damages in Florida. More complicated computer simulation techniques have since replaced this methodology. The old methodology contained two problems. One was the relative uncertainty inherent in hurricane prediction. This creates problems for actuaries who are not able to predict accurately whether there is a chance of a major hurricane hitting Florida in the near future or decades from now.

The second problem facing actuaries was the difficulty of predicting the amount of development that would occur in an area. The old methodology failed to note the increased development that occurred in Florida and other coastal states in the 1980s. Thus, the destruction of Andrew emphasized the reality of insurance overexposure to hurricanes not only in Florida but throughout coastal states. As Campbell pointed out: ''People in the industry are now more concerned about events so large that they threaten the solvency of insurance markets as a whole. . . . The question of insurability has become a public policy issue, beyond the possibility of insolvency of individual insurance firms. Some in the industry would turn to government as insurer of last resort . . . '' (1997:7).

After Hurricane Andrew, the state stepped in and took charge of the insurance situation occurring in Florida. First, the state passed a moratorium on cancellations and nonrenewals of residential property insurance policies. The moratorium allowed insurance companies to cancel or nonrenew only 5% of their policies in Florida and only 10% from one county for reasons of hurricane risk. However, no limitation was placed on their ability to cancel or non-renew policies under its underwriting rules for any reason other than hurricane risk. The final phase of the moratorium concludes in November 1999. The passage of this moratorium was an effort on the part of the state to allow stabilization of the insurance market and an orderly adjustment to exposure problems occurring within the insurance industry.

However, the moratorium was not enough to keep hundreds of thousands of homeowners from losing their insurance coverage. Therefore, in November 1992 the state legislature created a market of last resort for residential property insurance, the Florida Residential Property and Casualty Joint Underwriting Association (JUA). In 1994 the state also created the Florida Property and Casualty Joint Underwriting Association (Condo-JUA), which provides insurance to condominiums that are unable to obtain private insurance. By September 1996, the JUA had grown to 937,000 policies. Since that time, there has been an aggressive effort to reduce the number of properties insured by the JUA and find private insurance for these residential properties. The JUA currently includes 600,000 policy holders, with more than half located in Dade, Broward, and Palm Beach counties in southeast Florida (Summer 1997).

Florida also has a coastal wind and hurricane insurance called the Florida Windstorm Underwriting Association (FWUA), which covers facilities in certain coastal areas where wind and hurricane coverage have been determined to be unavailable in the private market. This determination is made during a series of public hearings. Since Hurricane Andrew, the number of FWUA policy holders has grown five times over and now includes more than 320,000 policy holders. The FWUA is a permanent insurance mechanism for high risk areas (Summer 1997).

In 1993, the Florida Legislature established the Florida Hurricane Catastrophe Fund, which acts as a reinsurance source for insurance companies serving Florida. Reinsurance reimburses insurers if hurricane losses reach a threshold level of loss. Most reinsurance is written in one of two ways. First, the reinsurer assumes a share of the risk in exchange for a share of the premiums or second, the reinsurer assumes a layer of risk (e.g., losses between $5 million and $10 million). In this way, reinsurance ''spreads risk from the primary insurer to other parties'' (Campbell 1997:9). The fund charges property insurers in Florida a premium for varying levels above the reimbursement threshold. The property insurer can select a 45, 75, or 90% reimbursement level and pay a premium based on the level chosen. However, all property insurers in the state must participate in the fund at some level. Florida law allows for the insurers to pass directly the cost of the premiums to policy holders.

Florida's insurance crisis also prompted scrutiny of the state's building code requirements and local code enforcement practices. Insurers and public officials alike began to question the existing building code system in Florida, particularly its administration and enforcement as well as the code itself, in light of widespread damage to structures during Hurricane Andrew. Many believe that inadequate administration and enforcement of building codes was a major factor contributing to the extent of structural damage [FEMA 1993; Insurance Institute for Property Loss Reduction 1995; Dade County Grand Jury 1992 (as cited in Getter, 1992)].

Currently, Florida law requires local governments and 14 state agencies to adopt one of four minimum building codes—the Standard Building Code, the One and Two Family Dwelling Code, the South Florida Building Code, and the EPCOT Code. Local governments are charged with enforcement of the codes and are permitted to amend the model codes as long as the amendments result in more stringent requirements. However, the Governor's Building Codes Study Commission, created in 1996, found that this system has led to a "patchwork of technical and administrative processes which allow for too many people to determine what codes are used, how those codes are administered and enforced, and interpreted, and to what level the participants...are educated, trained and disciplined" (Governor's Building Codes Study Commission 1997:44). Its recommendations resulted in sweeping reforms in 1998 to the state's Building Construction Standards statute (Chapter 553, Florida Statutes). In particular, changes to the law now call for development of a single, statewide code to replace the various state and local building codes that presently exist.

The state legislature directed the Florida Building Commission to develop and submit the Florida Building Code for approval in 2000. It is scheduled to take effect in 2001. Thereafter, the Florida Building Commission will maintain the code and approve amendments to it. The code will contain special provisions (such as wind load requirements) for construction in coastal areas. It is hoped that a unified, uniform code will diminish inconsistencies in the administration and enforcement of building codes and thereby reduce potential for structural damage from natural hazards, a goal shared by insurers and public officials alike.

V. CONCLUSION

With steady population growth in Florida's coastal areas, it is certain that hazard mitigation will continue to represent a major policy concern of the state. Since the 1970s, the state has developed and implemented a number of local mandates, regulations, and incentives to promote hazard mitigation within coastal communities and ensure that growth and development does not further exacerbate their vulnerability to natural hazards. As a whole, these actions embody Florida's approach to hazard mitigation in coastal areas and provide the basis for local initiatives.

Perhaps the greatest strength of Florida's hazard mitigation program is the consistent policy basis that it provides for local planning and regulation in coastal areas. All cities and counties must address common policies relating to land use, resource protection, emergency management, and postdisaster redevelopment. They must enforce minimum standards pertaining to construction in the Coastal Building Zone and seaward of the CCCL. The state's uniform building code, to be adopted in 2000, will further enhance consistency in the state's hazard mitigation program. In addition, the state's increasing commitment to providing funds for local mitigation activities improves the ability of cities and counties to meet and exceed these minimum requirements. The several mitigation funding sources and programs created since Hurricane Andrew undoubtedly have raised awareness about the value of planning for hazards and will provide the tools to support this process.

One of the greatest constraints on Florida's ability to mitigate hazards stems from the fact that many coastal areas are developed already and land use patterns in the high hazard areas are established. The only mitigation opportunities available to these areas are postdisaster redevelopment or redevelopment for economic reasons. Planning for these potential opportunities is vital, yet most communities in Florida fail to develop plans that outline specific strategies to acquire lands, relocate structures, or reduce densities in high hazard areas when these opportunities arise. Furthermore, the state has not enforced aggressively the postdisaster planning requirements for coastal cities and counties. Finally, implementing these types of strategies often requires government acquisition of property and land values in Florida's coastal areas tend to render acquisition financially infeasible.

REFERENCES

Ayscue J.K. (1996). *Hurricane Damage to Residential Structures: Risk and Mitigation*. Natural Hazards Research Working Paper #94. Boulder, CO: University of Colorado.

Beatley T., Brower D.T., Schwab A.K. (1994). *An Introduction to Coastal Zone Management*. Washington, DC: Island Press.

Burby, R.J., French S.P. (1985). *Flood Plain Land Use Management: A National Assessment*. Boulder, CO: Westview Press, Inc.

Bush D.M., Pilkey O.H. Jr., Neal W.L. (1996). *Living by the Rules of the Sea*. Durham, NC: Duke University Press.

Campbell J. (1997). The search for protection against natural disasters. *Federal Reserve Bank of Boston Regional Review*, Summer, 6–11.

Code of Federal Regulations (1998). Washington, D.C.: U.S. General Services Administration, National Archives and Records Service, Office of the Federal Register.

Congressional Research Service (1993). *A Descriptive Analysis of Federal Relief, Insurance, and Loss Reduction Programs for Natural Hazards*. U.S. Government Printing Office, Washington, D.C., 1993.

DeGrove J.M. (1998). Critical area programs in Florida: Creative balancing of growth and the environment. *Journal of Urban and Contemporary Law* 34, 51–97.

DeGrove J.M. (1992). *Planning and Growth Management in the States*. Cambridge, MA: Lincoln Institute of Land Policy.

DeGrove J.M., Stroud N.E. (1988). New development and future trends in local government comprehensive planning. *Stetson Law Rev* 17:573–605.

Deyle R.E., Smith R.A. (1994). Storm hazard mitigation and post-storm redevelopment policies. Department of Urban and Regional Planning, Tallahassee, FL: Florida State University.

Deyle R.E., Smith R.A. (1998). Local government compliance with state planning mandates. *American Planning Association Journal* 64; 457–469.

Drabek T.E., (1991). The evolution of emergency management. In:Drabek T.E., Hoetmer G.J. (eds.), *Emergency Management: Principles and Practices for Local Government*. Washington, DC: International City Management Association, pp. 3–29.

Environmental Land Management Study (ELMS III) Committee (1992). *Building Successful Communities (Final Report)*. Tallahassee, FL: State of Florida.

Federal Emergency Management Agency (1996). *The National Mitigation Strategy.* ⟨http://www.fema.gov⟩.

Federal Emergency Management Agency (1997). *The National Mitigation Strategy: Partnerships for Building Safer Communities.* Washington, D.C.: FEMA.

Federal Emergency Management Agency (1998). The National Flood Insurance Act of 1968. ⟨http://www.fema.gov/nfip/theact.htm⟩.

''Flood insurance revamped''(1994). *Natural Hazards Observer*, November 8.

Florida Administrative Code Annotated (1998). Atlanta, GA: Darby Printing Company.

Florida Center for Public Management (1997). *Florida Assessment of Coastal Trends.* Tallahassee, FL: Florida Department of Community Affairs, Florida Coastal Management Program.

Florida Department of Community Affairs (1997). *The Local Mitigation Strategy: A Guidebook for Florida Cities and Counties.* Tallahassee, FL: Florida Department of Community Affairs.

Florida Department of Community Affairs (1999). *Breaking the Cycle.* Tallahassee, FL: Florida Department of Community Affairs.

Florida Department of Environmental Protection (1993). *A Statewide Inventory and Identification of the Beach Erosion Problem Areas in Florida.* Beaches and Shores Technical and Design Memorandum 89-1. Tallahassee, FL: Author, Florida Department of Environmental Protection.

Florida State University, Institute of Science and Public Affairs (1992). *The Florida Atlas.* Tallahassee, FL: Board of Regents of the State of Florida.

Florida Statutes (1998). Tallahassee, FL: State of Florida.

Getter, Lisa (1992). ''Inspections: A breakdown in the system.'' *The Miami Herald*, December 20.

Godschalk D.R. (1991). Disaster mitigation and hazard management. In: Drabek T.E., Hoetmer G.J. (eds.), *Emergency Management: Principles and Practices for Local Government.* Washington, DC: International City Management Association, pp 131–160.

Godschalk D.R., Beatley T.E., Berke P., Brower D.J., Kaiser E.J. (1999). *Natural Hazard Mitigation: Recasting Disaster Policy and Planning.* Washington, DC: Island Press.

Governor's Building Codes Study Commission. (1997). *Five Foundations for a Better Built Environment.* Tallahassee, FL: Author.

Insurance Institute for Property Loss Reduction and Insurance Research Council (1995). Coastal *Exposure and Community Protection.* Boston: Insurance Research Council, Inc., and Insurance Institute for Property Loss Reduction.

Mittler E. (1997). *A Case Study of Florida's Emergency Management Since Hurricane Andrew.* Natural Hazards Research Working Paper #98. Boulder; CO: University of Colorado.

National Research Council (1989). *Reducing Disaster's Toll: The United States Decade for Natural Disaster Reduction.* Washington, DC: National Academy Press.

Platt R. (1996). Hazard mitigation: Cornerstone or grains of sand? *Natural Hazards Observer* 21, 10–11.

Sheets R.C. (1995). Stormy weather. *Forum for Applied Research and Public Policy* 10, 5–14.

Smith, Dennis (1999). Planning Manager, Florida Department of Community Affairs.

Sumner D.Y. (1997). Testimony of Daniel Y. Summer, General Counsel, Florida Department of Insurance, Before the Subcommittee on Housing and Community Opportunity. ⟨http://www.house.gov/banking/62497sum.htm⟩

United States Code (1998). Washington, DC: Office of the Law Revision Counsel of the House of Representatives.

University of Florida, Bureau of Economic and Business Research (1997). *Florida Statistical Abstract.* Gainesville, FL: University of Florida.

University of Florida, Bureau of Economic and Business Research (1998). *Florida Statistical Abstract.* Gainesville, FL: University of Florida.

Williams J.M., Duedall I.W. (1997). *Florida Hurricanes and Tropical Storms*, rev ed. Gainesville, FL: University of Florida, Florida Sea Grant College Program.

44
Planning for Prevention

Emergency Preparedness and Planning to Lessen the Potential for Crisis

Jack Pinkowski Wayne Huizenga Graduate School of Business and Entrepreneurship, Nova Southeastern University, Fort Lauderdale, Florida

I. INTRODUCTION

Preparing for crisis and emergency management requires preplanning and anticipating needs in many forms. Typically it focuses on needs assessment in terms of training personnel, evaluating hazards, and securing equipment. It also includes encouraging preventive measures to reduce the dangers that would necessitate an emergency response.

However, some emergencies with substantial potential for human disaster cannot realistically be eliminated by human intervention. These include earthquakes, tsunamis, volcanic eruptions, tornadoes, and hurricanes. Yet, planning can reduce the impacts of natural disasters on human lives by government intervention and emergency preparedness. This can be accomplished through such measures as advanced weather forecasting, seismic activity monitoring, and preplanned evacuation procedures. Most important, it also may embrace prohibitions on land use. This approach addresses a government obligation to not allow citizens to put themselves in harms way.

Realistically, many hazardous conditions that ultimately require an emergency management response and which can result in human tragedy are man made situations. Accordingly, they are not solely subject to the vagaries of climatological or natural phenomenon. These hazards include nuclear generating plants, nuclear waste sites, hazardous-materials storage facilities, landfills, and brown fields. The environmental degradation and pollution of natural resources that result from accidents at such locations have been catastrophic. Yet, these consequences are not inevitable. Nonetheless, the potential for disasters related to these sites are often produced because of what society has permitted to happen. It includes what facilities governments have allowed to be constructed as well as unanticipated consequences of these decisions. The potential for disaster from permitted land uses may also evolve over time, becoming hazardous when once they were not.

Whether potentially dangerous initially or a result of changes over time, hazardous land uses may adjoin environmentally pristine areas or residential neighborhoods where they now pose potential dangers to human life. Because modern society has allowed the potential for disaster to be produced, presumably it can disallow the potential for disaster by better land use planning. Some might argue that legislators almost never seem to deal with ideals; they need disasters (Hoban and Brooks, 1996, p. 153). This chapter intends to highlight the nature of potential hazards that planning has not prevented so that new planning may provide options to correct the reality of these situations before they involve disasters.

Especially pertinent are situations that have developed subsequent to original, prudent planning efforts but which have changed through no intentional fault of government planners. Although these situations now represent the potential for disaster, planning may still be possible to reduce the risks to human life and environmental contamination. The objective herein, is to offer a proposed solution by planning for prevention to lesson the potential for crisis in these situations. An essential component of this proposal for action must include consideration of possible reasons for inaction heretofore. Apropos this discussion are criticisms that societies tolerate particular hazardous circumstances, or merely socially offensive ones, on a selective basis. This selectively allows the burdens of potential disasters to be carried disproportionately by certain groups based upon their race, class, or ethnic identity.

II. SITING OF UNWANTED LAND USES

Unwanted land uses in general are those that because of their nature have been called LULUs (Bowman and Crews-Meyer, 1997), i.e., locally unwanted land uses, and NIMBY syndromes, i.e., not in my backyard. Such monikers express societal preferences for not only dangerous but also obnoxious facilities where they can negatively affect the quality of life. These consequences include potentially life-threatening hazards as well as those of appearance, smell, or inconvenience that translate into lower property values. Not in my backyard was the clarion call of protesters in 1982 when American attention was drawn to a proposed landfill for polychlorinated biphenyls (PCBs) in Warren County, North Carolina. The county has a predominantly black population and the effort to choose it as the site of what was described as a new PCB dumping ground elicited accusations that these attempts are a new form of racial discrimination. Reverend Benjamin Chavis Jr. coined the phrase ''environmental racism'' (Godsil, 1991) to describe such intentions assuming that the imposition of the choice of location on minorities is racially motivated.

Chavis used the term to refer to both intentional and unintentional affects that may result from allowing hazardous materials in communities that are demographically composed of racial minorities. However, from a legal standpoint this is still controversial. The U.S. Supreme Court requires proof of ''purposeful and invidious discrimination'' to find a violation of the 14th Amendment (*Washington v. Davis*, 1976) which affords all U.S. citizens equal protection under the law. Yet, employment discrimination law in the United States uses a different standard. It relies on the consequences of circumstances rather than purposeful intent. Federal employment statutes such as Title VII of the Civil Rights Act of 1964 prohibit the use of any employment criterion that ''disparately impacts employees on the basis of race.'' There is no specific law that defines the abridgement of civil rights in terms of environmental degradation or community impacts. Perhaps this is so because environmental legislation is usually drafted in response to particular incidents. Accordingly, clear standards by which emergency planners may assess potential hazards in terms of the potentially disparate impact on economic or racial minorities are not to be explicitly found in the law. Therefore, local standards, options, and solutions may be more important.

III. EVIDENCE FOR DISPARATE RACIAL IMPACT

The essence of the problem remains that regardless of whether hazardous sitings are intentional or unintentional, the consequences including pollution, hazards of toxic wastes, adverse health conditions, and the potential for deadly disasters are falling disproportionately on communities of color and low-income communities (Bullard, 1994). Institute, West Virginia, is an example of a hazardous situation that has been allowed to exist even after the dangerous nature of the potential for disaster has been made well known. It is the location of a Union Carbide plant that produces the same deadly chemical that caused a widely publicized human disaster when the chemicals leaked from the company's facility in Bhopal, India. The neighborhood surrounding the U.S. plant is composed predominately of poor citizens and minorities (McKinney, 1985).

Affluent communities have the means to lobby against such sitings when they are proposed and deliberated. Local residents in affluent communities may even be environmental activists themselves. Consequently, developers, corporations, and planners often choose the path of least resistance and place such facilities in predominantly poor and minority communities where they do not face the same opposition. They can even tout the advantages of these new industries as contributing to job creation and enhancing the tax base. Robert D. Bullard (1990) suggests that polluting industries are eager to relocate to poor, minority areas. Millions of urban and rural blacks are geographically isolated in economically depressed and environmentally polluted areas away from the expanding job centers and value the possibility of new jobs rather than the health risks involved with such economic development (Bullard and Wright, 1987).

Efforts to gain new jobs for communities put pressures on leaders to relax enforcement of pollution standards and environmental regulations. New environmental problems may even have been created as a consequence of the 1970s push for economic growth in the promotion of what was described as the "new South." Accordingly, the promise of jobs and a broadened tax base in economically depressed communities are often seen as an acceptable tradeoff for the potential health and environmental risks (Bullard, 1990). Industrial entities, like landfill operators and trash haulers, have come to view the black community in the South as a pushover.

Hazardous industrial plants, nuclear waste dumps, municipal incinerators, land fills, potentially explosive chemical tank farms, and similar land uses are allowed by appropriate zoning regulations for such locations. The nearby residents, including African-Americans, Hispanics, Native Americans, Asians, migrant farm workers, and others comprising a lower socioeconomic order, live in housing approved and authorized by zoning regulations pertaining to the land uses of their parcels. They may not know that they are not safe there.

In fact, many of these citizens also comprise the workforce of the industries that stand to pollute the environment. Several realities converge to define the demographics of such communities: These people have no choice; they need the work and consequently accept the risks out of economic necessity or ignorance; they are drawn to the affordable housing that is correspondingly cheaper adjoining hazardous facilities; and limited resources make choosing safer options difficult. They may not have a personal vehicle; they must walk to work instead of paying for transportation. These workers take what jobs they can find and live with whatever housing they find nearby out of necessity.

Blacks are described as lacking community organization and environmental consciousness (Collette, 1985). Statistical differences as to race have been reported for the level of awareness of environmental causes (Taylor, 1989). Taylor attributes racial differences to the limited economic means that makes environmental activism prohibitive. It constitutes a concern and action gap that limits mobilization of black groups around environmental issues. The reasons for this difference may include factors such as the lack of perceived access to decision-making elites, the failure to recognize advocacy channels that are affordable or costless, psychological factors, and even the inability to mobilize meager financial resources because of other considerations.

Following Abraham Maslow's classic "hierarchy of needs" theory, environmental issues are a luxury that cannot be of particular concern until more basic needs of food and shelter are met (Maslow, 1975). Consequently, individuals in lower socioeconomic groups—blacks, other nonwhites, and poor whites—typically accept lower physical living conditions out of financial necessity, not by choice.

The United Church of Christ, Commission for Racial Justice, reports from its survey, "Toxic Wastes and Race in the United States" (1987), these salient conclusions:

1. Race is the most significant variable associated with the location of hazardous waste sites.
2. The highest concentrations of commercial hazardous facilities are located in communities with the highest composition of racial and ethnic minorities.
3. The percentage of the minority population in communities with at least one commercial hazardous waste facility is twice the average minority percentage in communities without such facilities.
4. Socioeconomic status is an important variable in the location of these sites.
5. Three out of five black and Hispanic Americans live in communities with one or more toxic waste sites.
6. Over 15 million African-Americans, over 8 million Hispanics, and over 50% of Asian/Pacific Islanders and Native Americans live in communities with one or more abandoned or uncontrolled toxic waste sites.

The Environmental Protection Agency (EPA) in its report, "Environmental Equity" (1992), concludes that socioeconomic conditions and race are major factors determining environmental discrimination. A General Accounting Office study (1983) discloses that three out of four sites in eight states that comprise its designated Southern Region for disposal of hazardous materials are in communities with majority black populations. At least 26% of these populations have incomes below the poverty level.

These examples pose challenging questions. Why not just move people away from the danger of hazardous sites? Is the reason for the demonstrated demographic bias attributable to anything but the lack of resistance of the local residents, their interest in their own well-being, or their color, or their poverty? Perhaps a more salient explanation is simple fiscal economics. There are so many potentially dangerous locations that the costs to move the residents or the hazards are more than taxpayers have been willing to accept. Nationwide estimates of toxic waste sites alone are as high as 300,000 facilities (McKinney, 1985). Accordingly, perhaps the most important element of any proposed solution is monetary.

IV. EVOLUTION OF LAND USE

Another consideration is necessary to appreciate the problems that now constitute the potential for disaster. Without any intentionality, prior planning has resulted in existing land uses that have become hazardous sites, as opposed to conscious choices concerning new sitings that are inherently hazardous. Love Canal, in Niagara Falls, New York, is an example that drew extensive media coverage. At Love Canal toxic fumes and poisonous material leaching from the ground caused property damage and health problems for nearby residents. These maladies include higher incidence of cancer, birth defects, spontaneous abortions, and other medical problems. Yet no one predicted that this would be the eventual byproduct of local industrial production until it was too late.

Historically, zoning was the solution that was intended to prevent unwanted land uses that could result in communities at risk. In retrospect, it may be to blame for discriminatory practices. The court decision in *Euclid v. Ambler Realty* (1926) established the legitimacy of neighborhood planning. Communities have relied on zoning to separate industrial uses from residential ones. Comprehensive plans have designated industrial areas and corresponding adjacent residential areas separated by buffer zones. However, in many cases subsequent changes in the nature of the industrial land use have adversely affected the residential uses in their proximity. Some communities have even become endangered because new industrial activities, which pose health risks, have moved into sites that were original approved for industry without prior consideration of the possibility that hazardous industries were not prohibited. Other communities that now face dangerous risks were properly zoned for industry adjacent to residential areas in order to serve the needs of the plants for a nearby, available workforce.

Powell Duffryn Terminals, Inc., in Savannah, Georgia, represents such a situation. It became a hazard through the evolution of its land use. The facility that is now a chemical storage tank farm is part of an industrial complex along the Savannah River. The area was planned as a large industrial zone that served in the 1940s for constructing Liberty Ships in the American war effort. To facilitate the mobilization of manpower for shipbuilding, housing units were constructed immediately adjacent to the shipyards. For national security reasons, management personnel and their families were provided accommodations within the complex to provide close and convenient housing. In April of 1995, the storage facility was the site of a massive explosion, fire, and hazardous-material spill that not only endangered the modern-day residents of the former shipbuilder's apartments but also posed a threat of disaster for almost five weeks to a substantial part of the now populated community that has grown up around the industrial tract. This incident is included as a case study in another chapter of this volume.

The waterfront industrial area that was once vital to American interests has involved into a general industrial zone with many commercial enterprises. The sector continues to be favored by city and county planners as an appropriate district for industrial use because of its history and its industrial nature. Its closeness to several alternative modes of cargo transportation make it a natural site for industry. The river, ocean, rail, and highway access contribute to a locale that can attract industrial firms whose taxes and jobs build the local economy. Government leaders have even historically offered tax incentives to keep and attract these businesses to this district. These concessions have included designating the industrial zone as unincorporated county jurisdiction rather than including its land in the city. They thereby reduce the tax burden for the industries and in turn create local jobs when firms make investments in the area.

However, the remainder of the contiguous area is now within city confines and its residential occupants pay taxes and receive public benefits from the city. Yet, by special agreement, Savannah city water and fire services are provided for the industries in the riverside zone that are actually outside of the city's jurisdiction with respect to enforcement of health, safety, zoning, or fire code regulations. The overbearing priority, is the fact that favorable opportunities are made available to these businesses in return for job creation and economic impact. But the workers who accept hazardous work do not have to live there and accordingly their families do not have to be subject to the hazards that the breadwinner accepts in order to provide for the family. Other workers, including the lowest, unskilled ones live within walking distance because they have little choice.

The residents adjacent to the tank farm are primarily the working poor, those who live on government assistance and cannot work, and the retired. The residential property manager describes their situation as follows: ''these are people with no place else to go...all of them are low income households; more than fifty percent are minorities'' (Ramsey, 1996). The situation in Savannah is no different from that in many areas of the country, especially the South. By happenstance, by fate, or by the failure of government intervention, residential areas that are next to and are threatened by toxic or hazardous land uses, where the uses once may have been safe, now find only poor residents, mostly minorities, who are drawn to these places to live. The attraction is primarily low-priced rents but possibly ignorance of the dangers and desperation for gainful employment contributes to the skewed social demographics.

V. INCIDENCE OF THE SOCIAL COSTS OF HAZARDOUS LAND USES

Communities in proximity to these facilities bear other social costs associated with living next to hazardous or unwanted land uses. These include noise from the industrial operations, truck and vehicle traffic over public streets to and from the location, noxious odors, and air pollution. In many cases these are 24-hours-a-day, seven-days-a-week problems. The inevitable result is that the combined external costs imposed on locales next to potentially hazardous sites drive property values down.

The residential areas that are now beleaguered by noise and air pollution, truck traffic problems, dusts, smells, drainage, etc., may also be subject to life threatening dangers now or in the future if the residents become exposed to toxic chemicals in the water, soil, or air because of new life-threatening industrial hazards next door. The new hazards will affect all of those who live in the household. Although the wage earner may accept nearby hazardous employment for him/herself, out of economic necessity, it also puts his/her family at risk, perhaps to a greater degree. The worker has some protection on the job by Occupational Safety and Health Administration (OSHA) federal regulations regarding work hazards. These protections lower the risks of exposure on the job. But the workers' children playing in the nearby playground or attending school across the street may suffer from toxic fumes without any physical protection. The entire family's future is at risk from a potential explosion like that at the Powell Duffryn plant. The considerations of social issues that speak to quality of life and potential for upward mobility take the search for a solution beyond the health issues.

Poor and minority communities have the most to gain from the enforcement of existing environmental regulations, and the passage of new ones, because they live in close proximity to the sources of the hazards. However, they bear a disproportionate share of the burden of the existing problems. Zoning and restrictive land use regulations have so far failed to segregate the disparate impact on black communities that result from industrial uses that exist next to neighborhoods comprised primarily of poor and racial minorities. The intended benefits from policies to recruit new industries, to expand the tax base, and to create new jobs have not proportionately benefited this segment of society.

Lessening demands on industry to comply with existing pollution and environmental regulations imposes costs on the poor and minority members of these communities by way of their safety. For the most part, the taxes that are raised through economic development that results in hazardous land use have not been redistributed to the poor minority communities to fight the problems that are still endemic there. These social ills in addition to health hazards include high crime rates, drug trafficking, deteriorating infrastructure, high unemployment, and widespread poverty. The fact that these social ills that have not been abated, ostensibly for lack of resources to adequately address the troubles, is in contradiction to the increase in jobs and the tax base touted as the benefit of new, even hazardous, industry to an area. Poor and minority citizens continue to bear the cost for the rest of society. The more affluent avoid paying the costs but reap the benefit of economic growth and increased prosperity. Citizens with greater financial means invest in these industrial concerns through stock and mutual fund ownership. The larger society also benefits by the availability of the products manufactured by the industries even though toxins and environmental hazards are produced as a byproduct of their operation. The cost of these external, secondary products is not equally shared by the entire society but falls hardest on those who live in danger near the facilities. Unfortunately, the financial benefits are also not shared proportionately between the haves and have-nots.

Being poor and part of the working class in America, whether white or a person of color, means that you are more likely to bear the social costs of toxins produced in an industrialized society. For example, along the Mississippi River for 100 miles between Baton Rouge and New Orleans, there are so many international petrochemical companies and documented high incidences of health problems and environmental degradation that the area has been called Cancer Alley (Nixon, 1997). Louisiana officials point to the industries as contributing billions of dollars to the local economy. But residents mention numerous towns along the Mississippi that have historically been home to descendants of slaves which are now no more than contaminated, toxic ghost towns (Nixon, 1997). Industries that are potential polluters are drawn to poor neighborhoods by lower land values and lower costs of doing business that includes lower labor rates. At the same time, political power and community resources to fight back are limited, or overwhelmed, by condescending advice generally in the form—"do not bite the hand that feeds you."

The greater economic and physical mobility of whites and the middle class make them less vulnerable to such assaults on their physical environment. The evolution of land uses also makes the promise of jobs in exchange for environmental risk a short-term solution. The real hazards of the industrial sites for the residential areas may not materialize for years after the jobs, often low paying, are gone as the communities mature and metamorphose into class-stratified areas of decline.

VI. POSSIBLE SOLUTIONS

Direct compensation, economic incentives, and massive funds for cleanups have been some of the approaches proposed to redress the unequal share of benefits and burdens of toxic hazards and pollution problems. The Superfund Amendment and Reauthorization

Act (SARA) of 1986 provides a source of billions of dollars for cleanup of toxic sites. The funds come from fines paid by toxic waste producers and are administered by the Environmental Protection Agency (EPA). But the results of even massive spending on cleanup of toxic sites, or emergency response to accidents that result from hazards associated with them, do not address the social ills that allow people, perhaps even motivates them, to continue to live in danger from exposure and emergencies that may come from such hazards.

A. Judicial Remedies

If the local citizens who enjoy economic benefit are not the same citizens who pay the incidence costs, there is not equal protection afforded all under the law. As previously cited, the equal-protection clause of the 14th Amendment is a legal remedy only if litigants can prove disparate impact by showing a ''state harbored, discriminatory purpose'' (Godsil, 1991, p. 397). But the 14th Amendment also states in part that ''no state shall deny to any person within its jurisdiction the equal protection of the laws.'' Referring to the letter of the law seems in itself to be contradictory.

Case law supports the statutory authority under §1983 for civil rights actions brought by individuals to enforce constitutional rights (*Monroe v. Pape*, 1961). There are two essential elements of such actions: [1] the conduct must be committed by a person acting under the color of state law; and [2] the conduct deprived a person of rights, privileges, and immunities secured by the Constitution or the laws of the United States (*Parratt v. Taylor*, 1981). Disparate impact is a standard of proof that relates to a ''statute, neutral on its face, that bears more heavily on one race than on another'' (*Washington v. Davis*, 1976, p. 241). However, the Davis case also held that ''invidious purpose'' was necessary to trigger strict scrutiny of a government action that is neutral on its face (Tribe, 1988).

The burden of proof that a land use siting is motivated by a discriminatory purpose is problematic. However, it may be proved by circumstantial evidence. The court, in *Village of Arlington Heights v. Metropolitan Housing Development Corp.* (1977), outlined five relevant factors as evidentiary sources: (1) the impact on one race vs. another; (2) historical background, e.g., a series of invidious actions; (3) the sequence of events preceding a decision; (4) any departures from normal procedures; and (5) legislative and administrative history, e.g., minutes of meetings and reports.

Two cases involving the siting of non-hazardous waste landfills have attempted to apply the equal protection doctrine to resolve the issue of hazards imposed on adjacent communities composed of minorities. These cases are *East Bibb Twiggs Neighborhood Assn. v. Macon-Bibb County Planning and Zoning Commission* (1989), and *Bean v. Southwestern Waste Management Corp.* (1979). Both cases address the issue of intentional racial impact and neighborhood decline but speak as well to hazards that ultimately can result in emergency response and permanent health damage. However, both cases failed to provide sufficient evidence to establish that racial discrimination motivated the siting even though the evidence did ascertain the disproportionate affects on minorities.

Perhaps future courts will interpret disparate impact regarding land use differently or Congress will pass legislation defining its intent, i.e., that disparate impact should be judged by the consequences. Also mentioned earlier, in employment discrimination cases the court interprets disparate impact differently. *Griggs v. Duke Power Co.* (1971) is the landmark case that established the emphasis on the *consequences* of employment practices, not simply the motivation that seems to be the standard in land use decisions. Accordingly, until future court or legislative action clarifies the double standard, minority communities that are overburdened by the potential harm inherent in neighboring land uses that may result in emergency management response will not find a ready cure from judicial action.

B. Nuisance Law

Another legal concept, with established precedence, that may be useful in formulating a solution is the authority of a community to impose regulations on certain land uses that pose a nuisance to other citizens. This follows from a principle of economics that suggests that the external costs to the community may be internalized by adding them to private costs. One way of doing this is through nuisance laws where courts award damages for property losses suffered by neighboring landowners as a result of another's actions. The remedies include ordering modification of the offending activity or even its relocation. This implies value judgments and results in relief to one party by imposing a cost on the other one. The court implicitly assigns a preference in the property rights of the prevailing party to be free of adjacent, disturbing land uses (Mandelker, 1971). Zoning regulations in general also assign an implicit property right to residential homeowners to be free of adjacent, disturbing industrial development (Mandelker, 1981). Therefore, there is foundation for a community to impose additional costs on offending land uses in order to provide remedies to those who bear the burden of the offences.

There are two obstacles to applying the nuisance law concept to hazardous land uses that create the potential for disaster and emergency response. The first is that the citizens who effectively bear the social costs are not necessarily landowners but instead are poor and usually renters. To benefit their landlords with compensatory relief would not solve the problems. The second problem is that the result of imposing additional costs on business landowners or industrial process operators may result in the operations closing and moving out of the area. The probable consequences make such proposed action, if taken independently, to be self-defeating. Accordingly, any solution based on nuisance law must break new ground to avoid its natural pitfalls.

Local comprehensive plans do not give preference to environmental priorities. Yet, to rectify the disparities between those who pay for potentially hazardous land uses and those who benefit is an issue more akin to nuisance law wherein the concern for equity is between adjacent, competing land uses. The motivation for any equitable solution should not make any difference between the siting of a new landfill or the evolution of a hazardous material storage facility and even a site where toxins are byproducts of production that result in negative externalities for the community. However, to merely exclude certain land uses is problematic. Some courts have ruled that suburban exclusionary zoning is unconstitutional (Mandelker, 1981). The Supreme Court looks askance on regulations whose official purpose is to keep communities green and quiet but whose effective result is to exclude new arrivals which benefits those already in communities (Easterbrook, 1999). Exclusionary zoning is seen as one of the tools to attempt to create or maintain racial separation.

Typical zoning review is more concerned with the issue of compatibility with surroundings (Preiser and Rohane, 1988). Courts see this as allowing communities to control appearance and ease due process concerns (Mandelker, 1993). Perhaps the issue speaks to the need for the formulation of clear guidelines by which to evaluate the impacts of hazardous sitings (Shirvani, 1985). These are presently lacking (Nasar and Grannis, 1999). Motivation and the intent of government action have been issues that the court has used to judge the appropriateness of zoning decisions. In *Village of Arlington Heights v. Metropolitan Housing Development Corp.* (1977), previously mentioned, it cautiously set out a five-part evaluation to ascertain whether government actions were intended to be racially discriminatory. This landmark case leads to the conclusion that an official action will not be held unconstitutional solely because it results in a racially disproportionate impact. Although disproportionate impact is not irrelevant, it is not the sole basis for concluding that the action is motivated by racial discrimination. Arlington Heights argued that their intent was not to discriminate against low-income groups but instead borne of a desire to protect property values.

Anthony Downs (1997) argues that the consequences of multiple actions with ostensibly good intentions, over time, have resulted in central cities containing more poor Americans when compared to suburban communities. This selective population migration results in draining fiscal resources from American cities and contributes to urban decline and social inequalities within urban areas. The consequence of the affects and impacts of decisions that result in increased concentrations of poor citizens often contribute to destructive neighborhood environments. They include higher rates of crime, more single-parent households, higher unemployment, inadequate newborn care, drug abuse, and increased truancy with a corresponding lack of interest in education (Downs, 1997). According to Downs, this spatial segregation of the poor from the nonpoor in metropolitan areas is not found in most other developed nations. He attributes this in part to suburban exclusionary zoning regarding multifamily housing, which costs less than single-family housing. The result is that low-income people live together in older, more concentrated, poverty areas, often under the potential danger from emergencies and hazardous material accidents at facilities that also become concentrated in their immediate environs.

Accordingly, legislative experience with distributive environmental land use policies has resulted in hesitancy. The result is a preference to avoid such controversies. Attempts such as the South Carolina Coastal Zone Management Act provide an erstwhile example. Based on the destructive experience from Hurricane Hugo on South Carolina coastal properties, planners attempted to protect homeowners against the perils of the environment. Their plan was to prohibit rebuilding any structure that was destroyed by coastal storms within an area that is referred to as the coastal setback zone. However, the prohibitions to rebuild on the coast are tantamount to taking private property because they result in land losing its value for residential purposes. *Lucas v. South Carolina Coastal Council* (1992) is the landmark decision that established that these actions, although motivated to protecting citizens from the environment, resulted in takings and court decisions against the policy makers. Therefore, it is likely that any retroactive zoning to correct nuisance land use, even if it poses the potential for disaster, would result in claims of property rights takings as well.

The case law on the protection of property rights is not as incongruous as discrimination law. The Fifth Amendment provides that "private property shall not be taken for public use without just compensation." The intention of the Founding Fathers was to ensure that government would be fair in allocating the burdens of government projects such as building roads and canals (Strong et al., 1996). However, property takings for public use with just compensation requires the payments of public funds to private landowners. If our interest is, as that of the Founding Fathers was, to fairly allocate the burdens of government projects, some mechanism must be agreed on to make the sitings of hazardous or noxious land uses equitable for all, especially from the point of view of the potential for disaster, emergency management, and social equity.

Another landmark case, *Dolan v. City of Tigard* (1994), leads to a taking of private property when the burden of a public benefit is placed solely on a private property owner without legitimate public purpose. Perhaps we need to first conclude that when minority and poor communities disproportionately bear the cost of pollution and environmental hazards, while the greater society benefits, it is also an unfair burden on these citizens. Society must determine the equity of planning that benefits the private property owner, who may be an industrial polluter, while imposing costs on members of the community who are predominantly poor and racial minorities. These costs include the potential for disaster, depressed economic opportunity, and health hazards. If those potential dangers become real emergency management situations, the costs, which can be very substantial, will come out of public funds. Although the private property owner who may be at fault for a disaster would be asked to recompense government authorities, there is no assurance that they would be willing or able to.

VII. CONCLUSION AND SUGGESTED SOLUTION

For reasons outlined above, judicial remedies, outright payments to firms or citizens, prohibitions of land use, and nuisance law all present difficulties in providing ready solutions to solving potentially disastrous hazardous or toxic problems. However, a possible remedy for these situations would be to create local, special taxing districts that incorporate the landowners of both the industrial sites and the low-rent residential parcels.

Special taxing districts are based on limited, specific objectives that rely on voluntary acceptance. Once accepted by the majority of parcel owners, participation becomes mandatory. They rely on a local tax surcharge on the owner of the property and the additional funds are used exclusively within the special taxing district to achieve objectives for which the district is established. These objectives have been used to fund business improvement districts in America's aging downtowns to restore the former main streets to vibrant shopping and tourist destinations. The pooled funds from the surcharge pay for such expenditures as extra police, common advertising, concentrated clean-up initiatives, and acquiring derelict properties that can be improved and contribute to a district with enhanced amenities.

This approach is similar to tax incremental financing that relies on the repayment of debt by increased property values that are the result of acquisitions or improvements funded by the new debt. But special taxing districts do not require debt and are not tied to increased property values to make them work. Primarily, money raised by the surcharge is directed within the district for goals that the district sets. In the case of mitigating against potentially disasters, it would be some way that is fair and equitable to the industrial property owner, the low-rent parcel landlords, and the occupants of endangered housing areas.

Local input and decision making is an essential ingredient. Perhaps the district could fund job retraining for underskilled workers so that they qualify for more highly skilled jobs in the district. It can also compensate property owners forced to close or move out of the district to reduce the inherent dangers of their land use. The money raised from special taxing districts can be applied to acquiring additional property to create or increase buffer zones in order to protect the surrounding residential areas from the potential dangers.

The identity of subject operators who handle hazardous materials that potentially represent disasters is readily available. The Superfund Amendment and Reauthorization Act of 1986 already requires each industrial site to report annually to environmental officials the amount of hazardous materials that their facility handles. These reporting entities can serve as the locus of potentially hazardous land use special districts. A zone can be established within one half-mile surrounding the perimeter of each reporting site. This distance is consistent with the suggestion of the court in *Bean v. Southern Waste Management Corp.* (482 F. Supp. at 677, S.D. Tex., 1979). The court stated that within this distance there was established "a substantial threat to irreparable injury" according to the evidence presented in that case. It concerned a waste dump in Houston in proximity to the predominantly black Smiley High School.

Justification for the establishment of such hazardous land use special districts can also be found in case law. The court in *Just v. Marinette County* (1972) elicited a reexamination of the concept of public benefit versus public harm. This case involved a motivation to protect the public from harm instead of an attempt to secure a benefit for the public. It involved a restriction on the use of a citizen's property as an exercise of the state's legitimate police power and its obligations under the concept of the public trust doctrine.

Impact fees paid by developers for costs imposed on communities by new subdivisions also are in the same vein as the concept of special tax districts in that the private firm who gains financial benefit contributes to the public costs associated with its private benefit. These public costs might be new schools, playgrounds, roads, fire services and, in this case, emergency management services.

Nuisance doctrine also dictates that a monetary value be placed on external costs. Instead of searching for a solution to these social and potential emergency management problems in the courts, this alternative that uses a tax mechanism may be more workable. It also can provide for taxable redistribution to achieve equity. Similar to the use to which impact fees are put, special taxing districts provide a means to apply extra financial resources where the burden is greatest. Another equitable consideration is that the funds are generated from those who benefit the most. Such districts would produce money from potentially disastrous industrial site owners and use the funds to attempt a remedy for problems that are caused by their location near residential neighborhoods. Accordingly, the costs of the land use burden will not fall disproportionately on the poor and minorities while they do not share in its benefits, which are instead at present distributed among the greater community at large.

Most important, this proposal allows for local choice and the expression of local preferences in accepting hazardous land use special districts and the allocation of funds that they would generate. These local decisions might be to move the residential units or to move the hazardous facilities. The revenue generated from the special tax district itself would provide funds to allow fair compensation to the property owners affected if local choice dictated such property changes.

Because this suggested solution is predicated on the assumption that there is economic benefit that is not currently fairly apportioned to its external social costs, government leaders may elect to sequester some of its existing tax receipts from these properties and apply them to new expenditures in targeted areas where the taxes are generated. Local governments may decide that they do not have a fair distribution of the taxes raised when they recruit new businesses to their jurisdiction. This is a way to help those most adversely affected by development in areas where they need it the most and, with respect to community planning, it may enable them to avoid potential disasters by planning for prevention.

REFERENCES

Bean v. Southwestern Waste Management Corp., 482 F. Supp. 673 (S.D. Tex. 1979).

Beasley, C. Jr. (1990). ''Of pollution and poverty, part 2: keeping watch in cancer alley.'' *Buzzworm: The Environmental Journal*, 2(4), 34–45.

Bowman, A.O'M., and Crews-Meyer, K.A. (1997). ''Locating southern LULUs: race, class, and environmental justice.'' *State and Local Government Review*, Spring, 110–119.

Bullard, R.D. (1994). *Dumping in Dixie* (2nd. ed.) xv. Boulder, CO: Westview Press.

Bullard, R.D. (1990). ''Ecological inequities and the new south: black communities under siege.'' *Journal of Ethnic Studies*, 17(4), 101–115.

Bullard, R.D., and Wright, B.H. (1987). ''Blacks and the environment.'' *Humboldt Journal of Social Relations*, 14 (Summer), 165–184.

Chatham County Emergency Management Agency. (1995). *Annex 17A Hazardous Material Emergency Response Plan*. Savannah, GA: Chatham County Emergency Management Agency.

Collette, W. (1985). ''Somewhere else, USA: fighting back against chemical dumpers.'' *Southern Neighborhoods*, 9 (September), 1–3.

Dolan v. City of Tigard. 512 U.S. 374 (1994).

Downs, A. (1997). ''Suburban-inner-city ecosystem urban decay is inextricably linked to the symbiosis of suburban and inner-city life.'' *Journal of Property Management*, 62, 60–66.

East Bibb Twiggs Neighborhood Assn. v. Macon-Bibb County Planning and Zoning Commission, 706 F. Supp. 880 (M.D. Ga. 1989).

Easterbrook, G. (1999). ''Suburban myth.'' *New Republic*, 220 (11), 18–21.

Godsil, R.D. (1991). ''Remedying environmental racism.'' *Michigan Law Review*, 90, 394–427.

Griggs v. Duke Power Co., 401 U.S. 424, 427 (1971).

Hoban, T.M., and Brooks, R.O. (1996). *Green Justice: The Environment and the Courts* (2nd ed.). Boulder, CO: Westview Press.

Just v. Marinette County, 56 Wis. 2d 7, 201 N.W. 2nd 761 (1972).

Keystone Bituminous Coal Association v. De Benedictis, 480 U.S. 470 (1987).

Lucas v. South Carolina Coastal Council, 505 U.S. 1003 (1992).

Mandelker, D.R. (1971). *The Zoning Dilemma*, 31–36. New York: McGraw-Hill.

Mandelker, D.R. (1981). *Environment and Equity: A Regulatory Challenge*. New York: McGraw-Hill.

Mandelker, D.R. (1993). *Land Use Law* (3rd ed.). Charlottesville, VA: Michie Co.

Maslow, A.H. (1975). *Motivation and Personality* (2nd ed.), 80–106. New York: Viking Press.

McKinney, G. (1985). ''Toxic hazards and blacks.'' *Black Enterprise* (Nov.), 19.

Monroe v. Pape, 365 U.S. 167 (1961).

Nasar, J.L., and Grannis, P. (1999). ''Design review reviewed: administrative versus discretionary methods.'' *Journal of the American Planning Association*, 65(4), 424–433.

Nixon, R. (1997). ''Uprising in Cancer Alley.'' *Progressive*, 61, 16.

Parratt v. Taylor, 451 U.S. 527, 535 (1981).

Preiser, W.F.E., and Rohane, K. (1988). A survey of aesthetic controls in English-speaking countries. In J. Nasar (ed.), *Environmental Aesthetics: Theory, Research, and Applications*, 422–433. New York: Cambridge.

Ramsey, T. (1996). Property manager, Oaktree Townhomes, personal interview, Feb. 21.

Shirvani, H. (1985). *The Urban Design Process*. New York: Van Nostrand–Reinhold.

Street, R.S., and Orozco, S. (1992). Battling toxic racism: el pueblo para el aire y agua limpio. In R.S. Street (ed.), *Organizing for Our Lives: New Voices from Rural Communities*, 20–32. Portland, OR: New Sage Press and California Rural Legal Assistance.

Strong, A.L., Mandelker, D.R., and Kelly, E.D. (1996). ''Property rights and takings.'' *Journal of the American Planning Association*, 62 (1), 5–16.

Taylor, D.E. (1989). ''Blacks and the environment: toward an explanation of the concern and action gap between blacks and whites.'' *Environment and Behavior*, 21(2), 175–205.

Tribe, L.H. (1988). *American Constitutional Law* (2nd ed.), 1451. Minneola, NY: Foundation Press.

United Church of Christ Commission for Racial Justice. (1987). *Toxic Wastes and Race in the United States: A National Report on the Racial and Socio-economic Characteristics of Communities with Hazardous Waste Sites*. New York: Public Data Access: Inquiries to the Commission.

U.S. General Accounting Office. (1983). *Siting of Hazardous Waste Landfills and Their Correlation with Racial and Economic Status of Surrounding Communities*. Washington: U.S. General Accounting Office.

Village of Arlington Heights v. Metropolitan Housing Development Corp., 429 U.S. 252 (1977).

Village of Euclid v. Ambler Realty Co., 272 U.S. 365 (1926).

Washington v. Davis, 426 U.S. 229 (1976): p. 242.

45

Managing Refugee-Assistance Crises in the Twenty-First Century

The Intercultural Communication Factor

Peter Koehn Department of Political Science, University of Montana, Missoula, Montana

Phyllis Bo-Yuen Ngai Department of Curriculum and Instruction, University of Montana, Missoula, Montana

I. INTRODUCTION

Most emergency assistance operations are complicated by institutional pluralism and interdependency (Siegel 1985:109–110). The inherently multicultural nature of refugee-assistance situations, coupled with the involvement of international agencies and nongovernmental organizations, adds to the complexity of the crisis management challenge. Although cultural and institutional pluralism are particularly pronounced when crises involve refugees who seek ''sanctuary in a totally unfamiliar culture'' (Cuny 1979:359), the diversity of existing human resource and host-community environments on the eve of the twenty-first century ensures that emergency assistance managers increasingly will be called upon to engage in intercultural communication.

Communication undergirds all aspects of crisis and emergency management. In this chapter, the authors first identify critical intercultural-communication needs and roles, with refugee-assistance operations providing the basis for analysis.[1] The following section presents practical guidelines for effective communication in each strategic situation. The suggested guidelines are rooted in intercultural-communication studies, but are specifically adapted to the challenging field conditions that characterize complex refugee-assistance crises. In a separate chapter prepared for this volume, the authors elaborate a training program designed to develop competency in intercultural communication among individuals who will be responsible for managing refugee-assistance crises in the next century.

A. Refugee-Assistance Crises: Preparing for the Twenty-First Century

In 2000, roughly 12 million officially recognized refugees, and 20–25 million de facto refugees who have been externally or internally displaced by violence, lived in vulnerable conditions around the world. Crises beget crises. In the case of refugees, it is failure to resolve an internal or international political conflict of one type or another peacefully that typically produces a crisis of emergency and/or development assistance. In the post–Cold War era, most refugees are the casualties of homeland political crises. They flee persecution and life-threatening situations that arise for a variety of reasons, including one's political opinions, expressions, and/or associations, religious convictions, and ethnic background (see Zolberg et al. 1989:236–243, 263–264; Koehn 1991; Loescher 1993:91). Today's refugees often are the victims of political, religious, and nationality conflicts in disintegrating or reconsolidating states (van Rooyen 1994:37–39; Eade and Williams 1995:813).

The elimination or mitigation of human disasters resulting from political persecution and violent conflicts would constitute the most effective means of resolving refugee crises.[2] It is safe to assume, however, that the processes of refugee formation will not be abated in the early decades of the new century (see Koehn 1991:7–57, 400–405; Loescher 1993: 4). In that case, management of the catastrophic situations requiring immediate action that arise from the presence of politically dislocated persons in countries of asylum will continue to demand attention. Refugee-assistance crises in the twentyfirst century are likely to remain distinguished by (1) extreme vulnerability and serious threats to survival prospects due to loss of access to material resources and to kinship-support systems (Chambers 1979:386; Bemak et al., 1996:248–249; Hansen 1979:369); (2) a narrow time frame for responding to multiple threats; (3) recurrent, rather than exceptional or occasional, emergency conditions that generate long-term community and cultural disruptions; (4) political complexity; and (5) a high probability that violence and forced dislocation will recur.

In this chapter, the authors focus on refugee assistance in countries of first asylum. The victims of political dislocation confront a state of perpetual crisis in first-asylum situations. They typically face an unending series of threats to their health, psychological well-being, physical safety, family life, economic security, and survival capacity. Concomitantly, the impact of assisting refugees further burdens and damages inadequate local infrastructures and environmental conditions in most first-asylum situations (see, for instance, Zetter 1995:1658–1659, 1661). Crisis management, therefore, needs to be broadly defined to include most aspects of refugee assistance along the relief-to-development continuum and to encompass returnees and the affected local population as well as the externally and internally dislocated (also see Koehn and Ojo 1997:116; McKelvey 1994:16; van Rooyen 1994:43; Zetter 1995:1658–1659, 1661, 1665; Anderson and Woodrow 1989: 73).

B. Multicultural Refugee-Assistance Environments

In countries of first asylum, persons involved in refugee-assistance crisis management find it necessary to interact in at least three overlapping multicultural environments. These are the internal workplace, interorganizational forums, and community relations.

Internally, international organizations, such as the United Nations High Commission for Refugees (UNHCR), and many nongovernmental organizations (NGOs) field a multinational staff of technical and administrative personnel that consists of employees hired from the local host community(ies) and assistants drawn from refugee communities working alongside expatriate professionals and, occasionally, volunteers. The multiethnic composition of most first-asylum countries also frequently results in multicultural staffing within the host-country government agencies assigned to work with refugees and with NGOs.

The importance of NGOs at the grass-roots level is gaining increasing recognition among scholars, governments, and donors (see Koehn and Ojo 1997:110–114, 119). Collectively, NGOs distribute approximately $10 billion per year in emergency relief and development assistance (Bennett 1995b:xi–xii; also see Koehn and Ojo 1999:5,12). Roughly 70% of all U.S. aid currently is channeled through NGOs. In mid-1997, the head of the U.S. Agency for International Development, J. Brian Atwood, noted that one priority for such U.S. aid to Africa is "crisis prevention or crisis mitigation . . . " (Atwood 1997:6).

Although NGOs are assuming increasing responsibilities as governmental bilateral and multilateral aid budgets shrink, persons working for humanitarian-assistance organizations in international crisis- and emergency-management capacities often lack the professional skills required to manage their organizations effectively and with success in realizing urgent goals (see Koehn and Ojo 1997:124). The growing need among multicultural NGOs for facility in intercultural communication and decision making can be illustrated with reference to the Association of Medical Doctors of Asia (AMDA).

AMDA, a multinational NGO established in 1984 by young doctors from Japan, India, and Thailand, provides health care for refugees and assists the victims of natural emergencies in Asia, Africa, and Central Europe. AMDA also serves as the Secretariat for the International Network of NGOs for Emergencies and Development formed under the 1994 Okayama Declaration. In their field sites, AMDA's Asian Multinational Medical Missions (AMMMs) operate on the basis of the "coexistence of diversity" (*sougo-fujo* in Japanese). An AMMM might consist of a physician from Nepal, a Filipina nurse, a midwife from Bangladesh, and a project coordinator from Japan (Yamamoto 1995:139). In serving the population of a refugee camp, an AMMM typically is assisted by a small expatriate fiscal and administrative staff. The expatriate team also depends heavily upon locally recruited personnel who serve in medical and support capacities. AMDA's experience to date with multicultural field staffs indicates that the cross-national professional standards adhered to by personnel in medical fields (including physicians, nurses, and paramedics) are relatively uniform, widely recognized, and of high quality. However, its managers and other administrators, who often exert an equal or even larger influence on project results in comparison with the AMMM's medical staff, typically lack standard qualifications and the communication and related skills required for crisis management in multicultural contexts (Yamamoto 1995:140). In refugee crises, nevertheless, professional as well as administrative staff members are challenged by barriers to intercultural communication.[3]

The nationally and culturally diverse employees of international, donor, non-governmental (indigenous and Northern), and host-state organizations also must regularly interact and consult with each other, and are expected to coordinate crisis-management initiatives with the responsible host-government authority as well as with the UNHCR (and/or another U.N. agency) and/or the UNHCR-designated lead NGO (or Coordinating Agency for International Assistance).[4] This communication interface, which presents the second crucial multicultural operational context in the management of refugee crises, can be harmonious, respectful, cooperative, and productive, or competitive, conflictual, and damaging (see Zetter 1995:1664, 1653; Riker 1995:49,51; Karadawi 1983:544–545; Aall 1979: 429–434; Minear and Guillot 1996:64; Anderson and Woodrow 1989:153, 255; Eade and Williams 1995:870).[5] The involvement of many NGOs in a complex crisis situation exacerbates the difficulties encountered in providing policy coordination, a comprehensive management overview, and useful networking among implementing agencies (Zetter 1995:1663).

Thirdly, the professional and administrative crisis-management staff of field organizations must work in partnership with displaced persons who have (often spontaneously) self-settled,[6] refugees living in official and planned resettlement areas or camps, political factions, and/or host-community populations—whose nationality and cultural background(s) usually differ from those possessed by most of the players in the two environments discussed above. Although the nature of agency-client interactions largely determines the outcome of crisis-management interventions (Koehn 1994b:103; Mazur 1987: 451–452), emergency managers often fail to consider the diverse community contexts they must operate within (Neal and Phillips 1995:332–333). Specifically, it is essential to be sensitive to local cultural requirements (Neal and Phillips 1995:333), emergent norms (Schneider 1992:135, 137–138), and potential intercultural conflicts (Karadawi 1983:540; Phillips 1993:101–104) in emergency-management situations. In order to succeed in managing refugee-assistance crises, field staff must be capable of understanding and working in partnership with populations possessing diverse cultural and religious backgrounds in situations where time and information are especially constrained (Yamamoto 1995:140; Phillips 1993:108; van Bergen 1995:27; Burge 1995:157).

To sum up, the overlapping multicultural relationships that characterize the three principal refugee-assistance environments present a complex challenge for crisis management. In these multiple connectivity settings, intercultural communication (nonverbal as well as verbal) assumes critical importance. Lack of effective communication and intercultural misunderstanding result in conflict, squandering of scarce resources, human suffering, and administratively induced disaster.

II. CRITICAL INTERCULTURAL COMMUNICATION NEEDS AND ROLES IN REFUGEE ASSISTANCE

All communication is culturally shaped and defined (Philipsen 1992). Communication and culture constantly interact and exert mutual influence in international cooperation efforts. The transmittal of intended information is rendered complex and risky by cultural and linguistic diversity (Dupont and Faure 1991). In crisis-management situations requiring intercultural interaction, differences in values, verbal and nonverbal styles, and notions of status can seriously impair communication competency. Cultural orientations can affect the process of achieving international or interethnic cooperation in at least four crucial ways: by shaping one's perception of reality, by out filtering inconsistent or unfamiliar information, by projecting unintended meaning onto the other communicator's verbal and/or nonverbal behavior, and by leading an ethnocentric person to adopt an incorrect explanation of motive (Cohen 1991).

Although of vital and growing importance, the role of intercultural communication is relatively unexplored in the crisis-management context. Using functional and temporal analysis, we are able to identify key focal points for intercultural communication in the management of refugee-assistance crises. On the basis of the analysis of crucial communication needs and roles presented in this section, the following part of our chapter will provide practical intercultural-communication guidelines for refugee-assistance practitioners.

A. Functional and Temporal Analysis

In the management of complex assistance crises, preparation for effective intercultural communication requires process awareness. The particular intra- and interinstitutional process at stake shapes demands for communication among the actors involved in each specific situation. Institutional processes and communicators are elucidated through functional and temporal analysis.

The strategic management of refugee assistance encompasses a wide range of vital functions. The key functions identified by the authors are needs assessment and vulnerability analysis, resource identification and mobilization, service provision, conflict management, training, and accountability.[7] These management functions must address both staff and clientele interests. Each function requires tailored and timely (see Anderson and Woodrow 1989:49) interventions of (1) information (collection and sharing), (2) authority (provision and allocation), (3) supplies and materials (arrangement and distribution), and (4) human resources (mobilization and utilization). In this discussion, temporal analysis will be limited to two broad action phases: immediate and advanced. The immediate phase roughly corresponds with emergency-response and -relief operations (see Karadawi 1983:541; Neldner 1979:396; Dynes 1983:654),[8] while the advanced stage encompasses settlement, community (re)establishment and recovery (Dynes 1983:654), economic adaptation and social integration, and repatriation.

Function 1: Needs Assessment and Vulnerabilities Analysis

Basic-needs assessment and vulnerabilities analysis are *information*-intensive activities. The goals are to articulate and convey reliable information about priority needs that is required for planning and decision making and to ensure that relief measures are linked to development and community self-reliance (see Anderson and Woodrow 1989:326–327; Eade and Williams 1995:825, 835). In the immediate phase, the staff of refugee-assistance agencies are deeply involved in the initiation of needs-assessment undertakings. Their involvement includes collecting basic and accurate data on crisis conditions (''what has happened''—Dynes 1983:655) through observation, conducting interviews with arriving refugees, undertaking surveys and constructing needs profiles, and initiating useful community-based information-gathering techniques such as rapid health appraisal. Since they are the exclusive source of urgently required information, refugees also play an instrumental role in the immediate-action phase. NGO staff typically are most active in the process of giving voice to pressing needs and concerns at the onset of a crisis (see, for instance, Zetter 1995:1656) and in focusing attention on vulnerabilities that, if not addressed, could result in future disasters (Anderson and Woodrow 1989:10–14, 47).

Staff participate less directly in information gathering during the advanced stage of needs assessment; they focus on interpreting, refining, and amending priorities based upon client input. Through methodologies such as participatory rural appraisal (see Eade and Williams 1995:130–131), the refugee community assumes the lead role in gathering information from and about newcomers and regarding changes in needs over time (Anderson and Woodrow 1989:48). Advocacy tends to be shared in the advanced stage of a crisis. Information exchange, dialogue, problem sharing, external briefings, constructing databases of NGO activities, and the communication of successful initiatives among government authorities, donor officials, and local and international NGO personnel takes place in established and newly created informal and formal forums (Riker 1995:30–49; Burge, 1995:151, 159; Bennett and Benson 1995:175; Bennett 1995a:15–22). Refugee and host communities articulate their concerns through local political structures, coordinating committees, and/or subcommittees (on the latter, see Eade and Williams 1995: 879).

In refugee assistance, as in other complex emergencies, the need for informed and rapid decision making requires extensive delegation of *authority* for needs assessment to the field level during the immediate-response phase. At this stage, individual refugees also are relied upon to articulate urgent needs. In the advanced phase, assistance personnel transfer needs-assessment authority and responsibility for project identification and selection to the refugee community and are expected to refrain from intervention. Once participatory community appraisal and early-warning systems are in place, refugees assume primary authority for identifying and ranking needs, and internally selected leaders are relied upon to communicate priorities to assistance agencies.

In the immediate phase of a refugee-assistance crisis, agency staff provide and distribute the *supplies and materials* required for needs assessment. With support from refugee assistants, they also initiate and organize planning activities. In the advanced phase, the refugee community assumes a larger direct role in the logistics of needs assessment.

The *human resources* required to conduct needs- and vulnerability-assessment exercises often are provided by refugee-assistance agencies in the immediate phase of a crisis, even when efforts to engage communities in identifying their own leadership structure are initiated at once (Eade and Williams 1995:879). In the advanced phase, agency staff confine their involvement to training in the methodology of assessment techniques such as participatory community appraisal, and the principal human resources involved are drawn from the affected communities.

Function 2: Resource Identification and Mobilization

Refugee-assistance crisis managers are challenged by immense resource needs. The task of assembling *information* regarding existing resources and distribution systems falls largely upon the staff of assistance agencies during the immediate phase of action (also see Yamamoto 1995:140; Anderson and Woodrow 1989:47; Riker 1995:23). Although typically initially dispossessed of personal or collective material assets, refugees often can offer access to vital information concerning local resources—particularly how potentially available contributions of community shelter, labor, and expertise are organized/allocated and can be mobilized (Dynes 1983:657–658). Refugee involvement in information gathering increases when they have succeeded in overcoming the initial disorientation that typically accompanies dislocation. Much of the information needed for sustained resource mobilization must be provided by refugees and hosts. Furthermore, involving community members in data gathering "can empower local people and increase their understanding of and ability to cope with their own situation" (Anderson and Woodrow 1989:45).

The formal *authority* to identify and secure material resources and human skills to be applied in addressing refugee crises rarely is delegated either within assistance agencies (see, for instance, Zetter 1995:1664) or to the client group. Lack of delegation in this functional area exists in both action phases. Gil Loescher (1993:186) adds that "in many cases, international organizations and NGOs have delayed assistance to people whose lives were at risk, either because governments have not given their consent or because no central authority exists to request and authorize outside aid." Out of necessity, therefore, industrious and entrepreneurial local staff members and resourceful refugees assume independent resource-mobilization roles in the face of the urgent and chaotic conditions that often prevail during the immediate assistance phase as well as during unanticipated and pressing situations that arise in the advanced phase.

The *supplies and materials* required for resource identification/mobilization and capabilities analysis tend to be commanded by agency staff during the immediate-action phase and largely retained even during the advanced stage of assistance. Individual refugees from the client community rarely are provisioned for resource mobilization. In the immediate postdisaster period of refugee assistance, supplies and materials are gathered locally; externally mobilized resources begin to arrive at a later date (see Neldner 1979: 396–397). The critical intercultural-communication challenge in both phases involves identifying and overcoming obstacles to the mobilization and effective distribution of supplies, materials, and skills that are available from diverse sources.

The *human resources* of value in conducting capabilities studies and in identifying prospective material resources are distributed among refugee-assistance agencies and client communities. Assistance staff are expected to begin to identify specific decision-making and task-performance capabilities at the immediate crisis stage (see Anderson and Woodrow 1989:47, 71). In the advanced phase, members of the refugee and host communities are expected to assume primary responsibility for these human-resource-identification functions.

Function 3: Service Provision

The most fundamental and encompassing responsibility in the management of refugee-assistance crises is basic-service provision. Before outsiders arrive, refugees and impacted-community members offer limited rescue and emergency assistance that frequently is unevenly distributed and not accurately concentrated relative to need (see Siegel 1985:108; Anderson and Woodrow 1989:50). In light of the broader overview they typically possess, once coordinating NGO and government staff appear on the scene, they usually are expected to play the lead role in sharing and applying essential *information* in a ''timely and synergetic'' manner (Riker 1995:44) that facilitates service provision in the dynamic environment that prevails during the initial stage. In the immediate-action phase, moreover, agency personnel generally command official sources of information about available services. However, extensive informal means of communication, including rumors, also exist within the community(ies) being served. In the advanced phase, staff share the dissemination of official information function with representatives of the refugee and host communities, and the informal circulation of information about service provision and/or lack of service provision persists.

In the immediate phase of refugee-assistance crises, *authority* within agencies is delegated to the field level to allow for rapid decision making and decisive action in terms of emergency-service provision. In some cases, authority to deliver services is shared with refugees and flexible emergent entities. For instance, the UNHCR's quick-impact projects (QIPs) are fast-disbursing, designed to evoke community participation, and implemented by NGOs (McKelvey 1994:15; van Rooyen 1994:44). In the advanced phase, the personnel of most agencies continue to possess considerable authority in the realm of service provision, although the refugee and host communities increasingly become directly involved through field-based coordinating structures (see Bennett 1995b:xxi).

At the outbreak of an emergency or disaster, the host community frequently will provide emergency supplies of food and shelter (see Zetter 1995:1655; Anderson and Woodrow 1989:50). After they arrive on the scene, agency staff tend to control mobilization and distribution of the *supplies and materials* that accompany service delivery during the immediate-action phase. One international or, more rarely, indigenous agency is likely to be responsible for the overall coordination of efforts (see Zetter 1995:1656). Refugees are likely to assume both official and informal roles in the recipient-registration process and in the distribution of supplies and materials at this stage when urgent and large-scale operations are involved (see, for instance, Anderson and Woodrow 1989:276). In the advanced phase, assistance-agency personnel attend to the logistics of arranging and distributing the supplies needed for service provision (see Eade and Williams 1995:962–969; Neldner 1979:397) and the refugee community assumes a central role in the distribution process.

The mobilization of *human resources* for urgent service projects during the immediate phase of a refugee-assistance crisis involves both agency staff and the refugee and host communities. Staff focus on recruiting and supporting personnel from outside the area (see, for instance, Anderson and Woodrow 1989:87, 327) and on applying their own expertise while refugees and hosts attempt to engage the participation of community members. During the advanced-action stage, reliance on external personnel is reduced and the refugee community is expected to become increasingly involved in and adept at mobilizing members to assist in the provision of vital services.

Function 4: Conflict Management

The refugee-assistance process is filled with potential for conflict and threats to security (see, for instance, Minear and Guillot 1996:65; Anderson and Woodrow 1989:303–312). Some of the conflicts that arise are healthy and result in improved decision making while others are destructive in terms of refugee assistance. The management of complex assistance crises is marked by the constant need for vigilance and culturally sensitive negotiation. Conflict management is important in both action phases.

In the immediate and advanced phases, both agency staff and members of the refugee community typically play vital roles in contributing *information* of value in the conflict-management process (see Yamamoto 1995:140). The level and type of conflict and threat determine which actors possess the information required by crisis managers.

Agency staff tend to retain formal *authority* for conflict management during the immediate stage of complex assistance crises. Although high-level NGO and government officers intervene on an occasional and selective basis, the authority to deal with conflicts is decentralized within agencies in order to facilitate rapid decision making and decisive action. In addition, one typically finds that community leaders perform important informal negotiation roles during the immediate-action phase. Later, agency staff discover that delegating authority for conflict management to the refugee community allows them to avoid becoming embroiled in distracting issues and facilitates the management of refugee assistance.

In both phases, the *supplies and materials* required for effective conflict management tend to be controlled by agency staff. However, as relations of trust are built over time, such resources are likely to be shared with refugee leaders who are active in informal negotiation and balance restoration.

In the immediate-crisis phase of refugee assistance, conflict managers tend to rely upon external arbitrators and mediators. For this reason, assistance-agency personnel initially are more involved in *human-resource* mobilization than are refugees. In the advanced phase, in contrast, local actors assume the most critical conflict-management roles and the refugee and host communities become centrally involved in identifying effective negotiators.

B. Path Analysis

In the management of refugee-assistance crises, the intercultural communication of required information occurs along vertical, horizontal, and informal paths. The discussion presented in this section includes reference to the semiformal connections, or networks, that are typically present within each path.[9]

1. Vertical Communication Paths

In refugee-assistance crisis management, there are three principal vertical-communication paths. The first connects NGO field offices with local, provincial/state, and national government offices, and with multinational agencies. The second involves hierarchical communication within NGO agencies and government organizations. The final vertical-communication path links impacted communities with NGO and government-assistance operations.

The multinational staff of refugee-assistance NGOs engage in constant communication concerning both policy and technical issues with local, regional, and national government offices as well as with multinational and bilateral donor agencies. These vertical-communication exchanges deal with a wide range of policy requirements and options, the needs of settled and spontaneous refugees and members of impacted communities, delicate land-use issues, resource and technical-assistance requests, human-rights concerns, repatriation prospects, protection and security issues, and evaluation efforts. In addition to information sharing, such interorganizational, intersectoral, and intercultural contacts are vital for negotiating consensus on plans and decisions that affect the work of persons from various organizations at different levels as well as in the allocation of needed resources (Siegel 1985:109, 111).

The second type of vertical communication involves hierarchical exchanges within government structures and non-governmental organizations. Intragovernmental communication patterns tend to be complex and cumbersome in many host countries. They are influenced by the system of local government, which can involve a mix of delegation, deconcentration, and devolution (see, for instance, Hyden et al. 1996:31). Vertical communication within multicultural NGOs generally involves field-office and in-country headquarters staff and poses special challenges in light of the limited opportunities available for face-to-face interaction among both administrative and technical personnel at different hierarchical levels and in distant geographic jurisdictions. Another important set of vertical-communication exchanges involves interactions among in-country NGO officials and out-of-country headquarters personnel and, in some cases, agency governing boards. This set of hierarchical-communication transfers emphasizes refugee-needs assessment, resource and technical-assistance requests, environmental protection, accountability, training, and the security and quality of life of assistance workers.

The third and most extensively multicultural set of vertical-communication exchanges links refugees and the local host population to local NGO and government personnel. Information transfers among these groups tend to be devoted to physical- and mental-health conditions, service and resource provision, environmental protection, repatriation, and community protection and security issues.

2. Horizontal Communication Paths

In the management of refugee-assistance crises, there are three basic types of horizontal communication. The first involves intra-agency interaction. The second concerns communication between refugee and local host communities and assistance personnel at the grass roots. The third type of horizontal communication consists of interagency contacts.

Intraagency horizontal exchanges focus on the coordination of staff efforts, collective decision making, working conditions, resource mobilization, accountability, connections among administrative, technical, and client considerations, conflict management, and the protection and security of refugees and staff. Such communication will be predominantly intercultural in multicultural assistance agencies. In particular, effective intercultural-communication links need to be forged among the NGO's expatriate staff, workers drawn from the local population, and refugee employees and volunteers.

In virtually all instances, the information exchanges that arise among members of refugee and local host communities and among both separately with agency staff, will require intercultural communication. These two-way horizontal-communication paths also require sensitivity to the special requirements of refugee women, young adults, the elderly, and the disabled (Koehn 1994a:60, 64, 73). Staff-community partnership relations rank among the most complex and important links in the management of refugee-assistance crises, where misunderstandings due to lack of effective intercultural communication are rife. Such grass-roots communication transfers are likely to encompass needs/vulnerabilities/capabilities assessment, collaborative-service provision, resource mobilization, land use, environmental protection, conflict management, and community protection and security. In this vital horizontal-communication realm, multicultural NGOs often perform a central facilitating role in network creation. The broad range of local, national, and international contacts developed by experienced NGO staff enables them "to take the initiative in putting people in touch with each other, meeting the costs for groups to get together, providing resource materials, and supporting the necessary follow-up" (Eade and Williams 1995:379).

In the interests of (1) coordinated action, (2) the effective utilization of scarce resources, and (3) sharing updates on recent developments and unmet needs, specialized networks are developed for rapid and reliable horizontal communication among NGOs and between local NGO personnel and the field officers of government agencies. These communication networks, which typically require intercultural competence, are found in the vital functional performance areas of needs and vulnerabilities assessment, resource mobilization, service provision, environmental protection, conflict management, repatriation, community and staff protection and security, training, and monitoring and evaluation.

3. Informal Communication Paths

Three major types of informal communication paths can be identified in refugee-assistance situations. The first is intraorganizational and occurs among the staff of NGO and government agencies. The second is limited to the refugee community. The third involves informal networks among refugees, members of the host population, emergent groups, and agency workers.

Although all three types of informal communication paths often parallel formal channels and require intercultural competency, the third deserves special attention because of its critical importance in the successful management of complex assistance crises and its fundamentally multicultural nature. Given the urgent requirements placed on crisis managers for reliable information and the preference for spontaneous interaction that exists among many client and host communities, the most effective channels of intercultural communication often are the novel and informal networks among refugees, agency workers, the host population, and flexible emergent groups that arise to fill unmet needs (Neal and Phillips 1995:328–331).

III. GUIDELINES FOR EFFECTIVE INTERCULTURAL COMMUNICATION IN REFUGEE ASSISTANCE CRISES

Guidelines for effective intercultural communication in refugee-assistance crisis management need to take into consideration prevailing cultural practices as well as the state of emergency conditions and the type of activity required. Therefore, the practical suggestions set forth in this section are derived in large measure from an analytical framework that has proven helpful in sharpening intercultural sensitivity and in differentiating among cultures for communication purposes. The framework (presented in Table 1, below) draws extensively from Edward Hall's high/low-context and high/low-contact insights and Geert Hofstede's (1982) individualistic/collectivistic, high/low–power-distance, masculine/feminine, and high/low–uncertainty-avoidant contributions. By applying this analytical framework, the authors are able to suggest guidelines for effective intercultural communication that are tailored to the temporal and functional dimensions of refugee-assistance crises presented above.

A. Analytical Framework

Edward Hall generally is credited with first distinguishing cultures as *high/low-context* cultures. *High-context communication* refers to exchanges in which most information either is conveyed by the physical interaction or internalized in the person, while "little is in the coded, explicit, transmitted parts of the message" Hall (1976:91). In the high-context culture, Myron Lustig and Jolene Koester (1993:133) explain, a great deal is "taken for granted and assumed to be shared . . . ." Low-context messages, in contrast, are elaborate, clearly communicated, and highly specific (Andersen 1988).

In addition, Hall (1966) characterized cultures which display considerable interpersonal closeness or immediacy as *contact* cultures and those which inhibit closeness as *noncontact*. According to Peter Andersen (1988), "contact cultures also differ in the degree of sensory stimulation people prefer. *High-contact* cultures create immediacy by increasing sensory input, while *low-contact* cultures prefer less sensory involvement."

Andersen (1988) further contends that the fundamental difference among cultures is their degree of individualism versus collectivism. While *individualistic* cultures are characterized by independence, privacy, and self-centeredness, *collectivist* cultures emphasize *we* and group relationships.

Power distance refers to the degree to which power, prestige, and wealth are unequally distributed. In *high–power-distance* cultures, power, wealth, and influence are concentrated in the hands of a few rather than relatively equitably distributed throughout the population as they are in *low–power-distance* cultures (Andersen 1988).

In *masculine* cultures, people regard power, competition, assertiveness, and materialism as important values (Gudykunst and Kim 1992). Members of masculine cultures admire displays of manliness (Lustig and Koester 1993). In *feminine* cultures, in contrast, people place more importance on nurturance, compassion, and quality of life. In feminine cultures, both men and women can express more diverse, less stereotyped sex-role behaviors (Andersen 1988).

An uncertainty-avoidance orientation concerns the cultural predisposition toward valuing risk and ambiguity, conformity, and rituals. Members of cultures characterized by *high uncertainty avoidance* tend to avoid risks and ambiguity. They also display emotions shared by other group members more openly than expressed by people in *low–uncertainty-avoidant* cultures. However, disagreement and non-conformity tend not to be expressed in high-uncertainty-avoidant cultures (see Andersen 1988).

Table 1 elaborates the basic variations in communication style that prevail under each of the six cultural dimensions that exert a powerful impact on intercultural communication. The analytical framework presented in Table 1, coupled with practical insights based on field reports, facilitates the articulation of specific intercultural-communication guidelines for refugee-assistance personnel who work in diverse multicultural environments. These guidelines are presented in the following sections.

B. Communication Guidelines Based on Functional and Temporal Analysis

The first set of guidelines for intercultural communication in refugee-assistance crises takes into consideration the temporal and functional requirements as well as the principal communicators identified above. In this section, the authors suggest practical communication guidelines aimed at both the immediate phase and the advanced phase of assistance for each of the four interventions (information, authority, supplies and materials, and human resources) involved in the six functions of needs-assessment, resource-identification and mobilization, service-provision, conflict-management, training, and accountability.[10] These guidelines draw upon and apply the insights presented in Table 1 in an effort to maximize intercultural-communication effectiveness in refugee-assistance crises. Given space limitations, the guidelines provided below are illustrative rather than exhaustive. They are principally directed toward the crisis-assistance staff of NGOs and government agencies. Those involved in managing complex assistance crises are encouraged to seek further guidance for specific multicultural-communication needs not covered here through continuous referral to the framework presented in Table 1.

Function 1: Needs Assessment

Information interventions—immediate phase

1. During the process of obtaining information for needs assessment and vulnerability analysis in immediate-crisis situations (see Eade and Williams 1995:952, for a checklist of information that is vital in conducting independent assessments of overall emergency conditions), staff members need to take into account refugees' willingness to disclose thoughts and feelings. Refugees from collectivistic cultures, high-contexts cultures, and ethnic-minority cultures will be less open with outsiders. Thus, to obtain accurate, in-depth information, NGO staff members are advised to communicate through a trusted interpreter selected from among the refugees. The interpreter not only should interpret verbal information, but also should report nonverbal observations. The latter provide especially valuable information concerning the needs of refugees with high-context cultural backgrounds.

Table 1 Cross-Cultural Communication Differences on Six Major Cultural Dimensions: An Analytical Framework

High Context	*Low Context*
• Tune in to nonverbal communication	• Verbal codes are prevalent
• Rely heavily on nonverbal cues to express disagreement	• Communicate in explicit code
• Prefer inaccuracy and evasion to painful decision	• Preoccupied with specifics and details
• Express opinions indirectly	• Prefer precise time schedule
• Nondisclosive	• Precise with verbal and nonverbal expressions
• Facal expressions, tensions, movements, speed of interaction, location of interaction have implicit meanings	• Used to literalness
• Prefer face-to-face over written	• Talkative
• Tend to avoid conflict	• Fast pace
• Deal with conflicts subtly	• Short meetings
	• Perceive conflicts as natural and not damaging
	• More willing to confront the party to conflict
High Uncertainty-Avoidant	*Low Uncertainty-Avoidant*
• Low tolerance for change	• Tolerate nonconformity and change
• Upset when uniformity breaks down	• Value risk and ambiguity
• Display normative emotion	• Uncomfortable with ritual or stylized behavior
• Tolerate disagreement with outsiders	• More flexible
• Tolerate disagreement if consensus is the ultimate goal	• Diversity of opinions are accepted
• Behavior is codified and rule-governed rankings	• Dislike rituals and ceremony
• More codified behavior across rankings	
• Emphasize importance of rituals ceremony	
High Power-Distance	*Low Power-Distance*
• Prohibit interclass contact	• Free interclass contact
• Speak with a tense voice, especially with superiors	• Use more relaxed voice
• Show more respect nonverbally to high-status people	• People in power try to look less powerful
• Sources more influential if higher status	• More careful listening by high-status persons
• Show only positive emotions to high status others, negative to low-status others	• Type of style is not important
• Downward communication dominates	• Not hesitant to complain to superior
• Elegant style more effective than inelegant	• More two-way communication
• Prefer serious- to humorous-style message	
Masculine	*Feminine*
• Machismo emphasized	• Express less stereotyped sex-role behavior
• Speak with louder voice	• Exhibit relaxed vocal pattern
• Value competitiveness and assertiveness	• Value compassion and nurturance
• Bargain with firm position	• More submissive and willing to compromise
• Women rely more on nonverbal communication	• Emphasize overall equality of life
• Tend toward more aggressive style	• More reflective
• Emphasize competition over cooperation	
• More impulsive	

Table 1 Continued

Individualistic	*Collectivistic*
• Smile more • Express emotions freely • More remote and distant proximally • More affiliative nonverbally • Value small talk and initial acquaintance • More open communication • More likely to use confrontational strategies when dealing with interpersonal problems • Rely more on non-face-to-face communication • More frank • A humorous style is preferred to a serious style • Emphasize individual achievement and competition among individuals • More communication among groups because in-group boundary is weak	• Suppress emotional displays that are contrary to the mood of the group • Work in close proximity • Stay further from opponents • Develop friendly working relationships • Behavior tends to be synchronized within the system • Communication is less open because social network is more fixed • Value compliance with norms • Prefer avoidance • Slow/moderate pace and long negotiation process • Defer commitment to firm agreements • Consult superiors and/or colleagues before finalizing a decision • Intergroup communication is minimal; unwilling to share information with out-groups • Emphasize cooperation within an organization, but competition between organizations
High-contact	*Low-contact*
• More expressive nonverbally • Sit face to face with counterparts • Prefer face-to-face meetings to written communication	• Less expressive nonverbally • Stand farther away • Compensate for lack of immediacy by relaxed postures and seating arrangement

Source: Adapted from Andersen (1988), Ngai (1996), and Triandis and Albert (1988).

2. Friendly, down-to-earth staff members are more likely to secure information about the negative as well as positive conditions facing refugees from high–power-distance cultures, who tend to hide negative feelings and assessments from high-status others.

Information interventions—advanced phase

1. Staff members need to devote sufficient time to familiarizing themselves with the customs, culture, and experiences of the refugees whom they aim to assist. In particular, this effort allows staff members to decode interview and observational information regarding high-context (implicit and at times symbolic) cultures more accurately and deeply.
2. Useful participatory needs- and capabilities-assessment techniques among groups with a high proportion of members who are not literate and do not speak the national language include "seasonal calendars, ranking of resources using a matrix, and diagrams to show social and political relationships in a village or community" (Eade and Williams 1995:255, 881–882; also see Hyden et al. 1996:44).

3. In many cultures, women are more likely to express their needs and vulnerabilities effectively when consulted separately by female members of survey and assessment teams and/or when provided with opportunities to communicate indirectly through "socio-drama, role-play, painting, dance, music and song . . ." (Eade and Williams 1995:882).
4. Data collected for needs-assessment purposes should be disaggregated to ensure that relief and development efforts are tailored to the specific social groups that exist within the refugee and host-community populations (Eade and Williams 1995:883).

Authority interventions—immediate phase

1. Quick two-way communication is vital in this phase of refugee-needs assessment. In particular, field-staff personnel and other refugee-assistance workers from high-power-distance cultures need to set aside the fear and formality of communicating with people of higher status and to be assertive in communicating urgent needs directly to government and higher authorities.

Authority interventions—advanced phase

1. At this stage, the process of collecting and reporting accurate and comprehensive information about needs principally involves collective action among refugees. Community leaders must explain the importance of reaching and supporting agreement on priority needs to refugees from individualistic and low–uncertainty-avoidant cultures who are prone to challenge authority.

Supplies and materials interventions—immediate phase

1. Staff members need to adjust the amount of detail involved when explaining the logistics required in mobilizing supplies and materials for needs assessment according to the cultural background of the refugees who take part in the process. Relatively ambiguous instructions will suffice for refugee assistants from low-uncertainty-avoidant cultures who desire few predetermined rules and value flexibility and creativity. Refugee assistants from high-context cultures will benefit from detailed, specific instructions and sound anticipatory plans when dealing with the logistics of needs assessment in the immediate phase.
2. Comprehensive needs assessment in emergency situations requires the coordination of knowledge regarding the current and planned material interventions of all organizations and groups involved in the relief effort (see Eade and Williams 1995:952). Special efforts must be undertaken and incentives provided in high-context cultures, therefore, that encourage members of host-country government and local non-governmental organizations to communicate fully across agency boundaries and in coordinating forums.

Supplies and materials interventions—advanced phase

1. When working with members from the refugee community, agency staff must be aware of cultural differences that shape the use of time. The communicative and scheduling behavior of people from collectivistic cultures tends to be synchronized within their community. Therefore, staff members need to understand community work rhythms that affect the supply of materials needed for needs

assessment and vulnerabilities analysis and to avoid pressuring members of collectivistic cultures to meet externally imposed deadlines. At the same time, they should communicate openly about the need for and value *to the community* of timely interventions.

Human-resource interventions—immediate phase

1. During the process of assigning human resources for needs-assessment purposes, NGO and host-government staff members need to devote special attention to matching cultural preferences for communicating individually/collectively and for adopting masculine or feminine roles with the predominant cultural orientation of the refugee and local communities that are at risk.

Human-resource interventions—advanced phase

1. In high–power-distance cultures, trainers are likely to find it helpful to utilize written forms of communication, including questionnaires, to elicit questions from refugee- and host-community trainees that will ensure comprehension of the needs- and vulnerability-assessment methodology.
2. Staff trainers should pay special attention to understanding the meanings of key nonverbal indicators of training needs conveyed by trainees from high-context cultures.

Function 2: Resource Identification and Mobilization

Information interventions—immediate phase

1. High-context messages regarding potentially available resources often create confusion or even distortion in intercultural communication. A simple, standardized information recording sheet can be used to help people from high-context cultures communicate explicitly and accurately. The sheet should be designed in a way that prompts the detailed and specific identification of existing community resources. In the same vein, all substantive decisions regarding resource provision in emergency situations that are communicated by telephone or in person should be properly logged and made part of the formal written record (Eade and Williams 1995:953).
2. Information gathered locally about the short-term supply of urgently needed resources should be organized in "a way that helps people diagnose the causes of their problems and begin to plan ways to overcome them" (Anderson and Woodrow 1989:47). Short narratives offer a useful way to organize information about resource needs and availability in high-context situations.

Information interventions—advanced phase

1. In order to collect comprehensive information concerning local resources and about existing and potential group mobilization, staff members need to identify and develop trusting relationships with community leaders. This is particularly important in collectivistic cultures because people tend to be unwilling to share information with out groups and intergroup communication is infrequent given the relatively fixed nature of social networks.

Authority interventions—immediate phase

1. Urgent, chaotic conditions require that high-level NGO and government personnel from high–power-distance cultures make a special effort to listen carefully to the messages communicated by field staff and reliable representatives of the refugee and local communities.
2. Given the difficulties involved in introducing new supplier relationships on short notice, persons who occupy boundary roles in interagency communication should concentrate immediate attention on facilitating the rapid exchange of information with persons in local authority positions "who are able to release materials and equipment" (Siegel 1985:108). Careful attention to cross-boundary communication is likely to be especially fruitful in relations with members of collectivistic cultures.

Authority interventions—advanced phase

1. Field workers, volunteers, and community leaders from high-power-distance cultures need to be assured that providing advice and suggestions about locally available resources to high-status sources is not disrespectful behavior and directly benefits the community.

Supplies and materials interventions—immediate phase

1. When confronting emergency conditions, agency staff from collectivistic cultures who are used to a slow or moderate working and communicating pace will need to be prepared to speed up the resource-distribution process to accommodate their coworkers from fast-paced, low-context cultures. At the same time, staff members from low-context cultures need to learn to be patient with counterparts and clients from slow-paced cultures.

Supplies and materials interventions—advanced phase

1. Disagreements over resource-distribution plans and timetables are likely to occur between NGO headquarters and field staff, and among field workers. Frequent and comprehensive information exchange will facilitate the process of reaching consensus, especially among actors from individualistic and low–uncertainty-avoidant cultures.
2. Agency staff should make certain that the introduction of any externally mobilized materials and/or tools is "consistent with local socio-cultural practices" (Hartkopf and Goodspeed 1979:445; Dynes 1983:659) and involves existing communication channels.
3. Bicultural participants in the suggested Global Refugee Corps could play a useful bridging role in managing the logistics of resource mobilization (see Koehn 1994a:76; 1994b:108–110).

Human-resource interventions—immediate phase

1. To avoid duplication in resource mobilization, communication in emergency situations should be directed through a multicultural and multilingual communications center (see Siegel 1985:108).

Human-resource interventions—advanced phase

1. Headquarters personnel with high-power-distance cultural backgrounds need to appreciate that upward communication from the field level yields indispensable information regarding the availability of local expertise for the mobilization of physical resources.
2. In general, the use of culturally familiar and acceptable communication styles is indispensable for success in mobilizing participation by refugees in development activity.

Function 3: Service Provision

Information interventions—immediate phase

1. To the extent possible, face-to-face communication allows staff to distribute information about available services more effectively to refugees from high-context cultures and high-contact cultures. Distributing the information in person also allows staff members to answer questions from refugees on the spot, to build trust, and to correct inaccurate rumors about available and non-available services.
2. Understanding the informal communication network that exists within the refugee community allows staff members to identify key individuals who can successfully distribute information regarding service provision to the entire group or subgroup.

Information interventions—advanced phase

1. When establishing long-term communication links with refugee communities in high-power-distance cultures, staff members should select some individuals from each social stratum since members tend to avoid interclass communication in ways that would distort service provision. Among refugees from collectivistic cultures, who tend to avoid communication with out-groups, staff should link with selected representatives from each ethnic group, clan, or extended family.
2. Attention to and skill in securing feedback concerning the receptive accuracy of one's cross-cultural messages will minimize unintended communications that jeopardize the provision of essential services (see Pedersen 1994:91).

Authority interventions—immediate phase

1. Given the frequent absence of advice and assistance from headquarters in emergency situations and the need to work with local government personnel from high-power-distance cultures, NGO staff members from low-power-distance (and feminine) cultures need to replace their normally respectful communication style with a more assertive approach in order to provide the victims of dislocation with emergency services under chaotic conditions.
2. Communicating through existing host- and refugee-community authority structures increases the speed of decision making about service provision (Dynes 1983:659). However, staff expectations for rapid decisions should be reduced when working with members of collectivistic, high-context, or high-power-distance cultures.

Authority interventions—advanced phase

1. When refugee and host communities in feminine cultures assume increasing authority for service provision, field workers and refugee assistants from masculine cultures must learn to tone down or soften their communication style and be ready to compromise.

Supplies and materials interventions—immediate phase

1. Given the logistical difficulties and added expense involved in importing supplies and materials from outside the area of operations as well as the inappropriate nature of many imported goods (Eade and William 1995:942–943), assistance staff are advised to communicate directly with a broad range of refugee- and host-community groups in an effort to identify and mobilize adequate supplies, materials, and equipment that are available locally, can be adapted easily to indigenous designs, and, whenever possible, are renewable (Hartkopf and Goodspeed 1979:445; Neldner 1979:398).
2. During emergency situations, agency staff members rely on refugees and host communities for quick distribution of supplies and materials. Refugees from high-context or collectivist cultures may not to be able to keep up with fast-pace, frequent instructions from agency staff. In this case, a pyramid communication structure will allow extensive information about supplies and equipment to flow from agency staff to a small number of competent intercultural refugee communicators, who, then, divide distribution tasks among a larger number of individuals or among groups of refugee helpers.
3. When working with masculine cultures, special efforts need to be made to involve women in distribution networks (Eade and Williams 1995:969).

Supplies and materials interventions—advanced phase

1. When many refugee volunteers are involved in large-scale service delivery operations, agency staff from high-uncertainty-avoidant cultures need to be prepared for the breakdown of uniformity. Instead of providing local assistants with rigid instructions regarding how to distribute the supplies and equipment needed for service provision, they should focus on verbal explanations of what is to be distributed and to whom, and allow for flexibility in terms of means of delivery.

Human-resource interventions—immediate phase

1. When external and internal human resources are mobilized for urgent service projects, agency staff members should see their role as that of an intercultural communication and coordination center. By serving as cultural interpreters, they can minimize confusion among all parties.

Human-resource interventions—advanced phase

1. Refugee assistants often play the crucial role of intercultural broker in the advanced-action phase. To ensure that the high-power distance community mobilizes competent and reliable participants for service provision, they must communicate with high-status community leaders who possess authority to assign responsibilities to a broad spectrum of community members.

Function 4: Conflict Management

Information interventions—immediate phase

1. In an emergency situation, arbitration is likely to be the most efficient conflict-management approach. The arbitrator should be a neutral third party who bases his or her decision on information obtained through formal and informal channels. In a high-power-distance community, a high-status arbitrator must rely on a staff member or a refugee whose status and affiliation are on a par with the information source. Otherwise, sources are not likely to disclose information perceived as unfavorable to high-status inquirers.

Information interventions–advanced phase

1. Mediation is the most effective approach for managing conflicts over the long run. During the advanced stage, specific information about the conflict at issue is crucial in helping the conflicting parties reach an agreement with one another. Information directly released by the conflicting parties themselves in front of their ''rivals'' can be especially useful in building understanding between them. Thus, the appointed mediator needs to raise questions that will facilitate dialogue among all parties—especially among those from high-context cultures who are inclined to avoid sharing their feelings.

Authority interventions—immediate phase

1. At the initial stage of an emergency, staff should focus on identifying host-community and refugee leaders who are capable of calming the parties involved in a conflict and the arbitrator should emphasize the value of ceasing hostilities and gradually adopting confidence-building measures.
2. Staff need to forge consensus among themselves on the parameters of ''unreasonable risk'' and to reach a collective decision about whether to withdraw from situations where their personal safety is threatened (Eade and Williams 1995: 974). In reaching such decisions, participants should bear in mind that the communicative strengths of staff members from high-context and collectivistic cultures include reflective consideration of group interests.

Authority interventions—advanced phase

1. When refugees from high-context cultures continue to turn to external authorities to act as arbitrators in intra- and intercommunity conflicts, agency managers need to communicate openly concerning ways to minimize and diminish external involvement in local conflict-resolution capacities.

Supplies and materials interventions—immediate phase

1. In high-context cultures, information regarding the supplies and materials available for the process of arbitrating conflicts will need to be communicated in terms that will encourage usage. Thus, in high-context cultures, where people are prone to avoid confronting conflicts, applications should be honored for material resources that facilitate ''optimizing coordination'' and/or restoring balance rather than ''resolving *conflicts*.''

Supplies and materials interventions—advanced phase

1. Agency staff should reduce the detail of the messages they distribute in order that community leaders become increasingly involved in reaching decisions concerning the allocation of supplies and materials needed for conflict mediation. This approach is particularly important when communicating with high-context cultures.

Human-resource interventions—immediate phase

1. In high-power-distance and collectivistic cultures, emphasis should be placed on identifying respected community members who are willing to serve in informal conflict-management roles.

Human-resource interventions—advanced phase

1. In the advanced phase, both agency staff and community leaders should seek to mobilize indigenous mediators who are skilled in intercultural communication. In masculine cultures, charismatic individuals are likely to become effective local mediators. In feminine cultures, caring and empathetic individuals will be most likely to succeed as indigenous mediators.

C. Communication Guidelines Based on Path Analysis

In the management of refugee-assistance crises, the intercultural communication of required information occurs along vertical, horizontal, and informal paths. This section provides guidelines for assistance personnel who, at one time or another, will need to communicate along all three paths. The operating principle behind this second set of intercultural-communication guidelines is that ''in emergency situations, there is a greater need for information.'' Therefore, crisis managers should endeavor ''to provide the mechanisms for increasing public information in as many forms as possible'' (Dynes 1983: 656–659).

Vertical-communication Paths

NGO field offices ↔ Local, provincial/state, and national government offices

1. Consideration should be given to placing priority on arranging opportunities for face-to-face communication when one or more parties come(s) from a collectivistic culture.
2. The decision to communicate on a one-on-one basis with multiple recipients, or with groups of multiple recipients, should be based on whether the *receptor* culture is individualistic or collectivistic.
3. In a high-power-distance culture, an NGO field worker should communicate with government officials through a high-level NGO official.
4. In a high-power-distance culture, expatriate NGO staff need to be prepared to serve as cross-cultural communication buffers that function to protect indigenous actors against political pressures from above that would undermine project effectiveness (Anderson and Woodrow 1989:76).
5. When working with government officials from a high-context culture, NGO representatives need to take the initiative to present detailed written options

and seek approval on acceptable items, rather than anticipate a direct, specific agreement from the other side.

6. When conflicts arises over fundamental issues such as land use, resource requests, or human-rights concerns, NGO staff need to consider whether national and local government representatives are from a high-context culture and prefer resolving the conflicts through a neutral third party so as not to lose face.

Vertical (hierarchical) networks within government structures

1. In multicultural operational settings, collectivistic ethnic-group members need to avoid the tendency to restrict communication to in-group members. Although they initially are likely to find communicating with strangers (who are their subordinates or supervisors) uncomfortable, focusing communication on professional matters will help break the ice.
2. Officials with high-uncertainty-avoidant cultural backgrounds should be trained to avoid being surprised or paralysed when encountering nonconformity in crisis-management situations.
3. Headquarters personnel from high-power-distance cultures need to learn not overlook the value of accurate decision making and planning based on information provided by field offices through upward communication.

Vertical (hierarchical) networks within NGO structures

1. Headquarters officials should take into consideration the needs of high-uncertainty-avoidant and/or collectivist field workers for frequent supportive communication with, and clear instructions from, headquarters staff.
2. In high-context cultures, in particular, written communications from headquarters to field personnel should emphasize general principles over detailed instructions and should involve simple rather than complex plans (Dynes 1983:656).
3. When relying on letter, fax, telex, and/or e-mail as the dominant channel of communication instead of lengthy face-to-face meetings and/or expensive telephone calls, headquarters personnel and field workers from high-context cultures consciously need to communicate with explicit, precise messages in order to prevent confusion.
4. When telephone calls and face-to-face meetings are rare, the *tone* of written communication assumes even greater importance. Written messages from headquarters that convey a supportive tone help to maintain the morale of field workers, especially those from feminine cultures, who are working in a stressful environment and frequently are unable to contact family and friends.

Refugees and local host community ↔ Local NGO and local government

1. Refugees from collectivistic cultures and/or high-power-distance cultures may not feel comfortable expressing themselves openly with outsiders or with foreigners of high status even when language fluency is not at issue. Thus, an interpreter selected from the refugee community can serve as a valuable communication facilitator and/or mediator.
2. NGO and government personnel from masculine cultures should take into consideration the unstable, traumatic mental state of refugees. Many refugees are likely to be disturbed by a loud, aggressive, and impulsive communication style. Relaxed vocal patterns are more likely to elicit cooperation.
3. NGO and government personnel from high-contact cultures need to refrain from

using touch to express concern or friendliness, especially toward refugees of the opposite sex. Powerless refugees from low-contact cultures are likely to interpret such nonverbal communication as harassment.

4. The local population in high-uncertainty-avoidant cultures require convincing reassurance that the arrival of refugees will not result in further deterioration of conditions that critically affect their lives. Local-assistance personnel need to be proactive by including host-community representatives in their input-communication networks. Frequent communication from NGO and government personnel informing local communities regarding the current refugee situation, NGO activities, government policies, and programs they are eligible to participate in, reduces the likelihood that hosts will be consumed by destructive fear and anger toward the victims of dislocation in their midst.

Horizontal-Communication Paths

Intraagency communication networks

1. While working side by side in emergency and pressure-filled situations that involve potential life and death decisions, NGO expatriate staff, workers drawn from the local population, and refugee employees are likely to encounter interpersonal conflicts owing to cultural clashes. For individualistic actors from low-context cultures, confronting parties to the conflict and resolving problems collaboratively constitutes an effective strategy. For collectivistic parties from high-context cultures, a mediator from a third culture is necessary to facilitate the conflict-resolution process.
2. Given that working partners from diverse cultures must manage crises through collaborative action, each one needs to use precise, direct, and frank communication immediately regarding the communication style that one prefers, and to make a determined effort to recognize the style(s) that others are most comfortable with. In the multicultural workplace, coworkers constantly are called upon to adjust ingrained communication practices and to be tolerant when others forget one's preferred ways.
3. Explicit messages minimize misunderstanding among refugee-assistance personnel. However, consideration must be given to staff from high-context cultures who will need time to learn to use low-context messages.
4. Staff members from masculine cultures may express sex-role stereotypes when working with coworkers in the field. Female field workers should use appropriate opportunities to educate their masculine-culture coworkers about gender equity as a means of preventing potential conflicts from festering.

Refugees ↔ Local host communities

1. Refugees, as the newcomers, need to learn nonverbal- as well as verbal-communication skills in order to interact effectively in the host society without being perceived as vulgar or abnormal by locals from high–uncertainty-avoidant cultures.
2. Persons from collectivistic cultures tend to avoid communication with strangers or out-groups. This communication shyness should not be interpreted as hostility. Community and refugee leaders need to pursue initiatives that will break the ice.

3. Refugee communicators must be trained to be sensitive to local cultural taboos. For instance, joking about certain subjects or mentioning certain words may violate local customs and jeopardize relations with the host community.

Refugees and local host communities ↔ NGO agency staff

1. Demonstrating respect for local capabilities through intercultural communication is more likely to result in sustainable project outcomes than is any other staff qualification (see Anderson and Woodrow 1989:76).
2. NGO staff need to be aware that the less powerful in masculine cultures, such as women, children, the elderly, and the disabled, tend to rely more on nonverbal communication than on explicit verbal or written messages.
3. In collectivistic cultures, warning messages usually are more effectively communicated through traditional social structures than through government agencies or impersonal media. In general, it is advisable for NGO staff to utilize existing social units (such as families, voluntary associations) and authority structures rather than to create new ones, and to enhance valued channels of communication rather than to replace them (see Dynes 1983:658–659).
4. Misunderstandings between NGO agency staff and refugees (or local host communities) are likely to arise in emergency situations. In such cases, it is particularly important that NGO agency staff members succeed in explaining their perspective to community representatives in order that the latter can resolve the misunderstanding with their own people. This communication channel is especially important in collectivistic cultures where community members tend to be suspicious of out-groups.

NGOs ↔ Field representatives of government agencies

1. Teamwork involving NGO staff members and government field officials requires parallel pace and coordinated time management on both sides. Team members from individualistic cultures who prefer to schedule one event at a time need to compromise with members of collectivistic cultures whose behavior tends to be synchronized.
2. NGO agency staff members and field representatives of national and local governments need to reach immediate agreement on what formal communication channel(s) both sides have access to and are committed to using in emergency situations. The most reliable channel could be face-to-face meetings if any staff members are from high-context or high-contact cultures.

Informal-Communication Paths

1. Informal communication networks often are most suitable when quick transmission is vital. In individualistic cultures, small talk provides a common informal-communication channel. In collectivistic cultures, information and rumors are likely to be shared informally within groups or subgroups. In high-context cultures, informal communication will include metaphors and nonverbal cues which are understood only by in-group members. In the multicultural workplace, these forms of informal communication will co-exist. All should be utilized.
2. Communication processes under disaster conditions must adapt to emergent community norms (Neal and Phillips 1995:329–330). In light of the complete

break that occurs with previous communication systems and widespread distrust of official communication channels, rumors serve an important information-transmission function among refugee populations. Although they typically are incomplete and even incorrect, rumors give the dislocated ''some guidance and structure in a highly unusual, uncertain situation'' (Schneider 1992:137). Particularly when dealing with refugees from high-power-distance cultures, agency staff are advised to concentrate on ''keynoting,'' or reinforcing rumors that provide some reliable temporary direction for dislocated populations and bring the ''milling'' process to an end (Schneider 1992:137).

3. Informal communication reaches deeper in a collectivistic community, where social networks are extensive and inclusive, than it penetrates in an individualistic culture. Among collectivist communities, folk media—including theatre, puppetry, story-telling, dance, ballets, and mime—can be a particularly effective means of transmitting development-oriented messages (Melkote 1991:210–214).
4. In high-uncertainty-avoidant cultures, government officials and NGO staff members should feed the informal as well as the formal communication network promptly to satisfy the need for certainty.
5. Stereotypes passed along the informal path often cause misunderstandings and lack of understanding. All actors should be trained to defuse rumors based on ethnic, religious, gender, age, and other stereotyping.

IV. CONCLUSION

In this chapter, the authors have explored the growing scope and importance of intercultural communication in the multinational and multicultural environment that conditions contemporary refugee assistance. After differentiating the primary intercultural-communication needs of the principal actors engaged in the management of complex crises according to specific functional imperatives, the time frame involved, and the communication path activated, we presented concrete suggestions for maximizing intentional communication among crisis managers from different cultures that are grounded in insights emerging from intercultural-communication studies. In light of space limitations, the specific guidelines set forth here can only illustrate the utility of the approach advanced by the authors. When confronting unique field situations that require emergency and crisis management, practitioners are encouraged to refine and expand upon the guidelines we have suggested by linking intercultural-communication needs analysis to culturally sensitive insights based on application of the analytical framework.

ENDNOTES

1. The authors acknowledge with gratitude the helpful comments and suggestions provided by practitioners in the refugee-assistance field, notably Osamu Kunii (Bureau of International Cooperation, International Medical Center of Japan, Ministry of Health and Welfare, Government of Japan) and Naomi Yodokawa (formerly Director of Operations at the Association of Medical Doctors of Asia's Croatia refugee-assistance site).
2. In this connection, Lionel Rosenblatt (1997:8) contends that ''humanitarian action without

political/military action does not resolve root causes'' (also see Loescher 1993:189, 197; Eade and Williams 1995:816). See his controversial proposal for the creation of an ''international rapid reaction force'' charged with protecting humanitarian-assistance workers, weeding out intimidators from the general refugee population, and preventing emergencies (such as the 1994 genocide in Rwanda) from exploding (Rosenblatt 1997:8; also see Minear and Guillot 1996:168–169).

3. In another telling case, Peter Woodrow reports on the multicultural perspectives faced by the staff of Catholic Relief Services working on a health-care project among Khmer refugees in Surin, Thailand. Woodrow notes that ''refugee workers, locally hired national staff, the expatriate staff (further divided among Third World and European/American people), the country office personnel in a capital city, and the headquarters staff in the U.S. or Europe: each had a different viewpoint'' (Anderson and Woodrow 1989:312).
4. See the informative case studies describing the complex and shifting relations that exist among these actors presented in Zetter (1995) and Juma (1995:99–114); also see Karadawi (1983: 543–544). Administrative reforms under consideration within the United Nations in 1997 would transfer responsibility for coordinating a wide range of additional emergency programs to UNHCR (*International Herald Tribune*, 4 June 1997, p. 10) and, thus, would place further demands for intercultural communication on its staff.
5. Also see Riker's discussion of the ''five main modes of interaction or exchange between the central government and NGOs'' (Riker 1995:29–35). In 1983, an official with 10 years of working experience in the Sudanese Refugee Commission reported that the opportunities for *dialogue* among NGO personnel and indigenous government professionals are ''rare'' and that, at times, the former appear to view the latter as ''an obstacle'' to their work (Karadawi 1983:538).
6. Kuhlman (1994:124) points out that ''most refugees in Africa are spontaneously settled.'' For instance, approximately 300,000 Rwandan refugees settled outside camps in the North Kivu Region of (then) Zaire in 1994 (Porignon, et al. 1995:357). Self-settlement also prevailed among refugees from Mozambique who fled to Malawi (Zetter 1995:1655) and among Eritrean refugees in Sudan (Karadawi 1983:538).
7. Due to space limitations, it has been necessary to withdraw the discussion of training and accountability from both the analysis and guidelines sections of this chapter. Interested readers can receive a copy of this discussion by submitting a request directly to the authors.
8. For instance, when approximately one million Rwandan refugees crossed into eastern Zaire over four days in July 1994, UNHCR had to arrange for ''water tankers to be flown in, food, medicine and soap to be airlifted and heavy equipment to be mobilized to bury the dead in the hard volcanic soil . . . '' (*Refugees* 105, 1996:18).
9. Deborah Eade and Suzanne Williams (1995:377) point out that ''networking enables groups and organizations to maximize or 'scale up' their impact by sharing their knowledge, complementing each others' work, and building links and alliances in a systematic way.''
10. See note 7.

REFERENCES

Aall, Cato (1979). ''Disastrous international relief failure: A report on Burmese refugees in Bangladesh from May to December 1978.'' *Disasters* 3(4), 429–434.

Andersen, Peter (1988). ''Explaining intercultural differences in nonverbal communication.'' In *Intercultural Communication: A Reader*, edited by Larry A. Samovar and Richard E. Porter. Belmont, CA: Wadsworth Publishing Company, pp. 272–282.

Anderson, Mary B.; and Woodrow, Peter J. (1989). *Rising from the Ashes: Development Strategies in Times of Disaster*. Boulder, CO: Westview Press.

Atwood, J. Brian (1997). ''Q & A: Helping Africa go the way of reforms.'' *International Herald Tribune* (20 May), 6.

Bemak, Fred; Chung, Rita Chi-Ying; and Bornemann, Thomas H. (1996). ''Counseling and psychotherapy with refugees.'' In *Counseling Across Cultures*, 4th ed., edited by Paul B. Pedersen, Juris G. Draguns, Walter J. Lonner, and Joseph E. Trimble. Thousand Oaks, CA: Sage Publications, pp. 243–265.

Bennett, Jon (1995a). ''Afghanistan: Cross-border NGO coordination, 1985–93.'' In *Meeting Needs: NGO Coordination in Practice*, edited by Jon Bennett. London: Earthscan Publications, pp. 1–23.

Bennett, Jon (1995b). ''Recent trends in relief aid: Structural crisis and the quest for a new consensus.'' In *Meeting Needs: NGO Coordination in Practice*, edited by Jon Bennett. London: Earthscan Publications, pp. xi–xxii.

Bennett, Jon; and Benson, Charlotte (1995). ''Cambodia: NGO cooperation in a changing aid country, 1979–94.'' In *Meeting Needs: NGO Coordination in Practice*, edited by Jon Bennett. London: Earthscan Publications, pp. 166–183.

Brislin, Richard; and Yoshida, Tomoko (1994). *Intercultural Communication Training: An Introduction*. Thousand Oaks, CA: Sage Publications.

Burge, Alun (1995). ''Central America: NGO coordination in El Salvador and Guatemala 1980–94.'' In *Meeting Needs: NGO Coordination in Practice*, edited by Jon Bennett. London: Earthscan Publications, pp. 145–165.

Chambers, Robert (1979). ''Rural refugees in Africa: What the eye does not see.'' *Disasters* 3(4), 381–392.

Cohen, Raymond (1991). *Negotiating Across Cultures*. Washington, D.C.: United States Institute of Peace.

Cuny, Frederick C. (1979). ''Research, planning and refugees.'' *Disasters* 3(4), 339–340.

Dupont, Christophe; and Faure, Guy-Olivier (1991). ''The negotiation process.'' In *International Negotiation*, edited by Viktor A. Kremenyuk. San Francisco: Jossey-Bass Publishers, pp. 40–57.

Dynes, Russell R. (1983). ''Problems in emergency planning.'' *Energy* 8(8–9), 653–660.

Eade, Deborah; and Williams, Suzanne (1995). *The Oxfam Handbook of Development and Relief.* Volumes I and II. Oxford: Oxfam.

Gudykunst, William B.; and Kim, Young Yun (1992). *Communicating with Strangers: An Approach to Intercultural Communication*, 2nd ed. New York: Random House.

Hall, Edward T. (1966). *The Hidden Dimension*. Garden City, NY: Doubleday & Company.

Hall, Edward T. (1976). *Beyond Culture*. Garden City, NY: Anchor Books.

Hansen, Art (1979). ''Once the running stops: Assimilation of Angolan refugees into Zambian border villages.'' *Disaster* 3(4): 369–374.

Hartkop, Volker H.; and Goodspeed, Charles H. (1979). ''Space enclosures for emergencies in developing countries.'' *Disasters* 3(4), 443–455.

Hofstede, Geert (1982). *Culture's Consequences*. Beverly Hills, CA: Sage Publications.

Hyden, Goran; Koehn, Peter; and Saleh, Turhan (1996). ''The challenge of decentralization in Eritrea.'' *Journal of African Policy Studies* 2(1), 31–51.

Juma, Monika K. (1995). ''Kenya: NGO coordination during the Somali refugee crisis, 1990–93.'' In *Meeting Needs: NGO Coordination in Practice*, edited by Jon Bennett. London: Earthscan Publications, pp. 89–115.

Karadawi, Ahmed (1983). ''Constraints on assistance to refugees: Some observations for the Sudan.'' *World Development* 11(6), 537–547.

Koehn, Peter (1991). *Refugees from Revolution: U.S. Policy and Third-World Migration*. Boulder, CO: Westview Press.

Koehn, Peter (compiler and editor) (1994a). *Final Report of the International Symposium ''Refugees and Development Assistance: Training for Voluntary Repatriation.''* Missoula, MT: Office of International Programs, University of Montana.

Koehn, Peter (1994b). ''Refugee settlement and repatriation in Africa: Development prospects and constraints.'' In *African Refugees: Development Aid and Repatriation*, edited by Howard Adelman and John Sorenson. Boulder, CO: Westview Press, pp. 97–116.

Koehn, Peter; and Ojo, Olatunde J.B. (1997). ''NGOs and GONGOs: Opportunities for development management in Africa in the 21st century.'' In *Subsaharan Africa in the 1990s: Challenges to Democracy and Development*, edited by Rukhsana A. Siddiqui. Westport, CT: Greenwood Praeger, pp. 109–128.

Koehn, Peter; and Ojo, Olatunde J.B. (1999). ''Introduction: Making Aid Work in the New Millennium.'' In *Making Aid Work: Innovative Approaches for Africa at the Turn of the Century.* Lanham, MD: University Press of America, pp. 1–14.

Kuhlman, Tom (1994). ''Organized versus spontaneous settlement of refugees in Africa.'' In *African Refugees: Development Aid and Repatriation*, edited by Howard Adelman and John Sorenson. Boulder, CO: Westview Press, pp. 117–142.

Loescher, Gil (1993). *Beyond Charity: International Cooperation and the Global Refugee Crisis.* Oxford: Oxford University Press.

Lustig, Myron; and Koester, Jolene (1993). *Intercultural Competence: Interpersonal Communication Across Cultures.* New York: Harper Collins.

Mazur, Robert E. (1987). ''Linking popular initiative and aid agencies: The case of refugees.'' *Development and Change* 18(4), 437–461.

McKelvey, Margaret (1994). ''From Afghanistan to Zimbabwe: Making refugee repatriation work.'' In *Final Report of the International Symposium ''Refugees and Development Assistance: Training for Voluntary Repatriation,''* edited by Peter Koehn. Missoula, MT: Office of International Programs, University of Montana, pp. 10–24.

Melkote, Srinivas R. (1991). *Communication for Development in the Third World.* New Delhi: Sage Publications.

Minear, Larry; and Guillot, Philippe. (1996). *Soldiers to the Rescue: Humanitarian Lessons from Rwanda.* Paris: Development Centre, Organisation for Economic Co-operation and Development.

Neal, David M.; and Phillips, Brenda D. (1995). ''Effective emergency management: Reconsidering the bureaucratic approach.'' *Disasters* 19(4), 327–337.

Neldner, Brian W. (1979). ''Settlement of rural refugees in Africa.'' *Disasters* 3(4), 393–402.

Ngai, Phyllis Bo-Yuen (1996). ''Nonverbal communication behavior of professional administrators from Ethiopia, Tanzania, Hong Kong, and China in negotiations with U.S. negotiators: Cross-cultural perspectives.'' Unpublished master's thesis. Missoula, MT: The University of Montana.

Pedersen, Paul (1994). *A Handbook for Developing Multicultural Awareness* 2nd ed. Alexandria, VA: American Counseling Association.

Philipsen, Gerry (1992). *Speaking Culturally.* Albany, NY: State University of New York Press.

Phillips, Brenda D. (1993). ''Cultural diversity in disasters: Sheltering, housing, and long term recovery.'' *International Journal of Mass Emergencies and Disasters* 11(1), 99–110.

Porignon, Denis; Noterman, Jean-Pierre; Hennart, Phillipe; Tonglet, René; Soron'Gane, Etienne M.; and Lokombe, Tarcisse E. (1995). ''The role of the Zairian health services in the Rwandan refugee crisis.'' *Disasters* 19(4), 356–360.

Riker, James V. (1995). ''Contending perspectives for interpreting government-NGO relations in South and Southeast Asia: Constraints, challenges and the search for common ground in rural development.'' In *Government-NGO Relations in Asia: Prospects and Challenges for People-Centred Development*, edited by Noeleen Heyzer, James V. Riker, and Antonio B. Quizon. New York: St. Martin's Press, pp. 15–55.

Rosenblatt, Lionel A. (1997). ''It's not so simple to make rules about humanitarian aid.'' *International Herald Tribune* (5–6 April), p. 8.

Schneider, Saundra K. (1992). ''Governmental response to disasters: The conflict between bureaucratic procedures and emergent norms.'' *Public Administration Review* 52(2), 135–145.

Siegel, Gilbert B. (1985). ''Human resource development for emergency management.'' *Public Administration Review* 45(2), 107–117.

van Bergen, J.E.A.M. (1995). ''District health care between quality assurance and crisis management: Possibilities within the limits, Mporokoso and Kaputa District, Zambia.'' *Tropical and Geographical Medicine* 47(1), 23–29.

van Rooyen, René (1994). ''Repatriation: A viable solution for the 90s?'' In *Final Report of the International Symposium ''Refugees and Development Assistance: Training for Voluntary Repatriation,''* edited by Peter Koehn. Missoula, MT: Office of International Programs, University of Montana, pp. 35–46.

Yamamoto, Hideki (1995). ''An NGO perspective on empowerment of humanitarian assistance.'' *International Education Forum* 15(2), 138–141.

Zetter, Roger (1995). ''Incorporation and exclusion: The life cycle of Malawi's refugee assistance program.'' *World Development* 23(10), 1653–1667.

Zolberg, Aristide R.; Suhrke, Astri; and Aguayo, Sergio (1989). *Escape from Violence: Conflict and the Refugee Crisis in the Developing World.* Oxford: Oxford University Press.

Index